THE BIG BOOK OF
JOBS

2005-2006
EDITION

THE BIG BOOK OF
JOBS

**The Editors of VGM Career Books & the United States
Department of Labor, Bureau of Labor Statistics**

VGM Career Books

*New York   Chicago   San Francisco   Lisbon   London   Madrid   Mexico City
Milan   New Delhi   San Juan   Seoul   Singapore   Sydney   Toronto*

The McGraw-Hill Companies

The edition of the *Occupational Outlook Handbook* appearing in Section Two, first published in 2004 by VGM Career Books, is an unabridged publication of Bulletin 2570, the Occupational Outlook Handbook, compiled by the United States Department of Labor, Bureau of Labor Statistics.

1 2 3 4 5 6 7 8 9 0   VLP/VLP   3 2 1 0 9 8 7 6 5 4

ISBN 0-07-143732-0
ISSN 1520-6092

McGraw-Hill books are available at special quantity discounts to use as premiums and sales promotions, or for use in corporate training programs. For more information, please write to the Director of Special Sales, Professional Publishing, McGraw-Hill, Two Penn Plaza, New York, NY 10121-2298. Or contact your local bookstore.

This book is printed on acid-free paper.

CONTENTS

Section One
The Job-Seekers Guide

Section Two
Occupational Outlook Handbook

CHAPTER 1

BEGINNING THE JOURNEY

The journey of 12,000 days starts with a single step—and 12,000 days is, on average, what most of us will devote to our work during the course of our lifetimes. If we live to the reasonable age of 70, we'll spend between 45 and 50 years in the work force—and many of us will work even longer. This means we're likely to have 10 to 15 jobs and as many as three to six different *careers* during the course of our working life.

After a few bleak years in terms of employment trends, prospects are finally looking up, according to *Business Week Online*'s Hiring Outlook 2004. Job growth in biotech and healthcare fields is robust. The technology sector is on the road to recovery, hiring again after a long dry spell. Consultants are in demand as companies struggle to find creative solutions and meet their fiscal goals. More lawyers are needed—especially those experienced in securities and white-collar crime—as lawsuits increase. Approximately 112,000 new positions were created during January 2004, making it the most remarkable month for job creation in four years.

Nevertheless, the jobless rate is estimated at 5.6 percent. Competition for open positions is still fierce, and the average job search lasts about four to six months. There is also the much-discussed trend of outsourcing, or "offshoring." In such an employer's market, it is more important than ever to build your arsenal with a fantastic resume and cover letter to set you apart from other applicants. The only way to succeed on this journey is to have a realistic map of today's work-world terrain.

Building Career Management Skills

No matter what your circumstances—whether you're a recent college graduate launching your first job search, a homemaker returning to work after raising a family, or a manager seeking to change career fields—you'll find practical strategies in the chapters that follow. These strategies will to help you build skills in researching career options and conducting an effective job search.

Today, career management skills are a necessity, not a luxury, as the statistics above indicate. The ability to manage your career may be the most important skill you acquire, because you simply can't practice the profession of your choice if you can't find a job.

Jobs Versus Careers

What's the difference between a career and a job? A job is a particular position you pursue, while a career is the broad field of endeavor that consists of a series of related jobs. When you hunt for a job, you're seeking something relatively specific, such as an opening for a personnel recruiter or benefits specialist. When you choose a career, you're committing to a comprehensive field of knowledge and skill, such as human resources management.

This distinction between a job and career is important. Sometimes you may work in jobs that are unrelated to your career field. Sometimes you may not know the precise job you want to pursue today, tomorrow, or next year, but you've identified the ideal career.

Looking Beyond the Obvious

Sadly, most of us wear blinders when it comes to exploring the exciting range of truly viable, rewarding careers. Some of the most obvious career choices most of us recognize are accountant, business manager, doctor, editor, engineer, journalist, lawyer, nurse, and teacher. Many of us choose from this limited list without much thought or exploration, simply because it's easy.

If, however, you understand the importance of making a thoughtful, well-considered career choice, you'll gladly invest the relatively small amount of time it takes to discover a career that suits you. As you learn about new career possibilities and make initial decisions, you must consider many things:

- What you're good at and what you like to do—which may not be the same
- What part of the country or world you want to live in
- What experiences you've had and what experiences you want to have
- Which personal values shape your daily life and how these values relate to the work you will do
- Whether you prefer to work alone or as part of a larger team
- How many hours a day or week you want to devote to work
- How much money you want or need to earn

You'll notice that compensation is the last thing in the list. That's because the career decisions you make must go well beyond the mere fact of income. Certainly we all want to earn a decent or even substantial income, but in reality, the factors that make a career desirable and satisfying differ widely from person to person.

We sometimes place inordinate emphasis on a particular career's income potential. Because it's quantifiable, money is an easy way to measure our success. Only *you* can determine what personal and professional rewards deliver the greatest satisfaction, but it's important to assess the entire picture consciously when you select a career.

It's no accident that in recent years, as a result of the dot.com crash among other factors, droves of highly paid managers and professionals have jumped off the fast track and switched careers. According to a study in *Fortune* magazine, at any moment, one-third of all college-educated adults would opt for a different line of work if given the chance. Every year, roughly 10 percent of the American work force acts on these desires and switches occupations. In many cases, these are people who've discovered a fundamental truth: money is important, but it isn't everything—and 12,000 days is a very long time to do work you don't love.

Using *The Big Book of Jobs*

The Big Book of Jobs is divided into two main sections. Section One provides an overview of the major steps involved in exploring career options, researching career details, and conducting your job search in an effective, practical manner. While the job search process can be complex and time-consuming, this section is organized in a logical sequence that parallels that process. The topics we'll address include:

- Chapter 1—Beginning the Journey
- Chapter 2—Exploring Career Options
- Chapter 3—Writing Polished Cover Letters
- Chapter 4—Creating Professional Resumes
- Chapter 5—Hunting for the Right Job
- Chapter 6—Mastering Job Interviews
- Chapter 7—Launching Your Career

The most effective way to use the first section of *The Big Book of Jobs* is to read through it, then return and study the particular chapters that hold special interest or immediacy for you. Throughout each chapter, you'll find practical strategies for success; summary lists of *dos* and *don'ts*; plus data, quotes, and advice from employers, career services professionals, and job seekers.

At the end of each chapter we've provided a list of additional resources so you can learn more about particular concepts or strategies. There are more than 3,100 books devoted to exploring career options, self-assessment, resume writing, job networking, and other skills and strategies linked to the job hunt. This book isn't intended to replace these resources; it's designed to provide an initial overview that will get you started on your career search journey.

Section Two of *The Big Book of Jobs* is the *Occupational Outlook Handbook*, which offers detailed descriptions of specific jobs and career fields. The data in this section is gathered by the United States Bureau of Labor Statistics and is updated every other year. It provides a comprehensive summary of different job categories, along with brief job descriptions, projected rate of growth, education and employment criteria, plus wage and salary information.

Stepping into the Future

Experts believe that our current global economy is experiencing greater, more radical change in a shorter period of time than the world has ever experienced. Few of us would argue, since we see the effects daily. As you step into the future, these changes can create fear and paralysis—or opportunity and a new vision.

Technology and the information superhighway have changed many things, including the way we work, the nature of work we perform, and the tools we use to find work. In the end, however, information and the ability to conduct your own effective, targeted career search are far more powerful tools than technology itself.

Your career search journey begins with the essential process of researching and identifying a viable career field. Your next step is to hunt for jobs designed to further your existing career or start a new one. Most of us will continue this pilgrimage until the day we retire. *The Big Book of Jobs* is an invaluable tool that will help you launch your journey into a puzzling, fascinating, ever-changing place—the world of work.

CHAPTER 2
EXPLORING CAREER OPTIONS

Occupational information is available everywhere. It's covered in the morning newspaper and on the Internet in articles describing companies, people at work, and employment trends. It's summarized in the classified section, where current job openings are advertised. It's on TV, where news items highlight people and their professions, and it's present in job search websites that specialize in providing people with cutting-edge career information. Information about careers is pervasive in our daily lives, as we encounter people through work, school, community, and social activities.

Yet for many of us it's difficult to identify a career that is desirable, suitable, and attainable—whether it's our first or fifth career search effort. Since 80 percent of all job terminations (both voluntary and involuntary) are the result of people filling positions for which they are not the best fit, the key to exploring the fullest range of options is to balance job facts with personal "fit."

This chapter will discuss some of the most common self-assessment tools and strategies designed to help you understand your own strengths and weaknesses, so you can explore jobs that are the best fit. It will also introduce you to fundamental career research resources that will help you begin to identify what employers and which career fields will allow you to use your strengths and personal qualities to best effect.

Searching for the Perfect Career

Some of you are destined to find the perfect career and to work in that field for the rest of your lives. I know several people like this. One had a single goal from earliest childhood: to go to medical school and become a doctor. Today he runs the helicopter emergency care-flight response team for a major hospital. For him, there was never any career but medicine. The only question was what specialty he'd pursue and what specific environment he'd work in.

Another friend, on the other hand, was torn between acting and creative writing, because he'd received recognition for both at an early age. Nonetheless, he was persuaded to go to college and pursue a "real" career such as journalism. However, the writing skills that made his plays dramatic and moving didn't translate well to writing articles filled with facts and details. When he recognized his mistake, he left college to pursue his passion, and for years he's happily made his living as a performer and playwright. Whether he's on stage or at his computer, he's practicing his chosen career as an entertainer.

Many of you face a different challenge, because as yet you have no idea what career might suit you best. Perhaps you're not certain what skills and abilities you have to offer. Perhaps you're not certain what careers use the skills and abilities you have or are interested in developing. The key to a successful career search effort is to balance both perspectives: what you can and want to do *versus* what employers expect in specific career fields. The only way most of us reconcile this dilemma is by first conducting an extensive self-assessment and then researching careers that match our personal profile.

Using Self-Assessment and Career Discovery Books

Career research and decision-making books fall into four general categories: (1) those that help you assess your personal arsenal of skills, abilities, knowledges, values, and interests and that suggest careers that might suit you; (2) those that describe careers in a specific work environment, such as the film industry or local government; (3) those that describe careers suited to people with particular skills or education, such as history or science; and (4) those targeted to people with practical experience who want to change careers. Each type has value for career seekers at different stages of the decision-making process.

If you are completely uncertain of the career options that best suit you, you will want to read one of the many books dedicated to self-assessment and career exploration. Such books will independently guide you through the process of identifying, analyzing, and connecting your skills and traits to potential careers. Richard Bolles' *What Color Is Your Parachute?* is a classic self-assessment career guide, useful both for the first-time job seeker and for the mature career changer.

There are many books available to help students and new graduates find a suitable career path. For those just entering the job market or those who don't know what they want, these resources enable you to identify your interests, talents, and potential skills and then to match them to possible jobs. They help you determine your dream job and what you need to do to get it. Two books that are valuable for students and new graduates are *Choose the Right Career* by Louise Welsh Schrank and *Discover What You're Best At* by Linda Gale.

Today there are many books aimed at people with practical work experience who wish to make a career change or toward people re-entering the workforce after an absence of some years. Some of these resources are designed to assist experienced workers "recareer"—that is, change career fields completely or radically redirect their career, building from the experience base they've acquired. Other resources are suited for job seekers and job changers who've just experienced a company layoff or downsizing program. Examples include *Do What You Are* and *Knock 'em Dead*. Often these books include valuable tips on handling your budget, explaining your career change to a potential employer, dealing with family pressures, and more.

Success Strategy

If you use one or more of these books to conduct a self-directed assessment, be sure to work through the exercises and answer any questions *in writing*. You could read 20 of these books and come no closer to identifying your personal career profile. Writing your responses to critical questions and recording details about your skills and abilities will bring you closer to an accurate self-profile in a shorter amount of time.

Using Career Planning and Counseling Agencies

Another way to develop a useful self-profile is to work with a career planning specialist. Virtually every two- or four-year college in the United States has a career counselor, as well as self-assessment and career research resources.

Career counselors do just that—they counsel and advise based on what they know about you (or what you've told them). Good career counselors can't and won't make a career decision for you, but they can direct you to and assist you in ac-

Success Strategy

Use all the free resources first. Then, if you remain completely stumped and unable to decipher a career path, consider investing in paid, one-on-one counseling services.

cessing special resources you may not be familiar with. Generally, you can meet with a career adviser employed by your community college or your local bureau of employment services free of charge. Other career counselors are employed by placement agencies or operate their own counseling firms and usually charge a fee for their services.

If you're a student, take advantage of all the services your career planning office offers. If you're not a student, your local community college career counselors may be willing to administer one or more self-assessment tools, which are designed to help you identify careers that match your strengths, interests, and values. Some of the most common assessment tools include:

• Campbell Interest & Skill Survey
• Career Assessment Inventory
• Self-Directed Search
• Myers-Briggs Personality Type Indicator

Private career counselors perform services similar to school-based counselors, and often their training and education will be similar. There are at least 228,000 private counselors in the United States, and many of them charge between $75 and $125 per session. Using a private career counselor can be costly but effective, particularly if you need highly specialized assistance or if you're truly stymied in your career research. Take time to verify the credentials of any counselor you choose. The National Board of Certified Counselors (800-398-5389) will provide a list of accredited counselors in your area.

What's the Difference?

Career planning, counseling, or advising—People or agencies performing these functions will help you assess your skills, interests, and abilities and guide your research into careers that match your unique personal qualities.

Job placement, outplacement, head hunters, search firms—People or agencies performing these functions help you search for a job in the particular career field you've identified.

Using Computerized Career-Matching Programs

Today most college career offices also offer computerized resources designed to help you assess your career potential and evaluate employment data through structured interaction with a custom program. Some of the more common computerized self-assessment and occupational assessment systems are:

- Career Information System (CIS)—A data-driven program that provides self-assessment and career options, plus local and state employment data.

- Discover— A user-friendly program that matches your self-assessment responses to possible occupations and helps guide you through long-range career planning scenarios.

- Guidance Information System (GIS)—Like CIS, a data-driven program with self-assessment, career matching, and employment data.

- SIGI PLUS—A user-friendly program that matches your responses to possible occupations and provides assistance in the career decision-making process.

Computerized career research has advantages and drawbacks. The computer program will ask you questions about your interests, abilities, values, and experiences; based on your replies, it will suggest career fields that might suit you.

This approach can shorten the research path and provide you with an immediate list of options to explore. However, since these programs usually provide a straight path between your interests and potential careers, they eliminate those accidental, thought-provoking discoveries that occur as you browse through a book full of career descriptions. As a result, computerized career matching is more valuable once you've narrowed your range to just a few career fields.

Use books, magazines, journals, federal and state employment publications, and computerized resources for the best mix of targeted information and intriguing discoveries. As you conduct your self-assessment, keep in mind the basic qualities and competencies that employers value and see how closely your profile matches today's workplace expectations.

Most Valued Workplace Competencies

Resources: Ability to identify, organize, plan, and allocate resources such as:

- Time
- Money
- Material and facilities
- Human resources

Interpersonal Skills: Ability to work and communicate with others, which includes the capacity to:

- Participate as member of a team
- Teach others new skills
- Serve clients/customers
- Exercise leadership
- Negotiate
- Work with diversity

Information: Acquires and uses information, which includes the ability to:

- Acquire and evaluate information
- Organize and maintain information
- Interpret and communicate information
- Use computers to process information

Systems: Understands complex inter-relationships, which includes the ability to:

- Understand systems
- Monitor and correct performance
- Improve or design systems

Technology: Works with a variety of technologies, which includes the ability to:

- Select technology
- Apply technology to tasks
- Maintain and troubleshoot equipment

(Adapted from US Department of Labor SCANS Report, 1991)

Researching Careers in the Information Age

Even with today's technological advances, books remain one of the largest career reference categories. There are a number of well-recognized books such as *The Big Book of Jobs* that summarize jobs by different categories and provide brief job descriptions. Other books focus on jobs for people with special interests or education, such as history buffs or film fanatics. Mainstream business magazines, professional journals, and industry publications consistently produce articles summarizing new career opportunities, growth fields, and changing employment trends. Thousands of people make their living advising career seekers on how to make a sound decision.

Moreover, practitioners, the people who do what you think you want to do, are certainly an invaluable, largely untapped resource.

Electronic and written forms of career information are readily available. Public and college libraries and your local bookstore all contain impressive quantities of career information. Career services offices in high schools, colleges, and universities also contain amazing research resources. Many companies and governmental agencies maintain internal libraries, so if you're employed, don't forget to check your organization's library for information about related careers. Professional and trade associations, such as the Association of Business Communicators or the International Association of City Managers, maintain career information related to their specialty; many will fax or mail career information and employment criteria if you request it. More and more libraries and career service offices also provide access to electronic databases, which allow you to tap into potentially unlimited career information resources.

Be sure to read the list of resources cited at the end of the chapter to find additional materials that might be helpful. Keep in mind that many of these book titles might also be available in other forms, such as CD-ROM or through an online service.

Useful Directories

Directory of Career Training & Development Programs

Lists a variety of management and executive training programs, including criteria for entry, duration of training, and more.

Directory of Corporate Affiliations

Includes profiles of more than 4,000 companies, including subsidiaries, divisions, and affiliates.

Moody's Manuals

Includes contact information and descriptions of companies on the New York or American Stock Exchange. Separate volumes cover industrial companies, banking and finance, public utilities, transportation, and municipal bonds.

Encyclopedia of Associations

Consists of several volumes that list the more than 20,000 professional and trade associations.

Standard and Poor's Register of Corporations

Lists 45,000 corporations and their officials.

Researching Occupational Descriptions and Trends

The federal government has produced the *Dictionary of Occupational Titles (DOT)* for more than 50 years. Originally designed to help employers standardize requirements among similar jobs, the *DOT* is a valuable resource for career seekers. It lists over 20,000 jobs and provides a brief description for each, including a nine-digit occupational code, the occupational title, the industry where the job occurs, alternate occupational titles, and a summary of tasks performed in this job.

The *DOT* is organized by job grouping, with similar jobs clustered together. If you examine any one page, you'll notice that the descriptions for different job titles may overlap. To find a *DOT* description, go to the alphabetical index located at the back of the volume. Note the corresponding code listed along with the job title, then find the listing in the book. Reading through the tasks associated with the jobs you're interested in will help you determine which jobs you will want to explore in more depth.

This is where the *Occupational Outlook Handbook* (in Section Two) is useful. It describes more than 270 job categories in detail. Like the *DOT*, occupation descriptions are clustered into similar categories. As a result, distinctly different positions, such as aircraft pilot, broadcast technician, and computer programmer, are grouped under the classification of "Technicians, Except Health." (Health-care technicians are grouped under another classification.) If the position you wish to read about is a common one, you can find it by scanning the Contents listing. If you have a very specific job in mind, turn to the Index (at the back of the book) and find the title that most closely matches your area of interest. The Index will suggest cross references as well.

Each listing includes this standard information:

- The occupational title—Describes the common occupational category
- *DOT* codes—Identifies cross-reference numbers for this occupation
- Nature of Work—Describes the occupation in detail
- Working Conditions—Describes the typical environment, number of hours worked in a day or week, and the time of day worked
- Employment—Describes the number of current positions and common industries utilizing these positions
- Training, Other Qualifications, and Advancement—Describes how to prepare for job entry and requirements for advancement
- Job Outlook—Describes the rate of growth anticipated and the industries where growth or decline are expected to occur
- Earnings—Describes the relative pay in different industry settings and details entry, median, and top pay ranges
- Related Occupations—Describes other career fields requiring similar skills and training

- Sources of Additional Information—Describes national associations, licensing, and educational sources related to this field

It's important to understand exactly what you're looking at when you use the *Occupational Outlook Handbook*. For example, there are currently about 4.1 million secretaries and administrative assistants in the United States. If you read the information on growth rates among non-specialized secretarial positions, you'll see that these jobs are expected to grow at a slower-than-average rate through the year 2012. However, if you read carefully, you'll also learn that certain secretarial specialties—legal and medical secretarial jobs, in particular—are expected to grow more quickly than average.

What does this mean for you? First, translate these job descriptions into something measurable. If an average occupational growth rate is 25 percent, you immediately know that opportunities for legal or medical secretaries will increase at a faster pace.

You should not reject a career field solely because it isn't experiencing enormous growth. In the case of general secretarial positions, if slower-than-average growth is 10 percent, roughly 300,000 job openings are expected to occur before 2007. If this is what you really want to do, go for it! After all, on an individual scale, you don't need 3,403,000 or even 34 job offers—you only need one viable offer to launch your career.

Using Career Description Books

Books that describe occupational opportunities in a specific field or area of personal passion are worth reading, since most of us have no concept of the varied, fascinating array of jobs available in any given field. For example, the next time you view a film, study the list of credits at the end. What's a gaffer? A key grip? A scumbler? A face caster? What do they do? To find out, examine one of the many industry-specific career books, such as *Careers for Film Buffs & Other Hollywood Types*. Similar books exist for many work environments, including the music industry, publishing, sports, state and local government, nonprofit organizations, and international business. You may also find the VGM Career Books series *Opportunities in . . .* and *VGM Professional Careers* useful in delineating the various positions available within different fields of work.

Books that describe careers suited to people with specific skills or education are helpful if you have or intend to pursue a degree in a particular field. These books will help you recognize the many ways your unique cluster of skills, knowledge, and abilities can be applied in the work world. Every liberal arts major has been asked the question, "What can you do with *that* major?" To develop an intelligent, informed answer, just examine one or more of the books dedicated to matching education with careers. Some examples include *Great Jobs for History Majors* and *Great Jobs for Foreign Language Majors*.

Using College Career Services Offices

Community college career offices are among the best—and often least acknowledged—resources available. While most four-year colleges focus on providing assistance to their own graduating seniors and alumni, community colleges often provide a wide range of services to both students and the public.

Typically, the career services office will have copies of the *DOT* and the *Occupational Outlook Handbook*, along with many specialized books on skill and interest assessment and careers suited to specific degree fields. In addition, you'll also find data on local employers, plus regional and state employment trends.

Current job descriptions and recruitment notices can give you a good feel for what employers are seeking in applicants. Magazines on careers and job search strategies will help guide you through the career search process. Plus, many career services offices will share the names and phone numbers of alumni willing to answer questions about their chosen profession or arrange a job shadowing or observation experience.

Using Public Employment Agencies

Virtually every state operates some form of public employment services bureau. Employment bureaus can typically provide data on local employers and regional employment trends, such as which jobs are increasing and which are on the decline. These agencies, however, may be able to provide more productive assistance when you've finished your research and are actively involved in a job hunt.

Researching Careers Online

While the number of job openings and recruitment announcements posted online is increasing, this isn't necessarily an enormous help in your career research phase. Often the same information is available in the job classifieds of newspapers, magazines, professional or trade journals, and recruitment bulletin boards. Realistically, employers who don't publicize job openings in the newspaper may be equally reluctant to publicize openings online.

The greatest advantage of online career research is that you are able to enter a key word combination and conduct a search for articles related to your field of interest. For example, you could conduct an online search for careers in advertising and identify hundreds of articles and books that contain information on these careers. A second advantage of online research is the ability to access these sources relatively easily and download or print articles from magazines and journals. There are a number of excellent resources available on electronic job searching, including the *Guide to Internet Job Searching*.

In some cases, you'll be able to access career information more rapidly when the publication is distributed electronically. In other cases, the hard copy of the magazine will be at the library or in your mailbox before the electronic version is available.

A Caution About Online Job Research

The sheer volume of online information may be daunting; for some, it can also be a major distraction and obstacle. Many career researchers become so enamored with the number of sources they locate that they become overwhelmed and immobilized. Others faithfully retrieve and print article after article—often without reading or absorbing the content.

It's better to have a firm grasp of the information you locate and to use this information in shaping a decision than track down and retrieve enormous quantities of information you can't mentally process.

Career research is an art, not a game where she who makes the most online hits *wins*.

Hands-on Job Discovery

Once you've identified a general career field (for example, medicine or communications) or a specific occupation (such as recreational therapist or public relations specialist), it's important to learn as much as you can about the practical realities of working in that arena. There are a number of ways you can accomplish this research and discovery phase. You can find full- or part-time employment or work as a volunteer in that field or industry. You can interview, observe, or shadow practitioners. You can arrange to complete part of your educational requirements in a specific work environment, through internships, co-operative work programs, or practicums.

Gaining Paid or Volunteer Work Experience

Working in your targeted career field is the best way to test how well you match the real requirements. If you're still in the research and discovery phase, you may not qualify for the actual position you desire. However, often you can land a full- or part-time position working in a less specialized position within your targeted work environment. For example, if you know you want to do something in the medical field, seek employment as a receptionist, maintenance person, or aide in a hospital, urgent care facility, doctor's office, or nursing home. You'll be able to learn about the working conditions, pay ranges, qualifications, personalities of your future colleagues, as well as about the rewards and pitfalls associated with working in medicine.

Volunteer experiences deliver similar value, but they often have an additional advantage. If you're trying to reposition yourself for a new career path or you're trying to test out a career field for which you're not yet fully qualified, many organizations use more flexible criteria for unpaid assistance, and often they'll provide basic training in vital areas. Future doctors can gain hands-on experience in hospitals and nursing homes. Future writers can gain experience working on newsletters, press releases, and internal communications. Future paralegals can gain experience working with court systems and legal documents, and future recreation therapists can gain experience working with the elderly or the physically challenged.

Volunteer opportunities are boundless. Each year, millions of hours are contributed by unpaid workers in the United States. To find out more about opportunities in your community, contact a specific organization directly or get in touch with your local city government, the Red Cross, or the United Way.

Combining Work and Education

One of the best times to gain direct work experience is while you're still in college. There are many ways to do this, but some degree programs actually offer the opportunity to earn college credit while you gain hands-on experience through internships, co-operative education programs, or practicums. This combination of work and education is the ideal way to spot matches or mismatches between your education, abilities and preferences, and real work expectations.

For example, a young man I know completed his business management degree without ever questioning the fact that he preferred jeans to business suits, solitude to unrelenting social interaction, and the outdoors to a comfortable but windowless office. If he had worked in a business environment—during the summers or part-time during the school year or through a co-op, internship, or practicum—he would have recognized these differences before he completed his education. As it was, he was forced to launch an extensive career research effort after futile months of hunting for a job with Fortune 500 companies. Once he acknowledged his real desires, he was able to conduct an honest self-assessment and redirect his search toward forestry and smaller companies dedicated to environmental concerns and agriculture.

The specifics of co-op, intern, and practicum experiences vary from college to college, but fundamentally they offer similar benefits.

Participating in Co-operative Education Programs

Co-operative education programs typically emphasize an extended work experience with one or more employers. Many colleges require co-op experience for graduation from specific programs, particularly in technical fields such as engineering and computer science. Students are placed in an ongoing position with an employer, in a field related to their long-term career goals. The employer, faculty adviser, and student work together to determine the type of on-the-job training and experience most valuable to the employer and the student.

Co-op students may study for one quarter, then work full-time the next quarter, and so on throughout their college career. Other co-op experiences are structured to allow students to spend roughly half their time in class and the other half on the job. The goal is to balance work and education, and to provide co-op participants with a realistic view of their career in action. Many co-op positions are paid, and many students use co-op earnings to pay for all or part of their college education.

Participating in Internships and Practicums

Internships and practicums are usually approached differently than a co-op experience. A company or organization will identify a specific project they want completed and will work with the faculty of a local college to identify students capable of successfully tackling all or part of the project. The students will complete the project tasks under the guidance of their faculty advisers and under the supervision of the organization.

Internships and practicums typically require a time commitment, whether it's one quarter or several, but usually the scope of the task is limited to ensure a clear beginning and ending point. For example, a group of students might work with production engineers to determine why airplane engine parts are rusting during storage and how the loss of parts due to excessive rust can be reduced or eliminated. The students would collect, analyze, and interpret data; they'd interview workers who manage the storage and handling process; they'd research methods for solving this problem; and then they would write a report summarizing their conclusions and recommendations for eliminating the problem.

Often, students receive credit toward their degree program in lieu of compensation; in some cases, however, they receive both. The organization wins because an important project has been completed. The students win because they've gained hands-on, practical, guided experience in the real world. And the school wins because their students have acquired a more fully developed education/work experience and are therefore more employable upon graduation.

Internships and practicums are becoming more common as both educators and employers seek ways to close the sometimes enormous gap between education and work. Internships and practicums are typically available at four-year colleges, but some of the most progressive two-year colleges are revamping their technical programs to incorporate internships and practicums into their already strong co-op tradition.

If you're in college or planning to attend college, talk to your academic adviser about opportunities for combining work and education. Even if a formal program doesn't exist, many schools will help you create a program that blends your education and career goals. You will also find a wealth of advice on internships in *Internship Success* by Marianne Ehrlich Green.

Interviewing, Observing, or Shadowing Practitioners

If you want to explore careers unrelated to your work or volunteer experience or you're working in the right field but you want to learn more about future career realities, develop a personal campaign of informational interviews, job observation, and shadowing experiences. You can choose to do just one type of exploration, such as informational interviews, or you can pursue some combination of the three.

Conducting Informational Interviews

Informational interviews are prescheduled interviews that you conduct with one or more persons employed in the field or fields you have targeted. The purpose of the informational interview is to learn the "straight scoop" from an actual practitioner. It's wise, therefore, to complete a substantial portion of your career research legwork before you begin scheduling informational interviews.

Informational interviews can be conducted over the phone or in person, but usually a face-to-face meeting is more valuable. Why? Because a face-to-face session provides the opportunity to form a genuine, solid connection with someone in your potential field and see the environment where your career is performed. Plus, you might have the opportunity to meet other people in the organization and gain a plant or facility tour.

You should never just walk into a company and ask to "speak with someone in Engineering." It's imperative that you approach the informational interview in a mature, professional manner, which means calling a pre-identified person, introducing yourself, explaining why you're calling, and arranging a time to meet. Many career search books describe this process in explicit detail, and some even provide a script to use in the contact call. Study several books and identify your best mix of strategies.

Preparing for Informational Interviews

- Write out the first two or three sentences you'll use to introduce yourself and practice this introduction out loud.
- List the goals you want to accomplish during your call. Some examples might be:
  - Date and time to meet
  - Acquiring company literature or information about your career field
  - Arranging a quick tour of the facility
- On the day of the informational interview:
  - Arrive early
  - Shake hands firmly
  - Take notes
  - Don't overstay your welcome (about an hour)
  - Leave a clean, current copy of your resume
- Follow up with a thank-you note.

Informational interviews are valuable experiences if you plan well. Typically, your contact person will rely on you to ask the questions and lead the discussion. Before the interview, outline the specific questions you want to ask and write them down. The person you speak with will not mind if you take notes during the interview; it shows that you are prepared and professional. Don't tape record informational interviews without specifically asking the contact person if it's okay.

Be sure to ask any questions about this career that have been puzzling you. While each of you will have different specific concerns, there are some core facts and questions you should consider including in your interview. First, you want to verify facts related to the person you're interviewing, such as:

- Their full name (and the correct spelling)
- Their exact job title (get their business card if you can)
- The complete company name
- The phone number, extension, and address

Cover the traditional "who, what, when, where, why, and how," but don't forget to ask *how much*. Focus on the obvious topic areas, such as education, personal qualities, job experience, career path, pay ranges, and working conditions. Some questions you might want to ask include:

1. How long have you held this position?
2. How long have you been in this career field?
3. What are the major duties, responsibilities, and goals of your position?
4. What level of education did you achieve?
5. What level of education is required?
6. What classes in (school or college) have been most valuable to you on the job?
7. Why did you decide to pursue this career?
8. What skills and personal qualities are critical for success?
9. What career path did you follow to get to this position?
10. Where does this job lead? What's the path for advancement?
11. Do all (fill in job title) work in similar settings?
12. What do you like most about your job or career field?
13. What do you like least about your job or career field?
14. What professional associations do you belong to?
15. Would it be valuable for me to join one of them now? Which one?
16. How much does a typical entry-level job pay?
17. How much does a typical mid-range job pay?
18. If you could only give me one piece of advice, what would it be?
19. Who else in (this field, related fields) might be willing to speak with me?
20. May I have their names, phone numbers, and addresses?
21. May I tell them you suggested I call?

After about an hour, thank your contact person for their time and the valuable information they've shared, stand up, and shake their hand. If you have a current resume, this is a good time to give it to them, then exit rapidly but with grace. In a day or two, send a brief thank-you note (a handwritten note is fine).

Generally, it's a good idea to talk to two or three people in your target career field. An accountant in a not-for-profit organization or in city government may not perform the same duties as an accountant in a corporation. Speaking with people in different organizations will help you piece together a more realistic picture of the profession.

Success Strategy

If you're seeking employment in a nontraditional field or if you have special requirements (such as a physical challenge or disability), try to speak to at least one person who faces a similar challenge. They may be able to share helpful insights into specific obstacles or advantages you might encounter.

Participating in Job Observations and Shadowing Experiences

Job observations and shadowing experiences are different from informational interviews in critical ways. Both involve a larger time commitment—from you and from your contact person—and both provide a direct encounter with the job as it's performed on a daily basis. A job observation experience involves watching someone in your target career field perform a typical series of tasks. For example, you may observe a lawyer present a case in court or ride along with police officers or firefighters to see them in action. The observation session can last a couple of hours or an entire work day. Traditionally, you're there solely to observe and ask questions (when it's not disruptive).

A shadowing experience, on the other hand, may extend over a period of time—from several days to a week or more. When you shadow someone in a particular job, you follow them throughout every event of their day. You have the chance to see how they plan their day in the morning and how they lead a problem-solving meeting in the afternoon. You may be invited to assist with routine paperwork or listen to nonconfidential phone conversations.

In both situations, take extensive notes and be as unobtrusive as possible, unless you're specifically invited to contribute your thoughts and talents. At the end of your time together, request a debrief session, so you can ask about intriguing points or perplexing situations.

Observation and shadowing experiences are invaluable. They allow you to see real people performing real work in a field that interests you. Once you've had this type of exposure, you're much more likely to know whether or not you've chosen a career that genuinely suits you.

Making a Decision

If you've done your research it will be easy to make a career decision, right? For many of us, the answer is, "Wrong." You've read about jobs, talked with career counselors, interviewed professionals in targeted fields, completed computerized assessments, and still you're confused. Maturity and hands-on experience doesn't always help. Perhaps you're re-entering the workforce after time out for child-rearing or family illness. Perhaps you've worked for years in one career field, and you know it's time for a change. You may know what you want to move away *from*, but what do you move *toward*?

Resolving Indecision

This state is commonly known as "indecision," but realistically it's more complex than that. Perhaps the more information you collect and the more people you consult, the more confused you become. Perhaps you're afraid to make a decision because it seems so final. Or maybe you've developed a clear idea of what you *don't* want to do, but you're still uncertain about what you *do* want to do. Your apparent inability to decide may be the natural result of too much information, too little information, or an as-yet unrefined vision.

If what you're experiencing feels like information overload, the first step is to stop collecting information. Take time to gain control of what you already know. Find two boxes and set aside a chunk of time to sort all the notes, computer printouts, and articles you've collected. Put everything related to careers you've rejected in one box and everything related to careers you're still considering in the other.

Now make two lists. One list should summarize all the pros and cons of jobs you've rejected. The other should summarize all the pros and cons of jobs you're still interested in. Then ask yourself: What is it about certain jobs that really appeal to me? Are there other jobs that might offer these opportunities? That require similar skills? That provide similar satisfaction? Note any ideas or new careers that occur to you and set a deadline for completing additional research focused solely on these few careers.

If you can't reach a decision because you still lack quality information, the solution is simple. Implement a more intense career research effort and make an effort to use all of the available resources to full advantage.

If you find you can't reach a decision because your long-term vision is fuzzy or you're suffering from genuine indecision, take steps to correct this state. Sue Johnston, author of *The Career Adventure*, recommends these action steps:

1. Determine if outside forces (family, friends, employers) are restricting your options through influence, money, or suggestion.

2. Decide you will be "in the game" and will accept responsibility for your own decisions.

3. Reduce any pressures that are blocking a decision. Recognize that change is almost certain and that life is fluid not linear.

4. Accept that you can change your decision as often as you like.

5. Refocus your attention on immediate action:
   • What can you do today to move closer to a decision?
   • What can you do tomorrow and next week?

6. Refine your plan and work it:
   • Collect more information
   • Review information you have
   • Interview select professionals
   • Observe people in the workplace

7. Set a deadline for making a decision, then stick with it.

If you treat your career research as a valuable and interesting journey of discovery, eventually you'll uncover a career field or specific job that interests you. And, Johnston notes, while it's possible to follow all the rules, make all the right decisions, do all the "right" things, you can still go wrong.

The saving grace is that few career decisions are ever final. If you've made the wrong choice—you're in the wrong career, for example, or you're practicing the right career with the wrong company—make a change.

Making the Most of Career Exploration

Clearly, there are innumerable ways to learn more about the types of careers available today and exciting new careers for the future. The number one problem isn't lack of opportunity, it's the limited, superficial research we conduct as we struggle to make one of life's major decisions.

Take the time to look beyond the obvious. Use general resources, such as *The Big Book of Jobs* and the *DOT,* to learn more about jobs and careers in general. Then begin to focus your research and browse through books about specific industries and specific career fields. Before you select an academic major, read books that describe what you might do with a degree in that field. If you're a student, schedule time with your career counselor and take advantage of every assessment and career matching tool your college career center offers. If you're not a student, contact your local community college career service center or employment services office and do the same.

Be sure to talk to people and ask questions. When you meet people who work in areas you're curious about or who have careers you've never heard of, ask them to describe their work to you. Most people are delighted to share insider lore with an interested listener. If what they reveal piques your interest, arrange an informational interview or a tour of their work facilities.

It's Hard Work

"This is not the answer most people want to hear," says career planning specialist Suzanne Sayre, "but there's no magic bullet. Finding the right career match takes hard work and sheer diligence."

Most of us expend more time, energy, and money researching the cost, performance, and benefits of a car we hope to buy than we do researching the career choices that shape our lives. Do your homework and "test drive" at least three careers before you make a decision. You'll be glad you did.

Learning More About Career Exploration

Barron-Tieger, Barbara and Tieger, Paul. *Do What You Are: Discover the Perfect Career for You.* Boston, Mass.: Little, Brown & Company, Inc., 2001.

Bolles, Richard Nelson, *The Three Boxes of Life, and How to Get Out of Them*, Berkeley, Calif.: Ten Speed Press, 1978.

Bolles, Richard Nelson. *What Color is Your Parachute?* Berkeley, Calif.: Ten Speed Press, 2004.

Camenson, Blythe. *Careers for History Buffs & Others Who Learn from the Past.* Chicago, Ill.: VGM Career Books, a division of The McGraw-Hill Companies, 2002.

DeGalan, Julie and Stephen Lambert. *Great Jobs for Foreign Language Majors.* Chicago, Ill.: VGM Career Books, a division of The McGraw-Hill Companies, 2000.

DeGalan, Julie and Stephen Lambert. *Great Jobs for History Majors.* Chicago, Ill.: VGM Career Books, a division of The McGraw-Hill Companies, 2001.

DeGalan, Julie and Stephen Lambert. *Great Jobs for Psychology Majors.* Chicago, Ill.: VGM Career Books, a division of The McGraw-Hill Companies, 2000.

Green, Marianne Ehrlich. *Internship Success.* Chicago, Ill.: VGM Career Books, a division of The McGraw-Hill Companies, 1998.

Greenspon, Jaq. *Careers for Film Buffs & Other Hollywood Types.* Chicago, Ill.: VGM Career Books, a division of The McGraw-Hill Companies, 1993.

Schrank, Louise Welsh. *Choose the Right Career.* Chicago, Ill.: VGM Career Books, a division of The McGraw-Hill Companies, 1998.

CHAPTER 3
WRITING POLISHED COVER LETTERS

Thus far a variety of methods have been introduced for conducting self-assessments, exploring career fields, and finding a career that suits you. Now it's time to put this foundation to use and begin developing your cover letter and resume, two of the tools you'll use in your job search.

Many job hunting resources will tell you to skip cover letters and resumes and use other means for landing a job. These alternate strategies do work well for high-energy, assertive job seekers who are approaching employers who value these traits. Nonetheless, in most job searches there comes a time when you must use the classic combination—a cover letter and resume—to market your skills to a potential employer.

In this chapter you will learn the basic elements of an effective cover letter and how to identify the skills and qualities employers value in job applicants. Included is a real cover letter sample, plus some suggestions for making this letter even more persuasive. In addition, the criteria for producing a crisp, professional cover letter and strategies for solving some of the most common problems you might encounter as you work to develop your cover letter will be presented.

Creating Effective Cover Letters

The cover letter is exactly what it sounds like: it's the covering document (the page the recipient sees first) for the resume. A well-crafted cover letter and resume work together to present the best and most persuasive picture of your experience, education, capabilities, and unique talents. (See Chapter 4 for a discussion of resumes.)

Cover letters are very personal documents that provide a word-based snapshot of who we are, what we've done, what we know, and what we're capable of doing. This is why they're so difficult to write. It's a challenge to hit the right balance.

You want to appear confident but not arrogant. You want to present factual content without providing overwhelming detail. You want to be persuasive without being pushy. And you want to seem qualified, accomplished, and capable—without slipping into the realm of fiction writing.

Cover letters, like most business communications, are governed by ritual. Their purpose is to express your interest in a current or possible job opening and to provide the employer with an interesting, accurate summary of your skills and abilities. This summary must be carefully designed to leverage the impact of your resume and illustrate how and why you're a strong candidate for the job.

There are two general types of cover letters:

- *Basic* ones serve to introduce you and your capabilities to the person who makes the hiring decision.

- *Persuasive* ones are attention-grabbing and work to influence the hiring decision maker.

The focus will be on the key elements of a solid, polished cover letter, but you will also find techniques for balancing information and persuasion.

Hitting the Right Note

Adopt a moderately formal style and tone for your cover letters. You don't want to seem too familiar or casual in your choice of language. You want to address the recipient using an honorific (Ms., Mr., Dr., etc.), rather than by their first name. If you know the recipient personally, it's acceptable to use their first name if this is how you address them in person. Avoid nicknames and relationship terms, such as *uncle* or *aunt*.

While some consider it acceptable to use contractions in their communications, you may want to omit them if they feel too casual for your taste. If you're uncertain about acceptable business letter formats, study the sample letters included in this chapter. For more information, examine one of the many business letter writing books available. Use caution when using a word processing package with preset letter templates; some of these templates are more appropriate for personal or casual communications than for something as important as your cover letter.

Using the Basic Cover Letter Pattern

There are three main elements to the cover letter. We'll review each in detail, but the essential elements are:

1. The *opening*—Tell the employers why you're contacting them.

2. The *body*—Tell them how you're qualified and why you're the best candidate.

3. The *closing*—Tell them how and when you'll follow up, then exit on a positive note.

Your opening paragraph should specify the position you're applying for or state the reason you're contacting that organization. Why? If there's a job vacancy, don't they know why you're writing? The truthful answer is *Yes* and *No*.

While they do know a job opening exists, employers often recruit for more than one position at a time, and sometimes the various openings are similar in title and qualifications. If you're applying for the engineering supervisor position, you want to make sure that's the position they consider you for—not engineering technician or another similar position they currently have available.

Moreover, today's employers are always pressed for time. They will *not* expend the effort and energy to determine which position best suits your background. That's your job, and you should let them know you've done your homework. Cite the specific job title and state how you learned of the opening (a job posting at the company personnel office, newspaper classified ad, college placement office, the Senior Vice President of Operations suggested you apply, and so on).

Success Strategy

Don't ever start your cover letter by saying "I'm interested in any job available" or "Please consider me for whatever positions are open." These statements indicate you've not done your research to determine what positions they're currently trying to fill, and employers don't have the time to determine what you're qualified for.

Many organizations track which resources (word of mouth, job postings, newspapers) produce the best candidates, and some organizations give existing employees rewards for recommending a qualified candidate who's eventually hired. Providing this type of information can be valuable to the employer, and you'll be considered for the correct position.

Use the first sentence of the body of your letter to catch the employer's attention. Effective attention-grabbers typically describe experience, skills, education, and the personal qualities that employers value and that relate to the position you seek. They use action verbs (*built*, *offer*) and descriptive modifiers (*essential*, *excellent*, *successful*).

The opening statement sets the stage for presenting your credentials—that is the skills, abilities, and personal attributes that will help you be successful in the job you're applying for. If you're responding to a job advertisement, address each key point the employer has identified. Many employers spend substantial thought and energy in identifying exactly what they want in the ideal candidate. By responding to their stated needs, you are communicating that you understand and value their priorities, and you're illustrating how closely you match their ideal.

Use one of two strategies for organizing this information:

1. Present your qualifications in the same order they were cited in the advertisement.

or

2. Present your strongest qualifications first, your next-strongest second, and so on until you've addressed the critical areas requested.

Feel free to mirror the language used in the ad. If an employer is requesting someone with team leadership capabilities, it's both logical and effective to say: "I have five years' experience working as the team leader of our product design process."

Knowing What to Include

Employers expect applicants to make strong, clear, positive statements about themselves in both the cover letter and resume. They neither expect nor want you to lie, however, which is a balance that some job seekers don't seem to understand. Present the facts of your education, experience, and achievements in a favorable light, but never promise something you can't deliver or claim degrees or accomplishments you don't have.

The best way to hit this honest but positive balance is to think in terms of features and benefits. Features are the specifics you bring to the job: experience, education, training, awards, skills, abilities, and so on. Most job applicants focus solely on features, using the cover letter to present a boring recital of degrees and job titles. This approach rarely lands you the interview.

Focusing on the benefit entails emphasizing what your features mean to the employer. For example, if you have precisely the background the employer appears to be seeking, present this as a features/benefit statement: "I have the five years of hands-on experience you've identified as critical, which means

I'll be productive from the moment I begin working with you." The first half of this statement presents features (*experience, education*), while the second half emphasizes the payoff for the employer (*productive from the start*). The point is to close the gap between the skills and abilities you offer and what that means for the employer.

How do you know what employers value? The job ad, recruitment notice, or phone conversation you had with the employer will reveal much about the desired competencies, requirements, and expectations. Respond to stated requirements first, then elaborate on special abilities only *you* can offer. Study the list here, as well as those in chapters 2 and 4, and try to match your experiences with what employers value.

Don't use the cover letter to recap every point in your resume; instead, highlight the experience, skills, and education you've summarized there. The idea is to make your cover letter work in tandem with your resume, but it's in the cover letter that you have the widest latitude to market your abilities. Don't hesitate to quote a compliment, cite an award, or share concrete results that illustrate who you are and the work you're capable of delivering. Some examples might include:

What Employers Value

Very Important
- Overall personality
- Honesty and integrity
- Enthusiasm
- Critical thinking abilities
- Written and verbal communication skills
- Motivation
- Confidence
- Appearance
- Academic major (for specialized positions)
- Negotiating and influencing skills
- Potential to meet employer's needs
- Life experiences
- Quality of education

Sometimes Important
- Leadership activities
- Test results
- Extracurricular activities
- Grade point average
- Business attitudes
- Computer literacy

—Job Interviewing

Cover Letter Dos

- Think like the decision-makers.
- Answer logical questions, such as why you're interested in this particular opportunity and why you're the best choice.
- Cite real examples, concrete outcomes, notable accomplishments and complimentary remarks from supervisors, subordinates, clients, colleagues, teachers.
- Highlight the critical points included in your resume.
- Use clear, unequivocal language.
- Mirror the words the employer used to describe the position.
- Limit your cover letter to one page if possible (maximum length should never exceed one and a half pages).
- Refer to yourself in the first person *I* instead of *one* or, worse yet, by name ("Jones is the one to hire").

- Compliment: *My manager said no one else could have produced these quality results in such a short time frame.*
- Award: *This project won an award from the International Association of Engineers.*
- Result: *Due to changes I made in inventory control, our plant has reduced operating costs by $1 million a year, for a total savings of $7 million.*

Naturally, these examples won't fit your precise circumstances, but you can use them to model your own persuasive statements.

In theory, employers will decide to call you for an interview based on how well you match the stated job qualifications. Realistically, however, many job advertisements paint the picture of an ideal and perfect candidate. Real candidates, like you, bring a different but valuable mix of skills and experiences to the table. Hence, a strong, positive closing paragraph can tilt you into the "call in" category even if your qualifications are a less-than-perfect match. Construct an effective closing paragraph that includes a summary remark, follow-up information, and some statement of appreciation. Two examples of closing paragraphs are:

"I believe that my training and strong work ethic will allow me to make a significant contribution to your company. Please let me know if you would like more information about my qualifications. . . . I hope you will consider me for any appropriate position, and I look forward to hearing from you."   —*Slam Dunk Cover Letters*, 32.

"My resume (enclosed) provides a sketch of my background and experience. If you would like more details, please contact me. . . . Thank you very much for your consideration. I admire the outstanding image your galleries have developed, and I hope that I can become a part of your organization."   —*Slam Dunk Cover Letters*, 55.

I know several employers who use follow-up as a means of screening candidates, so if you state you'll call on a specific day, do so. Try to avoid Monday and Friday, as Monday tends to be a hectic, start-up day and Friday is when people scramble to wrap up the week's affairs.

Knowing What to Omit

There are many truthful statements that should *not* be included in a cover letter. Remember, the challenge of the cover letter is to think like the employer. Don't imply you'll accept any position available, because the employer will interpret this to mean you are desperate or lack direction. Don't state you can start work tomorrow or immediately, because the employer will translate this to mean you're unemployed or unprofessional enough to quit an existing job without the minimum expected two-weeks notice.

Don't include personal details, such as your recent divorce or the fact that you're filing for bankruptcy. Employers want vital, competent employees. Few will schedule interviews with people who are unprofessional enough to highlight their weaknesses, however temporary, in their cover letters.

Don't criticize your current or past employers, even if they were the worst employer imaginable. There's a great Boss Collective out there, so, in general, employers will choose not to hire someone who's openly critical of another employer and willing to put this criticism into writing. Also, be sure to avoid any phrase which could be read as a threat, such as "You'll regret it if you don't contact me today." What you're trying to convey is how valuable you can be to the organization. What the employer sees is someone who's too aggressive and volatile. Again, think like the employer: Would you interview or hire someone who sounds threatening?

Analyzing Sample Cover Letters

Since the best way to learn how to write a cover letter is to do it, some samples are provided that will show you how a cover letter is formatted and organized and what it should contain.

Cover Letter Don'ts

- Don't expect employers will intuitively know which job you're applying for.
- Don't assume employers will "read between the lines"—they won't.
- Don't lie about your education, experience, or achievements.
- Don't be chummy, cocky, or arrogant.
- Don't plead, beg, or share sob stories.
- Don't include threats or negative motivators.
- Don't repeat every detail you've included in your resume.

Look at the sample cover letter and examine its strengths and weaknesses. Then study the rewritten letter and note the differences. The first letter is strong, but the second version is even stronger and more persuasive. Now, write and rewrite your own cover letter until it's as strong as the second example.

Examining a Successful Cover Letter

This letter illustrates many of the elements we've identified as critical to a successful cover letter. In terms of the basic elements, Samuel Jackson, the applicant, has taken the time to identify a specific position with a particular company. He knows and uses the manager's name and title. He's produced his letter in a traditional, easy-to-read full block format. He has included his phone number and e-mail, so the human resources manager can easily contact him.

In terms of the content and structure of the letter, Jackson has followed the basic pattern: identified the position he's interested in, described his experience, and indicated a specific date for follow-up. He summarizes the amount of time he's worked as a civil engineer, and he quotes compliments he's received about his work.

Overall, this letter is generally effective. However, there are some obvious points he's omitted and areas where he could more clearly describe his experience, abilities, and future value to the company.

Jackson has neglected to date his letter, which is a sloppy oversight. He provides no concrete information that explains what he's learned or accomplished in three years as a civil engineer. He doesn't describe his technical capabilities, so it appears that he has three years' experience but few skills or accomplishments. And Jackson's letter contains five paragraphs, four of which consist of one lonely sentence each.

Typical Cover Letter

15468 Ash Street
San Antonio, Texas 96707
(123) 555-4379
sjackson@xxx.com

Jordan Debaji
Human Resources Manager
Debaji & Whitford Engineering Inc.
476 Ritt Avenue
San Antonio, Texas 89768

Dear Mr. Debaji: ✦

As you suggested during our telephone conversation on May 28, I am submitting my resume for the position of Junior Engineer. ✦
✦
With three years' experience as a civil engineer, I have developed a solid understanding of the business yet am eager to continue growing and expanding my knowledge of the industry. I have worked on a variety of projects and received compliments on my work habits and ethics, as well as my ability to interact with clients. ✦

I feel that not only would your company provide me with new and exciting challenges, but my experience, energy, and skills will be of benefit to you.
✦
I may be reached at (123) 555-4739 and will contact you on June 11 to answer any questions you may have. ✦

I look forward to hearing from you.

Sincerely,

Samuel Jackson

Strengths
+ Uses traditional block format
+ Includes phone number
+ Addressed to specific person
+ Verifies position and why contact is being made
+ Summarizes years of experience
+ Cites others' comments
+ Suggests benefit
+ Notes follow up on specific date

Weaknesses
− Missing a date
− Lacks examples
− Omits technical skills
− Lacks substance, examples
− Uses series of one-sentence paragraphs

Bottom Line
• Good start
• Add highlights of skills, accomplishments, projects

Examining the Rewritten Cover Letter

Here we take a look at a rewrite of Jackson's original letter. The purpose is to illustrate how a basic, solid letter can become more convincing when the missing details are provided.

In terms of basic elements, we've retained the original format, but we've dated the letter. We've also added additional information to identify both the features and benefits of Jackson's experience and education. Plus, we've restructured the cluster of sentences so the letter now contains four paragraphs, only one of which has a one-sentence structure.

In terms of content, we've provided examples of the type of work Jackson performed and described project outcomes to indicate his accomplishments. We've summarized his technical skills, then related these skills to the value he can bring to a new employer. As you can see, many of the changes are relatively simple ones. Nonetheless, they substantially improve the amount of information conveyed in the cover letter and serve to increase the letter's overall persuasive impact.

Solving Common Problems

Applying for a Position Without a Contact Name

If you are responding to a newspaper ad or if for any reason you cannot track down the name and position title of the person to whom you should address your cover letter and resume, please *don't* use the phrases "To Whom it May Concern," "Dear Sir," or "Dear Madam or Sir." The first approach implies you've produced a thousand cover letters without addresses or specific salutations and, hence, aren't particularly interested in the actual company that receives your letter. The second approach is rightly viewed as sexist and inappropriate, and the third is simply outdated.

When you cannot locate a person's name or you're responding to a blind ad in the newspaper, use a salutation like this:

- Dear Hiring Executive:

- Dear Human Resources Director:

- Dear Customer Service Manager:

Substituting a reasonable job or position title for a specific name is more professional and it avoids unintentional offense.

Eliminating Grammar and Spelling Problems

It's quite easy to send out a cover letter that contains a spelling or grammar error. Some uninitiated job seekers won't view this as a problem, but it is. Why? Your cover letter should illustrate your very best writing and communicating skills. If your best work contains errors, what is the quality of your everyday work like?

Many employers automatically bypass applicants whose cover letters or resumes contain errors. You can avoid making mistakes by taking the time to check your work carefully. If you've produced your letter on a word processor or computer, be sure to run a spellcheck. Then print out a hard copy and proofread it ruthlessly. Look up the correct spelling of any word that's not familiar. Next, have someone you know scrutinize your letter for errors in spelling, grammar, or flow of ideas. Be sure to select someone whose writing skills are strong or you'll only introduce new problems.

Use popular grammar-checking software programs with caution. I've found several instances where the grammar checking program suggests a change that is quite simply wrong. The quickest way to correct common grammar problems is to streamline and simplify. Break any long, complex sentences into two or three short sentences; you'll often solve knotty grammar problems at the same time.

Designing Professional Cover Letters

You've written, revised, and rewritten your cover letter. You've proofed it and had someone competent check it as well. Now you're ready to produce the final version you'll send with your resume.

It's time to be *strong*. While computers offer enormous layout possibilities, avoid the temptation to produce a flashy cover letter incorporating six different fonts in a variety of sizes and styles. Employers are practical people who've seen it all. You want to stand out for all the right reasons—not the wrong ones. Review the cover letter dos and don'ts, and be sure you haven't succumbed to the common pitfalls.

Using the KISS Approach

The more simple and direct your layout is, the more likely it will suit a wide variety of organizations that you might choose to contact. Because a simple straightforward format is easier to

Rewritten Cover Letter

15468 Ash Street
San Antonio, Texas 96707
(123) 555-4379
sjackson@xxx.com

June 1, 2004 ✔

Jordan Debaji
Human Resources Manager
Debaji & Whitford Engineering Inc.
476 Ritt Avenue
San Antonio, Texas 89768

Dear Mr. Debaji:

As you suggested during our telephone conversation on May 28, I am submitting my resume for the position of Junior Engineer.

With three years' experience as a civil engineer, I have developed a solid understanding of the business and have worked on a variety of projects. Recently, for example, I was the project assistant on the successful downtown street resurfacing effort, so I assisted in planning street closings and ✔ traffic control, managing work teams, and evaluating work quality. I prepared budget and design information for presentation to city council and was complimented on my ability to work ✔ well with the city engineering staff. In spite of an exceptionally rainy season, we completed this project on time and within budget. ✔

As a result of this and other projects summarized in my resume, I have sharpened my engineering skills and gained experience in project management, team leadership, and budget control. I ✔ feel that not only would your company provide me with new and exciting challenges, but my experience, energy, and skills will be of benefit to you.

I may be reached at (123) 555-4739 and will contact you on June 11 to answer any questions you may have. I look forward to hearing from you. ✔

Sincerely,

Samuel Jackson

Fixes
- Add letter date
- Provide work example
- Summarize technical skills
- Balance excitement with substance
- Consolidate one sentence paragraphs

Bottom Line
- Highlights skills, accomplishments, projects
- Result: this version is stronger and more persuasive

update and customize, you'll be more inclined to do this vital task when called for, rather than settle for what you used last time. In short, keep it simple and straightforward (KISS), and you'll produce a polished, professional cover letter that will help you get job interviews.

Keep in mind that many employers complain that the cover letters and resumes they receive have lots of flash but little substance. If you focus on presenting your skills in the clearest, most persuasive way, you can't go wrong. Review the sample cover letters and study one of the many books packed with cover letter examples to get fresh and effective ideas.

Cover Letter Basics

- Type or print on top-quality paper.
- Use crisp, black letter-quality print.
- Avoid dot-matrix print (some employers will not read dot-matrix submissions).
- Verify it's absolutely free from spelling, grammar, and punctuation errors.
- Use a simple, traditional business letter format (full block or modified block works well).
- Use an easy-to-read serif font, such as Times New Roman or CG Times.
- While font size varies, stick to the 10–12 pt. range.

Producing Your Cover Letter

Produce your cover letter and resume on good quality, matching paper stock. Your local copy center or office supply store will have a supply of "resume" paper you can choose from. Avoid paper printed with clouds, designs, or border patterns. It's difficult to read text superimposed on patterned paper (so employers won't), and the border patterns are too cute and too distracting.

One factor many applicants forget is that employers often make multiple copies of each resume and cover letter they receive, then circulate the copies to critical decision makers throughout the organization. Dark (such as medium gray), flecked, and patterned papers do not reproduce well.

Dark paper tones may reproduce as a solid gray or black, which will make the type unreadable. Speckled and flecked papers can be attractive, but when they're copied, the specks become black spots that look messy and interfere with the ap-

pearance of individual characters. Patterned paper can produce similar unprofessional results, because the copier will reproduce both the text you've typed and the shadows of the background pattern. The crisp, striking letter you mailed is reduced to a smudgy, unreadable document.

Before you buy reams of expensive paper, purchase a small sample package, print or type your letter on it, and then make copies to verify that the paper you've selected produces clean, crisp copies without flecks, specks, swirls, or a background color. Remember: keep it simple and straightforward (KISS).

Making Cover Letters Work

Cover letters can be powerful, persuasive tools if you take the time and effort to construct them properly. As we've seen, they must capture—and keep—employers' attention by presenting information they value. Cover letters should respond to the employers' identified job criteria and priorities, by connecting the facts and achievements detailed in your resume with the requirements of the job and company. The most effective cover letters are word-based snapshots that help employers picture you in the job they need to fill.

Cover letters can be challenging to write, and it's easy to miss the target. If you follow the guidelines outlined in this chapter and study the samples provided, you'll be able to avoid a real-life cover letter catastrophe and make your cover letters work for you.

Avoid Layout Problems

- Don't center all of the text. It's difficult to read and looks amateurish.
- Don't use more than one font in a cover letter.
- Don't use lots of bold, underlines, capitalization, and italics for emphasis.
- Don't write a letter in all capitals—ever.
- Don't use your existing employer's letterhead or stationery.
- Don't use clip art or flashy logos.

Cover Letter Catastrophes

Virtually every organization maintains a file of favorite resumes and cover letters. Contrary to what you might expect, these are the worst submissions, not the best. Some of the more memorable examples:

- Were written in pencil on paper torn from a spiral notebook—raggedy edges intact
- Were submitted on paper torn from a scratch pad
- Concluded with "you'll regret it if you don't hire me"
- Consisted of a 12-page cover letter and resume package replete with photos of the applicant and a horse
- Were submitted on purple, bright pink, or emergency yellow paper

In case you wondered, not one of these applicants was invited to an interview.

Learning More About Cover Letters

Rowh, Mark. *Slam-Dunk Cover Letters.* Chicago: VGM Career Books, a division of The McGraw-Hill Companies, 2004.

Yate, Martin. *Cover Letters that Knock 'em Dead.* Holbrook, Mass.: Adams Media Corparation, 2002.

Yate, Martin. *Knock 'em Dead 2004.* Holbrook, Mass.: Adams Media Corporation, 2004.

CHAPTER 4
CREATING PROFESSIONAL RESUMES

The purpose of a resume is to provide a potential employer with a concise summary of your education, experience, accomplishments, and abilities—but a resume alone won't land you a job. The true goal of the resume and cover letter combination is to gain an interview. How you perform in the interview and how your credentials stack up against other job contenders will determine whether or not you receive a job offer.

Developing a powerful resume is important, for the simple reason that employers are swamped by them. Before you can gain an interview, you must take the time and energy to develop a custom, polished resume tailored to showcase your talents. You must provide sufficient information to make it clear you're a desirable candidate without providing so much information your resume becomes lengthy, cumbersome, or confusing.

Since every decision maker is also an individual, there's no surefire style or content that will ensure you'll land an interview. For that reason, most job seekers find that it's valuable to have more than one resume stashed in their file and ready to send. For example, a simple chronological resume is handy when you're applying for a position directly related to what you've studied or to work you've performed for the past few years. A functional resume is useful when you're seeking a job in a different work environment (e.g., changing from the public sector to the private sector) or when you're changing career fields.

In this chapter, we've provided simple worksheets to help you compile your qualifications in preparation for developing a resume. We've described the basic elements of a professional resume and illustrated the three most common resume types. Plus, we've summarized dos and don'ts and shared strategies for solving the most common problems.

Assembling a Professional Qualifications File

One of your first steps will be to locate information about your education, background, accomplishments, training, professional certifications, memberships, awards, and references and put them in one place. Invest in an expanding file and start to assemble your professional qualifications file today. Buy one with lots of room to grow; as the years pass you will be adding to your file to keep it current.

Label each section according to the type of information you'll need to build your resume. The categories and types of information needed will typically include:

- Work Experience—Job descriptions, letters of acceptance and resignation, performance reviews, and samples of work

- Education—Degrees, diplomas, notes about dates attended; certified copies of transcripts and grade reports

- Training—Copies of certificates of completion for on-the-job training or notes about training received

- Honors—Honors, awards, and special recognition received at work or school

- Activities—Notes about personal and professional activities, such as volunteer activities

- Certificates and Licenses—Professional licenses, certificates, and notes about criteria for attaining certification or a license

- Professional Memberships—Records of professional associations, membership duration, and criteria

- Special Skills—Records of special projects completed and skills honed through self-directed learning or acquired through hobbies

- References—Copies of letters of reference from employers and teachers; lists of names, titles, addresses, and phone numbers of professional colleagues and personal contacts willing to provide a reference for you

Even if you don't need all of these categories right now, build a "home" for them in your qualifications file. As your career evolves and time passes, you'll have a convenient place to retain important information about your professional development. In addition to the categories above, keep copies of old resumes and cover letters. This gives you a starting point and a way to refresh your memory if you're revamping a resume after some time has passed.

The following pages include simple worksheets to help you extract key points from your files and compile them in a form that will be easy to use in developing your resume. Many people try to skip this interim compilation process, and their resume usually suffers as a result. They forget key facts and those major achievements or items that could help distinguish them from other applicants. It's important to take the time to build your resume one step at a time.

Capturing Your Work Experience

Your goal is to find a new job, so your work experience or the equivalent is the most important information to collect and summarize. Use the worksheet provided to record the critical details of your past employment. Be very accurate in the details you note. Include all of the information you can find (or remember) about each job. Focus on primary duties and responsibilities and be sure to capture those that relate most closely to your immediate career goal.

Feel free to include more information and detail about your most recent jobs and to reduce the amount of detail related to jobs that occurred early in your career. If you have relatively little job experience, list all the jobs you've held, including internships, co-op positions, and part-time or summer employment. Employers value employees who know how to work, so even unrelated job experience is more valuable than none at all.

In your actual resume, you'll list your work experience in reverse chronological order. As you fill out the worksheets, start with your most recent position as Job 1, your next most recent as Job 2, and so on.

Capturing Your Education

Education is the second most important feature of your resume. Many employers use education and employment as the primary factors for deciding whom to hire. Be sure to note details about degrees and certificates you received, major areas of concentration, and honors and achievements. If you participated in any special projects or programs, include those details with Honors and Awards.

Education • Degree 1
School
Major/ Concentration
Degree
Dates

Education • Degree 2
School
Major/ Concentration
Degree
Dates

Work Experience • Job 1

Job Title

Dates

Employer

Address

Major duties

Special Projects

Achievements

Rewards

Compliments

Work Experience • Job 2

Job Title

Dates

Employer

Address

Major duties

Special Projects

Achievements

Rewards

Compliments

Capturing Your Honors and Awards

During the course of your work experience and education, you may have received some type of award or recognition for your contributions or accomplishments. Identify your membership in honorary societies, achievements in sports or academic areas, and participation in special programs that carry prestige.

Honors • Awards
Honor
Organization
Dates
Honor
Organization
Dates

Capturing Your Activities

If you have been or still are active in social organizations, clubs, or community service organizations, this is a good place to note these activities. If you've worked as a volunteer or participated in a one-time volunteer event, these items should also be included. Activities that illustrate leadership and a commitment to community welfare might include serving as a troop leader, working in your local school system as a mentor for troubled teenagers, or organizing a community drive to assist a neighbor whose home was destroyed by fire.

Activities
Organization
Activities
Accomplishments
Organization
Activities
Accomplishments

Capturing Your Certificates and Licenses

Even if the career or position you want to apply for doesn't require special licensing, it's smart to include this type of information. Most certification and licensing procedures require some form of specialized study and training, which may conclude with a test or examination. Be sure you verify the exact dates and names of the licensing agencies.

Certificates • Licenses

Name of License
Licensing Agency
Date Issued
Name of License
Licensing Agency
Date Issued

Capturing Your Professional Memberships

Use this section to record your involvement in professional associations, trade organizations, and similar groups. Include any special projects or leadership roles you occupied in the organization and cite specific outcomes if they are relevant. If you were the Program Chair and your new approach to program content increased participation by 20 percent, this is an impressive accomplishment to add to your resume.

Membership in a professional association directly related to your career objective is always an advantage. If you've let a professional membership lapse, it may be worth your time and money to renew it now.

Professional Memberships

Organization
Offices Held
Dates
Activities
Accomplishments
Organization
Offices Held
Dates
Activities
Accomplishments

Building a Basic Resume

Certain elements of your resume are nonnegotiable. That is, if you ignore or omit them you send a clear message to potential employers that you don't understand their decision-making process. Other elements are more flexible, which allows you to tailor your content to suit the employer and your own style.

Resumes consist of a variety of category labels—experience, education, accomplishments, and so on—accompanied by brief descriptions. Resumes are one of the few formal writing examples where sentence fragments and tickler phrases are not only acceptable but desirable. The style should emphasize short, punchy statements, facts and figures, and examples. Action verbs produce the best resumes, and it's completely possible to write an effective, direct resume without ever using the word *I*.

Knowing What to Include

There are four essential elements that must be included in any professional resume. These are the *heading*, *work experience*, *education*, and a note about *references*.

The heading is placed at the top of your resume and should contain your full name, your complete home address, and a telephone number (including the area code). If you're employed, don't include your current office number unless you are 100 percent certain that receiving phone calls from possible employers will not affect your employment situation. If you do not have a phone number or are relocating and your phone number will be changing, include a contact number where the employer can leave a message for you. Pick someone who will take messages in a professional manner and pass them on to you.

Essential Versus Optional Elements

Essential	Optional
• Name	• Job Objective
• Address	• Honors
• Phone Number	• Special Skills
• Work Experience	• Professional Memberships
• Education	• Activities
• Note about References	• Certificates and Licenses

Whichever resume pattern you select, you'll need to include work experience in some fashion. To help you organize this information, summarize your current or last job, your job title, the organization's name, the year you started, and a list of tasks performed, projects completed, and results accomplished. Develop this same type of information for every job you've held. Use the worksheets provided or create your own. Match your summary of experience and qualifications against the list of skills and qualities employers value provided here. (Refer also to the lists in Chapters 2 and 3.) This will help you emphasize the most important points.

Skills and Qualities Employers Value

Basic Skills
- Reading
- Writing
- Mathematics
- Listening
- Speaking

Thinking Skills
- Creative thinking
- Decision making
- Problem solving
- Seeing things in the mind's eye
- Knowing how to learn
- Reasoning

Personal Qualities
- Responsible
- Has self-esteem
- Sociable
- Self-managing
- Demonstrates honesty/integrity

Adapted from US Department of Labor *SCANS* Report, 1991

Detail the education you've received, keeping in mind that no employer wants to read a list of every class you've taken or every training program you've attended. Work to capture the highlights of your education, emphasizing those factors most closely related to your targeted job.

It's important to include a note that indicates you have professional, personal, or educational references to offer. Employers may want to speak with someone who has worked with you or who knows your capabilities. Don't list full contact names and phone numbers; just note that references are available. The sample resumes illustrate how to handle this.

Knowing What to Omit

If you ask 10 people what to leave out of a resume, you'll probably receive 20 different answers. Some items or information should never appear on your resume. These items include:

- Personal data, such as age, race, religion, martial status, non-related physical limitations, or sexual orientation

- Detailed lists of employment or character references

- Photographs

- Philosophical revelations or political statements

Some details are more difficult to determine. Among the items you might consider omitting are:

- High school education if you've received an associates or bachelor's degree

- High school activities if you've been out of school for 10 years

- Extensive details of hobbies or personal interests

- Part-time or summer jobs held during high school and college if you've been out of school for several years

Leaving out information about recent jobs can be problematic, particularly if your employment was terminated by the employer. A potential employer who learns of such an omission may believe you're hiding important information about your work record. When deciding what to omit, use sound judgment.

Using Active Descriptions

Professional recruiters and experienced hiring decision makers may spend as little as 20 to 90 seconds reviewing your cover letter and resume before they make the decision to call you in for an interview—or move to the next candidate's package.

In order to get an interview, you must construct and deliver a cover letter and resume that are focused, well-structured, short, and to the point. You'll want to highlight critical pieces of information in your resume (using bold lettering, bullets, or italics) to identify major sections and call the reader's attention to the most important content.

Action verbs and direct sentence structure are pivotal to success. Action words indicate movement, accomplishment, and initiative. Notice the difference between the two phrases that follows:

- Was responsible for administering budget programs and monitoring profit/loss ratio.

versus

- Managed budget to improve profit/loss ratio.

The first phrase is sadly typical of many resumes. It implies responsibility, but shows little action and does not focus on purpose or results. In the second phrase, the writer clearly supervises the budgeting process and is directly involved in improving profit/loss ratios. The change is a simple one, but the end result is a dramatically more readable, powerful, and persuasive resume. Adopting this approach has many benefits. It will increase your chances of being called in for an interview, it will reduce the number of words you use to describe your work and accomplishments, and it will speak to the employer who's seeking an action-oriented employee.

Study the list of action words and take a moment to examine the sample resumes in this chapter. Then strive to see how many dull phrases you can eliminate by using these words.

Active Words		
administered	dissected	planned
advised	documented	prepared
analyzed	edited	presented
arranged	executed	produced
assembled	expanded	programmed
billed	gathered	published
built	handled	purchased
channeled	hired	recommended
collected	implemented	recorded
communicated	improved	reduced
compiled	increased	represented
completed	inspected	researched
conducted	introduced	reviewed
coordinated	invented	saved
counseled	investigated	screened
created	maintained	sold
cut	managed	suggested
decided	motivated	supervised
decreased	negotiated	taught
designed	operated	tested
developed	ordered	trained
directed	organized	typed
distributed	performed	wrote

Analyzing Sample Resumes

There are three widely accepted resume patterns: the *chronological*, the *functional*, and the *combination* resume. Each approach has advantages and disadvantages for presenting your unique experience and background information in the most effective manner.

As we've discussed, some elements of a resume are required, while others are optional. Four elements are common to all three resume structures, although the manner in which they are addressed differs greatly. These elements are:

- Heading—Provide your name, address, and phone number.
- Work Experience—Cite positions, dates, and company name in reverse chronological order, accompanied by brief descriptions of duties and accomplishments.
- Education—List degrees and institutions in reverse chronological order. Include a brief description of achievements related to each degree if appropriate.
- References—Note that references are available on request. Don't list reference contact names on your resume.

Examining a Chronological Resume

The chronological resume is just that—a recap of your experience based on time and sequence of events. This type of resume is most effective when your education and experience are closely related and your goal is to advance within the same career field. For example, if you have a degree in urban planning and hands-on experience as a city planner and your long-range goal is to become a director of urban planning, the chronological resume allows you to highlight your accomplishments and unwavering commitment to this field.

A classic chronological resume consists of these elements, usually presented in roughly this sequence:

- Heading—Provide your name, address, and phone number.
- Objective—State what position you're targeting and the value of what you can contribute.
- Work Experience—Cite positions, dates, and company name in reverse chronological order, accompanied by brief descriptions of duties and accomplishments.
- Education—List degrees and institutions in reverse chronological order. Include a brief description of achievements related to each degree if appropriate.
- Honors—List honors and commendations, plus appropriate details.
- Activities—Cite organizations and community and civic activities in reverse chronological order. Note accomplishments related to these activities.
- Certificates and Licenses—List certificates and licenses. Cite first those that are still in effect.
- Professional Memberships—Identify professional memberships, placing the most relevant ones first. Note accomplishments, leadership positions, and so on.
- Special Skills—Summarize any special skills relevant to your targeted career.
- References—Note that references are available on request. Don't list reference contact names on your resume.

Keep in mind that you probably won't need to use each category cited. Include the information that is accurate and honest for your individual history and omit any topic that doesn't apply.

Study the sample chronological resume on page 31. Don't feel compelled to copy this format, but do take note of the way information is presented. Take time to compare this resume with the other samples in this chapter and with other chronological resumes published in the many books available on resumes.

Examining a Functional Resume

The functional resume highlights specific activities in which you have education and experience, while it de-emphasizes your linear educational and work experience. Some typical business functions are finance, accounting, purchasing, operations, production, recruitment, wages and benefits management, labor relations, engineering, and research and design.

A functional resume, therefore, will emphasize skills and accomplishments in a few select functions and relate these to the desired career goal. Functional resumes are powerful tools when they're used properly. They allow you to consolidate and emphasize experience you've gained during your education, at work, as a volunteer, through hobbies, and more.

A typical functional resume would include the following categories:

- Heading—Provide your name, address, and phone number.
- Summary of Qualifications—State what position you're targeting and the value of what you can contribute.
- Accomplishments—Summarize skills, results, outcomes, recognition, dollars saved and/or increased profits organized by the appropriate function or skill area.
- Employment History—Cite positions, dates, and company name in reverse chronological order.
- Education—List degrees and institutions in reverse chronological order. Include a brief description of achievements related to each degree if appropriate.
- References—Note that references are available on request. Don't list reference contact names on your resume.

If you compare this list and the sample provided with the chronological or combination resume, you'll see the differences quite clearly.

Sample Chronological Resume

Charles Andawa

4783 West Maple • Baltimore, Maryland 21233 • 301-555-2983

Objective: A position in Chemical Engineering with an environmental engineering organization.

Experience:

1999–
present
Senior Project Manager, PPD, Inc., Baltimore, MD
Report to Senior Vice President of Engineering. Supervise 32 employees. Direct, supervise, administer, and manage several projects from inception to start-up, including new chemical process equipment manufacturing. Assist Sales Department in reviewing the system process design, scheduling, engineering, and costs before final proposal is presented to client.

Conceived, initiated, and developed chemical formations for non-toxic solutions for use in oil recovery and recycling. Formulated empirical equations and design criteria for the system, which resulted in increasing company sales seven-fold over the last five years.

Instituted procedures for project document handling, filing, and project communication, including project status summaries to management and clients.

Trained project engineers and project managers to design and manage projects.

Participated in developing service-system study concept to introduce PPD's name into new markets, which increased sales by 50% in that market.

1993–
1999
Senior Project and Process Engineer, Moreland Chemical, Annapolis, MD
Project experience included pulp liquor evaporation system operations, sand reclamation systems, waste wood utilization to manufacture charcoal, sewage sludge oxidation, waste oxidation, and heat recovery. Responsible for planning, scheduling, process design, and specifications.

Held complete process and project responsibility of four projects from proposal stage through plant start-up, including budgeting. Supervised 23 chemical and physical engineers and laboratory technicians.

1991–
1993
Process and Plant Engineer, Cecero's, Inc., Annapolis, MD
Major responsibilities included chemical plant trouble-shooting, process studies, process development, project cost estimation, equipment design, equipment sizing, selection and purchasing, utility optimization, air and water pollution controls, boiler and incinerator operations, and coordination of plant work with production department.

1988–
1991
Process Development Engineer, US Chemical Co., Philadelphia, PA
Worked on a solvent exchange and through-air drying of tissue paper. Operated the high speed pacer machine to test the through-air drying concept.

Education: B.S., M.S., Chemical Engineering, Minnesota Technical University, Houghton, MN, 1988

References available by request

Sample Functional Resume

Judith W. Swensen

4422 Kennet Avenue • Jubal, Tennessee 37232 • 615/555-4876

Summary of Qualifications

Experienced in providing comprehensive environmental assistance to mining operations and exploration projects. Maintains an awareness of all federal environmental regulations to assess compliance of subsidiary companies. Conducts detailed environment audits at mining and terminal locations.

Accomplishments

Solid Waste Disposal

As disposal methods analyst, charged with determining best possible disposal method at each subsidiary mine. Methods chosen are site-specific and depend upon depth to groundwater, percentage and types of heavy metals present in the coal ash, column leachate test results of coal ash alone and coal ash mixed with coarse coal refuse. Presently looking into utilization of coal ash for construction of concrete block stoppings and timbers for roof control in underground mines.

Mine Drainage Treatment

Since June 1993, I have been developing methods to economically and effectively treat Acid Mine Drainage (AMD) via the use of microbial troughs and anoxic drains. Thus far, the procedures have progressed rapidly toward successful conclusion and development.

Assisted subsidiaries with effective economical methods of controlling Acid Mine Drainage from coal refuse piles and ensuring reclamation success.

Conducted research with Tennessee State University to determine methods of refuse pre-treatment to eliminate future AMD and have successfully installed two systems.

Employment History

Senior Environmental Specialist, 2000 to present
Smoky Mountain Mining company, Memphis, Tennessee

Graduate Assistant/Lab Technician, 1997 to 2000
University of Tennessee, chemical Engineering Department

Education

University of Tennessee
Ph.D., Chemical Engineering, 2000
B.S., Chemistry and Physics, 1992

References provided on request

Examining a Combination Resume

The combination resume includes elements of both the functional and chronological resume. Its purpose is to respond in a very results-oriented way to the requirements of a specific job advertisement or a particular type of career opportunity. Of the three resume styles, the combination resume tends to be the most persuasive, since each element of the resume is structured to respond as closely as possible to the requirements of a specific position or field.

As a result, the combination resume might include an overview of one's experiences, highlighting skills related to the desired position or field, followed by a description of functional expertise and a quick recap of your job history. A typical functional resume would include the following categories:

- Heading—Provide your name, address, and phone number.
- Objective—Identify the position you're targeting and the value of what you can contribute.
- Professional Profile—Summarize career highlights, including skills, accomplishments, results achieved, and personal qualities.
- Employment History—Cite positions, dates, and company name and include a brief description of tasks and notable results. List in reverse chronological order.
- Education—List degrees and institutions in reverse chronological order. Include a brief description of achievements related to each degree if appropriate.
- References—Note that references are available on request. Don't list reference contact names on your resume.

Again, contrast the combination resume with the functional and chronological structures. Choose the type of resume that will allow you to showcase your abilities to best effect.

Solving Common Problems

As you develop your resume it's important to remember that few people have perfect work records. Perhaps you've lost your job due to layoffs or cutbacks; perhaps you left work to raise your children or return to school; perhaps you quit an unbearable situation or you were fired. All of these challenges can be handled gracefully, if you take the time to think through the best way to present the information.

Dealing with Gaps in Employment

In the past, a job applicant may well have been judged negatively for not having a perfectly stable, nonstop work history. Luckily, times have changed. Almost every employer today understands that perfectly competent people may lose their job because a company is sold, streamlined, or reorganized. If this is your situation, make it clear on your resume or in your cover letter that you're unemployed due to company cutbacks, then briefly explain the specifics. You might also want to take more time and space in your cover letter and resume to emphasize your special talents, qualifications, and accomplishments.

If you have major gaps in your employment, avoid using a chronological structure, as this will merely emphasize every "hole" in your employment history. Review the examples for combination and functional resumes and present your work history in one of these formats. This gives you two advantages. First, you highlight your skills, results, and accomplishments. Second, you downplay the amount of time you were out of the work force.

Overcoming Limited Experience

If you've never held a full-time, responsible position, it's easy to feel as if you'll never land a job. Whether you're a student graduating from high school or college or a full-time homemaker launching your first paid career, there's hope. The key is to make the most of the experience you *do* have and work even harder to develop a superb cover letter and resume package.

When you're developing your Professional Qualifications File, take time to list every activity, volunteer effort, unpaid work experience, and club or organization you've been involved with. Search for ways to define the results and outcomes you accomplished in these unpaid capacities.

For example, perhaps you organized a community coalition to persuade the city council to restructure the zoning regulations governing your neighborhood. This is valuable experience, which you should examine carefully for job-related skills and abilities. Ask yourself:

- What did I learn?
- How did I keep people motivated?
- How did I coordinate activities and responsibilities?
- Did I learn to delegate tasks to qualified individuals?
- Did I acquire the ability to read and understand complex zoning codes?
- Did I gain media exposure through the newspapers or TV?

Sample Combination Resume

Eleanor Wiler

6749 Deer Bluff Drive • Huber Heights, Ohio 45424 • 513/555-8259

Objective: Senior Pricing Analyst position that requires proven skills in cost reduction and profit protection

Profile:
- Increased divisional profits by $14 million
- Saved $7.6 million in 1 year by reducing expenses 20%
- Over 7 years, saved $1 million per year by revamping operational costs
- Created stockroom cycle count program that reduced costs by 50%
- Designed database that reconciled $17 million out-of-balance account and eliminated future out-of-balance accounts

Experience: **Senior Pricing Analyst,** NCR Corporation (2000 to present)
Analyze sales bids to determine competitive pricing and profit margin. Summarize analysis and recommend "go/no go" action to Executive Vice President of Sales. Accomplishments include:
- Created contribution margin models which accurately predicted break-even & profit points, making division profitable for first time in several years
- Model produced $14 million increase in profits (2% on $700 million total)

Senior Analyst, AT&T Corporation, Global Information Systems (1995–2000)
In various positions prepared annual budgets and expense forecasts for $32 million division, prepared bid pricing and gross margin analyses, developed profitability models for market program evaluation, and supervised administrative personnel. Accomplishments included:

- Cut $7.6 million from annual budget
- Eliminated $1 million in sales training expenses

Plant, Inventory & Revenue Analyst, NCR Corporation (1992–1995)
In various positions developed stockroom cycle count program, organized and executed physical inventories, reconciled inventory and invoicing detail. Accomplishments included:
- Implemented alternate-year physical inventory program, which slashed costs by 50%
- Developed analysis model which reconciled $17 million imbalance for in-transit accounts

Internships
Advanced Drainage Systems, Inc., 1991–1992
IBM Corporation, 1991

Education: **Masters in Business Administration**
University of Dayton, Dayton, Ohio
Anticipate completion in 2002

B.S., Business Administration
The Ohio State University, Columbus, Ohio
Graduated Cum Laude (3.65) in 1992
Majors: Finance and Economics

Excellent references available on request

- Did I save the city and citizens money?

- Did I receive any compliments, awards, or commendations?

These and similar questions will help you identify valuable experience that parallels the skills, abilities, and personal qualities today's employers are seeking. Homemakers, in many instances, are masters of many functions, ranging from budget planning and money management to nutrition and medical emergency skills.

If you're having difficulty identifying what makes you marketable to potential employers, sit down with a friend or academic advisor and ask for their insights. Often others can see the valuable skills, abilities, knowledge, and personal qualities that we overlook or take for granted.

Designing Professional Resumes

Those who make hiring decisions have their own personal preferences, so there's no way to know exactly what strategies they love best. Since many employers spend only 20 to 90 *seconds* reviewing a resume before they make their decision to contact or not contact you for an interview, the physical appearance and design of your resume package take on great importance.

Using the KISS Approach

Adopt some basic ground rules for effective resumes and they'll serve you well. Remember that white space isn't a nicety; it's essential for readability as well as visual appeal. Keep your resumes and cover letters simple and straightforward (KISS). Eliminate visual clutter and fussy details, because they only distract the reader and obscure the important points you're trying to convey.

Be sure not to sacrifice the quality of your content for the sake of a pretty layout. Follow these basic rules to produce a clean, readable resume:

1. Provide healthy margins at the top, bottom, and sides; usually 1" to 1½" is perfect.

2. Leave space between major sections.

3. Limit your selection of fonts and type styles to one or two and stick with them throughout your resume.

4. Use bold or all capital letters to highlight section headings.

5. Use the same type and treatments for the similar items. For example, if you emphasize the heading **Employment** with bold print, don't switch to italics for a similar heading, *Education*.

6. Use the same sequence or structure for similar items. For example, if you put your degree, university, description,

and year attained in the education section, list employment in a parallel sequence of job title, company, description, and employment dates.

7. Limit your resume to one or two pages. Stick to one page if you have only one degree or a few years' experience. Two are acceptable when you have the substantive work experience to justify it.

8. Use a combination of bulleted lists and small descriptive paragraphs. This is one time sentence fragments are acceptable.

Most employers emphasize content over flashy layouts. Your goal is to produce a clear, crisp presentation of experience and qualifications. Your layout should assist you in this goal, but it should not become a goal in and of itself.

To find a resume layout that suits you, study the examples we've provided and emulate the features that you like. Browse through books on resume writing and find a layout that appeals to you and allows you to showcase your experience to best effect. Show your resume to people who can share *informed* opinions and advice. Friends and relatives who work in business or a career services counselor at your local college are good options.

Success Strategy

Avoid the resume templates provided in standard word processing packages. Over the course of a week or two, employers may receive many resumes presented in the same layout you chose. How can you convince an employer you're the best candidate when you look just like a hundred others? Take the time to develop a resume model that works for *you*.

Submitting Electronic Applications

Some employers encourage applicants to submit their resume or their resume and cover letter electronically. The advantages to this strategy are obvious. It's fast and easy for the employer. Sometimes it's also fast and easy for the applicant, although not all of us have ready access to fax machines and e-mail capabilities.

If you intend to submit your resume by fax, it's doubly important to pay attention to your layout. Fax machines distort the image as it's transmitted and very small print can become unreadable. Also, some machines will not handle graphic elements, such as special text treatments.

The best way to determine if your resume will be readable at the receiving end is to test it. Fax it to a friend or pay to have it faxed from one location to another. (There are many copy and mailbox stores that will fax material, based on a standard rate per page.) Examine the printout for readability and determine if the format you used remains pleasing, then modify the font size and layout as necessary.

When submitting your resume electronically, either by posting it on the Internet or sending it via e-mail, be sure to ascertain what format is acceptable. If your resume must be in ASCII format, you will need to make some modifications to your existing resume's format. Page layout characteristics such as centering, tabs, and bullets cannot be used; neither can font attributes such as boldface or italics. The only way to make headings or other important information stand out is through the use of all caps. The easiest way to remove formatting from your existing resume is to save it (under a different name) as a text-only file. Once you've done this, you can modify the layout of your resume (keeping the above restrictions in mind) to make it more appealing and readable. If you are able to e-mail your resume as an attachment, you may not need to make any changes to its format.

If you submit an electronic (fax or e-mail) version of your resume, you might also want to drop a printed copy in the mail along with a copy of your cover letter. This ensures that the employer receives a crisp, readable version of your resume and your cover letter.

Making Resumes Work

Effective, professional resumes achieve a balance of brevity and detail. If typical employers spend only a minute or so reviewing your resume, they must be able to quickly identify the key points you want them to read and understand. Special text treatments, such as bold or italic category titles, will draw the employer's eye to the most important details. When you studied the samples we provided, you probably noticed they had very simple, straightforward layouts. This simplicity, coupled with a strong emphasis on results, is why these resumes have been so successful.

While you don't have to redo your resume each time you submit it, you should consider developing at least two versions of your resume and keep copies readily available. Then when you discover the perfect job opening, you will quickly be able to send the one that's most appropriate. This strategy allows you to focus your efforts on constructing a powerful cover letter that highlights your resume and is geared specifically to that position.

Learning More About Resumes

Bloch, Deborah P. *How to Write a Winning Resume*, fourth edition. Chicago, Ill.: VGM Career Books, a division of The McGraw-Hill Companies, 1999.

Yate, Martin. *Knock 'em Dead 2004*. Holbrook, Mass.: Adams Media Corporation, 2004.

Yate, Martin. *Resumes that Knock 'em Dead*. Holbrook, Mass.: Adams Media Corporation, 2004.

CHAPTER 5
HUNTING FOR THE RIGHT JOB

A recent U.S. Department of Labor study involving 10.4 million men and women who found jobs revealed some interesting facts. When all categories (except farm workers) are examined—from professionals and administrators to construction workers and mechanics—nearly two-thirds found their jobs through some form of networking. The next most successful approach was responding to job advertisements and recruitment announcements.

Job Search Strategies

Percent of Jobs Found	Source Used
63.4%	Networking
13.9%	Advertisements
12.2%	Employment agencies
10.5%	Other sources

—Job Search Networking

These statistics send a clear message to today's job seekers. To be successful, your job search strategy must link time-tested traditional tools, like responding to job ads, with progressive techniques such as networking and electronic job application. The challenge is to use each of these techniques professionally and effectively.

This chapter describes how to combine various job-hunting strategies in a manner that's effective for you. We'll review methods for finding job leads and organizing your search and explore practical tips for using networking to enhance your job hunt.

Finding Job Leads

Everyone knows someone or has heard of someone who sent 100 resumes to 100 employers and never heard from any of them. Why not? The answer is simple. Randomly bombarding employers with resumes through the mail is roughly as effective as dropping resumes from an airplane—and hoping somehow this will get you a job.

It's far more effective to send fewer resumes to targeted employers. One way to identify these employers is through industry specific directories and registers. Today, there are also many commercial books that describe the top 100 companies, employers by industry, employers by city, state, or region, and more. The level of detail varies widely, so it is well worth the time to browse through several. Some directories list employers, their products and services, and the skills they seek in employees. Others provide extensive data on profits and product mixes and identify key officers within the company. (See Chapter 2 for a list of suggested directories.)

Succeeding in Your Hunt

For most of us, job hunting isn't our favorite activity. It's demanding work, and sometimes when we're in the midst of it every day seems to bring a new opportunity for rejection or discouragement. As a veteran of career planning and placement, Del Vaughan has seen many people succeed—and many others fail—in the job hunting process. Vaughan finds that the factors that distinguish those who succeed are simple but powerful. Those who succeed are more likely to:

1. Treat every day of their job hunt as if it were their job.

2. Make everyone they know aware that they're looking for a job.

3. Research companies and study the job market, so they understand who they want to work for and why.

4. Take the time to target a specific career field and know clearly the type of job they're hunting for.

5. Have a clear plan of action for doing the job once they find it.

Quite simply, those who succeed are the ones who embrace the challenges of the job hunt as a necessary step in their path to success. They avoid dejection when rejection occurs by recognizing that it's part of the natural marketing process. They develop substantial quantities of leads in order to locate the best opportunities available. In *Job Interviewing for College Students*, John D. Shingleton describes the following approach as a proven marketing method. He recommends that you generate 100 leads for every two job offers you hope to elicit.

The Job Lead Process

Develop 100 leads
To generate 25 possible employers
Producing 15 definite prospects
Resulting in 10 interviews
Yielding 2 offers

1 Job Accepted

Pursuing Traditional Job Leads

In order to have job leads to pursue, you first must find them. It's at this stage of the process that many job seekers begin to unravel. How do you identify job leads? How do you identify employers who are hiring and learn what they are seeking in an employee?

Again, you must do your legwork and explore every possible resource. Some opportunities you'll eliminate, because the employer needs someone with qualifications vastly different from yours. Others you'll eliminate because the job doesn't interest you or the hours or the commute are unappealing.

The key is to identify and pursue *leads*, not jobs. Every month (barring a major economic depression), there are between two and three million jobs vacant in the United States. When you place your job hunt into this framework, generating 100 leads (for every two offers you hope to receive) sounds relatively manageable.

Job Opening Advertisements

Job openings are published in a variety of places and in a variety of ways. Advertisements appear in your local newspaper, but they also appear in a variety of other publications. *The New York Times*, *The Wall Street Journal*, and *The National Business Employment Weekly* are just a few of the national newspapers that include job advertisements from companies all over the country and from around the world. But don't overlook your own local newspaper. Most papers publish a special employ-

ment edition one day a week, in addition to the Sunday advertisements. In some cities the employment edition contains even more job announcements than the Sunday version.

Trade association and professional journals typically include job opportunities sections, and with these you have the added benefit that most of these jobs are related to the specific field the journal represents. Some employers won't place ads in the newspaper, but they will recruit through their trade publication.

Job advertisements or recruitment notices are also posted in many locations around your community. Many employers who place ads in newspapers and journals also issue job opening announcements to organizations such as:

- The chamber of commerce
- State employment bureaus
- Local government offices
- Federal government offices
- Job placement offices in two- and four-year colleges
- Agencies and organizations devoted to women and minority affairs
- Professional associations related to their industry or specialty

Companies typically post openings near their own personnel offices, as well as at other key locations in the organization. If you're employed at a company, you may learn of new opportunities available at other company locations or in different departments. If you're not employed, contact targeted companies to find out how you can review their job openings. Some keep a notebook of all current openings at the front desk, just so job seekers like you can browse through it.

Directories of Companies and Professions

Check your local or college library or community college placement office, which frequently contain many business and career opportunity directories. Some directories identify companies that hire people with specific skills or recruit people for specialized training programs, such as entry-level management or executive training programs. Others provide general descriptions of the company's products, services, profits, and total number of employees—along with officers' names and contact addresses. (See Chapter 2.) Directories are a useful way to identify companies you hadn't thought of contacting. Moreover, they can help remind you of all the job opportunities there are out in the world.

Public and Private Employment Agencies

Don't overlook your local public employment agency, which is likely to have listings of job openings. In recent years, the type of jobs listed with these agencies has expanded to include more technical, specialist, medical, and professional fields. If nothing else, the public agency is another place to access local employer information and elicit contact names and addresses.

Private employment agencies are a little different. First, the agency must get paid in order to stay in business. Essentially, there are two ways technical, professional, and managerial search firms get paid:

- You pay them to find you a job.

or

- An employer pays them to find them a qualified employee.

If you're considering working with a private employment agency, check the agency's credentials carefully. You'll want to determine if it has a successful track record placing people like you with solid companies. You'll want to verify who pays for the search effort. And, while most search firms are honest and reputable, be certain you understand the full ramifications of any agreement before you sign it. The job-search underground continues to generate horror stories of costly search agreements that drain job seekers' budgets long before a viable job materializes.

College Placement and Alumni Offices

Most community and four-year colleges publicly post job openings received from local employers. While some announcements are targeted to the new graduate with little experience, others require more extensive experience and education. If you're a student or alumnus, all of the office's services will probably be available to you. These may include access to job announcements posted on bulletin boards, shared over phone lines and accessed through online searches.

Services for non-students can vary widely, but almost all community college placement offices will allow you to browse through their job postings and use their library resources. A few select community colleges are connected to state-wide online job networks, which are available for anyone to use. Openings throughout the state are posted online and instructions for submitting your application are provided.

If you're a college graduate and are seeking a new job, contact your alumni affairs office. Some employers share employment announcements with alumni offices in the hopes of attracting applications from alumni with experience.

Professional Associations

Virtually every trade or profession has some type of association. Joining an appropriate national association, even if there's no local or regional group, can have value. Most associations produce newsletters, which often include job openings directed specifically to the profession or career field. You'll also receive a membership directory that lists the names, companies, and contact numbers for people in your field. Attending association meetings is another good way to network both during and after the job hunt.

Job Fairs

In fields where there is great demand, such as computer science and electronic technology, promoters or employment agencies will sometimes hold a job fair. These fairs consist of displays, presentations, and (sometimes) on-the-spot interviews from a large number of employers needing people with particular skills. Martin Yate, the author of *Knock 'em Dead*, suggests that you find out how many exhibitors are expected, then take twice that number of resumes. Job fairs provide an intense opportunity for collecting information about companies, learning about job openings and salary ranges, and expanding your network.

Locating Job Opportunities Online

Because online technology is changing daily, we'll focus on the broad opportunities available for job seekers. In *What Color Is Your Parachute?* Richard Bolles suggests that online job searches sound desirable, but the benefits have yet to be proven.

Value of Online Strategies	
• Posting your resume	3%
• Finding technical openings, posted by employers	10%
• Finding nontechnical openings, posted by employers	1%
• Getting job-hunting or career counseling assistance	6%
• Finding company information useful in the job hunt	8%
• Making useful contacts	30%
Adapted from *What Color Is Your Parachute?*	

First, it's theoretically possible to conduct your entire job hunt online: you can research employers, identify job openings, and submit your resume. Many dedicated online job networks require little technological know-how to access and utilize them. Others, particularly the more specialized databases, promote jobs where computer skills are presumed to be an essential, basic requirement. You may well want to use online search strategies if they appeal to you or if you're in a computer-focused or technically driven career field.

A variety of employers post jobs online. The Federal Job Opportunities Board lists openings with the federal government and this list is updated nightly. A variety of online service providers have job ad databases, and because "space" limitations are moot, many employers will provide more detail than they might in a newspaper notice.

You can also post your resume online through a variety of services. Some are primarily databases designed to sort and classify individuals in particular fields or with specific skills. Other services encompass a broader range, such as professional or managerial positions. Electronic placement firms typically charge both employers and job seekers. Employers are charged to access the files or to receive a select list of candidates who meet the employer's criteria, and job seekers pay a fee to have their resume and qualifications entered into the database and shared with employers.

If you have the skill, you can design a Web page promoting your abilities and announcing your availability for the right job opportunity. To learn more about the pros and cons of online job searches, read one of the many books on this topic. *Guide to Internet Job Searching*, for example, provides detailed information on mining Internet resources for job leads.

Building a Job-Search Network

Networking is a job search and career advancement strategy that's widely touted but frequently misunderstood. We'll focus on the job search angle, but many of the suggestions on networking can continue to be applied after you've launched your career.

Networking is the process of informing family, friends, teachers, fellow students, colleagues, and acquaintances that you're looking for a job in a particular field or for a position that requires your particular skills. To pay off, your networking efforts must, by definition, define the type of job you are qualified for, seeking, or interested in finding. This means you must have some knowledge of your skills, interests, values, and abilities, and you must be able to communicate this message concisely to a variety of people. To make networking truly productive, you must work to expand your network to include people in the companies or professions you've targeted.

Developing a Networking Statement

It's not *who* you know, it's *what* you do about who you know. To network effectively, follow these basic steps. First, develop a concise description of the type of position you are interested in and qualified for. This statement should clearly identify your education and background, two or three of your greatest strengths, the type of job(s) you are interested in, and a few examples by job title. An effective networking statement might be:

> I have a degree in management and hands-on experience in the theater. I've been told I'm well-organized and exceptionally effective dealing with everyone from the backstage crew to the star performers in stage productions. I'm interested in a position as stage manager, theater or facilities manager, or perhaps a management position with a performing arts organization. (56 words)

Read the statement several times, then construct a similar "networking blurb" of your own. Continue to refine it until you can say it easily, clearly, and with the fewest number of words. Networking, like any advertising and marketing effort, means the message must be clear, concise, understandable, and memorable.

Why is this so important? You are the key to successful networking. If your statement or your attitude indicates that you're willing to consider anything, contacts will either not bring any openings to your attention, because they don't understand what you can do, or they'll faithfully inform you of every opening they hear about, no matter how remote the relationship to your job goals.

Developing a Plan

The second step in effective networking requires some planning. Sit down with a pad and pen and ask yourself these questions:

- Who do I know?
- What do they do?
- How can I contact them?

Generate this list as fast as you can, without taking time to assess how valuable each person's assistance might be. (Remember that, in theory, in today's instant connection environment, it takes only six or seven connections to reach anyone anywhere in the world.)

Once you've identified as many people as you can, go through your list of names and identify those people you believe can and will be most helpful to you. Your Aunt Susan, the bank vice president, might be a top priority contact, because you're her favorite niece and she'll work hard to help you make the right connections. Your management instructor might be a top priority contact, because she's on the board of the local arts council. Your drama coach might be another top priority contact, because he's directly connected with the theater and hears of openings before they're made public.

Go through your entire list of contact names and assign a *1, 2*, or *3* (or *A, B*, or *C*) to indicate top, second, and third tier contact priorities. As new people occur to you, add them to your list and assign a priority.

Implementing Your Plan

Obviously, it's most important to contact your top priority connections first. Because of who they are, or what they do, or how much they care for you, they're most likely to take your networking efforts seriously. You can contact them by letter, by phone, or face-to-face. Make your first contacts with people you can approach easily, so you can practice your statement and your strategy.

When you make your contacts, address these issues:

- Introduce yourself and explain why you're contacting them

- Identify any person or organization that forms a bond or connection (e.g., Dr. Johnson, my management professor, suggested I call you…")

- Share your networking statement

- Ask if they know of any openings in their organization or in other organizations for which you might be qualified

- Ask if you can send them a resume

- Ask if they know anyone else you should contact

Set a goal that for each networking contact you initiate you'll acquire at least one name and phone number of a new contact. In this way, you'll continue to build your web of connections until eventually you land a job.

Making It Work

If your identifiable network isn't as strong as you would like, there are some simple steps you can take to expand it. Join a professional association related to your career goal. Volunteer time in an organization for which you'd like to work. Join a committee, public action coalition, or board that relates to your career goal. Contact your alma mater and get a list of graduates who are currently employed in your desired field. Study your newspaper and attend a speech, presentation, or workshop related to your career objective. Learn to introduce yourself with a firm handshake, a steady gaze, and your networking blurb.

Do your homework. Read the daily papers for your city or the city where you hope to relocate. Re-read the section in this book on making the most of career resources. If you didn't take the time to conduct informational interviews, job observations, and shadowing experiences, do so now. It's an effective, goal-oriented way of networking.

As you begin to initiate contacts with people, commit to a professional, disciplined schedule of follow-up. If someone can't meet with you but spends time with you on the phone, drop a handwritten note in the mail thanking your contact for taking time from his or her busy schedule to help you. If someone provides a lead, place a phone call or drop a note to let him or her know what happened as a result of the lead. Follow-up calls and notes put your name in front of a networking contact one more time in a gracious way. Follow-up calls and notes provide a vehicle for including your resume, if you haven't shared it with them earlier. What's more, follow-up calls and notes show that you are a professional, disciplined person who has both skill *and* savvy. As a result, you may well be the person they choose to contact when an unexpected opening occurs in their own company.

It's important to be flexible and open to unexpected opportunities. P. J. Mattia landed her position as a production manager through her network. Here's what happened:

> I was to have lunch with the "friend of a friend" I had recently met. He called me to cancel our appointment because his video production manager had quit and he needed to find someone to fill the job. I said, "Hire me," and he did! (*Job Hunting* 51)

As you pursue your networking strategy, make sure your resume is current and share it with your contacts. Take it to networking meetings and lunches, informational interviews, and professional association meetings. If you make a contact over the phone, send a follow-up note and include your resume.

Networking only works if *you* do. When you've initiated a contact or handed your resume to someone, your network task isn't finished—it's just begun. Plan to do one thank-you contact and one follow-up contact with each person you directly encounter. Remember to ask everyone you contact for additional names and phone numbers or addresses, so your networking web will continue to grow and remain dynamic.

If you approach this endeavor as a fascinating learning opportunity, you'll manage your networking program with enthusiasm and eventual success. And when you *do* land a position, take the time to recontact everyone who helped you along the way. Let them know what position you've accepted and how they can reach you, and thank them one last time for their interest and effort on your behalf. This simple strategy can help solidify your newly expanded network, and if you ever need or want to contact them again in the future, you will have handled the relationship with grace and professional savvy.

- Follow-up is critical.
- Be flexible and open to unexpected opportunities.
- Develop a current resume and cover letter—and use them.
- Keep an up-to-date, accurate log of people, positions, companies, and contact information.
- Accept responsibility for making networking work for you.

Success Strategy

"Treat the job hunt like a job. If you do, you'll be organized, prepared and focused," says Del Vaughan, Director of Career Planning & Placement. "Getting a job *is* a job."

Pursuing Job Leads

Once you've identified job leads, you need to actively pursue those that hold the greatest appeal. Ideally, you'll tailor each cover letter to each job and each employer. Your cover letter should directly respond to the requirements you've uncovered through a job ad, networking contact, or another source. In addition, use your cover letter to highlight special skills, qualities, and achievements only you can offer. Review Chapter 3 to refresh your skills in writing cover letters.

Enclose your resume with your cover letter. At a minimum, your resume should showcase work experience, accomplishments, education, and training. Review Chapter 4 if you need to revamp your resume.

For decades, there has been a running debate about whether to staple or clip your cover letter to your resume. My personal preference is to staple them. When you're replying to an ad, it's likely the employer will receive many resumes and cover letters. Your items won't become separated by accident if they arrive stapled together. If you prefer paper clips, then use them instead.

It's wise to mail your cover letter and resume in a full-sized business envelope (9 × 12 inches). These critical pieces, which you've worked so hard to polish and perfect, will arrive flat and readable, rather than permanently creased. Also, when a stack of mail arrives, many people will open large envelopes first. Your resume and cover letter may receive just a bit more attention as a result.

Use every resource available to identify as many viable job leads as possible. Pursue the leads that interest you most, remembering that you may need to explore 50 to 100 leads to elicit one or two job offers. Build your network and use it to identify the hidden jobs many employers never advertise. Education and experience are essential, but we all know bright, talented people who just haven't made it. In the final analysis, persistence and self-responsibility are the qualities of the successful job hunter.

Learning More About Job Hunting

Bolles, Richard Nelson. *What Color Is Your Parachute?* Berkeley, Calif.: Ten Speed Press, 2004.

Marler, Patty and Mattia, Jan Bailey. *Job Hunting Made Easy.* Chicago, Ill.: VGM Career Books, a division of The McGraw-Hill Companies, 1996.

Riley, Margaret, Frances Roehm, and Steve Oserman. *Guide to Internet Job Searching, 2004–5.* Chicago, Ill.: Co-published by the Public Library Association and VGM Career Books, a division of The McGraw-Hill Companies, 2004.

Yate, Martin. *Knock 'em Dead 2004.* Holbrook, Mass.: Adams Media Corporation, 2004.

CHAPTER 6

MASTERING JOB INTERVIEWS

While a resume and cover letter are useful tools for seeking employment, realistically, they only get you in the door. The employment interview is the primary hire/no hire point in the job-seeking process. It's critical, therefore, to be as prepared as possible for the interview session and the questions you're likely to be asked.

As you developed your cover letter and resume, you had a chance to evaluate your own strengths and weaknesses. This type of review is an essential early step in preparing for the job interview process.

In this chapter, we'll discuss how to fully prepare for an interview, what to expect, and questions you might want to ask. We'll review how to handle difficult questions and what to wear to look and feel your most confident. We've also provided tips on talking about money issues, evaluating and accepting job offers, and wrapping up your job hunt once you've found the best job match.

Preparing for an Interview

Knowing What to Expect

Since every employer has a different hiring strategy, it's impossible to know exactly which questions and what approach they'll adopt. However, nearly half of a typical interview will focus on you and your education, experience, background, attitudes, and career objectives. There's no excuse to be unprepared for a job interview, because you already know the answers to at least half the questions.

As you study the list of typical questions, begin to prepare your responses. It's best to write the question, followed by your concise, honest reply. Do this until you've drafted a response to each question. Review your written answers and revise them to focus on the most important facts you want to bring to the interviewer's attention. As you practice drafting

---

Typical Questions Employers Ask

- Tell me about yourself.
- Why are you interested in this position?
- Why should we hire you?
- What are your strengths and weaknesses?
- Why did you choose to major in _____ ?
- What goals have you established for yourself?
- Have you ever used drugs?
- How did you like your last employer?
- Where do you expect to be in five or ten years?
- What do you know about our organization?
- What qualifications do you have that would make you particularly qualified for this job?
- How did you happen to apply for this job?
- Tell me about your experience (in school, in the armed services, on your internship, on your last job)?
- When are you available for employment?
- Have I missed anything?

—Job Interviewing

---

replies, work to connect experiences and examples from your resume to the job for which you're applying. Ideally, all your answers should focus on these objectives:

- Responding to the employer's question
- Revealing positive skills, knowledges, and abilities you're able to contribute
- Relating your experience to the specific job opening

Once you've drafted your replies, practice reading them aloud. This step will help you identify obvious omissions, extremely wordy responses, or situations where you've really not responded to the question. Reread the skills and qualities employers value in Chapters 2 and 3 to make sure your replies focus on the employers' needs, not your own.

You may need to read and edit your responses several times in order to develop the proper balance of concise detail. After you've prepared and practiced your interview responses, have a friend or relative ask you the questions in random order and practice responding to them again. Make notes and refine your replies based on your practice performance and the feedback you receive.

Savvy companies believe that hiring good people is one of the most important things they do, so their employment processes may be highly refined, sophisticated, and demanding. You may be asked to participate in several interviews, each with its own unique structure. The one-on-one interview is the classic approach, but group interviews and serial interviews are also common in both large and small companies. In addition to the number of people involved, there are different interviewing strategies, such as structured, situation, or stress interviews.

To avoid being surprised when you arrive at your destination, ask what type of interview process the organization will be using and how many interviewers will be involved. It's easy to ask these questions when the organization contacts you to schedule the interview. Knowing what type of interview you're facing will allow you to prepare more effectively and increase the chance that you'll perform well the day of the interview.

Kinds of Interviews

One-on-One Interview

This is the classic interview format. Typically, the interviewer is a personnel recruiter or the manager responsible for the vacant position.

Group Interview

Two or more people may team up to interview applicants. In some organizations, the personnel manager and the supervising manager will interview together. In other organizations, a variety of managers, staff, and search committee members may be involved.

Structured Interview

The structured interview follows a prescribed set of questions that are posed to every applicant interviewed. Theoretically, this allows a number of interviewers to screen quantities of candidates while still maintaining some means of comparing the quality of responses from one candidate to another.

Continued

Unstructured Interview

This approach is open-ended and allows for more give and take. It also allows more room for error, so if the interviewer hasn't asked about important points, be sure to bring them up yourself.

Situation Interview

Some employers prefer to pose problems rather than ask questions. Hence, after the preliminaries, the interview will describe problem situations and ask you to describe how you would handle them.

Stress Interview

Just as it sounds, stress interview questions are designed to assess your abilities under pressure. Take each question one at a time and stay calm.

Adapted from *Job Interviewing*

Identifying Questions to Ask

Since half the interview can be anticipated, what does the other half consist of? Typically, employers will ask their own favorite questions, and you'll have an opportunity to ask your own.

It's easy to assume that employers will ask the "right" questions because they're more experienced at this. The truth is, many employers don't ask the questions that allow you to showcase your best skills and abilities. This means that it is often up to you to bring these points out and to get clarification on any point that is puzzling you.

Make a list of any questions you want to discuss with the interviewer. Memorize this list or take it with you to refer to during the interview. The employer expects you to have questions about the job, the company, and your fit with the position. Review the following list of some of the more common questions applicants ask during job interviews and develop your own questions. You'll have concerns that are specific to you, the job, and the company.

Questions You Might Ask

- Who was the last person to hold this job, and what is he or she doing now?
- Who will be my immediate supervisor?

Continued

- What are the possibilities for promotion?
- What is the organizational structure and where does this position fit in?
- What is the extent of travel required on this job?
- What is the starting salary for this position?
- What is the current financial condition of the organization?
- Specifically, what will my duties be (if not already discussed)?
- Do you have a training program for this position? If so, please briefly explain the program?
- I'm interested in this position. When will I hear from you regarding further action on my application?

—Job Interviewing

Choosing What to Wear

In *The Career Adventure*, Susan Johnston points out there are many variables controlled by you, and one of these is your appearance. Most employers are interested in credible, competent professionals, and since they don't know you, employers often judge these qualities based on appearance and behavior.

There are countless books on "dress for success" strategies, so feel free to read more about the options you might want to consider. Here, we'll cover the basic attire that's most appropriate for the broadest range of jobs and work environments. Keep in mind that interviewers assume you're putting your best foot forward, so if you appear untidy or wear inappropriate clothes, they'll fear the worst for your day-to-day job attire.

Men, quite frankly, have it easier in this arena, since male business attire has changed little during the past 100 years. Wear a dark suit (navy or charcoal grey), a white or ivory shirt, and a conservative tie. Shine your shoes, wear dark colored socks, and wear your hair neatly combed. Distribute your wallet, checkbook, pen, keys, and change among the various pockets of your suit so your appearance isn't downgraded by bulging pockets and clanking change.

Since women's fashions change drastically from year to year, it's easy to fall victim to trendy designs that aren't appropriate for many work environments. Most businesses are relatively conservative, so in general you can't go wrong with classic, classy attire. Select a well-tailored skirt suit in a solid, dark fabric and wear a white or ivory blouse of simple design. Select a skirt that is long enough and full enough to allow you to walk, sit, and bend with comfort and modesty. Wear hose that match your skin tone and plain, closed-toe flats or low-heeled pumps. Wear your hair in a neat, tidy style and if you

must carry a purse, make it a small shoulder bag so you can shake hands readily. Avoid see-through fabrics, plunging necklines, mini-skirts, skirts with slits, patterned hosiery, noisy jewelry, and overdone makeup.

Well before your scheduled interview, try on the clothes you will wear and study your appearance in a full-length mirror. Observe how your clothes move as you walk, stand still, and sit. Eliminate any clutter or awkward details. Check your jacket, skirt, or trouser hems for length and trailing threads. Make sure your clothes fit you well, without puckers, pulls, or baggy spots, and that the combination you've chosen is comfortable and attractive. Crush the fabric in your hand to see if it wrinkles easily, because your goal is to arrive at your interview looking clean, crisp, and professional.

If you're uncertain how to dress for an interview, err on the side of conservative attire. Both men and women should wear the minimum of jewelry. If you're seeking a creative position in a field like design, marketing, or theater, you can add drama and flair with small details, such as a unique scarf or dashing necktie. Carry your materials (extra copies of your resume, reference letters or contact names and numbers, your calendar, a pad, and pens) in a pad-folio or briefcase.

Success Strategy

If money is a concern, buy one good suit and make that your "interview" suit. Look for quality fabric and classic tailoring. Identify exactly what accessories (shoes, shirt or blouse, necktie or jewelry) complement your suit and communicate quality and professionalism.

Whenever an employer invites you for an interview, you'll know exactly what you'll wear. You'll also be free to focus your energy on the real issue—handling the interview questions well.

Behaving like a Professional

If you approach a job interview as if it were an important meeting, you'll be able to keep your interview stress-level under control. It's also helpful to remember that one of the most important tasks managers perform is hiring and supervising good people. You and the interviewer have complementary goals: to determine if you're the best person for the job and to determine if this is the best job for you. Keep this thought in the forefront of your mind, and you'll be more successful in your efforts to make the interview a cooperative exploration of the mutual "fit."

Whether you're a woman or a man, you should shake the interviewers' hands and look directly at them. (Carry your briefcase or notebook in your left hand so you won't have to juggle it to free your right hand.) Repeat each interviewer's name as you are introduced and say something simple such as "It's a pleasure to meet you." Carry yourself with confidence (not arrogance) and be yourself. You don't want them to hire some artificial personality you projected during the interview; you want them to hire the real you.

If you're with an experienced interviewer, he or she will work to draw information from you. Inexperienced interviewers will sometimes let you do all the talking, or they will talk so much you have little chance to showcase your talents. Try to spend at least half the time during the interview listening and observing the interviewers.

Take brief notes when important points are covered. The interview is a meeting, remember? In any other meeting, you'd take notes to identify what was discussed, key decisions, and who agreed to do what. Do the same here. Otherwise, you'll return home and realize you've forgotten everyone's name or you're a bit fuzzy on who's supposed to call whom next week.

Responding to Tough Questions

By definition, a tough interview question is any question you find difficult or impossible to answer. Several excellent books devote all or part of their discussion to strategies for handling stress interviews, challenging questions, or penetrating probes. Several suggested resources are listed at the end of this chapter.

For sound strategies on handling questions that may verge on illegality, read Martin Yate's book, *Knock 'em Dead*. In it, he also identifies "illegal" questions versus those that touch on the same topic but are generally permissible. We've summarized a few of these here.

Remember, large companies have teams of well-trained interviewers. In many smaller companies, the person doing the interviewing is often the manager who's seeking a new employee, and this manager may inadvertently ask borderline questions. As in all steps of the job hunting process, you must use your own judgment whether to respond or not. If you have doubts about questions you were asked during an interview, you may want to check with a lawyer.

Difficult Questions

"Illegal"	Permissible
Does your religion allow you to work on Saturdays?	This job requires work on Saturdays. Is that a problem?
What is your ancestry? National origin?	Are you a U.S. citizen or a resident alien with the right to work in the U.S.?
What is your native language?	In what languages are you fluent?
How old are you? How old are your children?	Are you over 18 years old?
Is that your maiden name? Are you married? Divorced? Single?	Have you ever worked for this company under a different name?
Do you wish to be addressed as Miss, Mrs., or Ms.?	How do you like to be addressed?

Adapted from *Knock 'em Dead*

Concluding the Interview

Conclude every interview with a clear plan of action in mind. Be sure you and the interviewers review these steps together and agree on the sequence and timing. You'll want to determine if you need to plan for additional interviews (with other managers in the organization or perhaps with your potential supervisor) and when these interviews might occur (this week, next week, within a month, etc.). Ask if they need more information, such as written references, contact names and numbers, or copies of your transcripts, before they can reach a decision. If you don't have the necessary materials with you, agree on a date when you will deliver or mail the necessary information.

If additional interviews are required, find out who will be in the interviews and how the interview will be structured (one-on-one, group or team interview, etc.). Ask when the company expects to make a final decision. This is your chance to learn as much about the next decision-making steps as possible, so make the most of it.

Be sure you let the employer know if you are interested in the position. This is called "asking for the job" and many employers use this one factor as an important method for selecting among top candidates. The candidate who says, "I'm truly excited about this opportunity and am eager to start working with you," often receives the job offer.

Before the interview is concluded, be certain you have the name and job title of every person involved in the interview. When the interview is concluded, stand up, look directly at the interviewers, and shake hands firmly. Thank them for their time and the information they shared. Reiterate that you're looking forward to hearing from them soon, then leave promptly and without fuss. On your way out of the building, be gracious to everyone you encounter.

Dealing with Money Issues

Sooner or later, the issue of money will arise. Many employers list a range of pay in their job advertisements and recruitment notices, but some do not. Job applicants tend to err in two ways: they avoid bringing up the topic of pay, or they bring it up at the wrong time. Here are some strategies for talking about pay and benefits in a professional, matter-of-fact way.

Researching Salary Ranges

Be sure to research salary ranges as part of your job interview preparation process. Once you're in the interview room, it's too late to find out how much the position pays at other companies. The exact amount an employer pays for particular jobs can be difficult to determine, but general salary ranges are easy to find if you do the legwork. The descriptions in *The Big Book of Jobs* include typical starting, mid-point, and top salary ranges, as well as the education and experience expected at each earning level.

To determine what a specific job is paid in your region, study the want ads in the newspaper for a week or two and plot the salary ranges stated in the ads. You may not be able to identify an exact figure for your target job, but you should be able to pin down a basic range of pay appropriate for that position. Pinpoint two figures: the minimum salary with benefits you would be willing and able to accept and a minimum salary without benefits. That way, you'll be prepared to discuss money issues like a pro.

Discussing Compensation and Benefits

Once an interviewer has asked you their target questions and described the position, many will naturally begin to discuss compensation and benefits. Listen carefully to the figures and conditions they disclose and let them fully make their case before you start asking questions. Be sure to keep your expression neutral—no matter how delighted or dejected the information may make you feel.

Keep in mind that employer-paid benefits, such as vacation, sick leave, holidays, and health insurance, carry a dollar value, too. A comprehensive package can add the equivalent of 20 to 35 percent to your basic pay rate. Conversely, the absence of employer-paid health care may mean you will need to negotiate for a higher salary in order to afford private insurance. Know the minimum salary range you'll accept, both with benefits and without, and evaluate the offer against those figures.

Some employers will wait for you to broach the topic of salary and benefits, so be prepared to do so. Many employers, however, react negatively if the *first* question you ask relates to salary. If you are nearing the end of your scheduled time together and money hasn't come up yet, ask two nonmonetary questions from your list. Then state, "We've discussed many aspects of the position, and I'm very interested. Could you tell me what the salary and benefits are?" By first asking questions not related to money, you communicate to the employer that you are genuinely interested in the organization and the job opportunity, not just the salary.

If possible, let the employer offer a figure first. It's easy to over- or under-price your skills and experience, particularly if you're just starting your career or you're switching from one field to another. Once the employer has detailed the compensation package and any benefits, take time to repeat the basic details out loud. This allows the interviewer to clarify any points you've misunderstood.

Following Up After the Interview

Sending a Thank-you Letter

The post-interview follow-up letter is invaluable. It's one more opportunity to expose interviewers to your name and gives you another chance to highlight your strengths and reaffirm your interest in the job. Follow-up notes are the sign of a courteous and savvy professional.

A typical follow-up letter can be typed, computer printed, or handwritten. Send one to everyone who interviewed you (if there were five people in the interview, send a personal note to each person) and mail it within two or three days of the interview.

What should you say? It's traditional to thank interviewers for their time and the information they shared. Recap your strengths and any special qualities that make you uniquely desirable for the position. Express your interest in the job and your eagerness to start work. If the interviewer asked you to forward references or other information, mention this and enclose the materials they requested along with your letter. Close courteously and be certain to include your full name along with a contact number and address.

Once you've sent a follow-up and any additional materials to that organization, continue to pursue other opportunities. A successful interview is not the same as a job offer, and you want to keep every lead alive until you finalize arrangements on a specific job with a specific employer.

Placing a Follow-up Call

If an employer agreed to contact you by a specific date and you don't hear from them, pick up the phone and call. Handle follow-up calls professionally. Don't be accusatory or desperate. Simply state your purpose clearly and briefly. For example, you might say, "You mentioned you'd contact me by such-and-so date. I'm still interested in the position and wanted to know if you'd reached a decision or if there was any additional information I could provide that would help with your decision-making process."

This strategy shows the employer that you take this opportunity seriously, you're interested in the job, and you're willing and able to take proactive, professional steps to accomplish your job-seeking goals.

Evaluating Job Offers

Sometimes it's a challenge to get even one offer of employment. At other times, you're faced with evaluating two or more offers from different employers, with different rates of pay, benefit packages, and long-term opportunities. If you have only one offer to consider and you're eager to work, you may feel tempted to accept the offer, even if the job or company is not a perfect fit for you. If, on the other hand, you have several offers to consider, it can be difficult to choose among them.

Making a Decision

Making a decision about a job offer is tricky, whichever situation you face. Most professionals advise job seekers to not accept an offer at the moment it's extended. Make sure you understand all of the details, then request time to consider the offer and agree on a date to respond to the employer. Some factors you'll want to evaluate are:

- The specific duties and responsibilities of the position
- The opportunities for advancement and promotion
- The potential for additional training and education
- The stability of the organization and the likelihood of near-term cutbacks
- The location of the organization
- The "personality" of the organization and how well you fit in
- The personality of your potential supervisor and how well you two might work together
- The work schedule (flexible, fixed, holidays off, work all holidays, etc.)
- The average expected work week ("full-time" employment can mean 32, 35, or 40 hours a week)
- The number of overtime hours expected (some salaried environments expect employees to work 60–70 hours a week)
- Other factors that interest or concern you (commuting distance or child care, for example)
- The starting salary
- The long-term salary potential
- The benefits package

First, assess how important each factor is to you. Then rate how closely the specific job offer matches your ideal. Keep in mind that your priorities may differ from those of your parents, teachers, and friends, so don't let their needs influence your decision. And, while income is important to all of us, try to avoid choosing a job solely because it pays the most. Job satisfaction is much more than pay. It's performing tasks you enjoy and can do well. It's working with people you admire, trust, and like. It's balancing personal and professional demands effectively. It's learning new skills and developing your best potential. It's receiving credit and recognition for your accomplishments. Pay and benefits are just one part of the total picture.

Accepting an Offer

Large organizations are likely to issue a job offer in writing. Smaller organizations often omit this step and rely on oral agreements. In either case, take the time to write a letter of acceptance. It provides you with the opportunity to review the position, salary, start date, job location, additional screening criteria (physical exam, drug tests, etc.), and other particulars you and the employer agreed upon.

A written summary of employment criteria and conditions accompanied by a written letter of acceptance provides both you and the employer with the opportunity to flag any items or areas where you've inadvertently misunderstood each other. You will thus be able to work together to resolve these issues before you start work, rather than face unpleasant surprises afterward.

Wrapping Up Your Job Search

Once you've accepted a position, contact every employer with whom you've interviewed recently and inform them of your decision. At the same time, or shortly after you've started your new job, take an evening or weekend and write notes to every person who provided a lead, advice, references, or assistance. Thank them for their efforts on your behalf, describe your new position briefly, and offer to reciprocate the assistance should they need it in the future.

If you've been working with a college placement office, be sure to let the administrators know of your success. Include particulars of your degree, job title, company name, contact number and address, and your starting salary range. This type of information is invaluable to placement offices because it helps them provide better assistance to future graduates.

Many job seekers neglect this final stage, but it's truly the mark of a professional. If you ever need assistance again, you'll feel more comfortable reviving contacts if you handled yourself with grace in the past.

It's easy to become unnerved—but don't let the thought of job interviewing bring your job hunt to a halt. As with every other phase of the job-seeking process, follow the guidelines and tackle each phase one step at a time.

Interviews can be delightful, enjoyable experiences if you approach them with the right attitude. Many years ago, I met Susan Johnston, author of *The Career Adventure*, in a job interview. She applied for a position with the organization where I worked, and I was on the interviewing team. Through accident or fate our paths continued to cross, and today she's a respected colleague and friend.

Interviewing can also be quite mysterious. Sometimes, you're certain your superb qualifications and polished delivery will prompt a job offer—and nothing happens. At other times, you're convinced you blew it and you'll never hear from that company again—but they call and offer you the job. Often you'll never know why one company wants you and another doesn't.

The Universal Hiring Rule

Employers hire the people they believe will deliver more in value than what they cost. The trick is learning how to explain this so clearly the employer is convinced . . . and you're hired.

—Del Vaughan,
Director of Career Planning & Placement
Sinclair Community College

As you work to master the interview process, keep Vaughan's universal hiring rule in mind. Your primary mission is to demonstrate to a potential employer that you'll add critical value to the organization. In the end, what employer can resist that?

Learning More About Job Interviewing

Deluca, Matthew J. *Best Answers to the 201 Most Frequently Asked Interview Questions*. New York, NY: McGraw-Hill Professional Publishing, 1997.

Martin, Carole. *Boost Your Interview IQ*. New York: McGraw-Hill, 2003.

Yate, Martin. *Knock 'em Dead*. Holbrook, Mass.: Adams Media Corporation, 2002.

CHAPTER 7
LAUNCHING YOUR CAREER

Some of you may just be starting your journey of 12,000 days and are working to identify your first career. Some of you are well down that path and are working to change jobs or re-career.

No matter what stage you're at, however, this book has provided practical strategies and new insights into the challenges of the career and job search. Whether you've landed a job or not, you've managed to conquer a process that frightens and immobilizes many people. Here's a quick review of what you've accomplished.

Reviewing Your Basic Action Plan

- Conduct a skill, interest, and value self-assessment.
- Develop a current self-profile.
- Identify a full range of career possibilities.
- Explore each career through research and hands-on contact.
- Identify a focused cluster of viable careers.
- Update your qualifications profile.
- Construct focused, effective cover letters.
- Design targeted, persuasive resume(s).
- Generate sufficient leads to elicit a number of job interviews.
- Evaluate job offers for alignment with career goals and personal values.
- Accept the best job offer—or continue the search.
- Launch your new (or next) career.

Mastering the Search

Once you've mastered this process, you'll be prepared to respond to the rapid and radical changes in today's work world. The key is to confront these changes with thoughtful, planned action and to recognize that every step of the process has value.

If you still feel pressured or even immobilized by the enormity of the career decision and job-seeking process, remember this rule. Few career decisions are fatal. So, you'll always be able to redirect your search, change your mind, build new skills, return to school, identify a new path, or restructure the balance of career and personal demands. Sometimes you won't like every facet of the choices you have to make, but you *will* have a choice.

Redirecting Your Energies

Many of the strategies that make the search process successful can also help you launch your career. It simply requires redirecting the energy and the focus. Networking is as vital to career success on the job as it is during the job search. Targeted, polished business communications are vital in today's information-driven environments, and the ability to construct concise results-based descriptions will add power to your messages on the job. Suggestions for negotiating compensation and benefits can be applied to other negotiations. The professionalism and self-confidence you learned to project in a job interview will serve you well as you move into your new work environment. Moreover, you've acquired critical planning and self-management skills that are essential for success.

Use these skills and they'll serve you well as you journey into the unpredictable but exciting world of work.

BIBLIOGRAPHY

Barron-Tieger, Barbara and Tieger, Paul. *Do What You Are: Discover the Perfect Career for You.* Boston, Mass.: Little, Brown & Company, Inc., 2001.

Bloch, Deborah P. *How to Have a Winning Job Interview* (3rd ed.). Chicago, Ill.: VGM Career Books, a division of The McGraw-Hill Companies, 1999.

Bloch, Deborah P. *How to Write a Winning Resume* (4th ed.). Chicago, Ill.: VGM Career Books, a division of The McGraw-Hill Companies, 1999.

Bolles, Richard Nelson. *The Three Boxes of Life, and How to Get Out of Them.* Berkeley, Calif.: Ten Speed Press, 1978.

Bolles, Richard Nelson. *What Color Is Your Parachute?* Berkeley, Calif.: Ten Speed Press, 2004.

Camenson, Blythe. *Careers for History Buffs & Others Who Learn from the Past.* Chicago, Ill.: VGM Career Books, a division of The McGraw-Hill Companies, 1994.

DeGalan, Julie and Stephen Lambert. *Great Jobs for Foreign Language Majors.* Chicago, Ill.: VGM Career Books, a division of The McGraw-Hill Companies, 2000.

DeGalan, Julie and Stephen Lambert. *Great Jobs for History Majors.* Chicago, Ill.: VGM Career Books, a division of The McGraw-Hill Companies, 2001.

DeGalan, Julie and Stephen Lambert. *Great Jobs for Psychology Majors.* Chicago, Ill.: VGM Career Books, a division of The McGraw-Hill Companies, 2000.

Greenspon, Jaq. *Careers for Film Buffs & Other Hollywood Types.* Chicago, Ill.: VGM Career Books, a division of The McGraw-Hill Companies, 1993.

Heitzman, William Ray. *Careers for Sports Nuts & Other Athletic Types.* Chicago, Ill.: VGM Career Books, a division of The McGraw-Hill Companies, 1998.

Johnston, Susan M. *The Career Adventure.* Scottsdale, Ariz.: Gorsuch Scarisbrick Publishers, 2001.

Kennedy, Joyce Lain and Morrow, Thomas J. *Electronic Job Search Revolution.* New York: John Wiley & Sons Inc., 1995.

"Managing Your Career," (special section). *Fortune Magazine*, January 15, 1996, pp. 33–78.

Marler, Patty and Jan Bailey Mattia. *Job Hunting Made Easy.* Chicago, Ill.: VGM Career Books, a division of The McGraw-Hill Companies, 1996.

Martin, Carole. *Boost Your Interview IQ.* New York: McGraw-Hill, 2003.

Resumes for Environmental Careers, 2nd ed. Chicago, Ill.: VGM Career Books, a division of The McGraw-Hill Companies, 2002.

Riley, Margaret, Frances Roehm, and Steve Oserman. *The Guide to Internet Job Searching, 2004–5.* Chicago, Ill.: Co-published by the Public Library Association and VGM Career Books, a division of The McGraw-Hill Companies, 2004.

Rowh, Mark. *Slam-Dunk Cover Letters.* Chicago: VGM Career Books, a division of The McGraw-Hill Companies, 2004.

Schrank, Louise Welsh. *Choose the Right Career.* Chicago, Ill.: VGM Career Books, a division of The McGraw-Hill Companies, 1998.

Shingleton, John D. *Job Interviewing for College Students.* Chicago, Ill.: VGM Career Books, a division of The McGraw-Hill Companies, 1996.

United States Department of Labor. *Occupational Outlook Handbook.* Chicago, Ill.: VGM Career Books, a division of The McGraw-Hill Companies, 2000–2001.

Wahlgren, Eric. "Hiring Outlook 2004, Part I." *Business Week*, Feb. 9, 2004. http://www.businessweek.com/careers/content/Feb2004/ca2004029_9743_ca004.htm.

"What Work Requires of Schools," *A SCANS Report for America 2000.* Secretary's Commission on Achieving Necessary Skills, US Department of Labor, 1991.

Yate, Martin. *Cover Letters that Knock 'em Dead.* Holbrook, Mass.: Adams Media Corporation, 2002.

Yate, Martin. *Knock 'em Dead 2004.* Holbrook, Mass.: Adams Media Corporation, 2004.

Yate, Martin. *Resumes that Knock 'em Dead.* Holbrook, Mass.: Adams Media Corporation, 2002.

Yeager, Dr. Neil M. *CareerMap: Deciding What You Want, Getting It, and Keeping It!* New York: John Wiley & Sons Inc., 1988.

Interviews

Johnston, Susan M., author of *The Career Adventure.* January 1996.

Sayre, Suzanne, Career Planning Specialist, Sinclair Community College, Dayton, Ohio. January 1996.

Vaughan, Del, Director of Career Planning and Placement, Sinclair Community College, Dayton, Ohio. February 1996.

NOTES

NOTES

NOTES

NOTES

NOTES

NOTES

Occupational Outlook Handbook 2004-2005

Compiled by
The United States Department of Labor

VGM Career Books

New York   Chicago   San Francisco   Lisbon   London   Madrid   Mexico City
Milan   New Delhi   San Juan   Seoul   Singapore   Sydney   Toronto

Publisher's Preface

McGraw-Hill is proud to bring you this special version of the *Occupational Outlook Handbook*. This important government publication, like the *Dictionary of Occupational Titles*, is an essential tool for all jobseekers.

First-time jobseekers can use *Occupational Outlook Handbook* to find out more about nearly 250 different types of careers. Vital information is given for each career field, including nature of the work, working conditions, employment, training, advancement opportunities, job outlook, earnings, and sources of additional information.

Experienced jobseekers should use this book to find the latest employment statistics for their career fields and the projected employment opportunities over the next several years. Those wishing to change careers will find helpful information on occupations related to their current experience; this information may indicate which new career areas to pursue.

Everyone can benefit from using the *Occupational Outlook Handbook*. Before making important career decisions, be sure to consult this publication for concise, comprehensive coverage of the employment picture in America today.

This McGraw-Hill edition is an unabridged publication of Bulletin 2570, the *Occupational Outlook Handbook, 2004–05 Edition*, compiled by the United States Department of Labor, Bureau of Labor Statistics.

1 2 3 4 5 6 7 8 9 0   VLP/VLP   3 2 1 0 9 8 7 6 5 4

ISBN 0-07-143175-8
ISSN 0082-9072

McGraw-Hill books are available at special quantity discounts to use as premiums and sales promotions, or for use in corporate training programs. For more information, please write to the Director of Special Sales, Professional Publishing, McGraw-Hill, Two Penn Plaza, New York, NY 10121-2298. Or contact your local bookstore.

This book is printed on acid-free paper.

Acknowledgments

The Bureau of Labor Statistics produced the Handbook under the general guidance and direction of Michael W. Horrigan, Assistant Commissioner for Occupational Statistics and Employment Projections, and Mike Pilot, Chief, Division of Occupational Outlook. Chester C. Levine and Jon Q. Sargent, Managers of Occupational Outlook Studies, provided planning and day-to-day direction.

Supervisors overseeing the research and preparation of material were Douglas Braddock, Theresa Cosca, Arlene K. Dohm, and Carolyn Veneri. Occupational analysts who contributed material were Azure Albeck, Andrew D. Alpert, Jill Auyer, Hall Dillon, Tamara Dillon, Erika Heaton, Elka Jones, Henry T. Kasper, Jonathan Kelinson, T. Alan Lacey, William Lawhorn, Mark Mittelhauser, Kevin M. McCarron, Roger Moncarz, Terry Schau, Lynn Shniper, Patricia Tate, and Ian Wyatt.

Editorial work was provided by Edith Baker, Monica Carpio, Monica Gabor, and Douglas Himes, under the supervision of Mary K. Rieg. Word processing support was provided by Monique Smith and Beverly A. Williams. Computer programming support was provided by David S. Frank, T. Alan Lacey, and Erik A. Savisaar. Cover and other art-work were designed by Keith Tapscott.

Photograph Credits

The Bureau of Labor Statistics wishes to express its appreciation for the cooperation and assistance of the many government and private sources—listed below—that either contributed photographs or made their facilities available to photographers working under contract to the U.S. Department of Labor. Situations portrayed in the photographs may not be free of every possible safety or health hazard. Depiction of company or trade name in no way constitutes endorsement by the Department of Labor.

Abacus Technology Corporation, Silver Spring, MD; Aggressive Construction; Black Magic Films; Burlington and Northern Railroad; Cape May—Lewes Ferry; Carlo Perlo, Dance Place; Citgo Gas, Gaithersburg, MD; Claims Administration Corporation, Rockville, MD; Craddock-Terry Inc., Farmville, VA; Cres Builders; Cynthia K. Reeser, Nutritionist, Women's Health Initiative; D.C. Vending Company; Dana A. Brown, Women's Exercise Research Center, George Washington University, Washington, DC; Darnestown Elementary School, Montgomery County, MD; David Hrupsa, First State Aerial Applicators, Felton, DE; Delaware Electric Cooperative; Department of Anthropology, Howard University, Washington, DC; Dravo Corporation, Pittsburgh, PA; Dr. Edna Medford, Department of History, Howard University, Washington, DC; Dr. Gary Felton, Agricultural Engineering Department, University of Maryland, College Park, MD; Dr. Larry Brown, Dupont Circle Chiropractic, Washington, DC; Fame Food Services, Wakefield, MD; Fannie Mae Computer Department, Washington, DC; Father Everett Pearson, Holy Name School, Washington, DC; Fitzgerald Pontiac, White Flint, MD; Food Service at the American University, Washington, DC; Gaithersburg Middle School, Montgomery County, MD; Gaithersburg Public Library, Montgomery County, MD; George Washington University Audio Visual Department, Washington, DC; George Washington University Hospital and Ambulatory Care Center, Washington, DC; Glenn Maurer and Associates; Holland Jewelers, Inc., Rehoboth Beach, DE; Information Technology Department, American Federation of Teachers, AFL-CIO; International Union of Bricklayers and Allied Craft Workers; Iona House and Sibley Hospital, Washington, DC; Jordana Pomeroy, Curator, National Museum of Women in the Arts; Julie Garrett, USDA Graduate School, Washington, DC; Kane County Cougars; Karen Ackoff, Smithsonian Institution, Washington, DC; Kathryn Morgan Lightcap, D.P.M., Lewes, DE; Kathy M. Perkins, At Your Fingertips, Washington, DC; Laurel Racetrack, Laurel, MD; Legal Services, Washington, DC; Legg, Mason, Wood, Walker, Inc.; Loudoun Pest Control, Leesburg, VA; Martha Tabor, Working Images Prints, Photographs, and Sculpture, Washington, DC; Maryland Applicators, Beltsville, MD; McAllister Towing, Baltimore, MD; McCutcheon's Apple Products, Inc.; Medical Records Corporation, Vienna, VA; Melvin M. Shapiro, Capitol Process Services; Midway Slots, Harrington, DE; Monilsen Animal Clinic, Madison Heights, VA; Montgomery County Police Department, Montgomery County, MD; National Institute of Standards and Technology, Gaithersburg, MD; National Zoo, Washington, DC; Patti Huntington, Singer; Penn Camera, Rockville, MD; Pierre L. Palian, D.D.S., and staff; Port of Seattle, Seattle, WA; Proctor S. Harvey, American Society of Landscape Architects, Lynchburg, VA; Public Production Group, Washington, DC; Rapp Funeral and Cremation Services; Red Cross Blood Bank, Baltimore, MD; Rev. Ruth Hamilton, Westminster Presbyterian Church, Washington, DC; Robbie Murray, Connie Rogers, Brandon Donaway, Sussex County Emergency Medical Services (Delaware); Robert M. Gable, CPA, Berry, Barlow, & Warrington, LLP, Certified Public Accountants; Robert Schwartz and Keith Peoples, Architects; Roush & Averill, Interior Designers, Gaithersburg, MD; Safeway, Gaithersburg, MD; Sandy Springs Friends School, Sandy Springs, MD; Seaport Transportation, Rehoboth Beach, DE; Shady Grove Adventist Hospital, Gaithersburg, MD; Siar Daires-Vollum, Paleontologist, Smithsonian Institution, Washington, DC; Sterling Optical, Gaithersburg, MD; Suburban Dental Laboratory, Inc.; Surgery Department, Children's National Medical Center, Washington, DC; Sussex County (Delaware) Engineering Department; Sussex County (Delaware) Finance Department; The Segal Company, Washington, DC; The Washington Times, Washington, DC; Triangle Tobacco Auction Warehouse, Upper Marlboro, MD; Trunnel Electric, Derwood, MD; Town of Rehoboth Beach, DE—Water Treatment Plant; United Air Temp, Rockville, MD; Urban Institute, Washington, DC; USDA Graduate School; Walter Reed Army Medical Hospital, Washington, DC; Washington Home, Washington, DC; Washington Metropolitan Area Transit Authority, Washington, DC; WETA Television and Radio, Washington, DC; William G. Grimm, Avorex Designs; William McGuire, Beltsville Agricultural Research Station, Beltsville, MD; Worker's Institute for Health and Safety, Washington, DC.

Contents

Service occupations

Sales and related occupations

Office and administrative support occupations

Additional Information About the 2002-12 Projections

Readers interested in more information about the projections; about the methods and assumptions that underlie them; or about details on economic growth, the labor force, or industry and occupational employment, should consult the February 2004 *Monthly Labor Review,* or the Winter 2003-04 *Occupational Outlook Quarterly.*

For more information about employment change, job openings, earnings, unemployment rates, and training requirements by occupation, consult *Occupational Projections and Training Data, 2004-05 Edition,* BLS Bulletin 2572.

For occupational information from an industry perspective, including discussions of some occupations and career paths that the *Occupational Outlook Handbook* does not cover, consult the *Career Guide to Industries, 2004-05 Edition,* BLS Bulletin 2571.

Tomorrow's Jobs

Making informed career decisions requires reliable information about opportunities in the future. Opportunities result from the relationships between the population, labor force, and the demand for goods and services.

Population ultimately limits the size of the labor force—individuals working or looking for work—which constrains how much can be produced. Demand for various goods and services determines employment in the industries providing them. Occupational employment opportunities, in turn, result from demand for skills needed within specific industries. Opportunities for medical assistants and other health care occupations, for example, have surged in response to rapid growth in demand for health services.

Examining the past and projecting changes in these relationships is the foundation of the Occupational Outlook Program. This chapter presents highlights of Bureau of Labor Statistics projections of the labor force and occupational and industry employment that can help guide your career plans. Sources of detailed information about the projections appear on page viii.

Population
Population trends affect employment opportunities in a number of ways. Changes in population influence the demand for goods and services. For example, a growing and aging population has increased the demand for health services. Equally important, population changes produce corresponding changes in the size and demographic composition of the labor force.

The U.S. population is expected to increase by 24 million over the 2002-12 period, at a slower rate of growth than during both the 1992-2002 and 1982-92 periods (chart 1). Continued growth will mean more consumers of goods and services, spurring demand for workers in a wide range of occupations and industries. The effects of population growth on various occupations will differ. The differences are partially accounted for by the age distribution of the future population.

The youth population, aged 16 to 24, will grow 7 percent over the 2002-12 period. As the baby boomers continue to age, the group aged 55 to 64 will increase by 43.6 percent or 11.5 million persons, more than any other group. Those aged 35 to 44 will decrease in size, reflecting the birth dearth following the baby boom generation.

Minorities and immigrants will constitute a larger share of the U.S. population in 2012. The number of Hispanics is projected to continue to grow much faster than those of all other racial and ethnic groups.

Labor force
Population is the single most important factor in determining the size and composition of the labor force—that is, people who are either working or looking for work. The civilian labor force is projected to increase by 17.4 million, or 12 percent, to 162.3 million over the 2002-12 period.

The U.S. workforce will become more diverse by 2012. White, non-Hispanic persons will continue to make up a decreasing share of the labor force, falling from 71.3 percent in 2002 to 65.5 percent in 2012 (chart 2). However, despite relatively slow growth, white, non-Hispanics will remain the largest group in the labor force in 2012. Hispanics are projected to account for an increasing share of the labor force by 2012, growing from 12.4 to 14.7 percent. By 2012, Hispanics will constitute a larger proportion of the labor force than will blacks, whose share will grow from 11.4 percent to 12.2 percent. Asians will continue to be the fastest growing of the four labor force groups.

The numbers of men and women in the labor force will grow, but the number of women will grow at a faster rate than the number of men. The male labor force is projected to grow by 10 percent from 2002 to 2012, compared with 14.3 percent for women. As a result, men's share of the labor force is expected to decrease from 53.5 to 52.5 percent, while women's share is expected to increase from 46.5 to 47.5 percent.

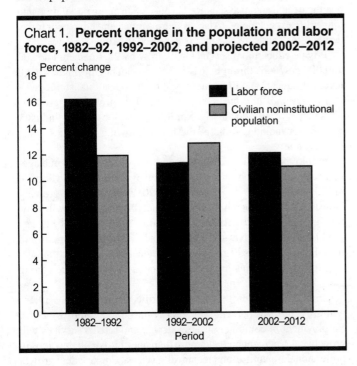

Chart 1. **Percent change in the population and labor force, 1982–92, 1992–2002, and projected 2002–2012**

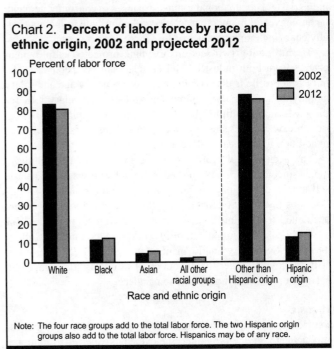

Chart 2. **Percent of labor force by race and ethnic origin, 2002 and projected 2012**

Note: The four race groups add to the total labor force. The two Hispanic origin groups also add to the total labor force. Hispanics may be of any race.

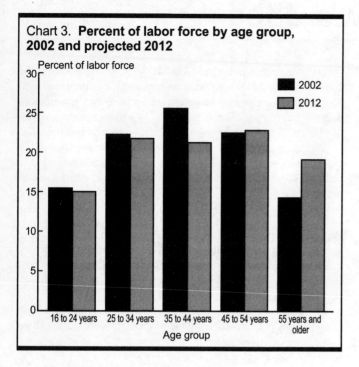

Chart 3. **Percent of labor force by age group, 2002 and projected 2012**

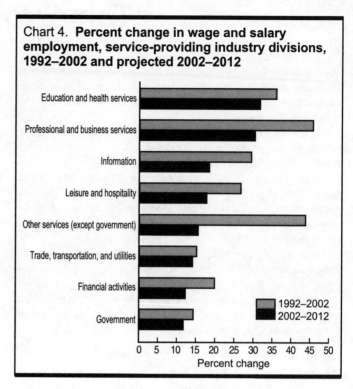

Chart 4. **Percent change in wage and salary employment, service-providing industry divisions, 1992–2002 and projected 2002–2012**

The youth labor force, aged 16 to 24, is expected to slightly decrease its share of the labor force to 15 percent by 2012. The primary working age group, between 25 and 54 years old, is projected to decline from 70.2 percent of the labor force in 2002 to 65.9 percent by 2012. Workers 55 and older, on the other hand, are projected to increase from 14.3 percent to 19.1 percent of the labor force between 2002 and 2012, due to the aging of the baby-boom generation (chart 3).

Employment

Total employment is expected to increase from 144 million in 2002 to 165 million in 2012, or by 14.8 percent. The 21 million jobs that will be added by 2012 will not be evenly distributed across major industrial and occupational groups. Changes in consumer demand, technology, and many other factors will contribute to the continually changing employment structure in the U.S. economy.

The following two sections examine projected employment change from both industrial and occupational perspectives. The industrial profile is discussed in terms of primary wage and salary employment. Primary employment excludes secondary jobs for those who hold multiple jobs. The exception is employment in agriculture, which includes self-employed and unpaid family workers in addition to wage and salary workers.

The occupational profile is viewed in terms of total employment—including primary and secondary jobs for wage and salary, self-employed, and unpaid family workers. Of the nearly 144 million jobs in the U.S. economy in 2002, wage and salary workers accounted for 132 million; self-employed workers accounted for 11.5 million; and unpaid family workers accounted for about 140,000. Secondary employment accounted for 1.7 million jobs. Self-employed workers held 9 out of 10 secondary jobs; wage and salary workers held most of the remainder.

Industry

Service-providing industries. The long-term shift from goods-producing to service-providing employment is expected to continue. Service-providing industries are expected to account for approxi-

mately 20.8 million of the 21.6 million new wage and salary jobs generated over the 2002-12 period (chart 4).

Education and health services. This industry supersector is projected to grow faster, 31.8 percent, and add more jobs than any other industry supersector. About 1 out of every 4 new jobs created in the U.S. economy will be in either the healthcare and social assistance or private educational services sectors.

Healthcare and social assistance—including private hospitals, nursing and residential care facilities, and individual and family services—will grow by 32.4 percent and add 4.4 million new jobs. Employment growth will be driven by increasing demand for healthcare and social assistance because of an aging population and longer life expectancies. Also, as more women enter the labor force, demand for childcare services is expected to grow.

Private educational services will grow by 28.7 percent and add 759,000 new jobs through 2012. Rising student enrollments at all levels of education will create demand for educational services.

Professional and business services. This group will grow by 30.4 percent and add nearly 5 million new jobs. This industry supersector includes some of the fastest growing industries in the U.S. economy.

Employment in administrative and support and waste management and remediation services will grow by 37 percent and add 2.8 million new jobs to the economy by 2012. The fastest growing industry in this sector will be employment services, which will grow by 54.3 percent and will contribute almost two-thirds of all new jobs in administrative and support and waste management and remediation services. Employment services ranks among the fastest growing industries in the Nation and is expected to be among those that provide the most new jobs.

Employment in professional, scientific, and technical services will grow by 27.8 percent and add 1.9 million new jobs by 2012. Employment in computer systems design and related services will grow by 54.6 percent and add more than one-third of all new jobs in professional, scientific, and technical services. Employment growth will be driven by the increasing reliance of businesses on information technology and the continuing importance of maintaining system and network security. Management, scientific, and technical consulting services also will grow very rapidly, by 55.4 percent, spurred by the increased use of new technology and computer software and the growing complexity of business.

Management of companies and enterprises will grow by 11.4 percent and add 195,000 new jobs.

Information. Employment in the information supersector is expected to increase by 18.5 percent, adding 632,000 jobs by 2012. Information contains some of the fast-growing computer-related industries such as software publishers; Internet publishing and broadcasting; and Internet service providers, Web search portals, and data processing services. Employment in these industries is expected to grow by 67.9 percent, 41.1 percent, and 48.2 percent, respectively. The information supersector also includes telecommunications, broadcasting, and newspaper, periodical, book, and directory publishers. Increased demand for residential and business land-line and wireless services, cable service, high-speed Internet connections, and software will fuel job growth among these industries.

Leisure and hospitality. Overall employment will grow by 17.8 percent. Arts, entertainment, and recreation will grow by 28 percent and add 497,000 new jobs by 2012. Most of these new job openings will come from the amusement, gambling, and recreation sector. Job growth will stem from public participation in arts, entertainment, and recreation activities—reflecting increasing incomes, leisure time, and awareness of the health benefits of physical fitness.

Accommodation and food services is expected to grow by 16.1 percent and add 1.6 million new jobs through 2012. Job growth will be concentrated in food services and drinking places, reflecting increases in population, dual-income families, and dining sophistication.

Trade, transportation, and utilities. Overall employment in this industry supersector will grow by 14.1 percent between 2002 and 2012. Transportation and warehousing is expected to increase by 914,000 jobs, or by 21.7 percent through 2012. Truck transportation will grow by 20.5 percent, adding 275,000 new jobs, while rail and water transportation are both projected to decline. The warehousing and storage and the couriers and messengers industries are projected to grow rapidly at 28.6 percent and 41.7 percent, respectively. Demand for truck transportation and warehousing services will expand as many manufacturers concentrate on their core competencies and contract out their product transportation and storage functions.

Employment in retail trade is expected to increase by 13.8 percent, from 15 million to 17.1 million. Increases in population, personal income, and leisure time will contribute to employment growth in this industry, as consumers demand more goods. Wholesale trade is expected to increase by 11.3 percent, growing from 5.6 million to 6.3 million jobs.

Employment in utilities is projected to decrease by 5.7 percent through 2012. Despite increased output, employment in electric power generation, transmission, and distribution and natural gas distribution is expected to decline through 2012 due to improved technology that increases worker productivity. However, employment in water, sewage, and other systems is expected to increase 46.4 percent by 2012. Jobs are not easily eliminated by technological gains in this industry because water treatment and waste disposal are very labor-intensive activities.

Financial activities. Employment is projected to grow 12.3 percent over the 2002-12 period. Real estate and rental and leasing is expected to grow by 18.4 percent and add 374,000 jobs by 2012. Growth will be due, in part, to increased demand for housing as the population grows. The fastest growing industry in the financial activities supersector will be commercial and industrial machinery and equipment rental and leasing, which will grow by 39.8 percent.

Finance and insurance is expected to increase by 590,000 jobs, or 10.2 percent, by 2012. Employment in securities, commodity contracts, and other financial investments and related activities is expected to grow 15.5 percent by 2012, reflecting the increased number of baby boomers in their peak savings years, the growth of tax-favorable retirement plans, and the globalization of the securities markets. Employment in credit intermediation and related services, including banks, will grow by 10.9 percent and add about half of all new jobs within finance and insurance. Insurance carriers and related activities is expected to grow by 7.5 percent and add 168,000 new jobs by 2012. The number of jobs within agencies, brokerages, and other insurance related activities is expected to grow about 14.5 percent, as many insurance carriers downsize their sales staffs and as agents set up their own businesses.

Government. Between 2002 and 2012, government employment, including that in public education and hospitals, is expected to increase by 11.8 percent, from 21.5 million to 24 million jobs. Growth in government employment will be fueled by growth in State and local educational services and the shift of responsibilities from the Federal Government to the State and local governments. Local government educational services is projected to increase 17.5 percent, adding over 1.3 million jobs. State government educational services also is projected to grow 17.5 percent, adding 388,000 jobs. Federal Government employment, including the Postal Service, is expected to increase by less than 1 percent as the Federal Government continues to contract out many government jobs to private companies.

Other services (except government). Employment will grow by 15.7 percent. More than 4 out of 10 new jobs in this supersector will

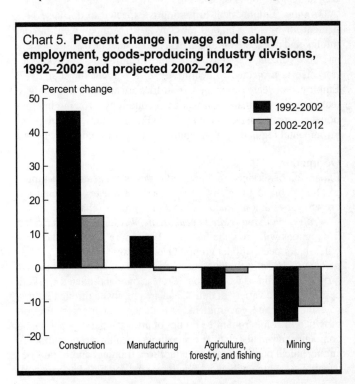

Chart 5. **Percent change in wage and salary employment, goods-producing industry divisions, 1992–2002 and projected 2002–2012**

be in religious organizations, which is expected to grow by 24.4 percent. Personal care services will be the fastest growing industry 27.6 percent. Also included among other services is private household employment, which is expected to decrease 7.2 percent.

Goods-producing industries. Employment in the goods-producing industries has been relatively stagnant since the early 1980s. Overall, this sector is expected to grow 3.3 percent over the 2002-12 period. Although employment is expected to increase more slowly than in the service-providing industries, projected growth among goods-producing industries varies considerably (chart 5).

Construction. Employment in construction is expected to increase by 15.1 percent, from 6.7 million to 7.7 million. Demand for new housing and an increase in road, bridge, and tunnel construction will account for the bulk of job growth in this supersector.

Manufacturing. Employment change in manufacturing will vary by individual industry, but overall employment in this supersector will decline by 1 percent or 157,000 jobs. For example, employment in plastics and rubber products manufacturing and machinery manufacturing is expected to grow by 138,000 and 120,000 jobs, respectively. Due to an aging population and increasing life expectancies, pharmaceutical and medicine manufacturing is expected to grow by 23.2 percent and add 68,000 jobs through 2012. However, productivity gains, job automation, and international competition will adversely affect employment in many other manufacturing industries. Employment in textile mills and apparel manufacturing will decline by 136,000 and 245,000 jobs, respectively. Employment in computer and electronic product manufacturing also will decline by 189,000 jobs through 2012.

Agriculture, forestry, fishing, and hunting. Overall employment in agriculture, forestry, fishing, and hunting is expected to decrease by 2 percent. Employment is expected to continue to decline due to advancements in technology. The only industry within this supersector expected to grow is support activities for agriculture and forestry, which includes farm labor contractors and farm management services. This industry is expected to grow by 18.4 percent and add 17,000 new jobs.

Mining. Employment in mining is expected to decrease 11.8 percent, or by some 60,000 jobs, by 2012. Employment in coal mining and metal ore mining is expected to decline by 30.2 percent and 38.8 percent, respectively. Employment in oil and gas extraction also is projected to decline by 27.8 percent through 2012. Employment decreases in these industries are attributable mainly to technology gains that boost worker productivity, growing international competition, restricted access to Federal lands, and strict environmental regulations that require cleaning of burning fuels.

Occupation

Expansion of service-providing industries is expected to continue, creating demand for many occupations. However, projected job growth varies among major occupational groups (chart 6).

Professional and related occupations. Professional and related occupations will grow the fastest and add more new jobs than any other major occupational group. Over the 2002-12 period, a 23.3-percent increase in the number of professional and related jobs is projected, a gain of 6.5 million. Professional and related workers perform a wide variety of duties, and are employed throughout private industry and government. About three-quarters of the job growth will come from three groups of professional occupations—computer and mathematical occupations, healthcare practitioners and technical occupations, and education, training, and library occupations—which will add 4.9 million jobs combined.

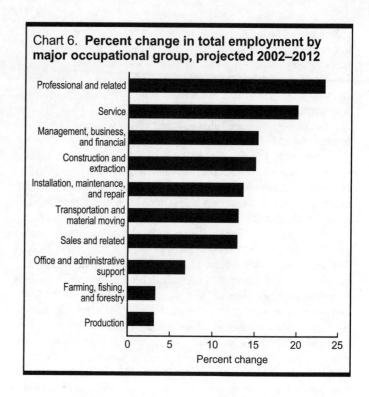

Chart 6. **Percent change in total employment by major occupational group, projected 2002–2012**

Service occupations. Service workers perform services for the public. Employment in service occupations is projected to increase by 5.3 million, or 20.1 percent, the second largest numerical gain and second highest rate of growth among the major occupational groups. Food preparation and serving related occupations are expected to add the most jobs among the service occupations, 1.6 million by 2012. However, healthcare support occupations are expected to grow the fastest, 34.5 percent, adding 1.1 million new jobs.

Management, business, and financial occupations. Workers in management, business, and financial occupations plan and direct the activities of business, government, and other organizations. Their employment is expected to increase by 2.4 million, or 15.4 percent, by 2012. Among managers, the numbers of computer and information systems managers and of preschool and childcare center/program educational administrators will grow the fastest, by 36.1 percent and 32 percent, respectively. General and operations managers will add the most new jobs, 376,000, by 2012. Farmers and ranchers are the only workers in this major occupational group whose numbers are expected to decline, losing 238,000 jobs. Among business and financial occupations, accountants and auditors and management analysts will add the most jobs, 381,000 combined. Management analysts also will be one of the fastest growing occupations in this group, along with personal financial advisors, with job increases of 30.4 percent and 34.6 percent, respectively.

Construction and extraction occupations. Construction and extraction workers construct new residential and commercial buildings, and also work in mines, quarries, and oil and gas fields. Employment of these workers is expected to grow 15 percent, adding 1.1 million new jobs. Construction trades and related workers will account for more than three-fourths of these new jobs, 857,000, by 2012. Many extraction occupations will decline, reflecting overall employment losses in the mining and oil and gas extraction industries.

Installation, maintenance, and repair occupations. Workers in installation, maintenance, and repair occupations install new equipment and maintain and repair older equipment. These occupations will add 776,000 jobs by 2012, growing by 13.6 percent. Automo-

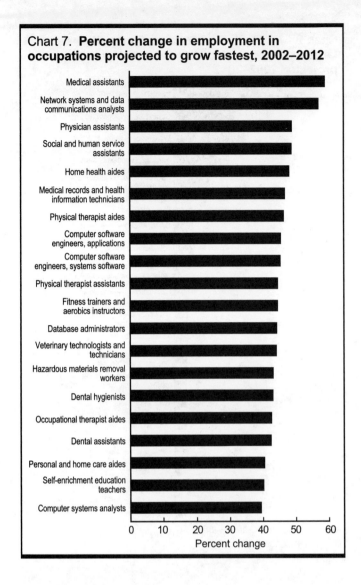

Chart 7. Percent change in employment in occupations projected to grow fastest, 2002–2012

Medical assistants
Network systems and data communications analysts
Physician assistants
Social and human service assistants
Home health aides
Medical records and health information technicians
Physical therapist aides
Computer software engineers, applications
Computer software engineers, systems software
Physical therapist assistants
Fitness trainers and aerobics instructors
Database administrators
Veterinary technologists and technicians
Hazardous materials removal workers
Dental hygienists
Occupational therapist aides
Dental assistants
Personal and home care aides
Self-enrichment education teachers
Computer systems analysts

Percent change: 0 10 20 30 40 50 60

public, and distributing information. Employment in these occupations is expected to grow by 6.8 percent, adding 1.6 million new jobs by 2012. Customer service representatives will add the most new jobs, 460,000. Desktop publishers will be among the fastest growing occupations in this group, increasing by 29.2 percent over the decade. Office and administrative support occupations account for 11 of the 20 occupations with the largest employment declines.

Farming, fishing, and forestry occupations. Farming, fishing, and forestry workers cultivate plants, breed and raise livestock, and catch animals. These occupations will grow 3.3 percent and add 35,000 new jobs by 2012. Agricultural workers, including farmworkers and laborers, accounted for the overwhelming majority of new jobs in this group. The numbers of both fishing and logging workers are expected to decline, by 26.8 percent and 3.2 percent, respectively.

Production occupations. Production workers are employed mainly in manufacturing, where they assemble goods and operate plants. Production occupations will have the slowest job growth among the major occupational groups, 3.2 percent, adding 354,000 jobs by 2012. Jobs will be created for many production occupations, including food processing workers, machinists, and welders, cutters, solderers, and brazers. Textile, apparel, and furnishings occupations, as well as assemblers and fabricators, will account for much of the job losses among production occupations.

Among all occupations in the economy, computer and healthcare occupations are expected to grow the fastest over the projection period (chart 7). In fact, healthcare occupations make up 10 of the 20 fastest growing occupations, while computer occupations account for 5 out of the 20 fastest growing occupations in the economy. In addition to high growth rates, these 15 computer and healthcare occupations combined will add more than 1.5 million new jobs. High growth rates among computer and healthcare occupations reflect projected rapid growth in the computer and data processing and health services industries.

The 20 occupations listed in chart 8 will account for more than one-third of all new jobs, 8 million combined, over the 2002-12 period. The occupations with the largest numerical increases cover a wider range of occupational categories than do those occupations with the fastest growth rates. Health occupations will account for some of these increases in employment, as well as occupations in education, sales, transportation, office and administrative support, and food service. Many of these occupations are very large, and will create more new jobs than will those with high growth rates. Only 2 out of the 20 fastest growing occupations—home health aides and personal and home care aides—also are projected to be among the 20 occupations with the largest numerical increases in employment.

Declining occupational employment stems from declining industry employment, technological advancements, changes in business practices, and other factors. For example, increased productivity and farm consolidations are expected to result in a decline of 238,000 farmers and ranchers over the 2002-12 period (chart 9). The majority of the 20 occupations with the largest numerical decreases are office and administrative support and production occupations, which are affected by increasing plant and factory automation and the implementation of office technology that reduces the needs for these workers. For example, employment of word processors and typists is expected to decline due to the proliferation of personal computers, which allows other workers to perform duties formerly assigned to word processors and typists.

tive service technicians and mechanics and general maintenance and repair workers will account for more than 4 in 10 new installation, maintenance, and repair jobs. The fastest growth rate will be among heating, air-conditioning, and refrigeration mechanics and installers, an occupation that is expected to grow 31.8 percent over the 2002-12 period.

Transportation and material moving occupations. Transportation and material-moving workers transport people and materials by land, sea, or air. The number of these workers should grow 13.1 percent, accounting for 1.3 million additional jobs by 2012. Among transportation occupations, motor vehicle operators will add the most jobs, 760,000. Rail transportation occupations are the only group in which employment is projected to decline, by 5.4 percent, through 2012. Material moving occupations will grow 8.9 percent and will add 422,000 jobs.

Sales and related occupations. Sales and related workers transfer goods and services among businesses and consumers. Sales and related occupations are expected to add 2 million new jobs by 2012, growing by 12.9 percent. The majority of these jobs will be among retail salespersons and cashiers, occupations that will add more than 1 million jobs combined.

Office and administrative support occupations. Office and administrative support workers perform the day-to-day activities of the office, such as preparing and filing documents, dealing with the

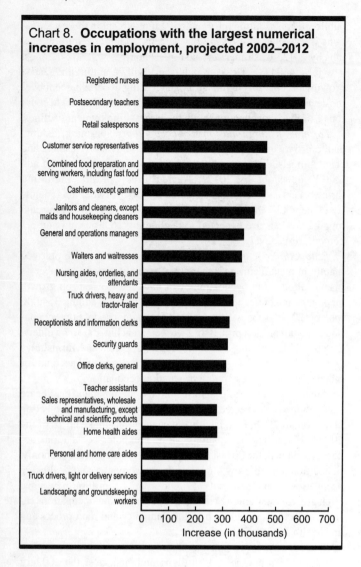

Chart 8. **Occupations with the largest numerical increases in employment, projected 2002–2012**

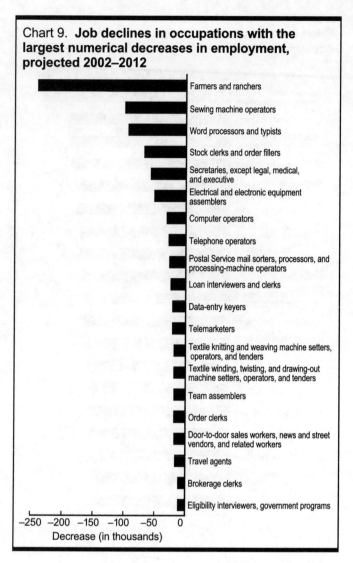

Chart 9. **Job declines in occupations with the largest numerical decreases in employment, projected 2002–2012**

Education and training

Education is essential in getting a high-paying job. In fact, for all but 1 of the 50 highest paying occupations, a college degree or higher is the most significant source of education or training. Air traffic controllers is the only occupation of the 50 highest paying for which this is not the case.

Among the 20 fastest growing occupations, a bachelor's or associate degree is the most significant source of education or training for 10 of them—network systems and data communications analysts; physician assistants; medical records and health information technicians; computer software engineers, applications; computer software engineers, systems software; physical therapist assistants; database administrators; veterinary technologists and technicians; dental hygienists; and computer systems analysts. On-the-job training is the most significant source of education or training for another 8 of the 20 fastest growing occupations—medical assistants, social and human service assistants, home health aides, physical therapist aides, hazardous materials removal workers, occupational therapist aides, dental assistants, and personal and home care aides. In contrast, on-the-job training is the most significant source of education or training for 17 of the 20 occupations with the largest numerical increases; 3 of these 20 occupations—registered nurses, postsecondary teachers, and general and operations

managers—have an associate or higher degree as the most significant source of education or training. On-the-job training also is the most significant source of education or training for 19 of the 20 occupations with the largest numerical decreases; one of these 20 occupations—travel agents—has a postsecondary vocational award as the most significant source of education or training. Table 1 lists the fastest growing occupations and occupations projected to have the largest numerical increases in employment between 2002 and 2012, by level of education or training.

Total job openings

Job openings stem from both employment growth and replacement needs (chart 10). Replacement needs arise as workers leave occupations. Some transfer to other occupations while others retire, return to school, or quit to assume household responsibilities. Replacement needs are projected to account for 60 percent of the approximately 56 million job openings between 2002 and 2012. Thus, even occupations projected to experience little or no growth or to decline in employment still may offer many job openings.

Professional and related occupations are projected to grow faster and add more jobs than any other major occupational group, with 6.5 million new jobs by 2012. Three-fourths of the job growth in professional and related occupations is expected among computer

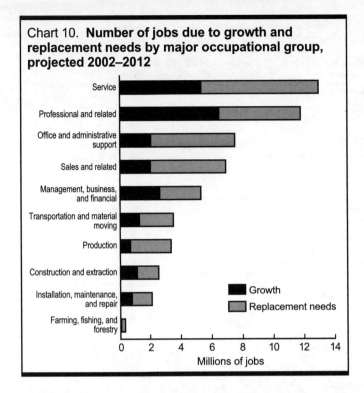

Chart 10. Number of jobs due to growth and replacement needs by major occupational group, projected 2002–2012

and mathematical occupations; healthcare practitioners and technical occupations; and education, training, and library occupations. With 5.3 million job openings due to replacement needs, professional and related occupations are the only major group projected to generate more openings from job growth than from replacement needs.

Service occupations are projected to have the largest number of total job openings, 13 million, reflecting high replacement needs. A large number of replacements will be necessary as young workers leave food preparation and service occupations. Replacement needs generally are greatest in the largest occupations and in those with relatively low pay or limited training requirements.

Office automation will significantly affect many individual office and administrative support occupations. Overall, these occupations are projected to grow more slowly than average, while some are projected to decline. Office and administrative support occupations are projected to create 7.5 million job openings over the 2002-12 period, ranking third behind service and professional and related occupations.

Farming, fishing, and forestry occupations are projected to have the fewest job openings, approximately 335,000. Because job growth is expected to be slow, and levels of retirement and job turnover high, more than 85 percent of these projected job openings are due to replacement needs.

Table 1.   Fastest growing occupations and occupations projected to have the largest numerical increases in employment between 2002 and 2012, by level of education or training

Fastest growing occupations	Education or training level	Occupations having the largest numerical job growth
	First professional degree	
Pharmacists		Lawyers
Veterinarians		Physicians and surgeons
Chiropractors		Pharmacists
Physicians and surgeons		Clergy
Optometrists		Veterinarians
	Doctoral degree	
Postsecondary teachers		Postsecondary teachers
Computer and information scientists, research		Clinical, counseling, and school psychologists
Medical scientists, except epidemiologists		Medical scientists, except epidemiologists
Clinical, counseling, and school psychologists		Computer and information scientists, research
Biochemists and biophysicists		Biochemists and biophysicists
	Master's degree	
Physical therapists		Physical therapists
Mental health and substance abuse social workers		Rehabilitation counselors
Rehabilitation counselors		Educational, vocational, and school counselors
Survey researchers		Mental health and substance abuse social workers
Epidemiologists		Market research analysts
	Bachelor's or higher degree, plus work experience	
Computer and information systems managers		General and operations managers
Education administrators, preschool and childcare center/program		Management analysts
Sales managers		Financial managers
Management analysts		Sales managers
Medical and health services managers		Computer and information systems managers
	Bachelor's degree	
Network systems and data communications analysts		Elementary school teachers, except special education
Physician assistants		Accountants and auditors
Computer software engineers, applications		Computer systems analysts
Computer software engineers, systems software		Secondary school teachers, except special and vocational education
Database administrators		Computer software engineers, applications
	Associate degree	
Medical records and health information technicians		Registered nurses
Physical therapist assistants		Computer support specialists
Veterinary technologists and technicians		Medical records and health information technicians
Dental hygienists		Dental hygienists
Occupational therapist assistants		Paralegals and legal assistants
	Postsecondary vocational award	
Fitness trainers and aerobics instructors		Preschool teachers, except special education
Preschool teachers, except special education		Licensed practical and licensed vocational nurses
Respiratory therapy technicians		Automotive service technicians and mechanics
Emergency medical technicians and paramedics		Hairdressers, hairstylists, and cosmetologists
Security and fire alarm systems installers		Fitness trainers and aerobics instructors
	Work experience in a related occupation	
Self-enrichment education teachers		First-line supervisors/managers of retail sales workers
Emergency management specialists		First-line supervisors/managers of food preparation and serving workers
Private detectives and investigators		First-line supervisors/managers of office and administrative support workers
First-line supervisors/managers of protective service workers, except police, fire, and corrections		First-line supervisors/managers of construction trades and extraction workers
Detectives and criminal investigators		Self-enrichment education teachers
	Long-term on-the-job training	
Heating, air-conditioning, and refrigeration mechanics and installers		Electricians
Audio and video equipment technicians		Police and sheriff's patrol officers
Tile and marble setters		Carpenters
Police and sheriff's patrol officers		Cooks, restaurant
Electricians		Plumbers, pipefitters, and steamfitters
	Moderate-term on-the-job training	
Medical assistants		Customer service representatives
Social and human service assistants		Truck drivers, heavy and tractor-trailer
Hazardous materials removal workers		Sales representatives, wholesale and manufacturing, except technical and scientific products
Dental assistants		Medical assistants
Residential advisors		Maintenance and repair workers, general
	Short-term on-the-job training	
Home health aides		Retail salespersons
Physical therapist aides		Combined food preparation and serving workers, including fast food
Occupational therapist aides		Cashiers, except gaming
Personal and home care aides		Janitors and cleaners, except maids and housekeeping cleaners
Security guards		Waiters and waitresses

Sources of Career Information

This section identifies sources of information about career planning, counseling, training, education, and financial aid. Handbook statements also include a section on sources of additional information, which lists organizations that can be contacted for more information about particular occupations including, in some cases, the required training and education.

Career information

Listed below are several places to begin collecting information on careers and job opportunities.

Personal contacts. The people close to you—your family and friends—can be extremely helpful in providing career information. They may be able to answer your questions directly or put you in touch with someone else who can. Networking can lead to meeting someone who can answer your questions about a specific career or company and provide inside information and other helpful hints. It is an effective way to learn the type of training they found necessary for a certain position, how they entered the field, their prospects for advancement, and what they like and dislike about the work.

Public libraries, career centers, and guidance offices. These institutions maintain a great deal of up-to-date material. To begin your library search, look at the computer listings under "vocations" or "careers," and then under specific fields. Check the periodicals section, where trade and professional magazines and journals about specific occupations and industries are located. Become familiar with the concerns and activities of potential employers by skimming their annual reports and other public documents. Occupational information on video cassettes and computerized information systems or the Internet can be valuable. Don't forget the librarians; they can be a great source and can save you valuable time by directing you to relevant information.

Check your school's career centers for resources such as individual counseling and testing, guest speakers, field trips, books, career magazines, and career days.

Always assess career guidance materials carefully. The information should be current and objective. Beware of materials that seem to glamorize the occupation, overstate the earnings, or exaggerate the demand for workers.

Counselors. These professionals are trained to help you discover your strengths and weaknesses, evaluate your goals and values, and determine what you would like in a career. Counselors will not tell you what to do. However, they may administer interest inventories and aptitude tests, interpret the results, and help you explore various options. Counselors also may discuss local job markets and the entry requirements and costs of schools, colleges, or training programs. Counselors are found in:

- High school guidance offices
- College career planning and placement offices
- Placement offices in private vocational or technical schools and institutions
- Vocational rehabilitation agencies

- Counseling services offered by community organizations
- Private counseling agencies and private practices
- State employment service offices

Before employing the services of a private counselor or agency, you may want to seek recommendations and check their credentials. The International Association of Counseling Services (IACS) accredits counseling services throughout the country. Most of these accredited services are college and university services restricted to students of those schools. To receive a listing of accredited services for your region, send a self-addressed, stamped, business-size envelope to:

➤ IACS, 101 South Whiting St., Suite 211, Alexandria, VA 22304. Telephone: (703) 823-9840. Internet: **http://www.iacsinc.org.**

The Directory of Counseling Services, an IACS publication providing employment counseling and other assistance, may be available in your library or school career counseling center. A list of certified career counselors—most of whom are private, for-fee counselors—by city or State is available from:

➤ National Board of Certified Counselors, 3 Terrace Way, Suite D, Greensboro, NC 27403-3660. Telephone: (336) 547-0607. Internet: **http://www.nbcc.org.**

Internet networks and resources. The growth of online listings has made countless resources instantly available at any time. Most companies, professional societies, academic institutions, and government agencies maintain Internet sites that highlight the organization's latest information and activities.

Listings may include information such as government documents, schedules of events, and job openings. Corporate and government Web sites often provide job application information, including links for submitting resumes. Listings for academic institutions often provide links to career counseling and placement services through career resource centers, as well as information on financing your education. Colleges and universities also offer online guides to campus facilities and admission requirements and procedures.

The career information available through the Internet provides much of the same information available through libraries, career centers, and guidance offices. However, no single network or resource will contain all desired information, so be prepared to search in a variety of places. As in a library search, look through various lists by field or discipline, or by using keywords.

Career sites can be an excellent place to obtain information about job opportunities. They provide a forum for employers to list job openings and for individuals to post their resumes. Some Internet sites also may provide an opportunity to research a particular industry or company.

A major portion of the U.S. Department of Labor's Labor Market Information System is the CareerOneStop site, which operates as a Federal-State partnership. This site includes America's Job Bank (AJB), America's Career InfoNet, and America's Service Locator. CareerOneStop, along with the National Tollfree Helpline (877-US2-JOBS) and the local One-Stop Career Centers in each State, combine to provide a wide range of workforce assistance and resources. Internet: **http://www.careeronestop.org.**

America's Job Bank (AJB), administered by the U.S. Department of Labor, lists more than 1 million job openings on any given day. These job openings are compiled by State employment service offices throughout the Nation. AJB is accessible at: **http://www.ajb.org.**

America's Career InfoNet is an especially useful site. It provides data on employment growth and wages by occupation; the knowledge, skills, and abilities required by an occupation; and links to employers. Internet: **http://www.acinet.org/acinet.**

America's Service Locator is a partnership between the U.S. Department of Labor, State governments, and local agencies to provide a comprehensive database of service providers accessible via telephone or the Internet by the public. Use of the database is free of charge and directs customers to a range of services available in their area, including unemployment benefits, job training, youth programs, seminars, education opportunities, and disabled or older worker programs, among others. Internet: **http://www.servicelocator.org.**

Career Voyages is the result of a collaboration between the U.S. Department of Labor and the U.S. Department of Education. It is designed to provide information on high-growth, high-demand occupations along with the skills and education needed to attain those jobs. Career Voyages is accessible at: **http://www.careervoyages.gov.**

Professional societies, trade associations, labor unions, business firms, and educational institutions. These organizations provide a variety of free or inexpensive career material. Many of these are listed in the sources of additional information section at the end of individual Handbook statements. For information on occupations not covered in the *Handbook*, consult directories in your library's reference section for the names of potential sources. You may start with *The Guide to American Directories* or *The Directory of Directories.* Another useful resource is *The Encyclopedia of Associations*, an annual publication listing trade associations, professional societies, labor unions, and fraternal and patriotic organizations.

The National Technical Information Service Audiovisual Center, a central source for audiovisual material produced by the U.S. Government, sells material on jobs and careers. For a catalog, contact:

➤ NTIS Audiovisual Center, Springfield, VA 22161. Telephone: (703) 605-6000 or (800) 553-6847. Internet: **http://www.ntis.gov/nac.**

Federal Government. Information on employment with the Federal Government is available from the U.S. Office of Personnel Management (OPM) through a telephone-based system. Consult your telephone directory under U.S. Government for a local number or call (703) 724-1850; Federal Relay Service: (800) 877-8339. The first number is not tollfree, and charges may result. Information also is available from the OPM Internet site: **http://www.usajobs.opm.gov.**

Information and resources for potential applicants and current employees pertaining to Federal employment of people with disabilities is available at: **http://www.opm.gov/disability.**

Organizations for specific groups. The organizations listed below provide information on career planning, training, or job opportunities prepared for specific groups. Consult directories in your library's reference center or a career guidance office for information on additional organizations associated with specific groups.

Disabled workers:
Counseling, training, and placement services for those with disabilities are available from the State Vocational Rehabilitation

Agency: Internet:

http://bccol02.ed.gov/Programs/EROD org_list.cfm?category_ID=SVR.

Information on employment opportunities for people with all types of disabilities is available from:

➤ National Organization on Disability, 910 Sixteenth St. NW., Suite 600, Washington, DC 20006. Telephone: (202) 293-5960. TTY: (202) 293-5968. Internet: **http://www.nod.org/economic.**

➤ Half the Planet Foundation, 1875 Eye St. NW., 12th Floor, Washington, DC 20006. Internet: **http://www.halftheplanet.org.**

➤ Job Accommodation Network (JAN). Internet: **http://ww.jan.wvu.edu.**

A comprehensive Federal Web site of disability-related resources is accessible at: **http://www.disabilityinfo.gov.**

Blind workers:
Information on the free national reference and referral service for the blind can be obtained by contacting:

➤ National Federation of the Blind, Job Opportunities for the Blind (JOB), 1800 Johnson St., Baltimore, MD 21230. Telephone: (410) 659-9314. Internet: **http://www.nfb.org.**

Older workers:

➤ National Council on the Aging, 300 D St. SW., Suite 8010, Washington, DC 20024. Telephone: (202) 479-1200. Internet: **http://www.ncoa.org.**

➤ National Caucus and Center on Black Aged, Inc., Senior Employment Programs, 1220 L St. NW., Suite 800, Washington, DC 20005. Telephone: (202) 637-8400. Fax: (202) 347-0895. Internet: **http://www.ncba-aged.org.**

Veterans:
Contact the nearest regional office of the U.S. Department of Labor Veterans' Employment and Training Service or:

➤ Credentialing Opportunities On-Line (COOL), which explains how Army soldiers can meet civilian certification and license requirements related to their Military Occupational Specialty (MOS). Internet: **https://www.cool.army.mil/index.htm.**

Women:

➤ Department of Labor, Women's Bureau, 200 Constitution Ave. NW., Washington, DC 20210. Telephone: (800) 827-5335. Internet: **http://www.dol.gov/wb.**

➤ Wider Opportunities for Women, 1001 Connecticut Ave. NW., Suite 930, Washington, DC 20036. Telephone: (202) 464-1596. Internet: **http://www.WOWonline.org.**

Federal laws, executive orders, and selected Federal grant programs bar discrimination in employment based on race, color, religion, sex, national origin, age, and handicap. Information on how to file a charge of discrimination is available from U.S. Equal Employment Opportunity Commission offices around the country. Their addresses and telephone numbers are listed in telephone directories under U.S. Government, EEOC. Telephone: (800) 669-4000 (TTY 1-800-669-6820). Internet: **http://www.eeoc.gov.**

Education and training information

Colleges, schools, and training institutes readily reply to requests for information about their programs. When contacting these institutions, you may want to keep in mind the following items:

- Admission requirements
- Courses offered
- Certificates or degrees awarded
- Cost
- Available financial aid
- Location and size of school
- Placement rate of graduates

Check with professional and trade associations for lists of schools that offer career preparation in a field in which you are interested. High school guidance offices and libraries usually have copies of the directories listed below, as well as college catalogs that can provide more information on specific institutions.

The U.S. Department of Education's IPEDS (Integrated Postsecondary Education Data System) program has an interactive school search system. You can search for any postsecondary school, focusing your search for a school based upon many factors: Number of students, type of school (2-year colleges, 4-year colleges, trade schools), public or privately funded institutions, instructional programs and fields of study (majors), accreditation, and geographic location. Once you've narrowed your choices, the site provides more detailed information on specific schools, including contact information. There also are links to other helpful sites. Internet: **http://nces.ed.gov/ipeds/cool/index.asp.**

The *Directory of Private Career Schools and Colleges of Technology*, put out by the Accrediting Commission of Career Schools and Colleges of Technology, is a helpful resource. Be sure to use the latest edition because these directories and catalogs are revised periodically.

Information about home or correspondence study programs appears in the *Directory of Accredited Institutions*. Send requests for the *Directory* and a list of other publications to:

➤ Distance Education and Training Council, 1601 18th St. NW., Washington, DC 20009-2529. Telephone: (202) 234-5100. Internet:**http://www.detc.org.**

Information about apprenticeships is available from local labor unions, school guidance counselors, and State employment offices or from:

➤ U.S. Department of Labor, Employment and Training Administration, 200 Constitution Ave. NW., Washington, DC 20210. Telephone: (202) 693-3812. Internet: **http://www.doleta.gov.**

Completing an internship is an excellent way for students and others to learn about an occupation and to make valuable contacts. Many employers offer internships that provide short-term or part-time job experience that can lead to a permanent position. Contact your school's career guidance center or employers directly regarding internship opportunities.

Financial aid information

Information about financial aid is available from a variety of sources. Contact your high school guidance counselor and college financial aid officer for information concerning qualifications and applications for scholarships, fellowships, grants, loans, and work-study programs. Every State administers financial aid programs; contact State Departments of Education for information. Banks and credit unions will provide information about student loans. You also may want to consult the directories and guides available in guidance offices and public libraries for sources of student financial aid.

The Federal Government provides grants, loans, work-study programs, and other benefits to students. Information about programs administered by the U.S. Department of Education is presented in The Student Guide to Federal Financial Aid Programs, updated annually. To receive a copy, write to:

➤ Federal Student Aid Information Center, c/o Federal Student Aid Programs,P.O. Box 84, Washington, DC 20044-0084. Telephone: (800) 433-3243. Internet: **http://www.ed.gov/offices/OSFAP/Students.**

The U.S. Department of Health and Human Services offers student loan, scholarship, and faculty loan repayment programs for health-related professions. For information, contact:

➤ HRSA, Bureau of Health Professions, Division of Student Assistance, Parklawn Bldg., Room 8-34, 5600 Fishers Lane, Rockville, MD 20857. Telephone: (888) 275-4772. Internet: **http://www.bhpr.hrsa.gov/dsa index.htm.**

College is Possible—a resource guide prepared by the Coalition of America's Colleges and Universities and the U.S. Department of Education—lists books, pamphlets, and Internet sites that help students prepare for, choose, and pay for college. It includes information on scholarships and is available in English and Spanish. Telephone: (800) 433-3243. Internet: **http://www.collegeispossible.org.**

The Armed Forces have several educational assistance programs. These include the Reserve Officers' Training Corps (ROTC), the new G.I. bill, and tuition assistance. Information can be obtained from military recruiting centers, located in most cities. Internet: **http://www.defenselink.mil/other_info/careers.html.**

State and local information

The *Handbook* provides information for the Nation as a whole. State or local area information is available from:

State Employment Security Agencies. These agencies develop detailed information about local labor markets, such as current and projected employment by occupation and industry, characteristics of the work force, and changes in State and local area economic activity. Listed below are the Internet addresses of these agencies and addresses and telephone numbers of the directors of research and analysis in these agencies.

Most States have career information delivery systems (CIDS). Look for these systems in secondary schools, postsecondary institutions, libraries, job training sites, vocational rehabilitation centers, and employment service offices. The public can use the systems' computers, printed material, microfiche, and tollfree hotlines to obtain information on occupations, educational opportunities, student financial aid, apprenticeships, and military careers. Ask counselors for specific locations.

State occupational projections also are available on the Internet: **http://www.projectionscentral.com**

Alabama
Chief, Labor Market Information Division, Department of Industrial Relations, 649 Monroe St., Room 427, Montgomery, AL 36131-2280. Telephone: (334) 242-8859. Internet: **http://www.dir.state.al.us/lmi**

Alaska
Chief, Research and Analysis Section, Department of Labor and Workforce Development, 1111 West 8th St., Juneau, AK 99802-5501. Telephone: (907) 465-6035. Internet: **http://aimis.labor.state.ak.us**

Arizona
Research Administrator, Department of Economic Security, 1789 West Jefferson St., 733A, Phoenix, AZ 85007-3295. Telephone: (602) 542-3871. Internet: **http://www.workforce.az.gov**

Arkansas
Director, Labor Market Information, Employment Security Department, P.O. Box 2981, Little Rock, AR 72203-2981. Telephone: (501) 682-3159. Internet: **http://www.state.ar.us/esd**

California
Chief, Labor Market Information Division, MIC57, Employment Development Department, 7000 Franklin Blvd., Building 1100, Sacramento, CA 95823. Telephone: (916) 262-2160. Internet: **http://www.calmis.cahwnet.gov**

Colorado
Director, Labor Market Information, Department of Labor and Employment, 1515 Arapahoe St., Tower 2, Suite 300, Denver, CO 80202-2117. Telephone: (303) 318-8898. Internet: **http://www.coworkforce.com/lmi**

Connecticut
Director, Employment Security Division, Research and Information, Department of Labor, 200 Folly Brook Blvd., Wethersfield, CT 06109-1114. Telephone: (860) 263-6255. Internet: **http://www.ctdol.state.ct.us/lmi/index.htm**

Delaware
Chief, Office of Occupational and Labor Market Information, Department of Labor, 4425 N. Market St.-Fox Valley Annex, Wilmington, DE 19809-1307. Telephone: (302) 761-8050. Internet: **http://www.oolmi.net**

District of Columbia
Chief, Office of Labor Market Research and Information, 64 New York Ave. NE., Suite 3035, Washington, D.C. 20002. Telephone: (202) 671-1633. Internet: **http://does.ci.washington.dc.us/info/labor_mkt.shtm**

Florida
Process Manager, Labor Market Statistics, Agency for Workforce Innovation, MSC G-020, 107 E. Madison St., Tallahassee, FL 32399-4111. Telephone: (850) 488-1048. Internet: **http://www.labormarketinfo.com**

Georgia
Director, Workforce Information and Analysis, Room 300, Department of Labor, 223 Courtland St., CWC Building, Atlanta, GA 30303. Telephone: (404) 232-3875. Internet: **http://www.dol.state.ga.us/lmi**

Guam
Director, Government of Guam, Sunny Plaza, 2nd Floor, 125 Tun Jesus Crisostomo, Tamuning, GU 96911. Telephone: (671) 647-7066.

Hawaii
Chief, Research and Statistics Office, Department of Labor and Industrial Relations, 830 Punchbowl St., Room 304, Honolulu, HI 96813. Telephone: (808) 586-8999. Internet: **http://www.state.hi.us/dlir/rs/loihi**

Idaho
Chief, Research and Analysis Bureau, Department of Labor, 317 Main St., Boise, ID 83735-0670. Telephone: (208) 334-6170. Internet: **http://www.labor.state.id.us/lmi/id-lmi.htm**

Illinois
Director, Economic Information and Analysis, Illinois Department of Employment Security, 401 South State St., 7th Floor-North, Chicago, IL 60605. Telephone: (312) 793-2316. Internet: **http://lmi.ides.state.il.us**

Indiana
Director, Labor Market Information - South E211, Department of Workforce Development, 10 North Senate Ave., Indianapolis, IN 46204-2277. Telephone: (317) 232-7460. Internet: **http://www.dwd.state.in.us**

Iowa
Division Administrator, Information and Policy Division, Iowa Workforce Development, 1000 East Grand Ave., Des Moines, IA 50319-0209. Telephone: (515) 281-0255. Internet: **http://www.state.ia.us/iwd**

Kansas
Chief, Labor Market Information Services, Department of Human Resources, 401 SW Topeka Blvd., Topeka, KS 66603-3182. Telephone: (785) 296-5058. Internet: **http://laborstats.hr.state.ks.us**

Kentucky
Manager, Research and Statistics Branch, Department for Employment Services, Workforce Development Cabinet, 275 East Main St., 2 W-G, Frankfort, KY 40621. Telephone: (502) 564-7976. Internet: **http://www.workforcekentucky.ky.gov**

Louisiana
Director, Research and Statistics Section, Department of Labor, 1001 North 23rd St., Baton Rouge, LA 70804-4094. Telephone: (225) 342-3141. Internet: **http://www.laworks.net**

Maine
Director, Division of Labor Market Information Services, Maine Department of Labor, 20 Union St., Augusta, ME 04330-6826. Telephone: (207) 287-2271. Internet: **http://www.state.me.us/labor/lmis/index.html**

Maryland
Director, Labor Market Analysis and Information, Department of Labor, Licensing and Regulations, 1100 North Eutaw St., Room 316, Baltimore, Md. 21201-2206. Telephone: (410) 767-2250. Internet: **http://www.dllr.state.md.us/lmi/index.htm**

Massachusetts
Assistant Director for Research, Division of Employment and Training, 19 Staniford St., Boston, MA 02114. Telephone: (617) 626-6556. Internet: **http://www.detma.org/lmiinfo.htm**

Michigan
Director, Labor Market Information Division, Department of Career Development, 3032 West Grand Blvd., 9th Floor, Detroit, MI 48202. Telephone: (313) 456-3090. Internet: **http://www.michlmi.org**

Minnesota
Labor Market Information Director, Department of Employment and Economic Development, 390 N. Robert St., 5th Floor, St. Paul, MN 55101. Telephone: (651) 296-4087. Internet: **http://www.mnwfc.org/lmi.htm**

Mississippi
Chief, Labor Market Information Division, Employment Security Commission, 1520 West Capitol St., Jackson, MS 39215-1699. Telephone: (601) 961-7424. Internet: **http://www.mesc.state.ms.us/lmi/index.html**

Missouri
Research Manager, Labor Market Information, Department of Economic Development, 301 West High St., Jefferson City, MO 65102. Telephone: (573) 751-3609. Internet: **http://www.works.state.mo.us/lmi**

Montana
Director, Research and Analysis, Department of Labor and Industry, 1327 Lockey and Roberts Sts., Helena, MT 59601. Telephone: (406) 444-2430. Internet: **http://rad.dli.state.mt.us**

Nebraska
Administrator, Labor Market Information Center, Nebraska Workforce Development, 550 South 16th St., Lincoln, NE 68508. Telephone: (402) 471-9964. Internet: **http://www.dol.state.ne.us/nelmi.htm**

Nevada
Chief, Research and Analysis, Department of Employment Training and Rehabilitation, 500 East Third St., Carson City, NV 89713-0020. Telephone: (775) 684-0387. Internet: **http://www.detr.state.nv.us/lmi/index.htm**

New Hampshire
Director, Economic and Labor Market Information, Department of Employment Security, 32 South Main St., Concord, NH 03301-4587. Telephone: (603) 228-4123. Internet: **http://www.nhworks.state.nh.us/lmipage.htm**

New Jersey
Director, Labor Market and Demographic Research, Department of Labor, John Fitch Plaza, 5th Floor, Trenton, NJ 08625. Telephone: (609) 292-0099. Internet: **http://www.state.nj.us/labor/lra**

New Mexico
Research Chief, Economic Research and Analysis, Department of Labor, 501 Mountain Rd., Albuquerque, NM 87102. Telephone: (505) 841-8645. Internet: **http://www.dol.state.nm.us/dol_lmif.html**

New York
Director, Division of Research and Statistics, New York State Department of Labor, State Campus, Building 12, Room 402, Albany, NY 12240-0020. Telephone: (518) 457-6369. Internet: **http://www.labor.state.ny.us**

North Carolina
Director, Labor Market Information Division, Employment Security Commission, 700 Wade Ave., Raleigh, NC 27605. Telephone: (919) 733-2936. Internet: **http://www.ncesc.com**

North Dakota
LMI Director, Research and Statistics, Job Service North Dakota, 1000 East Divide, Bismarck, ND 58501. Telephone: (701) 328-2868.Internet: **http://www.state.nd.us/jsnd warehouse.htm?bookmark=warehouse**

Ohio
Director, Labor Market Information Division, Department of Job and Family Services, 4300 Kimberly Pkwy., 3rd Floor, Columbus, OH 43232. Telephone: (614) 752-9494. Internet: **http://lmi.state.oh.us**

Oklahoma
Director, Economic Research and Analysis, Employment Security Commission, 2401 N. Lincoln, Room 402-1, Oklahoma City, OK 73105. Telephone: (405) 557-7265. Internet: **http://www.oesc.state.ok.us/lmi/default.htm**

Oregon
Manager, Workforce and Economic Research, Oregon Employment Department, 875 Union St., NE., Room 207, Salem, OR 97311-9986. Telephone: (503) 947-1212. Internet: **http://olmis.emp.state.or.us**

Pennsylvania
Director, Center for Workforce Information and Analysis, Department of Labor and Industry, Seventh and Forster Sts., Room 220, Harrisburg, PA 17121-0001. Telephone: (717) 787-3266. Internet: **www.dli.state.pa.us/workforceinfo**

Puerto Rico
Director, Bureau of Labor Statistics, Department of Labor and Human Resources, 505 Munoz Rivera Ave., 17th Floor, Hato Rey, PR 00918. Telephone: (787) 754-5340.

Rhode Island
Director, Labor Market Information, Department of Employment and Training, 1511 Pontiac Ave., Cranston, RI 02920. Telephone: (401) 462-8767. Internet: **http://www.dlt.ri.gov/lmi**

South Carolina
Director, Labor Market Information Division, Employment Security Commission, 631 Hampton St., Columbia, SC 29201. Telephone: (803) 737-2660. Internet: **http://www.sces.org/lmi/index.asp**

South Dakota
Director, Labor Market Information Division, Department of Labor, 420 S. Roosevelt St., Aberdeen, SD 57401-5131. Telephone: (605) 626-2314. Internet: **http://www.state.sd.us/dol/lmic/index.htm**

Tennessee
Director, Research and Statistics Division, Department of Labor and Workforce Development, 500 James Robertson Pkwy., 11th Floor, Nashville, TN 37245-1000. Telephone: (615) 741-2284. Internet: **http://www.state.tn.us/labor-wfd/lmi.htm**

Texas
Director, Labor Market Information, Texas Workforce Commission, 9001 North IH-35, Suite 103A, Austin, TX 75753. Telephone: (512) 491-4802. Internet: **http://www.tracer2.com**

Utah
LMI Director, Workforce Information, Department of Workforce Services, 140 East 300 South, Salt Lake City, UT 84111. Telephone: (801) 526-9401. Internet: **http://jobs.utah.gov/wi**

Vermont
Chief, Research and Analysis, Department of Employment and Training, 5 Green Mountain Dr., Montpelier, VT 05602. Telephone: (802) 828-4153. Internet: **http://www.vtlmi.info**

Virgin Islands
Chief, Bureau of Labor Statistics, Department of Labor, 53-A, 54 A and B, Kronprindsens Gade, Charlotte Amalie, VI 00801. Telephone: (340) 776-3700.

Virginia
Director, Economic Information Services, Virginia Employment Commission, 703 East Main St., Richmond, VA 23219. Telephone: (804) 786-7496. Internet: **http://www.vec.state.va.us/index.cfm?loc=lbrmkt&info=lmi**

Washington
Director, Labor Market and Economic Analysis, Employment Security Department, 605 Woodland Square Loop, Lacey, WA 98506. Telephone: (360) 438-4804. Internet: **http://www.wa.gov/esd/lmea**

West Virginia
Director, Research Information and Analysis Division, Bureau of Employment Programs, 112 California Ave., Room 107, Charleston, WV 25305-0112. Telephone: (304) 558-2660. Internet: **http://www.state.wv.us/bep/lmi/default.htm**

Wisconsin
Director, Bureau of Workforce Information, Department of Workforce Development, 201 E. Washington Ave., Madison, WI 53702. Telephone: (608) 267-9705. Internet: **http://www.dwd.state.wi.us/dwelmi**

Wyoming
Manager, Research and Planning, Department of Employment, 246 South Center St., 2nd floor, Casper, WY 82601. Telephone: (307) 473-3807. Internet: **http://wydoe.state.wy.us**

Finding a Job and Evaluating a Job Offer

Finding information on available jobs

It takes some people a great deal of time and effort to find a job they enjoy. Others may walk right into an ideal employment situation. Do not be discouraged if you have to pursue many leads. Friends, neighbors, teachers, and counselors may know of available jobs in your field of interest. Read the classified ads. Consult State employment service offices and consider private employment agencies. You also may contact employers directly.

```
╔══════════════════════════════════════════════════╗
║       Where to learn about job openings           ║
║                                                    ║
║  Personal contacts                                 ║
║  School career planning and placement offices      ║
║  Employers                                         ║
║  Classified ads                                    ║
║      —National and local newspapers                ║
║      —Professional journals                        ║
║      —Trade magazines                              ║
║  Internet networks and resources                   ║
║  State employment service offices                  ║
║  Federal Government                                ║
║  Professional associations                         ║
║  Labor unions                                      ║
║  Private employment agencies and career consultants║
║  Community agencies                                ║
╚══════════════════════════════════════════════════╝
```

Job search methods

Personal contacts. Your family, friends, and acquaintances may offer one of the most effective ways to find a job. They may help you directly or put you in touch with someone else who can. Such networking can lead to information about specific job openings, many of which may not be publicly posted.

School career planning and placement offices. High school and college placement offices help their students and alumni find jobs. They set up appointments and allow recruiters to use their facilities for interviews. Placement offices usually have a list of part-time, temporary, and summer jobs offered on campus. They also may have lists of jobs for regional, nonprofit, and government organizations. Students can receive career counseling and testing and job search advice. At career resource libraries, they may attend workshops on such topics as job search strategy, resume writing, letter writing, and effective interviewing; critique drafts of resumes and watch videotapes of mock interviews; explore files of resumes and references; and attend job fairs conducted by the placement office.

Employers. Through your library and Internet research, develop a list of potential employers in your desired career field. Employer Web sites often contain lists of job openings. Websites and business directories can provide you with information on how to apply for a position or whom to contact. Even if no open positions are posted, do not hesitate to contact the employer and the relevant department. Set up an interview with someone working in the same area in which you wish to work. Ask them how they got started, what they enjoy or dislike about the work, what type of qualifications are necessary for the job, and what type of personality suc-

ceeds in that position. Even if they don't have a position available, they may be able to put you in contact with other people who might hire you, and they can keep you in mind if a position opens up. Make sure to send them your resume and a cover letter. If you are able to obtain an interview, be sure to send a thank-you note. Directly contacting employers is one of the most successful means of job hunting.

Classified ads. The "Help Wanted" ads in newspapers list numerous jobs. You should realize, however, that many other job openings are not listed, and that the classified ads sometimes do not give all of the important information. They may offer little or no description of the job, working conditions, or pay. Some ads do not identify the employer. They may simply give a post office box to which you can mail your resume, making followup inquiries very difficult. Some ads offer out-of-town jobs; others advertise employment agencies rather than actual employment opportunities.

When using classified ads, keep the following in mind:

- Do not rely solely on the classifieds to find a job; follow other leads as well.

- Answer ads promptly, because openings may be filled quickly, even before the ad stops appearing in the paper.

- Read the ads every day, particularly the Sunday edition, which usually includes the most listings.

- Beware of "no experience necessary" ads. These ads often signal low wages, poor working conditions, or commission work.

- Keep a record of all ads to which you have responded, including the specific skills, educational background, and personal qualifications required for the position.

Internet networks and resources. The Internet provides a variety of information, including job listings and job search resources and techniques. However, no single Web site or resource will contain all of the information available on employment or career opportunities, so be prepared to search for what you need. Remember that job listings may be posted by field or discipline, so begin your search using keywords. Some Web sites provide national or local classified listings and allow jobseekers to post their resumes online. Other sites offer advice on how to search for a job, prepare for an interview, or write your resume. When searching employment databases on the Internet, it usually is possible to send your resume to an employer by e-mail or to post it online.

State employment service offices. The State employment service, sometimes called the Job Service, operates in coordination with the U.S. Department of Labor's Employment and Training Administration. Local offices, found nationwide, help jobseekers to find jobs and help employers to find qualified workers at no cost to either. To find the office nearest you, look in the State government telephone listings under "Job Service" or "Employment."

Job matching and referral. At the State employment service office, an interviewer will determine if you are "job ready" or if you need help from counseling and testing services to assess your occupational aptitudes and interests and to help you choose and prepare for a career. After you are "job ready," you may examine available job listings and select openings that interest you. A staff member can then describe the job openings in detail and arrange for interviews with prospective employers.

America's Job Bank, sponsored by the U.S. Department of Labor, is an Internet site that allows you to search through a database of more than 1 million jobs nationwide, create and post your resume online, and set up an automated job search. The database contains a wide range of mostly full-time private sector jobs that are available all over the country. Jobseekers can access America's Job Bank at: **http://www.ajb.org**. Computers with access to the Internet are available to the public in any local public employment service office, school, library, or military installation.

Using Internet Resources to Plan your Future, a U.S. Department of Labor publication, offers advice on organizing your Internet job search. It is primarily intended to provide instruction for jobseekers on how to use the Internet to their best advantage, but recruiters and other career service industry professionals will find information here to help them also. How to Use the Internet in your Job Search; The Job Search Process; and the Career-Related Pages, other U.S. Department of Labor Internet publications, each discusses specific steps that jobseekers can follow to identify employment opportunities. Included are daily tips and hints, plus a large database of links and job search engines. Many Department of Labor and other publications for jobseekers are available at: **http://safetynet.doleta.gov/netsourc.htm**. Check with your State employment service office, or order a copy of these and other publications from the U.S. Government Printing Office's Superintendent of Documents. Telephone: (202) 512-1800. Internet: **http://bookstore.gpo.gov or http://www.doleta.gov.**

Services for special groups. By law, veterans are entitled to priority for job placement at State employment service centers. If you are a veteran, a veterans' employment representative can inform you of available assistance and help you to deal with problems.

State employment service offices refer people to opportunities available under the Workforce Investment Act (WIA) of 1998. WIA reforms Federal employment, adult education, and vocational rehabilitation programs to create an integrated, "one-stop" system of workforce investment and education activities for adults and youths. Services are provided to employers and jobseekers, including adults, dislocated workers, and youths. WIA's primary purpose is to increase the employment, retention, skills, and earnings of participants. These programs help to prepare people to participate in the State's workforce, increase their employment and earnings potential, improve their educational and occupational skills, and reduce their dependency on welfare, which will improve the quality of the workforce and enhance the productivity and competitiveness of the Nation's economy.

Federal Government. Information on obtaining a position with the Federal Government is available from the U.S. Office of Personnel Management (OPM) through a telephone-based system. Consult your telephone directory under U.S. Government for a local number or call the Federal Relay Service for the hearing impaired (800) 877-8339. The first number is not tollfree, and charges may result. Information also is available from the OPM Internet site at: **http://www.usajobs.opm.gov.**

Professional associations. Many professions have associations that offer employment information, including career planning, educational programs, job listings, and job placement. To use these ser-

vices, associations usually require that you be a member; information can be obtained directly from an association through the Internet, by telephone, or by mail.

Labor unions. Labor unions provide various employment services to members, including apprenticeship programs that teach a specific trade or skill. Contact the appropriate labor union or State apprenticeship council for more information.

Private employment agencies and career consultants. These agencies can be helpful, but they are in business to make money. Most operate on a commission basis, with the fee dependent upon a percentage of the salary paid to a successful applicant. You or the hiring company will pay the fee. Find out the exact cost and who is responsible for paying associated fees before using the service.

Although employment agencies can help you save time and contact employers who otherwise might be difficult to locate, the costs may outweigh the benefits if you are responsible for the fee. Contacting employers directly often will generate the same type of leads that a private employment agency will provide. Consider any guarantees that the agency offers when determining if the service is worth the cost.

Community agencies. Many nonprofit organizations, including religious institutions and vocational rehabilitation agencies, offer counseling, career development, and job placement services, generally targeted to a particular group, such as women, youths, minorities, ex-offenders, or older workers.

Applying for a job

Resumes and application forms. Resumes and application forms are two ways to provide employers with written evidence of your qualifications and skills. Generally, the same information appears on both the resume and the application form, but the way in which it is presented differs. Some employers prefer a resume and others require an application form. The accompanying box presents the basic information you should include in your resume.

There are many ways of organizing a resume. Depending on the job, you should choose the format that best highlights your skills, training, and experience. It may be helpful to look in a variety of books and publications at your local library or bookstore for different examples.

What Usually Goes Into a Resume

- Name, address, e-mail address, and telephone number.
- Employment objective. State the type of work or specific job you are seeking.
- Education, including school name and address, dates of attendance, curriculum, and highest grade completed or degree awarded. Consider including any courses or areas of focus that might be relevant to the position.
- Experience, paid and volunteer. For each job, include the job title, name and location of employer, and dates of employment. Briefly describe your job duties.
- Special skills, computer skills, proficiency in foreign languages, achievements, and membership in organizations.
- Keep it short; only one page for less experienced applicants.
- Avoid long paragraphs; use bullets to highlight key skills and accomplishments.
- Have a friend review your resume for any spelling or grammatical errors.
- Print it on high quality paper.

When you fill out an application form, make sure you fill it out completely and follow all instructions. Do not omit any requested information and make sure that the information you provide is correct.

Cover letters. A cover letter is sent with a resume or application form, as a way of introducing yourself to prospective employers. It should capture the employer's attention, follow a business letter format, and usually should include the following information:

● The name and address of the specific person to whom the letter is addressed.
● Your main qualifications for the position.
● Request for an interview.
● Your home and work telephone numbers.

Interviewing. An interview gives you the opportunity to showcase your qualifications to an employer, so it pays to be well prepared. The information in the accompanying box provides some helpful hints.

Job interview tips

Preparation:
  Learn about the organization.
  Have a specific job or jobs in mind.
  Review your qualifications for the job.
  Prepare answers to broad questions about yourself.
  Review your resume.
  Practice an interview with a friend or relative.
  Arrive before the scheduled time of your interview.

Personal appearance:
  Be well groomed.
  Dress appropriately.
  Do not chew gum or smoke.

The interview:
  Relax and answer each question concisely.
  Respond promptly.
  Use good manners.
  Learn the name of your interviewer and shake hands as
    you meet.
  Use proper English—avoid slang.
  Be cooperative and enthusiastic.
  Ask questions about the position and the organization.
  Thank the interviewer when you leave and, as a followup,
    in writing.

Test (if employer gives one):
  Listen closely to instructions.
  Read each question carefully.
  Write legibly and clearly.
  Budget your time wisely and don't dwell on one question.

Information to bring to an interview:
  Social Security card.
  Government-issued identification (driver's license).
  Resume. Although not all employers require applicants
    to bring a resume, you should be able to furnish the
    interviewer information about your education, training, and
    previous employment.
  References. Employers typically require three references.
    Get permission before using anyone as a reference. Make
    sure that they will give you a good reference. Try to avoid
    using relatives as references.

Evaluating a job offer

Once you receive a job offer, you are faced with a difficult decision and must evaluate the offer carefully. Fortunately, most organizations will not expect you to accept or reject an offer immediately.

There are many issues to consider when assessing a job offer. Will the organization be a good place to work? Will the job be interesting? Are there opportunities for advancement? Is the salary fair? Does the employer offer good benefits? If you have not already figured out exactly what you want, the following discussion may help you to develop a set of criteria for judging job offers, whether you are starting a career, reentering the labor force after a long absence, or planning a career change.

The organization. Background information on an organization can help you to decide whether it is a good place for you to work. Factors to consider include the organization's business or activity, financial condition, age, size, and location.

You generally can get background information on an organization, particularly a large organization, on its Internet site or by telephoning its public relations office. A public company's annual report to the stockholders tells about its corporate philosophy, history, products or services, goals, and financial status. Most government agencies can furnish reports that describe their programs and missions. Press releases, company newsletters or magazines, and recruitment brochures also can be useful. Ask the organization for any other items that might interest a prospective employee. If possible, speak to current or former employees of the organization.

Background information on the organization may be available at your public or school library. If you cannot get an annual report, check the library for reference directories that may provide basic facts about the company, such as earnings, products and services, and number of employees. Some directories widely available in libraries include:

● *Dun & Bradstreet's Million Dollar Directory*
● *Standard and Poor's Register of Corporations*
● *Moody's Industrial Manual*
● *Thomas Register of American Manufacturers*
● *Wards Business Directory*

Stories about an organization in magazines and newspapers can tell a great deal about its successes, failures, and plans for the future. You can identify articles on a company by looking under its name in periodical or computerized indexes in libraries. However, it probably will not be useful to look back more than 2 or 3 years.

The library also may have government publications that present projections of growth for the industry in which the organization is classified. Long-term projections of employment and output for detailed industries, covering the entire U.S. economy, are developed by the Bureau of Labor Statistics and revised every 2 years— see the February 2004 Monthly Labor Review for the most recent projections, covering the 2002-12 period, on the Internet at: **http://www.bls.gov/opub/mlr/mlrhome.htm**. Trade magazines also may include articles on the trends for specific industries.

Career centers at colleges and universities often have information on employers that is not available in libraries. Ask a career-center representative how to find out about a particular organization.

Does the organization's business or activity match your own interests and beliefs?
It is easier to apply yourself to the work if you are enthusiastic about what the organization does.

How will the size of the organization affect you?

Large firms generally offer a greater variety of training programs and career paths, more managerial levels for advancement, and better employee benefits than do small firms. Large employers also may have more advanced technologies. However, many jobs in large firms tend to be highly specialized.

Jobs in small firms may offer broader authority and responsibility, a closer working relationship with top management, and a chance to clearly see your contribution to the success of the organization.

Should you work for a relatively new organization or one that is well established?

New businesses have a high failure rate, but for many people, the excitement of helping to create a company and the potential for sharing in its success more than offset the risk of job loss. However, it may be just as exciting and rewarding to work for a young firm that already has a foothold on success.

Does it make a difference if the company is private or public?

An individual or a family may control a privately owned company and key jobs may be reserved for relatives and friends. A board of directors responsible to the stockholders controls a publicly owned company and key jobs usually are open to anyone.

Is the organization in an industry with favorable long-term prospects?

The most successful firms tend to be in industries that are growing rapidly.

Nature of the job. Even if everything else about the job is attractive, you will be unhappy if you dislike the day-to-day work. Determining in advance whether you will like the work may be difficult. However, the more you find out about the job before accepting or rejecting the offer, the more likely you are to make the right choice. Actually working in the industry and, if possible, for the company would provide considerable insight. You can gain work experience through part-time, temporary, or summer jobs, or through internship or work-study programs while in school, all of which can lead to permanent job offers.

Where is the job located?

If the job is in another section of the country, you need to consider the cost of living, the availability of housing and transportation, and the quality of educational and recreational facilities in that section of the country. Even if the job location is in your area, you should consider the time and expense of commuting.

Does the work match your interests and make good use of your skills?

The duties and responsibilities of the job should be explained in enough detail to answer this question.

How important is the job in this company?

An explanation of where you fit in the organization and how you are supposed to contribute to its overall objectives should give you an idea of the job's importance.

Are you comfortable with the hours?

Most jobs involve regular hours—for example, 40 hours a week, during the day, Monday through Friday. Other jobs require night, weekend, or holiday work. In addition, some jobs routinely require overtime to meet deadlines or sales or production goals, or to better serve customers. Consider the effect that the work hours will have on your personal life.

How long do most people who enter this job stay with the company?

High turnover can mean dissatisfaction with the nature of the work or something else about the job.

Opportunities offered by employers. A good job offers you opportunities to learn new skills, increase your earnings, and rise to positions of greater authority, responsibility, and prestige. A lack of opportunities can dampen interest in the work and result in frustration and boredom.

The company should have a training plan for you. What valuable new skills does the company plan to teach you?

The employer should give you some idea of promotion possibilities within the organization. What is the next step on the career ladder? If you have to wait for a job to become vacant before you can be promoted, how long does this usually take? When opportunities for advancement do arise, will you compete with applicants from outside the company? Can you apply for jobs for which you qualify elsewhere within the organization, or is mobility within the firm limited?

Salaries and benefits. Wait for the employer to introduce these subjects. Some companies will not talk about pay until they have decided to hire you. In order to know if their offer is reasonable, you need a rough estimate of what the job should pay. You may have to go to several sources for this information. Try to find family, friends, or acquaintances who recently were hired in similar jobs. Ask your teachers and the staff in placement offices about starting pay for graduates with your qualifications. Help-wanted ads in newspapers sometimes give salary ranges for similar positions. Check the library or your school's career center for salary surveys such as those conducted by the National Association of Colleges and Employers or various professional associations.

If you are considering the salary and benefits for a job in another geographic area, make allowances for differences in the cost of living, which may be significantly higher in a large metropolitan area than in a smaller city, town, or rural area.

You also should learn the organization's policy regarding overtime. Depending on the job, you may or may not be exempt from laws requiring the employer to compensate you for overtime. Find out how many hours you will be expected to work each week and whether you receive overtime pay or compensatory time off for working more than the specified number of hours in a week.

Also take into account that the starting salary is just that—the start. Your salary should be reviewed on a regular basis; many organizations do it every year. How much can you expect to earn after 1, 2, or 3 or more years? An employer cannot be specific about the amount of pay if it includes commissions and bonuses.

Benefits also can add a lot to your base pay, but they vary widely. Find out exactly what the benefit package includes and how much of the cost you must bear.

National, State, and metropolitan area data from the Bureau's National Compensation Survey are available from:

➤ Bureau of Labor Statistics, Office of Compensation Levels and Trends, 2 Massachusetts Ave. NE., Room 4175, Washington, DC 20212-0001. Telephone: (202) 691-6199. Internet: **http://www.bls.gov/ncs**.

Data on earnings by detailed occupation from the Occupational Employment Statistics (OES) Survey are available from:

➤ Bureau of Labor Statistics, Office of Occupational Statistics and Employment Projections, 2 Massachusetts Ave. NE., Room 2135, Washington, DC 20212-0001. Telephone: (202) 691-6569. Internet: **http://www.bls.gov/oes**.

Occupational Information Included in the *Handbook*

The *Occupational Outlook Handbook* is best used as a reference; it is not meant to be read from cover to cover. Instead, start by looking at the table of contents, in which related occupations are grouped in clusters, or look in the alphabetical index in the back of the *Handbook* for specific occupations that interest you. For any occupation that sounds interesting, use the Handbook to learn about the type of work that is performed in the occupation, the working conditions, the education and training requirements, the possibilities for advancement, earnings in the occupation, the job outlook, and related occupations. Each occupational statement, or description, in the *Handbook* follows a standard format, making it easier for you to compare occupations.

Two previous sections—"Tomorrow's Jobs" and "Sources of Career Information"—highlight the forces that are likely to determine employment opportunities in industries and occupations through the year 2012 and indicate where to obtain additional information. The current section is an overview of how the occupational statements are developed and organized. It highlights information presented in each section of a *Handbook* statement and the source of the information, gives examples of specific occupations in some cases, and offers some hints on how to interpret the information provided.

Unless otherwise noted, the source of employment and earnings data presented in the *Handbook* is the Bureau of Labor Statistics. Nearly all *Handbook* statements cite employment and earnings data from the Occupational Employment Statistics (OES) survey. Some statements include data from outside sources. OES data may be used to compare earnings among occupations; however, outside data may not be used in this manner, because characteristics of these data vary widely.

About those numbers at the beginning of each statement

The numbers in parentheses that appear just below the title of every detailed occupational statement are from the Occupational Information Network (O*NET)—a system used by State employment service offices to classify applicants and job openings, and by some career information centers and libraries to file occupational information.

Occupational Information Network Coverage, a section beginning on page 665, cross-references O*NET codes to occupations covered in the *Handbook*. O*NET codes are based on the 2000 Standard Occupational Classification (SOC) system.

Significant Points
This section highlights key occupational characteristics discussed in the statement.

Nature of the Work
This section discusses what workers do on the job, what tools and equipment they use, and how closely they are supervised. Individual job duties may vary by industry or employer. For instance, workers in larger firms tend to be more specialized, whereas those in smaller firms often have a wider variety of duties. Most occupations have several levels of skills and responsibilities through which

workers may progress. Beginners may start as trainees performing routine tasks under close supervision. Experienced workers usually undertake more difficult tasks and are expected to perform with less supervision.

Some statements mention common alternative job titles or occupational specialties. For example, the statement on accountants and auditors discusses a few specialties, such as public accountants, management accountants, and internal auditors. Some statements—such as that on advertising, marketing, promotions, public relations, and sales managers—discuss titles or specialties that are detailed OES survey occupations. For these occupations, such as sales managers or marketing managers, separate employment projections are developed and their O*NET codes appear at the beginning of the statement.

Information in this section may be updated for several reasons. One is the emergence of occupational specialties. For instance, Webmasters—who are responsible for the technical aspects of operating a Web site—constitute a specialty within computer systems analysts, database administrators, and computer scientists. Information also may be updated due to changing technology that affects the way in which a job is performed. For example, the Internet allows purchasers to acquire supplies with a click of the mouse, saving time and money. Furthermore, job duties may be affected by modifications to business practices, such as organizational restructuring or changes in response to government regulations. An example is paralegals and legal assistants, who are increasingly being utilized by law firms in order to lower costs and increase the efficiency and quality of legal services.

Many sources are consulted in researching changes to the nature of the work section or any other section of a Handbook statement. Usual sources include articles in newspapers, magazines, and professional journals. Useful information also appears on the Web sites of professional associations, unions, and trade groups. Information found on the Internet or in periodicals is verified through interviews with individuals employed in the occupation, professional associations, unions, and others with occupational knowledge, such as university professors and counselors in career assistance centers.

Working Conditions
This section identifies the typical hours worked, the workplace environment, physical activities and susceptibility to injury, special equipment, and the extent of travel required. In many occupations, people work regular business hours—40 hours a week, Monday through Friday—but many do not. For example, waiters and waitresses often work evenings and weekends.

The work setting can range from a hospital, to a mall, to an offshore oil rig. Truck drivers might be susceptible to injury, while paramedics have high job-related stress. Semiconductor processors may wear protective clothing or equipment, some construction laborers do physically demanding work, and top executives may travel frequently.

Information on various worker characteristics, such as the average number of hours worked per week, is obtained from the Current Population Survey (CPS)—a survey of households conducted by the U.S. Census Bureau for BLS.

Employment

This section reports the number of jobs that the occupation provided in 2002, the key industries in which those jobs were found, and the number or proportion of self-employed workers in the occupation, if significant. Self-employed workers accounted for about 8 percent of the workforce in 2002; however, they were concentrated in a small number of occupations, such as farmers and ranchers, childcare workers, lawyers, health practitioners, and the construction trades.

BLS develops the National Employment Matrix, which presents current and projected employment for 284 detailed industries and 725 detailed occupations over the 2002–12 period. Data in the matrix come primarily from the OES survey, which reports employment of wage and salary workers for each occupation in almost all industries. The CPS survey provides information on the total number of self-employed and unpaid family workers in each occupation. The CPS also provides employment data on agriculture and private households. The Office of Personnel Management (OPM) furnishes employment data on Federal Government workers.

Because total employment in each occupation combines data from several different sources, employment numbers cited in the *Handbook* often differ from employment data provided by the OES, CPS, and other employment surveys. This may be a source of confusion for some readers.

When significant, the geographic distribution of jobs and the proportion of part-time workers (those working less than 35 hours a week) are mentioned, reflecting CPS data. On the basis of OES survey data, some *Handbook* statements, such as those on textile, apparel, and furnishings occupations, list States that employ substantial numbers of workers in the occupation.

Training, Other Qualifications, and Advancement

After knowing what a job is all about, it is important to understand how to train for it. This section describes the most significant sources of education and training, including the education or training preferred by employers, the typical length of training, and the possibilities for advancement. Job skills sometimes are acquired through high school, informal on-the-job training, formal training (including apprenticeships), the U.S. Armed Forces, home study, hobbies, or previous work experience. For example, sales experience is particularly important for many sales jobs. Many professional jobs, on the other hand, require formal postsecondary education—postsecondary vocational or technical training, or college, postgraduate, or professional education.

In addition to training requirements, the *Handbook* mentions desirable skills, aptitudes, and personal characteristics. For some entry-level jobs, personal characteristics are more important than formal training. Employers generally seek people who read, write, and speak well; compute accurately; think logically; learn quickly; get along with others; and demonstrate dependability.

Some occupations require certification or licensing to enter the field, to advance in the occupation, or to practice independently. Certification or licensing generally involves completing courses and passing examinations. Many occupations increasingly are requiring workers to participate in continuing education or training in relevant skills, either to keep up with the changes in their job or to improve their advancement opportunities.

Revisions to the training section may focus on changes in educational, certification, or licensing requirements, such as an increase in the number of hours of required training or in the number of States requiring a license. Information also is updated if new skills are needed to complete the job, such as those arising from the adoption of new technology.

Information in this section comes from personal interviews with individuals employed in the occupation or from Web sites, published training materials, and interviews with the organizations that grant the degree, certification, or license. Some occupations have numerous professional designations granted by different organizations. Generally, the most widely recognized organizations are listed in the *Handbook*.

Some statements list the number of training programs. For example, the statement on pharmacists indicates the number of colleges of pharmacy accredited by the American Council on Pharmaceutical Education. The minimum requirements for Federal Government employment cited in some statements are based on standards set by the U.S. Office of Personnel Management.

Job Outlook

In planning for the future, it is important to consider potential job opportunities. This section describes the factors that will result in employment growth or decline. Projecting occupational employment is the final step in the employment projections process. (A more detailed description of the projections process is discussed in the *Handbook* section entitled "Assumptions and Methods Used in Preparing Employment Projections.") The job outlook section reflects the occupational projections in the National Employment Matrix. Each occupation is assigned a descriptive phrase on the basis of its projected percent change in employment over the 2002–12 period. (All of the phrases are listed at the end of this section.)

A number of factors are examined in developing employment projections and updating the job outlook section. One factor is job growth or decline in industries that employ a significant percentage of workers in the occupation. If workers are concentrated in a rapidly growing industry, their employment will likely also grow quickly. For example, the growing need for business expertise is fueling demand for consulting services. Hence, management, scientific, and technical consulting services is projected to be among the fastest growing industries through 2012. Projected rapid growth in this industry helps to spur faster than average growth in employment of management analysts.

Demographic changes, which affect what services are required, can influence occupational growth or decline. For example, an aging population demands more healthcare workers, from registered nurses to pharmacists.

Technological change is another key factor. New technology can either create new job opportunities or eliminate jobs by making workers obsolete. The Internet has increased the demand for workers in the computer and information technology fields, such as computer support specialists and systems administrators. However, the Internet also has adversely affected travel agents, because many people now book tickets, hotels, and rental cars online.

Another factor affecting job growth or decline is changes in business practices, such as the outsourcing of work or the restructuring of businesses. In the past few years, insurance carriers have been outsourcing sales and claims adjuster jobs to large, 24-hour call centers in order to reduce costs. Corporate restructuring also has made many organizations "flatter," resulting in fewer middle management positions.

The substitution of one product or service for another can affect employment projections. For example, consumption of plastic products has grown as they have been substituted for metal goods in many consumer and manufactured products in recent years. The process is likely to continue and should result in stronger demand for machine operators in plastics than in metal.

Competition from foreign trade usually has a negative impact on employment. Often, foreign manufacturers can produce goods

U.S. manufacturers cannot compete. Increased international competition is a major reason for the decline in employment among textile, apparel, and furnishings workers.

In some cases, the *Handbook* mentions that an occupation is likely to provide numerous job openings or, in others, that an occupation likely will afford relatively few openings. This information reflects the projected change in employment, as well as replacement needs. Large occupations that have high turnover, such as food and beverage serving occupations, generally provide the most job openings—reflecting the need to replace workers who transfer to other occupations or who stop working.

Some *Handbook* statements discuss the relationship between the number of jobseekers and the number of job openings. (The phrases used to describe that relationship appear at the end of this section.) In some occupations, there is a rough balance between jobseekers and job openings, resulting in good opportunities. In other occupations, employers may report difficulty finding qualified applicants, resulting in excellent job opportunities. Still other occupations are characterized by a surplus of applicants, leading to keen competition for jobs. On the one hand, limited training facilities, salary regulations, or undesirable aspects of the work—as in the case of private household workers—can result in an insufficient number of entrants to fill all job openings. On the other hand, glamorous or potentially high-paying occupations, such as actors or musicians, generally have surpluses of jobseekers. Variation in job opportunities by industry, educational attainment, size of firm, or geographic location also may be discussed. Even in crowded fields, job openings do exist. Good students or highly qualified individuals should not be deterred from undertaking training for, or seeking entry into, those occupations.

Earnings

This section discusses typical earnings and how workers are compensated—by means of annual salaries, hourly wages, commissions, piece rates, tips, or bonuses. Within every occupation, earnings vary by experience, responsibility, performance, tenure, and geographic area. Almost every statement in the *Handbook* contains 2002 OES-survey earnings data for wage and salary workers. Information on earnings in the major industries in which the occupation is employed, also supplied by the OES survey, may be given as well.

In addition to presenting earnings data from the OES survey, some statements contain additional earnings data from non-BLS sources. Starting and average salaries of Federal workers are based on 2003 data from the U.S. Office of Personnel Management. The National Association of Colleges and Employers supplies information on average salary offers in 2003 for students graduating with a bachelor's, master's, or Ph.D. degree in certain fields. A few statements contain additional earnings information from other sources, such as unions, professional associations, and private companies. These data sources are cited in the text.

Benefits account for a significant portion of total compensation costs to employers. Benefits such as paid vacation, health insurance, and sick leave may not be mentioned, because they are so widespread. Although not as common as traditional benefits, flexible hours and profit-sharing plans may be offered to attract and

---

Key phrases in the *Handbook*

This box explains how to interpret the key phrases used to describe projected changes in employment. It also explains the terms used to describe the relationship between the number of job openings and the number of jobseekers. The description of this relationship in a particular occupation reflects the knowledge and judgment of economists in the BLS Office of Occupational Statistics and Employment Projections.

Changing employment between 2002 and 2012

If the statement reads:	Employment is projected to:
Grow much faster than average	increase 36 percent or more
Grow faster than average	increase 21 to 35 percent
Grow about as fast as average	increase 10 to 20 percent
Grow more slowly than average	increase 3 to 9 percent
Little or no growth	increase 0 to 2 percent
Decline	decrease 1 percent or more

Opportunities and competition for jobs

If the statement reads:	Job openings compared with jobseekers may be:
Very good to excellent opportunities	More numerous
Good or favorable opportunities	In rough balance
May face, or can expect, keen competition	Fewer

---

retain highly qualified workers. Less common benefits also include childcare, tuition for dependents, housing assistance, summers off, and free or discounted merchandise or services. For certain occupations, the percentage of workers affiliated with a union is listed. These data come from the CPS survey.

Related Occupations

Occupations involving similar duties, skills, interests, education, and training are listed.

Sources of Additional Information

No single publication can describe all aspects of an occupation. Thus, the *Handbook* lists the mailing addresses of associations, government agencies, unions, and other organizations that can provide occupational information. In some cases, tollfree telephone numbers and Internet addresses also are listed. Free or relatively inexpensive publications offering more information may be mentioned; some of these publications also may be available in libraries, in school career centers, in guidance offices, or on the Internet. Most of the organizations listed in this section were sources of information on the nature of the work, training, and job outlook discussed in the *Handbook*.

For additional sources of information, also read the earlier chapter, "Sources of Career Information."

Management and Business and Financial Operations Occupations

Management Occupations

Administrative Services Managers

(0*NET 11-3011.00)

Significant Points

- Administrative services managers work in private industry and government and have a wide range of responsibilities, experience, earnings, and education.

- Applicants face keen competition due to the substantial supply of competent, experienced workers seeking managerial jobs.

Nature of the Work

Administrative services managers perform a broad range of duties in virtually every sector of the economy. They coordinate and direct support services to organizations as diverse as insurance companies, computer manufacturers, and government offices. These workers manage the many services that allow organizations to operate efficiently, such as secretarial and reception, administration, payroll, conference planning and travel, information and data processing, mail, materials scheduling and distribution, printing and reproduction, records management, telecommunications management, security, parking, and personal property procurement, supply, and disposal.

Specific duties for these managers vary by degree of responsibility and authority. First-line administrative services managers directly supervise a staff that performs various support services. Mid-level managers, on the other hand, develop departmental plans, set goals and deadlines, implement procedures to improve productivity and customer service, and define the responsibilities of supervisory-level managers. Some mid-level administrative services managers oversee first-line supervisors from various departments, including the clerical staff. Mid-level managers also may be involved in the hiring and dismissal of employees, but they generally have no role in the formulation of personnel policy. Some of these managers advance to upper level positions, such as vice president of administrative services, which are discussed in the *Handbook* statement on top executives.

In small organizations, a single administrative services manager may oversee all support services. In larger ones, however, first-line administrative services managers often report to mid-level managers who, in turn, report to owners or top-level managers. As the size of the firm increases, administrative services managers are more likely to specialize in specific support activities. For example, some administrative services managers work primarily as office managers, contract administrators, or unclaimed property officers. In many cases, the duties of these administrative services managers are similar to those of other managers and supervisors, some of which are discussed in other *Handbook* statements.

Because of the range of administrative services required by organizations, the nature of these managerial jobs also varies significantly. Administrative services managers who work as contract administrators, for instance, oversee the preparation, analysis, negotiation, and review of contracts related to the purchase or sale of equipment, materials, supplies, products, or services. In addition, some administrative services managers acquire, distribute, and store supplies, while others dispose of surplus property or oversee the disposal of unclaimed property.

Administrative services managers who work as facility managers plan, design, and manage buildings and grounds in addition to people. They are responsible for coordinating the physical workplace with the people and work of an organization. This task requires integrating the principles of business administration, architecture, and behavioral and engineering science. Although the specific tasks assigned to facility managers vary substantially depending on the organization, the duties fall into several categories, relating to operations and maintenance, real estate, project planning and management, communication, finance, quality assessment, facility function, technology integration, and management of human and environmental factors. Tasks within these broad categories may include space and workplace planning, budgeting, purchase and sale of real estate, lease management, renovations, or architectural planning and design. Facility managers may suggest and oversee renovation projects for a variety of reasons, ranging from improving

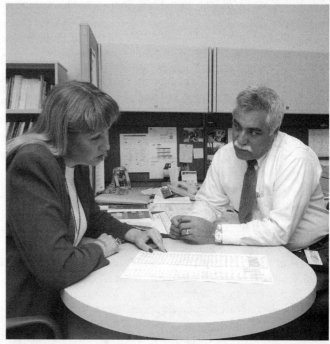

Administrative services managers coordinate and direct support services that allow organizations to operate efficiently.

efficiency to ensuring that facilities meet government regulations and environmental, health, and security standards. Additionally, facility managers continually monitor the facility to ensure that it remains safe, secure, and well-maintained. Often, the facility manager is responsible for directing staff, including maintenance, grounds, and custodial workers.

Working Conditions

Administrative services managers generally work in comfortable offices. Managers involved in contract administration and personal property procurement, use, and disposal may travel between their home office, branch offices, vendors' offices, and property sales sites. Also, facility managers who are responsible for the design of workspaces may spend time at construction sites and may travel between different facilities while monitoring the work of maintenance, grounds, and custodial staffs. However, new technology has increased the number of managers who telecommute from home or other offices, and teleconferencing has reduced the need for travel.

Most administrative services managers work a standard 40-hour week. However, uncompensated overtime frequently is required to resolve problems and meet deadlines. Facility managers often are "on call" to address a variety of problems that can arise in a facility during nonwork hours.

Employment

Administrative services managers held about 321,000 jobs in 2002. About 9 out of 10 worked in service-providing industries, including Federal, State, and local government, health services, financial services, professional, scientific, and technical services, and education. Most of the remaining workers worked in manufacturing industries.

Training, Other Qualifications, and Advancement

Educational requirements for these managers vary widely, depending on the size and complexity of the organization. In small organizations, experience may be the only requirement needed to enter a position as office manager. When an opening in administrative services management occurs, the office manager may be promoted to the position based on past performance. In large organizations, however, administrative services managers normally are hired from outside and each position has formal education and experience requirements. Some administrative services managers have advanced degrees.

Specific requirements vary by job responsibility. For first-line administrative services managers of secretarial, mailroom, and related support activities, many employers prefer an associate degree in business or management, although a high school diploma may suffice when combined with appropriate experience. For managers of audiovisual, graphics, and other technical activities, postsecondary technical school training is preferred. Managers of highly complex services, such as contract administration, generally need at least a bachelor's degree in business, human resources, or finance. Regardless of major, the curriculum should include courses in office technology, accounting, business mathematics, computer applications, human resources, and business law. Most facility managers have an undergraduate or graduate degree in engineering, architecture, construction management, business administration, or facility management. Many have a background in real estate, construction, or interior design, in addition to managerial experience.

Whatever the manager's educational background, it must be accompanied by related work experience reflecting demonstrated ability. For this reason, many administrative services managers have advanced through the ranks of their organization, acquiring work experience in various administrative positions before assuming first-line supervisory duties. All managers who oversee departmental supervisors should be familiar with office procedures and equipment. Managers of personal property acquisition and disposal need experience in purchasing and sales, and knowledge of a variety of supplies, machinery, and equipment. Managers concerned with supply, inventory, and distribution should be experienced in receiving, warehousing, packaging, shipping, transportation, and related operations. Contract administrators may have worked as contract specialists, cost analysts, or procurement specialists. Managers of unclaimed property often have experience in insurance claims analysis and records management.

Persons interested in becoming administrative services managers should have good communication skills and be able to establish effective working relationships with many different people, ranging from managers, supervisors, and professionals, to clerks and blue-collar workers. They should be analytical, detail-oriented, flexible, and decisive. They must also be able to coordinate several activities at once, quickly analyze and resolve specific problems, and cope with deadlines.

Most administrative services managers in small organizations advance by moving to other management positions or to a larger organization. Advancement is easier in large firms that employ several levels of administrative services managers. Attainment of the Certified Administrative Manager (CAM) designation offered by the Institute of Certified Professional Managers, through work experience and successful completion of examinations, can increase a manager's advancement potential. In addition, a master's degree in business administration or related field enhances a first-level manager's opportunities to advance to a mid-level management position, such as director of administrative services, and eventually to a top-level management position, such as executive vice president for administrative services. Those with enough money and experience can establish their own management consulting firm. Advancement of facility managers is based on the practices and size of individual companies. Some facility managers transfer from other departments within the organization or work their way up from technical positions. Others advance through a progression of facility management positions that offer additional responsibilities. Completion of the competency-based professional certification program offered by the International Facility Management Association can give prospective candidates an advantage. In order to qualify for this Certified Facility Manager (CFM) designation, applicants must meet certain educational and experience requirements.

Job Outlook

Employment of administrative services managers is projected to grow about as fast as the average for all occupations through 2012. Like persons seeking other managerial positions, applicants face keen competition because there are more competent, experienced workers seeking jobs than there are positions available. However, demand should be strong for facility managers because businesses increasingly are realizing the importance of maintaining, securing, and efficiently operating their facilities, which are very large investments for most organizations. Administrative services managers employed in management services and management consulting also should be in demand, as public and private organizations continue to streamline and, in some cases, contract out administrative services functions in an effort to cut costs.

At the same time, continuing corporate restructuring and increasing utilization of office technology should result in a flatter organizational structure with fewer levels of management, reducing the need for some middle management positions. This should adversely affect administrative services managers who oversee first-line mangers. Because many administrative services managers have a wide range of responsibilities, however, the effects of these changes on employment should be less severe than for other middle managers who specialize in only certain functions. In addition to new administrative services management jobs created over the 2002-12 projection period, many job openings will stem from the need to replace workers who transfer to other jobs, retire, or stop working for other reasons.

Earnings

Earnings of administrative services managers vary greatly depending on the employer, the specialty, and the geographic area. In general, however, median annual earnings of administrative services managers in 2002 were $52,500. The middle 50 percent earned between $36,190 and $74,590. The lowest 10 percent earned less than $26,120, and the highest 10 percent earned more than $99,870. Median annual earnings in the industries employing the largest numbers of these managers in 2002 are shown below:

Management of companies and enterprises	$66,700
Elementary and secondary schools	59,220
Colleges, universities, and professional schools	56,960
State government	55,710
Local government	51,570

In the Federal Government, contract specialists in nonsupervisory, supervisory, and managerial positions earned an average of $66,309 a year in 2003. Corresponding averages were $63,509 for facilities operations, $62,552 for industrial property managers, $58,880 for property disposal specialists, $62,751 for administrative officers, and $52,824 for support services administrators.

Related Occupations

Administrative services managers direct and coordinate support services and oversee the purchase, use, and disposal of personal property. Occupations with similar functions include office and administrative support worker supervisors and managers; cost estimators; property, real estate, and community association managers; purchasing managers, buyers, and purchasing agents; and top executives.

Sources of Additional Information

For information about careers and education and degree programs in facility management, as well as the Certified Facility Manager designation, contact:

➤ International Facility Management Association, 1 East Greenway Plaza, Suite 1100, Houston, TX 77046-0194. Internet: **http://www.ifma.org**

General information regarding facility management and a list of facility management education and degree programs may be obtained from:

➤ Association of Higher Education Facilities Officers, 1643 Prince St., Alexandria, VA 22314-2818. Internet: **http://www.appa.org**

For information about the Certified Manager or Certified Administrative Manager designations, contact:

➤ Institute of Certified Professional Managers, James Madison University, College of Business, Harrisonburg, VA 22807. Internet: **http://cob.jmu.edu/icpm**

Advertising, Marketing, Promotions, Public Relations, and Sales Managers

(0*NET 11-2011.00, 11-2021.00, 11-2022.00, 11-2031.00)

Significant Points

● Keen competition for jobs is expected.

● College graduates with related experience, a high level of creativity, and strong communication skills should have the best job opportunities.

● High earnings, substantial travel, and long hours, including evenings and weekends, are common.

Nature of the Work

The objective of any firm is to market and sell its products or services profitably. In small firms, the owner or chief executive officer might assume all advertising, promotions, marketing, sales, and public relations responsibilities. In large firms, which may offer numerous products and services nationally or even worldwide, an executive vice president directs overall advertising, promotions, marketing, sales, and public relations policies. (Executive vice presidents are included in the *Handbook* statement on top executives.) Advertising, marketing, promotions, public relations, and sales managers coordinate the market research, marketing strategy, sales, advertising, promotion, pricing, product development, and public relations activities.

Managers oversee advertising and promotion staffs, which usually are small, except in the largest firms. In a small firm, managers may serve as a liaison between the firm and the advertising or promotion agency to which many advertising or promotional functions are contracted out. In larger firms, advertising managers oversee in-house account, creative, and media services departments. The *account executive* manages the account services department, assesses the need for advertising, and, in advertising agencies, maintains the accounts of clients. The creative services department develops the subject matter and presentation of advertising. The *creative director* oversees the copy chief, art director, and associated staff. The *media director* oversees planning groups that select the communication media—for example, radio, television, newspapers, magazines, Internet, or outdoor signs—to disseminate the advertising.

Promotions managers supervise staffs of promotion specialists. They direct promotion programs that combine advertising with purchase incentives to increase sales. In an effort to establish closer contact with purchasers—dealers, distributors, or consumers—promotion programs may involve direct mail, telemarketing, television or radio advertising, catalogs, exhibits, inserts in newspapers, Internet advertisements or Web sites, instore displays or product endorsements, and special events. Purchase incentives may include discounts, samples, gifts, rebates, coupons, sweepstakes, and contests.

Marketing managers develop the firm's detailed marketing strategy. With the help of subordinates, including *product development managers* and *market research managers,* they determine the demand for products and services offered by the firm and its competitors. In addition, they identify potential markets—for example, business firms, wholesalers, retailers, government, or the general public. Marketing managers develop pricing strategy with an eye towards maximizing the firm's share of the market and its profits while ensuring that the firm's customers are satisfied. In collaboration with sales, product development, and other managers, they monitor trends that indicate the need for new products and services and oversee product development. Marketing managers work with advertising and promotion managers to promote the firm's products and services and to attract potential users.

Public relations managers supervise public relations specialists. (See the *Handbook* statement on public relations specialists.) These managers direct publicity programs to a targeted public. They often specialize in a specific area, such as crisis management—or in a specific industry, such as healthcare. They use every available communication medium in their effort to maintain the support of the specific group upon whom their organization's success depends, such as consumers, stockholders, or the general public. For example, public relations managers may clarify or justify the firm's point of view on health or environmental issues to community or special interest groups.

Public relations managers also evaluate advertising and promotion programs for compatibility with public relations efforts and serve as the eyes and ears of top management. They observe social, economic, and political trends that might ultimately affect the firm and make recommendations to enhance the firm's image based on those trends.

Public relations managers may confer with labor relations managers to produce internal company communications—such as newsletters about employee-management relations—and with financial managers to produce company reports. They assist company executives in drafting speeches, arranging interviews, and maintaining other forms of public contact; oversee company archives; and respond to information requests. In addition, some handle special events such as sponsorship of races, parties introducing new products, or other activities the firm supports in order to gain public attention through the press without advertising directly.

Sales managers direct the firm's sales program. They assign sales territories, set goals, and establish training programs for the sales representatives. (See the *Handbook* statement on sales representatives, wholesale and manufacturing.) Managers advise the sales representatives on ways to improve their sales performance. In large, multiproduct firms, they oversee regional and local sales managers and their staffs. Sales managers maintain contact with dealers and distributors. They analyze sales statistics gathered by their staffs to determine sales potential and inventory requirements and monitor the preferences of customers. Such information is vital to develop products and maximize profits.

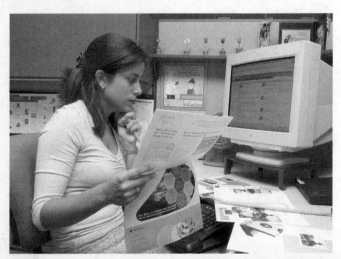

Advertising, marketing, promotions, public relations, and sales managers coordinate market research, marketing strategy, sales, advertising, promotion, pricing, product development, and public relations activities.

Working Conditions

Advertising, marketing, promotions, public relations, and sales managers work in offices close to those of top managers. Long hours, including evenings and weekends are common. About 44 percent of advertising, marketing, and public relations managers worked more than 40 hours a week in 2002. Working under pressure is unavoidable when schedules change and problems arise, but deadlines and goals must still be met.

Substantial travel may be involved. For example, attendance at meetings sponsored by associations or industries often is mandatory. Sales managers travel to national, regional, and local offices and to various dealers and distributors. Advertising and promotions managers may travel to meet with clients or representatives of communications media. At times, public relations managers travel to meet with special interest groups or government officials. Job transfers between headquarters and regional offices are common, particularly among sales managers.

Employment

Advertising, marketing, promotions, public relations, and sales managers held about 700,000 jobs in 2002. The following tabulation shows the distribution of jobs by occupational specialty:

Sales managers	343,000
Marketing managers	203,000
Advertising and promotions managers	85,000
Public relations managers	69,000

These managers were found in virtually every industry. Sales managers held almost half of the jobs; most were employed in manufacturing, wholesale and retail trade, and finance and insurance industries. Marketing managers held more one-fourth of the jobs; manufacturing, and professional, scientific, and technical services industries employed more than one-third of marketing managers. More than one-third of advertising and promotions managers worked in professional, scientific, and technical services, and information industries, including advertising and related services, and publishing industries. Most public relations managers were employed in services industries, such as other services (except government), professional, scientific, and technical services, finance and insurance, health care and social assistance services, and educational services.

Training, Advancement, and Other Qualifications

A wide range of educational backgrounds is suitable for entry into advertising, marketing, promotions, public relations, and sales managerial jobs, but many employers prefer those with experience in related occupations plus a broad liberal arts background. A bachelor's degree in sociology, psychology, literature, journalism, or philosophy, among other subjects, is acceptable. However, requirements vary, depending upon the particular job.

For marketing, sales, and promotions management positions, some employers prefer a bachelor's or master's degree in business administration with an emphasis on marketing. Courses in business law, economics, accounting, finance, mathematics, and statistics are advantageous. In highly technical industries, such as computer and electronics manufacturing, a bachelor's degree in engineering or science, combined with a master's degree in business administration, is preferred.

For advertising management positions, some employers prefer a bachelor's degree in advertising or journalism. A course of study should include marketing, consumer behavior, market research, sales, communication methods and technology, and visual arts—for example, art history and photography.

For public relations management positions, some employers prefer a bachelor's or master's degree in public relations or journalism. The applicant's curriculum should include courses in advertising, business administration, public affairs, public speaking, political science, and creative and technical writing.

For all these specialties, courses in management and completion of an internship while in school are highly recommended. Familiarity with word processing and database applications also is important for many positions. Computer skills are vital because marketing, product promotion, and advertising on the Internet are increasingly common. The ability to communicate in a foreign language may open up employment opportunities in many rapidly growing areas around the country, especially in cities with large Spanish-speaking populations.

Most advertising, marketing, promotions, public relations, and sales management positions are filled by promoting experienced staff or related professional personnel. For example, many managers are former sales representatives, purchasing agents, buyers, or product, advertising, promotions, or public relations specialists. In small firms, where the number of positions is limited, advancement to a management position usually comes slowly. In large firms, promotion may occur more quickly.

Although experience, ability, and leadership are emphasized for promotion, advancement can be accelerated by participation in management training programs conducted by many large firms. Many firms also provide their employees with continuing education opportunities, either in-house or at local colleges and universities, and encourage employee participation in seminars and conferences, often provided by professional societies. In collaboration with colleges and universities, numerous marketing and related associations sponsor national or local management training programs. Course subjects include brand and product management, international marketing, sales management evaluation, telemarketing and direct sales, interactive marketing, promotion, marketing communication, market research, organizational communication, and data processing systems procedures and management. Many firms pay all or part of the cost for those who successfully complete courses.

Some associations offer certification programs for these managers. Certification—a sign of competence and achievement in this field—is particularly important in a competitive job market. While relatively few advertising, marketing, promotions, public relations, and sales managers currently are certified, the number of managers who seek certification is expected to grow. For example, Sales and Marketing Executives International offers a management certification program based on education and job performance. The Public Relations Society of America offers a certification program for public relations practitioners based on years of experience and performance on an examination.

Persons interested in becoming advertising, marketing, promotions, public relations, and sales managers should be mature, creative, highly motivated, resistant to stress, flexible, and decisive. The ability to communicate persuasively, both orally and in writing, with other managers, staff, and the public is vital. These managers also need tact, good judgment, and exceptional ability to establish and maintain effective personal relationships with supervisory and professional staff members and client firms.

Because of the importance and high visibility of their jobs, advertising, marketing, promotions, public relations, and sales managers often are prime candidates for advancement to the highest ranks. Well-trained, experienced, successful managers may be promoted to higher positions in their own, or other, firms. Some become top executives. Managers with extensive experience and sufficient capital may open their own businesses.

Job Outlook

Advertising, marketing, promotions, public relations, and sales manager jobs are highly coveted and will be sought by other managers or highly experienced professionals, resulting in keen competition. College graduates with related experience, a high level of creativity, and strong communication skills should have the best job opportunities. Employers will particularly seek those who have the computer skills to conduct advertising, marketing, promotions, public relations, and sales activities on the Internet.

Employment of advertising, marketing, promotions, public relations, and sales managers is expected to increase faster than the average for all occupations through 2012, spurred by intense domestic and global competition in products and services offered to consumers. However, projected employment growth varies by industry. For example, employment is projected to grow much faster than average in scientific, professional, and related services such as computer systems design and related services and advertising and related services, as businesses increasingly hire contractors for these services instead of additional full-time staff. On the other hand, little or no change in employment is expected in many manufacturing industries.

Earnings

Median annual earnings in 2002 were $57,130 for advertising and promotions managers, $78,250 for marketing managers, $75,040 for sales managers, and $60,640 for public relations managers. Earnings ranged from less than $30,310 for the lowest 10 percent of advertising and promotions managers, to more than $145,600 for the highest 10 percent of marketing and sales managers.

Median annual earnings advertising and promotions managers in 2002 in the advertising and related services industry were $72,630.

Median annual earnings in the industries employing the largest numbers of marketing managers in 2002 were as follows:

Computer systems design and related services	$96,440
Management of companies and enterprises	90,750
Depository credit intermediation	65,960

Median annual earnings in the industries employing the largest numbers of sales managers in 2002 were as follows:

Computer systems design and related services	$102,520
Automobile dealers	91,350
Management of companies and enterprises	87,800
Insurance carriers	80,540
Traveler accommodation	44,560

Median annual earnings of public relations managers in 2002 in colleges, universities, and professional schools were $55,510.

According to a National Association of Colleges and Employers survey, starting salaries for marketing majors graduating in 2003 averaged $34,038; starting salaries for advertising majors averaged $29,495.

Salary levels vary substantially, depending upon the level of managerial responsibility, length of service, education, firm size, location, and industry. For example, manufacturing firms usually pay these managers higher salaries than do nonmanufacturing firms. For sales managers, the size of their sales territory is another important determinant of salary. Many managers earn bonuses equal to 10 percent or more of their salaries.

Related Occupations

Advertising, marketing, promotions, public relations, and sales managers direct the sale of products and services offered by their firms and the communication of information about their firms' activities. Other workers involved with advertising, marketing, promotions, public relations, and sales include actors, producers, and directors; artists and related workers; demonstrators, product promoters, and models; market and survey researchers; public relations specialists; sales representatives, wholesale and manufacturing; and writers and editors.

Sources of Additional Information

For information about careers in advertising management, contact:
➤ American Association of Advertising Agencies, 405 Lexington Ave., New York, NY 10174-1801. Internet: **http://www.aaaa.org**

Information about careers and professional certification in public relations management is available from:
➤ Public Relations Society of America, 33 Irving Place, New York, NY 10003-2376. Internet: **http://www.prsa.org**

Computer and Information Systems Managers

(0*NET 11-3021.00)

Significant Points

- Projected job growth stems primarily from rapid growth among computer-related occupations.

- Employers prefer managers with formal education and advanced technical knowledge acquired through computer-related work experience.

- Job opportunities should be best for applicants with a master's degree in business administration or management information systems with technology as a core component.

Nature of the Work

The need for organizations to incorporate existing and future technologies in order to remain competitive has become a more pressing issue over the last several yearsg. As electronic commerce becomes more common, how and when companies use technology are critical issues. Computer and information systems managers play a vital role in the technological direction of their organizations. They do everything from constructing the business plan to overseeing network security to directing Internet operations.

Computer and information systems managers plan, coordinate, and direct research and design the computer-related activities of firms. They help determine both technical and business goals in consultation with top management, and make detailed plans for the accomplishment of these goals. For example, working with their staff, they may develop the overall concepts of a new product or service, or may identify how an organization's computing capabilities can effectively aid project management.

Computer and information systems managers direct the work of systems analysts, computer programmers, support specialists, and other computer-related workers. These managers plan and coordinate activities such as installation and upgrading of hardware and software, programming and systems design, development of computer networks, and implementation of Internet and intranet sites. They are increasingly involved with the upkeep and maintenance and security of networks. They analyze the computer and informa-

tion needs of their organization, from an operational and strategic perspective, and determine immediate and long-range personnel and equipment requirements. They assign and review the work of their subordinates, and stay abreast of the latest technology in order to assure the organization does not lag behind competitors.

The duties of computer and information systems managers vary with their specific titles. *Chief technology officers*, for example, evaluate the newest and most innovative technologies and determine how these can help their organization. The chief technology officer, who often reports to the organization's chief information officer, manages and plans technical standards and tends to the daily information technology issues of the firm. (Chief information officers are covered in a separate *Handbook* statement on top executives.) Because of the rapid pace of technological change, chief technology officers must constantly be on the lookout for developments that could benefit their organization. They are responsible for demonstrating to a company how information technology can be used as a competitive tool that not only cuts costs, but also increases revenue and maintains or increases competitive advantage.

Management information systems (MIS) directors manage information systems and computing resources for their entire organization. They may also work under the chief information officer and plan and direct the work of subordinate information technology employees. These managers oversee a variety of user services such as an organization's help desk, which employees can call with questions or problems. MIS directors also may make hardware and software upgrade recommendations based on their experience with an organization's technology. Helping to assure the availability, continuity, and security of data and information technology services are key responsibilities for these workers.

Project managers develop requirements, budgets, and schedules for their firm's information technology projects. They coordinate such projects from development through implementation, working with internal and external clients, vendors, consultants, and computer specialists. These managers are increasingly involved in projects that upgrade the information security of an organization.

LAN/WAN (Local Area Network/Wide Area Network) *managers* provide a variety of services, from design to administration, of an organization's local area network, which connects staff within an organization. These managers direct the network, and its related computing environment, including hardware, systems software, applications software, and all other computer-related configurations.

Computer and information system managers need strong communication skills. They coordinate the activities of their unit with those of other units or organizations. They confer with top executives; financial, production, marketing, and other managers; and contractors and equipment and materials suppliers.

Working Conditions

Computer and information systems managers spend most of their time in an office. Most work at least 40 hours a week and may have to work evenings and weekends to meet deadlines or solve unexpected problems. Some computer and information systems managers may experience considerable pressure in meeting technical goals within short timeframes or tight budgets. As networks continue to expand and more work is done remotely, computer and information system managers have to communicate with and oversee offsite employees using modems, laptops, e-mail, and the Internet.

Like other workers who sit continuously in front of a keyboard, computer and information system managers are susceptible to eyestrain, back discomfort, and hand and wrist problems such as carpal tunnel syndrome.

Computer and information systems managers supervise information systems and computing resources for their entire organization.

Employment

Computer and information systems managers held about 284,000 jobs in 2002. About 2 in 5 works in service-providing industries, mainly in computer systems design and related services. This industry provides services related to the commercial use of computers on a contract basis, including custom computer programming services; computer systems integration design services; computer facilities management services, including computer systems or data-processing facilities support services for clients; and other computer-related services, such as disaster recovery services and software installation. Other large employers include insurance and financial services firms, government agencies, and manufacturers.

Training, Other Qualifications, and Advancement

Strong technical knowledge is essential for computer and information systems managers, who must understand and guide the work of their subordinates, yet also explain the work in nontechnical terms to senior management and potential customers. Therefore, these management positions usually require work experience and formal education similar to that of other computer occupations.

Many computer and information systems managers have experience as systems analysts; others may have experience as computer support specialists, programmers, or other information technology professionals. A bachelor's degree usually is required for management positions, although employers often prefer a graduate degree, especially a master's degree in business administration (MBA) with

technology as a core component. This degree differs from a traditional MBA in that there is a heavy emphasis on information technology in addition to the standard business curriculum. This is becoming important because more computer and information systems managers are making important technology decisions as well as business decisions for their organizations. Some universities specialize in offering degrees in management information systems, which blend technical core subjects with business, accounting, and communications courses. A few computer and information systems managers may have only an associate degree if they have sufficient experience and were able to learn additional skills on the job. To aid their professional advancement, though, many managers with an associate degree eventually earn a bachelor's or master's degree while working.

Computer and information systems managers need a broad range of skills. In addition to technical skills, employers also seek managers with strong business skills. Employers want managers who have experience with the specific software or technology to be used on the job, as well as a background in either consulting or business management. The expansion of electronic commerce has elevated the importance of business insight, because many managers are called upon to make important business decisions. Managers need a keen understanding of people, management processes, and customers' needs.

Computer and information systems managers must possess strong interpersonal, communication, and leadership skills because they are required to interact not only with their staff, but also with other people inside and outside their organization. They also must possess team skills to work on group projects and other collaborative efforts. Computer and information systems managers increasingly interact with persons outside their organization, reflecting their emerging role as vital parts of their firm's executive team.

Computer and information systems managers may advance to progressively higher leadership positions in their field. Some may become managers in non-technical areas such as marketing, human resources, or sales. In high technology firms, managers in non-technical areas often must possess the same specialized knowledge as do managers in technical areas.

Job Outlook

Employment of computer and information systems managers is expected to grow much faster than the average for all occupations through the year 2012. Technological advancements will boost the employment of computer-related workers; as a result, the demand for managers to direct these workers also will increase. In addition, job openings will result from the need to replace managers who retire or move into other occupations. Opportunities for obtaining a management position will be best for workers possessing an MBA with technology as a core component, or a management information systems degree, advanced technical knowledge, and strong communication and administrative skills.

Despite the recent downturn in the economy, especially in technology-related sectors, the outlook for computer and information systems managers remains strong. In order to remain competitive, firms will continue to install sophisticated computer networks and set up more complex Internet and intranet sites. Keeping a computer network running smoothly is essential to almost every organization. Firms will be more willing to hire managers who can accomplish that.

The security of computer networks will continue to increase in importance as more business is conducted over the Internet. The security of the Nation's entire electronic infrastructure has come under renewed focus in light of recent threats. Organizations need to understand how their systems are vulnerable and how to protect their infrastructure and Internet sites from hackers, viruses, and other acts of cyber-terrorism. The emergence of "cyber-security" as a key issue facing most organizations should lead to strong growth for computer managers. Firms will increasingly hire cyber-security experts to fill key leadership roles in their information technology departments, because the integrity of their computing environment is of the utmost concern. As a result, there will be a high demand for managers proficient in computer security issues.

Due to the explosive growth of electronic commerce and the capacity of the Internet to create new relationships with customers, the role of computer and information systems managers will continue to evolve in the future. Persons in these jobs will continue to become more vital to their companies. The expansion of the wireless Internet will spur the need for computer and information systems managers with both business savvy and technical proficiency.

Opportunities for those who wish to become computer and information systems managers should be closely related to the growth of the occupations they supervise and the industries in which they are found. (See the statements on computer programmers; computer software engineers; computer support specialists and systems administrators; and computer systems analysts, database administrators, and computer scientists elsewhere in the *Handbook*.)

Earnings

Earnings for computer and information systems managers vary by specialty and level of responsibility. Median annual earnings of these managers in 2002 were $85,240. The middle 50 percent earned between $64,150 and $109,950. The lowest 10 percent earned less than $47,440, and the highest 10 percent earned more than $140,440. Median annual earnings in the industries employing the largest numbers of computer and information systems managers in 2002 were:

Computer systems design and related services	$94,240
Management of companies and enterprises	91,710
Insurance carriers	89,920
Depository credit intermediation	75,160
Colleges, universities, and professional schools	68,100

According to Robert Half International, average starting salaries in 2003 for high-level information technology managers ranged from $82,750 to $151,500. According to a 2003 survey by the National Association of Colleges and Employers, starting salary offers for those with an MBA, a technical undergraduate degree, and 1 year or less of experience averaged $54,643; for those with a master's degree in management information systems/business data processing, the starting salary averaged $43,750.

In addition, computer and information systems managers, especially those at higher levels, often receive more employment-related benefits—such as expense accounts, stock option plans, and bonuses—than do non-managerial workers in their organizations.

Related Occupations

The work of computer and information systems managers is closely related to that of computer programmers; computer software engineers; computer systems analysts, database administrators, and computer scientists; and computer support specialists and systems administrators. Computer and information systems managers also have some high-level responsibilities similar to those of top executives.

Sources of Additional Information

For information about a career as a computer and information systems manager, contact the sources of additional information for the various computer occupations discussed elsewhere in the *Handbook*.

Construction Managers

(0*NET 11-9021.00)

Significant Points

- Construction managers must be available—often 24 hours a day—to deal with delays, bad weather, or emergencies at the jobsite.
- Employers prefer individuals who combine construction industry work experience with a bachelor's degree in construction science, construction management, or civil engineering.
- Good employment opportunities are expected; however, employment can be sensitive to the short-term nature of many construction projects and to cyclical fluctuations in construction activity.

Nature of the Work

Construction managers plan and coordinate construction projects. They may have job titles such as constructor, construction superintendent, general superintendent, project engineer, project manager, general construction manager, or executive construction manager. Construction managers may be owners or salaried employees of a construction management or contracting firm, or may work under contract or as a salaried employee of the owner, developer, contractor, or management firm overseeing the construction project. They may plan and direct a whole project or just a part of a project. The *Handbook* uses the term "construction manager" to describe salaried or self-employed managers who oversee construction supervisors and workers.

In contrast with the *Handbook* definition, "construction manager" is defined more narrowly within the construction industry to denote a management firm, or an individual employed by such a firm, involved in managerial oversight of a construction project. Under this definition, construction managers usually represent the owner or developer along with other workers throughout the project. Although they usually play no direct role in the actual construction of a structure, they typically schedule and coordinate all design and construction processes, including the selection, hiring, and oversight of specialty trade contractors.

Managers who work in the construction industry, such as general managers, project engineers, and others, increasingly are called *constructors*. Constructors manage, coordinate, and supervise the construction process from the conceptual development stage through final construction on a timely and economical basis. Given designs for buildings, roads, bridges, or other projects, constructors oversee the organization, scheduling, and implementation of the project to execute those designs. They are responsible for coordinating and managing people, materials, and equipment; budgets, schedules, and contracts; and safety of employees and the general public.

On large projects, several different management systems may be used. In the general contractor system, the owner hires a general contractor to manage all activities. Working for the general contractor, construction managers oversee the completion of all construction in accordance with the engineer's and architect's drawings and specifications and prevailing building codes. They arrange for trade contractors to perform specialized craftwork or other specified construction work. On small projects, such as remodeling a home, a self-employed construction manager or skilled trades worker who directs and oversees employees often is referred to as the construction "contractor." In the construction management system, the owner hires a firm to oversee all aspects of the project. The management firm will then hire a general contractor to run the construction process and oversee construction of the structure. The major difference from the general contractor system is that the hired management firm, rather than the owner, works with the individual construction manager. In the design-build system, the owners, architects, general contractors, and major subcontractors are brought together to cooperatively plan and design the project. The design-build group may be from an individual firm or a conglomeration of separate entities. The construction manager participates during the design process and may be in charge of the construction project once the design is agreed upon.

Large construction projects, such as an office building or industrial complex, are too complicated for one person to manage. These projects are divided into many segments: Site preparation, including land clearing and earth moving; sewage systems; landscaping and road construction; building construction, including excavation and laying of foundations, as well as erection of structural framework, floors, walls, and roofs; and building systems, including fire-protection, electrical, plumbing, air-conditioning, and heating. Construction managers may be in charge of one or more of these activities. Construction managers often work with engineers, architects, and others who are involved in the construction process.

Construction managers evaluate and determine appropriate construction methods and the most cost-effective plan and schedule. They divide all required construction site activities into logical steps, budgeting the time required to meet established deadlines. This may require sophisticated estimating and scheduling techniques and use of computers with specialized software. (See the statement on cost estimators elsewhere in the *Handbook*.) They oversee the selection of trade contractors to complete specific pieces of the project—which could include everything from structural metalworking and plumbing to painting and carpet installation. Construction managers determine the labor requirements and, in some cases, supervise or monitor the hiring and dismissal of workers. They oversee the performance of all trade contractors and are responsible for ensuring that all work is completed on schedule.

Construction managers direct and monitor the progress of construction activities, sometimes through construction supervisors or other construction managers. They oversee the delivery and use of materials, tools, and equipment; and the quality of construction, worker productivity, and safety. They are responsible for obtaining all necessary permits and licenses and, depending upon the contractual arrangements, direct or monitor compliance with building and safety codes and other regulations. They may have several subordinates, such as assistant managers or superintendents, field engineers, or crew supervisors, reporting to them.

Construction managers regularly review engineering and architectural drawings and specifications to monitor progress and ensure compliance with plans and schedules. They track and control construction costs against the project budget to avoid cost overruns. Based upon direct observation and reports by subordinate supervisors, managers may prepare daily reports of progress and requirements for labor, material, machinery, and equipment at the construction site. They meet regularly with owners, other constructors, trade contractors, vendors, architects, engineers, and others to monitor and coordinate all phases of the construction project.

Working Conditions

Construction managers work out of a main office from which the overall construction project is monitored, or out of a field office at

Construction managers are responsible for coordinating and managing people, materials, and equipment; budgets, schedules, and contracts; and the safety of employees and the general public.

the construction site. Advances in telecommunications and Internet access allow construction managers to be onsite without being out of contact of the office. Management decisions regarding daily construction activities generally are made at the jobsite. Managers usually travel when the construction site is in another State or when they are responsible for activities at two or more sites. Management of overseas construction projects usually entails temporary residence in another country.

Construction managers may be "on call"—often 24 hours a day—to deal with delays, bad weather, or emergencies at the site. Most work more than a standard 40-hour week because construction may proceed around-the-clock. They may have to work this type of schedule for days, even weeks, to meet special project deadlines, especially if there are delays.

Although the work usually is not considered inherently dangerous, construction managers must be careful while performing onsite services.

Employment

Construction managers held 389,000 jobs in 2002. Almost half were self-employed. Most of the rest were employed in the construction industry, 15 percent by specialty trade contractors—for example, plumbing, heating and air-conditioning, and electrical contractors—and 21 percent by general building contractors. Architectural, engineering and related services firms, as well as local governments, employed others.

Training, Other Qualifications, and Advancement

Persons interested in becoming a construction manager need a solid background in building science, business, and management, as well as related work experience within the construction industry. They need to understand contracts, plans, and specifications, and to be knowledgeable about construction methods, materials, and regulations. Familiarity with computers and software programs for job costing, online collaboration, scheduling, and estimating also is important.

Traditionally, persons advance to construction management positions after having substantial experience as construction craftworkers—carpenters, masons, plumbers, or electricians, for example—or after having worked as construction supervisors or as owners of independent specialty contracting firms overseeing workers in one or more construction trades. However, employers—particularly large construction firms—increasingly prefer individuals who combine industry work experience with a bachelor's degree in construction science, construction management, or civil engineering. Practical industry experience also is very important, whether it is acquired through internships, cooperative education programs, or work experience in the industry.

Construction managers should be flexible and work effectively in a fast-paced environment. They should be decisive and work well under pressure, particularly when faced with unexpected occurrences or delays. The ability to coordinate several major activities at once, while analyzing and resolving specific problems, is essential, as is an understanding of engineering, architectural, and other construction drawings. Good oral and written communication skills also are important, as are leadership skills. Managers must be able to establish a good working relationship with many different people, including owners, other managers, designers, supervisors, and craftworkers.

Advancement opportunities for construction managers vary depending upon an individual's performance and the size and type of company for which they work. Within large firms, managers may eventually become top-level managers or executives. Highly experienced individuals may become independent consultants; some serve as expert witnesses in court or as arbitrators in disputes. Those with the required capital may establish their own construction management services, specialty contracting, or general contracting firm.

Many colleges and universities offer 4-year degree programs in construction management, construction science, and construction engineering. These programs include courses in project control and development, site planning, design, construction methods, construction materials, value analysis, cost estimating, scheduling, contract administration, accounting, business and financial management, safety, building codes and standards, inspection procedures, engineering and architectural sciences, mathematics, statistics, and information technology. Graduates from 4-year degree programs usually are hired as assistants to project managers, field engineers, schedulers, or cost estimators. An increasing number of graduates in related fields—engineering or architecture, for example—also enter construction management, often after acquiring substantial experience on construction projects or after completing graduate studies in construction management or building science.

Several colleges and universities offer a master's degree program in construction management or construction science. Master's degree recipients, especially those with work experience in construction, typically become construction managers in very large construction or construction management companies. Often, individuals who hold a bachelor's degree in an unrelated field seek a master's degree in order to work in the construction industry. Some construction managers obtain a master's degree in business administration or finance to further their career prospects. Doctoral degree recipients usually become college professors or conduct research.

Many individuals also attend training and educational programs sponsored by industry associations, often in collaboration with postsecondary institutions. A number of 2-year colleges throughout the country offer construction management or construction technology programs.

There is a growing movement towards certification of construction managers to ensure that a construction manager has a certain body of knowledge, abilities, and experience. Both the American Institute of Constructors (AIC) and the Construction Management Association of America (CMAA) have established voluntary certification programs for construction managers. Requirements combine written examinations with verification of education and professional experience. AIC awards the Associate Constructor (AC) and Certified Professional Constructor (CPC) designations to candidates who meet its requirements and pass appropriate construction examinations. CMAA awards the Certified Construction Manager (CCM) designation to practitioners who meet its requirements through work performed in a construction management firm and by passing a technical examination. Applicants for the CMAA certification also must complete a self-study course that covers a broad range of topics central to construction management, including the professional role of a construction manager, legal issues, and allocation of risk. Although certification is not required to work in the construction industry, voluntary certification can be valuable because it provides evidence of competence and experience.

Job Outlook
Good employment opportunities for construction managers are expected through 2012 because the number of job openings should be sufficient to accommodate the number of qualified managers seeking to enter the occupation. Because the construction industry often is seen as having dirty, strenuous, and hazardous working conditions, even for managers, many potential managers choose other types of careers.

Employment of construction managers is projected to increase about as fast as the average for all occupations through 2012, as the level and complexity of construction activity continues to grow. Prospects in construction management, architectural and engineering services, and construction contracting firms should be best for persons who have a bachelor's or higher degree in construction science, construction management, or civil engineering, as well as practical experience working in construction. Employers prefer applicants with previous construction work experience who can combine a strong background in building technology with proven supervisory or managerial skills. In addition to those arising from job growth, many openings should result annually from the need to replace workers who transfer to other occupations or leave the labor force.

The increasing complexity of construction projects should boost demand for management-level personnel within the construction industry, as sophisticated technology and the proliferation of laws setting standards for buildings and construction materials, worker safety, energy efficiency, and environmental protection have further complicated the construction process. Advances in building materials and construction methods; the need to replace much of the Nation's infrastructure; and the growing number of multipurpose buildings, electronically operated "smart" buildings, and energy-efficient structures will further add to the demand for more construction managers. However, employment of construction managers can be sensitive to the short-term nature of many projects and to cyclical fluctuations in construction activity.

Earnings
Earnings of salaried construction managers and self-employed independent construction contractors vary depending upon the size and nature of the construction project, its geographic location, and economic conditions. In addition to typical benefits, many salaried construction managers receive benefits such as bonuses and use of company motor vehicles.

Median annual earnings of construction managers in 2002 were $63,500. The middle 50 percent earned between $48,720 and $84,080. The lowest 10 percent earned less than $38,130, and the highest 10 percent earned more than $112,810. Median annual earnings in the industries employing the largest numbers of construction managers in 2002 were:

Nonresidential building construction	$66,280
Foundation, structure, and building exterior contractors	60,020
Building finishing contractors	59,950
Residential building construction	59,900
Other specialty trade contractors	58,860

According to a 2003 salary survey by the National Association of Colleges and Employers, candidates with a bachelor's degree in construction science/management received job offers averaging $42,229 a year.

Related Occupations

Construction managers participate in the conceptual development of a construction project and oversee its organization, scheduling, and implementation. Other workers who perform similar functions include architects, except landscape and naval; civil engineers; cost estimators; landscape architects; and engineering and natural sciences managers.

Sources of Information

For information about constructor certification, contact:
➤ American Institute of Constructors, 466 94th Ave. North, St. Petersburg, FL 33702. Internet: **http://www.constructorcertification.org or http://www.aicnet.org**

For information about construction management and construction manager certification, contact:
➤ Construction Management Association of America, 7918 Jones Branch Dr., Suite 540, McLean, VA 22102-3307. Internet: **http://www.cmaanet.org**

Information on accredited construction science and management educational programs and accreditation requirements is available from:
➤ American Council for Construction Education, 1300 Hudson Lane, Suite 3, Monroe, LA 71201. Internet: **http://www.acce-hq.org**

Education Administrators

(0*NET 11-9031.00, 11-9032.00, 11-9033.00, 11-9039.99)

Significant Points

● Many jobs require a master's or doctoral degree and experience in a related occupation, such as a teacher or admissions counselor.

● Strong interpersonal and communication skills are essential because much of an administrator's job involves working and collaborating with others.

● Job outlook is expected to be excellent because a large proportion of education administrators are expected to retire over the next 10 years.

Nature of the Work

Smooth operation of an educational institution requires competent administrators. *Education administrators* provide instructional leadership as well as manage the day-to-day activities in schools, preschools, daycare centers, and colleges and universities. They also direct the educational programs of businesses, correctional institutions, museums, and job training and community service organiza-

tions. (College presidents and school superintendents are covered in the *Handbook* statement on general managers and top executives.) Education administrators set educational standards and goals and establish the policies and procedures to carry them out. They also supervise managers, support staff, teachers, counselors, librarians, coaches, and others. They develop academic programs; monitor students' educational progress; train and motivate teachers and other staff; manage guidance and other student services; administer recordkeeping; prepare budgets; handle relations with parents, prospective and current students, employers, and the community; and perform many other duties. In an organization such as a small daycare center, one administrator may handle all these functions. In universities or large school systems, responsibilities are divided among many administrators, each with a specific function.

Those who manage elementary, middle, and secondary schools are called *principals*. They set the academic tone and hire, evaluate, and help improve the skills of teachers and other staff. Principals confer with staff to advise, explain, or answer procedural questions. They visit classrooms, observe teaching methods, review instructional objectives, and examine learning materials. They actively work with teachers to develop and maintain high curriculum standards, develop mission statements, and set performance goals and objectives. Principals must use clear, objective guidelines for teacher appraisals, because pay often is based on performance ratings.

Principals also meet and interact with other administrators, students, parents, and representatives of community organizations. Decisionmaking authority has increasingly shifted from school district central offices to individual schools. Thus, parents, teachers, and other members of the community play an important role in setting school policies and goals. Principals must pay attention to the concerns of these groups when making administrative decisions.

Principals prepare budgets and reports on various subjects, including finances and attendance, and oversee the requisition and allocation of supplies. As school budgets become tighter, many principals have become more involved in public relations and fundraising to secure financial support for their schools from local businesses and the community.

Principals must take an active role to ensure that students meet national, State, and local academic standards. Many principals develop school/business partnerships and school-to-work transition programs for students. Increasingly, principals must be sensitive to the needs of the rising number of non-English speaking and culturally diverse students. Growing enrollments, which are leading to overcrowding at many existing schools, also are a cause for concern. When addressing problems of inadequate resources, administrators serve as advocates for the building of new schools or the repair of existing ones. During summer months, principals are responsible for planning for the upcoming year, overseeing summer school, participating in workshops for teachers and administrators, supervising building repairs and improvements, and working to be sure the school has adequate staff for the school year.

Schools continue to be involved with students' emotional welfare as well as their academic achievement. As a result, principals face responsibilities outside the academic realm. For example, in response to the growing numbers of dual-income and single-parent families and teenage parents, schools have established before- and after-school childcare programs or family resource centers, which also may offer parenting classes and social service referrals. With the help of community organizations, some principals have established programs to combat increases in crime, drug and alcohol abuse, and sexually transmitted diseases among students.

Assistant principals aid the principal in the overall administration of the school. Some assistant principals hold this position for several years to prepare for advancement to principal jobs; others are career assistant principals. They are primarily responsible for scheduling student classes, ordering textbooks and supplies, and coordinating transportation, custodial, cafeteria, and other support services. They usually handle student discipline and attendance problems, social and recreational programs, and health and safety matters. They also may counsel students on personal, educational, or vocational matters. With the advent of site-based management, assistant principals are playing a greater role in ensuring the academic success of students by helping to develop new curriculums, evaluating teachers, and dealing with school-community relations—responsibilities previously assumed solely by the principal. The number of assistant principals that a school employs may vary, depending on the number of students.

In preschools and childcare centers, education administrators are the director or supervisor of the school or center. Their job is similar to that of other school administrators in that they oversee daily activities and operation of the schools, hire and develop staff, and make sure that the school meets required regulations.

Administrators in school district central offices oversee public schools under their jurisdiction. This group includes those who direct subject-area programs such as English, music, vocational education, special education, and mathematics. They supervise instructional coordinators and curriculum specialists, and work with them to evaluate curriculums and teaching techniques and improve them. (Instructional coordinators are covered elsewhere in the *Handbook*.) Administrators also may oversee career counseling programs and testing that measures students' abilities and helps to place them in appropriate classes. Others may also direct programs such as school psychology, athletics, curriculum and instruction, and professional development. With site-based management, administrators have transferred primary responsibility for many of these programs to the principals, assistant principals, teachers, instructional coordinators, and other staff in the schools.

In colleges and universities, *academic deans, deans of faculty, provosts,* and *university deans* assist presidents, make faculty appointments, develop budgets, and establish academic policies and programs. They also direct and coordinate the activities of deans of individual colleges and chairpersons of academic departments. Fundraising also is becoming an essential part of their job.

College or university department heads or *chairpersons* are in charge of departments that specialize in particular fields of study, such as English, biological science, or mathematics. In addition to teaching, they coordinate schedules of classes and teaching assignments; propose budgets; recruit, interview, and hire applicants for teaching positions; evaluate faculty members; encourage faculty development; serve on committees; and perform other administrative duties. In overseeing their departments, chairpersons must consider and balance the concerns of faculty, administrators, and students.

Higher education administrators also direct and coordinate the provision of student services. *Vice presidents of student affairs or student life, deans of students,* and *directors of student services* may direct and coordinate admissions, foreign student services, health and counseling services, career services, financial aid, and housing and residential life, as well as social, recreational, and related programs. In small colleges, they may counsel students. In larger colleges and universities, separate administrators may handle each of these services. *Registrars* are custodians of students' records. They register students, record grades, prepare student transcripts, evaluate academic records, assess and collect tuition and fees, plan and implement commencement, oversee the preparation of college catalogs and schedules of classes, and analyze enrollment and demographic statistics. *Directors of admissions* manage the process of recruiting, evaluating, and admitting students, and work closely with *financial aid directors*, who oversee scholarship, fellowship, and loan programs. Registrars and admissions officers at most institutions need computer skills because they use electronic student information systems. For example, for those whose institutions present information—such as college catalogs and schedules—on the Internet, knowledge of online resources, imaging, and other computer skills is important. *Athletic directors* plan and direct intramural and intercollegiate athletic activities, seeing to publicity for athletic events, preparation of budgets, and supervision of coaches. Other increasingly important administrators direct fundraising, public relations, distance learning, and technology.

Working Conditions

Education administrators hold leadership positions with significant responsibility. Most find working with students extremely rewarding, but as the responsibilities of administrators have increased in recent years, so has the stress. Coordinating and interacting with faculty, parents, students, community members, business leaders, and State and local policymakers can be fast-paced and stimulating, but also stressful and demanding. Principals and assistant principals, whose varied duties include discipline, may find working with difficult students challenging. The pressures associated with education administrator jobs have multiplied in recent years, as workers in these positions are increasingly being held accountable for ensuring that their schools meet recently imposed State and Federal guidelines for student performance and teacher qualifications, and as they must cope with the additional challenges presented by current budget shortfalls,.

Many education administrators work more than 40 hours a week, often including school activities at night and on weekends. Most administrators work 11 or 12 months out of the year. Some jobs include travel.

Employment

Education administrators held about 427,000 jobs in 2002. About 2 in 10 worked for private education institutions, and 6 in 10 worked for State and local governments, mainly in schools, colleges and universities, and departments of education. Less than 5 percent were self-employed. The rest worked in child daycare centers, religious

Strong interpersonal and communication skills are essential for education administrators.

organizations, job training centers, and businesses and other organizations that provided training for their employees.

Training, Other Qualifications, and Advancement

Most education administrators begin their careers in related occupations, and prepare for a job in education administration by completing a master's or doctoral degree. Because of the diversity of duties and levels of responsibility, their educational backgrounds and experience vary considerably. Principals, assistant principals, central office administrators, academic deans, and preschool directors usually have held teaching positions before moving into administration. Some teachers move directly into principal positions; others first become assistant principals, or gain experience in other central office administrative jobs at either the school or district level in positions such as department head, curriculum specialist, or subject matter advisor. In some cases, administrators move up from related staff jobs such as recruiter, guidance counselor, librarian, residence hall director, or financial aid or admissions counselor.

To be considered for education administrator positions, workers must first prove themselves in their current jobs. In evaluating candidates, supervisors look for leadership, determination, confidence, innovativeness, and motivation. The ability to make sound decisions and to organize and coordinate work efficiently is essential. Because much of an administrator's job involves interacting with others—such as students, parents, teachers, and the community—a person in such a position must have strong interpersonal skills and be an effective communicator and motivator. Knowledge of leadership principles and practices, gained through work experience and formal education, is important. A familiarity with computer technology is a necessity for principals, who are required to gather information and coordinate technical resources for their students, teachers, and classrooms.

In most public schools, principals, assistant principals, and school administrators in central offices need a master's degree in education administration or educational supervision. Some principals and central office administrators have a doctorate or specialized degree in education administration. In private schools, which are not subject to State licensure requirements, some principals and assistant principals hold only a bachelor's degree; however, the majority have a master's or doctoral degree. Most States require principals to be licensed as school administrators. License requirements vary by State. National standards for school leaders, including principals and supervisors, have been developed by the Interstate School Leaders Licensure Consortium. Many States use these national standards as guidelines to assess beginning principals for licensure. Increasingly, on-the-job training, often with a mentor, is required for new school leaders. Some States require administrators to take continuing education courses to keep their license, thus ensuring that administrators have the most up-to-date skills. The number and types of courses required to maintain licensure vary by State.

Educational requirements for administrators of preschools and childcare centers vary depending on the setting of the program and the State of employment. Administrators who oversee school-based preschool programs are often required to have at least a bachelor's degree. Child care directors are generally not required to have a degree; however, most States require a credential such as the Child Development Associate credential (CDA) sponsored by the Council for Professional Recognition or other credential specifically designed for administrators. The National Child Care Association, offers a National Administration Credential, which some recent college graduates voluntarily earn to better qualify for positions as childcare center directors.

Academic deans and chairpersons usually have a doctorate in their specialty. Most have held a professorship in their department before advancing. Admissions, student affairs, and financial aid directors and registrars sometimes start in related staff jobs with bachelor's degrees—any field usually is acceptable—and obtain advanced degrees in college student affairs, counseling, or higher education administration. A Ph.D. or Ed.D. usually is necessary for top student affairs positions. Computer literacy and a background in accounting or statistics may be assets in admissions, records, and financial work.

Advanced degrees in higher education administration, educational supervision, and college student affairs are offered in many colleges and universities. The National Council for Accreditation of Teacher Education and the Educational Leadership Constituent Council accredit these programs. Education administration degree programs include courses in school leadership, school law, school finance and budgeting, curriculum development and evaluation, research design and data analysis, community relations, politics in education, and counseling. Educational supervision degree programs include courses in supervision of instruction and curriculum, human relations, curriculum development, research, and advanced teaching courses.

Education administrators advance through promotion to more responsible administrative positions or by transferring to more responsible positions at larger schools or systems. They also may become superintendents of school systems or presidents of educational institutions.

Job Outlook

Employment of education administrators is projected to grow faster than the average for all occupations through 2012. As education and training take on greater importance in everyone's lives, the need for people to administer education programs will grow. Job opportunities for many of these positions should also be excellent because a large proportion of education administrators are expected to retire over the next 10 years.

A significant portion of growth will stem from growth in the private and for-profit segments of education. Many of these schools cater to working adults, many of whom might not ordinarily participate in postsecondary education. These schools allow students to earn a degree, receive job-specific training or update their skills, in a convenient manner, such as through part-time programs or distance learning. As the number of these schools continues to grow, more administrators will be needed to oversee them.

Enrollments of school-age children will also have an impact on the demand for education administrators. The U.S. Department of Education projects enrollment of elementary and secondary school students to grow between 5 and 7 percent over the next decade. Preschool and childcare center administrators are expected to experience substantially more growth as enrollments in formal child care programs continues to expand as fewer private households care for young children. Additionally, if mandatory preschool becomes more widespread more preschool directors will be needed. The number of postsecondary school students is projected to grow more rapidly than other student populations, creating significant demand for administrators at that level. In addition, enrollments are expected to increase the fastest in the West and South, where the population is growing, and to decline or remain stable in the Northeast and the Midwest. School administrators also are in greater demand in rural and urban areas, where pay is generally lower than in the suburbs.

Principals and assistant principals should have favorable job prospects. A sharp increase in responsibilities in recent years has made the job more stressful, and has discouraged teachers from taking positions in administration. Principals are now being held more accountable for the performance of students and teachers, while at the same time they are required to adhere to a growing number of government regulations. In addition, overcrowded classrooms, safety issues, budgetary concerns, and teacher shortages in some areas all are creating additional stress for administrators. The increase in pay is often not high enough to entice people into the field.

Job prospects also are expected to be favorable for college and university administrators, particularly those seeking nonacademic positions. Colleges and universities may be subject to funding shortfalls during economic downturns, but increasing enrollments over the projection period will require that institutions replace the large numbers of administrators who retire, and even hire additional administrators. While competition among faculty for prestigious positions as academic deans and department heads is likely to remain keen, fewer applicants are expected for nonacademic administrative jobs, such as director of admissions or student affairs. Furthermore, many people are discouraged from seeking administrator jobs by the requirement that they have a master's or doctoral degree in education administration—as well as by the opportunity to earn higher salaries in other occupations.

Earnings

In 2002, elementary and secondary school administrators had median annual earnings of $71,490; postsecondary school administrators had median annual earnings of $64,640, while preschool and childcare center administrators earned a median of $33,340 per year. Salaries of education administrators depend on several factors, including the location and enrollment level in the school or school district. According to a survey of public schools, conducted by the Educational Research Service, average salaries for principals and assistant principals in the 2002-03 school year were as follows:

Directors, managers, coordinators, and supervisors, finance and business	$81,451
Principals:	
Elementary school	75,291
Jr. high/middle school	80,708
Senior high school	86,452
Assistant principals:	
Elementary school	$62,230
Jr. high/middle school	67,288
Senior high school	70,874

According to the College and University Professional Association for Human Resources, median annual salaries for selected administrators in higher education in 2001-02 were as follows:

Academic deans:	
Business	$107,414
Graduate programs	100,391
Education	100,227
Arts and sciences	98,780
Health-related professions	89,234
Nursing	88,386
Continuing education	84,457
Occupational or vocational education	73,595
Other administrators:	
Dean of students	$70,012
Director, admissions and registrar	61,519
Director, student financial aid	57,036
Director, annual giving	49,121
Director, student activities	41,050

Benefits for education administrators are generally very good. Many get 4 or 5 weeks vacation every year and have generous health and pension packages. Many colleges and universities offer free tuition to employees and their families.

Related Occupations

Education administrators apply organizational and leadership skills to provide services to individuals. Workers in related occupations include administrative services managers; office and administrative support worker supervisors and managers; human resource, training, and labor relations managers and specialists; and archivists, curators, and museum technicians. Education administrators also work with students and have backgrounds similar to those of counselors; librarians; instructional coordinators; teachers—preschool, kindergarten, elementary, middle, and secondary; and teachers—postsecondary.

Sources of Additional Information

For information on principals and other management staff in public schools, contact:

➤ Educational Research Service, 2000 Clarendon Boulevard, Arlington, VA 22201-2908. Internet: **http://www.ers.org**

For information on principals, contact:

➤ The National Association of Elementary School Principals, 1615 Duke St., Alexandria, VA 22314-3483. Internet: **http://www.naesp.org**

➤ The National Association of Secondary School Principals, 1904 Association Drive, Reston, VA 20191-1537. Internet: **http://www.nassp.org**

For information on collegiate registrars and admissions officers, contact:

➤ American Association of Collegiate Registrars and Admissions Officers, One Dupont Circle NW., Suite 520, Washington, DC 20036-1171. Internet: **http://www.aacrao.org**

For information on professional development and graduate programs for college student affairs administrators, contact:

➤ NASPA, Student Affairs Administrators in Higher Education, 1875 Connecticut Ave. NW., Suite 418, Washington, DC 20009. Internet: **http://www.naspa.org**

Engineering and Natural Sciences Managers

(0*NET 11-9041.00, 11-9121.00)

Significant Points

● Most engineering and natural sciences managers have previous experience as engineers, scientists, or mathematicians.

● Projected employment growth for engineering and natural sciences managers should be closely related to those for the engineers and scientists they supervise and the industries in which they are found.

● Opportunities will be best for workers with advanced technical knowledge and strong communication and business management skills.

Nature of the Work

Engineering and natural sciences managers plan, coordinate, and direct research, design, and production activities. They may supervise engineers, scientists, and technicians, along with support personnel. These managers use advanced technical knowledge of engineering and science to oversee a variety of activities. They determine scientific and technical goals within broad outlines provided by top executives, who are discussed elsewhere in the *Handbook*. These goals may include improving manufacturing processes, advancing scientific research, or developing new products. Managers make detailed plans to accomplish these goals—for example, they may develop the overall concepts of a new product or identify technical problems preventing the completion of a project.

To perform effectively, they also must possess knowledge of administrative procedures, such as budgeting, hiring, and supervision. These managers propose budgets for projects and programs and determine staff, training, and equipment needs. They hire and assign scientists, engineers, and support personnel to carry out specific parts of each project. They also supervise the work of these employees, review their output, and establish administrative procedures and policies—including environmental standards, for example.

In addition, these managers use communication skills extensively. They spend a great deal of time coordinating the activities of their unit with those of other units or organizations. They confer with higher levels of management; with financial, production, marketing, and other managers; and with contractors and equipment and materials suppliers.

Engineering managers supervise people who design and develop machinery, products, systems, and processes; or direct and coordinate production, operations, quality assurance, testing, or maintenance in industrial plants. Many are plant engineers, who direct and coordinate the design, installation, operation, and maintenance of equipment and machinery in industrial plants. Others manage research and development teams that produce new products and processes or improve existing ones.

Natural sciences managers oversee the work of life and physical scientists, including agricultural scientists, chemists, biologists, geologists, medical scientists, and physicists. These managers direct research and development projects and coordinate activities such as testing, quality control, and production. They may work on basic research projects or on commercial activities. Science managers sometimes conduct their own research in addition to managing the work of others.

Working Conditions

Engineering and natural sciences managers spend most of their time in an office. Some managers, however, also may work in laboratories, where they may be exposed to the same conditions as research scientists, or in industrial plants, where they may be exposed to the same conditions as production workers. Most managers work at least 40 hours a week and may work much longer on occasion to meet project deadlines. Some may experience considerable pressure to meet technical or scientific goals on a short deadline or within a tight budget.

Employment

Engineering and natural sciences managers held about 257,000 jobs in 2002. About 26 percent worked in professional, scientific, and technical services industries, primarily for firms providing architectural, engineering, and related services; computer systems design and related services; and scientific research and development services. Manufacturing industries employed 35 percent of engineering and natural sciences managers. Manufacturing industries with the largest employment include those producing computer and electronic equipment, machinery, transportation equipment, including aerospace products and parts, and chemicals, including pharmaceuticals. Other large employers include government agencies and telecommunications and utilities companies.

Engineering and natural sciences managers provide guidance to employees and oversee day-to-day operations of the organization.

Training, Other Qualifications, and Advancement

Strong technical knowledge is essential for engineering and natural sciences managers, who must understand and guide the work of their subordinates and explain the work in nontechnical terms to senior management and potential customers. Therefore, these management positions usually require work experience and formal education similar to those of engineers, scientists, or mathematicians.

Most engineering managers begin their careers as engineers, after completing a bachelor's degree in the field. To advance to higher level positions, engineers generally must assume management responsibility. To fill management positions, employers seek engineers who possess administrative and communications skills in addition to technical knowledge in their specialty. Many engineers gain these skills by obtaining a master's degree in engineering management or a master's degree in business administration (MBA). Employers often pay for such training. In large firms, some courses required in these degree programs may be offered on site. Engineers who prefer to manage in technical areas should get a master's degree in engineering management, while those interested in nontechnical management should get an MBA.

Many science managers begin their careers as scientists, such as chemists, biologists, geologists, or mathematicians. Most scientists or mathematicians engaged in basic research have a Ph.D.; some in applied research and other activities may have a bachelor's or master's degree. Science managers must be specialists in the work they supervise. In addition, employers prefer managers with good communication and administrative skills. Graduate programs allow scientists to augment their undergraduate training with instruction in other fields, such as management or computer technology. Given the rapid pace of scientific developments, science managers must continuously upgrade their knowledge.

Engineering and natural sciences managers may advance to progressively higher leadership positions within their discipline. Some may become managers in nontechnical areas such as marketing, human resources, or sales. In high technology firms, managers in nontechnical areas often must possess the same specialized knowledge as do managers in technical areas. For example, employers in an engineering firm may prefer to hire experienced engineers as sales workers because the complex services offered by the firm can be marketed only by someone with specialized engineering knowledge. Such sales workers could eventually advance to jobs as sales managers.

Job Outlook

Employment of engineering and natural sciences managers is expected to have average growth through the year 2012—in line with projected employment growth in engineering and most sciences. However, many additional jobs will result from the need to replace managers who retire or move into other occupations. Opportunities for obtaining a management position will be best for workers with advanced technical knowledge and strong communication skills. In addition, business management skills are important because engineering and natural sciences managers are involved in their firm's financial, production, and marketing activities.

Projected employment growth for engineering and natural sciences managers should be closely related to the growth of the occupations they supervise and the industries in which they are found. For example, opportunities for managers should be better in rapidly growing areas of engineering—such as electrical, computer, and biomedical engineering—than in more slowly growing areas of engineering or physical science, such as aerospace and petroleum engineering. (See the statements on engineers and on life and physical scientists, elsewhere in the *Handbook*.) In addition, many employers are finding it more efficient to contract engineering and science management services to outside companies and consultants, creating good opportunities for managers in management services and management, scientific, and technical consulting firms.

Earnings

Earnings for engineering and natural sciences managers vary by specialty and level of responsibility. Median annual earnings of engineering managers were $90,930 in 2002. The middle 50 percent earned between $72,480 and $114,050. The lowest 10 percent earned less than $57,840, and the highest 10 percent earned more than $141,380. Median annual earnings in the industries employing the largest numbers of engineering managers in 2002 were:

Navigational, measuring, electromedical, and control instruments manufacturing	$101,290
Management of companies and enterprises	98,000
Aerospace product and parts manufacturing	97,420
Federal Government	90,030
Architectural, engineering, and related services	89,520

Median annual earnings of natural sciences managers were $82,250 in 2002. The middle 50 percent earned between $60,000 and $111,070. The lowest 10 percent earned less than $45,640, and the highest 10 percent earned more than $144,590. Median annual earnings in the industries employing the largest numbers of natural sciences managers in 2002 were:

Scientific research and development services	$101,690
Federal Government	77,020

A survey of manufacturing firms, conducted by Abbot, Langer & Associates, found that engineering department managers and superintendents earned a median annual income of $89,271 in 2003, while research and development managers earned $86,412.

In addition, engineering and natural sciences managers, especially those at higher levels, often receive more benefits—such as expense accounts, stock option plans, and bonuses—than do non-managerial workers in their organizations.

Related Occupations

The work of engineering and natural sciences managers is closely related to that of engineers; mathematicians; and physical and life scientists, including agricultural and food scientists, biological and medical scientists, conservation scientists and foresters, atmospheric scientists, chemists and materials scientists, environmental scientists and geoscientists, and physicists and astronomers. It also is related to the work of other managers, especially top executives.

Sources of Additional Information

For information about a career as an engineering and natural sciences manager, contact the sources of additional information for engineers, life scientists, and physical scientists that are listed at the end of statements on these occupations elsewhere in the *Handbook*.

Farmers, Ranchers, and Agricultural Managers

(O*NET 11-9011.01, 11-9011.02, 11-9011.03, 11-9012.00)

Significant Points

- Modern farming requires knowledge of new developments in agriculture, and work experience acquired through growing up on a farm or through a small number of internships now available.

- Overall employment is projected to decline because of increasing productivity and consolidation of farms.

- Aquaculture and horticulture should provide better employment opportunities.

- Developments in value-added marketing and organic farming are making small-scale farming economically viable again.

Nature of the Work

American farmers, ranchers, and agricultural managers direct the activities of one of the world's largest and most productive agricultural sectors. They produce enough food and fiber to meet the needs of the United States and produce a surplus for export.

Farmers and ranchers own and operate mainly family-owned farms. They may also lease land from a landowner and operate it as a working farm. The type of farm they operate determines their specific tasks. On crop farms—farms growing grain, cotton, and other fibers, fruit, and vegetables—farmers are responsible for preparing, tilling, planting, fertilizing, cultivating, spraying, and harvesting. After the harvest, they make sure the crops are properly packaged, stored, or marketed. Livestock, dairy, and poultry farmers must feed, and care for the animals and keep barns, pens, coops, and other farm buildings clean and in good condition. They also plan and oversee breeding and marketing activities. Horticultural specialty farmers oversee the production of ornamental plants, nursery products—such as flowers, bulbs, shrubbery, and sod—and fruits and vegetables grown in greenhouses. Aquaculture farmers raise fish and shellfish in marine, brackish, or fresh water, usually in ponds, floating net pens, raceways, or recirculating systems. They stock, feed, protect, and otherwise manage aquatic life sold for consumption or used for recreational fishing.

Responsibilities of farmers and ranchers range from caring for livestock, to operating machinery, to maintaining equipment and facilities. The size of the farm or ranch often determines which of these tasks farmers and ranchers will handle themselves. Operators of small farms usually perform all tasks, physical and administrative. They keep records for management and tax purposes, service machinery, maintain buildings, and grow vegetables and raise animals. Operators of large farms, on the other hand, have employees who help with the physical work that small-farm operators do themselves. Although employment on most farms is limited to the farmer and one or two family workers or hired employees, some large farms have 100 or more full-time and seasonal workers. Some of these employees are in nonfarm occupations, working as truck drivers, sales representatives, bookkeepers, and computer specialists.

Agricultural managers manage the day-to-day activities of one or more farms, ranches, nurseries, timber tracts, greenhouses, and other agricultural establishments for farmers, absentee landowners, or corporations. Their duties and responsibilities vary widely, but are concentrated on the business aspects of running a farm. On small farms, they may oversee the entire operation, while on large farms they may oversee a single activity, such as marketing. Agricultural managers usually do not perform production activities; instead they hire and supervise farm and livestock workers, who perform most of the daily production tasks. In these cases, managers may establish output goals; determine financial constraints; monitor production and marketing; hire, assign, and supervise workers; determine crop transportation and storage requirements; and oversee maintenance of the property and equipment.

Farmers, ranchers, and agricultural managers make many managerial decisions. Farm output is strongly influenced by the weather, disease, fluctuations in prices of domestic and foreign farm products, and Federal farm programs. In crop production operations, farmers and managers usually determine the best time to plant seed, apply fertilizer and chemicals, harvest, and market. They use different strategies to protect themselves from unpredictable changes in the markets for agricultural products. Many farmers and managers carefully plan the combination of crops they grow so that if the price of one crop drops, they will have sufficient income from another to make up for the loss. While most farm output is sold to middlemen—primarily food processing companies—some farmers, particularly operators of smaller farms, may choose to sell their goods directly through farmers' markets, or use cooperatives to reduce their financial risk and to gain a larger share of consumers' expenditures on food. For example, in Community Supported Agriculture (CSA), cooperatives sell to consumers shares of a harvest prior to the planting season, thus freeing the farmer from having to bear all the financial risks and ensuring the farmer a market for the produce of the coming season.

Farmers, ranchers, and agricultural managers also negotiate with banks and other credit lenders to get the best financing deals for their equipment as well as their livestock and seed. They must also keep abreast of constantly changing prices for their products and be able to manage the risk of fluctuating prices. Those who plan ahead may be able to store their crops or keep their livestock to take advantage of better prices later in the year. Those who participate in the risky futures market, where contracts on agricultural goods are bought and sold at specified prices in the future, can minimize the risk of sudden price changes by buying futures contracts that guarantee they will get at least a certain price for their agricultural goods when they are ready to sell.

Like other businesses, farming operations have become more complex in recent years, so many farmers use computers to keep financial and inventory records. They also use computer databases and spreadsheets to manage breeding, dairy, and other farm operations.

Working Conditions
The work of farmers, ranchers, and agricultural managers is often strenuous; work hours are frequently long; and they rarely have days off during the planting, growing, and harvesting seasons. Nevertheless, for those who enter farming or ranching, the disadvantages are outweighed by the quality of life in a rural area, working outdoors, being self-employed, and making a living working the land. Farmers and farm managers on crop farms usually work from sunrise to sunset during the planting and harvesting seasons. During the rest of the year they plan next season's crops, market their output, and repair machinery; some may earn additional income by working a second job off the farm.

On livestock producing farms and ranches, work goes on throughout the year. Animals, unless they are grazing, must be fed and watered every day, and dairy cows must be milked two or three times a day. Many livestock and dairy farmers monitor and attend to the health of their herds, which may include assisting in the birthing of animals. Such farmers rarely get the chance to get away unless they hire an assistant or arrange for a temporary substitute.

Farmers who grow produce and perishables have different demands on their time. For example, organic farmers must maintain cover crops during the cold months, which keep them occupied with farming beyond the typical growing season.

Farm work also can be hazardous. Tractors and other farm machinery can cause serious injury, and workers must be constantly alert on the job. The proper operation of equipment and handling of chemicals is necessary to avoid accidents and protect the environment.

On very large farms, farmers spend substantial time meeting with farm managers or farm supervisors in charge of various activities. Professional farm managers overseeing several farms may divide their time between traveling to meet farmers or landowners and planning the farm operations in their offices. As farming practices and agricultural technology become more sophisticated, farmers and farm managers are spending more time in offices and at computers, where they electronically manage many aspects of their businesses. Some farmers also spend time at conferences, particularly during the winter months, exchanging information.

Employment
Farmers, ranchers, and agricultural managers held nearly 1.4 million jobs in 2002. About 84 percent were self-employed. Most farmers, ranchers, and agricultural managers oversee crop production activities, while others manage livestock and dairy production. A smaller number are involved in agricultural services, such as contract harvesting and farm labor contracting.

The soil, topography of the land, and climate determine the type of farming and ranching done in a particular area. For example, California, Wisconsin, New York, and Pennsylvania lead the country in milk production, while Iowa, Ohio, Pennsylvania, and California

Getting a crop to market is a prime responsibility of farmers and agricultural managers.

lead in egg production. Texas, California, Mississippi, Georgia, and Arizona are the biggest cotton producers; and Kansas, North Dakota, Washington, and Montana are the biggest wheat producers.

Training, Other Qualifications, and Advancement

Growing up on a family farm and participating in agricultural programs for young people (sponsored by the National FFA Organization, formerly known as the Future Farmers of America, or the 4-H youth educational programs, or other educational opportunities offered by the Extension Service) are important sources of training for those interested in pursuing agriculture as a career. However, modern farming requires increasingly complex scientific, business, and financial decisions. Therefore, even people who were raised on farms must acquire the appropriate education.

Not all agricultural managers grew up on farms or ranches. For these people, a bachelor's degree in business with a concentration in agriculture is important. In addition to formal education, they need several years of work experience in the different aspects of farm and ranch operations in order to qualify for an agricultural manager position.

Students should select the college most appropriate to their specific interests and location. In the United States, all State university systems have one land-grant university with a school of agriculture. Common programs of study include agronomy, dairy science, agricultural economics and business, horticulture, crop and fruit science, and animal science. For students interested in aquaculture, formal programs are available, and include coursework in fisheries biology, fish culture, hatchery management and maintenance, and hydrology. Whatever one's interest, the college curriculum should include courses in agricultural production, marketing, and economics.

Professional status can be enhanced through voluntary certification as an Accredited Farm Manager (AFM) by the American Society of Farm Managers and Rural Appraisers. Certification requires several years of farm management experience, the appropriate academic background—a bachelor's degree or, preferably, a master's degree in a field of agricultural science—and the passing of courses and examinations relating to business, financial, and legal aspects of farm and ranch management.

Farmers, ranchers, and agricultural managers need to keep abreast of continuing advances in agricultural methods both in the United States and abroad, as well as changes in governmental regulations that may impact methods or markets for particular crops. Besides print journals that inform the agricultural community, the spread of the Internet allows quick access to the latest developments in areas such as agricultural marketing, legal arrangements, or growing crops, vegetables, and livestock. Electronic mail, on-line journals, and newsletters from agricultural organizations also speed the exchange of information directly between farming associations and individual farmers.

Farmers, ranchers, and agricultural managers also must have enough technical knowledge of crops, growing conditions, and plant diseases to make decisions ensuring the successful operation of their farms. A rudimentary knowledge of veterinary science, as well as animal husbandry, is important for livestock and dairy farmers. Knowledge of the relationship between farm operations—for example, the use of pesticides—and environmental conditions is essential. Mechanical aptitude and the ability to work with tools of all kinds are also valuable skills for the operator of a small farm, who often maintains and repairs machinery or farm structures.

Farmers, ranchers, and agricultural managers need the managerial skills necessary to organize and operate a business. A basic knowledge of accounting and bookkeeping is essential in keeping financial records, while knowledge of credit sources is vital for buying seed, fertilizer, and other inputs necessary for planting. It is also necessary to be familiar with complex safety regulations and requirements of governmental agricultural support programs. Computer skills are increasingly important, especially on large farms, where computers are widely used for recordkeeping and business analysis. For example, some farmers, ranchers, and agricultural managers use personal computers to access the Internet to get the latest information on prices of farm products and other agricultural news. Additionally, skills in personnel management, communication, and conflict resolution are equally important in the operation of a farm or ranch business.

High school training should include courses in mathematics and in biology and other life sciences. Completion of a 2-year degree, and preferably a 4-year bachelor's degree program in a college of agriculture, is becoming increasingly important. But even after obtaining formal education, novices may need to spend time working under an experienced farmer to learn how to put into practice the skills learned through academic training. A small number of farms offer, on a formal basis, apprenticeships to help young people acquire such practical skills.

Job Outlook

Market pressures and low prices for many agricultural goods, will cause more farms to go out of business over the 2002-2012 period. The complexity of modern farming and keen competition among farmers leaves little room for the marginally successful farmer. Therefore, the long-term trend toward consolidation of farms into fewer and larger farms is expected to continue over the 2002-12 period, and result in the continued decline in employment of self-employed farmers and ranchers and slower than average growth in employment of salaried agricultural managers. As land, machinery, seed, and chemicals become more expensive, only well capitalized farmers and corporations are able to acquire many of the farms that become available. It is the larger, more productive farms that are better able to withstand the adverse effects of climate and price fluctuations upon farm output and income and to cover operating costs for livestock, feed, seed, and fuel, for example. Larger farms also have advantages in competing for government subsidies and payments.

In addition, the agriculture sector continues to produce more with fewer workers. Increasing productivity in the U.S. agricultural production industry is expected to allow greater domestic consumption needs and export requirements to be met with fewer farmers, ranchers, and agricultural managers overall. The overwhelming majority of job openings for self-employed farmers and ranchers will result from the need to replace farmers who retire or leave the occupation for economic or other reasons.

Despite the expected continued consolidation of farm land and the projected decline in overall employment of farmers, ranchers, and agricultural managers, an increasing number of small-scale farmers have developed successful market niches that involve personalized, direct contact with their customers. Many are finding opportunities in organic food production, as more consumers demand food grown without pesticides or chemicals. Others use farmers' markets that cater directly to urban and suburban consumers, allowing the farmers to capture a greater share of consumers' food dollars. Some small-scale farmers, such as some dairy farmers, belong to collectively owned marketing cooperatives that process and sell their product. Other farmers participate in community-supported agriculture cooperatives that allow consumers to directly buy a share of the farmer's harvest.

Aquaculture also should continue to provide some new employment opportunities over the 2002-12 period. Overfishing has resulted in declining ocean catches even as public demand for the consumption of seafood continues to grow. This has spurred the growth of aquaculture farms that raise selected aquatic species—such as shrimp, salmon, trout and catfish—in pens or ponds. Aquaculture's presence in even landlocked States has increased as farmers attempt to diversify and cater to the growing demand for fish by consumers. Additionally, growing consumer demand for horticulture products, such as flowers and ornamentals, trees, shrubs, and other non-edibles, is expected to produce better employment opportunities for greenhouse and nursery farmers and managers.

Earnings

Incomes of farmers and ranchers vary greatly from year to year because prices of farm products fluctuate depending upon weather conditions and other factors that influence the quantity and quality of farm output and the demand for those products. A farm that shows a large profit in one year may show a loss in the following year. Farmers, however, often receive government subsidies or other payments that supplement their incomes and reduce some of the risk of farming. Price supports for dairy farmers, though, are being phased out and may result in lower incomes for these farmers. Many farmers—primarily operators of small farms—have income from off-farm business activities or careers, often greater than that of their farm income.

Full-time, salaried farm managers had median annual earnings of $43,740 in 2002. The middle half earned between $32,620 and $59,330. The highest paid 10 percent earned more than $81,100, and the lowest paid 10 percent earned less than $24,410.

Farmers and self-employed farm managers make their own provisions for benefits. As members of farm organizations, they may derive benefits such as group discounts on health and life insurance premiums.

Related Occupations

Farmers, ranchers, and agricultural managers strive to improve the quality of agricultural products and the efficiency of farms. Others whose work is related to agricultural products include agricultural engineers, agricultural and food scientists, agricultural workers, and purchasing agents and buyers of farm products.

Sources of Additional Information

For general information about farming and agricultural occupations, contact:
➤ Center for Rural Affairs, P.O. Box 406, Walthill, NE 68067. Internet: **http://www.cfra.org**
➤ National FFA Organization, The National FFA Center, Attention Career Information Requests, P.O. Box 68690, Indianapolis, IN 46268-0960. Internet: **http://www.ffa.org**

For information about certification as an accredited farm manager, contact:
➤ American Society of Farm Managers and Rural Appraisers, 950 Cherry St., Suite 508, Denver, CO 80222. Internet: **http://www.asfmra.org**

For information on the USDA's program to help small farmers get started, contact:
➤ Small Farm Program, U.S. Department of Agriculture, Cooperative State, Research, Education, and Extension Service, Stop 2220, Washington, DC 20250-2220. Internet: **http://www.reeusda.gov/smallfarm/**

For information on aquaculture, education, training, or Community Supported Agriculture, contact:
➤ Alternative Farming System Information Center (AFSIC), National Agricultural Library USDA, 10301 Baltimore Ave., Room 132, Beltsville, MD 20705-2351. Internet: **http://www.nal.usda.gov/afsic**
➤ Appropriate Technology Transfer for Rural Areas, P.O. Box 3657, Fayetteville, AR 72702. Internet: **http://www.attra.org**

Financial Managers

(0*NET 11-3031.01, 11-3031.02)

Significant Points

● A bachelor's degree in finance, accounting, or a related field is the minimum academic preparation, but many employers increasingly seek graduates with a master's degree.

● Employment will grow as the economy expands and increases the need for workers with financial expertise.

Nature of the Work

Almost every firm, government agency, and organization has one or more financial managers who oversee the preparation of financial reports, direct investment activities, and implement cash management strategies. As computers are increasingly used to record and organize data, many financial managers are spending more time developing strategies and implementing the long-term goals of their organization.

The duties of financial managers vary with their specific titles, which include controller, treasurer or finance officer, credit manager, cash manager, and risk and insurance manager. *Controllers* direct the preparation of financial reports that summarize and forecast the organization's financial position, such as income statements, balance sheets, and analyses of future earnings or expenses. Controllers also are in charge of preparing special reports required by regulatory authorities. Often, controllers oversee the accounting, audit, and budget departments. *Treasurers* and *finance officers* direct the organization's financial goals, objectives, and budgets. They oversee the investment of funds and manage associated risks, supervise cash management activities, execute capital-raising strategies to support a firm's expansion, and deal with mergers and acquisitions. *Credit managers* oversee the firm's issuance of credit. They establish credit-rating criteria, determine credit ceilings, and monitor the collections of past-due accounts. Managers specializing in international finance develop financial and accounting systems for the banking transactions of multinational organizations.

Cash managers monitor and control the flow of cash receipts and disbursements to meet the business and investment needs of the firm. For example, cashflow projections are needed to determine whether loans must be obtained to meet cash requirements or whether surplus cash should be invested in interest-bearing instruments. *Risk and insurance managers* oversee programs to minimize risks and losses that might arise from financial transactions and business operations undertaken by the institution. They also manage the organization's insurance budget.

Financial institutions, such as commercial banks, savings and loan associations, credit unions, and mortgage and finance companies, employ additional financial managers who oversee various functions, such as lending, trusts, mortgages, and investments, or programs, including sales, operations, or electronic financial services. These managers may be required to solicit business, authorize loans, and direct the investment of funds, always adhering to Federal and State laws and regulations. (Chief financial officers and other executives are included with top executives elsewhere in the *Handbook*.)

Branch managers of financial institutions administer and manage all of the functions of a branch office, which may include hiring personnel, approving loans and lines of credit, establishing a rapport with the community to attract business, and assisting customers with account problems. Financial managers who work for financial institutions must keep abreast of the rapidly growing array of financial services and products.

In addition to the general duties described above, all financial managers perform tasks unique to their organization or industry. For example, government financial managers must be experts on the government appropriations and budgeting processes, whereas healthcare financial managers must be knowledgeable about issues surrounding healthcare financing. Moreover, financial managers must be aware of special tax laws and regulations that affect their industry.

Financial managers play an increasingly important role in mergers and consolidations, and in global expansion and related financing. These areas require extensive, specialized knowledge on the part of the financial manager to reduce risks and maximize profit. Financial managers increasingly are hired on a temporary basis to advise senior managers on these and other matters. In fact, some small firms contract out all accounting and financial functions to companies that provide these services.

The role of the financial manager, particularly in business, is changing in response to technological advances that have significantly reduced the amount of time it takes to produce financial reports. Financial managers now perform more data analysis and use it to offer senior managers ideas on how to maximize profits. They often work on teams, acting as business advisors to top management. Financial managers need to keep abreast of the latest computer technology in order to increase the efficiency of their firm's financial operations.

Working Conditions

Financial managers work in comfortable offices, often close to top managers and to departments that develop the financial data these managers need. They typically have direct access to state-of-the-art computer systems and information services. Financial managers commonly work long hours, often up to 50 or 60 per week. They generally are required to attend meetings of financial and economic associations and may travel to visit subsidiary firms or to meet customers.

Employment

Financial managers held about 599,000 jobs in 2002. While the vast majority is employed in private industry, nearly 1 in 10 work for the different branches of government. In addition, although they can be found in every industry, approximately 1 out of 4 are employed by insurance and finance establishments, such as banks, savings institutions, finance companies, credit unions, and securities dealers.

Training, Other Qualifications, and Advancement

A bachelor's degree in finance, accounting, economics, or business administration is the minimum academic preparation for financial managers. However, many employers now seek graduates with a master's degree, preferably in business administration, economics, finance, or risk management. These academic programs develop analytical skills and provide knowledge of the latest financial analysis methods and technology.

Experience may be more important than formal education for some financial manager positions—notably, branch managers in banks. Banks typically fill branch manager positions by promoting

Financial managers develop strategies and implement the long-term goals of an organization.

experienced loan officers and other professionals who excel at their jobs. Other financial managers may enter the profession through formal management training programs offered by the company.

Continuing education is vital for financial managers, who must cope with the growing complexity of global trade, changes in Federal and State laws and regulations, and the proliferation of new and complex financial instruments. Firms often provide opportunities for workers to broaden their knowledge and skills by encouraging employees to take graduate courses at colleges and universities or attend conferences related to their specialty. Financial management, banking, and credit union associations, often in cooperation with colleges and universities, sponsor numerous national and local training programs. Persons enrolled prepare extensively at home and then attend sessions on subjects such as accounting management, budget management, corporate cash management, financial analysis, international banking, and information systems. Many firms pay all or part of the costs for employees who successfully complete courses. Although experience, ability, and leadership are emphasized for promotion, advancement may be accelerated by this type of special study.

In some cases, financial managers also may broaden their skills and exhibit their competency by attaining professional certification. There are many different associations that offer professional certification programs. For example, the Association for Investment Management and Research confers the Chartered Financial Analyst designation on investment professionals who have a bachelor's degree, pass three sequential examinations, and meet work experience requirements. The Association for Financial Professionals (AFP) confers the Certified Cash Manager credential to those who pass a computer-based exam and have a minimum of 2 years of relevant experience. The Institute of Management Accountants offers a Certified in Financial Management designation to members with a BA and at least 2 years of work experience who pass the institute's four-part examination and fulfill continuing education requirements. Also, financial managers who specialize in accounting may earn the Certified Public Accountant (CPA) or Certified Management Accountant (CMA) designations. (See accountants and auditors elsewhere in the *Handbook.*)

Candidates for financial management positions need a broad range of skills. Interpersonal skills are important because these jobs involve managing people and working as part of a team to solve problems. Financial managers must have excellent communication skills to explain complex financial data. Because financial managers work extensively with various departments in their firm, a broad overview of the business is essential.

Financial managers should be creative thinkers and problem-solvers, applying their analytical skills to business. They must be comfortable with the latest computer technology. As financial operations increasingly are affected by the global economy, financial managers must have knowledge of international finance. Proficiency in a foreign language also may be important.

Because financial management is critical for efficient business operations, well-trained, experienced financial managers who display a strong grasp of the operations of various departments within their organization are prime candidates for promotion to top management positions. Some financial managers transfer to closely related positions in other industries. Those with extensive experience and access to sufficient capital may start their own consulting firms.

Job Outlook

Employment of financial managers is expected to grow about as fast as the average for all occupations through 2012. Growth is expected to be steady and will increase in line with the growth of the economy as a whole. However, jobseekers are likely to face keen competition for jobs, as the number of job openings is expected to be less than the number of applicants. Candidates with expertise in accounting and finance, particularly those with a master's degree, should enjoy the best job prospects. Strong computer skills and knowledge of international finance are important; so are excellent communication skills, because financial management jobs involve working on strategic planning teams.

As the economy expands, job growth for financial managers will stem from both the expansion of established companies and from the creation of new businesses. Over the short term, employment in this occupation is negatively impacted by economic downturns, during which companies are more likely to close departments, or even go out of business—decreasing the need for financial managers. Mergers, acquisitions, and corporate downsizing also are likely to adversely affect employment of financial managers. However, the growing need for financial expertise as the economy expands will ensure job growth over the next decade.

The banking industry, which employs more than 1 out of 10 financial managers, will continue to consolidate, although at a slower rate than in previous years. In spite of this trend, employment of bank branch managers is expected to increase as banks begin to refocus on the importance of their existing branches and as new branches are created to service a growing population. As banks expand the range of products and services they offer to include insurance and investment products, branch managers with knowledge in these areas will be needed. As a result, candidates who are licensed to sell insurance or securities will have the most favorable prospects.

Despite the current downturn in the securities and commodities industry, the long-run prospects for financial managers in that industry should be favorable, as more will be needed to handle increasingly complex financial transactions and manage a growing amount of investments. Financial managers also will be needed to handle mergers and acquisitions, raise capital, and assess global financial transactions. Risk managers, who assess risks for insurance and investment purposes, also will be in demand.

Some companies may hire financial managers on a temporary basis, to see the organization through a short-term crisis or to offer suggestions for boosting profits. Other companies may contract out all accounting and financial operations. Even in these cases, however, financial managers may be needed to oversee the contracts.

Computer technology has reduced the time and staff required to produce financial reports. As a result, forecasting earnings, profits, and costs, and generating ideas and creative ways to increase profitability will become a major role of corporate financial managers over the next decade. Financial managers who are familiar with computer software that can assist them in this role will be needed.

Earnings

Median annual earnings of financial managers were $73,340 in 2002. The middle 50 percent earned between $52,490 and $100,660. The lowest 10 percent had earnings of less than $39,120, while the top 10 percent earned over $142,260. Median annual earnings in the industries employing the largest numbers of financial managers in 2002 were as follows:

Securities and commodity contracts intermediation and brokerage	$125,220
Management of companies and enterprises	88,310
Nondepository credit intermediation	78,400
Local government	63,090
Depository credit intermediation	58,790

According to a 2002 survey by Robert Half International, a staffing services firm specializing in accounting and finance professionals, directors of finance earned between $75,000 and $204,500, and corporate controllers earned between $54,000 and $138,750.

The Association for Financial Professionals' 14th annual compensation survey showed that financial officers' average total compensation in 2002, including bonuses and deferred compensation, was $130,900. Selected financial manager positions had average total compensation as follows:

Vice president of finance	$183,500
Treasurer	150,600
Assistant vice president–finance	141,300
Controller/comptroller	134,300
Director	113,600
Assistant treasurer	111,900
Assistant controller/comptroller	115,500
Manager	84,500
Cash manager	64,700

Large organizations often pay more than small ones, and salary levels also can depend on the type of industry and location. Many financial managers in both public and private industry receive additional compensation in the form of bonuses, which also vary substantially by size of firm. Deferred compensation in the form of stock options is becoming more common, especially for senior level executives.

Related Occupations

Financial managers combine formal education with experience in one or more areas of finance, such as asset management, lending, credit operations, securities investment, or insurance risk and loss control. Workers in other occupations requiring similar training and skills include accountants and auditors; budget analysts; financial analysts and personal financial advisors; insurance underwriters; loan counselors and officers; securities, commodities, and financial services sales agents; and real estate brokers and sales agents.

Sources of Additional Information

For information about careers and certification in financial management, contact:

➤ Financial Management Association International, College of Business Administration, University of South Florida, Tampa, FL 33620-5500. Internet: **http://www.fma.org**

For information about careers in financial and treasury management and the Certified Cash Manager program, contact:

➤ Association for Financial Professionals, 7315 Wisconsin Ave., Suite 600 West, Bethesda, MD 20814. Internet: **http://www.afponline.org**

For information about the Chartered Financial Analyst program, contact:

➤ Association for Investment Management and Research, P.O. Box 3668, 560 Ray Hunt Dr., Charlottesville, VA 22903-0668. Internet: **http://www.aimr.org**

For information about the Certified in Financial Management designation, contact:

➤ Institute of Management Accountants, 10 Paragon Drive, Montvale, NJ, 07645-1759. Internet: **http://www.imanet.org/**

Food Service Managers

(0*NET 11-9051.00)

Significant Points

- Many experienced food and beverage preparation and service workers are promoted into managerial positions; however, applicants with a bachelor's or an associate degree in restaurant and institutional food service management should have the best job opportunities.

- Most new jobs will arise in food services and drinking places as the number of establishments increases along with the population.

- Job opportunities for salaried food service managers should be better than for self-employed managers, because more restaurant managers will be employed by larger companies to run multi-outlet establishments.

Nature of the Work

Food service managers are responsible for the daily operations of restaurants and other establishments that prepare and serve meals and beverages to customers. Besides coordinating activities among various departments, such as kitchen, dining room, and banquet operations, food service managers ensure that customers are satisfied with their dining experience. In addition, they oversee the inventory and ordering of food, equipment, and supplies and arrange for the routine maintenance and upkeep of the restaurant, its equipment, and facilities. Managers generally are responsible for all of the administrative and human-resource functions of running the business, including recruiting new employees and monitoring employee performance and training.

In most full-service restaurants and institutional food service facilities, the management team consists of a *general manager*, one or more *assistant managers*, and *an executive chef*. The executive chef is responsible for all food preparation activities, including running kitchen operations, planning menus, and maintaining quality standards for food service. In limited-service eating places, such as sandwich shops, coffee bars, or fast-food establishments, managers, not executive chefs, are responsible for supervising routine food preparation operations. Assistant managers in full-service facilities generally oversee service in the dining rooms and banquet areas. In larger restaurants and fast-food or other food service facilities that serve meals daily and maintain longer hours, individual assistant managers may supervise different shifts of workers. In smaller restaurants, formal titles may be less important, and one person may undertake the work of one or more food service positions. For example, the executive chef also may be the general manager or even sometimes an owner. (For additional information on these other workers, see the *Handbook* statements on top executives and chefs, cooks, and food preparation workers.)

One of the most important tasks of food service managers is assisting executive chefs as they select successful menu items. This task varies by establishment depending on the seasonality of menu items, the frequency with which restaurants change their menus, and the introduction of daily or weekly specials. Many restaurants rarely change their menus while others make frequent alterations. Managers or executive chefs select menu items, taking into account the likely number of customers and the past popularity of dishes. Other issues considered when planning a menu include whether there was any unserved food left over from prior meals that should not be wasted, the need for variety, and the seasonal availability of foods. Managers or executive chefs analyze the recipes of the dishes to determine food, labor, and overhead costs and to assign prices to various dishes. Menus must be developed far enough in advance that supplies can be ordered and received in time.

Managers or executive chefs estimate food needs, place orders with distributors, and schedule the delivery of fresh food and supplies. They plan for routine services or deliveries, such as linen services or the heavy cleaning of dining rooms or kitchen equipment, to occur during slow times or when the dining room is closed. Managers also arrange for equipment maintenance and repairs, and coordinate a variety of services such as waste removal and pest control. Managers or executive chefs receive deliveries and check the contents against order records. They inspect the quality of fresh meats, poultry, fish, fruits, vegetables, and baked goods to ensure that expectations are met. They meet with representatives from restaurant supply companies and place orders to replenish stocks of tableware, linens, paper products, cleaning supplies, cooking utensils, and furniture and fixtures.

Managers must be good communicators. They need to speak well, often in several languages, with a diverse clientele and staff. They must motivate employees to work as a team, to ensure that food and service meet appropriate standards. Managers also must ensure that written supply orders are clear and unambiguous.

Managers interview, hire, train, and, when necessary, fire employees. Retaining good employees is a major challenge facing food service managers. Managers recruit employees at career fairs, contact schools that offer academic programs in hospitality or culinary arts, and arrange for newspaper advertising to attract additional applicants. Managers oversee the training of new employees and explain the establishment's policies and practices. They schedule work hours, making sure that enough workers are present to cover each shift. If employees are unable to work, managers may have to call in alternates to cover for them or fill in themselves when needed. Some managers may help with cooking, clearing tables, or other tasks when the restaurant becomes extremely busy.

Food service managers ensure that diners are served properly and in a timely manner. They investigate and resolve customers' complaints about food quality or service. They monitor orders in the kitchen to determine where backups may occur, and they work with the chef to remedy any delays in service. Managers direct the cleaning of the dining areas and the washing of tableware, kitchen utensils, and equipment to comply with company and government sanitation standards. Managers also monitor the actions of their employees and patrons on a continual basis to ensure the personal safety of everyone. They make sure that health and safety standards and local liquor regulations are obeyed.

In addition to their regular duties, food service managers perform a variety of administrative assignments, such as keeping employee work records, preparing the payroll, and completing paperwork to comply with licensing laws and reporting requirements of tax, wage and hour, unemployment compensation, and Social Security laws. Some of this work may be delegated to an assistant manager or bookkeeper, or it may be contracted out, but most general managers retain responsibility for the accuracy of business records. Managers also maintain records of supply and equipment purchases and ensure that accounts with suppliers are paid.

Technology influences the jobs of food service managers in many ways, enhancing efficiency and productivity. Many restaurants use computers to track orders, inventory, and the seating of patrons. Point-of-service (POS) systems allow servers to key in a customer's order, either at the table, using a hand-held device, or from a computer terminal in the dining room, and send the order to the kitchen instantaneously so preparation can begin. The same system totals and prints checks, functions as a cash register, connects to credit card authorizers, and tracks sales. To minimize food costs and spoilage, many managers use inventory-tracking software to compare the record of sales from the POS with a record of the current inventory. Some establishments enter an inventory of standard ingredients and suppliers into their POS system. When supplies of particular ingredients run low, they can be ordered directly from the supplier using preprogrammed information. Computers also allow restaurant and food service managers to keep track of employee schedules and paychecks more efficiently.

Food service managers use the Internet to track industry news, find recipes, conduct market research, purchase supplies or equipment, recruit employees, and train staff. Internet access also makes service to customers more efficient. Many restaurants maintain Web sites that include menus and online promotions, provide information about the restaurant's location, and offer patrons the option to make a reservation.

Managers tally the cash and charge receipts received and balance them against the record of sales. They are responsible for depositing the day's receipts at the bank or securing them in a safe place. Finally, managers are responsible for locking up the establishment, checking that ovens, grills, and lights are off, and switching on alarm systems.

Working Conditions

Food service managers are among the first to arrive in the morning and the last to leave at night. Long hours—12 to 15 per day, 50 or more per week, and sometimes 7 days a week—are common. Managers of institutional food service facilities, such as school, factory, or office cafeterias, work more regular hours because the operating hours of these establishments usually conform to the operating hours of the business or facility they serve. However, hours for many managers are unpredictable.

Managers should be calm, flexible, and able to work through emergencies, such as a fire or flood, in order to ensure everyone's safety. Managers also should be able to fill in for absent workers on short notice. Managers often experience the pressures of simultaneously coordinating a wide range of activities. When problems occur, it is the manager's responsibility to resolve them with minimal disruption to customers. The job can be hectic, and dealing with irate customers or uncooperative employees can be stressful.

Managers also may experience the typical minor injuries of other restaurant workers, such as muscle aches, cuts, or burns. They might endure physical discomfort from moving tables or chairs to accommodate large parties, receiving and storing daily supplies from vendors, or making minor repairs to furniture or equipment.

Employment

Food service managers held about 386,000 jobs in 2002. Most managers were salaried, but about one-third were self-employed in independent restaurants or other small food service establishments. Almost three-fourths of all salaried jobs for food service managers were in full-service restaurants or limited-service eating places, such as fast-food restaurants and cafeterias. Other salaried jobs were in drinking places (alcoholic beverages) and in special food services— an industry that includes food service contractors who supply food services at institutional, governmental, commercial, or industrial locations. A small number of salaried jobs were in traveler accommodation (hotels); educational services; amusement, gambling, and recreation industries; nursing care facilities; and hospitals. Jobs are located throughout the country, with large cities and tourist areas providing more opportunities for full-service dining positions.

Food service managers check orders to ensure adequate inventories of food and other supplies.

Training, Other Qualifications, and Advancement

Most food service management companies and national or regional restaurant chains recruit management trainees from 2- and 4-year college hospitality management programs. Restaurant chains prefer to hire people with degrees in restaurant and institutional food service management, but they often hire graduates with degrees in other fields who have demonstrated interest and aptitude. Some restaurant and food service manager positions—particularly self-service and fast-food—are filled by promoting experienced food and beverage preparation and service workers. Waiters, waitresses, chefs, and fast-food workers demonstrating potential for handling increased responsibility sometimes advance to assistant manager or management trainee jobs. Executive chefs need extensive experience working as chefs, and general managers need prior restaurant experience, usually as assistant managers.

A bachelor's degree in restaurant and food service management provides particularly strong preparation for a career in this occupation. A number of colleges and universities offer 4-year programs in restaurant and hotel management or institutional food service management. For those not interested in pursuing a 4-year degree, community and junior colleges, technical institutes, and other institutions offer programs in the field leading to an associate degree or other formal certification. Both 2- and 4-year programs provide instruction in subjects such as nutrition, sanitation, and food planning and preparation, as well as accounting, business law and management, and computer science. Some programs combine classroom and laboratory study with internships providing on-the-job experience. In addition, many educational institutions offer culinary programs in food preparation. Such training can lead to a career as a cook or chef and provide a foundation for advancement to an executive chef position.

Most restaurant chains and food service management companies have rigorous training programs for management positions. Through a combination of classroom and on-the-job training, trainees receive instruction and gain work experience in all aspects of the operation of a restaurant or institutional food service facility. Areas include food preparation, nutrition, sanitation, security, company policies and procedures, personnel management, record-keeping, and preparation of reports. Training on use of the restaurant's computer system is increasingly important as well. Usually, after 6 months or a year, trainees receive their first permanent assignment as an assistant manager.

Most employers emphasize personal qualities when hiring managers. For example, self-discipline, initiative, and leadership ability are essential. Managers must be able to solve problems and concentrate on details. They need good communication skills to deal with customers and suppliers, as well as to motivate and direct their staff. A neat and clean appearance is important, because managers must convey self-confidence and show respect in dealing with the public. Food service management can be physically demanding, so good health and stamina also are important.

The certified Foodservice Management Professional (FMP) designation is a measure of professional achievement for food service managers. Although not a requirement for employment or advancement in the occupation, voluntary certification provides recognition of professional competence, particularly for managers who acquired their skills largely on the job. The National Restaurant Association Educational Foundation awards the FMP designation to managers who achieve a qualifying score on a written examination, complete a series of courses that cover a range of food service management topics, and meet standards of work experience in the field.

Willingness to relocate often is essential for advancement to positions with greater responsibility. Managers typically advance to larger establishments or regional management positions within restaurant chains. Some eventually open their own food service establishments.

Job Outlook

Employment of food service managers is expected to grow about as fast as the average for all occupations through 2012. In addition to job openings arising out of employment growth, the need to replace managers who transfer to other occupations or stop working will create many job opportunities. Applicants with a bachelor's or an associate degree in restaurant and institutional food service management should have the best job opportunities.

Projected employment growth varies by industry. Most new jobs will arise in full-service restaurants and limited-service eating places as the number of these establishments increases along with the population. Manager jobs in special food services, an industry that includes food service contractors, will increase as hotels, schools, healthcare facilities, and other businesses contract out their food services to firms in this industry. Food service manager jobs still are expected to increase in hotels, schools, and health-care facilities, but growth will be slowed as contracting out becomes more common.

Job opportunities should be better for salaried managers than for self-employed managers. More new restaurants are affiliated with national chains than are independently owned and operated. As this trend continues, fewer owners will manage restaurants themselves, and more restaurant managers will be employed by larger companies to run individual establishments.

Earnings

Median annual earnings of salaried food service managers were $35,790 in 2002. The middle 50 percent earned between $27,910 and $47,120. The lowest 10 percent earned less than $21,760, and the highest 10 percent earned more than $67,490. Median annual earnings in the industries employing the largest numbers of food service managers in 2002 were as follows:

Special food services	$40,720
Traveler accommodation	39,210
Full-service restaurants	37,280
Nursing care facilities	33,910
Limited-service eating places	33,590
Elementary and secondary schools	31,210

In addition to receiving typical benefits, most salaried food service managers are provided free meals and the opportunity for additional training, depending on their length of service.

Related Occupations

Food service managers direct the activities of a hospitality-industry business and provide a service to customers. Other managers and supervisors in hospitality-oriented businesses include gaming managers, lodging managers, sales worker supervisors, and first-line supervisors or managers of food preparation and serving workers.

Sources of Additional Information

Information about a career as a food service manager, 2- and 4-year college programs in restaurant and food service management, and certification as a Foodservice Management Professional is available from:

➤ National Restaurant Association Educational Foundation, 175 West Jackson Blvd., Suite 1500, Chicago, IL 60604-2702. Internet: **http://www.nraef.org**

General information on hospitality careers may be obtained from:
➤ The International Council on Hotel, Restaurant, and Institutional Education, 2613 North Parham Rd., 2nd Floor, Richmond, VA 23294. Internet: **http://www.chrie.org**

Additional information about job opportunities in food service management may be obtained from local employers and from local offices of State employment services agencies.

Funeral Directors

(O*NET 11-9061.00)

Significant Points

- Funeral directors must be licensed by their State.
- Job opportunities should be good, particularly for those who also embalm; however, mortuary science graduates may have to relocate to find jobs.

Nature of the Work
Funeral practices and rites vary greatly among cultures and religions. Among the many diverse groups in the United States, funeral practices usually share some common elements—removing the deceased to a mortuary, preparing the remains, performing a ceremony that honors the deceased and addresses the spiritual needs of the family, and final disposition of the remains. Funeral directors arrange and direct these tasks for grieving families.

Funeral directors also are called morticians or undertakers. This career may not appeal to everyone, but those who work as funeral directors take great pride in their ability to provide efficient and appropriate services. They also comfort the family and friends of the deceased.

Funeral directors arrange the details and handle the logistics of funerals. They interview the family to learn what family members desire with regard to the nature of the funeral, the clergy members or other persons who will officiate, and the final disposition of the remains. Sometimes, the deceased leaves detailed instructions for his or her own funeral. Together with the family, funeral directors establish the location, dates, and times of wakes, memorial services, and burials. They arrange for a hearse to carry the body to the funeral home or mortuary.

Funeral directors also prepare obituary notices and have them placed in newspapers, arrange for pallbearers and clergy, schedule the opening and closing of a grave with a representative of the cemetery, decorate and prepare the sites of all services, and provide transportation for the remains, mourners, and flowers between sites. They also direct preparation and shipment of remains for out-of-State burial.

Most funeral directors also are trained, licensed, and practicing embalmers. Embalming is a sanitary, cosmetic, and preservative process through which the body is prepared for interment. If more than 24 hours elapses between death and interment, State laws usually require that the remains be refrigerated or embalmed.

When embalming a body, funeral directors wash the body with germicidal soap and replace the blood with embalming fluid to preserve the tissues. They may reshape and reconstruct disfigured or maimed bodies using materials, such as clay, cotton, plaster of paris, and wax. They also may apply cosmetics to provide a natural appearance, and then dress the body and place it in a casket. Funeral directors maintain records such as embalming reports, and itemized lists of clothing or valuables delivered with the body. In large funeral homes, an embalming staff of two or more, plus several apprentices may be employed.

Funeral services may take place in a home, house of worship, or funeral home, or at the gravesite or crematory. Services may be nonreligious, but often they reflect the religion of the family, so funeral directors must be familiar with the funeral and burial customs of many faiths, ethnic groups, and fraternal organizations. For example, members of some religions seldom have the bodies of the deceased embalmed or cremated.

Burial in a casket is the most common method of disposing of remains in this country, although entombment also occurs. Cremation, which is the burning of the body in a special furnace, is increasingly selected because it can be less expensive, and is becoming more appealing. Memorial services can be held anywhere, and at any time, sometimes months later when all relatives and friends can get together. Even when the remains are cremated, many people still want a funeral service.

A funeral service followed by cremation need not be any different from a funeral service followed by a burial. Usually cremated remains are placed in some type of permanent receptacle, or urn, before being committed to a final resting place. The urn may be buried, placed in an indoor or outdoor mausoleum or columbarium, or interred in a special urn garden that many cemeteries provide for cremated remains.

Funeral directors handle the paperwork involved with the person's death, such as submitting papers to State authorities so that a formal certificate of death may be issued and copies distributed to the heirs. They may help family members apply for veterans' burial benefits, and notify the Social Security Administration of the death. Also, funeral directors may apply for the transfer of any pensions, insurance policies, or annuities on behalf of survivors.

Funeral directors also prearrange funerals. Increasingly, they arrange funerals in advance of need to provide peace of mind by ensuring that the client's wishes will be taken care of in a way that is satisfying to the person and to those who will survive.

Most funeral homes are small, family-run businesses, and the funeral directors are either owner-operators or employees of the operation. Funeral directors, therefore, are responsible for the success and the profitability of their businesses. Directors keep records of expenses, purchases, and services rendered; prepare and send invoices for services; prepare and submit reports for unemployment insurance; prepare Federal, State, and local tax forms; and prepare itemized bills for customers. Funeral directors increasingly are using computers for billing, bookkeeping, and marketing. Some are beginning to use the Internet to communicate with clients who are preplanning their funerals, or to assist clients by developing electronic obituaries and guestbooks. Directors strive to foster a cooperative spirit and friendly attitude among employees and a compassionate demeanor towards the families. A growing number of funeral directors also are involved in helping individuals adapt to changes in their lives following a death through aftercare services or support group activities.

Most funeral homes have a chapel, one or more viewing rooms, a casket-selection room, and a preparation room. An increasing number also have a crematory on the premises. Equipment may include a hearse, a flower car, limousines, and, sometimes, an ambulance. Funeral homes usually stock a selection of caskets and urns for families to purchase or rent.

Working Conditions

Funeral directors often work long, irregular hours, and the occupation can be highly stressful. Many work on an on-call basis, because they may be needed to remove remains in the middle of the night. Shiftwork sometimes is necessary because funeral home hours include evenings and weekends. In smaller funeral homes, working hours vary, but in larger homes employees usually work 8 hours a day, 5 or 6 days a week.

Funeral directors occasionally come into contact with the remains of persons who had contagious diseases, but the possibility of infection is remote if strict health regulations are followed.

To show proper respect and consideration for the families and the dead, funeral directors must dress appropriately. The profession usually requires short, neat haircuts and trim beards, if any, for men. Suits, ties, and dresses are customary for a conservative look.

Employment

Funeral directors held about 24,000 jobs in 2002. Eleven percent were self-employed. Nearly all worked in the death care services industry.

Training, Other Qualifications, and Advancement

Funeral directors must be licensed in all States. Licensing laws vary from State to State, but most require applicants to be 21 years old, have 2 years of formal education that includes studies in mortuary science, serve a 1-year apprenticeship, and pass a qualifying examination. After becoming licensed, new funeral directors may join the staff of a funeral home. Funeral directors who embalm must be licensed in all States, and some States issue a single license for funeral directors who embalm. In States that have separate licensing requirements, most people in the field obtain both licenses. Persons interested in a career as a funeral director should contact their State licensing board for specific requirements.

College programs in mortuary science usually last from 2 to 4 years; the American Board of Funeral Service Education accredits about 50 mortuary science programs. A small number of community and junior colleges offer 2-year programs, and a few colleges and universities offer both 2-year and 4-year programs. Mortuary science programs include courses in anatomy, physiology, pathology, embalming techniques, restorative art, business management, accounting and use of computers in funeral home management, and client services. They also include courses in the social sciences and legal, ethical, and regulatory subjects, such as psychology, grief

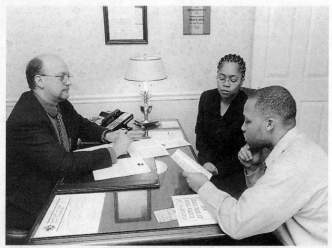

Funeral directors explain, arrange, and handle the details of funerals with clients.

counseling, oral and written communication, funeral service law, business law, and ethics.

Many State and national associations offer continuing education programs designed for licensed funeral directors. These programs address issues in communications, counseling, and management. More than 30 States have requirements that funeral directors receive continuing education credits in order to maintain their licenses.

Apprenticeships must be completed under the direction of an experienced and licensed funeral director. Depending on State regulations, apprenticeships last from 1 to 3 years and may be served before, during, or after mortuary school. Apprenticeships provide practical experience in all facets of the funeral service, from embalming to transporting remains.

State board licensing examinations vary, but they usually consist of written and oral parts and include a demonstration of practical skills. Persons who want to work in another State may have to pass the examination for that State; however, some States have reciprocity arrangements and will grant licenses to funeral directors from another State without further examination.

High school students can start preparing for a career as a funeral director by taking courses in biology and chemistry and participating in public speaking or debate clubs. Part-time or summer jobs in funeral homes consist mostly of maintenance and cleanup tasks, such as washing and polishing limousines and hearses, but these tasks can help students to become familiar with the operation of funeral homes.

Important personal traits for funeral directors are composure, tact, and the ability to communicate easily with the public. They also should have the desire and ability to comfort people in a time of sorrow.

Advancement opportunities are best in larger funeral homes—funeral directors may earn promotions to higher paying positions such as branch manager or general manager. Some directors eventually acquire enough money and experience to establish their own funeral home businesses.

Job Outlook

Employment opportunities for funeral directors are expected to be good, particularly for those who also embalm. However, mortuary science graduates may have to relocate to find jobs.

Employment of funeral directors is projected to increase more slowly than the average for all occupations through the year 2012, as the population and the number of deaths increase. The need to replace funeral directors who retire or leave the occupation for other reasons will account for more job openings than will employment growth. Typically, a number of mortuary science graduates leave the profession shortly after becoming licensed funeral directors to pursue other career interests, and this trend is expected to continue. Also, funeral directors are older, on average, than workers in most other occupations, and should be retiring in greater numbers between 2002 and 2012.

Earnings

Median annual earnings for funeral directors were $43,380 in 2002. The middle 50 percent earned between $33,540 and $58,140. The lowest 10 percent earned less than $24,950, and the top 10 percent more than $84,060.

Salaries of funeral directors depend on the number of years of experience in funeral service, the number of services performed, the number of facilities operated, the area of the country, the size of the community, and the level of formal education. Funeral directors in large cities earn more than their counterparts in small towns and rural areas.

Related Occupations

The job of a funeral director requires tact, discretion, and compassion when dealing with grieving people. Others who need these qualities include members of the clergy, social workers, psychologists, physicians and surgeons, and other health-diagnosing and -treating practitioners.

Sources of Additional Information

For a list of accredited mortuary science programs and information on the funeral service profession, write to:

➤ The National Funeral Directors Association, 13625 Bishop's Dr., Brookfield, WI 53005. Internet: **http://www.nfda.org**

For information about college programs in mortuary science, scholarships, and funeral service as a career, contact:

➤ The American Board of Funeral Service Education, 38 Florida Ave., Portland, ME 04103. Internet: **http://www.abfse.org/index.html**

Human Resources, Training, and Labor Relations Managers and Specialists

(0*NET 11-3040.00, 11-3041.00, 11-3042.00, 11-3049.99, 13-1071.01, 13-1071.02, 13-1072.00, 13-1073.00, 13-1079.99)

Significant Points

● Entry-level jobs are filled by college graduates who have majored in a wide range of fields.

● For many specialized jobs, previous experience is an asset; for more advanced positions, including those of managers, arbitrators, and mediators, it is essential.

● Keen competition for jobs is expected due to the abundant supply of qualified college graduates and experienced workers.

Nature of the Work

Attracting the most qualified employees and matching them to the jobs for which they are best suited is important for the success of any organization. However, many enterprises are too large to permit close contact between top management and employees. Human resources, training, and labor relations managers and specialists provide this link. In the past, these workers have been associated with performing the administrative function of an organization, such as handling employee benefits questions or recruiting, interviewing, and hiring new personnel in accordance with policies and requirements that have been established in conjunction with top management. Today's human resources workers juggle these tasks and, increasingly, consult top executives regarding strategic planning. They have moved from behind-the-scenes staff work to leading the company in suggesting and changing policies. Senior management is recognizing the importance of the human resources department to their financial success.

In an effort to improve morale and productivity and to limit job turnover, they also help their firms effectively use employee skills, provide training opportunities to enhance those skills, and boost employees' satisfaction with their jobs and working conditions. Although some jobs in the human resources field require only limited contact with people outside the office, dealing with people is an essential part of the job.

In a small organization, a *human resources generalist* may handle all aspects of human resources work, and thus require a broad range of knowledge. The responsibilities of human resources generalists can vary widely, depending on their employer's needs. In a large corporation, the top human resources executive usually develops and coordinates personnel programs and policies. (Executives are included in the *Handbook* statement on top executives.) These policies usually are implemented by a director or manager of human resources and, in some cases, a director of industrial relations.

The *director of human resources* may oversee several departments, each headed by an experienced manager who most likely specializes in one personnel activity, such as employment, compensation, benefits, training and development, or employee relations.

Employment and placement managers oversee the hiring and separation of employees and supervise various workers, including equal employment opportunity specialists and recruitment specialists. *Employment, recruitment,* and *placement specialists* recruit and place workers.

Recruiters maintain contacts within the community and may travel extensively, often to college campuses, to search for promising job applicants. Recruiters screen, interview, and sometimes test applicants. They also may check references and extend job offers. These workers must be thoroughly familiar with the organization and its personnel policies in order to discuss wages, working conditions, and promotional opportunities with prospective employees. They also must keep informed about equal employment opportunity (EEO) and affirmative action guidelines and laws, such as the Americans with Disabilities Act.

EEO officers, representatives, or *affirmative action coordinators* handle EEO matters in large organizations. They investigate and resolve EEO grievances, examine corporate practices for possible violations, and compile and submit EEO statistical reports.

Employer relations representatives, who usually work in government agencies, maintain working relationships with local employers and promote the use of public employment programs and services. Similarly, *employment interviewers*—whose many job titles include *personnel consultants, personnel development specialists,* and *human resources coordinators*—help to match employers with qualified jobseekers.

Compensation, benefits, and job analysis specialists conduct programs for employers and may specialize in specific areas such as position classifications or pensions. *Job analysts,* sometimes called *position classifiers,* collect and examine detailed information about job duties in order to prepare job descriptions. These descriptions explain the duties, training, and skills that each job requires. Whenever a large organization introduces a new job or reviews existing jobs, it calls upon the expert knowledge of the job analyst.

Occupational analysts conduct research, usually in large firms. They are concerned with occupational classification systems and study the effects of industry and occupational trends upon worker relationships. They may serve as technical liaison between the firm and other firms, government, and labor unions.

Establishing and maintaining a firm's pay system is the principal job of the *compensation manager.* Assisted by staff specialists, compensation managers devise ways to ensure fair and equitable pay rates. They may conduct surveys to see how their firm's rates compare with others and to see that the firm's pay scale complies with changing laws and regulations. In addition, compensation managers often oversee their firm's performance evaluation system, and they may design reward systems such as pay-for-performance plans.

Employee benefits managers and specialists handle the company's employee benefits program, notably its health insurance and pension plans. Expertise in designing and administering benefits programs continues to take on importance as employer-provided benefits account for a growing proportion of overall compensation costs, and as benefit plans increase in number and complexity. For example, pension benefits might include savings and thrift, profit-sharing, and stock ownership plans; health benefits might include long-term catastrophic illness insurance and dental insurance. Familiarity with health benefits is a top priority for employee benefits managers and specialists, as more firms struggle to cope with the rising cost of healthcare for employees and retirees. In addition to health insurance and pension coverage, some firms offer employees life and accidental death and dismemberment insurance, disability insurance, and relatively new benefits designed to meet the needs of a changing workforce, such as parental leave, child and elder care, long-term nursing home care insurance, employee assistance and wellness programs, and flexible benefits plans. Benefits managers must keep abreast of changing Federal and State regulations and legislation that may affect employee benefits.

Employee assistance plan managers, also called *employee welfare managers*, are responsible for a wide array of programs covering occupational safety and health standards and practices; health promotion and physical fitness, medical examinations, and minor health treatment, such as first aid; plant security; publications; food service and recreation activities; carpooling and transportation programs, such as transit subsidies; employee suggestion systems; childcare and elder care; and counseling services. Childcare and elder care are increasingly important due to growth in the number of dual-income households and the elderly population. Counseling may help employees deal with emotional disorders, alcoholism, or marital, family, consumer, legal, and financial problems. Some employers offer career counseling as well. In large firms, certain programs, such as those dealing with security and safety, may be in separate departments headed by other managers.

Training and development managers and specialists conduct and supervise training and development programs for employees. Increasingly, management recognizes that training offers a way of developing skills, enhancing productivity and quality of work, and building worker loyalty to the firm. Training is widely accepted as a method of improving employee morale, but this is only one of the reasons for its growing importance. Other factors include the complexity of the work environment, the rapid pace of organizational and technological change, and the growing number of jobs in fields that constantly generate new knowledge. In addition, advances in learning theory have provided insights into how adults learn, and how training can be organized most effectively for them.

Training managers provide worker training either in the classroom or onsite. This includes setting up teaching materials prior to the class, involving the class, and issuing completion certificates at the end of the class.

Training specialists plan, organize, and direct a wide range of training activities. Trainers respond to corporate and worker service requests. They consult with onsite supervisors regarding available performance improvement services and conduct orientation sessions and arrange on-the-job training for new employees. They help rank-and-file workers maintain and improve their job skills, and possibly prepare for jobs requiring greater skill. They help supervisors improve their interpersonal skills in order to deal effectively with employees. They may set up individualized training plans to strengthen an employee's existing skills or teach new ones.

Training specialists in some companies set up leadership or executive development programs among employees in lower level positions. These programs are designed to develop potential executives to replace those leaving the organization. Trainers also lead programs to assist employees with transitions due to mergers and acquisitions, as well as technological changes. In government-supported training programs, training specialists function as case managers. They first assess the training needs of clients, then guide them through the most appropriate training method. After training, clients may either be referred to employer relations representatives or receive job placement assistance.

Planning and program development is an important part of the training specialist's job. In order to identify and assess training needs within the firm, trainers may confer with managers and supervisors or conduct surveys. They also periodically evaluate training effectiveness.

Depending on the size, goals, and nature of the organization, trainers may differ considerably in their responsibilities and in the methods they use. Training methods include on-the-job training; operating schools that duplicate shop conditions for trainees prior to putting them on the shop floor; apprenticeship training; classroom training; and electronic learning, which may involve interactive Internet-based training, multimedia programs, distance learning, satellite training, other computer-aided instructional technologies, videos, simulators, conferences, and workshops.

An organization's *director of industrial relations* forms labor policy, oversees industrial labor relations, negotiates collective bargaining agreements, and coordinates grievance procedures to handle complaints resulting from management disputes with unionized employees. The director of industrial relations also advises and collaborates with the director of human resources, other managers, and members of their staff, because all aspects of personnel policy—such as wages, benefits, pensions, and work practices—may be involved in drawing up a new or revised union contract.

Labor relations managers and their staffs implement industrial labor relations programs. When a collective bargaining agreement is up for negotiation, labor relations specialists prepare information for management to use during negotiation, a process that requires the specialist to be familiar with economic and wage data and to have extensive knowledge of labor law and collective bargaining trends. The labor relations staff interprets and administers the contract with respect to grievances, wages and salaries, employee welfare, healthcare, pensions, union and management practices, and other contractual stipulations. As union membership continues to decline in most industries, industrial relations personnel are working more often with employees who are not members of a labor union.

Dispute resolution—attaining tacit or contractual agreements—has become increasingly important as parties to a dispute attempt to avoid costly litigation, strikes, or other disruptions. Dispute resolution also has become more complex, involving employees, management, unions, other firms, and government agencies. Specialists involved in dispute resolution must be highly knowledgeable and experienced, and often report to the director of industrial relations. *Conciliators*, or *mediators*, advise and counsel labor and management to prevent and, when necessary, resolve disputes over labor agreements or other labor relations issues. *Arbitrators*, sometimes called umpires or referees, decide disputes that bind both labor and management to specific terms and conditions of labor contracts. Labor relations specialists who work for unions perform many of the same functions on behalf of the union and its members.

Other emerging specialties include those of *international human resources managers*, who handle human resources issues related to a company's foreign operations, and *human resources information system specialists*, who develop and apply computer programs to process personnel information, match jobseekers with job openings, and handle other personnel matters.

Working Conditions

Personnel work usually takes place in clean, pleasant, and comfortable office settings. Arbitrators and mediators may work out of their homes. Many human resources, training, and labor relations managers and specialists work a standard 35- to 40-hour week. However, longer hours might be necessary for some workers—for example, labor relations managers and specialists, arbitrators, and mediators—when contract agreements are being prepared and negotiated.

Although most human resources, training, and labor relations managers and specialists work in the office, some travel extensively. For example, recruiters regularly attend professional meetings and visit college campuses to interview prospective employees; arbitrators and mediators often must travel to the site chosen for negotiations.

Employment

Human resources, training, and labor relations managers and specialists held about 677,000 jobs in 2002. The following tabulation shows the distribution of jobs by occupational specialty:

Training and development specialists	209,000
Human resources managers	202,000
Employment, recruitment, and placement specialists	175,000
Compensation, benefits, and job analysis specialists	91,000

Human resources, training, and labor relations managers and specialists were employed in virtually every industry. About 3,800 specialists were self-employed, working as consultants to public and private employers.

The private sector accounted for almost 8 out of 10 salaried jobs, including 11 percent in professional, scientific, and technical services and 10 percent each in manufacturing industries; health care and social assistance; finance and insurance firms; and administrative and support services.

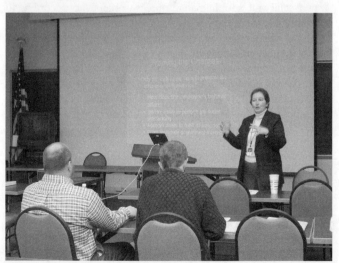

Keen competition for jobs as human resources workers is expected due to the abundant supply of qualified college graduates and experienced workers.

Government employed about 18 percent of human resources managers and specialists. They handled the recruitment, interviewing, job classification, training, salary administration, benefits, employee relations, and other matters related to the Nation's public employees.

Training, Other Qualifications, and Advancement

Because of the diversity of duties and levels of responsibility, the educational backgrounds of human resources, training, and labor relations managers and specialists vary considerably. In filling entry-level jobs, many employers seek college graduates who have majored in human resources, personnel administration, or industrial and labor relations. Other employers look for college graduates with a technical or business background or a well-rounded liberal arts education.

Many colleges and universities have programs leading to a degree in personnel, human resources, or labor relations. Some offer degree programs in personnel administration or human resources management, training and development, or compensation and benefits. Depending on the school, courses leading to a career in human resources management may be found in departments of business administration, education, instructional technology, organizational development, human services, communication, or public administration, or within a separate human resources institution or department.

Because an interdisciplinary background is appropriate in this field, a combination of courses in the social sciences, business, and behavioral sciences is useful. Some jobs may require a more technical or specialized background in engineering, science, finance, or law, for example. Most prospective human resources specialists should take courses in compensation, recruitment, training and development, and performance appraisal, as well as courses in principles of management, organizational structure, and industrial psychology. Other relevant courses include business administration, public administration, psychology, sociology, political science, economics, and statistics. Courses in labor law, collective bargaining, labor economics, labor history, and industrial psychology also provide a valuable background for the prospective labor relations specialist. As in many other fields, knowledge of computers and information systems also is useful.

An advanced degree is increasingly important for some jobs. Many labor relations jobs require graduate study in industrial or labor relations. A strong background in industrial relations and law is highly desirable for contract negotiators, mediators, and arbitrators; in fact, many people in these specialties are lawyers. A background in law also is desirable for employee benefits managers and others who must interpret the growing number of laws and regulations. A master's degree in human resources, labor relations, or in business administration with a concentration in human resources management is highly recommended for those seeking general and top management positions.

For many specialized jobs in the human resources field, previous experience is an asset; for more advanced positions, including those of managers as well as arbitrators and mediators, it is essential. Many employers prefer entry-level workers who have gained some experience through an internship or work-study program while in school. Personnel administration and human resources development require the ability to work with individuals as well as a commitment to organizational goals. This field also demands other skills that people may develop elsewhere—using computers, selling, teaching, supervising, and volunteering, among others. The field offers clerical workers opportunities for advancement to professional positions. Responsible positions sometimes are filled by experienced individuals from other fields, including business, government, education, social services administration, and the military.

The human resources field demands a range of personal qualities and skills. Human resources, training, and labor relations managers and specialists must speak and write effectively. The growing diversity of the workforce requires that they work with or supervise people with various cultural backgrounds, levels of education, and experience. They must be able to cope with conflicting points of view, function under pressure, and demonstrate discretion, integrity, fair-mindedness, and a persuasive, congenial personality.

The duties given to entry-level workers will vary, depending on whether the new workers have a degree in human resource management, have completed an internship, or have some other type of human resources-related experience. Entry-level employees commonly learn the profession by performing administrative duties — helping to enter data into computer systems, compiling employee handbooks, researching information for a supervisor, or answering the phone and handling routine questions. Entry-level workers often enter formal or on-the-job training programs in which they learn how to classify jobs, interview applicants, or administer employee benefits. They then are assigned to specific areas in the personnel department to gain experience. Later, they may advance to a managerial position, overseeing a major element of the personnel program—compensation or training, for example.

Exceptional human resources workers may be promoted to director of personnel or industrial relations, which can eventually lead to a top managerial or executive position. Others may join a consulting firm or open their own business. A Ph.D. is an asset for teaching, writing, or consulting work.

Most organizations specializing in human resources offer classes intended to enhance the marketable skills of their members. Some organizations offer certification programs, which are signs of competence and can enhance one's advancement opportunities. For example, the International Foundation of Employee Benefit Plans confers a designation to persons who complete a series of college-level courses and pass exams covering employee benefit plans. The Society for Human Resources Management has two levels of certification; both require experience and a passing score on a comprehensive exam.

Job Outlook

The abundant supply of qualified college graduates and experienced workers should create keen competition for jobs. Overall employment of human resources, training, and labor relations managers and specialists is expected to grow faster than the average for all occupations through 2012. In addition to openings due to growth, many job openings will arise from the need to replace workers who transfer to other occupations or leave the labor force.

Legislation and court rulings setting standards in various areas—occupational safety and health, equal employment opportunity, wages, health, pensions, and family leave, among others—will increase demand for human resources, training, and labor relations experts. Rising healthcare costs should continue to spur demand for specialists to develop creative compensation and benefits packages that firms can offer prospective employees. Employment of labor relations staff, including arbitrators and mediators, should grow as firms become more involved in labor relations, and attempt to resolve potentially costly labor-management disputes out of court. Additional job growth may stem from increasing demand for specialists in international human resources management and human resources information systems.

Demand may be particularly strong for certain specialists. For example, employers are expected to devote greater resources to job-specific training programs in response to the increasing complexity of many jobs, the aging of the workforce, and technological advances that can leave employees with obsolete skills. This should result in particularly strong demand for training and development specialists. In addition, increasing efforts throughout industry to recruit and retain quality employees should create many jobs for employment, recruitment, and placement specialists.

Among industries, firms involved in management, consulting, and employment services should offer many job opportunities, as businesses increasingly contract out personnel functions or hire personnel specialists on a temporary basis in order to deal with the increasing cost and complexity of training and development programs. Demand also should increase in firms that develop and administer complex employee benefits and compensation packages for other organizations.

Demand for human resources, training, and labor relations managers and specialists also are governed by the staffing needs of the firms for which they work. A rapidly expanding business is likely to hire additional human resources workers—either as permanent employees or consultants—while a business that has experienced a merger or a reduction in its workforce will require fewer human resources workers. Also, as human resources management becomes increasingly important to the success of an organization, some small and medium-size businesses that do not have a human resources department may assign employees various human resources duties together with other unrelated responsibilities. In any particular firm, the size and the job duties of the human resources staff are determined by the firm's organizational philosophy and goals, skills of its workforce, pace of technological change, government regulations, collective bargaining agreements, standards of professional practice, and labor market conditions.

Job growth could be limited by the widespread use of computerized human resources information systems that make workers more productive. Like that of other workers, employment of human resources, training, and labor relations managers and specialists, particularly in larger firms, may be adversely affected by corporate downsizing, restructuring, and mergers.

Earnings

Annual salary rates for human resources workers vary according to occupation, level of experience, training, location, and size of the firm, and whether they are union members. Median annual earnings of human resources managers were $64,710 in 2002. The middle 50 percent earned between $47,420 and $88,100. The lowest 10 percent earned less than $36,280, and the highest 10 percent earned more than $114,300. Median annual earnings in the industries employing the largest numbers of human resources managers in 2002 were:

Management of companies and enterprises	$77,690
Local government	65,590
General medical and surgical hospitals	61,720
Depository credit intermediation	60,030

Median annual earnings of training and development specialists were $42,800 in 2002. The middle 50 percent earned between $32,050 and $56,890. The lowest 10 percent earned less than $24,760, and the highest 10 percent earned more than $72,530. Median annual earnings in the industries employing the largest numbers of training and development specialists in 2002 were:

Management of companies and enterprises	$49,660
Insurance carriers	45,830
Local government	43,740
State government	40,960
Federal Government	37,560

Median annual earnings of employment, recruitment, and placement specialists were $39,410 in 2002. The middle 50 percent earned between $30,390 and $54,130. The lowest 10 percent earned less than $24,440, and the highest 10 percent earned more than $73,940. Median annual earnings in 2002 were $34,850 in employment services, the industry employing the largest numbers of these specialists.

Median annual earnings of compensation, benefits, and job analysis specialists were $45,100 in 2002. The middle 50 percent earned between $35,000 and $57,230. The lowest 10 percent earned less than $28,160, and the highest 10 percent earned more than $72,250. Median annual earnings in 2002 were $48,870 in local government, the industry employing the largest numbers of these specialists.

According to a 2003 salary survey conducted by the National Association of Colleges and Employers, bachelor's degree candidates majoring in human resources, including labor relations, received starting offers averaging $35,400 a year.

The average salary for human resources managers employed by the Federal Government was $66,886 in 2003; for employee relations specialists, $63,345; for labor relations specialists, $72,915; and for employee development specialists, $68,735. Salaries were slightly higher in areas where the prevailing local pay level was higher. There are no formal entry-level requirements for managerial positions. Applicants must possess a suitable combination of educational attainment, experience, and record of accomplishment.

Related Occupations
All human resources occupations are closely related. Other workers with skills and expertise in interpersonal relations include counselors, education administrators, public relations specialists, lawyers, psychologists, social and human service assistants, and social workers.

Sources of Additional Information
For information about human resource management careers and certification, contact:
➤ Society for Human Resource Management, 1800 Duke St., Alexandria, VA 22314. Internet: **http://www.shrm.org**

For information about careers in employee training and development and certification, contact:
➤ American Society for Training and Development, 1640 King St., Box 1443, Alexandria, VA 22313. Internet: **http://www.astd.org**

For information about careers and certification in employee compensation and benefits, contact:
➤ International Foundation of Employee Benefit Plans, 18700 W. Bluemound Rd., P.O. Box 69, Brookfield, WI 53008-0069. Internet: **http://www.ifebp.org**

For information about academic programs in industrial relations, write to:
➤ Industrial Relations Research Association, 121 Labor and Industrial Relations, University of Illinois, 504 E. Armory, Champaign, IL 61820. Internet: **http://www.irra.uiuc.edu**

Information about personnel careers in the healthcare industry is available from:
➤ American Society for Healthcare Human Resources Administration, One North Franklin, 31st Floor, Chicago, IL 60606. Internet: **http://www.ashhra.org**

Industrial Production Managers

(O*NET 11-3051.00)

Significant Points

● While there is no standard preparation, a college degree is required.

● Applicants with a college degree in industrial engineering, management, or business administration, and particularly those with an undergraduate engineering degree and a master's degree in business administration or industrial management, enjoy the best job prospects.

● Projected slower-than-average growth in employment reflects increasing productivity.

Nature of the Work
Industrial production managers coordinate the resources and activities required to produce millions of goods every year in the United States. Although their duties vary from plant to plant, industrial production managers share many of the same major responsibilities. These responsibilities include production scheduling, staffing, procurement and maintenance of equipment, quality control, inventory control, and the coordination of production activities with those of other departments.

The primary mission of industrial production managers is planning the production schedule within budgetary limitations and time constraints. They do this by analyzing the plant's personnel and capital resources to select the best way of meeting the production quota. Industrial production managers determine, often using mathematical formulas, which machines will be used, whether new machines need to be purchased, whether overtime or extra shifts are necessary, and what the sequence of production will be. They monitor the production run to make sure that it stays on schedule and correct any problems that may arise.

As production techniques have evolved beyond traditional mass assembly lines, industrial production managers have adapted to "lean" production techniques. Many manufacturers have adopted lean production techniques, while some others use a combination of lean and mass production techniques. In a traditional assembly line, each worker is responsible for only a small portion of the assembly, repeating that task on every product. Lean production employs teams to build and assemble products in stations or cells. When companies use stations, one worker may work alone with handtools and various parts to complete a large portion of the assembly process. Rather than specializing in a specific task, workers are capable of performing all jobs within a team. Without the constraints of the traditional assembly line, companies can be more flexible in their production process, more easily changing production levels on different product lines.

The increased flexibility of lean manufacturing enables industrial production managers to experiment with ways of improving the assembly and manufacturing process. As companies strive to minimize inventory, they want to maintain only a limited stock of finished products. Employing manufacturing cells and stations, companies can more quickly react to changes in customer demand so that limited inventories will not get too low.

Industrial production managers also must monitor product standards. Inspecting samples of finished goods and recording defects enables managers to statistically analyze quality control problems.

While traditional quality control programs reacted only to problems that reached a certain significant level, newer management techniques and programs, such as ISO 9000, Total Quality Management (TQM), or Six Sigma, emphasize continuous quality improvement. If the problem relates to the quality of work performed in the plant, the manager may implement better training programs or reorganize the manufacturing process, often based upon the suggestions of employee teams. If the cause is substandard materials or parts from outside suppliers, companies may work with their suppliers to improve their quality.

Because the work of many departments is related, managers work closely with heads of other departments such as sales, procurement, and logistics to plan and implement company goals, policies, and procedures. For example, the production manager works with the procurement department to ensure that plant inventories are maintained at their optimal level. This is vital to a firm's operation because maintaining the inventory of materials necessary for production ties up the firm's financial resources, yet insufficient quantities cause delays in production. A breakdown in communications between the production manager and the purchasing department can cause slowdowns and a failure to meet production schedules. Just-in-time production techniques have reduced inventory levels, making constant communication among the manager, suppliers, and purchasing departments even more important. Computers play an integral part in this coordination. They also are used to provide up-to-date information on inventory, the status of work in progress, and quality standards.

Production managers usually report to the plant manager or the vice president for manufacturing, and may act as liaison between executives and first-line supervisors. (Information about top executives may be found elsewhere in the *Handbook*.) In many plants, one production manager is responsible for all aspects of production. In large plants with several operations—aircraft assembly, for example—there are managers in charge of each operation, such as machining, assembly, or finishing.

Working Conditions

Most industrial production managers divide their time between production areas and their offices. While in the production area, they must follow established health and safety practices and wear the required protective clothing and equipment. The time in the office, which often is located near production areas, usually is spent meeting with subordinates or other department managers, analyzing production data, and writing and reviewing reports.

Most industrial production managers work more than 40 hours a week, especially when production deadlines must be met. In facilities that operate around-the-clock, managers often work late shifts and may be called at any hour to deal with emergencies. This could mean going to the plant to resolve the problem, regardless of the hour, and staying until the situation is under control. Dealing with production workers as well as superiors when working under the pressure of production deadlines or emergency situations can be stressful. Corporate restructuring has eliminated levels of management and support staff, thus shifting more responsibilities to production managers and compounding this stress.

Employment

Industrial production managers held about 182,000 jobs in 2002. Almost all are employed in manufacturing industries, including the plastics product manufacturing, printing and related support activities, motor vehicle parts manufacturing, and semiconductor and other

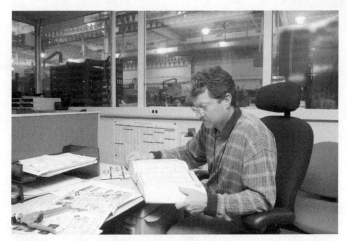

Industrial production managers often work near the factory floor.

electronic component manufacturing industries. Production managers work in all parts of the country, but jobs are most plentiful in areas where manufacturing is concentrated.

Training, Other Qualifications, and Advancement

Because of the diversity of manufacturing operations and job requirements, there is no standard preparation for this occupation. However, a college degree is required, even for those who have worked their way up through the ranks. Many industrial production managers have a college degree in business administration, management, industrial technology, or industrial engineering. Others have a master's degree in industrial management or business administration (MBA). Some are former production-line supervisors who have been promoted. Although many employers prefer candidates with a business or engineering background, some companies hire well-rounded liberal arts graduates.

As production operations become more sophisticated, increasing numbers of employers are looking for candidates with graduate degrees in industrial management or business administration. Combined with an undergraduate degree in engineering, either of these graduate degrees is considered particularly good preparation. Managers who do not have graduate degrees often take courses in decision sciences, which provide them with techniques and mathematical formulas that can be used to maximize efficiency and improve quality. Companies also are placing greater importance on a candidate's interpersonal skills. Because the job requires the ability to compromise, persuade, and negotiate, successful production managers must be well-rounded and have excellent communication skills.

Those who enter the field directly from college or graduate school often are unfamiliar with the firm's production process. As a result, they may spend their first few months in the company's training program. These programs familiarize trainees with the production process, company policies, and the requirements of the job. In larger companies, they also may include assignments to other departments, such as purchasing and accounting. A number of companies hire college graduates as first-line supervisors and later promote them.

Some industrial production managers have worked their way up through the ranks, perhaps after having worked as first-line supervisors. These workers already have an intimate knowledge of the production process and the firm's organization. To be selected for promotion, however, they must obtain a college degree, must demonstrate leadership qualities, and usually must take company-sponsored courses in management skills and communication techniques.

In addition to formal training, industrial production managers must keep informed of new production technologies and management practices. Many belong to professional organizations and attend trade shows at which new equipment is displayed; they also attend industry conferences and conventions at which changes in production methods and technological advances are discussed. Some take courses to become certified in various quality and management systems.

Industrial production managers with a proven record of superior performance may advance to plant manager or vice president for manufacturing. Others transfer to jobs with more responsibilities at larger firms. Opportunities also exist for consultants. (For more information, see the statement on management analysts elsewhere in the *Handbook*.)

Job Outlook

Employment of industrial production managers is expected to grow more slowly than the average for all occupations through 2012. However, a number of job openings will stem from the need to replace workers who transfer to other occupations or leave the labor force. Applicants with a college degree in industrial engineering, management, or business administration, and particularly those with an undergraduate engineering degree and a master's degree in business administration or industrial management, enjoy the best job prospects. Employers also are likely to seek candidates who have excellent communication skills and who are personable, flexible, and eager to enhance their knowledge and skills through ongoing training.

Although manufacturing output is projected to rise, increases in productivity among industrial production managers and the workers they supervise will limit growth in employment of these managers. Productivity gains among managers will stem from the increasing use of computers for scheduling, planning, and coordination. Productivity gains among workers will limit both the number of employees in factories and the need for supervision. In addition, more emphasis on quality in the production process has redistributed some of the production manager's oversight responsibilities to supervisors and workers on the production line. Because production managers are so essential to the efficient operation of a plant, they have not been greatly affected by recent efforts to flatten management structures. Nevertheless, this trend has led production managers to assume more responsibilities and has limited the creation of more employment opportunities.

Earnings

Median annual earnings for industrial production managers were $67,320 in 2002. The middle 50 percent earned between $50,710 and $88,880. The lowest 10 percent earned less than $38,980, and the highest 10 percent earned more than $114,750. Median annual earnings in the manufacturing industries employing the largest numbers of industrial production managers in 2002 were:

Management of companies and enterprises	$89,570
Semiconductor and other electronic component manufacturing	78,070
Motor vehicle parts manufacturing	73,570
Plastics products manufacturing	60,720
Printing and related support activities	59,270

Related Occupations

Industrial production managers oversee production staff and equipment, ensure that production goals and quality standards are being met, and implement company policies. Occupations requiring simi-

lar training and skills are engineers, management analysts, operations research analysts, top executives, and industrial engineers, including health and safety.

Sources of Additional Information

For more information on industrial production management, contact local manufacturers or schools with programs in industrial management.

Lodging Managers

(0*NET 11-9081.00)

Significant Points

- As in other hotel occupations, night and weekend work is common.
- Employment is projected to grow more slowly than average.
- College graduates with degrees in hotel or restaurant management should have the best job opportunities.

Nature of the Work

A comfortable room, good food, and a helpful staff can make being away from home an enjoyable experience for both vacationing families and business travelers. While most lodging managers work in traditional hotels and motels, some work in other lodging establishments, such as camps, inns, boardinghouses, dude ranches, and recreational resorts. In full-service hotels, lodging managers help their guests have a pleasant stay by providing many of the comforts of home, including cable television, fitness equipment, and voice mail, as well as specialized services such as health spas. For business travelers, lodging managers often schedule available meeting rooms and electronic equipment, including slide projectors and fax machines.

Lodging managers are responsible for keeping their establishments efficient and profitable. In a small establishment with a limited staff, the manager may oversee all aspects of operations. However, large hotels may employ hundreds of workers, and the general manager usually is aided by a number of assistant managers assigned to the various departments of the operation. In hotels of every size, managerial duties vary significantly by job title.

General managers, for example, have overall responsibility for the operation of the hotel. Within guidelines established by the owners of the hotel or executives of the hotel chain, the general manager sets room rates, allocates funds to departments, approves expenditures, and establishes expected standards for guest service, decor, housekeeping, food quality, and banquet operations. Managers who work for chains also may organize and staff a newly built hotel, refurbish an older hotel, or reorganize a hotel or motel that is not operating successfully. In order to fill entry-level service and clerical jobs in hotels, some managers attend career fairs.

Resident managers live in hotels and are on call 24 hours a day to resolve problems or emergencies. In general, though, they typically work an 8- to 10 hour day and oversee the day-to-day operations of the hotel. In many hotels, the general manager also is the resident manager.

Executive housekeepers ensure that guest rooms, meeting and banquet rooms, and public areas are clean, orderly, and well maintained. They also train, schedule, and supervise the work of housekeepers, inspect rooms, and order cleaning supplies.

Front office managers coordinate reservations and room assignments, as well as train and direct the hotel's front desk staff. They ensure that guests are treated courteously, complaints and problems are resolved, and requests for special services are carried out. Front office managers may adjust charges posted on a customer's bill.

Convention services managers coordinate the activities of various departments in larger hotels to accommodate meetings, conventions, and special events. They meet with representatives of groups or organizations to plan the number of rooms to reserve, the desired configuration of the meeting space, and the banquet services. During the meeting or event, they resolve unexpected problems and monitor activities to ensure that hotel operations conform to the expectations of the group.

Assistant managers help run the day-to-day operations of the hotel. In large hotels, they may be responsible for activities such as personnel, accounting, office administration, marketing and sales, purchasing, security, maintenance, and pool, spa, or recreational facilities. In smaller hotels, these duties may be combined into one position. Assistant managers may adjust charges on a hotel guest's bill when a manager is unavailable.

Computers are used extensively by lodging managers and their assistants to keep track of guests' bills, reservations, room assignments, meetings, and special events. In addition, computers are used to order food, beverages, and supplies, as well as to prepare reports for hotel owners and top-level managers. Managers work with computer specialists to ensure that the hotel's computer system functions properly. Should the hotel's computer system fail, managers must continue to meet the needs of hotel guests and staff.

Working Conditions

Because hotels are open around the clock, night and weekend work is common. Many lodging managers work more than 40 hours per week. Managers who live in the hotel usually have regular work schedules, but they may be called to work at any time. Some employees of resort hotels are managers during the busy season and have other duties during the rest of the year.

Lodging managers sometimes experience the pressures of coordinating a wide range of functions. Conventions and large groups of tourists may present unusual problems. Moreover, dealing with irate guests can be stressful. The job can be particularly hectic for front office managers during check-in and check-out time. Computer failures can further complicate an already busy time.

Employment

Lodging managers held about 69,000 jobs in 2002. Self-employed managers—primarily owners of small hotels and motels—held about 50 percent of these jobs. Companies that manage hotels and motels under contract employed some managers.

Training, Other Qualifications, and Advancement

Hotels increasingly emphasize specialized training. Postsecondary training in hotel or restaurant management is preferred for most hotel management positions, although a college liberal arts degree may be sufficient when coupled with related hotel experience. Internships or part-time or summer work are an asset to students seeking a career in hotel management. The experience gained and the contacts made with employers can greatly benefit students after graduation. Most bachelor's degree programs include work-study opportunities.

Community colleges, junior colleges, and some universities offer associate's, bachelor's, and graduate degree programs in hotel

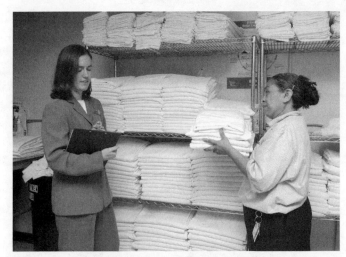

Lodging managers establish standards for guest services.

or restaurant management. Combined with technical institutes, vocational and trade schools, and other academic institutions, over 800 educational facilities have programs leading to formal recognition in hotel or restaurant management. Hotel management programs include instruction in hotel administration, accounting, economics, marketing, housekeeping, food service management and catering, and hotel maintenance engineering. Computer training also is an integral part of hotel management training, due to the widespread use of computers in reservations, billing, and housekeeping management.

Additionally, over 450 high schools in 45 States offer the Lodging Management Program created by the Educational Institute of the American Hotel and Lodging Association. This is a two-year program offered to high school juniors and seniors, which teaches management principles and leads to a professional certification called the "Certified Rooms Division Specialist". Many colleges and universities grant participants credit towards a post-secondary degree in hotel management.

Lodging managers must be able to get along with many different people, even in stressful situations. They must be able to solve problems and concentrate on details. Initiative, self-discipline, effective communication skills, and the ability to organize and direct the work of others also are essential for managers at all levels.

In the past, many managers were promoted from the ranks of front desk clerks, housekeepers, waiters, chefs, and hotel sales workers. Although some employees still advance to hotel management positions without education beyond high school, postsecondary education is preferred. Restaurant management training or experience also is a good background for entering hotel management, because the success of a hotel's food service and beverage operations often is important to the profitability of the entire establishment.

Graduates of hotel or restaurant management programs usually start as trainee assistant managers. Some large hotels sponsor specialized on-the-job management training programs that allow trainees to rotate among various departments and gain a thorough knowledge of the hotel's operation. Other hotels may help finance formal training in hotel management for outstanding employees. Newly built hotels, particularly those without established on-the-job training programs, often prefer to hire applicants who have hotel management experience.

Large hotel and motel chains may offer better opportunities for advancement than small, independently owned establishments, but relocation every several years often is necessary for advancement.

The large chains have more extensive career ladder programs and offer managers the opportunity to transfer to another hotel or motel in the chain or to the central office. Career advancement can be accelerated by the completion of certification programs offered by various associations. These programs usually require a combination of course work, examinations, and experience. For example, outstanding lodging managers may advance to higher level manager positions. (For more information, see the statement on top executives elsewhere in the *Handbook*.)

Job Outlook

Employment of lodging managers is expected to grow more slowly than the average for all occupations through 2012. Additional job openings are expected to occur as experienced managers transfer to other occupations or leave the labor force, in part because of the long hours and stressful working conditions. Job opportunities are expected to be best for persons with college degrees in hotel or restaurant management.

Increasing business travel and domestic and foreign tourism will drive employment growth of lodging managers. Managerial jobs are not expected to grow as rapidly as the hotel industry overall, however. As the industry consolidates, many chains and franchises will acquire independently owned establishments and increase the numbers of economy-class rooms to accommodate bargain-conscious guests. Economy hotels offer clean, comfortable rooms and front desk services without costly extras such as restaurants and room service. Because there are not as many departments in these hotels, fewer managers will be needed. Similarly, the increasing number of extended-stay hotels will temper demand for managers because, in these establishments, management is not required to be available 24 hours a day. In addition, front desk clerks increasingly are assuming some responsibilities previously reserved for managers, further limiting the employment growth of managers and their assistants.

Additional demand for managers is expected in suite hotels, because some guests—especially business customers—are willing to pay higher prices for rooms with kitchens and suites that provide the space needed to conduct meetings. In addition, large full-service hotels—offering restaurants, fitness centers, large meeting rooms, and play areas for children, among other amenities—will continue to provide many trainee and managerial opportunities.

Earnings

Median annual earnings of lodging managers were $33,970 in 2002. The middle 50 percent earned between $26,110 and $44,670. The lowest 10 percent earned less than $20,400, while the highest 10 percent earned more than $59,420.

Salaries of lodging managers vary greatly according to their responsibilities and the segment of the hotel industry in which they are employed, as well as the location and region where the hotel is located. Managers may earn bonuses of up to 25 percent of their basic salary in some hotels and also may be furnished with lodging, meals, parking, laundry, and other services. In addition to providing typical benefits, some hotels offer profit-sharing plans and educational assistance to their employees.

Related Occupations

Other occupations concerned with organizing and directing a business in which customer service is the cornerstone of their success include food service managers, gaming managers, sales worker supervisors, and property, real estate, and community association managers.

Sources of Additional Information

For information on careers and scholarships in hotel management, contact
➤ American Hotel and Lodging Association, 1201 New York Ave. NW., #600, Washington, DC 20005-3931.

Information on careers in the lodging industry and on professional development and training programs may be obtained from:
➤ Educational Institute of the American Hotel and Lodging Association, 800 N. Magnolia Ave., Suite 1800, Orlando, FL 32853-1126. Internet: **http://www.ei-ahla.org**

For information on educational programs, including correspondence courses, in hotel and restaurant management, write to:
➤ International Council on Hotel, Restaurant, and Institutional Education, 2613 North Parham Rd., 2nd Floor, Richmond, VA 23294-4442. Internet: **http://www.chrie.org**

Information on careers in housekeeping management may be obtained from:
➤ International Executive Housekeepers Association, Inc., 1001 Eastwind Dr., Suite 301, Westerville, OH 43081. **Internet: http://www.ieha.org**

Medical and Health Services Managers

(O*NET 11-9111.00)

Significant Points

- Earnings of medical and health services managers are high, but long work hours are common.
- A master's degree is the standard credential for most positions, although a bachelor's degree is adequate for some entry-level positions in smaller facilities.
- Employment will grow fastest in practitioners' offices and in home healthcare services.
- Applicants with work experience in healthcare and strong business and management skills should have the best opportunities.

Nature of the Work

Healthcare is a business and, like every other business, it needs good management to keep it running smoothly. The occupation, medical and health services manager, encompasses all individuals who plan, direct, coordinate, and supervise the delivery of healthcare. Medical and health services managers include specialists and generalists. Specialists are in charge of specific clinical departments or services, while generalists manage or help to manage an entire facility or system.

The structure and financing of healthcare is changing rapidly. Future medical and health services managers must be prepared to deal with evolving integrated healthcare delivery systems, technological innovations, an increasingly complex regulatory environment, restructuring of work, and an increased focus on preventive care. They will be called upon to improve efficiency in healthcare facilities and the quality of the healthcare provided. Increasingly, medical and health services managers will work in organizations in which they must optimize efficiency of a variety of interrelated services—for example, those ranging from inpatient care to outpatient followup care.

Large facilities usually have several assistant administrators to aid the top administrator and to handle daily decisions. Assistant administrators may direct activities in clinical areas such as nursing, surgery, therapy, medical records, or health information. (Managers in nonhealth areas, such as administrative services, computer and information systems, finance, and human resources, are not included in this statement. For information about them, see the statements on management occupations elsewhere in the *Handbook*.)

In smaller facilities, top administrators handle more of the details of daily operations. For example, many nursing home administrators manage personnel, finance, facility operations, and admissions, and have a larger role in resident care.

Clinical managers have more specific responsibilities than do generalists, and have training or experience in a specific clinical area. For example, directors of physical therapy are experienced physical therapists, and most health information and medical record administrators have a bachelor's degree in health information or medical record administration. Clinical managers establish and implement policies, objectives, and procedures for their departments; evaluate personnel and work; develop reports and budgets; and co-ordinate activities with other managers.

In group medical practices, managers work closely with physicians. Whereas an office manager may handle business affairs in small medical groups, leaving policy decisions to the physicians themselves, larger groups usually employ a full-time administrator to help formulate business strategies and coordinate day-to-day business.

A small group of 10 to 15 physicians might employ 1 administrator to oversee personnel matters, billing and collection, budgeting, planning, equipment outlays, and patient flow. A large practice of 40 to 50 physicians may have a chief administrator and several assistants, each responsible for different areas.

Medical and health services managers in managed care settings perform functions similar to those of their counterparts in large group practices, except that they may have larger staffs to manage. In addition, they may do more work in the areas of community outreach and preventive care than do managers of a group practice.

Some medical and health services managers oversee the activities of a number of facilities in health systems. Such systems may contain both inpatient and outpatient facilities and offer a wide range of patient services.

Working Conditions

Most medical and health services managers work long hours. Facilities such as nursing care facilities and hospitals operate around the clock, and administrators and managers may be called at all hours to deal with problems. They also may travel to attend meetings or inspect satellite facilities.

Some managers work in comfortable, private offices; others share space with other managers or staff. They may spend considerable time walking, to consult with coworkers.

Employment

Medical and health services managers held about 244,000 jobs in 2002. About 37 percent worked in hospitals, and another 17 percent worked in offices of physicians or nursing care facilities. The remainder worked mostly in home healthcare services, Federal government healthcare facilities, ambulatory facilities run by State and local governments, outpatient care centers, insurance carriers, and community care facilities for the elderly.

Medical and health services managers plan, direct, coordinate, and supervise the delivery of healthcare.

Training, Other Qualifications, and Advancement

Medical and health services managers must be familiar with management principles and practices. A master's degree in health services administration, long-term care administration, health sciences, public health, public administration, or business administration is the standard credential for most generalist positions in this field. However, a bachelor's degree is adequate for some entry-level positions in smaller facilities and at the departmental level within healthcare organizations. Physicians' offices and some other facilities may substitute on-the-job experience for formal education.

For clinical department heads, a degree in the appropriate field and work experience may be sufficient for entry. However, a master's degree in health services administration or a related field may be required to advance. For example, nursing service administrators usually are chosen from among supervisory registered nurses with administrative abilities and a graduate degree in nursing or health services administration.

Bachelor's, master's, and doctoral degree programs in health administration are offered by colleges, universities, and schools of public health, medicine, allied health, public administration, and business administration. In 2003, 67 schools had accredited programs leading to the master's degree in health services administration, according to the Accrediting Commission on Education for Health Services Administration.

Some graduate programs seek students with undergraduate degrees in business or health administration; however, many graduate programs prefer students with a liberal arts or health profession background. Candidates with previous work experience in healthcare also may have an advantage. Competition for entry to these programs is keen, and applicants need above-average grades to gain admission. Graduate programs usually last between 2 and 3 years. They may include up to 1 year of supervised administrative experience, and course work in areas such as hospital organization and management, marketing, accounting and budgeting, human resources administration, strategic planning, health economics, and health information systems. Some programs allow students to specialize in one type of facility—hospitals, nursing care facilities, mental health facilities, or medical groups. Other programs encourage a generalist approach to health administration education.

New graduates with master's degrees in health services administration may start as department managers or as staff employees. The level of the starting position varies with the experience of the applicant and the size of the organization. Hospitals and other health facilities offer postgraduate residencies and fellowships, which usually are staff positions. Graduates from master's degree programs also take jobs in large group medical practices, clinics, mental health facilities, nursing care corporations, and consulting firms.

Graduates with bachelor's degrees in health administration usually begin as administrative assistants or assistant department heads in larger hospitals. They also may begin as department heads or assistant administrators in small hospitals or nursing care facilities.

All States and the District of Columbia require nursing care facility administrators to have a bachelor's degree, pass a licensing examination, complete a State-approved training program, and pursue continuing education. A license is not required in other areas of medical and health services management.

Medical and health services managers often are responsible for millions of dollars' worth of facilities and equipment and hundreds of employees. To make effective decisions, they need to be open to different opinions and good at analyzing contradictory information. They must understand finance and information systems, and be able to interpret data. Motivating others to implement their decisions requires strong leadership abilities. Tact, diplomacy, flexibility, and communication skills are essential because medical and health services managers spend most of their time interacting with others.

Medical and health services managers advance by moving into more responsible and higher paying positions, such as assistant or associate administrator, or by moving to larger facilities.

Job Outlook

Employment of medical and health services managers is expected to grow faster than the average for all occupations through 2012, as the health services industry continues to expand and diversify. Opportunities will be especially good in offices of physicians and other health practitioners, home healthcare services, and outpatient care centers. Applicants with work experience in the healthcare field and strong business and management skills should have the best opportunities.

Hospitals will continue to employ the most medical and health services managers over the projection period. However, the number of new jobs created in hospitals is expected to increase at a slower rate than in many other industries, as hospitals focus on controlling costs and increasing the utilization of clinics and other alternate care sites. Medical and health services managers with experience in large facilities will enjoy the best job opportunities, as hospitals become larger and more complex.

Employment will grow the fastest in practitioners' offices and in home healthcare agencies. Many services previously provided in hospitals will continue to shift to these sectors, especially as medical technologies improve. Demand in medical group practice management will grow as medical group practices become larger and more complex. Medical and health services managers will need to deal with the pressures of cost containment and financial accountability, as well as with the increased focus on preventive care. They also will become more involved in trying to improve the health of their communities. Managers with specialized experience in a particular field, such as reimbursement, should have good opportunities.

Medical and health services managers also will be employed by healthcare management companies who provide management services to hospitals and other organizations, as well as to specific departments such as emergency, information management systems, managed care contract negotiations, and physician recruiting.

Earnings

Median annual earnings of medical and health services managers were $61,370 in 2002. The middle 50 percent earned between $47,910 and $80,150.The lowest 10 percent earned less than $37,460, and the highest 10 percent earned more than $109,080. Median annual earnings in the industries employing the largest numbers of medical and health services managers in 2002 were as follows:

General medical and surgical hospitals	$65,950
Home health care services	56,320
Outpatient care centers	55,650
Offices of physicians	55,600
Nursing care facilities	55,320

Earnings of medical and health services managers vary by type and size of the facility, as well as by level of responsibility. For example, the Medical Group Management Association reported that, in 2002, median salaries for administrators were $78,258 in practices with fewer than 7 physicians; $92,727 in practices with 7 to 25 physicians; and $125,988 in practices with more than 26 physicians.

According to a survey by *Modern Healthcare* magazine, median annual compensation in 2003 for managers of selected clinical departments was $71,800 in respiratory care, $79,000 in physical therapy, $84,500 in home healthcare, $85,100 in laboratory services, $89,100 in rehabilitation services, $89,500 in medical imaging/diagnostic radiology, and $98,400 in nursing services. Salaries also varied according to size of facility and geographic region.

Related Occupations

Medical and health services managers have training or experience in both health and management. Other occupations requiring knowledge of both fields are insurance underwriters and social and community service managers.

Sources of Additional Information

Information about undergraduate and graduate academic programs in this field is available from:
➤ Association of University Programs in Health Administration, 730 11th St. NW., Washington, DC 20001-4510. Internet: **http://www.aupha.org**

For a list of accredited graduate programs in medical and health services administration, contact:
➤ Accrediting Commission on Education for Health Services Administration, 730 11th St. NW., Washington, DC 20001-4510. Internet: **http://www.acehsa.org**

For information about career opportunities in long-term care administration, contact:
➤ American College of Health Care Administrators, 300 N. Lee St., Suite 301, Alexandria, VA 22314. Internet: **http://www.achca.org**

For information about career opportunities in medical group practices and ambulatory care management, contact:
➤ Medical Group Management Association, 104 Inverness Terrace East, Englewood, CO 80112-5306.

For information about medical and healthcare office managers, contact:
➤ Professional Association of Health Care Office Management, 461 East Ten Mile Rd., Pensacola, FL 32534-9712.

Property, Real Estate, and Community Association Managers

(O*NET 11-9141.00)

Significant Points

- Many enter the occupation as onsite managers of apartment buildings, office complexes, or community associations, or as employees of property management firms or community association management companies.

- Forty-six percent of property, real estate, and community association managers are self-employed.

- Opportunities should be best for those with college degrees in business administration or related fields, as well as professional designations.

Nature of the Work

Buildings can be homes, stores, or offices to those who use them. To businesses and investors, properly managed real estate is a potential source of income and profits, and, to homeowners, it is a way to preserve and enhance resale values. Property, real estate, and community association managers maintain and increase the value of real estate investments. *Property and real estate managers* oversee the performance of income-producing commercial or residential properties, and ensure that real estate investments achieve their expected revenues. *Community association managers* manage the common property and services of condominiums, cooperatives, and planned communities through their homeowners' or community associations.

When owners of apartments, office buildings, or retail or industrial properties lack the time or expertise needed for day-to-day management of their real estate investments or homeowners' associations, they often hire a property or real estate manager, or community association manager. The manager is employed either directly by the owner or indirectly through a contract with a property management firm.

Generally, property and real estate managers handle the financial operations of the property, ensuring that rent is collected and that mortgages, taxes, insurance premiums, payroll, and maintenance bills are paid on time. In community associations, although homeowners pay no rent and pay their own real estate taxes and mortgages, community association managers must collect association dues. Some property managers, called *asset property managers*, supervise the preparation of financial statements and periodically report to the owners on the status of the property, occupancy rates, dates of lease expirations, and other matters.

Often, property managers negotiate contracts for janitorial, security, groundskeeping, trash removal, and other services. When contracts are awarded competitively, managers solicit bids from several contractors and recommend to the owners which bid to accept. They monitor the performance of contractors and investigate and resolve complaints from residents and tenants when services are not properly provided. Managers also purchase supplies and equipment for the property and make arrangements with specialists for repairs that cannot be handled by regular property maintenance staff.

In addition to these duties, property managers must understand and comply with provisions of legislation, such as the Americans with Disabilities Act and the Federal Fair Housing Amendment Act, as well as local fair housing laws. They must ensure that their renting and advertising practices are not discriminatory and that the property itself complies with all of the local, State, and Federal regulations and building codes.

Onsite property managers are responsible for day-to-day operations for one piece of property, such as an office building, shopping center, community association, or apartment complex. To ensure that the property is safe and properly maintained, onsite managers routinely inspect the grounds, facilities, and equipment to determine if repairs or maintenance are needed. They meet not only with current residents when handling requests for repairs or trying to resolve complaints, but also with prospective residents or tenants to show vacant apartments or office space. Onsite managers also are responsible for enforcing the terms of rental or lease agreements, such as rent collection, parking and pet restrictions, and termination-of-lease procedures. Other important duties of onsite managers include keeping accurate, up-to-date records of income and expenditures from property operations and submitting regular expense reports to the asset property manager or owners.

Property managers who do not work onsite act as a liaison between the onsite manager and the owner. They also market vacant space to prospective tenants through the use of a leasing agent or by advertising or other means, and establish rental rates in accordance with prevailing local economic conditions.

Some property and real estate managers, often called *real estate asset managers*, act as the property owners' agent and adviser for the property. They plan and direct the purchase, development, and disposition of real estate on behalf of the business and investors. These managers focus on long-term strategic financial planning rather than on day-to-day operations of the property.

When deciding to acquire property, real estate asset managers take several factors into consideration, such as property values, taxes, zoning, population growth, transportation, and traffic volume and patterns. Once a site is selected, they negotiate contracts for the purchase or lease of the property, securing the most beneficial terms. Real estate asset managers periodically review their company's real estate holdings and identify properties that are no longer financially profitable. They then negotiate the sale of or terminate the lease on such properties.

Property and real estate managers who work for homebuilders, real estate developers, and land development companies acquire land and plan construction of shopping centers, houses, apartments, office buildings, or industrial parks. They negotiate with representatives of local governments, other businesses, community and public interest groups, and public utilities to eliminate obstacles to the development of land and to gain support for a planned project. It sometimes takes years to win approval for a project and, in the process, managers may have to modify plans for the project many times. Once cleared to proceed with a project, managers may help to negotiate short-term loans to finance the construction of the project, and later negotiate long-term permanent mortgage loans. They then help to choose, assist, and advise the architectural firms that draw up detailed plans and the construction companies that build the project.

In many respects, the work of community association managers parallels that of property managers. They collect monthly assessments, prepare financial statements and budgets, negotiate with contractors, and help to resolve complaints. In other respects, however, the work of these managers differs from that of other residential property and real estate managers. Community association managers interact on a daily basis with homeowners and other residents, rather than with renters. Hired by the volunteer board of directors of the association, they administer the daily affairs, and oversee the maintenance of property and facilities that the homeowners own and use jointly through the association. They also assist the board and owners in complying with association and government rules and regulations.

Some associations encompass thousands of homes and employ their own onsite staff and managers. In addition to administering the associations' financial records and budget, managers may be responsible for the operation of community pools, golf courses, and community centers, and for the maintenance of landscaping and parking areas. Community association managers also may meet with the elected boards of directors to discuss and resolve legal issues or disputes that may affect the owners, as well as to review any proposed changes or improvements by homeowners to their properties, to make sure that they comply with community guidelines.

Working Conditions

Offices of most property, real estate, and community association managers are clean, modern, and well lighted. However, many managers spend a major portion of their time away from their desks. Onsite managers, in particular, may spend a large portion of their workday away from their office, visiting the building engineer, showing apartments, checking on the janitorial and maintenance staff, or

Property, real estate, and community association managers manage, maintain, and increase the value of real estate investments.

investigating problems reported by tenants. Property and real estate managers frequently visit the properties they oversee, sometimes on a daily basis when contractors are doing major repair or renovation work. Real estate asset managers may spend time away from home while traveling to company real estate holdings or searching for properties to acquire.

Property, real estate, and community association managers often must attend evening meetings with residents, property owners, community association boards of directors, or civic groups. Not surprisingly, many managers put in long workweeks, especially before financial and tax reports are due. Some apartment managers are required to live in the apartment complexes where they work so that they are available to handle any emergency that occurs, even when they are off duty. They usually receive compensatory time off for working nights or weekends. Many apartment managers receive time off during the week so that they are available on weekends to show apartments to prospective residents.

Employment

Property, real estate, and community association managers held about 293,000 jobs in 2002. Forty percent worked for real estate agents and brokers, lessors of real estate, or property management firms. Others worked for real estate development companies, government agencies that manage public buildings, and corporations with extensive holdings of commercial properties. Forty-six percent of property, real estate, and community association managers were self-employed.

Training, Other Qualifications, and Advancement

Most employers prefer to hire college graduates for property management positions. Entrants with degrees in business administration, accounting, finance, real estate, public administration, or related fields are preferred, but those with degrees in the liberal arts also may qualify. Good speaking, writing, computer, and financial skills, as well as an ability to tactfully deal with people, are essential in all areas of property management.

Many people enter property management as onsite managers of apartment buildings, office complexes, or community associations, or as employees of property management firms or community association management companies. As they acquire experience working under the direction of a property manager, they may advance to positions with greater responsibility at larger properties. Those who excel as onsite managers often transfer to assistant property manager positions in which they can acquire experience handling a broad range of property management responsibilities.

Previous employment as a real estate sales agent may be an asset to onsite managers because it provides experience useful in showing apartments or office space. In the past, those with backgrounds in building maintenance have advanced to onsite manager positions on the strength of their knowledge of building mechanical systems, but this is becoming less common as employers place greater emphasis on administrative, financial, and communication abilities for managerial jobs.

Although many people entering jobs such as assistant property manager do so by having previously gained onsite management experience, employers increasingly hire inexperienced college graduates with bachelor's or master's degrees in business administration, accounting, finance, or real estate for these positions. Assistants work closely with a property manager and learn how to prepare budgets, analyze insurance coverage and risk options, market property to prospective tenants, and collect overdue rent payments. In time, many assistants advance to property manager positions.

The responsibilities and compensation of property, real estate, and community association managers increase as they manage more and larger properties. Most property managers are responsible for several properties at a time. As their careers advance, they gradually are entrusted with larger properties that are more complex to manage. Many specialize in the management of one type of property, such as apartments, office buildings, condominiums, cooperatives, homeowner associations, or retail properties. Managers who excel at marketing properties to tenants may specialize in managing new properties, while those who are particularly knowledgeable about buildings and their mechanical systems might specialize in the management of older properties requiring renovation or more frequent repairs. Some experienced managers open their own property management firms.

Persons most commonly enter real estate asset manager jobs by transferring from positions as property managers or real estate brokers. Real estate asset managers must be good negotiators, adept at persuading and handling people, and good at analyzing data in order to assess the fair market value of property or its development potential. Resourcefulness and creativity in arranging financing are essential for managers who specialize in land development.

Many employers encourage attendance at short-term formal training programs conducted by various professional and trade associations active in the real estate field. Employers send managers to these programs to improve their management skills and expand their knowledge of specialized subjects, such as the operation and maintenance of building mechanical systems, enhancement of property values, insurance and risk management, personnel management, business and real estate law, community association risks and liabilities, tenant relations, communications, and accounting and financial concepts. Managers also participate in these programs to prepare themselves for positions of greater responsibility in property management. Completion of these programs, related job experience, and a satisfactory score on a written examination lead to certification, or the formal award of a professional designation, by the sponsoring association. (Some organizations offering such programs are listed as sources of additional information at the end of this statement.) In addition to these qualifications, some associations require their members to adhere to a specific code of ethics. In some States, community association managers must be licensed.

Managers of public housing subsidized by the Federal Government are required to be certified, but many property, real estate, and community association managers, who work with all types of property, choose to earn a professional designation voluntarily because it represents formal recognition of their achievements and status in the occupation. Real estate asset managers who buy or sell property are required to be licensed by the State in which they practice.

Job Outlook

Employment of property, real estate, and community association managers is projected to increase about as fast as the average for all occupations through the year 2012. Additional job openings are expected to occur as managers transfer to other occupations or leave the labor force. Opportunities should be best for those with a college degree in business administration, real estate, or a related field, and for those who attain a professional designation.

Job growth among onsite property managers in commercial real estate is expected to accompany the projected expansion of the real estate and rental and leasing industry. An increase in the Nation's stock of apartments, houses, and offices also should require more property managers. Developments of new homes increasingly are being organized with community or homeowner associations that provide community services and oversee jointly owned common areas, requiring professional management. To help properties become more profitable or to enhance the resale values of homes, more commercial and residential property owners are expected to place their investments in the hands of professional managers.

The changing demographic composition of the population also should create more jobs for property, real estate, and community association managers. The number of older people will grow during the 2000-12 projection period, increasing the need for various types of suitable housing, such as assisted-living facilities and retirement communities. Accordingly, there will be demand for property and real estate managers to operate these facilities, and especially for those who have a background in the operation and administrative aspects of running a health unit.

Earnings

Median annual earnings of salaried property, real estate, and community association managers were $36,880 in 2002. The middle 50 percent earned between $25,470 and $56,000 a year. The lowest 10 percent earned less than $17,450, and the highest 10 percent earned more than $86,650 a year. Median annual earnings of salaried property, real estate, and community association managers in the largest employing industries in 2002 were as follows:

Local government	$50,340
Offices of real estate agents and brokers	37,820
Activities related to real estate	35,750
Lessors of real estate	31,190

Many resident apartment managers and onsite association managers receive the use of an apartment as part of their compensation package. Managers often are reimbursed for the use of their personal vehicles, and managers employed in land development often receive a small percentage of ownership in the projects that they develop.

Related Occupations

Property, real estate, and community association managers plan, organize, staff, and manage the real estate operations of businesses. Workers who perform similar functions in other fields include administrative services managers, education administrators, food service managers, lodging managers, medical and health services managers, real estate brokers and sales agents, and urban and regional planners.

Sources of Additional Information

General information about education and careers in property management is available from:
➤ Institute of Real Estate Management, 430 N. Michigan Ave., Chicago, IL 60611. Internet: **http://www.irem.org**

For information on careers and certification programs in commercial property management, contact:
➤ Building Owners and Managers Institute, 1521 Ritchie Hwy., Arnold, MD 21012.

For information on careers and professional designation and certification programs in residential property management and community association management, contact:
➤ Community Associations Institute, 225 Reinekers Ln., Suite 300, Alexandria, VA 22314. Internet: **http://www.caionline.org**
➤ National Board of Certification for Community Association Managers, P.O. Box 25037, Alexandria, VA 22313. Internet: **http://www.nbccam.org**

Purchasing Managers, Buyers, and Purchasing Agents

(0*NET 11-3061.00, 13-1021.00, 13-1022.00, 13-1023.00)

Significant Points

- Forty-two percent are employed in wholesale trade or manufacturing establishments.

- Some firms promote qualified employees to these positions, while other employers recruit college graduates; regardless of academic preparation, new employees need 1 to 5 years to learn the specifics of their employer's business.

- Overall employment is expected to be slower than the average, but the projected change in employment varies significantly by occupational specialty.

- Opportunities should be best for those with a college degree.

Nature of the Work

Purchasing managers, buyers, and purchasing agents seek to obtain the highest quality merchandise at the lowest possible purchase cost for their employers. In general, *purchasers* buy goods and services for use by their company or organization, whereas *buyers* typically buy items for resale. Purchasers and buyers determine which commodities or services are best, choose the suppliers of the product or service, negotiate the lowest price, and award contracts that ensure that the correct amount of the product or service is received at the appropriate time. In order to accomplish these tasks successfully, purchasing managers, buyers, and purchasing agents study sales records and inventory levels of current stock, identify foreign and domestic suppliers, and keep abreast of changes affecting both the supply of, and demand for, needed products and materials.

Purchasing managers, buyers, and purchasing agents evaluate suppliers on the basis of price, quality, service support, availability, reliability, and selection. To assist them in their search for the right suppliers, they review catalogs, industry and company publications, directories, and trade journals. Much of this information is now available on the Internet. They research the reputation and history of the suppliers and may advertise anticipated purchase actions in order to solicit bids. At meetings, trade shows, conferences, and suppliers' plants and distribution centers, they examine products and services, assess a supplier's production and distribution capabilities, and discuss other technical and business considerations that influence the purchasing decision. Once all of the necessary information on suppliers is gathered, orders are placed and contracts are awarded to those suppliers who meet the purchaser's needs. Contracts often are for several years and may stipulate the price or a narrow range of prices, allowing purchasers to reorder as necessary. Other specific job duties and responsibilities of purchasing managers, buyers, and purchasing agents vary by employer and by the type of commodities or services to be purchased.

Purchasing specialists employed by government agencies or manufacturing firms usually are called purchasing directors, managers, or agents; buyers or industrial buyers; or contract specialists. These workers acquire materials, parts, machines, supplies, services, and other inputs to the production of a final product. Some purchasing managers specialize in negotiating and supervising supply contracts, and are called contract or supply managers. Purchasing agents and managers obtain items ranging from raw materials, fab-ricated parts, machinery, and office supplies to construction services and airline tickets. The flow of work—or even the entire production process—can be slowed or halted if the right materials, supplies, or equipment are not on hand when needed. To be effective, purchasing specialists must have a working technical knowledge of the goods or services to be purchased.

In large industrial organizations, a distinction often is drawn between the work of a buyer or purchasing agent and that of a purchasing manager. Purchasing agents and buyers commonly focus on routine purchasing tasks, often specializing in a commodity or group of related commodities, such as steel, lumber, cotton, grains, fabricated metal products, or petroleum products. Purchasing agents usually track market conditions, price trends, or futures markets. Purchasing managers usually handle the more complex or critical purchases and may supervise a group of purchasing agents handling other goods and services. Whether a person is titled purchasing manager, buyer, or purchasing agent depends more on specific industry and employer practices than on specific job duties.

Changing business practices have altered the traditional roles of purchasing or supply management specialists in many industries. For example, manufacturing companies increasingly involve workers in this occupation at most stages of product development because of their ability to forecast a part's or material's cost, availability, and suitability for its intended purpose. Furthermore, potential problems with the supply of materials may be avoided by consulting the purchasing department in the early stages of product design.

Businesses also might enter into integrated supply contracts. These contracts increase the importance of selecting the right supplier, because agreements are larger in scope and longer in duration. Integrated supply incorporates all members of the supply chain, including the supplier, transportation companies, and the retailer. A major responsibility of most purchasers is to work out problems that may occur with a supplier, because the success of the relationship affects the buying firm's performance.

Purchasing specialists often work closely with other employees in their own organization when deciding on purchases, an arrangement sometimes called team buying. For example, before submitting an order, they may discuss the design of custom-made products with company design engineers, talk about problems involving the quality of purchased goods with quality assurance engineers and production supervisors, or mention shipment problems to managers in the receiving department.

Contract specialists and managers at various levels of government award contracts for an array of items, including office and building supplies, services for the public, and construction projects. For example, they may oversee the contract for cleaning services of a government office building to verify that the work is being done on schedule and on budget, even though the cleaners are not government employees. They may use sealed bids to award contracts, but usually establish negotiated agreements for complex items. Often, purchasing specialists in government place solicitations for services and accept bids and offers through the Internet. Government purchasing agents and managers must follow strict laws and regulations in their work, in order to avoid any appearance of impropriety. These legal requirements are occasionally changed, so agents and contract specialists must keep abreast of the latest regulations.

Purchasing specialists who buy finished goods for resale are employed by wholesale and retail establishments, where they commonly are known as buyers or merchandise managers. Wholesale and retail buyers are an integral part of a complex system of distribution and merchandising that caters to the vast array of consumer needs and desires. Wholesale buyers purchase goods directly from manufacturers or from other wholesale firms for resale to retail firms, commercial establishments, institutions, and other organizations. In retail firms, buyers purchase goods from wholesale firms or directly from manufacturers for resale to the public. Buyers largely determine which products their establishment will sell. Therefore, it is essential that they have the ability to predict what will appeal to consumers. They must constantly stay informed of the latest trends, because failure to do so could jeopardize profits and the reputation of their company. Buyers also follow ads in newspapers and other media to check competitors' sales activities, and they watch general economic conditions to anticipate consumer buying patterns. Buyers working for large and medium-sized firms usually specialize in acquiring one or two lines of merchandise, whereas buyers working for small stores may purchase the establishment's complete inventory.

The use of private-label merchandise and the consolidation of buying departments have increased the responsibilities of retail buyers. Private-label merchandise, produced for a particular retailer, requires buyers to work closely with vendors to develop and obtain the desired product. The downsizing and consolidation of buying departments increases the demands placed on buyers because, although the amount of work remains unchanged, there are fewer people to accomplish it. The result is an increase in the workloads and levels of responsibility for all.

Many merchandise managers assist in the planning and implementation of sales promotion programs. Working with merchandise executives, they determine the nature of the sale and purchase items accordingly. Merchandise managers may work with advertising personnel to create an ad campaign. For example, they may determine in which media the advertisement will be placed—newspapers, direct mail, television, or some combination of all three. In addition, merchandise managers often visit the selling floor to ensure that goods are properly displayed. Often, assistant buyers are responsible for placing orders and checking shipments.

Computers continue to have a major effect on the jobs of purchasing managers, buyers, and purchasing agents. In manufacturing and service industries, computers handle most of the routine tasks, enabling purchasing workers to concentrate mainly on the analytical and qualitative aspects of the job. Computers are used to obtain instant and accurate product and price listings, to track inventory levels, to process orders, and to help determine when to make purchases. Computers also maintain lists of bids and offers, record the history of supplier performance, and issue purchase orders.

Computerized systems have dramatically simplified many of the acquisition functions and improved the efficiency of determining which products are selling. For example, cash registers connected to computers, known as point-of-sale terminals, allow organizations to maintain instant access to current sales and inventory records. The information contained therein can then be used to produce sales reports that reflect customer buying habits. The ability to find out quickly which products or combinations of products are selling well enables buyers and supply managers to increase sales and reduce costs. Buyers can gain instant access to the specifications for thousands of commodities, inventory records, and their customers' purchase records to avoid overpaying for goods and to avoid shortages of popular goods or surpluses of goods that do not sell as well. Firms are linked with manufacturers and wholesalers by electronic purchasing systems, the Internet, or Extranets. These systems permit faster selection, customization, and ordering of products, and they allow buyers to concentrate better on selecting goods and suppliers.

Working Conditions

Most purchasing managers, buyers, and purchasing agents work in comfortable offices. They frequently work more than the standard 40-hour week, because of special sales, conferences, or production deadlines. Evening and weekend work also is common, before holiday and back-to-school seasons for those working in retail trade. Consequently, many retail firms discourage the use of vacation time during peak periods.

Buyers and merchandise managers often work under great pressure. Because wholesale and retail stores are so competitive, buyers need physical stamina to keep up with the fast-paced nature of their work.

Many purchasing managers, buyers, and purchasing agents travel at least several days a month. Purchasers for worldwide manufacturing companies and large retailers, as well as buyers of high fashion, may travel outside the United States.

Employment

Purchasing managers, buyers, and purchasing agents held about 527,000 jobs in 2002. Forty-two percent worked in the wholesale trade and manufacturing industries, and another 15 percent worked in retail trade. The remainder worked mostly in service establishments, such as hospitals, or different levels of government. A small number were self-employed.

The following tabulation shows the distribution of employment by occupational specialty:

Purchasing agents, except wholesale, retail, and farm products	245,000
Wholesale and retail buyers, except farm products	155,000
Purchasing managers	108,000
Purchasing agents and buyers, farm products	19,000

Training, Other Qualifications, and Advancement

Qualified persons may begin as trainees, purchasing clerks, expediters, junior buyers, or assistant buyers. Retail and wholesale firms prefer to hire applicants who have a college degree and who are familiar with the merchandise they sell and with wholesaling and retailing practices. Some retail firms promote qualified employees to assistant buyer positions; others recruit and train college graduates as assistant buyers. Most employers use a combination of methods.

Purchasing managers, buyers, and purchasing agents work to get the best merchandise at the lowest cost.

Educational requirements tend to vary with the size of the organization. Large stores and distributors, especially those in wholesale and retail trade, prefer applicants who have completed a bachelor's degree program with a business emphasis. Many manufacturing firms put yet a greater emphasis on formal training, preferring applicants with a bachelor's or master's degree in engineering, business, economics, or one of the applied sciences. A master's degree is essential for advancement to many top-level purchasing manager jobs.

Regardless of academic preparation, new employees must learn the specifics of their employers' business. Training periods vary in length, with most lasting 1 to 5 years. In wholesale and retail establishments, most trainees begin by selling merchandise, supervising sales workers, checking invoices on material received, and keeping track of stock. As they progress, retail trainees are given increased buying-related responsibilities.

In manufacturing, new purchasing employees often are enrolled in company training programs and spend a considerable amount of time learning about their firm's operations and purchasing practices. They work with experienced purchasers to learn about commodities, prices, suppliers, and markets. In addition, they may be assigned to the production planning department to learn about the material requirements system and the inventory system the company uses to keep production and replenishment functions working smoothly.

Purchasing managers, buyers, and purchasing agents must know how to use both word processing and spreadsheet software, as well as the Internet. Other important qualities include the ability to analyze technical data in suppliers' proposals; good communication, negotiation, and mathematical skills; knowledge of supply-chain management; and the ability to perform financial analyses.

Persons who wish to become wholesale or retail buyers should be good at planning and decisionmaking and have an interest in merchandising. Anticipating consumer preferences and ensuring that goods are in stock when they are needed requires resourcefulness, good judgment, and self-confidence. Buyers must be able to make decisions quickly and to take risks. Marketing skills and the ability to identify products that will sell also are very important. Employers often look for leadership ability, too, because buyers spend a large portion of their time supervising assistant buyers and dealing with manufacturers' representatives and store executives.

Experienced buyers may advance by moving to a department that manages a larger volume or by becoming a merchandise manager. Others may go to work in sales for a manufacturer or wholesaler.

An experienced purchasing agent or buyer may become an assistant purchasing manager in charge of a group of purchasing professionals before advancing to purchasing manager, supply manager, or director of materials management. At the top levels, duties may overlap with other management functions, such as production, planning, logistics, and marketing.

Regardless of industry, continuing education is essential for advancement. Many purchasers participate in seminars offered by professional societies and take college courses in supply management. Professional certification is becoming increasingly important, especially for those just entering the occupation.

In private industry, recognized marks of experience and professional competence are the Accredited Purchasing Practitioner (APP) and Certified Purchasing Manager (CPM) designations, conferred by the Institute for Supply Management, and the Certified Purchasing Professional (CPP) and Certified Professional Purchasing Manager (CPPM) designations, conferred by the American Purchasing Society. In Federal, State, and local government, the indications of professional competence are Certified Professional Public Buyer (CPPB) and Certified Public Purchasing Officer, (CPPO), conferred by the National Institute of Governmental Purchasing. Most of these certifications are awarded only after work-related experience and education requirements are met, and written or oral exams are successfully completed.

Job Outlook

Overall employment of purchasing managers, buyers, and purchasing agents is expected to be slower than the average through the year 2012. Offsetting some declines for purchasing workers in the manufacturing sector will be increases in the services sector. Companies in the services sector, which have typically made purchases on an ad hoc basis, are beginning to realize that centralized purchasing offices may be more efficient. Demand for purchasing workers will be limited by improving software, which has eliminated much of the paperwork involved in ordering and procuring supplies, the increased use of credit cards by some employees to purchase supplies without using the services of the procurement or purchasing office, and the growing number of purchases being made electronically. Despite slower-than-average growth, some job openings will result from the need to replace workers who transfer to other occupations or leave the labor force.

The projected change in employment varies significantly by occupational specialty. Employment of purchasing managers is expected to grow more slowly than the average through 2012. The use of the Internet to conduct electronic commerce has made information easier to obtain, thus increasing the productivity of purchasing managers. The Internet also allows both large and small companies to bid on contracts. Exclusive supply contracts and long-term contracting have allowed companies to negotiate with fewer suppliers less frequently.

Employment of wholesale and retail buyers, except farm products, also is projected to grow more slowly than the average. In the retail industry, mergers and acquisitions have forced buying departments to consolidate. In addition, larger retail stores are removing their buying departments from regional markets and centralizing them at their headquarters

In contrast, employment of purchasing agents, except wholesale, retail, and farm products, is expected to increase about as fast as the average for all occupations through 2012. Despite the greater use of electronic transactions, purchases of complex equipment are more difficult both to automate and to transact electronically. Employment of purchasing agents and buyers, farm products, also is projected to increase about as fast as the average for all occupations, as the need to evaluate the quality and freshness of farm products limits the ease of making purchases electronically.

Persons who have a bachelor's degree in business should have the best chance of obtaining a buyer position in wholesale or retail trade or within government. A bachelor's degree, combined with industry experience and knowledge of a technical field, will be an advantage for those interested in working for a manufacturing or industrial company. Government agencies and larger companies usually require a master's degree in business or public administration for top-level purchasing positions.

Earnings

Median annual earnings of purchasing managers were $59,890 in 2002. The middle 50 percent earned between $43,670 and $81,950 a year. The lowest 10 percent earned less than $32,330, and the highest 10 percent earned more than $108,140 a year.

Median annual earnings for purchasing agents and buyers, farm products were $40,900 in 2002. The middle 50 percent earned between $31,390 and $55,440 a year. The lowest 10 percent earned less than $23,850, and the highest 10 percent earned more than $76,740 a year.

Median annual earnings for wholesale and retail buyers, except farm products, were $40,780 in 2002. The middle 50 percent earned between $30,040 and $55,670 a year. The lowest 10 percent earned less than $23,270, and the highest 10 percent earned more than $76,070 a year. Median annual earnings in the industries employing the largest numbers of wholesale and retail buyers, except farm products, in 2002 were as follows:

Management of companies and enterprises	$49,150
Grocery and related product wholesalers	42,850
Machinery, equipment, and supplies merchant wholesalers	37,920
Building material and supplies dealers	35,910

Median annual earnings for purchasing agents, except wholesale, retail, and farm products, were $45,090 in 2002. The middle 50 percent earned between $34,820 and $58,780 a year. The lowest 10 percent earned less than $27,950, and the highest 10 percent earned more than $73,990 a year. Median annual earnings in the industries employing the largest numbers of purchasing agents, except of wholesale, retail, and farm products, in 2002 were as follows:

Federal Government	$58,410
Aerospace product and parts manufacturing	52,900
Management of companies and enterprises	50,790
Local government	42,450
General medical and surgical hospitals	34,420

Purchasing managers, buyers, and purchasing agents receive the same benefits package as other workers, including vacations, sick leave, life and health insurance, and pension plans. In addition to receiving standard benefits, retail buyers often earn cash bonuses based on their performance and may receive discounts on merchandise bought from their employer.

Related Occupations

Workers in other occupations who need a knowledge of marketing and the ability to assess consumer demand include those in advertising, marketing, promotions, and public relations, as well as sales managers; food service managers: insurance sales agents; lodging managers; sales engineers; and sales representatives, wholesale and manufacturing.

Sources of Additional Information

Further information about education, training, employment, and certification for purchasing careers is available from any of the following sources:

➤ American Purchasing Society, North Island Center, Suite 203, 8 East Galena Blvd., Aurora, IL 60506. Internet: **http://www.american-purchasing.com**
➤ Institute for Supply Management, P.O. Box 22160, Tempe, AZ 85285-2160. Internet: **http://www.ism.ws**
➤ National Institute of Governmental Purchasing, Inc., 151 Spring St., Suite 300, Herndon, VA 20170-5223. Internet: **http://www.nigp.org**

Top Executives

(0*NET 11-1011.01, 11-1011.02, 11-1021.00, 11-1031.00)

Significant Points

● Top executives are among the highest paid workers; however, long hours, considerable travel, and intense pressure to succeed are common.

● The formal education and experience of top executives varies as widely as the nature of their responsibilities.

● Keen competition is expected because the prestige and high pay attract a large number of qualified applicants.

● Most government chief executives and legislators are elected; local government managers are appointed.

Nature of the Work

All organizations have specific goals and objectives that they strive to meet. Top executives devise strategies and formulate policies to ensure that these objectives are met. Although they have a wide range of titles—such as chief executive officer, chief operating officer, board chair, president, vice president, school superintendent, county administrator, or tax commissioner—all formulate policies and direct the operations of businesses and corporations, nonprofit institutions, governments, and other organizations.

A corporation's goals and policies are established by the *chief executive officer* in collaboration with other top executives, who are overseen by a board of directors. In a large corporation, the chief executive officer meets frequently with subordinate executives to ensure that operations are conducted in accordance with these policies. The chief executive officer of a corporation retains overall accountability; however, a chief operating officer may be delegated several responsibilities, including the authority to oversee executives who direct the activities of various departments and implement the organization's policies on a day-to-day basis. In publicly held and nonprofit corporations, the board of directors ultimately is accountable for the success or failure of the enterprise, and the chief executive officer reports to the board.

The nature of other high-level executives' responsibilities depends upon the size of the organization. In large organizations, the duties of such executives are highly specialized. Some managers, for instance, are responsible for the overall performance of one aspect of the organization, such as manufacturing, marketing, sales, purchasing, finance, personnel, training, administrative services, computer and information systems, property management, transportation, or the legal services department. (Some of these and other management occupations are discussed elsewhere in this section of the *Handbook*.)

In smaller organizations, such as independent retail stores or small manufacturers, a partner, owner, or general manager often is responsible for purchasing, hiring, training, quality control, and day-to-day supervisory duties.

Chief financial officers direct the organization's financial goals, objectives, and budgets. They oversee the investment of funds and manage associated risks, supervise cash management activities, execute capital-raising strategies to support a firm's expansion, and deal with mergers and acquisitions.

Chief information officers are responsible for the overall technological direction of their organizations. They are increasingly involved in the strategic business plan of a firm as part of the executive team. To perform effectively, they also need knowledge of administrative procedures, such as budgeting, hiring, and supervision. These managers propose budgets for projects and programs, and make decisions on staff training and equipment purchases. They hire and assign computer specialists, information technology workers, and support personnel to carry out specific parts of the projects. They supervise the work of these employees, review their output, and establish administrative procedures and policies. Chief information officers also provide organizations with the vision to master information technology as a competitive tool.

Chief executives and legislators at the Federal, State, and local levels direct government activities and pass laws that affect us daily. These officials consist of the President and Vice President of the United States; members of Congress; State governors and lieutenant governors; members of the State legislators; county chief executives and commissioners; city, town, and township council members; mayors; and city, county, town, and township managers. (Many small communities have top government officials who are volunteers and receive no salary. These individuals are not included in the employment or salary data cited in this *Handbook* statement.)

Most chief executives are elected by their constituents, but many managers are hired by a local government executive, council, or commission, to whom they are directly responsible. These officials formulate and establish government policy and develop Federal, State, or local laws and regulations.

Chief executives, government—like their counterparts in the private sector—have overall responsibility for the operation of their organizations. Working with legislators, they set goals and arrange programs to attain them. These executives also appoint department heads, who oversee the civil servants who carry out programs enacted by legislative bodies. As in the private sector, government chief executives oversee budgets and ensure that resources are used properly and that programs are carried out as planned.

Chief executive officers carry out a number of other important functions, such as meeting with legislators and constituents to determine the level of support for proposed programs. In addition, they often nominate citizens to boards and commissions, encourage business investment, and promote economic development in their communities. To do all of these varied tasks effectively, chief executives of large governments rely on a staff of highly skilled aides to research issues that concern the public. Executives who control small governmental bodies, however, often do this work by themselves.

Legislators are elected officials who develop, enact, or amend laws. They include U.S. Senators and Representatives, State senators and representatives, and county, city, and town commissioners and council members. Legislators introduce, examine, and vote on bills to pass official legislation. In preparing such legislation, they study staff reports and hear testimony from constituents, representatives of interest groups, board and commission members, and others with an interest in the issue under consideration. They usually must approve budgets and the appointments of nominees for leadership posts whose names are submitted by the chief executive. In some bodies, the legislative council appoints the city, town, or county manager.

General and operations managers plan, direct, or coordinate the operations of companies or public and private sector organizations. Their duties include formulating policies, managing daily operations, and planning the use of materials and human resources, but are too diverse and general in nature to be classified in any one area of management or administration, such as personnel, purchasing, or administrative services. In some organizations, the duties of general and operations managers may overlap the duties of chief executive officers.

Working Conditions

Top executives typically have spacious offices and numerous support staff. General managers in large firms or nonprofit organizations usually have comfortable offices close to those of the top executives to whom they report. Long hours, including evenings and weekends, are standard for most top executives and general managers, although their schedules may be flexible.

Substantial travel between international, national, regional, and local offices to monitor operations and meet with customers, staff, and other executives often is required of managers and executives. Many managers and executives also attend meetings and conferences sponsored by various associations. The conferences provide an opportunity to meet with prospective donors, customers, contractors, or government officials and allow managers and executives to keep abreast of technological and managerial innovations.

In large organizations, job transfers between local offices or subsidiaries are common for persons on the executive career track. Top executives are under intense pressure to succeed; depending on the organization, this may mean earning higher profits, providing better service, or attaining fundraising and charitable goals. Executives in charge of poorly performing organizations or departments usually find their jobs in jeopardy.

The working conditions of legislators and government chief executives vary with the size and budget of the governmental unit. Time spent at work ranges from a few hours a week for some local

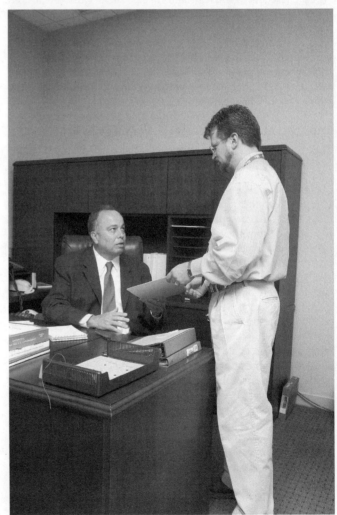

Top executives devise strategies, formulate policies, and direct operations to ensure that an organization's objectives are met.

leaders to stressful weeks of 60 or more hours for members of the U.S. Congress. Similarly, some jobs require only occasional out-of-town travel, while others involve long periods away from home, such as when attending sessions of the legislature.

U.S. Senators and Representatives, governors and lieutenant governors, and chief executives and legislators in municipalities work full time, year-round, as do most county and city managers. Many State legislators work full time on government business while the legislature is in session (usually for 2 to 6 months a year or every other year) and work only part time when the legislature is not in session. Some local elected officials work a schedule that is officially designated as part time, but actually is the equivalent of a full-time schedule when unpaid duties are taken into account. In addition to their regular schedules, most chief executives are on call to handle emergencies.

Employment

Top executives held about 2.7 million jobs in 2002. Employment by detailed occupation was distributed as follows:

General and operations managers	2,049,000
Chief executives	553,000
Legislators	67,000

Top executives are found in every industry, but service-providing industries, including government, employ almost 8 out of 10.

Chief executives and legislators in the Federal Government consist of the 100 Senators, 435 Representatives, and the President and Vice President. State governors, lieutenant governors, legislators, chief executives, professional managers, and council and commission members of local governments make up the remainder.

Government chief executives and legislators who do not hold full-time, year-round positions often continue to work in the occupation that they held before being elected.

Training, Other Qualifications, and Advancement

The formal education and experience of top executives varies as widely as the nature of their responsibilities. Many top executives have a bachelor's or higher degree in business administration or liberal arts. College presidents typically have a doctorate in the field in which they originally taught, and school superintendents often have a master's degree in education administration. (For information on lower level managers in educational services, see the *Handbook* statement on education administrators.) A brokerage office manager needs a strong background in securities and finance, and department store executives generally have extensive experience in retail trade.

Some top executives in the public sector have a background in public administration or liberal arts. Others might have a background related to their jobs. For example, a health commissioner might have a graduate degree in health services administration or business administration. (For information on lower level managers in health services, see the *Handbook* statement on medical and health services managers.)

Because many top executive positions are filled by promoting experienced, lower level managers when an opening occurs, many top managers have been promoted from within the organization. In industries such as retail trade or transportation, for instance, it is possible for individuals without a college degree to work their way up within the company and become managers. However, many companies prefer that their top executives have specialized backgrounds and, therefore, hire individuals who have been managers in other organizations.

Top executives must have highly developed personal skills. An analytical mind able to quickly assess large amounts of information and data is very important, as is the ability to consider and evaluate the interrelationships of numerous factors. Top executives also must be able to communicate clearly and persuasively. Other qualities critical for managerial success include leadership, self-confidence, motivation, decisiveness, flexibility, sound business judgment, and determination.

Advancement may be accelerated by participation in company training programs that impart a broader knowledge of company policy and operations. Managers also can help their careers by becoming familiar with the latest developments in management techniques at national or local training programs sponsored by various industry and trade associations. Managers who have experience in a particular field, such as accounting or engineering, may attend executive development programs to facilitate their promotion to an even higher level. Participation in conferences and seminars can expand knowledge of national and international issues influencing the organization and can help the participants to develop a network of useful contacts.

General managers may advance to top executive positions, such as executive vice president, in their own firm or they may take a corresponding position in another firm. They may even advance to peak corporate positions such as chief operating officer or chief executive officer. Chief executive officers often become members of the board of directors of one or more firms, typically as a director of their own firm and often as chair of its board of directors. Some top executives establish their own firms or become independent consultants.

Apart from meeting minimum age, residency, and citizenship requirements, candidates for a legislative position have no established training or qualifications. Candidates come from a wide variety of occupations—such as lawyer, private sector manager or executive, or business owner—but many do have some political experience as staffers or members of government bureaus, boards, or commissions. Successful candidates usually become well known through their political campaigns and some have built voter name recognition through their work with community religious, fraternal, or social organizations.

Increasingly, candidates target information to voters through advertising paid for by their respective campaigns, so fundraising skills are essential for candidates. Management-level work experience and public service help to develop the fundraising, budgeting, public speaking, and problem-solving skills that are needed to run an effective political campaign. Candidates must make decisions quickly, sometimes on the basis of limited or contradictory information. They also should be able to inspire and motivate their constituents and staff. Additionally, they must know how to reach compromises and satisfy conflicting demands of constituents. National, State, and some local campaigns require massive amounts of energy and stamina, traits vital to successful candidates.

Virtually all town, city, and county managers have at least a bachelor's degree, and many hold a higher degree. A master's degree in public administration is recommended, including courses in public financial management and legal issues in public administration. Working in management support positions in government is a prime source of the experience and personal contacts required to eventually secure a manager position. For example, applicants often gain experience as management analysts or assistants in government departments, working for committees, councils, or chief executives. In this capacity, they learn about planning, budgeting, civil engineering, and other aspects of running a government. With sufficient experience, they may be hired to manage a small government.

Generally, a town, city, or county manager is first hired by a smaller community. Advancement often takes the form of securing positions with progressively larger towns, cities, or counties. A broad knowledge of local issues, combined with communication skills and the ability to compromise, are essential for advancement in this field.

Advancement opportunities for elected officials are not clearly defined. Because elected positions normally require a period of residency and because local public support is critical, officials usually advance to other offices only in the jurisdictions where they live. For example, council members may run for mayor or for a position in the State government, and State legislators may run for governor or for the U.S. Congress. Many officials are not politically ambitious, however, and do not seek advancement. Others lose their bids for reelection or voluntarily leave the occupation. A lifetime career as a government chief executive or legislator is rare.

Job Outlook

Keen competition is expected for top executive positions, with the prestige and high pay attracting a large number of qualified applicants. Because this is a large occupation, numerous openings will occur each year as executives transfer to other positions, start their own businesses, or retire. However, many executives who leave their jobs transfer to other executive positions, which tend to limit the number of job openings for new entrants.

Experienced managers whose accomplishments reflect strong leadership qualities and the ability to improve the efficiency or competitive position of an organization will have the best opportunities. In an increasingly global economy, experience in international economics, marketing, information systems, and knowledge of several languages also may be beneficial.

Employment of top executives—including chief executives, general and operations managers, and legislators—is expected to grow about as fast as the average for all occupations through 2012. Because top managers are essential to the success of any organization, they should be more immune to automation and corporate restructuring—factors that are expected to adversely affect employment of lower level managers. Projected employment growth of top executives varies by industry, reflecting the projected change in industry employment over the 2002-12 period. For example, employment growth is expected to be faster than average in professional, scientific, and technical services and administrative and support services. However, employment is projected to decline in some manufacturing industries.

Few new governments at any level are likely to be formed, and the number of chief executives and legislators in existing governments rarely changes. However, some increase will occur at the local level as counties, cities, and towns take on professional managers or move from volunteer to paid career executives to deal with population growth, Federal regulations, and long-range planning.

Elections give newcomers the chance to unseat incumbents or to fill vacated positions. The level of competition in elections varies from place to place. There tends to be less competition in small communities that offer part-time positions with low or no salaries and little or no staff, compared with large municipalities with prestigious full-time positions offering high salaries, staff, and greater exposure.

Earnings

Top executives are among the highest paid workers in the U.S. economy. However, salary levels vary substantially depending upon the level of managerial responsibility, length of service, and type, size, and location of the firm. For example, a top manager in a very large corporation can earn significantly more than a counterpart in a small firm.

Median annual earnings of general and operations managers in 2002 were $68,210. The middle 50 percent earned between $45,720 and $104,970. Because the specific responsibilities of general and operations managers vary significantly within industries, earnings also tend to vary considerably. Median annual earnings in the industries employing the largest numbers of general and operations managers in 2002 were:

Management of companies and enterprises	$94,600
Building equipment contractors	74,550
Depository credit intermediation	68,110
Local government	60,470
Grocery stores	44,980

Median annual earnings of chief executives in 2002 were $126,260. Median annual earnings in the industries employing the largest numbers of chief executives in 2002 were:

Management of companies and enterprises	$145,600
Architectural, engineering, and related services	133,880
Depository credit intermediation	123,220
Colleges, universities, and professional schools	103,120
Local government	73,990

Salaries vary substantially by type and level of responsibilities and by industry. According to a survey by Abbott, Langer & Associates, the median income of chief executive officers in the nonprofit sector was $81,000 in 2003, but some of the highest paid made $600,000.

In addition to salaries, total compensation often includes stock options, dividends, and other performance bonuses. The use of executive dining rooms and company aircraft and cars, expense allowances, and company-paid insurance premiums and physical examinations also are among benefits commonly enjoyed by top executives in private industry. A number of chief executive officers also are provided with company-paid club memberships, a limousine with chauffeur, and other amenities.

Median annual earnings of legislators were $15,220 in 2002. The middle 50 percent earned between $13,180 and $38,540. The lowest 10 percent earned less than $12,130, and the highest 10 percent earned more than $69,380.

Earnings of public administrators vary widely, depending on the size of the governmental unit and on whether the job is part time, full time and year round, or full time for only a few months a year. Salaries range from little or nothing for a small-town council member to $400,000 a year for the President of the United States.

The National Conference of State Legislatures reports that the annual salary for rank-and-file legislators in the 40 States that paid an annual salary ranged from $10,000 to more than $99,000 in 2003. In eight States, legislators received a daily salary plus an additional allowance for living expenses while legislatures were in session.

The Council of State Governments reports in its *Book of the States, 2002-2003* that gubernatorial annual salaries ranged from $50,000 in American Samoa to $179,000 in New York. In addition to a salary, most governors received benefits such as transportation and an official residence. In 2003, U.S. Senators and Representatives earned $154,700, the Senate and House Majority and Minority leaders earned $171,900, and the Vice President was paid $198,600.

Related Occupations

Top executives plan, organize, direct, control, and coordinate the operations of an organization and its major departments or programs. The members of the board of directors and lower-level managers also are involved in these activities. Many other management occupations have similar responsibilities; however, they are concentrated in specific industries or are responsible for a specific department within an organization. A few examples are administrative services managers, education administrators, financial managers, food service managers, and advertising, marketing, promotions, public relations, and sales managers.

Sources of Additional Information

For a variety of information on top executives, including educational programs and job listings, contact:

➤ American Management Association, 1601 Broadway, 6th Floor, New York, NY 10019. Internet: **http://www.amanet.org**
➤ Institute of Certified Professional Managers, James Madison University, MSC 5504, Harrisonburg, VA 22807. Internet: **http://cob.jmu.edu/icpm/**

➤ International Public Management Association for Human Resources, 1617 Duke St., Alexandria, VA 22314. Internet: **http://www.ipma-hr.org**
➤ National Management Association, 2210 Arbor Blvd., Dayton, OH 45439. Internet: **http://www.nma1.org**

Information on appointed officials in local government can be obtained from:

➤ Council of State Governments, P.O. Box 11910, 2760 Research Park Dr., Lexington, KY 40578-1910. Internet: **http://www.statesnews.org**
➤ National Association of Counties, 440 First St. NW., 8th Floor, Washington, DC 20001. Internet: **http://www.naco.org**
➤ National Conference of State Legislatures, 7700 East First Place, Denver, CO 80230. Internet: **http://www.ncsl.org**
➤ National League of Cities, 1301 Pennsylvania Ave. NW., Washington, DC 20004. Internet: **http://www.nlc.org**

For information on executive financial management careers and certification, contact:

➤ Financial Executives International, 200 Campus Dr., P.O. Box 674, Florham Park, NJ 07932-0674. Internet: **http://www.fei.org**
➤ Financial Management Association International, College of Business Administration, University of South Florida, 4202 East Fowler Ave., BSN 3331, Tampa, FL 33620-5500. Internet: **http://www.fma.org**

Business and Financial Operations Occupations

Accountants and Auditors

(0*NET 13-2011.01, 13-2011.02)

Significant Points

● Most jobs require at least a bachelor's degree in accounting or a related field.

● Overall job opportunities should be favorable, although jobseekers who obtain professional recognition through certification or licensure, a master's degree, proficiency in accounting and auditing computer software, or specialized expertise will have an advantage.

● An increase in the number of businesses, changing financial laws and regulations, and increased scrutiny of company finances will drive growth of accountants and auditors.

Nature of the Work

Accountants and auditors help to ensure that the Nation's firms are run efficiently, its public records kept accurately, and its taxes paid properly and on time. They perform these vital functions by offering an increasingly wide array of business and accounting services to their clients. These services include public, management, and government accounting, as well as internal auditing. Beyond the fundamental tasks of the occupation—preparing, analyzing, and verifying financial documents in order to provide information to clients—many accountants now are required to possess a wide range of knowledge and skills. Accountants and auditors are broadening the services they offer to include budget analysis, financial and investment planning, information technology consulting, and limited legal services.

Specific job duties vary widely among the four major fields of accounting: *public, management, government, and internal.*

Public accountants perform a broad range of accounting, auditing, tax, and consulting activities for their clients, who may be corporations, governments, nonprofit organizations, or individuals. For example, some public accountants concentrate on tax matters, such as advising companies of the tax advantages and disadvantages of certain business decisions and preparing individual income tax returns. Others offer advice in areas such as compensation or employee healthcare benefits, the design of accounting and data-processing systems, and the selection of controls to safeguard assets. Still others audit clients' financial statements and report to investors and authorities that the statements have been correctly prepared and reported. Public accountants, many of whom are Certified Public Accountants (CPAs), generally have their own businesses or work for public accounting firms.

Some public accountants specialize in forensic accounting—investigating and interpreting white collar crimes such as securities fraud and embezzlement, bankruptcies and contract disputes, and other complex and possibly criminal financial transactions, such as money laundering by organized criminals. Forensic accountants combine their knowledge of accounting and finance with law and investigative techniques in order to determine if illegal activity is going on. Many forensic accountants work closely with law enforcement personnel and lawyers during investigations and often appear as expert witnesses during trials.

In response to the recent accounting scandals, new Federal legislation restricts the nonauditing services that public accountants can provide to clients. If an accounting firm audits a client's financial statements, that same firm cannot provide advice in the areas of human resources, technology, investment banking, or legal matters, although accountants may still advise on tax issues, such as establishing a tax shelter. Accountants may still advise other clients in these areas, or may provide advice within their own firm.

Management accountants—also called cost, managerial, industrial, corporate, or private accountants—record and analyze the financial information of the companies for which they work. Other responsibilities include budgeting, performance evaluation, cost management, and asset management. Usually, management accountants are part of executive teams involved in strategic planning or new-product development. They analyze and interpret the financial information that corporate executives need to make sound business decisions. They also prepare financial reports for nonmanagement groups, including stockholders, creditors, regulatory agencies, and tax authorities. Within accounting departments, they may work in various areas, including financial analysis, planning and budgeting, and cost accounting.

Government accountants and auditors work in the public sector, maintaining and examining the records of government agencies and auditing private businesses and individuals whose activities are subject to government regulations or taxation. Accountants employed by Federal, State, and local governments guarantee that revenues are received and expenditures are made in accordance with laws and regulations. Those who are employed by the Federal Government may work as Internal Revenue Service agents or in financial management, financial institution examination, or budget analysis and administration.

Internal auditors verify the accuracy of their organization's internal records and check for mismanagement, waste, or fraud. Internal auditing is an increasingly important area of accounting and auditing. Internal auditors examine and evaluate their firms' financial and information systems, management procedures, and internal controls to ensure that records are accurate and controls are adequate to protect against fraud and waste. They also review company operations—evaluating their efficiency, effectiveness, and compliance with corporate policies and procedures, laws, and government

Accountants and auditors carefully analyze financial data and prepare financial reports and tax returns for clients.

regulations. There are many types of highly specialized auditors, such as electronic data-processing, environmental, engineering, legal, insurance premium, bank, and healthcare auditors. As computer systems make information timelier, internal auditors help managers to base their decisions on actual data, rather than personal observation. Internal auditors also may recommend controls for their organization's computer system to ensure the reliability of the system and the integrity of the data.

Computers are rapidly changing the nature of the work for most accountants and auditors. With the aid of special software packages, accountants summarize transactions in standard formats for financial records and organize data in special formats for financial analysis. These accounting packages greatly reduce the amount of tedious manual work associated with data management and recordkeeping. Computers enable accountants and auditors to be more mobile and to use their clients' computer systems to extract information from databases and the Internet. As a result, a growing number of accountants and auditors with extensive computer skills specialize in correcting problems with software or in developing software to meet unique data management and analytical needs. Accountants also are beginning to perform more technical duties, such as implementing, controlling, and auditing systems and networks, and developing technology plans and budgets.

Increasingly, accountants also are assuming the role of a personal financial advisor. They not only provide clients with accounting and tax help, but also help them develop personal budgets, manage assets and investments, plan for retirement, and recognize and reduce exposure to risks. This role is a response to client demands for a single trustworthy individual or firm to meet all of their financial needs. However, accountants are restricted from providing these services to clients whose financial statements they also prepare. (See financial analysts and personal financial advisors elsewhere in the *Handbook*.)

Working Conditions

Most accountants and auditors work in a typical office setting. Self-employed accountants may be able to do part of their work at home. Accountants and auditors employed by public accounting firms and government agencies may travel frequently to perform audits at branches of their firm, clients' places of business, or government facilities.

Most accountants and auditors generally work a standard 40-hour week, but many work longer hours, particularly if they are self-employed and have numerous clients. Tax specialists often work long hours during the tax season.

Employment

Accountants and auditors held about 1.1 million jobs in 2002. They worked throughout private industry and government, but 1 out of 5 wage and salary accountants worked for accounting, tax preparation, bookkeeping, and payroll services firms. Approximately 1 out of 10 accountants or auditors were self-employed.

Many accountants and auditors are unlicensed management accountants, internal auditors, or government accountants and auditors; however, a large number are licensed Certified Public Accountants. Most accountants and auditors work in urban areas, where public accounting firms and central or regional offices of businesses are concentrated.

Some individuals with backgrounds in accounting and auditing are full-time college and university faculty; others teach part time while working as self-employed accountants or employed as accountants for private industry or government. (Elsewhere in the *Handbook* see teachers—postsecondary.)

Training, Other Qualifications, and Advancement

Most accountant and auditor positions require at least a bachelor's degree in accounting or a related field. Beginning accounting and auditing positions in the Federal Government, for example, usually require 4 years of college (including 24 semester hours in accounting or auditing) or an equivalent combination of education and experience. Some employers prefer applicants with a master's degree in accounting, or with a master's degree in business administration with a concentration in accounting.

Previous experience in accounting or auditing can help an applicant get a job. Many colleges offer students an opportunity to gain experience through summer or part-time internship programs conducted by public accounting or business firms. In addition, practical knowledge of computers and their applications in accounting and internal auditing is a great asset for jobseekers in the accounting field.

Professional recognition through certification or licensure provides a distinct advantage in the job market. CPAs are licensed by a State Board of Accountancy. The vast majority of States require CPA candidates to be college graduates, but a few States substitute a number of years of public accounting experience for a college degree. As of early 2003, based on recommendations made by the American Institute of Certified Public Accountants (AICPA), 42 States and the District of Columbia required CPA candidates to complete 150 semester hours of college coursework—an additional 30 hours beyond the usual 4-year bachelor's degree. Another five States—Arizona, Minnesota, New Mexico, New York, and Virginia—have adopted similar legislation that will become effective between 2004 and 2009. Colorado, Delaware, New Hampshire, and Vermont are the only States that do not require 150 semester hours. Many schools have altered their curricula accordingly with most programs offering masters degrees as part of the 150 hours, and prospective accounting majors should carefully research accounting curricula and the requirements of any States in which they hope to become licensed.

All States use the four-part Uniform CPA Examination prepared by the AICPA. The 2-day CPA examination is rigorous, and only about one-quarter of those who take it each year passes every part they attempt. Candidates are not required to pass all four parts at once, but most States require candidates to pass at least two parts for partial credit and to complete all four sections within a certain period. Most States also require applicants for a CPA certificate to have some accounting experience. In May 2004, the CPA exam will become computerized and offered quarterly at various testing centers throughout the United States.

The AICPA also offers members with valid CPA certificates the option to receive the Accredited in Business Valuation (ABV), Certified Information Technology Professional (CITP), or Personal Financial Specialist (PFS) designations. The addition of these designations to the CPA distinguishes those accountants with a certain level of expertise in the nontraditional areas in which accountants are practicing more frequently. The ABV designation requires a written exam, as well as completion of a minimum of 10 business valuation projects that demonstrate a candidate's experience and competence. The CITP requires payment of a fee, a written statement of intent, and the achievement of a set number of points awarded for business experience and education. Those who do not meet the required number of points may substitute a written exam. Candidates for the PFS designation also must achieve a certain level of points, based on experience and education, and must pass a written exam and submit references.

Nearly all States require CPAs and other public accountants to complete a certain number of hours of continuing professional education before their licenses can be renewed. The professional associations representing accountants sponsor numerous courses, seminars, group study programs, and other forms of continuing education.

Accountants and auditors also can seek to obtain other forms of credentials from professional societies on a voluntary basis. Voluntary certification can attest to professional competence in a specialized field of accounting and auditing. It also can certify that a recognized level of professional competence has been achieved by accountants and auditors who have acquired some skills on the job, without the formal education or public accounting work experience needed to meet the rigorous standards required to take the CPA examination.

The Institute of Management Accountants (IMA) confers the Certified Management Accountant (CMA) designation upon applicants who complete a bachelor's degree or attain a minimum score on specified graduate school entrance exams. Applicants, who must have worked at least 2 years in management accounting, also must pass a four-part examination, agree to meet continuing education requirements, and comply with standards of professional conduct. The CMA program is administered by the Institute of Certified Management Accountants, an affiliate of the IMA.

Graduates from accredited colleges and universities who have worked for 2 years as internal auditors and have passed a four-part examination may earn the Certified Internal Auditor (CIA) designation from the Institute of Internal Auditors (IIA). The IIA recently implemented three new specialty designations—Certification in Control Self—Assessment (CCSA), Certified Government Auditing Professional (CGAP), and Certified Financial Services Auditor (CFSA). Requirements are similar to those of the CIA. The Information Systems Audit and Control Association confers the Certified Information Systems Auditor (CISA) designation upon candidates who pass an examination and have 5 years of experience in auditing information systems. Auditing or data-processing experience and a college education may be substituted for up to 2 years of work experience in this program. For instance, an internal auditor might be a CPA, CIA, and CISA.

The Accreditation Council for Accountancy and Taxation, a satellite organization of the National Society of Public Accountants, confers three designations—Accredited Business Accountant (ABA), Accredited Tax Advisor (ATA), and Accredited Tax Preparer (ATP)—on accountants specializing in tax preparation for small- and medium-sized businesses. Candidates for the ABA must pass an exam, while candidates for the ATA and ATP must complete the required coursework and pass an exam. Often, a practitioner will hold multiple licenses and designations.

The Association of Government Accountants grants the Certified Government Financial Manager (CGFM) designation for accountants, auditors, and other government financial personnel at the Federal, State, and local levels. Candidates must have a minimum of a bachelor's degree, 24 hours of study in financial management, and 2 years' experience in government, and must pass a series of three exams. The exams cover topics in governmental environment; governmental accounting, financial reporting, and budgeting; and financial management and control.

Persons planning a career in accounting should have an aptitude for mathematics and be able to analyze, compare, and interpret facts and figures quickly. They must be able to clearly communicate both written and verbally the results of their work to clients and managers. Accountants and auditors must be good at working with people, as well as with business systems and computers. At a minimum, accountants should be familiar with basic accounting software packages. Because financial decisions are made based on their statements and services, accountants and auditors should have high standards of integrity.

Capable accountants and auditors may advance rapidly; those having inadequate academic preparation may be assigned routine jobs and find promotion difficult. Many graduates of junior colleges and business and correspondence schools, as well as book-keepers and accounting clerks who meet the education and experience requirements set by their employers, can obtain junior accounting positions and advance to positions with more responsibilities by demonstrating their accounting skills on the job.

Beginning public accountants usually start by assisting with work for several clients. They may advance to positions with more responsibility in 1 or 2 years, and to senior positions within another few years. Those who excel may become supervisors, managers, or partners; open their own public accounting firm; or transfer to executive positions in management accounting or internal auditing in private firms.

Management accountants often start as cost accountants, junior internal auditors, or trainees for other accounting positions. As they rise through the organization, they may advance to accounting manager, chief cost accountant, budget director, or manager of internal auditing. Some become controllers, treasurers, financial vice presidents, chief financial officers, or corporation presidents. Many senior corporation executives have a background in accounting, internal auditing, or finance.

In general, public accountants, management accountants, and internal auditors have much occupational mobility. Practitioners often shift into management accounting or internal auditing from public accounting, or between internal auditing and management accounting. However, it is less common for accountants and auditors to move from either management accounting or internal auditing into public accounting.

Job Outlook
Employment of accountants and auditors is expected to grow about as fast as the average for all occupations through the year 2012. An increase in the number of businesses, changing financial laws and regulations, and increased scrutiny of company finances will drive growth. In addition to openings resulting from growth, the need to replace accountants and auditors who retire or transfer to other occupations will produce numerous job openings in this large occupation.

As the economy grows, the number of business establishments will increase, requiring more accountants and auditors to set up books, prepare taxes, and provide management advice. As these businesses grow, the volume and complexity of information developed by accountants and auditors regarding costs, expenditures, and taxes will increase as well. Increased need for accountants and auditors will arise from changes in legislation related to taxes, financial reporting standards, business investments, mergers, and other financial matters. The growth of international business also has led to more demand for accounting expertise and services related to international trade and accounting rules, as well as to international mergers and acquisitions. These trends should create more jobs for accountants and auditors.

As a result of the recent accounting scandals, Federal legislation was enacted to increase penalties, and make company executives personally responsible for falsely reporting financial information. These changes should lead to increased scrutiny of company finances and accounting procedures, and should create opportunities for accountants and auditors, particularly Certified Public Accountants, to more thoroughly audit financial records. In order to ensure finances comply with the law before public accountants conduct au-

dits, management accountants and internal auditors will increasingly be needed to discover and eliminate fraud. And, in an effort to make government agencies more efficient and accountable, demand for government accountants should increase.

Increased awareness of financial crimes such as embezzlement, bribery, and securities fraud will also increase the demand for forensic accountants to detect illegal financial activity by individuals, companies, and organized crime rings. Computer technology has made these crimes easier to commit, and it is on the rise. But, development of new computer software and electronic surveillance technology has also made tracking down financial criminals easier, thus increasing the ease and likelihood that forensic accountants will discover their crimes. As success rates of investigations grow, demand will also grow for forensic accountants.

The changing role of accountants and auditors also will spur job growth, although this growth will be limited as a result of financial scandals. In response to demand, some accountants were offering more financial management and consulting services as they assumed a greater advisory role and developed more sophisticated accounting systems. Since Federal legislation now prohibits accountants from providing nontraditional services to clients whose books they audit, opportunities for accountants to do non-audit work could be limited. However, accountants will still be able to advise on other financial matters for clients that are not publicly traded companies, and for nonaudit clients, but growth in these areas will be slower than in the past. Also, due to the increasing popularity of tax preparation firms and computer software, accountants will shift away from tax preparation. As computer programs continue to simplify some accounting-related tasks, clerical staff will increasingly handle many routine calculations.

Overall, job opportunities for accountants and auditors should be favorable. After most States instituted the 150-hour rule for CPAs, enrollment in accounting programs declined; however, enrollment is slowly beginning to grow again as more students are attracted to the profession because of the attention from the accounting scandals. Those who pursue a CPA should have excellent job prospects. However, many accounting graduates are instead pursuing other certifications such as the CMA and CIA, so competition could be greater in management accounting and internal auditing than in public accounting. Regardless of specialty, accountants and auditors who have earned professional recognition through certification or licensure should have the best job prospects. Applicants with a master's degree in accounting, or a master's degree in business administration with a concentration in accounting, also will have an advantage. In the aftermath of the accounting scandals, professional certification is even more important in order to ensure that accountants' credentials and ethics are sound.

Proficiency in accounting and auditing computer software, or expertise in specialized areas such as international business, specific industries, or current legislation, may be helpful in landing certain accounting and auditing jobs. In addition, employers increasingly seek applicants with strong interpersonal and communication skills. Because many accountants work on teams with others from different backgrounds, they must be able to communicate accounting and financial information clearly and concisely. Regardless of one's qualifications, however, competition will remain keen for the most prestigious jobs in major accounting and business firms.

Earnings
In 2002, the median wage and salary annual earnings of accountants and auditors were $47,000. The middle half of the occupation earned between $37,210 and $61,630. The top 10 percent of accountants and auditors earned more than $82,730, and the bottom

10 percent earned less than $30,320. In 2002, median annual earnings in the industries employing the largest numbers of accountants and auditors were:

Federal Government	$51,070
Accounting, tax preparation, bookkeeping, and payroll services	49,520
Management of companies and enterprises	49,110
Local government	44,690
State government	42,680

According to a salary survey conducted by the National Association of Colleges and Employers, bachelor's degree candidates in accounting received starting offers averaging $40,647 a year in 2003; master's degree candidates in accounting were initially offered $42,241.

According to a 2003 salary survey conducted by Robert Half International, a staffing services firm specializing in accounting and finance, accountants and auditors with up to 1 year of experience earned between $29,500 and $40,500. Those with 1 to 3 years of experience earned between $34,000 and $49,500. Senior accountants and auditors earned between $41,000 and $61,500; managers earned between $47,500 and $78,750; and directors of accounting and auditing earned between $66,750 and $197,500 a year. The variation in salaries reflects differences in size of firm, location, level of education, and professional credentials.

In the Federal Government, the starting annual salary for junior accountants and auditors was $23,442 in 2003. Candidates who had a superior academic record might start at $29,037, while applicants with a master's degree or 2 years of professional experience usually began at $35,519. Beginning salaries were slightly higher in selected areas where the prevailing local pay level was higher. Accountants employed by the Federal Government in nonsupervisory, supervisory, and managerial positions averaged $69,370 a year in 2003; auditors averaged $73,247.

Related Occupations

Accountants and auditors design internal control systems and analyze financial data. Others for whom training in accounting is valuable include budget analysts; cost estimators; loan officers; financial analysts and personal financial advisors; tax examiners, collectors, and revenue agents; bill and account collectors; and bookkeeping, accounting, and auditing clerks. Recently, accountants have assumed the role of management analysts and are involved in the design, implementation, and maintenance of accounting software systems. Others who perform similar work include computer programmers, computer software engineers, and computer support specialists and systems administrators.

Sources of Additional Information

Information on accredited accounting programs can be obtained from:
➤ AACSB International—Association to Advance Collegiate Schools of Business, 600 Emerson Rd., Suite 300, St. Louis, MO 63141. Internet: http://www.aacsb.edu/accreditation/AccreditedMembers.asp

Information about careers in certified public accounting and CPA standards and examinations may be obtained from:
➤ American Institute of Certified Public Accountants, 1211 Avenue of the Americas, New York, NY 10036. Internet: http://www.aicpa.org

Information on CPA licensure requirements by State may be obtained from:
➤ National Association of State Boards of Accountancy, 150 Fourth Ave. North, Suite 700, Nashville, TN 37219-2417. Internet: http://www.nasba.org

Information on careers in management accounting and the CMA designation may be obtained from:

➤ Institute of Management Accountants, 10 Paragon Dr., Montvale, NJ 07645-1760. Internet: http://www.imanet.org

Information on the Accredited in Accountancy, Accredited Business Accountant, Accredited Tax Advisor, or Accredited Tax Preparer designations may be obtained from:
➤ Accreditation Council for Accountancy and Taxation, 1010 North Fairfax St., Alexandria, VA 22314. Internet: http://www.acatcredentials.org

Information on careers in internal auditing and the CIA designation may be obtained from:
➤ The Institute of Internal Auditors, 247 Maitland Ave., Altamonte Springs, FL 32701-4201. Internet: http://www.theiia.org

Information on careers in information systems auditing and the CISA designation may be obtained from:
➤ Information Systems Audit and Control Association, 3701 Algonquin Rd., Suite 1010, Rolling Meadows, IL 60008. Internet: http://www.isaca.org

Information on careers in government accounting and the CGFM designation may be obtained from:
➤ Association of Government Accountants, 2208 Mount Vernon Ave., Alexandria, VA 22301. Internet: http://www.agacgfm.org

Information on obtaining an accounting or auditing position with the Federal Government is available from the U.S. Office of Personnel Management (OPM) through a telephone-based system. Consult your telephone directory under U.S. Government for a local number or call (703) 724-1850; Federal Relay Service: (800) 877-8339. The first number is not tollfree, and charges may result. Information also is available from the OPM Internet site: http://www.usajobs.opm.gov.

Budget Analysts

(0*NET 13-2031.00)

Significant Points

● Almost half of all budget analysts work in Federal, State, and local governments.

● While a bachelor's degree generally is the minimum educational requirement, many employers prefer or require a master's degree.

● Competition for jobs is expected.

Nature of the Work

Deciding how to efficiently distribute limited financial resources is an important challenge in all organizations. In most large and complex organizations, this task would be nearly impossible without budget analysts. These workers play the primary role in the development, analysis, and execution of budgets, which are used to allocate current resources and estimate future financial requirements. Without effective budget analysis and feedback about budgetary problems, many private and public organizations could become bankrupt.

Budget analysts can be found in private industry, nonprofit organizations, and the public sector. In private sector firms, a budget analyst examines, analyzes, and seeks new ways to improve efficiency and increase profits. Although analysts working in nonprofit and governmental organizations usually are not concerned with profits, they still try to find the most efficient distribution of funds and other resources among various departments and programs.

Budget analysts have many responsibilities in these organizations, but their primary task is providing advice and technical assistance in the preparation of annual budgets. At the beginning of each budget cycle, managers and department heads submit proposed operational and financial plans to budget analysts for review. These plans outline prospective programs, including proposed funding increases and new initiatives, estimated costs and expenses, and capital expenditures needed to finance these programs.

Analysts examine the budget estimates or proposals for completeness, accuracy, and conformance with established procedures, regulations, and organizational objectives. Sometimes, they employ cost-benefit analysis to review financial requests, assess program tradeoffs, and explore alternative funding methods. They also examine past and current budgets and research economic and financial developments that affect the organization's spending. This process enables analysts to evaluate proposals in terms of the organization's priorities and financial resources.

After this initial review process, budget analysts consolidate the individual departmental budgets into operating and capital budget summaries. These summaries contain comments and statements that support or argue against funding requests. Budget summaries then are submitted to senior management or, as is often the case in local and State governments, to appointed or elected officials. Budget analysts then help the chief operating officer, agency head, or other top managers analyze the proposed plan and devise possible alternatives if the projected results are unsatisfactory. The final decision to approve the budget, however, usually is made by the organization head in a private firm or by elected officials, such as the State legislative body, in government.

Throughout the remainder of the year, analysts periodically monitor the budget by reviewing reports and accounting records to determine if allocated funds have been spent as specified. If deviations appear between the approved budget and actual performance, budget analysts may write a report providing reasons for the variations, along with recommendations for new or revised budget procedures. In order to avoid or alleviate deficits, they may recommend program cuts or reallocation of excess funds. They also inform program managers and others within their organization of the status and availability of funds in different budget accounts. Before any changes are made to an existing program or a new one is implemented, a budget analyst assesses the program's efficiency and effectiveness. Analysts also may be involved in long-range planning activities such as projecting future budget needs.

The amount of data and information that budget analysts are able to analyze has greatly increased through the use of computerized financial software programs. The analysts also make extensive use of spreadsheet, database, and word processing software.

Almost half of all budget analysts work in Federal, State, and local governments.

Budget analysts have seen their role broadened as limited funding has led to downsizing and restructuring throughout private industry and government. Not only do they develop guidelines and policies governing the formulation and maintenance of the budget, but they also measure organizational performance, assess the effects of various programs and policies on the budget, and help to draft budget-related legislation. In addition, budget analysts sometimes conduct training sessions for company or government agency personnel regarding new budget procedures.

Working Conditions
Budget analysts usually work in a comfortable office setting. Long hours are common among these workers, especially during the initial development and midyear and final reviews of budgets. The pressure of deadlines and tight work schedules during these periods can be stressful, and analysts usually are required to work more than the routine 40 hours a week.

Budget analysts spend the majority of their time working independently, compiling and analyzing data, and preparing budget proposals. Nevertheless, their schedule sometimes is interrupted by special budget requests, meetings, and training sessions. Some budget analysts travel to obtain budget details and explanations of various programs from coworkers, or to personally observe funding allocation.

Employment
Budget analysts held 62,000 jobs throughout private industry and government in 2002. Federal, State, and local governments are major employers, accounting for 46 percent of budget analyst jobs. About 1 in 5 worked for the Federal government. Many other budget analysts worked in manufacturing, financial services, or management services. Other major employers include schools and hospitals.

Training, Other Qualifications, and Advancement
Private firms and government agencies generally require candidates for budget analyst positions to have at least a bachelor's degree, but many prefer or require a master's degree. Within the Federal Government, a bachelor's degree in any field is sufficient for an entry-level budget analyst position, but, again, those with master's degrees are preferred. State and local governments have varying requirements, but a bachelor's degree in one of many areas—accounting, finance, business or public administration, economics, political science, statistics, or a social science such as sociology—may qualify one for entry into the occupation. Many States, especially larger, more urban States, require a master's degree. Sometimes, a degree in a field closely related to that of the employing industry or organization, such as engineering, may be preferred. Some firms prefer candidates with a degree in business because business courses emphasize quantitative and analytical skills. Many government employers prefer candidates with strong analytic and policy analysis backgrounds that may be obtained through such majors as political science, economics, public administration, or public finance. Occasionally, budget-related or finance-related work experience can be substituted for formal education.

Because developing a budget involves manipulating numbers and requires strong analytical skills, courses in statistics or accounting are helpful, regardless of the prospective budget analyst's major field of study. Financial analysis is automated in almost every organization and, therefore, familiarity with word processing and the financial software packages used in budget analysis often is required. Software packages commonly used by budget analysts include electronic spreadsheet, database, and graphics software.

Employers usually prefer job candidates who already possess these computer skills.

In addition to analytical and computer skills, those seeking a career as a budget analyst must be able to work under strict time constraints. Strong oral and written communication skills are essential for analysts because they must prepare, present, and defend budget proposals to decision makers.

Entry-level budget analysts may receive some formal training when they begin their jobs, but most employers feel that the best training is obtained by working through one complete budget cycle. During the cycle, which typically is 1 year, analysts become familiar with the various steps involved in the budgeting process. The Federal Government, on the other hand, offers extensive on-the-job and classroom training for entry-level trainees. In addition to on-the-job training, budget analysts are encouraged to participate in the various classes offered throughout their careers.

Some government budget analysts employed at the Federal, State, or local level may earn the Certified Government Financial Manager (CGFM) designation granted by the Association of Government Accountants. Other government financial officers also may earn this designation. Candidates must have a minimum of a bachelor's degree, 24 hours of study in financial management, and 2 years of experience in government, and must pass a series of three exams. The exams cover topics on the organization and structure of government; governmental accounting, financial reporting and budgeting; and financial management and control.

Budget analysts start their careers with limited responsibilities. In the Federal Government, for example, beginning budget analysts compare projected costs with prior expenditures, consolidate and enter data prepared by others, and assist higher grade analysts by doing research. As analysts progress in their careers, they begin to develop and formulate budget estimates and justification statements, perform indepth analyses of budget requests, write statements supporting funding requests, advise program managers and others on the status and availability of funds for different budget activities, and present and defend budget proposals to senior managers.

Beginning analysts usually work under close supervision. Capable entry-level analysts can be promoted into intermediate-level positions within 1 to 2 years, and then into senior positions within a few more years. Progressing to a higher level means added budgetary responsibility and can lead to a supervisory role. Because of the importance and high visibility of their jobs, senior budget analysts are prime candidates for promotion to management positions in various parts of the organization.

Job Outlook

Competition for budget analyst jobs is expected over the 2002-12 projection period. Candidates with a master's degree should have the best job opportunities. Familiarity with computer financial software packages also should enhance a jobseeker's employment prospects.

Employment of budget analysts is expected to grow about as fast as the average for all occupations through 2012. Employment growth will be driven by the continuing demand for sound financial analysis in both public and private sector organizations. In addition to employment growth, many job openings will result from the need to replace experienced budget analysts who transfer to other occupations or leave the labor force.

The expanding use of computer applications in budget analysis increases worker productivity by enabling analysts to process more data in less time. However, because budget analysts now have much more data available to them, their jobs are becoming more complicated. In addition, as businesses and other organizations become more complex and specialized, budget planning and financial control will demand greater attention. These factors should offset any adverse effects of computer applications on employment of budget analysts.

In coming years, all types of organizations will continue to rely heavily on budget analysts to examine, analyze, and develop budgets. Because of the importance of financial analysis performed by budget analysts, employment of these workers has remained relatively unaffected by downsizing in the Nation's workplaces. In addition, because financial and budget reports must be completed during both periods of economic growth and slowdowns, budget analysts usually are less subject to layoffs than are many other workers during economic downturns.

Earnings

Salaries of budget analysts vary widely by experience, education, and employer. Median annual earnings of budget analysts in 2002 were $52,480. The middle 50 percent earned between $42,000 and $66,180. The lowest 10 percent earned less than $34,580, and the highest 10 percent earned more than $82,720.

According to a 2002 survey conducted by Robert Half International—a staffing services firm specializing in accounting and finance—starting salaries of financial, budget, treasury, and cost analysts in small companies ranged from $29,750 to $36,250. In large companies, starting salaries ranged from $33,500 to $41,250.

In the Federal Government, budget analysts usually started as trainees earning $23,442 or $29,037 a year in 2003. Candidates with a master's degree might begin at $35,519. Beginning salaries were slightly higher in selected areas where the prevailing local pay level was higher. The average annual salary in 2003 for budget analysts employed by the Federal Government in nonsupervisory, supervisory, and managerial positions was $62,400.

Related Occupations

Budget analysts review, analyze, and interpret financial data; make recommendations for the future; and assist in the implementation of new ideas and financial strategies. Other workers who have similar duties include accountants and auditors, cost estimators, economists, financial analysts and personal financial advisors, financial managers, loan counselors and officers, and management analysts.

Sources of Additional Information

Information about career opportunities as a budget analyst may be available from your State or local employment service.

Information on careers in government financial management and the CGFM designation may be obtained from:

➤ Association of Government Accountants, 2208 Mount Vernon Ave., Alexandria, VA 22301. Internet: **http://www.agacgfm.org**

Information on careers in budget analysis at the State government level may be obtained from:

➤ National Association of State Budget Officers, Hall of the States Building, Suite 642, 444 North Capitol St. NW., Washington, DC 20001. Internet: **http://www.nasbo.org**

Information on obtaining a budget analyst position with the Federal Government is available from the U.S. Office of Personnel Management (OPM) through a telephone-based system. Consult your telephone directory under U.S. Government for a local number or call (703) 724-1850; Federal Relay Service: (800) 877-8339. The first number is not tollfree, and charges may result. Information also is available from the OPM Internet site: **http://www.usajobs.opm.gov**.

Claims Adjusters, Appraisers, Examiners, and Investigators

(0*NET 13-1031.01, 13-1031.02, 13-1032.00)

Significant Points

- Adjusters and examiners investigate insurance claims, negotiate settlements, and authorize payments; investigators deal with claims where there is a question of liability and where fraud or criminal activity is suspected.

- Most employers prefer to hire college graduates.

- Competition will be keen for jobs as investigators, because this occupation attracts many qualified people.

Nature of the Work

Individuals and businesses purchase insurance policies to protect against monetary losses. In the event of a loss, policyholders submit claims, or requests for payment, as compensation for their loss. Adjusters, examiners, and investigators work primarily for property and casualty insurance companies, for whom they handle a wide variety of claims for property damage, liability, and bodily injury. Their main role is to investigate the claims, negotiate settlements, and authorize payments to claimants, but they must always be mindful not to violate the claimant's rights under Federal and State privacy laws. They must determine whether the customer's insurance policy covers the loss and how much of the loss should be paid to the claimant. Although many adjusters, appraisers, examiners, and investigators have overlapping functions and may even perform the same job, the insurance industry generally assigns specific roles to each of these claims workers.

Adjusters plan and schedule the work required to process a claim that would follow, for example, an automobile accident or damage to one's home caused by a storm. They investigate claims by interviewing the claimant and witnesses, consulting police and hospital records, and inspecting property damage to determine the extent of the company's liability. Adjusters may also consult with other professionals, such as accountants, architects, construction workers, engineers, lawyers, and physicians, who can offer a more expert evaluation of a claim. The information gathered, including photographs and written or taped statements, is set down in a report that is then used to evaluate a claim. When the policyholder's claim is legitimate, the claims adjuster negotiates with the claimant and settles the claim. When claims are contested, adjusters will work with attorneys and expert witnesses to defend the insurer's position.

Many companies centralize the claims-adjusting operation in a claims center, where the cost of repair is determined and a check is issued immediately. More complex cases, usually involving bodily injury, are referred to senior adjusters. Some adjusters work with multiple types of insurance; however, most specialize in homeowner claims, business losses, automotive damage, or workers' compensation.

Claimants can opt not to rely on the services of their insurance company's adjuster and may instead choose to hire a public adjuster. Public adjusters assist clients in preparing and presenting claims to insurance companies and try to negotiate a fair settlement. They perform the same services as adjusters who work directly for companies; however, they work in the best interests of the client, rather than the insurance company.

Claims examiners within property and casualty insurance firms may have duties similar to those of an adjuster, but often their pri-

mary job is to review the claims submitted to ensure that proper guidelines have been followed. They may assist adjusters with complex and complicated claims or when a disaster suddenly greatly increases the volume of claims. Most claims examiners work for life or health insurance companies. In health insurance companies, examiners review health-related claims to see whether costs are reasonable based on the diagnosis. The examiners are provided with guides that supply information on the average period of disability, the expected treatments, and the average hospital stay, for patients with the various ailments for which a claim may be submitted. Examiners check claim applications for completeness and accuracy, interview medical specialists, and consult policy files to verify the information reported in a claim. Examiners will then either authorize the appropriate payment or refer the claim to an investigator for a more thorough review. Claims examiners usually specialize in group or individual insurance plans and in hospital, dental, or prescription drug claims.

In life insurance, claims examiners review the causes of death, particularly in the case of an accident, because most life insurance policies pay additional benefits if a death is accidental. Claims examiners also may review new applications for life insurance to make sure that applicants have no serious illnesses that would make them a high risk to insure and thus disqualify them from obtaining insurance.

Another occupation that plays an important role in the accurate settlement of claims is that of the *appraiser*, whose role is to assess the cost or value of an insured item. The majority of appraisers employed by insurance companies and independent adjusting firms are *auto damage appraisers*. These appraisers inspect damaged vehicles after an accident and estimate the cost of repairs. This information is then relayed to the adjuster, who incorporates the appraisal into the settlement. Auto damage appraisers are valued by insurance companies because they can provide an unbiased judgment of repair costs. Otherwise, the companies would have to rely on auto mechanics' estimates, which might be unreasonably high.

Many claims adjusters and auto damage appraisers are equipped with laptop computers from which they can download the necessary forms and files from insurance company databases. Many adjusters and appraisers use digital cameras, which allow photographs of the damage to be sent to the company via the Internet. Many also input information about the damage directly into their computers, where software programs produce estimates of damage on standard forms. These new technologies allow for faster and more efficient processing of claims.

When adjusters or examiners suspect fraud, they refer the claim to an investigator. *Insurance investigators* in an insurance company's Special Investigative Unit handle claims in which a company suspects fraudulent or criminal activity, such as arson cases, false workers' disability claims, staged accidents, or unnecessary medical treatments. The severity of insurance fraud cases can vary greatly, from claimants simply overstating the damage to a vehicle to complicated fraud rings responsible for many claimants supported by dishonest doctors, lawyers, and even insurance personnel.

Investigators usually start with a database search to obtain background information on claimants and witnesses. Investigators can access certain personal information and identify Social Security numbers, aliases, driver's license numbers, addresses, phone numbers, criminal records, and past claims histories to establish whether a claimant has ever attempted insurance fraud. Then, investigators may visit claimants and witnesses to obtain a recorded statement, take photographs, and inspect facilities, such as a doctor's office, to determine whether they have a proper license. Investigators often consult with legal counsel and can be expert witnesses in court cases.

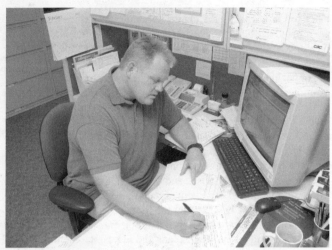

Claims adjusters, appraisers, examiners, and investigators gather facts related to insurance claims.

Often, investigators also perform surveillance work. For example, in a case involving fraudulent workers' compensation claims, an investigator may covertly observe the claimant for several days or even weeks. If the investigator observes the subject performing an activity that is ruled out by injuries stated in a workers' compensation claim, the investigator would take video or still photographs to document the activity and report it to the insurance company.

Working Conditions

Working environments of claims adjusters, appraisers, examiners, and investigators vary greatly. Most claims examiners employed by life and health insurance companies work a standard 5-day, 40-hour week in a typical office environment. Many claims adjusters and auto damage appraisers, however, often work outside the office, inspecting damaged buildings and automobiles. Adjusters who inspect damaged buildings must be wary of potential hazards such as collapsed roofs and floors, as well as weakened structures.

In general, adjusters are able to arrange their work schedules to accommodate evening and weekend appointments with clients. This accommodation sometimes results in adjusters working irregular schedules or more than 40 hours a week, especially when there are a lot of claims. Some report to the office every morning to get their assignments, while others simply call in from home and spend their days traveling to claim sites. New technology, such as laptop computers and cellular telephones, is making telecommuting easier for claims adjusters and auto damage appraisers. Many adjusters work inside their office only a few hours a week, while others conduct their business entirely out of their home and automobile. Occasionally, experienced adjusters must be away from home for days—for example, when they travel to the scene of a disaster such as a tornado, hurricane, or flood—to work with local adjusters and government officials. Adjusters often are called to work in the event of such emergencies and may have to work 50 or 60 hours a week until all claims are resolved.

Insurance investigators often work irregular hours because of the need to conduct surveillance and contact people who are not available during normal working hours. Early morning, evening, and weekend work is common. Some days, investigators will spend all day in the office doing database searches, making telephone calls, and writing reports. Other times, they may be away performing surveillance activities or interviewing witnesses. Some of the work can involve confrontation with claimants and others involved in a case, so the job can be stressful and dangerous.

Employment

Adjusters, appraisers, examiners, and investigators held about 241,000 jobs in 2002. Of these, more than 14,000 were jobs held by auto damage insurance appraisers. Insurance carriers employed nearly 60 percent of claims adjusters, appraisers, examiners, and investigators; more than 20 percent were employed by insurance agencies and brokerages, and private claims adjusting companies. Around 2 percent of adjusters, appraisers, examiners, and investigators were self-employed.

Training, Other Qualifications, and Advancement

Training and entry requirements vary widely for claims adjusters, appraisers, examiners, and investigators. Although many in these occupations do not have a college degree, most companies prefer to hire college graduates. No specific college major is recommended, but a variety of backgrounds can be an asset. A claims adjuster, for example, who has a business or an accounting background might specialize in claims of financial loss due to strikes, equipment breakdowns, or damage to merchandise. College training in architecture or engineering is helpful in adjusting industrial claims, such as those involving damage from fires or other accidents. Some claims adjusters and examiners apply expertise acquired through specialized professional training to adjust claims. A legal background can be beneficial to someone handling workers' compensation and product liability cases. A medical background is useful for those examiners working on medical and life insurance claims.

Because they often work closely with claimants, witnesses, and other insurance professionals, claims adjusters and examiners must be able to communicate effectively with others. Knowledge of computer applications also is extremely important. In addition, a valid driver's license and a good driving record are required for workers for whom travel is an important aspect of their job. Some companies require applicants to pass a series of written aptitude tests designed to measure communication, analytical, and general mathematical skills.

Licensing requirements for these workers vary by State. Some States have very few requirements, while others require the completion of prelicensing education or a satisfactory score on a licensing exam. Completion of the requirements to earn a voluntary professional designation may in some cases be substituted for the exam requirement. In some States, claims adjusters employed by insurance companies can work under the company license and need not become licensed themselves. Separate or additional requirements may apply for public adjusters. For example, some States require public adjusters to file a surety bond.

Continuing education (CE) in claims is very important for claims adjusters, appraisers, examiners, and investigators because new Federal and State laws and court decisions frequently affect how claims are handled or who is covered by insurance policies. Also, examiners working on life and health claims must be familiar with new medical procedures and prescription drugs. Some States that require licensing also require a certain number of CE credits per year in order to renew the license. These credits can be obtained from a number of sources. Many companies offer training sessions to inform their employees of industry changes. Many schools and associations give courses and seminars on various topics having to with claims. Correspondence courses via the Internet are making long-distance learning possible. Workers also can earn CE credits by writing articles for claims publications or by giving lectures and presentations. In addition, many adjusters and examiners choose to earn professional certifications and designations for independent recognition of their professional expertise. Although requirements for these designations vary, many entail at least 5 to 10 years' experience in the claims field and passing examinations; in addition, a certain number of CE credits must be earned each year to retain the designation.

For auto damage appraiser jobs, insurance companies and independent adjusting firms typically prefer to hire persons with experience as an estimator or manager of an auto-body repair shop. An appraiser must know how to repair vehicles in order to identify and estimate damage, and technical skills are essential. While auto damage appraisers do not require a college education, most companies prefer to hire persons with formal training. Many vocational colleges offer 2-year programs in auto-body repair on how to estimate and repair damaged vehicles. Some States require auto damage appraisers to be licensed, and certification also may be required or preferred. Basic computer skills are an important qualification for many auto damage appraiser positions. As with adjusters and examiners, continuing education is important because of the continual introduction of new car models and repair techniques.

Most insurance companies prefer to hire former law enforcement officers or private investigators as insurance investigators. Many experienced claims adjusters or examiners also become investigators. Licensing requirements vary among States. Most employers look for individuals with ingenuity who are persistent and assertive. Investigators should not be afraid of confrontation, should communicate well, and should be able to think on their feet. Good interviewing and interrogation skills also are important and usually are acquired in earlier careers in law enforcement.

Beginning claims adjusters, appraisers, examiners, and investigators work on small claims under the supervision of an experienced worker. As they learn more about claims investigation and settlement, they are assigned larger, more complex claims. Trainees are promoted as they demonstrate competence in handling assignments and progress in their coursework. Employees who demonstrate competence in claims work or administrative skills may be promoted to more responsible managerial or administrative jobs. Similarly, claims investigators may rise to supervisor or manager of the investigations department. Once they achieve a certain level of expertise, many choose to start their own independent adjusting or auto damage appraising firms.

Job Outlook

Employment of claims adjusters, appraisers, examiners, and investigators is expected to grow about as fast as the average for all occupations over the 2002-12 period. Opportunities will be best for those with a college degree. Numerous job openings also will result from the need to replace workers who transfer to other occupations or leave the labor force.

Many insurance carriers are downsizing their claims staff in an effort to contain costs. Larger companies are relying more on customer service representatives in call centers to handle the recording of the necessary details of the claim, allowing adjusters to spend more of their time investigating claims. New technology also is reducing the amount of time it takes for an adjuster to complete a claim, thereby increasing the number of claims that one adjuster can handle. However, as long as more insurance policies are being sold to accommodate a growing population, there will be a need for adjusters, appraisers, examiners, and investigators. Further, as the elderly population increases, there will be a greater need for healthcare, resulting in more claims.

Despite recent gains in productivity resulting from technological advances, these jobs are not easily automated. Adjusters still are needed to contact policyholders, inspect damaged property, and consult with experts. Although the number of claims in litigation and the number and complexity of insurance fraud cases are ex-

pected to increase over the next decade, demand for insurance investigators is not expected to grow significantly, because technology such as the Internet, which reduces the amount of time it takes to perform background checks, will allow investigators to handle more cases. Competition for investigator jobs will remain keen because the occupation attracts many qualified people, including retirees from law enforcement and military careers, as well as experienced claims adjusters and examiners who choose to get their investigator license.

As with claims adjusters, examiners, and investigators, employment of auto damage appraisers should grow about as fast as the average for all occupations. Insurance companies and agents continue to sell growing numbers of auto insurance policies, leading to more claims being filed that require the attention of an auto damage appraiser. The work of this occupation is not easily automated, because most appraisals require an on-site inspection. However, employment growth will be limited by industry downsizing and the implementation of new technology that is making auto damage appraisers more efficient. In addition, some insurance companies are opening their own repair facilities, which may reduce the need for auto damage appraisers.

Earnings

Earnings of claims adjusters, examiners, and investigators vary significantly. Median annual earnings were $43,020 in 2002. The middle 50 percent earned between $ 33,120 and $ 56,170. The lowest 10 percent earned less than $ 26,680, and the highest 10 percent earned more than $ 71,350.

Many claims adjusters, especially those who work for insurance companies, receive additional bonuses or benefits as part of their job. Adjusters often are furnished a laptop computer, a cellular telephone, and a company car or are reimbursed for the use of their own vehicle for business purposes.

Median annual earnings of auto damage insurance appraisers were $42,630 in 2002. The middle 50 percent earned between $34,570 and $52,360. The lowest 10 percent earned less than $27,410, and the highest 10 percent earned more than $60,470.

Related Occupations

Property-casualty insurance adjusters and life and health insurance examiners must determine the validity of a claim and negotiate a settlement. They also are responsible for determining how much to reimburse the client. Occupations similar to those of claims adjusters, appraisers, examiners, and investigators include cost estimators; bill and account collectors; medical records and health information technicians; billing and posting clerks; and credit authorizers, checkers, and clerks, as well as bookkeeping, accounting, and auditing clerks.

In determining the validity of a claim, insurance adjusters must inspect the damage in order to assess the magnitude of the loss. Workers who perform similar duties include fire inspectors and investigators and construction and building inspectors.

To ensure that company practices and procedures are followed, property and casualty examiners review insurance claims to which a claims adjuster has already proposed a settlement. Others in occupations that review documents for accuracy and compliance with a given set of rules and regulations are tax examiners and revenue agents, as well as accountants and auditors.

Insurance investigators detect and investigate fraudulent claims and criminal activity. Their work is similar to that of private detectives and investigators.

Like automotive body and related repairers and automotive service technicians and mechanics, auto damage appraisers must be familiar with the structure and functions of various automobiles and their parts.

Sources of Additional Information

General information about a career as a claims adjuster, an appraiser, an examiner, or an investigator is available from the home offices of many life, health, and property and casualty insurance companies.

Information about licensing requirements for claims adjusters may be obtained from the department of insurance in each State.

For information about professional designation and training programs, contact:

➤ Insurance Institute of America, 720 Providence Rd., P.O. Box 3016, Malvern, PA 19355-0716. Internet: **http://www.aicpcu.org**

➤ The American College, 270 South Bryn Mawr Ave., Bryn Mawr, PA 19010-2196. Internet: **http://www.amercoll.edu**

➤ International Claim Association, 1255 23rd St., NW., Washington, DC 20037. Internet: **http://www.claim.org**

Information on careers in auto damage appraising can be obtained from

➤ Independent Automotive Damage Appraisers Association, P.O. Box 12291 Columbus, GA 31917-2291. Internet: **http://www.iada.org**

Cost Estimators

(0*NET 13-1051.00)

Significant Points

● Over half work in the construction industry and another 20 percent are employed in manufacturing industries.

● Growth of the construction industry will be the driving force behind the demand for cost estimators.

● In construction and manufacturing, job prospects should be best for those with industry work experience and a bachelor's degree in a related field.

Nature of the Work

Accurately forecasting the cost of future projects is vital to the survival of any business. Cost estimators develop the cost information that business owners or managers need to make a bid for a contract or to determine if a proposed new product will be profitable. They also determine which endeavors are making a profit.

Regardless of the industry in which they work, estimators compile and analyze data on all of the factors that can influence costs—such as materials, labor, location, and special machinery requirements, including computer hardware and software. Job duties vary widely depending on the type and size of the project.

The methods of and motivations for estimating costs can differ greatly by industry. On a construction project, for example, the estimating process begins with the decision to submit a bid. After reviewing various preliminary drawings and specifications, the estimator visits the site of the proposed project. The estimator needs to gather information on access to the site and availability of electricity, water, and other services, as well as on surface topography and drainage. The information developed during the site visit usually is recorded in a signed report that is included in the final project estimate.

After the site visit is completed, the estimator determines the quantity of materials and labor the firm will need to furnish. This process, called the quantity survey or "takeoff," involves completing standard estimating forms, filling in dimensions, number of units, and other information. A cost estimator working for a general contractor, for example, will estimate the costs of all items the contractor must provide. Although subcontractors will estimate their costs as part of their own bidding process, the general contractor's cost estimator often analyzes bids made by subcontractors as well. Also during the takeoff process, the estimator must make decisions concerning equipment needs, sequence of operations, crew size, and physical constraints at the site. Allowances for the waste of materials, inclement weather, shipping delays, and other factors that may increase costs also must be incorporated in the estimate.

On completion of the quantity surveys, the estimator prepares a cost summary for the entire project, including the costs of labor, equipment, materials, subcontracts, overhead, taxes, insurance, markup, and any other costs that may affect the project. The chief estimator then prepares the bid proposal for submission to the owner.

Construction cost estimators also may be employed by the project's architect or owner to estimate costs or to track actual costs relative to bid specifications as the project develops. In large construction companies employing more than one estimator, it is common practice for estimators to specialize. For example, one may estimate only electrical work and another may concentrate on excavation, concrete, and forms.

In manufacturing and other firms, cost estimators usually are assigned to the engineering, cost, or pricing departments. The estimators' goal in manufacturing is to accurately estimate the costs associated with making products. The job may begin when management requests an estimate of the costs associated with a major redesign of an existing product or the development of a new product or production process. When estimating the cost of developing a new product, for example, the estimator works with engineers, first reviewing blueprints or conceptual drawings to determine the machining operations, tools, gauges, and materials that would be required for the job. The estimator then prepares a parts list and determines whether it is more efficient to produce or to purchase the parts. To do this, the estimator must initiate inquiries for price information from potential suppliers. The next step is to determine the cost of manufacturing each component of the product. Some high-technology products require a tremendous amount of computer programming during the design phase. The cost of software development is one of the fastest growing and most difficult activities to estimate. Some cost estimators now specialize in estimating only computer software development and related costs.

The cost estimator then prepares time-phase charts and learning curves. Time-phase charts indicate the time required for tool design and fabrication, tool "debugging"—finding and correcting all problems—manufacturing of parts, assembly, and testing. Learning curves graphically represent the rate at which performance improves with practice. These curves are commonly called "cost reduction" curves because many problems—such as engineering changes, rework, parts shortages, and lack of operator skills—diminish as the number of parts produced increases, resulting in lower unit costs.

Using all of this information, the estimator then calculates the standard labor hours necessary to produce a predetermined number of units. Standard labor hours are then converted to dollar values, to which are added factors for waste, overhead, and profit to yield the unit cost in dollars. The estimator then compares the cost of purchasing parts with the firm's cost of manufacturing them to determine which is cheaper.

Computers play an integral role in cost estimation because estimating often involves complex mathematical calculations and requires advanced mathematical techniques. For example, to undertake a parametric analysis (a process used to estimate project costs

Although estimators normally work a 40-hour week, overtime is common. Cost estimators often work under pressure and stress, especially when facing bid deadlines. Inaccurate estimating can cause a firm to lose out on a bid or to lose money on a job that was not accurately estimated.

Employment

Cost estimators held about 188,000 jobs in 2002. About 53 percent were in the construction industry, and another 20 percent were in manufacturing industries. The remainder worked in a wide range of other industries.

Cost estimators work throughout the country, usually in or near major industrial, commercial, and government centers, and in cities and suburban areas undergoing rapid change or development.

Training, Other Qualifications, and Advancement

Job entry requirements for cost estimators vary by industry. In the construction industry, employers increasingly prefer individuals with a degree in building construction, construction management, construction science, engineering, or architecture. However, most construction estimators also have considerable construction experience, gained through work in the industry, internships, or cooperative education programs. Applicants with a thorough knowledge of construction materials, costs, and procedures in areas ranging from heavy construction to electrical work, plumbing systems, or masonry work have a competitive edge.

In manufacturing industries, employers prefer to hire individuals with a degree in engineering, physical science, operations research, mathematics, or statistics; or in accounting, finance, business, economics, or a related subject. In most industries, great emphasis is placed on experience involving quantitative techniques.

Cost estimators should have an aptitude for mathematics, be able to quickly analyze, compare, and interpret detailed and sometimes poorly defined information, and be able to make sound and accurate judgments based on this knowledge. Assertiveness and self-confidence in presenting and supporting their conclusions are important, as are strong communications and interpersonal skills, because estimators may work as part of a project team alongside managers, owners, engineers, and design professionals. Cost estimators also need knowledge of computers, including word-processing and spreadsheet packages. In some instances, familiarity with special estimation software or programming skills also may be required.

Regardless of their background, estimators receive much training on the job because every company has its own way of handling estimates. Working with an experienced estimator, they become familiar with each step in the process. Those with no experience reading construction specifications or blueprints first learn that aspect of the work. They then may accompany an experienced estimator to the construction site or shop floor, where they observe the work being done, take measurements, or perform other routine tasks. As they become more knowledgeable, estimators learn how to tabulate quantities and dimensions from drawings and how to select the appropriate material prices.

For most estimators, advancement takes the form of higher pay and prestige. Some move into management positions, such as project manager for a construction firm or manager of the industrial engineering department for a manufacturer. Others may go into business for themselves as consultants, providing estimating services for a fee to government or to construction or manufacturing firms.

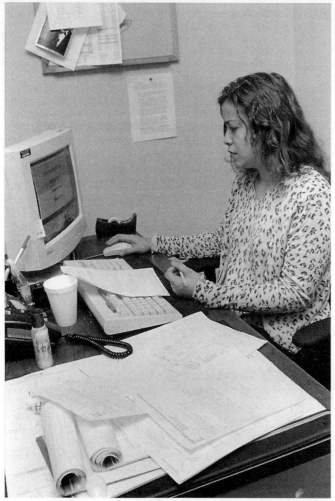

Cost estimators develop and analyze data on factors that influence costs in order to determine whether a proposed new product or contract will be profitable.

on a per unit basis, subject to the specific requirements of a project), cost estimators use a computer database containing information on costs and conditions of many other similar projects. Although computers cannot be used for the entire estimating process, they can relieve estimators of much of the drudgery associated with routine, repetitive, and time-consuming calculations. Computers also are used to produce all of the necessary documentation with the help of word-processing and spreadsheet software, leaving estimators more time to study and analyze projects.

Operations research, production control, cost, and price analysts who work for government agencies may do significant amounts of cost estimating in the course of their regular duties. In addition, the duties of construction managers also may include estimating costs. (For more information, see the statements on operations research analysts and construction managers elsewhere in the *Handbook*.)

Working Conditions

Although estimators spend most of their time in an office, construction estimators must make visits to project worksites that can be dusty, dirty, and occasionally hazardous. Likewise, estimators in manufacturing must spend time on the factory floor where it also can be noisy and dirty. In some industries, frequent travel between a firm's headquarters and its subsidiaries or subcontractors may be required.

Many colleges and universities include cost estimating as part of bachelor's and associate degree curriculums in civil engineering, industrial engineering, and construction management or construction engineering technology. In addition, cost estimating is a significant part of many master's degree programs in construction science or construction management. Organizations representing cost estimators, such as the Association for the Advancement of Cost Engineering (AACE International) and the Society of Cost Estimating and Analysis (SCEA), also sponsor educational and professional development programs. These programs help students, estimators-in-training, and experienced estimators stay abreast of changes affecting the profession. Specialized courses and programs in cost estimating techniques and procedures also are offered by many technical schools, community colleges, and universities.

Voluntary certification can be valuable to cost estimators because it provides professional recognition of the estimator's competence and experience. In some instances, individual employers may even require professional certification for employment. Both AACE International and SCEA administer certification programs. To become certified, estimators usually must have between 2 and 8 years of estimating experience and must pass an examination. In addition, certification requirements may include publication of at least one article or paper in the field.

Job Outlook

Overall employment of cost estimators is expected to grow about as fast as the average for all occupations through the year 2012. In addition to openings created by growth, some job openings will arise from the need to replace workers who transfer to other occupations or leave the labor force. In construction and manufacturing—the primary employers of cost estimators—job prospects should be best for those with industry work experience and a bachelor's degree in a related field.

Growth of the construction industry, in which 53 percent of all cost estimators are employed, will be the driving force behind the demand for these workers. Construction and repair of highways, streets, and bridges, as well as construction of more subway systems, airports, water and sewage systems, and electric power plants and transmission lines, will stimulate demand for many more cost estimators. The increasing population and its changing demographics that will boost the demand for residential construction and remodeling also will spur demand for cost estimators. As the population ages, the demand for nursing and extended care facilities will increase. School construction and repair also will add to the demand for cost estimators. Job prospects in construction should be best for cost estimators with a degree in construction management or construction science, engineering, or architecture, and who have practical experience in various phases of construction or in a specialty craft area.

Employment of cost estimators in manufacturing will also grow, but not as fast as in construction as firms continue to use their services to identify and control operating costs. Experienced estimators with degrees in engineering, science, mathematics, business administration, or economics should have the best job prospects in manufacturing.

Earnings

Salaries of cost estimators vary widely by experience, education, size of firm, and industry. Median annual earnings of cost estimators in 2002 were $47,550. The middle 50 percent earned between $36,440 and $62,040. The lowest 10 percent earned less than $28,670, and the highest 10 percent earned more than $79,240.

Median annual earnings in the industries employing the largest numbers of cost estimators in 2002 were:

Nonresidential building construction	$53,820
Building equipment contractors	50,240
Foundation, structure, and building exterior contractors	47,630
Residential building construction	47,180
Building finishing contractors	45,630

College graduates with degrees in fields that provide a strong background in cost estimating, such as engineering or construction management, could start at a higher level. According to a 2003 salary survey by the National Association of Colleges and Employers, bachelor's degree candidates with degrees in construction science/management received job offers averaging $42,229 a year.

Related Occupations

Other workers who quantitatively analyze information include accountants and auditors; budget analysts; claims adjusters, appraisers, examiners, and investigators; economists; financial analysts and personal financial advisors; insurance underwriters; loan counselors and officers; market and survey researchers; and operations research analysts. In addition, the duties of industrial production managers and construction managers also may involve analyzing costs.

Sources of Additional Information

Information about career opportunities, certification, educational programs, and cost estimating techniques may be obtained from:
➤ Association for the Advancement of Cost Engineering (AACE International), 209 Prairie Ave., Suite 100, Morgantown, WV 26501. Internet: **http://www.aacei.org**
➤ Society of Cost Estimating and Analysis, 101 S. Whiting St., Suite 201, Alexandria, VA 22304. Internet: **http://www.sceaonline.net**

Financial Analysts and Personal Financial Advisors

(O*NET 13-2051.00, 13-2052.00)

Significant Points

- A college degree and good interpersonal skills are among the most important qualifications for these workers.

- Although both occupations will benefit from an increase in investing by individuals, personal financial advisors will benefit more.

- Financial analysts will face keen competition for jobs, especially at top securities firms, where pay can be lucrative.

Nature of the Work

Financial analysts and personal financial advisors provide analysis and guidance to businesses and individuals to help them with their investment decisions. Both types of specialist gather financial information, analyze it, and make recommendations to their clients. However, their job duties differ because of the type of investment information they provide and the clients they work for. *Financial analysts* assess the economic performance of companies and industries for firms and institutions with money to invest. *Personal financial advisors* generally assess the financial needs of individuals, providing them a wide range of options.

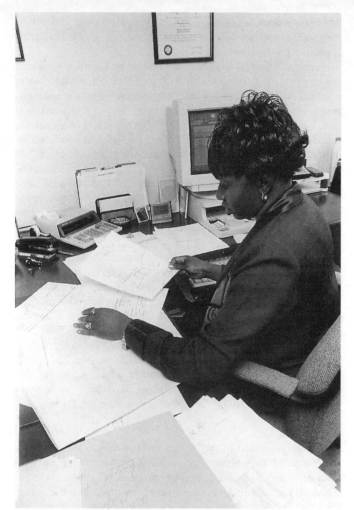

Financial analysts and personal financial advisors gather and analyze information, and then make recommendations to businesses or individuals with money to invest.

Financial analysts, also called *securities analysts* and *investment analysts*, work for banks, insurance companies, mutual and pension funds, securities firms, and other businesses, helping these companies or their clients make investment decisions. Financial analysts read company financial statements and analyze commodity prices, sales, costs, expenses, and tax rates in order to determine a company's value and project future earnings. They often meet with company officials to gain a better insight into a company's prospects and to determine the company's managerial effectiveness. Usually, financial analysts study an entire industry, assessing current trends in business practices, products, and industry competition. They must keep abreast of new regulations or policies that may affect the industry, as well as monitor the economy to determine its effect on earnings.

Financial analysts use spreadsheet and statistical software packages to analyze financial data, spot trends, and develop forecasts. On the basis of their results, they write reports and make presentations, usually making recommendations to buy or sell a particular investment or security. Senior analysts may actually make the decision to buy or sell for the company or client if they are the ones responsible for managing the assets. Other analysts use the data to measure the financial risks associated with making a particular investment decision.

Financial analysts in investment banking departments of securities or banking firms often work in teams, analyzing the future pros-

pects of companies that want to sell shares to the public for the first time. They also ensure that the forms and written materials necessary for compliance with Securities and Exchange Commission regulations are accurate and complete. They may make presentations to prospective investors about the merits of investing in the new company. Financial analysts also work in mergers and acquisitions departments, preparing analyses on the costs and benefits of a proposed merger or takeover.

Some financial analysts, called *ratings analysts*, evaluate the ability of companies or governments that issue bonds to repay their debt. On the basis of their evaluation, a management team assigns a rating to a company's or government's bonds. Other financial analysts perform budget, cost, and credit analysis as part of their responsibilities.

Personal financial advisors, also called *financial planners* or *financial consultants*, use their knowledge of investments, tax laws, and insurance to recommend financial options to individuals in accordance with their short-term and long-term goals. Some of the issues that planners address are retirement and estate planning, funding for college, and general investment options. While most planners offer advice on a wide range of topics, some specialize in areas such as retirement and estate planning or risk management.

An advisor's work begins with a consultation with the client, from whom the advisor obtains information on the client's finances and financial goals. The advisor then develops a comprehensive financial plan that identifies problem areas, makes recommendations for improvement, and selects appropriate investments compatible with the client's goals, attitude toward risk, and expectation or need for a return on the investment. Sometimes this plan is written, but, more often, it is in the form of verbal advice. Financial advisors usually meet with established clients at least once a year to update them on potential investments and to determine whether the clients have been through any life changes—such as marriage, disability, or retirement—that might affect their financial goals. Financial advisors also answer questions from clients regarding changes in benefit plans or the consequences of a change in their job or career.

Some advisors buy and sell financial products, such as mutual funds or insurance, or refer clients to other companies for products and services—for example, the preparation of taxes or wills. A number of advisors take on the responsibility of managing the clients' investments for them.

Finding clients and building a customer base is one of the most important parts of a financial advisor's job. Referrals from satisfied clients are an important source of new business. Many advisors also contact potential clients by giving seminars or lectures or meet clients through business and social contacts.

Working Conditions

Financial analysts and personal financial advisors usually work indoors in safe, comfortable offices or their own homes. Many of these workers enjoy the challenge of helping firms or people make financial decisions. However, financial analysts may face long hours, frequent travel to visit companies and talk to potential investors, and the pressure of deadlines. Much of their research must be done after office hours, because their day is filled with telephone calls and meetings. Personal financial advisors usually work standard business hours, but they also schedule meetings with clients in the evenings or on weekends. Many teach evening classes or hold seminars in order to bring in more clients.

Employment

Financial analysts and personal financial advisors held 298,000 jobs in 2002; financial analysts accounted for almost 6 in 10 of the total. Many financial analysts work at the headquarters of large financial companies, several of which are based in New York City. Nineteen percent of financial analysts work for securities and commodity brokers, exchanges, and investment services firms; and 17 percent work for depository and nondepository institutions, including banks, savings institutions, and mortgage bankers and brokers. The remainder work primarily for insurance carriers; accounting, tax preparation, bookkeeping, and payroll services; management, scientific, and technical consulting services; and State and local government agencies.

Approximately 38 percent of personal financial advisors are self-employed, operating small investment advisory firms, usually in urban areas. About 31 percent of personal financial advisors are employed by securities and commodity brokers, exchanges, and investment services firms. Another 14 percent are employed by depository and nondepository institutions, including banks, savings institutions, and credit unions. A small number work for insurance carriers and insurance agents, brokers, and services.

Training, Other Qualifications, and Advancement

A college education is required for financial analysts and is strongly preferred for personal financial advisors. Most companies require financial analysts to have at least a bachelor's degree in business administration, accounting, statistics, or finance. Coursework in statistics, economics, and business is required, and knowledge of accounting policies and procedures, corporate budgeting, and financial analysis methods is recommended. A master of business administration is desirable. Advanced courses in options pricing or bond valuation and knowledge of risk management also are suggested.

Employers usually do not require a specific field of study for personal financial advisors, but a bachelor's degree in accounting, finance, economics, business, mathematics, or law provides good preparation for the occupation. Courses in investments, taxes, estate planning, and risk management also are helpful. Programs in financial planning are becoming more widely available in colleges and universities. However, many financial planners enter the field after working in a related occupation, such as accountant, auditor, insurance sales agent, lawyer, or securities, commodities, and financial services sales agent.

Mathematical, computer, analytical, and problem-solving skills are essential qualifications for financial analysts and personal financial advisors. Good communication skills also are necessary, because these workers must present complex financial concepts and strategies in easy-to-understand language to clients and other professionals. Self-confidence, maturity, and the ability to work independently are important as well.

Financial analysts must be detail oriented, motivated to seek out obscure information, and familiar with the workings of the economy, tax laws, and money markets. Strong interpersonal skills and sales ability are crucial to the success of both financial analysts and personal financial advisors.

Although not required for financial analysts or personal financial advisors to practice, certification can enhance one's professional standing and is strongly recommended by many financial companies. Financial analysts may receive the title Chartered Financial Analyst (CFA), sponsored by the Association of Investment Management and Research. To qualify for CFA designation, applicants must hold a bachelor's degree, must have 3 years of work experience in a related field, and must pass a series of three examinations.

The essay exams, administered once a year for 3 years, cover subjects such as accounting, economics, securities analysis, asset valuation, and portfolio management.

Personal financial advisors may obtain the Certified Financial Planner credential, often referred to as CFP (R), demonstrating to potential customers that a planner has extensive training and competency in the area of financial planning. The CFP (R) certification, issued by the Certified Financial Planner Board of Standards, Inc., requires relevant experience, the completion of education requirements, the passage of a comprehensive examination, and adherence to an enforceable code of ethics. Personal financial advisors may also obtain the Chartered Financial Consultant (ChFC) designation, issued by the American College in Bryn Mawr, Pennsylvania, which requires experience and the completion of an eight-course program of study. Both designations have a continuing education requirement.

A license is not required to work as a personal financial advisor, but advisors who sell stocks, bonds, mutual funds, insurance, or real estate may need licenses to perform these additional services. Also, if legal advice is provided, a license to practice law may be required. Financial advisors who do not provide these additional services often refer clients to those qualified to provide them.

Financial analysts may advance by becoming portfolio managers or financial managers, directing the investment portfolios of their companies or of clients. Personal financial advisors who work in firms also may move into managerial positions, but most advisors advance by accumulating clients and managing more assets.

Job Outlook

Increased investment by businesses and individuals is expected to result in faster-than-average employment growth of financial analysts and personal financial advisors through 2012. Both occupations will benefit as baby boomers save for retirement and as a generally better educated and wealthier population requires investment advice. In addition, people are living longer and must plan to finance more years of retirement. The globalization of the securities markets will increase the need for analysts and advisors to help investors make financial choices.

Deregulation of the financial services industry is also expected to spur demand for financial analysts and personal financial advisors. Since 1999, banks, insurance companies, and brokerage firms have been allowed to broaden their financial services. Many firms are adding investment advice to their list of services and are expected to increase their hiring of personal financial advisors. Numerous banks are now entering the securities brokerage and investment banking fields and will increasingly need the skills of financial analysts in these areas.

Employment of personal financial advisors is expected to grow faster than the average for all occupations through the year 2012. The rapid expansion of self-directed retirement plans, such as 401(k) plans, is expected to continue. As the number and complexity of investments rises, more individuals will look to financial advisors to help manage their money. Financial advisors who have either the CFP (R) certification or ChFC designation are expected to have the best opportunities.

Employment of financial analysts is expected to grow about as fast as the average for all occupations through the year 2012. As the number of mutual funds and the amount of assets invested in the funds increase, mutual-fund companies will need increased numbers of financial analysts to recommend which financial products the funds should buy or sell.

Financial analysts also will be needed in the investment banking field, where they help companies raise money and work on corporate mergers and acquisitions. However, growth in demand for financial analysts to do company research will be constrained by the implementation of reform proposals calling for investment firms to subsidize independent research boutiques and separate research from investment banking. Firms may try to contain the costs of reform by eliminating research jobs.

Demand for financial analysts in investment banking fluctuates because investment banking is sensitive to changes in the stock market. In addition, further consolidation in the financial services industry may eliminate some financial analyst positions, dampening overall employment growth somewhat. Competition is expected to be keen for these highly lucrative positions, with many more applicants than jobs.

Earnings

Median annual earnings of financial analysts were $57,100 in 2002. The middle 50 percent earned between $43,660 and $76,620. The lowest 10 percent earned less than $34,570, and the highest 10 percent earned more than $108,060. Median annual earnings in the industries employing the largest numbers of financial analysts in 2002 were as follows:

Other financial investment activities	$74,860
Management of companies and enterprises	60,670
Securities and commodity contracts intermediation and brokerage	58,540
Nondepository credit intermediation	51,700
Depository credit intermediation	51,570

Median annual earnings of personal financial advisors were $56,680 in 2002. The middle 50 percent earned between $36,180 and $100,540. Median annual earnings in the industries employing the largest number of personal financial advisors in 2002 were as follows:

Other financial investment activities	$74,260
Securities and commodity contracts intermediation and brokerage	68,110
Depository credit intermediation	51,030

Many financial analysts receive a bonus in addition to their salary, and the bonus can add substantially to their earnings. Usually, the bonus is based on how well their predictions compare to the actual performance of a benchmark investment. Personal financial advisors who work for financial services firms are generally paid a salary plus bonus. Advisors who work for financial-planning firms or who are self-employed either charge hourly fees for their services or charge one set fee for a comprehensive plan, based on its complexity. Advisors who manage a client's assets usually charge a percentage of those assets. A majority of advisors receive commissions for financial products they sell, in addition to charging a fee.

Related Occupations

Other jobs requiring expertise in finance and investment or in the sales of financial products include accountants and auditors; financial managers; insurance sales agents; real estate brokers and sales agents; and securities, commodities, and financial services sales representatives.

Sources of Additional Information

For information on a career in financial planning, contact:
➤ The Financial Planning Association, 4100 E. Mississippi Ave., Denver, CO 80246-3053. Internet: **http://www.fpanet.org**

For information about the Certified Financial Planner, CFP (R), certification, contact:
➤ Certified Financial Planner Board of Standards, Inc., 1670 Broadway, Suite 600, Denver, CO 80202-4809. Internet: **http://www.cfp.net/become**

For information about the Chartered Financial Consultant (ChFC) designation, contact:
➤ The American College, 270 South Bryn Mawr Ave., Bryn Mawr, PA 19010. Internet: **http://www.amercoll.edu**

For information on a career as a financial analyst, contact:
➤ American Academy of Financial Management, 102 Beverly Dr., Metairie, LA 70001. Internet: **http://www.financialanalyst.org**
➤ Association of Investment Management and Research, P.O. Box 3668, 560 Ray C. Hunt Dr., Charlottesville, VA 22903. Internet: **http://www.aimr.org**

Insurance Underwriters

(0*NET 13-2053.00)

Significant Points

- Because insurance is considered a necessity for people and businesses, there will always be a need for underwriters.

- Most large insurance companies prefer college graduates who have a degree in business administration or finance with courses in accounting; however, a bachelor's degree in any field—plus courses in business law and accounting—may be sufficient to qualify.

Nature of the Work

Insurance companies protect individuals and organizations from financial loss by assuming billions of dollars in risks each year. Underwriters are needed to identify and calculate the risk of loss from policyholders, establish appropriate premium rates, and write policies that cover these risks. An insurance company may lose business to competitors if the underwriter appraises risks too conservatively, or it may have to pay excessive claims if the underwriting actions are too liberal.

With the aid of computers, underwriters analyze information in insurance applications to determine if a risk is acceptable and will not result in a loss. Applications are often supplemented with reports from loss-control consultants, medical reports, data vendors, and actuarial studies. Underwriters then must decide whether to issue the policy and the appropriate premium to charge. In making this determination, underwriters serve as the main link between the insurance carrier and the insurance agent. On occasion, they accompany sales agents to make presentations to prospective clients.

Technology plays an important role in an underwriter's job. Underwriters use computer applications called "smart systems" to manage risks more efficiently and accurately. These systems automatically analyze and rate insurance applications, recommend acceptance or denial of the risk, and adjust the premium rate in accordance with the risk. With these systems, underwriters are better equipped to make sound decisions and avoid excessive losses.

The Internet also has affected the work of underwriters. Many insurance carriers' computer systems are now linked to different databases on the Internet that allow immediate access to information—such as driving records—necessary in determining a potential client's risk. This reduces the amount of time and paperwork necessary for an underwriter to complete a risk assessment.

Most underwriters specialize in one of three major categories of insurance—life, health, or property and casualty. Life and health insurance underwriters may further specialize in group or individual policies.

Insurance underwriters review insurance applications and decide whether to issue a policy.

Property and casualty underwriters usually specialize in either commercial or personal insurance, and then by type of risk insured, such as fire, homeowners, automobile, marine, liability, or workers' compensation. In cases where casualty companies provide insurance through a single "package" policy, covering various types of risks, the underwriter must be familiar with different lines of insurance. For business insurance, the underwriter often must be able to evaluate the firm's entire operation in appraising its application for insurance.

An increasing proportion of insurance sales, particularly in life and health insurance, is being made through group contracts. A standard group policy insures everyone in a specified group through a single contract at a standard premium rate. The group underwriter analyzes the overall composition of the group to assure that the total risk is not excessive. Another type of group policy provides members of a group—a labor union, for example—with individual policies reflecting their needs. These usually are casualty policies, such as those covering automobiles. The casualty underwriter analyzes the application of each group member and makes individual appraisals. Some group underwriters meet with union or employer representatives to discuss the types of policies available to their group.

Working Conditions
Underwriters have desk jobs that require no unusual physical activity. Their offices usually are comfortable and pleasant. Although underwriters typically work a standard 40-hour week, more are working longer hours due to the downsizing of many insurance companies. Most underwriters are based in a home or regional branch office, but they occasionally attend meetings away from home for several days. Construction and marine underwriters frequently travel to inspect worksites and assess risks.

Employment
Insurance underwriters held about 102,000 jobs in 2002. The majority of underwriters—about 64 percent—work for insurance companies called "carriers." Most of the remaining underwriters work in insurance agencies or for organizations that offer insurance services to insurance companies and policyholders. A small number of underwriters work in agencies owned and operated by banks, mortgage companies, and real estate firms.

Most underwriters are based in the insurance company's home office, but some, mostly in the property and casualty area, work out of regional branch offices of the insurance company. These underwriters usually have the authority to underwrite most risks and determine an appropriate rating without consulting the home office.

Training, Other Qualifications, and Advancement
For entry-level underwriting jobs, most large insurance companies prefer college graduates who have a degree in business administration or finance, with courses or experience in accounting. However, a bachelor's degree in almost any field—plus courses in business law and accounting—provides a good general background and may be sufficient to qualify. Because computers are an integral part of most underwriters' jobs, computer skills are essential.

New employees usually start as underwriter trainees or assistant underwriters. They may help collect information on applicants and evaluate routine applications under the supervision of an experienced risk analyst. Property and casualty trainees study claims files to become familiar with factors associated with certain types of losses. Many larger insurers offer work-study training programs, lasting from a few months to a year. As trainees gain experience, they are assigned policy applications that are more complex and cover greater risks. These require the use of computers for more efficient analysis and processing.

Underwriting can be a satisfying career for people who enjoy analyzing information and paying attention to detail. In addition, underwriters must possess good judgment in order to make sound decisions. Excellent communication and interpersonal skills also are essential, as much of the underwriter's work involves dealing with agents and other insurance professionals.

Continuing education is necessary for advancement. Insurance companies usually pay tuition for underwriting courses that their trainees successfully complete; some also offer salary incentives. Independent study programs for experienced property and casualty underwriters also are available. The Insurance Institute of America offers a program called "Introduction to Underwriting" for beginning underwriters, and the specialty designation, Associate in Commercial Underwriting (AU), the second formal step in developing a career in underwriting business insurance policies. Those interested in developing a career underwriting personal insurance policies may earn the Associate in Personal Insurance (API) designation. To earn either the AU or API designation, underwriters complete a series of courses and examinations that generally lasts 1 to 2 years.

The American Institute for Chartered Property Casualty Underwriters awards the designation Chartered Property and Casualty Underwriter, or CPCU, the third and final stage of development for an underwriter. Earning the more advanced CPCU designation takes about four years, and requires passing eight examinations covering risk management; insurance operations and regulations; business and insurance law; financial management; financial institutions; and a three course concentration in either personal or commercial insurance coverage. Although the CPCU may be mainly for underwriters, it is also meant for everyone working in all aspects of property and casualty insurance. The American College offers the Chartered Life Underwriter (CLU) designation and the Registered Health Underwriter (RHU) designation for all life and health insurance professionals.

Experienced underwriters who complete courses of study may advance to senior underwriter or underwriting manager positions. Some underwriting managers are promoted to senior managerial jobs. Some employers require a master's degree to achieve this level. Other underwriters are attracted to the earnings potential of sales and therefore obtain State licenses to sell insurance and related financial products as agents or brokers.

Job Outlook

Employment of underwriters is expected to grow as fast as the average for all occupations through 2012. Underwriting software will continue to make workers more productive; however, because computer software does not do away with the need for human skills, underwriter employment will increase as economic and population growth result in increased insurance needs by businesses and individuals. In addition, job openings will be generated to replace underwriters who transfer or leave the occupation.

Insurance carriers are always assessing new risks and offering policies to meet changing circumstances. Underwriters are particularly needed in the area of product development, where underwriters assess risks and set the premiums for new lines of insurance. One new line of insurance being offered by life insurance carriers that may provide job opportunities for underwriters is long term care insurance.

Demand for underwriters is also expected to improve as insurance carriers try to restore profitability to make up for an unusually large number of underwriting losses in recent years. As the carriers' returns on their investments have declined, insurers are placing more emphasis on underwriting to generate revenues. This renewed interest in underwriting will result in favorable job opportunities for underwriters in the near term.

Employment of underwriters has historically been relatively steady. Overall, the best prospects for underwriter jobs will be for persons with the right skills and credentials, such as excellent computer and communication skills coupled with a background in finance. Because insurance is considered a necessity for people and businesses, there will always be a need for underwriters. It is a profession that is less subject to recession and layoffs than other fields.

Earnings

Median annual earnings of insurance underwriters were $45,590 in 2002. The middle 50 percent earned between $35,190 and $60,890 a year. The lowest 10 percent earned less than $28,840, while the highest 10 percent earned over $79,400. Median annual earnings in insurance carriers were $46,690, while earnings in agencies, brokerages, and other insurance related activities were $43,560.

Insurance companies usually provide better than average benefits, including employer-financed group life and health insurance, and retirement plans.

Related Occupations

Underwriters make decisions on the basis of financial and statistical data. Other workers with the same type of responsibility include accountants and auditors, actuaries, budget analysts, cost estimators, financial analysts and personal financial advisors, financial managers, loan counselors and officers, and credit analysts. Other related jobs in the insurance industry include insurance sales agents and claims adjusters, appraisers, examiners, and investigators.

Sources of Additional Information

Information about a career as an insurance underwriter is available from the home offices of many life, health, and property-casualty insurance companies.

Information about the property-casualty insurance field can be obtained by contacting:
➤ The Insurance Information Institute, 110 William St., New York, NY 10038. Internet: **http://www.iii.org**

Information on careers in the life insurance field can be obtained from:
➤ LIMRA International, P.O. Box 203, Hartford, CT 06141.

Information on the underwriting function and the CPCU and AU designations can be obtained from:
➤ The American Institute for Chartered Property and Casualty Underwriters/Insurance Institute of America, 720 Providence Rd., P.O. Box 3016, Malvern, PA 19355-0716. Internet: **http://www.aicpcu.org**

Information on the CLU and RHU designations can be obtained from:
➤ The American College, 270 South Bryn Mawr Ave., Bryn Mawr, PA, 19010-2196. Internet: **http://www.amercoll.edu**

Loan Counselors and Officers

(0*NET 13-2071.00, 13-2072.00)

Significant Points

- Loan officer positions generally require a bachelor's degree in finance, economics, or a related field; training or experience in banking, lending, or sales is advantageous.

- Average employment growth is expected for loan officers despite rising demand for loans, because technology is making loan processing and approval simpler and faster.

- Earnings often fluctuate with the number of loans generated, rising substantially when the economy is good and interest rates are low.

Nature of the Work

For many individuals, taking out a loan may be the only way to afford a house, car, or college education. For businesses, loans likewise are essential to start many companies, purchase inventory, or invest in capital equipment. *Loan officers* facilitate this lending by finding potential clients and assisting them in applying for loans. Loan officers also gather personal information about clients and businesses to ensure that an informed decision is made regarding the creditworthiness of the borrower and the probability of repayment. *Loan counselors* provide guidance to prospective loan applicants who have problems qualifying for traditional loans. The guidance they provide may include determining the most appropriate type of loan for a particular customer, and explaining specific requirements and restrictions associated with the loan. Some of the functions of a loan counselor also may be performed by a loan officer. Within some institutions, such as credit unions, loan counselor is an alternate title for loan officer.

Loan officers usually specialize in commercial, consumer, or mortgage loans. Commercial or business loans help companies pay for new equipment or expand operations; consumer loans include home equity, automobile, and personal loans; mortgage loans are made to purchase real estate or to refinance an existing mortgage. As banks and other financial institutions begin to offer new types of loans and a growing variety of financial services, loan officers will have to keep abreast of these new product lines so that they can meet their customers' needs.

In many instances, loan officers act as salespeople. Commercial loan officers, for example, contact firms to determine their needs for loans. If a firm is seeking new funds, the loan officer will try to persuade the company to obtain the loan from his or her institution. Similarly, mortgage loan officers develop relationships with commercial and residential real estate agencies so that, when an individual or firm buys a property, the real estate agent might recommend contacting a specific loan officer for financing.

Once this initial contact has been made, loan officers guide clients through the process of applying for a loan. This process begins with a formal meeting or telephone call with a prospective client, during which the loan officer obtains basic information about the purpose of the loan and explains the different types of loans and credit terms that are available to the applicant. Loan officers answer questions about the process and sometimes assist clients in filling out the application.

After a client completes the application, the loan officer begins the process of analyzing and verifying the information on the application to determine the client's creditworthiness. Often, loan officers can quickly access the client's credit history by computer and obtain a credit "score." This score represents the creditworthiness of a person or business as assigned by a software program that makes the evaluation. In cases in which a credit history is not available or in which unusual financial circumstances are present, the loan officer may request additional financial information from the client or, in the case of commercial loans, copies of the company's financial statements. With this information, loan officers who specialize in evaluating a client's creditworthiness—often called loan underwriters—may conduct a financial analysis or other risk assessment. Loan officers include this information and their written comments in a loan file, which is used to analyze whether the prospective loan meets the lending institution's requirements. Loan officers then decide, in consultation with their managers, whether to grant the loan. If the loan is approved, a repayment schedule is arranged with the client.

A loan may be approved that would otherwise be denied if the customer can provide the lender with appropriate collateral—property pledged as security for the repayment of a loan. For example, when lending money for a college education, a bank may insist that borrowers offer their home as collateral. If the borrowers were ever unable to repay the loan, the home would be seized under court order and sold to raise the necessary money.

Some loan officers, referred to as *loan collection officers*, contact borrowers with delinquent loan accounts to help them find a method of repayment in order to avoid their defaulting on the loan. If a repayment plan cannot be developed, the loan collection officer initiates collateral liquidation, in which the lender seizes the collateral used to secure the loan—a home or car, for example—and sells it to repay the loan.

Loan officers meet with prospective clients to discuss different types of loans and credit terms that are available.

Working Conditions

Working as a loan officer usually involves considerable travel. For example, commercial and mortgage loan officers frequently work away from their offices and rely on laptop computers, cellular telephones, and pagers to keep in contact with their offices and clients. Mortgage loan officers often work out of their home or car, visiting offices or homes of clients while completing loan applications. Commercial loan officers sometimes travel to other cities to prepare complex loan agreements. Consumer loan officers and loan counselors, however, are likely to spend most of their time in an office.

Most loan officers and counselors work a standard 40-hour week, but many work longer, depending on the number of clients and the demand for loans. Mortgage loan officers can work especially long hours because they are free to take on as many customers as they choose. Loan officers usually carry a heavy caseload and sometimes cannot accept new clients until they complete current cases. They are especially busy when interest rates are low, a condition that triggers a surge in loan applications.

Employment

Loan counselors and officers together held about 255,000 jobs in 2002. The majority of this employment consisted of loan officers—nearly 88 percent—with the remaining 31,000 jobs being held by loan counselors. Approximately 40 percent of loan officers and counselors were employed by commercial banks, savings institutions, and credit unions. Mortgage and consumer finance companies employed an additional 33 percent. Loan officers are employed throughout the Nation, but most work in urban and suburban areas. At some banks, particularly in rural areas, the branch or assistant manager often handles the loan application process.

Training, Other Qualifications, and Advancement

Loan officer positions generally require a bachelor's degree in finance, economics, or a related field. Most employers prefer applicants who are familiar with computers and their applications in banking. For commercial or mortgage loan officer jobs, training or experience in sales is highly valued by potential employers. Loan officers without college degrees usually advance to these positions from other jobs in an organization after acquiring several years of work experience in various other occupations, such as teller or customer service representative.

There are currently no specific licensing requirements for loan counselors and officers working in banks or credit unions. Training and licensing requirements for loan counselors and officers who work in mortgage banks or brokerages vary by State. These criteria also may vary depending on whether workers are employed by a mortgage bank or mortgage brokerage.

Various banking-related associations and private schools offer courses and programs for students interested in lending, as well as for experienced loan officers who want to keep their skills current. Completion of these courses and programs generally enhances one's employment and advancement opportunities.

Persons planning a career as a loan officer or counselor should be capable of developing effective working relationships with others, confident in their abilities, and highly motivated. For public relations purposes, loan officers must be willing to attend community events as representatives of their employer.

Capable loan officers and counselors may advance to larger branches of the firm or to managerial positions, while less capable workers—and those having weak academic preparation—could be assigned to smaller branches and might find promotion difficult without obtaining training to upgrade their skills. Advancement beyond a loan officer position usually includes supervising other loan officers and clerical staff.

Job Outlook

Employment of loan counselors and officers is projected to increase as fast as the average for all occupations through 2012. College graduates and those with banking, lending, or sales experience should have the best job prospects. Employment growth stemming from economic expansion and population increases—factors that generate demand for loans—will be partially offset by increased automation that speeds lending processes and by the spread of alternative methods of applying for and obtaining loans. Job opportunities for workers in these occupations are influenced by the volume of loan applications, which is determined largely by interest rates and by the overall level of economic activity. However, besides those resulting from growth, additional job openings will result from the need to replace workers who retire or otherwise leave the occupation permanently.

The use of credit scoring has made the loan evaluation process much simpler than in the past, and even unnecessary in some cases. Credit scoring allows loan officers, particularly loan underwriters, to evaluate many more loans in much less time, thus increasing loan officers' efficiency. In addition, the mortgage application process has become highly automated and standardized. This simplification has enabled online mortgage loan vendors to offer loan shopping services over the Internet. Online vendors accept loan applications from customers over the Internet and determine which lenders have the best interest rates for particular loans. With this knowledge, customers can go directly to the lending institution, thereby bypassing mortgage loan brokers. Shopping for loans on the Internet—though currently not a widespread practice—is expected to become more common over the next 10 years, particularly for mortgages, thus reducing demand for loan officers.

Although loans remain a major source of revenue for banks, demand for new loans fluctuates and affects the income and employment opportunities of loan officers. When the economy is on the upswing or when interest rates decline dramatically, there is a surge in real estate buying and mortgage refinancing that requires loan officers to work long hours processing applications and induces lenders to hire additional loan officers. Loan officers often are paid by commission on the value of the loans they place, and some have high earnings when demand for mortgages is high. When the real estate market slows, loan officers often suffer a decline in earnings and may even be subject to layoffs. The same applies to commercial loan officers, whose workloads increase during good economic times as companies seek to invest more in their businesses. In difficult economic conditions, loan collection officers are likely to see an increase in the number of delinquent loans.

Earnings

Median annual earnings of loan counselors were $32,010 in 2002. The middle 50 percent earned between $26,330 and $41,660. The lowest 10 percent earned less than $22,800, while the top 10 percent earned more than $57,400.

Median annual earnings of loan officers were $43,980 in 2002. The middle 50 percent earned between $32,360 and $62,160. The lowest 10 percent earned less than $25,790, while the top 10 percent earned more than $88,450. Median annual earnings in the industries employing the largest numbers of loan officers in 2002 were:

Activities related to credit intermediation	$47,240
Management of companies and enterprises	46,420
Nondepository credit intermediation	44,770
Depository credit intermediation	41,450

The form of compensation for loan officers varies. Most loan officers are paid a commission that is based on the number of loans they originate. In this way, commissions are used to motivate loan officers to bring in more loans. Some institutions pay only salaries, while others pay their loan officers a salary plus a commission or bonus based on the number of loans originated. Banks and other lenders sometimes offer their loan officers free checking privileges and somewhat lower interest rates on personal loans.

According to a salary survey conducted by Robert Half International, a staffing services firm specializing in accounting and finance, mortgage loan officers earned between $36,000 and $45,750 in 2002; consumer loan officers with 1 to 3 years of experience earned between $42,250 and $56,750; and commercial loan officers with 1 to 3 years of experience made between $48,000 and $64,500. With over 3 years of experience, commercial loan officers made between $66,000 and $92,000, and consumer loan officers earned between $55,500 and $75,750. Earnings of loan officers with graduate degrees or professional certifications were approximately 10 to 15 percent higher than these figures. Loan officers who are paid on a commission basis usually earn more than those on salary only, and those who work for smaller banks generally earn less than those employed by larger institutions.

Related Occupations

Loan officers help the public manage financial assets and secure loans. Occupations that involve similar functions include those of securities and financial services sales representatives, personal financial advisors, real estate brokers and sales agents, and insurance sales agents.

Sources of Additional Information

Information about a career as a mortgage loan officer can be obtained from:

➤ Mortgage Bankers Association of America, 1919 Pennsylvania Ave., NW., Washington, DC 20006-3438. Internet: **http://www.mbaa.org**

State bankers' associations can furnish specific information about job opportunities in their State. Also, individual banks can supply information about job openings and the activities, responsibilities, and preferred qualifications of their loan officers.

Management Analysts

(0*NET 13-1111.00)

Significant Points

- Thirty percent are self-employed, about one and a half times the average for other management, business, and financial occupations.

- Most positions in private industry require a master's degree and additional years of specialized experience; a bachelor's degree is sufficient for entry-level government jobs.

- Despite projected faster-than-average employment growth, intense competition is expected for jobs.

Nature of the Work

As business becomes more complex, the Nation's firms are continually faced with new challenges. Firms increasingly rely on management analysts to help them remain competitive amidst these changes. Management analysts, often referred to as *management consultants* in private industry, analyze and propose ways to improve an organization's structure, efficiency, or profits. For example, a small but rapidly growing company that needs help improving the system of control over inventories and expenses may decide to employ a consultant who is an expert in just-in-time inventory management. In another case, a large company that has recently acquired a new division may hire management analysts to help reorganize the corporate structure and eliminate duplicate or nonessential jobs. In recent years, information technology and electronic commerce have provided new opportunities for management analysts. Companies hire consultants to develop strategies for entering and remaining competitive in the new electronic marketplace. (For information on computer specialists working in consulting, see the following statements elsewhere in the *Handbook*: Computer software engineers; systems analysts, computer scientists, and database administrators; and computer programmers.)

Firms providing management analysis range in size from a single practitioner to large international organizations employing thousands of consultants. Some analysts and consultants specialize in a specific industry, such as healthcare or telecommunications, while others specialize by type of business function, such as human resources, marketing, logistics, or information systems. In government, management analysts tend to specialize by type of agency. The work of management analysts and consultants varies with each client or employer, and from project to project. Some projects require a team of consultants, each specializing in one area. In other projects, consultants work independently with the organization's managers. In all cases, analysts and consultants collect, review, and analyze information in order to make recommendations to managers.

Both public and private organizations use consultants for a variety of reasons. Some lack the internal resources needed to handle a project, while others need a consultant's expertise to determine what resources will be required and what problems may be encountered if they pursue a particular opportunity. To retain a consultant, a company first solicits proposals from a number of consulting firms specializing in the area in which it needs assistance. These proposals include the estimated cost and scope of the project, staffing requirements, references from a number of previous clients, and a completion deadline. The company then selects the proposal that best suits its needs.

After obtaining an assignment or contract, management analysts first define the nature and extent of the problem. During this phase, they analyze relevant data, which may include annual revenues, employment, or expenditures, and interview managers and employees while observing their operations. The analyst or consultant then develops solutions to the problem. In the course of preparing their recommendations, they take into account the nature of the organization, the relationship it has with others in the industry, and its internal organization and culture. Insight into the problem often is gained by building and solving mathematical models.

Once they have decided on a course of action, consultants report their findings and recommendations to the client. These suggestions usually are submitted in writing, but oral presentations regarding findings also are common. For some projects, management analysts are retained to help implement the suggestions they have made.

Management analysts in government agencies use the same skills as their private-sector colleagues to advise managers on many types of issues, most of which are similar to the problems faced by private firms. For example, if an agency is planning to purchase personal computers, it must first determine which type to buy, given its budget and data processing needs. In this case, management analysts would assess the prices and characteristics of various machines and determine which best meets the agency's needs.

Management analysts frequenty work in teams to complete projects.

Working Conditions

Management analysts usually divide their time between their offices and the client's site. In either situation, much of an analyst's time is spent indoors in clean, well-lit offices. Because they must spend a significant portion of their time with clients, analysts travel frequently.

Analysts and consultants generally work at least 40 hours a week. Uncompensated overtime is common, especially when project deadlines are approaching. Analysts may experience a great deal of stress as a result of trying to meet a client's demands, often on a tight schedule.

Self-employed consultants can set their workload and hours and work at home. On the other hand, their livelihood depends on their ability to maintain and expand their client base. Salaried consultants also must impress potential clients to get and keep clients for their company.

Employment

Management analysts held about 577,000 jobs in 2002. Thirty percent of these workers were self-employed, about one and a half times the average for other management, business, and financial occupations. Management analysts are found throughout the country, but employment is concentrated in large metropolitan areas. Most work in management, scientific, and technical consulting firms, in computer systems design and related services firms, and for Federal, State, and local governments. The majority of those working for the Federal Government are in the U.S. Department of Defense.

Training, Other Qualifications, and Advancement

Educational requirements for entry-level jobs in this field vary widely between private industry and government. Most employers in private industry generally seek individuals with a master's degree in business administration or a related discipline. Some employers also require additional years of experience in the field in which the worker plans to consult, in addition to a master's degree. Some will hire workers with a bachelor's degree as a research analyst or associate. Research analysts usually need to pursue a master's degree in order to advance to a consulting position. Most government agencies hire people with a bachelor's degree and no pertinent work experience for entry-level management analyst positions.

Few universities or colleges offer formal programs of study in management consulting; however, many fields of study provide a suitable educational background for this occupation because of the wide range of areas addressed by management analysts. These include most academic programs in business and management, such as accounting and marketing, as well as economics, computer and information sciences, and engineering. In addition to the appropriate formal education, most entrants to this occupation have years of experience in management, human resources, information technology, or other specialties. Analysts also routinely attend conferences to keep abreast of current developments in their field.

Management analysts often work with minimal supervision, so they need to be self-motivated and disciplined. Analytical skills, the ability to get along with a wide range of people, strong oral and written communication skills, good judgment, time management skills, and creativity are other desirable qualities. The ability to work in teams also is an important attribute as consulting teams become more common.

As consultants gain experience, they often become solely responsible for a specific project, taking on more responsibility and managing their own hours. At the senior level, consultants may supervise lower level workers and become more involved in seeking out new business. Those with exceptional skills may eventually become a partner in the firm. Others with entrepreneurial ambition may open their own firm.

A high percentage of management consultants are self-employed, partly because business startup costs are low. Self-employed consultants also can share office space, administrative help, and other resources with other self-employed consultants or small consulting firms, thus reducing overhead costs. Because many small consulting firms fail each year for lack of managerial expertise and clients, persons interested in opening their own firm must have good organizational and marketing skills and several years of consulting experience.

The Institute of Management Consultants USA, Inc. (IMC USA) offers a wide range of professional development programs and resources, such as meetings and workshops, which can be helpful for management consultants. The IMC USA also offers the Certified Management Consultant (CMC) designation to those who meet minimum levels of education and experience, submit client reviews, and pass an interview and exam covering the IMC USA's Code of Ethics. Management consultants with a CMC designation must be recertified every 3 years. Certification is not mandatory for management consultants, but it may give a jobseeker a competitive advantage.

Job Outlook

Despite projected rapid employment growth, keen competition is expected for jobs as management analysts. Because analysts can come from such diverse educational backgrounds, the pool of applicants from which employers can draw is quite large. Furthermore, the independent and challenging nature of the work, combined with high earnings potential, makes this occupation attractive to many. Job opportunities are expected to be best for those with a graduate degree, industry expertise, and a talent for salesmanship and public relations.

Employment of management analysts is expected to grow faster than the average for all occupations through 2012, as industry and government increasingly rely on outside expertise to improve the performance of their organizations. Job growth is projected in very large consulting firms with international expertise and in smaller consulting firms that specialize in specific areas, such as biotechnology, healthcare, information technology, human resources, engineering, and marketing. Growth in the number of individual practitioners may be hindered, however, by increasing use of consulting teams, which permits examination of a variety of different issues and problems within an organization.

Employment growth of management analysts and consultants has been driven by a number of changes in the business environment that have forced firms to take a closer look at their operations. These changes include developments in information technology and the growth of electronic commerce. Traditional companies hire analysts to help design intranets or company Web sites, or establish online businesses. New Internet start-up companies hire analysts not only to design Web sites, but also to advise them in more traditional business practices, such as pricing strategies, marketing, and inventory and human resource management. In order to offer clients better quality and a wider variety of services, consulting firms are partnering with traditional computer software and technology firms. Also, many computer firms are developing consulting practices of their own in order to take advantage of this expanding market. Although information technology consulting should remain one of the fastest growing consulting areas, the volatility of the computer services industry necessitates that the most successful management analysts have knowledge of traditional business practices in addition to computer applications, systems integration, and Web design and management skills.

The growth of international business also has contributed to an increase in demand for management analysts. As U.S. firms expand their business abroad, many will hire management analysts to help them form the right strategy for entering the market; advise on legal matters pertaining to specific countries; or help with organizational, administrative, and other issues, especially if the U.S. company is involved in a partnership or merger with a local firm. These trends provide management analysts with more opportunities to travel or work abroad, but also require them to have a more comprehensive knowledge of international business and foreign cultures and languages.

Furthermore, as international and domestic markets have become more competitive, firms have needed to use resources more efficiently. Management analysts increasingly are sought to help reduce costs, streamline operations, and develop marketing strategies. As this process continues and businesses downsize, even more opportunities will be created for analysts to perform duties that previously were handled internally. Finally, management analysts also will be in greater demand in the public sector, as Federal, State, and local government agencies seek ways to become more efficient.

Though management consultants are continually expanding their services, employment growth could be hampered by increasing competition for clients from occupations that do not traditionally perform consulting work, such as accountants, financial analysts, lawyers, and computer systems analysts. Furthermore, economic downturns also can have adverse effects on employment for some management consultants. In these times, businesses look to cut costs and consultants can be considered excess expense. On the other hand, some consultants might experience an increase in work during recessions because they advise businesses on how to cut costs and remain profitable.

Earnings

Salaries for management analysts vary widely by years of experience and education, geographic location, sector of expertise, and size of employer. Generally, management analysts employed in large firms or in metropolitan areas have the highest salaries. Median annual wage and salary earnings of management analysts in 2002 were $60,340. The middle 50 percent earned between $46,160 and $83,590. The lowest 10 percent earned less than $35,990, and the highest 10 percent earned more than $115,670. Median annual earnings in the industries employing the largest numbers of management analysts and consultants in 2002 were:

Management, scientific, and technical consulting services	$71,790
Computer systems design and related services	66,120
Federal Government	65,480
Insurance carriers	51,780
State government	47,340

According to a 2002 survey by the Association of Management Consulting Firms, earnings—including bonuses and profit sharing—averaged $47,826 for research associates in member firms; $61,496 for entry-level consultants, $78,932 for management consultants, $112,716 for senior consultants, $168,998 for junior partners, and $254,817 for senior partners.

Salaried management analysts usually receive common benefits such as health and life insurance, a retirement plan, vacation, and sick leave, as well as less common benefits such as profit sharing and bonuses for outstanding work. In addition, all travel expenses usually are reimbursed by the employer. Self-employed consultants have to maintain their own office and provide their own benefits.

Related Occupations

Management analysts collect, review, and analyze data; make recommendations; and implement their ideas. Occupations with similar duties include accountants and auditors; budget analysts; cost estimators; financial analysts and personal financial advisors; operations research analysts; economists; and market and survey researchers. Some management analysts specialize in information technology and work with computers, as do systems analysts, computer scientists, and database administrators. Most management analysts also have managerial experience similar to that of administrative services managers; advertising, marketing, promotions, public relations, and sales managers; financial managers; human resources, training, and labor relations managers and specialists; and top executives.

Sources of Additional Information

Information about career opportunities in management consulting is available from:
➤ Association of Management Consulting Firms, 380 Lexington Ave., Suite 1700, New York, NY 10168. Internet: **http://www.amcf.org**

Information about the Certified Management Consultant designation can be obtained from:
➤ Institute of Management Consultants USA, Inc., 2025 M St. NW., Suite 800, Washington DC 20036. Internet: **http://www.imcusa.org**

Information on obtaining a management analyst position with the Federal Government is available from the Office of Personnel Management (OPM) through a telephone-based system. Consult your telephone directory under U.S. Government for a local number or call (703) 724-1850; Federal Relay Service: (800) 877-8339. The first number is not tollfree, and charges may result. Information also is available from the OPM Internet site: **http://www.usajobs.opm.gov**.

Tax Examiners, Collectors, and Revenue Agents

(0*NET 13-2081.00)

Significant Points

- Tax examiners, collectors, and revenue agents work for Federal, State, and local governments.
- A bachelor's degree in accounting is becoming the standard source of training; in State and local government, an associate degree in accounting or related tax and accounting work experience may be sufficient.
- Employment is expected to grow more slowly than average over the 2002-12 projection period.
- Because of the relatively small number of openings, jobseekers can expect to face competition.

Nature of the Work

Taxes are one of the certainties of life. And, as long as governments collect taxes, there will be jobs for tax examiners, collectors, and revenue agents. These workers ensure that governments obtain revenues from businesses and citizens by reviewing tax returns, conducting audits, identifying taxes payable, and collecting overdue tax dollars.

Tax examiners do similar work, whether they are employed at the Federal, State, or local government level. They review filed tax returns for accuracy and determine whether tax credits and deductions are allowed by law. Because many States assess individual income taxes based on the taxpayer's reported Federal adjusted gross income, tax examiners working for the Federal Government report to the States adjustments or corrections they make. State tax examiners then determine whether the adjustments affect the taxpayer's State tax liability. At the local level, tax examiners often have additional duties, but an integral part of the work still includes the need to determine the factual basis for claims for refunds.

Tax examiners usually deal with the simplest tax returns—those filed by individual taxpayers with few deductions or those filed by small businesses. At the entry level, many tax examiners perform clerical duties, such as reviewing tax returns and entering them into a computer system for processing. If there is a problem, tax examiners may contact the taxpayer to resolve it.

Tax examiners also review returns for accuracy, checking taxpayers' math and making sure that the amounts that they report match those reported from other sources, such as employers and banks. In addition, the examiners verify that Social Security numbers match names and that taxpayers have correctly interpreted the instructions on the tax forms.

Much of a tax examiner's job involves making sure that tax credits and deductions claimed by taxpayers are legitimate. Tax examiners contact the taxpayer by mail or telephone to address discrepancies and request supporting documentation. They may notify the taxpayer of any overpayment or underpayment and either issue a refund or request further payment. If a taxpayer owes additional taxes, tax examiners adjust the total amount by assessing fees, interest, and penalties and notify the taxpayer of the total liability. Although most tax examiners deal with uncomplicated returns, some may work in more complex tax areas such as pensions or business net-operating losses.

Revenue agents specialize in tax-related accounting work for the U.S. Internal Revenue Service (IRS) and for equivalent agencies at the State and local government levels. Like tax examiners, they audit returns for accuracy. However, revenue agents handle complicated income, sales, and excise tax returns of businesses and large corporations. As a result, their work differs in a number of ways from that of tax examiners.

Entry-level revenue agents at the Federal level usually audit tax returns of small businesses whose market specializations are similar. As they develop expertise in an industry, such as construction, retail sales, or finance, insurance, and real estate, revenue agents work with tax returns of larger corporations.

Many experienced revenue agents specialize; for example, they may focus exclusively on multinational businesses. But all revenue agents working for the Federal Government must keep abreast of the lengthy, complex, and frequently changing tax code. Computer technology has simplified the research process, allowing revenue agents Internet access to relevant legal bulletins, IRS notices, and tax-related court decisions.

At the State level, revenue agents have duties similar to those of their counterparts in the Federal Government. State revenue agents use revenue adjustment reports forwarded by the IRS to determine whether adjustments made by Federal revenue agents affect a taxpayer's taxable income in the eyes of the States. In addition, State agents consider the sales and income taxes for their own States.

At the local level, revenue agents have varying titles and duties, but they still perform field audits or office audits of financial records for business firms. In some cases, local revenue agents also examine financial records of individuals. These local agents, like their State counterparts, rely on the information contained in Federal tax returns. However, local agents also must be knowledgeable enough to apply local tax laws regarding income, utility fees, or school taxes.

Collectors, also called revenue officers in the IRS, deal with delinquent accounts. The process of collecting a delinquent account starts with the revenue agent or tax examiner sending a report to the taxpayer. If the taxpayer makes no effort to resolve the delinquent account, the case is assigned to a collector. When a collector takes a case, he or she first sends the taxpayer a notice. The collector then works with the taxpayer on how to settle the debt.

In cases in which taxpayers fail to file a tax return, Federal collectors may request that the IRS prepare the return on a taxpayer's behalf. In other instances, collectors are responsible for verifying claims that delinquent taxpayers cannot pay their taxes. They investigate these claims by researching court information for the status of liens, mortgages, or financial statements; locating assets through third parties, such as neighbors or local departments of motor vehicles; and requesting legal summonses for other records. Ultimately, collectors must decide whether the IRS should take a lien, or a claim on an asset—such as a bank account, real estate, or an automobile—to settle a debt. Collectors also have the discretion to garnish wages—that is, take a portion of earned wages—to collect owed taxes.

A big part of a collector's job at the Federal level is imposing and following up on delinquent taxpayers' payment deadlines. For each case file, collectors also must maintain records including contacts, telephone numbers, and actions taken.

At the entry level, many tax examiners perform clerical duties, such as reviewing tax returns and entering them into a computer system for processing.

Like tax examiners and revenue agents, collectors use computers to maintain files. Computer technology also gives collectors data access to help them identify high-risk debtors—those who are unlikely to pay or are likely to flee.

Collectors at the IRS usually work independently. However, they call on experts when tax examiners or revenue agents find fraudulent returns, or when a property seizure will involve complex legal steps.

At the State level, collectors decide whether to take action on the basis of their own States' tax returns. Collection work may be handled over the telephone or be turned over to a collector who specializes in obtaining settlements. These collectors contact people directly and have authority to issue subpoenas and request seizures of property. At the local levels, collectors have less power than do their State and Federal counterparts. Although they can start the processes leading to seizure of property and garnishment of wages, they must go through the local court system.

Working Conditions

Tax examiners, collectors, and revenue agents generally work a 40-hour week, although some overtime might be needed during the tax season. State and local tax examiners, who also may review sales, gasoline, and cigarette taxes, may have a steadier workload year-round. Stress can result from the need to work under a deadline in checking returns and evaluating taxpayer claims. Collectors also must face the unpleasant task of confronting delinquent taxpayers.

Tax examiners, collectors, and revenue agents work in clean, well-lighted offices, either in cubicles or at desks. Sometimes travel is necessary. Revenue agents at both the Federal and State levels spend a significant portion of their time in the offices of private firms accessing tax-related records. Some agents may be permanently stationed in the offices of large corporations with complicated tax structures. Agents at the local level usually work in city halls or municipal buildings. Collectors travel to local courthouses; county and municipal seats of government; businesses; and taxpayers' homes to look up records, search for assets, and settle delinquent accounts.

Employment

In 2002, tax examiners, revenue agents, and collectors held about 75,000 jobs at all levels of government. About half worked for the Federal Government, one-third for State governments, and the remainder in local governments. Among those employed by the IRS, tax examiners and revenue agents predominate because of the need to examine or audit tax returns. Collectors make up a smaller proportion, because most disputed tax liabilities do not require enforced collection.

Training, Other Qualifications, and Advancement

Tax examiners, collectors, and revenue agents work with confidential financial and personal information; therefore, trustworthiness is crucial for maintaining the confidentiality of individuals and businesses. Applicants for Federal Government jobs must submit to a background investigation.

A degree in accounting is becoming the standard source of training for tax examiners, collectors, and revenue agents. A bachelor's degree generally is required for employment with the Federal Government. In State and local governments, prospective workers may be able to enter the occupation with an associate degree in accounting, or a combination of related tax and accounting work experience with some college-level business classes. For more advanced entry-level positions, applicants must have a bachelor's degree; demonstrate specialized experience working with tax records, tax laws and regulations, documents, financial accounts, or similar records; or have some combination of postsecondary education and specialized experience.

Tax examiners must be able to understand fundamental tax regulations and procedures, pay attention to detail, and cope well with deadlines. After they are hired, tax examiners receive some formal training. Additionally, annual employer-provided updates keep tax examiners current with changes in procedures or regulations.

Revenue agents need strong analytical, organizational, and time management skills. They also must be able to work independently because they spend so much time away from their home office, and must keep current with changes in the tax code and laws. Newly hired revenue agents expand their accounting knowledge and remain up to date by consulting auditing manuals and other sources for detailed information about individual industries. Additionally, employers continually offer training in new auditing techniques and tax-related issues and court decisions.

Collectors need good interpersonal and communication skills because they deal directly with the public and because their reports are scrutinized when the IRS must legally justify attempts to seize assets. They also must be able to act independently and to exercise good judgment in deciding when and how to collect a debt. Appli-

cants for collector jobs need experience demonstrating knowledge and understanding of business and financial practices, or knowledge of credit operations and practices related to the collection of delinquent accounts.

Entry-level collectors receive formal and on-the-job training under an instructor's guidance before working independently. Collectors usually complete initial training by the end of their second year of service but may receive advanced technical instruction as they gain seniority and take on more difficult cases. Also, collectors are encouraged to continue their professional education by attending meetings to exchange information about how changes in tax laws affect collection methods.

Advancement potential within Federal, State, and local agencies varies for tax examiners, revenue agents, and collectors. For related jobs outside government, experienced workers can take a licensing exam administered by the Federal Government to become enrolled agents—nongovernment tax professionals authorized to represent taxpayers before the IRS.

As revenue agents gain experience, they may specialize in an industry, work with larger corporations, and cover increasingly complex tax returns. Some revenue agents also specialize in assisting in criminal investigations, auditing the books of known or suspected criminals such as drug dealers or money launderers; some agents work with grand juries to help secure indictments. Others become international agents, assessing taxes on companies with subsidiaries abroad.

Collectors who demonstrate leadership skills and a thorough knowledge of collection activities may advance to supervisory or managerial collector positions, in which they oversee the activities of other collectors. It is only these higher supervisors and managers who may authorize the more serious actions against individuals and businesses. The more complex collection attempts, which usually are directed at larger businesses, are reserved for collectors at these higher levels.

Job Outlook

Employment of tax examiners, collectors, and revenue agents is projected to grow more slowly than average during the 2002-12 projection period. Job openings will stem primarily from the need to replace those workers who retire or leave the occupation for other reasons. Because of the relatively small number of openings, jobseekers can expect to face competition.

The number of tax returns filed will continue to increase as the labor force grows. Dampening this effect, however, is a decrease in the proportion of tax returns selected for audit and collection. Because much of the work done by tax examiners and revenue agents is now computerized, productivity has increased, limiting the need for more tax examiners, collectors, and revenue agents. Many State and local governments, as well as the Federal Government, may increasingly contract out their tax collection functions to private sector collection agencies in order to reduce costs.

Employment at the State and local levels may fluctuate with the overall state of the economy. When the economy is contracting, State and local governments are likely to freeze hiring and lay off workers in response to budgetary constraints. Employment growth is more likely to occur in Southern and Western States that are experiencing large population increases. Opportunities at the Federal level could arise from the relaxing of budget constraints imposed on the IRS, the primary employer of these workers.

Earnings

In 2002, median annual earnings for all tax examiners, collectors, and revenue agents was $42,250. The middle 50 percent earned between $31,250 and $59,670. The bottom 10 percent earned less than $23,950, and the top 10 percent earned more than $74,600.

However, median earnings vary considerably depending on the level of government. At the Federal level, 2002 median annual earnings for tax examiners, collectors, and revenue agents were $50,820; at the State level, they were $41,000; and at the local level, they were $28,710. Earnings also vary by occupational specialty. For example, in the Federal Government in 2003, tax examiners earned an average of $34,002, revenue agents earned $75,816, and tax specialists earned $53,083.

Related Occupations

Tax examiners, collectors, and revenue agents analyze and interpret financial data. Occupations with similar responsibilities include accountants and auditors, budget analysts, cost estimators, financial analysts and personal financial advisors, financial managers, and loan counselors and officers.

Sources of Additional Information

Information on obtaining a position as a tax examiner, collector, or revenue agent with the Federal Government is available from the U.S. Office of Personnel Management (OPM) through a telephone-based system. Consult your telephone directory under U.S. Government for a local number or call (703) 724-1850; Federal Relay Service: (800) 877-8339. The first number is not tollfree, and charges may result. Information also is available from the OPM Internet site: **http://www.usajobs.opm.gov**.

State or local government personnel offices can provide information about tax examiner, collector, or revenue agent jobs at those levels of government.

Professional and Related Occupations

Computer and Mathematical Occupations

Actuaries

(O*NET 15-2011.00)

Significant Points

- A strong background in mathematics is essential.
- About 6 out of 10 actuaries are employed in the insurance industry.
- Employment opportunities will be good despite the limited number of openings in this small occupation, as stringent qualifying requirements limit the number of new entrants.

Nature of the Work

One of the main functions of actuaries is to help businesses assess the risk of certain events occurring and formulate policies that minimize the cost of that risk. For this reason, actuaries are essential to the insurance industry. Actuaries assemble and analyze data to estimate the probability and likely cost of the occurrence of an event such as death, sickness, injury, disability, or loss of property. Actuaries also address financial questions, including those involving the level of pension contributions required to produce a certain retirement income level and the way in which a company should invest resources to maximize return on investments in light of potential risk. Using their broad knowledge of statistics, finance, and business, actuaries help design insurance policies, pension plans, and other financial strategies in a manner which will help ensure that the plans are maintained on a sound financial basis.

Most actuaries are employed in the insurance industry, specializing in life and health insurance or property and casualty insurance. They produce probability tables which determine the likelihood that a potential future event will generate a claim. From these tables, they estimate the amount a company can expect to pay in claims. For example, property and casualty actuaries calculate the expected amount of claims resulting from automobile accidents, which varies depending on the insured person's age, sex, driving history, type of car, and other factors. Actuaries ensure that the price, or premium, charged for such insurance will enable the company to cover claims and other expenses. This premium must be profitable, yet competitive with other insurance companies. Within the life and health insurance fields, actuaries are helping to develop long-term-care insurance and annuity policies, the latter a growing investment tool for many individuals.

Actuaries in other financial services industries manage credit and help price corporate security offerings. They also devise new investment tools to help their firms compete with other financial services companies. Pension actuaries working under the provisions of the Employee Retirement Income Security Act (ERISA) of 1974 evaluate pension plans covered by that Act and report on the plans' financial soundness to participants, sponsors, and Federal regulators. Actuaries working in govern-ment help manage social programs such as Social Security and Medicare.

Actuaries may help determine company policy and may need to explain complex technical matters to company executives, government officials, shareholders, policyholders, or the public in general. They may testify before public agencies on proposed legislation affecting their businesses or explain changes in contract provisions to customers. They also may help companies develop plans to enter new lines of business or new geographic markets with existing lines of business by forecasting demand in competitive settings.

Both staff actuaries employed by businesses and consulting actuaries provide advice to clients on a contract basis. The duties of most consulting actuaries are similar to those of other actuaries. For example, some may evaluate company pension plans by calculating the future value of employee and employer contributions and determining whether the amounts are sufficient to meet the future needs of retirees. Others help companies reduce their insurance costs by lowering the level of risk the companies take on. For instance, they may provide advice on how to lessen the risk of injury on the job, which will lower worker's compensation costs. Consulting actuaries sometimes testify in court regarding the value of the potential lifetime earnings of a person who is disabled or killed in an accident, the current value of future pension benefits (in divorce cases), or other values arrived at by complex calculations. Many consulting actuaries work in reinsurance, a field in which one insurance company arranges to share a large prospective liability policy with another insurance company in exchange for a percentage of the premium.

Working Conditions

Actuaries have desk jobs, and their offices usually are comfortable and pleasant. They often work at least 40 hours a week. Some actuaries, particularly consulting actuaries, may travel to

Actuaries analyze the probability that an adverse event will occur.

meet with clients. Consulting actuaries also may experience more erratic employment and be expected to work more than 40 hours per week.

Employment

Actuaries held about 15,000 jobs in 2002, with more than 1 in 2 actuaries employed by insurance carriers. Others work for pension funds and insurance agents and brokers. A growing number of actuaries work for firms providing a variety of corporate services, especially management and public relations, or for firms offering consulting services. A relatively small number of actuaries are employed by security and commodity brokers or by government agencies.

Training, Other Qualifications, and Advancement

Actuaries need a strong background in mathematics and general business. Applicants for beginning actuarial jobs usually have a bachelor's degree in mathematics, actuarial science, statistics, or a business-related discipline, such as economics, finance, or accounting. About 100 colleges and universities offer an actuarial science program, and most offer a degree in mathematics, statistics, economics, or finance. Some companies hire applicants without specifying a major, provided that the applicant has a working knowledge of mathematics, including calculus, probability, and statistics, and has demonstrated this knowledge by passing one or two actuarial exams required for professional designation. Courses in economics, accounting, finance, and insurance also are useful. Companies increasingly prefer well-rounded individuals who, in addition to having acquired a strong technical background, have some training in liberal arts and business and possess strong communication skills.

In addition to knowledge of mathematics, computer skills are becoming increasingly important. Actuaries should be able to develop and use spreadsheets and databases, as well as standard statistical analysis software. Knowledge of computer programming languages, such as Visual Basic, also is useful.

Two professional societies sponsor programs leading to full professional status in their specialty. The first, the Society of Actuaries (SOA), administers a series of actuarial examinations in the life insurance, health benefits systems, retirement systems, and finance and investment fields. The Casualty Actuarial Society (CAS), as the name indicates, gives a series of examinations in the property and casualty field, which includes fire, accident, medical malpractice, worker's compensation, and personal injury liability.

The first four exams in the SOA and CAS examination series are jointly sponsored by the two societies and cover the same material. For this reason, students do not need to commit themselves to a specialty until they have taken the initial examinations, which test an individual's competence in probability, calculus, statistics, and other branches of mathematics. The first few examinations help students evaluate their potential as actuaries. Many prospective actuaries begin taking the exams in college with the help of self-study guides and courses. Those who pass one or more examinations have better opportunities for employment at higher starting salaries than those who do not.

After graduating from college, most prospective actuaries gain on-the job experience at an insurance company or consulting firm, while at the same time working to complete the examination process. Actuaries are encouraged to finish the entire series of examinations as soon as possible, advancing first to the Associate level (with an ASA or ACAS designation) and then to the Fellowship level (FSA or FCAS designation). Advanced topics in the casualty field include investment and assets, dynamic financial analysis, and valuation of insurance. Candidates in the SOA examination series must choose a specialty-group and health benefits, individual life and annuities, pensions, investments, or finance. Examinations are given twice a year, in the spring and the fall. Although many companies allot time to their employees for study, home study is required to pass the examinations, and many actuaries study for months to prepare for each examination. It is likewise common for employers to pay the hundreds of dollars for examination fees and study materials. Most actuaries reach the Associate level within 4 to 6 years and the Fellowship level a few years later.

Specific requirements apply to pension actuaries, who verify the financial status of defined benefit pension plans for the Federal Government. These actuaries must be enrolled by the Joint Board for the Enrollment of Actuaries. To qualify for enrollment, applicants must meet certain experience and examination requirements, as stipulated by the Board.

To perform their duties effectively, actuaries must keep up with current economic and social trends and legislation, as well as with developments in health, business, finance, and economics that could affect insurance or investment practices. Good communication and interpersonal skills also are important, particularly for prospective consulting actuaries.

Beginning actuaries often rotate among different jobs in an organization to learn various actuarial operations and phases of insurance work, such as marketing, underwriting, and product development. At first, they prepare data for actuarial projects or perform other simple tasks. As they gain experience, actuaries may supervise clerks, prepare correspondence, draft reports, and conduct research. They may move from one company to another early in their careers as they advance to higher positions.

Advancement depends largely on job performance and the number of actuarial examinations passed. Actuaries with a broad knowledge of the insurance, pension, investment, or employee benefits fields can rise to administrative and executive positions in their companies. Actuaries with supervisory ability may advance to management positions in other areas, such as underwriting, accounting, data processing, marketing, and advertising. Some actuaries assume college and university faculty positions. (See the statement on teachers—postsecondary elsewhere in the *Handbook*.)

Job Outlook

Employment of actuaries is expected to grow as fast as the average for all occupations through 2012. Employment opportunities should remain good for those who qualify, because the stringent qualifying examination system restricts the number of candidates. Employment growth in the insurance industry is expected to continue at a stable pace, while more significant job growth is likely in some other industries. In addition, a small number of jobs will open up each year to replace actuaries who leave the occupation to retire or who find new jobs.

Steady demand by the insurance industry—the largest employer of actuaries—should ensure that actuary jobs in this key industry will not decrease over the projection period. Although relatively few new jobs will be created, actuaries will continue to be needed to develop, price, and evaluate a variety of insurance products and calculate the costs of new risks. Recently, employment of actuaries in life insurance had begun to decline, but the growing popularity of annuities, a financial product offered primarily by life insurance companies, has resulted in some job growth in this specialty. Also, new actuarial positions have been created in property-casualty insurance to analyze evolving risks, such as terrorism.

Some new employment opportunities for actuaries should also become available in the health-care field as health-care issues and Medicare reform continue to receive growing attention. Increased regulation of managed health-care companies and the desire to contain health-care costs will continue to provide job opportunities for actuaries, who will also be needed to evaluate the risks associated with new medical issues, such as genetic testing and the impact of new diseases. Others in this field are involved in drafting health-care legislation.

A significant proportion of new actuaries will find employment with consulting firms. Companies that may not find it cost effective to hire their own actuaries are increasingly hiring consulting actuaries to analyze various risks. Other areas with notable growth prospects are information services and accounting services. Also, because actuarial skills are increasingly seen as useful to other industries that deal with risk, such as the airline and the banking industries, additional job openings may be created in these industries.

The best job prospects for entry-level positions will be for those candidates who have passed at least one or two of the initial actuarial exams. Candidates with additional knowledge or experience, such as computer programming skills, will be particularly attractive to employers. Most jobs in this occupation are located in urban areas, but opportunities vary by geographic location. Opportunities should be best in Illinois, New Jersey, New York, and Connecticut—the four States in which about one-third of all actuary jobs are concentrated.

Earnings
Median annual earnings of actuaries were $69,970 in 2002. The middle 50 percent earned between $50,510 and $99,820. The lowest 10 percent had earnings of less than $39,700, while the top 10 percent earned more than $137,650.

According to the National Association of Colleges and Employers, annual starting salaries for graduates with a bachelor's degree in actuarial science averaged $40,396 in 2003.

Insurance companies and consulting firms give merit increases to actuaries as they gain experience and pass examinations. Some companies also offer cash bonuses for each professional designation achieved. A 2003 survey by Life Office Management Association, Inc., of the largest U.S. insurance and financial services companies indicated that the average base salary for an entry-level actuary was $46,991. Associate actuaries, who direct and provide leadership in the design, pricing, and implementation of insurance products, received an average salary of $99,446. Actuaries at the highest technical level without managerial responsibilities reportedly were paid an average of $104,235.

Related Occupations
Actuaries need a strong background in mathematics, statistics, and related fields. Other workers whose jobs involve related skills include accountants and auditors, budget analysts, economists, market and survey researchers, financial analysts and personal financial advisors, insurance underwriters, mathematicians, and statisticians.

Sources of Additional Information
Career information on actuaries specializing in pensions is available from
➤ American Society of Pension Actuaries, 4245 N. Fairfax Dr., Suite 750, Arlington, VA 22203. Internet: **http://www.aspa.org**

For information about actuarial careers in life and health insurance, employee benefits and pensions, and finance and investments, contact
➤ Society of Actuaries (SOA), 475 N. Martingale Rd., Suite 800, Schaumburg, IL 60173-2226. Internet: **http://www.soa.org**

For information about actuarial careers in property and casualty insurance, contact
➤ Casualty Actuarial Society (CAS), 1100 N. Glebe Rd., Suite 600, Arlington, VA 22201. Internet: **http://www.casact.org**

The SOA and CAS jointly sponsor a Web site for those interested in pursuing an actuarial career. Internet: **http://www.BeAnActuary.org**

For general facts about actuarial careers, contact
➤ American Academy of Actuaries, 1100 17th St. NW., 7th Floor, Washington, DC 20036. Internet: **http://www.actuary.org/index.htm**

Computer Programmers

(O*NET 15-1021.00)

Significant Points

● Nearly half of all computer programmers held a bachelor's degree in 2002; about 1 in 5 held a graduate degree.

● Employment is expected to grow much more slowly than that of other computer specialists.

● Prospects should be best for college graduates with knowledge of a variety of programming languages and tools; those with less formal education or its equivalent in work experience should face strong competition for programming jobs.

Nature of the Work
Computer programmers write, test, and maintain the detailed instructions, called programs, that computers must follow to perform their functions. They also conceive, design, and test logical structures for solving problems by computer. Many technical innovations in programming—advanced computing technologies and sophisticated new languages and programming tools—have redefined the role of a programmer and elevated much of the programming work done today. Job titles and descriptions may vary, depending on the organization. In this occupational statement, *computer programmer* refers to individuals whose main job function is programming; this group has a wide range of responsibilities and educational backgrounds.

Computer programs tell the computer what to do—which information to identify and access, how to process it, and what equipment to use. Programs vary widely depending upon the type of information to be accessed or generated. For example, the instructions involved in updating financial records are very different from those required to duplicate conditions on board an aircraft for pilots training in a flight simulator. Although simple programs can be written in a few hours, programs that use complex mathematical formulas, whose solutions can only be approximated, or that draw data from many existing systems may require more than a year of work. In most cases, several programmers work together as a team under a senior programmer's supervision.

Programmers write programs according to the specifications determined primarily by computer software engineers and systems analysts. (Separate statements on computer software engineers and on computer systems analysts, database administrators, and computer scientists appear elsewhere in the *Handbook*.) After the design process is complete, it is the job of the programmer to convert that design into a logical series of instructions that the computer can follow. The programmer then codes these instructions in a conventional programming language, such as COBOL; an artificial intelligence language, such as Prolog; or one of the most advanced object-oriented languages such as Java, C++, or Smalltalk. Different programming languages are used depending on the purpose of the program. COBOL, for example, is commonly used for business applications, whereas Fortran (short for "formula translation") is used in science and engineering. C++ is widely used for both scientific and business applications. Many programmers at the enterprise level are also expected to know platform-specific languages used in database programming. Programmers generally know more than one programming language and, because many languages are similar, they often can learn new languages relatively easily. In practice, programmers often are referred to by the language they know, as are Java programmers, or the type of function they perform or environment in which they work, which is the case for database programmers, mainframe programmers, or Web programmers.

Many programmers update, repair, modify, and expand existing programs. When making changes to a section of code, called a *routine*, programmers need to make other users aware of the task that the routine is to perform. They do this by inserting comments in the coded instructions, so that others can understand the program. Many programmers use computer-assisted software engineering (CASE) tools to automate much of the coding process. These tools enable a programmer to concentrate on writing the unique parts of the program, because the tools automate various pieces of the program being built. CASE tools generate whole sections of code automatically, rather than line by line. Programmers also utilize libraries of pre-written code, which can then be modified or customized for a specific application. This also yields more reliable and consistent programs and increases programmers' productivity by eliminating some routine steps.

Programmers test a program by running it to ensure that the instructions are correct and that the program produces the desired outcome. If errors do occur, the programmer must make the appropriate change and recheck the program until it produces the correct results. This process is called testing and debugging. Programmers may continue to fix these problems throughout the life of a program. Programmers working in a mainframe environment, which involves a large centralized computer, may prepare instructions for a computer operator who will run the program. (A separate statement on computer operators appears elsewhere in the *Handbook*.) They also may contribute to a manual for persons who will be using the program.

Programmers often are grouped into two broad types—applications programmers and systems programmers. *Applications programmers* write programs to handle a specific job, such as a program to track inventory within an organization. They may also revise existing packaged software or customize generic applications called middleware. *Systems programmers*, on the other hand, write programs to maintain and control computer systems software, such as operating systems, networked systems, and database systems. These workers make changes in the sets of instructions that determine how the network, workstations, and central processing unit of the system handle the various jobs they have been given, and how they communicate with peripheral equipment such as terminals, printers, and disk drives. Because of their knowledge of the entire computer system, systems programmers often help applications programmers to determine the source of problems that may occur with their programs.

Programmers in software development companies may work directly with experts from various fields to create software—either programs designed for specific clients or packaged software for general use—ranging from games and educational software to programs for desktop publishing and financial planning. Much of this type of programming takes place in the preparation of packaged software, which constitutes one of the most rapidly growing segments of the computer services industry.

In some organizations, particularly small ones, workers commonly known as *programmer-analysts* are responsible for both the systems analysis and the actual programming work. (A more detailed description of the work of programmer-analysts is presented in the statement on computer systems analysts, database administrators, and computer scientists elsewhere in the *Handbook*.) Advanced programming languages and new object-oriented programming capabilities are increasing the efficiency and productivity of both programmers and users. The transition from a mainframe environment to one that is based primarily on personal computers (PCs) has blurred the once rigid distinction between the programmer and the user. Increasingly, adept end-users are taking over many of the tasks previously performed by programmers. For example, the growing use of packaged software, such as spreadsheet and database management software packages, allows users to write simple programs to access data and perform calculations.

Working Conditions

Programmers generally work in offices in comfortable surroundings. Many programmers may work long hours or weekends to meet deadlines or fix critical problems that occur during off hours. Given the technology available, telecommuting is becoming common for a wide range of computer professionals,

Computer programmers write, test, and maintain the detailed instructions that computers follow.

including computer programmers. As computer networks expand, more programmers are able to make corrections or fix problems remotely by using modems, e-mail, and the Internet to connect to a customer's computer.

Like other workers who spend long periods in front of a computer terminal typing at a keyboard, programmers are susceptible to eyestrain, back discomfort, and hand and wrist problems, such as carpal tunnel syndrome.

Employment

Computer programmers held about 499,000 jobs in 2002. Programmers are employed in almost every industry, but the largest concentrations are in computer systems design and related services and in software publishers, which includes firms that write and sell software. Large numbers of programmers also can be found in management of companies and enterprises, telecommunications companies, manufacturers of computer and electronic equipment, financial institutions, insurance carriers, educational institutions, and government agencies.

A large number of computer programmers are employed on a temporary or contract basis or work as independent consultants, as companies demand expertise with new programming languages or specialized areas of application. Rather than hiring programmers as permanent employees and then laying them off after a job is completed, employers can contract with temporary help agencies, consulting firms, or directly with programmers themselves. A marketing firm, for example, may require the services of several programmers only to write and debug the software necessary to get a new customer resource management system running. This practice also enables companies to bring in people with a specific set of skills—usually in one of the latest technologies—as it applies to their business needs. Bringing in an independent contractor or consultant with a certain level of experience in a new or advanced programming language, for example, enables an establishment to complete a particular job without having to retrain existing workers. Such jobs may last anywhere from several weeks to a year or longer. There were 18,000 self-employed computer programmers in 2002.

Training, Other Qualifications, and Advancement

While there are many training paths available for programmers, mainly because employers' needs are so varied, the level of education and experience employers seek has been rising, due to the growing number of qualified applicants and the specialization involved with most programming tasks. Bachelor's degrees are commonly required, although some programmers may qualify for certain jobs with 2-year degrees or certificates. The associate degree is an increasingly attractive entry-level credential for prospective computer programmers. Most community colleges and many independent technical institutes and proprietary schools offer an associate degree in computer science or a related information technology field.

Employers are primarily interested in programming knowledge, and computer programmers can become certified in a programming language such as C++ or Java. College graduates who are interested in changing careers or developing an area of expertise also may return to a 2-year community college or technical school for additional training. In the absence of a degree, substantial specialized experience or expertise may be needed. Even when hiring programmers with a degree, employers appear to be placing more emphasis on previous experience.

Some computer programmers hold a college degree in computer science, mathematics, or information systems, whereas others have taken special courses in computer programming to supplement their degree in a field such as accounting, inventory control, or another area of business. As the level of education and training required by employers continues to rise, the proportion of programmers with a college degree should increase in the future. As indicated by the following tabulation, 65 percent of computer programmers had a bachelor's or higher degree in 2002.

	Percent
High school graduate or equivalent or less	7.7
Some college, no degree	15.2
Associate degree	11.6
Bachelor's degree	48.6
Graduate degree	16.7

Required skills vary from job to job, but the demand for various skills generally is driven by changes in technology. Employers using computers for scientific or engineering applications usually prefer college graduates who have degrees in computer or information science, mathematics, engineering, or the physical sciences. Graduate degrees in related fields are required for some jobs. Employers who use computers for business applications prefer to hire people who have had college courses in management information systems (MIS) and business and who possess strong programming skills. Although knowledge of traditional languages still is important, employers are placing increasing emphasis on newer, object-oriented programming languages and tools, such as C++ and Java. Additionally, employers are seeking persons familiar with fourth- and fifth-generation languages that involve graphic user interface (GUI) and systems programming. Employers also prefer applicants who have general business skills and experience related to the operations of the firm. Students can improve their employment prospects by participating in a college work-study program or by undertaking an internship.

Most systems programmers hold a 4-year degree in computer science. Extensive knowledge of a variety of operating systems is essential for such workers. This includes being able to configure an operating system to work with different types of hardware and having the skills needed to adapt the operating system to best meet the needs of a particular organization. Systems programmers also must be able to work with database systems, such as DB2, Oracle, or Sybase.

When hiring programmers, employers look for people with the necessary programming skills who can think logically and pay close attention to detail. The job calls for patience, persistence, and the ability to work on exacting analytical work, especially under pressure. Ingenuity, creativity, and imagination also are particularly important when programmers design solutions and test their work for potential failures. The ability to work with abstract concepts and to do technical analysis is especially important for systems programmers, because they work with the software that controls the computer's operation. Because programmers are expected to work in teams and interact directly with users, employers want programmers who are able to communicate with nontechnical personnel.

Entry-level or junior programmers may work alone on simple assignments after some initial instruction, or they may be assigned to work on a team with more experienced programmers. Either way, beginning programmers generally must work under close supervision. Because technology changes so rapidly, programmers must continuously update their knowledge and skills by taking courses sponsored by their employer or by software vendors, or offered through local community colleges and universities.

For skilled workers who keep up to date with the latest technology, the prospects for advancement are good. In large organizations, programmers may be promoted to lead programmer and be given supervisory responsibilities. Some applications programmers may move into systems programming after they gain experience and take courses in systems software. With general business experience, programmers may become programmer-analysts or systems analysts or be promoted to a managerial position. Other programmers, with specialized knowledge and experience with a language or operating system, may work in research and development on multimedia or Internet technology, for example. As employers increasingly contract out programming jobs, more opportunities should arise for experienced programmers with expertise in a specific area to work as consultants.

Certification is a way to demonstrate a level of competence, and may provide a jobseeker with a competitive advantage. In addition to language-specific certificates that a programmer can obtain, product vendors or software firms also offer certification and may require professionals who work with their products to be certified. Voluntary certification also is available through other various organizations.

Job Outlook

Employment of programmers is expected to grow about as fast as the average for all occupations through 2012. Jobs for both systems and applications programmers should be most plentiful in data processing service firms, software houses, and computer consulting businesses. These types of establishments are part of computer systems design and related services and software publishers, which are projected to be among the fastest growing industries in the economy over the 2002-12 period. As organizations attempt to control costs and keep up with changing technology, they will need programmers to assist in conversions to new computer languages and systems. In addition, numerous job openings will result from the need to replace programmers who leave the labor force or transfer to other occupations such as manager or systems analyst.

Employment of programmers, however, is expected to grow much more slowly than that of other computer specialists. With the rapid gains in technology, sophisticated computer software now has the capability to write basic code, eliminating the need for more programmers to do this routine work. The consolidation and centralization of systems and applications, developments in packaged software, advances in programming languages and tools, and the growing ability of users to design, write, and implement more of their own programs means that more of the programming functions can be transferred from programmers to other types of workers. Furthermore, as the level of technological innovation and sophistication increases, programmers are likely to face increasing competition from programming businesses overseas, to which much routine work can be contracted out at a lower cost.

Nevertheless, employers will continue to need programmers who have strong technical skills and who understand an employer's business and its programming requirements. This means that programmers will have to keep abreast of changing programming languages and techniques. Given the importance of networking and the expansion of client/server, Web-based, and wireless environments, organizations will look for programmers who can support data communications and help to implement electronic commerce and Intranet strategies. Demand for programmers with strong object-oriented programming capabilities and technical specialization in areas such as client/server programming, wireless applications, multimedia technology, and graphic user interface (GUI) should arise from the expansion of intranets, extranets, and Internet applications. Programmers also will be needed to create and maintain expert systems and embed these technologies in more products. Finally, growing emphasis on cyber-security will lead to increased demand for programmers who are familiar with digital security issues and skilled in using appropriate security technology.

As programming tasks become increasingly sophisticated and additional levels of skill and experience are demanded by employers, graduates of 2-year programs and people with less than a 2-year degree or its equivalent in work experience should face strong competition for programming jobs. Competition for entry-level positions, however, also can affect applicants with a bachelor's degree. Prospects should be best for college graduates with knowledge of, and experience working with, a variety of programming languages and tools—including C++ and other object-oriented languages such as Java, as well as newer, domain-specific languages that apply to computer networking, database management, and Internet application development. Obtaining vendor-specific or language-specific certification also can provide a competitive edge. Because demand fluctuates with employers' needs, jobseekers should keep up to date with the latest skills and technologies. Individuals who want to become programmers can enhance their prospects by combining the appropriate formal training with practical work experience.

Earnings

Median annual earnings of computer programmers were $60,290 in 2002. The middle 50 percent earned between $45,960 and $78,140 a year. The lowest 10 percent earned less than $35,080; the highest 10 percent earned more than $96,860. Median annual earnings in the industries employing the largest numbers of computer programmers in 2002 were:

Professional and commercial equipment and supplies merchant wholesalers	$70,440
Software publishers	66,870
Computer systems design and related services	65,640
Management of companies and enterprises	59,850
Data processing, hosting, and related services	59,300

According to the National Association of Colleges and Employers, starting salary offers for graduates with a bachelor's degree in computer programming averaged $45,558 a year in 2003.

According to Robert Half International, a firm providing specialized staffing services, average annual starting salaries in 2003 ranged from $51,500 to $80,500 for applications development programmers/analysts, and from $55,000 to $87,750 for software developers. Average starting salaries for mainframe systems programmers ranged from $53,250 to $68,750 in 2003.

Related Occupations

Other professional workers who deal extensively with data include computer software engineers; computer systems analysts, database administrators, and computer scientists; statisticians; mathematicians; engineers; financial analysts and personal financial advisors; accountants and auditors; actuaries; and operations research analysts.

Sources of Additional Information
State employment service offices can provide information about job openings for computer programmers. Municipal chambers of commerce are an additional source of information on an area's largest employers.

Further information about computer careers is available from:

➤ Association for Computing Machinery (ACM), 1515 Broadway, New York, NY 10036. Internet: **http://www.acm.org**

➤ Institute of Electrical and Electronics Engineers Computer Society, Headquarters Office, 1730 Massachusetts Ave. NW., Washington, DC 20036-1992. Internet: **http://www.computer.org**

➤ National Workforce Center for Emerging Technologies, 3000 Landerholm Circle SE., Bellevue, WA 98007. Internet: **http://www.nwcet.org**

Computer Software Engineers

(0*NET 15-1031.00, 15-1032.00)

Significant Points

● Computer software engineers are projected to be one of the fastest growing occupations over the 2002-12 period.

● Highly favorable opportunities are expected for college graduates with at least a bachelor's degree in computer engineering or computer science and with practical work experience.

● Computer software engineers must continually strive to acquire new skills in conjunction with the rapid changes in computer technology.

Nature of the Work
The explosive impact of computers and information technology on our everyday lives has generated a need to design and develop new computer software systems and to incorporate new technologies in a rapidly growing range of applications. The tasks performed by workers known as computer software engineers evolve quickly, reflecting new areas of specialization or changes in technology, as well as the preferences and practices of employers. Computer software engineers apply the principles and techniques of computer science, engineering, and mathematical analysis to the design, development, testing, and evaluation of the software and systems that enable computers to perform their many applications. (A separate statement on computer hardware engineers appears elsewhere in the *Handbook*.)

Software engineers working in applications or systems development analyze users' needs and design, construct, test, and maintain computer applications software or systems. Software engineers can be involved in the design and development of many types of software, including software for operating systems and network distribution, and compilers, which convert programs for execution on a computer. In programming, or coding, software engineers instruct a computer, line by line, how to perform a function. They also solve technical problems that arise. Software engineers must possess strong programming skills, but are more concerned with developing algorithms and analyzing and solving programming problems than with actually writing code. (A separate statement on computer programmers appears elsewhere in the *Handbook*.)

Computer applications software engineers analyze users' needs and design, construct, and maintain general computer applications software or specialized utility programs. These workers use different programming languages, depending on the purpose of the program. The programming languages most often used are C, C++, and Java, with Fortran and COBOL used less commonly. Some software engineers develop both packaged systems and systems software or create customized applications.

Computer systems software engineers coordinate the construction and maintenance of a company's computer systems and plan their future growth. Working with a company, they coordinate each department's computer needs—ordering, inventory, billing, and payroll recordkeeping, for example—and make suggestions about its technical direction. They also might set up the company's intranets—networks that link computers within the organization and ease communication among the various departments.

Systems software engineers work for companies that configure, implement, and install complete computer systems. They may be members of the marketing or sales staff, serving as the primary technical resource for sales workers and customers. They also may be involved in product sales and in providing their customers with continuing technical support.

Computer software engineers often work as part of a team that designs new hardware, software, and systems. A core team may comprise engineering, marketing, manufacturing, and design people who work together until the product is released.

Working Conditions
Computer software engineers normally work in well-lighted and comfortable offices or computer laboratories in which computer equipment is located. Most software engineers work at least 40 hours a week; however, due to the project-oriented nature of the work, they also may have to work evenings or weekends to meet deadlines or solve unexpected technical problems. Like other workers who sit for hours at a computer, typing on a keyboard, software engineers are susceptible to eyestrain, back

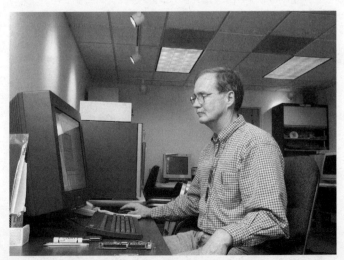

Computer software engineers design, create, and modify computer applications.

discomfort, and hand and wrist problems such as carpal tunnel syndrome.

As they strive to improve software for users, many computer software engineers interact with customers and coworkers. Computer software engineers who are employed by software vendors and consulting firms, for example, spend much of their time away from their offices, frequently traveling overnight to meet with customers. They call on customers in businesses ranging from manufacturing plants to financial institutions.

As networks expand, software engineers may be able to use modems, laptops, e-mail, and the Internet to provide more technical support and other services from their main office, connecting to a customer's computer remotely to identify and correct developing problems.

Employment

Computer software engineers held about 675,000 jobs in 2002. About 394,000 were computer applications software engineers, and about 281,000 were computer systems software engineers. Although they are employed in most industries, the largest concentration of computer software engineers, about 30 percent, is in computer systems design and related services. Many computer software engineers also work for establishments in other industries, such as government agencies, manufacturers of computers and related electronic equipment, and colleges and universities.

Employers of computer software engineers range from startup companies to established industry leaders. The proliferation of Internet, e-mail, and other communications systems expands electronics to engineering firms traditionally associated with unrelated disciplines. Engineering firms specializing in building bridges and power plants, for example, hire computer software engineers to design and develop new geographic data systems and automated drafting systems. Communications firms need computer software engineers to tap into growth in the personal communications market. Major communications companies have many job openings for both computer software applications and computer systems engineers.

An increasing number of computer software engineers are employed on a temporary or contract basis, with many being self-employed, working independently as consultants. Some consultants work for firms that specialize in developing and maintaining client companies' Web sites and intranets. Consulting opportunities for software engineers should grow as businesses need help managing, upgrading, and customizing increasingly complex computer systems. About 21,000 computer software engineers were self-employed in 2002.

Training, Other Qualifications, and Advancement

Most employers prefer to hire persons who have at least a bachelor's degree and broad knowledge of, and experience with, a variety of computer systems and technologies. Usual degree concentrations for applications software engineers are computer science or software engineering; for systems software engineers, usual concentrations are computer science or computer information systems. Graduate degrees are preferred for some of the more complex jobs.

Academic programs in software engineering emphasize software and may be offered as a degree option or in conjunction with computer science degrees. Increasing emphasis on computer security suggests that software engineers with advanced degrees that include mathematics and systems design will be sought after by software developers, government agencies, and consulting firms specializing in information assurance and security. Students seeking software engineering jobs enhance their employment opportunities by participating in internship or co-op programs offered through their schools. These experiences provide the students with broad knowledge and experience, making them more attractive candidates to employers. Inexperienced college graduates may be hired by large computer and consulting firms that train new hires in intensive, company-based programs. In many firms, new employees are mentored, and their mentors have an input into the new hires' evaluations.

For systems software engineering jobs that require workers who have a college degree, a bachelor's degree in computer science or computer information systems is typical. For systems engineering jobs that place less emphasis on workers having a computer-related degree, computer training programs leading to certification are offered by systems software vendors, including Microsoft, Novell, and Oracle. These programs usually last from 1 to 4 weeks, but the worker is not required to attend classes in order to sit for a certification exam; several study guides also are available to help prepare for the exams. Nonetheless, many training authorities feel that program certification alone is not sufficient for most software engineering jobs.

Professional certification is now offered by the Institute of Electrical and Electronics Engineers (IEEE) Computer Society. To be classified as a Certified Software Development Professional, individuals need a bachelor's degree and work experience that demonstrates that they have mastered a relevant body of knowledge, and must pass a written exam.

Persons interested in jobs as computer software engineers must have strong problem-solving and analytical skills. They also must be able to communicate effectively with team members, other staff, and the customers they meet. Because they often deal with a number of tasks simultaneously, they must be able to concentrate and pay close attention to detail.

As is the case with most occupations, advancement opportunities for computer software engineers increase with experience. Entry-level computer software engineers are likely to test and verify ongoing designs. As they become more experienced, computer software engineers may be involved in designing and developing software. Eventually, they may advance to become a project manager, manager of information systems, or chief information officer. Some computer software engineers with several years of experience or expertise find lucrative opportunities working as systems designers or independent consultants or starting their own computer consulting firms.

As technological advances in the computer field continue, employers demand new skills. Computer software engineers must continually strive to acquire such skills if they wish to remain in this extremely dynamic field. To help them keep up with the changing technology, continuing education and professional development seminars are offered by employers and software vendors, colleges and universities, private training institutions, and professional computing societies.

Job Outlook

Computer software engineers are projected to be one of the fastest growing occupations from 2002 to 2012. Rapid employment growth in the computer systems design and related services industry, which employs the greatest number of computer software engineers, should result in highly favorable opportunities for those college graduates with at least a bachelor's degree in computer engineering or computer science and practical experience working with computers. Employers will continue to seek computer professionals with strong programming, systems analysis, interpersonal, and business skills.

Despite the recent downturn among firms specializing in information technology, employment of computer software engineers is expected to increase much faster than the average for all occupations, as businesses and other organizations adopt and integrate new technologies and seek to maximize the efficiency of their computer systems. Job growth will not be as rapid as during the previous decade, however, as the software industry begins to mature and as routine software engineering work is increasingly outsourced overseas. Competition among businesses will continue to create an incentive for increasingly sophisticated technological innovations, and organizations will need more computer software engineers to implement these changes. In addition to jobs created through employment growth, many job openings will result annually from the need to replace workers who move into managerial positions, transfer to other occupations, or leave the labor force.

Demand for computer software engineers will increase as computer networking continues to grow. For example, the expanding integration of Internet technologies and the explosive growth in electronic commerce—doing business on the Internet—have resulted in rising demand for computer software engineers who can develop Internet, intranet, and World Wide Web applications. Likewise, expanding electronic data-processing systems in business, telecommunications, government, and other settings continue to become more sophisticated and complex. Growing numbers of systems software engineers will be needed to implement, safeguard, and update systems and resolve problems. Consulting opportunities for computer software engineers also should continue to grow as businesses seek help to manage, upgrade, and customize their increasingly complex computer systems.

New growth areas will continue to arise from rapidly evolving technologies. The increasing uses of the Internet, the proliferation of Web sites, and "mobile" technology such as the wireless Internet have created a demand for a wide variety of new products. As individuals and businesses rely more on hand-held computers and wireless networks, it will be necessary to integrate current computer systems with this new, more mobile technology. Also, information security concerns have given rise to new software needs. Concerns over "cyber security" should result in businesses and government continuing to invest heavily in security software that protects their networks and vital electronic infrastructure from attack. The expansion of this technology in the next 10 years will lead to an increased need for computer engineers to design and develop the software and systems to run these new applications and that will allow them to be integrated into older systems.

As with other information technology jobs, employment growth of computer software engineers may be tempered somewhat by an increase in contracting out of software development abroad. Firms may look to cut costs by shifting operations to foreign countries with highly educated workers who have strong technical skills.

Earnings

Median annual earnings of computer applications software engineers who worked full time in 2002 were about $70,900. The middle 50 percent earned between $55,510 and $88,660. The lowest 10 percent earned less than $44,830, and the highest 10 percent earned more than $109,800. Median annual earnings in the industries employing the largest numbers of computer applications software engineers in 2002 were:

Software publishers	$76,450
Navigational, measuring, electromedical, and control instruments manufacturing	75,890
Computer systems design and related services	71,890
Architectural, engineering, and related services	70,090
Management of companies and enterprises	67,260

Median annual earnings of computer systems software engineers who worked full time in 2002 were about $74,040. The middle 50 percent earned between $58,500 and $91,160. The lowest 10 percent earned less than $45,890, and the highest 10 percent earned more than $111,600. Median annual earnings in the industries employing the largest numbers of computer systems software engineers in 2002 are shown below:

Scientific research and development services	$82,270
Software publishers	77,120
Navigational, measuring, electromedical, and control instruments manufacturing	76,200
Computer systems design and related services	73,460
Wired telecommunications carriers	68,510

According to the National Association of Colleges and Employers, starting salary offers for graduates with a bachelor's degree in computer engineering averaged $51,343 in 2003, and those with a master's degree averaged $64,200. Starting salary offers for graduates with a bachelor's degree in computer science averaged $47,109.

According to Robert Half International, starting salaries for software engineers in software development ranged from $64,250 to $97,000 in 2003.

In addition to typical benefits, computer software engineers may be provided with profit sharing, stock options, and a company car with a mileage allowance.

Related Occupations

Other workers who use mathematics and logic extensively include computer systems analysts, database administrators, and computer scientists; computer programmers; financial analysts and personal financial advisors; computer hardware engineers; computer support specialists and systems administrators; statisticians; mathematicians; management analysts; actuaries; and operations research analysts.

Sources of Additional Information

Additional information on a career in computer software engineering is available from any of the following sources:
➤ Association for Computing Machinery (ACM), 1515 Broadway, New York, NY 10036. Internet: **http://www.acm.org**
➤ Institute of Electronics and Electrical Engineers Computer Society, Headquarters Office, 1730 Massachusetts Ave. NW., Washington, DC 20036-1992. Internet: **http://www.computer.org**
➤ National Workforce Center for Emerging Technologies, 3000 Landerholm Circle SE., Bellevue, WA 98007. Internet: **http://www.nwcet.org**

Computer Support Specialists and Systems Administrators

(0*NET 15-1041.00, 15-1071.00)

Significant Points

- Computer support specialists and systems administrators are projected to be among the fastest growing occupations over the 2002-12 period.

- There are many paths of entry to these occupations.

- Job prospects should be best for college graduates who are up to date with the latest skills and technologies; certifications and practical experience are essential for persons without degrees.

Nature of the Work

In the last decade, computers have become an integral part of everyday life, used for a variety of reasons at home, in the workplace, and at schools. And almost every computer user encounters a problem occasionally, whether it is the disaster of a crashing hard drive or the annoyance of a forgotten password. The explosion of computer use has created a high demand for specialists to provide advice to users, as well as day-to-day administration, maintenance, and support of computer systems and networks.

Computer support specialists provide technical assistance, support, and advice to customers and other users. This occupational group includes *technical support specialists* and *help-desk technicians*. These troubleshooters interpret problems and provide technical support for hardware, software, and systems. They answer telephone calls, analyze problems using automated diagnostic programs, and resolve recurrent difficulties. Support specialists may work either within a company that uses computer systems or directly for a computer hardware or software vendor. Increasingly, these specialists work for help-desk or support services firms, where they provide computer support to clients on a contract basis.

Technical support specialists are troubleshooters, providing valuable assistance to their organization's computer users. Because many nontechnical employees are not computer experts, they often run into computer problems that they cannot resolve on their own. Technical support specialists install, modify, clean, and repair computer hardware and software. They also may work on monitors, keyboards, printers, and mice.

Technical support specialists answer telephone calls from their organizations' computer users and may run automatic diagnostics programs to resolve problems. They also may write training manuals and train computer users how to properly use new computer hardware and software. In addition, technical support specialists oversee the daily performance of their company's computer systems and evaluate software programs for usefulness.

Help-desk technicians assist computer users with the inevitable hardware and software questions not addressed in a product's instruction manual. Help-desk technicians field telephone calls and e-mail messages from customers seeking guidance on technical problems. In responding to these requests for guidance, help-desk technicians must listen carefully to the customer, ask questions to diagnose the nature of the problem, and then patiently walk the customer through the problem-solving steps.

Help-desk technicians deal directly with customer issues, and companies value them as a source of feedback on their products. These technicians are consulted for information about what gives customers the most trouble, as well as other customer concerns. Most computer support specialists start out at the help desk.

Network or *computer systems administrators* design, install, and support an organization's LAN (local-area network), WAN (wide-area network), network segment, Internet, or intranet system. They provide day-to-day onsite administrative support for software users in a variety of work environments, including professional offices, small businesses, government, and large corporations. They maintain network hardware and software, analyze problems, and monitor the network to ensure its availability to system users. These workers gather data to identify customer needs and then use that information to identify, interpret, and evaluate system and network requirements. Administrators also may plan, coordinate, and implement network security measures.

Systems administrators are the information technology employees responsible for the efficient use of networks by organizations. They ensure that the design of an organization's computer site allows all of the components, including computers, the network, and software, to fit together and work properly. Furthermore, they monitor and adjust performance of existing networks and continually survey the current computer site to determine future network needs. Administrators also troubleshoot problems as reported by users and automated network monitoring systems and make recommendations for enhancements in the implementation of future servers and networks.

In some organizations, *computer security specialists* may plan, coordinate, and implement the organization's information security. These workers may be called upon to educate users on computer security, install security software, monitor the network for security breaches, respond to cyber attacks, and in some cases, gather data and evidence to be used in prosecuting cyber crime. This and other growing specialty occupations reflect the increasing emphasis on client-server applications, the expansion of Internet and intranet applications, and the demand for more end-user support.

Working Conditions

Computer support specialists and systems administrators normally work in well-lit, comfortable offices or computer laboratories. They usually work about 40 hours a week, but that may include being "on call" via pager or telephone for rotating evening or weekend work if the employer requires computer support over extended hours. Overtime may be necessary when unexpected technical problems arise. Like other workers who type on a keyboard for long periods, computer support specialists and systems administrators are susceptible to eyestrain, back discomfort, and hand and wrist problems such as carpal tunnel syndrome.

Due to the heavy emphasis on helping all types of computer users, computer support specialists and systems administrators constantly interact with customers and fellow employees as they answer questions and give valuable advice. Those who work as consultants are away from their offices much of the time, sometimes spending months working in a client's office.

As computer networks expand, more computer support specialists and systems administrators may be able to connect to a customer's computer remotely, using modems, laptops, e-mail, and the Internet, to provide technical support to computer users.

Computer support specialists provide technical assistance, support, and advice to computer users.

This capability would reduce or eliminate travel to the customer's workplace. Systems administrators also can administer and configure networks and servers remotely, although this practice is not as common as it is with computer support specialists.

Employment

Computer support specialists and systems administrators held about 758,000 jobs in 2002. Of these, about 507,000 were computer support specialists and about 251,000 were network and computer systems administrators. Although they worked in a wide range of industries, 35 percent of all computer support specialists and systems administrators were employed in professional and business services industries, principally in computer systems design and related services. Other organizations that employed substantial numbers of these workers include banks, government agencies, insurance companies, educational institutions, and wholesale and retail vendors of computers, office equipment, appliances, and home electronic equipment. Many computer support specialists also worked for manufacturers of computers, semiconductors, and other electronic components.

Employers of computer support specialists and systems administrators range from startup companies to established industry leaders. With the continued development of the Internet, telecommunications, and e-mail, industries not typically associated with computers—such as construction—increasingly need computer-related workers. Small and large firms across all industries are expanding or developing computer systems, creating an immediate need for computer support specialists and systems administrators.

Training, Other Qualifications, and Advancement

Due to the wide range of skills required, there are many paths of entry to a job as a computer support specialist or systems administrator. While there is no universally accepted way to prepare for a job as a computer support specialist, many employers prefer to hire persons with some formal college education. A bachelor's degree in computer science or information systems is a prerequisite for some jobs; however, other jobs may require only a computer-related associate degree. For systems administrators, many employers seek applicants with bachelor's degrees, although not necessarily in a computer-related field.

Many companies are becoming more flexible about requiring a college degree for support positions because of the explo-

sive demand for specialists. However, certification and practical experience demonstrating these skills will be essential for applicants without a degree. Completion of a certification training program, offered by a variety of vendors and product makers, may help some people to qualify for entry-level positions. Relevant computer experience may substitute for formal education.

Beginning computer support specialists usually work for organizations that deal directly with customers or in-house users. Then, they may advance into more responsible positions in which they use what they have learned from customers to improve the design and efficiency of future products. Job promotions usually depend more on performance than on formal education. Eventually, some computer support specialists become applications developers, designing products rather than assisting users. Computer support specialists at hardware and software companies often enjoy great upward mobility; advancement sometimes comes within months of initial employment.

Entry-level network and computer systems administrators are involved in routine maintenance and monitoring of computer systems, typically working behind the scenes in an organization. After gaining experience and expertise, they often are able to advance into more senior-level positions, in which they take on more responsibilities. For example, senior network and computer systems administrators may present recommendations to management on matters related to a company's network. They also may translate the needs of an organization into a set of technical requirements, based on the available technology. As with support specialists, administrators may become software engineers, actually involved in the designing of the system or network and not just the day-to-day administration.

Persons interested in becoming a computer support specialist or systems administrator must have strong problem-solving, analytical, and communication skills because troubleshooting and helping others are vital parts of the job. The constant interaction with other computer personnel, customers, and employees requires computer support specialists and systems administrators to communicate effectively on paper, via e-mail, or in person. Strong writing skills are useful when preparing manuals for employees and customers.

As technology continues to improve, computer support specialists and systems administrators must keep their skills current and acquire new ones. Many continuing education programs are offered by employers, hardware and software vendors, colleges and universities, and private training institutions. Professional development seminars offered by computing services firms also can enhance one's skills and advancement opportunities.

Job Outlook

Employment of computer support specialist is expected to increase faster than the average for all occupations through 2012, as organizations continue to adopt and integrate increasingly sophisticated technology. Job growth will continue to be driven by the continued expansion of the computer system design and related services industry, which is projected to remain one of the fastest growing industries in the U.S. economy, despite recent job losses. Job growth will not be as explosive as during the previous decade, however, as these jobs are being increasingly outsourced overseas.

Employment growth among computer support specialists reflects the rapid pace of improved technology. As computers and software become more complex, support specialists will be needed to provide technical assistance to customers and other users. New mobility technologies, such as the wireless Internet, will continue to create a demand for these workers to familiarize and educate computer users. Consulting opportunities for computer support specialists also should continue to grow as businesses increasingly need help managing, upgrading, and customizing more complex computer systems. However, growth in employment of support specialists may be tempered somewhat as firms continue to cut costs by shifting more routine work abroad to countries where workers are highly skilled but labor costs are lower. Physical location is not as important for these workers as it is for others, because computer support specialists can provide assistance remotely and support services can be provided around the clock.

Employment of systems administrators is expected to increase much faster than average as firms will continue to invest heavily in securing computer networks. Companies are looking for workers knowledgeable about the function and administration of networks. Such employees have become increasingly hard to find as systems administration has moved from being a separate function within corporations to one that forms a crucial element of business in an increasingly high-technology economy. Also, demand for computer security specialists will grow as businesses and government continue to invest heavily in "cyber-security," protecting vital computer networks and electronic infrastructure from attack.

The growth of electronic commerce means that more establishments use the Internet to conduct their business online. This translates into a need for information technology specialists who can help organizations use technology to communicate with employees, clients, and consumers. Explosive growth in these areas also is expected to fuel demand for specialists knowledgeable about network, data, and communications security.

Job prospects should be best for college graduates who are up to date with the latest skills and technologies, particularly if they have supplemented their formal education with some relevant work experience. Employers will continue to seek computer specialists who possess a strong background in fundamental computer skills, combined with good interpersonal and communication skills. Due to the rapid growth in demand for computer support specialists and systems administrators, those who have strong computer skills but do not have a bachelor's degree should continue to qualify for some entry-level positions. However, certifications and practical experience are essential for persons without degrees.

Earnings
Median annual earnings of computer support specialists were $39,100 in 2002. The middle 50 percent earned between $29,760 and $51,680. The lowest 10 percent earned less than $23,060, and the highest 10 percent earned more than $67,550. Median annual earnings in the industries employing the largest numbers of computer support specialists in 2002 were:

Professional and commercial equipment and supplies merchant wholesalers	$46,740
Software publishers	42,870
Computer systems design and related services	41,110
Management of companies and enterprises	40,850
Elementary and secondary schools	33,480

Median annual earnings of network and computer systems administrators were $54,810 in 2002. The middle 50 percent earned between $43,290 and $69,530. The lowest 10 percent earned less than $34,460, and the highest 10 percent earned more than $86,440. Median annual earnings in the industries employing the largest numbers of network and computer systems administrators in 2002 were:

Wired telecommunications carriers	$59,710
Computer systems design and related services	58,790
Management of companies and enterprises	58,610
Data processing, hosting, and related services	56,140
Elementary and secondary schools	48,350

According to Robert Half International, starting salaries in 2003 ranged from $27,500 to $56,500 for help-desk support staff, and from $51,000 to $67,250 for more senior technical support specialists. For systems administrators, starting salaries in 2003 ranged from $49,000 to $70,250.

Related Occupations
Other computer-related occupations include computer programmers; computer software engineers; and computer systems analysts, database administrators, and computer scientists.

Sources of Additional Information
For additional information about a career as a computer support specialist, contact:
➤ Association of Computer Support Specialists, 218 Huntington Rd., Bridgeport, CT 06608. Internet: **http://www.acss.org**
➤ Association of Support Professionals, 122 Barnard Ave., Watertown, MA 02472.

For additional information about a career as a systems administrator, contact:
➤ System Administrators Guild, 2560 9th St., Suite 215, Berkeley, CA 94710. Internet: **http://www.sage.org**

Further information about computer careers is available from:
➤ National Workforce Center for Emerging Technologies, 3000 Landerholm Circle SE., Bellevue, WA 98007. Internet: **http://www.nwcet.org**

Computer Systems Analysts, Database Administrators, and Computer Scientists

(O*NET 15-1011.00, 15-1051.00, 15-1061.00, 15-1081.00, 15-1099.99)

Significant Points

- Education requirements range from a 2-year degree to a graduate degree.
- Employment is expected to increase much faster than the average as organizations continue to adopt increasingly sophisticated technologies.
- Job prospects are favorable.

Nature of the Work
The rapid spread of computers and information technology has generated a need for highly trained workers to design and develop new hardware and software systems and to incorporate new technologies. These workers—computer systems analysts, database administrators, and computer scientists—include a wide

range of computer specialists. Job tasks and occupational titles used to describe these workers evolve rapidly, reflecting new areas of specialization or changes in technology, as well as the preferences and practices of employers.

Systems analysts solve computer problems and apply computer technology to meet the individual needs of an organization. They help an organization to realize the maximum benefit from its investment in equipment, personnel, and business processes. Systems analysts may plan and develop new computer systems or devise ways to apply existing systems' resources to additional operations. They may design new systems, including both hardware and software, or add a new software application to harness more of the computer's power. Most systems analysts work with specific types of systems—for example, business, accounting, or financial systems, or scientific and engineering systems—that vary with the kind of organization. Some systems analysts also are known as *systems developers* or *systems architects.*

Systems analysts begin an assignment by discussing the systems problem with managers and users to determine its exact nature. Defining the goals of the system and dividing the solutions into individual steps and separate procedures, systems analysts use techniques such as structured analysis, data modeling, information engineering, mathematical model building, sampling, and cost accounting to plan the system. They specify the inputs to be accessed by the system, design the processing steps, and format the output to meet users' needs. They also may prepare cost-benefit and return-on-investment analyses to help management decide whether implementing the proposed technology will be financially feasible.

When a system is accepted, systems analysts determine what computer hardware and software will be needed to set the system up. They coordinate tests and observe the initial use of the system to ensure that it performs as planned. They prepare specifications, flow charts, and process diagrams for computer programmers to follow; then, they work with programmers to "debug," or eliminate, errors from the system. Systems analysts who do more indepth testing of products may be referred to as *software quality assurance analysts.* In addition to running tests, these individuals diagnose problems, recommend solutions, and determine whether program requirements have been met.

In some organizations, *programmer-analysts* design and update the software that runs a computer. Because they are responsible for both programming and systems analysis, these workers must be proficient in both areas. (A separate statement on computer programmers appears elsewhere in the *Handbook.*) As this dual proficiency becomes more commonplace, these analysts increasingly work with databases, object-oriented programming languages, as well as client-server applications development and multimedia and Internet technology.

One obstacle associated with expanding computer use is the need for different computer systems to communicate with each other. Because of the importance of maintaining up-to-date information-accounting records, sales figures, or budget projections, for example—systems analysts work on making the computer systems within an organization, or among organizations, compatible so that information can be shared among them. Many systems analysts are involved with "networking," connecting all the computers internally—in an individual office, department, or establishment—or externally, because many organiza-

tions now rely on e-mail or the Internet. A primary goal of networking is to allow users to retrieve data from a mainframe computer or a server and use it on their desktop computer. Systems analysts must design the hardware and software to allow the free exchange of data, custom applications, and the computer power to process it all. For example, analysts are called upon to ensure the compatibility of computing systems between and among businesses to facilitate electronic commerce.

Networks come in many variations, so *network systems and data communications analysts* are needed to design, test, and evaluate systems such as local area networks (LANs), wide area networks (WANs), the Internet, intranets, and other data communications systems. Systems can range from a connection between two offices in the same building to globally distributed networks, voice mail, and e-mail systems of a multinational organization. Network systems and data communications analysts perform network modeling, analysis, and planning; they also may research related products and make necessary hardware and software recommendations. *Telecommunications specialists* focus on the interaction between computer and communications equipment. These workers design voice and data communication systems, supervise the installation of those systems, and provide maintenance and other services to clients after the system is installed.

The growth of the Internet and the expansion of the World Wide Web (the graphical portion of the Internet) have generated a variety of occupations related to the design, development, and maintenance of Web sites and their servers. For example, *webmasters* are responsible for all technical aspects of a Web site, including performance issues such as speed of access, and for approving the content of the site. *Internet developers* or W*eb developers*, also called W*eb designers*, are responsible for day-to-day site design and creation.

Computer scientists work as theorists, researchers, or inventors. Their jobs are distinguished by the higher level of theoretical expertise and innovation they apply to complex problems and the creation or application of new technology. Those employed by academic institutions work in areas ranging from complexity theory, to hardware, to programming-language design. Some work on multidisciplinary projects, such as developing and advancing uses of virtual reality, extending human-

Computer systems analysts solve computer problems and use computer technology to meet the needs of an organization.

computer interaction, or designing robots. Their counterparts in private industry work in areas such as applying theory, developing specialized languages or information technologies, or designing programming tools, knowledge-based systems, or even computer games.

With the Internet and electronic business generating large volumes of data, there is a growing need to be able to store, manage, and extract data effectively. *Database administrators* work with database management systems software and determine ways to organize and store data. They identify user requirements, set up computer databases, and test and coordinate modifications to the systems. An organization's database administrator ensures the performance of the system, understands the platform on which the database runs, and adds new users to the system. Because they also may design and implement system security, database administrators often plan and coordinate security measures. With the volume of sensitive data generated every second growing rapidly, data integrity, backup systems, and database security have become increasingly important aspects of the job of database administrators.

Working Conditions

Computer systems analysts, database administrators, and computer scientists normally work in offices or laboratories in comfortable surroundings. They usually work about 40 hours a week—the same as many other professional or office workers do. However, evening or weekend work may be necessary to meet deadlines or solve specific problems. Given the technology available today, telecommuting is common for computer professionals. As networks expand, more work can be done from remote locations through modems, laptops, electronic mail, and the Internet.

Like other workers who spend long periods in front of a computer terminal typing on a keyboard, computer systems analysts, database administrators, and computer scientists are susceptible to eyestrain, back discomfort, and hand and wrist problems such as carpal tunnel syndrome or cumulative trauma disorder.

Employment

Computer systems analysts, database administrators, and computer scientists held about 979,000 jobs in 2002; including about 89,000 who were self-employed. Employment was distributed among the following detailed occupations:

Computer systems analysts 468,000
Network systems and data communications analysts 186,000
Database administrators 110,000
Computer and information scientists, research 23,000
All other computer specialists 192,000

Although they are increasingly employed in every sector of the economy, the greatest concentration of these workers is in the computer systems design and related services industry. Firms in this industry provide services related to the commercial use of computers on a contract basis, including custom computer programming services; computer systems integration design services; computer facilities management services, including computer systems or data-processing facilities support services for clients; and other computer-related services, such as disaster recovery services and software installation. Many computer systems analysts, database administrators, and computer scientists are employed by Internet service providers, web search portals, and data-processing, hosting, and related services firms. Others work for government, manufacturers of computer and electronic products, insurance companies, financial institutions, and universities.

A growing number of computer specialists, such as systems analysts and network and data communications analysts, are employed on a temporary or contract basis; many of these individuals are self-employed, working independently as contractors or consultants. For example, a company installing a new computer system may need the services of several systems analysts just to get the system running. Because not all of the analysts would be needed once the system is functioning, the company might contract for such employees with a temporary help agency or a consulting firm or with the systems analysts themselves. Such jobs may last from several months up to 2 years or more. This growing practice enables companies to bring in people with the exact skills the firm needs to complete a particular project, rather than having to spend time or money training or retraining existing workers. Often, experienced consultants then train a company's in-house staff as a project develops.

Training, Other Qualifications, and Advancement

Rapidly changing technology requires an increasing level of skill and education on the part of employees. Companies look for professionals with an ever-broader background and range of skills, including not only technical knowledge, but also communication and other interpersonal skills. This shift from requiring workers to possess solely sound technical knowledge emphasizes workers who can handle various responsibilities. While there is no universally accepted way to prepare for a job as a systems analyst, computer scientist, or database administrator, most employers place a premium on some formal college education. A bachelor's degree is a prerequisite for many jobs; however, some jobs may require only a 2-year degree. Relevant work experience also is very important. For more technically complex jobs, persons with graduate degrees are preferred.

For systems analyst, programmer-analyst, and database administrator positions, many employers seek applicants who have a bachelor's degree in computer science, information science, or management information systems (MIS). MIS programs usually are part of the business school or college and differ considerably from computer science programs, emphasizing business and management-oriented course work and business computing courses. Employers are increasingly seeking individuals with a master's degree in business administration (MBA), with a concentration in information systems, as more firms move their business to the Internet. For some network systems and data communication analysts, such as webmasters, an associate's degree or certificate is sufficient, although more advanced positions might require a computer-related bachelor's degree. For computer and information scientists, a doctoral degree generally is required due to the highly technical nature of their work.

Despite employers' preference for those with technical degrees, persons with degrees in a variety of majors find employment in these computer occupations. The level of education and type of training that employers require depend on their needs. One factor affecting these needs is changes in technology. Employers often scramble to find workers capable of implementing "hot" new technologies. Those workers with formal education or experience in information security, for example, are in demand because of the growing need for their skills and services. Another factor driving employers' needs is the timeframe during which a project must be completed.

Most community colleges and many independent technical institutes and proprietary schools offer an associate's degree in computer science or a related information technology field. Many of these programs may be more geared toward meeting the needs of local businesses and are more occupation specific than are 4-year degree programs. Some jobs may be better suited to the level of training that such programs offer. Employers usually look for people who have broad knowledge and experience related to computer systems and technologies, strong problem-solving and analytical skills, and good interpersonal skills. Courses in computer science or systems design offer good preparation for a job in these computer occupations. For jobs in a business environment, employers usually want systems analysts to have business management or closely related skills, while a background in the physical sciences, applied mathematics, or engineering is preferred for work in scientifically oriented organizations. Art or graphic design skills may be desirable for webmasters or Web developers.

Jobseekers can enhance their employment opportunities by participating in internship or co-op programs offered through their schools. Because many people develop advanced computer skills in a non-computer-related occupation and then transfer those skills to a computer occupation, a background in the industry in which the person's job is located, such as financial services, banking, or accounting, can be important. Others have taken computer science courses to supplement their study in fields such as accounting, inventory control, or other business areas. For example, a financial analyst who is proficient in computers might become a computer support specialist in financial systems development, while a computer programmer might move into a systems analyst job.

Computer systems analysts, database administrators, and computer scientists must be able to think logically and have good communication skills. Because they often deal with a number of tasks simultaneously, the ability to concentrate and pay close attention to detail is important. Although these computer specialists sometimes work independently, they frequently work in teams on large projects. They must be able to communicate effectively with computer personnel, such as programmers and managers, as well as with users or other staff who may have no technical computer background.

Computer scientists employed in private industry may advance into managerial or project leadership positions. Those employed in academic institutions can become heads of research departments or published authorities in their field. Systems analysts may be promoted to senior or lead systems analyst. Those who show leadership ability also can become project managers or advance into management positions such as manager of information systems or chief information officer. Database administrators may advance into managerial positions, such as chief technology officer, on the basis of their experience managing data and enforcing security. Computer specialists with work experience and considerable expertise in a particular sub-

ject or a certain application may find lucrative opportunities as independent consultants or may choose to start their own computer consulting firms.

Technological advances come so rapidly in the computer field that continuous study is necessary to keep one's skills up to date. Employers, hardware and software vendors, colleges and universities, and private training institutions offer continuing education. Additional training may come from professional development seminars offered by professional computing societies.

Certification is a way to demonstrate a level of competence in a particular field. Some product vendors or software firms offer certification and require professionals who work with their products to be certified. Many employers regard these certifications as the industry standard. For example, one method of acquiring enough knowledge to get a job as a database administrator is to become certified in a specific type of database management. Voluntary certification also is available through various organizations associated with computer specialists. Professional certification may afford a jobseeker a competitive advantage.

Job Outlook

Computer systems analysts, database administrators, and computer scientists are expected to be among the fastest growing occupations through 2012. Employment of these computer specialists is expected to grow much faster than the average for all occupations as organizations continue to adopt and integrate increasingly sophisticated technologies. Job increases will be driven by very rapid growth in computer system design and related services, which is projected to be one of the fastest-growing industries in the U.S. economy. In addition, many job openings will arise annually from the need to replace workers who move into managerial positions or other occupations or who leave the labor force. Job growth will not be as rapid as during the previous decade, however, as the information technology sector begins to mature and as routine work is increasingly outsourced overseas.

Despite the recent economic downturn among information technology firms, workers in the occupation should still enjoy favorable job prospects. The demand for networking to facilitate the sharing of information, the expansion of client-server environments, and the need for computer specialists to use their knowledge and skills in a problem-solving capacity will be major factors in the rising demand for computer systems analysts, database administrators, and computer scientists. Moreover, falling prices of computer hardware and software should continue to induce more businesses to expand their computerized operations and integrate new technologies into them. In order to maintain a competitive edge and operate more efficiently, firms will keep demanding computer specialists who are knowledgeable about the latest technologies and are able to apply them to meet the needs of businesses.

Increasingly, more sophisticated and complex technology is being implemented across all organizations, which should fuel the demand for these computer occupations. There is a growing demand for system analysts to help firms maximize their efficiency with available technology. Expansion of electronic commerce—doing business on the Internet—and the continuing need to build and maintain databases that store critical information on customers, inventory, and projects are fueling demand for database administrators familiar with the latest technology. Also, the increasing importance being placed on "cybersecurity"—the protection of electronic information—will result in a need for workers skilled in information security.

The development of new technologies usually leads to demand for various kinds of workers. The expanding integration of Internet technologies into businesses, for example, has resulted in a growing need for specialists who can develop and support Internet and intranet applications. The growth of electronic commerce means that more establishments use the Internet to conduct their business online. The introduction of the wireless Internet, known as WiFi, creates new systems to be analyzed and new data to be administered. The spread of such new technologies translates into a need for information technology professionals who can help organizations use technology to communicate with employees, clients, and consumers. Explosive growth in these areas also is expected to fuel demand for specialists who are knowledgeable about network, data, and communications security.

As technology becomes more sophisticated and complex, employers demand a higher level of skill and expertise from their employees. Individuals with an advanced degree in computer science or computer engineering or with an MBA with a concentration in information systems should enjoy highly favorable employment prospects. College graduates with a bachelor's degree in computer science, computer engineering, information science, or MIS also should enjoy favorable prospects for employment, particularly if they have supplemented their formal education with practical experience. Because employers continue to seek computer specialists who can combine strong technical skills with good interpersonal and business skills, graduates with non-computer-science degrees, but who have had courses in computer programming, systems analysis, and other information technology areas, also should continue to find jobs in these computer fields. In fact, individuals with the right experience and training can work in these computer occupations regardless of their college major or level of formal education.

Earnings

Median annual earnings of computer systems analysts were $62,890 in 2002. The middle 50 percent earned between $49,500 and $78,350 a year. The lowest 10 percent earned less than $39,270, and the highest 10 percent earned more than $93,400. Median annual earnings in the industries employing the largest numbers of computer systems analysts in 2002 were as follows:

Federal Government	$68,370
Computer systems design and related services	67,690
Data processing, hosting, and related services	64,560
Management of companies and enterprises	63,390
Insurance carriers	59,510

Median annual earnings of database administrators were $55,480 in 2002. The middle 50 percent earned between $40,550 and $75,100. The lowest 10 percent earned less than $30,750, and the highest 10 percent earned more than $92,910. In 2002, median annual earnings of database administrators employed in computer system design and related services were $66,650,

and, for those in management of companies and enterprises, earnings were $59,620.

Median annual earnings of network systems and data communication analysts were $58,420 in 2002. The middle 50 percent earned between $44,850 and $74,290. The lowest 10 percent earned less than $34,880, and the highest 10 percent earned more than $92,110. Median annual earnings in the industries employing the largest numbers of network systems and data communications analysts in 2002 were as follows:

Computer systems design and related services	$65,800
Management of companies and enterprises	63,050
State government	45,110

Median annual earnings of computer and information scientists, research, were $77,760 in 2002. The middle 50 percent earned between $58,630 and $98,490. The lowest 10 percent earned less than $42,890, and the highest 10 percent earned more than $121,650. Median annual earnings of computer and information scientists employed in computer systems design and related services in 2002 were $78,730.

Median annual earnings of all other computer specialists were $54,070 in 2002. Median annual earnings of all other computer specialists employed in computer system design and related services were $49,590, and, for those in scientific research and development services, earnings were $70,150 in 2002.

According to the National Association of Colleges and Employers, starting offers for graduates with a master's degree in computer science averaged $62,806 in 2003. Starting offers averaged $47,109 for graduates with a bachelor's degree in computer science; $45,346 for those with a degree in computer programming; $41,118 for those with a degree in computer systems analysis; $40,556 for those with a degree in management information systems; and $38,282 for those with a degree in information sciences and systems.

According to Robert Half International, starting salaries in 2003 ranged from $69,750 to $101,750 for database administrators. Salaries for networking and Internet-related occupations ranged from $45,500 to $65,750 for LAN administrators and from $51,250 to $73,750 for Internet /Intranet developers. Starting salaries for security professionals ranged from $62,500 to $91,750 in 2003.

Related Occupations

Other workers who use logic and creativity to solve business and technical problems are computer programmers, computer software engineers, computer and information systems managers, financial analysts and personal financial advisors, urban and regional planners, engineers, mathematicians, statisticians, operations research analysts, management analysts, and actuaries.

Sources of Additional Information

Further information about computer careers is available from any of the following organizations:

➤ Association for Computing Machinery (ACM), 1515 Broadway, New York, NY 10036. Internet: **http://www.acm.org**

➤ Institute of Electrical and Electronics Engineers Computer Society, Headquarters Office, 1730 Massachusetts Ave. NW., Washington, DC 20036-1992. Internet: **http://www.computer.org**

➤ National Workforce Center for Emerging Technologies, 3000 Landerholm Circle SE., Bellevue, WA 98007. Internet: **http://www.nwcet.org**

Mathematicians

(0*NET 15-2021.00)

Significant Points

- A Ph.D. degree in mathematics usually is the minimum education needed, except in the Federal Government.

- Employment is expected to contract, reflecting the decline in the number of jobs with the title mathematician; competition will be keen for the limited number of jobs.

- Master's and Ph.D. degree holders with a strong background in mathematics and a related discipline, such as computer science or engineering, should have better employment opportunities in related occupations.

Nature of the Work

Mathematics is one of the oldest and most fundamental sciences. Mathematicians use mathematical theory, computational techniques, algorithms, and the latest computer technology to solve economic, scientific, engineering, physics, and business problems. The work of mathematicians falls into two broad classes—theoretical (pure) mathematics and applied mathematics. These classes, however, are not sharply defined, and often overlap.

Theoretical mathematicians advance mathematical knowledge by developing new principles and recognizing previously unknown relationships between existing principles of mathematics. Although these workers seek to increase basic knowledge without necessarily considering its practical use, such pure and abstract knowledge has been instrumental in producing or furthering many scientific and engineering achievements. Many theoretical mathematicians are employed as university faculty, and divide their time between teaching and conducting research. (See the statement on teachers—postsecondary, elsewhere in the *Handbook*.)

Applied mathematicians, on the other hand, use theories and techniques, such as mathematical modeling and computational methods, to formulate and solve practical problems in business, government, and engineering, and in the physical, life, and social sciences. For example, they may analyze the most efficient way to schedule airline routes between cities, the effect and safety of new drugs, the aerodynamic characteristics of an experimental automobile, or the cost-effectiveness of alternative manufacturing processes. Applied mathematicians working in industrial research and development may develop or enhance mathematical methods when solving a difficult problem. Some mathematicians, called cryptanalysts, analyze and decipher encryption systems designed to transmit military, political, financial, or law enforcement-related information in code.

Applied mathematicians start with a practical problem, envision the separate elements of the process under consideration, and then reduce the elements to mathematical variables. They often use computers to analyze relationships among the variables and solve complex problems by developing models with alternative solutions.

Much of the work in applied mathematics is done by individuals with titles other than mathematician. In fact, because

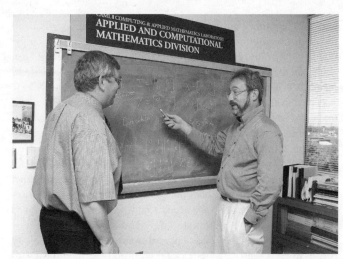

Mathematicians often use theory to explain mathematical relationships in the real world.

mathematics is the foundation upon which so many other academic disciplines are built, the number of workers using mathematical techniques is much greater than the number formally designated as mathematicians. For example, engineers, computer scientists, physicists, and economists are among those who use mathematics extensively. Some professionals, including statisticians, actuaries, and operations research analysts, actually are specialists in a particular branch of mathematics. Frequently, applied mathematicians are required to collaborate with other workers in their organizations to achieve common solutions to problems. (For more information, see the statements on actuaries, operations research analysts, and statisticians elsewhere in the *Handbook*.)

Working Conditions

Mathematicians usually work in comfortable offices. They often are part of an interdisciplinary team that may include economists, engineers, computer scientists, physicists, technicians, and others. Deadlines, overtime work, special requests for information or analysis, and prolonged travel to attend seminars or conferences may be part of their jobs. Mathematicians who work in academia usually have a mix of teaching and research responsibilities. These mathematicians often conduct research alone, or are aided by graduate students interested in the topic being researched.

Employment

Mathematicians held about 2,900 jobs in 2002. In addition, about 20,000 persons held full-time mathematics faculty positions in colleges and universities in 2002, according to the American Mathematical Society.

Many nonfaculty mathematicians work for Federal or State governments. The U.S. Department of Defense is the primary Federal employer, accounting for about three-fourths of the mathematicians employed by the Federal Government. Most other mathematicians employed by the Federal Government work for the National Aeronautics and Space Administration (NASA). In the private sector, major employers include insurance carriers, scientific research and development services, and management, scientific, and technical consulting services. Within manufacturing, the aerospace and pharmaceutical industries are the key employers. Some mathematicians also work for investment banks, insurance companies, and securities and commodity exchanges.

Training, Other Qualifications, and Advancement

A Ph.D. degree in mathematics usually is the minimum education needed for prospective mathematicians, except in the Federal Government. In the Federal Government, entry-level job candidates usually must have a 4-year degree with a major in mathematics or a 4-year degree with the equivalent of a mathematics major—24 semester hours of mathematics courses.

In private industry, candidates for mathematician jobs typically need a master's or Ph.D. degree. Most of the positions designated for mathematicians are in research and development laboratories, as part of technical teams. Research scientists in such positions engage either in basic research on pure mathematical principles or in applied research on developing or improving specific products or processes. The majority of those with a bachelor's or master's degree in mathematics who work in private industry do so not as mathematicians, but in related fields such as computer science, where they have titles such as computer programmer, systems analyst, or systems engineer.

A bachelor's degree in mathematics is offered by most colleges and universities. Mathematics courses usually required for this degree include calculus, differential equations, and linear and abstract algebra. Additional courses might include probability theory and statistics, mathematical analysis, numerical analysis, topology, discrete mathematics, and mathematical logic. Many colleges and universities urge or require students majoring in mathematics to take courses in a field that is closely related to mathematics, such as computer science, engineering, life science, physical science, or economics. A double major in mathematics and another related discipline is particularly desirable to many employers. High school students who are prospective college mathematics majors should take as many mathematics courses as possible while in high school.

In 2003, about 225 colleges and universities offered a master's degree as the highest degree in either pure or applied mathematics; about 200 offered a Ph.D. degree in pure or applied mathematics. In graduate school, students conduct research and take advanced courses, usually specializing in a subfield of mathematics.

For jobs in applied mathematics, training in the field in which the mathematics will be used is very important. Mathematics is used extensively in physics, actuarial science, statistics, engineering, and operations research. Computer science, business and industrial management, economics, finance, chemistry, geology, life sciences, and behavioral sciences are likewise dependent on applied mathematics. Mathematicians also should have substantial knowledge of computer programming, because most complex mathematical computation and much mathematical modeling are done on a computer.

Mathematicians need good reasoning ability and persistence in order to identify, analyze, and apply basic principles to technical problems. Communication skills are important, as mathematicians must be able to interact and discuss proposed solutions with people who may not have an extensive knowledge of mathematics.

Job Outlook

Competition is keen for the limited number of jobs as mathematicians. Employment of mathematicians is expected to decline through 2012, reflecting the decline in the number of jobs with the title mathematician. However, master's and Ph.D. degree holders with a strong background in mathematics and a related

discipline, such as engineering or computer science, should have better opportunities. Many of these workers have job titles that reflect their occupation, such as systems analyst, rather than the title mathematician, reflecting their primary educational background.

Advancements in technology usually lead to expanding applications of mathematics, and more workers with knowledge of mathematics will be required in the future. However, jobs in industry and government often require advanced knowledge of related scientific disciplines in addition to mathematics. The most common fields in which mathematicians study and find work are computer science and software development, physics, engineering, and operations research. More mathematicians also are becoming involved in financial analysis. Mathematicians must compete for jobs, however, with people who have degrees in these other disciplines. The most successful jobseekers will be able to apply mathematical theory to real-world problems, and possess good communication, teamwork, and computer skills.

Private industry jobs require at least a master's degree in mathematics or in one of the related fields. Bachelor's degree holders in mathematics usually are not qualified for most jobs, and many seek advanced degrees in mathematics or a related discipline. However, bachelor's degree holders who meet State certification requirements may become primary or secondary school mathematics teachers. (For additional information, see the statement on teachers—preschool, kindergarten, elementary, middle, and secondary, elsewhere in the *Handbook*.)

Holders of a master's degree in mathematics will face very strong competition for jobs in theoretical research. Because the number of Ph.D. degrees awarded in mathematics continues to exceed the number of university positions available, many of these graduates will need to find employment in industry and government.

Earnings

Median annual earnings of mathematicians were $76,470 in 2002. The middle 50 percent earned between $56,160 and $91,520. The lowest 10 percent had earnings of less than $38,930, while the highest 10 percent earned over $112,780.

According to a 2003 survey by the National Association of Colleges and Employers, starting salary offers averaged $40,512 a year for mathematics graduates with a bachelor's degree, and $42,348 for those with a master's degree. Doctoral degree candidates averaged $55,485.

In early 2003, the average annual salary for mathematicians employed by the Federal Government in supervisory, nonsupervisory, and managerial positions was $80,877; that for mathematical statisticians was $83,472; and for cryptanalysts, the average was $78,662.

Related Occupations

Other occupations that require extensive knowledge of mathematics or, in some cases, a degree in mathematics include actuaries; statisticians; computer programmers; computer systems analysts, database administrators, and computer scientists; computer software engineers; and operations research analysts. A strong background in mathematics also facilitates employment as teachers—postsecondary; teachers—preschool, kindergarten, middle, elementary, and secondary; engineers; economists; market and survey researchers; financial analysts and personal financial advisors; and physicists and astronomers.

Sources of Additional Information

For more information about careers and training in mathematics, especially for doctoral-level employment, contact:

➤ American Mathematical Society, 201 Charles St., Providence, RI 02940. Internet: http://www.ams.org

For specific information on careers in applied mathematics, contact:

➤ Society for Industrial and Applied Mathematics, 3600 University City Science Center, Philadelphia, PA 19104-2688. Internet: http://www.siam.org

Information on obtaining a mathematician position with the Federal Government is available from the Office of Personnel Management (OPM) through a telephone-based system. Consult your telephone directory under U.S. Government for a local number or call (703) 724-1850; Federal Relay Service: (800) 877-8339. The first number is not tollfree, and charges may result. Information also is available from the OPM Internet site: http://www.usajobs.opm.gov.

Operations Research Analysts

(0*NET 15-2031.00)

Significant Points

- Employers generally prefer applicants with at least a master's degree in operations research or a closely related field, such as computer science, engineering, business, mathematics, information systems, or management science.

- Employment growth is projected to be slower than average, reflecting slow growth in the number of jobs with the title "operations research analyst."

- Individuals with a master's or Ph.D. degree in management science or operations research should have good job opportunities as operations research analysts or in closely related occupations, such as systems analysts, computer scientists, or management analysts.

Nature of the Work

Operations research and *management science* are terms that are used interchangeably to describe the discipline of applying advanced analytical techniques to help make better decisions and to solve problems. The procedures of operations research have given effective assistance during wartime missions, such as deploying radar, searching for enemy submarines, and getting supplies where they were most needed. New analytical methods have been developed and numerous peacetime applications have emerged, leading to the use of operations research in many industries and occupations.

The prevalence of operations research in the Nation's economy reflects the growing complexity of managing large organizations that require the effective use of money, materials, equipment, and people. Operations research analysts help determine better ways to coordinate these elements by applying analytical methods from mathematics, science, and engineering. They solve problems in different ways and propose alternative solutions to management, which then chooses the course of action that best meets the organization's goals. In general, operations research analysts may be concerned with diverse issues such as

top-level strategy, planning, forecasting, resource allocation, performance measurement, scheduling, the design of production facilities and systems, supply chain management, pricing, transportation and distribution, and the analysis of large databases.

The duties of the operations research analyst vary according to the structure and management philosophy of the employer or client. Some firms centralize operations research in one department; others use operations research in each division. Operations research analysts also may work closely with senior managers to identify and solve a variety of problems. Some organizations contract operations research services with a consulting firm. Economists, systems analysts, mathematicians, industrial engineers, and others may apply operations research techniques to address problems in their respective fields. (These occupations are discussed elsewhere in the *Handbook*.)

Regardless of the type or structure of the client organization, operations research in its classical role entails a similar set of procedures in carrying out analysis to support management's quest to improve performance. Managers begin the process by describing the symptoms of a problem to the analyst, who then formally defines the problem. For example, an operations research analyst for an auto manufacturer may be asked to determine the best inventory level for each of the parts needed on a production line and to ascertain the optimal number of windshields to be kept in inventory. Too many windshields would be wasteful and expensive, while too few could result in an unintended halt in production.

Operations research analysts study such problems, breaking them into their components. Analysts then gather information about each of the components from a variety of sources. To determine the most efficient amount of inventory to be kept on hand, for example, operations research analysts might talk with engineers about production levels, discuss purchasing arrangements with buyers, and examine storage-cost data provided by the accounting department.

With the relevant information in hand, the analyst is ready to select the most appropriate analytical technique. Analysts can use any of several techniques, including simulation, linear and nonlinear programming, dynamic programming, queuing and other stochastic-process models, Markov decision processes, econometric methods, data envelopment analysis, neural networks, expert systems, decision analysis, and the analytic hierarchy process. Nearly all of these techniques, however, involve the construction of a mathematical model that attempts to describe the system being studied. The use of models enables the analyst to assign values to the different components and clarify the relationships among them. The values can be altered to examine what may happen to the system under different circumstances.

In most cases, the computer program developed to solve the model must be modified and run repeatedly to obtain different solutions. A model for airline flight scheduling, for example, might include variables for the cities to be connected, the amount of fuel required to fly the routes, projected levels of passenger demand, varying ticket and fuel prices, pilot scheduling, and maintenance costs. By locating the right combination of values for the variable, the analyst is able to produce the best flight schedule consistent with particular assumptions.

Upon concluding the analysis, the operations research analyst presents management with recommendations based on the results. Additional computer runs to consider different assumptions may be needed before the analyst presents the final

Operations research analysts study organizational efficiency and suggest ways to improve an organization's performance.

recommendation. Once management reaches a decision, the analyst usually works with others in the organization to ensure the plan's successful implementation.

Working Conditions

Operations research analysts generally work regular hours in an office environment. Because they work on projects that are of immediate interest to top management, operations research analysts often are under pressure to meet deadlines and work more than a 40-hour week.

Employment

Operations research analysts held about 61,700 jobs in 2002. Major employers include telecommunication companies, aerospace manufacturers, computer systems design firms, financial institutions, insurance carriers, engineering and management services firms, and Federal and State governments. More than 4 out of 5 operations research analysts in the Federal Government work for the Department of Defense, and many in private industry work directly or indirectly on national defense. About 1 out of 5 analysts works in architectural, engineering, or related services; computer systems design and related services; management, scientific, and technical consulting services; and scientific research and development firms that offer consulting services in the field of operations research.

Training, Other Qualifications, and Advancement

Employers generally prefer applicants with at least a master's degree in operations research or a closely related field, such as computer science, engineering, business, mathematics, information systems, or management science, coupled with a bachelor's degree in computer science or a quantitative discipline, such as economics, mathematics, or statistics. Dual graduate degrees in operations research and computer science are especially attractive to employers. Operations research analysts also must be able to think logically and work well with people, and employers prefer workers with good oral and written communication skills.

In addition to supporting formal education in one manner or another, employers often sponsor training for experienced workers, helping them keep up with new developments in operations

research techniques and computer science. Some analysts attend advanced university classes on these subjects at their employer's expense.

Because computers are the most important tools for performing in-depth analysis, training and experience in programming are required. Operations research analysts typically need to be proficient in database collection and management, programming, and the development and use of sophisticated software packages.

Beginning analysts usually perform routine work under the supervision of more experienced analysts. As the novices gain knowledge and experience, they are assigned more complex tasks and given greater autonomy to design models and solve problems. Operations research analysts advance by assuming positions as technical specialists or supervisors. The skills acquired by operations research analysts are useful for a variety of higher level management jobs, so experienced analysts may leave the field to assume nontechnical managerial or administrative positions. Operations research analysts with significant experience may become consultants, and some may even open their own consulting practice.

Job Outlook

Employment of operations research analysts is expected to grow more slowly than the average for all occupations through 2012, reflecting slow growth in the number of jobs with the title "operations research analyst." Job opportunities in operations research should be good, however, because organizations throughout the economy will strive to improve their productivity, effectiveness, and competitiveness and because of the extensive availability of data, computers, and software. Many jobs in operations research have other titles, such as "operations analyst," "management analyst," "systems analyst," and "policy analyst." Individuals who hold a master's or Ph.D. degree in operations research, management science, or a closely related field should find good job opportunities because the number of openings generated by employment growth and the need to replace those leaving the occupation are expected to exceed the number of persons graduating with those credentials.

Organizations face pressure today from growing domestic and international competition and must work to make their operations as effective as possible. As a result, businesses will increasingly rely on operations research analysts to optimize profits by improving productivity and reducing costs. As new technology is introduced into the marketplace, operations research analysts will be needed to determine how to utilize the technology in the best way.

Opportunities for operations research analysts exist in almost every industry because of the diversity of applications for their work. However, opportunities should be especially good in highly competitive industries, such as manufacturing, transportation, telecommunications, and finance. As businesses and government agencies continue to contract out jobs to cut costs, many operations research analysts also will find opportunities as consultants, either working for a consulting firm or setting up their own practice. Opportunities in the military will exist as well, but will depend on the size of future military budgets. As the military develops new weapons systems and strategies, military leaders will rely on operations research analysts to test and evaluate their accuracy and effectiveness. (See the *Handbook* statement on job opportunities in the Armed Forces.)

Earnings

Median annual earnings of operations research analysts were $56,920 in 2002. The middle 50 percent earned between $43,220 and $74,460. The lowest 10 percent had earnings of less than $34,140, while the highest 10 percent earned more than $92,430.

The average annual salary for operations research analysts in the Federal Government in nonsupervisory, supervisory, and managerial positions was $83,740 in 2003.

Related Occupations

Operations research analysts apply advanced analytical methods to large, complicated problems. Workers in other occupations that stress advanced analysis include computer systems analysts, database administrators, and computer scientists; computer programmers; engineers; mathematicians; statisticians; economists; and market and survey researchers. Because its goal is improved organizational effectiveness, operations research also is closely allied to managerial occupations, such as computer and information systems managers, and management analysts.

Sources of Additional Information

Information on career opportunities for operations research analysts is available from
➤ Institute for Operations Research and Management Science, 901 Elkridge Landing Rd., Suite 400, Linthicum, MD 21090. Internet: **http://www.informs.org**

For information on operations research careers in the Armed Forces and the U.S. Department of Defense, contact
➤ Military Operations Research Society, 1703 N. Beauregard St., Suite 450, Alexandria, VA 22311. Internet: **http://www.mors.org**

Information on obtaining an operations research analyst position with the Federal Government is available from the Office of Personnel Management (OPM) through a telephone-based system. Consult your telephone directory under U.S. Government for a local number or call (703) 724-1850; Federal Relay Service: (800) 877-8339. The first number is not tollfree, and charges may result. Information also is available from the OPM Internet site: **http://www.usajobs.opm.gov**.

Statisticians

(O*NET 15-2041.00)

Significant Points

● Many individuals with degrees in statistics enter jobs that do not have the title statistician.

● A master's degree in statistics or mathematics is the minimum educational requirement for most jobs as a statistician.

● Although slower than average growth is expected in employment of statisticians, job opportunities should remain favorable for individuals with degrees in statistics.

Nature of the Work

Statistics is the scientific application of mathematical principles to the collection, analysis, and presentation of numerical data. Statisticians contribute to scientific inquiry by applying their mathematical and statistical knowledge to the design of surveys and experiments; collection, processing, and analysis of data; and interpretation of the results. Statisticians may apply their knowledge of statistical methods to a variety of subject areas, such as biology, economics, engineering, medicine, public health, psychology, marketing, education, and sports. Many economic, social, political, and military decisions cannot be made without the use of statistical techniques, such as the design of experiments to gain Federal approval of a newly manufactured drug.

One technique that is especially useful to statisticians is sampling—obtaining information about a population of people or group of things by surveying a small portion of the total. For example, to determine the size of the audience for particular programs, television-rating services survey only a few thousand families, rather than all viewers. Statisticians decide where and how to gather the data, determine the type and size of the sample group, and develop the survey questionnaire or reporting form. They also prepare instructions for workers who will collect and tabulate the data. Finally, statisticians analyze, interpret, and summarize the data using computer software.

In business and industry, statisticians play an important role in quality control and in product development and improvement. In an automobile company, for example, statisticians might design experiments to determine the failure time of engines exposed to extreme weather conditions by running individual engines until failure and breakdown. Working for a pharmaceutical company, statisticians might develop and evaluate the results of clinical trials to determine the safety and effectiveness of new medications. And, at a computer software firm, statisticians might help construct new statistical software packages to analyze data more accurately and efficiently. In addition to product development and testing, some statisticians also are involved in deciding what products to manufacture, how much to charge for them, and to whom the products should be marketed. Statisticians also may manage assets and liabilities, determining the risks and returns of certain investments.

Statisticians also are employed by nearly every government agency. Some government statisticians develop surveys that measure population growth, consumer prices, or unemployment. Other statisticians work for scientific, environmental, and agricultural agencies, and may help to determine the amount of pesticides in drinking water, the number of endangered species living in a particular area, or the number of people afflicted with a particular disease. Statisticians also are employed in national

Statisticians work in many different fields, organizing surveys, collecting data, and analyzing the results.

defense agencies, determining the accuracy of new weapons and the likely effectiveness of defense strategies.

Because statistical specialists are employed in so many work areas, specialists who use statistics often have different professional designations. For example, a person using statistical methods on economic data may have the title econometrician, while statisticians in public health and medicine may hold titles such as biostatistician, biometrician, or epidemiologist.

Working Conditions
Statisticians usually work regular hours in comfortable offices. Some statisticians travel to provide advice on research projects, supervise and set up surveys, or gather statistical data. Some may have duties that vary widely, such as designing experiments or performing fieldwork in various communities. Statisticians who work in academia generally have a mix of teaching and research responsibilities.

Employment
Statisticians held about 20,000 jobs in 2002. Eighteen percent of these jobs were in the Federal Government, where statisticians were concentrated in the Departments of Commerce, Agriculture, and Health and Human Services. Another 16 percent were found in State and local governments, including State colleges and universities. Most of the remaining jobs were in private industry, especially in scientific research and development services; office administrative services; insurance carriers; management, scientific, and technical consulting services; and business, professional, labor, and political organizations; and pharmaceutical and medicine manufacturing. In addition, many professionals with a background in statistics were among the 20,000 full-time mathematics faculty in colleges and universities in 2002, according to the American Mathematical Society. (See the statement on teachers—postsecondary, elsewhere in the *Handbook*.)

Training, Other Qualifications, and Advancement
Although more employment opportunities are becoming available to individuals with a bachelor's degree in statistics, a master's degree in statistics or mathematics is usually the minimum educational requirement for most statistician jobs. Research and academic positions in institutions of higher education, for example, require at least a master's degree, and usually a Ph.D., in statistics. Beginning positions in industrial research often require a master's degree combined with several years of experience.

The training required for employment as an entry-level statistician in the Federal Government, however, is a bachelor's degree, including at least 15 semester hours of statistics or a combination of 15 hours of mathematics and statistics, if at least 6 semester hours are in statistics. Qualifying as a mathematical statistician in the Federal Government requires 24 semester hours of mathematics and statistics, with a minimum of 6 semester hours in statistics and 12 semester hours in an area of advanced mathematics, such as calculus, differential equations, or vector analysis.

Many other schools also offered degrees in mathematics, operations research, and other fields that included a sufficient number of courses in statistics to qualify graduates for some beginning positions in the Federal Government. Required subjects for statistics majors include differential and integral calculus, statistical methods, mathematical modeling, and probability theory. Additional courses that undergraduates should take include linear algebra, design and analysis of experiments, applied multivariate analysis, and mathematical statistics.

In 2002, approximately 140 universities offered a master's degree program in statistics or biostatistics, and about 90 offered a doctoral degree program. Many other schools also offered graduate-level courses in applied statistics for students majoring in biology, business, economics, education, engineering, psychology, and other fields. Acceptance into graduate statistics programs does not require an undergraduate degree in statistics, although good training in mathematics is essential.

Because computers are used extensively for statistical applications, a strong background in computer science is highly recommended. For positions involving quality and productivity improvement, training in engineering or physical science is useful. A background in biological, chemical, or health science is important for positions involving the preparation and testing of pharmaceutical or agricultural products. Courses in economics and business administration are helpful for many jobs in market research, business analysis, and forecasting.

Good communications skills are important for prospective statisticians in industry, who often need to explain technical matters to persons without statistical expertise. An understanding of business and the economy also is valuable for those who plan to work in private industry.

Beginning statisticians generally are supervised by an experienced statistician. With experience, they may advance to positions with more technical responsibility and, in some cases, supervisory duties. However, opportunities for promotion are greater for persons with advanced degrees. Master's and Ph.D. degree holders usually enjoy independence in their work and become qualified to engage in research, develop statistical methods, or, after a number of years of experience in a particular area, become statistical consultants.

Job Outlook
Slower than average growth is expected in employment of statisticians over the 2002-12 period. However, job opportunities should remain favorable for individuals with degrees in statistics, although many of these positions will not carry the explicit job title statistician. This is especially true of jobs that involve the analysis and interpretation of data from other disciplines such as economics, biological science, psychology, or computer software engineering. Despite the limited number of jobs resulting from growth, a number of openings will become available as statisticians transfer to other occupations or retire or leave the work force for other reasons.

Among graduates with a master's degree in statistics, those with a strong background in an allied field, such as finance, biology, engineering, or computer science, should have the best prospects of finding jobs related to their field of study. Federal agencies will hire statisticians in many fields, including demography, agriculture, consumer and producer surveys, Social Security, healthcare, and environmental quality. Competition for entry-level positions in the Federal Government is expected to be strong for persons just meeting the minimum qualification standards for statisticians, because the Federal Government is one of the few employers that considers a bachelor's degree to be an adequate entry-level qualification. Those who meet State certification requirements may become high school statistics teachers. (For additional information, see the statement on teachers—preschool, kindergarten, elementary, middle, and secondary elsewhere in the *Handbook*.)

Manufacturing firms will hire statisticians with master's and doctoral degrees for quality control of various products, including pharmaceuticals, motor vehicles, aircraft, chemicals, and food. For example, pharmaceutical firms employ statisticians to assess the safety and effectiveness of new drugs. To address global product competition, motor vehicle manufacturers will need statisticians to improve the quality of automobiles, trucks, and their components by developing and testing new designs. Statisticians with knowledge of engineering and the physical sciences will find jobs in research and development, working with teams of scientists and engineers to help improve design and production processes to ensure consistent quality of newly developed products. Many statisticians also will find opportunities developing statistical software for computer software manufacturing firms.

Business firms will rely heavily on workers with a background in statistics to forecast sales, analyze business conditions, and help to solve management problems in order to maximize profits. In addition, consulting firms increasingly will offer sophisticated statistical services to other businesses. Because of the widespread use of computers in this field, statisticians in all industries should have good computer programming skills and knowledge of statistical software.

Earnings

Median annual earnings of statisticians were $57,080 in 2002. The middle 50 percent earned between $40,510 and $76,500. The lowest 10 percent had earnings of less than $30,380, while the highest 10 percent earned more than $91,680.

The average annual salary for statisticians in the Federal Government in nonsupervisory, supervisory, and managerial positions was $75,979 in 2003, while mathematical statisticians averaged $83,472. According to a 2003 survey by the National Association of Colleges and Employers, starting salary offers for mathematics/statistics graduates with a bachelor's degree averaged $40,512 a year.

Related Occupations

People in a wide range of occupations work with statistics. Among these are actuaries; mathematicians; operations research analysts; computer systems analysts, database administrators, and computer scientists; computer programmers; computer software engineers; engineers; economists; market and survey researchers; financial analysts and personal financial advisors; and life, physical, and social scientists.

Sources of Additional Information

For information about career opportunities in statistics, contact:
➤ American Statistical Association, 1429 Duke St., Alexandria, VA 22314. Internet: **http://www.amstat.org**

For more information on doctoral-level careers and training in mathematics, a field closely related to statistics, contact:
➤ American Mathematical Society, 201 Charles St., Providence, RI 02940. Internet: **http://www.ams.org**

Information on obtaining a statistician position with the Federal Government is available from the Office of Personnel Management (OPM) through a telephone-based system. Consult your telephone directory under U.S. Government for a local number or call (703) 724-1850; Federal Relay Service: (800) 877-8339. The first number is not tollfree, and charges may result. Information also is available from the OPM Internet site: **http://www.usajobs.opm.gov**.

Architects, Surveyors, and Cartographers

Architects, Except Landscape and Naval

(O*NET 17-1011.00)

Significant Points

- More than 1 in 5 architects was self-employed—about three times the proportion for all professional and related occupations.

- Licensing requirements include a professional degree in architecture, a period of practical training, and passing all divisions of the Architect Registration Examination.

- Architecture graduates may face competition, especially for jobs in the most prestigious firms; opportunities will be best for those with experience working for a firm while still in school and for those with knowledge of computer-aided design and drafting technology.

Nature of the Work

People need places in which to live, work, play, learn, worship, meet, govern, shop, and eat. These places may be private or public; indoors or outdoors; or rooms, buildings, or complexes; and together, they make up neighborhoods, towns, suburbs, and cities. *Architects*—licensed professionals trained in the art and science of building design—transform these needs into concepts and then develop the concepts into images and plans of buildings that can be constructed by others.

Architects design the overall aesthetic and look of buildings and other structures, but the design of a building involves far more than its appearance. Buildings also must be functional, safe, and economical and must suit the needs of the people who use them. Architects consider all these factors when they design buildings and other structures.

Architects provide professional services to individuals and organizations planning a construction project. They may be involved in all phases of development, from the initial discussion with the client through the entire construction process. Their duties require specific skills—designing, engineering, managing, supervising, and communicating with clients and builders. Architects spend a great deal of time explaining their ideas to clients, construction contractors, and others. Successful architects must be able to communicate their unique vision persuasively.

The architect and client discuss the objectives, requirements, and budget of a project. In some cases, architects provide various predesign services—conducting feasibility and environmental impact studies, selecting a site, or specifying the requirements the design must meet. For example, they may determine space requirements by researching the numbers and types of

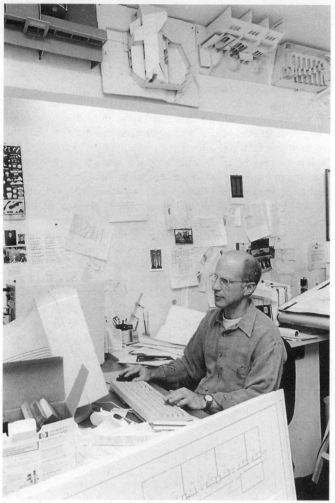

Architects update plans after receiving feedback from other professionals.

potential users of a building. The architect then prepares drawings and a report presenting ideas for the client to review.

After discussing and agreeing on the initial proposal, architects develop final construction plans that show the building's appearance and details for its construction. Accompanying these plans are drawings of the structural system; air-conditioning, heating, and ventilating systems; electrical systems; communications systems; plumbing; and, possibly, site and landscape plans. The plans also specify the building materials and, in some cases, the interior furnishings. In developing designs, architects follow building codes, zoning laws, fire regulations, and other ordinances, such as those requiring easy access by disabled persons. Throughout the planning stage, they make necessary changes. Although they have traditionally used pencil and paper to produce design and construction drawings, architects are increasingly turning to computer-aided design and drafting (CADD) technology for these important tasks. Continual revision of plans on the basis of client needs and budget constraints is often necessary.

Architects may also assist clients in obtaining construction bids, selecting contractors, and negotiating construction contracts. As construction proceeds, they may visit building sites to make sure that contractors follow the design, adhere to the schedule, use the specified materials, and meet work quality standards. The job is not complete until all construction is finished, required tests are conducted, and construction costs are paid. Sometimes, architects also provide postconstruction services, such as facilities management. They advise on energy efficiency measures, evaluate how well the building design adapts to the needs of occupants, and make necessary improvements.

Architects design a wide variety of buildings, such as office and apartment buildings, schools, churches, factories, hospitals, houses, and airport terminals. They also design complexes such as urban centers, college campuses, industrial parks, and entire communities. In addition, they may advise on the selection of building sites, prepare cost analysis and land-use studies, and do long-range planning for land development.

Architects sometimes specialize in one phase of work. Some specialize in the design of one type of building—for example, hospitals, schools, or housing. Others focus on planning and predesign services or construction management and do minimal design work. They often work with engineers, urban planners, interior designers, landscape architects, and other professionals. In fact, architects spend a great deal of their time coordinating information from, and the work of, others engaged in the same project. Many architects—particularly at larger firms—use the Internet and e-mail to update designs and communicate changes efficiently. Architects also use the Internet to research product specifications and government regulations.

During the required training period leading up to licensing as architects, entry-level workers are called interns. This training period, which generally lasts 3 years, gives them practical work experience in preparation for the Architect Registration Examination (ARE). Typical duties may include preparing construction drawings on CADD, building models, or assisting in the design of one part of a project.

Working Conditions
Architects usually work in a comfortable environment. Most of their time is spent in offices consulting with clients, developing reports and drawings, and working with other architects and engineers. However, they often visit construction sites to review the progress of projects.

Architects may occasionally be under stress, working nights and weekends to meet deadlines. In 2002, more than half of all full-time architects worked more than 40 hours a week.

Employment
Architects held about 113,000 jobs in 2002. Almost 2 out of 3 jobs were in architectural, engineering, and related services—mostly in architectural firms with fewer than five workers. A small number worked for residential and nonresidential building construction firms and for government agencies responsible for housing, planning, or community development, such as the U.S. Departments of Defense and Interior, and the General Services Administration. About 1 in 5 architects was self-employed.

Training, Other Qualifications, and Advancement
All States and the District of Columbia require individuals to be licensed (registered) before they may call themselves architects or contract to provide architectural services. Nevertheless, many architecture school graduates work in the field while they are in the process of becoming licensed. However, a licensed architect is required to take legal responsibility for all work. Licensing requirements include a professional degree in architecture, a period of practical training or internship, and passage of all divisions of the ARE.

In most States, the professional degree in architecture must be from one of the 113 schools of architecture that have degree programs accredited by the National Architectural Accrediting Board (NAAB). However, State architectural registration boards set their own standards, so graduation from a non-NAAB-accredited program may meet the educational requirement for licensing in a few States. Three types of professional degrees in architecture are available through colleges and universities. The majority of all architectural degrees are from 5-year Bachelor of Architecture programs, intended for students entering university-level studies from high school or with no previous architectural training. In addition, a number of schools offer a 2-year Master of Architecture program for students with a preprofessional undergraduate degree in architecture or a related area, or a 3- or 4-year Master of Architecture program for students with a degree in another discipline.

The choice of degree depends upon each individual's preference and educational background. Prospective architecture students should consider the available options before committing to a program. For example, although the 5-year Bachelor of Architecture program offers the fastest route to the professional degree, courses are specialized, and if the student does not complete the program, transferring to program offered by another discipline may be difficult. A typical program includes courses in architectural history and theory, building design, structures, technology, construction methods, professional practice, math, physical sciences, and liberal arts. Central to most architectural programs is the design studio, where students put into practice the skills and concepts learned in the classroom. During the final semester of many programs, students devote their studio time to creating an architectural project from beginning to end, culminating in a three-dimensional model of their design.

Many schools of architecture also offer postprofessional degrees for those who already have a bachelor's or master's degree in architecture or other areas. Although graduate education beyond the professional degree is not required for practicing architects, it may be for research, teaching, and certain specialties.

High school students interested in a career in architecture should take courses in English, history, art, social studies, mathematics, physics, and computer science. Students should also visit the design studio of a school of architecture or tour the offices of a local firm. In addition, many schools of architecture offer summer programs for high school students.

Architects must be able to communicate their ideas visually to their clients. Artistic and drawing ability is helpful, but not essential, to such communication. More important are a visual orientation and the ability to conceptualize and understand spatial relationships. Good communication skills, the ability to work independently or as part of a team, and creativity are important qualities for anyone interested in becoming an architect. Computer literacy also is required for writing specifications, for two- and three-dimensional drafting, and for financial management. Knowledge of CADD is helpful and will become essential as architectural firms continue to adopt that technology. Recently, the profession recognized National CAD Standards (NCS); architecture students who master NCS may have an advantage in the job market.

All State architectural registration boards require a training period before candidates may sit for the ARE and become licensed. Most States have adopted the training standards established by the Intern Development Program, a branch of the American Institute of Architects and the National Council of Architectural Registration Boards (NCARB). These standards stipulate broad and diversified training under the supervision of a licensed architect over a 3-year period. New graduates usually begin as interns in architectural firms, where they assist in preparing architectural documents or drawings. Some States allow some of the training to occur in the offices of related professionals, such as engineers or general contractors. Architecture students who complete internships in architectural firms while still in school can count some of that time toward the required 3-year training period.

Interns may research building codes and materials or write specifications for building materials, installation criteria, the quality of finishes, and other, related details. After completing the on-the-job training period, interns are eligible to sit for the ARE. The examination tests candidates' knowledge, skills, and ability to provide the various services required in the design and construction of buildings. Nine critical areas are covered. Candidates who pass the ARE and meet all standards established by their State board are licensed to practice in that State.

Several States require continuing education to maintain a license, and many more States are expected to adopt mandatory continuing education. Requirements vary by State, but usually involve the completion of a certain number of credits every year or two through seminars, workshops, formal university classes, conferences, self-study courses, or other sources.

A growing number of architects voluntarily seek certification by the NCARB, which can facilitate an individual's becoming licensed to practice in additional States. Certification is awarded after independent verification of the candidate's educational transcripts, employment record, and professional references. Certification is the primary requirement for reciprocity of licensing among State Boards that are NCARB members.

After becoming licensed and gaining experience, architects take on increasingly responsible duties, eventually managing entire projects. In large firms, architects may advance to supervisory or managerial positions. Some architects become partners in established firms; others set up their own practices. Graduates with degrees in architecture also enter related fields, such as graphic, interior, or industrial design; urban planning; real estate development; civil engineering; and construction management.

Job Outlook

Prospective architects may face competition for entry-level positions, especially if the number of architectural degrees awarded remains at current levels or increases. Employment of architects is projected to grow about as fast as the average for all occupations through 2012, and additional job openings will stem from the need to replace architects who retire, transfer to new occupations, or leave the labor force permanently for other reasons. However, many individuals are attracted to this occupation, and the number of applicants often exceeds the number of available jobs, especially in the most prestigious firms. Prospective architects who gain career-related experience in an architectural firm while they are still in school and who know CADD technology—especially that which conforms to the new national standards—will have a distinct advantage in obtaining an intern position after graduation.

Employment of architects is strongly tied to the level of local construction, particularly nonresidential structures such as office buildings, shopping centers, schools, and healthcare facilities. Employment in nonresidential construction is expected to grow because the replacement and renovation of many industrial plants and buildings has been delayed for years and a large number of structures will have to be replaced or remodeled, particularly in urban areas where space for new buildings is becoming limited. On the other hand, technology enhancements will dampen demand for new commercial construction as nontraditional work and retail environments, such as teleconferencing, home offices, telecommuting, and electronic shopping, proliferate.

Demographic trends and changes in healthcare delivery will influence the demand for certain institutional structures and should also provide more jobs for architects in the future. A growing and aging population will drive demand for the construction of adult daycare, assisted-living, and other outpatient facilities, all of which are preferable, less costly alternatives to hospitals and nursing homes. Similarly, the construction of schools will increase to accommodate growth in the school-aged population. Additions to existing schools (especially colleges and universities), as well as overall modernization, will continue to add to demand for architects through 2012.

Demand for residential construction is also expected to continue to grow. As the baby boomers reach their peak earning years and can afford to spend more on housing, demand for larger homes with more amenities, as well as for second homes, will continue to rise. Some older, more affluent, members of the baby-boom generation will want townhouses and condominiums in conveniently located suburban and urban settings. At the same time, as the "echo boomers" (the children of the baby boomers) start to augment the younger age groups, the demand for starter homes and rental apartments also should increase.

Growth in demand for new-home construction will be tempered by consumers' preference to perform home improvements and renovations—especially in attractive, established neighborhoods—rather than construct new homes. Many starter homes will be remodeled to appeal to more affluent, space- and amenity-hungry buyers. Also, as buyers trade up, some may prefer to remodel existing homes, rather than construct new homes.

Because construction—particularly office and retail construction—is sensitive to cyclical changes in the economy, architects will face especially strong competition for jobs or clients during recessions, and layoffs may ensue. Those involved in the design of institutional buildings, such as schools, hospitals, nursing homes, and correctional facilities, will be less affected by fluctuations in the economy.

Even in times of overall good job opportunities, however, there may be areas of the country with poor opportunities. Architects who are licensed to practice in one State must meet the licensing requirements of other States before practicing elsewhere. Obtaining licensure in other States, after initially receiving licensure in one State, is known as "reciprocity" and is much easier if an architect has received certification from the NCARB.

Earnings

Median annual earnings of wage and salary architects were $56,620 in 2002. The middle 50 percent earned between $44,030 and $74,460. The lowest 10 percent earned less than $36,280, and the highest 10 percent earned more than $92,350.

Earnings of partners in established architectural firms may fluctuate because of changing business conditions. Some architects may have difficulty establishing their own practices and may go through a period when their expenses are greater than their income, requiring substantial financial resources.

Related Occupations

Architects design buildings and related structures. Construction managers, like architects, also plan and coordinate activities concerned with the construction and maintenance of buildings and facilities. Others who engage in similar work are landscape architects, civil engineers, urban and regional planners, and designers, including interior designers, commercial and industrial designers, and graphic designers.

Sources of Additional Information

Information about education and careers in architecture can be obtained from:
➤ The American Institute of Architects, 1735 New York Ave. NW., Washington, DC 20006. Internet: **http://www.aia.org**
➤ Intern Development Program, National Council of Architectural Registration Boards, Suite 1100K, 1801 K Street NW., Washington, D.C. 20006-1310. Internet: **http://www.ncarb.org**

Landscape Architects

(0*NET 17-1012.00)

Significant Points

- Almost 23 percent are self-employed—more than 3 times the proportion for all professionals.

- A bachelor's degree in landscape architecture is the minimum requirement for entry-level jobs; many employers prefer to hire landscape architects who also have completed at least one internship.

- A growing demand for incorporating natural elements into man-made environments, along with the need to meet a wide array of environmental restrictions, will increase the demand for landscape architects.

Nature of the Work

Everyone enjoys attractively designed residential areas, public parks and playgrounds, college campuses, shopping centers, golf courses, parkways, and industrial parks. Landscape architects design these areas so that they are not only functional, but also beautiful, and compatible with the natural environment. They plan the location of buildings, roads, and walkways, and the arrangement of flowers, shrubs, and trees.

Landscape architects work for many types of organizations—from real estate development firms starting new projects to municipalities constructing airports or parks—and they often are involved with the development of a site from its conception. Working with architects, surveyors, and engineers, landscape architects help determine the best arrangement of roads and buildings. They also collaborate with environmental scientists, foresters, and other professionals to find the best way to conserve or restore natural resources. Once these decisions are made, landscape architects create detailed plans indicating new topography, vegetation, walkways, and other landscaping details, such as fountains and decorative features.

In planning a site, landscape architects first consider the nature and purpose of the project and the funds available. They analyze the natural elements of the site, such as the climate, soil, slope of the land, drainage, and vegetation; observe where sunlight falls on the site at different times of the day and examine the site from various angles; and assess the effect of existing buildings, roads, walkways, and utilities on the project.

After studying and analyzing the site, landscape architects prepare a preliminary design. To account for the needs of the client as well as the conditions at the site, they frequently make changes before a final design is approved. They also take into account any local, State, or Federal regulations, such as those protecting wetlands or historic resources. In preparing designs, computer-aided design (CAD) has become an essential tool for most landscape architects. Many landscape architects also use video simulation to help clients envision the proposed ideas and plans. For larger scale site planning, landscape architects also use geographic information systems technology, a computer mapping system.

Throughout all phases of the planning and design, landscape architects consult with other professionals involved in the project. Once the design is complete, they prepare a proposal for the client. They produce detailed plans of the site, including written reports, sketches, models, photographs, land-use studies, and cost estimates, and submit them for approval by the client and by regulatory agencies. When the plans are approved, landscape architects prepare working drawings showing all existing and proposed features. They also outline in detail the methods of construction and draw up a list of necessary materials. Although many landscape architects monitor the installation of their design, the developer's project general contractor or a landscape contractor usually directs the actual construction and installation of plantings.

Some landscape architects work on a variety of projects. Others specialize in a particular area, such as residential development, street and highway beautification, waterfront improvement projects, parks and playgrounds, or shopping centers. Still others work in regional planning and resource management; feasibility, environmental impact, and cost studies; or site construction. Increasingly, landscape architects are becoming involved with projects in environmental remediation, such as preservation and restoration of wetlands. Historic landscape preservation and restoration is another important area where landscape architects are increasingly playing an important role.

Most landscape architects do at least some residential work, but relatively few limit their practice to individual homeowners. Residential landscape design projects usually are too small to provide suitable income compared with larger commercial or multiunit residential projects. Some nurseries offer residential landscape design services, but these services often are performed by lesser qualified landscape designers, or others with training and experience in related areas.

Landscape architects who work for government agencies do site and landscape design for government buildings, parks, and other public lands, as well as park and recreation planning in national parks and forests. In addition, they prepare environmental impact statements and studies on environmental issues such as public land-use planning. Some restore degraded land, such as mines or landfills. Other architects use their skills in traffic-calming, the "art" of slowing traffic down through use of traffic design, enhancement of the physical environment, and greater attention to aesthetics.

Working Conditions
Landscape architects spend most of their time in offices creating plans and designs, preparing models and cost estimates, doing research, or attending meetings with clients and other professionals involved in a design or planning project. The remainder of their time is spent at the site. During the design and planning stage, landscape architects visit and analyze the site to verify that the design can be incorporated into the landscape. After the plans and specifications are completed, they may spend additional time at the site observing or supervising the construction. Those who work in large national or regional firms may spend considerably more time out of the office traveling to sites away from the local area.

Salaried employees in both government and landscape architectural firms usually work regular hours; however, they may work overtime to meet a project deadline. Hours of self-employed landscape architects vary depending on the demands of the projects on which they are working.

Employment
Landscape architects held about 23,000 jobs in 2002. About 4 out of 10 workers were employed in firms that provide architectural, engineering, and related services. The Federal Government also employs these workers, primarily in the U.S. Departments of Agriculture, Defense, and Interior. Almost 1 of every 4 landscape architects was self-employed.

Employment of landscape architects is concentrated in urban and suburban areas throughout the country; some landscape architects work in rural areas, particularly those employed by the Federal Government to plan and design parks and recreation areas.

Landscape architects often visit the worksite to check that plans are implemented properly.

Training, Other Qualifications, and Advancement
A bachelor's or master's degree in landscape architecture usually is necessary for entry into the profession. The bachelor's degree in landscape architecture takes 4 or 5 years to complete. There also are two types of accredited master's degree programs. The most common type of master's degree is a 3-year first professional degree program designed for students with an undergraduate degree in another discipline. The second type is of master's degree is a 2-year second professional degree program for students who have a bachelor's degree in landscape architecture and who wish to teach or specialize in some aspect of landscape architecture, such as regional planning or golf course design.

In 2002, 58 colleges and universities offered 75 undergraduate and graduate programs in landscape architecture that were accredited by the Landscape Architecture Accreditation Board of the American Society of Landscape Architects. College courses required in these programs usually include technical subjects such as surveying, landscape design and construction, landscape ecology, site design, and urban and regional planning. Other courses include history of landscape architecture, plant and soil science, geology, professional practice, and general management. Many landscape architecture programs also are adding courses that address environmental issues, a growing concern of landscape architects. The design studio is another important aspect of many landscape architecture curriculums. Whenever possible, students are assigned real projects, providing them with valuable hands-on experience. While working on these projects, students become more proficient in the use of computer-aided design, geographic information systems, and video simulation.

In 2002, 46 States required landscape architects to be licensed or registered. Licensing is based on the Landscape Architect Registration Examination (L.A.R.E.), sponsored by the Council of Landscape Architectural Registration Boards and administered over a 3-day period. Admission to the exam usually requires a degree from an accredited school plus 1 to 4 years of work experience under the supervision of a registered landscape architect, although standards vary from State to State. Currently, 15 States require the passage of a State examination in addition to the L.A.R.E. to satisfy registration requirements. State examinations, which usually are 1 hour in length and completed at the end of the L.A.R.E., focus on laws, environmental regulations, plants, soils, climate, and any other characteristics unique to the State.

Because State requirements for licensure are not uniform, landscape architects may not find it easy to transfer their registration from one State to another. However, those who meet the national standards of graduating from an accredited program, serving 3 years of internship under the supervision of a registered landscape architect, and passing the L.A.R.E. can satisfy requirements in most States. Through this means, a landscape architect can obtain certification from the Council of Landscape Architectural Registration Boards, and so gain reciprocity (the right to work) in other States.

In the Federal Government, candidates for entry positions should have a bachelor's or master's degree in landscape architecture. The Federal Government does not require its landscape architects to be licensed.

Persons planning a career in landscape architecture should appreciate nature, enjoy working with their hands, and possess strong analytical skills. Creative vision and artistic talent also are desirable qualities. Good oral communication skills are essential; landscape architects must be able to convey their ideas to other professionals and clients and to make presentations before large groups. Strong writing skills also are valuable, as is knowledge of computer applications of all kinds, including word processing, desktop publishing, and spreadsheets. Landscape architects use these tools to develop presentations, proposals, reports, and land impact studies for clients, colleagues, and superiors. The ability to draft and design using CAD software is essential. Many employers recommend that prospective landscape architects complete at least one summer internship with a landscape architecture firm in order to gain an understanding of the day-to-day operations of a small business, including how to win clients, generate fees, and work within a budget.

In States where licensure is required, new hires may be called "apprentices" or "intern landscape architects" until they become licensed. Their duties vary depending on the type and size of the employing firm. They may do project research or prepare working drawings, construction documents, or base maps of the area to be landscaped. Some are allowed to participate in the actual design of a project. However, interns must perform all work under the supervision of a licensed landscape architect. Additionally, all drawings and specifications must be signed and sealed by the licensed landscape architect, who takes legal responsibility for the work. After gaining experience and becoming licensed, landscape architects usually can carry a design through all stages of development. After several years, they may become project managers, taking on the responsibility for meeting schedules and budgets, in addition to overseeing the project design. Later, they may become associates or partners of a firm, with a proprietary interest in the business.

Many landscape architects are self-employed because start-up costs, after an initial investment in CAD software, are relatively low. Self-discipline, business acumen, and good marketing skills are important qualities for those who choose to open their own business. Even with these qualities, however, some may struggle while building a client base.

Those with landscape architecture training also qualify for jobs closely related to landscape architecture, and may, after gaining some experience, become construction supervisors, land or environmental planners, or landscape consultants.

Job Outlook
Employment of landscape architects is expected to increase faster than the average for all occupations through the year 2012. Their expertise will be highly sought after in the planning and development of new residential, commercial, and other types of construction, to meet the needs of a growing population. With land costs rising and the public demanding more beautiful spaces, the importance of good site planning and landscape design grows. Also, new construction is increasingly contingent upon compliance with environmental regulations, land use zoning, and water restrictions, spurring demand for landscape architects to help plan sites and integrate man-made structures with the natural environment in the least disruptive way. Landscape architects also will be increasingly involved in preserving and restoring wetlands and other environmentally sensitive sites. However, opportunities will vary from year to year, and by geographic region, depending on local economic conditions. During a recession, when real estate sales and construction slow down, landscape architects may face layoffs and greater competition for jobs. The need to replace landscape architects who retire or leave the labor force will produce some additional job openings.

Continuation of the Transportation Equity Act for the Twenty-First Century is expected to spur employment for landscape architects, particularly within State and local governments. This Act, known as TEA-21, provides funds for surface transportation and transit programs, such as interstate highway construction and maintenance and environment-friendly pedestrian and bicycle trails. Budget tightening in the Federal Government might restrict hiring in the U.S. Forest Service and the National Park Service, agencies that traditionally employ the most landscape architects in the Federal Government. Instead, such agencies may increasingly contract out for landscape architecture services, providing additional employment opportunities in private landscape architecture firms.

In addition to the work related to new development and construction, landscape architects are expected to be involved in historic preservation, land reclamation, and refurbishment of existing sites. They are also doing more residential design work as households spend more on landscaping than in the past. Because landscape architects can work on many different types of projects, they may have an easier time than other design professionals finding employment when traditional construction slows down.

New graduates can expect to face competition for jobs in the largest and most prestigious landscape architecture firms, but should face good job opportunities overall as demand increases, while the number of graduates of landscape architecture holds steady or goes up slightly. Opportunities will be best for landscape architects who develop strong technical skills—such as computer design—and communication skills, as well as knowledge of environmental codes and regulations. Those with additional training or experience in urban planning increase their opportunities for employment in landscape architecture firms that specialize in site planning as well as landscape design. Many employers prefer to hire entry-level landscape architects who have internship experience, which significantly reduces the amount of on-the-job training required.

Earnings

In 2002, median annual earnings for landscape architects were $47,400. The middle 50 percent earned between $36,140 and $62,470. The lowest 10 percent earned less than $28,730 and the highest 10 percent earned over $79,620. Architectural, engineering, and related services employed more landscape architects than any other group of industries, and there the median annual earnings were $46,980 in 2002.

In 2003, the average annual salary for all landscape architects in the Federal Government in nonsupervisory, supervisory, and managerial positions was $68,959.

Because many landscape architects work for small firms or are self-employed, benefits tend to be less generous than those provided to workers in large organizations.

Related Occupations

Landscape architects use their knowledge of design, construction, land-use planning, and environmental issues to develop a landscape project. Others whose work requires similar skills are architects, except landscape and naval; surveyors, cartographers, photogrammetrists, and surveying technicians; civil engineers; and urban and regional planners. Landscape architects also must know how to grow and use plants in the landscape. Some conservation scientists and foresters and biological and medical scientists study plants in general and do related work, while environmental scientists and geoscientists work in the area of environmental remediation.

Sources of Additional Information

Additional information, including a list of colleges and universities offering accredited programs in landscape architecture, is available from:
➤ American Society of Landscape Architects, Career Information, 636 Eye St. NW., Washington, DC 20001-3736. Internet: **http://www.asla.org**

General information on registration or licensing requirements is available from:
➤ Council of Landscape Architectural Registration Boards, 144 Church Street NW., Suite 201, Vienna, VA 22180-4550. Internet: **http://www.clarb.org**

Surveyors, Cartographers, Photogrammetrists, and Surveying Technicians

(O*NET 17-1021.00, 17-1022.00, 17-3031.01, 17-3031.02)

Significant Points

● Almost 2 out of 3 jobs were in architectural, engineering, and related services.

● Opportunities will be best for surveyors, cartographers, and photogrammetrists who have at least a bachelor's degree and strong technical skills.

● Computer skills enhance employment opportunities.

Nature of the Work

Several different types of workers are responsible for measuring and mapping the earth's surface. Traditional *land surveyors* establish official land, air space, and water boundaries. They write descriptions of land for deeds, leases, and other legal documents; define airspace for airports; and measure construction and mineral sites. Other surveyors provide data relevant to the shape, contour, location, elevation, or dimension of land or land features. *Cartographers* compile geographic, political, and cultural information and prepare maps of large areas. *Photogrammetrists* measure and analyze aerial photographs that are subsequently used to prepare detailed maps and drawings. *Surveying technicians* assist land surveyors by operating survey instruments and collecting information in the field and by performing computations and computer-aided drafting in offices. *Mapping technicians* calculate mapmaking information from field notes. They also draw topographical maps and verify their accuracy.

Land surveyors manage survey parties who measure distances, directions, and angles between points and elevations of points, lines, and contours on, above, and below the earth's surface. They plan the fieldwork, select known survey reference points, and determine the precise location of important features in the survey area. Surveyors research legal records, look for evidence of previous boundaries, and analyze the data to determine the location of boundary lines. They also record the results of surveys, verify the accuracy of data, and prepare plots, maps, and reports. Surveyors who establish boundaries must be licensed by the State in which they work. Known as professional land surveyors, they are sometimes called to provide expert testimony in court cases concerning matters pertaining to surveying.

A survey party gathers the information needed by the land surveyor. A typical survey party consists of a party chief and one or more surveying technicians and helpers. The party chief, who may be either a land surveyor or a senior surveying technician, leads day-to-day work activities. Surveying technicians assist the party chief by adjusting and operating surveying instruments, such as the theodolite (used to measure horizontal and vertical angles) and electronic distance-measuring equipment. Surveying technicians or assistants position and hold the vertical rods, or targets, that the theodolite operator sights on to measure angles, distances, or elevations. In addition, they may hold measuring tapes, if electronic distance-measuring equipment is not used. Surveying technicians compile notes, make sketches, and enter the data obtained from surveying instruments into computers. Survey parties also may include laborers or helpers who perform less skilled duties, such as clearing brush from sight lines, driving stakes, or carrying equipment.

New technology is changing the nature of the work of surveyors and surveying technicians. On larger projects, surveyors are increasingly using the Global Positioning System (GPS), a satellite system that locates points on the earth to a high degree of precision by using radio signals transmitted via satellites. To use this system, a surveyor places a satellite signal receiver—a small instrument mounted on a tripod—on a desired point. The receiver simultaneously collects information from several satellites to establish a precise position. The receiver also can be placed in a vehicle for tracing out road systems. Because receivers now come in different sizes and shapes, and because the cost of receivers has fallen, much more surveying work can be done with GPS. Surveyors then must interpret and check the results produced by the new technology.

Cartographers measure, map, and chart the earth's surface. Their work involves everything from performing geographical research and compiling data to actually producing maps. Cartographers collect, analyze, and interpret both spatial data—such as latitude, longitude, elevation, and distance—and nonspatial data—for example, population density, land-use patterns, annual precipitation levels, and demographic characteristics. They prepare maps in either digital or graphic form, using information provided by geodetic surveys, aerial photographs, and satellite data. *Photogrammetrists* prepare detailed maps and drawings from aerial photographs, usually of areas that are inaccessible, difficult, or less cost efficient to survey by other methods. *Map editors* develop and verify the contents of maps, using aerial photographs and other reference sources. Some States require photogrammetrists to be licensed as professional land surveyors.

Some surveyors perform specialized functions closer to those of cartographers than to those of traditional surveyors. For example, *geodetic surveyors* use high-accuracy techniques, including satellite observations (remote sensing), to measure large areas of the earth's surface. *Geophysical prospecting surveyors* mark sites for subsurface exploration, usually in relation to petroleum. *Marine or hydrographic surveyors* survey harbors, rivers, and other bodies of water to determine shorelines, the topography of the bottom, water depth, and other features.

Surveyors select known survey reference points and determine the precise location of important features in the survey area.

The work of surveyors and cartographers is changing because of advancements in technology, including not only the GPS, but also new earth resources data satellites, improved aerial photography, and geographic information systems (GIS)—computerized data banks of spatial data, along with the hardware, software, and staff needed to use them. These systems are capable of assembling, integrating, analyzing, and displaying data identified according to location. A GIS typically is used to handle maps which combine information that is useful for environmental studies, geology, engineering, planning, business marketing, and other disciplines. As more of these systems are developed, a new type of mapping scientist is emerging from the older specialties of photogrammetrist and cartographer: the *geographic information specialist* combines the functions of mapping science and surveying into a broader field concerned with the collection and analysis of geographic data.

Working Conditions

Surveyors usually work an 8-hour day, 5 days a week, and may spend a lot of time outdoors. Sometimes they work longer hours during the summer, when weather and light conditions are most suitable for fieldwork. Seasonal demands for longer hours are related to demand for specific surveying services. Home purchases traditionally are related to the start and end of the school year; construction is related to the materials to be used (unlike wood framing, concrete and asphalt are restricted by outside temperatures); and aerial photography is most effective when the leaves are off the trees.

Land surveyors and technicians engage in active, sometimes strenuous, work. They often stand for long periods, walk considerable distances, and climb hills with heavy packs of instruments and other equipment. They also can be exposed to all types of weather. Traveling often is part of the job, and land surveyors and technicians may commute long distances, stay away from home overnight, or temporarily relocate near a survey site.

Although surveyors can spend considerable time indoors, planning surveys, analyzing data, and preparing reports and maps, cartographers and photogrammetrists spend virtually all of their time in offices and seldom visit the sites they are mapping.

Employment

Surveyors, cartographers, photogrammetrists, and surveying technicians held about 124,000 jobs in 2002. Architectural, engineering, and related services firms—including firms that provided surveying and mapping services to other industries on a contract basis—provided about two-thirds of jobs for these workers. Federal, State, and local governmental agencies provided almost 1 in 6 jobs. Major Federal Government employers are the U.S. Geological Survey (USGS), the Bureau of Land Management (BLM), the Army Corps of Engineers, the Forest Service (USFS), the National Oceanic and Atmospheric Administration (NOAA), the National Imagery and Mapping Agency (NIMA), and the Federal Emergency Management Agency (FEMA). Most surveyors in State and local government work for highway departments and urban planning and redevelopment agencies. Construction firms, mining and oil and gas extraction companies, and utilities also employ surveyors, cartographers, photogrammetrists, and surveying technicians. Only a small number were self-employed in 2002.

Training, Other Qualifications, and Advancement

Most people prepare for a career as a licensed surveyor by combining postsecondary school courses in surveying with extensive on-the-job training. However, as technology advances, a 4-year college degree is increasingly becoming a prerequisite. About 50 universities now offer 4-year programs leading to a B.S. degree in surveying. Junior and community colleges, technical institutes, and vocational schools offer 1-, 2-, and 3-year programs in both surveying and surveying technology.

All 50 States and all U.S. territories (Puerto Rico, Guam, the Mariana Islands, and the Virgin Islands) license land surveyors. For licensure, most State licensing boards require that individuals pass a written examination given by the National Council of Examiners for Engineering and Surveying. Most States also require surveyors to pass a written examination prepared by the State licensing board. In addition, candidates must meet varying standards of formal education and work experience in the field.

In the past, many with little formal training in surveying started as members of survey crews and worked their way up to become licensed surveyors. However, because of advancing technology and rising licensing standards, formal education requirements are increasing. Specific requirements vary among States. Generally, the quickest route to licensure is a combination of 4 years of college, up to 4 years of experience under the supervision of an experienced surveyor (a few States do not require any such experience), and passing the licensing examinations. An increasing number of States require a bachelor's degree in surveying or in a closely related field, such as civil engineering or forestry (with courses in surveying), regardless of the number of years of experience. Many states also have a continuing education requirement.

High school students interested in surveying should take courses in algebra, geometry, trigonometry, drafting, mechanical drawing, and computer science. High school graduates with no formal training in surveying usually start as apprentices. Beginners with postsecondary school training in surveying usually can start as technicians or assistants. With on-the-job experience and formal training in surveying—either in an institutional program or from a correspondence school—workers may advance to senior survey technician, then to party chief, and, in some cases, to licensed surveyor (depending on State licensing requirements).

The National Society of Professional Surveyors, a member organization of the American Congress on Surveying and Mapping, has a voluntary certification program for surveying technicians. Technicians are certified at four levels requiring progressive amounts of experience, in addition to the passing of written examinations. Although not required for State licensure, many employers require certification for promotion to positions with greater responsibilities.

Surveyors should have the ability to visualize objects, distances, sizes, and abstract forms. They must work with precision and accuracy, because mistakes can be costly. Members of a survey party must be in good physical condition, because they work outdoors and often carry equipment over difficult terrain. They need good eyesight, coordination, and hearing to communicate verbally and manually (using hand signals). Surveying is a cooperative operation, so good interpersonal skills and the ability to work as part of a team are important. Good office skills also are essential, because surveyors must be able to research old deeds and other legal papers and prepare reports that document their work.

Cartographers and photogrammetrists usually have a bachelor's degree in a field such as engineering, forestry, geography, or a physical science. Although it is possible to enter these positions through previous experience as a photogrammetric or cartographic technician, nowadays most cartographic and photogrammetric technicians have had some specialized postsecondary school training. With the development of GIS, cartographers and photogrammetrists need additional education and stronger technical skills—including more experience with computers—than in the past.

The American Society for Photogrammetry and Remote Sensing has a voluntary certification program for photogrammetrists. To qualify for this professional distinction, individuals must meet work experience standards and pass an oral or a written examination.

Job Outlook

Overall employment of surveyors, cartographers, photogrammetrists, and surveying technicians is expected to grow about as fast as the average for all occupations through the year 2012. The widespread availability and use of advanced technologies, such as GPS, GIS, and remote sensing, will continue to increase both the accuracy and productivity of these workers, resulting in modest overall growth in employment. However, job openings will continue to result from the need to replace workers who transfer to other occupations or who leave the labor force altogether.

Employment of surveying and mapping technicians is expected to grow faster than the average for all occupations through 2012. The short training period needed to learn to operate the equipment, the current lack of any formal testing or licensing, the growing demand for people to do basic GIS-related data-entry work, and relatively lower wages all encourage demand for these technicians. However, many persons possess the basic skills needed to qualify for the jobs that are available, so competition for job openings may result.

As technologies become more complex, opportunities will be best for surveyors, cartographers, and photogrammetrists who have at least a bachelor's degree and strong technical skills. Increasing demand for geographic data, as opposed to traditional surveying services, will mean better opportunities for cartographers and photogrammetrists who are involved in the development and use of geographic and land information systems. New technologies, such as GPS and GIS, also may enhance employment opportunities for surveyors, as well as for those surveying technicians who have the educational background and who have acquired technical skills that enable them to work with the new systems. At the same time, upgraded licensing requirements will continue to limit opportunities for professional advancement for those without bachelor's degrees.

Opportunities for surveyors, cartographers, and photogrammetrists should remain concentrated in architectural, engineering, and related services firms. However, nontraditional areas, such as urban planning, emergency preparedness, and natural resource exploration and mapping, also should provide employment growth, particularly with regard to producing maps for the management of emergencies and updating maps with the newly available technology. Continued growth in construction through 2012 will require surveyors to lay out streets, shopping centers, housing developments, factories, office buildings, and recreation areas, while setting aside flood plains, wetlands, wildlife habitats, and environmentally sensitive areas for protection.

However, employment may fluctuate from year to year along with construction activity or with mapping needs for land and resource management.

Earnings

Median annual earnings of cartographers and photogrammetrists were $42,870 in 2002. The middle 50 percent earned between $32,580 and $55,610. The lowest 10 percent earned less than $25,810 and the highest 10 percent earned more than $69,320.

Median annual earnings of surveyors were $39,970 in 2002. The middle 50 percent earned between $29,320 and $53,440. The lowest 10 percent earned less than $22,260, and the highest 10 percent earned more than $67,700. Median hourly earnings of surveyors employed in architectural, engineering, and related services were $38,370 in 2002.

Median annual earnings of surveying and mapping technicians were $29,230 in 2002. The middle 50 percent earned between $22,640 and $39,070 in 2002. The lowest 10 percent earned less than $18,490, and the highest 10 percent earned more than $48,970. Median annual earnings of surveying and mapping technicians employed in architectural, engineering, and related services were $27,130 in 2002, while those employed by local governments had median annual earnings of $33,680.

In 2003, land surveyors in nonsupervisory, supervisory, and managerial positions in the Federal Government earned an average salary of $62,980; cartographers, $67,989; geodetic technicians, $55,374; surveying technicians, $33,316; and cartographic technicians, $43,517.

Related Occupations

Surveying is related to the work of civil engineers, architects, and landscape architects because an accurate survey is the first step in land development and construction projects. Cartography and geodetic surveying are related to the work of environmental scientists and geoscientists, who study the earth's internal composition, surface, and atmosphere. Cartography also is related to the work of geographers and urban and regional planners, who study and decide how the earth's surface is to be used.

Sources of Additional Information

For career information on surveyors, cartographers, photogrammetrists, and surveying technicians, contact:
➤ The American Congress on Surveyong and Mapping, Suite #403, 6 Montgomery Village Ave., Gaithersburg, MD 20879. Internet: **http://www.acsm.net**

Information about career opportunities, licensure requirements, and the surveying technician certification program is available from:
➤ National Society of Professional Surveyors, Suite #403, 6 Montgomery Village Ave., Gaithersburg, MD 20879. Internet: **http://www.acsm.net/nsps**

For information on a career as a geodetic surveyor, contact:
➤ American Association of Geodetic Surveying (AAGS), Suite #403, 6 Montgomery Village Ave., Gaithersburg, MD 20879. Internet: **http://www.acsm.net/aags**

General information on careers in photogrammetry and remote sensing is available from:
➤ ASPRS: The Imaging and Geospatial Information Society, 5410 Grosvenor Ln., Suite 210, Bethesda, MD 20814-2160. Internet: **http://www.asprs.org**

Engineers

(0*NET 17-2011.00, 17-2021.00, 17-2031.00, 17-2041.00, 17-2051.00, 17-2061.00, 17-2071.00, 17-2072.00, 17-2081.00, 17-2111.01, 17-2111.02, 17-2111.03, 17-2112.00, 17-2121.01, 17-2121.02, 17-2131.00, 17-2141.00, 17-2151.00, 17-2161.00, 17-2171.00, 17-2199.99)

Significant Points

- Overall, job opportunities in engineering are expected to be good, but will vary by specialty.
- A bachelor's degree is required for most entry-level jobs.
- Starting salaries are significantly higher than those of college graduates in other fields.
- Continuing education is critical to keep abreast of the latest technology.

Nature of the Work

Engineers apply the theories and principles of science and mathematics to research and develop economical solutions to technical problems. Their work is the link between perceived social needs and commercial applications. Engineers design products, machinery to build those products, plants in which those products are made, and the systems that ensure the quality of the products and the efficiency of the workforce and manufacturing process. Engineers design, plan, and supervise the construction of buildings, highways, and transit systems. They develop and implement improved ways to extract, process, and use raw materials, such as petroleum and natural gas. They develop new materials that both improve the performance of products and take advantage of advances in technology. They harness the power of the sun, the Earth, atoms, and electricity for use in supplying the Nation's power needs, and create millions of products using power. They analyze the impact of the products they develop or the systems they design on the environment and on people using them. Engineering knowledge is applied to improving many things, including the quality of healthcare, the safety of food products, and the operation of financial systems.

Engineers consider many factors when developing a new product. For example, in developing an industrial robot, engineers determine precisely what function the robot needs to perform; design and test the robot's components; fit the components together in an integrated plan; and evaluate the design's overall effectiveness, cost, reliability, and safety. This process applies to many different products, such as chemicals, computers, gas turbines, helicopters, and toys.

In addition to design and development, many engineers work in testing, production, or maintenance. These engineers supervise production in factories, determine the causes of breakdowns, and test manufactured products to maintain quality. They also estimate the time and cost to complete projects. Some move into engineering management or into sales. In sales, an engineering background enables them to discuss technical aspects and assist in product planning, installation, and use. (See the statements on engineering and natural sciences managers, and sales engineers, elsewhere in the *Handbook*.)

Most engineers specialize. More than 25 major specialties are recognized by professional societies, and the major branches have numerous subdivisions. Some examples include structural and transportation engineering, which are subdivisions of civil engineering; and ceramic, metallurgical, and polymer engineering, which are subdivisions of materials engineering. Engineers also may specialize in one industry, such as motor vehicles, or in one field of technology, such as turbines or semiconductor materials.

This statement, which contains an overall discussion of engineering, is followed by separate statements on 14 branches of engineering: Aerospace; agricultural; biomedical; chemical; civil; computer hardware; electrical and electronics, except computer; environmental; industrial, including health and safety; materials; mechanical; mining and geological, including mining safety; nuclear; and petroleum engineering. (Computer software engineers are discussed elsewhere in the *Handbook*.) Some branches of engineering not covered in detail in the *Handbook*, but for which there are established college programs, include architectural engineering—the design of a building's internal support structure; and marine engineering—the design and installation of ship machinery and propulsion systems.

Engineers in each branch have a base of knowledge and training that can be applied in many fields. Electronics engineers, for example, work in the medical, computer, communications, and missile guidance fields. Because there are many separate problems to solve in a large engineering project, engineers in one field often work closely with specialists in other scientific, engineering, and business occupations.

Engineers use computers to produce and analyze designs; to simulate and test how a machine, structure, or system operates; and to generate specifications for parts. Using the Internet or related communications systems, engineers can collaborate on designs with other engineers around the country or even abroad. Many engineers also use computers to monitor product quality and control process efficiency. They spend a great deal of time writing reports and consulting with other engineers, as complex projects often require an interdisciplinary team of engineers. Supervisory engineers are responsible for major components or entire projects.

Working Conditions

Most engineers work in office buildings, laboratories, or industrial plants. Others may spend time outdoors at construction sites and oil and gas exploration and production sites, where they monitor or direct operations or solve onsite problems. Some engineers travel extensively to plants or worksites.

Many engineers work a standard 40-hour week. At times, deadlines or design standards may bring extra pressure to a job, sometimes requiring engineers to work longer hours.

Employment

In 2002 engineers held 1.5 million jobs. The following tabulation shows the distribution of employment by engineering specialty.

Specialty	Employment	Percent
Total, all engineers	1,478,000	100
Electrical and electronics	292,000	19.8
Civil	228,000	15.4
Mechanical	215,000	14.5
Industrial, including health and safety	194,000	13.1
Aerospace	78,000	5.3
Computer hardware	74,000	5.0
Environmental	47,000	3.2
Chemical	33,000	2.2
Materials	24,000	1.6
Nuclear	16,000	1.1
Petroleum	14,000	0.9
Biomedical	7,600	0.5
Mining and geological, including mining safety	5,200	0.4
Marine engineers and naval architects	4,900	0.3
Agricultural	2,900	0.2
All other engineers	243,000	16.4

Almost 4 in 10 of all engineering jobs were found in manufacturing industries, such as transportation and equipment manufacturing and computer and electronic product manufacturing. About 354,000 wage and salary jobs were in the professional, scientific, and technical service industry, primarily in architectural, engineering, and related services and in scientific research and development services, where firms designed construction projects or did other engineering work on a contractual basis. Engineers also worked in the construction and transportation, telecommunications, and utilities industries.

Federal, State, and local governments employed about 192,000 engineers in 2002. About 88,000 of these were in the Federal Government, mainly in the U.S. Departments of Defense, Transportation, Agriculture, Interior, and Energy, and in the National Aeronautics and Space Administration. Most engineers in State and local government agencies worked in highway and public works departments. In 2002, about 55,000 engineers were self-employed, many as consultants.

Engineers are employed in every State, in small and large cities, and in rural areas. Some branches of engineering are concentrated in particular industries and geographic areas, as discussed later in this chapter.

Training, Other Qualifications, and Advancement

A bachelor's degree in engineering is required for almost all entry-level engineering jobs. College graduates with a degree in a physical science or mathematics occasionally may qualify for some engineering jobs, especially in specialties in high demand. Most engineering degrees are granted in electrical, electronics, mechanical, or civil engineering. However, engineers trained in one branch may work in related branches. For example, many aerospace engineers have training in mechanical engineering. This flexibility allows employers to meet staffing needs in new technologies and specialties in which engineers may be in short supply. It also allows engineers to shift to fields with better employment prospects or to those that more closely match their interests.

Most engineering programs involve a concentration of study in an engineering specialty, along with courses in both mathematics and science. Most programs include a design course, sometimes accompanied by a computer or laboratory class or both.

In addition to the standard engineering degree, many colleges offer 2- or 4-year degree programs in engineering technology. These programs, which usually include various hands-on laboratory classes that focus on current issues, prepare students for practical design and production work, rather than for jobs that require more theoretical and scientific knowledge. Graduates of 4-year technology programs may get jobs similar to those obtained by graduates with a bachelor's degree in engineering. Engineering technology graduates, however, are not qualified to register as professional engineers under the same terms as graduates with degrees in engineering. Some employers regard technology program graduates as having skills between those of a technician and an engineer.

Graduate training is essential for engineering faculty positions and many research and development programs, but is not required for the majority of entry-level engineering jobs. Many engineers obtain graduate degrees in engineering or business administration to learn new technology and broaden their education. Many high-level executives in government and industry began their careers as engineers.

About 340 colleges and universities offer bachelor's degree programs in engineering that are accredited by the Accreditation Board for Engineering and Technology (ABET), and about 240 colleges offer accredited bachelor's degree programs in engineering technology. ABET accreditation is based on an examination of an engineering program's student achievement, program improvement, faculty, curricular content, facilities, and institutional commitment. Although most institutions offer programs in the major branches of engineering, only a few offer programs in the smaller specialties. Also, programs of the same title may vary in content. For example, some programs emphasize industrial practices, preparing students for a job in industry, whereas others are more theoretical and are designed to prepare students for graduate work. Therefore, students should investigate curricula and check accreditations carefully before selecting a college.

Admissions requirements for undergraduate engineering schools include a solid background in mathematics (algebra, geometry, trigonometry, and calculus) and science (biology, chemistry, and physics), and courses in English, social studies, humanities, and computer and information technology. Bachelor's degree programs in engineering typically are designed to last 4 years, but many students find that it takes between 4 and 5 years to complete their studies. In a typical 4-year college curriculum, the first 2 years are spent studying mathematics, basic sciences, introductory engineering, humanities, and social sciences. In the last 2 years, most courses are in engineering, usually with a concentration in one branch. For example, the last 2 years of an aerospace program might include courses in fluid mechanics, heat transfer, applied aerodynamics, analytical mechanics, flight vehicle design, trajectory dynamics, and aerospace propulsion systems. Some programs offer a general engineering curriculum; students then specialize in graduate school or on the job.

Some engineering schools and 2-year colleges have agreements whereby the 2-year college provides the initial engineering education, and the engineering school automatically admits students for their last 2 years. In addition, a few engineering schools have arrangements whereby a student spends 3 years in a liberal arts college studying pre-engineering subjects and

2 years in an engineering school studying core subjects, and then receives a bachelor's degree from each school. Some colleges and universities offer 5-year master's degree programs. Some 5-year or even 6-year cooperative plans combine classroom study and practical work, permitting students to gain valuable experience and to finance part of their education.

All 50 States and the District of Columbia require licensure for engineers who offer their services directly to the public. Engineers who are licensed are called Professional Engineers (PE). This licensure generally requires a degree from an ABET-accredited engineering program, 4 years of relevant work experience, and successful completion of a State examination. Recent graduates can start the licensing process by taking the examination in two stages. The initial Fundamentals of Engineering (FE) examination can be taken upon graduation. Engineers who pass this examination commonly are called Engineers in Training (EIT) or Engineer Interns (EI). After acquiring suitable work experience, EITs can take the second examination, the Principles and Practice of Engineering exam. Several States have imposed mandatory continuing education requirements for relicensure. Most States recognize licensure from other States provided that the manner in which the initial license was obtained meets or exceeds their licensure requirements. Many civil, electrical, mechanical, and chemical engineers are licensed PEs.

Engineers should be creative, inquisitive, analytical, and detail-oriented. They should be able to work as part of a team and to communicate well, both orally and in writing. Communication abilities are important because engineers often interact with specialists in a wide range of fields outside engineering.

Beginning engineering graduates usually work under the supervision of experienced engineers and, in large companies, also may receive formal classroom or seminar-type training. As new engineers gain knowledge and experience, they are assigned more difficult projects with greater independence to develop designs, solve problems, and make decisions. Engineers may advance to become technical specialists or to supervise a staff or team of engineers and technicians. Some may eventually become engineering managers or enter other managerial or sales jobs. (See the statements under management and business and financial operations occupations, and sales and related occupations, elsewhere in the *Handbook*.)

Job Outlook
Overall engineering employment is expected to increase more slowly than the average for all occupations over the 2002-12 period. Engineers tend to be concentrated in slow-growing manufacturing industries, a factor which tends to hold down their employment growth. Also, many employers are increasing their use of engineering services performed in other countries. Despite this, overall job opportunities in engineering are expected to be good because the number of engineering graduates should be in rough balance with the number of job openings over this period. Expected changes in employment and, thus, job opportunities vary by specialty. Projections range from a decline in employment of mining and geological engineers, petroleum engineers, and nuclear engineers to much faster than average growth among environmental engineers.

Competitive pressures and advancing technology will force companies to improve and update product designs and to optimize their manufacturing processes. Employers will rely on engineers to further increase productivity, as investment in plant and equipment increases to expand output of goods and services. New computer and communications systems have improved the design process, enabling engineers to produce and analyze various product designs much more rapidly than in the past and to collaborate on designs with other engineers throughout the world. Despite these widespread applications, computer technology is not expected to limit employment opportunities. Finally, additional engineers will be needed to improve or build new roads, bridges, water and pollution control systems, and other public facilities.

There is a large number of well-trained, often English-speaking engineers available in many countries who are willing to work at much lower salaries than U.S. engineers. The rise of the Internet and other electronic communications systems has made it relatively easy for much of the engineering work previously done by engineers in this country to be done by engineers in other countries, a factor that will tend to hold down employment growth.

Compared with most other workers, a smaller proportion of engineers leave their jobs each year. Nevertheless, many job openings will arise from replacement needs, reflecting the large size of this profession. Numerous job openings will be created by engineers who transfer to management, sales, or other professional occupations; additional openings will arise as engineers retire or leave the labor force for other reasons.

Many engineers work on long-term research and development projects or in other activities that continue even during economic slowdowns. In industries such as electronics and aerospace, however, large cutbacks in defense expenditures and government research and development funds in the past, as well as the trend toward contracting out engineering work to engineering services firms, both domestic and foreign, have resulted in significant layoffs of engineers.

It is important for engineers, like those working in other technical occupations, to continue their education throughout their careers because much of their value to their employer depends on their knowledge of the latest technology. Although the pace of technological change varies by engineering specialty and industry, advances in technology have significantly affected every engineering discipline. Engineers in high-technology areas, such as advanced electronics or information technology, may find that technical knowledge can become outdated rapidly. Even those who continue their education are vulnerable to layoffs if the particular technology or product in which they have specialized becomes obsolete. By keeping current in their field, engineers are able to deliver the best solutions and greatest value to their employers. Engineers who have not kept current in their field may find themselves passed over for promotions or vulnerable to layoffs, should they occur. On the other hand, it often is these high-technology areas that offer the greatest challenges, the most interesting work, and the highest salaries. Therefore, the choice of engineering specialty and employer involves an assessment not only of the potential rewards but also of the risk of technological obsolescence.

Related Occupations

Engineers apply the principles of physical science and mathematics in their work. Other workers who use scientific and mathematical principles include architects, except landscape and naval; engineering and natural sciences managers; computer and information systems managers; mathematicians; drafters; engineering technicians; sales engineers; science techni-

cians; and physical and life scientists, including agricultural and food scientists, biological scientists, conservation scientists and foresters, atmospheric scientists, chemists and materials scientists, environmental scientists and geoscientists, and physicists and astronomers.

Sources of Additional Information

High school students interested in obtaining information about careers in engineering should visit the JETS Web site: **http://www.jets.org**.
➤ JETS-Guidance, 1420 King St., Suite 405, Alexandria, VA 22314-2794.

Information on ABET-accredited engineering programs is available from:
➤ The Accreditation Board for Engineering and Technology, Inc., 111 Market Place, Suite 1050, Baltimore, MD 21202-4012. Internet: **http://www.abet.org**

Those interested in information on the Professional Engineer licensure should contact:
➤ The National Society of Professional Engineers, 1420 King St., Alexandria, VA 22314-2794. Internet: **http://www.nspe.org**
➤ National Council of Examiners for Engineers and Surveying, P.O. Box 1686, Clemson, SC 29633-1686. Internet: **http://www.ncees.org**

Information on general engineering education and career resources is available from:
➤ American Society for Engineering Education, 1818 N St. NW., Suite 600, Washington, DC 20036-2479. Internet: **http://www.asee.org**

Information on obtaining an engineering position with the Federal Government is available from the Office of Personnel Management (OPM) through a telephone-based system. Consult your telephone directory under U.S. Government for a local number or call (703) 724-1850; Federal Relay Service: (800) 877-8339. The first number is not tollfree, and charges may result. Information also is available from the OPM Internet site **http://www.usajobs.opm.gov**

Non-high school students wanting more detailed information on an engineering specialty should contact societies representing the individual branches of engineering. Each can provide information about careers in the particular branch. The individual statements that follow also provide other detailed information on aerospace; agricultural; biomedical; chemical; civil; computer hardware; electrical and electronics, except computer; environmental; industrial, including health and safety; materials; mechanical; mining and geological, including mining safety; nuclear; and petroleum engineering.

Aerospace Engineers

(O*NET 17-2011.00)

Nature of the Work

Aerospace engineers create extraordinary machines, from airplanes that weigh over a half a million pounds to spacecraft that travel over 17,000 miles an hour. They design, develop, and test aircraft, spacecraft, and missiles and supervise the manufacture of these products. Aerospace engineers who work with aircraft are called *aeronautical engineers*, and those working specifically with spacecraft are *astronautical engineers*.

Aerospace engineers develop new technologies for use in aviation, defense systems, and space exploration, often specializing in areas such as structural design, guidance, navigation and control, instrumentation and communication, or produc-

Aerospace engineers prepare a space vehicle for launch.

tion methods. They often use computer-aided design (CAD) software, robotics, and lasers and advanced electronic optics. They also may specialize in a particular type of aerospace product, such as commercial transports, military fighter jets, helicopters, spacecraft, or missiles and rockets. Aerospace engineers may be experts in aerodynamics, thermodynamics, celestial mechanics, propulsion, acoustics, or guidance and control systems.

Aerospace engineers typically are employed in the aerospace product and parts industry, although their skills are becoming increasingly valuable in other fields. For example, in the motor vehicles manufacturing industry, aerospace engineers design vehicles that have lower air resistance and, thus, increased fuel efficiency.

Employment

Aerospace engineers held about 78,000 jobs in 2002. Most worked in the aerospace product and parts manufacturing industries. Federal Government agencies, primarily the U.S. Department of Defense and the National Aeronautics and Space Administration, provided 10 percent of jobs. Architectural, engineering and related services, scientific research and development services, and navigational, measuring, electromedical, and control instruments manufacturing industry firms accounted for most of the remaining jobs.

Job Outlook

Employment of aerospace engineers is expected to decline over the projection period. Foreign competition and the slowdown in air travel will limit the number of new jobs for aerospace engineers related to the design and production of commercial aircraft over the projection period. Despite the expected decline in employment, favorable opportunities are expected for aerospace engineers through 2012 because the number of degrees granted in aerospace engineering has declined greatly over the last decade due to the perceived lack of opportunities in this occupation. The decline in degree production has reached the point that the number trained in aerospace engineering may not be adequate to replace the large numbers of aerospace engineers who are expected to leave the occupation, especially due to retirement, over the 2002-12 period. Some employment opportunities also will occur in industries not typically associated with aerospace, such as motor vehicle manufacturing.

Earnings

Median annual earnings of aerospace engineers were $72,750 in 2002. The middle 50 percent earned between $59,520 and $88,310. The lowest 10 percent earned less than $49,640, and the highest 10 percent earned more than $105,060. Median annual earnings in the industries employing the largest numbers of aerospace engineers in 2002 were:

Federal government	$81,830
Architectural, engineering, and related services	74,890
Aerospace product and parts manufacturing	70,920

According to a 2003 salary survey by the National Association of Colleges and Employers, bachelor's degree candidates in aerospace engineering received starting salary offers averaging $48,028 a year, master's degree candidates were offered $61,162, and Ph.D. candidates were offered $68,406.

Sources of Additional Information

For further information about careers in the aerospace industry, contact:

➤ Aerospace Industries Association, 1250 Eye St. NW., Suite 1200, Washington, DC 20005-3924. Internet: **http://www.aia-aerospace.org**

➤ American Institute of Aeronautics and Astronautics, Inc., 1801 Alexander Bell Dr., Suite 500, Reston, VA 20191-4344. Internet: **http://www.aiaa.org**

See the introduction to the section on engineers for information on working conditions, training requirements, and other sources of additional information.

Agricultural Engineers

(O*NET 17-2021.00)

Nature of the Work

Agricultural engineers apply knowledge of engineering technology and biological science to agriculture. (See biological scientists and agricultural and food scientists elsewhere in the *Handbook*.) They design agricultural machinery and equipment and agricultural structures. Some specialties include power systems and machinery design; structures and environment; and food and bioprocess engineering. They develop ways to conserve soil and water and to improve the processing of agricultural products. Agricultural engineers work in research and development, production, sales, or management.

Employment

About one third of the 2,900 agricultural engineers employed in 2002 worked for professional, scientific, and technical services, supplying consultant services to farmers and farm-related industries. Others worked in a wide variety of industries, including crops and livestock as well as manufacturing and government.

Job Outlook

Employment of agricultural engineers is expected to increase about as fast as the average for all occupations through 2012. The growing interest in worldwide standardization of agricultural equipment should result in increased employment of agricultural engineers. Job opportunities also should result from the increasing demand for agricultural products, the continued efforts for more efficient agricultural production, and the increasing emphasis on the conservation of resources. In addition to those resulting from employment growth, job openings will

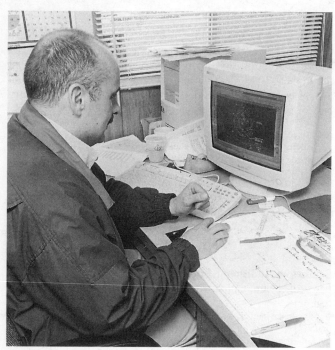

Agricultural engineers apply knowledge of engineering technology and biological science to agriculture.

be created by the need to replace agricultural engineers who transfer to other occupations or leave the labor force.

Earnings

Median annual earnings of agricultural engineers were $50,700 in 2002. The middle 50 percent earned between $40,320 and $70,100. The lowest 10 percent earned less than $35,590, and the highest 10 percent earned more than $87,220.

According to a 2003 salary survey by the National Association of Colleges and Employers, bachelor's degree candidates in agricultural engineering received starting offers averaging $42,987 a year, and master's degree candidates, on average, were offered $54,000.

Sources of Additional Information

Information on a career as an agricultural engineer can be obtained from:

➤ American Society of Agricultural Engineers, 2950 Niles Rd., St. Joseph, MI 49085-9659. Internet: **http://www.asae.org**

See the introduction to the section on engineers for information on working conditions, training requirements, and other sources of additional information.

Biomedical Engineers

(0*NET 17-2031.00)

Nature of the Work

By combining biology and medicine with engineering, biomedical engineers develop devices and procedures that solve medical and health-related problems. Many do research, along with life scientists, chemists, and medical scientists, to develop and evaluate systems and products for use in the fields of biology and health, such as artificial organs, prostheses (artificial devices that replace missing body parts), instrumentation, medi-

cal information systems, and health management and care delivery systems. (See biological scientists, medical scientists, and chemists and materials scientists elsewhere in the *Handbook*.) Biomedical engineers design devices used in various medical procedures, such as the computers used to analyze blood or the laser systems used in corrective eye surgery. They develop artificial organs, imaging systems such as magnetic resonance, ultrasound, and x-ray, and devices for automating insulin injections or controlling body functions. Most engineers in this specialty require a sound background in one of the basic engineering specialties, such as mechanical or electronics engineering, in addition to specialized biomedical training. Some specialties within biomedical engineering include biomaterials, biomechanics, medical imaging, rehabilitation engineering, and orthopedic engineering.

Unlike many other engineering specialties, a graduate degree is recommended or required for many entry-level jobs.

Employment

Biomedical engineers held about 7,600 jobs in 2002. Manufacturing industries employed 38 percent of all biomedical engineers, primarily in the pharmaceutical and medicine manufacturing and medical instruments and supplies industries. Many others worked for hospitals. Some also worked for government agencies or as independent consultants.

Many biomedical engineers conduct research to develop and evaluate systems and products for use in the fields of biology and health.

Job Outlook

Employment of biomedical engineers is expected to increase faster than the average for all occupations through 2012. The aging of the population and the focus on health issues will increase the demand for better medical devices and equipment designed by biomedical engineers. For example, computer-assisted surgery and molecular, cellular, and tissue engineering are being more heavily researched and are developing rapidly. In addition, the rehabilitation and orthopedic engineering specialties are growing quickly, increasing the need for biomedical engineers. Along with the demand for more sophisticated medical equipment and procedures is an increased concern for cost efficiency and effectiveness that also will boost demand for biomedical engineers. However, because of the growing interest in this field, the number of degrees granted in biomedical engineering has increased greatly, leading to the potential for competition for jobs.

Earnings

Median annual earnings of biomedical engineers were $60,410 in 2002. The middle 50 percent earned between $58,320 and $88,830. The lowest 10 percent earned less than $48,450, and the highest 10 percent earned more than $107,520.

According to a 2003 salary survey by the National Association of Colleges and Employers, bachelor's degree candidates in biomedical engineering received starting offers averaging $39,126 a year, and master's degree candidates, on average, were offered $61,000.

Sources of Additional Information

For further information about biomedical engineering careers, contact:
➤ Biomedical Engineering Society, 8401 Corporate Dr., Suite 225, Landover, MD 20785-2224. Internet: **http://www.bmes.org**

See the introduction to the section on engineers for information on working conditions, training requirements, and other sources of additional information.

Chemical Engineers

(0*NET 17-2041.00)

Nature of the Work

Chemical engineers build a bridge between science and manufacturing, applying the principles of chemistry and engineering to solve problems involving the production or use of chemicals. They design equipment and develop processes for large-scale chemical manufacturing, plan and test methods of manufacturing products and treating byproducts, and supervise production. Chemical engineers also work in a variety of manufacturing industries other than chemical manufacturing, such as those producing electronics, photographic equipment, clothing, and pulp and paper. They also work in the healthcare, biotechnology, and business services industries.

The knowledge and duties of chemical engineers overlap many fields. Chemical engineers apply principles of chemistry, physics, mathematics, and mechanical and electrical engineer-

In addition to working in the chemical industry, chemical engineers are employed in a variety of other manufacturing industries and professional, scienitfic, and technical services firms.

ing. (See chemists and materials scientists; physicists and astronomers; mechanical engineers; electrical and electronics engineers, except computer; and mathematicians elsewhere in the *Handbook*.) They frequently specialize in a particular chemical process such as oxidation or polymerization. Others specialize in a particular field, such as materials science, or the development of specific products such as fertilizers and pesticides, automotive plastics, or chlorine bleach. They must be aware of all aspects of chemicals manufacturing and how it affects the environment, the safety of workers, and customers. Because chemical engineers use computer technology to optimize all phases of research and production, they need to understand how to apply computer skills to chemical process analysis, automated control systems, and statistical quality control.

Employment

Chemical engineers held about 33,000 jobs in 2002. Manufacturing industries employed 55 percent of all chemical engineers, primarily in the chemicals, electronics, petroleum refining, paper, and related industries. Most others worked for professional, scientific, or technical services firms that design chemical plants or perform research and development or other services, mainly for chemical companies.

Job Outlook

Little or no growth in employment of chemical engineers is expected though 2012. Although overall employment in the chemical manufacturing industry is expected to decline, chemical companies will continue to research and develop new chemicals and more efficient processes to increase output of existing chemicals. Among manufacturing industries, pharmaceuticals may provide the best opportunities for jobseekers. Many of the jobs for chemical engineers, however, will be in nonmanufacturing industries, especially services industries such as research and testing services. Even though no new jobs due to growth are expected to be created, many openings will result from the need to replace chemical engineers who transfer to other occupations or leave the labor force.

Earnings

Median annual earnings of chemical engineers were $72,490 in 2002. The middle 50 percent earned between $58,320 and $88,830. The lowest 10 percent earned less than $48,450, and the highest 10 percent earned more than $107,520.

According to a 2003 salary survey by the National Association of Colleges and Employers, bachelor's degree candidates in chemical engineering received starting offers averaging $52,384 a year, master's degree candidates averaged $57,857, and Ph.D. candidates averaged $70,729.

Sources of Additional Information

Information on careers, employment, education, training, conferences, and publications on chemical engineering is available from:
➤ American Institute of Chemical Engineers, 3 Park Ave., New York, NY 10016-5901. Internet: **http://www.aiche.org**

Additional information on careers in chemical engineering is available from:
➤ American Chemical Society, Department of Career Services, 1155 16th St. NW., Washington, DC 20036. Internet: **http://www.chemistry.org/portal/Chemistry**

See the introduction to the section on engineers for information on working conditions, training requirements, and other sources of additional information.

Civil Engineers

(0*NET 17-2051.00)

Nature of the Work

Civil engineers design and supervise the construction of roads, buildings, airports, tunnels, dams, bridges, and water supply and sewage systems. Civil engineering, considered one of the oldest engineering disciplines, encompasses many specialties. The major specialties within civil engineering are structural, water resources, environmental, construction, transportation, and geotechnical engineering.

Many civil engineers hold supervisory or administrative positions, from supervisor of a construction site to city engineer. Others may work in design, construction, research, and teaching.

Employment

Civil engineers held about 228,000 jobs in 2002. More than 4 in 10 were employed by firms providing architectural, engineering, and related services, primarily developing designs for new construction projects. Almost one-third of the jobs were in Federal, State, and local government agencies. The construction industry accounted for most of the remaining employment. About 15,000 civil engineers were self-employed, many as consultants.

Civil engineers usually work near major industrial and commercial centers, often at construction sites. Some projects are situated in remote areas or in foreign countries. In some jobs, civil engineers move from place to place to work on different projects.

Job Outlook

Employment of civil engineers is expected to increase more slowly than the average for all occupations through 2012.

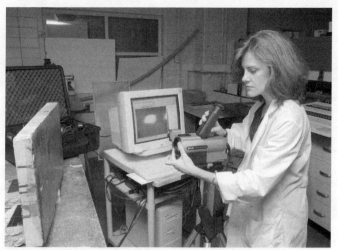

Some civil engineers do research on building materials.

Spurred by general population growth and an increased emphasis on infrastructure and security, more civil engineers will be needed to design and construct safe and higher capacity transportation, water supply, and pollution control systems, and large buildings and building complexes. They also will be needed to repair or replace existing roads, bridges, and other public structures. In addition to those arising from job growth, openings will result from the need to replace civil engineers who transfer to other occupations or leave the labor force.

Because construction and related industries—including those providing design services—employ many civil engineers, employment opportunities will vary by geographic area and may decrease during economic slowdowns, when construction often is curtailed.

Earnings

Median annual earnings of civil engineers were $60,070 in 2002. The middle 50 percent earned between $48,360 and $74,700. The lowest 10 percent earned less than $39,960, and the highest 10 percent earned more than $91,010. Median annual earnings in the industries employing the largest numbers of civil engineers in 2002 were:

Federal government	$67,410
Local government	62,210
Architectural, engineering, and related services	59,060
State government	58,350
Nonresidential building construction	54,190

According to a 2003 salary survey by the National Association of Colleges and Employers, bachelor's degree candidates in civil engineering received starting offers averaging $41,669 a year; master's degree candidates received an average offer of $47,245, and Ph.D. candidates were offered $69,079, on average, as an initial salary.

Sources of Additional Information

General information about civil engineers, as well as career, education, and related information, can be obtained from:
➤ American Society of Civil Engineers, 1801 Alexander Bell Dr., Reston, VA 20191-4400. Internet: **http://www.asce.org**

See the introduction to the section on engineers for information on working conditions, training requirements, and other sources of additional information.

Computer Hardware Engineers

(0*NET 17-2061.00)

Nature of the Work
Computer hardware engineers research, design, develop, and test computer hardware and supervise its manufacture and installation. Hardware refers to computer chips, circuit boards, computer systems, and related equipment such as keyboards, modems, and printers. (Computer software engineers—often simply called computer engineers—design and develop the software systems that control computers. These workers are covered elsewhere in the *Handbook*.) The work of computer hardware engineers is very similar to that of electronics engineers, but, unlike electronics engineers, computer hardware engineers work exclusively with computers and computer-related equipment. (See electrical and electronics engineers elsewhere in the *Handbook*.) In addition to design and development duties, computer hardware engineers may supervise the manufacture and installation of computers and computer-related equipment. The rapid advances in computer technology are largely a result of the research, development, and design efforts of computer hardware engineers. To keep up with technological advances, these engineers must continually update their knowledge.

Employment
The number of computer hardware engineers is relatively small compared with the number of computer-related workers who work with software or computer applications. Computer hardware engineers held about 74,000 jobs in 2002. Almost 40 percent worked in computer and electronic product manufacturing. Almost one-quarter worked in professional, scientific, and technical services firms, many of which provided services to the computer industry. Many of the rest were employed in the telecommunications.

Job Outlook
Computer hardware engineers may face competition for jobs because the number of degrees granted in this field has increased rapidly and because employment is expected to grow more slowly than average. Although the use of information technology continues to expand rapidly, the manufacture of computer hardware is expected to be adversely affected by intense foreign competition. Also, this industry is expected to continue to experience very high levels of productivity growth, which will even affect computer hardware engineers. The utilization of foreign computer hardware engineering services also will serve to limit growth. In addition to job openings arising from employment growth, other vacancies will result from the need to replace workers who move into managerial positions, transfer to other occupations, or leave the labor force.

Earnings
Median annual earnings of computer hardware engineers were $72,150 in 2002. The middle 50 percent earned between $56,490 and $91,730. The lowest 10 percent earned less than $46,190, and the highest 10 percent earned more than $114,880. Median annual earnings in the industries employing the largest numbers of computer hardware engineers in 2002 were:

Semiconductor and other electronic component manufacturing $76,600
Computer and peripheral equipment manufacturing 75,300
Computer systems designs and related services 74,320

According to the National Association of Colleges and Employers, starting salary offers in 2003 for bachelor's degree candidates in computer engineering averaged $51,343 a year; master's degree candidates averaged $64,200.

Sources of Additional Information
For further information on careers, education, certification, publications, and conferences related to computer hardware engineers, contact:
➤ IEEE Computer Society, 1730 Massachusetts Ave. NW., Washington, DC 20036-1992. Internet: **http://www.computer.org**

See the introduction to the section on engineers for information on working conditions, training requirements, and other sources of additional information.

The work of computer hardware engineers is similar to that of electronics engineers, but, unlike electronics engineers, computer hardware engineers work exclusively with computers and computer-related equipment.

Electrical and Electronics Engineers

(0*NET 17-2071.00, 17-2072.00)

Nature of the Work
From the global positioning system that can continuously provide the location of a vehicle to giant electric power generators, electrical and electronics engineers are responsible for a wide range of technologies. Electrical and electronics engineers design, develop, test, and supervise the manufacture of electrical and electronic equipment. Some of this equipment includes broadcast and communications systems; electric motors, machinery controls, lighting, and wiring in buildings, automobiles, aircraft, and radar and navigation systems; and power generating, controlling, and transmission devices used by electric utilities. Many electrical and electronics engineers also work in areas closely related to computers. However, engineers whose work is related exclusively to computer hardware are considered computer hardware engineers, another engineering specialty covered elsewhere in the *Handbook*.

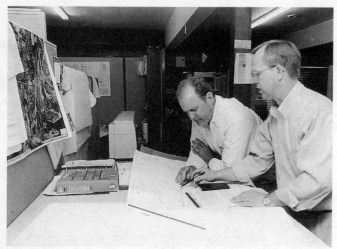

Electrical and electronics engineering graduates should have favorable employment opportunities.

Electrical and electronics engineers specialize in different areas such as power generation, transmission, and distribution; communications; and electrical equipment manufacturing, or a specialty within one of these areas—industrial robot control systems or aviation electronics, for example. Electrical and electronics engineers design new products, write performance requirements, and develop maintenance schedules. They also test equipment, solve operating problems, and estimate the time and cost of engineering projects.

Employment

Electrical and electronics engineers held about 292,000 jobs in 2002, making up the largest branch of engineering. Most jobs were in professional, scientific, and technical services firms, government agencies, and manufacturers of computer and electronic products and machinery. Wholesale trade, communications, and utilities firms accounted for most of the remaining jobs.

Job Outlook

Electrical and electronics engineering graduates should have favorable employment opportunities. The number of job openings resulting from employment growth and the need to replace electrical engineers who transfer to other occupations or leave the labor force is expected to be in rough balance with the supply of graduates.

Employment of electrical and electronics engineers is expected to increase more slowly than the average for all occupations through 2012. Although rising demand for electrical and electronic goods, including advanced communications equipment, defense-related electronic equipment, and consumer electronics products should increase, foreign competition for electronic products and increasing use of engineering services performed in other countries will act to limit employment growth Job growth is expected to be fastest in services industries—particularly consulting firms that provide electronic engineering expertise.

Continuing education is important for electrical and electronics engineers. Engineers who fail to keep up with the rapid changes in technology risk becoming more susceptible to layoffs or, at a minimum, more likely to be passed over for advancement.

Earnings

Median annual earnings of electrical engineers were $68,180 in 2002. The middle 50 percent earned between $54,550 and $84,670. The lowest 10 percent earned less than $44,780, and the highest 10 percent earned more than $100,980. Median annual earnings in the industries employing the largest numbers of electrical engineers in 2002 were:

Scientific research and development services	$77,410
Semiconductor and other electronic component manufacturing	72,670
Electric power generation, transmission, and distribution	71,640
Navigational, measuring, electromedical, and control instruments manufacturing	70,430
Architectural, engineering, and related services	66,980

Median annual earnings of electronics engineers, except computer, were $69,930 in 2002. The middle 50 percent earned between $55,930 and $85,980. The lowest 10 percent earned less than $46,310, and the highest 10 percent earned more than $103,860. Median annual earnings in the industries employing the largest numbers of electronics engineers in 2002 were:

Federal government	$78,830
Architectural, engineering, and related services	72,850
Navigational, measuring, electromedical, and control instruments manufacturing	70,950
Semiconductor and other electronic component manufacturing	70,800
Wired telecommunications carriers	62,670

According to a 2003 salary survey by the National Association of Colleges and Employers, bachelor's degree candidates in electrical/electronics and communications engineering received starting offers averaging $49,794 a year; master's degree candidates averaged $64,556; and Ph.D. candidates averaged $74,283.

Sources of Additional Information

Information on careers and employment, education, publications, and conferences related to electrical and electronics engineers is available from:
➤ Institute of Electrical and Electronics Engineers, 445 Hoes Lane, Piscataway, NJ 08855-1331. Internet: **http://www.ieee.org**

See the introduction to the section on engineers for information on working conditions, training requirements, and other sources of additional information.

Environmental Engineers

(0*NET 17-2081.00)

Nature of the Work

Using the principles of biology and chemistry, environmental engineers develop solutions to environmental problems. They are involved in water and air pollution control, recycling, waste disposal, and public health issues. Environmental engineers conduct hazardous-waste management studies in which they evaluate the significance of the hazard, offer analysis on treatment and containment, and develop regulations to prevent mishaps. They design municipal water supply and industrial wastewater treatment systems. They conduct research on proposed environmental projects, analyze scientific data, and perform quality control checks.

Many environmental engineers work as consultants, helping their clients to comply with regulations and to clean up hazardous sites.

Environmental engineers are concerned with local and worldwide environmental issues. They study and attempt to minimize the effects of acid rain, global warming, automobile emissions, and ozone depletion. They also are involved in the protection of wildlife.

Many environmental engineers work as consultants, helping their clients to comply with regulations and to clean up hazardous sites.

Employment

Environmental engineers held about 47,000 jobs in 2002. Almost half worked in professional, scientific, and technical services and about 15,000 were employed in Federal, State, and local government agencies. Most of the rest worked in various manufacturing industries.

Job Outlook

Environmental engineering graduates should have favorable job opportunities. Employment of environmental engineers is expected to increase much faster than the average for all occupations through 2012. Much of the expected growth will be due to the emergence of this occupation as a widely recognized engineering specialty rather than as an area that other engineering specialties, such as civil engineers, specialize in. More environmental engineers will be needed to comply with environmental regulations and to develop methods of cleaning up existing hazards. A shift in emphasis toward preventing problems rather than controlling those that already exist, as well as increasing public health concerns, also will spur demand for environmental engineers. However, political factors determine the job outlook for environmental engineers more than that for other engineers. Looser environmental regulations would reduce job opportunities; stricter regulations would enhance opportunities.

Even though employment of environmental engineers should be less affected by economic conditions than that of most other types of engineers, a significant economic downturn could reduce the emphasis on environmental protection, reducing employment opportunities. Environmental engineers need to keep abreast of a range of environmental issues to ensure their steady employment because their area of focus may change frequently—for example, from hazardous waste cleanup to the prevention of water pollution.

Earnings

Median annual earnings of environmental engineers were $61,410 in 2002. The middle 50 percent earned between $47,650 and $77,360. The lowest 10 percent earned less than $38,640, and the highest 10 percent earned more than $91,510. Median annual earnings in the industries employing the largest numbers of environmental engineers in 2002 were:

Architectural, engineering, and related services	$58,620
Management, scientific, and technical consulting services	57,800
State government	54,160

According to a 2003 salary survey by the National Association of Colleges and Employers, bachelor's degree candidates in environmental/environmental health engineering received starting offers averaging $44,702 a year.

Sources of Additional Information

Further information about environmental engineering careers, training, and certification can be obtained from:
➤ American Academy of Environmental Engineers, 130 Holiday Court, Suite 100, Annapolis, MD 21401. Internet: **http://www.aaee.net**

See the introduction to the section on engineers for information on working conditions, training requirements, and other sources of additional information.

Industrial Engineers, Including Health and Safety

(0*NET 17-2111.01, 17-2111.02, 17-2111.03, 17-2112.00)

Nature of the Work

Industrial engineers determine the most effective ways to use the basic factors of production—people, machines, materials, information, and energy—to make a product or to provide a service. They are the bridge between management goals and operational performance. They are more concerned with in-

Most industrial engineers work in manufacturing.

creasing productivity through the management of people, methods of business organization, and technology than are engineers in other specialties, who generally work more with products or processes. Although most industrial engineers work in manufacturing industries, they may also work in consulting services, healthcare, and communications.

To solve organizational, production, and related problems most efficiently, industrial engineers carefully study the product and its requirements, use mathematical methods such as operations research to meet those requirements, and design manufacturing and information systems. They develop management control systems to aid in financial planning and cost analysis and design production planning and control systems to coordinate activities and ensure product quality. They also design or improve systems for the physical distribution of goods and services. Industrial engineers determine which plant location has the best combination of raw materials availability, transportation facilities, and costs. Industrial engineers use computers for simulations and to control various activities and devices, such as assembly lines and robots. They also develop wage and salary administration systems and job evaluation programs. Many industrial engineers move into management positions because the work is closely related.

The work of health and safety engineers is similar to that of industrial engineers in that it deals with the entire production process. Health and safety engineers promote worksite or product safety and health by applying knowledge of industrial processes, as well as mechanical, chemical, and psychological principles. They must be able to anticipate, recognize, and evaluate hazardous conditions as well as develop hazard control methods. They also must be familiar with the application of health and safety regulations.

Employment

Industrial engineers, including health and safety, held about 194,000 jobs in 2002. Six in 10 of these jobs were in manufacturing industries, and an additional 1 in 10 worked in professional, scientific, and technical services firms, many of whom provide consulting services to manufacturing firms. Because their skills can be used in almost any type of organization, industrial engineers are more widely distributed among industries than are other engineers.

Job Outlook

Overall employment of industrial engineers, including health and safety, is projected to increase as fast as the average for all occupations through 2012. In addition, many openings will be created by the need to replace industrial engineers who transfer to other occupations or leave the labor force. Employment of industrial engineers is expected to increase as fast as the average while that of health and safety engineers is expected to grow more slowly than average.

Because the main function of industrial and health and safety engineers is to make a higher quality product as efficiently and as safely as possible, their services should be in demand in the manufacturing sector as firms seek to reduce costs and increase productivity. The concern for health and safety within work environments should increase the need for health and safety engineers.

Earnings

Median annual earnings of industrial engineers were $62,150 in 2002. The middle 50 percent earned between $50,160 and $75,440. The lowest 10 percent earned less than $40,380, and the highest 10 percent earned more than $90,420. Median annual earnings in the manufacturing industries employing the largest numbers of industrial engineers in 2002 were:

Semiconductor and other electronic component manufacturing	$67,460
Navigational, measuring, electromedical, and control instruments manufacturing	65,470
Architectural, engineering, and related services	64,020
Aerospace products and parts manufacturing	63,630
Motor vehicle parts manufacturing	62,610

Median annual earnings of health and safety engineers were $58,010 in 2002. The middle 50 percent earned between $46,580 and $71,980. The lowest 10 percent earned less than $37,230, and the highest 10 percent earned more than $87,250.

According to a 2003 salary survey by the National Association of Colleges and Employers, bachelor's degree candidates in industrial/manufacturing engineering received starting offers averaging about $47,051 a year and master's degree candidates averaged $54,565 a year.

Sources of Additional Information

For further information about industrial engineering careers, education, and training, contact:
➤ Institute of Industrial Engineers, 3577 Parkway Lane, Suite 200, Norcross, GA 30092. Internet: **http://www.iienet.org**

Information on careers, education, accreditation and certification, and salaries of safety engineers is available from:
➤ American Society of Safety Engineers, 1800 E Oakton St., Des Plaines, IL 60018. Internet: **http://www.asse.org**

Information on certification, accreditation, careers, and safety-related degree programs for safety professionals, including safety engineers, is available from:
➤ Board of Certified Safety Professionals, 208 Burwash Ave., Savoy, Il 61874. Internet: **http://www.bcsp.org**

See the introduction to the section on engineers for information on working conditions, training requirements, and other sources of additional information.

Materials Engineers

(O*NET 17-2131.00)

Nature of the Work

Materials engineers are involved in the extraction, development, processing, and testing of the materials used to create a diversity of products, from computer chips and television screens to golf clubs and snow skis. They work with metals, ceramics, plastics, semiconductors, and combinations of materials called composites to create new materials that meet certain mechanical, electrical, and chemical requirements. They also are involved in selecting materials for new applications.

There are numerous new developments within materials engineering that make it possible to manipulate and use materials in various ways. For example, materials engineers have developed the ability to create and then study materials at an atomic level using advanced processes to replicate the characteristics of materials and their components with computers.

Most metallurgical engineers work in 1 of the 3 main branches of metallurgy—extractive or chemical, physical, and process. Extractive metallurgists are concerned with removing metals from ores and refining and alloying them to produce suitable inputs for a number of industrial processes. Physical metallurgists study the nature, structure, and physical properties of metals and their alloys to find the best methods of processing basic materials into final products. Process metallurgists develop and improve metalworking processes such as casting, forging, rolling, and drawing. Most materials engineers specialize in a particular material. For example, metallurgical engineers specialize in metals, while ceramic engineers develop ceramic materials and the processes for making ceramic materials into useful products. Ceramics include all nonmetallic, inorganic materials that generally require high temperatures in their processing. Ceramic engineers work on products as diverse as glassware, automobile and aircraft engine components, fiberoptic communication lines, tile, and electric insulators.

Employment

Materials engineers held about 24,000 jobs in 2002. Because materials are building blocks for other goods, materials engineers are widely distributed among manufacturing industries. In fact, 68 percent of materials engineers worked in manufacturing industries, primarily computer and electronic products, transportation equipment, fabricated metal products, primary metal production, and machinery manufacturing. They also worked in services industries such as professional, scientific, and technical services. Most remaining materials engineers worked for Federal and State governments.

Job Outlook

Employment of materials engineers is expected to grow more slowly than the average for all occupations through 2012. Although many of the manufacturing industries in which materials engineers are concentrated are expected to experience declines in employment, more materials engineers will be needed to develop new materials for electronics, biotechnology, and plastics products. As manufacturing firms contract for their materials engineering needs, employment growth is expected in professional, scientific, and technical services industries. In addition to those arising from employment growth, job openings will result from the need to replace materials engineers who transfer to other occupations or leave the labor force.

Earnings

Median annual earnings of materials engineers were $62,590 in 2002. The middle 50 percent earned between $49,810 and $77,500. The lowest 10 percent earned less than $39,360, and the highest 10 percent earned more than $92,690.

According to a 2003 salary survey by the National Association of Colleges and Employers, bachelor's degree candidates in materials engineering received starting offers averaging $44,680 a year.

Sources of Additional Information

For information on careers, education, accreditation, and other topics related to materials engineers, contact:
➤ The Minerals, Metals, & Materials Society, 184 Thorn Hill Rd., Warrendale, PA 15086. Internet: **http://www.tms.org**
➤ ASM International, 9639 Kinsman Rd., Materials Park, OH 44073-0002. Internet: **http://www.asm-intl.org**

See the introduction to the section on engineers for information on working conditions, training requirements, and other sources of additional information.

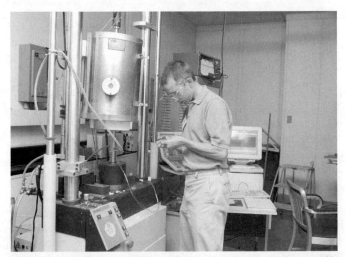

Because materials are building blocks for other goods, materials engineers are widely distributed among manufacturing industries.

Mechanical Engineers

(O*NET 17-2141.00)

Nature of the Work

Mechanical engineers research, develop, design, manufacture, and test tools, engines, machines, and other mechanical devices. They work on power-producing machines such as electric generators, internal combustion engines, and steam and gas turbines. They also develop power-using machines such as refrigeration and air-conditioning equipment, machine tools, material handling systems, elevators and escalators, industrial production equipment, and robots used in manufacturing. Mechanical engineers also design tools that other engineers need for their work. The field of nanotechnology, which involves the creation of high-performance materials and components by integrating atoms and molecules, is introducing entirely new principles to the design process.

Some mechanical engineers specialize in developing new energy systems.

Computers assist mechanical engineers by accurately and efficiently performing computations, and by permitting the modeling and simulation of new designs as well as facilitating changes to existing designs. Computer-Aided Design (CAD) and Computer-Aided Manufacturing (CAM) are used for design data processing and for turning the design into a product.

Mechanical engineers work in many industries, and their work varies by industry and function. Some specialize in energy systems; applied mechanics; automotive design; manufacturing; materials; plant engineering and maintenance; pressure vessels and piping; and heating, refrigeration, and air-conditioning systems. Mechanical engineering is one of the broadest engineering disciplines. Mechanical engineers may work in production operations in manufacturing or agriculture, maintenance, or technical sales; many are administrators or managers.

Employment
Mechanical engineers held about 215,000 jobs in 2002. More than half of the jobs were in manufacturing—mostly in machinery, transportation equipment, computer and electronic products, and fabricated metal products manufacturing industries. Architectural, engineering, and related services, and the Federal Government provided many of the remaining jobs.

Job Outlook
Employment of mechanical engineers is projected to grow more slowly than the average for all occupations though 2012. Although overall employment in manufacturing industries—where employment of mechanical engineers is concentrated—is expected to decrease slightly, employment of mechanical engineers in manufacturing should increase more rapidly as the demand for improved machinery and machine tools grows and as industrial machinery and processes become increasingly complex. Also, emerging technologies in biotechnology, materials science, and nanotechnology will create new job opportunities for mechanical engineers. Additional opportunities for mechanical engineers will arise because a degree in mechanical engineering often can be applied in other engineering specialties. In addition to job openings arising from growth, many openings should result from the need to replace workers who transfer to other occupations or leave the labor force.

Earnings
Median annual earnings of mechanical engineers were $62,880 in 2002. The middle 50 percent earned between $50,800 and $78,040. The lowest 10 percent earned less than $41,490, and the highest 10 percent earned more than $93,430. Median annual earnings in the industries employing the largest numbers of mechanical engineers in 2002 were:

Federal government	$72,500
Architectural, engineering, and related services	65,610
Navigational, measuring, electromedical, and control instruments manufacturing	65,430
Aerospace products and parts manufacturing	65,160
Other general puropse machinery manufacturing	55,850

According to a 2003 salary survey by the National Association of Colleges and Employers, bachelor's degree candidates in mechanical engineering received starting offers averaging $48,585 a year, master's degree candidates had offers averaging $54,565, and Ph.D. candidates were initially offered $69,904.

Sources of Additional Information
General information about mechanical engineers as well as information on careers, education, and training is available from:
➤ The American Society of Mechanical Engineers, 3 Park Ave., New York, NY 10016. Internet: **http://www.asme.org**

Information about heating, refrigeration, and air-conditioning engineering, a mechanical engineering specialty, is available from:
➤ American Society of Heating, Refrigerating, and Air-Conditioning Engineers, Inc., 1791 Tullie Circle NE., Atlanta, GA 30329. Internet: **http://www.ashrae.org**

Information about automotive engineering, a mechanical engineering specialty, is available from:
➤ Society of Automotive Engineers, 400 Commonwealth Dr., Warrendale, PA 15096-0001. Internet: **http://www.sae.org**

See the introduction to the section on engineers for information on working conditions, training requirements, and other sources of additional information.

Mining and Geological Engineers, Including Mining Safety Engineers

(0*NET 17-2151.00)

Nature of the Work
Mining and geological engineers find, extract, and prepare coal, metals, and minerals for use by manufacturing industries and utilities. They design open pit and underground mines, often using computers; supervise the construction of mine shafts and tunnels in underground operations; and devise methods for transporting minerals to processing plants. Mining engineers are responsible for the safe, economical, and environmentally sound operation of mines. Some mining engineers work with geologists and metallurgical engineers to locate and appraise new ore deposits. Others develop new mining equipment or direct mineral processing operations to separate minerals from the dirt, rock, and other materials with which they are mixed. Mining engineers frequently specialize in the mining of one mineral or metal, such as coal or gold. With increased emphasis on protecting the environment, many mining engineers work to solve problems related to land reclamation and water and air pollution.

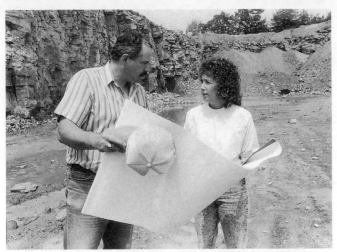

Mining engineers frequently specialize in the mining of one mineral or metal, such as coal or gold.

Mining safety engineers use their knowledge of mine design and practices to ensure the safety of workers and to comply with State and Federal safety regulations. They inspect walls and roof surfaces, test air samples, and examine mining equipment for compliance with safety practices.

Employment

Mining and geological engineers, including mining safety engineers, held about 5,200 jobs in 2002. While about 4 out of 10 mining engineers worked in the mining industry, over one-third worked in professional, scientific, and technical services firms, mostly providing consulting and other services to the mining industry. Most of the rest worked in State or Federal government.

Mining engineers often are employed at the location of natural deposits, often near small communities, and sometimes outside the United States. Those in research and development, management, consulting, or sales, however, often are located in metropolitan areas.

Job Outlook

Despite a projected decline in employment, very good employment opportunities are expected in this small occupation. A significant number of mining engineers currently employed are approaching retirement age, which should create some job openings over the 2002-12 period. In addition, relatively few schools offer mining engineering programs, and the small number of graduates is not expected to increase.

Favorable job opportunities also may be available worldwide as mining operations around the world recruit graduates of U.S. mining engineering programs. As a result, some graduates should expect to travel frequently, or even live abroad.

Employment of mining and geological engineers, including mining safety engineers, is projected to decline through 2012. Most of the industries in which mining engineers are concentrated—such as coal, metal, and copper mining—are expected to experience declines in employment.

Earnings

Median annual earnings of mining and geological engineers, including mining safety engineers, were $61,770 in 2002. The middle 50 percent earned between $48,250 and $77,160. The lowest 10 percent earned less than $36,720, and the highest 10 percent earned more than $93,660.

According to a 2003 salary survey by the National Association of Colleges and Employers, bachelor's degree candidates in mining and mineral engineering (including geological) received starting offers averaging $44,326 a year.

Sources of Additional Information

For more information on careers, education, accreditation, and related topics for mining engineers, contact:
➤ The Society for Mining, Metallurgy, and Exploration, Inc., 8307 Shaffer Parkway, P.O. Box 277002, Littleton, CO 80127. Internet: **http://www.smenet.org**

See the introduction to the section on engineers for information on working conditions, training requirements, and other sources of additional information.

Nuclear Engineers

(O*NET 17-2161.00)

Nature of the Work

Nuclear engineers research and develop the processes, instruments, and systems used to derive benefits from nuclear energy and radiation. They design, develop, monitor, and operate nuclear plants used to generate power. They may work on the nuclear fuel cycle—the production, handling, and use of nuclear fuel and the safe disposal of waste produced by the generation of nuclear energy—or on the production of fusion energy. Some specialize in the development of nuclear power sources for spacecraft; others find industrial and medical uses for radioactive materials, such as equipment to diagnose and treat medical problems.

Employment

Nuclear engineers held about 16,000 jobs in 2002. Almost half were employed in utilities, one-quarter in professional, scientific, and technical services firms, and 14 percent in the Federal Government. Many Federally employed nuclear engineers were civilian employees of the U.S. Navy, and most of the rest worked for the U.S. Department of Energy.

Job Outlook

Good opportunities should exist for nuclear engineers because the small number of nuclear engineering graduates is likely to

Almost half of all nuclear engineers work in utilities.

be in rough balance with the number of job openings. Because this is a small occupation, projected job growth will generate few openings; consequently, most openings will result from the need to replace nuclear engineers who transfer to other occupations or leave the labor force.

Little or no growth in employment of nuclear engineers is expected through 2012. Due to public concerns over the cost and safety of nuclear power, no commercial nuclear powerplants have been built in the United States for many years. Nevertheless, nuclear engineers will be needed to operate existing plants. In addition, nuclear engineers may be needed to research and develop future nuclear power sources. They also will be needed to work in defense-related areas, to develop nuclear medical technology, and to improve and enforce waste management and safety standards.

Earnings

Median annual earnings of nuclear engineers were $81,350 in 2002. The middle 50 percent earned between $67,970 and $92,930. The lowest 10 percent earned less than $58,350, and the highest 10 percent earned more than $111,260. In the Federal Government, nuclear engineers in supervisory, nonsupervisory, and management positions earned an average of $73,769 a year in 2003.

According to a 2003 salary survey by the National Association of Colleges and Employers, bachelor's degree candidates in nuclear engineering received starting offers averaging $50,104 a year.

Sources of Additional Information

Information on careers and related topics for nuclear engineers is available from:
➤ American Nuclear Society, 555 North Kensington Ave., LaGrange Park, IL 60526. Internet: **http://www.ans.org**

See the introduction to the section on engineers for information on working conditions, training requirements, and other sources of additional information.

Petroleum Engineers

(0*NET 17-2171.00)

Nature of the Work

Petroleum engineers search the world for reservoirs containing oil or natural gas. Once these resources are discovered, petroleum engineers work with geologists and other specialists to understand the geologic formation and properties of the rock containing the reservoir, determine the drilling methods to be used, and monitor drilling and production operations. They design equipment and processes to achieve the maximum profitable recovery of oil and gas. Petroleum engineers rely heavily on computer models to simulate reservoir performance using different recovery techniques. They also use computer models for simulations of the effects of various drilling options.

Because only a small proportion of oil and gas in a reservoir will flow out under natural forces, petroleum engineers develop and use various enhanced recovery methods. These include injecting water, chemicals, gases, or steam into an oil reservoir to force out more of the oil, and computer-controlled drilling or fracturing to connect a larger area of a reservoir to a single well. Because even the best techniques in use today recover only a

Even though employment is expected to decline, favorable opportunities are expected for petroleum engineers because the number of job openings is likely to exceed the relatively small number of graduates.

portion of the oil and gas in a reservoir, petroleum engineers research and develop technology and methods to increase recovery and lower the cost of drilling and production operations.

Employment

Petroleum engineers held about 14,000 jobs in 2002, mostly in oil and gas extraction, professional, scientific and technical services, and petroleum refining. Employers include major oil companies and hundreds of smaller, independent oil exploration, production, and service companies.

Most petroleum engineers work where oil and gas are found. Large numbers are employed in Texas, Louisiana, Oklahoma, Alaska, and California, including offshore sites. Many American petroleum engineers also work overseas in oil-producing countries.

Job Outlook

Employment of petroleum engineers is expected to decline through 2012 because most of the potential petroleum-producing areas in the United States already have been explored. Even so, favorable opportunities are expected for petroleum engineers because the number of job openings is likely to exceed the relatively small number of graduates. All job openings should result from the need to replace petroleum engineers who transfer to other occupations or leave the labor force.

Petroleum engineers work around the world and, in fact, the best employment opportunities may be in other countries. Many foreign employers seek U.S.-trained petroleum engineers, and many U.S. employers maintain overseas branches where petroleum engineers work.

Earnings
Median annual earnings of petroleum engineers were $83,370 in 2002. The middle 50 percent earned between $63,390 and $105,920. The lowest 10 percent earned less than $49,010, and the highest 10 percent earned more than $127,950.

According to a 2003 salary survey by the National Association of Colleges and Employers, bachelor's degree candidates in petroleum engineering received starting offers averaging $55,987 year.

Sources of Additional Information
For further information on careers, education, and salaries for petroleum engineers, contact:
➤ Society of Petroleum Engineers, P.O. Box 833836, Richardson, TX 75083-3836. Internet: **http://www.spe.org**

See the introduction to the section on engineers for information on working conditions, training requirements, and other sources of additional information.

Drafters and Engineering Technicians

Drafters

(0*NET 17-3011.01, 17-3011.02, 17-3012.01, 17-3012.02, 17-3013.00)

Significant Points

- The type and quality of postsecondary drafting programs vary considerably; prospective students should be careful in selecting a program.

- Opportunities should be best for individuals with at least 2 years of postsecondary training in drafting and considerable skill and experience using computer-aided design and drafting (CADD) systems.

- Demand for particular drafting specialties varies geographically, depending on the needs of local industry.

Nature of the Work
Drafters prepare technical drawings and plans used by production and construction workers to build everything from manufactured products, such as toys, toasters, industrial machinery, and spacecraft, to structures, such as houses, office buildings, and oil and gas pipelines. Their drawings provide visual guidelines, show the technical details of the products and structures, and specify dimensions, materials, and procedures. Drafters fill in technical details, using drawings, rough sketches, specifications, codes, and calculations previously made by engineers, surveyors, architects, or scientists. For example, they use their knowledge of standardized building techniques to draw in the details of a structure. Some drafters use their knowledge of engineering and manufacturing theory and standards to draw the parts of a machine in order to determine design elements, such as the numbers and kinds of fasteners needed to assemble the machine. Drafters use technical handbooks, tables, calculators, and computers to complete their work.

Traditionally, drafters sat at drawing boards and used pencils, pens, compasses, protractors, triangles, and other drafting devices to prepare a drawing manually. Most drafters now use computer-aided design and drafting (CADD) systems to prepare drawings. Consequently, some drafters are referred to as *CADD operators*. CADD systems employ computer workstations to create a drawing on a video screen. The drawings are stored electronically to facilitate revisions and create duplications easily. These systems also permit drafters to quickly prepare variations of a design. Although drafters use CADD extensively, it is only a tool: Persons who produce technical drawings with CADD still function as drafters and need the knowledge of traditional drafters, in addition to CADD skills. Despite the near-universal use of CADD systems, manual drafting and sketching still is used in certain applications.

Drafting work has many specialties, and titles may denote a particular discipline of design or drafting.

Aeronautical drafters prepare engineering drawings detailing plans and specifications used in the manufacture of aircraft, missiles, and related parts.

Architectural drafters draw architectural and structural features of buildings and other structures. These workers may specialize in a type of structure, such as residential or commercial, or in a kind of material used, such as reinforced concrete, masonry, steel, or timber.

Civil drafters prepare drawings and topographical and relief maps used in major construction or civil engineering projects, such as highways, bridges, pipelines, flood control projects, and water and sewage systems.

Electrical drafters prepare wiring and layout diagrams used by workers who erect, install, and repair electrical equipment

Most drafters now use computer-aided design drafting (CADD) systems to prepare drawings.

and wiring in communication centers, powerplants, electrical distribution systems, and buildings.

Electronics drafters draw wiring diagrams, circuit board assembly diagrams, schematics, and layout drawings used in the manufacture, installation, and repair of electronic devices and components.

Mechanical drafters prepare detail and assembly drawings of a wide variety of machinery and mechanical devices, indicating dimensions, fastening methods, and other requirements.

Process piping or *pipeline drafters* prepare drawings used in the layout, construction, and operation of oil and gas fields, refineries, chemical plants, and process piping systems.

Working Conditions

Most drafters work a standard 40-hour week; only a small number work part time. Drafters usually work in comfortable offices furnished to accommodate their tasks. They may sit at adjustable drawing boards or drafting tables when doing manual drawings, although most drafters work at computer terminals much of the time. Because they spend long periods in front of computer terminals doing detailed work, drafters may be susceptible to eyestrain, back discomfort, and hand and wrist problems.

Employment

Drafters held about 216,000 jobs in 2002. Architectural and civil drafters held about half of all jobs for drafters, mechanical drafters held about a third of all jobs, and the rest of all jobs were held by electrical and electronics drafters.

Almost half of all jobs for drafters were in architectural, engineering, and related services firms that design construction projects or do other engineering work on a contract basis for other industries. More than a quarter of jobs were in manufacturing industries, such as machinery manufacturing, including metalworking and other general machinery; fabricated metal products manufacturing, including architectural and structural metals; computer and electronic products manufacturing, including navigational, measuring, electromedical, and control instruments; and transportation equipment manufacturing, including aerospace products and parts manufacturing, as well as ship and boat building. Most of the rest were employed in construction, government, wholesale trade, utilities, and employment services. Only a small number were self-employed in 2002.

Training, Other Qualifications, and Advancement

Employers prefer applicants who have completed postsecondary school training in drafting, which is offered by technical institutes, community colleges, and some 4-year colleges and universities. Employers are most interested in applicants with well-developed drafting and mechanical-drawing skills; knowledge of drafting standards, mathematics, science, and engineering technology; and a solid background in computer-aided design and drafting techniques. In addition, communication and problem-solving skills are important.

Training and course work differ somewhat within the drafting specialties. The initial training for each specialty is similar. All incorporate math and communication skills, for example, but course work relating to the specialty varies. In an electronics drafting program, for example, students learn how to depict electronic components and circuits in drawings.

Many types of publicly and privately operated schools provide some form of training in drafting. The kind and quality of programs vary considerably; therefore, prospective students should be careful in selecting a program. They should contact prospective employers regarding their preferences and ask schools to provide information about the kinds of jobs that are obtained by the school's graduates, the types and conditions of the instructional facilities and equipment, and the faculty's qualifications.

Technical institutes offer intensive technical training, but less general education than do junior and community colleges. Certificates or diplomas based on the completion of a certain number of course hours may be awarded. Many technical institutes offer 2-year associate degree programs, which are similar to, or part of, the programs offered by community colleges or State university systems. Their programs vary considerably in both length and type of courses offered. Some area vocational-technical schools are postsecondary public institutions that serve local students and emphasize the type of training preferred by local employers. Many offer introductory drafting instruction. Most require a high school diploma or its equivalent for admission. Other technical institutes are run by private, often for-profit, organizations, sometimes called proprietary schools.

Community colleges offer curricula similar to those in technical institutes, but include more courses on theory and liberal arts. Often, there is little or no difference between technical institute and community college programs. However, courses taken at community colleges are more likely than those given at technical institutes to be accepted for credit at 4-year colleges. After completing a 2-year associate degree program, graduates may obtain jobs as drafters or continue their education in a related field at 4-year colleges. Most 4-year colleges usually do not offer training in drafting, but college courses in engineering, architecture, and mathematics are useful for obtaining a job as a drafter.

Technical training obtained in the Armed Forces also can be applied in civilian drafting jobs. Some additional training may be necessary, depending on the technical area or military specialty.

The American Design Drafting Association (ADDA) has established a certification program for drafters. Although employers usually do not require drafters to be certified, certification demonstrates an understanding of nationally recognized practices and standards of knowledge. Individuals who wish to become certified must pass the Drafter Certification Test, which is administered periodically at ADDA-authorized sites. Applicants are tested on their knowledge and understanding of basic drafting concepts, such as geometric construction, working drawings, and architectural terms and standards.

Individuals planning careers in drafting should take courses in mathematics, science, computer technology, design, and computer graphics, as well as any high school drafting courses available. Mechanical ability and visual aptitude also are important. Prospective drafters should be able to draw well and perform detailed work accurately and neatly. Artistic ability is helpful in some specialized fields, as is knowledge of manufacturing and construction methods. In addition, prospective drafters should have good interpersonal skills, because they work closely with engineers, surveyors, architects, other professionals, and, sometimes, customers.

Entry-level or junior drafters usually do routine work under close supervision. After gaining experience, they may become intermediate-level drafters and progress to more difficult work with less supervision. At the intermediate level, they may need to exercise more judgment and perform calculations when preparing and modifying drawings. Drafters may eventually advance to senior drafter, designer, or supervisor. Many employers pay for continuing education, and, with appropriate college degrees, drafters may go on to become engineering technicians, engineers, or architects.

Job Outlook
Employment of drafters is expected to grow more slowly than the average for all occupations through 2012. Industrial growth and increasingly complex design problems associated with new products and manufacturing processes will increase the demand for drafting services. Further, drafters are beginning to break out of the traditional drafting role and increasingly do work traditionally performed by engineers and architects, thus also increasing demand for drafters. However, the greater use of CADD equipment by drafters, as well as by architects and engineers, should limit demand for lesser skilled drafters, resulting in slower-than-average overall employment growth. Most job openings are expected to arise from the need to replace drafters who transfer to other occupations, leave the labor force, or retire.

Opportunities should be best for individuals with at least 2 years of postsecondary training in a drafting program that provides strong technical skills, as well as considerable experience with CADD systems. CADD has increased the complexity of drafting applications while enhancing the productivity of drafters. It also has enhanced the nature of drafting by creating more possibilities for design and drafting. As technology continues to advance, employers will look for drafters with a strong background in fundamental drafting principles, a higher level of technical sophistication, and an ability to apply their knowledge to a broader range of responsibilities.

Demand for particular drafting specialties varies throughout the country because employment usually is contingent upon the needs of local industry. Employment of drafters remains highly concentrated in industries that are sensitive to cyclical changes in the economy, such as manufacturing and architectural and engineering services. During recessions, drafters may be laid off. However, a growing number of drafters should continue to find employment on a temporary or contract basis as more companies turn to the employment services industry to meet their changing needs.

Earnings
Earnings for drafters vary by specialty and level of responsibility. Median annual earnings of architectural and civil drafters were $37,330 in 2002. The middle 50 percent earned between $30,170 and $45,500. The lowest 10 percent earned less than $24,570, and the highest 10 percent earned more than $56,260. Median annual earnings for architectural and civil drafters in architectural, engineering, and related services were $36,780.

Median annual earnings of mechanical drafters were $40,730 in 2002. The middle 50 percent earned between $32,100 and $51,950. The lowest 10 percent earned less than $25,950, and the highest 10 percent earned more than $64,780. Median annual earnings for mechanical drafters in architectural, engineering, and related services were $41,170.

Median annual earnings of electrical and electronics drafters were $41,090 in 2002. The middle 50 percent earned between $32,060 and $53,440. The lowest 10 percent earned less than $25,710, and the highest 10 percent earned more than $68,000. In architectural, engineering, and related services, median annual earnings for electrical and electronics drafters were $39,760.

Related Occupations
Other workers who prepare or analyze detailed drawings and make precise calculations and measurements include architects, except landscape and naval; landscape architects; designers; engineers; engineering technicians; science technicians; and surveyors, cartographers, photogrammetrists, and surveying technicians.

Sources of Additional Information
Information on schools offering programs in drafting and related fields is available from:
➤ Accrediting Commission of Career Schools and Colleges of Technology, 2101 Wilson Blvd., Suite 302, Arlington, VA 22201. Internet: **http://www.accsct.org**

Information about certification is available from:
➤ American Design Drafting Association, 105 E. Main St., Newbern, TN 38059. Internet: **http://www.adda.org**

Engineering Technicians

(0*NET 17-3021.00, 17-3022.00, 17-3023.01, 17-3023.02, 17-3023.03, 17-3024.00, 17-3025.00, 17-3026.00, 17-3027.00)

Significant Points

- Electrical and electronic engineering technicians make up 42 percent of all engineering technicians.
- Because the type and quality of training programs vary considerably, prospective students should carefully investigate training programs before enrolling.
- Opportunities will be best for individuals with an associate degree or extensive job training in engineering technology.

Nature of the Work
Engineering technicians use the principles and theories of science, engineering, and mathematics to solve technical problems in research and development, manufacturing, sales, construction, inspection, and maintenance. Their work is more limited in scope and more practically oriented than that of scientists and engineers. Many engineering technicians assist engineers and scientists, especially in research and development. Others work in quality control—inspecting products and processes, conducting tests, or collecting data. In manufacturing, they may assist in product design, development, or production. Although many workers who repair or maintain various types of electrical, electronic, or mechanical equipment are called technicians, these workers are covered in the *Handbook* section on installation, maintenance, and repair occupations.

Engineering technicians who work in research and development build or set up equipment, prepare and conduct experiments, collect data, calculate or record results, and help engineers or scientists in other ways, such as making prototype versions of newly designed equipment. They also assist in design work, often using computer-aided design (CAD) equipment.

Most engineering technicians specialize in certain areas, learning skills and working in the same disciplines as engineers. Occupational titles, therefore, tend to reflect those of engineers.

Aerospace engineering and operations technicians install, construct, maintain, and test systems used to test, launch, or track aircraft and space vehicles. They may calibrate test equipment and determine causes of equipment malfunctions. Using computer and communications systems, aerospace engineering and operations technicians often record and interpret test data.

Chemical engineering technicians usually are employed in industries producing pharmaceuticals, chemicals, and petroleum products, among others. They work in laboratories as well as processing plants. They help to develop new chemical products and processes, test processing equipment and instrumentation, gather data, and monitor quality.

Civil engineering technicians help civil engineers to plan and build highways, buildings, bridges, dams, wastewater treatment systems, and other structures, and to do related research. Some estimate construction costs and specify materials to be used, and some may even prepare drawings or perform land-surveying duties. Others may set up and monitor instruments used to study traffic conditions. (Cost estimators; drafters; and surveyors, cartographers, photogrammetrists, and surveying technicians are covered elsewhere in the *Handbook*.)

Electrical and electronics engineering technicians help to design, develop, test, and manufacture electrical and electronic equipment such as communication equipment, radar, industrial and medical measuring or control devices, navigational equipment, and computers. They may work in product evaluation and testing, using measuring and diagnostic devices to adjust, test, and repair equipment. (Workers whose jobs are limited to repairing electrical and electronic equipment, who often are referred to as electronics technicians, are included with electrical and electronics installers and repairers elsewhere in the *Handbook*.)

Electrical and electronic engineering technology also is applied to a wide variety of systems such as communication and process controls. *Electromechanical engineering technicians* combine fundamental principles of mechanical engineering technology with knowledge of electrical and electronic circuits to design, develop, test, and manufacture electrical and computer-controlled mechanical systems.

Environmental engineering technicians work closely with environmental engineers and scientists in developing methods and devices used in the prevention, control, or correction of environmental hazards. They inspect and maintain equipment affecting air pollution and recycling. Some inspect water and wastewater treatment systems to ensure that pollution control requirements are met.

Many engineering technicians assist engineers and scientists, especially in research and development.

Industrial engineering technicians study the efficient use of personnel, materials, and machines in factories, stores, repair shops, and offices. They prepare layouts of machinery and equipment, plan the flow of work, make statistical studies, and analyze production costs.

Mechanical engineering technicians help engineers to design, develop, test, and manufacture industrial machinery, consumer products, and other equipment. They may assist in product tests—by setting up instrumentation for auto crash tests, for example. They may make sketches and rough layouts, record data, make computations, analyze results, and write reports. When planning production, mechanical engineering technicians prepare layouts and drawings of the assembly process and of parts to be manufactured. They estimate labor costs, equipment life, and plant space. Some test and inspect machines and equipment or work with engineers to eliminate production problems.

Working Conditions
Most engineering technicians work at least 40 hours a week in laboratories, offices, or manufacturing or industrial plants, or on construction sites. Some may be exposed to hazards from equipment, chemicals, or toxic materials.

Employment
Engineering technicians held 478,000 jobs in 2002. 204,000 of these were electrical and electronics engineering technicians, as indicated by the following tabulation.

Electrical and electronic engineering technicians	204,000
Civil engineering technicians	92,000
Industrial engineering technicians	62,000
Mechanical engineering technicians	55,000
Electro-mechanical technicians	31,000
Environmental engineering technicians	19,000
Aerospace engineering and operations technicians	15,000

About 39 percent of all engineering technicians worked in manufacturing, mainly in the computer and electronic equipment, transportation equipment, and machinery manufacturing industries. Another 20 percent worked in professional, scientific, and technical service industries, mostly in engineering or business services companies that do engineering work on contract for government, manufacturing firms, or other organizations.

In 2002, the Federal Government employed 11,000 engineering technicians. State governments employed 34,000, and local governments employed 24,000.

Training, Other Qualifications, and Advancement
Although it may be possible to qualify for certain engineering technician jobs without formal training, most employers prefer to hire someone with at least a 2-year associate degree in engineering technology. Training is available at technical institutes, community colleges, extension divisions of colleges and universities, and public and private vocational-technical schools, and in the Armed Forces. Persons with college courses in science, engineering, and mathematics may qualify for some positions but may need additional specialized training and experience. Although employers usually do not require engineering technicians to be certified, such certification may provide jobseekers a competitive advantage.

Prospective engineering technicians should take as many high school science and math courses as possible to prepare for postsecondary programs in engineering technology. Most 2-year associate degree programs accredited by the Technology Accreditation Commission of the Accreditation Board for Engineering and Technology (TAC/ABET) require, at a minimum, college algebra and trigonometry, and one or two basic science courses. Depending on the specialty, more math or science may be required.

The type of technical courses required also depends on the specialty. For example, prospective mechanical engineering technicians may take courses in fluid mechanics, thermodynamics, and mechanical design; electrical engineering technicians may need classes in electric circuits, microprocessors, and digital electronics; and those preparing to work in environmental engineering technology need courses in environmental regulations and safe handling of hazardous materials.

Because many engineering technicians assist in design work, creativity is desirable. Because these workers often are part of a team of engineers and other technicians, good communication skills and the ability to work well with others also are important.

Engineering technicians usually begin by performing routine duties under the close supervision of an experienced technician, technologist, engineer, or scientist. As they gain experience, they are given more difficult assignments with only general supervision. Some engineering technicians eventually become supervisors.

Many publicly and privately operated schools provide technical training; the type and quality of training varies considerably. Therefore, prospective students should be careful in selecting a program. They should contact prospective employers regarding their preferences and ask schools to provide information about the kinds of jobs obtained by graduates, instructional facilities and equipment, and faculty qualifications. Graduates of ABET-accredited programs usually are recognized to have achieved an acceptable level of competence in the mathematics, science, and technical courses required for this occupation.

Technical institutes offer intensive technical training through application and practice, but less theory and general education than do community colleges. Many offer 2-year associate degree programs, and are similar to or part of a community college or State university system. Other technical institutes are run by private, often for-profit organizations, sometimes called proprietary schools. Their programs vary considerably in length and types of courses offered, although some are 2-year associate degree programs.

Community colleges offer curriculums that are similar to those in technical institutes, but that may include more theory and liberal arts. There may be little or no difference between programs at technical institutes and community colleges, as both offer associate degrees. After completing the 2-year program, some graduates get jobs as engineering technicians, while others continue their education at 4-year colleges. However, there is a difference between an associate degree in pre-engineering and one in engineering technology. Students who enroll in a 2-year pre-engineering program may find it very difficult to find work as an engineering technician should they decide not to enter a 4-year engineering program, because pre-engineering programs usually focus less on hands-on applications and more on academic preparatory work. Conversely, graduates of 2-year engineering technology programs may not receive credit for some of the courses they have taken if they choose to transfer to a 4-year engineering program. Colleges with these 4-year programs usually do not offer engineering technician training, but college courses in science, engineering, and mathematics are useful for obtaining a job as an engineering technician. Many 4-year colleges offer bachelor's degrees in engineering technology, but graduates of these programs often are hired to work as technologists or applied engineers, not technicians.

Area vocational-technical schools, another source of technical training, include postsecondary public institutions that serve local students and emphasize training needed by local employers. Most require a high school diploma or its equivalent for admission.

Other training in technical areas may be obtained in the Armed Forces. Many military technical training programs are highly regarded by employers. However, skills acquired in military programs are often narrowly focused, so they may not be useful in civilian industry, which often requires broader training. Therefore, some additional training may be needed, depending on the acquired skills and the kind of job.

The National Institute for Certification in Engineering Technologies (NICET) has established a voluntary certification program for engineering technicians. Certification is available at various levels, each level combining a written examination in 1 of about 30 specialties with a certain amount of job-related experience, a supervisory evaluation, and a recommendation.

Job Outlook

Opportunities will be best for individuals with an associate degree or extensive job training in engineering technology. As technology becomes more sophisticated, employers will continue to look for technicians who are skilled in new technology and require a minimum of additional job training. An increase in the number of jobs related to public health and safety should create job opportunities for engineering technicians with the appropriate certification.

Overall employment of engineering technicians is expected to increase about as fast as the average for all occupations through 2012. Competitive pressures will force companies to improve and update manufacturing facilities and product designs, resulting in more jobs for engineering technicians. However, the growing use of advanced technologies, such as computer simulation and computer-aided design and drafting will continue to increase productivity and limit job growth. In addition to growth, many job openings will stem from the need to replace technicians who retire or leave the labor force.

As is the case for engineers, employment of engineering technicians is influenced by local and national economic conditions. As a result, the employment outlook varies with industry and specialization. Growth in the largest specialty—electrical and electronics engineering technicians—is expected to be about as fast as the average, and there will also be many jobs created by the need to replace technicians who retire or leave the labor force. Employment of environmental engineering technicians is expected to grow faster than average, partly due to increased demand for environmental protection and partly due to recognition of environmental engineering technicians as a separate occupation.

Earnings

Median annual earnings of engineering technicians by specialty is shown in the following tabulation.

Aerospace engineering and operations technicians	$51,650
Electrical and electronic engineering technicians	42,950
Industrial engineering technicians.....................................	41,910
Mechanical engineering technicians	41,280
Electro-mechanical technicians	38,120
Civil engineering technicians	37,720
Environmental engineering technicians	36,850

Median annual earnings of electrical and electronics engineering technicians were $42,950 in 2002. The middle 50 percent earned between $33,760 and $53,200. The lowest 10 percent earned less than $26,770, and the highest 10 percent earned more than $64,070. Median annual earnings in the industries employing the largest numbers of electrical and electronics engineering technicians in 2002 are shown below.

Federal government..	$58,520
Wired telecommunications carriers	49,610
Architectural, engineering, and related services	43,670
Semiconductor and other electronic component manufacturing..	40,110
Navigational, measuring, electromedical, and control instruments manufacturing	39,760

Median annual earnings of civil engineering technicians were $37,720 in 2002. The middle 50 percent earned between $29,030 and $47,260. The lowest 10 percent earned less than $23,080, and the highest 10 percent earned more than $56,910. Median annual earnings in the industries employing the largest numbers of civil engineering technicians in 2002 are shown below.

Local government	42,120
Architectural, engineering, and related services	36,930
State government	34,800

In 2002, the average annual salary for aerospace engineering and operations technicians in the aerospace products and parts manufacturing industry was $54,530, and the average annual salary for environmental engineering technicians in the architectural, engineering, and related services industry was $32,690. The average annual salary for industrial engineering technicians in the semiconductor and other electronic component manufacturing industry was $38,230. In the architectural, engineering, and related services industry, the average annual salary for mechanical engineering technicians was $42,090.

Related Occupations

Engineering technicians apply scientific and engineering principles usually acquired in postsecondary programs below the baccalaureate level. Similar occupations include science technicians; drafters; surveyors, cartographers, photogrammetrists, and surveying technicians; and broadcast and sound engineering technicians and radio operators.

Sources of Additional Information

High school students interested in obtaining information about careers in engineering technology should visit the JETS Web site: **http://www.jets.org**.
➤ JETS-Guidance, 1420 King St., Suite 405, Alexandria, VA 22314-2794.

Information on ABET-accredited engineering technology programs is available from:
➤ Accreditation Board for Engineering and Technology, Inc., 111 Market Place, Suite 1050, Baltimore, MD 21202. Internet: **http://www.abet.org**

Information on certification of engineering technicians as well as job and career information is available from:
➤ National Institute for Certification in Engineering Technologies (NICET), 1420 King St., Alexandria, VA 22314-2794. Internet: **http://www.nicet.org**

Life Scientists

Agricultural and Food Scientists

(0*NET 19-1011.00, 19-1012.00, 19-1013.01, 19-1013.02)

Significant Points

● Almost 4 in 10 salaried agricultural and food scientists work for Federal, State, or local governments.

● A bachelor's degree in agricultural science is sufficient for some jobs in applied research; a master's or doctoral degree is required for basic research.

● Slower-than-average job growth is projected because of limited growth in the Federal Government and modest growth in State and local governments, the largest employers of these scientists.

Nature of the Work

The work of agricultural and food scientists plays an important part in maintaining the Nation's food supply by ensuring agricultural productivity and the safety of the food supply. Agricultural scientists study farm crops and animals, and develop ways of improving their quantity and quality. They look for ways to improve crop yield with less labor, control pests and weeds more safely and effectively, and conserve soil and water. They research methods of converting raw agricultural commodities into attractive and healthy food products for consumers.

Agricultural science is closely related to biological science, and agricultural scientists use the principles of biology, chemistry, physics, mathematics, and other sciences to solve problems in agriculture. They often work with biological scientists on basic biological research and on applying to agriculture the advances in knowledge brought about by biotechnology.

In the past two decades, rapid advances in basic biological knowledge related to genetics spurred growth in the field of biotechnology. Some agricultural and food scientists use this technology to manipulate the genetic material of plants and crops, attempting to make organisms more productive or resistant to disease. These advances in biotechnology have opened up research opportunities in many areas of agricultural and food science, including commercial applications in agriculture, environmental remediation, and the food industry.

Many agricultural scientists work in basic or applied research and development. Others manage or administer research and development programs, or manage marketing or production operations in companies that produce food products or agricultural chemicals, supplies, and machinery. Some agricultural scientists are consultants to business firms, private clients, or government.

Depending on the agricultural or food scientist's area of specialization, the nature of the work performed varies.

Food science. Food scientists and technologists usually work in the food processing industry, universities, or the Federal Government, and help to meet consumer demand for food products that are healthful, safe, palatable, and convenient. To do this, they use their knowledge of chemistry, physics, engineering, microbiology, biotechnology, and other sciences to develop new or better ways of preserving, processing, packaging, storing, and delivering foods. Some food scientists engage in basic research, discovering new food sources; analyzing food content to determine levels of vitamins, fat, sugar, or protein; or searching for substitutes for harmful or undesirable additives, such as nitrites. They also develop ways to process, preserve, package, or store food according to industry and government regulations. Traditional food processing research into functions involving baking, blanching, canning, drying, evaporation, and pasteurization will continue to be conducted and will find new applications. Other food scientists enforce government regulations, inspecting food processing areas and ensuring that sanitation, safety, quality, and waste management standards are met. Food technologists generally work in product development, applying the findings from food science research to the selection, preservation, processing, packaging, distribution, and use of safe, nutritious, and wholesome food.

Plant science. Agronomy, crop science, entomology, and plant breeding are included in plant science. Scientists in these disciplines study plants and their growth in soils, helping producers of food, feed, and fiber crops to continue to feed a growing population while conserving natural resources and maintaining the environment. Agronomists and crop scientists not only help increase productivity, but also study ways to improve the nutritional value of crops and the quality of seed, often through biotechnology. Some crop scientists study the breeding, physiology, and management of crops and use genetic engineering to develop crops resistant to pests and drought. Entomologists conduct research to develop new technologies to control or eliminate pests in infested areas and to prevent the spread of harmful pests to new areas, as well as technologies that are compatible with the environment. They also conduct research or engage in oversight activities aimed at halting the spread of insect-borne disease.

Soil science. Soil scientists study the chemical, physical, biological, and mineralogical composition of soils as they relate to plant or crop growth. They also study the responses of various soil types to fertilizers, tillage practices, and crop rotation. Many soil scientists who work for the Federal Government conduct soil surveys, classifying and mapping soils. They provide information and recommendations to farmers and other landowners regarding the best use of land, plant growth, and methods to avoid or correct problems such as erosion. They may also consult with engineers and other technical personnel working on construction projects about the effects of, and solutions to, soil problems. Because soil science is closely related to environmental science, persons trained in soil science also apply their knowledge to ensure environmental quality and effective land use.

Animal science. Animal scientists work to develop better, more efficient ways of producing and processing meat, poultry, eggs, and milk. Dairy scientists, poultry scientists, animal breed-

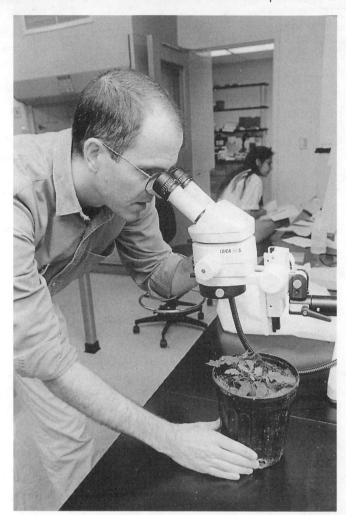

The work of agricultural and food scientists plays an important part in maintaining the Nation's food supply.

ers, and other scientists in related fields study the genetics, nutrition, reproduction, growth, and development of domestic farm animals. Some animal scientists inspect and grade livestock food products, purchase livestock, or work in technical sales or marketing. As extension agents or consultants, animal scientists advise agricultural producers on how to upgrade animal housing facilities properly, lower mortality rates, handle waste matter, or increase production of animal products, such as milk or eggs.

Working Conditions

Agricultural scientists involved in management or basic research tend to work regular hours in offices and laboratories. The work environment for those engaged in applied research or product development varies, depending on the discipline of agricultural science and on the type of employer. For example, food scientists in private industry may work in test kitchens while investigating new processing techniques. Animal scientists working for Federal, State, or university research stations may spend part of their time at dairies, farrowing houses, feedlots, or farm animal facilities or outdoors conducting research associated with livestock. Soil and crop scientists also spend time outdoors conducting research on farms and agricultural research stations. Entomologists work in laboratories, insectories, or agricultural research stations, and also may spend time outdoors studying or collecting insects in their natural habitat.

Employment

Agricultural and food scientists held about 18,000 jobs in 2002. In addition, several thousand persons held agricultural science faculty positions in colleges and universities. (See the statement on postsecondary teachers elsewhere in the *Handbook.*)

Almost 4 in 10 salaried agricultural and food scientists work for Federal, State, or local governments. One out of 6 worked for the Federal Government in 2002, mostly in the U.S. Department of Agriculture. Another 1 in 6 worked for State governments at State agricultural colleges or agricultural research stations. Some worked for agricultural service companies; others worked for commercial research and development laboratories, seed companies, pharmaceutical companies, wholesale distributors, and food products companies. Over 1,600 agricultural scientists were self-employed in 2002, mainly as consultants.

Training, Other Qualifications, and Advancement

Training requirements for agricultural scientists depend on their specialty and on the type of work they perform. A bachelor's degree in agricultural science is sufficient for some jobs in applied research or for assisting in basic research, but a master's or doctoral degree is required for basic research. A Ph.D. in agricultural science usually is needed for college teaching and for advancement to administrative research positions. Degrees in related sciences such as biology, chemistry, or physics or in related engineering specialties also may qualify persons for some agricultural science jobs.

All States have a land-grant college that offers agricultural science degrees. Many other colleges and universities also offer agricultural science degrees or some agricultural science courses. However, not every school offers all specialties. A typical undergraduate agricultural science curriculum includes communications, mathematics, economics, business, and physical and life sciences courses, in addition to a wide variety of technical agricultural science courses. For prospective animal scientists, these technical agricultural science courses might include animal breeding, reproductive physiology, nutrition, and meats and muscle biology. Graduate students typically specialize in a subfield of agricultural science, such as animal breeding and genetics, crop science, or horticulture science, depending on their interest and the kind of work they wish to do. For example, those interested in doing genetic and biotechnological research in the food industry need to develop a strong background in life and physical sciences, such as cell and molecular biology, microbiology, and inorganic and organic chemistry. However, students normally need not specialize at the undergraduate level. In fact, undergraduates who are broadly trained have greater flexibility when changing jobs than if they had narrowly defined their interests.

Students preparing as food scientists take courses such as food chemistry, food analysis, food microbiology, food engineering, and food processing operations. Those preparing as crop or soil scientists take courses in plant pathology, soil chemistry, entomology, plant physiology, and biochemistry, among others. Advanced degree programs include classroom and fieldwork, laboratory research, and a thesis or dissertation based on independent research.

Agricultural and food scientists should be able to work independently or as part of a team and be able to communicate clearly and concisely, both orally and in writing. Most of these scientists also need an understanding of basic business principles, and the ability to apply basic statistical techniques. Employers increasingly prefer job applicants who are able to apply computer skills to determine solutions to problems, to collect and analyze data, and to control various processes.

The American Society of Agronomy offers certification programs in crop science, agronomy, crop advising, soil science, plant pathology, and weed science. To become certified, applicants must pass designated examinations and have at least 2 years of experience with at least a bachelor's degree in agriculture or 4 years of experience with no degree. To become a certified crop advisor, however, candidates do not need a degree.

Agricultural scientists who have advanced degrees usually begin in research or teaching. With experience, they may advance to jobs such as supervisors of research programs or managers of other agriculture-related activities.

Job Outlook

Employment of agricultural and food scientists is expected to grow more slowly than the average for all occupations through 2012. This projection reflects limited growth in the Federal Government and modest growth in State and local governments. The need to replace agricultural and food scientists who retire or otherwise leave the occupation permanently will account for many more job openings than will projected growth.

Past agricultural research has resulted in the development of higher yielding crops, crops with better resistance to pests and plant pathogens, and chemically based fertilizers and pesticides. Research is still necessary, particularly as insects and diseases continue to adapt to pesticides and as soil fertility and water quality continue to need improvement, resulting in job opportunities in biotechnology. Agricultural scientists are using new avenues of research in biotechnology to develop plants and food crops that require less fertilizer, fewer pesticides and herbicides, and even less water for growth.

Biotechnological research, including studies and approaches relying on the tools of genomics, will continue to offer possibilities for the development of new food products. This research will allow agricultural and food scientists to develop techniques to detect and control food pathogens, and should lead to better understanding of other physiological responses of pathogens in food environments.

Agricultural scientists will be needed to balance increased agricultural output with protection and preservation of soil, water, and ecosystems. They will increasingly encourage the practice of "sustainable agriculture" by developing and implementing plans to manage pests, crops, soil fertility and erosion, and animal waste in ways that reduce the use of harmful chemicals and do little damage to the natural environment.

Further food research will result in more job opportunities for food scientists and technologists. This research will be stimulated by a heightened public focus on diet, health, and food safety, as well as domestic and global issues such as increasing world population, availability and cost of usable water, loss of arable land, deforestation, environmental pollution, and climate change.

Those with doctorates in agricultural and food science may face competition for jobs, due to an increase in the number of graduates and the limited numbers of research and teaching positions. Opportunities may be more numerous for those with a master's degree, particularly for graduates seeking basic research positions in a laboratory. Most of these positions, however, entail working under the guidance and direction of a Ph.D. scientist.

Graduates with a bachelor's degree should have opportunities, although not necessarily as an agricultural or food scientist.

A bachelor's degree in agricultural science is useful for managerial jobs in businesses that deal with ranchers and farmers, such as feed, fertilizer, seed, and farm equipment manufacturers; retailers or wholesalers; and farm credit institutions. In some cases, persons with a 4-year degree can provide consulting services, or become a certified crop advisor, providing crop management recommendations to farmers to help them meet their objectives. Bachelor's degree holders also can work in some applied research and product development positions, but usually only in certain subfields, such as food science and technology, and the Federal Government hires bachelor's degree holders to work as soil scientists. Four-year degrees also may help persons enter occupations such as farmer, or farm or ranch manager; cooperative extension service agent; agricultural products inspector; or purchasing or sales agent for agricultural commodity or farm supply companies.

Employment of agricultural and food scientists is relatively stable during periods of economic recession. Layoffs are less likely among agricultural and food scientists than in some other occupations because food is a staple item and its demand fluctuates very little with economic activity.

Earnings

Median annual earnings of agricultural and food scientists were $48,670 in 2002. The middle 50 percent earned between $35,770 and $65,990. The lowest 10 percent earned less than $28,750, and the highest 10 percent earned more than $85,460.

The average Federal salary for employees in nonsupervisory, supervisory, and managerial positions in 2003 was $82,729 in animal science and $68,846 in agronomy.

According to the National Association of Colleges and Employers, beginning salary offers in 2003 for graduates with a bachelor's degree in animal sciences averaged $30,026 a year; plant sciences, $28,203 a year; and in other agricultural sciences, $29,971 a year.

Related Occupations

The work of agricultural scientists is closely related to that of other scientists, including biological scientists, chemists, and conservation scientists and foresters. It also is related to the work of managers of agricultural production, such as farmers, ranchers, and agricultural managers. Certain specialties of agricultural science also are related to other occupations. For example, the work of animal scientists is related to that of veterinarians, and horticulturists perform duties similar to those of landscape architects.

Sources of Additional Information

Information on careers in agricultural science is available from:
➤ American Society of Agronomy, Crop Science Society of America, Soil Science Society of America, 677 S. Segoe Rd., Madison, WI 53711-1086. Internet: **http://www.agronomy.org**
➤ Food and Agricultural Careers for Tomorrow, Purdue University, 1140 Agricultural Administration Bldg., West Lafayette, IN 47907-1140.

For information on careers in food technology, write to:
➤ Institute of Food Technologists, Suite 300, 221 N. LaSalle St., Chicago IL 60601-1291. Internet: **http://www.ift.org**

Information on acquiring a job as an agricultural scientist with the Federal Government is available from the Office of Personnel Management through a telephone-based system. Consult your telephone directory under U.S. Government for a local number or call (703) 724-1850; Federal Relay Service: (800) 877-8339. The first number is not tollfree, and charges may result. Information also is available from the Internet site **http://www.usajobs.opm.gov**.

Biological Scientists

(0*NET 19-1020.01, 19-1021.01, 19-1021.02, 19-1022.00, 19-1023.00, 19-1029.99)

Significant Points

● A Ph.D. degree usually is required for independent research, but a master's degree is sufficient for some jobs in applied research or product development; a bachelor's degree is adequate for some nonresearch jobs.

● Doctoral degree holders face considerable competition for independent research positions, particularly in universities; holders of bachelor's or master's degrees in biological science can expect better opportunities in nonresearch positions.

● Biotechnological research and development will continue to drive employment growth.

Nature of the Work

Biological scientists study living organisms and their relationship to their environment. They research problems dealing with life processes. Most specialize in some area of biology such as zoology (the study of animals) or microbiology (the study of microscopic organisms). (Medical scientists, whose work is closely related to that of biological scientists, are discussed elsewhere in the *Handbook*.)

Many biological scientists work in research and development. Some conduct basic research to advance knowledge of living organisms, including viruses, bacteria, and other infectious agents. Basic biological research continues to provide the building blocks necessary to develop solutions to human health problems, and to preserve and repair the natural environment. Biological scientists mostly work independently in private industry, university, or government laboratories, often exploring new areas of research or expanding on specialized research started in graduate school. Those who are not wage and salary workers in private industry typically submit grant proposals to obtain funding for their projects. Colleges and universities, private industry, and Federal Government agencies, such as the National Institutes of Health and the National Science Foundation, contribute to the support of scientists whose research proposals are determined to be financially feasible and to have the potential to advance new ideas or processes.

Biological scientists who work in applied research or product development use knowledge provided by basic research to develop new drugs and treatments, increase crop yields, and protect and clean up the environment. They usually have less autonomy than basic researchers to choose the emphasis of their research, relying instead on market-driven directions based on the firm's products and goals. Biological scientists doing applied research and product development in private industry may be required to describe their research plans or results to nonscientists who are in a position to veto or approve their ideas, and they must understand the potential cost of their work and its impact on business. Scientists increasingly are working as part of teams, interacting with engineers, scientists of other disciplines, business managers, and technicians. Some biological scientists also work with customers or suppliers and manage budgets.

Those who conduct research usually work in laboratories and use electron microscopes, computers, thermal cyclers, or a wide variety of other equipment. Some conduct experiments using laboratory animals or greenhouse plants. This is particularly true of botanists, physiologists, and zoologists. For some biological scientists, research also is performed outside of laboratories. For example, a botanist might do research in tropical rain forests to see what plants grow there, or an ecologist might study how a forest area recovers after a fire. Some marine biologists also work outdoors, often on research vessels from which they study various marine organisms such as marine plankton or fish.

Some biological scientists work in managerial or administrative positions, usually after spending some time doing research and learning about the firm, agency, or project. They may plan and administer programs for testing foods and drugs, for example, or direct activities at zoos or botanical gardens. Some work as consultants to business firms or to government, while others test and inspect foods, drugs, and other products.

Recent advances in biotechnology and information technology are transforming the industries in which biological scientists work. In the 1980s, swift advances in basic biological knowledge related to genetics and molecules spurred growth in the field of biotechnology. Biological scientists using this technology manipulate the genetic material of animals or plants, attempting to make organisms more productive or resistant to disease. Research using biotechnology techniques, such as recombining DNA, has led to the production of important substances, including human insulin and growth hormone. Many other substances not previously available in large quantities are starting to be produced by biotechnological means; some may be useful in treating cancer and other diseases. Today, many biological scientists are involved in biotechnology. Those who work on the Human Genome project continue to isolate genes and determine their functionality. This work continues to lead to the discovery of the genes associated with specific diseases and inherited traits, such as certain types of cancer or obesity. These advances in biotechnology have opened up research opportunities in almost all areas of biology, including commercial applications in agriculture, environmental remediation, and the food and chemical industries.

Many biological scientists work in research and development, often in offices and laboratories.

Most biological scientists are further classified by the type of organism they study or by the specific activity they perform, although recent advances in the understanding of basic life processes at the molecular and cellular levels have blurred some traditional classifications.

Aquatic biologists study micro-organisms, plants, and animals living in water. *Marine biologists* study salt water organisms, and *limnologists* study fresh water organisms. Much of the work of marine biology centers on molecular biology, the study of the biochemical processes that take place inside living cells. Marine biologists sometimes are mistakenly called oceanographers, but oceanography is the study of the physical characteristics of oceans and the ocean floor. (See the statement on environmental scientists and geoscientists elsewhere in the *Handbook*.)

Biochemists study the chemical composition of living things. They analyze the complex chemical combinations and reactions involved in metabolism, reproduction, growth, and heredity. Biochemists and molecular biologists do most of their work in the field of biotechnology, which involves understanding the complex chemistry of life.

Botanists study plants and their environment. Some study all aspects of plant life, including algae, fungi, lichens, mosses, ferns, conifers, and flowering plants; others specialize in areas such as identification and classification of plants, the structure and function of plant parts, the biochemistry of plant processes, the causes and cures of plant diseases, the interaction of plants with other organisms and the environment, and the geological record of plants.

Microbiologists investigate the growth and characteristics of microscopic organisms such as bacteria, algae, or fungi. Most microbiologists specialize in environmental, food, agricultural, or industrial microbiology; virology (the study of viruses); or immunology (the study of mechanisms that fight infections). Many microbiologists use biotechnology to advance knowledge of cell reproduction and human disease.

Physiologists study life functions of plants and animals, both in the whole organism and at the cellular or molecular level, under normal and abnormal conditions. Physiologists often specialize in functions such as growth, reproduction, photosynthesis, respiration, or movement, or in the physiology of a certain area or system of the organism.

Biophysicists study the application of principles of physics, such as electrical and mechanical energy and related phenomena, to living cells and organisms.

Zoologists and wildlife biologists study animals and wildlife—their origin, behavior, diseases, and life processes. Some experiment with live animals in controlled or natural surroundings, while others dissect dead animals in order to study their structure. They also may collect and analyze biological data to determine the environmental effects of current and potential use of land and water areas. Zoologists usually are identified by the animal group studied—ornithologists (birds), mammalogists (mammals), herpetologists (reptiles), and ichthyologists (fish).

Ecologists study the relationships among organisms and between organisms and their environments, and the effects of influences such as population size, pollutants, rainfall, temperature, and altitude. Utilizing knowledge of various scientific disciplines, they may collect, study, and report data on the quality of air, food, soil, and water.

Agricultural and food scientists, who are sometimes referred to as biological scientists, are discussed elsewhere in the *Handbook*.

Working Conditions

Biological scientists usually work regular hours in offices or laboratories and usually are not exposed to unsafe or unhealthy conditions. Those who work with dangerous organisms or toxic substances in the laboratory must follow strict safety procedures to avoid contamination. Many biological scientists such as botanists, ecologists, and zoologists take field trips that involve strenuous physical activity and primitive living conditions. Biological scientists in the field may work in warm or cold climates, in all kinds of weather. In their research, they may dig, chip with a hammer, scoop with a net, and carry equipment in a backpack. They also may climb, stand, kneel, or dive.

The work of a marine biologist varies dramatically, depending on the type of work involved. Some work in a laboratory, while others work on research ships. Marine biologists who work underwater must practice safe diving while working around sharp coral reefs and hazardous marine life. Although some marine biologists obtain their specimens from the sea, many still spend a good deal of their time in laboratories and offices, conducting tests, running experiments, recording results, and compiling data.

Some biological scientists depend on grant money to support their research. They may be under pressure to meet deadlines and to conform to rigid grant-writing specifications when preparing proposals to seek new or extended funding.

Employment

Biological scientists held about 75,000 jobs in 2002. Almost half of all biological scientists were employed by Federal, State, and local governments. Federal biological scientists worked mainly for the U.S. Departments of Agriculture, Interior, and Defense, and for the National Institutes of Health. Most of the rest worked in scientific research and testing laboratories, the pharmaceutical and medicine manufacturing industry, or hospitals.

In addition, many biological scientists held biology faculty positions in colleges and universities. (See the statement on teachers—postsecondary elsewhere in the *Handbook*.)

Training, Other Qualifications, and Advancement

A Ph.D. degree usually is necessary for independent research, industrial research, and college teaching, and for advancement to administrative positions. A master's degree is sufficient for some jobs in basic research, applied research or product development, management, or inspection; it may also qualify one to work as a research technician or as a teacher in an aquarium. The bachelor's degree is adequate for some nonresearch jobs. For example, some graduates with a bachelor's degree start as biological scientists in testing and inspection, or get jobs related to biological science, such as technical sales or service representatives. In some cases, graduates with a bachelor's degree are able to work in a laboratory environment on their own projects, but this is unusual. Some may work as research assistants, while others become biological laboratory technicians or, with courses in education, high school biology teachers. (See the statements on clinical laboratory technologists and technicians; science technicians; and teachers-preschool, kindergarten, elementary, middle, and secondary elsewhere in the *Handbook*.) Many with a bachelor's degree in biology enter medical, dental, veterinary, or other health profession schools.

In addition to required courses in chemistry and biology, undergraduate biological science majors usually study allied disciplines such as mathematics, physics, and computer science.

Computer courses are essential, as employers prefer job applicants who are able to apply computer skills to modeling and simulation tasks and to operate computerized laboratory equipment. Those interested in studying the environment also should take courses in environmental studies and become familiar with current legislation and regulations. Prospective biological scientists who hope to work as marine biologists should have at least a bachelor's degree in a biological or marine science. However, students should not overspecialize in undergraduate study, as knowledge of marine biology often is acquired in graduate study. Most colleges and universities offer bachelor's degrees in biological science, and many offer advanced degrees. Curriculums for advanced degrees often emphasize a subfield such as microbiology or botany, but not all universities offer all curriculums. Larger universities frequently have separate departments specializing in different areas of biological science. For example, a program in botany might cover agronomy, horticulture, or plant pathology. Advanced degree programs include classroom and fieldwork, laboratory research, and a thesis or dissertation.

Biological scientists with a Ph.D. often take temporary postdoctoral research positions that provide specialized research experience. In private industry, some may become managers or administrators within the field of biology; others leave biology for nontechnical managerial, administrative, or sales jobs.

Biological scientists should be able to work independently or as part of a team and be able to communicate clearly and concisely, both orally and in writing. Those in private industry, especially those who aspire to management or administrative positions, should possess strong business and communication skills and be familiar with regulatory issues and marketing and management techniques. Those doing field research in remote areas must have physical stamina. Biological scientists also must have patience and self-discipline to conduct long and detailed research projects.

Job Outlook

Despite projected as fast as average job growth for biological scientists over the 2002-12 period, doctoral degree holders can expect to face competition for basic research positions. The Federal Government funds much basic research and development, including many areas of medical research that relate to biological science. Recent budget increases at the National Institutes of Health have led to large increases in Federal basic research and development expenditures, with research grants growing both in number and in dollar amount. At the same time, the number of newly trained scientists has continued to increase at least as fast as available research funds, so both new and established scientists have experienced difficulty winning and renewing research grants. Currently, about 1 in 3 grant proposals are approved for long-term research projects. If the number of advanced degrees awarded continues to grow, as seems likely based on enrollment trends, this competitive situation will persist. Additionally, applied research positions in private industry may become more difficult to obtain if increasing numbers of scientists seek jobs in private industry because of the competitive job market for independent research positions in universities and for college and university faculty.

Opportunities for those with a bachelor's or master's degree in biological science are expected to be better. The number of science-related jobs in sales, marketing, and research management, for which non-Ph.D.s usually qualify, is expected to exceed the number of independent research positions. Non-Ph.D.s also may fill positions as science or engineering technicians or health technologists and technicians. Some may become high school biology teachers.

Biological scientists enjoyed very rapid gains in employment between the mid-1980s and mid-1990s, in part reflecting increased staffing requirements in new biotechnology companies. Employment growth should slow somewhat as increases in the number of new biotechnology firms slow and existing firms merge or are absorbed into larger ones. However, much of the basic biological research done in recent years has resulted in new knowledge, including the isolation and identification of genes. Biological scientists will be needed to take this knowledge to the next stage, which is the understanding of how certain genes function within an entire organism, so that gene therapies can be developed to treat diseases. Even pharmaceutical and other firms not solely engaged in biotechnology use biotechnology techniques extensively, spurring employment increases for biological scientists. Expected expansion of research related to health issues, such as AIDS, cancer, and Alzheimer's disease, also should create more jobs for these scientists. In addition, efforts to discover new and improved ways to clean up and preserve the environment will continue to add to job growth. More biological scientists, including some botanists, will be needed to determine the environmental impact of industry and government actions and to prevent or correct environmental problems, while some will find opportunities in environmental regulatory agencies. Botanists also will use their expertise to advise lawmakers on legislation for environmental protection and for ways to save environmentally sensitive areas. There will continue to be demand for biological scientists specializing in botany, zoology, and marine biology, but opportunities will be limited because of the small size of these fields.

Biological scientists are less likely to lose their jobs during recessions than are those in many other occupations because many are employed on long-term research projects. However, an economic downturn could influence the amount of money allocated to new research and development efforts, particularly in areas of risky or innovative research. An economic downturn could also limit the possibility of extension or renewal of existing projects.

Earnings

Median annual earnings of biochemists and biophysicists were $60,390 in 2002. The middle 50 percent earned between $43,110 and $82,080. The lowest 10 percent earned less than $33,930, and the highest 10 percent earned more than $102,930. Median annual earnings of microbiologists were $51,020 in 2002. The middle 50 percent earned between $39,100 and $67,420. The lowest 10 percent earned less than $31,250, and the highest 10 percent earned more than $87,060. Median annual earnings of zoologists and wildlife biologists were $47,740 in 2002. The middle 50 percent earned between $37,100 and $58,040. The lowest 10 percent earned less than $29,260, and the highest 10 percent earned more than $71,270. Median annual earnings of biochemists and biophysicists employed in scientific research and development services were $64,390 in 2002.

According to the National Association of Colleges and Employers, beginning salary offers in 2003 averaged $29,456 a year for bachelor's degree recipients in biological and life sciences; $33,600 for master's degree recipients; and $42,244 for doctoral degree recipients.

In the Federal Government in 2003, general biological scientists in nonsupervisory, supervisory, and managerial positions earned an average salary of $66,262; microbiologists, $73,513; ecologists, $65,207; physiologists, $85,181; geneticists, $78,652; zoologists, $90,178; and botanists, $55,727.

Related Occupations

Many other occupations deal with living organisms and require a level of training similar to that of biological scientists. These include medical scientists, agricultural and food scientists, and conservation scientists and foresters, as well as health occupations such as physicians and surgeons, dentists, and veterinarians.

Sources of Additional Information

For information on careers in the biological sciences, contact:
➤ American Institute of Biological Sciences, Suite 200, 1444 I St. NW., Washington, DC 20005. Internet: **http://www.aibs.org**

For information on careers in biochemistry or biological sciences, contact:
➤ Federation of American Societies for Experimental Biology, 9650 Rockville Pike, Bethesda, MD 20814. Internet: **http://www.faseb.org**

For information on careers in microbiology, contact:
➤ American Society for Microbiology, Office of Education and Training—Career Information, 1325 Massachusetts Ave. NW., Washington, DC 20005. Internet: **http://www.asmusa.org**

Information on obtaining a biological scientist position with the Federal Government is available from the U.S. Office of Personnel Management (OPM) through a telephone-based system. Consult your telephone directory under U.S. Government for a local number or call (703) 724-1850; Federal Relay Service: (800) 877-8339. The first number is not tollfree, and charges may result. Information also is available from the OPM Internet site: **http://www.usajobs.opm.gov**.

Conservation Scientists and Foresters

(0*NET 19-1031.01, 19-1031.02, 19-1031.03, 19-1032.00)

Significant Points

● Nearly two-thirds of salaried conservation scientists and foresters work for Federal, State, or local governments.

● A bachelor's degree in forestry, range management, or a related discipline is the minimum educational requirement.

● Slower-than-average job growth is projected because of limited growth in government and in forestry and logging; most employment opportunities will be in private sector consulting.

Nature of the Work

Forests and rangelands supply wood products, livestock forage, minerals, and water; serve as sites for recreational activities; and provide habitats for wildlife. Conservation scientists and foresters manage, develop, use, and help to protect these and other natural resources.

Foresters manage forested lands for a variety of purposes. Those working in private industry may manage company forest land or procure timber from private landowners. Company forests usually are managed to produce a sustainable supply of wood for company mills. Procurement foresters contact local forest owners and gain permission to take inventory of the type, amount, and location of all standing timber on the property, a process known as timber cruising. Foresters then appraise the timber's worth, negotiate its purchase, and draw up a contract for procurement. Next, they subcontract with loggers or pulpwood cutters for tree removal, aid in road layout, and maintain close contact with the subcontractor's workers and the landowner to ensure that the work meets the landowner's requirements, as well as Federal, State, and local environmental specifications. Forestry consultants often act as agents for the forest owner, performing these duties and negotiating timber sales with industrial procurement foresters.

Throughout the forest management and procurement processes, foresters consider the economics as well as the environmental impact on natural resources. To do this, they determine how to conserve wildlife habitats, creek beds, water quality, and soil stability, and how best to comply with environmental regulations. Foresters must balance the desire to conserve forested ecosystems for future generations with the need to use forest resources for recreational or economic purposes.

Through a process called regeneration, foresters also supervise the planting and growing of new trees. They choose and prepare the site, using controlled burning, bulldozers, or herbicides to clear weeds, brush, and logging debris. They advise on the type, number, and placement of trees to be planted. Foresters then monitor the seedlings to ensure healthy growth and to determine the best time for harvesting. If they detect signs of disease or harmful insects, they consult with forest pest management specialists to decide on the best course of treatment. Foresters who work for Federal and State governments manage public forests and parks and work with private landowners to protect and manage forest land outside of the public domain. They may also design campgrounds and recreation areas.

Foresters use a number of tools to perform their jobs. Clinometers measure the height, diameter tapes measure the diameter, and increment borers and bark gauges measure the growth of trees so that timber volumes can be computed and growth rates estimated. Remote sensing (aerial photographs and other imagery taken from airplanes and satellites) and Geographic Information Systems (GIS) data often are used for mapping large forest areas and for detecting widespread trends of forest and land use. Once the map is generated, the data are digitized to create a computerized inventory of information required to manage the forest land and its resources. Moreover, hand-held computers, Global Positioning Satellite (GPS), and World Wide Web-based applications are used extensively.

Range managers, also called *range conservationists*, *range ecologists*, or *range scientists*, study, manage, improve, and protect rangelands to maximize their use without damaging the environment. Rangelands cover about 1 billion acres of the United States, mostly in Western States and Alaska. They contain many natural resources, including grass and shrubs for animal grazing, wildlife habitats, water from vast watersheds, recreation facilities, and valuable mineral and energy resources. Range managers may inventory soils, plants, and animals, develop resource management plans, help to restore degraded ecosystems, or assist in managing a ranch. For example, they may help ranchers attain optimum livestock production by determining the number and kind of animals to graze, the grazing system to use, and the best season for grazing. At the same time, however, range managers maintain soil stability and vegetation for other uses such as wildlife habitats and outdoor recreation. They also plan and implement revegetation of disturbed sites.

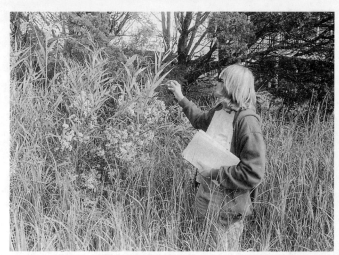

Conservation scientists and foresters often work outdoors, sometimes in isolated areas.

Soil and water conservationists provide technical assistance to farmers, ranchers, forest managers, State and local agencies, and others concerned with the conservation of soil, water, and related natural resources. They develop programs for private landowners designed to make the most productive use of land without damaging it. Soil conservationists also assist landowners by visiting areas with erosion problems, finding the source of the problem, and helping landowners and managers develop management practices to combat it. Water conservationists also assist private landowners and Federal, State, and local governments by advising on a broad range of natural resource topics— specifically, issues of water quality, preserving water supplies, groundwater contamination, and management and conservation of water resources.

Foresters and conservation scientists often specialize in one area, such as wildlife management, urban forestry, wood technology, native species, or forest economics.

Working Conditions
Working conditions vary considerably. Although some of the work is solitary, foresters and conservation scientists also deal regularly with landowners, loggers, forestry technicians and aides, farmers, ranchers, government officials, special interest groups, and the public in general. Some foresters and conservation scientists work regular hours in offices or labs. Others may split their time between fieldwork and office work, while independent consultants and especially new, less experienced workers spend the majority of their time outdoors overseeing or participating in hands-on work.

The work can be physically demanding. Some foresters and conservation scientists work outdoors in all types of weather, sometimes in isolated areas. Other foresters may need to walk long distances through densely wooded land to carry out their work. Foresters also may work long hours fighting fires. Conservation scientists often are called to prevent erosion after a forest fire, and they provide emergency help after floods, mudslides, and tropical storms.

Employment
Conservation scientists and foresters held about 33,000 jobs in 2002. Nearly one-third of all workers were employed by the Federal Government, many in the U.S. Department of Agriculture (USDA). Foresters were concentrated in the USDA's Forest

Service; soil conservationists were employed primarily in the USDA's Natural Resource Conservation Service. Most range managers worked in the U.S. Department of the Interior's Bureau of Land Management, the Natural Resource Conservation Service, or the Forest Service. Another 20 percent of conservation scientists and foresters worked for State governments, and about 10 percent worked for local governments. The remainder worked in private industry, mainly in support activities for agriculture and forestry or in wood product manufacturing. Some were self-employed as consultants for private landowners, Federal and State governments, and forestry-related businesses.

Although conservation scientists and foresters work in every State, employment of foresters is concentrated in the Western and Southeastern States, where many national and private forests and parks, and most of the lumber and pulpwood-producing forests, are located. Range managers work almost entirely in the Western States, where most of the rangeland is located. Soil conservationists, on the other hand, are employed in almost every county in the country. Besides the jobs described above, some foresters and conservation scientists held faculty positions in colleges and universities. (See the statement on teachers—postsecondary elsewhere in the *Handbook*.)

Training, Other Qualifications, and Advancement

A bachelor's degree in forestry, range management, or a related discipline is the minimum educational requirement for careers in forestry or conservation science. In the Federal Government, a combination of experience and appropriate education occasionally may substitute for a 4-year forestry degree, but job competition makes this difficult.

Sixteen States have mandatory licensing or voluntary registration requirements that a forester must meet in order to acquire the title "professional forester" and practice forestry in the State. Of those 16 States, 7 have mandatory licensing; 5 have mandatory registration, and the remaining 4 States have optional registration. Both licensing and registration requirements usually entail completing a 4-year degree in forestry and several years of forestry work experience. Candidates pursuing licensing also must pass a comprehensive written exam.

Foresters who wish to perform specialized research or teach should have an advanced degree, preferably a Ph.D.

Most land-grant colleges and universities offer bachelor's or higher degrees in forestry; about 110 of these degree programs at around 50 educational institutions are accredited by the Society of American Foresters. Curriculums stress four components: Ecology, measurement of forest resources, management of forest resources, and public policy. Students should balance general science courses such as ecology, biology, tree physiology, taxonomy, and soil formation with technical forestry courses, such as forest inventory or wildlife habitat assessment, remote sensing, land surveying, GPS technology, integrated forest resource management, silviculture, and forest protection. In addition, communications skills, mathematics, statistics, and computer science courses also are recommended. Many forestry curriculums include advanced computer applications such as GIS and resource assessment programs. Courses in resource policy and administration, specifically forest economics and business administration, supplement the student's scientific and technical knowledge. Forestry curriculums increasingly include courses on best management practices, wetlands analysis, and sustainability and regulatory issues in response to the growing focus on protecting forested lands during timber harvesting operations. Prospective foresters should have a strong grasp of

Federal, State, and local policy issues and of increasingly numerous and complex environmental regulations that affect many forestry-related activities. Many colleges require students to complete a field session either in a camp operated by the college or in a cooperative work-study program with a Federal or State agency or private industry. All schools encourage students to take summer jobs that provide experience in forestry or conservation work.

A bachelor's degree in range management or range science is the usual minimum educational requirement for range managers; graduate degrees usually are required for teaching and research positions. More than 30 colleges and universities offer degrees in range management that are accredited by the Society of Range Management. A number of other schools offer degree programs in range science or in a closely related discipline with a range management or range science option. Specialized range management courses combine plant, animal, and soil sciences with principles of ecology and resource management. Desirable electives include economics, statistics, forestry, hydrology, agronomy, wildlife, animal husbandry, computer science, and recreation. Selection of a minor in range management, such as wildlife ecology, watershed management, animal science, or agricultural economics, can often enhance qualifications for certain types of employment. The Society for Range Management offers certification as a professional rangeland manager (CPRM). Candidates seeking certification must have at least a bachelor's degree in range science or a closely related field, have a minimum of 5 years of full-time work experience, and pass a comprehensive written exam.

Very few colleges and universities offer degrees in soil conservation. Most soil conservationists have degrees in environmental studies, agronomy, general agriculture, hydrology, or crop or soil science; a few have degrees in related fields such as wildlife biology, forestry, and range management. Programs of study usually include 30 semester hours in natural resources or agriculture, including at least 3 hours in soil science.

In addition to meeting the demands of forestry and conservation research and analysis, foresters and conservation scientists generally must enjoy working outdoors, be physically hardy, and be willing to move to where the jobs are. They also must work well with people and have good communication skills.

Recent forestry and range management graduates usually work under the supervision of experienced foresters or range managers. After gaining experience, they may advance to more responsible positions. In the Federal Government, most entry-level foresters work in forest resource management. An experienced Federal forester may supervise a ranger district, and may advance to forest supervisor, to regional forester, or to a top administrative position in the national headquarters. In private industry, foresters start by learning the practical and administrative aspects of the business and acquiring comprehensive technical training. They are then introduced to contract writing, timber harvesting, and decisionmaking. Some foresters work their way up to top managerial positions within their companies. Foresters in management usually leave the fieldwork behind, spending more of their time in an office, working with teams to develop management plans and supervising others. After gaining several years of experience, some foresters may become consulting foresters, working alone or with one or several partners. They contract with State or local governments, private landowners, private industry, or other forestry consulting groups.

Soil conservationists usually begin working within one county or conservation district and, with experience, may advance to the area, State, regional, or national level. Also, soil conservationists can transfer to related occupations, such as farm or ranch management advisor or land appraiser.

Job Outlook

Employment of conservation scientists and foresters is expected to grow more slowly than the average for all occupations through 2012. Growth should be strongest in private sector consulting firms and in scientific research and development services. Demand will be spurred by a continuing emphasis on environmental protection, responsible land management, and water-related issues. Job opportunities for conservation scientists will arise because government regulations, such as those regarding the management of storm water and coastlines, have created demand for persons knowledgeable about runoff and erosion on farms and in cities and suburbs. Soil and water quality experts will be needed as States design initiatives to improve water resources by preventing pollution by agricultural producers and industrial plants.

Fewer opportunities for conservation scientists and foresters are expected in Federal and State Government, mostly due to budgetary constraints and the trend among governments toward contracting functions out to private consulting firms. Also, Federal land management agencies, such as the USDA Forest Service, have de-emphasized their timber programs and increasingly focused on wildlife, recreation, and sustaining ecosystems, thereby spurring demand for other life and social scientists rather than for foresters. However, departures of foresters who retire or leave the Government for other reasons will result in some job openings between 2002 and 2012. A small number of new jobs will result from the need for range and soil conservationists to provide technical assistance to owners of grazing land through the Natural Resource Conservation Service.

Reductions in timber harvesting on public lands, most of which are located in the Northwest and California, also will dampen job growth for private industry foresters in these regions. Opportunities will be better for foresters in the Southeast, where much forested land is privately owned. Salaried foresters working for private industry—such as paper companies, sawmills, and pulpwood mills—and consulting foresters will be needed to provide technical assistance and management plans to landowners.

Scientific research and development services have increased their hiring of conservation scientists and foresters in recent years in response to demand for professionals to prepare environmental impact statements and erosion and sediment control plans, monitor water quality near logging sites, and advise on tree harvesting practices required by Federal, State, or local regulations. Hiring in these firms should continue during the 2002-12 period, although at a slower rate than over the last 10 years.

Earnings

Median annual earnings of conservation scientists in 2002 were $50,340. The middle 50 percent earned between $39,300 and $61,440. The lowest 10 percent earned less than $30,630, and the highest 10 percent earned more than $70,770.

Median annual earnings of foresters in 2002 were $46,730. The middle 50 percent earned between $36,330 and $56,890. The lowest 10 percent earned less than $29,690, and the highest 10 percent earned more than $69,600.

In 2003, most bachelor's degree graduates entering the Federal Government as foresters, range managers, or soil conserva-

tionists started at $23,442 or $29,037, depending on academic achievement. Those with a master's degree could start at $35,519 or $42,976. Holders of doctorates could start at $51,508. Beginning salaries were slightly higher in selected areas where the prevailing local pay level was higher. In 2003, the average Federal salary for foresters in nonsupervisory, supervisory, and managerial positions was $59,233; for soil conservationists, $57,084; and for rangeland managers, $53,657.

According to the National Association of Colleges and Employers, graduates with a bachelor's degree in conservation and renewable natural resources received an average starting salary offer of $29,715 in 2003.

In private industry, starting salaries for students with a bachelor's degree were comparable with starting salaries in the Federal Government, but starting salaries in State and local governments were usually lower.

Conservation scientists and foresters who work for Federal, State, and local governments and large private firms generally receive more generous benefits than do those working for smaller firms.

Related Occupations

Conservation scientists and foresters manage, develop, and protect natural resources. Other workers with similar responsibilities include environmental engineers; agricultural and food scientists; biological scientists; environmental scientists and geoscientists; and farmers, ranchers, and agricultural managers.

Sources of Additional Information

For information about the forestry profession and lists of schools offering education in forestry, send a self-addressed, stamped business envelope to:
➤ Society of American Foresters, 5400 Grosvenor Lane, Bethesda, MD 20814, or visit the society's Web site: **http://www.safnet.org**

For information about career opportunities in forestry in the Federal Government, contact:
➤ Chief, U.S. Forest Service, U.S. Department of Agriculture, P.O. Box 96090, Washington, DC 20090-6090. Internet: **http://www.fs.fed.us**

Information about a career as a range manager, as well as a list of schools offering training, is available from:
➤ Society for Range Management, 445 Union Blvd., Suite 230, Lakewood, CO 80228-1259. Internet: **http://www.rangelands.org/ScriptContent/Index.cfm**

Medical Scientists

(O*NET 19-1041.00, 19-1042.00)

Significant Points

- Epidemiologists typically require a master's degree in public health or, in some cases, a medical degree; other medical scientists need a Ph.D. degree in a biological science.

- Competition is expected for most positions.

- Most medical scientists work in research and development.

Nature of the Work

Medical scientists research human diseases in order to improve human health. Most medical scientists work in research and development. Some conduct basic research to advance knowledge of living organisms, including viruses, bacteria, and other infectious agents. Past research has resulted in the development of vaccines, medicines, and treatments for many diseases. Basic medical research continues to provide the building blocks necessary to develop solutions to human health problems. Medical scientists also engage in clinical investigation, technical writing, drug application review, patent examination, or related activities.

Medical scientists study biological systems to understand the causes of disease and other health problems and to develop treatments. They try to identify changes in a cell or chromosomes that signal the development of medical problems, such as different types of cancer. For example, a medical scientist involved in cancer research may formulate a combination of drugs that will lessen the effects of the disease. Medical scientists who are also physicians can administer these drugs to patients in clinical trials, monitor their reactions, and observe the results. Those who are not physicians normally collaborate with a physician who deals directly with patients. Medical scientists examine the results of clinical trials and, if necessary, adjust the dosage levels to reduce negative side effects or to try to induce even better results. In addition to developing treatments for health problems, medical scientists attempt to discover ways to prevent health problems, such as affirming the link between smoking and lung cancer, or between alcoholism and liver disease.

Many medical scientists work independently in private industry, university, or government laboratories, often exploring new areas of research or expanding on specialized research that they started in graduate school. Medical scientists working in colleges and universities, hospitals, and nonprofit medical research organizations typically submit grant proposals to obtain funding for their projects. Colleges and universities, private industry, and Federal Government agencies, such as the National Institutes of Health and the National Science Foundation, contribute to the support of scientists whose research proposals are determined to be financially feasible and have the potential to advance new ideas or processes.

Medical scientists who work in applied research or product development use knowledge provided by basic research to develop new drugs and medical treatments. They usually have less autonomy than basic researchers to choose the emphasis of their research, relying instead on market-driven directions based on the firm's products and goals. Medical scientists doing applied research and product development in private industry may be required to express their research plans or results to nonscientists who are in a position to veto or approve their ideas, and they must understand the impact of their work on business. Scientists increasingly work as part of teams, interacting with engineers, scientists of other disciplines, business managers, and technicians.

Medical scientists who conduct research usually work in laboratories and use electron microscopes, computers, thermal cyclers, or a wide variety of other equipment. Some may work directly with individual patients or larger groups as they administer drugs and monitor and observe the patients during clinical trials. Medical scientists who are also physicians may administer gene therapy to human patients, draw blood, excise tissue, or perform other invasive procedures.

Some medical scientists work in managerial, consulting, or administrative positions, usually after spending some time doing research and learning about the firm, agency, or project. In the 1980s, swift advances in basic medical knowledge related to genetics and molecules spurred growth in the field of biotechnology. Medical scientists using this technology manipu-

late the genetic material of animals, attempting to make organisms more productive or resistant to disease. Research using biotechnology techniques, such as recombining DNA, has led to the discovery of important drugs, including human insulin and growth hormone. Many other substances not previously available in large quantities are now produced by biotechnological means; some may be useful in treating diseases such as Parkinson's or Alzheimer's. Today, many medical scientists are involved in the science of genetic engineering—isolating, identifying, and sequencing human genes and then determining their functionality. This work continues to lead to the discovery of the genes associated with specific diseases and inherited traits, such as certain types of cancer or obesity. These advances in biotechnology have opened up research opportunities in almost all areas of medical science.

Some medical scientists specialize in epidemiology. This branch of medical science investigates and describes the determinants of disease, disability, and other health outcomes and develops the means for prevention and control. Epidemiologists may study many different diseases such as tuberculosis, influenza, or cholera, often focusing on epidemics.

Epidemiologists can be separated into two groups, research and clinical. Research epidemiologists conduct basic and advanced research on infectious diseases that affect the entire body, such as AIDS or typhus—attempting to eradicate or control these diseases. Others may focus only on localized infections of the brain, lungs, or digestive tract, for example. Research epidemiologists work at colleges and universities, schools of public health, medical schools, and research and development services firms. For example, Government agencies such as the Department of Defense may contract with a research firm's epidemiologists to evaluate the incidence of malaria in certain parts of the world. While some perform consulting services, other research epidemiologists may work as college and university faculty.

Clinical epidemiologists work primarily in consulting roles at hospitals, informing the medical staff of infectious outbreaks and providing containment solutions. These clinical epidemiologists sometimes are referred to as infection control professionals. Consequently, many epidemiologists in this specific area often are physicians. Epidemiologists who are not physicians often collaborate with physicians to find ways to contain diseases and outbreaks. In addition to traditional duties of studying and controlling diseases, clinical epidemiologists also may

Most medical scientists conduct basic research to advance knowledge of living organisms.

be required to develop standards and guidelines for the treatment and control of communicable diseases. Some clinical epidemiologists may work in outpatient settings.

Working Conditions

Medical scientists typically work regular hours in offices or laboratories and usually are not exposed to unsafe or unhealthy conditions. Those who work with dangerous organisms or toxic substances in the laboratory must follow strict safety procedures to avoid contamination. Medical scientists also spend time working in clinics and hospitals administering drugs and treatments to patients in clinical trials. On occasion, epidemiologists may be required to work evenings and weekends to attend meetings and hearings for medical investigations.

Some medical scientists depend on grant money to support their research. They may be under pressure to meet deadlines and to conform to rigid grant-writing specifications when preparing proposals to seek new or extended funding.

Employment

Medical scientists, including epidemiologists, held about 62,000 jobs in 2002. Medical scientists accounted for 58,000 of the total; epidemiologists, 3,900. In addition, many medical scientists held faculty positions in colleges and universities, but they are classified as college or university faculty. (See teachers—postsecondary elsewhere in the *Handbook*.)

Almost 30 percent of medical scientists were employed in scientific research and development services firms, another 24 percent worked in Government, 14 percent in pharmaceutical and medicine manufacturing, 13 percent in private hospitals, and most of the remainder worked in private educational services and ambulatory health care services. About 1,000 were self-employed.

Among epidemiologists, nearly 45 percent were employed in Government, another 20 percent worked in management, scientific, and technical consulting services firms, 14 percent in private hospitals, and 12 percent in scientific research and development services firms.

Training, Other Qualifications, and Advancement

A Ph.D. degree in a biological science is the minimum education required for most prospective medical scientists, except epidemiologists, because the work of medical scientists is almost entirely research oriented. A Ph.D. degree qualifies one to do research on basic life processes or on particular medical problems or diseases, and to analyze and interpret the results of experiments on patients. Some medical scientists obtain a medical degree instead of a Ph.D., but may not be licensed physicians because they have not taken the State licensing examination or completed a residency program, typically because they prefer research to clinical practice. Medical scientists who administer drug or gene therapy to human patients, or who otherwise interact medically with patients—drawing blood, excising tissue, or performing other invasive procedures—must be licensed physicians. To be licensed, physicians must graduate from an accredited medical school, pass a licensing examination, and complete 1 to 7 years of graduate medical education. (See physicians and surgeons elsewhere in the *Handbook*.) It is particularly helpful for medical scientists to earn both Ph.D. and medical degrees.

Students planning careers as medical scientists should have a bachelor's degree in a biological science. In addition to required courses in chemistry and biology, undergraduates should study allied disciplines such as mathematics, physics, and computer science, or courses in their field of interest. Once they have completed undergraduate studies, they can then select a specialty area for their advanced degree, such as cytology, genomics, or pathology. In addition to formal education, medical scientists usually spend several years in a postdoctoral position before they apply for permanent jobs. Postdoctoral work provides valuable laboratory experience, including experience in specific processes and techniques such as gene splicing, which is transferable to other research projects. In some institutions, the postdoctoral position can lead to a permanent job.

Medical scientists should be able to work independently or as part of a team and be able to communicate clearly and concisely, both orally and in writing. Those in private industry, especially those who aspire to consulting and administrative positions, should possess strong communication skills so they can provide instruction and advice to physicians and other healthcare professionals.

The minimum educational requirement for epidemiology is a master's degree from a school of public health. Some jobs require a Ph.D. or medical degree, depending on the work performed. Epidemiologists who work in hospitals and healthcare centers often must have a medical degree with specific training in infectious diseases. Currently, 134 infectious disease training programs exist in 42 States. Some employees in research epidemiology positions are required to be licensed physicians, as they are required to administer drugs in clinical trials.

Epidemiologists who perform laboratory tests often require the knowledge and expertise of a licensed physician in order to administer drugs to patients in clinical trials. Epidemiologists who are not physicians frequently work closely with one.

Very few students select epidemiology for undergraduate study. Undergraduates, nonetheless, should study biological sciences and should have a solid background in chemistry, mathematics, and computer science. Once a student is prepared for graduate studies, he or she can choose a specialty within epidemiology. For example, those interested in studying environmental epidemiology should focus on environmental coursework, such as water pollution, air pollution, or pesticide use. The core work of environmental studies includes toxicology and molecular biology, and students may continue with advanced coursework in environmental or occupational epidemiology. Some epidemiologists are registered nurses and medical technologists seeking advancement.

Job Outlook

Employment of medical scientists is expected to grow faster than the average for all occupations through 2012. Despite projected rapid job growth for medical scientists, doctoral degree holders can expect to face considerable competition for basic research positions. The Federal Government funds much basic research and development, including many areas of medical research. Recent budget increases at the National Institutes of Health have led to large increases in Federal basic research and development expenditures, with the number of grants awarded to researchers growing in number and dollar amount. At the same time, the number of newly trained medical scientists has continued to increase at least as fast as employment opportunities, so both new and established scientists have experienced greater difficulty winning and renewing research grants. If the number of advanced degrees awarded continues to grow unabated, as expected, this competitive situation is likely to persist.

Medical scientists enjoyed rapid gains in employment between the mid-1980s and mid-1990s, in part reflecting increased staffing requirements in new biotechnology companies. Employment growth should slow somewhat as increases in the number of new biotechnology firms slow and existing firms merge or are absorbed into larger ones. However, much of the basic medical research done in recent years has resulted in new knowledge, including the isolation and identification of new genes. Medical scientists will be needed to take this knowledge to the next stage, which is understanding how certain genes function within an entire organism, so that gene therapies can be developed to treat diseases. Even pharmaceutical and other firms not solely engaged in biotechnology are expected to increasingly use biotechnology techniques, thus creating employment for medical scientists.

Expected expansion in research related to health issues such as AIDS, cancer, and Alzheimer's disease also should result in employment growth. Although medical scientists greatly contributed to developing many vaccines and antibiotics, more medical research will be required to better understand these and other epidemics and to improve human health.

Opportunities in epidemiology also should be highly competitive, as the number of available positions remains limited. However, an increasing focus on monitoring patients at hospitals and healthcare centers to ensure positive patient outcomes will contribute to job growth. In addition, a heightened awareness of bioterrorism and infectious diseases such as West Nile Virus or SARS should also spur demand for these workers. As hospitals enhance their infection control programs, many will seek to boost the quality and quantity of their staff. Besides job openings due to employment growth, additional openings will result as workers leave the labor force or transfer to other occupations. Because employment of epidemiologists is somewhat tied to the healthcare industry, industry conditions will influence occupational demand.

Medical scientists and some epidemiologists are less likely to lose their jobs during recessions than are those in many other occupations because they are employed on long-term research projects. However, a recession could influence the amount of money allocated to new research and development efforts, particularly in areas of risky or innovative medical research. A recession also could limit the possibility of extension or renewal of existing projects.

Earnings

Median annual earnings of medical scientists, except epidemiologists, were $56,980 in 2002. The middle 50 percent earned between $40,180 and $82,720. The lowest 10 percent earned less than $29,980, and the highest 10 percent earned more than $114,640. Median annual earnings in the industries employing the largest numbers of medical scientists in 2002 were:

Pharmaceutical and medicine manufacturing	$72,330
Scientific research and development services	61,470
General medical and surgical hospitals	50,660
Colleges, universities, and professional schools	35,520

Median annual earnings of epidemiologists were $53,840 in 2002. The middle 50 percent earned between $44,900 and $66,510. The lowest 10 percent earned less than $35,910, and the highest 10 percent earned more than $85,930.

Related Occupations

Many other occupations deal with living organisms and require a level of training similar to that of medical scientists. These include biological scientists, agricultural and food scientists, and health occupations such as physicians and surgeons, dentists, and veterinarians.

Sources of Additional Information

For a brochure entitled *Is a Career in the Pharmaceutical Sciences Right for Me?*, contact:
➤ American Association of Pharmaceutical Scientists (AAPS), 2107 Wilson Blvd., Suite #700, Arlington, VA 22201.

For a career brochure entitled *A Million and One*, contact:
➤ American Society for Microbiology, Education Department, 1752 N St. NW., Washington, D.C. 20036-2804. Internet: **http://www.asmusa.org**

For information on infectious diseases training programs, contact:
➤ Infectious Diseases Society of America, Guide to Training Programs, 66 Canal Center Plaza, Suite # 600, Alexandria, VA 22314. Internet: **http://www.idsociety.org**

Information on obtaining a medical scientist position with the Federal Government is available from the Office of Personnel Management (OPM) through a telephone-based system. Consult your telephone directory under U.S. Government for a local number or call (703) 724-1850; Federal Relay Service: (800) 877-8339. The first number is not tollfree, and charges may result. Information also is available from the OPM Internet site: **http://www.usajobs.opm.gov**.

Physical Scientists

Atmospheric Scientists

(0*NET 19-2021.00)

Significant Points

● Almost 4 in 10 atmospheric scientists work for the Federal Government, which is the largest employer of such workers.

● A bachelor's degree in meteorology, or in a closely related field with courses in meteorology, is the minimum educational requirement; a master's degree is necessary for some positions, and a Ph.D. is required for most research positions.

Nature of the Work

Atmospheric science is the study of the atmosphere—the blanket of air covering the Earth. *Atmospheric scientists*, commonly called *meteorologists*, study the atmosphere's physical characteristics, motions, and processes, and the way in which it affects the rest of our environment. The best known application of this knowledge is in forecasting the weather. Aside from predicting the weather, scientists also attempt to identify and interpret climate trends, understand past weather, and analyze today's weather. However, weather information and meteorological research also are applied in air-pollution control, agriculture, forestry, air and sea transportation, defense, and the study of possible trends in the Earth's climate, such as global warming, droughts, or ozone depletion.

Atmospheric scientists who forecast the weather, known professionally as *operational meteorologists*, are the largest group of specialists. They study information on air pressure, temperature, humidity, and wind velocity; and apply physical and mathematical relationships to make short-range and long-range weather forecasts. Their data come from weather satellites, weather radars, sensors, and weather stations in many parts of the world. Meteorologists use sophisticated computer models of the world's atmosphere to make long-term, short-term, and local-area forecasts. More accurate instruments for measuring and observing weather conditions, as well as high-speed computers to process and analyze weather data, have revolutionized weather forecasting. Using satellite data, climate theory, and sophisticated computer models of the world's atmosphere, meteorologists can more effectively interpret the results of these models to make local-area weather predictions. These forecasts inform not only the general public, but also those who need accurate weather information for both economic and safety reasons, such as the shipping, air transportation, agriculture, fishing, forestry, and utilities industries.

The use of weather balloons, launched a few times a day to measure wind, temperature, and humidity in the upper atmosphere, is currently supplemented by sophisticated atmospheric monitoring equipment that transmits data as frequently as every few minutes. Doppler radar, for example, can detect airflow patterns in violent storm systems—allowing forecasters to better predict tornadoes and other hazardous winds, and to monitor the storms' direction and intensity. Combined radar and satellite observations allow meteorologists to predict flash floods.

Some atmospheric scientists work in research. *Physical meteorologists*, for example, study the atmosphere's chemical and physical properties; the transmission of light, sound, and radio waves; and the transfer of energy in the atmosphere. They also study factors affecting the formation of clouds, rain, and snow; the dispersal of air pollutants over urban areas; and other weather phenomena, such as the mechanics of severe storms. *Synoptic meteorologists* develop new tools for weather forecasting using computers and sophisticated mathematical models of atmospheric activity. *Climatologists* study climactic variations spanning hundreds or even millions of years. They also may collect, analyze, and interpret past records of wind, rainfall, sunshine, and temperature in specific areas or regions. Their studies are

Atmospheric scientists utilize sophisticated instruments and high-speed computers to predict weather and identify climate trends.

used to design buildings, plan heating and cooling systems, and aid in effective land use and agricultural production. Environmental problems, such as pollution and shortages of fresh water, have widened the scope of the meteorological profession. *Environmental meteorologists* study these problems and may evaluate and report on air quality for environmental impact statements. Other research meteorologists examine the most effective ways to control or diminish air pollution.

Working Conditions
Most weather stations operate around the clock, 7 days a week. Jobs in such facilities usually involve night, weekend, and holiday work, often with rotating shifts. During weather emergencies, such as hurricanes, operational meteorologists may work overtime. Operational meteorologists also are often under pressure to meet forecast deadlines. Weather stations are found everywhere—at airports, in or near cities, and in isolated and remote areas. Some atmospheric scientists also spend time observing weather conditions and collecting data from aircraft. Weather forecasters who work for radio or television stations broadcast their reports from station studios, and may work evenings and weekends. Meteorologists in smaller weather offices often work alone; in larger ones, they work as part of a team. Meteorologists not involved in forecasting tasks work regular hours, usually in offices. Those who work for private consulting firms or for companies analyzing and monitoring emissions to improve air quality usually work with other scientists or engineers; fieldwork and travel may be common for these workers.

Employment
Atmospheric scientists held about 7,700 jobs in 2002. The Federal Government was the largest single employer of civilian meteorologists, accounting for about 2,900. The National Oceanic and Atmospheric Administration (NOAA) employed most Federal meteorologists in National Weather Service stations throughout the Nation; the remainder of NOAA's meteorologists worked mainly in research and development or management. The U.S. Department of Defense employed several hundred civilian meteorologists. Others worked for professional, scientific, and technical services firms, including private weather consulting services; radio and television broadcasting; air carriers; and State government.

Although several hundred people teach atmospheric science and related courses in college and university departments of meteorology or atmospheric science, physics, earth science, or geophysics, these individuals are classified as college or university faculty, rather than atmospheric scientists. (See the statement on postsecondary teachers elsewhere in the *Handbook*.)

In addition to civilian meteorologists, hundreds of Armed Forces members are involved in forecasting and other meteorological work. (See the statement on job opportunities in the Armed Forces elsewhere in the *Handbook*.)

Training, Other Qualifications, and Advancement
A bachelor's degree in meteorology or atmospheric science, or in a closely related field with courses in meteorology, usually is the minimum educational requirement for an entry-level position as an atmospheric scientist.

The preferred educational requirement for entry-level meteorologists in the Federal Government is a bachelor's degree—not necessarily in meteorology—with at least 24 semester hours of meteorology courses, including 6 hours in the analysis and prediction of weather systems, 6 hours of atmospheric dynamics and thermodynamics, 3 hours of physical meteorology, and 2 hours of remote sensing of the atmosphere or instrumentation. Other required courses include 3 semester hours of ordinary differential equations, 6 hours of college physics, and at least 9 hours of courses appropriate for a physical science major—such as statistics, chemistry, physical oceanography, physical climatology, physical hydrology, radiative transfer, aeronomy, advanced thermodynamics, advanced electricity and magnetism, light and optics, and computer science. Sometimes, a combination of education and appropriate experience may be substituted for a degree.

Although positions in operational meteorology are available for those with only a bachelor's degree, obtaining a second bachelor's degree or a master's degree enhances employment opportunities and advancement potential. A master's degree usually is necessary for conducting applied research and development, and a Ph.D. is required for most basic research positions. Students planning on a career in research and development need not necessarily major in atmospheric science or meteorology as an undergraduate. In fact, a bachelor's degree in mathematics, physics, or engineering provides excellent preparation for graduate study in atmospheric science.

Because atmospheric science is a small field, relatively few colleges and universities offer degrees in meteorology or atmospheric science, although many departments of physics, earth science, geography, and geophysics offer atmospheric science and related courses. Prospective students should make certain that courses required by the National Weather Service and other employers are offered at the college they are considering. Computer science courses, additional meteorology courses, a strong background in mathematics and physics, and good communication skills are important to prospective employers. Many programs combine the study of meteorology with another field, such as agriculture, oceanography, engineering, or physics. For example, hydrometeorology is the blending of hydrology (the science of Earth's water) and meteorology, and is the field concerned with the effect of precipitation on the hydrologic cycle and the environment. Students who wish to become broadcast meteorologists for radio or television stations should develop excellent communication skills through courses in speech, journalism, and related fields. Those interested in air quality work should take courses in chemistry and supplement their technical training with coursework in policy or government affairs. Prospective meteorologists seeking opportunities at weather consulting firms should possess knowledge of business, statistics, and economics, as an increasing emphasis is being placed on long-range seasonal forecasting to assist businesses.

Beginning atmospheric scientists often do routine data collection, computation, or analysis, and some basic forecasting. Entry-level operational meteorologists in the Federal Government usually are placed in intern positions for training and experience. During this period, they learn about the Weather Service's forecasting equipment and procedures, and rotate to different offices to learn about various weather systems. After completing the training period, they are assigned a permanent duty station. Experienced meteorologists may advance to supervisory or administrative jobs, or may handle more complex forecasting jobs. After several years of experience, some meteorologists establish their own weather consulting services.

The American Meteorological Society offers professional certification of consulting meteorologists, administered by a Board of Certified Consulting Meteorologists. Applicants must meet formal education requirements (though not necessarily have a college degree), pass an examination to demonstrate thorough meteorological knowledge, have a minimum of 5 years of experience or a combination of experience plus an advanced degree, and provide character references from fellow professionals.

Job Outlook

Employment of atmospheric scientists is projected to increase about as fast as the average for all occupations through 2012. The National Weather Service has completed an extensive modernization of its weather forecasting equipment and finished all hiring of meteorologists needed to staff the upgraded stations. The Service has no plans to increase the number of weather stations or the number of meteorologists in existing stations. Employment of meteorologists in other Federal agencies is expected to remain stable.

On the other hand, job opportunities for atmospheric scientists in private industry are expected to be better than for those in the Federal Government over the 2002-12 period. As research leads to continuing improvements in weather forecasting, demand should grow for private weather consulting firms to provide more detailed information than has formerly been available, especially to weather-sensitive industries. Farmers, commodity investors, radio and television stations, and utilities, transportation, and construction firms can greatly benefit from additional weather information more closely targeted to their needs than the general information provided by the National Weather Service. Additionally, research on seasonal and other long-range forecasting is yielding positive results, which should spur demand for more atmospheric scientists to interpret these forecasts and advise weather-sensitive industries. However, because many customers for private weather services are in industries sensitive to fluctuations in the economy, the sales and growth of private weather services depend on the health of the economy.

There will continue to be demand for atmospheric scientists to analyze and monitor the dispersion of pollutants into the air to ensure compliance with Federal environmental regulations outlined in the Clean Air Act of 1990, but related employment increases are expected to be small. Opportunities in broadcasting are rare and highly competitive, making for very few job openings.

Earnings

Median annual earnings of atmospheric scientists in 2002 were $60,200. The middle 50 percent earned between $39,970 and $76,880. The lowest 10 percent earned less than $30,220, and the highest 10 percent earned more than $92,430.

The average salary for meteorologists in nonsupervisory, supervisory, and managerial positions employed by the Federal Government was about $74,528 in 2003. Meteorologists in the Federal Government with a bachelor's degree and no experience received a starting salary of $23,442 or $29,037, depending on their college grades. Those with a master's degree could start at $35,519 or $42,976; those with the Ph.D., at $51,508. Beginning salaries for all degree levels are slightly higher in areas of the country where the prevailing local pay level is higher.

Related Occupations

Workers in other occupations concerned with the physical environment include environmental scientists and geoscientists, physicists and astronomers, mathematicians, and civil, chemical, and environmental engineers.

Sources of Additional Information

Information about careers in meteorology is available on the Internet from:

<>American Meteorological Society. Internet: **http://www.ametsoc.org/ AMS. Phone: (617)-227-2425.**

Information on obtaining a meteorologist position with the Federal Government is available from the U.S. Office of Personnel Management through a telephone-based system. Consult your telephone directory under U.S. Government for a local number or call (703) 724-1850; Federal Relay Service: (800) 877-8339. The first number is not tollfree, and charges may result. Information also is available from the Internet site: **http://www.usajobs.opm.gov.**

Chemists and Materials Scientists

(0*NET 19-2031.00, 19-2032.00)

Significant Points

- A bachelor's degree in chemistry or a related discipline is the minimum educational requirement; however, many research jobs require a Ph.D.

- Job growth will be concentrated in pharmaceutical and medicine manufacturing companies and in scientific research and development services firms.

- Graduates with a master's degree, and particularly those with a Ph.D., will enjoy better opportunities than those with a bachelor's degree.

Nature of the Work

Everything in the environment, whether naturally occurring or of human design, is composed of chemicals. Chemists and materials scientists search for and use new knowledge about chemicals. Chemical research has led to the discovery and development of new and improved synthetic fibers, paints, adhesives, drugs, cosmetics, electronic components, lubricants, and thousands of other products. Chemists and materials scientists also develop processes that save energy and reduce pollution, such as improved oil refining and petrochemical processing methods. Research on the chemistry of living things spurs advances in medicine, agriculture, food processing, and other fields.

Materials scientists research and study the structures and chemical properties of various materials to develop new products or enhance existing ones. They also determine ways to strengthen or combine materials or develop new materials for use in a variety of products. Materials science encompasses the natural and synthetic materials used in a wide range of products and structures, from airplanes, cars, and bridges to clothing and household goods. Companies whose products are made of metals, ceramics, and rubber employ most materials scientists. Other applications of materials science include studies of superconducting materials, graphite materials, integrated-circuit chips, and fuel cells. Materials scientists, applying chemistry and physics, study all aspects of these materials. Chemistry plays an increasingly dominant role in materials science, because it provides information about the structure and composition of materials. Materials scientists often specialize in specific areas such as ceramics or metals.

Many chemists and materials scientists work in research and development (R&D). In basic research, they investigate properties, composition, and structure of matter and the laws that govern the combination of elements and reactions of substances. In applied R&D, they create new products and processes or improve existing ones, often using knowledge gained from basic research. For example, synthetic rubber and plastics resulted from research on small molecules uniting to form large ones, a process called polymerization. R&D chemists and materials scientists use computers and a wide variety of sophisticated laboratory instrumentation for modeling and simulation in their work.

The use of computers to analyze complex data has had the dramatic impact of allowing chemists and materials scientists to practice combinatorial chemistry. This technique makes and tests large quantities of chemical compounds simultaneously in order to find compounds with certain desired properties. As an integral part of drug and materials discovery, combinatorial chemistry speeds up materials design and R&D, permitting useful compounds to be developed more quickly and inexpensively than was formerly possible. Combinatorial chemistry has allowed chemists to produce thousands of compounds each year and to assist in the completion of the sequencing of human genes. Today, chemists are working with life scientists to translate this knowledge into viable new drugs.

Chemists also work in production and quality control in chemical manufacturing plants. They prepare instructions for plant workers that specify ingredients, mixing times, and temperatures for each stage in the process. They also monitor automated processes to ensure proper product yield, and test samples of raw materials or finished products to make certain that they meet industry and government standards, including the regulations governing pollution. Chemists report and document test results and analyze those results in hopes of further improving existing theories or developing new test methods.

Chemists often specialize. *Analytical chemists* determine the structure, composition, and nature of substances by examining and identifying the various elements or compounds that make up a substance. These chemists are absolutely crucial to the pharmaceutical industry because pharmaceutical companies need to know the identity of compounds that they hope to turn into drugs. Furthermore, they study the relations and interactions of the parts of compounds and develop analytical techniques. They also identify the presence and concentration of chemical pollutants in air, water, and soil. *Organic chemists* study the chemistry of the vast number of carbon compounds that make up all living things. Organic chemists who synthesize elements or simple compounds to create new compounds or substances that have different properties and applications have developed many commercial products, such as drugs, plastics, and elastomers (elastic substances similar to rubber). *Inorganic chemists* study compounds consisting mainly of elements other than carbon, such as those in electronic components. *Physical and theoretical chemists* study the physical characteristics of atoms and molecules and the theoretical properties of matter, and investigate how chemical reactions work. Their research may result in new and better energy sources. *Macromolecular chemists* study the behavior of atoms and molecules. *Medicinal chemists* study the structural properties of compounds intended for applications to human medicine. *Materials chemists* study and develop new materials to improve existing products or make new ones. In fact, virtually all chemists are involved in this quest in one way or another. Developments in the field of chemistry that involve life sciences will expand, resulting in more interaction among biologists, engineers, and chemists. (*Bio-*

chemists, whose work encompasses both biology and chemistry, are discussed in the *Handbook* s tatement on biological scientists.)

Working Conditions

Chemists and materials scientists usually work regular hours in offices and laboratories. R&D chemists and materials scientists spend much time in laboratories, but also work in offices when they do theoretical research or plan, record, and report on their lab research. Although some laboratories are small, others are large enough to incorporate prototype chemical manufacturing facilities as well as advanced equipment for chemists. In addition to working in a laboratory, materials scientists also work with engineers and processing specialists in industrial manufacturing facilities. After a material is sold, materials scientists often help customers tailor the material to suit their needs. Chemists do some of their work in a chemical plant or outdoors—while gathering water samples to test for pollutants, for example. Some chemists are exposed to health or safety hazards when handling certain chemicals, but there is little risk if proper procedures are followed.

Employment

Chemists and materials scientists held about 91,000 jobs in 2002. About 44 percent of all chemists and material scientists are employed in manufacturing firms—mostly in the chemical manufacturing industry, which includes firms that produce plastics and synthetic materials, drugs, soaps and cleaners, pesticides and fertilizers, paint, industrial organic chemicals, and other chemical products. About 15 percent of chemists and material scientists work in scientific research and development services; another 13 percent work in architectural, engineering, and related services. In addition, thousands of persons with a background in chemistry and materials science hold teaching positions in high schools and in colleges and universities. (See the statements on teachers—postsecondary, and teachers—preschool, kindergarten, elementary, middle, and secondary elsewhere in the *Handbook*.)

Chemists and materials scientists are employed in all parts of the country, but they are mainly concentrated in large industrial areas.

The use of computers allows chemists to test large quantities of chemical compounds with desired properties.

Training, Other Qualifications, and Advancement

A bachelor's degree in chemistry or a related discipline usually is the minimum educational requirement for entry-level chemist jobs. However, many research jobs require a master's degree, or more often a Ph.D. While some materials scientists hold a degree in materials science, a bachelor's degree in chemistry, physics, or electric engineering also is accepted. Similar to chemists, many R&D jobs require a Ph.D. in materials science or a related science.

Many colleges and universities offer a bachelor's degree program in chemistry; about 620 are approved by the American Chemical Society (ACS). The number of colleges that offer a degree program in materials science is small, but gradually increasing. Several hundred colleges and universities also offer advanced degree programs in chemistry; around 320 master's programs and about 190 doctoral programs are ACS-approved.

Students planning careers as chemists and materials scientists should take courses in science and mathematics, should like working with their hands building scientific apparatus and performing laboratory experiments, and should like computer modeling. Perseverance, curiosity, and the ability to concentrate on detail and to work independently are essential. Interaction among specialists in this field is increasing, especially for chemists in drug development. One type of chemist often relies on the findings of another type of chemist. For example, an organic chemist must understand findings on the identity of compounds prepared by an analytical chemist.

In addition to required courses in analytical, inorganic, organic, and physical chemistry, undergraduate chemistry majors usually study biological sciences, mathematics, and physics. Those interested in the environmental field also should take courses in environmental studies and become familiar with current legislation and regulations. Computer courses are essential, because employers prefer job applicants who are able to apply computer skills to modeling and simulation tasks and operate computerized laboratory equipment. This is increasingly important as combinatorial chemistry techniques are more widely applied. Additionally, courses in statistics are useful because both chemists and materials scientists need the ability to apply basic statistical techniques.

Because R&D chemists and materials scientists are increasingly expected to work on interdisciplinary teams, some understanding of other disciplines, including business and marketing or economics, is desirable, along with leadership ability and good oral and written communication skills. Experience, either in academic laboratories or through internships, fellowships, or work-study programs in industry, also is useful. Some employers of research chemists, particularly in the pharmaceutical industry, prefer to hire individuals with several years of postdoctoral experience.

Graduate students typically specialize in a subfield of chemistry, such as analytical chemistry or polymer chemistry, depending on their interests and the kind of work they wish to do. For example, those interested in doing drug research in the pharmaceutical industry usually develop a strong background in synthetic organic chemistry. However, students normally need not specialize at the undergraduate level. In fact, undergraduates who are broadly trained have more flexibility when job hunting or changing jobs than if they had narrowly defined their interests. Most employers provide new graduates additional training or education.

In government or industry, beginning chemists with a bachelor's degree work in quality control, perform analytical testing, or assist senior chemists in R&D laboratories. Many employers prefer chemists and materials scientists with a Ph.D., or at least a master's degree, to lead basic and applied research. Nonetheless, relevant work experience is an asset. Chemists who hold a Ph.D. and have previous industrial experience may be particularly attractive to employers because such people are more likely to understand the complex regulations that apply to the pharmaceutical industry. Within materials science, a broad background in various sciences is preferred. This broad base may be obtained through degrees in physics, engineering, or chemistry. While many companies prefer hiring Ph.D.s, many materials scientists have bachelor's and master's degrees.

Job Outlook

Employment of chemists is expected to grow about as fast as the average for all occupations through 2012. Job growth will be concentrated in pharmaceutical and medicine manufacturing and in scientific research and development services firms. The chemical industry, the major employer of chemists, should face continued demand for goods such as new and better pharmaceuticals and personal care products, as well as for more specialty chemicals designed to address specific problems or applications. To meet these demands, some chemical firms will continue to devote money to research and development—through in-house teams or outside contractors—spurring employment growth of chemists. Those with at least a master's degree, and particularly those with a Ph.D., will enjoy better opportunities than those with just a bachelor's degree for most research and upper management positions. Opportunities for individuals with a bachelor's degree are expected to be more competitive. The number of science-related jobs in sales, marketing, and middle management, for which bachelor's and master's degree holders may qualify, are expected to be fewer as companies continue to streamline their operations. Some bachelor's and master's degree holders become chemical technicians or technologists or high school chemistry teachers.

Within the chemical industry, job opportunities are expected to be most plentiful in pharmaceutical and biotechnology firms. Biotechnological research, including studies of human genes, continues to offer possibilities for the development of new drugs and products to combat illnesses and diseases that have previously been unresponsive to treatments derived by traditional chemical processes. Stronger competition among drug companies and an aging population are contributing to the need for innovative and improved drugs discovered through scientific research.

Employment in the remaining segments of the chemical industry is expected to decline as companies downsize and turn to outside contractors to provide specialized services. As a result, scientific research and development services firms will experience healthy growth. To control costs, some chemical companies, including drug manufacturers, are increasingly turning to these firms to perform specialized research and other work formerly done by in-house chemists. Despite downsizing, some job openings will result from the need to replace chemists who retire or otherwise leave the labor force. Quality control will continue to be an important issue in chemical manufacturing and other industries that use chemicals in their manufacturing processes. Chemists also will be needed to develop and improve the technologies and processes used to produce chemicals for all purposes, and to monitor and measure air and water pollutants to ensure compliance with local, State, and Federal environmental regulations. Environmental research will offer many new opportunities for chemists and materials scientists. To satisfy public concerns and to comply with government regulations, the chemical industry will continue to invest billions of dollars each year in technology that reduces pollution and cleans up existing wastesites. Chemists also are needed to find ways to use less energy and to discover new sources of energy.

During periods of economic recession, layoffs of chemists may occur—especially in the industrial chemicals industry. This industry provides many of the raw materials to the auto manufacturing and construction industries, both of which are vulnerable to temporary slowdowns during recessions.

Earnings

Median annual earnings of chemists in 2002 were $52,890. The middle 50 percent earned between $39,410 and $71,710. The lowest 10 percent earned less than $30,980, and the highest 10 percent earned more than $92,170. Median annual earnings of materials scientists in 2002 were $64,590. The middle 50 percent earned between $46,280 and $86,240. The lowest 10 percent earned less than $33,480, and the highest 10 percent earned more than $107,400. Median annual earnings in the industries employing the largest numbers of chemists in 2002 were:

Federal government	$72,010
Scientific research and development services	60,400
Pharmaceutical and medicine manufacturing	53,070
Architectural, engineering, and related services	38,780

The American Chemical Society reports that the median salary of all of its members with a bachelor's degree was $32,800 a year in 2002; for those with a master's degree, it was $50,000; and for those with a Ph.D., it was $68,000. Median salaries were highest for those working in private industry; those in academia earned the least. According to an ACS survey of recent graduates, inexperienced chemistry graduates with a bachelor's degree earned a median starting salary of $31,000 in 2002; those with a master's degree earned a median salary of $45,000; and those with a Ph.D. made median earnings of $67,500. Among bachelor's degree graduates, those who had completed internships or had other work experience while in school commanded the highest starting salaries.

In 2003, chemists in nonsupervisory, supervisory, and managerial positions in the Federal Government averaged $76,857 a year.

Related Occupations

The research and analysis conducted by chemists and materials scientists is closely related to work done by agricultural and food scientists, biological scientists, medical scientists, chemical engineers, materials engineers, physicists, and science technicians.

Sources of Additional Information

General information on career opportunities and earnings for chemists is available from:
❖American Chemical Society, Education Division, 1155 16th St. NW., Washington, DC 20036. Internet: **http://www.acs.org**

For general information on materials science, contact:
❖Materials Research Society (MRS), 506 Keystone Dr., Warrendale, PA 15086-7573. Internet: **http://www.mrs.org**

Information on obtaining a position as a chemist with the Federal Government is available from the Office of Personnel Management (OPM) through a telephone-based system. Consult your telephone directory under U.S. Government for a local number or call (703) 724-1850; Federal Relay Service: (800) 877-8339. The first number is not tollfree, and charges may result. Information also is available from the OPM Internet site: **http://www.usajobs.opm.gov.**

Environmental Scientists and Geoscientists

(O*NET 19-2041.00, 19-2042.01, 19-2043.00)

Significant Points

● Work at remote field sites is common.

● Federal, State, and local governments employ nearly one-half of all environmental scientists and geoscientists.

● A bachelor's degree is adequate for a few entry-level jobs, but a master's degree is usually the minimum educational requirement; a Ph.D. degree is required for most high-level research positions.

● Employment of geoscientists is expected to grow as fast as average, while environmental scientists and hydrologists will experience faster than average growth.

Nature of the Work

Environmental scientists and geoscientists use their knowledge of the physical makeup and history of the Earth to protect the environment; locate water, mineral, and energy resources; predict future geologic hazards; and offer advice on construction and land-use projects.

Environmental scientists conduct research to identify and abate or eliminate sources of pollutants that affect people, wildlife, and their environments. These workers analyze and report measurements and observations of air, water, soil, and other sources and make recommendations on how best to clean and preserve the environment. Understanding the issues involved in protecting the environment—degradation, conservation, recycling, and replenishment—is central to the work of environmental scientists, who often use their skills and knowledge to design and monitor waste disposal sites, preserve water supplies, and reclaim contaminated land and water to comply with Federal environmental regulations.

Many environmental scientists do work and have training that is similar to other physical or life scientists, but is applied to environmental areas. Many specialize in some specific area, such as environmental ecology and conservation, environmental chemistry, environmental biology, or fisheries science. Most environmental scientists are further classified by the specific activity they perform (although recent advances in the understanding of basic life processes within the ecosystem have blurred some traditional classifications). For example, *environmental ecologists* study the relationships between organisms and their environments and the effects of influences such as population size, pollutants, rainfall, temperature, and altitude. Utilizing their knowledge of various scientific disciplines, they may collect, study, and report data on air, food, soil, and water. *Ecological modelers* study ecosystems, the control of environmental pollution, and the management of resources. These environmental scientists may use mathematical modeling, systems analy-

sis, thermodynamics, and computer techniques. *Environmental chemists* may study the toxicity of various chemicals—how those chemicals affect plants, animals, and people. *Geochemists* study the nature and distribution of chemical elements in ground water and Earth materials.

Some environmental scientists work in managerial positions, usually after spending some time performing research or learning about environmental laws and regulations. Many work as consultants to business firms or to government agencies, helping them comply with environmental policy, particularly with regard to ground-water contamination and flood control. Environmental scientists who determine policy may help identify how human behavior can be modified in the future to avoid such problems as ground-water contamination and depletion of the ozone layer.

Geoscientists study the composition, structure, and other physical aspects of the Earth. With the use of sophisticated instruments and by analyzing the composition of the earth and water, geoscientists study the Earth's geologic past and present. Many geoscientists are involved in searching for oil and gas, while others work closely with environmental scientists in preserving and cleaning up the environment.

Geoscientists usually study, and are subsequently classified into, one of several closely related fields of geoscience. *Geologists* study the composition, processes, and history of the Earth. They try to find out how rocks were formed and what has happened to them since their formation. They also study the evolution of life by analyzing plant and animal fossils. *Geophysicists* use the principles of physics, mathematics, and chemistry to study not only the Earth's surface, but also its internal composition; ground and surface waters; atmosphere; oceans; and magnetic, electrical, and gravitational forces.

Oceanographers use their knowledge of geology and geophysics, in addition to biology and chemistry, to study the world's oceans and coastal waters. They study the motion and circulation of the ocean waters; the physical and chemical properties of the oceans; and how these properties affect coastal areas, climate, and weather. Oceanographers are further broken down according to their areas of expertise. For example, *physical oceanographers* study the ocean tides, waves, currents, temperatures, density, and salinity. They examine the interaction of various forms of energy, such as light, radar, sound, heat, and wind, with the sea, in addition to investigating the relationship between the sea, weather, and climate. *Chemical oceanographers* study the distribution of chemical compounds and chemical interactions that occur in the ocean and on the sea floor. They may investigate how pollution affects the chemistry of the ocean. *Geological and geophysical oceanographers* study the topographic features and the physical makeup of the ocean floor. Their knowledge can help companies find oil and gas off coastal waters. (*Biological oceanographers*, often called marine biologists, study the distribution and migration patterns of the many diverse forms of sea life in the ocean, but because they are considered biological scientists, they are not covered in this statement on environmental scientists and geoscientists. See instead the statement on biological scientists elsewhere in the *Handbook*.)

Geoscientists can spend a large part of their time in the field, identifying and examining rocks, studying information collected by remote sensing instruments in satellites, conducting geological surveys, constructing field maps, and using instruments to measure the Earth's gravity and magnetic field. For example, they often perform seismic studies, which involve bouncing energy waves off buried rock layers, to search for oil and gas or to understand the structure of subsurface rock layers. Seismic signals generated by an earthquake are used to determine the earthquake's location and intensity. In laboratories, geologists and geophysicists examine the chemical and physical properties of specimens. They study fossil remains of animal and plant life or experiment with the flow of water and oil through rocks.

Numerous specialties that further differentiate the type of work geoscientists do fall under the two major disciplines of geology and geophysics. For example, *petroleum geologists* explore for oil and gas deposits by studying and mapping the subsurface of the ocean or land. They use sophisticated geophysical instrumentation and computers to interpret geological information. *Engineering geologists* apply geologic principles to the fields of civil and environmental engineering, offering advice on major construction projects and assisting in environmental remediation and natural hazard reduction projects. *Mineralogists* analyze and classify minerals and precious stones according to their composition and structure. They study the environment surrounding rocks in order to find new mineral resources. *Paleontologists* study fossils found in geological formations to trace the evolution of plant and animal life and the geologic history of the Earth. *Stratigraphers* examine the formation and layering of rocks to understand the environment in which they were formed. *Volcanologists* investigate volca-

Some environmental scientists and geoscientists spend the majority of their time in an office; but many others divide their time between fieldwork and laboratory work.

noes and volcanic phenomena to try to predict the potential for future eruptions and possible hazards to human health and welfare. *Hydrologists* study the quantity, distribution, circulation, and physical properties of underground and surface waters. They examine the form and intensity of precipitation, its rate of infiltration into the soil, its movement through the earth, and its return to the ocean and atmosphere. The work hydrologists do is particularly important in environmental preservation, remediation, and flood control.

Geophysicists specialize in areas such as geodesy, seismology, or magnetic geophysics. *Geodesists* study the Earth's size, shape, gravitational field, tides, polar motion, and rotation. *Seismologists* interpret data from seismographs and other geophysical instruments to detect earthquakes and locate earthquake-related faults. *Geomagnetists* measure the Earth's magnetic field and use measurements taken over the past few centuries to devise theoretical models that explain the Earth's origin. *Paleomagnetists* interpret fossil magnetization in rocks and sediments from the continents and oceans to record the spreading of the sea floor, the wandering of the continents, and the many reversals of polarity that the Earth's magnetic field has undergone through time. Other geophysicists study atmospheric sciences and space physics. (See the statements on atmospheric scientists, and physicists and astronomers, elsewhere in the *Handbook*.)

Working Conditions

Some environmental scientists and geoscientists spend the majority of their time in an office, but many others divide their time between fieldwork and office or laboratory work. Many environmental scientists, such as environmental ecologists, environmental chemists, and hydrologists, often take field trips that involve physical activity. Environmental scientists in the field may work in warm or cold climates, in all kinds of weather. In their research, they may dig or chip with a hammer, scoop with a net, and carry equipment in a backpack. Oceanographers may spend considerable time at sea on academic research ships. Fieldwork often requires working long hours. Geologists frequently travel to remote field sites by helicopter or four-wheel-drive vehicles and cover large areas on foot. An increasing number of exploration geologists and geophysicists work in foreign countries, sometimes in remote areas and under difficult conditions. Travel often is required to meet with prospective clients or investors.

Environmental scientists and geoscientists in research positions with the Federal Government or in colleges and universities frequently are required to design programs and write grant proposals in order to continue their data collection and research. Environmental scientists and geoscientists in consulting jobs face similar pressures to market their skills and write proposals so that they will have steady work.

Employment

Environmental scientists and geoscientists held about 101,000 jobs in 2002. Environmental scientists accounted for 65,000 of the total; geoscientists, 28,000; and hydrologists, 8,000. Many more individuals held environmental science and geoscience faculty positions in colleges and universities, but they are classified as college and university faculty. (See the statement on teachers-postsecondary elsewhere in the *Handbook*.)

About 47 percent of environmental scientists were employed in State and local governments, 14 percent in architectural, engineering and related services, 13 percent in management, scientific, and technical consulting services, and 9 percent in the Federal Government. About 1,900 were self-employed.

Among geoscientists, 30 percent were employed in architectural, engineering, and related services, and 15 percent worked for oil and gas extraction companies. In 2002, the Federal Government employed about 3,000 geoscientists, including geologists, geophysicists, and oceanographers, mostly within the U.S. Department of the Interior for the U.S. Geological Survey (USGS) and within the U.S. Department of Defense. Another 3,400 worked for State agencies, such as State geological surveys and State departments of conservation. Nearly 3 percent of geoscientists were self-employed, most as consultants to industry or government.

Approximately 32 percent of hydrologists worked in the Federal Government in 2002, another 21 percent in architectural, engineering, and related services, 17 percent worked in management, scientific, and technical consulting services, and 16 percent for State governments.

Training, Other Qualifications, and Advancement
A bachelor's degree is adequate for a few entry-level positions, but environmental scientists and geoscientists increasingly need a master's degree in a natural science. A master's degree also is the minimum educational requirement for most entry-level research positions in private industry, Federal agencies, and State geological surveys. A doctoral degree is necessary for most high-level research positions.

Many environmental scientists earn degrees in life science, chemistry, geology, geophysics, atmospheric science, or physics and then, either through further education or through their research interests and work experience, apply their education to environmental areas. Others earn a degree in environmental science. A bachelor's degree in environmental science offers an interdisciplinary approach to the natural sciences, with an emphasis on biology, chemistry, and geology. In addition, undergraduate environmental science majors should focus on data analysis and physical geography, particularly if they are interested in studying pollution abatement, water resources, or ecosystem protection, restoration, or management. Those students interested in working in the environmental or regulatory fields, either in environmental consulting firms or for Federal or State governments, should take courses in hydrology, hazardous waste management, environmental legislation, chemistry, fluid mechanics, and geologic logging. An understanding of environmental regulations and government permit issues also is valuable for those planning to work in mining and oil and gas extraction. Hydrologists and environmental scientists should have some knowledge of the potential liabilities associated with some environmental work. Students interested in the field of hydrology should take courses in the physical sciences, geophysics, chemistry, engineering science, soils, mathematics, aquatic biology, atmospheric science, meteorology, geology, oceanography, or the management or conservation of water resources. In some cases, graduates with a bachelor's degree in a hydrologic science are qualified for positions in environmental consulting and planning regarding water quality or waste-water treatment. Curricula for advanced degrees often emphasize the natural sciences, but not all universities offer all curricula.

Traditional geoscience courses emphasizing classical geologic methods and topics (such as mineralogy, petrology, paleontology, stratigraphy, and structural geology) are important for all geoscientists. Persons studying physics, chemistry, biology, mathematics, engineering, or computer science may also qualify for some geoscience positions if their course work includes study in geology or natural sciences.

Computer skills are essential for prospective environmental scientists and geoscientists; students who have some experience with computer modeling, data analysis and integration, digital mapping, remote sensing, and geographic information systems will be the most prepared entering the job market. A knowledge of the Global Information System (GIS) and Global Positioning System (GPS)—a locator system that uses satellites—also is very helpful. Some employers seek applicants with field experience, so a summer internship may be beneficial to prospective geoscientists.

Environmental scientists and geoscientists must have excellent interpersonal skills, because they usually work as part of a team with other scientists, engineers, and technicians. Strong oral and written communication skills also are important, because writing technical reports and research proposals, as well as communicating research results to others, are important aspects of the work. Because many jobs require foreign travel, knowledge of a second language is becoming an important attribute to employers. Geoscientists must be inquisitive, be able to think logically, and have an open mind. Those involved in fieldwork must have physical stamina.

Environmental scientists and geoscientists often begin their careers in field exploration or as research assistants or technicians in laboratories or offices. They are given more difficult assignments as they gain experience. Eventually, they may be promoted to project leader, program manager, or some other management and research position.

Job Outlook
Overall employment of environmental scientists and geoscientists is expected to grow about as fast as the average for all occupations through 2012. Driving job growth will be public policy, which will force companies and organizations to comply with environmental laws and regulations, particularly those regarding ground-water contamination, clean air, and flood control.

Projected employment growth varies by occupational specialty. Environmental scientists and hydrologists are expected to grow faster than average. A general heightened awareness regarding the need to monitor the quality of the environment, to interpret the impact of human actions on terrestrial and aquatic ecosystems, and to develop strategies for ecosystem restoration are all increasingly important issues that will drive demand for environmental scientists. Issues related to water conservation, deteriorating coastal environments, and rising sea levels also will stimulate employment growth of these workers. As the population increases and moves to more environmentally sensitive locations, environmental scientists and hydrologists will be needed to assess building sites for potential geologic hazards, to mitigate the effects of natural hazards such as floods, tornadoes, and earthquakes, and to address issues related to pollution control and waste disposal. Hydrologists and environmental scientists also will be needed to conduct research on hazardous-waste sites in order to determine the impact of hazardous pollutants on soil and ground water so that engineers can design remediation systems. Demand is growing for environmental scientists who understand both the science and engineering aspects of waste remediation.

In contrast to employment of environmental scientists and hydrologists, that of geoscientists is expected to grow about as fast as the average for all occupations. In the past, employment of geologists and some other geoscientists has been cyclical and largely affected by the price of oil and gas. When prices were low, oil and gas producers curtailed exploration activities and laid off geologists. When prices were higher, companies had the funds and incentive to renew exploration efforts and hire geoscientists in large numbers. In recent years, a growing worldwide demand for oil and gas and for new exploration and recovery techniques—particularly in deep water and previously inaccessible sites—has returned a modicum of stability to the petroleum industry. Growth in this area, though, will be limited due to increasing efficiencies in finding oil and gas. Geoscientists who speak a foreign language and who are willing to work abroad should enjoy the best opportunities. An expected increase in highway building and other infrastructure projects will be a source of jobs for engineering geologists. The need to replace geoscientists who retire also will result in job openings over the next decade.

Earnings
Median annual earnings of environmental scientists were $47,600 in 2002. The middle 50 percent earned between $36,820 and $62,400. The lowest 10 percent earned less than $29,920, and the highest 10 percent earned more than $78,200.

Median annual earnings of geoscientists were $67,470 in 2002. The middle 50 percent earned between $48,370 and $102,120; the lowest 10 percent, less than $36,580 and the highest 10 percent more than $133,310.

Median annual earnings of hydrologists were $56,530 in 2002, with the middle 50 percent earning between $44,080 and $70,160, the lowest 10 percent less than $36,790, and the highest 10 percent more than $86,620.

Median annual earnings in the industries employing the largest number of environmental scientists in 2002 were as follows:

Federal Government	$66,190
Management, scientific, and technical consulting services	45,560
Local government	45,270
Architectural, engineering, and related services	44,590
State government	44,580

According to the National Association of Colleges and Employers, beginning salary offers in 2003 for graduates with bachelor's degrees in geology and related sciences averaged about $32,828 a year; graduates with a master's degree averaged $47,981, and graduates with a doctoral degree averaged $61,050.

In 2003, the Federal Government's average salary for geologists in managerial, supervisory, and nonsupervisory positions was $76,389 for geologists, $86,809 for geophysicists, $70,525 for hydrologists, and $79,023 for oceanographers.

The petroleum, mineral, and mining industries are vulnerable to recessions and to changes in oil and gas prices, among other factors, and usually release workers when exploration and drilling slow down. Consequently, they offer higher salaries, but less job security, than do other industries.

Related Occupations
Many geoscientists work in the petroleum and natural gas industry, an industry that also employs many other workers in the scientific and technical aspects of petroleum and natural gas exploration and extraction. Among these other workers are engineering technicians, science technicians, petroleum engineers, surveyors, cartographers, photogrammetrists, and surveying technicians. Also, some physicists, chemists, and atmospheric sci-

entists—as well as mathematicians, computer systems analysts, database administrators, and computer scientists—perform related work both in petroleum and natural gas exploration and extraction and in environment-related activities.

Sources of Additional Information
Information on training and career opportunities for geologists is available from either of the following organizations:
◆American Geological Institute, 4220 King St., Alexandria, VA 22302-1502. Internet: **http://www.agiweb.org**
◆American Association of Petroleum Geologists, P.O. Box 979, Tulsa, OK 74101. Internet: **http://www.aapg.org**

A packet of free career information and a list of education and training programs in oceanography and related fields, priced at $6.00, is available from
◆Marine Technology Society, 5565 Sterrett Place, Suite 108, Columbia, MD 21004. Telephone: (410) 884-5330. Internet: **http://www.mtsociety.org**

Information on applying for a job as a geologist, a geophysicist, a hydrologist, or an oceanographer with the Federal Government may be obtained through a telephone-based system from the Office of Personnel Management. Consult your telephone directory under "U.S. Government" for a local number, or call (703) 724-1850 or Federal Relay Service (800) 877-8339. This number is not toll free, and charges may accrue. Information also is available from the Internet site **http://www.usajobs.opm.gov**.

Physicists and Astronomers

(0*NET 19-2011.00, 19-2012.00)

Significant Points

● Scientific research and development services firms and the Federal Government employ 3 out of 5 physicists and astronomers.

● Most jobs are in basic research and development, usually requiring a doctoral degree; master's degree holders qualify for many jobs in applied research and development, while bachelor's degree holders may qualify as technicians or research assistants.

● Ph.D. graduates will face competition for basic research jobs.

Nature of the Work
Physicists explore and identify basic principles governing the structure and behavior of matter, the generation and transfer of energy, and the interaction of matter and energy. Some physicists use these principles in theoretical areas, such as the nature of time and the origin of the universe; others apply their physics knowledge to practical areas, such as the development of advanced materials, electronic and optical devices, and medical equipment.

Physicists design and perform experiments with lasers, particle accelerators, telescopes, mass spectrometers, and other equipment. Based on observations and analysis, they attempt to discover and explain laws describing the forces of nature, such as gravity, electromagnetism, and nuclear interactions. Physicists also find ways to apply physical laws and theories to problems in nuclear energy, electronics, optics, materials, communications, aerospace technology, and medical instrumentation.

Astronomy is sometimes considered a subfield of physics. *Astronomers* use the principles of physics and mathematics to learn about the fundamental nature of the universe, including the sun, moon, planets, stars, and galaxies. They also apply their knowledge to solve problems in navigation, space flight, and satellite communications, and to develop the instrumentation and techniques used to observe and collect astronomical data.

Most physicists work in research and development. Some do basic research to increase scientific knowledge. Physicists who conduct applied research build upon the discoveries made through basic research and work to develop new devices, products, and processes. For example, basic research in solid-state physics led to the development of transistors and, then, integrated circuits used in computers.

Physicists also design research equipment. This equipment often has additional unanticipated uses. For example, lasers are used in surgery, microwave devices are used in ovens, and measuring instruments can analyze blood or the chemical content of foods. A small number of physicists work in inspection, testing, quality control, and other production-related jobs in industry.

Much physics research is done in small or medium-sized laboratories. However, experiments in plasma, nuclear, and high energy and in some other areas of physics require extremely large, expensive equipment, such as particle accelerators. Physicists in these subfields often work in large teams. Although physics research may require extensive experimentation in laboratories, research physicists still spend time in offices planning, recording, analyzing, and reporting on research.

Almost all astronomers do research. Some are theoreticians, working on the laws governing the structure and evolution of astronomical objects. Others analyze large quantities of data gathered by observatories and satellites, and write scientific papers or reports on their findings. Some astronomers actually operate large space- or ground-based telescopes, usually as part of a team. However, astronomers may spend only a few weeks each year making observations with optical telescopes, radio telescopes, and other instruments. For many years, satellites and other space-based instruments, such as the Hubble space telescope, have provided tremendous amounts of astronomical data. New technology resulting in improvements in analytical

Most physicist and astronomer jobs are in basic research and development, usually requiring a doctoral degree.

techniques and instruments, such as computers and optical telescopes and mounts, is leading to a resurgence in ground-based research. A small number of astronomers work in museums housing planetariums. These astronomers develop and revise programs presented to the public, and may direct planetarium operations.

Physicists generally specialize in one of many subfields— elementary particle physics, nuclear physics, atomic and molecular physics, physics of condensed matter (solid-state physics), optics, acoustics, space physics, plasma physics, or the physics of fluids. Some specialize in a subdivision of one of these subfields. For example, within condensed matter physics, specialties include superconductivity, crystallography, and semiconductors. However, all physics involves the same fundamental principles, so specialties may overlap, and physicists may switch from one subfield to another. Also, growing numbers of physicists work in interdisciplinary fields, such as biophysics, chemical physics, and geophysics.

Working Conditions
Physicists often work regular hours in laboratories and offices. At times, however, those who are deeply involved in research may work long or irregular hours. Most do not encounter unusual hazards in their work. Some physicists temporarily work away from home at national or international facilities with unique equipment, such as particle accelerators. Astronomers who make observations using ground-based telescopes may spend long periods in observatories; this work usually involves travel to remote locations and may require long hours, including nightwork.

Physicists and astronomers whose work depends on grant money often are under pressure to write grant proposals to keep their work funded.

Employment
Physicists and astronomers held about 14,000 jobs in 2002. Jobs for astronomers accounted for only 7 percent of the total. Nearly one-third of physicists and astronomers worked for scientific research and development services firms. The Federal Government employed 29 percent, mostly in the U.S. Department of Defense, but also in the National Aeronautics and Space Administration (NASA), and in the U.S. Departments of Commerce, Health and Human Services, and Energy. Other physicists and astronomers worked in colleges and universities in nonfaculty, usually research, positions, or for State governments, information technology companies, pharmaceutical and medicine manufacturing companies, or electronic equipment manufacturers.

Besides the jobs described above, many physicists and astronomers held faculty positions in colleges and universities. (See the statement on teachers—postsecondary elsewhere in the *Handbook*.)

Although physicists and astronomers are employed in all parts of the country, most work in areas in which universities, large research and development laboratories, or observatories are located.

Training, Other Qualifications, and Advancement
Because most jobs are in basic research and development, a doctoral degree is the usual educational requirement for physicists and astronomers. Additional experience and training in a postdoctoral research appointment, although not required, is important for physicists and astronomers aspiring to permanent

positions in basic research in universities and government laboratories. Many physics and astronomy Ph.D. holders ultimately teach at the college or university level.

Master's degree holders usually do not qualify for basic research positions but do qualify for many kinds of jobs requiring a physics background, including positions in manufacturing and applied research and development. Increasingly, many master's degree programs specifically prepare students for physics-related research and development that does not require a Ph.D. degree. These master's degree programs teach students specific research skills that can be used in private industry jobs. A master's degree may suffice for teaching jobs in high schools or at 2-year colleges.

Those with bachelor's degrees in physics are rarely qualified to fill positions in research or in teaching at the college level. They are, however, usually qualified to work as technicians or research assistants in engineering-related areas, in software development and other scientific fields, or in setting up computer networks and sophisticated laboratory equipment. Some may qualify for applied research jobs in private industry or nonresearch positions in the Federal Government. Some become science teachers in secondary schools.Astronomy bachelor's or master's degree holders often enter a field unrelated to astronomy, and they are qualified to work in planetariums running science shows, to assist astronomers doing research, and to operate space-based and ground-based telescopes and other astronomical instrumentation. (See the statements on engineers; environmental scientists and geoscientists; computer programmers; computer systems analysts, database administrators, and computer scientists; and computer software engineers, elsewhere in the *Handbook*.)

More than 500 colleges and universities offer a bachelor's degree in physics. Undergraduate programs provide a broad background in the natural sciences and mathematics. Typical physics courses include electromagnetism, optics, thermodynamics, atomic physics, and quantum mechanics.

About 180 colleges and universities have departments offering Ph.D. degrees in physics. More than 70 additional colleges offer a master's as their highest degree in physics. Graduate students usually concentrate in a subfield of physics, such as elementary particles or condensed matter. Many begin studying for their doctorate immediately after receiving their bachelor's degree.

About 70 universities grant degrees in astronomy, either through an astronomy, physics, or combined physics/astronomy department. Currently, more than 30 departments are combined with the physics department and nearly 40 are administered separately. With fewer than 40 doctoral programs in astronomy, applicants face considerable competition for available slots. Those planning a career in astronomy should have a very strong physics background. In fact, an undergraduate degree in either physics or astronomy is excellent preparation, followed by a Ph.D. in astronomy.

Mathematical ability, problem-solving and analytical skills, an inquisitive mind, imagination, and initiative are important traits for anyone planning a career in physics or astronomy. Prospective physicists who hope to work in industrial laboratories applying physics knowledge to practical problems should broaden their educational background to include courses outside of physics, such as economics, information technology, and business management. Good oral and written communication skills also are important because many physicists work as part of a team, write research papers or proposals, or

have contact with clients or customers with nonphysics backgrounds.

Many physics and astronomy Ph.D. holders begin their careers in a postdoctoral research position, in which they may work with experienced physicists as they continue to learn about their specialty and develop ideas and results to be used in later work. Initial work may be under the close supervision of senior scientists. After some experience, physicists perform increasingly complex tasks and work more independently. Those who develop new products or processes sometimes form their own companies or join new firms to exploit their own ideas.

Job Outlook
Employment of physicists and astronomers is expected to grow more slowly than the average for all occupations through 2012. Federal research expenditures are the major source of physics-related and astronomy-related research funds, especially for basic research. Although these expenditures are expected to steadily increase over the 2002-12 projection period, resulting in some growth in employment and opportunities, the limited research funds available still will result in competition among Ph.D. holders for basic research jobs. The need to replace physicists and astronomers who retire or otherwise leave the occupation permanently will account for most expected job openings.

Although research and development budgets in private industry will continue to grow, many research laboratories in private industry are expected to continue to reduce basic research, which includes much physics research, in favor of applied or manufacturing research and product and software development. Nevertheless, persons with a physics background continue to be in demand in the areas of information technology, semiconductor technology, and other applied sciences. This trend is expected to continue; however, many of the new workers will have job titles such as computer software engineer, computer programmer, engineer, and systems developer, rather than physicist.

Through the 1990s, the number of doctorates granted in physics was much greater than the number of job openings for physicists, resulting in keen competition, particularly for research positions in colleges and universities and in research and development centers. Competitive conditions have eased somewhat because the number of doctorate degrees awarded has been dropping for several years, in line with declining enrollment in graduate physics programs. Recent increases in undergraduate physics enrollments, however, may again lead to growth in enrollments in graduate physics programs, meaning that, toward the end of the projection period, there may be an increase in the number of doctoral degrees granted that will intensify the competition for job openings.

Opportunities may be more numerous for those with a master's degree, particularly graduates from programs preparing students for applied research and development, product design, and manufacturing positions in private industry. Many of these positions, however, will have titles other than physicist, such as engineer or computer scientist.

Persons with only a bachelor's degree in physics or astronomy are not qualified to enter most physicist or astronomer research jobs but may qualify for a wide range of positions related to engineering, mathematics, computer science, and environmental science. Those who meet State certification requirements can become high school physics teachers, an occupation in strong demand in many school districts. Most States require new teachers to obtain a master's degree in education within a certain time. (See the statement on teachers—preschool, kindergarten, elementary, middle, and secondary elsewhere in the *Handbook*.) Despite competition for traditional physics and astronomy research jobs, individuals with a physics degree at any level will find their knowledge of science and mathematics useful for entry to many other occupations.

Earnings

Median annual earnings of physicists were $85,020 in 2002. The middle 50 percent earned between $66,680 and $107,410. The lowest 10 percent earned less than $50,350, and the highest 10 percent earned more than $129,250.

Median annual earnings of astronomers were $81,690 in 2002. The middle 50 percent earned between $53,390 and $106,230; the lowest 10 percent, less than $40,140, and the highest 10 percent more than $126,320.

According to a 2003 National Association of Colleges and Employers survey, the average annual starting salary offer to physics doctoral degree candidates was $55,485.

The American Institute of Physics reported a median annual salary of $95,000 in 2002 for its full time members with Ph.D.'s (excluding those in postdoctoral positions); the median was $87,000 for those with master's degrees, and $78,000 for bachelor's degree holders. Those working in temporary postdoctoral positions earned significantly less.

The average annual salary for physicists employed by the Federal Government was $95,685 in 2003; for astronomy and space scientists, it was $100,591.

Related Occupations

The work of physicists and astronomers relates closely to that of engineers; chemists and materials scientists; atmospheric scientists; environmental scientists and geoscientists; computer systems analysts, computer scientists, and database administrators; computer programmers; and mathematicians.

Sources of Additional Information

General information on career opportunities in physics is available from:

◇►American Institute of Physics, Career Services Division and Education and Employment Division, One Physics Ellipse, College Park, MD 20740-3843. Internet: **http://www.aip.org**

►The American Physical Society, One Physics Ellipse, College Park, MD 20740-3844. Internet: **http://www.aps.org**

Social Scientists and Related Occupations

Economists

(0*NET 19-3011.00)

Significant Points

- Quantitative skills are important in all economics specialties.

- Employment of economists is expected to grow about as fast as the average; most new jobs will arise in private industry, including economic research and consulting firms.

- Candidates who hold a master's or Ph.D. degree in economics will have the best employment prospects and advancement opportunities.

Nature of the Work

Economists study how society distributes scarce resources such as land, labor, raw materials, and machinery to produce goods and services. They conduct research, collect and analyze data, monitor economic trends, and develop forecasts. They research issues such as energy costs, inflation, interest rates, exchange rates, business cycles, taxes, or employment levels.

Economists devise methods and procedures for obtaining the data they need. For example, sampling techniques may be used to conduct a survey, and various mathematical modeling techniques may be used to develop forecasts. Preparing reports, including tables and charts, on research results is an important part of an economist's job. Presenting economic and statistical concepts in a clear and meaningful way is particularly important for economists whose research is directed toward making policies for an organization. Some economists might also provide economic analysis to the media.

Many economists specialize in a particular area of economics, although general knowledge of basic economic principles is useful in each area. *Microeconomists* study the supply and demand decisions of individuals and firms, such as how profits can be maximized and how much of a good or service consumers will demand at a certain price. *Industrial/organizational economists* study the market structure of particular industries in terms of the number of competitors, and the market decisions of competitive firms and monopolies. These economists may also be concerned with antitrust policy and its impact on market structure. *Macroeconomists* study historical trends in the whole economy and forecast future trends in areas such as unemployment, inflation, economic growth, productivity, and investment. Closely related to macroeconomists are *monetary or financial economists*, who study the money and banking system and the effects of rising interest rates. *International economists* study international financial markets, exchange rates, and the effects of various trade policies such as tariffs. *Labor* or *demographic economists* study the supply and demand for labor and the determination of wages. These economists also try to explain the reasons for unemployment, and the effects on labor markets of changing demographic trends such as an aging population and increasing immigration. *Public finance* economists primarily are involved in studying the role of the government in the economy and the effects of tax cuts, budget deficits, and welfare policies. *Econometricians* are involved in all areas of economics and use mathematical techniques such as calculus, game theory, and regression analysis to formulate economic models. These models help to explain economic relationships and are used to develop forecasts related to the nature and length of business cycles, the effects of a specific rate of inflation on the economy, the effects of tax legislati on on unemployment levels, and other economic phenomena. Many economists have applied these fundamental areas of economics to more narrow areas with specific applications such as health, education, agriculture, urban and regional economics, law, history, energy, and the environment.

Most economists are concerned with practical applications of economic policy, and work for a variety of organizations. Economists working for corporations are involved primarily in microeconomic issues, such as forecasting consumer demand and sales of the firm's products. Economists working for corporations might also analyze their competitors' growth and market share and advise their company on how to handle the competition. Other economists working for corporations monitor legislation passed by Congress, such as environmental and worker safety regulations, and assess its impact on their business. Corporations with many international branches or subsidiaries might employ economists to monitor the economic situations in countries where they do business, or to provide a risk assessment of a country into which the company might expand.

Corporations that are too small or that do not have sufficient funding might hire economists working in economic consulting or research firms to perform the same tasks as staff economists. Economists in consulting firms also perform much of the macroeconomic analysis and forecasting that is completed in the United States. These economists collect data on various indicators, maintain databases, analyze historical trends, and develop models to forecast growth, inflation, unemployment,

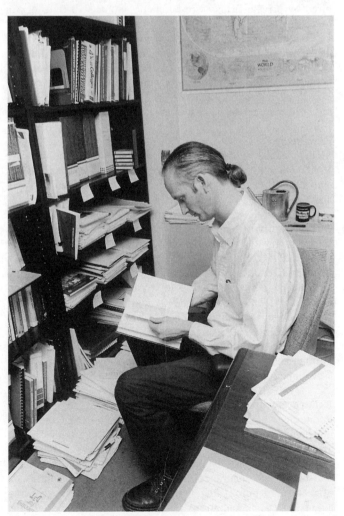

Economists frequently conduct research, write reports and articles, and present findings to clients and colleagues.

or interest rates. These analyses and forecasts are frequently published in newspapers and journal articles.

Another large employer of economists is government. Economists in the Federal Government administer most of the surveys and collect most of the economic data in the United States. For example, economists in the U.S. Department of Commerce collect and analyze data on the production, distribution, and consumption of commodities produced in the United States and overseas, while economists employed by the U.S. Department of Labor collect and analyze data on the domestic economy, including those having to do with prices, wages, employment, productivity, and safety and health. Economists who work for government agencies also assess economic conditions in the United States or abroad in order to estimate the economic effects of specific changes in legislation or public policy. Government economists advise policy makers in areas such as telecommunications deregulation, Social Security revamping, the effects of tax cuts on the budget deficit, and the effectiveness of imposing tariffs on imported steel. An economist working in State or local government might analyze data on the growth of school-age or prison populations, and on employment and unemployment rates, in order to project future spending needs.

Working Conditions
Economists have structured work schedules. They often work alone, writing reports, preparing statistical charts, and using computers, but they also may be an integral part of a research team. Most work under pressure of deadlines and tight schedules, which may require overtime. Their routine may be interrupted by special requests for data, and by the need to attend meetings or conferences. Frequent travel may be necessary.

Employment
Economists held about 16,000 jobs in 2002. Private industry employed 53 percent of salaried economists, particularly in scientific research and development firms; management, scientific, and technical consulting firms; banks and securities firms, and business, professional, labor, and political organizations. A wide range of government agencies provided the remaining jobs. The U.S. Departments of Labor, Agriculture, and State are the largest Federal employers of economists. A number of economists combine a full-time job in government, academia, or business with part-time or consulting work in another setting. A little over 11 percent of economists are self-employed.

Employment of economists is concentrated in large cities. Some work abroad for companies with major international operations, for U.S. Government agencies, and for international organizations, such as the World Bank, International Monetary fund, and United Nations.

Besides the jobs described above, many economists hold faculty positions in colleges and universities. Economics faculties have flexible work schedules, and may divide their time among teaching, research, consulting, and administration. (See the statement on teachers—postsecondary elsewhere in the *Handbook*.)

Training, Other Qualifications, and Advancement
A master's or Ph.D. degree in economics is required for many private sector economist jobs, and for advancement to more responsible positions. Economics includes many specialties at the graduate level, such as advanced economic theory, econometrics, international economics, and labor economics. Students should select graduate schools strong in specialties in

which they are interested. Undergraduate economics majors can choose from a variety of courses, ranging from microeconomics, macroeconomics, and econometrics, to more philosophical courses, such as the history of economic thought. Because of the importance of quantitative skills to economists, courses in mathematics, statistics, econometrics, sampling theory and survey design, and computer science are extremely helpful. Some schools help graduate students find internships or part-time employment in government agencies, economic consulting or research firms, or financial institutions prior to graduation.

In the Federal Government, candidates for entry-level economist positions must have a bachelor's degree with a minimum of 21 semester hours of economics and 3 hours of statistics, accounting, or calculus.

Whether working in government, industry, research organizations, or consulting firms, economists with a bachelor's degree usually qualify for most entry-level positions as a research assistant, for administrative or management trainee positions, or for various sales jobs. A master's degree usually is required to qualify for more responsible research and administrative positions. Many businesses, research and consulting firms, and government agencies seek individuals who have strong computer and quantitative skills and can perform complex research. A Ph.D. is necessary for top economist positions in many organizations. Many corporation and government executives have a strong background in economics.

A master's degree is usually the minimum requirement for a job as an instructor in junior and community colleges. In most colleges and universities, however, a Ph.D. is necessary for appointment as an instructor. A Ph.D. and extensive publications in academic journals are required for a professorship, tenure, and promotion.

Aspiring economists should gain experience gathering and analyzing data, conducting interviews or surveys, and writing reports on their findings while in college. This experience can prove invaluable later in obtaining a full-time position in the field, because much of the economist's work, especially in the beginning, may center on these duties. With experience, economists eventually are assigned their own research projects. Related job experience, such as work as a stock or bond trader, might be advantageous.

Those considering careers as economists should be able to pay attention to details because much time is spent on precise data analysis. Patience and persistence are necessary qualities because economists must spend long hours on independent study and problem solving. Economists must be able to present their findings, both orally and in writing, in a clear, concise manner.

Job Outlook

Employment of economists is expected to grow about as fast as the average for all occupations through 2012. Many job openings are likely to result from the need to replace experienced workers who transfer to other occupations or who retire or leave the labor force for other reasons.

Opportunities for economists should be best in private industry, especially in scientific research and development, and consulting firms, as more companies contract out for economic research services. Rising demand for economists should stem from the growing complexity of the global economy, competition, and increased reliance on quantitative methods for analyzing and forecasting business, sales, and other economic trends. A greater need for economic analyses in virtually every industry could result in additional jobs for economists, although some corporations are eliminating some or all of their economist positions in favor of hiring economic consultants. Employment of economists in the Federal Government should decline, but not by as much as other occupations in the Federal workforce. Average employment growth is expected among economists in State and local government.

A master's or Ph.D. degree, coupled with a strong background in economic theory, mathematics, statistics, and econometrics, provides the basis for acquiring any specialty within the economics field. Those skilled in quantitative techniques and their application to economic modeling and forecasting, and who have good communications skills, should have the best job opportunities. Like those in many other disciplines, however, Ph.D. holders are likely to face keen competition for tenured teaching positions in colleges and universities.

Bachelor's degree holders may face competition for the limited number of economist positions for which they qualify. They will qualify for a number of other positions, however, in which they can take advantage of their economic knowledge by conducting research, developing surveys, or analyzing data. Many graduates with bachelor's degrees will find jobs in industry and business as management or sales trainees, or as administrative assistants. Bachelor's degree holders with good quantitative skills and a strong background in mathematics, statistics, survey design, and computer science also may be hired by private firms as researchers. Some will find jobs in government.

Candidates who meet State certification requirements may become high school economics teachers. The demand for secondary school economics teachers is expected to grow, as economics becomes an increasingly important and popular course. (See the statement on teachers—preschool, kindergarten, elementary, middle, and secondary elsewhere in the *Handbook*.)

Earnings

Median annual wage and salary earnings of economists were $68,550 in 2002. The middle 50 percent earned between $50,560 and $90,710. The lowest 10 percent earned less than $38,690, and the highest 10 percent earned more than $120,440.

The Federal Government recognizes education and experience in certifying applicants for entry-level positions. The entrance salary for economists having a bachelor's degree was about $23,442 a year in 2003; however, those with superior academic records could begin at $29,037. Those having a master's degree could qualify for positions at an annual salary of $35,519. Those with a Ph.D. could begin at $42,976, while some individuals with experience and an advanced degree could start at $51,508. Starting salaries were slightly higher in selected areas where the prevailing local pay was higher. The average annual salary for economists employed by the Federal Government was $81,852 a year in 2003.

Related Occupations

Economists are concerned with understanding and interpreting financial matters, among other subjects. Other jobs in this area include accountants and auditors; actuaries; budget analysts; financial analysts and personal financial advisors; financial managers; insurance underwriters; loan counselors and officers; and purchasing managers, buyers, and purchasing agents. Other occupations involved in market research and data collection are management analysts, as well as market and survey researchers.

Sources of Additional Information

For information on careers in business economics, contact:

➤ National Association for Business Economics, 1233 20th St. NW., Suite 505, Washington, DC 20036.

Information on obtaining a position as an economist with the Federal Government is available from the U.S. Office of Personnel Management (OPM) through a telephone-based system. Consult your telephone directory under U.S. Government for a local number or call (703) 724-1850; Federal Relay Service: (800) 877-8339. The first number is not tollfree, and charges may result. Information also is available from the OPM Internet site: **http://www.usajobs.opm.gov**.

Market and Survey Researchers

(O*NET 19-3021.00, 19-3022.00)

Significant Points

- Strong demand is expected for market and survey researchers.

- A master's degree is the minimum requirement for many private sector jobs.

- Quantitative skills are critical.

Nature of the Work

Market, or *marketing, research analysts* are concerned with the potential sales of a product or service. They analyze statistical data on past sales to predict future sales. They gather data on competitors and analyze prices, sales, and methods of marketing and distribution. Market research analysts devise methods and procedures for obtaining the data they need. They often design telephone, mail, or Internet surveys to assess consumer preferences. Some surveys are conducted as personal interviews by going door-to-door, leading focus group discussions, or setting up booths in public places such as shopping malls. Trained interviewers, under the market research analyst's direction, usually conduct the surveys.

After compiling the data, market research analysts evaluate them and make recommendations to their client or employer based upon their findings. They provide a company's management with information needed to make decisions on the promotion, distribution, design, and pricing of products or services. The information may also be used to determine the advisability of adding new lines of merchandise, opening new branches, or otherwise diversifying the company's operations. Market research analysts might also develop advertising brochures and commercials, sales plans, and product promotions such as rebates and giveaways.

Survey researchers design and conduct surveys for a variety of clients such as corporations, government agencies, political candidates, and service providers. They use surveys to collect information that is used for research, making fiscal or policy decisions, measuring policy effectiveness, and improving customer satisfaction. Analysts may conduct opinion research to determine public attitudes on various issues, which may help political or business leaders and others assess public support for their electoral prospects or social policies. Like market research analysts, survey researchers may use a variety of mediums to conduct surveys, such as the Internet, personal or telephone

Market and survey researchers conduct research and design surveys.

interviews, or mail questionnaires. They also may supervise interviewers who conduct surveys in person or over the telephone.

Survey researchers design surveys in many different formats, depending upon the scope of research and method of collection. Interview surveys, for example, are common because they can increase survey participation rates. Survey researchers may consult with economists, statisticians, market research analysts, or other data users in order to design surveys. They also may present survey results to clients.

Working Conditions

Market and survey researchers generally have structured work schedules. Some often work alone, writing reports, preparing statistical charts, and using computers, but they also may be an integral part of a research team. Market researchers who conduct personal interviews will have frequent contact with the public. Most work under pressure of deadlines and tight schedules, which may require overtime. Their routine may be interrupted by special requests for data, as well as by the need to attend meetings or conferences. Travel may be necessary.

Employment

Market and survey researchers held about a total of 155,000 jobs in 2002. Most of these jobs were held by market research analysts, who held 135,000 jobs. Private industry provided about 97 percent of salaried market research analyst jobs. Because of the applicability of market research to many industries, market research analysts are employed in most industries. The industries which employ the largest number of market research analysts are management, scientific, and technical consulting firms, insurance carriers, computer systems design and related firms, software publishers, securities and commodities brokers, and advertising and related firms. Survey researchers held about 20,000 jobs in 2002. Survey researchers were mainly employed by professional, scientific, and technical services firms, including management, scientific and technical consulting firms, and scientific research and development firms; employment services, State government, and internet service providers and web search portals. A number of market and survey researchers combine a full-time job in government, academia, or business with part-time or consulting work in another setting. About 8 percent of market and survey researchers are self-employed.

Besides the jobs described above, many market and survey researchers held faculty positions in colleges and universities. Marketing faculties have flexible work schedules and may divide their time among teaching, research, consulting, and administration. (See the statement on teachers—postsecondary elsewhere in the *Handbook*.)

Training, Other Qualifications, and Advancement

A master's degree is the minimum requirement for many private sector market and survey research jobs, and for advancement to more responsible positions. Market and survey researchers may earn advanced degrees in business administration, marketing, statistics, communications, or some closely related discipline. Some schools help graduate students find internships or part-time employment in government agencies, consulting firms, financial institutions, or marketing research firms prior to graduation.

In addition to courses in business, marketing, and consumer behavior, prospective market and survey researchers should take other liberal arts and social science courses, including economics, psychology, English, and sociology. Because of the importance of quantitative skills to market and survey researchers, courses in mathematics, statistics, sampling theory and survey design, and computer science are extremely helpful.

Bachelor's degree holders who majored in marketing and related fields may qualify for many entry-level positions that might or might not be related to market and survey research. These positions include research assistant, administrative or management trainee, marketing interviewer, and salesperson, among others. Many businesses, research and consulting firms, and government agencies seek individuals who have strong computer and quantitative skills and can perform complex research. Many corporation and government executives have a strong background in marketing.

In addition to being required for most market and survey research jobs in business and industry, a master's degree is usually the minimum requirement for a job as an instructor in junior and community colleges. In most colleges and universities, however, a Ph.D. is necessary for appointment as an instructor. A Ph.D. and extensive publications in academic journals are required for a professorship, tenure, and promotion.

Aspiring market and survey researchers should gain experience gathering and analyzing data, conducting interviews or surveys, and writing reports on their findings while in college. This experience can prove invaluable later in obtaining a full-time position in the field, because much of the work, in the beginning, may center on these duties. With experience, market and survey researchers eventually are assigned their own research projects.

Those considering careers as market and survey researchers should be able to pay attention to details because much time is spent on precise data analysis. Patience and persistence are necessary qualities because market and survey researchers must spend long hours on independent study and problem solving. At the same time, they must work well with others, because they often oversee interviews of a wide variety of individuals. Communication skills are very important because market and survey researchers must be able to present their findings both orally and in writing, in a clear, concise manner.

Job Outlook

Employment of market and survey researchers is expected to grow faster than the average for all occupations through 2012.

Many job openings are likely to result from the need to replace experienced workers who transfer to other occupations or who retire or leave the labor force for other reasons. Opportunities should be best for those with a master's or Ph.D. degree in marketing or a related field and strong quantitative skills.

Demand for market research analysts should be strong because of an increasingly competitive economy. Marketing research provides organizations valuable feedback from purchasers, allowing companies to evaluate consumer satisfaction and more effectively plan for the future. As companies seek to expand their market and as consumers become better informed, the need for marketing professionals will increase. As globalization of the marketplace continues, market researchers will also be increasingly utilized to analyze foreign markets and competition for goods and services.

Market research analysts should have opportunities in a wide range of employment settings, particularly in marketing research firms, as companies find it more profitable to contract for marketing research services rather than support their own marketing department. Increasingly, marketing research analysts are not only collecting and analyzing information, but are also helping the client implement their ideas and recommendations. Other organizations, including computer systems design companies, financial services organizations, healthcare institutions, advertising firms, manufacturing firms producing consumer goods, and insurance companies may offer job opportunities for market research analysts. Survey researchers will be needed to meet the growing demand for market and opinion research, as an increasingly competitive economy requires businesses to more effectively and efficiently allocate advertising funds.

Bachelor's degree holders may face competition for the limited number of market and survey research jobs for which they are eligible. However, they will qualify for a number of other positions, however, in which they can take advantage of their knowledge in conducting research, developing surveys, or analyzing data. Some graduates with bachelor's degrees will find jobs in industry and business as management or sales trainees or as administrative assistants. Bachelor's degree holders with good quantitative skills, including a strong background in mathematics, statistics, survey design, and computer science, may be hired by private firms as research assistants or interviewers.

Ph.D. degree holders in marketing and related fields should have a range of opportunities in industry and consulting firms. As in many other disciplines, however, Ph.D. holders are likely to face keen competition for tenured teaching positions in colleges and universities.

Earnings

Median annual earnings of market research analysts in 2002 were $53,810. The middle 50 percent earned between $38,760 and $76,310. The lowest 10 percent earned less than $29,390, and the highest 10 percent earned more than $100,160. Median annual earnings in the industries employing the largest numbers of market research analysts in 2002 were as follows:

Management of companies and enterprises	$56,750
Insurance carriers	46,700
Other professional, scientific, and technical services	46,380
Management, scientific, and technical consulting services	44,580

Median annual earnings of survey researchers in 2002 were $22,200. The middle 50 percent earned between $17,250 and $38,530. The lowest 10 percent earned less than $15,140, and the highest 10 percent earned more than $57,080. Median annual earnings of survey researchers in 2002 in other professional, scientific, and technical services were $19,610.

Related Occupations

Market and survey researchers do research to find out how well the market receives products or services. This may include planning, implementation, and analysis of surveys to determine people's needs and preferences. Other jobs using these skills include economists, psychologists, sociologists, statisticians, and urban and regional planners.

Sources of Additional Information

For information about careers and salaries in market and survey research, contact:

➤ Marketing Research Association, 1344 Silas Deane Hwy., Suite 306, Rocky Hill, CT 06067-0230. Internet: **http://www.mra-net.org**
➤ Council of American Survey Research Organizations, 3 Upper Devon, Port Jefferson, NY 11777. Internet: **http://www.casro.org**

Psychologists

(O*NET 19-3031.01, 19-3031.02, 19-3031.03, 19-3032.00)

Significant Points

● More than 1 out of 4 psychologists are self-employed, nearly four times the average for professional workers.

● Most specialists, including clinical and counseling psychologists, need a doctoral degree; school and industrial-organizational psychologists need a master's degree.

● Opportunities in psychology are limited for those with only a bachelor's degree.

Nature of the Work

Psychologists study the human mind and human behavior. Research psychologists investigate the physical, cognitive, emotional, or social aspects of human behavior. Psychologists in health service provider fields provide mental health care in hospitals, clinics, schools, or private settings. Psychologists employed in applied settings such as business, industry, government or non-profits provide training, conduct research, design systems, and act as advocates for psychology.

Like other social scientists, psychologists formulate hypotheses and collect data to test their validity. Research methods vary depending on the topic under study. Psychologists sometimes gather information through controlled laboratory experiments or by administering personality, performance, aptitude, and intelligence tests. Other methods include observation, interviews, questionnaires, clinical studies, and surveys.

Psychologists apply their knowledge to a wide range of endeavors, including health and human services, management, education, law, and sports. In addition to working in a variety of settings, psychologists usually specialize in one of a number of different areas.

Clinical psychologists—who constitute the largest specialty—most often work in counseling centers, independent or group practices, hospitals, or clinics. They help mentally and emotionally disturbed clients adjust to life and may help medical and surgical patients deal with illnesses or injuries. Some clinical psychologists work in physical rehabilitation settings, treating patients with spinal cord injuries, chronic pain or illness, stroke, arthritis, and neurological conditions. Others help people deal with times of personal crisis, such as divorce or the death of a loved one.

Clinical psychologists often interview patients and give diagnostic tests. They may provide individual, family, or group psychotherapy, and design and implement behavior modification programs. Some clinical psychologists collaborate with physicians and other specialists to develop and implement treatment and intervention programs that patients can understand and comply with. Other clinical psychologists work in universities and medical schools, where they train graduate students in the delivery of mental health and behavioral medicine services. Some administer community mental health programs.

Areas of specialization within clinical psychology include health psychology, neuropsychology, and geropsychology. *Health psychologists* promote good health through health maintenance counseling programs designed to help people achieve goals, such as to stop smoking or lose weight. *Neuropsychologists* study the relation between the brain and behavior. They often work in stroke and head injury programs. *Geropsychologists* deal with the special problems faced by the elderly. The emergence and growth of these specialties reflects the increasing participation of psychologists in providing direct services to special patient populations.

Often, clinical psychologists will consult with other medical personnel regarding the best treatment for patients, especially treatment that includes medications. Clinical psychologists generally are not permitted to prescribe medications to treat patients; only psychiatrists and other medical doctors may prescribe medications. (See the statement on physicians and surgeons elsewhere in the *Handbook.*) However, one State, New Mexico, has passed legislation allowing clinical psychologists who undergo additional training to prescribe medication, and similar proposals have been made in additional States.

Counseling psychologists use various techniques, including interviewing and testing, to advise people on how to deal with problems of everyday living. They work in settings such as university counseling centers, hospitals, and individual or group practices. (Also see the statements on counselors and social workers elsewhere in the *Handbook.*)

School psychologists work in elementary and secondary schools or school district offices to resolve students' learning and behavior problems. They collaborate with teachers, parents, and school personnel to improve classroom management strategies or parenting skills, counter substance abuse, work with students with disabilities or gifted and talented students, and improve teaching and learning strategies. They may evaluate the effectiveness of academic programs, behavior management procedures, and other services provided in the school setting.

Industrial-organizational psychologists apply psychological principles and research methods to the workplace in the interest of improving productivity and the quality of worklife. They also are involved in research on management and marketing problems. They conduct applicant screening, training and development, counseling, and organizational development and analysis. An industrial psychologist might work with management to reorganize the work setting to improve productivity or quality of life in the workplace. They frequently act as consultants, brought in by management in order to solve a particular problem.

Developmental psychologists study the physiological, cognitive, and social development that takes place throughout life. Some specialize in behavior during infancy, childhood, and adolescence, or changes that occur during maturity or old age. They also may study developmental disabilities and their effects. Increasingly, research is developing ways to help elderly people remain independent as long as possible.

Social psychologists examine people's interactions with others and with the social environment. They work in organizational consultation, marketing research, systems design, or other applied psychology fields. Prominent areas of study include group behavior, leadership, attitudes, and perception.

Experimental or *research psychologists* work in university and private research centers and in business, nonprofit, and governmental organizations. They study behavior processes using human beings and animals, such as rats, monkeys, and pigeons. Prominent areas of study in experimental research include motivation, thought, attention, learning and memory, sensory and perceptual processes, effects of substance abuse, and genetic and neurological factors affecting behavior.

Working Conditions

A psychologist's subfield and place of employment determine working conditions. Clinical, school, and counseling psychologists in private practice have their own offices and set their own hours. However, they often offer evening and weekend hours to accommodate their clients. Those employed in hospitals, nursing homes, and other health facilities may work shifts including evenings and weekends, while those who work in schools and clinics generally work regular hours.

Psychologists employed as faculty by colleges and universities divide their time between teaching and research and also may have administrative responsibilities. Many have part-time consulting practices. Most psychologists in government and industry have structured schedules.

Increasingly, many psychologists work as part of a team and consult with other psychologists and professionals. Many experience pressures due to deadlines, tight schedules, and overtime work. Their routine may be interrupted frequently. Travel usually is required, in order to attend conferences or conduct research.

Employment

Psychologists held about 139,000 jobs in 2002. Educational institutions employed about 3 out of 10 salaried psychologists in positions other than teaching, such as counseling, testing, research, and administration. Three out of 10 were employed in health care, primarily in offices of mental health practitioners and in outpatient care facilities, private hospitals, nursing and residential care facilities, and individual and family service organizations. Government agencies at the State and local levels employed 1 in 10 psychologists, primarily in public hospitals, clinics, correctional facilities, and other settings. Some psychologists work in, research organizations, management consulting firms, marketing research firms, religious organizations, and other businesses.

After several years of experience, some psychologists—usually those with doctoral degrees—enter private practice or set up private research or consulting firms. More than 1 out of 4 psychologists were self-employed.

In addition to the jobs described above, many psychologists held faculty positions at colleges and universities, and as high school psychology teachers. (See the statements on teachers—

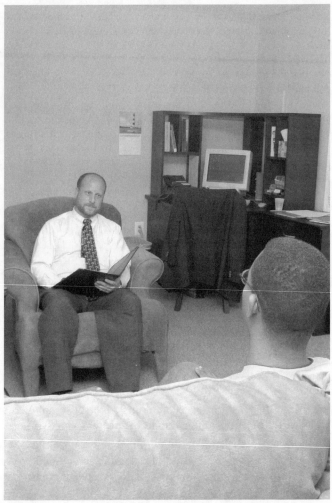

Because psychologists interact with people daily, they must possess good communication and interpersonal skills.

postsecondary and teachers—preschool, kindergarten, elementary, middle, and secondary elsewhere in the *Handbook*.)

Training, Other Qualifications, and Advancement

A doctoral degree usually is required for employment as an independent licensed clinical or counseling psychologist. Psychologists with a Ph.D. qualify for a wide range of teaching, research, clinical, and counseling positions in universities, healthcare services, elementary and secondary schools, private industry, and government. Psychologists with a Doctor of Psychology (Psy.D.) degree usually work in clinical positions or in private practices.

A doctoral degree usually requires 5 to 7 years of graduate study. The Ph.D. degree culminates in a dissertation based on original research. Courses in quantitative research methods, which include the use of computer-based analysis, are an integral part of graduate study and are necessary to complete the dissertation. The Psy.D. may be based on practical work and examinations rather than a dissertation. In clinical or counseling psychology, the requirements for the doctoral degree usually include at least a 1-year internship.

Persons with a master's degree in psychology may work as industrial-organizational psychologists or school psychologists. They also may work as psychological assistants, under the supervision of doctoral-level psychologists, and conduct research or psychological evaluations. A master's degree in psychology requires at least 2 years of full-time graduate study. Requirements usually include practical experience in an applied setting and a master's thesis based on an original research project. Competition for admission to graduate programs is keen. Some universities require applicants to have an undergraduate major in psychology. Others prefer only coursework in basic psychology with courses in the biological, physical, and social sciences; and statistics and mathematics.

A bachelor's degree in psychology qualifies a person to assist psychologists and other professionals in community mental health centers, vocational rehabilitation offices, and correctional programs. They may work as research or administrative assistants or become sales or management trainees in business. Some work as technicians in related fields, such as marketing research.

In the Federal Government, candidates having at least 24 semester hours in psychology and one course in statistics qualify for entry-level positions. However, competition for these jobs is keen because this is one of the few areas in which one can work as a psychologist without an advanced degree.

The American Psychological Association (APA) presently accredits doctoral training programs in clinical, counseling, and school psychology. The National Council for Accreditation of Teacher Education, with the assistance of the National Association of School Psychologists, also is involved in the accreditation of advanced degree programs in school psychology. The APA also accredits institutions that provide internships for doctoral students in school, clinical, and counseling psychology.

Psychologists in independent practice or those who offer any type of patient care—including clinical, counseling, and school psychologists—must meet certification or licensing requirements in all States and the District of Columbia. Licensing laws vary by State and by type of position and require licensed or certified psychologists to limit their practice to areas in which they have developed professional competence through training and experience. Clinical and counseling psychologists usually require a doctorate in psychology, completion of an approved internship, and 1 to 2 years of professional experience. In addition, all States require that applicants pass an examination. Most State licensing boards administer a standardized test, and many supplement that with additional oral or essay questions. Most States certify those with a master's degree as school psychologists after completion of an internship. Some States require continuing education for license renewal.

The National Association of School Psychologists (NASP) awards the Nationally Certified School Psychologist (NCSP) designation, which recognizes professional competency in school psychology at a national level, rather than at a State level. Currently, 22 States recognize the NCSP and allow those with the certification to transfer credentials from one State to another without taking a new State certification exam. In those States that recognize the NCSP, the requirements for State licensure and the NCSP often are the same or similar. Requirements for the NCSP include completion of 60 graduate semester hours in school psychology; a 1,200-hour internship, 600 hours of which must be completed in a school setting; and a passing score on the National School Psychology Examination.

The American Board of Professional Psychology (ABPP) recognizes professional achievement by awarding specialty certification, primarily in clinical psychology, clinical neuropsychology, and counseling, forensic, industrial-organizational, and school psychology. Candidates for ABPP certification need a doctorate in psychology, postdoctoral training in their specialty, 5 years of experience, professional endorsements, and a passing grade on an examination.

Aspiring psychologists who are interested in direct patient care must be emotionally stable, mature, and able to deal effectively with people. Sensitivity, compassion, good communication skills, and the ability to lead and inspire others are particularly important qualities for persons wishing to do clinical work and counseling. Research psychologists should be able to do detailed work independently and as part of a team. Patience and perseverance are vital qualities because achieving results from psychological treatment of patients or from research usually takes a long time.

Job Outlook

Overall employment of psychologists is expected to grow faster than the average for all occupations through 2012, due to increased demand for psychological services in schools, hospitals, social service agencies, mental health centers, substance abuse treatment clinics, consulting firms, and private companies. Clinical, counseling, and school psychologists will grow faster than the average, while industrial-organizational psychologists will have average growth.

Among the specialties in this field, school psychologists may enjoy the best job opportunities. Growing awareness of how students' mental health and behavioral problems, such as bullying, affect learning is increasing demand for school psychologists to offer student counseling and mental health services. Clinical and counseling psychologists will be needed to help people deal with depression and other mental disorders, marriage and family problems, job stress, and addiction. The rise in healthcare costs associated with unhealthy lifestyles, such as smoking, alcoholism, and obesity, has made prevention and treatment more critical. The increase in the number of employee assistance programs, which help workers deal with personal problems, also should spur job growth in clinical and counseling specialties. Industrial-organizational psychologists will be in demand to help to boost worker productivity and retention rates in a wide range of businesses. Industrial-organizational psychologists will help companies deal with issues such as workplace diversity and antidiscrimination policies. Companies also will use psychologists' expertise in survey design, analysis, and research to develop tools for marketing evaluation and statistical analysis.

Demand should be particularly strong for persons holding doctorates from leading universities in applied specialties, such as counseling, health, and school psychology. Psychologists with extensive training in quantitative research methods and computer science may have a competitive edge over applicants without this background.

Master's degree holders in fields other than school or industrial-organizational psychology will face keen competition for jobs, because of the limited number of positions that require only a master's degree. Master's degree holders may find jobs as psychological assistants or counselors, providing mental health services under the direct supervision of a licensed psychologist. Still others may find jobs involving research and data collection and analysis in universities, government, or private companies.

Opportunities directly related to psychology will be limited for bachelor's degree holders. Some may find jobs as assistants in rehabilitation centers, or in other jobs involving data collection and analysis. Those who meet State certification requirements may become high school psychology teachers.

Earnings

Median annual earnings of wage and salary clinical, counseling, and school psychologists in 2002 were $51,170. The middle 50 percent earned between $38,560 and $66,970. The lowest 10 percent earned less than $30,090, and the highest 10 percent earned more than $87,060. Median annual earnings in the industries employing the largest numbers of clinical, counseling, and school psychologists in 2002 were as follows:

Offices of other health practitioners	$59,600
Elementary and secondary schools	54,480
Offices of physicians	51,140
Outpatient care centers	44,010
Individual and family services	37,490

Median annual earnings of wage and salary industrial-organizational psychologists in 2002 were $63,710. The middle 50 percent earned between $48,540 and $81,880. The lowest 10 percent earned less than $36,620, and the highest 10 percent earned more than $112,660.

Related Occupations

Psychologists are trained to conduct research and teach, evaluate, counsel, and advise individuals and groups with special needs. Others who do this kind of work include clergy, counselors, physicians and surgeons, social workers, sociologists, and special education teachers.

Sources of Additional Information

For information on careers, educational requirements, financial assistance, and licensing in all fields of psychology, contact:
➤ American Psychological Association, 750 1st St. NE., Washington, DC 20002. Internet: **http://www.apa.org**

For information on careers, educational requirements, certification, and licensing of school psychologists, contact:
➤ National Association of School Psychologists, 4340 East West Hwy., Suite 402, Bethesda, MD 20814. Internet: **http://www.nasponline.org**

Information about State licensing requirements is available from:
➤ Association of State and Provincial Psychology Boards, P.O. Box 241245, Montgomery, AL 36124-1245. Internet: **http://www.asppb.org**

Information about psychology specialty certifications is available from:
➤ American Board of Professional Psychology, Inc., 514 East Capitol Ave., Jefferson City, MO 65101. Internet: **http://www.abpp.org**

Urban and Regional Planners

(O*NET 19-3051.00)

Significant Points

● Local governments employ 7 out of 10 urban and regional planners.

● Most entry-level jobs require a master's degree; bachelor's degree holders may find some entry-level positions, but advancement opportunities are limited.

● Most new jobs will arise in affluent, rapidly growing urban and suburban communities.

Nature of the Work

Planners develop long-term and short-term plans to use land for the growth and revitalization of urban, suburban, and rural communities, while helping local officials make decisions concerning social, economic, and environmental problems. Because local governments employ the majority of urban and regional planners, they often are referred to as community, regional, or city planners.

Planners promote the best use of a community's land and resources for residential, commercial, institutional, and recreational purposes. Planners may be involved in various other activities, including making decisions relating to establishing alternative public transportation systems, developing resources, and protecting ecologically sensitive regions. Urban and regional planners address issues such as traffic congestion, air pollution, and the effects of growth and change on a community. They may formulate plans relating to the construction of new school buildings, public housing, or other kinds of infrastructure. Some planners are involved in environmental issues ranging from pollution control to wetland preservation, forest conservation, and the location of new landfills. Planners also may be involved in drafting legislation on environmental, social, and economic issues, such as sheltering the homeless, planning a new park, or meeting the demand for new correctional facilities.

Planners examine proposed community facilities, such as schools, to be sure that these facilities will meet the changing demands placed upon them over time. They keep abreast of economic and legal issues involved in zoning codes, building codes, and environmental regulations. They ensure that builders and developers follow these codes and regulations. Planners also deal with land-use issues created by population movements. For example, as suburban growth and economic development create more new jobs outside cities, the need for public transportation that enables workers to get to those jobs increases. In response, planners develop transportation models and explain their details to planning boards and the general public.

Before preparing plans for community development, planners report on the current use of land for residential, business, and community purposes. Their reports include information on the location and capacity of streets, highways, airports, water and sewer lines, schools, libraries, and cultural and recreational sites. They also provide data on the types of industries in the community, the characteristics of the population, and employment and economic trends. Using this information, along with input from citizens' advisory committees, planners design the layout of land uses for buildings and other facilities such as subway lines and stations. Planners prepare reports showing how their programs can be carried out and what they will cost.

Planners use computers to record and analyze information and to prepare reports and recommendations for government executives and others. Computer databases, spreadsheets, and analytical techniques are widely utilized to project program costs and forecast future trends in employment, housing, transportation, or population. Computerized geographic information systems enable planners to map land areas, to overlay maps with geographic variables such as population density, and to combine or manipulate geographic information to produce alternative plans for land use or development.

Urban and regional planners help to determine the locations of housing developments, businesses, schools, and hospitals in a community.

Urban and regional planners often confer with land developers, civic leaders, and public officials and may function as mediators in community disputes, presenting alternatives that are acceptable to opposing parties. Planners may prepare material for community relations programs, speak at civic meetings, and appear before legislative committees and elected officials to explain and defend their proposals.

In large organizations, planners usually specialize in a single area, such as transportation, demography, housing, historic preservation, urban design, environmental and regulatory issues, or economic development. In small organizations, planners do various kinds of planning.

Working Conditions

Urban and regional planners often travel to inspect the features of land under consideration for development or regulation, including its current use and the types of structures on it. Some local government planners involved in site development inspections spend most of their time in the field. Although most planners have a scheduled 40-hour workweek, they frequently attend evening or weekend meetings or public hearings with citizens' groups. Planners may experience the pressure of deadlines and tight work schedules, as well as political pressure generated by interest groups affected by proposals related to urban development and land use.

Employment

Urban and regional planners held about 32,000 jobs in 2002. About 7 out of 10 were employed by local governments. Companies involved with architectural, engineering, and related services, as well as management, scientific, and technical consulting services, employ an increasing proportion of planners in the private sector. Others are employed in State government agencies dealing with housing, transportation, or environmental protection, and a small number work for the Federal Government.

Training, Other Qualifications, and Advancement

For jobs as urban and regional planners, employers prefer workers who have advanced training. Most entry-level jobs in Fed-

eral, State, and local government agencies require a master's degree from an accredited program in urban or regional planning or a master's degree in a related field, such as urban design or geography. A bachelor's degree from an accredited planning program, coupled with a master's degree in architecture, landscape architecture, or civil engineering, is good preparation for entry-level planning jobs in various areas, including urban design, transportation, and the environment. A master's degree from an accredited planning program provides the best training for a wide range of planning fields. Although graduates from one of the limited number of accredited bachelor's degree programs qualify for some entry-level positions, their advancement opportunities often are limited, unless they acquire an advanced degree.

Courses in related disciplines, such as architecture, law, earth sciences, demography, economics, finance, health administration, geographic information systems, and management, are highly recommended. Because familiarity with computer models and statistical techniques is important, courses in statistics and computer science also are recommended.

In 2003, 67 colleges and universities offered an accredited master's degree program, and 13 offered an accredited bachelor's degree program, in urban or regional planning. Accreditation for these programs is from the Planning Accreditation Board, which consists of representatives of the American Institute of Certified Planners, the American Planning Association, and the Association of Collegiate Schools of Planning. Most graduate programs in planning require a minimum of 2 years of study.

Specializations most commonly offered by planning schools are environmental planning, land use and comprehensive planning, economic development, housing, historic preservation, and social planning. Other popular offerings include community development, transportation, and urban design. Graduate students spend considerable time in studios, workshops, and laboratory courses learning to analyze and solve planning problems. They often are required to work in a planning office part time or during the summer. Local government planning offices frequently offer students internships, providing experience that proves invaluable in obtaining a full-time planning position after graduation.

The American Institute of Certified Planners, a professional institute within the American Planning Association, grants certification to individuals who have the appropriate combination of education and professional experience and who pass an examination. Certification may be helpful for promotion.

Planners must be able to think in terms of spatial relationships and visualize the effects of their plans and designs. They should be flexible and be able to reconcile different viewpoints and make constructive policy recommendations. The ability to communicate effectively, both orally and in writing, is necessary for anyone interested in this field.

After a few years of experience, planners may advance to assignments requiring a high degree of independent judgment, such as designing the physical layout of a large development or recommending policy and budget options. Some public-sector planners are promoted to community planning director and spend a great deal of time meeting with officials, speaking to civic groups, and supervising a staff. Further advancement occurs through a transfer to a larger jurisdiction with more complex problems and greater responsibilities or into related occupations, such as director of community or director of economic development.

Job Outlook
Employment of urban and regional planners is expected to grow about as fast as the average for all occupations through 2012. Employment growth will be driven by the need for State and local governments to provide public services such as regulation of commercial development, the environment, transportation, housing, and land use and development for an expanding population. Nongovernmental initiatives dealing with historic preservation and redevelopment will provide additional openings. Some job openings also will arise from the need to replace experienced planners who transfer to other occupations, retire, or leave the labor force for other reasons. Graduates with a degree from an accredited program should have an advantage in the job market.

Most planners work for local governments with limited resources and many demands for services. When communities need to cut expenditures, planning services may be cut before basic services, such as police, firefighting, and education. Budget constraints could limit job growth in government; as a result, the number of openings for consulting positions in private industry is expected to grow more rapidly than the number of openings in government.

Most new jobs for urban and regional planners will arise in affluent, rapidly expanding communities. Local governments need planners to address an array of problems associated with population growth. For example, new housing developments require roads, sewer systems, fire stations, schools, libraries, and recreation facilities that must be planned for in the midst of a consideration of budgetary constraints. Smalltown chambers of commerce, economic development authorities, and tourism bureaus may hire planners, preferably with some background in marketing and public relations.

Earnings
Median annual earnings of urban and regional planners were $49,880 in 2002. The middle 50 percent earned between $39,210 and $62,710. The lowest 10 percent earned less than $31,830, and the highest 10 percent earned more than $76,700. Median annual earnings in local government, the industry employing the largest number of urban and regional planners, were $48,950.

Related Occupations
Urban and regional planners develop plans for the growth of urban, suburban, and rural communities. Others whose work is similar include architects, civil engineers, environmental engineers, landscape architects, and geographers.

Sources of Additional Information
Information on careers, salaries, and certification in urban and regional planning is available from
➤ American Planning Association, Education Division, 122 South Michigan Ave., Suite 1600, Chicago, IL 60603-6107. Internet: **http://www.planning.org**
➤ Information on accredited urban and regional planning programs is available from
➤ Association of Collegiate Schools of Planning, 6311 Mallard Trace, Tallahassee, FL 32312. Internet: **http://www.acsp.org**

Social Scientists, Other

(O*NET 19-3041.00, 19-3091.01, 19-3091.02, 19-3092.00, 19-3093.00, 19-3094.00)

Significant Points

● The educational attainment of social scientists is among the highest of all occupations.

● Anthropologists and archaeologists, geographers, and sociologists will experience average growth, but slower-than-average growth is expected for historians and political scientists because they enjoy fewer opportunities outside of government and academic settings.

● Competition for jobs will remain keen for all specialties because many of these social scientists compete for jobs with other workers, such as psychologists, statisticians, or market and survey researchers.

Nature of the Work
The major social science occupations covered in this statement include anthropologists, archaeologists, geographers, historians, political scientists, and sociologists. (Economists, market and survey researchers, psychologists, and urban and regional planners are covered elsewhere in the *Handbook*.)

Social scientists study all aspects of society—from past events and achievements to human behavior and relationships among groups. Their research provides insights that help us understand different ways in which individuals and groups make decisions, exercise power, and respond to change. Through their studies and analyses, social scientists suggest solutions to social, business, personal, governmental, and environmental problems.

Research is a major activity of many social scientists, who use various methods to assemble facts and construct theories. Applied research usually is designed to produce information that will enable people to make better decisions or manage their affairs more effectively. Interviews and surveys are widely used to collect facts, opinions, or other information. Information collection takes many forms, including living and working among the population being studied; performing field investigations; analyzing historical records and documents; experimenting with human or animal subjects in a laboratory; administering standardized tests and questionnaires; and preparing and interpreting maps and computer graphics. The work of specialists in social science varies greatly, although specialists in one field may find that their research overlaps work being conducted in another discipline.

Anthropologists study the origin and the physical, social, and cultural development and behavior of humans. They may study the way of life, archaeological remains, language, or physical characteristics of people in various parts of the world. Some compare the customs, values, and social patterns of different cultures. Anthropologists usually concentrate in sociocultural anthropology, archaeology, linguistics, or biophysical anthropology. Sociocultural anthropologists study the customs, cultures, and social lives of groups in settings that vary from unindustrialized societies to modern urban centers.

Archaeologists recover and examine material evidence, such as ruins, tools, and pottery remaining from past human cultures, in order to determine the history, customs, and living habits of earlier civilizations. Linguistic anthropologists study the role of, and changes in, language over time in various cultures. Biophysical anthropologists study the evolution of the human body, look for the earliest evidences of human life, and analyze how culture and biology influence one another. Most anthropologists specialize in a particular region of the world.

Geographers analyze distributions of physical and cultural phenomena on local, regional, continental, and global scales. Economic geographers study the distribution of resources and economic activities. Political geographers are concerned with the relationship of geography to political phenomena, whereas cultural geographers study the geography of cultural phenomena. Physical geographers study variations in climate, vegetation, soil, and landforms and their implications for human activity. Urban and transportation geographers study cities and metropolitan areas, while regional geographers study the physical, economic, political, and cultural characteristics of regions ranging in size from a congressional district to entire continents. Medical geographers study health-care delivery systems, epidemiology (the study of the causes and control of epidemics), and the effect of the environment on health. (Some occupational classification systems include geographers under physical scientists rather than social scientists.)

Increasingly, geographers are utilizing geographic information systems (GIS) technology to create computerized maps that can track information such as population growth, traffic patterns, environmental hazards, natural resources, and weather patterns. They then use the information to advise governments on the development of houses, roads, or landfills.

Historians research, analyze, and interpret the past. They use many sources of information in their research, including government and institutional records, newspapers and other periodicals, photographs, interviews, films, and unpublished manuscripts such as personal diaries and letters. Historians usually specialize in a country or region, a particular period, or a particular field, such as social, intellectual, cultural, political, or diplomatic history. Biographers collect detailed information on individuals. Other historians help study and preserve archival materials, artifacts, and historic buildings and sites.

Political scientists study the origin, development, and operation of political systems and public policy. They conduct research on a wide range of subjects, such as relations between the United States and other countries, the institutions and political life of nations, the politics of small towns or a major metropolis, and the decisions of the U.S. Supreme Court. Studying topics such as public opinion, political decisionmaking, ideology, and public policy, they analyze the structure and operation of governments, as well as various political entities. Depending on the topic, a political scientist might conduct a public-opinion survey, analyze election results, analyze public documents, or interview public officials.

Sociologists study society and social behavior by examining the groups and social institutions people form, as well as various social, religious, political, and business organizations. They also study the behavior of, and interaction among, groups, trace their origin and growth, and analyze the influence of group activities on individual members. Sociologists are concerned with the characteristics of social groups, organizations, and institutions; the ways individuals are affected by each other and by the groups to which they belong; and the effect of social traits such as sex, age, or race on a person's daily life. The results of sociological research aid educators, lawmakers, administra-

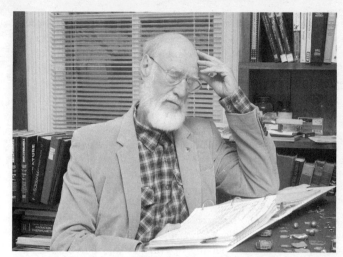
Many social scientists conduct research and write reports.

tors, and others interested in resolving social problems and formulating public policy.

Most sociologists work in one or more specialties, such as social organization, stratification, and mobility; racial and ethnic relations; education; family; social psychology; urban, rural, political, and comparative sociology; sex roles and relations; demography; gerontology; criminology; and sociological practice.

Working Conditions
Most social scientists have regular hours. Generally working behind a desk, either alone or in collaboration with other social scientists, they read and write research articles or reports. Many experience the pressures of writing and publishing, as well as those associated with deadlines and tight schedules, and sometimes they must work overtime, for which they usually are not remunerated. Social scientists often work as an integral part of a research team, among whose members good communications skills are important. Travel may be necessary to collect information or attend meetings. Social scientists on foreign assignment must adjust to unfamiliar cultures, climates, and languages.

Some social scientists do fieldwork. For example, anthropologists, archaeologists, and geographers may travel to remote areas, live among the people they study, learn their languages, and stay for long periods at the site of their investigations. They may work under rugged conditions, and their work may involve strenuous physical exertion.

Social scientists employed by colleges and universities usually have flexible work schedules, often dividing their time among teaching, research, writing, consulting, or administrative responsibilities.

Employment
Social scientists held about 17,000 jobs in 2002. Many worked as researchers, administrators, and counselors for a wide range of employers, including Federal, State, and local governments; educational institutions; social assistance agencies; scientific research and development firms; and management, scientific, and technical consulting firms. Other employers included architectural, engineering, and related firms; civic and social associations; museums; and business, professional, labor, political, and similar organizations.

Many individuals with training in a social science discipline teach in colleges and universities and in secondary and elementary schools. (For more information, see teachers—postsecondary and teachers—preschool, kindergarten, elementary, middle, and secondary elsewhere in the *Handbook*.) The proportion of social scientists who teach varies by specialty—for example, the academic world usually is a more important source of jobs for graduates in history than for graduates in most other social science fields.

Training, Other Qualifications, and Advancement

The educational attainment of social scientists is among the highest of all occupations. The Ph.D. or equivalent degree is a minimum requirement for most positions in colleges and universities and is important for advancement to many top-level nonacademic research and administrative posts. Graduates with master's degrees in applied specialties usually have better opportunities outside of colleges and universities, although the situation varies by field. Graduates with a master's degree in a social science may qualify for teaching positions in community colleges. Bachelor's degree holders have limited opportunities and, in most social science occupations, do not qualify for "professional" positions. The bachelor's degree does, however, provide a suitable background for many different kinds of entry-level jobs, such as research assistant, administrative aide, or management or sales trainee. With the addition of sufficient education courses, social science graduates also can qualify for teaching positions in secondary and elementary schools.

Training in statistics and mathematics is essential for many social scientists. Mathematical and quantitative research methods increasingly are being used in geography, political science, and other fields. The ability to utilize computers for research purposes is mandatory in most disciplines. Most geographers also will need to be familiar with GIS technology.

Many social science students find that internships or field experience is beneficial. Numerous local museums, historical societies, government agencies, and other organizations offer internships or volunteer research opportunities. A few archeological field schools instruct future anthropologists, archeologists, and historians in how to excavate historical sites.

Depending on their jobs, social scientists may need a wide range of personal characteristics. Because they constantly seek new information about people, things, and ideas, intellectual curiosity and creativity are fundamental personal traits. The ability to think logically and methodically is important to a political scientist comparing, for example, the merits of various forms of government. Objectivity, openmindedness, and systematic work habits are important in all kinds of social science research. Perseverance is essential for an anthropologist, who might spend years accumulating artifacts from an ancient civilization. Excellent written and oral communication skills are necessary for all these professionals.

Job Outlook

Overall employment of social scientists is expected to grow about as fast as the average for all occupations through 2012. However, growth rates will vary by specialty. Anthropologists and archaeologists, geographers, and sociologists will experience average employment growth. However, employment of historians and political scientists will grow more slowly than average because these workers enjoy fewer opportunities outside of government and academic settings.

Despite projected job growth, competition will remain keen for social science positions. Many jobs in policy, research, or marketing, for which social scientists qualify, are not advertised exclusively as social scientist positions. Because of the wide range of skills and knowledge possessed by social scientists discussed in this *Handbook* statement, many compete for jobs with other workers, such as market and survey researchers, psychologists, engineers, urban and regional planners, and statisticians.

A few social scientists will find opportunities as university faculty, although competition for these jobs also will remain keen. Usually, there are more graduates than available faculty positions, although retirements among faculty are expected to rise in the next few years. The growing importance and popularity of social science subjects in secondary schools is strengthening the demand for social science teachers at that level.

Anthropologists and sociologists will find opportunities performing policy research for consulting firms, nonprofit organizations, and social service agencies in such areas as crime, ethnic conflict, public health, and refugee policy. These social scientists also will be employed by various companies in product development, marketing, and advertising. Others are employed in human resources in conflict resolution and in issues relating to diverse workforces. As construction projects increase, archaeologists will be needed to perform preliminary excavations in order to preserve historical artifacts.

Geographers will have opportunities to utilize their skills to advise government, real-estate developers, utilities, and telecommunications firms on where to build new roads, buildings, power plants, and cable lines. Geographers also will advise on environmental matters, such as where to build a landfill or preserve wetland habitats. As the use of GIS technology expands, geographers will find numerous job opportunities applying GIS technology in non-traditional areas, such as emergency assistance, where GIS can track locations of ambulances, police, and fire rescue units and their proximity to the emergency. GIS technology will also be utilized in areas of growing importance, such as homeland security and defense.

Historians and political scientists also will find jobs in policy or research. Opportunities in government will be limited as government contracts out more work to the private sector or cuts research grants and funding for museums. Historians may find opportunities with historic preservation societies as public interest in preserving and restoring historical sites increases. Political scientists will be able to utilize their knowledge of political institutions to further the interests of nonprofit, political lobbying, and social organizations.

Earnings

Median annual earnings of social scientists (excluding economists, market and survey researchers, psychologists, and urban and regional planners) were $52,280 in 2002. Anthropologists and archeologists had median annual earnings of $38,620; geographers, $53,420; historians, $42,030; political scientists, $80,560; and sociologists, $53,160.

In the Federal Government, social scientists with a bachelor's degree and no experience could start at $23,442 or $29,307 a year in 2003, depending on their college records. Those with a master's degree could start at $35,519, and those with a Ph.D. degree could begin at $42,976, while some individuals with experience and an advanced degree could start at $51,508.

Beginning salaries were slightly higher in selected areas of the country where the prevailing local pay level was higher.

Related Occupations

Social scientists' duties and training outlined in this statement are similar to those of other occupations covered elsewhere in the *Handbook*, including other social science occupations—economists, market and survey researchers, psychologists, and urban and regional planners. Many social scientists conduct surveys, study social problems, teach, and work in museums, performing tasks similar to those of statisticians; counselors; social workers; teachers—postsecondary; teachers—preschool, kindergarten, elementary, middle, and secondary; and archivists, curators, and museum technicians.

Political scientists are concerned with the function of government, including the legal system, as are lawyers; paralegals; and judges, magistrates, and other judicial workers. Many political scientists analyze and report on current events, much as do news analysts, reporters, and correspondents.

Along with conservation scientists and foresters, atmospheric scientists, and environmental scientists and geoscientists, geographers are concerned with the earth's environment and natural resources. Geographers also use GIS computer technology to make maps. Other occupations with similar duties are surveyors, cartographers, photogrammetrists, and surveying technicians; and computer systems analysts, database administrators, and computer scientists.

Sources of Additional Information

Detailed information about economists and market and survey researchers, psychologists, and urban and regional planners is presented elsewhere in the *Handbook*.

For information about careers in anthropology, contact
➤ American Anthropological Association, 2200 Wilson Blvd., Suite 600, Arlington, VA 22201. Internet: **http://www.aaanet.org**

For information about careers in archaeology, contact either of the following organizations:
➤ Society for American Archaeology, 900 2nd St. NE., Suite 12, Washington, DC 20002-3557. Internet: **http://www.saa.org**
➤ Archaeological Institute of America, 656 Beacon St., Boston, MA 02215-2006. Internet: **http://www.archaeological.org**

For information about careers in geography, contact
➤ Association of American Geographers, 1710 16th St. NW., Washington, DC 20009-3198. Internet: **http://www.aag.org**

Information on careers for historians is available from
➤ American Historical Association, 400 A St. SE., Washington, DC 20003-3889. Internet: **http://www.theaha.org**

For information about careers in political science, contact either of the following sources:
➤ American Political Science Association, 1527 New Hampshire Ave. NW., Washington, DC 20036-1206. Internet: **http://www.apsanet.org**
➤ National Association of Schools of Public Affairs and Administration, 1120 G St. NW., Suite 730, Washington, DC 20005-3869. Internet: **http://www.naspaa.org**

Information about careers in sociology is available from
➤ American Sociological Association, 1307 New York Ave. NW., Suite 700, Washington, DC 20005-4712. Internet: **http://www.asanet.org**

Science Technicians

(0*NET 19-4011.01, 19-4011.02, 19-4021.00, 19-4031.00, 19-4041.01, 19-4041.02, 19-4051.01, 19-4051.02, 19-4091.00, 19-4092.00, 19-4093.00)

Significant Points

- Science technicians in production jobs can be employed on day, evening, or night shifts.

- Many employers prefer applicants who have at least 2 years of specialized training or an associate degree.

- Job opportunities are expected to be best for graduates of applied science technology programs.

- Job growth will be concentrated in pharmaceutical manufacturing, chemical manufacturing, and biotechnological research and development firms.

Nature of the Work

Science technicians use the principles and theories of science and mathematics to solve problems in research and development and to help invent and improve products and processes. However, their jobs are more practically oriented than those of scientists. Technicians set up, operate, and maintain laboratory instruments, monitor experiments, make observations, calculate and record results, and often develop conclusions. They must keep detailed logs of all of their work-related activities. Those who work in production monitor manufacturing processes and may be involved in ensuring quality by testing products for

proper proportions of ingredients, for purity, or for strength and durability.

As laboratory instrumentation and procedures have become more complex in recent years, the role of science technicians in research and development has expanded. In addition to performing routine tasks, many technicians also develop and adapt laboratory procedures to achieve the best results, interpret data, and devise solutions to problems, under the direction of scientists. Moreover, technicians must master the laboratory equipment so that they can adjust settings when necessary and recognize when equipment is malfunctioning.

The increasing use of robotics to perform many routine tasks has freed technicians to operate more sophisticated laboratory equipment. Science technicians make extensive use of computers, computer-interfaced equipment, robotics, and high-technology industrial applications, such as biological engineering.

Most science technicians specialize, learning skills and working in the same disciplines in which scientists work. Occupational titles, therefore, tend to follow the same structure as those for scientists. *Agricultural technicians* work with agricultural scientists in food, fiber, and animal research, production, and processing. Some conduct tests and experiments to improve the yield and quality of crops or to increase the resistance of plants and animals to disease, insects, or other hazards. Other agricultural technicians do animal breeding and nutrition work. *Food science technicians* assist food scientists and technologists in research and development, production technology, and quality control. For example, food science technicians may conduct tests on food additives and preservatives to ensure FDA compliance on factors such as color, texture, and nutrients. They analyze, record, and compile test results; order supplies to maintain laboratory inventory; and clean and sterilize laboratory equipment.

Biological technicians work with biologists studying living organisms. Many assist scientists who conduct medical research—helping to find a cure for cancer or AIDS, for example. Those who work in pharmaceutical companies help develop and manufacture medicinal and pharmaceutical preparations. Those working in the field of microbiology generally work as lab assistants, studying living organisms and infectious agents. Biological technicians also analyze organic substances, such as blood, food, and drugs, and some examine evidence in a forensic science laboratory. Biological technicians working in biotechnology labs use the knowledge and techniques gained from basic research by scientists, including gene splicing and recombinant DNA, and apply them in product development.

Chemical technicians work with chemists and chemical engineers, developing and using chemicals and related products and equipment. Generally, there are two types of chemical technicians—research and development technicians who work in experimental laboratories, and process control technicians who work in manufacturing or other industrial plants. Many research and development chemical technicians conduct a variety of laboratory procedures, from routine process control to complex research projects. For example, they may collect and analyze samples of air and water to monitor pollution levels or produce compounds through complex organic synthesis. Most process technicians work in manufacturing, where they test packaging for design, integrity of materials, and environmental acceptability. Often, process technicians who work in plants also focus on quality assurance: there, they monitor product quality or production processes and develop new production techniques. A few work in shipping to provide technical support and expertise for these functions.

Environmental science and protection technicians perform laboratory and field tests to monitor environmental resources and determine the contaminants and sources of pollution. They may collect samples for testing or be involved in abating, controlling, or remediating sources of environmental pollutants. Some are responsible for waste management operations, control and management of hazardous materials inventory, or general activities involving regulatory compliance.

Forensic science technicians investigate crimes by collecting and analyzing physical evidence. Often, they specialize in areas such as DNA analysis or firearm examination, performing tests on weapons or substances such as fiber, hair, tissue, or body fluids to determine significance to the investigation. They also prepare reports to document their findings and the laboratory techniques used, and may provide information and expert opinion to investigators. When criminal cases come to trial, forensic science technicians often provide testimony, as expert witnesses, on specific laboratory findings by identifying and classifying substances, materials, and other evidence collected at the crime scene.

Forest and conservation technicians compile data on the size, content, and condition of forest land tracts. These workers usually work in a forest under the supervision of a forester, conducting specific tasks such as measuring timber, supervising harvesting operations, assisting in roadbuilding operations, and locating property lines and features. They also may gather basic information, such as species and population of trees, disease

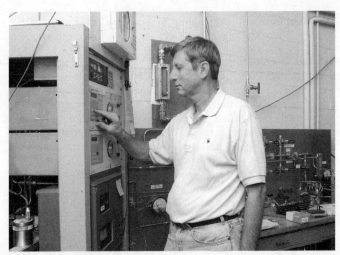

Many science technicians make extensive use of computers, computer-interfaced equipment, robotics, and high-technology industrial applications.

and insect damage, tree seedling mortality, and conditions that may cause fire danger. Forest and conservation technicians also train and lead forest and conservation workers in seasonal activities, such as planting tree seedlings, putting out forest fires, and maintaining recreational facilities.

Geological and petroleum technicians measure and record physical and geologic conditions in oil or gas wells, using advanced instruments lowered into wells or by analysis of the mud from wells. In oil and gas exploration, these technicians collect and examine geological data or test geological samples to determine petroleum and mineral and element composition using scanning electron microscopes. Some petroleum technicians, called *scouts*, collect information about oil and gas well drilling operations, geological and geophysical prospecting, and land or lease contracts.

Nuclear technicians operate nuclear test and research equipment, monitor radiation, and assist nuclear engineers and physicists in research. Some also operate remote control equipment to manipulate radioactive materials or materials to be exposed to radioactivity.

Other science technicians collect weather information or assist oceanographers.

Working Conditions

Science technicians work under a wide variety of conditions. Most work indoors, usually in laboratories, and have regular hours. Some occasionally work irregular hours to monitor experiments that cannot be completed during regular working hours. Production technicians often work in 8-hour shifts around the clock. Others, such as agricultural, forest and conservation, geological and petroleum, and environmental science and protection technicians, perform much of their work outdoors, sometimes in remote locations.

Some science technicians may be exposed to hazards from equipment, chemicals, or toxic materials. Chemical technicians sometimes work with toxic chemicals or radioactive isotopes, nuclear technicians may be exposed to radiation, and biological technicians sometimes work with disease-causing organisms or radioactive agents. Forensic science technicians often are exposed to human body fluids and firearms. However, these working conditions pose little risk, if proper safety procedures are followed. For forensic science technicians, collecting evidence from crime scenes can be distressing and unpleasant.

Employment

Science technicians held about 208,000 jobs in 2002. As indicated by the following tabulation, chemical and biological technicians accounted for over half of all jobs:

Chemical technicians	69,000
Biological technicians	48,000
Environmental science and protection technicians, including health	28,000
Agricultural and food science technicians	20,000
Forest and conservation technicians	19,000
Geological and petroleum technicians	11,000
Forensic science technicians	8,400
Nuclear technicians	5,700

Chemical technicians held jobs in a wide range of manufacturing and service industries, but were concentrated in chemical manufacturing, where they held 26,000 jobs. About 17,000 worked in professional, scientific, or technical services firms; about 17,000 biological technicians also worked in professional, scientific, or technical services firms. Most other biological technicians worked in pharmaceutical and medicine manufacturing or for Federal, State, or local governments. Significant numbers of environmental science and protection technicians also worked for State and local governments and professional, scientific, and technical services firms. Almost two-thirds of forest and conservation technicians held jobs in the Federal Government; another 20 percent worked for State governments. Around 22 percent of agricultural and food science technicians worked for food processing companies; most of the rest worked for scientific research and development services firms and State governments. Over one-fifth of all geological and petroleum technicians worked for oil and gas extraction companies, and forensic science technicians worked primarily for State and local governments.

Training, Other Qualifications, and Advancement

There are several ways to qualify for a job as a science technician. Many employers prefer applicants who have at least 2 years of specialized training or an associate degree in applied science or science-related technology. Because employers' preferences vary, however, some science technicians have a bachelor's degree in chemistry, biology, or forensic science, or have taken several science and math courses at 4-year colleges.

Many technical and community colleges offer associate degrees in a specific technology or a more general education in science and mathematics. A number of 2-year associate degree programs are designed to provide easy transfer to a 4-year college or university, if desired. Technical institutes usually offer technician training, but provide less theory and general education than do technical or community colleges. The length of programs at technical institutes varies, although 1-year certificate programs and 2-year associate degree programs are common.

More than 20 colleges or universities offer a bachelor's degree program in forensic science; more than 10 additional schools offer a bachelor's of science in chemistry, biochemistry, or genetic engineering with an emphasis on forensic science; a few additional schools offer a bachelor's of science degree with an emphasis in a specialty area, such as criminalistics, pathology, jurisprudence, odontology, toxicology, or forensic accounting.

In contrast to some other science technician positions that require only a 2-year degree, a 4-year degree in forensics science is usually necessary to work in the field. Knowledge and understanding of legal procedures also can be helpful. Forestry and conservation technicians can choose from more than 20 associate degree programs in forest technology accredited by the Society of American Foresters.

Most chemical process technicians have a 2-year degree, usually an associate degree in process technology, although in some cases a high school diploma is sufficient. They usually receive additional on-the-job training. Entry-level workers whose college training encompasses extensive hands-on experience with a variety of diagnostic laboratory equipment usually require less on-the-job training. Those with a high school diploma typically begin work as trainees under the direct supervision of a more experienced process technician. Many with only a high school diploma eventually earn a 2-year degree in process technology, often paid for by their employer.

Some schools offer cooperative-education or internship programs, allowing students the opportunity to work at a local company or other workplace while attending classes in alternate terms. Participation in such programs can significantly enhance a student's employment prospects.

Persons interested in careers as science technicians should take as many high school science and math courses as possible. Science courses taken beyond high school, in an associate or bachelor's degree program, should be laboratory oriented, with an emphasis on bench skills. A solid background in applied basic chemistry, physics, and math is vital. Because computers often are used in research and development laboratories, technicians should have strong computer skills. Communication skills also are important; technicians often are required to report their findings both orally and in writing. Additionally, technicians should be able to work well with others, because teamwork is common. Organizational ability, an eye for detail, and skill in interpreting scientific results also are important. High mechanical aptitude, attention to detail, and analytical thinking are all important characteristics of science technicians.

Prospective science technicians can acquire good career preparation through 2-year formal training programs that combine the teaching of scientific principles and theory with practical hands-on application in a laboratory setting with up-to-date equipment. Graduates of 4-year bachelor's degree programs in science who have considerable experience in laboratory-based courses, have completed internships, or have held summer jobs in laboratories also are well qualified for science technician positions and are preferred by some employers. However, those with a bachelor's degree who accept technician jobs generally cannot find employment that uses their advanced academic education.

Technicians usually begin work as trainees in routine positions, under the direct supervision of a scientist or a more experienced technician. Job candidates whose training or educational background encompasses extensive hands-on experience with a variety of laboratory equipment, including computers and related equipment, usually require a short period of on-the-job training. As they gain experience, technicians take on more responsibility and carry out assignments under only general supervision, and some eventually become supervisors. However, technicians employed at universities often have their fortunes tied to those of particular professors; when professors retire or leave, these technicians face uncertain employment prospects.

Job Outlook

Overall employment of science technicians is expected to increase about as fast as the average for all occupations through the year 2012. Continued growth of scientific and medical research, particularly research related to biotechnology, as well as the development and production of technical products, should stimulate demand for science technicians in many industries. The increase in the number of biological technicians will be about as fast as average, as the growing number of agricultural and medicinal products developed using biotechnology techniques will boost demand for these workers. Also, stronger competition among pharmaceutical companies and an aging population are expected to contribute to the need for innovative and improved drugs, further spurring demand for biological technicians. Fastest employment growth of biological technicians should occur in the pharmaceutical and medicine manufacturing industry and in scientific research and development services firms.

Job growth for chemical technicians is projected to grow more slowly than average. The chemical manufacturing industry, the major employer of chemical technicians, will experience a decline in overall employment as companies downsize and turn to outside contractors to provide specialized services. Job opportunities are expected to be more plentiful in pharmaceutical and medicine manufacturing as the public continues to demand newer and better pharmaceuticals. To meet this demand, pharmaceutical manufacturing firms are expected to continue to devote money to research and development, either through in-house teams, or, increasingly, by contracting to scientific research and development services firms, spurring employment growth of chemical technicians in that industry. An increasing focus on quality assurance will require a greater number of process technicians, further stimulating demand for these workers.

Employment of environmental science and protection technicians should grow much faster than average to help regulate waste products; to collect air, water, and soil samples for measuring levels of pollutants; to monitor compliance with environmental regulations; and to clean up contaminated sites.

There will be limited demand for forest and conservation technicians at the Federal and State government levels, leading to slower-than-average growth, due to general downsizing and reductions in timber harvesting on Federal lands. However, increased emphasis on specific conservation issues, such as environmental protection, water resources preservation, and control of exotic and invasive pests, may provide some employment opportunities.

Employment of agricultural and food science technicians should grow more slowly than average, mainly due to limited growth in agriculture and the food processing industry. However, research will still be necessary, particularly biotechnological research in the private sector, as it becomes increasingly important to balance greater agricultural output with protection and preservation of soil, water, and the ecosystem. Specifically, research will be needed to combat insects and diseases as they continue to adapt to pesticides and as soil fertility and water quality continue to need improvement.

Jobs for forensic science technicians are expected to increase about as fast as average. Crime scene technicians who work for State Public Safety Departments may experience favorable employment prospects if the number of qualified applicants remains low.

Little or no growth in employment of geological and petroleum technicians is expected because employment in the oil and gas extraction and mining industries, among the largest employers of geological and petroleum technicians, is expected to decline. Job opportunities will be more favorable in professional, scientific, and technical services firms, as geological and petroleum technicians will be needed to consult companies regarding environmental policy and Federal Government mandates, such as those requiring lower sulfur emissions.

Job opportunities are expected to be best for graduates of applied science technology programs who are well trained on equipment used in industrial and government laboratories and production facilities. As the instrumentation and techniques used in industrial research, development, and production become increasingly more complex, employers are seeking individuals with highly developed technical and communication skills.

Along with opportunities created by growth, many job openings should arise from the need to replace technicians who retire or leave the labor force for other reasons. During periods of economic recession, layoffs of science technicians may occur.

Earnings

Median hourly earnings of science technicians in 2002 were as follows:

Nuclear technicians	$28.84
Forensic science technicians	19.73
Geological and petroleum technicians	18.96
Chemical technicians	18.00
Environmental science and protection technicians, including health	16.98
Biological technicians	15.73
Forest and conservation technicians	14.90
Agricultural and food science technicians	13.74

In 2003, the average annual salary in nonsupervisory, supervisory, and managerial positions in the Federal Government was $30,440 for biological science technicians; $44,068 for physical science technicians; $55,374 for geodetic technicians; $40,781 for hydrologic technicians; and $52,585 for meteorological technicians.

Related Occupations

Other technicians who apply scientific principles at a level usually acquired in 2-year associate degree programs include engineering technicians, broadcast and sound engineering technicians and radio operators, drafters, and health technologists and technicians, especially clinical laboratory technologists and technicians, diagnostic medical sonographers, and radiologic technologists and technicians.

Sources of Additional Information

For information about a career as a chemical technician, contact:
➤ American Chemical Society, Education Division, Career Publications, 1155 16th St. NW., Washington, DC 20036. Internet: **http://www.acs.org**

For career information and a list of undergraduate, graduate, and doctoral programs in forensic sciences, contact:
➤ American Academy of Forensic Sciences, P.O. Box 669, Colorado Springs, CO, 80901. Internet: **http://www.aafs.org**

For general education information on forestry technicians and lists of schools offering education in forestry, send a self-addressed, stamped business envelope to:
➤ Society of American Foresters, 5400 Grosvenor Ln., Bethesda, MD 20814. Internet: **http://www.safnet.org**

Community and Social Services Occupations

Clergy

(0*NET 21-2011.00)

Significant Points

- Many denominations require that clergy complete a bachelor's degree and a graduate-level program of theological study; others will admit anyone who has been "called" to the vocation.

- Individuals considering a career in the clergy should realize they are choosing not only a career but also a way of life; members of the clergy typically work irregular hours and many put in longer than average work days.

- Opportunities are expected in all faiths, but in some denominations competition is likely for positions leading large urban worship groups.

Nature of the Work

Religious beliefs—such as Buddhist, Christian, Jewish, or Moslem—are significant influences in the lives of millions of Americans, and prompt many to participate in organizations that reinforce their faith. Even within a religion many denominations may exist, with each group having unique traditions and responsibilities assigned to its clergy. For example, Christianity has more than 70 denominations, while Judaism has 4 major branches, as well as groups within each branch, with diverse customs.

Clergy are religious and spiritual leaders, and teachers and interpreters of their traditions and faith. Most members of the clergy serve in a pulpit. They organize and lead regular religious services and officiate at special ceremonies, including confirmations, weddings, and funerals. They may lead worshipers in prayer, administer the sacraments, deliver sermons, and read from sacred texts such as the Bible, Torah, or Koran. When not conducting worship services, clergy organize, supervise, and lead religious education programs for their congregations. Clergy visit the sick or bereaved to provide comfort and counsel persons who are seeking religious or moral guidance or who are troubled by family or personal problems. They also may work to expand the membership of their congregations and solicit donations to support their activities and facilities.

Clergy who serve large congregations often share their duties with associates or more junior clergy. Senior clergy may spend considerable time on administrative duties. They oversee the management of buildings, order supplies, contract for services and repairs, and supervise the work of staff and volunteers. Associate or assistant members of the clergy sometimes specialize in an area of religious service, such as music, education, or youth counseling. Clergy also work with committees and officials, elected by the congregation, who guide the management of the congregation's finances and real estate.

Other members of the clergy serve their religious communities in ways that do not call for them to hold positions in congregations. Some serve as chaplains in the U.S. Armed Forces and in hospitals, while others help to carry out the missions of religious community and social services agencies. A few members of the clergy serve in administrative or teaching posts in schools at all grade levels, including seminaries.

Working Conditions

Members of the clergy typically work irregular hours and many put in longer than average work days. Those who do not work in congregational settings may have more routine schedules. In 2002, almost one-fifth of full-time clergy worked 60 or more hours a week, more than 3 times that of all workers in professional occupations. Although many of their activities are sedentary and intellectual in nature, clergy frequently are called on short notice to visit the sick, comfort the dying and their families, and provide counseling to those in need. Involvement in community, administrative, and educational activities sometimes require clergy to work evenings, early mornings, holidays, and weekends.

Because of their roles as leaders regarding spiritual and morality issues, some members of the clergy often feel obligated to address and resolve both societal problems and the personal problems of their congregants, which can lead to stress.

Training, Other Qualifications, and Advancement

Educational requirements for entry into the clergy vary greatly. Similar to other professional occupations, about 3 out of 4 members of the clergy have completed at least a bachelor's degree. Many denominations require that clergy complete a bachelor's degree and a graduate-level program of theological study; others will admit anyone who has been "called" to the vocation. Some faiths do not allow women to become clergy; however, others, mainly in Protestant churches, do. Men and women considering careers in the clergy should consult their religious leaders to verify specific entrance requirements.

Individuals considering a career in the clergy should realize they are choosing not only a career but also a way of life. In fact, most members of the clergy remain in their chosen vocation throughout their lives; in 2002, almost 10 percent of clergy were 65 or older, compared with only 3 percent of workers in all occupations.

Religious leaders must exude confidence and motivation, while remaining tolerant and able to listen to the needs of others. They should be capable of making difficult decisions, working under pressure, and living up to the moral standards set by their faith and community.

The sections that follow provide more detailed information on the three largest groups of clergy: Protestant ministers, Rabbis, and Roman Catholic priests.

Sources of Additional Information

For more information on careers in the ministry, contact the association affiliated with a particular denomination.

The following website provides links to many of these denominations. Internet:
http://www.hirr.hartsem.edu/org/faith_denominations_homepages.html

Protestant Ministers

(0*NET 21-2011.00)

Significant Points

- Entry requirements vary greatly; many denominations require a bachelor's degree followed by study at a theological seminary, whereas others have no formal educational requirements.
- Competition for positions will vary among denominations and geographic regions.

Nature of the Work

Protestant ministers lead their congregations in worship services and administer the various rites of the church, such as baptism, confirmation, and Holy Communion. The services that ministers conduct differ among the numerous Protestant denominations and even among congregations within a denomination. In many denominations, ministers follow a traditional order of worship; in others, they adapt the services to the needs of youth and other groups within the congregation. Most services include Bible readings, hymn singing, prayers, and a sermon. In some denominations, Bible readings by members of the congregation and individual testimonials constitute a large part of the service. In addition to these duties, ministers officiate at weddings, funerals, and other occasions.

Each Protestant denomination has its own hierarchical structure. Some ministers are responsible only to the congregation they serve, whereas others are assigned duties by elder ministers or by the bishops of the diocese they serve. In some denominations, ministers are reassigned to a new pastorate by a central governing body or diocese every few years.

Ministers who serve small congregations usually work personally with parishioners. Those who serve large congregations may share specific aspects of the ministry with one or more associates or assistants, such as a minister of education or a minister of music.

Employment

There are many denominations; however, most ministers are employed by the five largest Protestant bodies—Baptist, Episcopalian, Lutheran, Methodist, and Presbyterian.

Protestant ministers are trained to administer a particular denomination's unique expression of worship.

Although most ministers are located in urban areas, many serve two or more smaller congregations in less densely populated areas. Some small churches increasingly employ part-time ministers who are seminary students, retired ministers, or holders of secular jobs. Unpaid pastors serve other churches with meager funds. In addition, some churches employ specially trained members of the laity to conduct nonliturgical functions.

Training and Other Qualifications

Educational requirements for entry into the Protestant ministry vary greatly. Many denominations require, or at least strongly prefer, a bachelor's degree followed by study at a theological seminary. However, some denominations have no formal educational requirements, and others ordain persons having various types of training from Bible colleges or liberal arts colleges. Many denominations now allow women to be ordained, but some do not. Persons considering a career in the ministry should first verify the ministerial requirements with their particular denomination.

In general, each large denomination has its own schools of theology that reflect its particular doctrine, interests, and needs. However, many of these schools are open to students from other denominations. Several interdenominational schools associated with universities give both undergraduate and graduate training covering a wide range of theological points of view.

In 2002, the Association of Theological Schools in the United States and Canada accredited 216 Protestant denominational theological schools. These schools only admit students who have received a bachelor's degree or its equivalent from an accredited college. After college graduation, many denominations require a 3-year course of professional study in one of these accredited schools, or seminaries, for the degree of Master of Divinity.

The standard curriculum for accredited theological schools consists of four major categories: Biblical studies, church history, theology and ethics, and practical theology. Other subjects taught include sociology and anthropology, comparative religions, spiritual formation, religion and the arts, and speech, among others. Many accredited schools require that students work under the supervision of a faculty member or experienced minister. Some institutions offer Doctor of Ministry degrees to students who have completed additional study—usually 2 or more years—and served at least 2 years as a minister. Scholarships and loans often are available for students of theological institutions.

Persons who have denominational qualifications for the ministry usually are ordained after graduation from a seminary or after serving a probationary pastoral period. Denominations that do not require seminary training ordain clergy at various appointed times. Some churches ordain ministers with only a high school education.

Women and men entering the clergy often begin their careers as pastors of small congregations or as assistant pastors in large churches. Pastor positions in large metropolitan areas or in large congregations often require many years of experience.

Job Outlook

Job opportunities as Protestant ministers should be best for graduates of theological schools. The degree of competition for positions will vary among denominations and geographic regions. For example, relatively favorable prospects are expected for ministers in evangelical churches. Competition, however, will be keen for responsible positions serving large, urban congregations. Ministers willing to work part time or for small, rural congregations should have better opportunities. Many job openings will stem from the need to replace ministers who retire, die, or leave the ministry.

For newly ordained Protestant ministers who are unable to find parish positions, employment alternatives include working in youth counseling, family relations, and social welfare organizations; teaching in religious educational institutions; or serving as chaplains in the Armed Forces, hospitals, universities, and correctional institutions.

Earnings
Salaries of Protestant clergy vary substantially, depending on experience, denomination, size and wealth of the congregation, and geographic location. For example, some denominations tie a minister's pay to the average pay of the congregation or the community. As a result, ministers serving larger, wealthier congregations often earned significantly higher salaries than those in smaller, less affluent areas or congregations. Ministers with modest salaries sometimes earn additional income from employment in secular occupations.

Sources of Additional Information
Persons who are interested in entering the Protestant ministry should seek the counsel of a minister or church guidance worker. Theological schools can supply information on admission requirements. For information on special requirements for ordination, prospective ministers also should contact the ordination supervision body of their particular denomination.

Rabbis

(0*NET 21-2011.00)

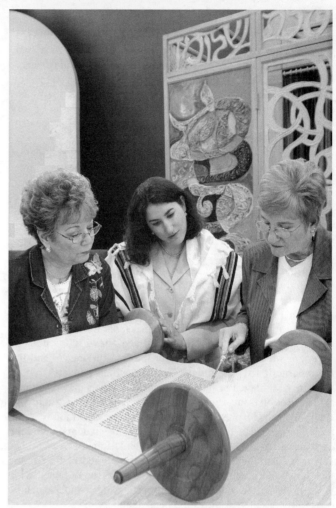

Newly ordained rabbis often begin as spiritual leaders of small congregations or as assistants to more experienced rabbis.

Significant Points

- Ordination usually requires completion of a college degree followed by a 4- to 6-year program at a Jewish seminary.

- Job opportunities for rabbis are expected in all four major branches of Judaism through the year 2012.

Nature of the Work
Rabbis serve Orthodox, Conservative, Reform, Reconstructionist, and unaffiliated Jewish congregations. Regardless of the branch of Judaism they serve or their individual points of view, all rabbis preserve the substance of Jewish religious worship. Congregations differ in the extent to which they follow the traditional form of worship—for example, in the wearing of head coverings, in the use of Hebrew as the language of prayer, and in the use of instrumental music or a choir. Additionally, the format of the worship service and, therefore, the ritual that the rabbi uses may vary even among congregations belonging to the same branch of Judaism.

Rabbis have greater independence in religious expression than other clergy, because of the absence of a formal religious hierarchy in Judaism. Instead, rabbis are responsible directly to the board of trustees of the congregation they serve. Those serving large congregations may spend considerable time in administrative duties, working with their staffs and committees.

Large congregations frequently have associate or assistant rabbis, who often serve as educational directors. All rabbis play a role in community relations. For example, many rabbis serve on committees, alongside business and civic leaders in their communities to help find solutions to local problems.

Rabbis also may write for religious and lay publications and teach in theological seminaries, colleges, and universities.

Employment
Although the majority of rabbis served congregations representing the four main branches of Judaism, many rabbis functioned in other settings. Some taught in Jewish studies programs at colleges and universities, whereas others served as chaplains in hospitals, colleges, or the military. Additionally, some rabbis held positions in one of the many social service or Jewish community agencies.

Although rabbis serve Jewish communities throughout the Nation, they are concentrated in major metropolitan areas with large Jewish populations.

Training, Other Qualifications, and Advancement
To become eligible for ordination as a rabbi, a student must complete a course of study in a seminary. Entrance requirements and the curriculum depend upon the branch of Judaism with which the seminary is associated. Most seminaries require applicants to be college graduates.

Jewish seminaries typically take 5 years for completion of studies, with an additional preparatory year required for students without sufficient grounding in Hebrew and Jewish studies. In addition to the core academic program, training generally includes fieldwork and internships providing hands-on experience and, in some cases, study in Jerusalem. Seminary graduates are awarded the title Rabbi and earn the Master of Arts in Hebrew Letters degree. After more advanced study, some earn the Doctor of Hebrew Letters degree.

In general, the curricula of Jewish theological seminaries provide students with a comprehensive knowledge of the Bible, the Torah, rabbinic literature, Jewish history, Hebrew, theology, and courses in education, pastoral psychology, and public speaking. Students receive extensive practical training in dealing with social problems in the community. Training for alternatives to the pulpit, such as leadership in community services and religious education, is increasingly stressed. Some seminaries grant advanced academic degrees in such fields as biblical and Talmudic research. All Jewish theological seminaries make scholarships and loans available.

Major rabbinical seminaries include the Jewish Theological Seminary of America, which educates rabbis for the Conservative branch; the Hebrew Union College—Jewish Institute of Religion, which educates rabbis for the Reform branch; and the Reconstructionist Rabbinical College, which educates rabbis in the newest branch of Judaism. Orthodox rabbis may be trained at The Rabbi Isaac Elchanan Theological Seminary and the Beth Medrash Govoha Seminary. The number of Orthodox seminaries is relatively high, but the number of students attending each seminary is low. In all cases, rabbinic training is rigorous. When students have become sufficiently learned in the Torah, the Bible, and other religious texts, they may be ordained with the approval of an authorized rabbi, acting either independently or as a representative of a rabbinical seminary.

Newly ordained rabbis usually begin as spiritual leaders of small congregations, assistants to experienced rabbis, directors of Hillel Foundations on college campuses, teachers in educational institutions, or chaplains in the U.S. Armed Forces. As a rule, experienced rabbis fill the pulpits of large, well-established Jewish congregations.

Job Outlook
Job opportunities for rabbis are expected in all four major branches of Judaism through the year 2012. Rabbis willing to work in small, underserved communities should have the best prospects.

Graduates of Orthodox seminaries who seek pulpits should have opportunities as growth in enrollments slows and as many graduates seek alternatives to the pulpit. Rapidly expanding membership is expected to create employment opportunities for Reconstructionist rabbis. Conservative and Reform rabbis should have job opportunities serving congregations or in other settings because of the large size of these two branches of Judaism.

Earnings
In addition to their annual salary, benefits received by rabbis may include housing, health insurance, and a retirement plan. Income varies widely, depending on the size and financial status of the congregation, as well as denominational branch and geographic location. Rabbis may earn additional income from gifts or fees for officiating at ceremonies such as bar or bat mitzvahs and weddings.

Sources of Additional Information
Persons who are interested in becoming rabbis should discuss their plans with a practicing rabbi. Information on the work of rabbis and allied occupations can be obtained from:
➤ Rabbinical Council of America, 305 7th Ave., New York, NY 10001. Internet: **http://www.rabbis.org** (Orthodox)
➤ The Jewish Theological Seminary of America, 3080 Broadway, New York, NY 10027. Internet: **http://www.jtsa.edu** (Conservative)
➤ Hebrew Union College-Jewish Institute of Religion, One West 4th St., New York, NY 10012. Internet: **http://www.huc.edu** (Reform)
➤ Reconstructionist Rabbinical College, 1299 Church Rd., Wyncote, PA 19095. Internet: **http://www.rrc.edu** (Reconstructionist)

Roman Catholic Priests

(O*NET 21-2011.00)

Significant Points

● Preparation generally requires 8 years of study beyond high school, usually including a college degree followed by 4 or more years of theology study at a seminary.

● The shortage of Roman Catholic priests is expected to continue, resulting in a very favorable outlook.

Nature of the Work
Priests in the Catholic Church may be categorized as either diocesan or religious. Both types of priests have the same priesthood faculties, acquired through ordination by a bishop. Differences lie in their way of life, type of work, and the Church authority to which they are responsible. *Diocesan priests* commit their lives to serving the people of a diocese, a church administrative region, and generally work in parishes, schools, or other Catholic institutions as assigned by the bishop of their diocese. Diocesan priests take oaths of celibacy and obedience. *Religious priests* belong to a religious order, such as the Jesuits, Dominicans, or Franciscans. In addition to the vows taken by diocesan priests, religious priests take a vow of poverty.

Diocesan priests attend to the spiritual, pastoral, moral, and educational needs of the members of their church. A priest's day usually begins with morning meditation and mass and may end with an individual counseling session or an evening visit to a hospital or home. Many priests direct and serve on church committees, work in civic and charitable organizations, and assist in community projects. Some counsel parishioners preparing for marriage or the birth of a child.

Religious priests receive duty assignments from their superiors in their respective religious orders. Some religious priests specialize in teaching, whereas others serve as missionaries in foreign countries, where they may live under difficult and primitive conditions. Other religious priests live a communal life in monasteries, where they devote their lives to prayer, study, and assigned work.

Both religious and diocesan priests hold teaching and administrative posts in Catholic seminaries, colleges and universities, and high schools. Priests attached to religious orders staff many of the Church's institutions of higher education and many high schools, whereas diocesan priests usually are concerned with the parochial schools attached to parish churches and with diocesan high schools. Members of religious orders do much of the missionary work conducted by the Catholic Church in this country and abroad.

Many priests work with civic and charitable organizations and assist in community projects.

Employment

According to *The Official Catholic Directory*, there were approximately 45,000 priests in 2002; about 30,000 were diocesan priests. Priests are found in nearly every city and town and in many rural communities; however, the majority is in metropolitan areas, where most Catholics reside.

Training and Other Qualifications

Men exclusively are ordained as priests. Women may serve in church positions that do not require priestly ordination. Preparation for the priesthood generally requires 8 years of study beyond high school, usually including a college degree followed by 4 or more years of theology study at a seminary.

Preparatory study for the priesthood may begin in the first year of high school, at the college level, or in theological seminaries after college graduation. Seven high-school seminary programs—four free-standing high school seminaries and three programs within Catholic high schools—provided a college preparatory program in 2002. Programs emphasize and support religious formation in addition to a regular, college-preparatory curriculum. Latin may be required, and modern languages are encouraged. In Hispanic communities, knowledge of Spanish is mandatory.

Those who begin training for the priesthood in college do so in one of 39 priesthood formation programs offered either through Catholic colleges or universities or in freestanding college seminaries. Preparatory studies usually include training in philosophy, religious studies, and prayer.

Today, most candidates for the priesthood have a 4-year degree from an accredited college or university, then attend one of 46 theological seminaries (also called theologates) and earn either the Master of Divinity or the Master of Arts degree. Thirty-four theologates primarily train diocesan priests, whereas 12 theologates provide information mostly for priesthood candidates from religious orders. (Slight variations in training reflect the differences in their expected duties.) Theology coursework includes sacred scripture; dogmatic, moral, and pastoral theology; homiletics (art of preaching); church history; liturgy (sacraments); and canon (church) law. Fieldwork experience usually is required.

Young men are never denied entry into seminaries because of lack of funds. In seminaries for diocesan priests, scholarships or loans are available, and contributions of benefactors and the Catholic Church finance those in religious seminaries—who have taken a vow of poverty and are not expected to have personal resources.

Graduate work in theology beyond that required for ordination also is offered at a number of American Catholic universities or at ecclesiastical universities around the world, particularly in Rome. Also, many priests do graduate work in fields unrelated to theology. Priests are encouraged by the Catholic Church to continue their studies, at least informally, after ordination. In recent years, the Church has stressed continuing education for ordained priests in the social sciences, such as sociology and psychology.

A newly ordained diocesan priest usually works as an assistant pastor. Newly ordained priests of religious orders are assigned to the specialized duties for which they have been trained. Depending on the talents, interests, and experience of the individual, many opportunities for additional responsibility exist within the Church.

Job Outlook

The shortage of Roman Catholic priests is expected to continue, resulting in a very favorable job outlook through the year 2012. Many priests will be needed in the years ahead to provide for the spiritual, educational, and social needs of the increasing number of Catholics. In recent years, the number of ordained priests has been insufficient to fill the needs of newly established parishes and other Catholic institutions and to replace priests who retire, die, or leave the priesthood. This situation is likely to continue, as seminary enrollments remain below the levels needed to overcome the current shortfall of priests.

In response to the shortage of priests, permanent deacons and teams of clergy and laity increasingly are performing certain traditional functions within the Catholic Church. The number of ordained deacons has increased 30 percent over the past 20 years, and this trend should continue. Throughout most of the country, permanent deacons have been ordained to preach and perform liturgical functions, such as baptisms, marriages, and funerals, and to provide service to the community. Deacons are not authorized to celebrate Mass, nor are they allowed to administer the Sacraments of Reconciliation and the Anointing of the Sick. Teams of clergy and laity undertake some liturgical and nonliturgical functions, such as hospital visits and religious teaching.

Earnings

Salaries of diocesan priests vary from diocese to diocese. According to a biennial survey of the National Federation of Priests' Council, low-end salaries averaged $15,291 per year in 2002; high-end salaries averaged $18,478 per year. In addition to a salary, diocesan priests receive a package of benefits that may include a car allowance, room and board in the parish rectory, health insurance, and a retirement plan.

Diocesan priests who do special work related to the church, such as teaching, usually receive a salary which is less than a lay person in the same position would receive. The difference between the usual salary for these jobs and the salary that the priest receives is called "contributed service." In some situations, housing and related expenses may be provided; in other cases, the priest must make his own arrangements. Some priests doing special work receive the same compensation that a lay person would receive.

Religious priests take a vow of poverty and are supported by their religious order. Any personal earnings are given to the order. Their vow of poverty is recognized by the Internal Revenue Service, which exempts them from paying Federal income tax.

Sources of Additional Information

Young men interested in entering the priesthood should seek the guidance and counsel of their parish priests and diocesan vocational office. For information regarding the different religious orders and the diocesan priesthood, as well as a list of the seminaries that prepare students for the priesthood, contact the diocesan director of vocations through the office of the local pastor or bishop.

Individuals seeking additional information about careers in the Catholic Ministry should contact their local diocese.

For information on training programs for the Catholic ministry, contact:
➤ Center for Applied Research in the Apostolate (CARA), Georgetown University, 2300 Wisconsin Ave. NW., Suite 400, Washington, DC 20007. Internet: **http://cara.georgetown.edu**

Counselors

(0*NET 21-1011.00, 21-1012.00, 21-1013.00, 21-1014.00, 21-1015.00))

Significant Points

- A master's degree is often required to be licensed or certified as a counselor.

- All but three States require some form of licensure or certification for practice outside of schools; all States require school counselors to hold a State school counseling certification.

Nature of the Work

Counselors assist people with personal, family, educational, mental health, and career decisions and problems. Their duties depend on the individuals they serve and on the settings in which they work.

Educational, vocational, and school counselors provide individuals and groups with career and educational counseling. In school settings—elementary through postsecondary—they are usually called school counselors and they work with students, including those considered to be at risk and those with special needs. They advocate for students and work with other individuals and organizations to promote the academic, career, and personal and social development of children and youths. School counselors help students evaluate their abilities, interests, talents, and personality characteristics in order to develop realistic academic and career goals. Counselors use interviews, counseling sessions, tests, or other methods in evaluating and advising students. They also operate career information centers and career education programs. High school counselors advise students regarding college majors, admission requirements, entrance exams, financial aid, trade or technical schools, and apprenticeship programs. They help students develop job search skills such as resume writing and interviewing techniques. College career planning and placement counselors assist alumni or students with career development and job-hunting techniques.

Elementary school counselors observe younger children during classroom and play activities and confer with their teachers and parents to evaluate the children's strengths, problems, or special needs. They also help students develop good study habits. Elementary school counselors do less vocational and academic counseling than do secondary school counselors.

School counselors at all levels help students understand and deal with social, behavioral, and personal problems. These counselors emphasize preventive and developmental counseling to provide students with the life skills needed to deal with problems before they occur and to enhance the student's personal, social, and academic growth. Counselors provide special services, including alcohol and drug prevention programs and conflict resolution classes. Counselors also try to identify cases of domestic abuse and other family problems that can affect a student's development. Counselors work with students individually, with small groups, or with entire classes. They consult and collaborate with parents, teachers, school administrators, school psychologists, medical professionals, and social workers in order to develop and implement strategies to help students be successful in the education system.

Vocational counselors who provide mainly career counseling outside the school setting are also referred to as *employment counselors* or *career counselors*. Their chief focus is helping individuals with their career decisions. Vocational counselors explore and evaluate the client's education, training, work history, interests, skills, and personality traits, and arrange for aptitude and achievement tests to assist in making career decisions. They also work with individuals to develop their job search skills, and they assist clients in locating and applying for jobs. In addition, career counselors provide support to persons experiencing job loss, job stress, or other career transition issues.

Rehabilitation counselors help people deal with the personal, social, and vocational effects of disabilities. They counsel people with disabilities resulting from birth defects, illness or disease, accidents, or the stress of daily life. They evaluate the strengths and limitations of individuals, provide personal and vocational counseling, and arrange for medical care, vocational training, and job placement. Rehabilitation counselors interview both individuals with disabilities and their families, evaluate school and medical reports, and confer and plan with physicians, psychologists, occupational therapists, and employers to determine the capabilities and skills of the individual. Conferring with the client, they develop a rehabilitation program that often includes training to help the person develop job skills. Rehabilitation counselors also work toward increasing the client's capacity to live independently.

Mental health counselors work with individuals, families, and groups to address and treat mental and emotional disorders and to promote optimum mental health. They are trained in a variety of therapeutic techniques used to address a wide range of issues, including depression, addiction and substance abuse, suicidal impulses, stress management, problems with self-esteem, issues associated with aging, job and career concerns, educational decisions, issues related to mental and emotional health, and family, parenting, and marital or other relationship problems. Mental health counselors often work closely with other mental health specialists, such as psychiatrists, psychologists, clinical social workers, psychiatric nurses, and school counselors. (Information on other mental health specialists appears in the *Handbook* statements on physicians and surgeons, psychologists, registered nurses, and social workers.)

Substance abuse and behavioral disorder counselors help people who have problems with alcohol, drugs, gambling, and eating disorders. They counsel individuals who are addicted to drugs, helping them identify behaviors and problems related to their addiction. These counselors hold sessions for one person, for families, or for groups of people.

Marriage and family therapists apply principles, methods, and therapeutic techniques to individuals, family groups, couples, or organizations for the purpose of resolving emotional conflicts. In doing so, they modify people's perceptions and behaviors, enhance communication and understanding among all family members, and help to prevent family and individual crises. Marriage and family therapists also may engage in psychotherapy of a nonmedical nature, with appropriate referrals to psychiatric resources, and in research and teaching in the overall field of human development and interpersonal relationships.

Other counseling specialties include gerontological, multicultural, and genetic counseling. A gerontological counselor provides services to elderly persons who face changing lifestyles because of health problems; the counselor helps families cope with the changes. A multicultural counselor helps employers adjust to an increasingly diverse workforce. Genetic counselors provide information and support to families who have members with birth defects or genetic disorders and to families who may be at risk for a variety of inherited conditions. These counselors identify families at risk, investigate the problem that is present in the family, interpret information about the disorder, analyze inheritance patterns and risks of recurrence, and review available options with the family.

Working Conditions

Most school counselors work the traditional 9- to 10-month school year with a 2- to 3-month vacation, although increasing numbers are employed on 10½- or 11-month contracts. They usually work the same hours that teachers do. College career planning and placement counselors work long and irregular hours during student recruiting periods.

Rehabilitation counselors usually work a standard 40-hour week. Self-employed counselors and those working in mental health and community agencies, such as substance abuse and behavioral disorder counselors, frequently work evenings to counsel clients who work during the day. Both mental health counselors and marriage and family therapists also often work flexible hours, to accommodate families in crisis or working couples who must have evening or weekend appointments.

Counselors must possess high physical and emotional energy to handle the array of problems they address. Dealing daily with these problems can cause stress. Because privacy is essential for confidential and frank discussions with clients, counselors usually have private offices.

Employment

Counselors held about 526,000 jobs in 2002. Employment was distributed among the counseling specialties as follows:

Educational, vocational, and school counselors	228,000
Rehabilitation counselors	122,000
Mental health counselors	85,000
Substance abuse and behavioral disorder counselors	67,000
Marriage and family therapists	23,000

Educational, vocational, and school counselors work primarily in elementary and secondary schools and colleges and universities. Other types of counselors work in a wide variety of public and private establishments, including health care facilities; job training, career development, and vocational rehabilitation centers; social agencies; correctional institutions; and residential care facilities, such as halfway houses for criminal offenders and group homes for children, the elderly, and the disabled. Some substance abuse and behavioral disorder counselors work in therapeutic communities where addicts live while undergoing treatment. Counselors also work in organizations engaged in community improvement and social change and work as well in drug and alcohol rehabilitation programs and State and local government agencies. A growing number of counselors are self-employed and

Counselors must be able to inspire respect, trust, and confidence in order to assist people with their problems.

working in group practices or private practice. This growth has been helped by laws allowing counselors to receive payments from insurance companies and the growing recognition that counselors are well-trained professionals.

Training, Other Qualifications, and Advancement

All States require school counselors to hold State school counseling certification and to have completed at least some graduate course work; most require the completion of a master's degree. Some States require public school counselors to have both counseling and teaching certificates and to have had some teaching experience before receiving certification. For counselors based outside of schools, 47 States and the District of Columbia had some form of counselor credentialing, licensure, certification, or registration that governed their practice of counseling. Requirements typically include the completion of a master's degree in counseling, the accumulation of 2 years or 3,000 hours of supervised clinical experience beyond the master's degree level, the passage of a State-recognized exam, adherence to ethical codes and standards, and the satisfaction of annual continuing education requirements.

Counselors must be aware of educational and training requirements that are often very detailed and that vary by area and by counseling specialty. Prospective counselors should check with State and local governments, employers, and national voluntary certification organizations in order to determine which requirements apply.

As mentioned, a master's degree is typically required to be licensed or certified as a counselor. A bachelor's degree often qualifies a person to work as a counseling aide, rehabilitation aide, or social service worker. Some States require counselors in public employment to have a master's degree; others accept a bachelor's degree with appropriate counseling courses. Counselor education programs in colleges and universities usually are in departments of education or psychology. Fields of study include college student affairs, elementary or secondary school counseling, education, gerontological counseling, marriage and family counseling, substance abuse counseling, rehabilitation counseling, agency or community counseling, clinical mental health counseling, counseling psychology, career counseling, and related fields. Courses are grouped into eight core areas: Human growth and development, social and cultural diversity, relationships, group work, career development, assessment, research and program evaluation, and professional identity. In an accredited master's degree program, 48 to 60 semester hours of graduate study, including a period of supervised clinical experience in counseling, are required for a master's degree.

In 2003, 176 institutions offered programs in counselor education—including career, community, gerontological, mental health, school, student affairs, and marriage and family counseling—that were accredited by the Council for Accreditation of Counseling and Related Educational Programs (CACREP). CACREP also recognizes many counselor education programs, apart from those in the 176 accredited institutions, that use alternative instruction methods, such as distance learning. Programs that use such alternative instruction methods are evaluated on the basis of the same standards for accreditation that CACREP applies to programs that employ the more traditional methods. Another organization, the Council on Rehabilitation Education (CORE), accredits graduate programs in rehabilitation counseling. Accredited master's degree programs include a minimum of 2 years of full-time study, including 600 hours of supervised clinical internship experience.

Many counselors elect to be nationally certified by the National Board for Certified Counselors, Inc. (NBCC), which grants the general practice credential "National Certified Counselor." To be certified, a counselor must hold a master's or higher degree, with a concentration in counseling, from a regionally accredited college or university; must have at least 2 years of supervised field experience in a counseling setting (graduates from counselor education programs accredited by CACREP are exempted); must provide two professional endorsements, one of which must be from a recent supervisor; and must have a passing score on the NBCC's National Counselor Examination for Licensure and Certification (NCE). This national certification is voluntary and is distinct from State certification. However, in some States, those who pass the national exam are exempted from taking a State certification exam. NBCC also offers specialty certification in school, clinical mental health, and addiction counseling. Beginning January 1, 2004, new candidates for NBCC's National Certified School counselor (NCSC) credential must pass a practical simulation examination in addition to fulfilling the current requirements. To maintain their certification, counselors retake and pass the NCE or complete 100 hours of acceptable continuing education credit every 5 years.

Another organization, the Commission on Rehabilitation Counselor Certification, offers voluntary national certification for rehabilitation counselors. Many employers require rehabilitation counselors to be nationally certified. To become certified, rehabilitation counselors usually must graduate from an accredited educational program, complete an internship, and pass a written examination. (Certification requirements vary according to an applicant's educational history. Employment experience, for example, is required for those with a counseling degree in a specialty other than rehabilitation.) After meeting these requirements, candidates are designated "Certified Rehabilitation Counselors." To maintain their certification, counselors must successfully retake the certification exam or complete 100 hours of acceptable continuing education credit every 5 years.

Other counseling organizations also offer certification in particular counseling specialties. Usually these are voluntary, but having one may enhance one's job prospects.

Some employers provide training for newly hired counselors. Others may offer time off or provide help with tuition if it is needed to complete a graduate degree. Counselors must participate in graduate studies, workshops, and personal studies to maintain their certificates and licenses.

Persons interested in counseling should have a strong interest in helping others and should possess the ability to inspire respect, trust, and confidence. They should be able to work independently or as part of a team. Counselors must follow the code of ethics associated with their respective certifications and licenses.

Prospects for advancement vary by counseling field. School counselors can move to a larger school; become directors or supervisors of counseling, guidance, or pupil personnel services; or, usually with further graduate education, become counselor educators, counseling psychologists, or school administrators. (See the statements on psychologists and education administrators elsewhere in the *Handbook*.) Some counselors choose to work for a State's department of education. For marriage and family therapists, doctoral education in family therapy emphasizes the training of supervisors, teachers, researchers, and clinicians in the discipline.

Counselors can become supervisors or administrators in their agencies. Some counselors move into research, consulting, or college teaching or go into private or group practice.

Job Outlook
Overall employment of counselors is expected to grow faster than the average for all occupations through 2012, and job opportunities should be very good because there are usually more job openings than graduates of counseling programs. In addition, numerous job openings will occur as many counselors retire or leave the profession.

Employment of educational, vocational, and school counselors is expected to grow as fast as the average for all occupations as a result of: increasing student enrollments, particularly in secondary and postsecondary schools; State legislation requiring counselors in elementary schools; and an expansion in the responsibilities of counselors. For example, counselors are becoming more involved in crisis and preventive counseling, helping students deal with issues ranging from drug and alcohol abuse to death and suicide. Although schools and governments realize the value of counselors in achieving academic success in their students, budget constraints at every school level will dampen job growth of school counselors. However, Federal grants and subsidies may fill in the gaps and allow the current ongoing reduction in student-to-counselor ratios to continue.

Demand for vocational or career counselors should grow as the notion of staying in one job over a lifetime continues to be rejected and replaced by the concept of managing one's own career and taking responsibility for it. In addition, changes in welfare laws that require beneficiaries to work will continue to create demand for counselors by State and local governments. Other opportunities for employment counselors will arise in private job-training centers that provide training and other services to laid-off workers, as well as to those seeking a new or second career or wanting to upgrade their skills.

Demand is expected to be strong for substance abuse and behavioral, mental health, and marriage and family therapists and for rehabilitation counselors, for a variety of reasons. For one, California and a few other States have recently passed laws requiring substance abuse treatment instead of jail for people caught possessing a drug. This shift will require more substance abuse counselors in those States. Second, the increasing availability of funds to build statewide networks to improve services for children and adolescents with serious emotional disturbances and for their family members should increase employment opportunities for counselors. Under managed care systems, insurance companies are increasingly providing for reimbursement of counselors as a less costly alternative to psychiatrists and psychologists. Also, legislation is pending that may provide counseling services to Medicare recipients.

The number of people who will need rehabilitation counseling is expected to grow as the population continues to age and as advances in medical technology continue to save lives that only a few years ago would have been lost. In addition, legislation requiring equal employment rights for people with disabilities will spur demand for counselors, who not only will help these people make a transition into the workforce, but also will help companies comply with the law.

Employment of mental health counselors and marriage and family therapists will grow as the Nation becomes more comfortable seeking professional help for a variety of health and personal and family problems. Employers also are increasingly offering employee assistance programs that provide mental health and alcohol and drug abuse services. More people are expected to use these services as society focuses on ways of developing mental well-being, such as controlling stress associated with job and family responsibilities.

Earnings
Median annual earnings of educational, vocational, and school counselors in 2002 were $44,100. The middle 50 percent earned between $33,160 and $56,770. The lowest 10 percent earned less than $24,930, and the highest 10 percent earned more than $70,320. School counselors can earn additional income working summers in the school system or in other jobs. Median annual earnings in the industries employing the largest numbers of educational, vocational, and school counselors in 2002 were as follows:

Educational, vocational, and school counselors	228,000
Rehabilitation counselors	122,000
Mental health counselors	85,000
Substance abuse and behavioral disorder counselors	67,000
Marriage and family therapists	23,000

Median annual earnings of substance abuse and behavioral disorder counselors in 2002 were $30,180. The middle 50 percent earned between $24,350 and $37,520. The lowest 10 percent earned less than $19,540, and the highest 10 percent earned more than $45,570.

Median annual earnings of mental health counselors in 2002 were $29,940. The middle 50 percent earned between $23,950 and $39,160. The lowest 10 percent earned less than $19,760, and the highest 10 percent earned more than 50,170.

Median annual earnings of rehabilitation counselors in 2002 were $25,840. The middle 50 percent earned between $20,350 and $34,000. The lowest 10 percent earned less than $16,840, and the highest 10 percent earned more than $44,940.

For substance abuse, mental health, and rehabilitation counselors, government employers generally pay the highest wages, followed by hospitals and social service agencies. Residential care facilities often pay the lowest wages.

Median annual earnings of marriage and family therapists in 2002 were $35,580. The middle 50 percent earned between $26,790 and $44,620. The lowest 10 percent earned less than 20,960, and the highest 10 percent earned more than $59,030. Median annual earnings in 2002 were $29,160 in individual and family social services, the industry employing the largest numbers of marriage and family therapists.

Self-employed counselors who have well-established practices, as well as counselors employed in group practices, usually have the highest earnings.

Related Occupations
Counselors help people evaluate their interests, abilities, and disabilities and deal with personal, social, academic, and career problems. Others who help people in similar ways include teachers, social and human service assistants, social workers, psychologists, physicians and surgeons, registered nurses, members of the clergy, occupational therapists, and human resources, training, and labor relations managers and specialists.

Sources of Additional Information
For general information about counseling, as well as information on specialties such as school, college, mental health, rehabilitation, multicultural, career, marriage and family, and gerontological counseling, contact:
➤ American Counseling Association, 5999 Stevenson Ave., Alexandria, VA 22304-3300. Internet: **http://www.counseling.org**

For information on accredited counseling and related training programs, contact:
➤ Council for Accreditation of Counseling and Related Educational Programs, American Counseling Association, 5999 Stevenson Ave., 4th floor, Alexandria, VA 22304. Internet: **http://www.counseling.org/cacrep**

For information on national certification requirements for counselors, contact:
➤ National Board for Certified Counselors, Inc., 3 Terrace Way, Suite D, Greensboro, NC 27403-3660. Internet: **http://www.nbcc.org**

State departments of education can supply information on those colleges and universities which offer guidance and counseling training that meets State certification and licensure requirements.

State employment service offices have information about job opportunities and about entrance requirements for counselors.

Probation Officers and Correctional Treatment Specialists

(0*NET 21-1092.00)

Significant Points
- State and local governments employ most workers.
- A bachelor's degree in social work, criminal justice, or a related field usually is required.
- Employment growth, which is projected to be about as fast as average, depends on government funding.

Nature of the Work
Many people who are convicted of crimes are placed on probation, instead of being sent to prison. During probation, offenders must stay out of trouble and meet various other requirements. *Probation officers*, who are called community supervision officers in some States, supervise people who have been placed on probation. *Correctional treatment specialists*, who may also be known as case managers, counsel prison inmates and help them plan for their release from incarceration.

Parole officers and *pretrial services officers* perform many of the same duties that probation officers perform. However, parole officers supervise offenders who have been released from prison on parole to ensure that they comply with the conditions of their parole. In some States, the job of parole and probation officer is combined. Pretrial services officers conduct pretrial investigations of criminal suspects when they are arrested by police. Their findings help to determine whether a suspect should be released before their trial. When suspects are released before their trial, pretrial services officers have the responsibility of supervising them to make sure they adhere to the terms of their release and that they show up for their trial. Occasionally, in the Federal courts system, probation officers perform the functions of pretrial services officers.

Probation officers supervise offenders on probation or parole through personal contact with the offenders and their families. Instead of requiring offenders to meet officers in their offices, many officers meet offenders in their homes and at their places of employment or therapy. Probation and parole agencies also seek the assistance of community organizations, such as religious institutions, neighborhood groups, and local residents, to monitor the behavior of many offenders. Some offenders are required to wear an electronic device so that probation officers can monitor their location and movements. Officers may arrange for offenders to get substance abuse rehabilitation or job training. Probation officers usually work with either adults or juveniles exclusively. Only in small, usually rural, jurisdictions do probation officers counsel both adults and juveniles.

Probation officers also spend much of their time working for the courts. They investigate the background of offenders brought before the court, write presentence reports, and make sentencing recommendations for each offender. Officers review sentencing recommendations with offenders and their families before submitting them to the court. Officers may be required to testify in court as to their findings and recommendations. They also attend court hearings to update the court on the offender's compliance with the terms of his or her sentence and on the offender's efforts at rehabilitation.

Correctional treatment specialists work in correctional institutions (jails and prisons) or in parole or probation agencies. In jails and prisons, they evaluate the progress of inmates. They also work with inmates, probation officers, and other agencies to develop parole and release plans. Their case reports are provided to the appropriate parole board when their clients are eligible for release. In addition, they plan education and training programs to improve offenders' job skills and provide them with coping, anger management, and drug or sexual abuse counseling either individually or in groups. They usually write treatment plans and summaries for each client. Correctional treatment specialists working in parole and probation agencies perform many of the same duties as their counterparts who work in correctional institutions.

Through personal contact with offenders and their families, probation officers supervise offenders who are on probation or parole.

The number of cases a probation officer or correctional treatment specialist handles at one time depends on the needs of offenders and the risks they pose. Higher risk offenders and those who need more counseling usually command more of the officer's time and resources. Caseload size also varies by agency jurisdiction. Consequently, officers may handle from 20 to more than 100 active cases at a time.

Computers, telephones, and fax machines enable the officers to handle the caseload. Probation officers may telecommute from their own homes. Other technological advancements, such as electronic monitoring devices and drug screening, also have assisted probation officers and correctional treatment specialists in supervising and counseling offenders.

Working Conditions
Probation officers and correctional treatment specialists work with criminal offenders, some of whom may be dangerous. In the course of supervising offenders, they usually interact with many other individuals, such as family members and friends of their clients, who may be angry, upset, or difficult to work with. Workers may be assigned to fieldwork in high crime areas or in institutions where there is a risk of violence or communicable disease. Probation officers and correctional treatment specialists are required to meet many deadlines, most of which are imposed by courts, which contributes to their heavy workloads.

In addition, extensive travel and fieldwork may be required to meet with offenders who are on probation or parole. Workers may be required to carry a firearm or other weapon for protection. They generally work a 40-hour workweek, but some may work longer. They may be on call 24 hours a day to supervise and assist offenders at any time. They also may be required to collect and transport urine samples of offenders for drug testing. All of these factors make for a stressful work environment. Although the high stress levels can make these jobs very difficult at times, this work also can be very rewarding. Many workers obtain personal satisfaction from counseling members of their community and helping them become productive citizens.

Employment
Probation officers and correctional treatment specialists held about 84,000 jobs in 2002. Most jobs are found in State or local governments. In some States, the State government employs all probation officers and correctional treatment specialists; in other States, local governments are the only employers. In still other States, both levels of government employ these workers. Jobs are more plentiful in urban areas. Probation officers and correctional treatment specialists who work for the Federal Government are employed by the U.S. courts and the U.S. Department of Justice's Bureau of Prisons.

Training, Other Qualifications, and Advancement
Background qualifications for probation officers and correctional treatment specialists vary by State, but a bachelor's degree in social work, criminal justice, or a related field from a 4-year college or university is usually required. Some employers require previous experience or a master's degree in criminal justice, social work, psychology, or a related field.

Applicants usually are administered written, oral, psychological, and physical examinations. Most probation officers and some correctional treatment specialists are required to complete a training program sponsored by their State government or the Federal Government, after which a certification test may be required.

Prospective probation officers or correctional treatment specialists should be in good physical and emotional condition. Most agencies require applicants to be at least 21 years old and, for Federal employment, not older than 37. Those convicted of felonies may not be eligible for employment in this occupation. Familiarity with the use of computers often is required due to the increasing use of computer technology in probation and parole work. Candidates also should be knowledgeable about laws and regulations pertaining to corrections. Probation officers and correctional treatment specialists should possess strong writing skills due to the large numbers of reports they are required to prepare.

Most probation officers and correctional treatment specialists work as trainees or on a probationary period for up to a year. After successfully completing the training period, workers obtain a permanent position. A typical agency has several levels of probation and parole officers and correctional treatment specialists, as well as supervisors. A graduate degree, such as a master's degree in criminal justice, social work, or psychology, may be helpful for advancement.

Job Outlook

Employment of probation officers and correctional treatment specialists is projected to grow about as fast as the average for all occupations through 2012. In addition to openings due to growth, many openings will be created by replacement needs, especially openings due to the large number of these workers who are expected to retire over the 2002-12 projection period. This occupation is not attractive to some potential entrants due to relatively low earnings, heavy workloads, and high stress.

Vigorous law enforcement is expected to result in a continuing increase in the prison population. Overcrowding in prisons also has increased the probation population, as judges and prosecutors search for alternate forms of punishment, such as electronic monitoring and day reporting centers. The number of offenders released on parole also is expected to increase to create room in prison for other offenders. The increasing prison, parole, and probation populations should spur demand for probation and parole officers and correctional treatment specialists. However, the job outlook depends primarily on the amount of government funding that is allocated to corrections, and especially to probation systems. Although community supervision is far less expensive than keeping offenders in prison, a change in political trends toward more imprisonment and away from community supervision could result in reduced employment opportunities.

Earnings

Median annual earnings of probation officers and correctional treatment specialists in 2002 were $38,360. The middle 50 percent earned between $30,770 and $50,550. The lowest 10 percent earned less than $25,810, and the highest 10 percent earned more than $62,520. In 2002, median annual earnings for probation officers and correctional treatment specialists employed in State government were $38,720; those employed in local government earned $39,450. Higher wages tend to be found in urban areas.

Related Occupations

Probation officers and correctional treatment specialists counsel criminal offenders as they reenter society. Other occupations that involve similar responsibilities include social workers, social and human service assistants, and counselors.

Probation officers and correctional treatment also play a major role in maintaining public safety. Other occupations related to corrections and law enforcement include police and detectives, correctional officers, and firefighting occupations.

Sources of Additional Information

For information about criminal justice job opportunities in your area, contact your State's Department of Corrections, Criminal Justice, or Probation.

Further information about probation officers and correctional treatment specialists is available from:
➤ American Probation and Parole Association, P.O. Box 11910, Lexington, KY 40578. Internet: **http://www.appa-net.org**
➤ American Correctional Association, 4380 Forbes Blvd., Lanham, MD 20706. Internet: **http://www.aca.org**

Social and Human Service Assistants

(0*NET 21-1093.00)

Significant Points

- While a bachelor's degree usually is not required, employers increasingly seek individuals with relevant work experience or education beyond high school.

- Employment is projected to grow much faster than average.

- Job opportunities should be excellent, particularly for applicants with appropriate postsecondary education, but pay is low.

Nature of the Work

Social and human service assistant is a generic term for people with a wide array of job titles, including human service worker, case management aide, social work assistant, community support worker, mental health aide, community outreach worker, life skill counselor, or gerontology aide. They usually work under the direction of professionals from a variety of fields, such as nursing, psychiatry, psychology, rehabilitative or physical therapy, or social work. The amount of responsibility and supervision they are given varies a great deal. Some have little direct supervision; others work under close direction.

Social and human service assistants provide direct and indirect client services to ensure that individuals in their care reach their maximum level of functioning. They assess clients' needs, establish their eligibility for benefits and services such as food stamps, Medicaid, or welfare, and help to obtain them. They also arrange for transportation and escorts, if necessary, and provide emotional support. Social and human service assistants monitor and keep case records on clients and report progress to supervisors and case managers.

Social and human service assistants play a variety of roles in a community. They may organize and lead group activities, assist clients in need of counseling or crisis intervention, or administer a food bank or emergency fuel program. In halfway houses, group homes, and government-supported housing programs, they assist adults who need supervision with personal hygiene and daily living skills. They review clients' records, ensure that they take correct doses of medication, talk with family members, and confer with medical personnel and other

Social and human service assistants provide direct and indirect client services to ensure that individuals in their care reach their maximum level of functioning.

caregivers to gain better insight into clients' backgrounds and needs. Social and human service assistants also provide emotional support and help clients become involved in their own well-being, in community recreation programs, and in other activities.

In psychiatric hospitals, rehabilitation programs, and outpatient clinics, social and human service assistants work with professional care providers, such as psychiatrists, psychologists, and social workers, to help clients master everyday living skills, communicate more effectively, and get along better with others. They support the client's participation in a treatment plan, such as individual or group counseling or occupational therapy.

Working Conditions

Working conditions of social and human service assistants vary. Some work in offices, clinics, and hospitals, while others work in group homes, shelters, sheltered workshops, and day programs. Many spend their time in the field visiting clients. Most work a 40-hour week, although some work in the evening and on weekends.

The work, while satisfying, can be emotionally draining. Understaffing and relatively low pay may add to the pressure. Turnover is reported to be high, especially among workers without academic preparation for this field.

Employment

Social and human service assistants held about 305,000 jobs in 2002. More than half worked in the health care and social assistance industries. Almost one third were employed by State and local governments, primarily in public welfare agencies and facilities for mentally disabled and developmentally challenged individuals.

Training, Other Qualifications, and Advancement

While a bachelor's degree usually is not required for entry into this occupation, employers increasingly seek individuals with relevant work experience or education beyond high school. Certificates or associate degrees in subjects such as social work, human services, gerontology, or one of the social or behavioral sciences meet most employers' requirements. Some jobs may require a bachelor's or master's degree in human services or a related field such as counseling, rehabilitation, or social work.

Human services degree programs have a core curriculum that trains students to observe patients and record information, conduct patient interviews, implement treatment plans, employ problem-solving techniques, handle crisis intervention matters, and use proper case management and referral procedures. General education courses in liberal arts, sciences, and the humanities also are part of the curriculum. Many degree programs require completion of a supervised internship.

Educational attainment often influences the kind of work employees may be assigned and the degree of responsibility that may be entrusted to them. For example, workers with no more than a high school education are likely to receive extensive on-the-job training to work in direct-care services, while employees with a college degree might be assigned to do supportive counseling, coordinate program activities, or manage a group home. Social and human service assistants with proven leadership ability, either from previous experience or as a volunteer in the field, often have greater autonomy in their work. Regardless of the academic or work background of employees, most employers provide some form of inservice training, such as seminars and workshops, to their employees.

There may be additional hiring requirements in group homes. For example, employers may require employees to have a valid driver's license or to submit to a criminal background investigation.

Employers try to select applicants who have effective communication skills, a strong sense of responsibility, and the ability to manage time effectively. Many human services jobs involve direct contact with people who are vulnerable to exploitation or mistreatment; therefore, patience, understanding, and a strong desire to help others are highly valued characteristics.

Formal education almost always is necessary for advancement. In general, advancement requires a bachelor's or master's degree in human services, counseling, rehabilitation, social work, or a related field.

Job Outlook

Job opportunities for social and human service assistants are expected to be excellent, particularly for applicants with appropriate postsecondary education. The number of social and human service assistants is projected to grow much faster than the average for all occupations between 2002 and 2012—ranking the occupation among the most rapidly growing. Many additional job opportunities will arise from the need to replace workers who advance into new positions, retire, or leave the workforce for other reasons. There will be more competition for jobs in urban areas than in rural areas, but qualified applicants should have little difficulty finding employment. Faced with rapid growth in the demand for social and human services many employers increasingly rely on social and human service assistants to undertake greater responsibility for delivering services to clients.

Opportunities are expected to be good in private social service agencies, which provide such services as adult daycare and meal delivery programs. Employment in private agencies will grow as State and local governments continue to contract out services to the private sector in an effort to cut costs. Demand for social services will expand with the growing elderly population, who are more likely to need these services. In addition, more social and human service assistants will be needed to provide services to pregnant teenagers, the homeless, the mentally disabled and developmentally challenged, and substance abusers. Some private agencies have been employing more social and human service assistants in place of social workers, who are more educated and, thus, more highly paid.

Job training programs also are expected to require additional social and human service assistants. As social welfare policies shift focus from benefit-based programs to work-based initiatives, there will be more demand for people to teach job skills to the people who are new to, or returning to, the workforce.

Residential care establishments should face increased pressures to respond to the needs of the mentally and physically disabled. Many of these patients have been deinstitutionalized and lack the knowledge or the ability to care for themselves. Also, more community-based programs, supported independent-living sites, and group residences are expected to be established to house and assist the homeless and the mentally and physically disabled. As substance abusers are increasingly being sent to treatment programs instead of prison, employment of social and human service assistants in substance abuse treatment programs also will grow.

The number of jobs for social and human service assistants in State and local governments will grow but not as fast as employment for social and human service assistants in other industries. Employment in the public sector may fluctuate with the level of funding provided by State and local governments. Also, some State and local governments are contracting out selected social services to private agencies in order to save money.

Earnings

Median annual earnings of social and human service assistants were $23,370 in 2002. The middle 50 percent earned between $18,670 and $29,520. The top 10 percent earned more than $37,550, while the lowest 10 percent earned less than $15,420.

Median annual earnings in the industries employing the largest numbers of social and human service assistants in 2002 were:

State government	$31,280
Local government	26,570
Individual and family services	22,210
Community food and housing, and emergency and other relief services	21,840
Residential mental retardation, mental health and substance abuse facilities	20,010

Related Occupations

Workers in other occupations that require skills similar to those of social and human service assistants include social workers; clergy; counselors; childcare workers; occupational therapist assistants and aides; physical therapist assistants and aides; and nursing, psychiatric, and home health aides.

Sources of Additional Information

Information on academic programs in human services may be found in most directories of 2- and 4-year colleges, available at libraries or career counseling centers.

For information on programs and careers in human services, contact:

➤ National Organization for Human Service Education, 375 Myrtle Ave., Brooklyn, NY 11205. Internet: **http://www.nohse.org**
➤ Council for Standards in Human Services Education, Harrisburg Area Community College, Human Services Program, One HACC Dr., Harrisburg, PA 17110-2999. Internet: **http://www.cshse.org**

Information on job openings may be available from State employment service offices or directly from city, county, or State departments of health, mental health and mental retardation, and human resources.

Social Workers

(0*NET 21-1021.00, 21-1022.00, 21-1023.00)

Significant Points

● While a bachelor's degree is the minimum requirement, a master's degree in social work or a related field has become the standard for many positions.

● Employment is projected to grow faster than average.

● Competition for jobs is expected in cities, but opportunities should be good in rural areas.

Nature of the Work

Social work is a profession for those with a strong desire to help improve people's lives. Social workers help people function the best way they can in their environment, deal with their relationships, and solve personal and family problems. Social workers often see clients who face a life-threatening disease or a social problem. These problems may include inadequate housing, unemployment, serious illness, disability, or substance abuse. Social workers also assist families that have serious domestic conflicts, including those involving child or spousal abuse.

Social workers often provide social services in health-related settings that now are governed by managed care organizations. To contain costs, these organizations are emphasizing short-term intervention, ambulatory and community-based care, and greater decentralization of services.

Most social workers specialize. Although some conduct research or are involved in planning or policy development, most social workers prefer an area of practice in which they interact with clients.

Child, family, and school social workers provide social services and assistance to improve the social and psychological functioning of children and their families and to maximize the family well-being and academic functioning of children. Some social workers assist single parents; arrange adoptions; and help find foster homes for neglected, abandoned, or abused children. In schools, they address such problems as teenage pregnancy, misbehavior, and truancy. They also advise teachers on how to cope with problem students. Some social workers may specialize in services for senior citizens. They run support groups for family caregivers or for the adult children of aging parents. Some advise elderly people or family members about choices in areas such as housing, transportation, and long-term care; they also coordinate and monitor services. Through employee assistance programs, they may help workers cope with job-related pressures or with personal problems that affect the quality of their work. Child, family, and school social workers typically work in individual and family services agencies, schools, or State or local governments. These social workers may be known as child welfare social workers, family services social workers, child protective services social workers, occupational social workers, or gerontology social workers.

Medical and public health social workers provide persons, families, or vulnerable populations with the psychosocial support needed to cope with chronic, acute, or terminal illnesses, such as Alzheimer's disease, cancer, or AIDS. They also advise family caregivers, counsel patients, and help plan for patients' needs after discharge by arranging for at-home services—from meals-on-wheels to oxygen equipment. Some work on interdis-

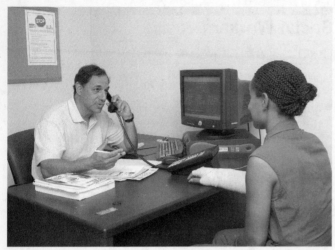

Social workers often see clients who face inadequate housing, unemployment, serious illness, disability, or substance abuse.

ciplinary teams that evaluate certain kinds of patients—geriatric or organ transplant patients, for example. Medical and public health social workers may work for hospitals, nursing and personal care facilities, individual and family services agencies, or local governments.

Mental health and substance abuse social workers assess and treat individuals with mental illness, or substance abuse problems, including abuse of alcohol, tobacco, or other drugs. Such services include individual and group therapy, outreach, crisis intervention, social rehabilitation, and training in skills of everyday living. They may also help plan for supportive services to ease patients' return to the community. Mental health and substance abuse social workers are likely to work in hospitals, substance abuse treatment centers, individual and family services agencies, or local governments. These social workers may be known as clinical social workers. (Counselors and psychologists, who may provide similar services, are discussed elsewhere in the *Handbook*.)

Other types of social workers include social work planners and policymakers, who develop programs to address such issues as child abuse, homelessness, substance abuse, poverty, and violence. These workers research and analyze policies, programs, and regulations. They identify social problems and suggest legislative and other solutions. They may help raise funds or write grants to support these programs.

Working Conditions

Full-time social workers usually work a standard 40-hour week; however, some occasionally work evenings and weekends to meet with clients, attend community meetings, and handle emergencies. Some, particularly in voluntary nonprofit agencies, work part time. Social workers usually spend most of their time in an office or residential facility, but also may travel locally to visit clients, meet with service providers, or attend meetings. Some may use one of several offices within a local area in which to meet with clients. The work, while satisfying, can be emotionally draining. Understaffing and large caseloads add to the pressure in some agencies. To tend to patient care or client needs, many hospitals and long-term care facilities are employing social workers on teams with a broad mix of occupations—including clinical specialists, registered nurses, and health aides.

Employment

Social workers held about 477,000 jobs in 2002. About 4 out of 10 jobs were in State or local government agencies, primarily in departments of health and human services. Most private sector jobs were in the health care and social assistance industry. Although most social workers are employed in cities or suburbs, some work in rural areas. The following tabulation shows 2002 employment by type of social worker.

Child, family, and school social workers	274,000
Medical and public health social workers	107,000
Mental health and substance abuse social workers	95,000

Training, Other Qualifications, and Advancement

A bachelor's degree in social work (BSW) degree is the most common minimum requirement to qualify for a job as a social worker; however, majors in psychology, sociology, and related fields may be adequate to qualify for some entry-level jobs, especially in small community agencies. Although a bachelor's degree is sufficient for entry into the field, an advanced degree has become the standard for many positions. A master's degree in social work (MSW) is typically required for positions in health settings and is required for clinical work. Some jobs in public and private agencies also may require an advanced degree, such as a master's degree in social services policy or administration. Supervisory, administrative, and staff training positions usually require an advanced degree. College and university teaching positions and most research appointments normally require a doctorate in social work (DSW or Ph.D.).

As of 2002, the Council on Social Work Education (CSWE) accredited 436 BSW programs and 149 MSW programs. The Group for the Advancement of Doctoral Education (GADE) listed 78 doctoral programs in social work (DSW or Ph.D.). BSW programs prepare graduates for direct service positions such as caseworker. They include courses in social work values and ethics, dealing with a culturally diverse clientele, at-risk-populations, promotion of social and economic justice, human behavior and the social environment, social welfare policy and services, social work practice, social research methods, and field education. Accredited BSW programs require a minimum of 400 hours of supervised field experience.

Master's degree programs prepare graduates for work in their chosen field of concentration and continue to develop the skills required to perform clinical assessments, manage large caseloads, and explore new ways of drawing upon social services to meet the needs of clients. Master's programs last 2 years and include a minimum of 900 hours of supervised field instruction, or internship. A part-time program may take 4 years. Entry into a master's program does not require a bachelor's in social work, but courses in psychology, biology, sociology, economics, political science, and social work are recommended. In addition, a second language can be very helpful. Most master's programs offer advanced standing for those with a bachelor's degree from an accredited social work program.

All States and the District of Columbia have licensing, certification, or registration requirements regarding social work practice and the use of professional titles. Although standards for licensing vary by State, a growing number of States are placing greater emphasis on communications skills, professional ethics, and sensitivity to cultural diversity issues. Additionally, the National Association of Social Workers (NASW) offers voluntary credentials. Social workers with an MSW may be eligible for the Academy of Certified Social Workers (ACSW), the Qualified Clinical Social Worker (QCSW), or the Diplomate in Clinical Social Work (DCSW) credential based on their professional experience. Credentials are particularly important for those in private practice; some health insurance providers require social workers to have them in order to be reimbursed for services.

Social workers should be emotionally mature, objective, and sensitive to people and their problems. They must be able to handle responsibility, work independently, and maintain good working relationships with clients and coworkers. Volunteer or paid jobs as a social work aide offer ways of testing one's interest in this field.

Advancement to supervisor, program manager, assistant director, or executive director of a social service agency or department is possible, but usually requires an advanced degree and related work experience. Other career options for social workers include teaching, research, and consulting. Some of these workers also help formulate government policies by analyzing and advocating policy positions in government agencies, in research institutions, and on legislators' staffs.

Some social workers go into private practice. Most private practitioners are clinical social workers who provide psychotherapy, usually paid for through health insurance or by the client themselves. Private practitioners must have at least a master's degree and a period of supervised work experience. A network of contacts for referrals also is essential. Many private practitioners work part time while they work full time elsewhere.

Job Outlook

Competition for social worker jobs is stronger in cities, where demand for services often is highest and training programs for social workers are prevalent. However, opportunities should be good in rural areas, which often find it difficult to attract and retain qualified staff. By specialty, job prospects may be best for those social workers with a background in gerontology and substance abuse treatment.

Employment of social workers is expected to increase faster than the average for all occupations through 2012. The rapidly growing elderly population and the aging baby boom generation will create greater demand for health and social services, resulting in particularly rapid job growth among gerontology social workers. Many job openings also will stem from the need to replace social workers who leave the occupation.

As hospitals continue to limit the length of patient stays, the demand for social workers in hospitals will grow more slowly than in other areas. Because hospitals are releasing patients earlier than in the past, social worker employment in home healthcare services is growing. However, the expanding senior population is an even larger factor. Employment opportunities for social workers with backgrounds in gerontology should be good in the growing numbers of assisted-living and senior-living communities. The expanding senior population will also spur demand for social workers in nursing homes, long-term care facilities, and hospices.

Employment of substance abuse social workers will grow rapidly over the 2002-12 projection period. Substance abusers are increasingly being placed into treatment programs instead of being sentenced to prison. As this trend grows, demand will increase for treatment programs and social workers to assist abusers on the road to recovery.

Employment of social workers in private social service agencies will increase. However, agencies increasingly will restructure services and hire more lower-paid social and human service assistants instead of social workers. Employment in State and local government agencies may grow somewhat in response to increasing needs for public welfare, family services, and child protection services; however, many of these services will be contracted out to private agencies. Employment levels in public and private social services agencies may fluctuate, depending on need and government funding levels.

Employment of school social workers also is expected to steadily grow. Expanded efforts to respond to rising student enrollments and continued emphasis on integrating disabled children into the general school population may lead to more jobs. Availability of State and local funding will be a major factor in determining the actual job growth in schools.

Opportunities for social workers in private practice will expand but growth may be somewhat hindered by restrictions that managed care organizations put on mental health services. The growing popularity of employee assistance programs is expected to spur some demand for private practitioners, some of whom provide social work services to corporations on a contractual basis. However, the popularity of employee assistance programs will fluctuate with the business cycle, as businesses are not likely to offer these services during recessions.

Earnings

Median annual earnings of child, family, and school social workers were $33,150 in 2002. The middle 50 percent earned between $26,310 and $42,940. The lowest 10 percent earned less than $21,270, and the top 10 percent earned more than $54,250. Median annual earnings in the industries employing the largest numbers of child, family, and school social workers in 2002 were:

Elementary and secondary schools	$44,100
Local government	38,140
State government	34,000
Individual and family services	29,150
Other residential care facilities	28,470

Median annual earnings of medical and public health social workers were $37,380 in 2002. The middle 50 percent earned between $29,700 and $46,540. The lowest 10 percent earned less than $23,840, and the top 10 percent earned more than $56,320. Median annual earnings in the industries employing the largest numbers of medical and public health social workers in 2002 were:

General medical and surgical hospitals	$42,730
Local government	37,620
State government	35,250
Nursing care facilities	33,330
Individual and family services	31,000

Median annual earnings of mental health and substance abuse social workers were $32,850 in 2002. The middle 50 percent earned between $25,940 and $42,160. The lowest 10 percent earned less than $21,050, and the top 10 percent earned more than $52,240. Median annual earnings in the industries employing the largest numbers of mental health and substance abuse social workers in 2002 were:

State government	$38,430
Local government	35,700
Psychiatric and substance abuse hospitals	34,610
Outpatient care centers	31,370
Individual and family services	31,300

Related Occupations

Through direct counseling or referral to other services, social workers help people solve a range of personal problems. Workers in occupations with similar duties include the clergy, counselors, probation officers and correctional treatment specialists, psychologists, and social and human services assistants.

Sources of Additional Information

For information about career opportunities in social work and voluntary credentials for social workers, contact:

➤ National Association of Social Workers, 750 First St. NE., Suite 700, Washington, DC 20002-4241. Internet: **http://www.socialworkers.org**

For a listing of accredited social work programs, contact:

➤ Council on Social Work Education, 1725 Duke St., Suite 500, Alexandria, VA 22314-3457. Internet: **http://www.cswe.org**

Information on licensing requirements and testing procedures for each State may be obtained from State licensing authorities, or from:

➤ Association of Social Work Boards, 400 South Ridge Pkwy., Suite B, Culpeper, VA 22701. Internet: **http://www.aswb.org**

Legal Occupations

Court Reporters

(0*NET 23-2091.00)

Significant Points

● Court reporters usually need a 2- or 4- year postsecondary school degree.

● Demand for realtime and broadcast captioning and translating will result in employment growth in the occupation.

● Job opportunities should be best for those with certification.

Nature of the Work

Court reporters typically take verbatim reports of speeches, conversations, legal proceedings, meetings, and other events when written accounts of spoken words are necessary for correspondence, records, or legal proof. Court reporters play a critical role not only in judicial proceedings, but at every meeting where the spoken word must be preserved as a written transcript. They are responsible for ensuring a complete, accurate, and secure legal record. In addition to preparing and protecting the legal record, many court reporters assist judges and trial attorneys in a variety of ways, such as organizing and searching for information in the official record or making suggestions to judges and attorneys regarding courtroom administration and procedure. Increasingly, court reporters are providing closed-captioning and realtime translating services to the deaf and hard-of-hearing community.

There are two main methods of court reporting: Stenotyping and voice writing. Using a stenotype machine, stenotypists document all statements made in official proceedings. The machine allows them to press multiple keys at a time to record combinations of letters representing sounds, words, or phrases. These symbols are then recorded on computer disks or CD-ROM, which are then translated and displayed as text in a process called computer-aided transcription. In all cases, accuracy is crucial because there is only one person creating an official transcript. In a judicial setting, for example, appeals often depend on the court reporter's transcript. Stenotype machines used for realtime captioning are linked directly to the computer. As the reporter keys in the symbols, they instantly appear as text on the screen. This process, called communications access realtime translation (CART), is used in courts, in classrooms, at meetings, and for closed captioning for the hearing-impaired on television.

The other method of court reporting is called voice writing. Using the voice-writing method, a court reporter speaks directly into a stenomask—a hand-held mask containing a microphone with a voice silencer. As the reporter repeats the testimony into the recorder, the mask and silencer prevent the reporter from being heard during testimony. Voice writers record everything that is said by judges, witnesses, attorneys, and other parties to a proceeding, including gestures and emotional reactions.

Some voice writers produce a transcript in real time, using computer speech recognition technology. Other voice writers prefer to translate their voice files after the proceeding is over, or they transcribe the files manually, without using speech recognition at all. In any event, speech recognition technology is allowing voice writers to pursue not only court reporting careers, but also careers as closed captioners, CART reporters for hearing-impaired individuals, and Internet streaming text or caption providers.

Court reporters that use either method are responsible for a number of duties both before and after transcribing events. First, they must create and maintain the computer dictionary that they use to translate stenographic strokes or voice record files into written text. They may customize the dictionary with parts of words, entire words, or terminology specific to the proceeding, program, or event—such as a religious service—they plan to transcribe. After documenting proceedings, court reporters must edit their CART translation for correct grammar, for accurate identification of proper names and places, and to ensure that the record or testimony is discernible. They usually prepare written transcripts, make copies, and provide information from the transcript to courts, counsels, parties, and the public upon request. Court reporters also develop procedures for easy storage and retrieval of all stenographic notes and files in paper or digital format.

Although many court reporters record official proceedings in the courtroom, others work outside the courtroom. For example, they may take depositions for attorneys in offices and document proceedings of meetings, conventions, and other private activities. Still others capture the proceedings taking place in government agencies at all levels, from the U.S. Congress to State and local governing bodies. Court reporters, both stenotypists and voice writers, who specialize in captioning live television programming for people with hearing loss are commonly known as *stenocaptioners*. They work for television networks or cable stations, captioning news, emergency broadcasts, sporting events, and other programming. With CART and broadcast captioning, the level of understanding gained by a person with

Court reporters play a critical role in courtrooms and at meetings in which every word spoken must be documented.

hearing loss depends entirely on the skill of the stenocaptioner. In an emergency, such as a tornado or a hurricane, people's safety may depend entirely on the accuracy of information provided in the form of captioning.

Medical transcriptionists, discussed elsewhere in the *Handbook,* have similar duties, but with a different focus. They translate and edit recorded dictation by physicians and other healthcare providers regarding their assessment and treatment of patients.

Working Conditions

The majority of court reporters work in comfortable settings, such as offices of attorneys, courtrooms, legislatures, and conventions. An increasing number of court reporters work from home-based offices as independent contractors, or freelancers.

Work in this occupation presents few hazards, although sitting in the same position for long periods can be tiring, and workers can suffer wrist, back, neck, or eye problems due to strain. Workers also risk repetitive motion injuries such as carpal tunnel syndrome. In addition, the pressure to be accurate and fast can be stressful.

Many official court reporters work a standard 40-hour week. Self-employed court reporters, or freelancers, usually work flexible hours, including part time, evenings, and weekends, or they can work on an on-call basis.

Employment

Court reporters held about 18,000 jobs in 2002. About 60 percent worked for State and local governments, a reflection of the large number of court reporters working in courts, legislatures, and various agencies. Most of the remaining wage and salary workers worked for court reporting agencies. Eleven percent of court reporters were self-employed.

Training, Other Qualifications, and Advancement

The amount of training required to become a court reporter varies with the type of reporting chosen. It usually takes less than a year to become a voice writer. In contrast, the average length of time it takes to become a stenotypist is 33 months. Training is offered by about 160 postsecondary vocational and technical schools and colleges. The National Court Reporters Association (NCRA) has approved about 82 programs, all of which offer courses in stenotype computer-aided transcription and realtime reporting. NCRA-approved programs require students to capture a minimum of 225 words per minute, a Federal Government requirement as well.

Some States require court reporters to be notary publics. Others require the certified court reporter (CCR) designation, for which a reporter must pass a State certification test administered by a board of examiners. The NCRA confers the entry-level designation "registered professional reporter" (RPR) upon those who pass a four-part examination and participate in mandatory continuing education programs. Although voluntary, the designation is recognized as a mark of distinction in the field. A reporter may obtain additional certifications that demonstrate higher levels of competency, such as "registered merit reporter" (RMR) or "registered diplomate reporter" (RDR). The RDR is the highest level of certification available to court reporters. In order to receive the designation, a court reporter must either have 5 consecutive years of experience as an RMR or be an RMR and hold a 4-year baccalaureate degree.

The NCRA also offers the designations "certified realtime reporter"(CRR), "certified broadcast captioner" (CBC), and "certified CART provider" (CCP). These designations promote and recognize competence in the specialized skill of converting the spoken word into the written word instantaneously.

Some States require voice writers to pass a test and to earn State licensure. As a substitute for State certification, the National Verbatim Reporters Association offers three national certifications to voice writers: "certified verbatim reporter" (CVR), the certificate of merit (CM), and "real-time verbatim reporter" (RVR). Earning these certifications may be sufficient to get licensed in the State. In order to get the CM or RVR, one must first earn the CVR. Candidates for the CVR must pass a written test covering punctuation, spelling, grammar, legal terminology, definitions, and more and also must pass, three five-minute dictation and transcription examinations that test for speed as well as accuracy. Passing the CM exam requires a higher level of speed and accuracy. The RVR measures the candidate's skill at realtime transcription. In order to retain these certifications, the voice writer must obtain continuing education credits. Credits are given for voice writer education courses, continuing legal education courses, and college courses.

In addition to possessing speed and accuracy, court reporters must have excellent listening skills, as well as good English grammar, vocabulary, and punctuation skills. Voice writers must learn to listen and speak simultaneously and very quickly, while also identifying speakers and describing peripheral activities in the courtroom or deposition room. They must be aware of business practices and current events as well as the correct spelling of names of people, places, and events that may be mentioned in a broadcast or in court proceedings. For those who work in courtrooms, an expert knowledge of legal terminology and criminal and appellate procedure is essential. Because capturing proceedings requires the use of computerized stenography or speech recognition equipment, court reporters must be knowledgeable about computer hardware and software applications.

With experience and education, court reporters can advance to administrative and management positions, consulting, or teaching.

Job Outlook

Employment of court reporters is projected to grow about as fast as the average for all occupations through 2012. Demand for court reporter services will be spurred by the continuing need for accurate transcription of proceedings in courts and in pretrial depositions and by the growing need to create captions for live or prerecorded television and to provide other realtime translating services for the deaf and hard-of-hearing community. Despite the good job prospects, fewer people are going into this profession, creating a shortage of court reporters—particularly stenographic typists—and making job opportunities very good to excellent. Because of this shortage, voice writers have become more widely accepted as speech recognition technology improves and error rates decline. Still, many courts hire only stenotypists to perform court reporting duties, and because of this practice, demand for these highly skilled reporters will remain high.

Federal legislation mandates that, by 2006, all new television programming must be captioned for the deaf and hard-of-hearing. In addition, the Americans with Disabilities Act gives deaf and hard-of-hearing students in colleges and universities the right to request access to realtime translation in their classes. Both of these factors are expected to increase demand for court reporters to provide realtime captioning and CART services. Although these services forgo transcripts and differ from traditional court reporting, which uses computer-aided transcription to turn spoken words into permanent text, they require the same skills that court reporters learn in their training.

Despite increasing numbers of civil and criminal cases, budget constraints are expected to limit the ability of Federal, State, and local courts to expand, thereby also limiting the demand for traditional court reporting services in courtrooms and other legal venues. Further, in efforts to keep costs down, many courtrooms have installed tape recorders to maintain records of proceedings. Some jurisdictions have found the error rates associated with tape recorders to be unacceptable, bringing court reporters back to their courtrooms despite budgetary issues. Still, despite the use of audiotape and videotape technology, court reporters can quickly turn spoken words into readable, searchable, permanent text, so they will continue to be needed to produce written legal transcripts and proceedings for publication.

Earnings

Court reporters had median annual earnings of $41,550 in 2002. The middle 50 percent earned between $29,770 and $55,360. The lowest paid 10 percent earned less than $23,120, and the highest paid 10 percent earned more than $73,440. Median annual earnings in 2002 were $40,720 for court reporters working in local government.

Both compensation and compensation methods for court reporters vary with the type of reporting job, the experience of the individual reporter, the level of certification achieved, and the region of the country the reporter works in. Official court reporters earn a salary and a per-page fee for transcripts. Many salaried court reporters supplement their income by doing additional freelance work. Freelance court reporters are paid per job and receive a per-page fee for transcripts. Communication access realtime translation providers are paid hourly. Stenocaptioners receive a salary and benefits if they work as employees of a captioning company; stenocaptioners working as independent contractors are paid hourly.

Related Occupations

A number of other workers type, record information, and process paperwork. Among these are secretaries and administrative assistants, medical transcriptionists, receptionists and information clerks, and human resources assistants, except payroll and timekeeping. Other workers who provide legal support include paralegals and legal assistants.

Sources of Additional Information

State employment service offices can provide information about job openings for court reporters. For information about careers, training, and certification in court reporting, contact any of the following sources:
➤ National Court Reporters Association, 8224 Old Courthouse Rd., Vienna, VA 22182. Internet: **http://www.ncraonline.org**
➤ United States Court Reporters Association, P.O. Box 465, Chicago, Il 60690-0465. Internet: **http://www.uscra.org**
➤ National Verbatim Reporters Association, 207 Third Avenue, Hattiesburg, MS 39401. Internet: **http://www.nvra.org**

Judges, Magistrates, and Other Judicial Workers

(O*NET 23-1021.00, 23-1022.00, 23-1023.00)

Significant Points

- A bachelor's degree and work experience are the minimum requirements for a judgeship or magistrate position, but most workers filling these positions also have law degrees.
- Judges and magistrates should encounter some competition for jobs.
- Demand for arbitrators, mediators, and conciliators is growing because of the high cost and long delays associated with litigation.

Nature of the Work

Judges, magistrates, and other judicial workers apply the law and oversee the legal process in courts according to local, State, and Federal statutes. They preside over cases concerning every aspect of society, from traffic offenses, to disputes over the management of professional sports, to issues concerning the rights of huge corporations, to questions over disconnecting life-support equipment connected to terminally ill persons. All judicial workers must ensure that trials and hearings are conducted fairly and that the court administers justice in a manner which safeguards the legal rights of all parties involved.

The most visible responsibility of judges is presiding over trials or hearings and listening as attorneys represent the parties present. Judges rule on the admissibility of evidence and the methods of conducting testimony, and they may be called upon to settle disputes between opposing attorneys. Also, they ensure that rules and procedures are followed, and if unusual circumstances arise for which standard procedures have not been established, they determine the manner in which the trial will proceed, on the basis of their interpretation of the law.

Judges often hold pretrial hearings for cases. They listen to allegations and determine whether the evidence presented merits a trial. In criminal cases, judges may decide that persons charged with crimes should be held in jail pending their trial, or they may set conditions for their release. In civil cases, they occasionally impose restrictions upon the parties until a trial is held.

In many trials, juries are selected to decide guilt or innocence in criminal cases or liability and compensation in civil cases. Judges instruct juries on applicable laws, direct them to deduce the facts from the evidence presented, and hear their verdict. When the law does not require a jury trial or when the parties waive their right to a jury, judges decide the cases. In such instances, in a criminal case, the judge determines guilt and imposes sentences; in civil cases, the judge awards relief— such as compensation for damages—to the parties to the lawsuit (called litigants). Judges also work outside the courtroom, "in chambers." In these, their private offices, judges read documents on pleadings and motions, research legal issues, write opinions, and oversee the court's operations. In some jurisdictions, judges also manage the courts' administrative and clerical staff.

Judges' duties vary according to the extent of their jurisdictions and powers. *General trial court judges* of the Federal and State court systems have jurisdiction over any case in their system. They usually try civil cases transcending the jurisdiction of lower courts and all cases involving felony offenses. Federal and State *appellate court judges*, although few in number, have the power to overrule decisions made by trial court or administrative law judges if they determine that legal errors were made in a case or if legal precedent does not support the judgment of the lower court. Appellate court judges rule on a small number of cases and rarely have direct contacts with litigants. Instead, they usually base their decisions on lower court records and lawyers' written and oral arguments.

Many State court judges preside in courts whose jurisdiction is limited by law to certain types of cases. A variety of titles are assigned to these judges; among the most common are *municipal court judge*, *county court judge*, *magistrate*, and *justice of the peace*. Traffic violations, misdemeanors, small-claims cases, and pretrial hearings constitute the bulk of the work of State court judges, but some States allow them to handle cases involving domestic relations, probate, contracts, and other selected areas of the law.

Administrative law judges, sometimes called *hearing officers* or *adjudicators*, are employed by government agencies to make determinations for administrative agencies. These judges make decisions, for example, on a person's eligibility for various Social Security or worker's compensation benefits, on protection of the environment, on the enforcement of health and safety regulations, on employment discrimination, and on compliance with economic regulatory requirements.

Arbitration, mediation, and conciliation—called appropriate dispute resolution (ADR)—are alternative processes that can be used to settle disputes between parties. All ADR hearings are private and confidential, and the processes are less formal than a court trial. If no settlement is reached through ADR, any statements made during the proceedings are inadmissible as evidence in any subsequent litigation.

During arbitration, opposing parties submit their dispute to one or more impartial persons, called arbitrators, for a final and binding decision. Arbitrators usually are attorneys or businesspersons with expertise in a particular field. The parties identify beforehand the issues to be resolved by arbitration, the scope of the relief to be awarded, and many of the procedural aspects of the process. Few awards are reviewed by the courts, because the parties have agreed to be bound by the decision of their arbitrator, although in some cases, it is prearranged that the award will be only advisory. Mediation involves an attempt by the parties to resolve their dispute with the aid of a neutral third party and generally is used when the parties wish to preserve their relationship. A mediator may offer suggestions, but resolution of the dispute rests with the parties themselves. Mediation proceedings are also confidential and private. If the parties are unable to reach a settlement, they are free to pursue other options. The parties usually decide in advance how they will contribute to the cost of mediation.

Conciliation is similar to mediation. The conciliator's role is to guide the parties to a settlement. The parties must decide in advance whether they will be bound by the conciliator's recommendations; they generally share equally in the cost of the conciliation.

Working Conditions

Judges, magistrates, and other judicial workers do most of their work in offices, law libraries, and courtrooms. Work in these occupations presents few hazards, although sitting in the same position in the courtroom for long periods can be tiring. Most judges wear robes when they are in a courtroom. Judges typically work a standard 40-hour week, but many work more than 50 hours per week. Some judges with limited jurisdiction are employed part time and divide their time between their judicial responsibilities and other careers.

Arbitrators, mediators, and conciliators usually work in private offices or meeting rooms; no public record is made of the proceedings.

Judges may be called upon to settle disputes between opposing attorneys.

Employment

Judges, magistrates, and magistrate judges held 27,000 jobs in 2002, primarily in State and local government. Administrative law judges, adjudicators, and hearing officers held about 19,000 jobs; 57 percent worked in State governments, 24 percent in the Federal Government, and 16 percent in local governments. Arbitrators, mediators, and conciliators held another 6,100 jobs. Approximately half worked for State and local governments. The remainder worked for labor organizations, law offices, insurance carriers, and other private companies and for organizations that specialize in providing dispute resolution services.

Training, Other Qualifications, and Advancement

A bachelor's degree and work experience usually constitute the minimum requirement for a judgeship or magistrate position. A number of lawyers become judges, and most judges have first been lawyers. In fact, Federal and State judges usually are required to be lawyers. About 40 States allow nonlawyers to hold limited-jurisdiction judgeships, but opportunities are better for those with law experience. Federal administrative law judges must be lawyers and pass a competitive examination administered by the U.S. Office of Personnel Management. Some State administrative law judges and other hearing officials are not required to be lawyers.

Federal administrative law judges are appointed by various Federal agencies, with virtually lifetime tenure. Federal magistrate judges are appointed by district judges—the life-tenured Federal judges of a district court—to serve in a United States district court for a period of 8 years. A part-time federal magistrate judge's term of office is 4 years. Some State judges are appointed, but the remainder are elected in partisan or nonpartisan State elections. Many State and local judges serve fixed renewable terms ranging from 4 or 6 years for some trial court judgeships to as long as 14 years or even life for other trial or appellate court judges. Judicial nominating commissions, composed of members of the bar and the public, are used to screen candidates for judgeships in many States and for some Federal judgeships.

All States have some type of orientation for newly elected or appointed judges. The Federal Judicial Center, American Bar Association, National Judicial College, and National Center for State Courts provide judicial education and training for judges and other judicial-branch personnel. General and continuing education courses usually last from a couple of days to 3 weeks in length. More than half of all States, as well as Puerto Rico, require judges to enroll in continuing education courses while serving on the bench.

Training and education requirements for arbitrators, mediators, and conciliators differ from those for judges. Mediators who practice in State- or court-funded mediation programs usually must meet specific training or experience standards, which vary by State and court. In most States, individuals who offer private mediation services do not need a license, certification, or specific course work; however, many private mediators and most of those affiliated with mediation organizations and programs have completed mediation training and agreed to comply with certain ethical standards. For example, the American Arbitration Association (AAA) requires mediators listed on its mediation panel to complete an AAA training course, receive recommendations from the trainers, and complete an apprenticeship.

Training for arbitrators, mediators, and conciliators is available through independent mediation programs, national and local mediation membership organizations, and postsecondary schools. In 2002, 16 colleges or universities in the United States offered master's degrees in dispute resolution or conflict management, and 2 offered doctoral degrees. Many more schools offer conflict-management specializations within other degree programs. Degrees in public policy, law, and related fields also provide good background for prospective arbitrators, mediators, and conciliators.

Job Outlook

Employment of judges and magistrates is expected to grow more slowly than the average through 2012. Budgetary pressures at all levels of government will hold down the hiring of judges, despite rising caseloads, particularly in Federal courts. Most job openings will arise as judges retire. However, additional openings occur when new judgeships positions are authorized by law or when judges are elevated to a higher judicial office.

Public concerns about crime and safety, as well as a public increasingly willing to go to court to settle disputes, should spur demand for judges. Not only has the quantity of a judge's work increased, but many cases have become more complex because of developments in information technology, medical science, e-commerce, and globalization. The prestige associated with serving on the bench should ensure competition for judge and magistrate positions. However, a growing number of judges and candidates for judgeships are choosing to forgo the bench and work in the private sector, where pay is significantly higher. This movement may lessen the competition somewhat. Becoming a judge also is often difficult because, not only must judicial candidates compete with other qualified people, but also, they frequently must also gain political support in order to be elected or appointed, and getting that support can be expensive.

Employment of arbitrators, mediators, and conciliators is expected to grow as fast as the average for all occupations through 2012. Many individuals and businesses try to avoid litigation, which can involve lengthy delays, high costs, unwanted publicity, and ill will. Arbitration and other alternatives to litigation usually are faster, less expensive, and more conclusive, spurring demand for the services of arbitrators, mediators, and conciliators. Administrative law judges are expected to experience little to no change in employment, due to a slowing of growth in the Federal sector.

Earnings

Judges, magistrate judges, and magistrates had median annual earnings of $94,070 in 2002. The middle 50 percent earned between $44,970 and $120,390. The top 10 percent earned more than $138,300, while the bottom 10 percent earned less than $24,250. Median annual earnings in the industries employing the largest numbers of judges, magistrate judges, and magistrates in 2002 were $112,720 in State government and $54,750 in local government. Administrative law judges, adjudicators, and hearing officers earned a median of $64,540, and arbitrators, mediators, and conciliators earned a median of $47,320.

In Federal courts, the following salaries apply: the Chief Justice of the United States Supreme Court earned $198,600, and the Associate Justices earned $190,100. Federal court of appeals judges earned $164,100 a year in 2001 while district court judges had salaries of $154,700, as did judges in the Court of Federal Claims and the Court of International Trade. Federal judges with limited jurisdiction, such as magistrates and bankruptcy court judges, had salaries of $142,324.

According to a survey by the National Center for State Courts, annual salaries of associate justices of States' highest courts averaged $120,100 in 2002 and ranged from about $89,381 to $170,319. Salaries of State intermediate appellate court judges averaged $116,064 and ranged from $91,469 to $159,657. Salaries of State judges of general jurisdiction trial courts averaged $109,811 and ranged from $82,600 to $150,000.

Most salaried judges are provided health and life insurance, and contributions to retirement plans are made on their behalf.

Related Occupations

Legal training and mediation skills are useful in many other occupations, including counselors; lawyers; paralegals and legal assistants; title examiners, abstractors, and searchers; law clerks; and detectives and criminal investigators.

Sources of Additional Information

Information on judges, magistrates, and other judicial workers may be obtained from

➤ National Center for State Courts, 300 Newport Ave., Williamsburg, VA 23185. Internet: **http://www.ncsconline.org**

Information on arbitrators, mediators, and conciliators may be obtained from

➤ American Arbitration Association, 335 Madison Ave., Floor 10, New York, NY 10017. Internet: **http://www.adr.org**

Lawyers

(0*NET 23-1011.00)

Significant Points

- Formal educational requirements for lawyers include a 4-year college degree, 3 years in law school, and the passing of a written bar examination.

- Competition for admission to most law schools is intense.

- Demand for lawyers will be spurred by the growth of legal action in such areas as health care, intellectual property, international law, elder law, environmental law, and sexual harassment.

Nature of the Work

The legal system affects nearly every aspect of our society, from buying a home to crossing the street. Lawyers form the backbone of this vital system, linking it to society in myriad ways. For that reason, they hold positions of great responsibility and are obligated to adhere to a strict code of ethics.

Lawyers, also called *attorneys*, act as both advocates and advisors in our society. As advocates, they represent one of the parties in criminal and civil trials by presenting evidence and arguing in court to support their client. As advisors, lawyers counsel their clients concerning their legal rights and obligations and suggest particular courses of action in business and personal matters. Whether acting as an advocate or an advisor, all attorneys research the intent of laws and judicial decisions and apply the law to the specific circumstances faced by their client.

The more detailed aspects of a lawyer's job depend upon his or her field of specialization and position. Although all lawyers are licensed to represent parties in court, some appear in court more frequently than others. Trial lawyers, who specialize in trial work, must be able to think quickly and speak with ease and authority. In addition, familiarity with courtroom rules and strategy is particularly important in trial work. Still, trial lawyers spend the majority of their time outside the courtroom, conducting research, interviewing clients and witnesses, and handling other details in preparation for trial.

Lawyers may specialize in a number of different areas, such as bankruptcy, probate, international, or elder law. Those specializing in environmental law, for example, may represent public-interest groups, waste disposal companies, or construction firms in their dealings with the U.S. Environmental Protection Agency (EPA) and other Federal and State agencies. These lawyers help clients prepare and file for licenses and applications for approval before certain activities may occur. In addition, they represent clients' interests in administrative adjudications.

Some lawyers concentrate in the growing field of intellectual property, helping to protect clients' claims to copyrights, artwork under contract, product designs, and computer programs. Still other lawyers advise insurance companies about the legality of insurance transactions, writing insurance policies to conform with the law and to protect companies from unwarranted claims. When claims are filed against insurance companies, these attorneys review the claims and represent the companies in court.

Most lawyers are found in private practice, where they concentrate on criminal or civil law. In criminal law, lawyers represent individuals who have been charged with crimes and argue their cases in courts of law. Attorneys dealing with civil law assist clients with litigation, wills, trusts, contracts, mortgages, titles, and leases. Other lawyers handle only public-interest cases—civil or criminal—which may have an impact extending well beyond the individual client.

Lawyers are sometimes employed full time by a single client. If the client is a corporation, the lawyer is known as "house counsel" and usually advises the company concerning legal issues related to its business activities. These issues might in-

Lawyers spend most of their time outside the courtroom, conducting research, interviewing clients and witnesses, and preparing paperwork.

volve patents, government regulations, contracts with other companies, property interests, or collective-bargaining agreements with unions.

A significant number of attorneys are employed at the various levels of government. Lawyers who work for State attorneys general, prosecutors, public defenders, and courts play a key role in the criminal justice system. At the Federal level, attorneys investigate cases for the U.S. Department of Justice and other agencies. Government lawyers also help develop programs, draft and interpret laws and legislation, establish enforcement procedures, and argue civil and criminal cases on behalf of the government.

Other lawyers work for legal-aid societies—private, nonprofit organizations established to serve disadvantaged people. These lawyers generally handle civil, rather than criminal, cases. A relatively small number of trained attorneys work in law schools. Most are faculty members who specialize in one or more subjects; however, some serve as administrators. Others work full time in nonacademic settings and teach part time. (For additional information, see the *Handbook* section on teachers—postsecondary.)

Lawyers are increasingly using various forms of technology to perform their varied tasks more efficiently. While all lawyers continue to use law libraries to prepare cases, some supplement their search of conventional printed sources with computer sources, such as the Internet and legal databases. Software is used to search this legal literature automatically and to identify legal texts relevant to a specific case. In litigation involving many supporting documents, lawyers may use computers to organize and index material. Lawyers also utilize electronic filing, videoconferencing, and voice-recognition technology to share information more effectively with other parties involved in a case.

Working Conditions

Lawyers do most of their work in offices, law libraries, and courtrooms. They sometimes meet in clients' homes or places of business and, when necessary, in hospitals or prisons. They may travel to attend meetings, gather evidence, and appear before courts, legislative bodies, and other authorities.

Salaried lawyers usually have structured work schedules. Lawyers who are in private practice may work irregular hours while conducting research, conferring with clients, or preparing briefs during nonoffice hours. Lawyers often work long hours, and of those who regularly work full time, about half work 50 hours or more per week. They may face particularly heavy pressure, especially when a case is being tried. Preparation for court includes keeping abreast of the latest laws and judicial decisions.

Although legal work generally is not seasonal, the work of tax lawyers and other specialists may be an exception. Because lawyers in private practice often can determine their own workload and the point at which they will retire, many stay in practice well beyond the usual retirement age.

Employment

Lawyers held about 695,000 jobs in 2002. About 3 out of 4 lawyers practiced privately, either in law firms or in solo practices. Most of the remaining lawyers held positions in government and with corporations and nonprofit organizations. For those working in government, the greatest number were em-

ployed at the local level. In the Federal Government, lawyers work for many different agencies, but are concentrated in the Departments of Justice, Treasury, and Defense. For those working outside of government, lawyers are employed as house counsel by public utilities, banks, insurance companies, real-estate agencies, manufacturing firms, and other business firms and nonprofit organizations. Some salaried lawyers also have part-time independent practices; others work part time as lawyers and full time in another occupation.

Training, Other Qualifications, and Advancement

To practice law in the courts of any State or other jurisdiction, a person must be licensed, or admitted to its bar, under rules established by the jurisdiction's highest court. All States require that applicants for admission to the bar pass a written bar examination; most jurisdictions also require applicants to pass a separate written ethics examination. Lawyers who have been admitted to the bar in one jurisdiction occasionally may be admitted to the bar in another without taking an examination if they meet the latter jurisdiction's standards of good moral character and have a specified period of legal experience. Federal courts and agencies set their own qualifications for those practicing before or in them.

To qualify for the bar examination in most States, an applicant usually must earn a college degree and graduate from a law school accredited by the American Bar Association (ABA) or the proper State authorities. ABA accreditation signifies that the law school—particularly its library and faculty—meets certain standards developed to promote quality legal education. ABA currently accredits 188 law schools; others are approved by State authorities only. With certain exceptions, graduates of schools not approved by the ABA are restricted to taking the bar examination and practicing in the State or other jurisdiction in which the school is located; most of these schools are in California. In 2002, eight States accepted the study of law in a law office as qualification for taking the bar examination; three jurisdictions—California, the District of Columbia, and New Mexico—now accept the study of law by correspondence. Several States require registration and approval of students by the State Board of Law Examiners, either before the students enter law school or during their early years of legal study.

Although there is no nationwide bar examination, 48 States, the District of Columbia, Guam, the Northern Mariana Islands, Puerto Rico, and the Virgin Islands require the 6-hour Multistate Bar Examination (MBE) as part of the overall bar examination; the MBE is not required in Louisiana and Washington. The MBE covers issues of broad interest, and sometimes a locally prepared State bar examination is given in addition to the MBE. The 3-hour Multistate Essay Examination (MEE) is used as part of the bar examination in several States. States vary in their use of MBE and MEE scores.

Many States have begun to require Multistate Performance Testing (MPT) to test the practical skills of beginning lawyers. This program has been well received, and many more States are expected to require performance testing in the future. Requirements vary by State, although the test usually is taken at the same time as the bar exam and is a one-time requirement.

The required college and law school education usually takes 7 years of full-time study after high school—4 years of undergraduate study, followed by 3 years of law school. Law school applicants must have a bachelor's degree to qualify for admission. To meet the needs of students who can attend only part time, a number of law schools have night or part-time divisions, which usually require 4 years of study; about 1 in 10 graduates from ABA-approved schools attended part time.

Although there is no recommended "prelaw" major, prospective lawyers should develop proficiency in writing and speaking, reading, researching, analyzing, and thinking logically—skills needed to succeed both in law school and in the profession. Regardless of major, a multidisciplinary background is recommended. Courses in English, foreign languages, public speaking, government, philosophy, history, economics, mathematics, and computer science, among others, are useful. Students interested in a particular aspect of law may find related courses helpful. For example, prospective patent lawyers need a strong background in engineering or science, and future tax lawyers must have extensive knowledge of accounting.

Acceptance by most law schools depends on the applicant's ability to demonstrate an aptitude for the study of law, usually through good undergraduate grades, the Law School Admission Test (LSAT), the quality of the applicant's undergraduate school, any prior work experience, and, sometimes, a personal interview. However, law schools vary in the weight they place on each of these and other factors.

All law schools approved by the ABA, except those in Puerto Rico, require applicants to take the LSAT. Nearly all law schools require applicants to have certified transcripts sent to the Law School Data Assembly Service, which then submits applicants' LSAT scores and their standardized records of college grades to the law schools of their choice. Both this service and the LSAT are administered by the Law School Admission Council. Competition for admission to many law schools—especially the most prestigious ones—generally is intense, with the number of applicants to most law schools greatly exceeding the number that can be admitted.

During the first year or year and a half of law school, students usually study core courses, such as constitutional law, contracts, property law, torts, civil procedure, and legal writing. In the remaining time, they may elect specialized courses in fields such as tax, labor, or corporate law. Law students often acquire practical experience by participating in school-sponsored legal clinic activities; in the school's moot court competitions, in which students conduct appellate arguments; in practice trials under the supervision of experienced lawyers and judges; and through research and writing on legal issues for the school's law journal.

A number of law schools have clinical programs in which students gain legal experience through practice trials and projects under the supervision of practicing lawyers and law school faculty. Law school clinical programs might include work in legal-aid clinics, for example, or on the staff of legislative committees. Part-time or summer clerkships in law firms, government agencies, and corporate legal departments also provide valuable experience. Such training can lead directly to a job after graduation and can help students decide what kind of practice best suits them. Clerkships may also be an important source of financial aid.

In 2001, law students in 52 jurisdictions were required to pass the Multistate Professional Responsibility Examination (MPRE), which tests their knowledge of the ABA codes on professional responsibility and judicial conduct. In some States, the MPRE may be taken during law school, usually after completing a course on legal ethics.

Law school graduates receive the degree of *juris doctor* (J.D.) as the first professional degree. Advanced law degrees may be desirable for those planning to specialize, research, or teach. Some law students pursue joint degree programs, which usually require an additional semester or year of study. Joint degree programs are offered in a number of areas, including law and business administration or public administration.

After graduation, lawyers must keep informed about legal and nonlegal developments that affect their practice. Currently, 40 States and jurisdictions mandate continuing legal education (CLE). Many law schools and State and local bar associations provide continuing education courses that help lawyers stay abreast of recent developments. Some States allow CLE credits to be obtained through participation in seminars on the Internet.

The practice of law involves a great deal of responsibility. Individuals planning careers in law should like to work with people and be able to win the respect and confidence of their clients, associates, and the public. Perseverance, creativity, and reasoning ability also are essential to lawyers, who often analyze complex cases and handle new and unique legal problems.

Most beginning lawyers start in salaried positions. Newly hired salaried attorneys usually start as associates and work with more experienced lawyers or judges. After several years of gaining more responsibilities, some lawyers are admitted to partnership in their firm or go into practice for themselves. Some experienced lawyers are nominated or elected to judgeships. (See the section on judges, magistrates, and other judicial workers elsewhere in the *Handbook*.) Others become full-time law school faculty or administrators; a growing number of these lawyers have advanced degrees in other fields as well.

Some attorneys use their legal training in administrative or managerial positions in various departments of large corporations. A transfer from a corporation's legal department to another department often is viewed as a way to gain administrative experience and rise in the ranks of management.

Job Outlook

Employment of lawyers is expected to grow about as fast as the average through 2012, primarily as a result of growth in the population and in the general level of business activities. Employment growth of lawyers also will result from growth in demand for legal services in such areas as elder, antitrust, environmental, and intellectual-property law. In addition, the wider availability and affordability of legal clinics and prepaid legal service programs should result in increased use of legal services by middle-income people.

Growth in demand will be somewhat mitigated, because, in an effort to reduce money spent on legal fees, many businesses increasingly are using large accounting firms and paralegals to perform some of the same functions that lawyers do. For example, accounting firms may provide employee-benefit counseling, process documents, or handle various other services previously performed by a law firm. Also, mediation and dispute resolution increasingly are being used as alternatives to litigation.

Competition for job openings should continue to be keen because of the large number of students graduating from law school each year. Graduates with superior academic records from well-regarded law schools will have the best job opportunities.

Perhaps as a result of competition for attorney positions, lawyers are increasingly finding work in nontraditional areas for which legal training is an asset, but not normally a requirement—for example, administrative, managerial, and business positions in banks, insurance firms, real-estate companies, government agencies, and other organizations. Employment opportunities are expected to continue to arise in these organizations at a growing rate.

As in the past, some graduates may have to accept positions in areas outside of their field of interest or for which they feel overqualified. Some recent law school graduates who have been unable to find permanent positions are turning to the growing number of temporary staffing firms that place attorneys in short-term jobs until they are able to secure full-time positions. This service allows companies to hire lawyers on an "as-needed" basis and permits beginning lawyers to develop practical skills while looking for permanent positions.

Due to the competition for jobs, a law graduate's geographic mobility and work experience assume greater importance. The willingness to relocate may be an advantage in getting a job, but, to be licensed in another State, a lawyer may have to take an additional State bar examination. In addition, employers are increasingly seeking graduates who have advanced law degrees and experience in a specialty, such as tax, patent, or admiralty law.

Employment growth for lawyers will continue to be concentrated in salaried jobs, as businesses and all levels of government employ a growing number of staff attorneys and as employment in the legal services industry grows. Most salaried positions are in urban areas where government agencies, law firms, and big corporations are concentrated. The number of self-employed lawyers is expected to decrease slowly, reflecting the difficulty of establishing a profitable new practice in the face of competition from larger, established law firms. Moreover, the growing complexity of law, which encourages specialization, along with the cost of maintaining up-to-date legal research materials, favors larger firms.

For lawyers who wish to work independently, establishing a new practice will probably be easiest in small towns and expanding suburban areas. In such communities, competition from larger, established law firms is likely to be less keen than in big cities, and new lawyers may find it easier to become known to potential clients.

Some lawyers are adversely affected by cyclical swings in the economy. During recessions, demand declines for some discretionary legal services, such as planning estates, drafting wills, and handling real-estate transactions. Also, corporations are less likely to litigate cases when declining sales and profits result in budgetary restrictions. Some corporations and law firms will not hire new attorneys until business improves, and these establishments may even cut staff to contain costs. Several factors, however, mitigate the overall impact of recessions on lawyers; during recessions, for example, individuals and corporations face other legal problems, such as bankruptcies, foreclosures, and divorces requiring legal action.

Earnings

In 2002, the median annual earnings of all lawyers was $90,290. The middle half of the occupation earned between $61,060 and $136,810. The lowest paid 10 percent earned less than $44,490; at least 10 percent earned more than $145,600. Median annual earnings in the industries employing the largest numbers of lawyers in 2002 are given in the following tabulation:

Management of companies and enterprises	$131,970
Federal government	98,790
Legal services	93,970
Local government	69,710
State government	67,910

Median salaries of lawyers 6 months after graduation from law school in 2001 varied by type of work, as indicated by table 1.

Table 1. Median salaries of lawyers 6 months after graduation, 2001

All graduates	$60,000
Type of work	
Private practice	90,000
Business/industry	60,000
Judicial clerkship and government	40,300
Academe	40,000

Source: *National Association of Law Placement*

Salaries of experienced attorneys vary widely according to the type, size, and location of their employer. Lawyers who own their own practices usually earn less than do those who are partners in law firms. Lawyers starting their own practice may need to work part time in other occupations to supplement their income until their practice is well established.

Most salaried lawyers are provided health and life insurance, and contributions are made on their behalf to retirement plans. Lawyers who practice independently are covered only if they arrange and pay for such benefits themselves.

Related Occupations

Legal training is necessary in many other occupations, including paralegal and legal assistant; law clerk; title examiner, abstractor, and searcher; arbitrator, mediator, and conciliator; judge, magistrate judge, and magistrate; and administrative law judge, adjudicator, and hearing officer.

Sources of Additional Information

Information on law schools and a career in law may be obtained from
➤ American Bar Association, 750 North Lake Shore Dr., Chicago, IL 60611. Internet: **http://www.abanet.org**

Information on the LSAT, the Law School Data Assembly Service, the law school application process, and the financial aid available to law students may be obtained from
➤ Law School Admission Council, P.O. Box 40, Newtown, PA 18940. Internet: **http://www.lsac.org**

Information on obtaining a job as a lawyer with the Federal Government is available from the Office of Personnel Management through a telephone-based system. Consult your telephone directory under "U.S. Government" for a local number, or call (703) 724-1850; Federal Relay Service: (800) 877-8339. The first number is not toll free, and charges may accrue. Information also is available from the Internet site **http://www.usajobs.opm.gov**.

The requirements for admission to the bar in a particular State or other jurisdiction also may be obtained at the State capital, from the clerk of the Supreme Court, or from the administrator of the State Board of Bar Examiners.

Paralegals and Legal Assistants

(O*NET 23-2011.00)

Significant Points

- While some paralegals train on the job, employers increasingly prefer graduates of postsecondary paralegal education programs; college graduates who have taken some paralegal courses are especially in demand in some markets.

- Paralegals are projected to grow faster than average, as law offices try to reduce costs by assigning them tasks formerly carried out by lawyers.

- Paralegals are employed by law firms, corporate legal departments, and various government offices and they may specialize in many different areas of the law.

Nature of the Work

While lawyers assume ultimate responsibility for legal work, they often delegate many of their tasks to paralegals. In fact, paralegals—also called legal assistants—continue to assume a growing range of tasks in the Nation's legal offices and perform many of the same tasks as lawyers. Nevertheless, they are still explicitly prohibited from carrying out duties which are considered to be the practice of law, such as setting legal fees, giving legal advice, and presenting cases in court.

One of a paralegal's most important tasks is helping lawyers prepare for closings, hearings, trials, and corporate meetings. Paralegals investigate the facts of cases and ensure that all relevant information is considered. They also identify appropriate laws, judicial decisions, legal articles, and other materials that are relevant to assigned cases. After they analyze and organize the information, paralegals may prepare written reports that attorneys use in determining how cases should be handled. Should attorneys decide to file lawsuits on behalf of clients, paralegals may help prepare the legal arguments, draft pleadings and motions to be filed with the court, obtain affidavits, and assist attorneys during trials. Paralegals also organize and track files of all important case documents and make them available and easily accessible to attorneys.

In addition to this preparatory work, paralegals also perform a number of other vital functions. For example, they help draft contracts, mortgages, separation agreements, and trust instruments. They also may assist in preparing tax returns and planning estates. Some paralegals coordinate the activities of other law office employees and maintain financial office records. Various additional tasks may differ, depending on the employer.

Paralegals are found in all types of organizations, but most are employed by law firms, corporate legal departments, and various government offices. In these organizations, they can work in many different areas of the law, including litigation, personal injury, corporate law, criminal law, employee benefits, intellectual property, labor law, bankruptcy, immigration, family law, and real estate. As the law has become more complex, paralegals have responded by becoming more specialized. Within specialties, functions often are broken down further so that paralegals may deal with a specific area. For example, paralegals specializing in labor law may deal exclusively with employee benefits.

The duties of paralegals also differ widely based on the type of organization in which they are employed. Paralegals who work for corporations often assist attorneys with employee contracts, shareholder agreements, stock-option plans, and employee benefit plans. They also may help prepare and file annual financial reports, maintain corporate minute books and record resolutions, and prepare forms to secure loans for the corporation. Paralegals often monitor and review government regulations to ensure that the corporation is aware of new requirements and it operates within the law.

The duties of paralegals who work in the public sector usually vary within each agency. In general, they analyze legal material for internal use, maintain reference files, conduct research for attorneys, and collect and analyze evidence for agency hearings. They may then prepare informative or explanatory material on laws, agency regulations, and agency policy for general use by the agency and the public. Paralegals employed in community legal-service projects help the poor, the aged, and others in need of legal assistance. They file forms, conduct research, prepare documents, and when authorized by law, may represent clients at administrative hearings.

Paralegals in small and medium-sized law firms usually perform a variety of duties that require a general knowledge of the law. For example, they may research judicial decisions on improper police arrests or help prepare a mortgage contract. Paralegals employed by large law firms, government agencies, and corporations, however, are more likely to specialize in one aspect of the law.

Computer use and technical knowledge has become essential to paralegal work. Computer software packages and the Internet are increasingly used to search legal literature stored in computer databases and on CD-ROM. In litigation involving many supporting documents, paralegals may use computer databases to retrieve, organize, and index various materials. Imaging software allows paralegals to scan documents directly into a database, while billing programs help them to track hours billed to clients. Computer software packages also may be used to perform tax computations and explore the consequences of possible tax strategies for clients.

Working Conditions

Paralegals employed by corporations and government usually work a standard 40-hour week. Although most paralegals work

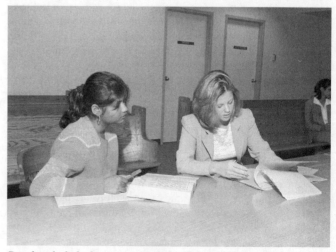

Paralegals help lawyers to prepare for closings, hearings, trials, and corporate meetings.

year round, some are temporarily employed during busy times of the year, then released when the workload diminishes. Paralegals who work for law firms sometimes work very long hours when they are under pressure to meet deadlines. Some law firms reward such loyalty with bonuses and additional time off.

These workers handle many routine assignments, particularly when they are inexperienced. As they gain experience, paralegals usually assume more varied tasks with additional responsibility. Paralegals do most of their work at desks in offices and law libraries. Occasionally, they travel to gather information and perform other duties.

Employment

Paralegals and legal assistants held about 200,000 jobs in 2002. Private law firms employed 7 out of 10 paralegals and legal assistants; most of the remainder worked for corporate legal departments and various levels of government. Within the Federal Government, the U.S. Department of Justice is the largest employer, followed by the Social Security Administration and the U.S. Department of Treasury. A small number of paralegals own their own businesses and work as freelance legal assistants, contracting their services to attorneys or corporate legal departments.

Training, Other Qualifications, and Advancement

There are several ways to become a paralegal. The most common is through a community college paralegal program that leads to an associate's degree. The other common method of entry, mainly for those who have a college degree, is through a certification program that leads to a certification in paralegal studies. A small number of schools also offer bachelor's and master's degrees in paralegal studies. Some employers train paralegals on the job, hiring college graduates with no legal experience or promoting experienced legal secretaries. Other entrants have experience in a technical field that is useful to law firms, such as a background in tax preparation for tax and estate practice, criminal justice, or nursing or health administration for personal injury practice.

Formal paralegal training programs are offered by an estimated 600 colleges and universities, law schools, and proprietary schools. Approximately 250 paralegal programs are approved by the American Bar Association (ABA). Although this approval is neither required nor sought by many programs, graduation from an ABA-approved program can enhance one's employment opportunities. The requirements for admission to these programs vary. Some require certain college courses or a bachelor's degree; others accept high school graduates or those with legal experience; and a few schools require standardized tests and personal interviews.

Paralegal programs include 2-year associate's degree programs, 4-year bachelor's degree programs, and certificate programs that can take only a few months to complete. Most certificate programs provide intensive paralegal training for individuals who already hold college degrees, while associate's and bachelor's degree programs usually combine paralegal training with courses in other academic subjects. The quality of paralegal training programs varies; the better programs usually include job placement. Programs increasingly include courses introducing students to the legal applications of computers, including how to perform legal research using the Internet. Many paralegal training programs include an internship in which students gain practical experience by working for several months in a private law firm, office of a public defender or attorney general, bank, corporate legal department, legal-aid organization, or government agency. Experience gained in internships is an asset when seeking a job after graduation. Prospective students should examine the experiences of recent graduates before enrolling in those programs.

Although most employers do not require certification, earning a voluntary certificate from a professional society may offer advantages in the labor market. The National Association of Legal Assistants, for example, has established standards for certification requiring various combinations of education and experience. Paralegals who meet these standards are eligible to take a 2-day examination, given three times each year at several regional testing centers. Those who pass this examination may use the designation Certified Legal Assistant (CLA). In addition, the Paralegal Advanced Competency Exam, established in 1996 and administered through the National Federation of Paralegal Associations, offers professional recognition to paralegals with a bachelor's degree and at least 2 years of experience. Those who pass this examination may use the designation Registered Paralegal (RP).

Paralegals must be able to document and present their findings and opinions to their supervising attorney. They need to understand legal terminology and have good research and investigative skills. Familiarity with the operation and applications of computers in legal research and litigation support also is increasingly important. Paralegals should stay informed of new developments in the laws that affect their area of practice. Participation in continuing legal education seminars allows paralegals to maintain and expand their legal knowledge.

Because paralegals frequently deal with the public, they should be courteous and uphold the ethical standards of the legal profession. The National Association of Legal Assistants, the National Federation of Paralegal Associations, and a few States have established ethical guidelines for paralegals to follow.

Paralegals usually are given more responsibilities and less supervision as they gain work experience. Experienced paralegals who work in large law firms, corporate legal departments, and government agencies may supervise and delegate assignments to other paralegals and clerical staff. Advancement opportunities also include promotion to managerial and other law-related positions within the firm or corporate legal department. However, some paralegals find it easier to move to another law firm when seeking increased responsibility or advancement.

Job Outlook

Paralegals and legal assistants are projected to grow faster than the average for all occupations through 2012. Some employment growth stems from law firms and other employers with legal staffs increasingly hiring paralegals to lower the cost and increase the availability and efficiency of legal services. The majority of job openings for paralegals in the future will be new jobs created by employment growth, but additional job openings will arise as people leave the occupation. Despite projections of fast employment growth, competition for jobs should continue as many people seek to go into this profession; however, highly skilled, formally trained paralegals have excellent employment potential.

Private law firms will continue to be the largest employers of paralegals, but a growing array of other organizations, such as corporate legal departments, insurance companies, real estate and title insurance firms, and banks hire paralegals. Corporations, in particular, are boosting their in-house legal departments to cut costs. Demand for paralegals also is expected to grow as an increasing population requires legal services, especially in areas such as intellectual property, healthcare, international, elder issues, criminal, and environmental law. The growth of prepaid legal plans also should contribute to the demand for legal services. Paralegal employment is expected to increase as organizations presently employing paralegals assign them a growing range of tasks, and as paralegals are increasingly employed in small and medium-sized establishments. A growing number of experienced paralegals are expected to establish their own businesses.

Job opportunities for paralegals will expand in the public sector as well. Community legal-service programs, which provide assistance to the poor, aged, minorities, and middle-income families, will employ additional paralegals to minimize expenses and serve the most people. Federal, State, and local government agencies, consumer organizations, and the courts also should continue to hire paralegals in increasing numbers.

To a limited extent, paralegal jobs are affected by the business cycle. During recessions, demand declines for some discretionary legal services, such as planning estates, drafting wills, and handling real estate transactions. Corporations are less inclined to initiate certain types of litigation when falling sales and profits lead to fiscal belt tightening. As a result, full-time paralegals employed in offices adversely affected by a recession may be laid off or have their work hours reduced. On the other hand, during recessions, corporations and individuals are more likely to face other problems that require legal assistance, such as bankruptcies, foreclosures, and divorces. Paralegals, who provide many of the same legal services as lawyers at a lower cost, tend to fare relatively better in difficult economic conditions.

Earnings

Earnings of paralegals and legal assistants vary greatly. Salaries depend on education, training, experience, type and size of employer, and geographic location of the job. In general, paralegals who work for large law firms or in large metropolitan areas earn more than those who work for smaller firms or in less populated regions. In addition to a salary, many paralegals receive bonuses. In 2002, full-time, wage and salary paralegals and legal assistants had median annual earnings, including bonuses of $37,950. The middle 50 percent earned between $30,020 and $48,760. The top 10 percent earned more than $61,150,

while the bottom 10 percent earned less than $24,470. Median annual earnings in the industries employing the largest numbers of paralegals in 2002 were as follows:

Federal government	$53,770
Legal services	36,780
Local government	36,030
State government	34,750

Related Occupations

Several other occupations call for a specialized understanding of the law and the legal system, but do not require the extensive training of a lawyer. These include law clerks; title examiners, abstractors, and searchers; claims adjusters, appraisers, examiners, and investigators; and occupational health and safety specialists and technicians.

Sources of Additional Information

General information on a career as a paralegal can be obtained from:
➤ Standing Committee on Legal Assistants, American Bar Association, 541 N. Fairbanks Ct,., Chicago, IL 60611. Internet: **http://www.abanet.org**

For information on the Certified Legal Assistant exam, schools that offer training programs in a specific State, and standards and guidelines for paralegals, contact:
➤ National Association of Legal Assistants, Inc., 1516 South Boston St., Suite 200, Tulsa, OK 74119. Internet: **http://www.nala.org**

Information on a career as a paralegal, schools that offer training programs, job postings for paralegals, the Paralegal Advanced Competency Exam, and local paralegal associations can be obtained from:
➤ National Federation of Paralegal Associations, P.O. Box 33108, Kansas City, MO 64114. Internet: **http://www.paralegals.org**

Information on paralegal training programs, including the pamphlet "How to Choose a Paralegal Education Program," may be obtained from:
➤ American Association for Paralegal Education, 407 Wekiva Springs Road, Suite 241, Longwood, FL 32779.. Internet: **http://www.aafpe.org**

Information on obtaining a position as a paralegal specialist with the Federal Government is available from the Office of Personnel Management (OPM) through a telephone-based system. Consult your telephone directory under U.S. Government for a local number or call (703) 724-1850; Federal Relay Service: (800) 877-8339. The first number is not tollfree, and charges may result. Information also is available from the OPM Internet site: **http://www.usajobs.opm.gov.**

Education, Training, Library, and Museum Occupations

Archivists, Curators, and Museum Technicians

(0*NET 25-4011.00, 25-4012.00, 25-4013.00)

Significant Points

● Employment in this occupation usually requires graduate education and related work experience.

● Keen competition is expected for the most desirable job openings, which generally attract a large number of applicants.

Nature of the Work

Archivists, curators, and museum technicians acquire and preserve important documents and other valuable items for permanent storage or display. They work for museums, governments, zoos, colleges and universities, corporations, and other institutions that require experts to preserve important records. They also describe, catalogue, analyze, exhibit, and maintain valuable objects and collections for the benefit of researchers and the public. These documents and collections may include works of art, transcripts of meetings, coins and stamps, living and preserved plants and animals, and historic buildings and sites.

Archivists and curators plan and oversee the arrangement, cataloguing, and exhibition of collections and, along with technicians and conservators, maintain collections. Archivists and curators may coordinate educational and public outreach programs, such as tours, workshops, lectures, and classes, and may work with the boards of institutions to administer plans and policies. They also may research topics or items relevant to their collections. Although some duties of archivists and curators are similar, the types of items they deal with differ: curators usually handle objects with cultural, biological, or historical significance, such as sculptures, textiles, and paintings, while archivists handle mainly records and documents that are retained because of their importance and potential value in the future.

Archivists collect, organize, and maintain control over a wide range of information deemed important enough for permanent safekeeping. This information takes many forms: photographs, films, video and sound recordings, computer tapes, and video and optical disks, as well as more traditional paper records, letters, and documents. Archivists work for a variety of organizations, including government agencies, museums, historical societies, corporations, and educational institutions that use or generate records of great potential value to researchers, exhibitors, genealogists, and others who would benefit from having access to original source material.

Archivists maintain records in accordance with accepted standards and practices, that ensure the long-term preservation and easy retrieval of the documents. Records may be saved on any medium, including paper, film, videotape, audiotape, electronic disk, or computer. They also may be copied onto some other format to protect the original and to make them more accessible to researchers who use the records. As various storage media evolve, archivists must keep abreast of technological advances in electronic information storage.

Archivists often specialize in an area of history or technology so they can more accurately determine what records in that area qualify for retention and should become part of the archives. Archivists also may work with specialized forms of records, such as manuscripts, electronic records, photographs, cartographic records, motion pictures, and sound recordings.

Computers are increasingly being used to generate and maintain archival records. Professional standards for the use of computers in handling archival records are still evolving. However, computers are expected to transform many aspects of archival collections as computer capabilities and the use of multimedia and the Internet expand and allow more records to be stored and exhibited electronically.

Curators administer the affairs of museums, zoos, aquariums, botanical gardens, nature centers, and historic sites. The head curator of the museum is usually called the *museum director*. Curators direct the acquisition, storage, and exhibition of collections, including negotiating and authorizing the purchase, sale, exchange, or loan of collections. They are also responsible for authenticating, evaluating, and categorizing the specimens in a collection. Curators oversee and help conduct the institution's research projects and related educational programs. However, an increasing part of a curator's duties involves fundraising and promotion, which may include the writing and reviewing of grant proposals, journal articles, and publicity materials, as well as attendance at meetings, conventions, and civic events.

Archivists and curators oversee the cataloguing and display of collections of artwork, documents, and other valuable items.

Most curators specialize in a particular field, such as botany, art, paleontology, or history. Those working in large institutions may be highly specialized. A large natural-history museum, for example, would employ separate curators for its collections of birds, fishes, insects, and mammals. Some curators maintain their collections, others do research, and others perform administrative tasks. In small institutions, with only one or a few curators, one curator may be responsible for multiple tasks, from maintaining collections to directing the affairs of the museum.

Conservators manage, care for, preserve, treat, and document works of art, artifacts, and specimens, work that may require substantial historical, scientific, and archaeological research. They use x rays, chemical testing, microscopes, special lights, and other laboratory equipment and techniques to examine objects and determine their condition, their need for treatment or restoration, and the appropriate method for preserving them. Conservators document their findings and treat items to minimize their deterioration or to restore them to their original state. Conservators usually specialize in a particular material or group of objects, such as documents and books, paintings, decorative arts, textiles, metals, or architectural material.

Museum technicians assist curators by performing various preparatory and maintenance tasks on museum items.   Some museum technicians also may assist curators with research. Archives technicians help archivists organize, maintain, and provide access to historical documentary materials.

Working Conditions

The working conditions of archivists and curators vary. Some spend most of their time working with the public, providing reference assistance and educational services. Others perform research or process records, which often means working alone or in offices with only a few people. Those who restore and install exhibits or work with bulky, heavy record containers may climb, stretch, or lift. Those in zoos, botanical gardens, and other outdoor museums or historic sites frequently walk great distances.

Curators who work in large institutions may travel extensively to evaluate potential additions to the collection, organize exhibitions, and conduct research in their area of expertise. However, travel is rare for curators employed in small institutions.

Employment

Archivists, curators, and museum technicians held about 22,000 jobs in 2002. About 35 percent were employed in museums, historical sites, and similar institutions, and 15 percent worked for State and private educational institutions, mainly college and university libraries. Nearly 40 percent worked in Federal, State, and local government. Most Federal archivists work for the National Archives and Records Administration; others manage military archives in the U.S. Department of Defense. Most Federal Government curators work at the Smithsonian Institution, in the military museums of the Department of Defense, and in archaeological and other museums and historic sites managed by the U.S. Department of the Interior. All State governments have archival or historical-record sections employing archivists. State and local governments also have numerous historical museums, parks, libraries, and zoos employing curators.

Some large corporations that have archives or record centers employ archivists to manage the growing volume of records created or maintained as required by law or necessary to the firms' operations. Religious and fraternal organizations, professional associations, conservation organizations, major private collectors, and research firms also employ archivists and curators.

Conservators may work under contract to treat particular items, rather than as regular employees of a museum or other institution. These conservators may work on their own as private contractors, or they may work as an employee of a conservation laboratory or regional conservation center that contracts their services to museums.

Training, Other Qualifications, and Advancement

Employment as an archivist, conservator, or curator usually requires graduate education and related work experience. While completing their formal education, many archivists and curators work in archives or museums to gain the "hands-on" experience that many employers seek.

Although most archivists have a variety of undergraduate degrees, a graduate degree in history or library science, with courses in archival science, is preferred by most employers. Some positions may require knowledge of the discipline related to the collection, such as business or medicine. Currently, no programs offer bachelor's or master's degrees in archival science. However, approximately 65 colleges and universities offer courses or practical training in archival science as part of their history, library science, or other curriculum. The Academy of Certified Archivists offers voluntary certification for archivists. The designation "Certified Archivist" is obtained by those with at least a master's degree and a year of appropriate archival experience. The certification process requires candidates to pass a written examination, and they must renew their certification periodically.

Archivists need research and analytical ability to understand the content of documents and the context in which they were created and to decipher deteriorated or poor-quality printed matter, handwritten manuscripts, or photographs and films. A background in preservation management is often required of archivists because they are responsible for taking proper care of their records. Archivists also must be able to organize large amounts of information and write clear instructions for its retrieval and use. In addition, computer skills and the ability to work with electronic records and databases are becoming increasingly important.

Many archives, including one-person shops, are very small and have limited opportunities for promotion. Archivists typically advance by transferring to a larger unit with supervisory positions. A doctorate in history, library science, or a related field may be needed for some advanced positions, such as director of a State archive.

For employment as a curator, most museums require a master's degree in an appropriate discipline of the museum's specialty—art, history, or archaeology—or museum studies. Many employers prefer a doctoral degree, particularly for curators in natural history or science museums. Earning two graduate degrees—in museum studies (museology) and a specialized subject—gives a candidate a distinct advantage in this competitive job market. In small museums, curatorial positions may be available to individuals with a bachelor's degree. For some positions, an internship of full-time museum work supplemented by courses in museum practices is needed.

Curatorial positions often require knowledge in a number of fields. For historic and artistic conservation, courses in chemistry, physics, and art are desirable. Since curators—particularly those in small museums—may have administrative and managerial responsibilities, courses in business administration, public relations, marketing, and fundraising also are recommended. Like archivists, curators need computer skills and the ability to work with electronic databases. Many curators are responsible for posting information on the Internet, so they also need to be familiar with digital imaging, scanning technology, and copyright law.

Curators must be flexible because of their wide variety of duties, among which are the design and presentation of exhibits. In small museums, curators need manual dexterity, to build exhibits or restore objects. Leadership ability and business skills are important for museum directors, while marketing skills are valuable in increasing museum attendance and fundraising.

In large museums, curators may advance through several levels of responsibility, eventually becoming the museum director. Curators in smaller museums often advance to larger ones. Individual research and publications are important for advancement in larger institutions.

When hiring conservators, employers look for a master's degree in conservation or in a closely related field, together with substantial experience. There are only a few graduate programs in museum conservation techniques in the United States. Competition for entry to these programs is keen; to qualify, a student must have a background in chemistry, archaeology or studio art, and art history, as well as work experience. For some programs, knowledge of a foreign language is also helpful. Conservation apprenticeships or internships as an undergraduate can enhance one's admission prospects. Graduate programs last 2 to 4 years, the latter years of which include internship training. A few individuals enter conservation through apprenticeships with museums, nonprofit organizations, and conservators in private practice. Apprenticeships should be supplemented with courses in chemistry, studio art, and history. Apprenticeship training, although accepted, usually is a more difficult route into the conservation profession.

Museum technicians usually need a bachelor's degree in an appropriate discipline of the museum's specialty, training in museum studies, or previous experience working in museums, particularly in the design of exhibits. Similarly, archives technicians usually need a bachelor's degree in library science or history, or relevant work experience. Technician positions often serve as a steppingstone for individuals interested in archival and curatorial work. Except in small museums, a master's degree is needed for advancement.

Relatively few schools grant a bachelor's degree in museum studies. More common are undergraduate minors or tracks of study that are part of an undergraduate degree in a related field, such as art history, history, or archaeology. Students interested in further study may obtain a master's degree in museum studies, offered in colleges and universities throughout the country. However, many employers feel that, while museum studies are helpful, a thorough knowledge of the museum's specialty and museum work experience are more important.

Continuing education, which enables archivists, curators, and museum technicians to keep up with developments in the field, is available through meetings, conferences, and workshops sponsored by archival, historical, and museum associations. Some larger organizations, such as the National Archives, offer such training in-house.

Job Outlook

Competition for jobs as archivists, curators, and museum technicians is expected to be keen because qualified applicants outnumber job openings. Graduates with highly specialized training, such as master's degrees in both library science and history, with a concentration in archives or records management and extensive computer skills should have the best opportunities for jobs as archivists. A curator job also is attractive to many people, and many applicants have the necessary training and knowledge of the subject, but there are only a few openings. Consequently, candidates may have to work part time, as an intern, or even as a volunteer assistant curator or research associate after completing their formal education. Substantial work experience in collection management, exhibit design, or restoration, as well as database management skills, will be necessary for permanent status. Job opportunities for curators should be best in art and history museums, since these are the largest employers in the museum industry.

The job outlook for conservators may be more favorable, particularly for graduates of conservation programs. However, competition is stiff for the limited number of openings in these programs, and applicants need a technical background. Students who qualify and successfully complete the program, have knowledge of a foreign language, and are willing to relocate will have an advantage over less qualified candidates.

Employment of archivists, curators, and museum technicians is expected to increase about as fast as the average for all occupations through 2012. Jobs are expected to grow as public and private organizations emphasize establishing archives and organizing records and information and as public interest in science, art, history, and technology increases. Museum and zoo attendance has been on the rise and is expected to continue increasing, which will generate demand for curators and museum technicians and conservators. However, museums and other cultural institutions can be subject to cuts in funding during recessions or periods of budget tightening, reducing demand for archivists and curators. Although the rate of turnover among archivists and curators is relatively low, the need to replace workers who leave the occupation or stop working will create some additional job openings.

Earnings

Median annual earnings of archivists, curators, and museum technicians in 2002 were $35,270. The middle 50 percent earned between $26,400 and $48,460. The lowest 10 percent earned less than $20,010, and the highest 10 percent earned more than $66,050.

Earnings of archivists and curators vary considerably by type and size of employer and often by specialty. Median annual earnings of archivists, curators, and museum technicians in 2002 were $33,720 in museums, historical sites, and similar institutions.. Salaries, though, of curators in large, well-funded museums can be several times higher than those in small ones. The average annual salary for archivists in the Federal Government in nonsupervisory, supervisory, and managerial positions was $69,706 in 2003; for museum curators, $70,100; museum specialists and technicians, $48,414; and for archives technicians, $37,067.

Related Occupations

The skills that archivists, curators, and museum technicians use in preserving, organizing, and displaying objects or information of historical interest are shared by artists and related workers; librarians; and anthropologists and archeologists, historians, and other social scientists.

Sources of Additional Information

For information on archivists and on schools offering courses in archival studies, contact

➤ Society of American Archivists, 527 South Wells St., 5th floor, Chicago, IL 60607-3922. Internet: **http://www.archivists.org**

For general information about careers as a curator and schools offering courses in museum studies, contact

➤ American Association of Museums, 1575 Eye St. NW., Suite 400, Washington, DC 20005. Internet: **http://www.aam-us.org**

For information about careers and education programs in conservation and preservation, contact

➤ American Institute for Conservation of Historic and Artistic Works, 1717 K St. NW., Suite 200, Washington, DC 20006. Internet: **http://aic.stanford.edu**

Instructional Coordinators

(0*NET 25-9031.00)

Significant Points

- Many instructional coordinators are former teachers or principals.
- A bachelor's degree is the minimum educational requirement, but a graduate degree is preferred.
- The need to meet new educational standards will create more demand for instructional coordinators to train teachers and develop new materials.

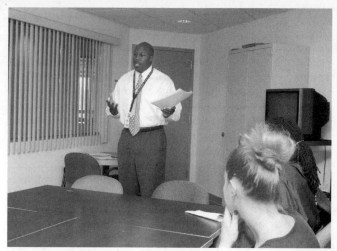

Instructional coordinators train teachers in the use of materials and equipment.

Nature of the Work

Instructional coordinators, also known as curriculum specialists, staff development specialists, or directors of instructional material, play a large role in improving the quality of education in the classroom. They develop instructional materials, train teachers, and assess educational programs in terms of quality and adherence to regulations and standards. They also assist in implementing new technology in the classroom. Instructional coordinators often specialize in specific subjects, such as reading, language arts, mathematics, or social studies.

Instructional coordinators evaluate how well a school's curriculum, or plan of study, meets students' needs. They research teaching methods and techniques and develop procedures to determine whether program goals are being met. To aid in their evaluation, they may meet with members of educational committees and advisory groups to learn about subjects—English, history, or mathematics, for example—and to relate curriculum materials to these subjects, to students' needs, and to occupations for which these subjects are good preparation. They also may develop questionnaires and interview school staff about the curriculum. Based on their research and observations of instructional practice, they recommend instruction and curriculum improvements.

Another duty instructional coordinators have is to review textbooks, software, and other educational materials and make recommendations on purchases. They monitor materials ordered and the ways in which teachers use them in the classroom. They also supervise workers who catalogue, distribute, and maintain a school's educational materials and equipment.

Instructional coordinators develop effective ways to use technology to enhance student learning. They monitor the introduction of new technology, including the Internet, into a school's curriculum. In addition, instructional coordinators might recommend installing educational computer software, such as interactive books and exercises designed to enhance student literacy and develop math skills. Instructional coordinators may invite experts—such as computer hardware, software, and library or media specialists—into the classroom to help integrate technological materials into a school's curriculum.

Many instructional coordinators plan and provide onsite education for teachers and administrators. They may train teachers about the use of materials and equipment or help them to improve their skills. Instructional coordinators also mentor new teachers and train experienced ones in the latest instructional methods. This role becomes especially important when a school district introduces new content, program innovations, or a different organizational structure. For example, when a State or

school district introduces standards or tests that must be met by students in order to pass to the next grade, instructional coordinators often must advise teachers on the content of the standards and provide instruction on implementing the standards in the classroom.

Working Conditions

Instructional coordinators, including those employed by school districts, often work year round, usually in offices or classrooms. Some spend much of their time traveling between schools meeting with teachers and administrators. The opportunity to shape and improve instructional curricula and work in an academic environment can be satisfying. However, some instructional coordinators find the work stressful because the occupation requires continual accountability to school administrators and it is not uncommon for people in this occupation to work long hours.

Employment

Instructional coordinators held about 98,000 jobs in 2002. More than 1 in 3 worked in local government education. About 1 in 5 worked in private education, and about 1 in 10 worked in State government education. The remainder worked mostly in the following industries: individual and family services; child daycare services; scientific research and development services; and management, scientific, and technical consulting services.

Training, Other Qualifications, and Advancement

The minimum educational requirement for instructional coordinators is a bachelor's degree, usually in education. Most employers, however, prefer candidates with a master's or higher degree. Many instructional coordinators have training in curriculum development and instruction, or in a specific academic field, such as mathematics or history. Instructional coordinators must have a good understanding of how to teach specific groups of students, in addition to expertise in developing educational materials. As a result, many persons transfer into instructional coordinator jobs after working for several years as teachers. Work experience in an education administrator position, such as principal or assistant principal, also is beneficial. Specific requirements for instructional coordinator jobs vary depending on the particular position or school district. They may also vary by State.

Helpful college courses may include those in curriculum development and evaluation, instructional approaches, or research design, which teaches how to create and implement research studies to determine the effectiveness of a given method of curriculum or instruction, or to measure and improve student performance. Moreover, instructional coordinators usually are required to take continuing education courses to keep their skills current. Topics for continuing education courses may include teacher evaluation techniques, curriculum training, new teacher induction, consulting and teacher support, and observation and analysis of teaching.

Instructional coordinators must be able to make sound decisions about curriculum options and to organize and coordinate work efficiently. They should have strong interpersonal and communication skills. Familiarity with computer technology also is important for instructional coordinators, who are increasingly involved in gathering and coordinating technical information for students and teachers.

Depending on experience and educational attainment, instructional coordinators may advance to higher positions in a school system, or to management or executive positions in private industry.

Job Outlook

Employment of instructional coordinators is expected to grow faster than the average for all occupations through the year 2012. Over the next decade, instructional coordinators will be instrumental in developing new curricula to meet the demands of a changing society and in training the teacher workforce. Although budget cuts, particularly in the near term, may negatively impact employment to some extent, a continuing emphasis on improving the quality of education is expected to result in a relatively steady and increasing demand for these workers. As increasing Federal, State and local standards impel more schools to focus on improving educational quality and student performance, growing numbers of coordinators will be needed to incorporate the standards into curriculums and make sure teachers and administrators are informed of the changes. Opportunities are expected to be best for those who specialize in subject areas that have been targeted for improvement by the No Child Left Behind Act—namely, reading, math, and science.

Instructional coordinators also will be needed to provide classes on using technology in the classroom, to keep teachers up-to-date on changes in their fields, and to demonstrate new teaching techniques. Additional job growth for instructional coordinators will stem from the increasing emphasis on lifelong learning and on programs for students with special needs, including those for whom English is a second language. These students often require more educational resources and consolidated planning and management within the educational system.

Earnings

Median annual earnings of instructional coordinators in 2002 were $47,350. The middle 50 percent earned between $34,450 and $62,460. The lowest 10 percent earned less than $25,880, and the highest 10 percent earned more than $76,820.

Related Occupations

Instructional coordinators are professionals involved in education and training and development, which requires organizational, administrative, teaching, research, and communication skills. Occupations with similar characteristics include preschool, kindergarten, elementary, middle, and secondary school teachers; postsecondary teachers; education administrators; counselors; and human resources, training, and labor relations managers and specialists.

Sources of Additional Information

Information on requirements and job opportunities for instructional coordinators is available from local school systems and State departments of education.

Librarians

(0*NET 25-4021.00)

Significant Points

- A master's degree in library science usually is required; special librarians often need an additional graduate or professional degree.

- A large number of retirements in the next decade is expected to result in many job openings for librarians to replace those who leave.

- Librarians increasingly use information technology to perform research, classify materials, and help students and library patrons seek information.

Nature of the Work

The traditional concept of a library is being redefined from a place to access paper records or books to one that also houses the most advanced media, including CD-ROM, the Internet, virtual libraries, and remote access to a wide range of resources. Consequently, librarians, or information professionals, increasingly are combining traditional duties with tasks involving quickly changing technology. Librarians assist people in finding information and using it effectively for personal and professional purposes. Librarians must have knowledge of a wide variety of scholarly and public information sources and must follow trends related to publishing, computers, and the media in order to oversee the selection and organization of library materials. Librarians manage staff and develop and direct information programs and systems for the public, to ensure that information is organized in a manner that meets users' needs.

Most librarian positions incorporate three aspects of library work: User services, technical services, and administrative services. Still, even librarians specializing in one of these areas have other responsibilities. Librarians in user services, such as reference and children's librarians, work with patrons to help them find the information they need. The job involves analyzing users' needs to determine what information is appropriate, as well as searching for, acquiring, and providing the information. The job also includes an instructional role, such as showing users how to access information. For example, librarians commonly help users navigate the Internet so they can search for relevant information efficiently. Librarians in technical services, such as acquisitions and cataloguing, acquire and prepare materials for use and often do not deal directly with the public. Librarians in administrative services oversee the management and planning of libraries: negotiate contracts for services, materials, and equipment; supervise library employees; perform public-relations and fundraising duties: prepare budgets; and direct activities to ensure that everything functions properly.

In small libraries or information centers, librarians usually handle all aspects of the work. They read book reviews, publishers' announcements, and catalogues to keep up with current literature and other available resources, and they select and purchase materials from publishers, wholesalers, and distributors. Librarians prepare new materials by classifying them by subject matter and describe books and other library materials to make them easy to find. Librarians supervise assistants, who prepare cards, computer records, or other access tools that direct users to resources. In large libraries, librarians often specialize in a single area, such as acquisitions, cataloguing, bibliography, reference, special collections, or administration. Teamwork is increasingly important to ensure quality service to the public.

Librarians also compile lists of books, periodicals, articles, and audiovisual materials on particular subjects; analyze collections; and recommend materials. They collect and organize books, pamphlets, manuscripts, and other materials in a specific field, such as rare books, genealogy, or music. In addition, they coordinate programs such as storytelling for children and literacy skills and book talks for adults; conduct classes; publicize services; provide reference help; write grants; and oversee other administrative matters.

Librarians are classified according to the type of library in which they work: A public library; school library media center; college, university, or other academic library; or special library. Some librarians work with specific groups, such as children, young adults, adults, or the disadvantaged. In school library media centers, librarians—often called school media specialists—help teachers develop curricula, acquire materials for classroom instruction, and sometimes team teach.

Librarians also work in information centers or libraries maintained by government agencies, corporations, law firms, advertising agencies, museums, professional associations, medical centers, hospitals, religious organizations, and research laboratories. They acquire and arrange an organization's information resources, which usually are limited to subjects of special interest to the organization. These special librarians can provide vital information services by preparing abstracts and indexes of current periodicals, organizing bibliographies, or analyzing background information and preparing reports on areas of particular interest. For example, a special librarian working for a corporation could provide the sales department with information on competitors or new developments affecting the field. A medical librarian may provide information about new medical treatments, clinical trials, and standard procedures to health professionals, patients, consumers, and corporations. Government document librarians, who work for government agencies and depository libraries in each of the States, preserve government publications, records, and other documents that make up a historical record of government actions and decisionmaking.

Many libraries have access to remote databases and maintain their own computerized databases. The widespread use of automation in libraries makes database-searching skills important to librarians. Librarians develop and index databases and help train users to develop searching skills for the information they need. Some libraries are forming consortiums with other librar-

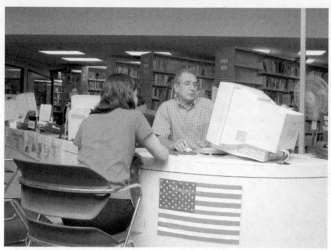

Librarians assist people in finding information and using it effectively.

ies through electronic mail. This practice allows patrons to submit information requests to several libraries simultaneously. The Internet also is expanding the amount of available reference information. Librarians must be aware of how to use these resources in order to locate information.

Librarians with computer and information systems skills can work as automated-systems librarians, planning and operating computer systems, and information architect librarians, designing information storage and retrieval systems and developing procedures for collecting, organizing, interpreting, and classifying information. These librarians analyze and plan for future information needs. (See the statements on computer support specialists and systems administrators; and systems analysts, computer scientists, and database administrators elsewhere in the *Handbook*.) The increasing use of automated information systems is enabling librarians to focus on administrative and budgeting responsibilities, grant writing, and specialized research requests, while delegating more technical and user services responsibilities to technicians. (See the statement on library technicians elsewhere in the *Handbook*.)

More and more, librarians are applying their information management and research skills to arenas outside of libraries—for example, database development, reference tool development, information systems, publishing, Internet coordination, marketing, web content management and design, and training of database users. Entrepreneurial librarians sometimes start their own consulting practices, acting as freelance librarians or information brokers and providing services to other libraries, businesses, or government agencies.

Working Conditions

Librarians spend a significant portion of time at their desks or in front of computer terminals; extended work at video display terminals can cause eyestrain and headaches. Assisting users in obtaining information or books for their jobs, homework, or recreational reading can be challenging and satisfying, but working with users under deadlines can be demanding and stressful. Some librarians lift and carry books, and some climb ladders to reach high stacks. Librarians in small organizations sometimes shelve books themselves.

More than 2 out of 10 librarians work part time. Public and college librarians often work weekends and evenings, as well as some holidays. School librarians usually have the same workday and vacation schedules as classroom teachers. Special librarians usually work normal business hours, but in fast-paced industries—such as advertising or legal services—they can work longer hours when needed.

Employment

Librarians held about 167,000 jobs in 2002. Most worked in school and academic libraries, but nearly a third worked in public libraries. The remainder worked in special libraries or as information professionals for companies and other organizations.

Training, Other Qualifications, and Advancement

A master's degree in library science (MLS) is necessary for librarian positions in most public, academic, and special libraries and in some school libraries. The Federal Government requires an MLS or the equivalent in education and experience. Many colleges and universities offer MLS programs, but employers often prefer graduates of the approximately 56 schools accredited by the American Library Association. Most MLS programs require a bachelor's degree; any liberal arts major is appropriate.

Most MLS programs take 1 year to complete; some take 2. A typical graduate program includes courses in the foundations of library and information science, including the history of books and printing, intellectual freedom and censorship, and the role of libraries and information in society. Other basic courses cover the selection and processing of materials, the organization of information, reference tools and strategies, and user services. Courses are adapted to educate librarians to use new resources brought about by advancing technology, such as online reference systems, Internet search methods, and automated circulation systems. Course options can include resources for children or young adults; classification, cataloguing, indexing, and abstracting; library administration; and library automation. Computer-related course work is an increasingly important part of an MLS degree. Some programs offer interdisciplinary degrees combining technical courses in information science with traditional training in library science.

The MLS degree provides general preparation for library work, but some individuals specialize in a particular area, such as reference, technical services, or children's services. A Ph.D. degree in library and information science is advantageous for a college teaching position or for a top administrative job in a college or university library or large library system.

Usually, an MLS also is required of librarians working in special libraries. In addition, most special librarians supplement their education with knowledge of the subject in which they are specializing, sometimes earning a master's, doctoral, or professional degree in the subject. Areas of specialization include medicine, law, business, engineering, and the natural and social sciences. For example, a librarian working for a law firm may also be a licensed attorney, holding both library science and law degrees. In some jobs, knowledge of a foreign language is needed.

State certification requirements for public school librarians vary widely. Most States require school librarians, often called library media specialists, to be certified as teachers and to have had courses in library science. An MLS is needed in some cases, perhaps with a library media specialization, or a master's in education with a specialty in school library media or

educational media. Some States require certification of public librarians employed in municipal, county, or regional library systems.

Librarians participate in continuing education and training once they are on the job, in order to keep abreast of new information systems brought about by changing technology.

Experienced librarians can advance to administrative positions, such as department head, library director, or chief information officer.

Job Outlook

Employment of librarians is expected to grow about as fast as the average for all occupations over the 2002-12 period. However, job opportunities are expected to be very good because a large number of librarians are expected to retire in the coming decade, creating many job openings. Also, the number of people going into this profession has fallen in recent years, resulting in more jobs than applicants in some cases. Colleges and universities report the greatest difficulty in hiring librarians, because the pay is often less than the prospective employees can get elsewhere.

Offsetting the need for librarians are government budget cuts and the increasing use of computerized information storage and retrieval systems. Both will result in the hiring of fewer librarians and the replacement of librarians with less costly library technicians. Computerized systems make cataloguing easier, allowing library technicians to perform the work. In addition, many libraries are equipped for users to access library computers directly from their homes or offices. That way, users can bypass librarians altogether and conduct research on their own. However, librarians will still be needed to manage staff, help users develop database-searching techniques, address complicated reference requests, and define users' needs.

Jobs for librarians outside traditional settings will grow the fastest over the decade. Nontraditional librarian jobs include working as information brokers and working for private corporations, nonprofit organizations, and consulting firms. Many companies are turning to librarians because of their research and organizational skills and their knowledge of computer databases and library automation systems. Librarians can review vast amounts of information and analyze, evaluate, and organize it according to a company's specific needs. Librarians also are hired by organizations to set up information on the Internet. Librarians working in these settings may be classified as systems analysts, database specialists and trainers, webmasters or web developers, or local area network (LAN) coordinators.

Earnings

Salaries of librarians vary according to the individual's qualifications and the type, size, and location of the library. Librarians with primarily administrative duties often have greater earnings. Median annual earnings of librarians in 2002 were $43,090. The middle 50 percent earned between $33,560 and $54,250. The lowest 10 percent earned less than $24,510, and the highest 10 percent earned more than $66,590. Median annual earnings in the industries employing the largest numbers of librarians in 2002 were as follows:

Elementary and secondary schools	$45,660
Colleges, universities, and professional schools	45,600
Local government	37,970
Other information services	37,770

The average annual salary for all librarians in the Federal Government in nonsupervisory, supervisory, and managerial positions was $70,238 in 2003.

Nearly one in three librarians is a member of a union or is covered under a union contract.

Related Occupations

Librarians play an important role in the transfer of knowledge and ideas by providing people with access to the information they need and want. Jobs requiring similar analytical, organizational, and communicative skills include archivists, curators, and museum technicians; and computer and information scientists, research. School librarians have many duties similar to those of schoolteachers. Librarians are increasingly storing, cataloguing, and accessing information with computers. Other jobs that use similar computer skills include systems analysts, computer scientists, and database administrators.

Sources of Additional Information

For information on a career as a librarian and information on accredited library education programs and scholarships, contact
➤ American Library Association, Office for Human Resource Development and Recruitment, 50 East Huron St., Chicago, IL 60611. Internet: **http://www.ala.org**

For information on a career as a special librarian, write to
➤ Special Libraries Association, 1700 18th St. NW., Washington, DC 20009. Internet: **http://www.sla.org**

Information on graduate schools of library and information science can be obtained from
➤ Association for Library and Information Science Education, 1009 Commerce Park Dr., Suite 150, PO Box 4219, Oak Ridge, TN 37839. Internet: **http://www.alise.org**

For information on a career as a law librarian, scholarship information, and a list of ALA-accredited schools offering programs in law librarianship, contact
➤ American Association of Law Libraries, 53 West Jackson Blvd., Suite 940, Chicago, IL 60604. Internet: **http://www.aallnet.org**

For information on employment opportunities for health sciences librarians and for scholarship information, credentialing information, and a list of MLA-accredited schools offering programs in health sciences librarianship, contact
➤ Medical Library Association, 65 E Wacker Place , Suite 1900, Chicago, IL 60601. Internet: **http://www.mlanet.org**

Information on acquiring a job as a librarian with the Federal Government may be obtained from the Office of Personnel Management through a telephone-based system. Consult your telephone directory under "U.S. Government" for a local number, or call (703) 724-1850 (Federal Relay Service (800) 877-8339). The first number is not toll free, and charges may result. Information also is available on the Internet at **http://www.usajobs.opm.gov**.

Information concerning requirements and application procedures for positions in the Library of Congress can be obtained directly from
➤ Human Resources Office, Library of Congress, 101 Independence Ave. SE., Washington, DC 20540-2231.

State library agencies can furnish information on scholarships available through their offices, requirements for certification, and general information about career prospects in the particular State of interest. Several of these agencies maintain job hot lines reporting openings for librarians.

State departments of education can furnish information on certification requirements and job opportunities for school librarians.

Library Technicians

(0*NET 25-4031.00)

Significant Points

- Training requirements range from a high school diploma to an associate's or bachelor's degree, but computer skills are needed for many jobs.

- Increasing use of computerized circulation and information systems should continue to spur job growth, but many libraries' budget constraints should moderate growth.

- Employment should grow rapidly in special libraries because growing numbers of professionals and other workers use those libraries.

Nature of the Work

Library technicians both help librarians acquire, prepare, and organize material and assist users in finding information. Library technicians usually work under the supervision of a librarian, although they work independently in certain situations. Technicians in small libraries handle a range of duties; those in large libraries usually specialize. As libraries increasingly use new technologies—such as CD-ROM, the Internet, virtual libraries, and automated databases—the duties of library technicians will expand and evolve accordingly. Library technicians are assuming greater responsibilities, in some cases taking on tasks previously performed by librarians. (See the statement on librarians elsewhere in the *Handbook*.)

Depending on the employer, library technicians can have other titles, such as library technical assistant or media aide. Library technicians direct library users to standard references, organize and maintain periodicals, prepare volumes for binding, handle interlibrary loan requests, prepare invoices, perform routine cataloguing and coding of library materials, retrieve information from computer databases, and supervise support staff.

The widespread use of computerized information storage and retrieval systems has resulted in technicians handling technical services—such as entering catalogue information into the library's computer—that were once performed by librarians. Technicians assist with customizing databases. In addition, technicians instruct patrons in how to use computer systems to access data. The increased automation of recordkeeping has reduced the amount of clerical work performed by library technicians. Many libraries now offer self-service registration and circulation areas with computers, decreasing the time library technicians spend manually recording and inputting records.

Some library technicians operate and maintain audiovisual equipment, such as projectors, tape recorders, and videocassette recorders, and assist users with microfilm or microfiche readers. They also design posters, bulletin boards, or displays.

Library technicians in school libraries encourage and teach students to use the library and media center. They also help teachers obtain instructional materials, and they assist students with special assignments. Some work in special libraries maintained by government agencies, corporations, law firms, advertising agencies, museums, professional societies, medical centers, and research laboratories, where they conduct literature searches, compile bibliographies, and prepare abstracts, usually on subjects of particular interest to the organization.

To extend library services to more patrons, many libraries operate bookmobiles, often run by library technicians. The technicians take trucks stocked with books, or bookmobiles, to designated sites on a regular schedule, frequently stopping at shopping centers, apartment complexes, schools, and nursing homes. Bookmobiles also may be used to extend library service to patrons living in remote areas. Depending on local conditions, the technicians may operate a bookmobile alone or may be accompanied by another library employee.

Library technicians who drive bookmobiles, answer patrons' questions, receive and check out books, collect fines, maintain the book collection, shelve materials, and occasionally operate audiovisual equipment to show slides or films. They participate, and may assist, in planning programs sponsored by the library, such as reader advisory programs, used-book sales, or outreach programs. Technicians who drive the bookmobile keep track of their mileage, the materials lent out, and the amount of fines collected. In some areas, they are responsible for maintenance of the vehicle and any photocopiers or other equipment in it. They record statistics on circulation and the number of people visiting the bookmobile. Technicians also may record requests for special items from the main library and arrange for the materials to be mailed or delivered to a patron during the next scheduled visit. Many bookmobiles are equipped with personal computers and CD-ROM systems linked to the main library system, allowing technicians to reserve or locate books immediately. Some bookmobiles now offer Internet access to users.

Working Conditions

Technicians answer questions and provide assistance to library users. Those who prepare library materials sit at desks or computer terminals for long periods and can develop headaches or eyestrain from working with the terminals. Some duties, like calculating circulation statistics, can be repetitive and boring. Others, such as performing computer searches with the use of local and regional library networks and cooperatives, can be interesting and challenging. Library technicians may lift and

Library technicians direct library users to standard references, organize and maintain periodicals, and perform routine cataloguing and coding of library materials.

carry books climb ladders to reach high stacks, and bend low to shelve books on bottom shelves.

Library technicians in school libraries work regular school hours. Those in public libraries and college and university (academic) libraries also work weekends, evenings and some holidays. Library technicians in special libraries usually work normal business hours, although they often work overtime as well.

The schedules of library technicians who drive bookmobiles depend on the size of the area being served. Some bookmobiles operate every day, while others go only on certain days. Some bookmobiles operate in the evenings and weekends, to give patrons as much access to the library as possible. Because library technicians who operate bookmobiles may be the only link some people have to the library, much of their work consists of helping the public. They may assist handicapped or elderly patrons to the bookmobile or shovel snow to ensure their safety. They may enter hospitals or nursing homes to deliver books to patrons who are bedridden.

Employment

Library technicians held about 119,000 jobs in 2002. Most worked in school, academic, or public libraries. Some worked in hospitals and for religious organizations, mainly parochial schools. The Federal Government—primarily the U.S. Department of Defense and the U.S. Library of Congress—and State and local governments also employed library technicians.

Training, Other Qualifications, and Advancement

Training requirements for library technicians vary widely, ranging from a high school diploma to specialized postsecondary training. Some employers hire individuals with work experience or other training; others train inexperienced workers on the job. Still other employers require that technicians have an associate's or bachelor's degree. Given the rapid spread of automation in libraries, computer skills are needed for many jobs. Knowledge of databases, library automation systems, online library systems, online public access systems, and circulation systems is valuable. Many bookmobile drivers are required to have a commercial driver's license.

Some 2-year colleges offer an associate-of-arts degree in library technology. Programs include both liberal arts and library-related study. Students learn about library and media organization and operation, as well as how to order, process, catalogue, locate, and circulate library materials and work with library automation. Libraries and associations offer continuing education courses to keep technicians abreast of new developments in the field.

Library technicians usually advance by assuming added responsibilities. For example, technicians often start at the circulation desk, checking books in and out. After gaining experience, they may become responsible for storing and verifying information. As they advance, they may become involved in budget and personnel matters in their departments. Some library technicians advance to supervisory positions and are in charge of the day-to-day operation of their departments.

Job Outlook

Employment of library technicians is expected to grow about as fast as the average for all occupations through 2012. In addition to jobs opening up through employment growth, some job openings will result from the need to replace library technicians who transfer to other fields or leave the labor force.

The increasing use of library automation is expected to continue to spur job growth among library technicians. Computerized information systems have simplified certain tasks, such as descriptive cataloguing, which can now be handled by technicians instead of librarians. For example, nowadays technicians can easily retrieve information from a central database and store it in the library's computer. Although efforts to contain costs could dampen employment growth of library technicians in school, public, and college and university libraries, cost containment efforts could also result in more hiring of library technicians than librarians. Growth in the number of professionals and other workers who use special libraries should result in good job opportunities for library technicians in those settings.

Earnings

Median annual earnings of library technicians in 2002 were $24,090. The middle 50 percent earned between $18,150 and $31,140. The lowest 10 percent earned less than $14,410, and the highest 10 percent earned more than $38,000. Median annual earnings in the industries employing the largest numbers of library technicians in 2002 were as follows:

Colleges, universities, and professional schools	$27,280
Local government	23,310
Elementary and secondary schools	21,770
Other information services	20,950

Salaries of library technicians in the Federal Government averaged $36,788 in 2003.

Related Occupations

Library technicians perform organizational and administrative duties. Workers in other occupations with similar duties include library assistants, clerical; information and record clerks; and medical records and health information technicians.

Sources of Additional Information

For information on training programs for library/media technical assistants, write to
➤ American Library Association, Office for Human Resource Development and Recruitment, 50 East Huron St., Chicago, IL 60611. Internet: http://www.ala.org

Information on acquiring a job as a library technician with the Federal Government may be obtained from the Office of Personnel Management through a telephone-based system. Consult your telephone directory under "U.S. Government" for a local number, or call (703) 724-1850 (Federal Relay Service (800) 877-8339). The first number is not toll free, and charges may result. Information also is available on the Internet at http://www.usajobs.opm.gov.

Information concerning requirements and application procedures for positions in the Library of Congress can be obtained directly from
➤ Human Resources Office, Library of Congress, 101 Independence Ave. SE., Washington, DC 20540-2231.

State library agencies can furnish information on requirements for technicians and general information about career prospects in the State. Several of these agencies maintain job hot lines reporting openings for library technicians.

State departments of education can furnish information on requirements and job opportunities for school library technicians.

Teacher Assistants

(O*NET 25-9041.00)

Significant Points

- About 4 in 10 teacher assistants work part time.
- Educational requirements range from a high school diploma to some college training.
- Workers with experience in special education, or who can speak a foreign language, will be especially in demand.

Nature of the Work

Teacher assistants provide instructional and clerical support for classroom teachers, allowing teachers more time for lesson planning and teaching. Teacher assistants tutor and assist children in learning class material using the teacher's lesson plans, providing students with individualized attention. Teacher assistants also supervise students in the cafeteria, schoolyard, and hallways, or on field trips. They record grades, set up equipment, and help prepare materials for instruction. Teacher assistants also are called teacher aides or instructional aides. Some assistants refer to themselves as paraeducators or paraprofessionals.

Some teacher assistants perform exclusively noninstructional or clerical tasks, such as monitoring nonacademic settings. Playground and lunchroom attendants are examples of such assistants. Most teacher assistants, however, perform a combination of instructional and clerical duties. They generally provide instructional reinforcement to children, under the direction and guidance of teachers. They work with students individually or in small groups—listening while students read, reviewing or reinforcing class lessons, or helping them find information for reports. At the secondary school level, teacher assistants often specialize in a certain subject, such as math or science. Teacher assistants often take charge of special projects and prepare equipment or exhibits, such as for a science demonstration. Some assistants work in computer laboratories, helping students using computers and educational software programs.

In addition to instructing, assisting, and supervising students, teacher assistants grade tests and papers, check homework, keep health and attendance records, do typing and filing, and duplicate materials. They also stock supplies, operate audiovisual equipment, and keep classroom equipment in order.

Many teacher assistants work extensively with special education students. As schools become more inclusive, integrating special education students into general education classrooms, teacher assistants in general education and special education classrooms increasingly assist students with disabilities. Teacher assistants attend to a disabled student's physical needs, including feeding, teaching good grooming habits, or assisting students riding the schoolbus. They also provide personal attention to students with other special needs, such as those from disadvantaged families, those who speak English as a second language, or those who need remedial education. Teacher assistants help assess a student's progress by observing performance and recording relevant data.

Teacher assistants also work with infants and toddlers who have developmental delays or other disabilities. Under the guidance of a teacher or therapist, teacher assistants perform exercises or play games to help the child develop physically and

Teacher assistants provide students with individual attention.

behaviorally. Some teacher assistants work with young adults to help them obtain a job or to apply for community services for the disabled.

Working Conditions
Approximately 4 in 10 teacher assistants work part time. However, even among full-time workers, nearly 40 percent work less than 8 hours per day. Most assistants who provide educational instruction work the traditional 9- to 10-month school year. Teacher assistants work in a variety of settings—including private homes and preschools, and local government offices, where they would deal with young adults—but most work in classrooms in elementary, middle, and secondary schools. They also work outdoors supervising recess when weather allows, and they spend much of their time standing, walking, or kneeling.

Seeing students develop and gain appreciation of the joy of learning can be very rewarding. However, working closely with students can be both physically and emotionally tiring. Teacher assistants who work with special education students often perform more strenuous tasks, including lifting, as they help students with their daily routine. Those who perform clerical work may tire of administrative duties, such as copying materials or typing.

Employment
Teacher assistants held almost 1.3 million jobs in 2002. Nearly 3 in 4 work for State and local government education institutions; mostly at the preschool and elementary school level. Private schools, daycare centers, and religious organizations hire most of the rest.

Training, Other Qualifications, and Advancement
Educational requirements for teacher assistants vary by State or school district and range from a high school diploma to some college training, although employers increasingly prefer applicants with some college training. Teacher assistants with instructional responsibilities usually require more training than do those who do not perform teaching tasks. In addition, as a

result of the No Child Left Behind Act of 2001, teacher assistants in Title 1 schools—those with a large proportion of students from low-income households—will be required to meet one of three requirements: have a minimum of 2 years of college, hold a 2-year or higher degree, or pass a rigorous state and local assessment. Many schools also require previous experience in working with children and a valid driver's license. Some schools may require the applicant to pass a background check.

A number of 2-year and community colleges offer associate degree programs that prepare graduates to work as teacher assistants. However, most teacher assistants receive on-the-job training. Those who tutor and review lessons with students must have a thorough understanding of class materials and instructional methods, and should be familiar with the organization and operation of a school. Teacher assistants also must know how to operate audiovisual equipment, keep records, and prepare instructional materials, as well as have adequate computer skills.

Teacher assistants should enjoy working with children from a wide range of cultural backgrounds, and be able to handle classroom situations with fairness and patience. Teacher assistants also must demonstrate initiative and a willingness to follow a teacher's directions. They must have good writing skills and be able to communicate effectively with students and teachers. Teacher assistants who speak a second language, especially Spanish, are in great demand for communicating with growing numbers of students and parents whose primary language is not English.

Advancement for teacher assistants—usually in the form of higher earnings or increased responsibility—comes primarily with experience or additional education. Some school districts provide time away from the job or tuition reimbursement so that teacher assistants can earn their bachelor's degrees and pursue licensed teaching positions. In return for tuition reimbursement, assistants are often required to teach a certain length of time for the school district.

Job Outlook
Employment of teacher assistants is expected to grow somewhat faster than the average for all occupations through 2012. Although school enrollments are projected to increase only slowly over the next decade, the student population for which teacher assistants are most needed—special education students and students for whom English is not their first language—is expected to increase more rapidly than the general school-age population. Legislation that requires students with disabilities and non-native English speakers to receive an education "equal" to that of other students, will generate jobs for teacher assistants to accommodate these students' special needs. Children with special needs require much personal attention, and special education teachers, as well as general education teachers with special education students, rely heavily on teacher assistants.

Additionally, a greater focus on educational quality and accountability, as required by the No Child Left Behind Act, is likely to lead to an increased demand for teacher assistants. Growing numbers of teacher assistants will be needed to help teachers prepare students for standardized testing and to provide extra assistance to students who perform poorly on standardized tests. An increasing number of afterschool programs and summer programs also will create new opportunities for teacher assistants. In addition to those stemming from employment growth, numerous job openings will arise as assistants transfer to other occupations or leave the labor force to assume family responsibilities, to return to school, or for other reasons characteristic of occupations that require limited formal education and offer relatively low pay.

Opportunities for teacher assistant jobs are expected to be best for persons with at least 2 years of formal education after high school. Persons who can speak a foreign language should be in particular demand in school systems with large numbers of students whose families do not speak English at home. Demand is expected to vary by region of the country. Areas in which the population and school enrollments are expanding rapidly, such as many communities in the South and West, should have rapid growth in the demand for teacher assistants.

Earnings
Median annual earnings of teacher assistants in 2002 were $18,660. The middle 50 percent earned between $14,880 and $23,600. The lowest 10 percent earned less than $12,900, and the highest 10 percent earned more than $29,050.

Teacher assistants who work part time ordinarily do not receive benefits. Full-time workers usually receive health coverage and other benefits.

In 2002, about 3 out of 10 teacher assistants belonged to unions—mainly the American Federation of Teachers and the National Education Association—which bargain with school systems over wages, hours, and the terms and conditions of employment.

Related Occupations
Teacher assistants who instruct children have duties similar to those of preschool, kindergarten, elementary, middle, and secondary school teachers, special education teachers, and school librarians. However, teacher assistants do not have the same level of responsibility or training. The support activities of teacher assistants and their educational backgrounds are similar to those of childcare workers, library technicians, and library assistants. Teacher assistants who work with children with disabilities perform many of the same functions as occupational therapy assistants and aides.

Sources of Additional Information
For information on teacher assistants, including training and certification, contact:
➤ American Federation of Teachers, Paraprofessional and School Related Personnel Division, 555 New Jersey Ave. NW., Washington, DC 20001.
➤ National Education Association, Educational Support Personnel division, 1201 16th Street, NW | Washington, DC 20036.

For information on a career as a teacher assistant, contact:
➤ National Resource Center for Paraprofessionals, 6526 Old Main Hill, Utah State University, Logan, UT 84322. Internet: **http://www.nrcpara.org**

Human resource departments of school systems, school administrators, and State departments of education also can provide details about employment opportunities and required qualifications for teacher assistant jobs.

Teachers—Adult Literacy and Remedial and Self-Enrichment Education
(0*NET 25-3011.00, 25-3021.00)

Significant Points
● Many adult literacy and remedial and self-enrichment teachers work part time and receive no benefits; unpaid volunteers also teach these subjects.
● Opportunities for teachers of English as a second language are expected to be very good, due to the expected increase in the number of residents with limited English skills who seek classes.
● Demand for self-enrichment courses is expected to rise with growing numbers of people who embrace lifelong learning and of retirees who have more free time to take classes.

Nature of the Work
Self-enrichment teachers teach courses that students take for pleasure or personal enrichment; these classes are not usually intended to lead to a particular degree or vocation. Self-enrichment teachers may instruct children or adults in a wide variety of areas, such as cooking, dancing, creative writing, photography, or personal finance. In contrast, *adult literacy and remedial education teachers* provide adults and out-of-school youths with the education they need to read, write, and speak English and to perform elementary mathematical calculations—basic skills that equip them to solve problems well enough to become active participants in our society, to hold a job, and to further their education. The instruction provided by these teachers can be divided into three principle categories: *remedial or adult basic education (ABE)*, which is geared toward adults whose skills are either at or below an eighth-grade level; *adult secondary education (ASE)*, which is geared towards students who wish to obtain their General Educational Development (GED) certificate or other high school equivalency credential; and *English literacy*, which provides instruction for adults with limited proficiency in English. Traditionally, the students in adult literacy and remedial (basic) education classes were made up primarily of those who did not graduate high school or who passed through school without the knowledge needed to meet their educational goals or to participate fully in today's high-skill society. Increasingly, however, students in these classes are immigrants or other people whose native language is not English. Educators who work with adult English-language learners are usually called *teachers of English as a second language (ESL)* or *teachers of English to speakers of other languages (ESOL)*.

Self-enrichment teachers, due to the wide range of classes and subjects they teach, may have styles and methods of instruction that differ greatly. The majority of self-enrichment classes are relatively informal and nonintensive in terms of instructional demands. Some classes, such as pottery or sewing, may be largely hands-on, requiring students to practice doing things themselves in order to learn. In that case, teachers may demonstrate methods or techniques for their class and subsequently supervise students' progress as they attempt to carry out the same or similar tasks or actions. Other classes, such as those involving financial planning or religion and spirituality, may be somewhat more academic in nature. Teachers of these classes are likely to rely more heavily on lectures and group discussions as methods of instruction. Classes offered through religious institutions, such as marriage preparation or classes in religion for children, may also be taught by self-enrichment teachers.

Many of the classes that self-enrichment educators teach are shorter in duration than classes taken for academic credit; some finish in 1 or 2 days to several weeks. These brief classes tend to be introductory in nature and generally focus on only one topic— for example, a cooking class that teaches students how to make bread. Some self-enrichment classes introduce children and youths to activities such as piano or drama, and may be designed to last anywhere from 1 week to several months. These and other self-enrichment classes may be scheduled to occur after school or during school vacations.

Remedial education teachers, more commonly called adult basic education teachers, teach basic academic courses in mathematics, languages, history, reading, writing, science, and other areas, using instructional methods geared toward adult learning. They teach these subjects to students 16 years of age and older who demonstrate the need to increase their skills in one or more of the subject areas mentioned. Classes are taught to appeal to a variety of learning styles and usually include large-group, small-group, and one-on-one instruction. Because the students often are at different proficiency levels for different subjects, adult basic education teachers must make individual assessments of each student's abilities beforehand. In many programs, the assessment is used to develop an individualized education plan for each student. Teachers are required to evaluate students periodically to determine their progress and potential for advancement to the next level.

Teachers in remedial or adult basic education may have to assist students in acquiring effective study skills and the self-confidence they need to reenter an academic environment. Teachers also may encounter students with a learning or physical disability that requires additional expertise. Teachers should possess an understanding of how to help these students achieve their goals, but they also may need to have the knowledge to detect challenges their students may have and provide them with access to a broader system of additional services that are required to address their challenges.

For students who wish to get a GED credential in order to get a job or qualify for postsecondary education, adult secondary education or GED teachers provide help in acquiring the necessary knowledge and skills to pass the test. The GED tests students in subject areas such as reading, writing, mathematics, science, and social studies, while at the same time measuring students' communication, information-processing, problem-solving, and critical-thinking skills. The emphasis in class is on acquiring the knowledge needed to pass the GED test, as well as preparing students for success in further educational endeavors.

ESOL teachers help adults to speak, listen, read, and write in English, often in the context of real-life situations to promote learning. More advanced students may concentrate on writing and conversational skills or focus on learning more academic or job-related communication skills. ESOL teachers teach adults who possess a wide range of cultures and abilities and who speak a variety of languages. Some of their students have a college degree and many advance quickly through the program owing to a variety of factors, such as their age, previous language experience, educational background, and native lan-

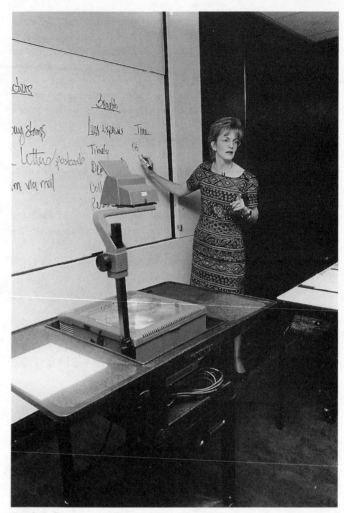

English literacy teachers often use real-life situations to promote learning.

guage. Others may need additional time due to these same factors. Because the teacher and students often do not share a common language, creativity is an important part of fostering communication in the classroom and achieving learning goals.

All adult literacy, remedial, and self-enrichment teachers must prepare lessons beforehand, do any related paperwork, and stay current in their fields. Attendance for students is mostly voluntary and course work is rarely graded. Many teachers also must learn the latest uses for computers in the classroom, as computers are increasingly being used to supplement instruction in basic skills and in teaching ESOL.

Working Conditions

A large number of adult literacy and remedial and self-enrichment education teachers work part time. Some have several part-time teaching assignments or work full time in addition to their part-time teaching job. Classes for adults are held on days and at times that best accommodate students who may have a job or family responsibilities. Similarly, self-enrichment classes for children are usually held after school or during school vacation periods.

Because many of these teachers work with adult students, they do not encounter some of the behavioral or social problems sometimes found with younger students. Adults attend by choice, are highly motivated, and bring years of experience to the classroom—attributes that can make teaching these students rewarding and satisfying. Self-enrichment teachers must have a great deal of patience, particularly when working with young children.

Employment
Teachers of adult literacy, remedial, and self-enrichment education held about 280,000 jobs in 2002. About 1 in 5 was self-employed. Many additional teachers worked as unpaid volunteers.

Nearly three-quarters, or 200,000, of the jobs were held by self-enrichment teachers. The largest numbers of these workers were employed by public and private educational institutions, religious organizations, and providers of social assistance and amusement and recreation services.

Adult literacy, basic education, and GED teachers and instructors held about 80,000 jobs. Many of the jobs are federally funded, with additional funds coming from State and local governments. The education industry employs the majority of these teachers, who work in adult learning centers, libraries, or community colleges. Others work for social service organizations such as job-training or residential care facilities. Still others work for State and local governments, providing basic education at juvenile detention and corrections institutions, among other places.

Training, Other Qualifications, and Advancement
The main qualification for self-enrichment teachers is expertise in their subject area; however, requirements may vary greatly with both the type of class taught and the place of employment. In some cases, a portfolio of one's work may be required. For example, to secure a job teaching a photography course, an applicant would need to show examples of previous work. Special certification may be required to teach some subjects, such as a Red Cross water safety instructor certificate to teach swimming. Some self-enrichment teachers are trained educators or other professionals who teach enrichment classes in their spare time. In some disciplines, such as art or music, specific teacher training programs are available. Prospective dance teachers, for example, may complete programs that prepare them to instruct any number of types of dance—from ballroom dancing to ballet. Self-enrichment teachers also should have good speaking skills and a talent for making the subject interesting. Patience and the ability to explain and instruct students at a basic level are important as well, particularly when one is working with children.

Requirements for teaching adult literacy and basic and secondary education vary by State and by program. Federally funded programs run by State and local governments require high accountability and student achievement standards. Those programs run by religious, community, or volunteer organizations, rather than State-run, federally funded programs, generally develop standards based on their own needs and organizational goals. Most State and local governments and educational institutions require that adult teachers have at least a bachelor's degree and, preferably, a master's degree. Some—especially school districts that hire adult education teachers—require an elementary or secondary school teaching certificate. A few have begun requiring a special certificate in ESOL or adult education. Teaching experience, especially with adults, also is preferred or required. Volunteers usually do not need a bachelor's degree, but often must attend a training program before they are allowed to work with students.

Most programs recommend that adult literacy and basic and secondary education teachers take classes or workshops on teaching adults, using technology to teach, working with learners from a variety of cultures, and teaching adults with learning disabilities. ESOL teachers also should have courses or training in second-language acquisition theory and linguistics. In addition, knowledge of the citizenship and naturalization process may be useful. Knowledge of a second language is not necessary to teach ESOL students, but can be helpful in understanding the students' perspectives. GED teachers should know what is required to pass the GED and be able to instruct students in the subject matter. Training for literacy volunteers usually consists of instruction on effective teaching practices, needs assessment, lesson planning, the selection of appropriate instructional materials, characteristics of adult learners, and cross-cultural awareness.

Adult education and literacy teachers must have the ability to work with a variety of cultures, languages, and educational and economic backgrounds. They must be understanding and respectful of their students' circumstances and be familiar with their concerns. All teachers, both paid and volunteer, should be able to communicate well and motivate their students.

Professional development among adult education and literacy teachers varies widely. Both part-time and full-time teachers are expected to participate in ongoing professional development activities in order to keep current on new developments in the field and to enhance skills already acquired. Each State's professional development system reflects the unique needs and organizational structure of that State. Attendance by teachers at professional development workshops and other activities is often outlined in State or local policy. Some teachers are able to access professional development activities through alternative delivery systems such as the Internet or distance learning.

Opportunities for advancement in these professions, particularly for adult education and literacy teachers, again vary from State to State and program to program. Some part-time teachers are able to move into full-time teaching positions or program administrator positions, such as coordinator or director, when such vacancies occur. Others may decide to use their classroom experience to move into policy work at a nonprofit organization or with the local, State, or Federal government or to perform research. Self-enrichment teachers also may advance to administrative positions or may even go on to start their own school or program. Experienced self-enrichment teachers may mentor new instructors and volunteers.

Job Outlook
Opportunities for jobs as adult literacy, remedial, and self-enrichment education teachers are expected to be favorable. Employment is expected to grow faster than the average for all occupations through 2012, and a large number of job openings is expected, due to the need to replace people who leave the occupation or retire.

Self-enrichment education teachers account for the largest proportion of jobs in these occupations. The need for self-enrichment teachers is expected to grow as more people embrace lifelong learning and as the baby boomers begin to retire and have more time to take classes. Subjects that are not easily researched on the Internet and those that provide hands-on experiences, such as cooking, crafts, and the arts, will be in greater demand. Also, classes on spirituality and self-improvement are expected to be popular.

As employers increasingly require a more literate workforce, workers' demand for adult literacy, basic education, and secondary education classes is expected to grow. Significant employment growth is anticipated especially for ESOL teachers, who will be needed by the increasing number of immigrants and other residents living in this country who need to learn, or enhance their skills in, English. In addition, a greater proportion of these groups is expected to take ESOL classes. Demand for ESOL teachers will be greatest in States such as California, Florida, Texas, and New York, due to their large populations of residents who have limited English skills. However, parts of the Midwest and Plains States have begun to attract large numbers of immigrants, making for especially good opportunities in those areas as well.

The demand for adult literacy and basic and secondary education often fluctuates with the economy. When the economy is good and workers are hard to find, employers relax their standards and hire workers without a degree or GED or those with limited proficiency in English. As the economy softens, more students find that they need additional education to get a job. However, adult education classes often are subject to changes in funding levels, which can cause the number of teaching jobs to fluctuate from year to year. In addition, factors such as immigration policies and the relative prosperity of the United States compared with other countries may have an impact on the number of immigrants entering this country and, consequently, on the demand for ESOL teachers.

Earnings

Median hourly earnings of self-enrichment teachers were $14.09 in 2002. The middle 50 percent earned between $9.86 and $19.69. The lowest 10 percent earned less than $7.37, and the highest 10 percent earned more than $26.49. Self-enrichment teachers are generally paid by the hour or for each class that they teach.

Median hourly earnings of adult literacy, remedial education, and GED teachers and instructors were $17.50 in 2002. The middle 50 percent earned between $13.21 and $24.00. The lowest 10 percent earned less than $10.08, and the highest 10 percent earned more than $34.30. Part-time adult literacy and remedial education and GED instructors are usually paid by the hour or for each class that they teach, and receive few benefits or none at all. Full-time teachers are generally paid a salary and receive health insurance and other benefits if they work for a school system or government.

Related Occupations

The work of adult literacy, remedial, and self-enrichment teachers is closely related to that of other types of teachers, especially preschool, kindergarten, elementary school, middle school, and secondary school teachers. In addition, adult literacy and basic and secondary education teachers require a wide variety of skills and aptitudes. Not only must they be able to teach and motivate students (including, at times, those with learning disabilities), but they also must often take on roles as advisers and mentors. Workers in other occupations that require these aptitudes include special-education teachers, counselors, and social workers. Self-enrichment teachers teach a wide variety of subjects that may be related to the work done by those in many other occupations, such as dancers and choreographers; artists and related workers; musicians, singers, and related workers; recreation and fitness workers; and athletes, coaches, umpires, and related workers.

Sources of Additional Information

Information on adult literacy, basic and secondary education programs, and teacher certification requirements is available from State departments of education, local school districts, and literacy resource centers. Information also may be obtained through local religious and charitable organizations.

For information on adult education and family literacy programs, contact
➤ The U.S. Department of Education, Office of Vocational and Adult Education, 4090 MES, 400 Maryland Ave. SW., Washington, DC 20202. Internet: **http://www.ed.gov/offices/OVAE**

For information on teaching English as a second language, contact
➤ The National Center for ESL Literacy Education, 4646 40th St. NW., Washington, DC 20016. Internet: **http://www.cal.org/ncle**

Teachers—Postsecondary

(O*NET 25-1011.00, 25-1021.00, 25-1022.00, 25-1031.00, 25-1032.00, 25-1041.00, 25-1042.00, 25-1043.00, 25-1051.00, 25-1052.00, 25-1053.00, 25-1054.00, 25-1061.00, 25-1062.00, 25-1063.00, 25-1064.00, 25-1065.00, 25-1066.00, 25-1067.00, 25-1069.99, 25-1071.00, 25-1072.00, 25-1081.00, 25-1082.00, 25-1111.00, 25-1112.00, 25-1113.00, 25-1121.00, 25-1122.00, 25-1123.00, 25-1124.00, 25-1125.00, 25-1126.00, 25-1191.00, 25-1192.00, 25-1193.00, 25-1194.00, 25-1199.99)

Significant Points

● Opportunities for college and university teaching jobs are expected to improve, but many new openings will be for part-time or non-tenure-track positions.

● Prospects for teaching jobs will continue to be better in academic fields that offer attractive alternative nonacademic job opportunities—health specialties, business, and computer science, for example—which attract fewer applicants for academic positions.

● Educational qualifications for postsecondary teacher jobs range from expertise in a particular field to a Ph.D, depending on the subject being taught and the type of educational institution.

● One out of eight postsecondary teachers is a graduate teaching assistant—and one out of ten is a vocational or career and technical education teacher.

Nature of the Work

Postsecondary teachers instruct students in a wide variety of academic and vocational subjects beyond the high school level that may lead to a degree or simply to improvement in one's knowledge or skills. These teachers include college and university faculty, postsecondary career and technical education teachers, and graduate teaching assistants.

College and university faculty make up the majority of postsecondary teachers. They teach and advise more than 15 million full- and part-time college students and perform a significant part of our Nation's research. Faculty also keep up with new developments in their field and may consult with government, business, nonprofit, and community organizations.

Faculty usually are organized into departments or divisions, based on academic subject or field. They usually teach several different related courses in their subject—algebra, calculus, and statistics, for example. They may instruct undergraduate or graduate students, or both. College and university faculty may give lectures to several hundred students in large halls, lead small seminars, or supervise students in laboratories. They prepare lectures, exercises, and laboratory experiments; grade exams and papers; and advise and work with students individually. In universities, they also supervise graduate students' teaching and research. College faculty work with an increasingly varied student population made up of growing shares of part-time, older, and culturally and racially diverse students.

Faculty keep abreast of developments in their field by reading current literature, talking with colleagues, and participating in professional conferences. They may also do their own research to expand knowledge in their field. They may perform experiments; collect and analyze data; and examine original documents, literature, and other source material. From this process, they arrive at conclusions, and publish their findings in scholarly journals, books, and electronic media.

Most college and university faculty extensively use computer technology, including the Internet; electronic mail; software programs, such as statistical packages; and CD-ROMs. They may use computers in the classroom as teaching aids and may post course content, class notes, class schedules, and other information on the Internet. Some faculty are increasingly using sophisticated telecommunications and videoconferencing equipment and the Internet to teach courses to students at remote sites. The use of e-mail, chat rooms, and other techniques has greatly improved communications between students and teachers and among students.

Most faculty members serve on academic or administrative committees that deal with the policies of their institution, departmental matters, academic issues, curricula, budgets, equipment purchases, and hiring. Some work with student and community organizations. Department chairpersons are faculty members who usually teach some courses but have heavier administrative responsibilities.

The proportion of time spent on research, teaching, administrative, and other duties varies by individual circumstance and type of institution. Faculty members at universities normally spend a significant part of their time doing research; those in 4-year colleges, somewhat less; and those in 2-year colleges, relatively little. The teaching load, however, often is heavier in 2-year colleges and somewhat lighter at 4-year institutions. Full professors at all types of institutions usually spend a larger portion of their time conducting research than do assistant professors, instructors, and lecturers.

Postsecondary vocational education teachers, also known as *postsecondary career and technical education teachers,* provide instruction for occupations that require specialized training, but may not require a 4-year degree, such as welder, dental hygienist, x-ray technician, auto mechanic, and cosmetologist. Classes often are taught in an industrial or laboratory setting where students are provided hands-on experience. For example, welding instructors show students various welding techniques and essential safety practices, watch them use tools and equipment, and have them repeat procedures until they meet the specific standards required by the trade. Increasingly, career and technical education teachers are integrating academic and vocational curriculums so that students obtain a variety of skills that can be applied to the "real world."

Career and technical education teachers have many of the same responsibilities that other college and university faculty have. They must prepare lessons, grade papers, attend faculty

Postsecondary teachers review current research to keep abreast of developments in their field.

meetings, and keep abreast of developments in their field. Career and technical education teachers at community colleges and career and technical schools also often play a key role in students' transition from school to work by helping to establish internship programs for students and by providing information about prospective employers.

Graduate teaching assistants, often referred to as *graduate TAs*, assist faculty, department chairs, or other professional staff at colleges and universities by performing teaching or teaching-related duties. In addition to their work responsibilities, assistants have their own school commitments, as they are also students who are working towards earning a graduate degree, such as a Ph.D. Some teaching assistants have full responsibility for teaching a course—usually one that is introductory in nature—which can include preparation of lectures and exams, and assigning final grades to students. Others provide assistance to faculty members, which may consist of a variety of tasks such as grading papers, monitoring exams, holding office hours or help-sessions for students, conducting laboratory sessions, or administering quizzes to the class. Teaching assistants generally meet initially with the faculty member whom they are going to assist in order to determine exactly what is expected of them, as each faculty member may have his or her own needs. For example, some faculty members prefer assistants to sit in on classes, while others assign them other tasks to do during class time. Graduate teaching assistants may work one-on-one with a faculty member or, for large classes, they may be one of several assistants.

Working Conditions

Postsecondary teachers usually have flexible schedules. They must be present for classes, usually 12 to 16 hours per week, and for faculty and committee meetings. Most establish regular office hours for student consultations, usually 3 to 6 hours per week. Otherwise, teachers are free to decide when and where they will work, and how much time to devote to course preparation, grading, study, research, graduate student supervision, and other activities.

Some teach night and weekend classes. This is particularly true for teachers at 2-year community colleges or institutions with large enrollments of older students who have full-time jobs or family responsibilities. Most colleges and universities require teachers to work 9 months of the year, which allows them the time to teach additional courses, do research, travel, or pursue nonacademic interests during the summer and school holidays. Colleges and universities usually have funds to support research or other professional development needs, including travel to conferences and research sites.

About 3 out of 10 college and university faculty worked part time in 2002. Some part-timers, known as "adjunct faculty," have primary jobs outside of academia—in government, private industry, or nonprofit research—and teach "on the side." Others prefer to work part-time hours or seek full-time jobs but are unable to obtain them due to intense competition for available openings. Some work part time in more than one institution. Many adjunct faculty are not qualified for tenure-track positions because they lack a doctoral degree.

University faculty may experience a conflict between their responsibilities to teach students and the pressure to do research and publish their findings. This may be a particular problem for young faculty seeking advancement in 4-year research universities. Also, recent cutbacks and the hiring of more part-time faculty have put a greater administrative burden on full-time faculty. Requirements to teach online classes also have added greatly to the workloads of postsecondary teachers. Many find that developing the courses to put online, plus learning how to operate the technology and answering large amounts of e-mail, is very time-consuming.

Like college and university faculty, there is usually a great deal of flexibility in graduate TAs' work schedules, which allows them the time to pursue their own academic coursework and studies. The number of hours that TAs work varies depending on their assignments. Work may be stressful, particularly when assistants are given full responsibility for teaching a class; however, these types of positions allow graduate students the opportunity to gain valuable teaching experience. This experience is especially helpful for those graduate teaching assistants who seek to become faculty members at colleges and universities after completing their degree.

Employment

Postsecondary teachers held nearly 1.6 million jobs in 2002. Most were employed in public and private 4-year colleges and universities and in 2-year community colleges. Postsecondary career and technical education teachers also are employed by schools and institutes that specialize in training people in a specific field, such as technology centers or culinary schools. Some career and technical education teachers work for State

and local governments and job training facilities. The following tabulation shows postsecondary teaching jobs in specialties having 20,000 or more jobs in 2002:

Graduate teaching assistants	128,000
Vocational education teachers	119,000
Health specialties teachers	86,000
Business teachers	67,000
Art, drama, and music teachers	58,000
English language and literature teachers	55,000
Education teachers	42,000
Biological science teachers	47,000
Mathematical science teachers	41,000
Nursing instructors and teachers	37,000
Computer science teachers	33,000
Engineering teachers	29,000
Psychology teachers	26,000

Training, Other Qualifications, and Advancement

The education and training required of postsecondary teachers varies widely, depending on the subject taught and educational institution employing them. Educational requirements for teachers are generally the highest at 4-year research universities but, at career and technical institutes, experience and expertise in a related occupation is the most valuable qualification.

Postsecondary teachers should communicate and relate well with students, enjoy working with them, and be able to motivate them. They should have inquiring and analytical minds, and a strong desire to pursue and disseminate knowledge. Additionally, they must be self-motivated and able to work in an environment in which they receive little direct supervision.

Training requirements for postsecondary career and technical education teachers vary by State and by subject. In general, teachers need a bachelor's or higher degree, plus work or other experience in their field. In some fields, a license or certificate that demonstrates one's qualifications may be all that is required. Teachers update their skills through continuing education, in order to maintain certification. They must also maintain ongoing dialogue with businesses to determine the most current skills needed in the workplace.

Four-year colleges and universities usually consider doctoral degree holders for full-time, tenure-track positions, but may hire master's degree holders or doctoral candidates for certain disciplines, such as the arts, or for part-time and temporary jobs. Most college and university faculty are in four academic ranks—professor, associate professor, assistant professor, and instructor. These positions usually are considered to be tenure-track positions. Most faculty members are hired as instructors or assistant professors. A smaller number of additional faculty members, called lecturers, are usually employed on contracts for a single academic term and are not on the tenure track.

In 2-year colleges, master's degree holders fill most full-time positions. However, with increasing competition for available jobs, institutions can be more selective in their hiring practices. Many 2-year institutions increasingly prefer job applicants to have some teaching experience or experience with distance learning. Preference also may be given to those holding dual master's degrees, because they can teach more subjects. In addition, with greater competition for jobs, master's degree holders may find it increasingly difficult to obtain employment as they are passed over in favor of candidates holding a Ph.D.

Doctoral programs take an average of 6 to 8 years of full-time study beyond the bachelor's degree, including time spent completing a master's degree and a dissertation. Some programs, such as those in the humanities, take longer to complete; others, such as those in engineering, usually are shorter. Candidates specialize in a subfield of a discipline—for example, organic chemistry, counseling psychology, or European history—but also take courses covering the entire discipline. Programs include 20 or more increasingly specialized courses and seminars plus comprehensive examinations on all major areas of the field. Candidates also must complete a dissertation—a written report on original research in the candidate's major field of study. The dissertation sets forth an original hypothesis or proposes a model and tests it. Students in the natural sciences and engineering usually do laboratory work; in the humanities, they study original documents and other published material. The dissertation is done under the guidance of one or more faculty advisors and usually takes 1 or 2 years of full-time work.

In some fields, particularly the natural sciences, some students spend an additional 2 years on postdoctoral research and study before taking a faculty position. Some Ph.D.s extend postdoctoral appointments, or take new ones, if they are unable to find a faculty job. Most of these appointments offer a nominal salary.

Obtaining a position as a graduate teaching assistant is a good way to gain college teaching experience. To qualify, candidates must be enrolled in a graduate school program. In addition, some colleges and universities require teaching assistants to attend classes or take some training prior to being given responsibility for a course.

Although graduate teaching assistants usually work at the institution and in the department where they are earning their degree, teaching or internship positions for graduate students at institutions that do not grant a graduate degree have become more common in recent years. For example, a program called Preparing Future Faculty, administered by the Association of American Colleges and Universities and the Council of Graduate Schools, has led to the creation of many now-independent programs that offer graduate students at research universities the opportunity to work as teaching assistants at other types of institutions, such as liberal arts or community colleges. Working with a mentor, the graduate students teach classes and learn how to improve their teaching techniques. They may attend faculty and committee meetings, develop a curriculum, and learn how to balance the teaching, research, and administrative roles that faculty play. These programs provide valuable learning opportunities for graduate students interested in teaching at the postsecondary level, and also help to make these students aware of the differences among the various types of institutions at which they may someday work.

For faculty, a major step in the traditional academic career is attaining tenure. New tenure-track faculty usually are hired as instructors or assistant professors, and must serve a period—usually 7 years—under term contracts. At the end of the period, their record of teaching, research, and overall contribution to the institution is reviewed; tenure is granted if the review is favorable. Those denied tenure usually must leave the institution. Tenured professors cannot be fired without just cause and due process. Tenure protects the faculty's academic freedom—the ability to teach and conduct research without fear of being fired for advocating unpopular ideas. It also gives both faculty and institutions the stability needed for effective research and teaching, and provides financial security for faculty. Some institutions have adopted post-tenure review policies to encourage ongoing evaluation of tenured faculty.

The number of tenure-track positions is expected to decline as institutions seek flexibility in dealing with financial matters and changing student interests. Institutions will rely more heavily on limited term contracts and part-time, or adjunct, faculty, thus shrinking the total pool of tenured faculty. In a trend that is expected to continue, some institutions now offer limited-term contracts to prospective faculty—typically 2-, 3-, or 5-year, full-time contracts. These contracts may be terminated or extended when they expire. Institutions are not obligated to grant tenure to the contract holders. In addition, some institutions have limited the percentage of faculty who can be tenured.

For most postsecondary teachers, advancement involves a move into administrative and managerial positions, such as departmental chairperson, dean, and president. At 4-year institutions, such advancement requires a doctoral degree. At 2-year colleges, a doctorate is helpful but not usually required, except for advancement to some top administrative positions. (Deans and departmental chairpersons are covered in the *Handbook* statement on education administrators, while college presidents are included in the *Handbook* statement on top executives.)

Job Outlook

Overall, employment of postsecondary teachers is expected to grow much faster than the average for all occupations through 2012. A significant proportion of these new jobs will be part-time positions. Good job opportunities are expected as retirements of current postsecondary teachers and continued increases in student enrollments create numerous openings for teachers at all types of postsecondary institutions.

Projected growth in college and university enrollment over the next decade stems largely from the expected increase in the population of 18- to 24-year-olds. Adults returning to college and an increase in foreign-born students also will add to the number of students, particularly in the fastest growing States of California, Texas, Florida, New York, and Arizona. In addition, workers' growing need to regularly update their skills will continue to create new opportunities for postsecondary teachers, particularly at community colleges and for-profit institutions that cater to working adults. However, many postsecondary educational institutions receive a significant portion of their funding from State and local governments, and, over the early years of the projection period, tight State and local budgets will limit the ability of many schools to expand. Nevertheless, a significant number of openings also is expected to arise due to the need to replace the large numbers of postsecondary teachers who are likely to retire over the next decade. Many postsecondary teachers were hired in the late 1960s and 1970s to teach the baby boomers, and they are expected to retire in growing numbers in the years ahead.

Postsecondary institutions are a major employer of workers holding doctoral degrees, and opportunities for Ph.D. recipients seeking jobs as postsecondary teachers are expected to be somewhat better than in previous decades. The number of earned doctorate degrees is projected to rise by only 4 percent over the 2002-12 period, sharply lower than the 10-percent increase over the previous decade. In spite of this positive trend, competition will remain tight for those seeking tenure-track positions at 4-year colleges and universities, as many of the job openings are expected to be either part-time or renewable, term appointments.

Opportunities for graduate teaching assistants are expected to be very good. Graduate enrollments over the 2002-12 period are projected to increase at a rate that is somewhat slower than that of the previous decade, while total undergraduate enrollments in degree-granting institutions are expected to increase at nearly twice the rate of the preceding decade, creating many teaching opportunities. Constituting more than 12 percent of all postsecondary teachers, graduate teaching assistants play an integral role in the postsecondary education system, and they are expected to continue to do so in the future.

Because one of the main reasons why students attend postsecondary institutions is to obtain a job, the best job prospects for postsecondary teachers are likely to be in fields where job growth is expected to be strong over the next decade. These will include fields such as business, health specialties, nursing, and computer and biological sciences. Community colleges and other institutions offering career and technical education have been among the most rapidly growing, and these institutions are expected to offer some of the best opportunities for postsecondary teachers.

Earnings

Median annual earnings of all postsecondary teachers in 2002 were $49,040. The middle 50 percent earned between $34,310 and $69,580. The lowest 10 percent earned less than $23,080, and the highest 10 percent earned more than $92,430.

Earnings for college faculty vary according to rank and type of institution, geographic area, and field. According to a 2002-03 survey by the American Association of University Professors, salaries for full-time faculty averaged $64,455. By rank, the average was $86,437 for professors, $61,732 for associate professors, $51,545 for assistant professors, $37,737 for instructors, and $43,914 for lecturers. Faculty in 4-year institutions earn higher salaries, on average, than do those in 2-year schools. In 2002-03, average faculty salaries in public institutions—$63,974—were lower than those in private independent institutions—$74,359—but higher than those in religiously affiliated private colleges and universities—$57,564. In fields with high-paying nonacademic alternatives-medicine, law, engineering, and business, among others—earnings exceed these averages. In others—such as the humanities and education—they are lower.

Many faculty members have significant earnings, in addition to their base salary, from consulting, teaching additional courses, research, writing for publication, or other employment. In addition, many college and university faculty enjoy some unique benefits, including access to campus facilities, tuition waivers for dependents, housing and travel allowances, and paid sabbatical leaves. Part-time faculty usually have fewer benefits than do full-time faculty.

Earnings for postsecondary career and technical education teachers vary widely by subject, academic credentials, experience, and region of the country. Part-time instructors usually receive few benefits.

Related Occupations

Postsecondary teaching requires the ability to communicate ideas well, motivate students, and be creative. Workers in other occupations that require these skills are teachers—preschool, kindergarten, elementary, middle, and secondary; education administrators; librarians; counselors; writers and editors; public relations specialists; and management analysts. Faculty research activities often are similar to those of scientists, as well as

to those of managers and administrators in industry, government, and nonprofit research organizations.

Sources of Additional Information

Professional societies related to a field of study often provide information on academic and nonacademic employment opportunities. Names and addresses of many of these societies appear in statements elsewhere in the *Handbook*.

Special publications on higher education, such as *The Chronicle of Higher Education*, list specific employment opportunities for faculty. These publications are available in libraries.

For information on the Preparing Future Faculty program, contact:

➤ Association of American Colleges and Universities, 1818 R St. NW., Washington, DC 20009. Internet: **http://www.aacu-edu.org**

For information on postsecondary career and technical education teaching positions, contact State departments of career and technical education.

General information on adult and career and technical education is available from:

➤ Association for Career and Technical Education, 1410 King St., Alexandria, VA 22314. Internet: **http://www.acteonline.org**

Teachers—Preschool, Kindergarten, Elementary, Middle, and Secondary

(O*NET 25-2011.00, 25-2012.00, 25-2021.00, 25-2022.00, 25-2023.00, 25-2031.00, 25-2032.00)

Significant Points

- Public school teachers must have at least a bachelor's degree, complete an approved teacher education program, and be licensed.

- Many States offer alternative licensing programs to attract people into teaching, especially for hard-to-fill positions.

- Excellent job opportunities are expected as a large number of teachers retire over the next 10 years, particularly at the secondary school level; opportunities will vary somewhat by geographic area and subject taught.

Nature of the Work

Teachers act as facilitators or coaches, using interactive discussions and "hands-on" approaches to help students learn and apply concepts in subjects such as science, mathematics, or English. They utilize "props" or "manipulatives" to help children understand abstract concepts, solve problems, and develop critical thought processes. For example, they teach the concepts of numbers or of addition and subtraction by playing board games. As the children get older, the teachers use more sophisticated materials, such as science apparatus, cameras, or computers.

To encourage collaboration in solving problems, students are increasingly working in groups to discuss and solve problems together. Preparing students for the future workforce is the major stimulus generating the changes in education. To be prepared, students must be able to interact with others, adapt to new technology, and think through problems logically.

Teachers provide the tools and the environment for their students to develop these skills.

Preschool, kindergarten, and elementary school teachers play a vital role in the development of children. What children learn and experience during their early years can shape their views of themselves and the world and can affect their later success or failure in school, work, and their personal lives. Preschool, kindergarten, and elementary school teachers introduce children to mathematics, language, science, and social studies. They use games, music, artwork, films, books, computers, and other tools to teach basic skills.

Preschool children learn mainly through play and interactive activities. *Preschool teachers* capitalize on children's play to further language and vocabulary development (using storytelling, rhyming games, and acting games), improve social skills (having the children work together to build a neighborhood in a sandbox), and introduce scientific and mathematical concepts (showing the children how to balance and count blocks when building a bridge or how to mix colors when painting). Thus, a less structured approach, including small-group lessons, one-on-one instruction, and learning through creative activities such as art, dance, and music, is adopted to teach preschool children. Play and hands-on teaching also are used in kindergarten classrooms, but there academics begin to take priority. Letter recognition, phonics, numbers, and awareness of nature and science, introduced at the preschool level, are taught primarily by *kindergarten teachers*.

Most *elementary school teachers* instruct one class of children in several subjects. In some schools, two or more teachers work as a team and are jointly responsible for a group of students in at least one subject. In other schools, a teacher may teach one special subject—usually music, art, reading, science, arithmetic, or physical education—to a number of classes. A small but growing number of teachers instruct multilevel classrooms, with students at several different learning levels.

Middle school teachers and *secondary school teachers* help students delve more deeply into subjects introduced in elementary school and expose them to more information about the world. Middle and secondary school teachers specialize in a specific subject, such as English, Spanish, mathematics, history, or biology. They also can teach subjects that are career oriented. *Vocational education teachers*, also referred to as career and technical or career-technology teachers, instruct and train students to work in a wide variety of fields, such as healthcare, business, auto repair, communications, and, increasingly, technology. They often teach courses that are in high demand by area employers, who may provide input into the curriculum and offer internships to students. Many vocational teachers play an active role in building and overseeing these partnerships. Additional responsibilities of middle and secondary school teachers may include career guidance and job placement, as well as followups with students after graduation. (Special education teachers—who instruct elementary and secondary school students who have a variety of disabilities—are discussed separately in this section of the *Handbook*.)

Teachers may use films, slides, overhead projectors, and the latest technology in teaching, including computers, telecommunication systems, and video discs. The use of computer resources, such as educational software and the Internet, exposes students to a vast range of experiences and promotes interactive learning. Through the Internet, students can communicate with students in other countries. Students also use the Internet for individual research projects and to gather information. Computers are used in other classroom activities as well, from solving math problems to learning English as a second language. Teachers also may use computers to record grades and perform other administrative and clerical duties. They must continually update their skills so that they can instruct and use the latest technology in the classroom.

Teachers often work with students from varied ethnic, racial, and religious backgrounds. With growing minority populations in most parts of the country, it is important for teachers to work effectively with a diverse student population. Accordingly, some schools offer training to help teachers enhance their awareness and understanding of different cultures. Teachers may also include multicultural programming in their lesson plans, to address the needs of all students, regardless of their cultural background.

Teachers design classroom presentations to meet students' needs and abilities. They also work with students individually. Teachers plan, evaluate, and assign lessons; prepare, administer, and grade tests; listen to oral presentations; and maintain classroom discipline. They observe and evaluate a student's performance and potential and increasingly are asked to use new assessment methods. For example, teachers may examine a portfolio of a student's artwork or writing in order to judge the student's overall progress. They then can provide additional assistance in areas in which a student needs help. Teachers also grade papers, prepare report cards, and meet with parents and school staff to discuss a student's academic progress or personal problems.

In addition to conducting classroom activities, teachers oversee study halls and homerooms, supervise extracurricular activities, and accompany students on field trips. They may identify students with physical or mental problems and refer the students to the proper authorities. Secondary school teachers occasionally assist students in choosing courses, colleges, and careers. Teachers also participate in education conferences and workshops.

In recent years, site-based management, which allows teachers and parents to participate actively in management decisions regarding school operations, has gained popularity. In many schools, teachers are increasingly involved in making decisions regarding the budget, personnel, textbooks, curriculum design, and teaching methods.

Teachers find that helping students to gain an appreciation of knowledge and learning can be very rewarding.

Working Conditions

Seeing students develop new skills and gain an appreciation of knowledge and learning can be very rewarding. However, teaching may be frustrating when one is dealing with unmotivated or disrespectful students. Occasionally, teachers must cope with unruly behavior and violence in the schools. Teachers may experience stress in dealing with large classes, students from disadvantaged or multicultural backgrounds, or heavy workloads. Inner-city schools in particular, may be run down and lack the amenities of schools in wealthier communities. Accountability standards also may increase stress levels, with teachers expected to produce students who are able to exhibit satisfactory performance on standardized tests in core subjects.

Teachers are sometimes isolated from their colleagues because they work alone in a classroom of students. However, some schools allow teachers to work in teams and with mentors to enhance their professional development.

Including school duties performed outside the classroom, many teachers work more than 40 hours a week. Part-time schedules are more common among preschool and kindergarten teachers. Although some school districts have gone to all-day kindergartens, most kindergarten teachers still teach two kindergarten classes a day. Most teachers work the traditional 10-month school year with a 2-month vacation during the summer. During the vacation break, those on the 10-month schedule may teach in summer sessions, take other jobs, travel, or pursue personal interests. Many enroll in college courses or workshops to continue their education. Teachers in districts with a year-round schedule typically work 8 weeks, are on vacation for 1 week, and have a 5-week midwinter break. Preschool teachers working in daycare settings often work year round.

Most States have tenure laws that prevent teachers from being fired without just cause and due process. Teachers may obtain tenure after they have satisfactorily completed a probationary period of teaching, normally 3 years. Tenure does not absolutely guarantee a job, but it does provide some security.

Employment

Preschool, kindergarten, elementary school, middle school, and secondary school teachers, except special education, held about 3.8 million jobs in 2002. Of the teachers in those jobs, about 1.5 million were elementary school teachers, 1.1 million were secondary school teachers, 602,000 were middle school teachers, 424,000 were preschool teachers, and 168,000 were kindergarten teachers. The majority of kindergarten, elementary school, middle school, and secondary school teachers, except special education worked in local government educational services. About 10 percent worked for private schools. Preschool teachers, except special education were most often employed in child daycare services (63 percent), religious organizations (9 percent), local government educational services (9 percent), and private educational services (7 percent). Employment of teachers is geographically distributed much the same as the population is.

Training, Other Qualifications, and Advancement

All 50 States and the District of Columbia require public school teachers to be licensed. Licensure is not required for teachers in private schools. Usually licensure is granted by the State Board of Education or a licensure advisory committee. Teachers may be licensed to teach the early childhood grades (usually preschool through grade 3); the elementary grades (grades 1 through 6 or 8); the middle grades (grades 5 through 8); a secondary-

education subject area (usually grades 7 through 12); or a special subject, such as reading or music (usually grades kindergarten through 12).

Requirements for regular licenses to teach kindergarten through grade 12 vary by State. However, all States require general education teachers to have a bachelor's degree and to have completed an approved teacher training program with a prescribed number of subject and education credits, as well as supervised practice teaching. Some States also require technology training and the attainment of a minimum grade point average. A number of States require that teachers obtain a master's degree in education within a specified period after they begin teaching.

Almost all States require applicants for a teacher's license to be tested for competency in basic skills, such as reading and writing, and in teaching. Almost all also require the teacher to exhibit proficiency in his or her subject. Nowadays, school systems are moving toward implementing performance-based systems for licensure, which usually require the teacher to demonstrate satisfactory teaching performance over an extended period in order to obtain a provisional license, in addition to passing an examination in one's subject. Most States require continuing education for renewal of the teacher's license. Many States have reciprocity agreements that make it easier for teachers licensed in one State to become licensed in another.

Many States offer alternative licensure programs for teachers who have bachelor's degrees in the subject they will teach, but who lack the necessary education courses required for a regular license. Alternative licensure programs originally were designed to ease shortages of teachers of certain subjects, such as mathematics and science. The programs have expanded to attract other people into teaching, including recent college graduates and those changing from another career to teaching. In some programs, individuals begin teaching quickly under provisional licensure. After working under the close supervision of experienced educators for 1 or 2 years while taking education courses outside school hours, they receive regular licensure if they have progressed satisfactorily. In other programs, college graduates who do not meet licensure requirements take only those courses that they lack and then become licensed. This approach may take 1 or 2 semesters of full-time study. States may issue emergency licenses to individuals who do not meet the requirements for a regular license when schools cannot attract enough qualified teachers to fill positions. Teachers who need to be licensed may enter programs that grant a master's degree in education, as well as a license.

In many States, vocational teachers have many of the same requirements for teaching as their academic counterparts. However, because knowledge and experience in a particular field are important criteria for the job, some States will license vocational education teachers without a bachelor's degree, provided they can demonstrate expertise in their field. A minimum number of hours in education courses may also be required.

Licensing requirements for preschool teachers also vary by State. Requirements for public preschool teachers are generally higher than those for private preschool teachers. Some States require a bachelor's degree in early childhood education, others require an associate's degree, and still others require certification by a nationally recognized authority. The Child Development Associate (CDA) credential, the most common type of certification, requires a mix of classroom training and experience working with children, along with an independent assessment of an individual's competence.

In some cases, teachers of kindergarten through high school may attain professional certification in order to demonstrate competency beyond that required for a license. The National Board for Professional Teaching Standards offers a voluntary national certification. To become nationally accredited, experienced teachers must prove their aptitude by compiling a portfolio showing their work in the classroom and by passing a written assessment and evaluation of their teaching knowledge. Currently, teachers may become certified in a variety of areas, on the basis of the age of the students and, in some cases, the subject taught. For example, teachers may obtain a certificate for teaching English language arts to early adolescents (aged 11 to 15), or they may become certified as early childhood generalists. All States recognize national certification, and many States and school districts provide special benefits to teachers holding such certification. Benefits typically include higher salaries and reimbursement for continuing education and certification fees. In addition, many States allow nationally certified teachers to carry a license from one State to another.

The National Council for Accreditation of Teacher Education currently accredits more than 550 teacher education programs across the United States. Generally, 4-year colleges require students to wait until their sophomore year before applying for admission to teacher education programs. Traditional education programs for kindergarten and elementary school teachers include courses—designed specifically for those preparing to teach—in mathematics, physical science, social science, music, art, and literature, as well as prescribed professional education courses, such as philosophy of education, psychology of learning, and teaching methods. Aspiring secondary school teachers most often major in the subject they plan to teach while also taking a program of study in teacher preparation. Teacher education programs are now required to include classes in the use of computers and other technologies in order to maintain their accreditation. Most programs require students to perform a student-teaching internship.

Many States now offer professional development schools—partnerships between universities and elementary or secondary schools. Students enter these 1-year programs after completion of their bachelor's degree. Professional development schools merge theory with practice and allow the student to experience a year of teaching firsthand, under professional guidance.

In addition to being knowledgeable in their subject, teachers must have the ability to communicate, inspire trust and confidence, and motivate students, as well as understand the students' educational and emotional needs. Teachers must be able to recognize and respond to individual and cultural differences in students and employ different teaching methods that will result in higher student achievement. They should be organized, dependable, patient, and creative. Teachers also must be able to work cooperatively and communicate effectively with other teachers, support staff, parents, and members of the community.

With additional preparation, teachers may move into positions as school librarians, reading specialists, curriculum specialists, or guidance counselors. Teachers may become administrators or supervisors, although the number of these positions is limited and competition can be intense. In some systems, highly qualified, experienced teachers can become senior or mentor teachers, with higher pay and additional responsibilities. They guide and assist less experienced teachers while keeping most of their own teaching responsibilities. Preschool teachers usually work their way up from assistant teacher, to teacher, to lead teacher—who may be responsible for the instruction of several classes—and, finally, to director of the center. Preschool teachers with a bachelor's degree frequently are qualified to teach kindergarten through grade 3 as well. Teaching at these higher grades often results in higher pay.

Job Outlook

Job opportunities for teachers over the next 10 years will vary from good to excellent, depending on the locality, grade level, and subject taught. Most job openings will be attributable to the expected retirement of a large number of teachers. In addition, relatively high rates of turnover, especially among beginning teachers employed in poor, urban schools, also will lead to numerous job openings for teachers. Competition for qualified teachers among some localities will likely continue, with schools luring teachers from other States and districts with bonuses and higher pay.

Through 2012, overall student enrollments, a key factor in the demand for teachers, are expected to rise more slowly than in the past. As the children of the baby-boom generation get older, smaller numbers of young children will enter school behind them, resulting in average employment growth for all teachers, from preschool through secondary grades. Projected enrollments will vary by region. Fast-growing States in the South and West—particularly California, Texas, Georgia, Idaho, Hawaii, Alaska, and New Mexico—will experience the largest enrollment increases. Enrollments in the Northeast and Midwest are expected to hold relatively steady or decline. The job market for teachers also continues to vary by school location and by subject taught. Many inner cities—often characterized by overcrowded, ill-equipped schools and higher-than-average poverty rates—and rural areas—characterized by their remote location and relatively low salaries—have difficulty attracting and retaining enough teachers, so job prospects should be better in these areas than in suburban districts. Currently, many school districts have difficulty hiring qualified teachers in some subject areas—mathematics, science (especially chemistry and physics), bilingual education, and foreign languages. Qualified vocational teachers, at both the middle school and secondary school levels, also are currently in demand in a variety of fields. Specialties that have an adequate number of qualified teachers include general elementary education, physical education, and social studies. Teachers who are geographically mobile and who obtain licensure in more than one subject should have a distinct advantage in finding a job. Increasing enrollments of minorities, coupled with a shortage of minority teachers, should cause efforts to recruit minority teachers to intensify. Also, the number of non-English-speaking students has grown dramatically, creating demand for bilingual teachers and for those who teach English as a second language. The number of teachers employed is dependent as well on State and local expenditures for education and on the enactment of legislation to increase the quality of education. A number of initiatives, such as reduced class size (primarily in the early elementary grades), mandatory preschool for 4-year-olds, and all-day kindergarten, have been implemented in a few States, but not nationwide. Additional teachers—particularly preschool and early elementary school teachers—will be needed if States or localities implement any of these measures. At the Federal level, legislation that is likely to affect teachers recently was put into place with the enactment of the No Child Left Behind Act. Although the full impact of this act is not yet known, its emphasis on ensuring that all schools hire and retain only qualified teachers, may lead to an increase in funding for schools that currently lack such teachers.

The supply of teachers is expected to increase in response to reports of improved job prospects, better pay, more teacher involvement in school policy, and greater public interest in education. In recent years, the total number of bachelor's and master's degrees granted in education has increased steadily. Because of a shortage of teachers in certain locations, and in anticipation of the loss of a number of teachers to retirement, many States have implemented policies that will encourage more students to become teachers. In addition, more teachers may be drawn from a reserve pool of career changers, substitute teachers, and teachers completing alternative certification programs.

Earnings

Median annual earnings of kindergarten, elementary, middle, and secondary school teachers ranged from $39,810 to $44,340 in 2002; the lowest 10 percent earned $24,960 to $29,850; the top 10 percent earned $62,890 to $68,530. Median earnings for preschool teachers were $19,270.

According to the American Federation of Teachers, beginning teachers with a bachelor's degree earned an average of $30,719 in the 2001-02 school year. The estimated average salary of all public elementary and secondary school teachers in the 2001-02 school year was $44,367. Private school teachers generally earn less than public school teachers.

In 2002, more than half of all elementary, middle, and secondary school teachers belonged to unions—mainly the American Federation of Teachers and the National Education Association—that bargain with school systems over wages, hours, and other terms and conditions of employment. Fewer preschool and kindergarten teachers were union members—about 15 percent in 2002.

Teachers can boost their salary in a number of ways. In some schools, teachers receive extra pay for coaching sports and working with students in extracurricular activities. Getting a master's degree or national certification often results in a raise in pay, as does acting as a mentor. Some teachers earn extra income during the summer by teaching summer school or performing other jobs in the school system.

Related Occupations

Preschool, kindergarten, elementary school, middle school, and secondary school teaching requires a variety of skills and aptitudes, including a talent for working with children; organizational, administrative, and recordkeeping abilities; research and communication skills; the power to influence, motivate, and train others; patience; and creativity. Workers in other occupations requiring some of these aptitudes include teachers—postsecondary; counselors; teacher assistants; education administrators; librarians; child care workers; public relations specialists; social workers; and athletes, coaches, umpires, and related workers.

Sources of Additional Information

Information on licensure or certification requirements and approved teacher training institutions is available from local school systems and State departments of education.

Information on the teaching profession and on how to become a teacher can be obtained from
➤ Recruiting New Teachers, Inc., 385 Concord Ave., Suite 103, Belmont, MA 02478. Internet: **http://www.rnt.org**

This organization also sponsors another Internet site that provides helpful information on becoming a teacher: Internet: **http://www.recruitingteachers.org**

Information on teachers' unions and education-related issues may be obtained from any of the following sources:
➤ American Federation of Teachers, 555 New Jersey Ave. NW., Washington, DC 20001.
➤ National Education Association, 1201 16th St. NW., Washington, DC 20036.

A list of institutions with accredited teacher education programs can be obtained from:
➤ National Council for Accreditation of Teacher Education, 2010 Massachusetts Ave. NW., Suite 500, Washington, DC 20036-1023. Internet: **http://www.ncate.org**

For information on vocational education and vocational education teachers, contact
➤ Association for Career and Technical Education, 1410 King St., Alexandria, VA 22314. Internet: **http://www.acteonline.org**

For information on careers in educating children and issues affecting preschool teachers, contact either of the following organizations:
➤ National Association for the Education of Young Children, 1509 16th St. NW., Washington, DC 20036. Internet: **http://www.naeyc.org**
➤ Council for Professional Recognition, 2460 16th St. NW., Washington, DC 20009-3575. Internet: **http://www.cdacouncil.org**

For information on teachers and the No Child Left Behind Act, contact
➤ U.S. Department of Education, 400 Maryland Avenue, SW., Washington, DC, 20202. Internet: **http://www.ed.gov**

Teachers—Special Education

(O*NET 25-2041.00, 25-2042.00, 25-2043.00)

Significant Points

● Excellent job prospects are expected due to rising enrollments of special education students and reported shortages of qualified teachers.

● A bachelor's degree, completion of an approved teacher preparation program, and a license are required to qualify; many States require a master's degree.

● Many States offer alternative licensure programs to attract people into these jobs.

Nature of the Work

Special education teachers work with children and youths who have a variety of disabilities. A small number of special education teachers work with students with mental retardation or autism, primarily teaching them life skills and basic literacy. However, the majority of special education teachers work with children with mild to moderate disabilities, using the general education curriculum, or modifying it, to meet the child's individual needs. Most special education teachers instruct students at the elementary, middle, and secondary school level, although some teachers work with infants and toddlers.

The various types of disabilities that qualify individuals for special education programs include specific learning disabilities, speech or language impairments, mental retardation, emotional disturbance, multiple disabilities, hearing impairments, orthopedic impairments, visual impairments, autism, combined deafness and blindness, traumatic brain injury, and other health impairments. Students are classified under one of the categories, and special education teachers are prepared to work with specific groups. Early identification of a child with special needs is an important part of a special education teacher's job. Early intervention is essential in educating children with disabilities.

Special education teachers use various techniques to promote learning. Depending on the disability, teaching methods can include individualized instruction, problem-solving assignments, and small-group work. When students need special accommodations in order to take a test, special education teachers see that appropriate ones are provided, such as having the questions read orally or lengthening the time allowed to take the test.

Special education teachers help to develop an Individualized Education Program (IEP) for each special education student. The IEP sets personalized goals for each student and is tailored to the student's individual learning style and ability. The program includes a transition plan outlining specific steps to prepare special education students for middle school or high school or, in the case of older students, a job or postsecondary study. Teachers review the IEP with the student's parents, school administrators, and, often, the student's general education teacher. Teachers work closely with parents to inform them of their child's progress and suggest techniques to promote learning at home.

Special education teachers design and teach appropriate curricula, assign work geared toward each student's ability, and grade papers and homework assignments. They are involved in the students' behavioral and academic development, helping the students develop emotionally, feel comfortable in social situations, and be aware of socially acceptable behavior. Preparing special education students for daily life after graduation also is an important aspect of the job. Teachers provide students with career counseling or help them learn routine skills, such as balancing a checkbook.

As schools become more inclusive, special education teachers and general education teachers are increasingly working together in general education classrooms. Special education teachers help general educators adapt curriculum materials and teaching techniques to meet the needs of students with disabilities. They coordinate the work of teachers, teacher assistants, and related personnel, such as therapists and social workers, to meet the requirements of inclusive special education programs. A large part of a special education teacher's job involves interacting with others. Special education teachers communicate frequently with parents, social workers, school psychologists, occupational and physical therapists, school administrators, and other teachers.

Special education teachers work in a variety of settings. Some have their own classrooms and teach only special education students; others work as special education resource teachers and offer individualized help to students in general education classrooms; still others teach together with general education teachers in classes composed of both general and special education students. Some teachers work with special education students for several hours a day in a resource room, separate from their general education classroom. Considerably fewer special education teachers work in residential facilities or tutor students in homebound or hospital environments.

Special education teachers who work with infants usually travel to the child's home to work with the child and his or her parents. Many of these infants have medical problems that slow or preclude normal development. Special education teachers show parents techniques and activities designed to stimulate

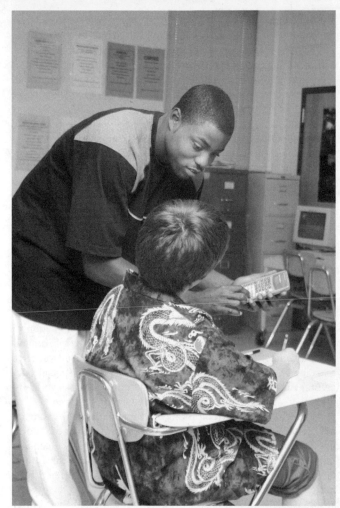

Special education teachers usually modify the general education curriculum to meet an individual student's needs.

the infant and encourage the growth of the child's skills. Toddlers usually receive their services at a preschool where special education teachers help them develop social, self-help, motor, language, and cognitive skills, often through the use of play.

Technology is playing an increasingly important role in special education. Teachers use specialized equipment such as computers with synthesized speech, interactive educational software programs, and audiotapes to assist children.

Working Conditions
Special education teachers enjoy the challenge of working with students with disabilities and the opportunity to establish meaningful relationships with them. Although helping these students can be highly rewarding, the work also can be emotionally and physically draining. Many special education teachers are under considerable stress due to heavy workloads and administrative tasks. They must produce a substantial amount of paperwork documenting each student's progress, and they work under the threat of litigation by students' parents if correct procedures are not followed or if the parents feel that their child is not receiving an adequate education. The physical and emotional demands of the job cause some special education teachers to leave the occupation.

Some schools offer year-round education for special education students, but most special education teachers work only the traditional 10-month school year.

Employment

Special education teachers held a total of about 433,000 jobs in 2002. A great majority, almost 90 percent, work in public schools. Another 7 percent work at private schools. About half work in elementary schools. A few worked for individual and social assistance agencies or residential facilities, or in homebound or hospital environments.

Training, Other Qualifications, and Advancement

All 50 States and the District of Columbia require special education teachers to be licensed. The State board of education or a licensure advisory committee usually grants licenses, and licensure varies by State. In many States, special education teachers receive a general education credential to teach kindergarten through grade 12. These teachers then train in a specialty, such as learning disabilities or behavioral disorders. Some States offer general special education licenses, while others license several different specialties within special education, and still others require teachers to obtain a general education license first and an additional license in special education afterwards.

All States require a bachelor's degree and the completion of an approved teacher preparation program with a prescribed number of subject and education credits and supervised practice teaching. Many States require a master's degree in special education, involving at least 1 year of additional course work, including a specialization, beyond the bachelor's degree.

Some States have reciprocity agreements allowing special education teachers to transfer their licenses from one State to another, but many still require that the teacher pass licensing requirements for the State in which they work. In the future, employers may recognize certification or standards offered by a national organization.

Many colleges and universities across the United States offer programs in special education, at the undergraduate, master's, and doctoral degree levels. Special education teachers usually undergo longer periods of training than do general education teachers. Most bachelor's degree programs are 4-year programs that include general and specialized courses in special education. However, an increasing number of institutions are requiring a 5th year or other postbaccalaureate preparation. Among the courses offered are educational psychology, legal issues of special education, and child growth and development; courses imparting knowledge and skills needed for teaching students with disabilities also are given. Some programs require specialization, while others offer generalized special education degrees or a course of study in several specialized areas. The last year of the program usually is spent student teaching in a classroom supervised by a certified teacher.

Alternative and emergency licenses are available in many States, due to the need to fill special education teaching positions. Alternative licenses are designed to bring college graduates and those changing careers into teaching more quickly. Requirements for an alternative license may be less stringent than for a regular license. Requirements vary by State. In some programs, individuals begin teaching quickly under a provisional license and can obtain a regular license by teaching under the supervision of licensed teachers for a period of 1 to 2 years while taking education courses. Emergency licenses are granted when States have difficulty finding licensed special education teachers to fill positions.

Special education teachers must be patient, able to motivate students, understanding of their students' special needs, and accepting of differences in others. Teachers must be creative and apply different types of teaching methods to reach students who are having difficulty learning. Communication and cooperation are essential traits, because special education teachers spend a great deal of time interacting with others, including students, parents, and school faculty and administrators.

Special education teachers can advance to become supervisors or administrators. They may also earn advanced degrees and become instructors in colleges that prepare others to teach special education. In some school systems, highly experienced teachers can become mentors to less experienced ones, providing guidance to those teachers while maintaining a light teaching load.

Job Outlook

Employment of special education teachers is expected to increase faster than the average for all occupations through 2012. Although slowdowns in student enrollments may constrain employment growth somewhat, additional positions for these workers will be created by continued increases in the number of special education students needing services, by legislation emphasizing training and employment for individuals with disabilities, and by educational reforms requiring higher standards for graduation. The need to replace special education teachers who switch to general education, change careers altogether, or retire will lead to additional job openings. At the same time, many school districts report shortages of qualified teachers. As a result, special education teachers should have excellent job prospects.

The job outlook varies by geographic area and specialty. Although many areas of the country report difficulty finding qualified applicants, positions in inner cities and rural areas usually are more plentiful than job openings in suburban or wealthy urban areas. Student populations, in general, also are expected to increase significantly in several States in the West and South, resulting in increased demand for special education teachers in those regions. In addition, job opportunities may be better in certain specialties—such as speech or language impairments and learning disabilities—because of large increases in the enrollment of special education students classified under those categories. Legislation encouraging early intervention and special education for infants, toddlers, and preschoolers has created a need for early childhood special education teachers. Bilingual special education teachers and those with multicultural experience also are needed to work with an increasingly diverse student population.

The number of students requiring special education services has grown steadily in recent years, a trend that is expected to continue. Learning disabilities will continue to be identified and diagnosed at earlier ages. In addition, medical advances have resulted in more children surviving serious accidents or illnesses, but with impairments that require special accommodations. The percentage of foreign-born special education students also is expected to grow, as teachers begin to recognize learning disabilities in that population. Finally, more parents are expected to seek special services for those of their children who have difficulty meeting the new, higher standards required of students.

Earnings

Median annual earnings in 2002 of special education teachers who worked primarily in preschools, kindergartens, and elementary schools were $42,690. The middle 50 percent earned between $34,160 and $54,340. The lowest 10 percent earned less than $28,680, and the highest 10 percent earned more than $67,810.

Median annual earnings in 2002 of middle school special education teachers were $41,350. The middle 50 percent earned between $33,460 and $52,370. The lowest 10 percent earned less than $28,560, and the highest 10 percent earned more than $65,070.

Median annual earnings in 2002 of special education teachers who worked primarily in secondary schools were $44,130. The middle 50 percent earned between $35,320 and $56,850. The lowest 10 percent earned less than $29,630, and the highest 10 percent earned more than $71,020.

In 2002, about 62 percent of special education teachers belonged to unions—mainly the American Federation of Teachers and the National Education Association—that bargain with school systems over wages, hours, and the terms and conditions of employment.

In most schools, teachers receive extra pay for coaching sports and working with students in extracurricular activities. Some teachers earn extra income during the summer, working in the school system or in other jobs.

Related Occupations

Special education teachers work with students who have disabilities and special needs. Other occupations involved with the identification, evaluation, and development of students with disabilities include psychologists, social workers, speech-language pathologists and audiologists, counselors, teacher assistants, occupational therapists, recreational therapists, and teachers—preschool, kindergarten, elementary, middle, and secondary.

Sources of Additional Information

For information on professions related to early intervention and education for children with disabilities, a list of accredited schools, information on teacher certification and financial aid, and general information on related personnel issues—including recruitment, retention, and the supply of, and demand for, special education professionals—contact
➤ National Clearinghouse for Professions in Special Education, Council for Exceptional Children, 1110 N. Glebe Rd., Suite 300, Arlington, VA 22201. Internet: **http://www.special-ed-careers.org**

To learn more about the special education teacher certification and licensing requirements in your State, contact your State's department of education.

Art and Design Occupations

Artists and Related Workers

(0*NET 27-1011.00, 27-1013.01, 27-1013.02, 27-1013.03, 27-1013.04, 27-1014.00)

Significant Points

● More than half of all artists and related workers were self-employed—almost eight times the proportion for all professional and related occupations.

● Artists usually develop their skills through a bachelor's degree program or other postsecondary training in art or design.

● Keen competition is expected for both salaried jobs and freelance work, because many talented people are attracted to the visual arts.

Nature of the Work

Artists create art to communicate ideas, thoughts, or feelings. They use a variety of methods—painting, sculpting, or illustration—and an assortment of materials, including oils, watercolors, acrylics, pastels, pencils, pen and ink, plaster, clay, and computers. Artists' works may be realistic, stylized, or abstract and may depict objects, people, nature, or events.

Artists generally fall into one of three categories. *Art directors* formulate design concepts and presentation approaches for visual communications media. *Fine artists, including painters, sculptors, and illustrators* create original artwork, using a variety of media and techniques. *Multi-media artists and animators* create special effects, animation, or other visual images on film, on video, or with computers or other electronic media. (Designers, including graphic designers, are discussed elsewhere in the *Handbook*.)

Art directors develop design concepts and review material that is to appear in periodicals, newspapers, and other printed or digital media. They decide how best to present the information visually, so that it is eye catching, appealing, and organized. Art directors decide which photographs or artwork to use and oversee the layout design and production of the printed material. They may direct workers engaged in artwork, layout design, and copywriting.

Fine artists typically display their work in museums, commercial art galleries, corporate collections, and private homes. Some of their artwork may be commissioned (done on request from clients), but most is sold by the artist or through private art galleries or dealers. The gallery and the artist predetermine how much each will earn from the sale. Only the most successful fine artists are able to support themselves solely through the sale of their works. Most fine artists must work in an unrelated field to support their art careers. Some work in museums or art galleries as fine-arts directors or as curators, planning and setting up art exhibits. Others work as art critics for newspapers or magazines or as consultants to foundations or institutional collectors.

Usually, fine artists specialize in one or two art forms, such as painting, illustrating, sketching, sculpting, printmaking, and restoring. *Painters, illustrators, cartoonists, and sketch artists* work with two-dimensional art forms, using shading, perspective, and color to produce realistic scenes or abstractions.

Illustrators typically create pictures for books, magazines, and other publications, and for commercial products such as textiles, wrapping paper, stationery, greeting cards, and calendars. Increasingly, illustrators work in digital format, preparing work directly on a computer.

Medical and *scientific illustrators* combine drawing skills with knowledge of biology or other sciences. Medical illustrators draw illustrations of human anatomy and surgical procedures. Scientific illustrators draw illustrations of animal and plant life, atomic and molecular structures, and geologic and planetary formations. The illustrations are used in medical and scientific publications and in audiovisual presentations for teaching purposes. Medical illustrators also work for lawyers, producing exhibits for court cases.

Cartoonists draw political, advertising, social, and sports cartoons. Some cartoonists work with others who create the idea or story and write the captions. Most cartoonists have comic, critical, or dramatic talents in addition to drawing skills.

Sketch artists create likenesses of subjects using pencil, charcoal, or pastels. Sketches are used by law enforcement agencies to assist in identifying suspects, by the news media to depict courtroom scenes, and by individual patrons for their own enjoyment.

Sculptors design three-dimensional artworks, either by molding and joining materials such as clay, glass, wire, plastic, fabric, or metal or by cutting and carving forms from a block of plaster, wood, or stone. Some sculptors combine various materials to create mixed-media installations. Some incorporate light, sound, and motion into their works.

Printmakers create printed images from designs cut or etched into wood, stone, or metal. After creating the design, the artist inks the surface of the woodblock, stone, or plate and uses a printing press to roll the image onto paper or fabric. Some make prints by pressing the inked surface onto paper by hand or by graphically encoding and processing data, using a computer.

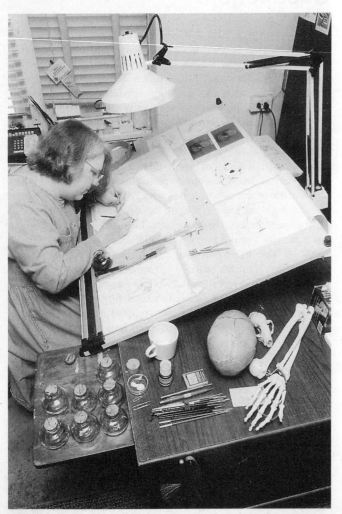

Medical illustrators combine drawing skills with knowledge of the biological sciences.

The digitized images are then printed on paper with the use of a computer printer.

Painting restorers preserve and restore damaged and faded paintings. They apply solvents and cleaning agents to clean the surfaces of the paintings, they reconstruct or retouch damaged areas, and they apply preservatives to protect the paintings. All this is highly detailed work and usually is reserved for experts in the field.

Multi-media artists and animators work primarily in motion picture and video industries, advertising, and computer systems design services. They draw by hand and use computers to create the large series of pictures that form the animated images or special effects seen in movies, television programs, and computer games. Some draw storyboards for television commercials, movies, and animated features. Storyboards present television commercials in a series of scenes similar to a comic strip and allow an advertising agency to evaluate proposed commercials with the company doing the advertising. Storyboards also serve as guides to placing actors and cameras on the television or motion picture set and to other details that need to be taken care of during the production of commercials.

Working Conditions

Many artists work in fine- or commercial-art studios located in office buildings, warehouses, or lofts. Others work in private studios in their homes. Some fine artists share studio space, where they also may exhibit their work. Studio surroundings usually are well lighted and ventilated; however, fine artists may be exposed to fumes from glue, paint, ink, and other materials and to dust or other residue from filings, splattered paint, or spilled fluids. Artists who sit at drafting tables or who use computers for extended periods may experience back pain, eyestrain, or fatigue.

Artists employed by publishing companies, advertising agencies, and design firms generally work a standard workweek. During busy periods, they may work overtime to meet deadlines. Self-employed artists can set their own hours, but may spend much time and effort selling their artwork to potential customers or clients and building a reputation.

Employment

Artists held about 149,000 jobs in 2002. More than half were self-employed. Of the artists who were not self-employed, many worked in advertising and related services; newspaper, periodical, book, and software publishers; motion picture and video industries; specialized design services; and computer systems design and related services. Some self-employed artists offered their services to advertising agencies, design firms, publishing houses, and other businesses on a contract or freelance basis.

Training, Other Qualifications, and Advancement

Training requirements for artists vary by specialty. Although formal training is not strictly necessary for fine artists, it is very difficult to become skilled enough to make a living without some training. Many colleges and universities offer programs leading to the Bachelor in Fine Arts (BFA) and Master in Fine Arts (MFA) degrees. Course work usually includes core subjects, such as English, social science, and natural science, in addition to art history and studio art.

Independent schools of art and design also offer postsecondary studio training in the fine arts leading to an Associate in Art or Bachelor in Fine Arts degree. Typically, these programs focus more intensively on studio work than do the academic programs in a university setting. The National Association of Schools of Art and Design accredits more than 200 postsecondary institutions with programs in art and design; most award a degree in art.

Formal educational programs in art also provide training in computer techniques. Computers are used widely in the visual arts, and knowledge and training in computer graphics and other visual display software are critical elements of many jobs in these fields.

Those who want to teach fine arts at public elementary or secondary schools must have a teaching certificate in addition to a bachelor's degree. An advanced degree in fine arts or arts administration is necessary for management or administrative positions in government or in foundations or for teaching in colleges and universities. (See the statements for teachers-postsecondary; and teachers-preschool, kindergarten, elementary, middle, and secondary school teachers elsewhere in the *Handbook*.)

Illustrators learn drawing and sketching skills through training in art programs and through extensive practice. Most employers prefer candidates with a bachelor's degree; however, some illustrators are contracted on the basis of portfolios of their past work.

Medical illustrators must have both a demonstrated artistic ability and a detailed knowledge of living organisms, surgical and medical procedures, and human and animal anatomy. A 4-year bachelor's degree combining art and premedical courses usually is preferred; a master's degree in medical illustration is recommended. This degree is offered in only five accredited schools in the United States.

Evidence of appropriate talent and skill, displayed in an artist's portfolio, is an important factor used by art directors, clients, and others in deciding whether to hire an individual or to contract out work. The portfolio is a collection of handmade, computer-generated, photographic, or printed samples of the artist's best work. Assembling a successful portfolio requires skills usually developed in a bachelor's degree program or through other postsecondary training in art or visual communications. Internships also provide excellent opportunities for artists to develop and enhance their portfolios.

Artists hired by advertising agencies often start with relatively routine work. While doing this work, however, they may observe and practice their skills on the side. Many artists freelance on a part-time basis while continuing to hold a full-time job until they are established. Others freelance part time while still in school, to develop experience and to build a portfolio of published work.

Freelance artists try to develop a set of clients who regularly contract for work. Some freelance artists are widely recognized for their skill in specialties such as magazine or children's book illustration. These artists may earn high incomes and can choose the type of work they do.

Fine artists advance professionally as their work circulates and as they establish a reputation for a particular style. Many of the most successful artists continually develop new ideas, and their work often evolves over time.

Job Outlook

Employment of artists and related workers is expected to grow about as fast as the average through the year 2012. Because the arts attract many talented people with creative ability, the number of aspiring artists continues to grow. Consequently, competition for both salaried jobs and freelance work in some areas is expected to be keen.

Art directors work in a variety of industries, such as advertising, public relations, publishing, and design firms. Despite an expanding number of opportunities, they should experience keen competition for the available openings.

Fine artists mostly work on a freelance, or commission, basis and may find it difficult to earn a living solely by selling their artwork. Only the most successful fine artists receive major commissions for their work. Competition among artists for the privilege of being shown in galleries is expected to remain acute, and grants from sponsors such as private foundations, State and local arts councils, and the National Endowment for the Arts should remain competitive. Nonetheless, studios, galleries, and individual clients are always on the lookout for artists who display outstanding talent, creativity, and style. Talented fine artists who have developed a mastery of artistic techniques and skills, including computer skills, will have the best job prospects.

The need for artists to illustrate and animate materials for magazines, journals, and other printed or electronic media will spur demand for illustrators and animators of all types. Growth in motion picture and video industries will provide new job opportunities for illustrators, cartoonists, and animators. Competition for most jobs, however, will be strong, because job opportunities are relatively few and the number of people interested in these positions usually exceeds the number of available openings. Employers should be able to choose from among the most qualified candidates.

Earnings

Median annual earnings of salaried art directors were $61,850 in 2002. The middle 50 percent earned between $44,740 and $85,010. The lowest 10 percent earned less than $32,410, and the highest 10 percent earned more than $115,570. Median annual earnings were $67,340 in advertising and related services.

Median annual earnings of salaried fine artists, including painters, sculptors, and illustrators, were $35,260 in 2002. The middle 50 percent earned between $23,970 and $48,040. The lowest 10 percent earned less than $16,900, and the highest 10 percent earned more than $73,560.

Median annual earnings of salaried multi-media artists and animators were $43,980 in 2002. The middle 50 percent earned between $33,970 and $61,120. The lowest 10 percent earned less than $25,830, and the highest 10 percent earned more than $85,160. Median annual earnings were $58,840 in motion picture and video industries.

Earnings for self-employed artists vary widely. Some charge only a nominal fee while they gain experience and build a reputation for their work. Others, such as well-established freelance fine artists and illustrators, can earn more than salaried artists. Many, however, find it difficult to rely solely on income earned from selling paintings or other works of art. Like other self-employed workers, freelance artists must provide their own benefits.

Related Occupations

Other workers who apply art skills include architects, except landscape and naval; archivists, curators, and museum technicians; designers; landscape architects; and photographers. Some computer-related occupations, including computer software engineers and desktop publishers, may require art skills.

Sources of Additional Information

For general information about art and design and a list of accredited college-level programs, contact:

➤ National Association of Schools of Art and Design, 11250 Roger Bacon Dr., Suite 21, Reston, VA 20190. Internet: **http://nasad.arts-accredit.org**

For information on careers in medical illustration, contact:

➤ Association of Medical Illustrators, 5475 Mark Dabling Blvd., Suite 108, Colorado Springs, CO 80918. Internet: **http://www.ami.org**

Designers

(O*NET 27-1021.00, 27-1022.00, 27-1023.00, 27-1024.00, 27-1025.00, 27-1026.00, 27-1027.01, 27-1027.02)

Significant Points

- Nearly one-third of designers were self-employed—almost five times the proportion for all professional and related occupations.

- Creativity is crucial in all design occupations; most designers need a bachelor's degree, and candidates with a master's degree hold an advantage.

- Keen competition is expected for most jobs, despite average projected employment growth, because many talented individuals are attracted to careers as designers.

Nature of the Work

Designers are people with a desire to create. They combine practical knowledge with artistic ability to turn abstract ideas into formal designs for the merchandise we buy, the clothes we wear, the Web sites we use, the publications we read, and the living and office space we inhabit. Designers usually specialize in a particular area of design, such as automobiles, industrial or medical equipment, home appliances, clothing and textiles, floral arrangements, publications, Web sites, logos, signage, movie or TV credits, interiors of homes or office buildings, merchandise displays, or movie, television, and theater sets.

The first step in developing a new design or altering an existing one is to determine the needs of the client, the ultimate function for which the design is intended, and its appeal to customers or users. When creating a design, designers often begin by researching the desired design characteristics, such as size, shape, weight, color, materials used, cost, ease of use, fit, and safety.

Designers then prepare sketches or diagrams—by hand or with the aid of a computer—to illustrate the vision for the design. After consulting with the client, a creative director, or a product development team, designers create detailed designs, using drawings, a structural model, computer simulations, or a full-scale prototype. Many designers use computer-aided design (CAD) tools to create and better visualize the final product. Computer models allow ease and flexibility in exploring a greater number of design alternatives, thus reducing design costs and cutting the time it takes to deliver a product to market. Industrial designers use computer-aided industrial design (CAID) tools to create designs and machine-readable instructions that communicate with automated production tools.

Designers sometimes supervise assistants who carry out their creations. Designers who run their own businesses also may devote a considerable amount of time to developing new business contacts, examining equipment and space needs, and performing administrative tasks, such as reviewing catalogues and ordering samples. The need for up-to-date computer and communications equipment is an ongoing consideration for many designers, especially those in industrial and graphic design.

Design encompasses a number of different fields. Many designers specialize in a particular area of design, whereas others work in more than one area.

Commercial and industrial designers develop countless manufactured products, including airplanes; cars; children's toys; computer equipment; furniture; home appliances; and medical, office, and recreational equipment. They combine artistic talent with research on the use of a product, on customer needs, and on marketing, materials, and production methods to create the most functional and appealing design that will be competitive with others in the marketplace. Industrial designers typically concentrate in a subspecialty such as kitchen appliances, auto interiors, or plastic-molding machinery.

Fashion designers design clothing and accessories. Some high-fashion designers are self-employed and design for individual clients. Other high-fashion designers cater to specialty stores or high-fashion department stores. These designers create original garments, as well as clothing that follows established fashion trends. Most fashion designers, however, work for apparel manufacturers, creating designs of men's, women's, and children's fashions for the mass market.

Floral designers cut and arrange live, dried, or artificial flowers and foliage into designs, according to the customer's order. They design arrangements by trimming flowers and arranging bouquets, sprays, wreaths, dish gardens, and terrariums. They may either meet with customers to discuss the arrangement or work from a written order. Floral designers make note of the occasion, the customer's preference with regard to the color and type of flower involved, the price of the completed order, the time at which the floral arrangement or plant is to be ready, and the place to which it is to be delivered. The variety of duties performed by floral designers depends on the size of the shop and the number of designers employed. In a small operation, floral designers may own their shops and do almost everything, from growing and purchasing flowers to keeping financial records.

Graphic designers plan, analyze, and create visual solutions to communications problems. They use a variety of print, electronic, and film media and technologies to execute a design that meet clients' communication needs. They consider cognitive, cultural, physical, and social factors in planning and executing designs appropriate for a given context. Graphic designers use computer software to develop the overall layout and production design of magazines, newspapers, journals, corporate reports, and other publications. They also produce promotional displays and marketing brochures for products and services, design distinctive logos for products and businesses, and develop signs and signage systems—called environmental graphics—for business and government. An increasing number of graphic designers are developing material for Internet Web pages, computer interfaces, and multimedia projects. Graphic designers also produce the credits that appear before and after television programs and movies.

Interior designers enhance the function, safety, and quality of interior spaces of private homes, public buildings, and business or institutional facilities, such as offices, restaurants, retail establishments, hospitals, hotels, and theaters. They also plan the interiors of existing structures that are undergoing renovation or expansion. Most interior designers specialize. For example, some may concentrate on residential design, while others focus on business design. Still others may specialize further by focusing on particular rooms, such as kitchens or baths. With a client's tastes, needs, and budget in mind, interior designers prepare drawings and specifications for non-load-bearing interior construction, furnishings, lighting, and finishes. Increasingly, designers are using computers to plan layouts, because computers make it easy to change plans to include ideas received from the client. Interior designers also design lighting and architectural details—such as crown molding, built-in bookshelves, or cabinets—coordinate colors, and select furniture, floor coverings, and window treatments. Interior designers must design space to conform to Federal, State, and local laws, including building codes. Designs for public areas also must meet accessibility standards for the disabled and the elderly.

Merchandise displayers and window dressers, or *visual merchandisers*, plan and erect commercial displays, such as those in windows and interiors of retail stores or at trade exhibitions. Those who work on building exteriors erect major store decorations, including building and window displays and lights. Those who design store interiors outfit store departments, arrange table displays, and dress mannequins. In large retail chains, store layouts typically are designed corporately, through a central design department. To retain the chain's visual identity and ensure that a particular image or theme is promoted in each store, designs are distributed to individual stores by e-mail, downloaded to computers equipped with the appropriate design software, and adapted to meet the size and dimension requirements of each individual store.

Set and exhibit designers create sets for movie, television, and theater productions and design special exhibition displays. Set designers study scripts, confer with directors and other designers, and conduct research to determine the historical period, fashion, and architectural styles appropriate for the production on which they work. They then produce sketches or scale models to guide in the construction of the actual sets or exhibit spaces. Exhibit designers work with curators, art and museum directors, and trade-show sponsors to determine the most effective use of available space.

Working Conditions

Working conditions and places of employment vary. Designers employed by manufacturing establishments, large corporations, or design firms generally work regular hours in well-lighted and comfortable settings. Designers in smaller design consulting firms, or those who freelance, generally work on a contract, or job, basis. They frequently adjust their workday to suit their clients' schedules and deadlines, meeting with the clients during evening or weekend hours when necessary. Consultants and self-employed designers tend to work longer hours and in smaller, more congested, environments.

Designers may transact business in their own offices or studios or in clients' homes or offices. They also may travel to other locations, such as showrooms, design centers, clients' exhibit sites, and manufacturing facilities. Designers who are paid by the assignment are under pressure to please clients and to find new ones in order to maintain a steady income. All designers sometimes face frustration when their designs are rejected or when their work is not as creative as they wish. With the increased speed and sophistication of computers and advanced communications networks, designers may form international design teams, serve a geographically more dispersed clientele, research design alternatives by using information on the Internet, and purchase supplies electronically, all with the aid of a computer in their workplace or studio.

Occasionally, industrial designers may work additional hours to meet deadlines. Similarly, graphic designers usually work regular hours, but may work evenings or weekends to meet production schedules. In contrast, set and exhibit designers work long and irregular hours; often, they are under pressure to make rapid changes. Merchandise displayers and window trimmers may spend much of their time designing displays in their office or studio, but those who also construct and install the displays may have to move lumber and heavy materials and perform some carpentry and painting. Fashion designers may work long hours to meet production deadlines or prepare for fashion shows. In addition, fashion designers may be required to travel to production sites across the United States and overseas. Interior designers generally work under deadlines and may put in extra hours to finish a job. Also, they typically carry heavy, bulky sample books to meetings with clients. Floral designers generally work regular hours in a pleasant work environment, but holiday, wedding, and funeral orders often require overtime.

Interior designers refer to swatches from sample books to plan the space and furnish the interiors of buildings.

Employment

Designers held about 532,000 jobs in 2002. Approximately one-third were self-employed. Employment was distributed as follows:

Graphic designers	212,000
Floral designers	104,000
Merchandise displayers and window trimmers	77,000
Interior designers	60,000
Commercial and industrial designers	52,000
Fashion designers	15,000
Set and exhibit designers	12,000

Salaried designers worked in a number of different industries, depending on their design specialty. Graphic designers, for example, worked primarily in specialized design services; newspaper, periodical, book, and directory publishers; and advertising and related services. Floral designers were concentrated in retail florists or floral departments of grocery stores. Merchandise displayers and window trimmers were dispersed across a variety of retailers and wholesalers. Interior designers generally worked in specialized design services or in retail furniture stores. Most commercial and industrial designers were employed in manufacturing or architectural, engineering, and related services. Fashion designers generally worked in apparel manufacturing or wholesale distribution of apparel, piece goods, and notions. Set and exhibit designers worked primarily for performing arts companies, movie and video industries, and radio and television broadcasting.

In 2002, a large proportion of designers were self-employed and did freelance work—full time or part time—in addition to holding a salaried job in design or in another occupation.

Training, Other Qualifications, and Advancement

Creativity is crucial in all design occupations. People in this field must have a strong sense of the esthetic—an eye for color and detail, a sense of balance and proportion, and an appreciation for beauty. Designers also need excellent communication and problem-solving skills. Despite the advancement of computer-aided design, sketching ability remains an important advantage in most types of design, especially fashion design. A good portfolio—a collection of examples of a person's best work—often is the deciding factor in getting a job.

A bachelor's degree is required for most entry-level design positions, except for floral design and visual merchandising. Esthetic ability is important in floral design and visual merchandising, but formal preparation typically is not necessary. Many candidates in industrial design pursue a master's degree to increase their chances of selection for open positions.

Interior design is the only design field subject to government regulation. According to the American Society of Interior Designers, 22 States and the District of Columbia register or license interior designers. Passing the National Council for Interior Design Qualification examination is required for registration or licensure in these jurisdictions. To be eligible to take the exam, an applicant must have at least 6 years of combined education and experience in interior design, of which at least 2 years constitute postsecondary education in design. Because registration or licensure is not mandatory in all States, membership in a professional association is an indication of an interior designer's qualifications and professional standing, and can aid in obtaining clients.

In fashion design, employers seek individuals with a 2- or 4-year degree who are knowledgeable in the areas of textiles, fabrics, and ornamentation, and about trends in the fashion world. Set and exhibit designers typically have college degrees in design. A Master of Fine Arts degree from an accredited university program further establishes one's design credentials. For set designers, membership in the United Scenic Artists, Local 829, is recognized nationally as the attainment of professional standing in the field.

Most floral designers learn their skills on the job. When employers hire trainees, they generally look for high school graduates who have a flair for arranging and a desire to learn. The completion of formal design training, however, is an asset for floral designers, particularly those interested in advancing to chief floral designer or in opening their own businesses. Vocational and technical schools offer programs in floral design, usually lasting less than a year, while 2- and 4-year programs in floriculture, horticulture, floral design, or ornamental horticulture are offered by community and junior colleges, colleges, and universities. The American Institute of Floral Designers offers an accreditation examination to its members as an indication of professional achievement in floral design.

Formal training for some design professions also is available in 2- and 3-year professional schools that award certificates or associate degrees in design. Graduates of 2-year programs normally qualify as assistants to designers, or they may enter a formal bachelor's degree program. The Bachelor of Fine Arts degree is granted at 4-year colleges and universities. The curriculum in these schools includes art and art history, principles of design, designing and sketching, and specialized studies for each of the individual design disciplines, such as garment construction, textiles, mechanical and architectural drawing, computerized design, sculpture, architecture, and basic engineering. A liberal arts education or a program that includes training in business or project management, together with courses in merchandising, marketing, and psychology, along with training in art, is recommended for designers who want to freelance. In addition, persons with training or experience in architecture qualify for some design occupations, particularly interior design.

Employers increasingly expect new designers to be familiar with computer-aided design software as a design tool. For example, industrial designers use computers extensively in the aerospace, automotive, and electronics industries. Interior designers use computers to create numerous versions of interior space designs—images can be inserted, edited, and replaced easily and without added cost—making it possible for a client to see and choose among several designs.

The National Association of Schools of Art and Design accredits more than 200 postsecondary institutions with programs in art and design. Most of these schools award a degree in art, and some award degrees in industrial, interior, textile, graphic, or fashion design. Many schools do not allow formal entry into a bachelor's degree program until a student has successfully finished a year of basic art and design courses. Applicants may be required to submit sketches and other examples of their artistic ability.

The Foundation for Interior Design Education Research also accredits interior design programs that lead to a bachelor's degree. There are about 120 accredited professional programs in the United States, located primarily in schools of art, architecture, and home economics.

Individuals in the design field must be creative, imaginative, and persistent and must be able to communicate their ideas in writing, visually, and verbally. Because tastes in style and fashion can change quickly, designers need to be well read, open to new ideas and influences, and quick to react to changing trends. Problem-solving skills and the ability to work independently and under pressure are important traits. People in this field need self-discipline to start projects on their own, to budget their time, and to meet deadlines and production schedules. Good business sense and sales ability also are important, especially for those who freelance or run their own business.

Beginning designers usually receive on-the-job training and normally need 1 to 3 years of training before they can advance to higher level positions. Experienced designers in large firms may advance to chief designer, design department head, or other supervisory positions. Some designers leave the occupation to become teachers in design schools or in colleges and universities. Many faculty members continue to consult privately or operate small design studios to complement their classroom activities. Some experienced designers open their own firms.

Job Outlook

Overall employment of designers is expected to grow about as fast as the average for all occupations through the year 2012 as the economy expands and consumers, businesses, and manufacturers continue to rely on the services provided by designers. However, designers in most fields—with the exception of floral design—are expected to face keen competition for available positions. Many talented individuals are attracted to careers as designers. Individuals with little or no formal education in design, as well as those who lack creativity and perseverance, will find it very difficult to establish and maintain a career in the occupation.

Among the design specialties, graphic designers are projected to provide the most new jobs. Demand for graphic designers should increase because of the rapidly expanding market for Web-based information and expansion of the video entertainment market, including television, movies, video, and made-for-Internet outlets.

Rising demand for interior design of private homes, offices, restaurants and other retail establishments, and institutions that care for the rapidly growing elderly population should spur employment growth of interior designers. New jobs for floral designers are expected to stem mostly from the relatively high replacement needs in retail florists that result from comparatively low starting pay and limited opportunities for advancement. The majority of new jobs for merchandise displayers and window trimmers will also result from the need to replace workers who retire, transfer to other occupations, or leave the labor force for other reasons.

Increased demand for industrial designers will stem from continued emphasis on the quality and safety of products, demand for new products that are easy and comfortable to use, and the development of high-technology products in medicine, transportation, and other fields. Demand for fashion designers should remain strong, because many consumers continue to seek new fashions and fresh styles of apparel. Employment growth for fashion designers will be slowed, however, by declines in the apparel manufacturing industries. Despite faster-than-average growth for set and exhibit designers, few job openings will result because the occupation is small.

Earnings

Median annual earnings for commercial and industrial designers were $52,260 in 2002. The middle 50 percent earned between $39,240 and $67,430. The lowest 10 percent earned less than $28,820, and the highest 10 percent earned more than $82,130. Median annual earnings were $61,530 in architectural, engineering, and related services.

Median annual earnings for fashion designers were $51,290 in 2002. The middle 50 percent earned between $35,550 and $75,970. The lowest 10 percent earned less than $25,350, and the highest 10 percent earned more than $105,280.

Median annual earnings for floral designers were $19,480 in 2002. The middle 50 percent earned between $15,880 and $23,560. The lowest 10 percent earned less than $13,440, and the highest 10 percent earned more than $29,830. Median annual earnings were $21,610 in grocery stores and $18,950 in florists.

Median annual earnings for graphic designers were $36,680 in 2002. The middle 50 percent earned between $28,140 and $48,820. The lowest 10 percent earned less than $21,860, and the highest 10 percent earned more than $64,160. Median annual earnings in the industries employing the largest numbers of graphic designers were as follows:

Advertising and related services	$39,510
Specialized design services	38,710
Printing and related support activities	31,800
Newspaper, periodical, book, and directory publishers	31,670

Median annual earnings for interior designers were $39,180 in 2002. The middle 50 percent earned between $29,070 and $53,060. The lowest 10 percent earned less than $21,240, and the highest 10 percent earned more than $69,640. Median annual earnings in the industries employing the largest numbers of interior designers were as follows:

Architectural, engineering, and related services	$41,680
Specialized design services	39,870
Furniture stores	36,320

Median annual earnings of merchandise displayers and window dressers were $22,550 in 2002. The middle 50 percent earned between $18,320 and $29,070. The lowest 10 percent earned less than $15,100, and the highest 10 percent earned more than $40,020. Median annual earnings were $22,130 in department stores.

Median annual earnings for set and exhibit designers were $33,870 in 2002. The middle 50 percent earned between $24,780 and $46,350. The lowest 10 percent earned less than $17,830, and the highest 10 percent earned more than $63,280.

The American Institute of Graphic Arts reported 2002 median annual earnings for graphic designers with increasing levels of responsibility. Staff-level graphic designers earned $40,000, while senior designers, who may supervise junior staff or have some decisionmaking authority that reflects their knowledge of graphic design, earned $55,000. Solo designers, who freelanced or worked under contract to another company, reported median earnings of $55,000. Design directors, the creative heads of design firms or in-house corporate design departments, earned $85,000. Graphic designers with ownership or partnership interests in a firm or who were principals of the firm in some other capacity earned $93,000.

Related Occupations

Workers in other occupations who design or arrange objects, materials, or interiors to enhance their appearance and function include artists and related workers; architects, except landscape and naval; engineers; landscape architects; and photographers. Some computer-related occupations, including computer software engineers and desktop publishers, require design skills.

Sources of Additional Information

For general information about art and design and a list of accredited college-level programs, contact:

➤ National Association of Schools of Art and Design, 11250 Roger Bacon Dr., Suite 21, Reston, VA 20190. Internet: **http://nasad.arts-accredit.org**

For information about graphic, communication, or interaction design careers, contact:

➤ American Institute of Graphic Arts, 164 Fifth Ave., New York, NY 10010. Internet: **http://www.aiga.org**

For information on degree, continuing education, and licensure programs in interior design and interior design research, contact:

➤ American Society for Interior Designers, 608 Massachusetts Ave. NE., Washington, DC 20002-6006. Internet: **http://www.asid.org**

For a list of schools with accredited programs in interior design, contact:

➤ Foundation for Interior Design Education Research, 146 Monroe Center NW., Suite 1318, Grand Rapids, MI 49503. Internet: **http://www.fider.org**

For information on careers, continuing education, and certification programs in the interior design specialty of residential kitchen and bath design, contact:

➤ National Kitchen and Bath Association, 687 Willow Grove St., Hackettstown, NJ 07840. Internet: **http://www.nkba.org/student**

For information about careers in floral design, contact:

➤ Society of American Florists, 1601 Duke St., Alexandria, VA 22314. Internet: **http://www.safnow.org**

Entertainers and Performers, Sports and Related Occupations

Actors, Producers, and Directors

(0*NET 27-2011.00, 27-2012.01, 27-2012.02,

27-2012.03, 27-2012.04, 27-2012.05)

Significant Points

● Actors endure long periods of unemployment, intense competition for roles, and frequent rejections in auditions.

● Formal training through a university or acting conservatory is typical; however, many actors, producers, and directors find work on the basis of their experience and talent alone.

● Because earnings for actors are erratic, many supplement their incomes by holding jobs in other fields.

Nature of the Work

Actors, producers, and directors express ideas and create images in theater, film, radio, television, and other performing arts media. They interpret a writer's script to entertain, inform, or instruct an audience. Although the most famous actors, producers, and directors work in film, network television, or theater in New York or Los Angeles, far more work in local or regional television studios, theaters, or film production companies, preparing advertising, public-relations, or independent, small-scale movie productions.

Actors perform in stage, radio, television, video, or motion picture productions. They also work in cabarets, nightclubs, theme parks, commercials, and "industrial" films produced for training and educational purposes. Most actors struggle to find steady work; only a few ever achieve recognition as stars. Some well-known, experienced performers may be cast in supporting roles. Others work as "extras," with no lines to deliver, or make brief, cameo appearances, speaking only one or two lines. Some actors do voiceover and narration work for advertisements, animated features, books on tape, and other electronic media. They also teach in high school or university drama departments, acting conservatories, or public programs.

Producers are entrepreneurs, overseeing the business and financial decisions of a motion picture, made-for-television feature, or stage production. They select scripts, approve the development of ideas for the production, arrange financing, and determine the size and cost of the endeavor. Producers hire or approve the selection of directors, principal cast members, and key production staff members. They also negotiate contracts with artistic and design personnel in accordance with collective bargaining agreements and guarantee payment of salaries, rent, and other expenses. Television and radio producers determine which programs, episodes, or news segments get aired. They may research material, write scripts, and oversee the production of individual pieces. Producers in any medium coordinate the activities of writers, directors, managers, and agents to ensure that each project stays on schedule and within budget.

Directors are responsible for the creative decisions of a production. They interpret scripts, express concepts to set and costume designers, audition and select cast members, conduct rehearsals, and direct the work of cast and crew. Directors cue

Directors, who are responsible for creative decisions, instruct actors and technicians on how to play a scene.

the performers and technicians to make entrances or to make light, sound, or set changes. They approve the design elements of a production, including the sets, costumes, choreography, and music.

Working Conditions

Actors, producers, and directors work under constant pressure. Many face stress from the continual need to find their next job. To succeed, actors, producers, and directors need patience and commitment to their craft. Actors strive to deliver flawless performances, often while working under undesirable and unpleasant conditions. Producers and directors organize rehearsals; meet with writers, designers, financial backers, and production technicians. They experience stress not only from these activities, but also from the need to adhere to budgets, union work rules, and production schedules.

Acting assignments typically are short term—ranging from 1 day to a few months—which means that actors frequently experience long periods of unemployment between jobs. The uncertain nature of the work results in unpredictable earnings and intense competition for even the lowest-paid jobs. Often, actors, producers, and directors must hold other jobs in order to sustain a living.

When performing, actors typically work long, irregular hours. For example, stage actors may perform one show at night while rehearsing another during the day. They also might travel with a show when it tours the country. Movie actors may work on location, sometimes under adverse weather conditions, and may spend considerable time in their trailers or dressing rooms waiting to perform their scenes. Actors who perform in a television series often appear on camera with little preparation time, because scripts tend to be revised frequently or even written moments before taping. Those who appear live or before a studio audience must be able to handle impromptu situations and calmly ad lib, or substitute, lines when necessary.

Evening and weekend work is a regular part of a stage actor's life. On weekends, more than one performance may be held per day. Actors and directors working on movies or television programs—especially those who shoot on location—may work in the early morning or late evening hours to film night scenes or tape scenes inside public facilities outside of normal business hours.

Actors should be in good physical condition and have the necessary stamina and coordination to move about theater stages and large movie and television studio lots. They also need to maneuver about complex technical sets while staying in character and projecting their voices audibly. Actors must be fit to endure heat from stage or studio lights and the weight of heavy costumes. Producers and directors ensure the safety of actors by conducting extra rehearsals on the set so that the actors can learn the layout of set pieces and props, by allowing time for warmups and stretching exercises to guard against physical and vocal injuries, and by providing an adequate number of breaks to prevent heat exhaustion and dehydration.

Employment

In 2002, actors, producers, and directors held about 139,000 jobs, primarily in motion picture and video, performing arts, and broadcast industries. Because many others were between jobs, the total number of actors, producers, and directors available for work was higher. Employment in the theater, and other performing arts companies, is cyclical—higher in the fall and spring seasons—and concentrated in New York and other major cities with large commercial houses for musicals and touring productions. Also, many cities support established professional regional theaters that operate on a seasonal or year-round basis. About one fourth of actors, producers, and directors are self-employed.

Actors, producers, and directors may find work in summer festivals, on cruise lines, and in theme parks. Many smaller, nonprofit professional companies, such as repertory companies, dinner theaters, and theaters affiliated with drama schools, acting conservatories, and universities, provide employment opportunities for local amateur talent and professional entertainers. Auditions typically are held in New York for many productions across the country and for shows that go on the road.

Employment in motion pictures and in films for television is centered in New York and Hollywood. However, small studios are located throughout the country. Many films are shot on location and may employ local professional and nonprofessional actors. In television, opportunities are concentrated in the network centers of New York and Los Angeles, but cable television services and local television stations around the country also employ many actors, producers, and directors.

Training, Other Qualifications, and Advancement

Persons who become actors, producers, and directors follow many paths. Employers generally look for people with the creative instincts, innate talent, and intellectual capacity to perform. Actors should possess a passion for performing and enjoy entertaining others. Most aspiring actors participate in high school and college plays, work in college radio stations, or perform with local community theater groups. Local and regional theater experience and work in summer stock, on cruise lines, or in theme parks helps many young actors hone their skills and earn qualifying credits toward membership in one of the actors' unions. Union membership and work experience in smaller communities may lead to work in larger cities, notably New York or Los Angeles. In television and film, actors and directors typically start in smaller television markets or with independent movie production companies and then work their way up to larger media markets and major studio productions. Intense competition, however, ensures that only a few actors reach star billing.

Formal dramatic training, either through an acting conservatory or a university program, generally is necessary; however, some people successfully enter the field without it. Most people studying for a bachelor's degree take courses in radio and television broadcasting, communications, film, theater, drama, or dramatic literature. Many continue their academic training and receive a Master of Fine Arts (MFA) degree. Advanced curricula may include courses in stage speech and movement, directing, playwriting, and design, as well as intensive acting workshops. The National Association of Schools of Theatre accredits 128 programs in theater arts.

Actors, regardless of experience level, may pursue workshop training through acting conservatories or by being mentored by a drama coach. Actors also research roles so that they can grasp concepts quickly during rehearsals and understand the story's setting and background. Sometimes actors learn a foreign language or train with a dialect coach to develop an accent to make their characters more realistic.

Actors need talent, creative ability, and training that will enable them to portray different characters. Because competition for parts is fierce, versatility and a wide range of related performance skills, such as singing, dancing, skating, juggling, or miming are especially useful. Experience in horseback riding, fencing, or stage combat also can lift some actors above the average and get them noticed by producers and directors. Actors must have poise, stage presence, the capability to affect an audience, and the ability to follow direction. Modeling experience also may be helpful. Physical appearance, such as possessing the right size, weight, or features, often is a deciding factor in being selected for particular roles.

Many professional actors rely on agents or managers to find work, negotiate contracts, and plan their careers. Agents generally earn a percentage of the pay specified in an actor's contract. Other actors rely solely on attending open auditions for parts. Trade publications list the times, dates, and locations of these auditions.

To become a movie extra, one usually must be listed by a casting agency, such as Central Casting, a no-fee agency that supplies extras to the major movie studios in Hollywood. Applicants are accepted only when the number of persons of a particular type on the list—for example, athletic young women, old men, or small children—falls below the foreseeable need. In recent years, only a very small proportion of applicants have succeeded in being listed.

There are no specific training requirements for producers. They come from many different backgrounds. Talent, experience, and business acumen are important determinants of success for producers. Actors, writers, film editors, and business managers commonly enter the field. Also, many people who start out as actors move into directing, while some directors might try their hand at acting. Producers often start in a theatrical management office, working for a press agent, managing director, or business manager. Some start in a performing arts union or service organization. Others work behind the scenes with successful directors, serve on boards of directors, or promote their own projects. No formal training exists for producers; however, a growing number of colleges and universities now offer degree programs in arts management and in managing nonprofits.

As the reputations and box-office draw of actors, producers, and directors grow, they might work on bigger budget productions, on network or syndicated broadcasts, or in more prestigious theaters. Actors may advance to lead roles and receive star billing. A few actors move into acting-related jobs, such as drama coaches or directors of stage, television, radio, or motion picture productions. Some teach drama privately or in colleges and universities.

Job Outlook

Employment of actors, producers, and directors is expected to grow about as fast as the average for all occupations through 2012. Although a growing number of people will aspire to enter these professions, many will leave the field early because the work—when it is available—is hard, the hours are long, and the pay is low. Competition for jobs will be stiff, in part because the large number of highly trained and talented actors auditioning for roles generally exceeds the number of parts that become available. Only performers with the most stamina and talent will find regular employment.

Expanding cable and satellite television operations, increasing production and distribution of major studio and independent films, and continued growth and development of interactive media, such as direct-for-Web movies and videos, should increase demand for actors, producers, and directors. However, greater emphasis on national, rather than local, entertainment productions may restrict employment opportunities in the broadcasting industry.

Venues for live entertainment, such as Broadway and Off-Broadway theaters, touring productions and repertory theaters in many major metropolitan areas, theme parks, and resorts, are expected to offer many job opportunities; however, prospects in these venues are more variable, because they fluctuate with economic conditions.

Earnings

Median annual earnings of salaried actors were $23,470 in 2002. The middle 50 percent earned between $15,320 and $53,320. The lowest 10 percent earned less than $13,330, and the highest 10 percent earned more than $106,360. Median annual earnings in the industries employing the largest numbers of actors were as follows:

Accounting, tax preparation, bookkeeping, and payroll services	$29,590
Performing arts companies	28,850
Motion picture and video industries	17,610

Minimum salaries, hours of work, and other conditions of employment are covered in collective bargaining agreements between the producers and the unions representing workers. The Actors' Equity Association (Equity) represents stage actors; the Screen Actors Guild (SAG) covers actors in motion pictures, including television, commercials, and films; and the American Federation of Television and Radio Artists (AFTRA) represents television and radio studio performers. While these unions generally determine minimum salaries, any actor or director may negotiate for a salary higher than the minimum.

Under terms of a joint SAG and AFTRA contract covering all unionized workers, motion picture and television actors with speaking parts earned a minimum daily rate of $678 or $2,352 for a 5-day week as of July 1, 2003. Actors also receive contributions to their health and pension plans and additional compensation for reruns and foreign telecasts of the productions in which they appear.

According to Equity, the minimum weekly salary for actors in Broadway productions as of June 30, 2003 was $1,354. Actors in Off-Broadway theaters received minimums ranging from $479 to $557 a week as of October 27, 2003, depending on the seating capacity of the theater. Regional theaters that operate under an Equity agreement pay actors $531 to $800 per week. For touring productions, actors receive an additional $111 per day for living expenses ($117 per day in larger, higher cost cities).

Some well-known actors—stars—earn well above the minimum; their salaries are many times the figures cited, creating the false impression that all actors are highly paid. For example, of the nearly 100,000 SAG members, only about 50 might be considered stars. The average income that SAG members earn from acting—less than $5,000 a year—is low because employment is erratic. Therefore, most actors must supplement their incomes by holding jobs in other occupations.

Many actors who work more than a set number of weeks per year are covered by a union health, welfare, and pension fund, which includes hospitalization insurance and to which employers contribute. Under some employment conditions, Equity and AFTRA members receive paid vacations and sick leave.

Median annual earnings of salaried producers and directors were $46,240 in 2002. The middle 50 percent earned between $31,990 and $70,910. The lowest 10 percent earned less than $23,300, and the highest 10 percent earned more than $119,760. Median annual earnings were $56,090 in motion picture and video industries and $38,480 in radio and television broadcasting.

Many stage directors belong to the Society of Stage Directors and Choreographers (SSDC), and film and television directors belong to the Directors Guild of America. Earnings of stage directors vary greatly. According to the SSDC, summer theaters offer compensation, including "royalties" (based on the number of performances), usually ranging from $2,500 to $8,000 for a 3- to 4-week run. Directing a production at a dinner theater generally will pay less than directing one at a summer theater, but has more potential for generating income from royalties. Regional theaters may hire directors for longer periods, increasing compensation accordingly. The highest-paid directors work on Broadway and commonly earn $50,000 per show. However, they also receive payment in the form of royalties—a negotiated percentage of gross box office receipts—that can exceed their contract fee for long-running box office successes.

Stage producers seldom get a set fee; instead, they get a percentage of a show's earnings or ticket sales.

Related Occupations

People who work in performing arts occupations that may require acting skills include announcers; dancers and choreographers; and musicians, singers, and related workers. Others working in film- and theater-related occupations are makeup artists, theatrical and performance; fashion designers; set and exhibit designers; and writers and authors. Producers share many responsibilities with those who work as top executives.

Sources of Additional Information

For general information about theater arts and a list of accredited college-level programs, contact:
➤ National Association of Schools of Theater, 11250 Roger Bacon Dr., Suite 21, Reston, VA 20190. Internet: **http://nast.arts-accredit.org**

For general information on actors, producers, and directors, contact any of the following organizations:
➤ Actors Equity Association, 165 West 46th St., New York, NY 10036. Internet: **http://www.actorsequity.org**
➤ Screen Actors Guild, 5757 Wilshire Blvd., Los Angeles, CA 90036-3600. Internet: **http://www.sag.org**
➤ American Federation of Television and Radio Artists—Screen Actors Guild, 4340 East-West Hwy., Suite 204, Bethesda, MD 20814-4411. Internet: **http://www.aftra.org** or **http://www.sag.org**

Athletes, Coaches, Umpires, and Related Workers

(0*NET 27-2021.00, 27-2022.00, 27-2023.00)

Significant Points

● Work hours are often irregular; travel may be extensive.

● Career-ending injuries are always a risk for athletes.

● Job opportunities for coaches, sports instructors, umpires, referees, and sports officials will be best in high school and other amateur sports.

● Competition for professional athlete jobs will continue to be extremely intense; athletes who seek to compete professionally must have extraordinary talent, desire, and dedication to training.

Nature of the Work

We are a nation of sports fans and sports players. Interest in watching sports continues at a high level and recreational participation in sports continues to grow. Some of those who participate in amateur sports dream of becoming paid professional athletes, coaches, or sports officials but very few beat the long and daunting odds of making a full-time living from professional athletics. Those athletes who do make it to professional levels find that careers are short and jobs are insecure. Even though the chances of employment as a professional athlete are slim, there are many opportunities for at least a part-time job related to athletics as a coach, instructor, referee, or umpire in amateur athletics and in high schools, colleges, and universities.

Athletes and *sports competitors* compete in organized, officiated sports events to entertain spectators. When playing a game, athletes are required to understand the strategies of their game while obeying the rules and regulations of the sport. The events in which they compete include both team sports—such as baseball, basketball, football, hockey, and soccer—and individual sports—such as golf, tennis, and bowling. As the type of sport varies, so does the level of play, ranging from unpaid high school athletics to professional sports, in which the best from around the world compete before international television audiences.

In addition to competing in athletic events, athletes spend many hours practicing skills and teamwork under the guidance of a coach or sports instructor. Most athletes spend hours in hard practices every day. They also spend additional hours viewing video tapes, in order to critique their own performances and techniques and to scout their opponents' tendencies and weaknesses to gain a competitive advantage. Some athletes may also be advised by *strength trainers* in an effort to gain muscle and stamina, while also preventing injury. Competition at all levels is extremely intense and job security is always precarious. As a result, many athletes train year round to maintain excellent form, technique, and peak physical condition. Very little downtime from the sport exists at the professional level. Athletes also must conform to regimented diets during the height of their sports season to supplement any physical training program. Many athletes push their bodies to the limit during both practice and play, so career-ending injury always is a risk. Even minor injuries to an athlete may put the player at risk of replacement.

Coaches organize, instruct, and teach amateur and professional athletes in fundamentals of individual and team sports. In individual sports, *instructors* may sometimes fill this role. Coaches train athletes for competition by holding practice sessions to perform drills and improve the athlete's skills and stamina. Using their expertise in the sport, coaches instruct the athlete on proper form and technique in beginning and, later, in advanced exercises attempting to maximize the players' physical potential. Along with overseeing athletes as they refine their individual skills, coaches also are responsible for managing the team during both practice sessions and competitions, and for instilling good sportsmanship, a competitive spirit, and teamwork. They may also select, store, issue, and inventory equipment, materials, and supplies. During competitions, for example, coaches substitute players for optimum team chemistry and success. In addition, coaches direct team strategy and may call specific plays during competition to surprise or overpower the opponent. To choose the best plays, coaches evaluate or "scout" the opposing team prior to the competition, allowing them to determine game strategies and practice specific plays.

Many coaches in high schools are primarily teachers of academic subjects who supplement their income by coaching part time. College coaches consider coaching a full-time discipline and may be away from home frequently as they travel to scout and recruit prospective players.

Sports instructors teach professional and nonprofessional athletes on an individual basis. They organize, instruct, train, and lead athletes of indoor and outdoor sports such as bowling, tennis, golf, and swimming. Because activities are as diverse as weight lifting, gymnastics, and scuba diving, and may include self-defense training such as karate, instructors tend to specialize in one or a few types of activities. Like coaches, sports instructors also may hold daily practice sessions and be responsible for any needed equipment and supplies. Using their knowledge of their sport, physiology, and corrective techniques, they determine the type and level of difficulty of exercises, prescribe specific drills, and correct the athlete's techniques. Some instructors also teach and demonstrate use of training apparatus, such as trampolines or weights, while correcting athletes' weaknesses and enhancing their conditioning. Using their expertise in the sport, sports instructors evaluate the athlete and the athlete's opponents to devise a competitive game strategy.

Coaches and sports instructors sometimes differ in their approach to athletes because of the focus of their work. For example, while coaches manage the team during a game to optimize its chance for victory, sports instructors—such as those who work for professional tennis players—often are not permitted to instruct their athletes during competition. Sports instructors spend more of their time with athletes working one-on-one, which permits them to design customized training programs for each individual. Motivating athletes to play hard challenges most coaches and sports instructors but is vital for the athlete's success. Many coaches and instructors derive great satisfaction working with children or young adults, helping them to learn new physical and social skills and to improve their physical condition, as well as helping them to achieve success in their sport.

Umpires, referees, and other sports officials officiate at competitive athletic and sporting events. They observe the play, detect infractions of rules, and impose penalties established by the sports' rules and regulations. Umpires, referees, and sports officials anticipate play and position themselves to best see the action, assess the situation, and determine any violations. Some sports officials, such as boxing referees, may work independently, while others such as umpires—the sports officials of baseball—work in groups. Regardless of the sport, the job is highly stressful because officials are often required to make a decision in a matter of a split second, sometimes resulting in strong disagreement among competitors, coaches, or spectators.

Professional *scouts* evaluate the skills of both amateur and professional athletes to determine talent and potential. As a sports intelligence agent, the scout's primary duty is to seek out top athletic candidates for the team he or she represents, ultimately contributing to team success. At the professional level, scouts typically work for scouting organizations, or as freelance scouts. In locating new talent, scouts perform their work in secrecy so as to not "tip off" their opponents about their interest in certain players. At the college level, the head scout is often an assistant coach, although freelance scouts may aid colleges by providing reports about exceptional players to coaches.

Athletes spend many hours practicing skills under the guidance of a coach or sports instructor.

Scouts at this level seek talented high school athletes by reading newspapers, contacting high school coaches and alumni, attending high school games, and studying videotapes of prospects' performances.

Working Conditions

Irregular work hours are the trademark of the athlete. They also are common for the coach, as well as umpires, referees, and other sports officials. Athletes, coaches, umpires, and related workers often work Saturdays, Sundays, evenings, and holidays. Athletes and full-time coaches usually work more than 40 hours a week for several months during the sports season, if not most of the year. Some coaches in educational institutions may coach more than one sport, particularly at the high school level.

Athletes, coaches, and sports officials who participate in competitions that are held outdoors may be exposed to all weather conditions of the season; those involved in events that are held indoors tend to work in climate-controlled comfort, often in arenas, enclosed stadiums, or gymnasiums. Athletes, coaches, and some sports officials frequently travel to sporting events by bus or airplane. Scouts also travel extensively in locating talent, often by automobile.

Employment

Athletes, coaches, umpires, and related workers held about 158,000 jobs in 2002. Coaches and scouts held 130,000 jobs; athletes, 15,000; and umpires, referees, and other sports officials, 14,000. Large proportions of athletes, coaches, umpires, and related workers worked part time—about 37 percent, while 17 percent maintained variable schedules. Many sports officials and coaches receive such a small and irregular payment for their services (occasional officiating at club games, for example) that they may not consider themselves employed in these occupations, even part time.

About 27 percent of workers in this occupation were self-employed, earning prize money or fees for lessons, scouting, or officiating assignments, and many other coaches and sports officials, although technically not self-employed, have such irregular or tenuous working arrangements that their working conditions resemble self-employment.

Among those employed in wage and salary jobs, 20 percent held jobs in private educational services. About 12 percent worked in amusement, gambling, and recreation industries, including golf and tennis clubs, gymnasiums, health clubs, judo and karate schools, riding stables, swim clubs, and other sports and recreation-related facilities. Another 7 percent worked in the spectator sports industry.

Training, Other Qualifications, and Advancement
Education and training requirements for athletes, coaches, umpires, and related workers vary greatly by the level and type of sport. Regardless of the sport or occupation, jobs require immense overall knowledge of the game, usually acquired through years of experience at lower levels. Athletes usually begin competing in their sports while in elementary or middle school and continue through high school and sometimes college. They play in amateur tournaments and on high school and college teams, where the best attract the attention of professional scouts. Most schools require that participating athletes maintain specific academic standards to remain eligible to play. Becoming a professional athlete is the culmination of years of effort. Athletes who seek to compete professionally must have extraordinary talent, desire, and dedication to training.

For high school coach and sports instructor jobs, schools usually prefer to hire teachers willing to take on the jobs part time. If no one suitable is found, they hire someone from outside. Some entry-level positions for coaches or instructors require only experience derived as a participant in the sport or activity. Many coaches begin their careers as assistant coaches to gain the necessary knowledge and experience needed to become a head coach. Head coaches at larger schools that strive to compete at the highest levels of a sport require substantial experience as a head coach at another school or as an assistant coach. To reach the ranks of professional coaching, it usually takes years of coaching experience and a winning record in the lower ranks.

Public secondary school head coaches and sports instructors at all levels usually must have a bachelor's degree. (For information on teachers, including those specializing in physical education, see the section on teachers—preschool, kindergarten, elementary, middle, and secondary elsewhere in the *Handbook.)* Those who are not teachers must meet State requirements for certification in order to become a head coach. Certification, however, may not be required for coach and sports instructor jobs in private schools. Degree programs specifically related to coaching include exercise and sports science, physiology, kinesiology, nutrition and fitness, physical education, and sports medicine.

For sports instructors, certification is highly desirable for those interested in becoming a tennis, golf, karate, or any other kind of instructor. Often, one must be at least 18 years old and CPR certified. There are many certifying organizations specific to the various sports, and their training requirements vary depending on their standards. Participation in a clinic, camp, or school usually is required for certification. Part-time workers and those in smaller facilities are less likely to need formal education or training.

Each sport has specific requirements for umpires, referees, and other sports officials. Referees, umpires, and other sports officials often begin their careers by volunteering for intramural, community, and recreational league competitions. For college refereeing, candidates must be certified by an officiating school and be evaluated during a probationary period. Some larger college conferences require officials to have certification and other qualifications, such as residence in or near the confer-

ence boundaries along with previous experience that typically includes several years officiating at high school, community college, or other college conference games.

Standards are even more stringent for officials in professional sports. For umpire jobs in professional baseball, for example, a high school diploma or equivalent is usually sufficient, plus 20/20 vision and quick reflexes. To qualify for the professional ranks, however, prospective candidates must attend professional umpire training school. Currently, there are two schools whose curriculums have been approved by the Professional Baseball Umpires Corporation (PBUC) for training. Top graduates are selected for further evaluation while officiating in a rookie minor league. Umpires then usually need 8 to 10 years of experience in various minor leagues before being considered for major league jobs. Football also is competitive, as candidates must have at least 10 years of officiating experience, with 5 of them at a collegiate varsity or minor professional level. For the National Football League (NFL), prospects are interviewed by clinical psychologists to determine levels of intelligence and ability to handle extremely stressful situations. In addition, the NFL's security department conducts thorough background checks. Potential candidates are likely to be interviewed by a panel from the NFL officiating department and are given a comprehensive examination on the rules of the sport.

Jobs as scouts require experience playing a sport at the college or professional level that enables them to spot young players who possess extraordinary athletic abilities and skills. Most beginning scout jobs are as part-time talent spotters in a particular area or region. Hard work and a record of success often lead to full-time jobs responsible for bigger territories. Some scouts advance to scouting director jobs or various administrative positions in sports.

Athletes, coaches, umpires, and related workers must relate well to others and possess good communication and leadership skills. Coaches also must be resourceful and flexible to successfully instruct and motivate individuals or groups of athletes.

Job Outlook
Employment of athletes, coaches, umpires, and related workers is expected to increase about as fast as the average for all occupations through the year 2012. Employment will grow as the general public continues to increasingly participate in organized sports as a form of entertainment, recreation, and physical conditioning. Job growth also will be driven by the increasing numbers of baby boomers approaching retirement, during which they are expected to become more active participants of leisure-time activities, such as golf and tennis, and require instruction. The large numbers of the children of baby boomers in high schools and colleges also will be active participants in athletics and require coaches and instructors.

Expanding opportunities are expected for coaches and instructors, as a higher value is being placed upon physical fitness in our society. Americans of all ages are engaging in more physical fitness activities, such as participating in amateur athletic competition and joining athletic clubs, and are being encouraged to participate in physical education. Employment of coaches and instructors also will increase with expansion of school and college athletic programs and growing demand for private sports instruction. Sports-related job growth within education also will be driven by the decisions of local school boards. Population growth dictates the construction of additional schools, particularly in the expanding suburbs. However, funding for athletic programs is often one of the first areas to be cut when budgets become tight, but the popularity of team sports often enables shortfalls to be offset somewhat by assistance from fundraisers, booster clubs, and parents. Persons who are State-certified to teach academic subjects in addition to physical education are likely to have the best prospects for obtaining coach and instructor jobs. The need to replace many high school coaches also will provide some coaching opportunities.

Competition for professional athlete jobs will continue to be extremely intense. Opportunities to make a living as a professional in individual sports such as golf or tennis may grow as new tournaments are established and prize money distributed to participants increases. Most professional athletes' careers last only several years due to debilitating injuries and age, so a large proportion of the athletes in these jobs is replaced every year, creating some job opportunities. However, a far greater number of talented young men and women dream of becoming a sports superstar and will be competing for a very limited number of job openings.

Opportunities should be best for persons seeking part-time umpire, referee, and other sports official jobs at the high school level, but competition is expected for higher paying jobs at the college level, and even greater competition for jobs in professional sports. Competition should be very keen for jobs as scouts, particularly for professional teams, as the number of available positions is limited.

Earnings

Median annual earnings of athletes were $45,320 in 2002. The lowest 10 percent earned less than $14,090, and the highest 10 percent earned more than $145,600. However, the highest paid professional athletes earn salaries far in excess of these estimates.

Median annual earnings of umpires and related workers were $20,540 in 2002. The middle 50 percent earned between $16,210 and $29,490. The lowest 10 percent earned less than $13,760, and the highest 10 percent earned more than $40,350.

Median annual earnings of coaches and scouts were $27,880 in 2002. The middle 50 percent earned between $17,890 and $42,250. The lowest 10 percent earned less than $13,370, and the highest 10 percent earned more than $60,230. Median annual earnings in the industries employing the largest numbers of coaches and scouts in 2002 were as follows:

Colleges, universities, and professional schools	$36,170
Other amusement and recreation industries	25,900
Elementary and secondary schools	24,740
Other schools and instruction	22,570

Earnings vary by education level, certification, and geographic region. Some instructors and coaches are paid a salary, while others may be paid by the hour, per session, or based on the number of participants.

Related Occupations

Athletes and coaches have extensive knowledge of physiology and sports, and instruct, inform, and encourage participants. Other workers with similar duties include dietitians and nutritionists; physical therapists; recreation and fitness workers; recreational therapists; and teachers—preschool, kindergarten, elementary, middle, and secondary.

Sources of Additional Information

For general information on coaching, contact:
➤ National High School Athletic Coaches Association, P.O. Box 4342, Hamden, CT 06514. Internet: **http://www.hscoaches.org**

For information about sports officiating for team and individual sports, contact:
➤ National Association of Sports Officials, 2017 Lathrop Ave., Racine, WI 53405. Internet: **http://www.naso.org**

Dancers and Choreographers

(O*NET 27-2031.00, 27-2032.00)

Significant Points

● Many dancers stop performing by their late thirties; however, some remain in the field as choreographers, dance teachers, or artistic directors.

● Most dancers begin formal training at an early age— between 5 and 15—and many have their first professional audition by age 17 or 18.

● Dancers and choreographers face intense competition—only the most talented find regular work.

Nature of the Work

From ancient times to the present, dancers have expressed ideas, stories, and rhythm with their bodies. They use a variety of dance forms that allow free movement and self-expression, including classical ballet, modern dance, and culturally specific dance styles. Many dancers combine performance work with teaching or choreography.

Dancers perform in a variety of settings, such as musical productions, and may present folk, ethnic, tap, jazz, and other popular kinds of dance. They also perform in opera, musical theater, television, movies, music videos, and commercials, in which they also may sing and act. Dancers most often perform as part of a group, although a few top artists perform solo.

Many dancers work with choreographers, who create original dances and develop new interpretations of existing dances.

Dancers spend considerable time warming up and practicing in rehearsal halls or dance studios.

Because few dance routines are written down, choreographers instruct performers at rehearsals to achieve the desired effect. In addition, choreographers often are involved in auditioning performers.

Working Conditions

Dance is strenuous. Many dancers stop performing by their late thirties because of the physical demands on the body. However, some continue to work in the field as choreographers, dance teachers and coaches, or artistic directors. Others move into administrative positions, such as company managers. A few celebrated dancers, however, continue performing beyond the age of 50.

Daily rehearsals require very long hours. Many dance companies tour for part of the year to supplement a limited performance schedule at home. Dancers who perform in musical productions and other family entertainment spend much of their time on the road; others work in nightclubs or on cruise ships. Most dance performances are in the evening, whereas rehearsals and practice take place during the day. As a result, dancers often work very long and late hours. Generally, dancers and choreographers work in modern and temperature-controlled facilities; however, some studios may be older and less comfortable.

Employment

Professional dancers and choreographers held about 37,000 jobs in 2002. Many others were between engagements, so that the total number of people available for work as dancers over the course of the year was greater. Dancers and choreographers worked in a variety of industries, such as private educational services, which includes dance studios and schools, as well as colleges and universities; food services and drinking establishments; performing arts companies, which includes dance, theater, and opera companies; and amusement and recreation venues, such as casinos and theme parks. Almost one fifth of dancers and choreographers are self-employed.

New York City is home to many major dance companies; however, full-time professional dance companies operate in most major cities.

Training, Other Qualifications, and Advancement

Training varies with the type of dance and is a continuous part of all dancers' careers. Many dancers and dance instructors believe that dancers should start with a good foundation in classical dance before selecting a particular dance style. Ballet training for women usually begins at 5 to 8 years of age with a private teacher or through an independent ballet school. Serious training traditionally begins between the ages of 10 and 12. Men often begin their ballet training between the ages of 10 and 15. Students who demonstrate potential in their early teens receive more intensive and advanced professional training. At about this time, students should begin to focus their training on a particular style and decide whether to pursue additional training through a dance company's school or a college dance program. Leading dance school companies often have summer training programs from which they select candidates for admission to their regular full-time training programs. Formal training for modern and culturally specific dancers often begins later than training in ballet; however, many folk dance forms are taught to very young children.

Many dancers have their first professional auditions by age 17 or 18. Training is an important component of profes-

sional dancers' careers. Dancers normally spend 8 hours a day in class and rehearsal, keeping their bodies in shape and preparing for performances. Their daily training period includes time to warm up and cool down before and after classes and rehearsals.

Because of the strenuous and time-consuming dance training required, some dancers view formal education as secondary. However, a broad, general education including music, literature, history, and the visual arts is helpful in the interpretation of dramatic episodes, ideas, and feelings. Dancers sometimes conduct research to learn more about the part they are playing.

Many colleges and universities award bachelor's or master's degrees in dance, typically through departments of music, theater, or fine arts. The National Association of Schools of Dance accredits 57 programs in dance. Many programs concentrate on modern dance, but some also offer courses in jazz, culturally specific, ballet, or classical techniques; dance composition, history, and criticism; and movement analysis.

A college education is not essential to obtaining employment as a professional dancer; however, many dancers obtain degrees in unrelated fields to prepare themselves for careers after dance. The completion of a college program in dance and education is essential in order to qualify to teach dance in college, high school, or elementary school. Colleges and conservatories sometimes require graduate degrees, but may accept performance experience. A college background is not necessary, however, for teaching dance or choreography in local recreational programs. Studio schools usually require teachers to have experience as performers.

Because of the rigorous practice schedules of most dancers, self-discipline, patience, perseverance, and a devotion to dance are essential for success in the field. Dancers also must possess good problem-solving skills and an ability to work with people. Good health and physical stamina also are necessary attributes. Above all, dancers must have flexibility, agility, coordination, grace, a sense of rhythm, a feeling for music, and a creative ability to express themselves through movement.

Dancers seldom perform unaccompanied, so they must be able to function as part of a team. They should also be highly motivated and prepared to face the anxiety of intermittent employment and rejections when auditioning for work. For dancers, advancement takes the form of a growing reputation, more frequent work, bigger and better roles, and higher pay.

Choreographers typically are older dancers with years of experience in the theater. Through their performance as dancers, they develop reputations that often lead to opportunities to choreograph productions.

Job Outlook

Dancers and choreographers face intense competition for jobs. Only the most talented find regular employment.

Employment of dancers and choreographers is expected to grow about as fast as the average for all occupations through 2012. The public's continued interest in dance will sustain larger dance companies; however, funding from public and private organizations is not expected to keep pace with rising production costs. For many small and midsize organizations, the result will be fewer performances and more limited employment opportunities. Although job openings will arise each year because dancers and choreographers retire or leave the occupation for other reasons, the number of applicants will continue to vastly exceed the number of job openings.

National dance companies should continue to provide jobs in this field. Opera companies and dance groups affiliated with colleges and universities and with television and motion pictures also will offer some opportunities. Moreover, the growing popularity of dance in recent years has resulted in increased opportunities to teach dance. Finally, music video channels will provide some opportunities for both dancers and choreographers.

Earnings

Median annual earnings of salaried dancers were $21,100 in 2002. The middle 50 percent earned between $14,570 and $34,660. The lowest 10 percent earned less than $12,880, and the highest 10 percent earned more than $53,350.

Median annual earnings of salaried choreographers were $29,470 in 2002. The middle 50 percent earned between $19,590 and $43,720. The lowest 10 percent earned less than $14,000, and the highest 10 percent earned more than $57,590. Median annual earnings were $29,820 in other schools and instruction, which includes dance studios and schools.

Dancers who were on tour received an additional allowance for room and board, as well as extra compensation for overtime. Earnings from dancing are usually low, because employment is part year and irregular. Dancers often supplement their income by working as guest artists with other dance companies, teaching dance, or taking jobs unrelated to the field.

Earnings of many professional dancers are governed by union contracts. Dancers in the major opera ballet, classical ballet, and modern dance corps belong to the American Guild of Musical Artists, Inc. of the AFL-CIO; those who appear on live or videotaped television programs belong to the American Federation of Television and Radio Artists; those who perform in films and on television belong to the Screen Actors Guild; and those in musical theater are members of the Actors' Equity Association. The unions and producers sign basic agreements specifying minimum salary rates, hours of work, benefits, and other conditions of employment. However, the contract each dancer signs with the producer of the show may be more favorable than the basic agreement.

Dancers and choreographers covered by union contracts are entitled to some paid sick leave, paid vacations, and various health and pension benefits, including extended sick pay and family-leave benefits provided by their unions. Employers contribute toward these benefits. Those not covered by union contracts usually do not enjoy such benefits.

Related Occupations

People who work in other performing arts occupations include actors, producers, and directors; and musicians, singers, and related workers. Those directly involved in the production of dance programs include set and exhibit designers; fashion designers; and barbers, cosmetologists, and other personal appearance workers. Like dancers, athletes, coaches, umpires, and related workers need strength, flexibility, and agility.

Sources of Additional Information

For general information about dance and a list of accredited college-level programs, contact:

➤ National Association of Schools of Dance, 11250 Roger Bacon Dr., Suite 21, Reston, VA 20190. Internet: **http://nasd.arts-accredit.org**

For information about dance and dance companies, contact:

➤ Dance/USA, 1156 15th St. NW., Suite 820, Washington, DC 20005. Internet: **http://www.danceusa.org**

Musicians, Singers, and Related Workers

(O*NET 27-2041.01, 27-2041.02, 27-2041.03, 27-2042.01, 27-2042.02)

Significant Points

● Part-time schedules and intermittent unemployment are common; many musicians supplement their income with earnings from other sources.

● Aspiring musicians begin studying an instrument or training their voices at an early age.

● Competition for jobs is keen; those who can play several instruments and perform a wide range of music styles should enjoy the best job prospects.

Nature of the Work

Musicians, singers, and related workers play musical instruments, sing, compose or arrange music, or conduct groups in instrumental or vocal performances. They may perform solo or as part of a group. Musicians, singers, and related workers entertain live audiences in nightclubs, concert halls, and theaters featuring opera, musical theater, or dance. Although most of these entertainers play for live audiences, many perform exclusively for recording or production studios. Regardless of the setting, musicians, singers, and related workers spend considerable time practicing, alone and with their band, orchestra, or other musical ensemble.

Musicians often gain their reputation or professional standing in a particular kind of music or performance. However, those who learn several related instruments, such as the flute and clarinet, and who can perform equally well in several musical styles, have better employment opportunities. Instrumental musicians, for example, may play in a symphony orchestra, rock group, or jazz combo one night, appear in another ensemble the next, and work in a studio band the following day. Some play a variety of string, brass, woodwind, or percussion instruments or electronic synthesizers.

Singers interpret music, using their knowledge of voice production, melody, and harmony. They sing character parts or perform in their own individual style. Singers are often classified according to their voice range—soprano, contralto, tenor, baritone, or bass—or by the type of music they sing, such as opera, rock, popular, folk, rap, or country and western.

Music directors conduct, direct, plan, and lead instrumental or vocal performances by musical groups, such as orchestras, choirs, and glee clubs. Conductors lead instrumental music groups, such as symphony orchestras, dance bands, show bands, and various popular ensembles. These leaders audition and select musicians, choose the music most appropriate for their talents and abilities, and direct rehearsals and performances. Choral directors lead choirs and glee clubs, sometimes working with a band or an orchestra conductor. Directors audition and select singers and lead them at rehearsals and performances in order to achieve harmony, rhythm, tempo, shading, and other desired musical effects.

Composers create original music such as symphonies, operas, sonatas, radio and television jingles, film scores, or popular songs. They transcribe ideas into musical notation, using harmony, rhythm, melody, and tonal structure. Although most

Singers interpret music, using their knowledge of voice production, melody, and harmony.

composers and songwriters practice their craft on instruments and transcribe the notes with pen and paper, some use computer software to compose and edit their music.

Arrangers transcribe and adapt musical compositions to a particular style for orchestras, bands, choral groups, or individuals. Components of music—including tempo, volume, and the mix of instruments needed—are arranged to express the composer's message. While some arrangers write directly into a musical composition, others use computer software to make changes.

Working Conditions

Musicians typically perform at night and on weekends. They spend much of their remaining time practicing or in rehearsal. Full-time musicians with long-term employment contracts, such as those with symphony orchestras or television and film production companies, enjoy steady work and less travel. Nightclub, solo, or recital musicians frequently travel to perform in a variety of local settings and may tour nationally or internationally. Because many musicians find only part-time or intermittent work, experiencing unemployment between engagements, they often supplement their income with other types of jobs. The stress of constantly looking for work leads many musicians to accept permanent, full-time jobs in other occupations, while working only part time as musicians.

Most instrumental musicians work closely with a variety of other people, including their colleagues, agents, employers, sponsors, and audiences. Although they usually work indoors, some perform outdoors for parades, concerts, and dances. In some nightclubs and restaurants, smoke and odors may be present, and lighting and ventilation may be inadequate.

Employment

Musicians, singers, and related workers held about 215,000 jobs in 2002. Almost 40 percent worked part time, and more than one third were self-employed. Many found jobs in cities in which entertainment and recording activities are concentrated, such as New York, Los Angeles, Chicago, and Nashville.

Musicians, singers, and related workers are employed in a variety of settings. Of those who earn a wage or salary, more than one half are employed by religious organizations and one fourth by performing arts companies, such as professional orchestras, small chamber music groups, opera companies, musical theater companies, and ballet troupes. Musicians and singers also perform in nightclubs and restaurants and for weddings and other events. Well-known musicians and groups may perform in concerts, appear on radio and television broadcasts, and make recordings and music videos. The Armed Forces also offer careers in their bands and smaller musical groups.

Training, Other Qualifications, and Advancement

Aspiring musicians begin studying an instrument at an early age. They may gain valuable experience playing in a school or community band or an orchestra or with a group of friends. Singers usually start training when their voices mature. Participation in school musicals or choirs often provides good early training and experience.

Musicians need extensive and prolonged training to acquire the necessary skills, knowledge, and ability to interpret music. Like other artists, musicians and singers continually strive to stretch themselves—exploring different forms of music. Formal training may be obtained through private study with an accomplished musician, in a college or university music program, or in a music conservatory. For university or conservatory study, an audition generally is necessary. The National Association of Schools of Music accredits nearly 600 college-level programs in music. Courses typically include musical theory, music interpretation, composition, conducting, and performance in a particular instrument or in voice. Music directors, composers, conductors, and arrangers need considerable related work experience or advanced training in these subjects.

Many colleges, universities, and music conservatories grant bachelor's or higher degrees in music. A master's or doctoral degree is usually required to teach advanced music courses in colleges and universities; a bachelor's degree may be sufficient to teach basic courses. A degree in music education qualifies graduates for a State certificate to teach music in public elementary or secondary schools. Musicians who do not meet public school music education requirements may teach in private schools and recreation associations or instruct individual students in private sessions.

Musicians must be knowledgeable about a broad range of musical styles, but keenly aware of the form that interests them most. This broader range of interest, knowledge, and training can help expand employment opportunities and musical abilities. Voice training and private instrumental lessons, taken especially when the individual is young, also help develop technique and enhance one's performance.

Young persons considering careers in music should have musical talent, versatility, creativity, poise, and a good stage presence. Because quality performance requires constant study and practice, self-discipline is vital. Moreover, musicians who play in concerts or in nightclubs and those who tour must have physical stamina to endure frequent travel and an irregular performance schedule. Musicians and singers always must make their performances look effortless; therefore, preparation and practice are important. They also must be prepared to face the anxiety of intermittent employment and of rejection when auditioning for work.

Advancement for musicians usually means becoming better known and performing for higher earnings. Successful musicians often rely on agents or managers to find them performing engagements, negotiate contracts, and develop their careers.

Job Outlook

Competition for jobs for musicians, singers, and related workers is expected to be keen. The vast number of persons with the desire to perform will exceed the number of openings. Talent alone is no guarantee of success: many people start out to become musicians or singers, but leave the profession because they find the work difficult, the discipline demanding, and the long periods of intermittent unemployment unendurable.

Overall employment of musicians, singers, and related workers is expected to grow about as fast as the average for all occupations through 2012. Most new wage and salary jobs for musicians will arise in religious organizations. Slower-than-average growth is expected for self-employed musicians, who generally perform in nightclubs, concert tours, and other venues. Although growth in demand for musicians will generate a number of job opportunities, many openings also will arise from the need to replace those who leave the field each year because they are unable to make a living solely as musicians or for other reasons.

Earnings

Median annual earnings of salaried musicians and singers were $36,290 in 2002. The middle 50 percent earned between $18,660 and $59,970. The lowest 10 percent earned less than $13,040, and the highest 10 percent earned more than $96,250. Median annual earnings were $43,060 in performing arts companies and $18,160 in religious organizations.

Median annual earnings of salaried music directors and composers were $31,310 in 2002. The middle 50 percent earned between $23,820 and $46,350. The lowest 10 percent earned less than $14,590, and the highest 10 percent earned more than $67,330.

Earnings often depend on the number of hours and weeks worked, a performer's professional reputation, and the setting. The most successful musicians earn performance or recording fees that far exceed the median earnings.

According to the American Federation of Musicians, weekly minimum salaries in major orchestras ranged from $734 to $1,925 during the 2002-03 performing season. Each orchestra works out a separate contract with its local union, with individual musicians eligible to negotiate a higher salary. Top orchestras have a season ranging from 24 to 52 weeks, with 18 orchestras reporting 52-week contracts. In regional orchestras, minimum salaries are often less, because fewer performances are scheduled. Community orchestras often have yet more limited levels of funding and offer salaries that are much lower for seasons of shorter duration. Regional orchestra musicians often are paid for their services, without any guarantee of future employment.

Although musicians employed by some symphony orchestras work under master wage agreements, which guarantee a season's work up to 52 weeks, many other musicians face relatively long periods of unemployment between jobs. Even when employed, many musicians and singers work part time in unrelated occupations. Thus, their earnings usually are lower than earnings in many other occupations. Moreover, because they may not work steadily for one employer, some performers cannot qualify for unemployment compensation, and few have typical benefits such as sick leave or paid vacations. For these reasons, many musicians give private lessons or take jobs unrelated to music to supplement their earnings as performers.

Many musicians belong to a local of the American Federation of Musicians. Professional singers who perform live often belong to a branch of the American Guild of Musical Artists; those who record for the broadcast industries may belong to the American Federation of Television and Radio Artists.

Related Occupations

Musical instrument repairers and tuners (part of precision instrument and equipment repairers) require technical knowledge of musical instruments. Others whose work involves music include actors, producers, and directors; announcers; and dancers and choreographers.

Sources of Additional Information

For general information about music and music teacher education and a list of accredited college-level programs, contact:
➤ National Association of Schools of Music, 11250 Roger Bacon Dr., Suite 21, Reston, VA 22091. Internet: **http://nasm.arts-accredit.org**

Media and Communication-Related Occupations

Announcers

(0*NET 27-3011.00, 27-3012.00)

Significant Points

- Competition for announcer jobs will continue to be keen.

- Jobs at small stations usually have low pay, but offer the best opportunities for beginners.

- Related work experience at a campus radio station or as an intern at a commercial station can be helpful in breaking into the occupation.

Nature of the Work

Announcers in radio and television perform a variety of tasks on and off the air. They announce station program information, such as program schedules and station breaks for commercials, or public service information, and they introduce and close programs. Announcers read prepared scripts or ad-lib commentary on the air, as they present news, sports, weather, time, and commercials. If a written script is required, they may do the research and writing. Announcers also interview guests and moderate panels or discussions. Some provide commentary for the audience during sporting events, at parades, and on other occasions. Announcers often are well known to radio and television audiences and may make promotional appearances and remote broadcasts for their stations.

Radio announcers often are called *disc jockeys* (*DJs*). Some disc jockeys specialize in one kind of music, announcing selections as they air them. Most DJs do not select much of the music they play (although they often did so in the past); instead, they follow schedules of commercials, talk, and music provided to them by management. While on the air, DJs comment on the music, weather, and traffic. They may take requests from listeners, interview guests, and manage listener contests.

Newscasters, or *anchors*, work at large stations and specialize in news, sports, or weather. (See the related statement on news analysts, reporters, and correspondents elsewhere in the *Handbook*.) *Show hosts* may specialize in a certain area of interest, such as politics, personal finance, sports, or health. They contribute to the preparation of the program's content, interview guests, and discuss issues with viewers, listeners, or the studio audience.

Announcers at smaller stations may cover all of these areas and tend to have more off-air duties as well. They may operate the control board, monitor the transmitter, sell commercial time to advertisers, keep a log of the station's daily programming, and produce advertisements and other recorded material. Advances in technology make it possible for announcers to do some work previously performed by broadcast technicians. At many music stations, the announcer is simultaneously responsible for both announcing and operating the control board, which is used to broadcast programming, commercials, and public-service announcements according to the station's schedule. (See the statement on broadcast and sound engineering technicians and radio operators elsewhere in the *Handbook*.) Public radio and television announcers are involved in station fundraising efforts.

Changes in technology have led to more remote operation of stations. Several stations in different locations of the same region may be operated from one office. Some stations operate without any staff overnight, playing programming from a satellite feed or using programming that was recorder earlier, including segments from announcers.

Announcers frequently participate in community activities. Sports announcers, for example, may serve as masters of ceremonies at sports club banquets or may greet customers at openings of sporting goods stores.

Although most announcers are employed in broadcasting, some are employed in the motion picture production industry. *Public address system announcers* provide information to the audience at sporting, performing arts, and other events. Some disc jockeys announce and play music at clubs, dances, restaurants, and weddings.

Working Conditions

Announcers usually work in well-lighted, air-conditioned, soundproof studios. The broadcast day is long for radio and TV stations—many are on the air 24 hours a day—so announcers

Some public-address system announcers work at sporting events.

can expect to work unusual hours. Many present early-morning shows, when most people are getting ready for work or commuting, while others do late-night programs.

Announcers often work within tight schedule constraints, which can be physically and mentally stressful. For many announcers, the intangible rewards—creative work, many personal contacts, and the satisfaction of becoming widely known—far outweigh the disadvantages of irregular and often unpredictable hours, work pressures, and disrupted personal lives.

Employment

Announcers held about 76,000 jobs in 2002. More than half were employed in broadcasting, but some were self-employed freelance announcers who sold their services for individual assignments to networks and stations or to advertising agencies and other independent producers. About a third of all announcers work part time.

Training, Other Qualifications, and Advancement

Entry into this occupation is highly competitive. Formal training in broadcasting from a college or technical school (private broadcasting school) is valuable. Most announcers have a bachelor's degree in a major such as communications, broadcasting, or journalism. Station officials pay particular attention to taped auditions that show an applicant's delivery and—in television—appearance and style on commercials, news, and interviews. Those hired by television stations usually start out as production assistants, researchers, or reporters and are given a chance to move into announcing if they show an aptitude for "on-air" work. A beginner's chance of landing an on-air job is remote, except possibly at a small radio station, as a substitute for a familiar announcer, or on the late-night shift at a larger station. In radio, newcomers usually start out taping interviews and operating equipment.

Announcers usually begin at a station in a small community and, if they are qualified, may move to a better paying job in a large city. They also may advance by hosting a regular program as a disc jockey, sportscaster, or other specialist. Competition is particularly intense for employment by networks, and employers look for college graduates with at least several years of successful announcing experience.

Announcers must have a pleasant and well-controlled voice, good timing, excellent pronunciation, and correct grammar. College broadcasting programs offer courses, such as voice and diction, to help students improve their vocal qualities. Television announcers need a neat, pleasing appearance as well. Knowledge of theater, sports, music, business, politics, and other subjects likely to be covered in broadcasts improves one's chances for success. Announcers also must be computer literate, because programming is created and edited by computer. Announcers need strong writing skills, because they normally write their own material. In addition, they should be able to ad-lib all or part of a show and to work under tight deadlines. The most successful announcers attract a large audience by combining a pleasing personality and voice with an appealing style.

High school and college courses in English, public speaking, drama, foreign languages, and computer science are valuable, and hobbies such as sports and music are additional assets. Students may gain valuable experience at campus radio or TV facilities and at commercial stations while serving as interns. Paid or unpaid internships provide students with hands-on training and the chance to establish contacts in the industry. Unpaid interns often receive college credit and are allowed to observe and assist station employees. Although the Fair Labor Standards Act limits the work unpaid interns may perform in a station, unpaid internships are the rule. Unpaid internships sometimes lead to paid internships, which are valuable because interns do work ordinarily performed by regular employees and may even go on the air.

Persons considering enrolling in a broadcasting school should contact personnel managers of radio and television stations, as well as broadcasting trade organizations, to determine the school's reputation for producing suitably trained candidates.

Job Outlook
Competition for jobs as announcers will be keen because the broadcasting field attracts many more jobseekers than there are jobs. Small radio stations are more inclined to hire beginners, but the pay is low. Applicants who have completed internships or have related work experience usually receive preference for available positions. Because competition for ratings is so intense in major metropolitan areas, large stations will continue to seek announcers who have proven that they can attract and retain a sizable audience.

Announcers who are knowledgeable in business, consumer, and health news may have an advantage over others. While specialization is more common at large stations and the networks, many small stations also encourage it.

Employment of announcers is expected to decline through 2012, due to the lack of growth of new radio and television stations and consolidation of existing stations, but some job openings will arise from the need to replace those who transfer to other kinds of work or leave the labor force. Some announcers leave the field because they cannot advance to better paying jobs. Changes in station ownership, format, and ratings frequently cause periods of unemployment for many announcers.

Increasing consolidation of radio and television stations, new technology, and the growth of alternative media sources, such as cable television and satellite radio, will contribute to the expected decline in employment of announcers. Consolidation in broadcasting may lead to an increased use of syndicated programming and programs originating outside a station's viewing or listening area. Digital technology is increasing the productivity of announcers, reducing the time required to edit material or perform other off-air technical and production work.

Earnings
Salaries in broadcasting vary widely, but generally are relatively low, except for announcers who work for large stations in major markets or for networks. Earnings are higher in television than in radio and higher in commercial than in public broadcasting.

Median hourly earnings of announcers in 2002 were $9.91. The middle 50 percent earned between $7.13 and $15.10. The lowest 10 percent earned less than $6.14, and the highest 10 percent earned more than $24.92. Median hourly earnings of announcers in 2002 were $9.86 in the radio and television broadcasting industry.

Related Occupations
The success of announcers depends upon how well they communicate. Others who must be skilled at oral communication include news analysts, reporters, and correspondents; interpreters and translators; salespersons and those in related occupations; and public-relations specialists. Many announcers also must entertain their audience, so their work is similar to other entertainment-related occupations, such as actors, producers, and directors; and musicians, singers, and related workers. Announcers perform a variety of duties, including some technical operations, like broadcast sound engineering technicians and radio operators.

Sources of Additional Information
General information on the broadcasting industry is available from
➤ National Association of Broadcasters, 1771 N St. NW., Washington, DC 20036. Internet: **http://www.nab.org**

Broadcast and Sound Engineering Technicians and Radio Operators

(O*NET 27-4011.00, 27-4012.00, 27-4013.00, 27-4014.00)

Significant Points

- Job applicants face strong competition for jobs in major metropolitan areas, where pay generally is higher; prospects are better in small cities and towns.

- Technical school, community college, or college training in electronics, computer networking, or broadcast technology provides the best preparation.

- About 32 percent work in broadcasting, mainly for radio and television stations, and 16 percent work in the motion picture and sound recording industries.

- Evening, weekend, and holiday work is common.

Nature of the Work
Broadcast and sound engineering technicians and radio operators set up, operate, and maintain a wide variety of electrical and electronic equipment involved in almost any radio or television broadcast, concert, play, musical recording, television show, or movie. With such a range of work, there are many specialized occupations within the field.

Audio and video equipment technicians set up and operate audio and video equipment, including microphones, sound speakers, video screens, projectors, video monitors, recording equipment, connecting wires and cables, sound and mixing boards, and related electronic equipment for concerts, sports events, meetings and conventions, presentations, and news conferences. They may also set up and operate associated spotlights and other custom lighting systems.

Broadcast technicians set up, operate, and maintain equipment that regulates the signal strength, clarity, and range of sounds and colors of radio or television broadcasts. They also operate control panels to select the source of the material. Technicians may switch from one camera or studio to another, from film to live programming, or from network to local programming.

Sound engineering technicians operate machines and equipment to record, synchronize, mix, or reproduce music, voices, or sound effects in recording studios, sporting arenas, theater productions, or movie and video productions.

Radio operators mainly receive and transmit communications using a variety of tools. They also are responsible for repairing equipment, using such devices as electronic testing equipment, handtools, and power tools. One of their major duties is to help to maintain communication systems in good condition.

Broadcast and sound engineering technicians and radio operators perform a variety of duties in small stations. In large stations and at the networks, technicians are more specialized, although job assignments may change from day to day. The terms "operator," "engineer," and "technician" often are used interchangeably to describe these jobs. Workers in these positions may monitor and log outgoing signals and operate transmitters; set up, adjust, service, and repair electronic broadcasting equipment; and regulate fidelity, brightness, contrast, volume, and sound quality of television broadcasts.

Technicians also work in program production. *Recording engineers* operate and maintain video and sound recording equipment. They may operate equipment designed to produce special effects, such as the illusions of a bolt of lightning or a police siren. *Sound mixers* or *rerecording mixers* produce the soundtrack of a movie or television program. After filming or recording is complete, they may use a process called "dubbing" to insert sounds. *Field technicians* set up and operate portable transmission equipment outside the studio. Television news coverage requires so much electronic equipment, and the technology is changing so rapidly, that many stations assign technicians exclusively to news.

Chief engineers, *transmission engineers*, and *broadcast field supervisors* oversee other technicians and maintain broadcasting equipment.

The transition to digital recording, editing, and broadcasting has greatly changed the work of broadcast and sound engineering technicians and radio operators. Software on desktop computers has replaced specialized electronic equipment in many recording and editing functions. Most radio and television stations have replaced video and audio tapes with computer hard drives and other computer data storage systems. Computer networks linked to the specialized equipment dominate modern broadcasting. This transition has forced technicians to learn computer networking and software skills. (See the

statement on computer support specialists and systems administrators elsewhere in the *Handbook*.)

Working Conditions

Broadcast and sound engineering technicians and radio operators generally work indoors in pleasant surroundings. However, those who broadcast news and other programs from locations outside the studio may work outdoors in all types of weather. Technicians doing maintenance may climb poles or antenna towers, while those setting up equipment do heavy lifting.

Technicians at large stations and the networks usually work a 40-hour week under great pressure to meet broadcast deadlines, and may occasionally work overtime. Technicians at small stations routinely work more than 40 hours a week. Evening, weekend, and holiday work is usual, because most stations are on the air 18 to 24 hours a day, 7 days a week. Even though a technician may not be on duty when the station is broadcasting, some technicians may be on call during nonwork hours; that is, they must handle any problems that occur when they are on call.

Those who work on motion pictures may be on a tight schedule and may work long hours to meet contractual deadlines.

Employment

Broadcast and sound engineering technicians and radio operators held about 93,000 jobs in 2002. Their employment was distributed among the following detailed occupations:

Audio and video equipment technicians	42,000
Broadcast technicians	5,000
Sound engineering technicians	13,000
Radio operators	3,000

About 32 percent worked in broadcasting (except Internet) and 16 percent worked in the motion picture and sound recording industries. Almost 1 in 10 were self-employed. Television stations employ, on average, many more technicians than do radio stations. Some technicians are employed in other industries, producing employee communications, sales, and training programs. Technician jobs in television are located in virtually all cities, whereas jobs in radio also are found in many small towns. The highest paying and most specialized jobs are concentrated in New York City, Los Angeles, Chicago, and Washington, DC—the originating centers for most network or news programs. Motion picture production jobs are concentrated in Los Angeles and New York City.

Training, Other Qualifications, and Advancement

The best way to prepare for a broadcast and sound engineering technician job is to obtain technical school, community college, or college training in electronics, computer networking, or broadcast technology. In the motion picture industry, people are hired as apprentice editorial assistants and work their way up to more skilled jobs. Employers in the motion picture industry usually hire experienced freelance technicians on a picture-by-picture basis. Reputation and determination are important in getting jobs.

Audio and video equipment technicians monitor and adjust sound and mixing boards.

Beginners learn skills on the job from experienced technicians and supervisors. They often begin their careers in small stations and, once experienced, move on to larger ones. Large stations usually hire only technicians with experience. Many employers pay tuition and expenses for courses or seminars to help technicians keep abreast of developments in the field.

Audio and video equipment technicians generally need a high school diploma. Many recent entrants have a community college degree or various other forms of postsecondary degrees, although that is not always a requirement. They may substitute on-the-job training for formal education requirements. Working in a studio, as an assistant, is a great way of gaining experience and knowledge.

Radio operators do not usually require any formal training. This is an entry-level position that generally requires on-the-job training.

The Federal Communications Commission no longer requires the licensing of broadcast technicians, as the Telecommunications Act of 1996 eliminated this licensing requirement. Certification by the Society of Broadcast Engineers is a mark of competence and experience. The certificate is issued to experienced technicians who pass an examination.

Prospective technicians should take high school courses in math, physics, and electronics. Building electronic equipment from hobby kits and operating a "ham," or amateur, radio are good experience, as is work in college radio and television stations.

Broadcast and sound engineering technicians and radio operators must have manual dexterity and an aptitude for working with electrical, electronic, and mechanical systems and equipment.

Experienced technicians can become supervisory technicians or chief engineers. A college degree in engineering is needed in order to become chief engineer at a large television station.

Job Outlook
People seeking entry-level jobs as technicians in broadcasting are expected to face strong competition in major metropolitan areas, where pay generally is higher and the number of qualified jobseekers typically exceeds the number of openings. There, stations seek highly experienced personnel. Prospects for entry-level positions usually are better in small cities and towns for beginners with appropriate training.

Overall employment of broadcast and sound engineering technicians and radio operators is expected to about as fast as the average for all occupations through the year 2012. Job growth in radio and television broadcasting will be limited by consolidation of ownership of radio and television stations, and by laborsaving technical advances such as computer-controlled programming and remotely controlled transmitters. Changes to Federal Communications Commission (FCC) regulations now allow a single owner for up to eight radio stations in a single large market, and rules changes under consideration may have a similar impact on the ownership of television stations. Owners of multiple stations often consolidate the stations into a single location, reducing employment because one or a few technicians can provide support to multiple stations. Technicians who know how to install transmitters will be in demand as television stations install digital transmitters. Although most television stations are broadcasting in both analog and digital for-

mats and plan to switch entirely to digital, radio stations are only beginning to broadcast digital signals.

Employment of broadcast and sound engineering technicians in the cable and pay television portion of the broadcasting industry should grow as the range of services is expanded to provide, such products as cable Internet access and video-on-demand. Employment of these workers in the motion picture industry will grow rapidly. However, job prospects are expected to remain competitive because of the large number of people who are attracted by the glamour of working in motion pictures.

Projected job growth varies among detailed occupations in this field. Employment of broadcast technicians is expected to grow about as fast as the average for all occupations through 2012, as advancements in technology enhance the capabilities of technicians to produce higher quality radio and television programming. Employment of radio operators is expected to decline as more stations operate transmitters that control programming remotely. Employment of audio and video equipment technicians and sound engineering technicians is expected to grow faster than the average for all occupations. Not only will these workers have to set up audio and video equipment, but it will be necessary for them to maintain and repair this equipment.

In addition to employment growth, job openings also will result from the need to replace experienced technicians who leave this field. Some of these workers leave for other jobs that require knowledge of electronics, such as computer repairer or industrial machinery repairer.

Earnings
Television stations usually pay higher salaries than do radio stations; commercial broadcasting usually pays more than public broadcasting; and stations in large markets pay more than those in small markets.

Median annual earnings of broadcast technicians in 2002 were $27,760. The middle 50 percent earned between $18,860 and $45,200. The lowest 10 percent earned less than $14,600, and the highest 10 percent earned more than $65,970.

Median annual earnings of sound engineering technicians in 2002 were $36,970. The middle 50 percent earned between $24,330 and $57,350. The lowest 10 percent earned less than $18,540, and the highest 10 percent earned more than $82,510.

Median annual earnings of audio and video equipment technicians in 2002 were $31,110. The middle 50 percent earned between $22,670 and $43,950. The lowest 10 percent earned less than $17,710, and the highest 10 percent earned more than $61,420.

Median annual earnings of radio operators in 2002 were $31,530. The middle 50 percent earned between $24,000 and $41,430. The lowest 10 percent earned less than $17,380, and the highest 10 percent earned more than $56,340.

Related Occupations
Broadcast and sound engineering technicians and radio operators need the electronics training necessary to operate technical equipment, and they generally complete specialized postsecondary programs. Occupations with similar characteristics include engineering technicians, science technicians, and

electrical and electronics installers and repairers. Broadcast and sound engineering technicians also may operate computer networks, as do computer support specialists and systems administrators. Broadcast technicians on some live radio and television programs are responsible for screening incoming calls, similar to the work of communications equipment operators.

Sources of Additional Information

For career information and links to employment resources, contact:

➤ National Association of Broadcasters, 1771 N St. NW., Washington, DC 20036. Internet: **http://www.nab.org**

For information on certification, contact:

➤ Society of Broadcast Engineers, 9247 North Meridian St., Suite 305, Indianapolis, IN 46260. Internet: **http://www.sbe.org**

Interpreters and Translators

(0*NET 27-3091.00)

Significant Points

- Twenty percent of these workers are self-employed.

- Work is often sporadic and many interpreters and translators work part time.

- Although training requirements can vary, almost all interpreters and translators have a bachelor's degree.

- Job outlook varies by specialty and language combination.

Nature of the Work

Interpreters and translators enable the cross-cultural communication necessary in today's society by converting one language into another. However, these language specialists do more than simply translate words—they relay concepts and ideas between languages. They must thoroughly understand the subject matter in which they work, so that they are able to convert information from one language, known as the source language, into another, the target language. In addition, they must remain sensitive to the cultures associated with their languages of expertise.

Interpreters and translators are often discussed together because they share some common traits. For example, both need a special ability, known as language combination. This enables them to be fluent in at least two languages—a native, or active, language and a secondary, or passive, language. Their active language is the one they know best and into which they interpret or translate, and their passive language is one of which they have nearly perfect knowledge.

Although some people do both, interpretation and translation are different professions. Each requires a distinct set of skills and aptitudes, and most people are better suited for one or the other. While interpreters often work into and from both languages, translators generally work only into their active language.

Interpreters convert one spoken language into another—or, in the case of sign-language interpreters, between spoken communication and sign language. This requires interpreters to pay attention carefully, understand what is communicated in both languages, and express thoughts and ideas clearly. Strong research and analytical skills, mental dexterity, and an exceptional memory also are important.

The first part of an interpreter's work begins before arriving at the jobsite. The interpreter must become familiar with the subject matter that the speakers will cover, a task that may involve research to create a list of common words and phrases associated with the topic. Next, the interpreter usually travels to the location where his or her services are needed. Physical presence may not be required for some work, such as telephone interpretation. But it is usually important that the interpreter see the communicators in order to hear and observe the person speaking and to relay the message to the other party.

There are two types of interpretation: simultaneous and consecutive. Simultaneous interpretation requires interpreters to listen and speak (or sign) at the same time. In simultaneous interpretation, the interpreter begins to convey a sentence being spoken while the speaker is still talking. Ideally, simultaneous interpreters should be so familiar with a subject that they are able to anticipate the end of the speaker's sentence. Because they need a high degree of concentration, simultaneous interpreters work in pairs, with each interpreting for 20- to 30-minute segments. This type of interpretation is required at international conferences and is sometimes used in the courts.

In contrast to simultaneous interpretation's immediacy, consecutive interpretation begins only after the speaker has verbalized a group of words or sentences. Consecutive interpreters often take notes while listening to the speakers, so they must develop some type of note-taking or shorthand system. This form of interpretation is used most often for person-to-person communication, during which the interpreter sits near both parties.

Translators convert written materials from one language into another. They must have excellent writing and analytical ability. And because the documents they translate must be as flawless as possible, they also need good editing skills.

Translators' assignments may vary in length, writing style, and subject matter. When they first receive text to convert into another language, translators usually read it in its entirety to get an idea of the subject. Next, they identify and look up any unfamiliar words. Translators also might do additional reading on the subject matter if they are unclear about anything in the text. However, they also consult with the text's originator or issuing agency to clarify unclear or unfamiliar ideas, words, or acronyms.

Translating involves more than replacing a word with its equivalent in another language; sentences and ideas must be manipulated to flow with the same coherence as those in the source document, so that the translation reads as though it originated in the target language. Translators also must bear in mind any cultural references that may need to be explained to the intended audience, such as colloquialisms, slang, and other expressions that do not translate literally. Some subjects may be more difficult than others to translate because words or passages may have multiple meanings that make several translations possible. Not surprisingly, translated work often goes through multiple revisions before final text is submitted.

The way in which translators do their jobs has changed with advancements in technology. Today, nearly all translation work is done on a computer, and most assignments are received and submitted electronically. This enables translators to work from almost anywhere, and a large percentage of them work from home. The Internet provides advanced research capabilities and valuable language resources, such as specialized dictionaries and glossaries. In some cases, use of machine-assisted translation—including memory tools that provide comparisons of previous translations with current work—helps save time and reduce repetition.

The services of interpreters and translators are needed in a number of subject areas. While these workers may not completely specialize in a particular field or industry, many do focus on one area of expertise. Some of the most common areas are described below; however, interpreters and translators also may work in a variety of other areas, including business, social services, or entertainment.

Conference interpreters work at conferences that involve non-English-speaking attendees. This work includes international business and diplomacy, although conference interpreters also may interpret for any organization that works with foreign language speakers. Employers prefer high-level interpreters who have at least two language combinations—for example, the ability to interpret from English to French and English to Spanish. For some positions, such as those with the United Nations, this qualification is mandatory.

Much of the interpreting performed at conferences is simultaneous; however, at some meetings with a small number of attendees, consecutive interpreting also may be used. Usually, interpreters sit in soundproof booths, listening to the speakers through headphones and interpreting into a microphone what is said. The interpreted speech is then relayed to the listener through headsets. When interpreting is needed for only one or two people, the *chuchotage*, or *whispering*, method may be used. The interpreter sits behind or next to the attendee and whispers a translation of the proceedings.

Guide or escort interpreters accompany either U.S. visitors abroad or foreign visitors in the United States to ensure that they are able to communicate during their stay. These specialists interpret on a variety of subjects, both on an informal basis and on a professional level. Most of their interpretation is consecutive, and work is generally shared by two interpreters when the assignment requires more than an 8-hour day. Frequent travel, often for days or weeks at a time, is common, a factor which some find particularly appealing.

Judiciary interpreters and translators help people appearing in court who are unable or unwilling to communicate in English. These workers must remain detached from the content of their work and not alter or modify the meaning or tone of what is said. Legal translators must be thoroughly familiar with the language and functions of the U.S. judicial system, as well as other countries' legal systems. Court interpreters work in a variety of legal settings, such as attorney-client meetings, preliminary hearings, depositions, trials, and arraignments. Success as a court interpreter requires an understanding of both legal terminology and colloquial language. In addition to interpreting what is said, court interpreters also may be required to translate written documents and read them aloud, also known as sight translation.

Literary translators adapt written literature from one language into another. They may translate any number of documents, including journal articles, books, poetry, and short stories. Literary translation is related to creative writing; literary translators must create a new text in the target language that reproduces the content and style of the original. Whenever possible, literary translators work closely with authors in order to best capture their intended meanings and literary characteristics.

This type of work often is done as a sideline by university professors; however, opportunities exist for well-established literary translators. As is the case with writers, finding a publisher is a critical part of the job. Most aspiring literary translators begin by submitting a short sample of their work, in the hope that it will be printed and give them recognition. For example, after receiving permission from the author, they might submit to a publishing house a previously unpublished short work, such as a poem or essay.

Localization translators constitute a relatively recent and rapidly expanding specialty. Localization involves the complete adaptation of a product for use in a different language and culture. At its earlier stages, this work dealt primarily with software localization, but the specialty has expanded to include the adaptation of Internet sites and products in manufacturing and other business sectors.

Translators working in localization need a solid grasp of the languages to be translated, a thorough understanding of technical concepts and vocabulary, and a high degree of knowledge about the intended target audience or users of the product. The goal of these specialists is for the product to appear as if it were originally manufactured in the country where it will be sold and supported. Because software often is involved, it is not uncommon for people who work in this area of translation to have a strong background in computer science or computer-related work experience.

Providing language services to healthcare patients with limited English proficiency is the realm of *medical interpreters and translators*. Medical interpreters help patients to communicate with doctors, nurses, and other medical staff. Translators working in this specialty primarily convert patient materials and informational brochures, issued by hospitals and medical facilities, into the desired language. Medical interpreters need a strong grasp of medical and colloquial terminology in both languages, along with cultural sensitivity regarding how the patient receives the information. They must remain detached but aware of the patient's feelings and pain.

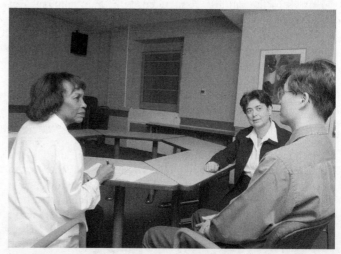

Interpreters help people who speak different languages to communicate with each other.

Sign language interpreters facilitate communication between people who are deaf or hard of hearing and people who can hear. Sign language interpreters must be fluent in English and American Sign Language (ASL), which combines signing, finger spelling, and specific body language. ASL has its own grammatical rules, sentence structure, idioms, historical contexts, and cultural nuances. Sign language interpreting, like foreign language interpreting, involves more than simply replacing a word of spoken English with a sign representing that word.

Most sign language interpreters either interpret, aiding communication between English and ASL, or transliterate, facilitating communication between English and contact signing—a form of signing that uses a more English language-based word order. Some interpreters specialize in oral interpreting for deaf or hard of hearing persons who lipread instead of sign. Other specialties include tactile signing, interpreting for persons who are deaf-blind; cued speech; and signing exact English.

Working Conditions

Working environments of interpreters and translators vary. Interpreters work in a variety of settings, such as hospitals, courtrooms and conference centers. They are required to travel to the site—whether it is a neighboring town or the other side of the world—where their services are needed. Interpreters who work over the telephone generally work on call or in call centers in urban areas and keep to a standard 5-day, 40-hour workweek. Interpreters for deaf students in schools usually work in a school setting and work 9 months out of the year. Translators usually work alone, and they must frequently perform under pressure of deadlines and tight schedules. Many translators choose to work at home; however, technology allows translators to work from virtually anywhere.

Because many interpreters and translators freelance, their schedules are often erratic, with extensive periods of no work interspersed with others requiring long, irregular hours. For those who freelance, a significant amount of time must be dedicated to looking for jobs. In addition, freelancers must manage their own finances, and payment for their services may not always be prompt. Freelancing, however, offers variety and flexibility, and allows many workers to choose which jobs to accept or decline.

The number of work-related accidents in these occupations is relatively low. The work can be stressful and exhausting and translation can be lonesome or dull. However, interpreters and translators may use their irregular schedules to pursue other interests, such as traveling, dabbling in a hobby, or working a second job. Many interpreters and translators enjoy what they do and value the ability to control their schedules and workloads.

Employment

Interpreters and translators held about 24,000 jobs in 2002. Because of the large number of people who work in the occupation sporadically, however, the actual number of interpreters and translators is probably significantly higher. Reflecting the diversity of employment options in the field, interpreters and translators are employed in a variety of industries. Nearly 3 in 10 worked in public and private educational institutions, such as schools, colleges, and universities. About 1 in 10 worked in healthcare, many of which worked for hospitals. More than 1 in 10 worked in other areas of government, such as Federal, State and local courts. Other employers of interpreters and translators include publishing companies, telephone companies, airlines, and interpreting and translating agencies.

More than 2 in 10 interpreters and translators are self-employed. To find work, these interpreters and translators may submit resumes to 100 or more employment agencies, and then wait to be contacted when an agency matches their skills with a job. After establishing a few regular clients, interpreters and translators often hear of subsequent jobs by word of mouth; or, they may receive enough work from a few clients to stay busy. Many who freelance in the occupation work only part time, relying on other sources of income to supplement earnings from interpreting or translation.

Training, Other Qualifications, and Advancement

The educational backgrounds of interpreters and translators vary. Knowing a language in addition to a native language is a given. Although it is not necessary to have been raised bilingual to succeed, many interpreters and translators grew up speaking two languages.

In high school, students can begin to prepare for these careers by taking a broad range of courses that include English writing and comprehension, foreign languages, and basic computer proficiency. Other helpful pursuits include spending time abroad, or comparable forms of direct contact with foreign cultures, and extensive reading on a variety of subjects in English and at least one other language.

Beyond high school, there are many educational options. Although a bachelor's degree is almost always required, interpreters and translators note that it is acceptable to major in something other than a language. However, specialized training in how to do the work is generally required. A number of formal programs in interpreting and translation are available at colleges nationwide and through nonuniversity training programs, conferences, and courses. Many people who work as conference interpreters or in more technical areas—such as localization, engineering, or finance—have master's degrees, while those working in the community as court or medical interpreters or translators are more likely to complete job-specific training programs.

There is currently no universal form of certification required of all interpreters and translators in the United States, but there are a variety of different tests that workers can take to demonstrate proficiency. The American Translators Association provides accreditation in more than 24 language combinations for its members; other options include a certification program offered by The Translators and Interpreters Guild. Many interpreters are not certified. Federal courts have certification for Spanish, Navaho, and Haitian Creole interpreters, and many State and municipal courts offer their own forms of certification. The National Association of Judiciary Interpreters and Translators also offers certification for court interpreting.

The U.S. Department of State has a three-test series for interpreters, including simple consecutive interpreting (escort), simultaneous interpreting (court/seminar), and conference-level interpreting (international conferences). These tests are not referred to directly as certification, but successful completion often indicates that a person has an adequate level of skill to work in the field.

Both the National Association of the Deaf and the Registry of Interpreters for the Deaf offer certification for sign interpreters and have recently collaborated to develop a joint exam.

Experience is an essential part of a successful career in either interpreting or translation. In fact, many agencies or companies use only the services of people who have worked in the field for 3 to 5 years or who have a degree in translation studies or both.

A good way for translators to learn firsthand about the profession is to start out working in-house for a company; however, such jobs are not very numerous. Advice for new entrants to the field is to begin getting experience whatever way they can—even if it means doing informal or unpaid work. Mentoring relationships and internships are other ways to build skills and confidence. Escort interpreting may offer an opportunity for inexperienced candidates to work alongside a more seasoned interpreter. Interpreters might also find it easier to break into areas with particularly high demand for language services, such as court or medical interpretation. Once interpreters and translators have gained sufficient experience, they may then move up to more difficult or prestigious assignments, may be given editorial responsibility, or may eventually manage or start their own translation agency.

Job Outlook

Employment of interpreters and translators is projected to grow faster than the average for all occupations over the 2002-12 period, reflecting growth in the industries employing interpreters and translators. Higher demand for interpreters and translators in recent years has resulted directly from the broadening of international ties and the increase in foreign language speakers in the United States. Both of these trends are expected to continue, contributing to relatively rapid growth in the number of jobs for interpreters and translators.

Technology has made the work of interpreters and translators easier. However, technology is not likely to have a negative impact on employment of interpreters and translators because such innovations are incapable of producing work comparable with work produced by these professionals.

Translators are most in demand for the languages referred to as "PFIGS"—Portuguese, French, Italian, German, and Spanish—and the principal Asian languages—Chinese, Japanese, and Korean. Current events and changing political environments, often difficult to foresee, sometimes increase the need for persons who can work with other languages.

Urban areas, especially those in California, New York, and Washington, DC, provide the largest numbers of employment possibilities, especially for interpreters; however, as the immigrant population spreads into more rural areas, jobs in smaller communities will become more widely available.

Job prospects for interpreters and translators vary by specialty. In particular, there should be strong demand for specialists in localization, driven by imports and exports, the expansion of the Internet, and demand in other technical areas such as medicine or law. Rapid employment growth among interpreters and translators in health services industries will be fueled by relatively recent guidelines regarding compliance with Title VI of the Civil Rights Act, which requires all healthcare providers receiving Federal aid to provide language services to non-English speakers. Similarly, the Americans with Disabilities Act and other laws, such as the Rehabilitation Act,

mandate that, in certain situations, an interpreter must be available for people who are deaf or hard of hearing. Given the lack of qualified candidates meeting these requirements, interpreters for the deaf will continue to have favorable employment prospects. On the other hand, job growth is expected to be limited for both conference interpreters and literary translators.

Earnings

Salaried interpreters and translators had median hourly earnings of $15.67 in 2002. The middle 50 percent earned between $11.97 and $20.33. The lowest 10 percent earned less than $9.37, and the highest 10 percent earned more than $25.99. Limited information suggests that highly skilled interpreters and translators—for example, high-level conference interpreters—working full time can earn more than $100,000 annually. Earnings depend on language, subject matter, skill, experience, education, certification, and type of employer, and salaries of interpreters and translators can vary widely. Interpreters and translators with language skills for which there is a greater demand, or for which there are relatively few people with the skills, often have higher earnings. According to a 2001 salary survey by the American Translators Association, Chinese and Japanese interpreters and translators earned the highest median hourly rates—ranging from $45 to $50 an hour. Interpreters and translators with specialized expertise, such as those working in software localization, also generally command higher rates. Individuals classified as language specialists for the Federal Government earned an average of $64,234 annually in 2003.

For those who are not salaried, earnings may fluctuate, depending on the availability of work. Furthermore, freelancers do not have any employer-paid benefits. Freelance interpreters usually earn an hourly rate, whereas translators who freelance typically earn a rate per word or per hour.

Related Occupations

Interpreters and translators use their multilingual skills, as do teachers of languages. These include teachers—preschool, kindergarten, elementary, middle, and secondary; teachers—postsecondary; teachers—special education; and teachers—adult literacy and remedial and self-enrichment education. The work of interpreters, particularly guide or escort interpreters, can be likened to that of tour and travel guides, in that they accompany individuals or groups on tours or to places of interest. Similarly, interpreters may share some common work characteristics with announcers, who also work in soundproof environments relaying information to listeners.

The work of translators is similar to that of writers and editors, in that they communicate information and ideas through the written word and prepare texts for publication or dissemination. Those working in localization of software have skills similar to those of computer software engineers, in that they analyze users' needs and design, create, and modify computer software, and many possess strong programming skills. Furthermore, interpreters or translators working in a legal or healthcare environment are required to have a knowledge of terms and concepts that is similar to that of professionals working in these fields, such as court reporters or medical transcriptionists.

Sources of Additional Information

Organizations dedicated to these professions can provide valuable advice and guidance for people interested in learning more about interpretation and translation. The language services division of local hospitals or courthouses also may be able to offer information about available opportunities.

For career information, contact the organizations listed below:

➤ American Translators Association, 225 Reinekers Lane, Suite 590, Alexandria, VA 22314. Internet: **http://www.atanet.org**
➤ The Translators and Interpreters Guild, 8611 Second Ave., Suite 203, Silver Spring, MD 20910. Internet: **http://www.ttig.org**
➤ U.S. Department of State, Office of Language Services, Room 2212, Washington, DC 20520.

For more detailed information by specialty, contact the association affiliated with that subject area:

➤ National Association of Judiciary Interpreters and Translators, 2150 N. 107th St., Suite 205, Seattle, WA 98133. Internet: **http://www.najit.org**
➤ American Literary Translators Association, PO Box 830688, Richardson, TX 75083. Internet: **http://www.literarytranslators.org**
➤ The Localisation Industry Standards Association, 7 Route du Monastère-CH-1173, Féchy, Switzerland. Internet: **http://www.lisa.org**
➤ Massachusetts Medical Interpreters Association, New England Medical Center, 750 Washington St., NEMC Box 271, Boston, MA 02111. Internet: **http://www.mmia.org**
➤ Registry of Interpreters for the Deaf, 333 Commerce St., Alexandria, VA 22314. Internet: **http://www.rid.org**

News Analysts, Reporters, and Correspondents

(0*NET 27-3021.00, 27-3022.00)

Significant Points

● Most employers prefer experienced individuals with a bachelor's degree in journalism or mass communications.

● Competition will be keen for jobs at large metropolitan and national newspapers, broadcast stations, and magazines; most entry-level openings arise at small broadcast stations and publications.

● Jobs often involve irregular hours, night and weekend work, and pressure to meet deadlines.

Nature of the Work

News analysts, reporters, and correspondents play a key role in our society. They gather information, prepare stories, and make broadcasts that inform us about local, State, national, and international events; present points of view on current issues; and report on the actions of public officials, corporate executives, special-interest groups, and others who exercise power.

News analysts examine, interpret, and broadcast news received from various sources. They also are called *newscasters* or *news anchors*. News anchors present news stories and introduce videotaped news or live transmissions from on-the-scene reporters. Some newscasters at large stations and networks specialize in a particular type of news, such as sports or weather. *Weathercasters*, also called weather reporters, report current and forecasted weather conditions. They gather information from national satellite weather services, wire services, and local and regional

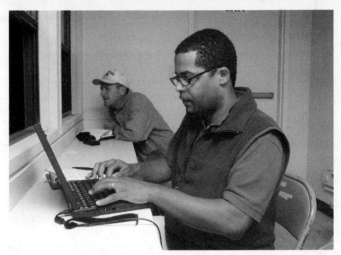

Reporters often travel to sporting events.

weather bureaus. Some weathercasters are trained meteorologists and can develop their own weather forecasts. (See the statement on atmospheric scientists elsewhere in the *Handbook*.) *Sportscasters* select, write, and deliver sports news. This may include interviews with sports personalities and coverage of games and other sporting events.

In covering a story, *reporters* investigate leads and news tips, look at documents, observe events at the scene, and interview people. Reporters take notes and also may take photographs or shoot videos. At their office, they organize the material, determine the focus or emphasis, write their stories, and edit accompanying video material. Many reporters enter information or write stories on laptop computers, and electronically submit the material to their offices from remote locations. In some cases, *newswriters* write a story from information collected and submitted by reporters. Radio and television reporters often compose stories and report "live" from the scene. At times, they later tape an introduction to or commentary on their story in the studio. Some journalists also interpret the news or offer opinions to readers, viewers, or listeners. In this role, they are called *commentators* or *columnists*.

General assignment reporters write about newsworthy occurrences, such as an accident, a political rally, the visit of a celebrity, or a company going out of business, as assigned. Large newspapers and radio and television stations assign reporters to gather news about specific topics or "beats," such as crime or education. Some reporters specialize in fields such as health, politics, foreign affairs, sports, theater, consumer affairs, social events, science, business, or religion. Investigative reporters cover stories that may take many days or weeks of information gathering. Some publications use teams of reporters instead of assigning specific beats, allowing reporters to cover a greater variety of stories. News teams may include reporters, editors, graphic artists, and photographers, working together to complete a story.

News *correspondents* report on news occurring in the large U.S. and foreign cities where they are stationed. Reporters on small publications cover all aspects of the news. They take photographs, write headlines, lay out pages, edit wire service stories, and write editorials. Some also solicit advertisements, sell subscriptions, and perform general office work.

Working Conditions

The work of news analysts, reporters, and correspondents is usually hectic. They are under great pressure to meet deadlines. Broadcasts sometimes are made with little or no time for preparation. Some news analysts, reporters, and correspondents work in comfortable, private offices; others work in large rooms filled with the sound of keyboards and computer printers, as well as the voices of other reporters. Curious onlookers, police, or other emergency workers can distract those reporting from the scene for radio and television. Covering wars, political uprisings, fires, floods, and similar events is often dangerous.

Working hours vary. Reporters on morning papers often work from late afternoon until midnight. Radio and television reporters usually are assigned to a day or evening shift. Magazine reporters usually work during the day.

Reporters sometimes have to change their work hours to meet a deadline, or to follow late-breaking developments. Their work demands long hours, irregular schedules, and some travel. Many stations and networks are on the air 24 hours a day, so newscasters can expect to work unusual hours.

Employment

News analysts, reporters, and correspondents held about 66,000 jobs in 2002. About 60 percent worked for newspaper, periodical, book, and directory publishers. Another 25 percent worked in radio and television broadcasting. About 4,100 news analysts, reporters, and correspondents were self-employed.

Training, Other Qualifications, and Advancement

Most employers prefer individuals with a bachelor's degree in journalism or mass communications, but some hire graduates with other majors. They look for experience on school newspapers or broadcasting stations and internships with news organizations. Large-city newspapers and stations also may prefer candidates with a degree in a subject-matter specialty such as economics, political science, or business. Some large newspapers and broadcasters may hire only experienced reporters.

Bachelor's degree programs in journalism are available at more than 400 colleges or universities. About three-fourths of the courses in a typical curriculum are in liberal arts; the remaining courses are in journalism. Examples of journalism courses are introductory mass media, basic reporting and copy editing, history of journalism, and press law and ethics. Students planning a career in broadcasting take courses in radio and television news and production. Those planning newspaper or magazine careers usually specialize in news-editorial journalism. To create a story for an online presentation, they need to know how to use computer software to combine online story text with audio and video elements and graphics.

Many community and junior colleges offer journalism courses or programs; credits may be transferable to 4-year journalism programs. About 120 schools offered a master's degree in journalism in 2002; about 35 schools offered a Ph.D. degree. Some graduate programs are intended primarily as preparation for news careers, while others prepare journalism teachers, researchers and theorists, and advertising and public relations workers.

High school courses in English, journalism, and social studies provide a good foundation for college programs. Useful college liberal arts courses include English with an emphasis on writing, sociology, political science, economics, history, and psychology. Courses in computer science, business, and speech are useful as well. Fluency in a foreign language is necessary in some jobs.

Although reporters need good word processing skills, computer graphics and desktop publishing skills also are useful. Computer-assisted reporting involves the use of computers to analyze data in search of a story. This technique and the interpretation of the results require computer skills and familiarity with databases. Knowledge of news photography also is valuable for entry-level positions, which sometimes combine the responsibilities of a reporter with those of a camera operator or photographer.

Employers report that practical experience is the most important part of education and training. Upon graduation many students have already gained much practical experience through part-time or summer jobs or through internships with news organizations. Most newspapers, magazines, and broadcast news organizations offer reporting and editing internships. Work on high school and college newspapers, at broadcasting stations, or on community papers or U.S. Armed Forces publications also provides practical training. In addition, journalism scholarships, fellowships, and assistantships awarded to college journalism students by universities, newspapers, foundations, and professional organizations are helpful. Experience as a stringer or freelancer—a part-time reporter who is paid only for stories printed—is advantageous.

Reporters should be dedicated to providing accurate and impartial news. Accuracy is important, both to serve the public and because untrue or libelous statements can lead to lawsuits. A nose for news, persistence, initiative, poise, resourcefulness, a good memory, and physical stamina are important, as is the emotional stability to deal with pressing deadlines, irregular hours, and dangerous assignments. Broadcast reporters and news analysts must be comfortable on camera. All reporters must be at ease in unfamiliar places and with a variety of people. Positions involving on-air work require a pleasant voice and appearance.

Most reporters start at small publications or broadcast stations as general assignment reporters or copy editors. Large publications and stations hire few recent graduates; as a rule, they require new reporters to have several years of experience.

Beginning reporters cover court proceedings and civic and club meetings, summarize speeches, and write obituaries. With experience, they report more difficult assignments, cover an assigned beat, or specialize in a particular field.

Some news analysts and reporters can advance by moving to larger newspapers or stations. A few experienced reporters become columnists, correspondents, writers, announcers, or public relations specialists. Others become editors in print journalism or program managers in broadcast journalism, who supervise reporters. Some eventually become broadcasting or publishing industry managers.

Job Outlook

Employment of news analysts, reporters, and correspondents is expected to grow more slowly than the average for all occupations through the year 2012—the result of mergers, consolidations, and closures of newspapers; decreased circulation; increased expenses; and a decline in advertising profits. In addition to consolidation of local newspaper and television and radio station ownership, increasing competition for viewers from cable networks also should limit employment growth. Some job growth is expected in new media areas, such as online newspapers and magazines. Job openings also will result from the need to replace workers who leave their occupations permanently. Some news analysts, reporters, and correspondents find the work too stressful and hectic or do not like the lifestyle, and transfer to other occupations.

Most opportunities will be with smalltown and suburban newspapers and radio and television stations. Competition will continue to be keen for more sought-after jobs on large metropolitan and national newspapers, broadcast stations and networks, and magazines. Talented writers who can handle highly specialized scientific or technical subjects have an advantage. Also, newspapers increasingly are hiring stringers and freelancers.

Journalism graduates have the background for work in closely related fields such as advertising and public relations, and many take jobs in these fields. Other graduates accept sales, managerial, or other nonmedia positions.

The number of job openings in the newspaper and broadcasting industries—in which news analysts, reporters, and correspondents are employed—is sensitive to economic ups and downs, because these industries depend on advertising revenue.

Earnings

Salaries for news analysts, reporters, and correspondents vary widely. Median annual earnings of news analysts, reporters, and correspondents were $30,510 in 2002. The middle 50 percent earned between $22,350 and $47,170. The lowest 10 percent earned less than $17,620, and the highest 10 percent earned more than $69,450. Median annual earnings of news analysts, reporters, and correspondents were $33,320 in radio and television broadcasting and $29,090 in newspaper, periodical, book, and directory publishers in 2002.

Related Occupations

News analysts, reporters, and correspondents must write clearly and effectively to succeed in their profession. Others for whom good writing ability is essential include writers and editors, and public relations specialists. Many news analysts, reporters, and correspondents also must communicate information orally. Others for whom oral communication skills are important are announcers, interpreters and translators, sales and related occupations, and teachers.

Sources of Additional Information

For information on broadcasting education and scholarship resources, contact:
➤ National Association of Broadcasters, 1771 N St. NW., Washington, DC 20036. Internet: **http://www.nab.org**

Information on careers in journalism, colleges and universities offering degree programs in journalism or communications, and journalism scholarships and internships may be obtained from:
➤ Dow Jones Newspaper Fund, Inc., P.O. Box 300, Princeton, NJ 08543-0300.

Information on union wage rates for newspaper and magazine reporters is available from:
➤ Newspaper Guild, Research and Information Department, 501 3rd St. NW., Suite 250, Washington, DC 20001.

For a list of schools with accredited programs in journalism and mass communications, send a stamped, self-addressed envelope to:
➤ Accrediting Council on Education in Journalism and Mass Communications, University of Kansas School of Journalism and Mass Communications, Stauffer-Flint Hall, 1435 Jayhawk Blvd., Lawrence, KS 66045. Internet: **http://www.ku.edu/~acejmc/STUDENT/STUDENT.SHTML**

Names and locations of newspapers and a list of schools and departments of journalism are published in the *Editor and Publisher International Year Book*, available in most public libraries and newspaper offices.

Photographers

(0*NET 27-4021.01, 27-4021.02)

Significant Points

- Competition for jobs is expected to be keen because the work is attractive to many people.

- Technical expertise, a "good eye," imagination, and creativity are essential.

- More than half of all photographers are self-employed; the most successful are able to adapt to rapidly changing technologies and are adept at operating a business.

Nature of the Work

Photographers produce and preserve images that paint a picture, tell a story, or record an event. To create commercial quality photographs, photographers need both technical expertise and creativity. Producing a successful picture requires choosing and presenting a subject to achieve a particular effect, and selecting the appropriate equipment. For example, photographers may enhance the subject's appearance with natural or artificial light, use a particular lens depending on the desired range or level of detail, or draw attention to a particular aspect of the subject by blurring the background.

Today, many cameras adjust settings such as shutter speed and aperture automatically. They also let the photographer adjust these settings manually, allowing greater creative and technical control over the picture-taking process. In addition to automatic and manual cameras, photographers use an array of film, lenses, and equipment—from filters, tripods, and flash attachments to specially constructed lighting equipment.

Photographers use either a traditional camera that records images on silver halide film that is developed into prints or a digital camera that electronically records images. Some photographers send their film to laboratories for processing. Color film requires expensive equipment and exacting conditions for correct processing and printing. (See the statement on photographic process workers and processing machine operators elsewhere in the *Handbook*.) Other photographers, especially those who use black and white film or who require special effects, prefer to develop and print their own photographs. Photographers who do their own film developing must have the technical skill to operate a fully equipped darkroom or the appropriate computer software to process prints digitally.

Portrait photographers take pictures of individuals or groups of people and often work in their own studios.

Recent advances in electronic technology now make it possible for the professional photographer to develop and scan standard 35mm or other types of film, and use flatbed scanners and photofinishing laboratories to produce computer-readable, digital images from film. After converting the film to a digital image, photographers can edit and electronically transmit images using a method as simple as e-mail or as advanced as a satellite phone. This makes it easier and faster to shoot, develop, and transmit pictures from remote locations.

Using computers and specialized software, photographers also can manipulate and enhance the scanned or digital image to create a desired effect. Images can be stored on portable memory devices including compact disks (CDs) or on new types of smaller "mini pocket" storage devices such as flash disks, which are small memory cards used in digital cameras. Digital technology also allows the production of larger, more colorful, and more accurate prints or images for use in advertising, photographic art, and scientific research. Some photographers use this technology to create electronic portfolios as well. Because much photography now involves the use of computer technology, photographers must have hands-on knowledge of computer editing software.

Some photographers specialize in areas such as portrait, commercial and industrial, scientific, news, or fine arts photography. *Portrait photographers* take pictures of individuals or groups of people and often work in their own studios. Some specialize in weddings, religious ceremonies, or school photographs and may work on location. Portrait photographers who are business owners arrange for advertising, schedule appointments, set and adjust equipment, develop and retouch negatives, and mount and frame pictures. They also purchase supplies, keep records, bill customers, and may hire and train employees.

Commercial and industrial photographers take pictures of various subjects, such as buildings, models, merchandise, artifacts, and landscapes. These photographs are used in a variety of media, including books, reports, advertisements, and catalogs. Industrial photographers often take pictures of equipment, machinery, products, workers, and company officials. The pictures are used for various purposes—for example, analysis of engineering projects, publicity, or records of equipment development or deployment, such as placement of an offshore rig. This photography frequently is done on location.

Scientific photographers take images of a variety of subjects to illustrate or record scientific or medical data or phenomena, using knowledge of scientific procedures. They typically possess additional knowledge in areas such as engineering, medicine, biology, or chemistry.

News photographers, also called *photojournalists*, photograph newsworthy people, places, and sporting, political, and community events for newspapers, journals, magazines, or television. Some news photographers are salaried staff; others are self-employed and are known as freelance photographers.

Fine arts photographers sell their photographs as fine artwork. In addition to technical proficiency, fine arts photographers need artistic talent and creativity.

Self-employed, or freelance, photographers may license the use of their photographs through stock photo agencies or contract with clients or agencies to provide photographs as necessary. Stock agencies grant magazines and other customers the right to purchase the use of photographs, and, in turn, pay the photographer on a commission basis. Stock photo agencies require an application from the photographer and a sizable portfolio. Once accepted, a large number of new submissions usually is required from the photographer each year.

Working Conditions

Working conditions for photographers vary considerably. Photographers employed in government and advertising agencies usually work a 5-day, 40-hour week. On the other hand, news photographers often work long, irregular hours and must be available to work on short notice. Many photographers work part-time or variable schedules.

Portrait photographers usually work in their own studios but also may travel to take photographs at the client's location, such as a school, a company office, or a private home. News and commercial photographers frequently travel locally, stay overnight on assignments, or travel to distant places for long periods.

Some photographers work in uncomfortable or even dangerous surroundings, especially news photographers covering accidents, natural disasters, civil unrest, or military conflicts. Many photographers must wait long hours in all kinds of weather for an event to take place and stand or walk for long periods while carrying heavy equipment. News photographers often work under strict deadlines.

Self-employment allows for greater autonomy, freedom of expression, and flexible scheduling. However, income can be uncertain and the continuous, time-consuming search for new clients can be stressful. Some self-employed photographers hire assistants who help seek out new business.

Employment

Photographers held about 130,000 jobs in 2002. More than half were self-employed, a much higher proportion than the average for all occupations. Some self-employed photographers have contracts with advertising agencies, magazines, or others to do individual projects at a predetermined fee, while others operate portrait studios or provide photographs to stock photo agencies.

Most salaried photographers work in portrait or commercial photography studios. Newspapers, magazines, television broadcasters, and advertising agencies employ most of the others. Most photographers work in metropolitan areas.

Training, Other Qualifications, and Advancement

Employers usually seek applicants with a "good eye," imagination, and creativity, as well as a good technical understanding of photography. Entry-level positions in photojournalism or in industrial or scientific photography generally require a college degree in journalism or photography. Freelance and portrait photographers need technical proficiency, whether gained through a degree program, vocational training, or extensive work experience.

Many universities, community and junior colleges, vocational-technical institutes, and private trade and technical schools offer photography courses. Basic courses in photography cover equipment, processes, and techniques. Bachelor's degree programs, especially those including business courses, provide a well-rounded education. Art schools offer useful training in design and composition.

Individuals interested in photography should subscribe to photographic newsletters and magazines, join camera clubs, and seek summer or part-time employment in camera stores, newspapers, or photo studios.

Photographers may start out as assistants to experienced photographers. Assistants learn to mix chemicals, develop film, and print photographs, and acquire the other skills necessary to run a portrait or commercial photography business. Freelance photographers also should develop an individual style of photography in order to differentiate themselves from the competition. Some photographers enter the field by submitting unsolicited photographs to magazines and to art directors at advertising agencies. For freelance photographers, a good portfolio of their work is critical.

Photographers need good eyesight, artistic ability, and good hand-eye coordination. They should be patient, accurate, and detail-oriented. Photographers should be able to work well with others, as they frequently deal with clients, graphic designers, or advertising and publishing specialists. Increasingly, photographers need to know how to use computer software programs and applications that allow them to prepare and edit images.

Portrait photographers need the ability to help people relax in front of the camera. Commercial and fine arts photographers must be imaginative and original. News photographers not only must be good with a camera, but also must understand the story behind an event so that their pictures match the story. They must be decisive in recognizing a potentially good photograph and act quickly to capture it.

Photographers who operate their own businesses, or freelance, need business skills as well as talent. These individuals must know how to prepare a business plan; submit bids; write contracts; market their work; hire models, if needed; get permission to shoot on locations that normally are not open to the public; obtain releases to use photographs of people; license and price photographs; secure copyright protection for their work; and keep financial records. Knowledge of licensing and copyright laws as well as contract negotiation procedures is especially important for self-employed photographers, in order to protect their rights and their work.

After several years of experience, magazine and news photographers may advance to photography or picture editor positions. Some photographers teach at technical schools, film schools, or universities.

Job Outlook

Photographers can expect keen competition for job openings because the work is attractive to many people. The number of individuals interested in positions as commercial and news photographers usually is much greater than the number of openings. Those who succeed in landing a salaried job or attracting enough work to earn a living by freelancing are likely to be the most creative, able to adapt to rapidly changing technologies, and adept at operating a business. Related work experience, job-related training, or some unique skill or talent—such as a background in computers or electronics—also are beneficial to prospective photographers.

Employment of photographers is expected to increase about as fast as the average for all occupations through 2012. Demand for portrait photographers should increase as the population grows. As the number of electronic versions of magazines, journals, and newspapers increases on the Internet, commercial photographers will be needed to provide digital images.

Job growth, however, will be constrained somewhat by the widespread use of digital photography and the falling price of digital equipment. Besides increasing photographers' productivity, improvements in digital technology reduce barriers of entry into this profession and allow more individual consumers and businesses to produce, store, and access photographic images on their own. Declines in the newspaper industry also will reduce demand for photographers to provide still images for print.

Earnings

Median annual earnings of salaried photographers were $24,040 in 2002. The middle 50 percent earned between $17,740 and $34,910. The lowest 10 percent earned less than $14,640, and the highest 10 percent earned more than $49,920. Median annual earnings in the industries employing the largest numbers of salaried photographers were $31,460 for newspapers and periodicals and $21,860 for other professional or scientific services.

Salaried photographers—more of whom work full time—tend to earn more than those who are self-employed. Because most freelance and portrait photographers purchase their own equipment, they incur considerable expense acquiring and maintaining cameras and accessories. Unlike news and commercial photographers, few fine arts photographers are successful enough to support themselves solely through their art.

Related Occupations

Other occupations requiring artistic talent and creativity include architects, except landscape and naval; artists and related workers; designers; news analysts, reporters, and correspondents; and television, video, and motion picture camera operators and editors.

Sources of Additional Information

Career information on photography is available from:
➤ Professional Photographers of America, Inc., 229 Peachtree St. NE., Suite 2200, Atlanta, GA 30303.
➤ National Press Photographers Association, Inc., 3200 Croasdaile Dr., Suite 306, Durham, NC 27705. Internet: **http://www.nppa.org**

Public Relations Specialists

(0*NET 27-3031.00)

Significant Points

- Although employment is projected to increase faster than average, keen competition is expected for entry-level jobs.

- Opportunities should be best for college graduates who combine a degree in public relations, journalism, or another communications-related field with a public relations internship or other related work experience.

- The ability to communicate effectively is essential.

Nature of the Work

An organization's reputation, profitability, and even its continued existence can depend on the degree to which its targeted "publics" support its goals and policies. Public relations specialists—also referred to as communications specialists and media specialists, among other titles—serve as advocates for businesses, nonprofit associations, universities, hospitals, and other organizations, and build and maintain positive relationships with the public. As managers recognize the growing importance of good public relations to the success of their organizations, they increasingly rely on public relations specialists for advice on the strategy and policy of such programs.

Public relations specialists handle organizational functions such as media, community, consumer, industry, and governmental relations; political campaigns; interest-group representation; conflict mediation; or employee and investor relations. They help an organization and its public adapt mutually to each other. However, public relations are not only about "telling the organization's story." Understanding the attitudes and concerns of consumers, employees, and various other groups also is a vital part of the job. To improve communication, public relations specialists establish and maintain cooperative relationships with representatives of community, consumer, employee, and public interest groups, and with representatives from print and broadcast journalism.

Informing the general public, interest groups, and stockholders of an organization's policies, activities, and accomplishments is an important part of a public relations specialist's job. The work also involves keeping management aware of public attitudes and the concerns of the many groups and organizations with which they must deal.

Media specialists draft press releases and contact people in the media who might print or broadcast their material. Many radio or television special reports, newspaper stories, and magazine articles start at the desks of public relations specialists. Sometimes, the subject is an organization and its policies towards its employees or its role in the community. Often, the subject is a public issue, such as health, energy, or the environment.

Public affairs specialists also arrange and conduct programs to keep up contact between organization representatives and the public. For example, they set up speaking engagements and often prepare speeches for company officials. These media specialists represent employers at community projects; make film, slide, or other visual presentations at meetings and school assemblies; and plan conventions. In addition, they are respon-

Public relations specialists serve as advocates for organizations and build and maintain positive relationships with the public.

sible for preparing annual reports and writing proposals for various projects.

In government, public relations specialists—who may be called press secretaries, information officers, public affairs specialists, or communication specialists—keep the public informed about the activities of government agencies and officials. For example, public affairs specialists in the U.S. Department of State keep the public informed of travel advisories and of U.S. positions on foreign issues. A press secretary for a member of Congress keeps constituents aware of the representative's accomplishments.

In large organizations, the key public relations executive, who often is a vice president, may develop overall plans and policies with other executives. In addition, public relations departments employ public relations specialists to write, research, prepare materials, maintain contacts, and respond to inquiries.

People who handle publicity for an individual or who direct public relations for a small organization may deal with all aspects of the job. They contact people, plan and research, and prepare materials for distribution. They also may handle advertising or sales promotion work to support marketing.

Working Conditions

Some public relations specialists work a standard 35- to 40-hour week, but unpaid overtime is common. Occasionally, they must be at the job or on call around the clock, especially if there is an emergency or crisis. Public relations offices are busy places; work schedules can be irregular and frequently interrupted. Schedules often have to be rearranged so that workers can meet deadlines, deliver speeches, attend meetings and community activities, or travel.

Employment

Public relations specialists held about 158,000 jobs in 2002. Public relations specialists are concentrated in service-providing industries such as advertising and related services; health care and social assistance; educational services; and government. Others worked for communications firms, financial institutions, and government agencies. About 11,000 public relations specialists were self-employed.

Public relations specialists are concentrated in large cities, where press services and other communications facilities are readily available and many businesses and trade associations have their headquarters. Many public relations consulting firms, for example, are in New York, Los Angeles, San Francisco, Chicago, and Washington, DC. There is a trend, however, for public relations jobs to be dispersed throughout the Nation, closer to clients.

Training, Other Qualifications, and Advancement

There are no defined standards for entry into a public relations career. A college degree combined with public relations experience, usually gained through an internship, is considered excellent preparation for public relations work; in fact, internships are becoming vital to obtaining employment. The ability to communicate effectively is essential. Many entry-level public relations specialists have a college major in public relations, journalism, advertising, or communication. Some firms seek college graduates who have worked in electronic or print journalism. Other employers seek applicants with demonstrated communication skills and training or experience in a field related to the firm's business—information technology, health, science, engineering, sales, or finance, for example.

Many colleges and universities offer bachelor's and postsecondary degrees in public relations, usually in a journalism or communications department. In addition, many other colleges offer at least one course in this field. A common public relations sequence includes courses in public relations principles and techniques; public relations management and administration, including organizational development; writing, emphasizing news releases, proposals, annual reports, scripts, speeches, and related items; visual communications, including desktop publishing and computer graphics; and research, emphasizing social science research and survey design and implementation. Courses in advertising, journalism, business administration, finance, political science, psychology, sociology, and creative writing also are helpful. Specialties are offered in public relations for business, government, and nonprofit organizations.

Many colleges help students gain part-time internships in public relations that provide valuable experience and training. The U.S. Armed Forces also can be an excellent place to gain training and experience. Membership in local chapters of the Public Relations Student Society of America (affiliated with the Public Relations Society of America) or the International Association of Business Communicators provides an opportunity for students to exchange views with public relations specialists and to make professional contacts that may help them find a job in the field. A portfolio of published articles, television or radio programs, slide presentations, and other work is an asset in finding a job. Writing for a school publication or television or radio station provides valuable experience and material for one's portfolio.

Creativity, initiative, good judgment, and the ability to express thoughts clearly and simply are essential. Decision making, problem-solving, and research skills also are important. People who choose public relations as a career need an outgoing personality, self-confidence, an understanding of human psychology, and an enthusiasm for motivating people. They should be competitive, yet able to function as part of a team and open to new ideas.

Some organizations, particularly those with large public relations staffs, have formal training programs for new employees. In smaller organizations, new employees work under the guidance of experienced staff members. Beginners often maintain files of material about company activities, scan newspapers and magazines for appropriate articles to clip, and assemble information for speeches and pamphlets. They also may answer calls from the press and public, work on invitation lists and details for press conferences, or escort visitors and clients. After gaining experience, they write news releases, speeches, and articles for publication or design and carry out public relations programs. Public relations specialists in smaller firms usually get all-around experience, whereas those in larger firms tend to be more specialized.

The Public Relations Society of America accredits public relations specialists who have at least 5 years of experience in the field and have passed a comprehensive 6-hour examination (5 hours written, 1 hour oral). The International Association of Business Communicators also has an accreditation program for professionals in the communication field, including public relations specialists. Those who meet all the requirements of the program earn the Accredited Business Communicator (ABC) designation. Candidates must have at least 5 years of experience in a communication field and pass a written and oral examination. They also must submit a portfolio of work samples demonstrating involvement in a range of communication projects and a thorough understanding of communication planning. Employers may consider professional recognition through accreditation a sign of competence in this field, which could be especially helpful in a competitive job market.

Promotion to supervisory jobs may come as public relations specialists show that they can handle more demanding assignments. In public relations firms, a beginner might be hired as a research assistant or account coordinator and be promoted to account executive, senior account executive, account manager, and, eventually, vice president. A similar career path is followed in corporate public relations, although the titles may differ. Some experienced public relations specialists start their own consulting firms. (For more information on public relations managers, see the *Handbook* statement on advertising, marketing, promotions, public relations, and sales managers.)

Job Outlook

Keen competition will likely continue for entry-level public relations jobs, as the number of qualified applicants is expected to exceed the number of job openings. Many people are attracted to this profession due to the high-profile nature of the work. Opportunities should be best for college graduates who combine a degree in journalism, public relations, advertising, or another communications-related field with a public relations internship or other related work experience. Applicants without the appropriate educational background or work experience will face the toughest obstacles.

Employment of public relations specialists is expected to increase faster than the average for all occupations through 2012. The need for good public relations in an increasingly competitive business environment should spur demand for public relations specialists in organizations of all types and sizes. The value of a company is measured not just by its balance sheet, but also by the strength of its relationships with those upon whom it depends for its success. And, in the wake of corporate scandals, more emphasis will be placed on improving the image of the client, as well as building public confidence.

Employment in public relations firms should grow as firms hire contractors to provide public relations services rather than support full-time staff. In addition to those arising from employment growth, job opportunities should result from the need to replace public relations specialists who take other jobs or who leave the occupation altogether.

Earnings
Median annual earnings for salaried public relations specialists were $41,710 in 2002. The middle 50 percent earned between $31,300 and $56,180; the lowest 10 percent earned less than $24,240, and the top 10 percent earned more than $75,100. Median annual earnings in the industries employing the largest numbers of public relations specialists in 2002 were:

Advertising and related services	$48,070
Local government	42,000
Business, professional, labor, political, and similar organizations	39,330
Colleges, universities, and professional schools	36,820

According to a joint survey conducted by the International Association of Business Communicators and the Public Relations Society of America, the median annual income for a public relations specialist was $66,800 in 2002.

Related Occupations
Public relations specialists create favorable attitudes among various organizations, special interest groups, and the public through effective communication. Other workers with similar jobs include advertising, marketing, promotions, public relations, and sales managers; demonstrators, product promoters, and models; news analysts, reporters, and correspondents; lawyers; market and survey researchers; sales representatives, wholesale and manufacturing; and police and detectives involved in community relations.

Sources of Additional Information
A comprehensive directory of schools offering degree programs, a sequence of study in public relations, a brochure on careers in public relations, and a $5 brochure entitled *Where Shall I go to Study Advertising and Public Relations?* are available from:
➤ Public Relations Society of America, Inc., 33 Irving Place, New York, NY 10003-2376. Internet: **http://www.prsa.org**

For information on accreditation for public relations professionals, contact:
➤ International Association of Business Communicators, One Hallidie Plaza, Suite 600, San Francisco, CA 94102.

Television, Video, and Motion Picture Camera Operators and Editors

(O*NET 27-4031.00, 27-4032.00)

Significant Points

● Workers acquire their skills through on-the-job or formal postsecondary training.

● Technical expertise, a "good eye," imagination, and creativity are essential.

● Keen competition for job openings is expected, because many talented peopled are attracted to the field.

● About one in five camera operators are self-employed.

Nature of the Work
Television, video, and motion picture camera operators produce images that tell a story, inform or entertain an audience, or record an event. *Film and video editors* edit soundtracks, film, and video for the motion picture, cable, and broadcast television industries. Some camera operators do their own editing.

Making commercial-quality movies and video programs requires technical expertise and creativity. Producing successful images requires choosing and presenting interesting material, selecting appropriate equipment, and applying a good eye and steady hand to assure smooth, natural movement of the camera.

Camera operators use television, video, or motion picture cameras to shoot a wide range of material, including television series, studio programs, news and sporting events, music videos, motion pictures, documentaries, and training sessions. Some camera operators film or videotape private ceremonies and special events. Those who record images on videotape are often called *videographers*. Many are employed by independent television stations, local affiliates, large cable and television networks, or smaller, independent production companies. *Studio camera operators* work in a broadcast studio and usually videotape their subjects from a fixed position. *News camera operators*, also called *electronic news gathering (ENG) operators*, work as part of a reporting team, following newsworthy events as they unfold. To capture live events, they must anticipate the action and act quickly. ENG operators may

Film and video editors edit soundtracks, film, and video.

need to edit raw footage on the spot for relay to a television affiliate for broadcast.

Camera operators employed in the entertainment field use motion picture cameras to film movies, television programs, and commercials. Those who film motion pictures are also known as *cinematographers*. Some specialize in filming cartoons or special effects. They may be an integral part of the action, using cameras in any of several different mounts. For example, the camera operator can be stationary and shoot whatever passes in front of the lens, or the camera can be mounted on a track, with the camera operator responsible for shooting the scene from different angles or directions. More recently, the introduction of digital cameras has enhanced the number of angles and the clarity that a camera operator can provide. Other camera operators sit on cranes and follow the action while crane operators move them into position. *Steadicam operators* mount a harness and carry the camera on their shoulders to provide a clear picture while they move about the action. Camera operators who work in the entertainment field often meet with directors, actors, editors, and camera assistants to discuss ways of filming, editing, and improving scenes.

Working Conditions

Working conditions for camera operators and editors vary considerably. Those employed in government, television and cable networks, and advertising agencies usually work a 5-day, 40-hour week. By contrast, ENG operators often work long, irregular hours and must be available to work on short notice. Camera operators and editors working in motion picture production also may work long, irregular hours.

ENG operators and those who cover major events, such as conventions or sporting events, frequently travel locally, stay overnight on assignments, or travel to distant places for longer periods. Camera operators filming television programs or motion pictures may travel to film on location.

Some camera operators—especially ENG operators covering accidents, natural disasters, civil unrest, or military conflicts—work in uncomfortable or even dangerous surroundings. Many camera operators must wait long hours in all kinds of weather for an event to take place and must stand or walk for long periods while carrying heavy equipment. ENG operators often work under strict deadlines.

Employment

Television, video, and motion picture camera operators held about 28,000 jobs in 2002, and film and video editors held about 19,000. About 1 in 5 camera operators were self-employed. Some self-employed camera operators contracted with television networks, documentary or independent filmmakers, advertising agencies, or trade show or convention sponsors to work on individual projects for a predetermined fee, often at a daily rate.

Most of the salaried camera operators were employed by television broadcasting stations or motion picture studios. More than half of the salaried film and video editors worked for motion picture studios. Most camera operators and editors worked in large metropolitan areas.

Training, Other Qualifications, and Advancement

Employers usually seek applicants with a "good eye," imagination, and creativity, as well as a good technical understanding of how the camera operates. Television, video, and motion picture camera operators and editors usually acquire their skills through on-the-job training or formal postsecondary training at vocational schools, colleges, universities, or photographic institutes. Formal education may be required for some positions.

Many universities, community and junior colleges, vocational-technical institutes, and private trade and technical schools offer courses in camera operation and videography. Basic courses cover equipment, processes, and techniques. Bachelor's degree programs, especially those including business courses, provide a well-rounded education.

Individuals interested in camera operations should subscribe to videographic newsletters and magazines, join clubs, and seek summer or part-time employment in cable and television networks, motion picture studios, or camera and video stores.

Camera operators in entry-level jobs learn to set up lights, cameras, and other equipment. They may receive routine assignments requiring adjustments to their cameras or decisions on what subject matter to capture. Camera operators in the film and television industries usually are hired for a project on the basis of recommendations from individuals such as producers, directors of photography, and camera assistants from previous projects or through interviews with the producer. ENG and studio camera operators who work for television affiliates usually start in small markets to gain experience.

Camera operators need good eyesight, artistic ability, and hand-eye coordination. They should be patient, accurate, and detail oriented. Camera operators also should have good communication skills and, if needed, the ability to hold a camera by hand for extended periods.

Camera operators who run their own businesses, or freelance, need business skills as well as talent. These individuals must know how to submit bids, write contracts, get permission to shoot on locations that normally are not open to the public, obtain releases to use film or tape of people, price their services, secure copyright protection for their work, and keep financial records.

With increased experience, operators may advance to more demanding assignments or to positions with larger or network television stations. Advancement for ENG operators may mean moving to larger media markets. Other camera operators and editors may become directors of photography for movie studios, advertising agencies, or television programs. Some teach at technical schools, film schools, or universities.

Job Outlook

Television, video, and motion picture camera operators and editors can expect keen competition for job openings because the work is attractive to many people. The number of individuals interested in positions as videographers and movie camera operators usually is much greater than the number of openings. Those who succeed in landing a salaried job or attracting enough work to earn a living by freelancing are likely to be the most creative, highly motivated, able to adapt to rapidly changing technologies, and adept at operating a business. Related work experience or job-related training also can benefit prospective camera operators.

Employment of camera operators and editors is expected to grow about as fast as the average for all occupations through 2012. Rapid expansion of the entertainment market, especially motion picture production and distribution, will spur growth of camera operators. In addition, computer and Internet services will provide new outlets for interactive productions. Growth will be tempered, however, by the increased off-shore production of motion pictures. Camera operators will be needed to film made-for-the-Internet broadcasts, such as live music videos, digital movies, sports features, and general information or entertainment programming. These images can be delivered directly into the home either on compact discs or over the Internet. Job growth also is expected in radio and television broadcasting.

Earnings

Median annual earnings for television, video, and motion picture camera operators were $32,720 in 2002. The middle 50 percent earned between $20,610 and $51,000. The lowest 10 percent earned less than $14,710, and the highest 10 percent earned more than $65,070. Median annual earnings were $46,540 in the motion picture and video industries and $25,830 in radio and television broadcasting.

Median annual earnings for film and video editors were $38,270 in 2002. The middle 50 percent earned between $26,780 and $55,300. The lowest 10 percent earned less than $20,030, and the highest 10 percent earned more than $78,070. Median annual earnings were $41,440 in the motion picture and video industries, which employ the largest numbers of film and video editors.

Many camera operators who work in film or video are freelancers whose earnings tend to fluctuate each year. Because most freelance camera operators purchase their own equipment, they incur considerable expense acquiring and maintaining cameras and accessories. Some camera operators belong to unions, including the International Alliance of Theatrical Stage Employees and the National Association of Broadcast Employees and Technicians.

Related Occupations

Related arts and media occupations include artists and related workers, broadcast and sound engineering technicians and radio operators, designers, and photographers.

Sources of Additional Information

Information about career and employment opportunities for camera operators and film and video editors is available from local offices of State employment service agencies, local offices of the relevant trade unions, and local television and film production companies that employ these workers.

Writers and Editors

(O*NET 27-3041.00, 27-3042.00, 27-3043.01, 27-3043.02, 27-3043.03, 27-3043.04)

Significant Points

- Most jobs in this occupation require a college degree in communications, journalism, or English, although a degree in a technical subject may be useful for technical-writing positions.

- The outlook for most writing and editing jobs is expected to be competitive, because many people with writing or journalism training are attracted to the occupation.

- Online publications and services are growing in number and sophistication, spurring the demand for writers and editors, especially those with Web experience.

Nature of the Work

Communicating through the written word, writers and editors generally fall into one of three categories. *Writers and authors* develop original fiction and nonfiction for books, magazines, trade journals, online publications, company newsletters, radio and television broadcasts, motion pictures, and advertisements. (Reporters and correspondents who collect and analyze facts about newsworthy events are described elsewhere in the *Handbook*.) *Editors* examine proposals and select material for publication or broadcast. They review and revise a writer's work for publication or dissemination. *Technical writers* develop technical materials, such as equipment manuals, appendices, or operating and maintenance instructions. They also may assist in layout work.

Most writers and editors have at least a basic familiarity with technology, regularly using personal computers, desktop or electronic publishing systems, scanners, and other electronic communications equipment. Many writers prepare material directly for the Internet. For example, they may write for electronic newspapers or magazines, create short fiction or poetry, or produce technical documentation that is available only online. Also, they may write text for Web sites. These writers should be knowledgeable about graphic design, page layout, and desktop publishing software. In addition, they should be familiar with interactive technologies of the Web so that they can blend text, graphics, and sound together.

Writers—especially of nonfiction—are expected to establish their credibility with editors and readers through strong research and the use of appropriate sources and citations. Sustaining high ethical standards and meeting publication deadlines are essential.

Creative writers, poets, and lyricists, including novelists, playwrights, and screenwriters, create original works—such as prose, poems, plays, and song lyrics—for publication or performance. Some works may be commissioned (at the request of a sponsor); others may be written for hire (on the basis of the completion of a draft or an outline).

Nonfiction writers either propose a topic or are assigned one, often by an editor or publisher. They gather information about the topic through personal observation, library and Internet research, and interviews. Writers then select the material they

Most writers and editors use computers and other communications equipment to compose and transmit written information.

want to use, organize it, and use the written word to express ideas and convey information. Writers also revise or rewrite sections, searching for the best organization or the right phrasing. *Copy writers* prepare advertising copy for use by publication or broadcast media or to promote the sale of goods and services. *Newsletter writers* produce information for distribution to association memberships, corporate employees, organizational clients, or the public.

Freelance writers sell their work to publishers, publication enterprises, manufacturing firms, public-relations departments, or advertising agencies. Sometimes, they contract with publishers to write a book or an article. Others may be hired to complete specific assignments, such as writing about a new product or technique.

Editors review, rewrite, and edit the work of writers. They may also do original writing. An editor's responsibilities vary with the employer and type and level of editorial position held. Editorial duties may include planning the content of books, technical journals, trade magazines, and other general-interest publications. Editors also decide what material will appeal to readers, review and edit drafts of books and articles, offer comments to improve the work, and suggest possible titles. In addition, they may oversee the production of the publications. In the book-publishing industry, an editor's primary responsibility is to review proposals for books and decide whether to buy the publication rights from the author.

Major newspapers and newsmagazines usually employ several types of editors. The *executive editor* oversees *assistant editors* who have responsibility for particular subjects, such as local news, international news, feature stories, or sports. Executive editors generally have the final say about what stories are published and how they are covered. The *managing editor* usually is responsible for the daily operation of the news department. *Assignment editors* determine which reporters will cover a given story. *Copy editors* mostly review and edit a reporter's copy for accuracy, content, grammar, and style.

In smaller organizations, such as small daily or weekly newspapers or membership or publications departments of nonprofit or similar organizations, a single editor may do everything or share responsibility with only a few other people. Executive and managing editors typically hire writers, reporters, and other employees. They also plan budgets and negotiate contracts with freelance writers, sometimes called "stringers" in the news industry. In broadcasting companies, *program directors* have similar responsibilities.

Editors and program directors often have assistants, many of whom hold entry-level jobs. These assistants, such as copy editors and *production assistants*, review copy for errors in grammar, punctuation, and spelling and check the copy for readability, style, and agreement with editorial policy. They suggest revisions, such as changing words and rearranging sentences, to improve clarity or accuracy. They also carry out research for writers and verify facts, dates, and statistics. Production assistants arrange page layouts of articles, photographs, and advertising; compose headlines; and prepare copy for printing. *Publication assistants* who work for publishing houses may read and evaluate manuscripts submitted by freelance writers, proofread printers' galleys, or answer letters about published material. Production assistants on small newspapers or in radio stations compile articles available from wire services or the Internet, answer phones, and make photocopies.

Technical writers put technical information into easily understandable language. They prepare operating and maintenance manuals, catalogs, parts lists, assembly instructions, sales promotion materials, and project proposals. Many technical writers work with engineers on technical subject matters to prepare written interpretations of engineering and design specifications and other information for a general readership. They plan and edit technical materials and oversee the preparation of illustrations, photographs, diagrams, and charts.

Science and medical writers prepare a range of formal documents presenting detailed information on the physical or medical sciences. They convey research findings for scientific or medical professions and organize information for advertising or public-relations needs. Many writers work with researchers on technical subjects to prepare written interpretations of data and other information for a general readership.

Working Conditions

Some writers and editors work in comfortable, private offices; others work in noisy rooms filled with the sound of keyboards and computer printers, as well as the voices of other writers tracking down information over the telephone. The search for information sometimes requires that the writer travel to diverse workplaces, such as factories, offices, or laboratories, but many find their material through telephone interviews, the library, and the Internet.

For some writers, the typical workweek runs 35 to 40 hours. However, writers occasionally work overtime to meet publication deadlines. Those who prepare morning or weekend publications and broadcasts work some nights and weekends. Freelance writers generally work more flexible hours, but their schedules must conform to the needs of the client. Deadlines and erratic work hours, often part of the daily routine in these jobs, may cause stress, fatigue, or burnout.

Changes in technology and electronic communications also affect a writer's work environment. For example, laptops allow writers to work from home or on the road. Writers and editors who use computers for extended periods may experience back pain, eyestrain, or fatigue.

Employment

Writers and editors held about 319,000 jobs in 2002. More than one-third were self-employed. Writers and authors held about 139,000 jobs; editors, about 130,000 jobs; and technical writers, about 50,000 jobs. More than one-half of jobs for writers and editors were salaried positions in the information sector, which includes newspaper, periodical, book, and directory publishers; radio and television broadcasting; software publishers; motion picture and sound recording industries; Internet service providers, web search portals, and data processing services; and Internet publishing and broadcasting. Substantial numbers also worked in advertising and related services, computer systems design and related services, and public and private educational services. Other salaried writers and editors worked in computer and electronic product manufacturing, government agencies, religious organizations, and business, professional, labor, political, and similar organizations.

Jobs with major book publishers, magazines, broadcasting companies, advertising agencies, and public-relations firms are concentrated in New York, Chicago, Los Angeles, Boston, Philadelphia, and San Francisco. Jobs with newspapers, business and professional journals, and technical and trade magazines are more widely dispersed throughout the country.

Thousands of other individuals work as freelance writers, earning some income from their articles, books, and, less commonly, television and movie scripts. Most support themselves with income derived from other sources.

Training, Other Qualifications, and Advancement

A college degree generally is required for a position as a writer or editor. Although some employers look for a broad liberal arts background, most prefer to hire people with degrees in communications, journalism, or English. For those who specialize in a particular area, such as fashion, business, or legal issues, additional background in the chosen field is expected. Knowledge of a second language is helpful for some positions.

Increasingly, technical writing requires a degree in, or some knowledge about, a specialized field—engineering, business, or one of the sciences, for example. In many cases, people with good writing skills can learn specialized knowledge on the job. Some transfer from jobs as technicians, scientists, or engineers. Others begin as research assistants or as trainees in a technical information department, develop technical communication skills, and then assume writing duties.

Writers and editors must be able to express ideas clearly and logically and should love to write. Creativity, curiosity, a broad range of knowledge, self-motivation, and perseverance also are valuable. Writers and editors must demonstrate good judgment and a strong sense of ethics in deciding what material to publish. Editors also need tact and the ability to guide and encourage others in their work.

For some jobs, the ability to concentrate amid confusion and to work under pressure is essential. Familiarity with electronic publishing, graphics, and video production equipment increasingly is needed. Online newspapers and magazines require knowledge of computer software used to combine online text with graphics, audio, video, and animation.

High school and college newspapers, literary magazines, community newspapers, and radio and television stations all provide valuable, but sometimes unpaid, practical writing experience. Many magazines, newspapers, and broadcast stations have internships for students. Interns write short pieces, conduct research and interviews, and learn about the publishing or broadcasting business.

In small firms, beginning writers and editors hired as assistants may actually begin writing or editing material right away. Opportunities for advancement can be limited, however. Many writers look for work on a short-term, project-by-project basis. Many small or not-for-profit organizations either do not have enough regular work or cannot afford to employ writers on a full-time basis. However, they routinely contract out work to freelance writers as needed.

In larger businesses, jobs usually are more formally structured. Beginners generally do research, fact checking, or copy editing. Advancement to full-scale writing or editing assignments may occur more slowly for newer writers and editors in larger organizations than for employees of smaller companies. Advancement often is more predictable, though, coming with the assignment of more important articles.

Job Outlook

Employment of writers and editors is expected to grow about as fast as the average for all occupations through the year 2012. The outlook for most writing and editing jobs is expected to be competitive, because many people with writing or journalism training are attracted to the occupation.

Employment of salaried writers and editors for newspapers, periodicals, book publishers, and nonprofit organizations is expected to increase as demand grows for these publications. Magazines and other periodicals increasingly are developing market niches, appealing to readers with special interests. Businesses and organizations are developing newsletters and websites, and more companies are experimenting with publishing materials directly for the Internet. Online publications and services are growing in number and sophistication, spurring the demand for writers and editors, especially those with Web experience. Advertising and public-relations agencies, which also are growing, should be another source of new jobs.

Opportunities should be best for technical writers and those with training in a specialized field. Demand for technical writers and writers with expertise in specialty areas, such as law, medicine, or economics, is expected to increase because of the continuing expansion of scientific and technical information and the need to communicate it to others. Developments and discoveries in the law, science, and technology generate demand for people to interpret technical information for a more general audience. Rapid growth and change in the high-technology and electronics industries result in a greater need for people to write users' guides, instruction manuals, and training materials. This work requires people who are not only technically skilled as writers, but also familiar with the subject area.

In addition to job openings created by employment growth, some openings will arise as experienced workers retire, transfer to other occupations, or leave the labor force. Replacement needs are relatively high in this occupation; many freelancers leave because they cannot earn enough money.

Earnings

Median annual earnings for salaried writers and authors were $42,790 in 2002. The middle 50 percent earned between $29,150 and $58,930. The lowest 10 percent earned less than $21,320, and the highest 10 percent earned more than $85,140. Median annual earnings were $54,520 in advertising and related services and $33,550 in newspaper, periodical, book, and directory publishers.

Median annual earnings for salaried editors were $41,170 in 2002. The middle 50 percent earned between $30,770 and $56,360. The lowest 10 percent earned less than $24,010, and the highest 10 percent earned more than $76,620. Median annual earnings in newspaper, periodical, book, and directory publishers were $40,280.

Median annual earnings for salaried technical writers were $50,580 in 2002. The middle 50 percent earned between $39,100 and $64,750. The lowest 10 percent earned less than $30,270, and the highest 10 percent earned more than $80,900. Median annual earnings in computer systems design and related services were $51,730.

According to the Society for Technical Communication, the median annual salary for entry level technical writers was $41,000 in 2002. The median annual salary for mid-level nonsupervisory technical writers was $49,900 and for senior-level non-supervisory technical writers, $66,000.

Related Occupations

Writers and editors communicate ideas and information. Other communications occupations include announcers; interpreters and translators; news analysts, reporters, and correspondents; and public relations specialists.

Sources of Additional Information

For information on careers in technical writing, contact:
➤ Society for Technical Communication, Inc., 901 N. Stuart St., Suite 904, Arlington, VA 22203. Internet: **http://www.stc.org**

Health Diagnosing and Treating Practitioners

Audiologists

(0*NET 29-1121.00)

Significant Points

● Employment of audiologists is expected to grow rapidly because the expanding population in older age groups is prone to medical conditions that result in hearing problems.

● More than half worked in healthcare facilities, and most others were employed by educational services.

● A master's degree in audiology is currently the standard credential; however, a clinical doctoral degree is expected to become the new standard.

Nature of the Work

Audiologists work with people who have hearing, balance, and related ear problems. They examine individuals of all ages and identify those with the symptoms of hearing loss and other auditory, balance, and related neural problems. They then assess the nature and extent of the problems and help the individuals manage them. Using audiometers, computers, and other testing devices, they measure the loudness at which a person begins to hear sounds, the ability to distinguish between sounds, and the impact of hearing loss or balance problems on an individual's daily life. Audiologists interpret these results and may coordinate them with medical, educational, and psychological information to make a diagnosis and determine a course of treatment.

Hearing disorders can result from a variety of causes including trauma at birth, viral infections, genetic disorders, exposure to loud noise, certain medications, or aging. Treatment may include examining and cleaning the ear canal, fitting and dispensing hearing aids, fitting and tuning cochlear implants, and audiologic rehabilitation. Audiologic rehabilitation emphasizes counseling on adjusting to hearing loss, training on the use of hearing instruments, and teaching communication strategies for use in a variety of listening environments. For example, they may provide instruction in lip reading. Audiologists also may recommend, fit, and dispense personal or large area amplification systems and alerting devices.

Audiologists provide direct clinical services to individuals with hearing or balance disorders. In audiology (hearing) clinics, they may independently develop and carry out treatment programs. Audiologists, in a variety of settings, work with other health professionals as a team in planning and implementing services for children and adults, from birth to old age. Audiologists keep records on the initial evaluation, progress, and discharge of clients. These records help pinpoint problems, track client progress, and justify the cost of treatment when applying for reimbursement.

Some audiologists specialize in work with the elderly, children, or hearing-impaired individuals who need special therapy programs. Others develop and implement ways to protect workers' ear from on-the-job injuries. They measure noise levels in workplaces and conduct hearing protection programs in factories, as well as in schools and communities.

Audiologists who work in private practice also manage the business aspects of running an office, such as developing a patient base, hiring employees, keeping records, and ordering equipment and supplies.

Audiologists may conduct research on types of—and treatment for—hearing, balance, and related disorders. Others design and develop equipment or techniques for diagnosing and treating these disorders.

Working Conditions

Audiologists usually work at a desk or table in clean, comfortable surroundings. The job is not physically demanding but does require attention to detail and intense concentration. The emotional needs of clients and their families may be demand-

Audiologists provide direct clinical services to individuals with hearing or balance disorders.

ing. Most full-time audiologists work about 40 hours per week, which may include weekends and evenings to meet the needs of patients. Some work part time. Those who work on a contract basis may spend a substantial amount of time traveling between facilities.

Employment
Audiologists held about 11,000 jobs in 2002. More than half of all jobs were in offices of physicians; hospitals; offices of other health practitioners, including audiologists; and outpatient care centers. About 1 in 5 jobs was in educational services, including elementary and secondary schools. Other jobs for audiologists were in health and personal care stores, including hearing aid stores; scientific research and development services; and State and local governments.

A small number of audiologists were self-employed in private practice. They provided hearing healthcare services in their own offices or worked under contract for schools, healthcare facilities, or other establishments.

Training, Other Qualifications, and Advancement
Of the 48 States that require a license to practice audiology, almost all require that individuals have a master's degree in audiology or the equivalent; however, a clinical doctoral degree is expected to become the new standard. A passing score on a national examination on audiology offered through the Praxis Series of the Educational Testing Service is needed, as well. Other requirements are 300 to 375 hours of supervised clinical experience and 9 months of postgraduate professional clinical experience. An additional examination may be required in order to dispense hearing aids. Forty States have continuing education requirements for licensure renewal. Medicaid, medicare, and private health insurers generally require practitioners to be licensed to qualify for reimbursement.

About 107 colleges and universities offer graduate programs in audiology in the United States. About 39 of these offer a Doctor of Audiology (Au.D.) degree. Requirements for admission to programs in audiology include courses in English, mathematics, physics, chemistry, biology, psychology, and communication sciences. Graduate course work in audiology includes anatomy; physiology; physics; genetics; normal and abnormal communication development; auditory, balance, and neural systems assessment and treatment; diagnosis and treatment; pharmacology; and ethics.

Audiologists can acquire the Certificate of Clinical Competence in Audiology (CCC-A) offered by the American Speech-Language-Hearing Association. To earn a CCC, a person must have a graduate degree and 375 hours of supervised clinical experience, complete a 36-week postgraduate clinical fellowship, and pass the Praxis Series examination in audiology, administered by the Educational Testing Service. According to the American Speech-Language-Hearing Association, as of 2007, audiologists will need to have a bachelor's degree and complete 75 hours of credit toward a doctoral degree in order to seek certification. As of 2012, audiologists will have to earn a doctoral degree in order to be certified.

Audiologists may also be certified through the American Board of Audiology. Applicants must earn a Master's or Doctoral degree in audiology from a regionally accredited college or university, achieve a passing score on a national examination in audiology, and demonstrate that they have completed a minimum of 2,000 hours of mentored professional

practice in a two-year period with a qualified audiologist. Certificants must apply for renewal every three years. They must demonstrate that they have earned 45 hours of approved continuing education within the three-year period. Beginning in the year 2007, all applicants must earn a doctoral degree in audiology.

Audiologists should be able to effectively communicate diagnostic test results, diagnoses, and proposed treatments in a manner easily understood by their clients. They must be able to approach problems objectively and provide support to clients and their families. Because a client's progress may be slow, patience, compassion, and good listening skills are necessary.

Job Outlook
Employment of audiologists is expected to grow faster than the average for all occupations through the year 2012. Because hearing loss is strongly associated with aging, rapid growth in the population age 55 and over will cause the number of persons with hearing impairment to increase markedly. In addition, members of the baby boom generation are now entering middle age, when the possibility of neurological disorders and associated hearing impairments increases. Medical advances are also improving the survival rate of premature infants and trauma and stroke victims, who then need assessment and possible treatment. Many States now require that all newborns be screened for hearing loss and receive appropriate early intervention services.

Employment in educational services will increase along with growth in elementary and secondary school enrollments, including enrollment of special education students. Federal law guarantees special education and related services to all eligible children with disabilities. Greater awareness of the importance of early identification and diagnosis of hearing disorders will also increase employment.

The number of audiologists in private practice will rise due to the increasing demand for direct services to individuals as well as increasing use of contract services by hospitals, schools, and nursing care facilities. Only a few job openings for audiologists will arise from the need to replace those who leave the occupation, because the occupation is small.

Earnings
Median annual earnings of audiologists were $48,400 in 2002. The middle 50 percent earned between $39,510 and $58,430. The lowest 10 percent earned less than $32,500, and the highest 10 percent earned more than $73,130.

According to a 2003 survey by the American Speech-Language-Hearing Association, the median annual salary for full-time certified audiologists who worked on a calendar-year basis, generally 11 or 12 months annually, was $52,000. For those who worked on an academic-year basis, usually 9 or 10 months annually, the median annual salary was $47,500. The median starting salary for certified audiologists with one to three years experience was $43,000 on a calendar-year basis. Certified audiologists who worked 25 or fewer hours per week had a median hourly salary of $28.00.

Related Occupations
Audiologists specialize in the prevention, diagnosis, and treatment of hearing problems. Workers in related occupations in-

clude occupational therapists, optometrists, physical therapists, psychologists, recreational therapists, rehabilitation counselors, and speech-language pathologists.

Sources of Additional Information
State licensing boards can provide information on licensure requirements. State departments of education can supply information on certification requirements for those who wish to work in public schools.

General information on careers in audiology is available from:
➤ American Speech-Language-Hearing Association, 10801 Rockville Pike, Rockville, MD 20852. Internet: **http://www.asha.org**
➤ Academy of Audiology, 11730 Plaza America Dr., Suite 300, Reston, VA 20190. Internet: **http://www.audiology.org**

Chiropractors

(0*NET 29-1011.00)

Significant Points

● Chiropractors must be licensed, requiring 2 to 4 years of undergraduate education, completion of a 4-year chiropractic college course, and passing scores on national and State examinations.

● Employment is expected to increase faster than average as a result of research and changing attitudes about alternative healthcare practices.

● Job prospects should be good; establishing a new practice will be easiest in areas with a low concentration of chiropractors.

● As with other types of independent practice, earnings for chiropractors are relatively low in the beginning, but increase as the practice grows.

Nature of the Work
Chiropractors, also known as *doctors of chiropractic* or *chiropractic physicians*, diagnose and treat patients whose health problems are associated with the body's muscular, nervous, and skeletal systems, especially the spine. Chiropractors believe that interference with these systems impairs the body's normal functions and lowers its resistance to disease. They also hold that spinal or vertebral dysfunction alters many important body functions by affecting the nervous system and that skeletal imbalance through joint or articular dysfunction, especially in the spine, can cause pain.

The chiropractic approach to healthcare is holistic, stressing the patient's overall health and wellness. It recognizes that many factors affect health, including exercise, diet, rest, environment, and heredity. Chiropractors provide natural, drugless, nonsurgical health treatments and rely on the body's inherent recuperative abilities. They also recommend changes in lifestyle—in eating, exercise, and sleeping habits, for example—to their patients. When appropriate, chiropractors consult with and refer patients to other health practitioners.

Like other health practitioners, chiropractors follow a standard routine to secure the information they need for diagnosis and treatment. They take the patient's medical history, conduct physical, neurological, and orthopedic examinations, and may

order laboratory tests. X rays and other diagnostic images are important tools because of the chiropractor's emphasis on the spine and its proper function. Chiropractors also employ a postural and spinal analysis common to chiropractic diagnosis.

In cases in which difficulties can be traced to the involvement of musculoskeletal structures, chiropractors manually adjust the spinal column. Some chiropractors use water, light, massage, ultrasound, electric, and heat therapy. They also may apply supports such as straps, tapes, and braces. Chiropractors counsel patients about wellness concepts such as nutrition, exercise, changes in lifestyle, and stress management, but do not prescribe drugs or perform surgery.

Some chiropractors specialize in sports injuries, neurology, orthopedics, pediatrics, nutrition, internal disorders, or diagnostic imaging.

Many chiropractors are solo or group practitioners who also have the administrative responsibilities of running a practice. In larger offices, chiropractors delegate these tasks to office managers and chiropractic assistants. Chiropractors in private practice are responsible for developing a patient base, hiring employees, and keeping records.

Working Conditions
Chiropractors work in clean, comfortable offices. Their average workweek is about 40 hours, although longer hours are not uncommon. Solo practitioners set their own hours, but may work evenings or weekends to accommodate patients.

A chiropractor manually adjusts the spine to relieve pressure.

Like other health practitioners, chiropractors are sometimes on their feet for long periods. Chiropractors who take x rays must employ appropriate precautions against the dangers of repeated exposure to radiation.

Employment

Chiropractors held about 49,000 jobs in 2002. Most chiropractors are in solo practice, although some are in group practice or work for other chiropractors. A small number teach, conduct research at chiropractic institutions, or work in hospitals and clinics.

Many chiropractors are located in small communities. There are geographic imbalances in the distribution of chiropractors, in part because many establish practices close to chiropractic institutions.

Training, Other Qualifications, and Advancement

All States and the District of Columbia regulate the practice of chiropractic and grant licenses to chiropractors who meet educational and examination requirements established by the State. Chiropractors can practice only in States where they are licensed. Some States have agreements permitting chiropractors licensed in one State to obtain a license in another without further examination, provided that their educational, examination, and practice credentials meet State specifications.

Most State boards require at least 2 years of undergraduate education; an increasing number are requiring a 4-year bachelor's degree. All boards require the completion of a 4-year program at an accredited chiropractic college leading to the Doctor of Chiropractic degree.

For licensure, most State boards recognize either all or part of the four-part test administered by the National Board of Chiropractic Examiners. State examinations may supplement the National Board tests, depending on State requirements.

To maintain licensure, almost all States require the completion of a specified number of hours of continuing education each year. Chiropractic associations and accredited chiropractic programs and institutions offer continuing education programs. Specialty councils within some chiropractic associations also offer programs leading to clinical specialty certification, called "diplomate" certification, in areas such as orthopedics, neurology, sports injuries, occupational and industrial health, nutrition, diagnostic imaging, thermography, and internal disorders.

In 2003, 16 chiropractic programs and 2 chiropractic institutions in the United States were accredited by the Council on Chiropractic Education. Applicants are required to have at least 90 semester hours of undergraduate study leading toward a bachelor's degree, including courses in English, the social sciences or humanities, organic and inorganic chemistry, biology, physics, and psychology. Many applicants have a bachelor's degree, which may eventually become the minimum entry requirement. Several chiropractic colleges offer prechiropractic study, as well as a bachelor's degree program. Recognition of prechiropractic education offered by chiropractic colleges varies among the State boards.

During the first 2 years, most chiropractic programs emphasize classroom and laboratory work in basic science subjects such as anatomy, physiology, public health, microbiology, pathology, and biochemistry. The last 2 years stress courses in manipulation and spinal adjustment and provide clinical experience in physical and laboratory diagnosis, neurology, orthopedics, geriatrics, physiotherapy, and nutrition. Chiropractic programs and institutions grant the degree of Doctor of Chiropractic.

Chiropractic requires keen observation to detect physical abnormalities. It also takes considerable manual dexterity, but not unusual strength or endurance, to perform adjustments. Chiropractors should be able to work independently and handle responsibility. As in other health-related occupations, empathy, understanding, and the desire to help others are good qualities for dealing effectively with patients.

Newly licensed chiropractors can set up a new practice, purchase an established one, or enter into partnership with an established practitioner. They also may take a salaried position with an established chiropractor, a group practice, or a healthcare facility.

Job Outlook

Job prospects are expected to be good for persons who enter the practice of chiropractic. Employment of chiropractors is expected to grow faster than the average for all occupations through the year 2012 as consumer demand for alternative healthcare grows. Chiropractors emphasize the importance of healthy lifestyles and do not prescribe drugs or perform surgery. As a result, chiropractic care is appealing to many health-conscious Americans. Chiropractic treatment of the back, neck, extremities, and joints has become more accepted as a result of research and changing attitudes about alternative, noninvasive healthcare practices. The rapidly expanding older population, with its increased likelihood of mechanical and structural problems, also will increase demand for chiropractors.

Demand for chiropractic treatment also is related to the ability of patients to pay, either directly or through health insurance. Although more insurance plans now cover chiropractic services, the extent of such coverage varies among plans. Increasingly, chiropractors must educate communities about the benefits of chiropractic care in order to establish a successful practice.

In this occupation, replacement needs arise almost entirely from retirements. Chiropractors usually remain in the occupation until they retire; few transfer to other occupations. Establishing a new practice will be easiest in areas with a low concentration of chiropractors.

Earnings

Median annual earnings of salaried chiropractors were $65,330 in 2002. The middle 50 percent earned between $44,140 and $102,400 a year.

Self-employed chiropractors usually earn more than salaried chiropractors. According to the American Chiropractic Association, in 2000, the average income for all chiropractors, including the self-employed, was about $81,500 after expenses. In chiropractic, as in other types of independent practice, earnings are relatively low in the beginning and increase as the practice grows. Geographic location and the characteristics and qualifications of the practitioner also may influence earnings. Self-employed chiropractors must provide for their own health insurance and retirement.

Related Occupations

Chiropractors treat patients and work to prevent bodily disorders and injuries. So do dentists, occupational therapists, optometrists, physical therapists, physicians and surgeons, podiatrists, and veterinarians.

Sources of Additional Information

General information on chiropractic as a career is available from:

➤ American Chiropractic Association, 1701 Clarendon Blvd., Arlington, VA 22209. Internet: **http://www.amerchiro.org**

➤ International Chiropractors Association, 1110 North Glebe Rd., Suite 1000, Arlington, VA 22201. Internet: **http://www.chiropractic.org**

➤ World Chiropractic Alliance, 2950 N. Dobson Rd., Suite 1, Chandler, AZ 85224-1802.

➤ Dynamic Chiropractic, P.O. Box 40109, Huntington, CA 92605-4109.

For a list of chiropractic programs and institutions, as well as general information on chiropractic education, contact:

➤ Council on Chiropractic Education, 8049 North 85th Way, Scottsdale, AZ 85258-4321. Internet: **http://www.cce-usa.org**.

For information on State education and licensure requirements, contact:

➤ Federation of Chiropractic Licensing Boards, 901 54th Ave., Suite 101, Greeley, CO 80634-4400. Internet: **http://www.fclb.org**

For information on admission requirements to a specific chiropractic college, as well as scholarship and loan information, contact the college's admissions office.

Dentists

(0*NET 29-1021.00, 29-1022.00, 29-1023.00, 29-1024.00, 29-1029.99)

Significant Points

● Most dentists are solo practitioners.

● Dentists usually complete at least 8 years of education beyond high school.

● Employment is projected to grow more slowly than average, and most job openings will result from the need to replace the large number of dentists expected to retire.

● Job prospects should be good.

Nature of the Work

Dentists diagnose, prevent, and treat problems with teeth or mouth tissue. They remove decay, fill cavities, examine x rays, place protective plastic sealants on children's teeth, straighten teeth, and repair fractured teeth. They also perform corrective surgery on gums and supporting bones to treat gum diseases. Dentists extract teeth and make models and measurements for dentures to replace missing teeth. They provide instruction on diet, brushing, flossing, the use of fluorides, and other aspects of dental care. They also administer anesthetics and write prescriptions for antibiotics and other medications.

Dentists use a variety of equipment, including x-ray machines, drills, and instruments such as mouth mirrors, probes, forceps, brushes, and scalpels. They wear masks, gloves, and safety glasses to protect themselves and their patients from infectious diseases.

Dentists in private practice oversee a variety of administrative tasks, including bookkeeping and buying equipment and supplies. They may employ and supervise dental hygienists, dental assistants, dental laboratory technicians, and receptionists. (These occupations are described elsewhere in the *Handbook*.)

Most dentists are general practitioners, handling a variety of dental needs. Other dentists practice in any of nine specialty areas. *Orthodontists*, the largest group of specialists, straighten teeth by applying pressure to the teeth with braces or retainers.

The next largest group, *oral and maxillofacial surgeons*, operates on the mouth and jaws. The remainder may specialize as *pediatric dentists* (focusing on dentistry for children); *periodontists* (treating gums and bone supporting the teeth); *prosthodontists* (replacing missing teeth with permanent fixtures, such as crowns and bridges, or removable fixtures, such as dentures); *endodontists* (performing root canal therapy); *public-health dentists* (promoting good dental health and preventing dental diseases within the community); *oral pathologists* (studying oral diseases); or *oral and maxillofacial radiologists* (diagnosing diseases in the head and neck through the use of imaging technologies).

Working Conditions

Most dentists work 4 or 5 days a week. Some work evenings and weekends to meet their patients' needs. Most full-time dentists work between 35 and 40 hours a week, but others work more. Initially, dentists may work more hours as they establish their practice. Experienced dentists often work fewer hours. A considerable number continue in part-time practice well beyond the usual retirement age.

Most dentists are solo practitioners, meaning that they own their own businesses and work alone or with a small staff. Some dentists have partners, and a few work for other dentists as associate dentists.

Employment

Dentists held about 153,000 jobs in 2002. About 2 in 5 dentists were self-employed. Almost all dentists work in private practice. According to the American Dental Association (ADA), about 80 percent of dentists in private practice are sole proprietors, and 13 percent belong to a partnership. A small number of salaried dentists work in hospitals and offices of physicians.

Training, Other Qualifications, and Advancement

All 50 States and the District of Columbia require dentists to be licensed. To qualify for a license in most States, a candidate must graduate from one of the 55 dental schools accredited by the ADA's Commission on Dental Accreditation in 2002 and also must pass written and practical examinations. Candidates may fulfill the written part of the State licensing requirements by passing the National Board Dental Examinations. Individual

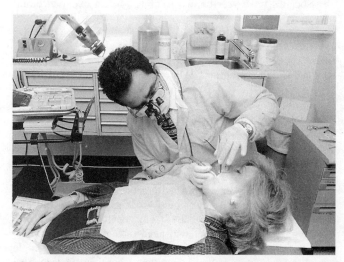

Most dentists are general practitioners, handling a variety of dental needs.

States or regional testing agencies administer the written or practical examinations.

Dental schools require a minimum of 2 years of college-level predental education, regardless of the major chosen. However, most dental students have at least a bachelor's degree. Predental education emphasizes course work in science, and many applicants to dental school major in a science such as biology or chemistry, while other applicants major in another subject and take many science courses as well. A small number of applicants are accepted to dental school after 2 or 3 years of college and complete their bachelor's degree while attending dental school.

All dental schools require applicants to take the Dental Admissions Test (DAT). When selecting students, schools consider scores earned on the DAT, applicants' grade point averages, and information gathered through recommendations and interviews. Competition for admission to dental school is keen.

Dental school usually lasts 4 academic years. Studies begin with classroom instruction and laboratory work in basic sciences, including anatomy, microbiology, biochemistry, and physiology. Beginning courses in clinical sciences, including laboratory techniques, also are provided at this time. During the last 2 years, students treat patients, usually in dental clinics, under the supervision of licensed dentists.

Most dental schools award the degree of Doctor of Dental Surgery (DDS). The rest award an equivalent degree, Doctor of Dental Medicine (DMD).

Currently, about 17 States license or certify dentists who intend to practice in a specialty area. Requirements include 2 to 4 years of postgraduate education and, in some cases, the completion of a special State examination. Most State licenses permit dentists to engage in both general and specialized practice. Dentists who want to teach or conduct research usually spend an additional 2 to 5 years in advanced dental training, in programs operated by dental schools or hospitals.

Dentistry requires diagnostic ability and manual skills. Dentists should have good visual memory, excellent judgment regarding space and shape, a high degree of manual dexterity, and scientific ability. Good business sense, self-discipline, and good communication skills are helpful for success in private practice. High school and college students who want to become dentists should take courses in biology, chemistry, physics, health, and mathematics.

Some dental school graduates work for established dentists as associates for a year or two in order to gain experience and save money to equip an office of their own. Most dental school graduates, however, purchase an established practice or open a new one immediately after graduation. According to the ADA, each year about 12 percent of new graduates enroll in postgraduate training programs to prepare for a dental specialty.

Job Outlook

Employment of dentists is expected to grow more slowly than the average for all occupations through 2012. Although employment growth will provide some job opportunities, most jobs will result from the need to replace the large number of dentists projected to retire. Job prospects should be good as new dentists take over established practices or start their own.

Demand for dental care should grow substantially through 2012. As members of the baby-boom generation advance into middle age, a large number will need maintenance on complicated dental work, such as bridges. In addition, elderly people are more likely to retain their teeth than were their predecessors, so they will require much more care than in the past. The younger generation will continue to need preventive checkups despite

treatments such as fluoridation of the water supply, which decreases the incidence of tooth decay. However, employment of dentists is not expected to grow as rapidly as the demand for dental services, because, as their practices expand, dentists are likely to hire more dental hygienists and dental assistants to handle routine services.

Dental care will focus more on prevention, including teaching people how to take better care of their teeth. Dentists will increasingly provide care that is aimed at preventing the loss of teeth—rather than simply providing treatments, such as fillings. Improvements in dental technology also will allow dentists to offer more effective and less painful treatment to their patients.

Earnings

Median annual earnings of salaried dentists were $123,210 in 2002. Earnings vary according to number of years in practice, location, hours worked, and specialty.

Self-employed dentists in private practice tend to earn more than salaried dentists. A relatively large proportion of dentists is self-employed. Like other business owners, these dentists must provide their own health insurance, life insurance, and retirement benefits.

Related Occupations

Dentists examine, diagnose, prevent, and treat diseases and abnormalities. So do chiropractors, optometrists, physicians and surgeons, podiatrists, psychologists, and veterinarians.

Sources of Additional Information

For information on dentistry as a career, a list of accredited dental schools, and a list of State boards of dental examiners, contact:

➤ American Dental Association, Commission on Dental Accreditation, 211 E. Chicago Ave., Chicago, IL 60611. Internet: **http://www.ada.org**

For information on admission to dental schools, contact:

➤ American Dental Education Association, 1625 Massachusetts Ave. NW., Suite 600, Washington, DC 20036. Internet: **http://www.adea.org**

Persons interested in practicing dentistry should obtain the requirements for licensure from the board of dental examiners of the State in which they plan to work.

Prospective dental students should contact the office of student financial aid at the schools to which they apply, in order to obtain information on scholarships, grants, and loans, including Federal financial aid.

Dietitians and Nutritionists

(O*NET 29-1031.00)

Significant Points

- Most jobs were in hospitals, nursing care facilities, and offices of physicians or other health practitioners.

- Dietitians and nutritionists need at least a bachelor's degree in dietetics, foods and nutrition, food service systems management, or a related area.

- Average employment growth is expected; however, growth may be constrained if employers substitute other workers for dietitians and if limitations are placed on insurance reimbursement for dietetic services.

Nature of the Work

Dietitians and nutritionists plan food and nutrition programs and supervise the preparation and serving of meals. They help to prevent and treat illnesses by promoting healthy eating habits and recommending dietary modifications, such as the use of less salt for those with high blood pressure or the reduction of fat and sugar intake for those who are overweight.

Dietitians manage food service systems for institutions such as hospitals and schools, promote sound eating habits through education, and conduct research. Major areas of practice include clinical, community, management, and consultant dietetics.

Clinical dietitians provide nutritional services for patients in institutions such as hospitals and nursing care facilities. They assess patients' nutritional needs, develop and implement nutrition programs, and evaluate and report the results. They also confer with doctors and other healthcare professionals in order to coordinate medical and nutritional needs. Some clinical dietitians specialize in the management of overweight patients or the care of critically ill or renal (kidney) and diabetic patients. In addition, clinical dietitians in nursing care facilities, small hospitals, or correctional facilities may manage the food service department.

Community dietitians counsel individuals and groups on nutritional practices designed to prevent disease and promote health. Working in places such as public health clinics, home health agencies, and health maintenance organizations, community dietitians evaluate individual needs, develop nutritional care plans, and instruct individuals and their families. Dietitians working in home health agencies provide instruction on grocery shopping and food preparation to the elderly, individuals with special needs, and children.

Increased public interest in nutrition has led to job opportunities in food manufacturing, advertising, and marketing. In these areas, dietitians analyze foods, prepare literature for distribution, or report on issues such as the nutritional content of recipes, dietary fiber, or vitamin supplements.

Management dietitians oversee large-scale meal planning and preparation in healthcare facilities, company cafeterias, prisons, and schools. They hire, train, and direct other dietitians and food service workers; budget for and purchase food, equipment, and supplies; enforce sanitary and safety regulations; and prepare records and reports.

Dietitians and nutritionists usually work in clean, well-lighted, and well-ventilated areas.

Consultant dietitians work under contract with healthcare facilities or in their own private practice. They perform nutrition screenings for their clients and offer advice on diet-related concerns such as weight loss or cholesterol reduction. Some work for wellness programs, sports teams, supermarkets, and other nutrition-related businesses. They may consult with food service managers, providing expertise in sanitation, safety procedures, menu development, budgeting, and planning.

Working Conditions

In 2002, most full-time dietitians and nutritionists worked a regular 40-hour week, although some worked weekends. About 1 in 4 worked part time.

Dietitians and nutritionists usually work in clean, well-lighted, and well-ventilated areas. However, some dietitians work in warm, congested kitchens. Many dietitians and nutritionists are on their feet for much of the workday.

Employment

Dietitians and nutritionists held about 49,000 jobs in 2002. More than half of all jobs were in hospitals, nursing care facilities, outpatient care centers, or offices of physicians and other health practitioners. State and local government agencies provided about 1 job in 5—mostly in correctional facilities, health departments, and other public health-related areas. Some dietitians and nutritionists were employed in special food services, an industry which includes firms that provide food services on contract to facilities such as colleges and universities, airlines, correctional facilities, and company cafeterias. Other jobs were in public and private educational services, community care facilities for the elderly (which includes assisted-living facilities), individual and family services, home healthcare services, and the Federal Government—mostly in the U.S. Department of Veterans Affairs.

Some dietitians were self-employed, working as consultants to facilities such as hospitals and nursing care facilities or providing dietary counseling to individual clients.

Training, Other Qualifications, and Advancement

High school students interested in becoming a dietitian or nutritionist should take courses in biology, chemistry, mathematics, health, and communications. Dietitians and nutritionists need at least a bachelor's degree in dietetics, foods and nutrition, food service systems management, or a related area. College students in these majors take courses in foods, nutrition, institution management, chemistry, biochemistry, biology, microbiology, and physiology. Other suggested courses include business, mathematics, statistics, computer science, psychology, sociology, and economics.

Of the 46 States and jurisdictions with laws governing dietetics, 30 require licensure, 15 require certification, and 1 requires registration. The Commission on Dietetic Registration of the American Dietetic Association (ADA) awards the Registered Dietitian credential to those who pass a certification exam after completing their academic coursework and supervised experience. Because practice requirements vary by State, interested candidates should determine the requirements of the State in which they want to work before sitting for any exam.

As of 2003, there were about 230 bachelor's and master's degree programs approved by the ADA's Commission on Accreditation for Dietetics Education (CADE). Supervised practice experience can be acquired in two ways. The first requires the completion of a CADE-accredited coordinated program. As of 2003, there were more than 50 accredited programs, which combined academic and supervised practice experience and generally lasted 4 to 5 years. The second option requires the completion of 900 hours of supervised practice experience in any of the 264 CADE-accredited/approved internships. These internships may be full-time programs lasting 6 to 12 months or part-time programs lasting 2 years. Students interested in research, advanced clinical positions, or public health may need an advanced degree.

Experienced dietitians may advance to assistant director, associate director, or director of a dietetic department or may become self-employed. Some dietitians specialize in areas such as renal or pediatric dietetics. Others may leave the occupation to become sales representatives for equipment, pharmaceutical, or food manufacturers.

Job Outlook

Employment of dietitians is expected to grow about as fast as the average for all occupations through 2012 as a result of increasing emphasis on disease prevention through improved dietary habits. A growing and aging population will boost the demand for meals and nutritional counseling in hospitals, nursing care facilities, schools, prisons, community health programs, and home healthcare agencies. Public interest in nutrition and increased emphasis on health education and prudent lifestyles will also spur demand, especially in management. In addition to employment growth, job openings will result from the need to replace experienced workers who leave the occupation.

On the one hand, the number of dietitian positions in nursing care facilities and in State government is expected to decline slightly, as these establishments continue to contract out food service operations. On the other hand, employment is expected to grow rapidly in contract providers of food services, outpatient care centers, and offices of physicians and other health practitioners.

Employment growth for dietitians and nutritionists may be constrained if some employers substitute other workers, such as health educators, food service managers, and dietetic technicians. Growth also may be curbed by limitations on insurance reimbursement for dietetic services.

Earnings

Median annual earnings of dietitians and nutritionists were $41,170 in 2002. The middle 50 percent earned between $33,210 and $49,830. The lowest 10 percent earned less than $25,520, and the highest 10 percent earned more than $58,700. In 2002, median annual earnings in general medical and surgical hospitals, the industry employing the largest number of dietitians and nutritionists, were $41,910.

According to the American Dietetic Association, median annual income for registered dietitians in 2002 varied by practice area as follows: $60,000 in consultation and business; $55,000 in food and nutrition management; $54,800 in education and research; $44,000 in clinical nutrition/ambulatory care; $43,300 in clinical nutrition/long-term care; $43,200 in community nutrition; and $40,800 in clinical nutrition/acute care. Salaries

also vary by years in practice, educational level, geographic region, and size of the community.

Related Occupations

Workers in other occupations who may apply the principles of food and nutrition include food service managers, health educators, and registered nurses.

Sources of Additional Information

For a list of academic programs, scholarships, and other information about dietetics, contact:
➤ The American Dietetic Association, 120 South Riverside Plaza, Suite 2000, Chicago, IL 60606-6995. Internet: **http://www.eatright.org**

Occupational Therapists

(O*NET 29-1122.00)

Significant Points

- Employment is projected to increase faster than the average, as rapid growth in the number of middle-aged and elderly individuals increases the demand for therapeutic services.

- A bachelor's degree in occupational therapy is the minimum educational requirement; beginning in 2007, however, a master's degree or higher will be required.

- Occupational therapists are increasingly taking on supervisory roles.

- More than a quarter of occupational therapists work part time.

Nature of the Work

Occupational therapists (OTs) help people improve their ability to perform tasks in their daily living and working environments. They work with individuals who have conditions that are mentally, physically, developmentally, or emotionally disabling. They also help them to develop, recover, or maintain daily living and work skills. Occupational therapists help clients not only to improve their basic motor functions and reasoning abilities, but also to compensate for permanent loss of function. Their goal is to help clients have independent, productive, and satisfying lives.

Occupational therapists assist clients in performing activities of all types, ranging from using a computer to caring for daily needs such as dressing, cooking, and eating. Physical exercises may be used to increase strength and dexterity, while other activities may be chosen to improve visual acuity and the ability to discern patterns. For example, a client with short-term memory loss might be encouraged to make lists to aid recall, and a person with coordination problems might be assigned exercises to improve hand-eye coordination. Occupational therapists also use computer programs to help clients improve decisionmaking, abstract-reasoning, problem-solving, and perceptual skills, as well as memory, sequencing, and coordination—all of which are important for independent living.

Therapists instruct those with permanent disabilities, such as spinal cord injuries, cerebral palsy, or muscular dystrophy, in the use of adaptive equipment, including wheelchairs, splints,

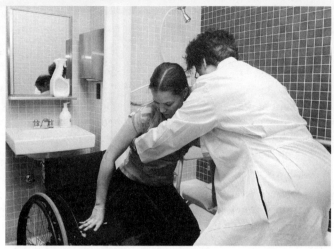

Occupational therapists help people improve their ability to perform tasks in their daily living and working environments.

and aids for eating and dressing. They also design or make special equipment needed at home or at work. Therapists develop computer-aided adaptive equipment and teach clients with severe limitations how to use that equipment in order to communicate better and control various aspects of their environment.

Some occupational therapists treat individuals whose ability to function in a work environment has been impaired. These practitioners arrange employment, evaluate the work environment, plan work activities, and assess the client's progress. Therapists also may collaborate with the client and the employer to modify the work environment so that the work can be successfully completed.

Occupational therapists may work exclusively with individuals in a particular age group or with particular disabilities. In schools, for example, they evaluate children's abilities, recommend and provide therapy, modify classroom equipment, and help children participate as fully as possible in school programs and activities. Occupational therapy also is beneficial to the elderly population. Therapists help the elderly lead more productive, active, and independent lives through a variety of methods, including the use of adaptive equipment.

Occupational therapists in mental-health settings treat individuals who are mentally ill, mentally retarded, or emotionally disturbed. To treat these problems, therapists choose activities that help people learn to engage in and cope with daily life. Activities include time management skills, budgeting, shopping, homemaking, and the use of public transportation. Occupational therapists also may work with individuals who are dealing with alcoholism, drug abuse, depression, eating disorders, or stress-related disorders.

Assessing and recording a client's activities and progress is an important part of an occupational therapist's job. Accurate records are essential for evaluating clients, for billing, and for reporting to physicians and other healthcare providers.

Working Conditions
Occupational therapists in hospitals and other healthcare and community settings usually worked a 40-hour week. Those in schools may participate in meetings and other activities during

and after the school day. In 2002, more than a quarter of occupational therapists worked part time.

In large rehabilitation centers, therapists may work in spacious rooms equipped with machines, tools, and other devices generating noise. The work can be tiring, because therapists are on their feet much of the time. Those providing home healthcare services may spend time driving from appointment to appointment. Therapists also face hazards such as back strain from lifting and moving clients and equipment.

Therapists increasingly are taking on supervisory roles. Due to rising healthcare costs, third-party payers are beginning to encourage occupational therapist assistants and aides to take more hands-on responsibility. By having assistants and aides work more closely with clients under the guidance of a therapist, the cost of therapy should decline.

Employment
Occupational therapists held about 82,000 jobs in 2002. About 1 in 10 occupational therapists held more than one job. The largest number of jobs was in hospitals. Other major employers were offices of other health practitioners (which includes offices of occupational therapists), public and private educational services, and nursing care facilities. Some occupational therapists were employed by home healthcare services, outpatient care centers, offices of physicians, individual and family services, community care facilities for the elderly, and government agencies.

A small number of occupational therapists were self-employed in private practice. These practitioners saw clients referred by physicians or other health professionals or provided contract or consulting services to nursing care facilities, schools, adult daycare programs, and home healthcare agencies.

Training, Other Qualifications, and Advancement
Currently, a bachelor's degree in occupational therapy is the minimum requirement for entry into this field. Beginning in 2007, however, a master's degree or higher will be the minimum educational requirement. As a result, students in bachelor's-level programs should complete their coursework and fieldwork before 2007. All States, Puerto Rico, and the District of Columbia regulate the practice of occupational therapy. To obtain a license, applicants must graduate from an accredited educational program and pass a national certification examination. Those who pass the exam are awarded the title "Occupational Therapist Registered (OTR)."

In 2003, entry-level education was offered in 38 bachelor's degree programs, 3 postbaccalaureate certificate programs for students with a degree other than occupational therapy, and 86 entry-level master's degree programs. There were 48 programs that offered a combined bachelor's and master's degree and 5 offered an entry-level doctoral degree. Most schools have full-time programs, although a growing number also offer weekend or part-time programs.

Occupational therapy coursework includes physical, biological, and behavioral sciences and the application of occupational therapy theory and skills. Completion of 6 months of supervised fieldwork also is required.

Persons considering this profession should take high school courses in biology, chemistry, physics, health, art, and the social sciences. College admissions offices also look favorably at paid or volunteer experience in the healthcare field.

Occupational therapists need patience and strong interpersonal skills to inspire trust and respect in their clients. Ingenuity and imagination in adapting activities to individual needs are assets. Those working in home healthcare services must be able to adapt to a variety of settings.

Job Outlook

Employment of occupational therapists is expected to increase faster than the average for all occupations through 2012. The impact of proposed Federal legislation imposing limits on reimbursement for therapy services may adversely affect the job market for occupational therapists in the near term. However, over the long run, the demand for occupational therapists should continue to rise as a result of growth in the number of individuals with disabilities or limited function who require therapy services. The baby-boom generation's movement into middle age, a period when the incidence of heart attack and stroke increases, will spur the demand for therapeutic services. Growth in the population 75 years and older—an age group that suffers from high incidences of disabling conditions—also will increase the demand for therapeutic services. In addition, medical advances now enable more patients with critical problems to survive—patients who ultimately may need extensive therapy.

Hospitals will continue to employ a large number of occupational therapists to provide therapy services to acutely ill inpatients. Hospitals also will need occupational therapists to staff their outpatient rehabilitation programs.

Employment growth in schools will result from the expansion of the school-age population and extended services for disabled students. Therapists will be needed to help children with disabilities prepare to enter special education programs.

Earnings

Median annual earnings of occupational therapists were $51,990 in 2002. The middle 50 percent earned between $42,910 and $ 61,620. The lowest 10 percent earned less than $35,130, and the highest 10 percent earned more than $74,390. Median annual earnings in the industries employing the largest numbers of occupational therapists in 2002 were as follows:

Offices of other health practitioners	$53,660
Nursing care facilities	53,930
General medical and surgical hospitals	53,210
Elementary and secondary schools	45,740

Related Occupations

Occupational therapists use specialized knowledge to help individuals perform daily living skills and achieve maximum independence. Other workers performing similar duties include audiologists, chiropractors, physical therapists, recreational therapists, rehabilitation counselors, respiratory therapists, and speech-language pathologists.

Sources of Additional Information

For more information on occupational therapy as a career, contact:

➤ American Occupational Therapy Association, 4720 Montgomery Lane, Bethesda, MD 20824-1220. Internet: **http://www.aota.org**

Optometrists

(0*NET 29-1041.00)

Significant Points

● Licensed optometrists must earn a Doctor of Optometry degree from an accredited optometry school and pass a written and a clinical State board examination.

● Admission to optometry school is competitive.

● Optometrists usually remain in practice until they retire, so relatively few job openings arise from the need to replace those who leave the occupation.

Nature of the Work

Optometrists, also known as *doctors of optometry,* or *ODs,* provide most primary vision care. They examine people's eyes to diagnose vision problems and eye diseases, and they test patients' visual acuity, depth and color perception, and ability to focus and coordinate the eyes. Optometrists prescribe eyeglasses and contact lenses and provide vision therapy and low-vision rehabilitation. Optometrists analyze test results and develop a treatment plan. They administer drugs to patients to aid in the diagnosis of vision problems and prescribe drugs to treat some eye diseases. Optometrists often provide preoperative and postoperative care to cataract patients, as well as patients who have had laser vision correction or other eye surgery. They also diagnose conditions due to systemic diseases such as diabetes and high blood pressure, referring patients to other health practitioners as needed.

Optometrists should not be confused with ophthalmologists or dispensing opticians. Ophthalmologists are physicians who perform eye surgery, and diagnose and treat eye diseases and injuries. Like optometrists, they also examine eyes and prescribe eyeglasses and contact lenses. Dispensing opticians fit and adjust eyeglasses and, in some States, may fit contact lenses according to prescriptions written by ophthalmologists or optometrists. (See the sections on physicians and surgeons; and opticians, dispensing, elsewhere in the *Handbook.*)

Most optometrists are in general practice. Some specialize in work with the elderly, children, or partially sighted persons who need specialized visual devices. Others develop and implement ways to protect workers' eyes from on-the-job strain or injury. Some specialize in contact lenses, sports vision, or vision therapy. A few teach optometry, perform research, or consult.

Most optometrists are private practitioners who also handle the business aspects of running an office, such as developing a patient base, hiring employees, keeping records, and ordering equipment and supplies. Optometrists who operate franchise optical stores also may have some of these duties.

Working Conditions

Optometrists work in places—usually their own offices—that are clean, well lighted, and comfortable. Most full-time optometrists work about 40 hours a week. Many work weekends and evenings to suit the needs of patients. Emergency calls, once uncommon, have increased with the passage of therapeutic-drug laws expanding optometrists' ability to prescribe medications.

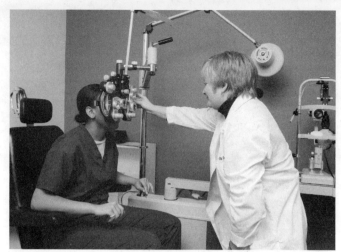

Most optometrists are private practitioners who also handle the business aspects of running an office.

Employment

Optometrists held about 32,000 jobs in 2002. The number of jobs is greater than the number of practicing optometrists because some optometrists hold two or more jobs. For example, an optometrist may have a private practice, but also work in another practice, in a clinic, or in a vision care center. According to the American Optometric Association, about two-thirds of practicing optometrists are in private practice. Although many optometrists practice alone, a growing number are in a partnership or group practice.

Salaried jobs for optometrists were primarily in offices of other health practitioners, including optometrists; offices of physicians, including ophthalmologists; or health and personal care stores, including optical goods stores. A small number of salaried jobs for optometrists were in hospitals; the Federal government; or outpatient care centers, including health maintenance organizations. Almost a third of optometrists were self-employed.

Training, Other Qualifications, and Advancement

All States and the District of Columbia require that optometrists be licensed. Applicants for a license must have a Doctor of Optometry degree from an accredited optometry school and pass both a written and a clinical State board examination. In many States, applicants can substitute the examinations of the National Board of Examiners in Optometry, usually taken during the student's academic career, for part or all of the written examination. Licenses are renewed every 1 to 3 years, and, in all States, continuing education credits are needed for renewal.

The Doctor of Optometry degree requires the completion of a 4-year program at an accredited optometry school, preceded by at least 3 years of preoptometric study at an accredited college or university. Most optometry students hold a bachelor's or higher degree. In 2002, 17 U.S. schools and colleges of optometry held an accredited status with the Accreditation Council on Optometric Education of the American Optometric Association.

Requirements for admission to schools of optometry include courses in English, mathematics, physics, chemistry, and biology. A few schools also require or recommend courses in psychology, history, sociology, speech, or business. Since a strong background in science is important, many applicants to optometry school major in a science such as biology or chemistry, while other applicants major in another subject and take many science courses as well. Applicants must take the Optometry Admissions Test, which measures academic ability and scientific comprehension. Most applicants take the test after their sophomore or junior year, allowing them an opportunity to take the test again and raise their score. A small number of applicants are accepted to optometry school after 3 years of college and complete their bachelor's degree while attending optometry school. Admission to optometry school is competitive.

Optometry programs include classroom and laboratory study of health and visual sciences, as well as clinical training in the diagnosis and treatment of eye disorders. Courses in pharmacology, optics, vision science, biochemistry, and systemic disease are included.

Business ability, self-discipline, and the ability to deal tactfully with patients are important for success. The work of optometrists requires attention to detail and manual dexterity.

Optometrists wishing to teach or do research may study for a master's or Ph.D. degree in visual science, physiological optics, neurophysiology, public health, health administration, health information and communication, or health education. One-year postgraduate clinical residency programs are available for optometrists who wish to specialize in family practice optometry, pediatric optometry, geriatric optometry, vision therapy, contact lenses, hospital-based optometry, primary care optometry, or ocular disease.

Job Outlook

Employment of optometrists is expected to grow about as fast as the average for all occupations through 2012, in response to the vision care needs of a growing and aging population. As baby boomers age, they will be more likely to visit optometrists and ophthalmologists because of the onset of vision problems in middle age, including those resulting from the extensive use of computers. The demand for optometric services also will increase because of growth in the oldest age group, with its increased likelihood of cataracts, glaucoma, diabetes, and hypertension. Greater recognition of the importance of vision care, rising personal incomes, and growth in employee vision care plans will spur employment growth, as well.

Employment of optometrists would grow more rapidly were it not for anticipated productivity gains that will allow each optometrist to see more patients. These expected gains stem from greater use of optometric assistants and other support personnel, who will reduce the amount of time optometrists need with each patient. Also, laser surgery that can correct some vision problems is available, but expensive. Optometrists will still be needed to perform preoperative and postoperative care for laser surgery; however, patients who successfully undergo this surgery may not require optometrists to prescribe glasses or contacts for several years.

In addition to growth, the need to replace optometrists who leave the occupation will create employment opportunities. Relatively few opportunities from this source are expected, however, because optometrists usually continue to practice until they retire; few transfer to other occupations.

Earnings

Median annual earnings of salaried optometrists were $86,090 in 2002. The middle 50 percent earned between $62,030 and $115,550. Median annual earnings of salaried optometrists in

2002 were $87,070 in offices of other health practitioners. Salaried optometrists tend to earn more initially than do optometrists who set up their own independent practice. In the long run, however, those in private practice usually earn more.

According to the American Optometric Association, median net annual income for all optometrists, including the self-employed, was $110,000 in 2002. The middle 50 percent earned between $82,500 and $156,500.

Related Occupations
Other workers who apply scientific knowledge to prevent, diagnose, and treat disorders and injuries are chiropractors, dentists, physicians and surgeons, podiatrists, and veterinarians.

Sources of Additional Information
For information on optometry as a career and a list of accredited optometric educational institutions, contact:
➤ Association of Schools and Colleges of Optometry, 6110 Executive Blvd., Suite 510, Rockville, MD 20852. Internet: **http://www.opted.org**

Additional career information is available from:
➤ American Optometric Association, Educational Services, 243 North Lindbergh Blvd., St. Louis, MO 63141-7881. Internet: **http://www.aoanet.org**

The Board of Optometry in each State can supply information on licensing requirements.

For information on specific admission requirements and sources of financial aid, contact the admissions officers of individual optometry schools.

Pharmacists

(0*NET 29-1051.00)

Significant Points

- Pharmacists are becoming more involved in drug therapy decisionmaking and patient counseling.

- A license is required; one must graduate from an accredited college of pharmacy and pass a State examination.

- Very good employment opportunities are expected.

- Earnings are very high, but some pharmacists work long hours, nights, weekends, and holidays.

Nature of the Work
Pharmacists dispense drugs prescribed by physicians and other health practitioners and provide information to patients about medications and their use. They advise physicians and other health practitioners on the selection, dosages, interactions, and side effects of medications. Pharmacists also monitor the health and progress of patients in response to drug therapy to ensure safe and effective use of medication. Pharmacists must understand the use, clinical effects, and composition of drugs, including their chemical, biological, and physical properties. Compounding—the actual mixing of ingredients to form powders, tablets, capsules, ointments, and solutions—is a small part of a pharmacist's practice, because most medicines are produced by pharmaceutical companies in a standard dosage and drug deliv-

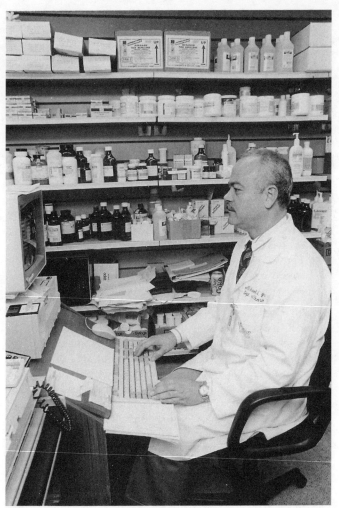

Pharmacists must check records to ensure that patients are not allergic to new medications.

ery form. Traditionally, most pharmacists work in a community setting, such as a retail drugstore, or in a healthcare facility, such as a hospital, nursing home, mental health institution, or neighborhood health clinic.

Pharmacists in community and retail pharmacies counsel patients and answer questions about prescription drugs, including questions regarding possible side effects or interactions among various drugs. They provide information about over-the-counter drugs and make recommendations after talking with the patient. They also may give advice about diet, exercise, or stress management, or about durable medical equipment and home healthcare supplies. They also may complete third-party insurance forms and other paperwork. Those who own or manage community pharmacies may sell non-health-related merchandise, hire and supervise personnel, and oversee the general operation of the pharmacy. Some community pharmacists provide specialized services to help patients manage conditions such as diabetes, asthma, smoking cessation, or high blood pressure. Some community pharmacists are also certified to administer vaccinations.

Pharmacists in healthcare facilities dispense medications and advise the medical staff on the selection and effects of drugs. They may make sterile solutions and buy medical supplies. They also assess, plan, and monitor drug programs or regimens. They counsel patients on the use of drugs while in the hospital, and on their use at home when the patients are discharged. Pharmacists also may evaluate drug use patterns and outcomes for patients in hospitals or managed care organizations.

Pharmacists who work in home healthcare monitor drug therapy and prepare infusions—solutions that are injected into patients—and other medications for use in the home.

Some pharmacists specialize in specific drug therapy areas, such as intravenous nutrition support, oncology (cancer), nuclear pharmacy (used for chemotherapy), geriatric pharmacy, and psychopharmacotherapy (the treatment of mental disorders with drugs).

Most pharmacists keep confidential computerized records of patients' drug therapies to ensure that harmful drug interactions do not occur. Pharmacists are responsible for the accuracy of every prescription that is filled, but they often rely upon pharmacy technicians and pharmacy aides to assist them in the dispensing process. Thus, the pharmacist may delegate prescription-filling and administrative tasks and supervise their completion. They also frequently oversee pharmacy students serving as interns in preparation for graduation and licensure.

Increasingly, pharmacists pursue nontraditional pharmacy work. Some are involved in research for pharmaceutical manufacturers, developing new drugs and therapies and testing their effects on people. Others work in marketing or sales, providing expertise to clients on a drug's use, effectiveness, and possible side effects. Some pharmacists also work for health insurance companies, developing pharmacy benefit packages and carrying out cost-benefit analyses on certain drugs. Other pharmacists work for the government and pharmacy associations. Finally, some pharmacists are employed full time or part time as college faculty, teaching classes and performing research in a wide range of areas.

Working Conditions

Pharmacists work in clean, well-lighted, and well-ventilated areas. Many pharmacists spend most of their workday on their feet. When working with sterile or potentially dangerous pharmaceutical products, pharmacists wear gloves and masks and work with other special protective equipment. Many community and hospital pharmacies are open for extended hours or around the clock, so pharmacists may work evenings, nights, weekends, and holidays. Consultant pharmacists may travel to nursing homes or other facilities to monitor patients' drug therapy.

About 19 percent of pharmacists worked part time in 2002. Most full-time salaried pharmacists worked about 40 hours a week. Some, including many self-employed pharmacists, worked more than 50 hours a week.

Employment

Pharmacists held about 230,000 jobs in 2002. About 62 percent work in community pharmacies that are either independently owned or part of a drugstore chain, grocery store, department store, or mass merchandiser. Most community pharmacists are salaried employees, but some are self-employed owners. About 22 percent of salaried pharmacists work in hospitals, and others work in clinics, mail-order pharmacies, pharmaceutical wholesalers, home healthcare agencies, or the Federal Government.

Training, Other Qualifications, and Advancement

A license to practice pharmacy is required in all States, the District of Columbia, and U.S. territories. To obtain a license, one must graduate from a college of pharmacy accredited by the American Council on Pharmaceutical Education (ACPE) and pass an examination. All States except California require the North American Pharmacist Licensure Exam (NAPLEX) and the Multistate Pharmacy Jurisprudence Exam (MPJE), both administered by the National Association of Boards of Pharmacy. California has its own pharmacist licensure exam. In addition to the NAPLEX and MPJE, some States require additional exams unique to their State. All States except California currently grant a license without extensive re-examination to qualified pharmacists already licensed by another State. In Florida, reexamination is not required if a pharmacist passed the NAPLEX and MPJE within 12 years of his or her application for license transfer. Many pharmacists are licensed to practice in more than one State. States may require continuing education for license renewal. Persons interested in a career as a pharmacist should check with State boards of pharmacy for details on examination requirements and license transfer procedures.

In 2002, 85 colleges of pharmacy were accredited to confer degrees by the American Council on Pharmaceutical Education. Pharmacy programs grant the degree of Doctor of Pharmacy (Pharm.D.), which requires at least 6 years of postsecondary study and the passing of the licensure examination of a State board of pharmacy. Courses offered at colleges of pharmacy are designed to teach students how to dispense prescriptions and communicate with patients and other health care providers about drug information and patient care. Students also learn professional ethics. In addition to classroom study, students in the Pharm.D. program are provided in-depth exposure to and active participation in a variety of pharmacy practice settings under the supervision of licensed pharmacists. The Pharm.D. degree has replaced the Bachelor of Pharmacy (B.Pharm.) degree, which is no longer offered to new students and will cease to be awarded after 2005.

The Pharm.D. is a 4-year program that requires at least 2 years of college study prior to admittance, although most applicants have 3 years prior to entering the program. Entry requirements usually include courses in mathematics and natural sciences, such as chemistry, biology, and physics, as well as courses in the humanities and social sciences. Approximately half of all colleges require the applicant to take the Pharmacy College Admissions Test (PCAT).

In 2003, the American Association of Colleges of Pharmacy (AACP) launched the Pharmacy College Application Service, known as PharmCAS, for students interested in applying to schools and colleges of pharmacy. This centralized service allows applicants to use a single Web-based application and one set of transcripts to apply to multiple Pharm.D. degree programs. A total of 43 pharmacy programs participated in 2003.

In the 2002-03 academic year, 66 colleges of pharmacy awarded the master of science degree or the Ph.D. degree. Both the master's and Ph.D. degrees are awarded after completion of a Pharm.D. degree. These degrees are designed for those who want more laboratory and research experience. Many master's and Ph.D. degree holders do research for a drug company or teach at a university. Other options for pharmacy graduates who are interested in further training include 1- or 2-year residency programs or fellowships. Pharmacy residencies are postgraduate training programs in pharmacy practice, and usually require the completion of a research study. Pharmacy fellowships are highly individualized programs designed to prepare participants to work in research laboratories. Some pharmacists who run their own pharmacy obtain a master's degree in business administration (MBA).

Areas of graduate study include pharmaceutics and pharmaceutical chemistry (physical and chemical properties of drugs and dosage forms), pharmacology (effects of drugs on the body), and pharmacy administration.

Prospective pharmacists should have scientific aptitude, good communication skills, and a desire to help others. They also must be conscientious and pay close attention to detail, because the decisions they make affect human lives.

In community pharmacies, pharmacists usually begin at the staff level. In independent pharmacies, after they gain experience and secure the necessary capital, some become owners or part owners of pharmacies. Pharmacists in chain drugstores may be promoted to pharmacy supervisor or manager at the store level, then to manager at the district or regional level, and later to an executive position within the chain's headquarters.

Hospital pharmacists may advance to supervisory or administrative positions. Pharmacists in the pharmaceutical industry may advance in marketing, sales, research, quality control, production, packaging, or other areas.

Job Outlook

Very good employment opportunities are expected for pharmacists over the 2002-12 period because the number of degrees granted in pharmacy is expected to be less than the number of job openings created by employment growth and the need to replace pharmacists who retire or otherwise leave the occupation. Recently, enrollments in pharmacy programs are rising as more students are attracted by high salaries and good job prospects. Despite this increase in enrollments, pharmacist jobs should still be more numerous than those seeking employment.

Employment of pharmacists is expected to grow faster than the average for all occupations through the year 2012, due to the increased pharmaceutical needs of a growing elderly population and increased use of medications. The growing numbers of middle-aged and elderly people—who, on average, use more prescription drugs than do younger people—will continue to spur demand for pharmacists in all employment settings. Other factors likely to increase the demand for pharmacists include scientific advances that will make more drug products available, new developments in genome research and medication distribution systems, increasingly sophisticated consumers seeking more information about drugs, and coverage of prescription drugs by a greater number of health insurance plans and by Medicare.

Community pharmacies are taking steps to manage increasing prescription volume. Automation of drug dispensing and greater employment of pharmacy technicians and pharmacy aides will help these establishments to dispense more prescriptions.

With its emphasis on cost control, managed care encourages the use of lower cost prescription drug distributors, such as mail-order firms and online pharmacies, for purchases of certain medications. Prescriptions ordered through the mail via the Internet are filled in a central location and shipped to the patient at a lower cost. Mail-order and online pharmacies typically use automated technology to dispense medication and employ fewer pharmacists. If the utilization of mail-order pharmacies increases rapidly, job growth among pharmacists could be limited.

Employment of pharmacists will not grow as fast in hospitals as in other industries, as hospitals reduce inpatient stays, downsize, and consolidate departments. The increase in outpatient surgeries means more patients are discharged and purchase medications through retail, supermarket, or mail-order pharmacies, rather than through the hospital. An aging population means more pharmacy services are required in nursing homes, assisted living facilities, and home care settings, where the most rapid job growth among pharmacists is expected.

New opportunities are emerging for pharmacists in managed-care organizations, where they may analyze trends and patterns in medication use for their populations of patients, and for pharmacists trained in research, disease management, and pharmacoeconomics—determining the costs and benefits of different drug therapies. Pharmacists also will have opportunities to work in research and development as well as sales and marketing for pharmaceutical manufacturing firms. New breakthroughs in biotechnology will increase the potential for drugs to treat diseases and expand the opportunities for pharmacists to conduct research and sell medications.

Job opportunities for pharmacists in patient care will arise as cost-conscious insurers and health systems continue to emphasize the role of pharmacists in primary and preventive health services. Health insurance companies realize that the expense of using medication to treat diseases and various health conditions often is considerably less than the potential costs for patients whose conditions go untreated. Pharmacists also can reduce the expenses resulting from unexpected complications due to allergic reactions or medication interactions.

Earnings

Median annual wage and salary earnings of pharmacists in 2002 were $77,050. The middle 50 percent earned between $66,210 and $87,250 a year. The lowest 10 percent earned less than $54,110, and the highest 10 percent earned more than $94,570 a year. Median annual earnings in the industries employing the largest numbers of pharmacists in 2002 were as follows:

Grocery stores	$78,270
Health and personal care stores	76,800
General medical and surgical hospitals	76,620

Related Occupations

Pharmacy technicians and pharmacy aides also work in pharmacies. Persons in other professions who may work with pharmaceutical compounds include biological scientists, medical scientists, and chemists and materials scientists. Increasingly, pharmacists are involved in patient care and therapy, work that they have in common with physicians and surgeons.

Sources of Additional Information

For information on pharmacy as a career, preprofessional and professional requirements, programs offered by colleges of pharmacy, and student financial aid, contact:

➤ American Association of Colleges of Pharmacy, 1426 Prince St., Alexandria, VA 22314. Internet: http://www.aacp.org

General information on careers in pharmacy is available from:

➤ American Society of Health-System Pharmacists, 7272 Wisconsin Ave., Bethesda, MD 20814. Internet: http://www.ashp.org

➤ National Association of Chain Drug Stores, 413 N. Lee St., P.O. Box 1417-D49, Alexandria, VA 22313-1480. Internet: http://www.nacds.org

Information on the North American Pharmacist Licensure Exam (NAPLEX) and the Multistate Pharmacy Jurisprudence Exam (MPJE) is available from:
➤ National Association of Boards of Pharmacy, 700 Busse Hwy., Park Ridge, IL 60068. Internet: **http://www.nabp.net**

State licensure requirements are available from each State's Board of Pharmacy. Information on specific college entrance requirements, curriculums, and financial aid is available from any college of pharmacy.

Physical Therapists

(0*NET 29-1123.00)

Significant Points

- Employment is expected to increase faster than the average, as growth in the number of individuals with disabilities or limited function spurs demand for therapy services.

- After graduating from an accredited physical therapist educational program, therapists must pass a licensure exam before they can practice.

- About two-thirds of physical therapists work either in hospitals or in offices of physical therapists.

Nature of the Work

Physical therapists (PTs) provide services that help restore function, improve mobility, relieve pain, and prevent or limit permanent physical disabilities of patients suffering from injuries or disease. They restore, maintain, and promote overall fitness and health. Their patients include accident victims and individuals with disabling conditions such as low-back pain, arthritis, heart disease, fractures, head injuries, and cerebral palsy.

Therapists examine patients' medical histories and then test and measure the patients' strength, range of motion, balance and coordination, posture, muscle performance, respiration, and motor function. They also determine patients' ability to be independent and reintegrate into the community or workplace after injury or illness. Next, physical therapists develop treatment plans describing a treatment strategy, its purpose, and its anticipated outcome. Physical therapist assistants, under the direction and supervision of a physical therapist, may be involved in implementing treatment plans with patients. Physical therapist aides perform routine support tasks, as directed by the therapist. (*Physical therapist assistants and aides* are discussed elsewhere in the *Handbook*.)

Treatment often includes exercise for patients who have been immobilized and lack flexibility, strength, or endurance. Physical therapists encourage patients to use their own muscles to increase their flexibility and range of motion before finally advancing to other exercises that improve strength, balance, coordination, and endurance. The goal is to improve how an individual functions at work and at home.

Physical therapists also use electrical stimulation, hot packs or cold compresses, and ultrasound to relieve pain and reduce swelling. They may use traction or deep-tissue massage to relieve pain. Therapists also teach patients to use assistive and adaptive devices, such as crutches, prostheses, and wheelchairs. They also may show patients exercises to do at home to expedite their recovery.

As treatment continues, physical therapists document the patient's progress, conduct periodic examinations, and modify treatments when necessary. Besides tracking the patient's progress, such documentation identifies areas requiring more or less attention.

Physical therapists often consult and practice with a variety of other professionals, such as physicians, dentists, nurses, educators, social workers, occupational therapists, speech-language pathologists, and audiologists.

Some physical therapists treat a wide range of ailments; others specialize in areas such as pediatrics, geriatrics, orthopedics, sports medicine, neurology, and cardiopulmonary physical therapy.

Working Conditions

Physical therapists practice in hospitals, clinics, and private offices that have specially equipped facilities, or they treat patients in hospital rooms, homes, or schools.

In 2002, most full-time physical therapists worked a 40-hour week; some worked evenings and weekends to fit their patients' schedules. More than 1 in 5 physical therapists worked part time. The job can be physically demanding because therapists often have to stoop, kneel, crouch, lift, and stand for long periods. In addition, physical therapists move heavy equipment and lift patients or help them turn, stand, or walk.

Physical therapists may use traction or deep-tissue massage to relieve pain.

Employment

Physical therapists held about 137,000 jobs in 2002. The number of jobs is greater than the number of practicing physical therapists, because some physical therapists hold two or more jobs. For example, some may work in a private practice, but also work part time in another healthcare facility.

About two-thirds of jobs for physical therapists were either in hospitals or in offices of other health practitioners (which includes offices of physical therapists). Other jobs were in home healthcare services, nursing care facilities, outpatient care centers, and offices of physicians. Some physical therapists were self-employed in private practices, seeing individual patients and contracting to provide services in hospitals, rehabilitation centers, nursing care facilities, home healthcare agencies, adult daycare programs, and schools. Physical therapists also teach in academic institutions and conduct research.

Training, Other Qualifications, and Advancement

All States require physical therapists to pass a licensure exam before they can practice, after graduating from an accredited physical therapist educational program.

According to the American Physical Therapy Association, there were 203 accredited physical therapist programs in 2003. Of the accredited programs, 113 offered master's degrees, and 90 offered doctoral degrees. All physical therapist programs seeking accreditation are required to offer degrees at the master's degree level and above, in accordance with the Commission on Accreditation in Physical Therapy Education.

Physical therapist programs start with basic science courses such as biology, chemistry, and physics and then introduce specialized courses, including biomechanics, neuroanatomy, human growth and development, manifestations of disease, examination techniques, and therapeutic procedures. Besides getting classroom and laboratory instruction, students receive supervised clinical experience. Among the courses that are useful when one applies to a physical therapist educational program are anatomy, biology, chemistry, social science, mathematics, and physics. Before granting admission, many professional education programs require experience as a volunteer in a physical therapy department of a hospital or clinic.

Physical therapists should have strong interpersonal skills in order to be able to educate patients about their physical therapy treatments. PTs also should be compassionate and possess a desire to help patients. Similar traits are needed to interact with the patient's family.

Physical therapists are expected to continue their professional development by participating in continuing education courses and workshops. In fact, a number of States require continuing education as a condition of maintaining one's licensure.

Job Outlook

Employment of physical therapists is expected to grow faster than the average for all occupations through 2012. The impact of proposed Federal legislation imposing limits on reimbursement for therapy services may adversely affect the short-term job outlook for physical therapists. However, over the long run, the demand for physical therapists should continue to rise as growth in the number of individuals with disabilities or limited function spurs demand for therapy services. The growing elderly population is particularly vulnerable to chronic and debilitating conditions that require therapeutic services. Also, the baby-boom generation is entering the prime age for heart attacks and strokes, increasing the demand for cardiac and physical rehabilitation. Further, young people will need physical therapy as technological advances save the lives of a larger proportion of newborns with severe birth defects.

Future medical developments also should permit a higher percentage of trauma victims to survive, creating additional demand for rehabilitative care. In addition, growth may result from advances in medical technology that could permit the treatment of more disabling conditions.

Widespread interest in health promotion also should increase demand for physical therapy services. A growing number of employers are using physical therapists to evaluate worksites, develop exercise programs, and teach safe work habits to employees in the hope of reducing injuries.

Earnings

Median annual earnings of physical therapists were $57,330 in 2002. The middle 50 percent earned between $48,480 and $70,050. The lowest 10 percent earned less than $40,200, and the highest 10 percent earned more than $86,260. Median annual earnings in the industries employing the largest numbers of physical therapists in 2002 were as follows:

Home health care services	$62,480
Offices of other health practitioners	58,510
Offices of physicians	57,640
Nursing care facilities	57,570
General medical and surgical hospitals	57,200

Related Occupations

Physical therapists rehabilitate persons with physical disabilities. Others who work in the rehabilitation field include audiologists, chiropractors, occupational therapists, recreational therapists, rehabilitation counselors, respiratory therapists, and speech-language pathologists.

Sources of Additional Information

Additional career information and a list of accredited educational programs in physical therapy are available from:
➤ American Physical Therapy Association, 1111 North Fairfax St., Alexandria, VA 22314-1488. Internet: **http://www.apta.org**

Physician Assistants

(0*NET 29-1071.00)

Significant Points

● The typical physician assistant program lasts about 2 years and requires at least 2 years of college and some healthcare experience for admission.

● Most applicants to physician assistant programs hold a bachelor's or master's degree.

● Job opportunities should be good, particularly in rural and inner city clinics.

● Earnings are high.

Nature of the Work

Physician assistants (PAs) provide healthcare services under the supervision of physicians. They should not be confused with medical assistants, who perform routine clinical and clerical tasks. (Medical assistants are discussed elsewhere in the *Handbook*.) PAs are formally trained to provide diagnostic, therapeutic, and preventive healthcare services, as delegated by a physician. Working as members of the healthcare team, they take medical histories, examine and treat patients, order and interpret laboratory tests and x rays, make diagnoses, and prescribe medications. They also treat minor injuries, by suturing, splinting, and casting. PAs record progress notes, instruct and counsel patients, and order or carry out therapy. In 47 States and the District of Columbia, physician assistants may prescribe medications. PAs also may have managerial duties. Some order medical and laboratory supplies and equipment and may supervise technicians and assistants.

Physician assistants work under the supervision of a physician. However, PAs may be the principal care providers in rural or inner city clinics, where a physician is present for only 1 or 2 days each week. In such cases, the PA confers with the supervising physician and other medical professionals as needed or as required by law. PAs also may make house calls or go to hospitals and nursing care facilities to check on patients, after which they report back to the physician.

The duties of physician assistants are determined by the supervising physician and by State law. Aspiring PAs should investigate the laws and regulations in the States in which they wish to practice.

Many PAs work in primary care specialties, such as general internal medicine, pediatrics, and family medicine. Others specialty areas include general and thoracic surgery, emergency medicine, orthopedics, and geriatrics. PAs specializing in surgery provide preoperative and postoperative care and may work as first or second assistants during major surgery.

Working Conditions

Although PAs usually work in a comfortable, well-lighted environment, those in surgery often stand for long periods, and others do considerable walking. Schedules vary according to the practice setting, and often depend on the hours of the supervising physician. The workweek of hospital-based PAs may include weekends, nights, or early morning hospital rounds to visit patients. These workers also may be on call. PAs in clinics usually work a 40-hour week.

Physician assistants conduct medical examinations under a physician's supervision.

Employment

Physician assistants held about 63,000 jobs in 2002. The number of jobs is greater than the number of practicing PAs because some hold two or more jobs. For example, some PAs work with a supervising physician, but also work in another practice, clinic, or hospital. According to the American Academy of Physician Assistants, almost 90 percent of certified PAs were in clinical practice in 2003.

More than half of jobs for PAs were in the offices of physicians or other health practitioners. About a quarter were in hospitals. The rest were mostly in outpatient care centers, the Federal government, educational services, and employment services.

Training, Other Qualifications, and Advancement

All States require that new PAs complete an accredited, formal education program. In 2002 there were about 133 accredited or provisionally accredited education programs for physician assistants. Sixty-eight of these programs offered a master's degree, and the rest offered either a bachelor's degree or an associate degree. Most PA graduates have at least a bachelor's degree.

Admission requirements vary, but many programs require 2 years of college and some work experience in the healthcare field. Students should take courses in biology, English, chemistry, mathematics, psychology, and the social sciences. Most applicants to PA programs hold a bachelor's or master's degree. Many PAs have backgrounds as registered nurses, while others come from varied backgrounds, including military corpsman/medics and allied health occupations such as respiratory therapists, physical therapists, and emergency medical technicians and paramedics.

PA programs usually last at least 2 years and are full time. Most programs are in schools of allied health, academic health centers, medical schools, or 4-year colleges; a few are in community colleges, the military, or hospitals. Many accredited PA programs have clinical teaching affiliations with medical schools.

PA education includes classroom instruction in biochemistry, pathology, human anatomy, physiology, microbiology, clinical pharmacology, clinical medicine, geriatric and home healthcare, disease prevention, and medical ethics. Students obtain supervised clinical training in several areas, including primary care medicine, inpatient medicine, surgery, obstetrics and gynecology, geriatrics, emergency medicine, psychiatry, and pediatrics. Sometimes, PA students serve one or more of these "rotations" under the supervision of a physician who is seeking to hire a PA. The rotations often lead to permanent employment.

All States and the District of Columbia have legislation governing the qualifications or practice of physician assistants. All jurisdictions require physician assistants to pass the Physician Assistants National Certifying Examination, administered by the National Commission on Certification of Physician Assistants (NCCPA) and open to graduates of accredited PA education programs. Only those successfully completing the examination may use the credential "Physician Assistant-Certified." In order to remain certified, PAs must complete 100 hours of continuing medical education every 2 years. Every 6 years, they must pass a recertification examination or complete an alternative program combining learning experiences and a take-home examination.

Some PAs pursue additional education in a specialty such as surgery, neonatology, or emergency medicine. PA postgraduate residency training programs are available in areas such as internal medicine, rural primary care, emergency medicine, surgery, pediatrics, neonatology, and occupational medicine. Candidates must be graduates of an accredited program and be certified by the NCCPA.

Physician assistants need leadership skills, self-confidence, and emotional stability. They must be willing to continue studying throughout their career to keep up with medical advances.

As they attain greater clinical knowledge and experience, PAs can advance to added responsibilities and higher earnings. However, by the very nature of the profession, clinically practicing PAs always are supervised by physicians.

Job Outlook
Employment of PAs is expected to grow much faster than the average for all occupations through the year 2012, due to anticipated expansion of the health services industry and an emphasis on cost containment, resulting in increasing utilization of PAs by physicians and healthcare institutions.

Physicians and institutions are expected to employ more PAs to provide primary care and to assist with medical and surgical procedures because PAs are cost-effective and productive members of the healthcare team. Physician assistants can relieve physicians of routine duties and procedures. Telemedicine—using technology to facilitate interactive consultations between physicians and physician assistants—also will expand the use of physician assistants. Job opportunities for PAs should be good, particularly in rural and inner city clinics, because those settings have difficulty attracting physicians.

Besides the traditional office-based setting, PAs should find a growing number of jobs in institutional settings such as hospitals, academic medical centers, public clinics, and prisons. Additional PAs may be needed to augment medical staffing in inpatient teaching hospital settings as the number of hours physician residents are permitted to work is reduced, encouraging hospitals to use PAs to supply some physician resident services. Opportunities will be best in States that allow PAs a wider scope of practice.

Earnings
Median annual earnings of physician assistants were $64,670 in 2002. The middle 50 percent earned between $49,640 and $77,280. The lowest 10 percent earned less than $35,410, and the highest 10 percent earned more than $90,350. Median annual earnings of physician assistants in 2002 were $65,910 in general medical and surgical hospitals and $64,170 in offices of physicians.

According to the American Academy of Physician Assistants, median income for physician assistants in full-time clinical practice in 2003 was about $72,457; median income for first-year graduates was about $63,437. Income varies by specialty, practice setting, geographical location, and years of experience.

Related Occupations
Other health workers who provide direct patient care that requires a similar level of skill and training include audiologists, occupational therapists, physical therapists, and speech-language pathologists.

Sources of Additional Information
For information on a career as a physician assistant, contact:

➤ American Academy of Physician Assistants Information Center, 950 North Washington St., Alexandria, VA 22314-1552. Internet: http://www.aapa.org

For a list of accredited programs and a catalog of individual PA training programs, contact:
➤ Association of Physician Assistant Programs, 950 North Washington St., Alexandria, VA 22314-1552. Internet: http://www.apap.org

For eligibility requirements and a description of the Physician Assistant National Certifying Examination, contact:
➤ National Commission on Certification of Physician Assistants, Inc., 6849-B Peachtree Dunwoody Rd., Atlanta, GA 30328. Internet: http://www.nccpa.net

Physicians and Surgeons

(O*NET 29-1061.00, 29-1062.00, 29-1063.00, 29-1064.00, 29-1065.00, 29-1066.00, 29-1067.00, 29-1069.99)

Significant Points

● Many physicians and surgeons work long, irregular hours; almost one-third of physicians worked 60 or more hours a week in 2002.

● New physicians are much less likely to enter solo practice and more likely to work as salaried employees of group medical practices, clinics, hospitals, or health networks.

● Formal education and training requirements are among the most demanding of any occupation, but earnings are among the highest.

Nature of the Work
Physicians and surgeons serve a fundamental role in our society and have an effect upon all our lives. They diagnose illnesses and prescribe and administer treatment for people suffering from injury or disease. Physicians examine patients, obtain medical histories, and order, perform, and interpret diagnostic tests. They counsel patients on diet, hygiene, and preventive healthcare.

There are two types of physicians: M.D.—Doctor of Medicine—and D.O.—Doctor of Osteopathic Medicine. M.D.s also are known as allopathic physicians. While both M.D.s and D.O.s may use all accepted methods of treatment, including drugs and surgery, D.O.s place special emphasis on the body's musculoskeletal system, preventive medicine, and holistic patient care. D.O.s are more likely than M.D.s to be primary care specialists although they can be found in all specialties. About half of D.O.s practice general or family medicine, general internal medicine, or general pediatrics.

Physicians work in one or more of several specialties, including, but not limited to, anesthesiology, family and general medicine, general internal medicine, general pediatrics, obstetrics and gynecology, psychiatry, and surgery.

Anesthesiologists. Anesthesiologists focus on the care of surgical patients and pain relief. Like other physicians, they evaluate and treat patients and direct the efforts of those on their staffs. Anesthesiologists confer with other physicians and surgeons about appropriate treatments and procedures before, during, and after operations. These critical specialists are responsible for maintenance of the patient's vital life functions—heart rate, body temperature, blood pressure, breathing—through continual monitoring and assessment during surgery.

Family and general practitioners. Family and general practitioners are often the first point of contact for people seeking health care, acting as the traditional family doctor. They assess and treat a wide range of conditions, ailments, and injuries, from sinus and respiratory infections to broken bones and scrapes. Family and general practitioners typically have a patient base of regular, long-term visitors. Patients with more serious conditions are referred to specialists or other healthcare facilities for more intensive care.

General internists. General internists diagnose and provide nonsurgical treatment for diseases and injuries of internal organ systems. They provide care mainly for adults who have a wide range of problems associated with the internal organs, such as the stomach, kidneys, liver, and digestive tract. Internists use a variety of diagnostic techniques to treat patients through medication or hospitalization. Like general practitioners, general internists are commonly looked upon as primary care specialists. They have patients referred to them by other specialists, in turn referring patients to those and yet other specialists when more complex care is required.

General pediatricians. Providing care from birth to early adulthood, pediatricians are concerned with the health of infants, children, and teenagers. They specialize in the diagnosis and treatment of a variety of ailments specific to young people and track their patients' growth to adulthood. Like most physicians, pediatricians work with different healthcare workers, such as nurses and other physicians, to assess and treat children with various ailments, such as muscular dystrophy. Most of the work of pediatricians, however, involves treating day-to-day illnesses that are common to children—minor injuries, infectious diseases, and immunizations—much as a general practitioner treats adults. Some pediatricians specialize in serious medical conditions and pediatric surgery, treating autoimmune disorders or serious chronic ailments.

Obstetricians and gynecologists. Obstetricians and gynecologists (ob/gyns) are specialists whose focus is women's health. They are responsible for general medical care for women, but also provide care related to pregnancy and the reproductive system. Like general practitioners, ob/gyns are concerned with the prevention, diagnosis, and treatment of general health problems, but they focus on ailments specific to the female anatomy, such as breast and cervical cancer, urinary tract and pelvic disorders, and hormonal disorders. Ob/gyns also specialize in childbirth, treating and counseling women throughout their pregnancy, from giving prenatal diagnoses to delivery and postpartum care. Ob/gyns track the health of, and treat, both mother and fetus as the pregnancy progresses.

Psychiatrists. Psychiatrists are the primary caregivers in the area of mental health. They assess and treat mental illnesses through a combination of psychotherapy, psychoanalysis, hospitalization, and medication. Psychotherapy involves regular discussions with patients about their problems; the psychiatrist helps them find solutions through changes in their behavioral patterns, the exploration of their past experiences, and group and family therapy sessions. Psychoanalysis involves long-term psychotherapy and counseling for patients. In many cases, medications are administered to correct chemical imbalances that may be causing emotional problems. Psychiatrists may also administer electroconvulsive therapy to those of their patients who do not respond to, or who cannot take, medications.

Surgeons. Surgeons are physicians who specialize in the treatment of injury, disease, and deformity through operations. Using a variety of instruments, and with patients under general or local anesthesia, a surgeon corrects physical deformities, repairs bone and tissue after injuries, or performs preventive surgeries on patients with debilitating diseases or disorders. Although a large number perform general surgery, many surgeons choose to specialize in a specific area. One of the most prevalent specialties is orthopedic surgery: the treatment of the skeletal system and associated organs. Others include neurological surgery (treatment of the brain and nervous system), ophthalmology (treatment of the eye), orthopedic surgery, otolaryngology (treatment of the ear, nose, and throat), and plastic or reconstructive surgery. Like primary care and other specialist physicians, surgeons also examine patients, perform and interpret diagnostic tests, and counsel patients on preventive health care.

A number of other medical specialists, including allergists, cardiologists, dermatologists, emergency physicians, gastroenterologists, pathologists, and radiologists, also work in clinics, hospitals, and private offices.

Working Conditions
Many physicians—primarily general and family practitioners, general internists, pediatricians, ob/gyns, and psychiatrists—work in small private offices or clinics, often assisted by a small staff of nurses and other administrative personnel. Increasingly, physicians are practicing in groups or healthcare organizations that provide backup coverage and allow for more time off. These physicians often work as part of a team coordinating care for a population of patients; they are less independent than solo practitioners of the past.

Surgeons and anesthesiologists typically work in well-lighted, sterile environments while performing surgery and often stand for long periods. Most work in hospitals or in surgical outpatient centers. Many physicians and surgeons work long, irregular hours. Almost one-third of physicians worked 60 hours or more a week in 2002. Physicians and surgeons must travel frequently between office and hospital to care for their patients. Those who are on call deal with many patients' concerns over the phone and may make emergency visits to hospitals or nursing homes.

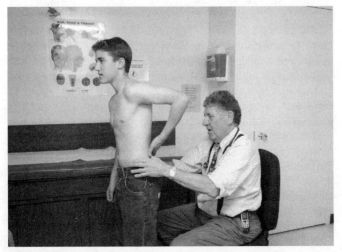

Physicians practice in a variety of specialties, including general pediatrics.

Employment

Physicians and surgeons held about 583,000 jobs in 2002; approximately 1 out of 6 was self-employed. About half of salaried physicians and surgeons were in office-based practice, and almost a quarter were employed by hospitals. Others practiced in Federal, State, and local government; educational services; and outpatient care centers.

A growing number of physicians are partners or salaried employees of group practices. Organized as clinics or as associations of physicians, medical groups can afford expensive medical equipment and realize other business advantages.

The New England and Middle Atlantic States have the highest ratio of physicians to population; the South Central States have the lowest. D.O.s are more likely than M.D.s to practice in small cities and towns and in rural areas. M.D.s tend to locate in urban areas, close to hospital and education centers.

Training and Other Qualifications

It takes many years of education and training to become a physician: 4 years of undergraduate school, 4 years of medical school, and 3 to 8 years of internship and residency, depending on the specialty selected. A few medical schools offer a combined undergraduate and medical school programs that last 6 rather than the customary 8 years.

Premedical students must complete undergraduate work in physics, biology, mathematics, English, and inorganic and organic chemistry. Students also take courses in the humanities and the social sciences. Some students volunteer at local hospitals or clinics to gain practical experience in the health professions.

The minimum educational requirement for entry into a medical school is 3 years of college; most applicants, however, have at least a bachelor's degree, and many have advanced degrees. There are 146 medical schools in the United States—126 teach allopathic medicine and award a Doctor of Medicine (M.D.) degree; 20 teach osteopathic medicine and award the Doctor of Osteopathic Medicine (D.O.) degree. Acceptance to medical school is highly competitive. Applicants must submit transcripts, scores from the Medical College Admission Test, and letters of recommendation. Schools also consider applicants' character, personality, leadership qualities, and participation in extracurricular activities. Most schools require an interview with members of the admissions committee.

Students spend most of the first 2 years of medical school in laboratories and classrooms, taking courses such as anatomy, biochemistry, physiology, pharmacology, psychology, microbiology, pathology, medical ethics, and laws governing medicine. They also learn to take medical histories, examine patients, and diagnose illnesses. During their last 2 years, students work with patients under the supervision of experienced physicians in hospitals and clinics, learning acute, chronic, preventive, and rehabilitative care. Through rotations in internal medicine, family practice, obstetrics and gynecology, pediatrics, psychiatry, and surgery, they gain experience in the diagnosis and treatment of illness.

Following medical school, almost all M.D.s enter a residency—graduate medical education in a specialty that takes the form of paid on-the-job training, usually in a hospital. Most D.O.s serve a 12-month rotating internship after graduation and before entering a residency, which may last 2 to 6 years.

All States, the District of Columbia, and U.S. territories license physicians. To be licensed, physicians must graduate from an accredited medical school, pass a licensing examination, and complete 1 to 7 years of graduate medical education. Although physicians licensed in one State usually can get a license to practice in another without further examination, some States limit reciprocity. Graduates of foreign medical schools generally can qualify for licensure after passing an examination and completing a U.S. residency.

M.D.s and D.O.s seeking board certification in a specialty may spend up to 7 years in residency training, depending on the specialty. A final examination immediately after residency or after 1 or 2 years of practice also is necessary for certification by the American Board of Medical Specialists or the American Osteopathic Association. There are 24 specialty boards, ranging from allergy and immunology to urology. For certification in a subspecialty, physicians usually need another 1 to 2 years of residency.

A physician's training is costly. More than 80 percent of medical students borrow money to cover their expenses.

People who wish to become physicians must have a desire to serve patients, be self-motivated, and be able to survive the pressures and long hours of medical education and practice. Physicians also must have a good bedside manner, emotional stability, and the ability to make decisions in emergencies. Prospective physicians must be willing to study throughout their career in order to keep up with medical advances.

Job Outlook

Employment of physicians and surgeons will grow about as fast as the average for all occupations through the year 2012 due to continued expansion of the health services industries. The growing and aging population will drive overall growth in the demand for physician services, as consumers continue to demand high levels of care using the latest technologies, diagnostic tests, and therapies.

Demand for physicians' services is highly sensitive to changes in consumer preferences, healthcare reimbursement policies, and legislation. For example, if changes to health coverage result in consumers facing higher out-of-pocket costs, they may demand fewer physician services. Demand for physician services may also be tempered by patients relying more on other healthcare providers—such as physician assistants, nurse practitioners, optometrists, and nurse anesthetists—for some healthcare services. In addition, new technologies will increase physician productivity. Telemedicine will allow physicians to treat patients or consult with other providers remotely. Increasing use of electronic medical records, test and prescription orders, billing, and scheduling will also improve physician productivity.

Opportunities for individuals interested in becoming physicians and surgeons are expected to be favorable. Reports of shortages in some specialties or geographic areas should attract new entrants, encouraging schools to expand programs and hospitals to expand available residency slots. However, because physician training is so lengthy, employment change happens gradually. In the short term, to meet increased demand, experienced physicians may work longer hours, delay retirement, or take measures to increase productivity, such as using more support staff to provide services. Opportunities should be particularly good in rural and low-income areas, because some physicians find these areas unattractive due to lower earnings potential, isolation from medical colleagues, or other reasons.

Unlike their predecessors, newly trained physicians face radically different choices of where and how to practice. New physicians are much less likely to enter solo practice and more likely to take salaried jobs in group medical practices, clinics, and health networks.

Earnings

Physicians have among the highest earnings of any occupation. According to the Medical Group Management Association's Physician Compensation and Production Survey, median total compensation for physicians in 2002 varied by specialty, as shown in table 1. Total compensation for physicians reflects the amount reported as direct compensation for tax purposes, plus all voluntary salary reductions. Salary, bonus and/or incentive payments, research stipends, honoraria, and distribution of profits were included in total compensation.

Table 1. Total compensation of physicians by specialty, 2002

Anesthesiology	$306,964
Surgery, general	255,438
Obstetrics/gynecology	233,061
Psychiatry	163,144
Internal medicine	155,530
Pediatrics/adolescent medicine	152,690
Family practice (without obstetrics)	150,267

SOURCE: *Medical Group Management Association, Physician Compensation and Production Report, 2003.*

Self-employed physicians—those who own or are part owners of their medical practice—generally have higher median incomes than salaried physicians. Earnings vary according to number of years in practice, geographic region, hours worked, and skill, personality, and professional reputation. Self-employed physicians and surgeons must provide for their own health insurance and retirement.

Related Occupations

Physicians work to prevent, diagnose, and treat diseases, disorders, and injuries. Professionals in other occupations requiring similar skills and critical judgment include chiropractors, dentists, optometrists, physician assistants, podiatrists, registered nurses, and veterinarians.

Sources of Additional Information

For a list of medical schools and residency programs, as well as general information on premedical education, financial aid, and medicine as a career, contact:
➤ Association of American Medical Colleges, Section for Student Services, 2450 N St. NW., Washington, DC 20037-1126. Internet: **http://www.aamc.org**
➤ American Association of Colleges of Osteopathic Medicine, 5550 Friendship Blvd., Suite 310, Chevy Chase, MD 20815-7231. Internet: **http://www.aacom.org**

For general information on physicians, contact:
➤ American Medical Association, Department of Communications and Public Relations, 515 N. State St., Chicago, IL 60610. Internet: **http://www.ama-assn.org**
➤ American Osteopathic Association, Division of Public Relations, 142 East Ontario St., Chicago, IL 60611. Internet: **http://www.aoa-net.org**

For information about various medical specialties, contact:
➤ American Society of Anesthesiologists, 520 N. Northwest Hwy., Park Ridge, IL 60068-2573. Internet: **http://www.asahq.org**
➤ American Board of Anesthesiology, 4101 Lake Boone Trail, Suite 510, Raleigh, NC 27607-7506. Internet: **http://www.abanes.org**
➤ Society of General Internal Medicine, 2501 M St. NW., Suite 575, Washington, DC 20037. Internet: **http://www.sgim.org**
➤ American Academy of Pediatrics, 141 Northwest Point Blvd., Elk Grove Village, IL 60007-1098. Internet: **http://www.aap.org**
➤ American Board of Obstetrics and Gynecology, 2915 Vine St., Dallas, TX 75204. Internet: **http://www.abog.org**
➤ American College of Obstetrics and Gynecologists, 409 12th St.SW., P.O. Box 96920, Washington, DC 20090-6920. Internet: **http://www.acog.org**
➤ American Psychiatric Association, 1000 Wilson Blvd., Suite 1825, Arlington, VA 22209-3901. Internet: **http://www.psych.org**
➤ American College of Surgeons, 633 North Saint Clair St., Chicago, IL 60611-3211. Internet: **http://www.facs.org**

Information on Federal scholarships and loans is available from the directors of student financial aid at schools of medicine.

Information on licensing is available from State boards of examiners.

Podiatrists

(0*NET 29-1081.00)

Significant Points

● Demand for podiatric care is expected to increase; however, only a limited number of job openings for podiatrists is expected because the occupation is small and most podiatrists remain in it until they retire.

● Podiatrists need a State license that requires the completion of at least 90 hours of undergraduate study, the completion of a 4-year program at a college of podiatric medicine, and in most States, a postdoctoral residency program of at least 1 year.

● Many podiatrists are solo practitioners, although more are entering partnerships with other podiatrists or other health practitioners; establishing a new practice will be most difficult in the areas surrounding colleges of podiatric medicine.

● Podiatrists enjoy very high earnings.

Nature of the Work

Americans spend a great deal of time on their feet. As the Nation becomes more active across all age groups, the need for foot care will become increasingly important to maintaining a healthy lifestyle.

The human foot is a complex structure. It contains 26 bones—plus muscles, nerves, ligaments, and blood vessels—and is designed for balance and mobility. The 52 bones in your feet make up about one-fourth of all the bones in your body. Podiatrists, also known as *doctors of podiatric medicine (DPMs)*, diagnose and treat disorders, diseases, and injuries of the foot and lower leg to keep this part of the body working properly.

Podiatrists treat corns, calluses, ingrown toenails, bunions, heel spurs, and arch problems; ankle and foot injuries, deformities, and infections; and foot complaints associated with diseases such as diabetes. To treat these problems, podiatrists prescribe drugs, order physical therapy, set fractures, and perform sur-

A podiatrist fits corrective inserts called orthotics.

gery. They also fit corrective inserts called orthotics, design plaster casts and strappings to correct deformities, and design custom-made shoes. Podiatrists may use a force plate to help design the orthotics. Patients walk across a plate connected to a computer that "reads" their feet, picking up pressure points and weight distribution. From the computer readout, podiatrists order the correct design or recommend another kind of treatment.

To diagnose a foot problem, podiatrists also order x rays and laboratory tests. The foot may be the first area to show signs of serious conditions such as arthritis, diabetes, and heart disease. For example, diabetics are prone to foot ulcers and infections due to poor circulation. Podiatrists consult with and refer patients to other health practitioners when they detect symptoms of these disorders.

Most podiatrists have a solo practice, although more are forming group practices with other podiatrists or health practitioners. Some specialize in surgery, orthopedics, primary care, or public health. Besides these board-certified specialties, podiatrists may practice other specialties, such as sports medicine, pediatrics, dermatology, radiology, geriatrics, or diabetic foot care.

Podiatrists who are in private practice are responsible for running a small business. They may hire employees, order supplies, and keep records, among other tasks. In addition, some educate the community on the benefits of foot care through speaking engagements and advertising.

Working Conditions

Podiatrists usually work in their own offices. They also may spend time visiting patients in nursing homes or performing surgery at hospitals or ambulatory surgical centers, but usually have fewer afterhours emergencies than other doctors have. Those with private practices set their own hours, but may work evenings and weekends to meet the needs of their patients.

Employment

Podiatrists held about 13,000 jobs in 2002. Most podiatrists were solo practitioners, although more are entering partnerships and multispecialty group practices. Solo practitioners were primarily unincorporated self-employed workers, although some were also incorporated wage and salary workers in offices of other health practitioners. Other podiatrists are employed in hospitals and the Federal government.

Training, Other Qualifications, and Advancement

All States and the District of Columbia require a license for the practice of podiatric medicine. Each State defines its own licensing requirements, although many States grant reciprocity to podiatrists who are licensed in another State. Generally, the applicant must be a graduate of an accredited college of podiatric medicine and pass written and oral examinations. Some States permit applicants to substitute the examination of the National Board of Podiatric Medical Examiners, given in the second and fourth years of podiatric medical college, for part or all of the written State examination. Most States also require the completion of a postdoctoral residency program of at least 1 year and continuing education for licensure renewal.

Prerequisites for admission to a college of podiatric medicine include the completion of at least 90 semester hours of undergraduate study, an acceptable grade point average, and suitable scores on the Medical College Admission Test (some colleges also may accept the Dental Admission Test or the Graduate Record Exam). All of the colleges require 8 semester hours each of biology, inorganic chemistry, organic chemistry, and physics, as well as 6 hours of English. The science courses should be those designed for premedical students. Potential podiatric medical students also are evaluated on the basis of extracurricular and community activities, personal interviews, and letters of recommendation. More than 90 percent of podiatric students have at least a bachelor's degree.

Colleges of podiatric medicine offer a 4-year program whose core curriculum is similar to that in other schools of medicine. During the first 2 years, students receive classroom instruction in basic sciences, including anatomy, chemistry, pathology, and pharmacology. Third- and fourth-year students have clinical rotations in private practices, hospitals, and clinics. During these rotations, they learn how to take general and podiatric histories, perform routine physical examinations, interpret tests and findings, make diagnoses, and perform therapeutic procedures. Graduates receive the degree of Doctor of Podiatric Medicine (DPM).

Most graduates complete a hospital residency program after receiving a DPM. Residency programs last from 1 to 3 years. Residents receive advanced training in podiatric medicine and surgery and serve clinical rotations in anesthesiology, internal medicine, pathology, radiology, emergency medicine, and orthopedic and general surgery. Residencies lasting more than 1 year provide more extensive training in specialty areas.

There are a number of certifying boards for the podiatric specialties of orthopedics, primary medicine, and surgery. Certification means that the DPM meets higher standards than those required for licensure. Each board requires advanced training, the completion of written and oral examinations, and experience as a practicing podiatrist. Most managed care organizations prefer board-certified podiatrists.

People planning a career in podiatry should have scientific aptitude, manual dexterity, interpersonal skills, and good business sense.

Podiatrists may advance to become professors at colleges of podiatric medicine, department chiefs in hospitals, or general health administrators.

Job Outlook

Employment of podiatrists is expected to grow about as fast as the average for all occupations through 2012. More people will turn to podiatrists for foot care as the number of injuries sustained by a more active and increasingly older population grows. Additional job openings will result from podiatrists who retire from the occupation, particularly members of the "baby-boom" generation. However, relatively few job openings from this source are expected because the occupation is small and most podiatrists remain in it until they retire.

Medicare and most private health insurance programs cover acute medical and surgical foot services, as well as diagnostic x rays and leg braces. Details of such coverage vary among plans. However, routine foot care—including the removal of corns and calluses—ordinarily is not covered, unless the patient has a systemic condition that has resulted in severe circulatory problems or areas of desensitization in the legs or feet. Like dental services, podiatric care is often discretionary and, therefore, more dependent on disposable income than some other medical services.

Employment of podiatrists would grow even faster were it not for continued emphasis on controlling the costs of specialty healthcare. Insurers will balance the cost of sending patients to podiatrists against the cost and availability of substitute practitioners, such as physicians and physical therapists. Opportunities will be better for board-certified podiatrists, because many managed care organizations require board certification. Opportunities for newly trained podiatrists will be better in group medical practices, clinics, and health networks than in a traditional solo practice. Establishing a practice will be most difficult in the areas surrounding colleges of podiatric medicine, because podiatrists are concentrated in these locations.

Earnings

Median annual earnings of salaried podiatrists were $94,870 in 2002. The middle 50 percent earned between $62,500 and $139,230 a year. According to a survey by the American Podiatric Medical Association, median net income for all podiatrists was $134,415 in 2001. Additionally, a survey by *Podiatric Magazine* reported median net income of $114,200 in 2003. Podiatrists in partnerships tended to earn higher net incomes than those in solo practice. Self-employed podiatrists must provide for their own health insurance and retirement.

Related Occupations

Other workers who apply scientific knowledge to prevent, diagnose, and treat disorders and injuries include chiropractors, dentists, optometrists, physicians and surgeons, and veterinarians.

Sources of Additional Information

For information on podiatric medicine as a career, contact:

➤ American Podiatric Medical Association, 9312 Old Georgetown Rd., Bethesda, MD 20814-1621. Internet: **http://www.apma.org**

Information on the colleges of podiatric medicine and their entrance requirements, curricula, and student financial aid is available from:

➤ American Association of Colleges of Podiatric Medicine, 15850 Crabbs Branch Way, Suite 320, Rockville, MD 20855-2622. Internet: **http://www.aacpm.org**

Recreational Therapists

(0*NET 29-1125.00)

Significant Points

- Overall employment of recreational therapists is expected to grow more slowly than the average for all occupations, but employment of therapists who work in community care facilities for the elderly and in residential mental retardation, mental health, and substance abuse facilities should grow faster than the average.

- Recreational therapists should be comfortable working with persons who are ill or who have disabilities.

- Opportunities should be best for persons with a bachelor's degree in therapeutic recreation or in recreation with a concentration in therapeutic recreation.

Nature of the Work

Recreational therapists, also referred to as *therapeutic recreation specialists*, provide treatment services and recreation activities to individuals with disabilities or illnesses. Using a variety of techniques, including arts and crafts, animals, sports, games, dance and movement, drama, music, and community outings, therapists treat and maintain the physical, mental, and emotional well-being of their clients. Therapists help individuals reduce depression, stress, and anxiety; recover basic motor functioning and reasoning abilities; build confidence; and socialize effectively so that they can enjoy greater independence, as well as reduce or eliminate the effects of their illness or disability. In addition, therapists help integrate people with disabilities into the community by teaching them how to use community resources and recreational activities. Recreational therapists should not be confused with recreation and fitness workers, who organize recreational activities primarily for enjoyment. (Recreation and fitness workers are discussed elsewhere in the *Handbook*.)

In acute healthcare settings, such as hospitals and rehabilitation centers, recreational therapists treat and rehabilitate individuals with specific health conditions, usually in conjunction or collaboration with physicians, nurses, psychologists, social workers, and physical and occupational therapists. In long-term and residential care facilities, recreational therapists use leisure activities—especially structured group programs—to improve and maintain their clients' general health and well-being. They also may provide interventions to prevent the cli-

With a variety of techniques, including the use of arts and crafts, recreational therapists treat clients and maintain their well-being.

ent from suffering further medical problems and complications related to illnesses and disabilities.

Recreational therapists assess clients on the basis of information the therapists learn from standardized assessments, observations, medical records, the medical staff, the clients' families, and the clients themselves. They then develop and carry out therapeutic interventions consistent with the clients' needs and interests. For example, clients who are isolated from others or who have limited social skills may be encouraged to play games with others, and right-handed persons with right-side paralysis may be instructed in how to adapt to using their unaffected left side to throw a ball or swing a racket. Recreational therapists may instruct patients in relaxation techniques to reduce stress and tension, stretching and limbering exercises, proper body mechanics for participation in recreation activities, pacing and energy conservation techniques, and individual as well as team activities. In addition, therapists observe and document a patient's participation, reactions, and progress.

Community-based recreational therapists may work in park and recreation departments, special-education programs for school districts, or programs for older adults and people with disabilities. Included in the last group are programs and facilities such as assisted-living, adult daycare, and substance abuse rehabilitation centers. In these programs, therapists use interventions to develop specific skills, while providing opportuni-

ties for exercise, mental stimulation, creativity, and fun. Although most therapists are employed in other areas, those who work in schools help counselors, teachers, and parents address the special needs of students, including easing disabled students' transition into adult life.

Working Conditions

Recreational therapists provide services in special activity rooms, but also plan activities and prepare documentation in offices. When working with clients during community integration programs, they may travel locally to instruct the clients regarding the accessibility of public transportation and other public areas, such as parks, playgrounds, swimming pools, restaurants, and theaters.

Therapists often lift and carry equipment, as well as lead recreational activities. Recreational therapists generally work a 40-hour week that may include some evenings, weekends, and holidays.

Employment

Recreational therapists held about 27,000 jobs in 2002. About a third of salaried jobs for therapists were in nursing care facilities and almost another third were in hospitals. Others worked in State and local government agencies and in community care facilities for the elderly, including assisted-living facilities. The rest worked primarily in residential mental retardation, mental health, and substance abuse facilities; individual and family services; Federal government agencies; educational services; and outpatient care centers. Only a small number of therapists were self-employed, generally contracting with long-term care facilities or community agencies to develop and oversee programs.

Training, Other Qualifications, and Advancement

A bachelor's degree in therapeutic recreation, or in recreation with a concentration in therapeutic recreation, is the usual requirement for entry-level positions. Persons may qualify for paraprofessional positions with an associate degree in therapeutic recreation or a healthcare-related field. An associate degree in recreational therapy; training in art, drama, or music therapy; or qualifying work experience may be sufficient for activity director positions in nursing homes.

Approximately 140 programs prepare students to become recreational therapists. Most offer bachelor's degrees, although some also offer associate, master's, or doctoral degrees. Programs include courses in assessment, treatment and program planning, intervention design, and evaluation. Students also study human anatomy, physiology, abnormal psychology, medical and psychiatric terminology, characteristics of illnesses and disabilities, professional ethics, and the use of assistive devices and technology.

Most employers prefer to hire candidates who are certified therapeutic recreation specialists. The National Council for Therapeutic Recreation Certification is the certificatory agency. To become certified, specialists must have a bachelor's degree, pass a written certification examination, and complete an internship of at least 480 hours. Additional requirements apply in order to maintain certification and to recertify.

Recreational therapists should be comfortable working with persons who are ill or who have disabilities. Therapists must be patient, tactful, and persuasive when working with people who have a variety of special needs. Ingenuity, a sense of humor, and imagination are needed to adapt activities to individual needs, and good physical coordination is necessary to demonstrate or participate in recreational activities.

Therapists may advance to supervisory or administrative positions. Some teach, conduct research, or consult for health or social services agencies.

Job Outlook

Overall employment of recreational therapists is expected to grow more slowly than the average for all occupations through the year 2012. In nursing care facilities—the largest industry employing recreational therapists—employment will grow slightly faster than the occupation as a whole, as the number of older adults continues to grow. Employment is expected to decline, however, in hospitals as services shift to outpatient settings and employers emphasize cost containment. Fast employment growth is expected in the residential and outpatient settings that serve disabled persons, the elderly, or those diagnosed with mental retardation, mental illness, or substance abuse problems—for example, community care facilities for the elderly (which includes assisted-living facilities); residential mental retardation, mental health, and substance abuse facilities; and individual and family services (which includes daycare centers for disabled persons and the elderly). Opportunities should be best for persons with a bachelor's degree in therapeutic recreation or in recreation with an option in therapeutic recreation.

Health services facilities will support a growing number of jobs in adult daycare and outpatient programs offering short-term mental health and alcohol or drug abuse services. Rehabilitation, home healthcare, and transitional programs will provide additional jobs.

The rapidly growing number of older adults is expected to spur job growth for recreational therapy professionals and paraprofessionals in assisted-living facilities, adult daycare programs, and other social assistance agencies. Continued growth also is expected in community residential care facilities, as well as daycare programs for individuals with disabilities.

Earnings

Median annual earnings of recreational therapists were $30,540 in 2002. The middle 50 percent earned between $23,180 and $38,620. The lowest 10 percent earned less than $18,130, and the highest 10 percent earned more than $47,180. In 2002, median annual earnings for recreational therapists were $25,010 in nursing care facilities.

Related Occupations

Recreational therapists primarily design activities to help people with disabilities lead more fulfilling and independent lives. Other workers who have similar jobs are occupational therapists, physical therapists, recreation and fitness workers, and rehabilitation counselors.

Sources of Additional Information

For information on how to order materials describing careers and academic programs in recreational therapy, contact either of the following sources:
➤ American Therapeutic Recreation Association, 1414 Prince St., Suite 204, Alexandria, VA 22314-2853. Internet: **http://www.atra-tr.org**
➤ National Therapeutic Recreation Society, 22377 Belmont Ridge Rd., Ashburn, VA 20148-4501. Internet:
http://www.nrpa.org/index.cfm?publicationID=21

Information on certification may be obtained from:
➤ National Council for Therapeutic Recreation Certification, 7 Elmwood Dr., New City, NY 10956. Internet: **http://www.nctrc.org**

Registered Nurses

(0*NET 29-1111.00)

Significant Points

● Registered nurses constitute the largest healthcare occupation, with 2.3 million jobs.

● More new jobs are expected to be created for registered nurses than for any other occupation.

● Job opportunities are expected to be very good.

● The three major educational paths to registered nursing are a bachelor's degree, an associate degree, and a diploma.

Nature of the Work

Registered nurses (RNs) work to promote health, prevent disease, and help patients cope with illness. They are advocates and health educators for patients, families, and communities. When providing direct patient care, they observe, assess, and record symptoms, reactions, and progress in patients; assist physicians during surgeries, treatments, and examinations; administer medications; and assist in convalescence and rehabilitation. RNs also develop and manage nursing care plans, instruct patients and their families in proper care, and help individuals and groups take steps to improve or maintain their health. While State laws govern the tasks that RNs may perform, it is usually the work setting that determines their daily job duties.

Hospital nurses form the largest group of nurses. Most are staff nurses, who provide bedside nursing care and carry out medical regimens. They also may supervise licensed practical nurses and nursing aides. Hospital nurses usually are assigned to one department, such as surgery, maternity, pediatrics, the emergency room, intensive care, or the treatment of cancer patients. Some may rotate among departments.

Office nurses care for outpatients in physicians' offices, clinics, ambulatory surgical centers, and emergency medical centers. They prepare patients for, and assist with, examinations; administer injections and medications; dress wounds and incisions; assist with minor surgery; and maintain records. Some also perform routine laboratory and office work.

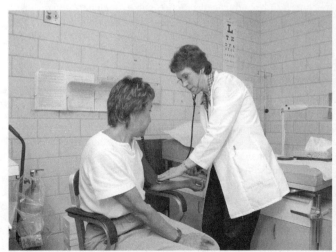

Registered nurses work to promote health, prevent disease, and help patients to cope with illness.

Nursing care facility nurses manage care for residents with conditions ranging from a fracture to Alzheimer's disease. Although they often spend much of their time on administrative and supervisory tasks, RNs also assess residents' health, develop treatment plans, supervise licensed practical nurses and nursing aides, and perform invasive procedures, such as starting intravenous fluids. They also work in specialty-care departments, such as long-term rehabilitation units for patients with strokes and head injuries.

Home health nurses provide nursing services to patients at home. RNs assess patients' home environments and instruct patients and their families. Home health nurses care for a broad range of patients, such as those recovering from illnesses and accidents, cancer, and childbirth. They must be able to work independently and may supervise home health aides.

Public health nurses work in government and private agencies, including clinics, schools, retirement communities, and other community settings. They focus on populations, working with individuals, groups, and families to improve the overall health of communities. They also work with communities to help plan and implement programs. Public health nurses instruct individuals, families, and other groups regarding health issues such as preventive care, nutrition, and childcare. They arrange for immunizations, blood pressure testing, and other health screening. These nurses also work with community leaders, teachers, parents, and physicians in community health education.

Occupational health nurses, also called *industrial nurses*, provide nursing care at worksites to employees, customers, and others with injuries and illnesses. They give emergency care, prepare accident reports, and arrange for further care if necessary. They also offer health counseling, conduct health examinations and inoculations, and assess work environments to identify potential or actual health problems.

Head nurses or *nurse supervisors* direct nursing activities, primarily in hospitals. They plan work schedules and assign duties to nurses and aides, provide or arrange for training, and visit patients to observe nurses and to ensure that the patients receive proper care. They also may ensure that records are maintained and equipment and supplies are ordered.

At the advanced level, *nurse practitioners* provide basic, primary healthcare. They diagnose and treat common acute illnesses and injuries. Nurse practitioners also can prescribe medications—but certification and licensing requirements vary by State. Other advanced practice nurses include *clinical nurse specialists, certified registered nurse anesthetists,* and *certified nurse midwives.* Advanced practice nurses must meet educational and clinical practice requirements beyond the basic nursing education and licensing required of all RNs.

Working Conditions
Most nurses work in well-lighted, comfortable healthcare facilities. Home health and public health nurses travel to patients' homes, schools, community centers, and other sites. Nurses may spend considerable time walking and standing. Patients in hospitals and nursing care facilities require 24-hour care; consequently, nurses in these institutions may work nights, weekends, and holidays. RNs also may be on call—available to work on short notice. Office, occupational health, and public health nurses are more likely to work regular business hours. More than 1 in 5 RNs worked part time in 2002 and nearly 1 in 10 held more than one job.

Nursing has its hazards, especially in hospitals, nursing care facilities, and clinics, in all three of which nurses may care for individuals with infectious diseases. Nurses must observe rigid standardized guidelines to guard against disease and other dangers, such as those posed by radiation, accidental needle sticks, chemicals used to sterilize instruments, and anesthetics. In addition, they are vulnerable to back injury when moving patients, shocks from electrical equipment, and hazards posed by compressed gases.

Employment
As the largest healthcare occupation, registered nurses held about 2.3 million jobs in 2002. Almost 3 out of 5 jobs were in hospitals, in inpatient and outpatient departments. Others worked in offices of physicians, nursing care facilities, home healthcare services, employment services, government agencies, and outpatient care centers. The remainder worked mostly in social assistance agencies and educational services, public and private. About 1 in 5 RNs worked part time.

Training, Other Qualifications, and Advancement
In all States and the District of Columbia, students must graduate from an approved nursing program and pass a national licensing examination in order to obtain a nursing license. Nurses may be licensed in more than one State, either by examination, by the endorsement of a license issued by another State, or through a multi-State licensing agreement. All States require periodic renewal of licenses, which may involve continuing education.

There are three major educational paths to registered nursing: a bachelor's of science degree in nursing (BSN), an associate degree in Nursing (ADN), and a diploma. BSN programs, offered by colleges and universities, take about 4 years to complete. In 2002, 678 nursing programs offered degrees at the bachelor's level. ADN programs, offered by community and junior colleges, take about 2 to 3 years to complete. About 700 RN programs in 2002 were at the ADN level. Diploma programs, administered in hospitals, last about 3 years. Only a small and declining number of programs offer diplomas. Generally, licensed graduates of any of the three types of educational programs qualify for entry-level positions as staff nurses.

Many ADN- and diploma-educated nurses later enter bachelor's programs to prepare for a broader scope of nursing practice. Often, they can find a staff nurse position and then take advantage of tuition reimbursement benefits to work toward a BSN by completing one of many RN-to-BSN programs.

Accelerated BSN programs also are available for individuals who have a bachelor's or higher degree in another field and who are interested in moving into nursing. In 2002, more than 110 of these programs were available. Accelerated BSN programs last 12 to 18 months and provide the fastest route to a BSN for individuals who already hold a degree. Accelerated master's degree programs in nursing also are available and take about 3 years to complete.

Individuals considering nursing should carefully weigh the advantages and disadvantages of enrolling in a BSN program, because, if they do, their advancement opportunities usually are broader. In fact, some career paths are open only to nurses with bachelor's or advanced degrees. A bachelor's degree often is necessary for administrative positions and is a prerequisite for admission to graduate nursing programs in research, consulting, teaching, or a clinical specialization.

Nursing education includes classroom instruction and supervised clinical experience in hospitals and other healthcare facilities. Students take courses in anatomy, physiology, microbiology, chemistry, nutrition, psychology and other behavioral sciences, and nursing. Course work also includes the liberal arts.

Supervised clinical experience is provided in hospital departments such as pediatrics, psychiatry, maternity, and surgery. A growing number of programs include clinical experience in nursing care facilities, public health departments, home health agencies, and ambulatory clinics.

Nurses should be caring, sympathetic, responsible, and detail oriented. They must be able to direct or supervise others, correctly assess patients' conditions, and determine when consultation is required. They need emotional stability to cope with human suffering, emergencies, and other stresses.

Experience and good performance can lead to promotion to more responsible positions. In management, nurses can advance to assistant head nurse or head nurse and, from there, to assistant director, director, and vice president. Increasingly, management-level nursing positions require a graduate or an advanced degree in nursing or health services administration. They also require leadership, negotiation skills, and good judgment. Graduate programs preparing executive-level nurses usually last about 2 years.

Within patient care, nurses can move into a nursing specialty such as clinical nurse specialist, nurse practitioner, certified nurse midwife, or certified registered nurse anesthetist. These positions require about 2 years of graduate education leading to a master's degree.

Some nurses move into the business side of health care. Their nursing expertise and experience on a healthcare team equip them with the ability to manage ambulatory, acute, home health, and chronic care services. Employers—including hospitals, insurance companies, pharmaceutical manufacturers, and managed care organizations, among others—need RNs for health planning and development, marketing, consulting, policy development, and quality assurance. Other nurses work as college and university faculty or conduct research.

Job Outlook

Job opportunities for RNs are expected to be very good. Employment of registered nurses is expected to grow faster than the average for all occupations through 2012, and because the occupation is very large, many new jobs will result. In fact, more new jobs are expected be created for RNs than for any other occupation. Thousands of job openings also will result from the need to replace experienced nurses who leave the occupation, especially as the median age of the registered nurse population continues to rise.

Faster-than-average growth will be driven by technological advances in patient care, which permit a greater number of medical problems to be treated, and an increasing emphasis on preventive care. In addition, the number of older people, who are much more likely than younger people to need nursing care, is projected to grow rapidly.

Employers in some parts of the country are reporting difficulty in attracting and retaining an adequate number of RNs, due primarily to an aging RN workforce and insufficient nursing school enrollments. Imbalances between the supply of, and demand for, qualified workers should spur efforts to attract and retain qualified RNs. For example, employers may restructure workloads, improve compensation and working conditions, and subsidize training or continuing education.

Employment in hospitals, the largest sector, is expected to grow more slowly than in most other healthcare sectors. While the intensity of nursing care is likely to increase, requiring more nurses per patient, the number of inpatients (those who remain in the hospital for more than 24 hours) is not likely to increase much. Patients are being discharged earlier and more procedures are being done on an outpatient basis, both inside and outside hospitals. Rapid growth is expected in hospital outpatient facilities, such as those providing same-day surgery, rehabilitation, and chemotherapy.

An increasing proportion of sophisticated procedures, which once were performed only in hospitals, are being performed in physicians' offices and in outpatient care centers, such as freestanding ambulatory surgical and emergency centers. Accordingly, employment is expected to grow faster than average in these places as healthcare in general expands.

Employment in nursing care facilities is expected to grow faster than average due to increases in the number of elderly, many of whom require long-term care. In addition, the financial pressure on hospitals to discharge patients as soon as possible should produce more admissions to nursing care facilities. Job growth also is expected in units that provide specialized long-term rehabilitation for stroke and head injury patients, as well as units that treat Alzheimer's victims.

Employment in home healthcare is expected to increase rapidly in response to the growing number of older persons with functional disabilities, consumer preference for care in the home, and technological advances that make it possible to bring increasingly complex treatments into the home. The type of care demanded will require nurses who are able to perform complex procedures.

In evolving integrated healthcare networks, nurses may rotate among various employment settings. Because jobs in traditional hospital nursing positions are no longer the only option, RNs will need to be flexible. Opportunities should be excellent, particularly for nurses with advanced education and training.

Earnings

Median annual earnings of registered nurses were $48,090 in 2002. The middle 50 percent earned between $40,140 and $57,490. The lowest 10 percent earned less than $33,970, and the highest 10 percent earned more than $69,670. Median annual earnings in the industries employing the largest numbers of registered nurses in 2002 were as follows:

Employment services	$55,980
General medical and surgical hospitals	49,190
Home health care services	45,890
Offices of physicians	44,870
Nursing care facilities	43,850

Many employers offer flexible work schedules, childcare, educational benefits, and bonuses.

Related Occupations

Workers in other healthcare occupations with responsibilities and duties related to those of registered nurses are emergency medical technicians and paramedics, occupational therapists, physical therapists, physician assistants, respiratory therapists, and social workers.

Sources of Additional Information

For information on a career as a registered nurse and nursing education, contact:

➤ National League for Nursing, 61 Broadway, New York, NY 10006. Internet: **http://www.nln.org**

For a list of BSN, graduate, and accelerated nursing programs, contact:

➤ American Association of Colleges of Nursing, 1 Dupont Circle NW., Suite 530, Washington, DC 20036. Internet: **http://www.aacn.nche.edu**

Information on registered nurses also is available from:

➤ American Nurses Association, 600 Maryland Ave. SW., Washington, DC 20024-2571. Internet: **http://www.nursingworld.org**

Respiratory Therapists

(0*NET 29-1126.00, 29-2054.00)

Significant Points

- An associate degree has become the general requirement for entry into this field.

- Hospitals will continue to employ the vast majority of respiratory therapists, but a growing number of therapists will work in other settings.

- Job opportunities will be very good, especially for therapists with cardiopulmonary care skills or experience working with newborns and infants.

Nature of the Work

Respiratory therapists and *respiratory therapy technicians*—also known as respiratory care practitioners—evaluate, treat, and care for patients with breathing or other cardiopulmonary disorders. Respiratory therapists, practicing under physician direction, assume primary responsibility for all respiratory care therapeutic treatments and diagnostic procedures, including the supervision of respiratory therapy technicians. Respiratory therapy technicians follow specific, well-defined respiratory care procedures, under the direction of respiratory therapists and physicians. In clinical practice, many of the daily duties of therapists and technicians overlap, although therapists generally have greater responsibility than technicians. For example, respiratory therapists will primarily consult with physicians and other healthcare staff to help develop and modify individual patient care plans. Respiratory therapists are also more likely to provide complex therapy requiring considerable independent judgment, such as caring for patients on life support in hospital intensive care units. In this statement, the term *respiratory therapists* includes both respiratory therapists and respiratory therapy technicians.

To evaluate patients, respiratory therapists interview them, perform limited physical examinations, and conduct diagnostic tests. For example, respiratory therapists test patients' breathing capacity and determine the concentration of oxygen and other gases in patients' blood. They also measure patients' pH, which indicates the acidity or alkalinity level of the blood. To evaluate a patient's lung capacity, respiratory therapists have the patient breathe into an instrument that measures the volume and flow of oxygen during inhalation and exhalation. By comparing the reading with the norm for the patient's age, height, weight, and sex, respiratory therapists can provide information that helps determine whether the patient has any lung deficien-

To evaluate patients, respiratory therapists test the capacity of the lungs and analyze their oxygen and carbon dioxide concentrations.

cies. To analyze oxygen, carbon dioxide, and pH levels, therapists draw an arterial blood sample, place it in a blood gas analyzer, and relay the results to a physician. Physicians rely on data provided by respiratory therapists to make treatment decisions.

Respiratory therapists treat all types of patients, ranging from premature infants whose lungs are not fully developed to elderly people whose lungs are diseased. Respiratory therapists provide temporary relief to patients with chronic asthma or emphysema, as well as emergency care to patients who are victims of a heart attack, stroke, drowning, or shock.

To treat patients, respiratory therapists use oxygen or oxygen mixtures, chest physiotherapy, and aerosol medications. When a patient has difficulty getting enough oxygen into their blood, therapists increase the patient's concentration of oxygen by placing an oxygen mask or nasal cannula on a patient and set the oxygen flow at the level prescribed by a physician. Therapists also connect patients who cannot breathe on their own to ventilators that deliver pressurized oxygen into the lungs. The therapists insert a tube into the patient's trachea, or windpipe; connect the tube to the ventilator; and set the rate, volume, and oxygen concentration of the oxygen mixture entering the patient's lungs.

Therapists perform regular checks on patients and equipment. If the patient appears to be having difficulty, or if the oxygen, carbon dioxide, or pH level of the blood is abnormal, therapists change the ventilator setting according to the doctor's orders or check the equipment for mechanical problems. In home care, therapists teach patients and their families to use ventilators and other life-support systems. In addition, therapists visit patients several times a month to inspect and clean equipment and to ensure its proper use. Therapists also make emergency visits if equipment problems arise.

Respiratory therapists perform chest physiotherapy on patients to remove mucus from their lungs and make it easier for them to breathe. For example, during surgery, anesthesia depresses respiration, so chest physiotherapy may be prescribed to help get the patient's lungs back to normal and to prevent congestion. Chest physiotherapy also helps patients suffering from lung diseases, such as cystic fibrosis, that cause mucus to collect in the lungs. Therapists place patients in positions that help drain mucus, and then they thump and vibrate the patients' rib cages and instruct the patients to cough.

Respiratory therapists also administer aerosols—liquid medications suspended in a gas that forms a mist which is inhaled—and teach patients how to inhale the aerosol properly to ensure its effectiveness.

In some hospitals, therapists perform tasks that fall outside their traditional role. Therapists' tasks are expanding into cardiopulmonary procedures such as taking electrocardiograms and administering stress tests, as well as other areas—for example, drawing blood samples from patients. Therapists also keep records of materials used and charges to patients.

Working Conditions

Respiratory therapists generally work between 35 and 40 hours a week. Because hospitals operate around the clock, therapists may work evenings, nights, or weekends. They spend long periods standing and walking between patients' rooms. In an emergency, therapists work under a great deal of stress. Respiratory therapists employed in home healthcare must travel frequently to the homes of patients.

Respiratory therapists are trained to work with gases stored under pressure that can be hazardous. Adherence to safety precautions and regular maintenance and testing of equipment minimize the risk of injury. As in many other health occupations, respiratory therapists run a risk of catching an infectious disease, but carefully following proper procedures minimizes this risk.

Employment

Respiratory therapists held about 112,000 jobs in 2002. More than 4 out of 5 jobs were in hospital departments of respiratory care, anesthesiology, or pulmonary medicine. Most of the remaining jobs were found in offices of physicians or other health practitioners, consumer goods rental firms that supply respiratory equipment for home use, nursing care facilities, and home healthcare services. Holding a second job is relatively common for respiratory therapists. About 17 percent held another job, compared with 5 percent of workers in all occupations.

Training, Other Qualifications, and Advancement

Formal training is necessary for entry into this field. Training is offered at the postsecondary level by colleges and universities, medical schools, vocational-technical institutes, and the Armed Forces. An associate degree has become the general requirement for entry into this field. Most programs award associate or bachelor's degrees and prepare graduates for jobs as advanced respiratory therapists. Other programs award associate degrees or certificates and lead to jobs as entry-level respiratory therapists. According to the Commission on Accreditation of Allied Health Education Programs (CAAHEP), 59 entry-level and 319 advanced respiratory therapy programs are presently accredited in the United States, including Puerto Rico.

Areas of study in respiratory therapy programs include human anatomy and physiology, pathophysiology, chemistry, physics, microbiology, pharmacology, and mathematics. Other courses deal with therapeutic and diagnostic procedures and tests, equipment, patient assessment, cardiopulmonary resuscitation, application of clinical practice guidelines, patient care outside of hospitals, cardiac and pulmonary rehabilitation, respiratory health promotion and disease prevention, and medical recordkeeping and reimbursement.

More than 40 States license respiratory care personnel. Aspiring respiratory care practitioners should check on licensure requirements with the board of respiratory care examiners for the State in which they plan to work. Also, most employers require respiratory therapists to maintain a cardiopulmonary resuscitation (CPR) certification.

The National Board for Respiratory Care (NBRC) offers voluntary certification and registration to graduates of programs accredited by CAAHEP or the Committee on Accreditation for Respiratory Care (CoARC). Two credentials are awarded to respiratory therapists who satisfy the requirements: Registered Respiratory Therapist (RRT) and Certified Respiratory Therapist (CRT). Graduates from accredited programs in respiratory therapy may take the CRT examination. CRTs who meet education and experience requirements can take two separate examinations leading to the award of the RRT credential. The CRT examination is the standard in the States requiring licensure.

Most employers require applicants for entry-level or generalist positions to hold the CRT or at least be eligible to take the certification examination. Supervisory positions and intensive-care specialties usually require the RRT or RRT eligibility.

Therapists should be sensitive to patients' physical and psychological needs. Respiratory care practitioners must pay attention to detail, follow instructions, and work as part of a team. In addition, operating advanced equipment requires proficiency with computers.

High school students interested in a career in respiratory care should take courses in health, biology, mathematics, chemistry, and physics. Respiratory care involves basic mathematical problem solving and an understanding of chemical and physical principles. For example, respiratory care workers must be able to compute dosages of medication and calculate gas concentrations.

Respiratory therapists advance in clinical practice by moving from general care to care of critical patients who have significant problems in other organ systems, such as the heart or kidneys. Respiratory therapists, especially those with 4-year degrees, may also advance to supervisory or managerial positions in a respiratory therapy department. Respiratory therapists in home healthcare and equipment rental firms may become branch managers. Some respiratory therapists advance by moving into teaching positions.

Job Outlook

Job opportunities are expected to be very good, especially for respiratory therapists with cardiopulmonary care skills or experience working with infants. Employment of respiratory therapists is expected to increase faster than the average for all occupations through the year 2012, because of substantial growth in numbers of the middle-aged and elderly population—a development that will heighten the incidence of cardiopulmonary disease.

Older Americans suffer most from respiratory ailments and cardiopulmonary diseases such as pneumonia, chronic bronchitis, emphysema, and heart disease. As their numbers increase, the need for respiratory therapists will increase as well. In addition, advances in treating victims of heart attacks, accident victims, and premature infants (many of whom are dependent on a ventilator during part of their treatment) will increase the demand for the services of respiratory care practitioners.

Although hospitals will continue to employ the vast majority of therapists, a growing number can expect to work outside of hospitals in home healthcare services, offices of physicians or other health practitioners, or consumer goods rental firms.

Earnings

Median annual earnings of respiratory therapists were $40,220 in 2002. The middle 50 percent earned between $34,430 and $46,130. The lowest 10 percent earned less than $30,270, and the highest 10 percent earned more than $54,030. In general medical and surgical hospitals, median annual earnings of respiratory therapists were $40,390 in 2002.

Median annual earnings of respiratory therapy technicians were $34,130 in 2002. The middle 50 percent earned between $28,460 and $41,140. The lowest 10 percent earned less than $23,230, and the highest 10 percent earned more than $47,800. Median annual earnings of respiratory therapy technicians employed in general medical and surgical hospitals were $34,210 in 2002.

Related Occupations

Under the supervision of a physician, respiratory therapists administer respiratory care and life support to patients with heart and lung difficulties. Other workers who care for, treat, or train people to improve their physical condition include registered nurses, occupational therapists, physical therapists, and radiation therapists.

Sources of Additional Information

Information concerning a career in respiratory care is available from:

➤ American Association for Respiratory Care, 9425 N. MacArthur Blvd., Suite 100, Irving, TX 75063-4706. Internet: **http://www.aarc.org**

For a list of accredited educational programs for respiratory care practitioners, contact:

➤ Commission on Accreditation for Allied Health Education Programs, 39 East Wacker Dr., Chicago, IL 60601. Internet: **http://www.caahep.org**
➤ Committee on Accreditation for Respiratory Care, 1248 Harwood Rd., Bedford, TX 76021-4244.

Information on gaining credentials in respiratory care and a list of State licensing agencies can be obtained from:

➤ National Board for Respiratory Care, Inc., 8310 Nieman Rd., Lenexa, KS 66214-1579. Internet: **http://www.nbrc.org**

Speech-Language Pathologists

(0*NET 29-1127.00)

Significant Points

● Employment of speech-language pathologists is expected to grow rapidly because the expanding population in older age groups is prone to medical conditions that result in speech, language, and swallowing problems.

● About half worked in educational services, and most others were employed by healthcare and social assistance facilities.

● A master's degree in speech-language pathology is the standard credential.

Nature of the Work

Speech-language pathologists, sometimes called *speech therapists*, assess, diagnose, treat, and help to prevent speech, language, cognitive, communication, voice, swallowing, fluency, and other related disorders.

Speech-language pathologists work with people who cannot make speech sounds, or cannot make them clearly; those with speech rhythm and fluency problems, such as stuttering; people with voice quality problems, such as inappropriate pitch or harsh voice; those with problems understanding and producing language; those who wish to improve their communication skills by modifying an accent; those with cognitive communication impairments, such as attention, memory, and problem solving disorders; and those with hearing loss who use hearing aids or cochlear implants in order to develop auditory skills and improve communication. They also work with people who have swallowing difficulties.

Speech and language difficulties can result from a variety of causes including stroke, brain injury or deterioration, developmental delays, cerebral palsy, cleft palate, voice pathology, mental retardation, hearing impairment, or emotional problems. Problems can be congenital, developmental, or acquired. Speech-language pathologists use written and oral tests, as well as special instruments, to diagnose the nature and extent of impairment and to record and analyze speech, language, and swallowing irregularities. Speech-language pathologists develop an individualized plan of care, tailored to each patient's needs. For individuals with little or no speech capability, speech-language pathologists may select augmentative or alternative communication methods, including automated devices and sign language, and teach their use. They teach these individuals how to make sounds, improve their voices, or increase their language skills to communicate more effectively. Speech-language pathologists help patients develop, or recover, reliable communication skills so patients can fulfill their educational, vocational, and social roles.

Most speech-language pathologists provide direct clinical services to individuals with communication or swallowing disorders. In speech and language clinics, they may independently develop and carry out treatment programs. In medical facilities, they may work with physicians, social workers, psychologists, and other therapists. Speech-language pathologists in schools

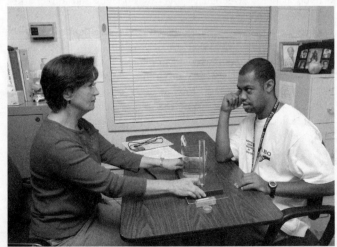

Most speech-language pathologists provide direct clinical services to individuals with communication or swallowing disorders.

develop individual or group programs, counsel parents, and may assist teachers with classroom activities.

Speech-language pathologists keep records on the initial evaluation, progress, and discharge of clients. This helps pinpoint problems, tracks client progress, and justifies the cost of treatment when applying for reimbursement. They counsel individuals and their families concerning communication disorders and how to cope with the stress and misunderstanding that often accompany them. They also work with family members to recognize and change behavior patterns that impede communication and treatment and show them communication-enhancing techniques to use at home.

Some speech-language pathologists conduct research on how people communicate. Others design and develop equipment or techniques for diagnosing and treating speech problems.

Working Conditions
Speech-language pathologists usually work at a desk or table in clean comfortable surroundings. In medical settings, they may work at the patient's bedside and assist in positioning the patient. In school settings they may participate in classroom activities. While the job is not physically demanding, it requires attention to detail and intense concentration. The emotional needs of clients and their families may be demanding. Most full-time speech-language pathologists work between 35 and 40 hours per week; some work part time. Those who work on a contract basis may spend a substantial amount of time traveling between facilities.

Employment
Speech-language pathologists held about 94,000 jobs in 2002. About half of jobs were in educational services, including preschools, elementary and secondary schools, and colleges and universities. Others were in hospitals; offices of other health practitioners, including speech-language pathologists; nursing care facilities; home healthcare services; individual and family services; outpatient care centers; child day care services; or other facilities.

A few speech-language pathologists are self-employed in private practice. They contract to provide services in schools, offices of physicians, hospitals, or nursing care facilities, or work as consultants to industry.

Training, Other Qualifications, and Advancement
Of the 46 States that regulate licensing, almost all require a master's degree or equivalent. A passing score on a national examination on speech-language pathology offered through the Praxis Series of the Educational Testing Service is needed, as well. Other requirements are 300 to 375 hours of supervised clinical experience and 9 months of postgraduate professional clinical experience. Thirty-eight States have continuing education requirements for licensure renewal. Medicaid, Medicare, and private health insurers generally require a practitioner to be licensed to qualify for reimbursement.

About 233 colleges and universities offer graduate programs in speech-language pathology. Courses cover anatomy and physiology of the areas of the body involved in speech, language, swallowing, and hearing; the development of normal speech, language, swallowing, and hearing; the nature of disorders; acoustics; and psychological aspects of communication. Graduate students also learn to evaluate and treat speech, lan-

guage, swallowing, and hearing disorders and receive supervised clinical training in communication disorders.

Speech-language pathologists can acquire the Certificate of Clinical Competence in Speech-Language Pathology (CCC-SLP) offered by the American Speech-Language-Hearing Association. To earn a CCC, a person must have a graduate degree and 375 hours of supervised clinical experience, complete a 36-week postgraduate clinical fellowship, and pass the Praxis Series examination in speech-language pathology administered by the Educational Testing Service (ETS).

Speech-language pathologists should be able to effectively communicate diagnostic test results, diagnoses, and proposed treatment in a manner easily understood by their clients. They must be able to approach problems objectively and provide support to clients and their families. Because a client's progress may be slow, patience, compassion, and good listening skills are necessary.

Job Outlook
Employment of speech-language pathologists is expected to grow faster than the average for all occupations through the year 2012. Members of the baby boom generation are now entering middle age, when the possibility of neurological disorders and associated speech, language, swallowing, and hearing impairments increases. Medical advances are also improving the survival rate of premature infants and trauma and stroke victims, who then need assessment and possible treatment. Many States now require that all newborns be screened for hearing loss and receive appropriate early intervention services.

In health services facilities, the impact of proposed Federal legislation imposing limits on reimbursement for therapy services may adversely affect the short-term job outlook for therapy providers. However, over the long run, the demand for therapists should continue to rise as growth in the number of individuals with disabilities or limited function spurs demand for therapy services.

Employment in educational services will increase along with growth in elementary and secondary school enrollments, including enrollment of special education students. Federal law guarantees special education and related services to all eligible children with disabilities. Greater awareness of the importance of early identification and diagnosis of speech, language, swallowing, and hearing disorders will also increase employment.

The number of speech-language pathologists in private practice will rise due to the increasing use of contract services by hospitals, schools, and nursing care facilities. In addition to job openings stemming from employment growth, a number of openings for speech-language pathologists will arise from the need to replace those who leave the occupation.

Earnings
Median annual earnings of speech-language pathologists were $49,450 in 2002. The middle 50 percent earned between $39,930 and $60,190. The lowest 10 percent earned less than $32,580, and the highest 10 percent earned more than $74,010. Median annual earnings in the industries employing the largest numbers of speech-language pathologists in 2002 were as follows:

Offices of other health practitioners	$53,090
General medical and surgical hospitals	52,940
Elementary and secondary schools	46,060

According to a 2003 survey by the American Speech-Language-Hearing Association, the median annual salary for full-time certified speech-language pathologists who worked on a calendar-year basis, generally 11 or 12 months annually, was $48,000. For those who worked on an academic-year basis, usually 9 or 10 months annually, the median annual salary was $44,800. Certified speech-language pathologists who worked 25 or fewer hours per week had a median hourly salary of $40.00. Starting salaries for certified speech-language pathologists with one to three years experience were $42,000 for those who worked on a calendar-year basis and $37,000 for those who worked on an academic-year basis.

Related Occupations

Speech-language pathologists specialize in the prevention, diagnosis, and treatment of speech and language problems. Workers in related occupations include audiologists, occupational therapists, optometrists, physical therapists, psychologists, recreational therapists, and rehabilitation counselors.

Sources of Additional Information

State licensing boards can provide information on licensure requirements. State departments of education can supply information on certification requirements for those who wish to work in public schools.

General information on careers in speech-language pathology is available from:

➤ American Speech-Language-Hearing Association, 10801 Rockville Pike, Rockville, MD 20852. Internet: **http://www.asha.org**

Veterinarians

(0*NET 29-1131.00)

Significant Points

- Graduation from an accredited college of veterinary medicine and a State license are required.

- Employment opportunities are expected to be very good, but competition for admission to veterinary school is keen.

- Veterinarians should have an affinity for animals and the ability to get along with animal owners.

Nature of the Work

Veterinarians play a major role in the healthcare of pets, livestock, and zoo, sporting, and laboratory animals. Some veterinarians use their skills to protect humans against diseases carried by animals and conduct clinical research on human and animal health problems. Others work in basic research, broadening the scope of fundamental theoretical knowledge and, in applied research, developing new ways to use knowledge.

Most veterinarians perform clinical work in private practices. More than one-half of these veterinarians predominately, or exclusively, treat small animals. Small-animal practitioners usually care for companion animals, such as dogs and cats, but also treat birds, reptiles, rabbits, and other animals that can be kept as pets. About one-fourth of all veterinarians work in mixed animal practices where they see pigs, goats, sheep, and some nondomestic animals, in addition to companion animals. Vet-

erinarians in clinical practice diagnose animal health problems; vaccinate against diseases, such as distemper and rabies; medicate animals suffering from infections or illnesses; treat and dress wounds; set fractures; perform surgery; and advise owners about animal feeding, behavior, and breeding.

A small number of private practice veterinarians work exclusively with large animals, focusing mostly on horses or cows; some also care for various kinds of food animals. These veterinarians usually drive to farms or ranches to provide veterinary services for herds or individual animals. Much of this work involves preventive care to maintain the health of the food animals. These veterinarians test for and vaccinate against diseases and consult with farm or ranch owners and managers on animal production, feeding, and housing issues. They also treat and dress wounds, set fractures, and perform surgery—including cesarean sections on birthing animals. Veterinarians also euthanize animals when necessary. Other veterinarians care for zoo, aquarium, or laboratory animals.

Veterinarians who treat animals use medical equipment, such as stethoscopes; surgical instruments; and diagnostic equipment, such as radiographic and ultrasound equipment. Veterinarians working in research use a full range of sophisticated laboratory equipment.

Veterinarians can contribute to human as well as animal health. A number of veterinarians work with physicians and scientists as they research ways to prevent and treat various human health

Most veterinarians perform clinical work in private practices on animals such as cats and dogs.

problems. For example, veterinarians contributed greatly in conquering malaria and yellow fever, solved the mystery of botulism, produced an anticoagulant used to treat some people with heart disease, and defined and developed surgical techniques for humans, such as hip and knee joint replacements and limb and organ transplants. Today, some determine the effects of drug therapies, antibiotics, or new surgical techniques by testing them on animals.

Some veterinarians are involved in food safety at various levels. Veterinarians who are livestock inspectors check animals for transmissible diseases, advise owners on treatment, and may quarantine animals. Veterinarians who are meat, poultry, or egg product inspectors examine slaughtering and processing plants, check live animals and carcasses for disease, and enforce government regulations regarding food purity and sanitation.

Working Conditions

Veterinarians often work long hours. Those in group practices may take turns being on call for evening, night, or weekend work; and solo practitioners can work extended and weekend hours, responding to emergencies or squeezing in unexpected appointments. The work setting often can be noisy.

Veterinarians in large-animal practice also spend time driving between their office and farms or ranches. They work outdoors in all kinds of weather, and may have to treat animals or perform surgery under unsanitary conditions. When working with animals that are frightened or in pain, veterinarians risk being bitten, kicked, or scratched.

Veterinarians working in nonclinical areas, such as public health and research, have working conditions similar to those of other professionals in those lines of work. In these cases, veterinarians enjoy clean, well-lit offices or laboratories and spend much of their time dealing with people rather than animals.

Employment

Veterinarians held about 58,000 jobs in 2002. About 28 percent were self-employed in solo or group practices. Most others were salaried employees of another veterinary practice. The Federal Government employed about 1,100 civilian veterinarians, chiefly in the U.S. Departments of Agriculture and Health and Human Services. Other employers of veterinarians are State and local governments, colleges of veterinary medicine, medical schools, research laboratories, animal food companies, and pharmaceutical companies. A few veterinarians work for zoos, but most veterinarians caring for zoo animals are private practitioners who contract with zoos to provide services, usually on a part-time basis.

In addition, many veterinarians hold veterinary faculty positions in colleges and universities. (See the statement on teachers—postsecondary elsewhere in the *Handbook*.)

Training, Other Qualifications, and Advancement

Prospective veterinarians must graduate from a 4-year program at an accredited college of veterinary medicine with a Doctor of Veterinary Medicine (D.V.M. or V.M.D.) degree and obtain a license to practice. There are 28 colleges in 26 States that meet accreditation standards set by the Council on Education of the American Veterinary Medical Association (AVMA). The prerequisites for admission vary by veterinary medical college. Many of these colleges do not require a bachelor's degree for entrance, but all require a significant number of credit hours—ranging from 45 to 90 semester hours—at the undergraduate level. How-

ever, most of the students admitted have completed an undergraduate program. Applicants without a bachelor's degree face a difficult task gaining admittance.

Preveterinary courses emphasize the sciences. Veterinary medical colleges typically require classes in organic and inorganic chemistry, physics, biochemistry, general biology, animal biology, animal nutrition, genetics, vertebrate embryology, cellular biology, microbiology, zoology, and systemic physiology. Some programs require calculus; some require only statistics, college algebra and trigonometry, or precalculus. Most veterinary medical colleges also require core courses, including some in English or literature, the social sciences, and the humanities. Increasingly, courses in practice management and career development are becoming a standard part of the curriculum to provide a foundation of general business knowledge for new graduates.

In addition to satisfying preveterinary course requirements, applicants also must submit test scores from the Graduate Record Examination (GRE), the Veterinary College Admission Test (VCAT), or the Medical College Admission Test (MCAT), depending on the preference of each college. Currently, 21 schools require the GRE, 5 require the VCAT, and 2 accept the MCAT.

Some veterinary medical colleges place heavy consideration on a candidate's veterinary and animal experience in admittance decisions. Formal experience, such as work with veterinarians or scientists in clinics, agribusiness, research, or some area of health science, is particularly advantageous. Less formal experience, such as working with animals on a farm or ranch or at a stable or animal shelter, also is helpful. Students must demonstrate ambition and an eagerness to work with animals.

There is keen competition for admission to veterinary school. The number of accredited veterinary colleges has largely remained the same since 1983, whereas the number of applicants has risen significantly. Only about 1 in 3 applicants was accepted in 2002. Most veterinary medical colleges are public, State-supported institutions and reserve the majority of their openings for instate residents, making admission for out-of-state applicants difficult.

While in veterinary medical college, students receive additional academic instruction in the basic sciences for the first 2 years. Later in the program, students are exposed to clinical procedures, such as diagnosing and treating animal diseases and performing surgery. They also do laboratory work in anatomy, biochemistry, medicine, and other scientific subjects. At most veterinary medical colleges, students who plan a career in research can earn both a D.V.M. degree and a Doctor of Philosophy (Ph.D.) degree at the same time.

Veterinary graduates who plan to work with specific types of animals typically choose to pursue additional education in 1 of 20 AVMA-recognized veterinary specialties—such as pathology, internal medicine, dentistry, ophthalmology, surgery, radiology, preventive medicine, or laboratory animal medicine—usually in the form of a 2-year internship. Interns receive a small salary but usually find that their internship experience leads to a higher beginning salary, relative to those of other starting veterinarians. Veterinarians who seek board certification in a specialty must also complete a 3- to 4-year residency program that provides intensive training in specialties, such as internal medicine, oncology, radiology, surgery, dermatology, anesthesiology, neurology, cardiology, ophthalmology, and exotic small-animal medicine.

All States and the District of Columbia require that veterinarians be licensed before they can practice. The only exemptions are for veterinarians working for some Federal agencies and some State governments. Licensing is controlled by the States and is not strictly uniform, although all States require successful completion of the D.V.M. degree—or equivalent education—and passage of a national board examination. The Educational Commission for Foreign Veterinary Graduates (ECFVG) grants certification to individuals trained outside the United States who demonstrate that they meet specified requirements for the English language and clinical proficiency. ECFVG certification fulfills the educational requirement for licensure in all States except Nebraska. Applicants for licensure satisfy the examination requirement by passing the North American Veterinary Licensing Exam (NAVLE). The NAVLE, administered by computer, takes 1 day to complete and consists of 360 multiple-choice questions, covering all aspects of veterinary medicine. The NAVLE also includes visual materials designed to test diagnostic skills, comprising 10 percent of the total examination.

The majority of States also require candidates to pass a State jurisprudence examination covering State laws and regulations. Some States also do additional testing on clinical competency. There are few reciprocal agreements between States, making it difficult for a veterinarian to practice in a different State without first taking another State examination.

Nearly all States have continuing education requirements for licensed veterinarians. Requirements differ by State and may involve attending a class or otherwise demonstrating knowledge of recent medical and veterinary advances.

Most veterinarians begin as employees in established practices. Despite the substantial financial investment in equipment, office space, and staff, many veterinarians with experience set up their own practice or purchase an established one.

Newly trained veterinarians can become U.S. Government meat and poultry inspectors, disease-control workers, animal welfare and safety workers, epidemiologists, research assistants, or commissioned officers in the U.S. Public Health Service or various branches of the U.S. Armed Forces. A State license may be required.

Prospective veterinarians must have good manual dexterity. They should have an affinity for animals and the ability to get along with animal owners, especially when working with pet owners, who tend to form a strong bond with their pet. Veterinarians who intend to go into private practice should possess excellent communication and business skills because they will need to successfully manage their practice and employees and will need to promote, market, and sell their services.

Job Outlook

Very good opportunities are expected because the number of graduates from veterinary school is not expected to increase significantly over the 2002-12 period. However, as mentioned earlier, there is keen competition for admittance to veterinary school. Employment of veterinarians is expected to increase faster than the average for all occupations through the year 2012. As pets are increasingly viewed as a member of the family, pet owners will be more willing to spend increasing amounts on advanced veterinary medical care, creating more demand for veterinarians.

Most veterinarians practice in animal hospitals or clinics and care primarily for companion animals. Recent trends indicate particularly strong interest in cats as pets. Faster growth of the cat population is expected to increase the demand for feline medicine and veterinary services, while demand for veterinary care for dogs should continue to grow at a more modest pace.

Pet owners are becoming more aware of the availability of advanced care and are more willing to pay for intensive veterinary care than in the past because many pet owners are more affluent, and because they consider their pet part of the family. More pet owners even purchase pet insurance, increasing the likelihood that a considerable amount of money will be spent on veterinary care for their pets. More pet owners also will take advantage of nontraditional veterinary services, such as preventive dental care.

New graduates continue to be attracted to small-animal medicine because they prefer to deal with pets and to live and work near heavily populated areas. This situation will not necessarily limit the ability of veterinarians to find employment or to set up and maintain a practice in a particular area. Rather, beginning veterinarians may take positions requiring evening or weekend work to accommodate the extended hours of operation that many practices are offering. Some veterinarians take salaried positions in retail stores offering veterinary services. Self-employed veterinarians usually have to work hard and long to build a sufficient client base.

The number of jobs for large-animal veterinarians is likely to grow more slowly than that for veterinarians in private practice who care for companion animals. Nevertheless, job prospects may be better for veterinarians who specialize in farm animals than for small-animal practitioners because of low earnings in the former specialty and because many veterinarians do not want to work in rural or isolated areas.

Continued support for public health and food safety, national disease control programs, and biomedical research on human health problems will contribute to the demand for veterinarians, although positions in these areas of interest are few in number. Homeland security also may provide opportunities for veterinarians involved in efforts to minimize animal diseases and prevent them from entering the country. Veterinarians with training in public health and epidemiology should have the best opportunities for a career in the Federal Government.

Earnings

Median annual earnings of veterinarians were $63,090 in 2002. The middle 50 percent earned between $49,050 and $85,770. The lowest 10 percent earned less than $38,000, and the highest 10 percent earned more than $123,370.

According to a survey by the American Veterinary Medical Association, average starting salaries of 2002 veterinary medical college graduates varied by type of practice as follows:

All private clinical practices	$46,339
Large animals, exclusively	48,303
Small animals, exclusively	48,178
Small animals, predominantly	46,582
Large animals, predominantly	45,087
Mixed animals	43,948
Equine (horses)	34,273

The average annual salary for veterinarians in the Federal Government in nonsupervisory, supervisory, and managerial positions was $72,208 in 2003.

Related Occupations

Veterinarians prevent, diagnose, and treat diseases, disorders, and injuries in animals. Those who do similar work for humans include chiropractors, dentists, optometrists, physicians and surgeons, and podiatrists. Veterinarians have extensive training in physical and life sciences, and some do scientific and medical research, closely paralleling the work of biological scientists and medical scientists.

Animal care and service workers and veterinary technologists and technicians work extensively with animals. Like veterinarians, they must have patience and feel comfortable with animals. However, the level of training required for these occupations is substantially less than that needed by veterinarians.

Sources of Additional Information
For additional information on careers in veterinary medicine, a list of U.S. schools and colleges of veterinary medicine, and accreditation policies, send a letter-size, self-addressed, stamped envelope to:
➤ American Veterinary Medical Association, 1931 N. Meacham Rd., Suite 100, Schaumburg, IL 60173-4360. Internet: **http://www.avma.org**

For information on veterinary education, write to:
➤ Association of American Veterinary Medical Colleges, 1101 Vermont Ave. NW., Suite 710, Washington, DC 20005. Internet: **http://www.aavmc.org**

For information on scholarships, grants, and loans, contact the financial aid officer at the veterinary schools to which you wish to apply.

Information on obtaining a veterinarian position with the Federal Government is available from the U.S. Office of Personnel Management (OPM) through a telephone-based system. Consult your telephone directory under U.S. Government for a local number or call (703) 724-1850; Federal Relay Service: (800) 877-8339. The first number is not tollfree, and charges may result. Information also is available from the OPM Internet site: **http://www.usajobs.opm.gov**.

Health Technologists and Technicians

Cardiovascular Technologists and Technicians

(0*NET 29-2031.00)

Significant Points

● Employment will grow faster than the average, but the number of job openings created will be low because the occupation is small.

● Employment of most specialties will grow, but fewer EKG technicians will be needed.

● About 3 out of 4 jobs were in hospitals.

Nature of the Work
Cardiovascular technologists and technicians assist physicians in diagnosing and treating cardiac (heart) and peripheral vascular (blood vessel) ailments. Cardiovascular technologists may specialize in three areas of practice—invasive cardiology, echocardiography, and vascular technology. Cardiovascular technicians who specialize in electrocardiograms (EKGs), stress testing, and Holter monitors are known as *cardiographic*, or *EKG technicians.*

Cardiovascular technologists specializing in invasive procedures are called *cardiology technologists.* They assist physicians with cardiac catheterization procedures in which a small tube, or catheter, is wound through a patient's blood vessel from a spot on the patient's leg into the heart. The procedure can determine whether a blockage exists in the blood vessels that supply the heart muscle. The procedure also can help to diagnose other problems. Part of the procedure may involve balloon angioplasty, which can be used to treat blockages of blood vessels or heart valves without the need for heart surgery. Cardiology technologists assist physicians as they insert a catheter with a balloon on the end to the point of the obstruction.

Technologists prepare patients for cardiac catheterization and balloon angioplasty by first positioning them on an examining table and then shaving, cleaning, and administering anesthesia

to the top of their leg near the groin. During the procedures, they monitor patients' blood pressure and heart rate with EKG equipment and notify the physician if something appears to be wrong. Technologists also may prepare and monitor patients during open-heart surgery and the implantation of pacemakers.

Cardiovascular technologists who specialize in echocardiography or vascular technology often run noninvasive tests using ultrasound instrumentation, such as Doppler ultrasound. Tests are called "noninvasive" if they do not require the insertion of probes or other instruments into the patient's body. The ultrasound instrumentation transmits high-frequency sound waves into areas of the patient's body and then processes reflected echoes of the sound waves to form an image. Technologists view the ultrasound image on a screen, and may record the image on videotape or photograph it for interpretation and diagnosis by a physician. As the instrument scans the image, technologists check the image on the screen for subtle differences between healthy and diseased areas, decide which images to include in the report to the physician, and judge if the images are satisfactory for diagnostic purposes. They also explain the procedure to patients, record any additional medical history the patient relates, select appropriate equipment settings, and change the patient's position as necessary. (See the statement on diagnostic medical sonographers elsewhere in the *Handbook* to learn more about other sonographers.)

Those who assist physicians in the diagnosis of disorders affecting the circulation are known as *vascular technologists* or *vascular sonographers.* They perform a medical history and evaluate pulses by listening to the sounds of the arteries for abnormalities. Then, they perform a noninvasive procedure using ultrasound instrumentation to record vascular information, such as vascular blood flow, blood pressure, limb volume changes, oxygen saturation, cerebral circulation, peripheral circulation, and abdominal circulation. Many of these tests are performed during or immediately after surgery.

Technologists who use ultrasound to examine the heart chambers, valves, and vessels are referred to as *cardiac sonographers*, or *echocardiographers.* They use ultrasound instrumentation to create images called echocardiograms. An echocardiogram may be performed while the patient is either resting or physically active. Technologists may administer medication to physically active patients to assess their heart function. Cardiac sonographers may also assist physicians who perform transesophageal echocardiography, which involves placing a tube in the patient's esophagus to obtain ultrasound images.

Cardiovascular technicians who obtain EKGs are known as *electrocardiograph* (or *EKG*) *technicians*. To take a basic EKG, which traces electrical impulses transmitted by the heart, technicians attach electrodes to the patient's chest, arms, and legs, and then manipulate switches on an EKG machine to obtain a reading. A printout is made for interpretation by the physician. This test is done before most kinds of surgery or as part of a routine physical examination, especially for persons who have reached middle age or who have a history of cardiovascular problems.

EKG technicians with advanced training perform Holter monitor and stress testing. For Holter monitoring, technicians place electrodes on the patient's chest and attach a portable EKG monitor to the patient's belt. Following 24 or more hours of normal activity by the patient, the technician removes a tape from the monitor and places it in a scanner. After checking the quality of the recorded impulses on an electronic screen, the technician usually prints the information from the tape so that a physician can interpret it later. Physicians use the output from the scanner to diagnose heart ailments, such as heart rhythm abnormalities or problems with pacemakers.

For a treadmill stress test, EKG technicians document the patient's medical history, explain the procedure, connect the patient to an EKG monitor, and obtain a baseline reading and resting blood pressure. Next, they monitor the heart's performance while the patient is walking on a treadmill, gradually increasing the treadmill's speed to observe the effect of increased exertion. Like vascular technologists and cardiac sonographers, cardiographic technicians who perform EKG, Holter monitor, and stress tests are known as "noninvasive" technicians.

Some cardiovascular technologists and technicians schedule appointments, type doctors' interpretations, maintain patient files, and care for equipment.

Working Conditions

Technologists and technicians generally work a 5-day, 40-hour week that may include weekends. Those in catheterization labs tend to work longer hours and may work evenings. They also may be on call during the night and on weekends.

Cardiovascular technologists and technicians spend a lot of time walking and standing. Those who work in catheterization labs may face stressful working conditions because they are in close contact with patients with serious heart ailments. Some patients, for example, may encounter complications from time to time that have life-or-death implications.

Employment

Cardiovascular technologists and technicians held about 43,000 jobs in 2002. About 3 out 4 jobs were in hospitals, primarily in cardiology departments. The remaining jobs were mostly in offices of physicians, including cardiologists; or in medical and diagnostic laboratories, including diagnostic imaging centers.

Training, Other Qualifications, and Advancement

Although a few cardiovascular technologists, vascular technologists, and cardiac sonographers are currently trained on the job,

most receive training in 2- to 4-year programs. Cardiovascular technologists, vascular technologists, and cardiac sonographers normally complete a 2-year junior or community college program. The first year is dedicated to core courses and is followed by a year of specialized instruction in either invasive, noninvasive cardiovascular, or noninvasive vascular technology. Those who are qualified in an allied health profession need to complete only the year of specialized instruction.

Graduates from the 29 programs accredited by the Joint Review Committee on Education in Cardiovascular Technology are eligible to obtain professional certification in cardiac catheterization, echocardiography, vascular ultrasound, and cardiographic techniques from Cardiovascular Credentialing International. Cardiac sonographers and vascular technologists also may obtain certification from the American Registry of Diagnostic Medical Sonographers.

For basic EKGs, Holter monitoring, and stress testing, 1-year certification programs exist, but most EKG technicians are still trained on the job by an EKG supervisor or a cardiologist. On-the-job training usually lasts about 8 to 16 weeks. Most employers prefer to train people already in the healthcare field—nursing aides, for example. Some EKG technicians are students enrolled in 2-year programs to become technologists, working part time to gain experience and make contact with employers.

Cardiovascular technologists and technicians must be reliable, have mechanical aptitude, and be able to follow detailed instructions. A pleasant, relaxed manner for putting patients at ease is an asset.

Job Outlook

Employment of cardiovascular technologists and technicians is expected to grow faster than the average for all occupations through the year 2012. Growth will occur as the population ages, because older people have a higher incidence of heart problems. Employment of vascular technologists and echocardiographers will grow as advances in vascular technology and sonography reduce the need for more costly and invasive procedures. However, fewer EKG technicians will be needed, as hospitals train nursing aides and others to perform basic EKG procedures. Individuals trained in Holter monitoring and stress testing are expected to have more favorable job prospects than are those who can perform only a basic EKG.

Some job openings for cardiovascular technologists and technicians will arise from replacement needs, as individuals trans-

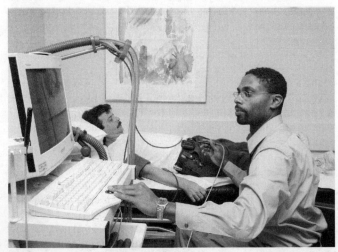

Cardiovascular technologists use ultrasound technology to produce images for diagnosis.

fer to other jobs or leave the labor force. However, job growth and replacement needs will produce relatively few job openings because the occupation is small.

Earnings

Median annual earnings of cardiovascular technologists and technicians were $36,430 in 2002. The middle 50 percent earned between $26,730 and $46,570. The lowest 10 percent earned less than $20,920, and the highest 10 percent earned more than $56,080. Median annual earnings of cardiovascular technologists and technicians in 2002 were $36,420 in offices of physicians and $35,800 in general medical and surgical hospitals.

Related Occupations

Cardiovascular technologists and technicians operate sophisticated equipment that helps physicians and other health practitioners to diagnose and treat patients. So do diagnostic medical sonographers, nuclear medicine technologists, radiation therapists, radiologic technologists and technicians, and respiratory therapists.

Sources of Additional Information

For general information about a career in cardiovascular technology, contact:
➤ Alliance of Cardiovascular Professionals, 4456 Thalia Landing Offices, Bldg. 2, 4356 Bonney Rd., Suite 103, Virginia Beach, VA 23452-1200. Internet: **http://www.acp-online.org**

For a list of accredited programs in cardiovascular technology, contact:
➤ Committee on Accreditation for Allied Health Education Programs, 39 East Wacker Dr., Chicago, IL 60601. Internet: **http://www.caahep.org**
➤ Joint Review Committee on Education in Cardiovascular Technology, 3525 Ellicott Mills Dr., Suite N, Ellicott City, MD 21043-4547.

For information on vascular technology, contact:
➤ Society of Vascular Ultrasound, 4601 Presidents Dr., Suite 260, Lanham, MD 20706-4381. Internet: **http://www.svunet.org**

For information on echocardiography, contact:
➤ American Society of Echocardiography, 1500 Sunday Dr., Suite 102, Raleigh, NC 27607. Internet: **http://www.asecho.org**

For information regarding registration and certification, contact:
➤ Cardiovascular Credentialing International, 1500 Sunday Dr., Suite 102, Raleigh, NC 27607. Internet: **http://www.cci-online.org**
➤ American Registry of Diagnostic Medical Sonographers, 51 Monroe St., Plaza East One, Rockville, MD 20850-2400. Internet: **http://www.ardms.org**

Clinical Laboratory Technologists and Technicians

(O*NET 29-2011.00, 29-2012.00)

Significant Points

● Clinical laboratory technologists usually have a bachelor's degree with a major in medical technology or in one of the life sciences; clinical laboratory technicians generally need either an associate degree or a certificate.

● Average employment growth is expected as the volume of laboratory tests increases with both population growth and the development of new types of tests.

● Job opportunities are expected to be excellent.

Nature of the Work

Clinical laboratory testing plays a crucial role in the detection, diagnosis, and treatment of disease. Clinical laboratory technologists, also referred to as clinical laboratory scientists or medical technologists, and clinical laboratory technicians, also known as medical technicians or medical laboratory technicians, perform most of these tests.

Clinical laboratory personnel examine and analyze body fluids, tissues, and cells. They look for bacteria, parasites, and other microorganisms; analyze the chemical content of fluids; match blood for transfusions; and test for drug levels in the blood to show how a patient is responding to treatment. These technologists also prepare specimens for examination, count cells, and look for abnormal cells. They use automated equipment and instruments capable of performing a number of tests simultaneously, as well as microscopes, cell counters, and other sophisticated laboratory equipment. Then they analyze the results and relay them to physicians. With increasing automation and the use of computer technology, the work of technologists and technicians has become less hands-on and more analytical.

The complexity of tests performed, the level of judgment needed, and the amount of responsibility workers assume depend largely on the amount of education and experience they have.

Clinical laboratory technologists generally have a bachelor's degree in medical technology or in one of the life sciences, or they have a combination of formal training and work experience. They perform complex chemical, biological, hematological, immunologic, microscopic, and bacteriological tests. Technologists microscopically examine blood, tissue, and other body substances. They make cultures of body fluid and tissue samples, to determine the presence of bacteria, fungi, parasites, or other microorganisms. Clinical laboratory technologists analyze samples for chemical content or a chemical reaction and determine blood glucose and cholesterol levels. They also type and cross match blood samples for transfusions.

Clinical laboratory technologists evaluate test results, develop and modify procedures, and establish and monitor programs, to ensure the accuracy of tests. Some clinical laboratory technologists supervise clinical laboratory technicians.

Technologists in small laboratories perform many types of tests, whereas those in large laboratories generally specialize. Technologists who prepare specimens and analyze the chemical and hormonal contents of body fluids are called clinical chemistry technologists. Those who examine and identify bacteria and other microorganisms are microbiology technologists. Blood bank technologists, or immunohematology technologists, collect, type, and prepare blood and its components for transfusions. Immunology technologists examine elements of the human immune system and its response to foreign bodies. Cytotechnologists prepare slides of body cells and examine these cells microscopically for abnormalities that may signal the beginning of a cancerous growth. Molecular biology technologists perform complex protein and nucleic acid testing on cell samples.

Clinical laboratory technicians perform less complex tests and laboratory procedures than technologists perform. Technicians may prepare specimens and operate automated analyzers, for example, or they may perform manual tests in accordance with detailed instructions. Like technologists, they may work in several areas of the clinical laboratory or specialize in just one. Histotechnicians cut and stain tissue specimens for microscopic examination by pathologists, and phlebotomists collect blood samples. They usually work under the supervision of medical and clinical laboratory technologists or laboratory managers.

Working Conditions

Hours and other working conditions of clinical laboratory technologists and technicians vary with the size and type of employment setting. In large hospitals or in independent laboratories that operate continuously, personnel usually work the day, evening, or night shift and may work weekends and holidays. Laboratory personnel in small facilities may work on rotating shifts, rather than on a regular shift. In some facilities, laboratory personnel are on call several nights a week or on weekends, in case of an emergency.

Clinical laboratory personnel are trained to work with infectious specimens. When proper methods of infection control and sterilization are followed, few hazards exist. Protective masks, gloves, and goggles are often necessary to ensure the safety of laboratory personnel.

Laboratories usually are well lighted and clean; however, specimens, solutions, and reagents used in the laboratory sometimes produce fumes. Laboratory workers may spend a great deal of time on their feet.

Employment

Clinical laboratory technologists and technicians held about 297,000 jobs in 2002. More than half of jobs were in hospitals. Most of the remaining jobs were in offices of physicians and in medical and diagnostic laboratories. A small proportion was in educational services; other ambulatory healthcare services, including blood and organ banks; outpatient care centers; and scientific research and development services.

Training, Other Qualifications, and Advancement

The usual requirement for an entry-level position as a clinical laboratory technologist is a bachelor's degree with a major in medical technology or in one of the life sciences; although it is possible to qualify through a combination of education, on-the-job, and specialized training. Universities and hospitals offer medical technology programs.

Bachelor's degree programs in medical technology include courses in chemistry, biological sciences, microbiology, mathematics, and statistics, as well as specialized courses devoted to knowledge and skills used in the clinical laboratory. Many programs also offer or require courses in management, business, and computer applications. The Clinical Laboratory Improvement Act requires technologists who perform highly complex tests to have at least an associate degree.

Medical and clinical laboratory technicians generally have either an associate degree from a community or junior college or a certificate from a hospital, a vocational or technical school, or one of the U.S. Armed Forces. A few technicians learn their skills on the job.

The National Accrediting Agency for Clinical Laboratory Sciences (NAACLS) fully accredits 467 programs for medical and clinical laboratory technologists, medical and clinical laboratory technicians, histotechnologists and histotechnicians, cytogenetic technologists, and diagnostic molecular scientists. NAACLS also approves 57 programs in phlebotomy and clinical assisting. Other nationally recognized accrediting agencies that accredit specific areas for clinical laboratory workers include the Commission on

Clinical laboratory technologists and technicians examine and analyze body fluids, tissues, and cells.

Accreditation of Allied Health Education Programs and the Accrediting Bureau of Health Education Schools.

Some States require laboratory personnel to be licensed or registered. Information on licensure is available from State departments of health or boards of occupational licensing. Certification is a voluntary process by which a nongovernmental organization, such as a professional society or certifying agency, grants recognition to an individual whose professional competence meets prescribed standards. Widely accepted by employers in the health industry, certification is a prerequisite for most jobs and often is necessary for advancement. Agencies certifying medical and clinical laboratory technologists and technicians include the Board of Registry of the American Society for Clinical Pathology, the American Medical Technologists, the National Credentialing Agency for Laboratory Personnel, and the Board of Registry of the American Association of Bioanalysts. These agencies have different requirements for certification and different organizational sponsors.

Clinical laboratory personnel need good analytical judgment and the ability to work under pressure. Close attention to detail is essential, because small differences or changes in test substances or numerical readouts can be crucial for patient care. Manual dexterity and normal color vision are highly desirable. With the widespread use of automated laboratory equipment, computer skills are important. In addition, technologists in particular are expected to be good at problem solving.

Technologists may advance to supervisory positions in laboratory work or may become chief medical or clinical laboratory technologists or laboratory managers in hospitals. Manufacturers of home diagnostic testing kits and laboratory equipment and supplies seek experienced technologists to work in product development, marketing, and sales. A graduate degree in medical technology, one of the biological sciences, chemistry, management, or education usually speeds advancement. A doctorate is needed to become a laboratory director; however, Federal regulation allows directors of moderately complex laboratories to have either a master's degree or a bachelor's degree, combined with the appropriate amount of training and experience. Technicians can become technologists through additional education and experience.

Job Outlook

Job opportunities are expected to be excellent, because the number of job openings is expected to continue to exceed the number of job seekers. Employment of clinical laboratory workers is expected to grow about as fast as the average for all occupations through the year 2012, as the volume of laboratory tests increases with both population growth and the development of new types of tests.

Technological advances will continue to have two opposing effects on employment through 2012. On the one hand, new, increasingly powerful diagnostic tests will encourage additional testing and spur employment. On the other hand, research and development efforts targeted at simplifying routine testing procedures may enhance the ability of nonlaboratory personnel— physicians and patients in particular—to perform tests now conducted in laboratories. Although hospitals are expected to continue to be the major employer of clinical laboratory workers, employment is expected to grow faster in medical and diagnostic laboratories, offices of physicians, and other ambulatory health care services, including blood and organ banks.

Although significant, job growth will not be the only source of opportunities. As in most occupations, many openings will result from the need to replace workers who transfer to other occupations, retire, or stop working for some other reason.

Earnings

Median annual earnings of medical and clinical laboratory technologists were $42,910 in 2002. The middle 50 percent earned between $36,400 and $50,820. The lowest 10 percent earned less than $30,530, and the highest 10 percent earned more than $58,000. Median annual earnings in the industries employing the largest numbers of medical and clinical laboratory technologists in 2002 were as follows:

General medical and surgical hospitals	$43,340
Medical and diagnostic laboratories	42,020
Offices of physicians	38,690

Median annual earnings of medical and clinical laboratory technicians were $29,040 in 2002. The middle 50 percent earned between $23,310 and $35,840. The lowest 10 percent earned less than $19,070, and the highest 10 percent earned more than $43,960. Median annual earnings in the industries employing the largest numbers of medical and clinical laboratory technicians in 2002 were as follows:

General medical and surgical hospitals	$30,500
Colleges, universities, and professional schools	30,350
Offices of physicians	27,820
Medical and diagnostic laboratories	27,550
Other ambulatory health care services	26,710

According to the American Society for Clinical Pathology, median annual wages of staff clinical laboratory technologists and technicians in 2002 varied by specialty as follows:

	Lowest	Average	Highest
Cytotechnologist	$41,454	$49,920	$54,600
Histotechnologist	33,280	41,122	45,760
Medical technologist	33,280	40,186	45,760
Histotechnician	28,413	34,549	38,667
Medical laboratory technician	27,040	31,928	35,776
Phlebotomist	18,720	21,944	25,168

Related Occupations

Clinical laboratory technologists and technicians analyze body fluids, tissue, and other substances, using a variety of tests. Similar or related procedures are performed by chemists and materials scientists, science technicians, and veterinary technologists and technicians.

Sources of Additional Information

For a list of accredited and approved educational programs for clinical laboratory personnel, contact:

➤ National Accrediting Agency for Clinical Laboratory Sciences, 8410 W. Bryn Mawr Ave., Suite 670, Chicago, IL 60631. Internet: **http://www.naacls.org**

Information on certification is available from the following organizations:

➤ American Association of Bioanalysts, Board of Registry, 917 Locust St., Suite 1100, St. Louis, MO 63101. Internet: **http://www.aab.org**
➤ American Medical Technologists, 710 Higgins Rd., Park Ridge, IL 60068.
➤ American Society for Clinical Pathology, Board of Registry, 2100 West Harrison St., Chicago, IL 60612. Internet: **http://www.ascp.org/bor**
➤ National Credentialing Agency for Laboratory Personnel, P.O. Box 15945-289, Lenexa, KS 66285. Internet: **http://www.nca-info.org**

Additional career information is available from the following sources:

➤ American Association of Blood Banks, 8101 Glenbrook Rd., Bethesda, MD 20814-2749. Internet: **http://www.aabb.org**
➤ American Society for Clinical Laboratory Science, 6701 Democracy Blvd., Suite 300, Bethesda, MD 20817. Internet: **http://www.ascls.org**
➤ American Society for Clinical Pathology, 2100 West Harrison St., Chicago, IL 60612. Internet: **http://www.ascp.org**
➤ American Society for Cytopathology, 400 West 9th St., Suite 201, Wilmington, DE 19801. Internet: **http://www.cytopathology.org**
➤ Clinical Laboratory Management Association, 989 Old Eagle School Rd., Wayne, PA 19087. Internet: **http://www.clma.org**

Dental Hygienists

(0*NET 29-2021.00)

Significant Points

● Most dental hygiene programs grant an associate degree; others offer a certificate, a bachelor's degree, or a master's degree.

● Job prospects are expected to remain excellent.

● Opportunities for part-time work and flexible schedules are common.

Nature of the Work

Dental hygienists remove soft and hard deposits from teeth, teach patients how to practice good oral hygiene, and provide other preventive dental care. Hygienists examine patients' teeth and gums, recording the presence of diseases or abnormalities. They remove calculus, stains, and plaque from teeth; perform root planing as a periodontal therapy; take and develop dental x rays; and apply cavity-preventive agents such as fluorides and pit and fissure sealants. In some States, hygienists administer anesthetics; place and carve filling materials, temporary fillings, and periodontal dressings; remove sutures; and smooth and polish metal restorations. Although hygienists may not diagnose diseases, they can prepare clinical and laboratory diagnostic tests for the dentist to interpret. Hygienists sometimes work chairside with the dentist during treatment.

Dental hygienists also help patients develop and maintain good oral health. For example, they may explain the relationship between diet and oral health or inform patients how to select toothbrushes and show them how to brush and floss their teeth.

Dental hygienists use hand and rotary instruments and ultrasonics to clean and polish teeth, x-ray machines to take dental pictures, syringes with needles to administer local anesthetics, and models of teeth to explain oral hygiene.

Working Conditions

Flexible scheduling is a distinctive feature of this job. Full-time, part-time, evening, and weekend schedules are widely available. Dentists frequently hire hygienists to work only 2 or 3 days a week, so hygienists may hold jobs in more than one dental office.

Dental hygienists work in clean, well-lighted offices. Important health safeguards include strict adherence to proper radiological procedures, and the use of appropriate protective devices when administering anesthetic gas. Dental hygienists also wear safety glasses, surgical masks, and gloves to protect themselves and patients from infectious diseases.

Employment

Dental hygienists held about 148,000 jobs in 2002. Because multiple jobholding is common in this field, the number of jobs exceeds the number of hygienists. More than half of all dental hygienists worked part time—less than 35 hours a week.

Almost all jobs for dental hygienists were in offices of dentists. A very small number worked for employment services or in offices of physicians.

Training, Other Qualifications, and Advancement

Dental hygienists must be licensed by the State in which they practice. To qualify for licensure, a candidate must graduate from an accredited dental hygiene school and pass both a written and clinical examination. The American Dental Association Joint Commission on National Dental Examinations administers the written examination, which is accepted by all States and the District of Columbia. State or regional testing agencies administer the clinical examination. In addition, most States require an examination on the legal aspects of dental hygiene practice. Alabama allows candidates to take its examinations if they have been trained through a State-regulated on-the-job program in a dentist's office.

In 2002, the Commission on Dental Accreditation accredited about 265 programs in dental hygiene. Most dental hygiene programs grant an associate degree, although some also offer a certificate, a bachelor's degree, or a master's degree. A minimum of an associate degree or certificate in dental hygiene is required for practice in a private dental office. A bachelor's or master's degree usually is required for research, teaching, or clinical practice in public or school health programs.

About half of the dental hygiene programs prefer applicants who have completed at least 1 year of college. However, requirements vary from one school to another. Schools offer laboratory, clinical, and classroom instruction in subjects such as anatomy, physiology, chemistry, microbiology, pharmacology, nutrition, radiography, histology (the study of tissue structure),

periodontology (the study of gum diseases), pathology, dental materials, clinical dental hygiene, and social and behavioral sciences.

Dental hygienists should work well with others and must have good manual dexterity, because they use dental instruments within a patient's mouth, with little room for error. High school students interested in becoming a dental hygienist should take courses in biology, chemistry, and mathematics.

Job Outlook

Employment of dental hygienists is expected to grow much faster than the average for all occupations through 2012, in response to increasing demand for dental care and the greater utilization of hygienists to perform services previously performed by dentists. Job prospects are expected to remain excellent. In fact, dental hygienists is expected to be one of the fastest growing occupations through the year 2012.

Population growth and greater retention of natural teeth will stimulate demand for dental hygienists. Older dentists, who have been less likely to employ dental hygienists, are leaving the occupation and will be replaced by recent graduates, who are more likely to employ one or even two hygienists. In addition, as dentists' workloads increase, they are expected to hire more hygienists to perform preventive dental care, such as cleaning, so that they may devote their own time to more profitable procedures.

Earnings

Median hourly earnings of dental hygienists were $26.59 in 2002. The middle 50 percent earned between $21.96 and $32.48 an hour. The lowest 10 percent earned less than $17.34, and the highest 10 percent earned more than $39.24 an hour.

Earnings vary by geographic location, employment setting, and years of experience. Dental hygienists may be paid on an hourly, daily, salary, or commission basis.

Benefits vary substantially by practice setting and may be contingent upon full-time employment. According to the American Dental Association, almost all full-time dental hygienists employed by private practitioners received paid vacation. The ADA also found that 9 out of 10 full-time and part-time dental hygienists received dental coverage. Dental hygienists who work for school systems, public health agen-

Dental hygienists use hand and rotary instruments and ultrasonics to clean and polish teeth.

cies, the Federal Government, or State agencies usually have substantial benefits.

Related Occupations

Other workers supporting health practitioners in an office setting include dental assistants, medical assistants, occupational therapist assistants and aides, physical therapist assistants and aides, physician assistants, and registered nurses.

Sources of Additional Information

For information on a career in dental hygiene, including educational requirements, contact:

➤ Division of Education, American Dental Hygienists' Association, 444 N. Michigan Ave., Suite 3400, Chicago, IL 60611. Internet: **http://www.adha.org**

For information about accredited programs and educational requirements, contact:

➤ Commission on Dental Accreditation, American Dental Association, 211 E. Chicago Ave., Suite 1814, Chicago, IL 60611. Internet: **http://www.ada.org**

The State Board of Dental Examiners in each State can supply information on licensing requirements.

Diagnostic Medical Sonographers

(0*NET 29-2032.00)

Significant Points

- More than half of all sonographers were employed by hospitals, and most of the rest worked in offices of physicians or in medical and diagnostic laboratories, including diagnostic imaging centers.

- Sonographers may train in hospitals, vocational-technical institutions, colleges and universities, and the Armed Forces.

- Sonographers should experience favorable job opportunities, as sonography becomes an increasingly attractive alternative to radiologic procedures.

Nature of the Work

Diagnostic imaging embraces several procedures that aid in diagnosing ailments. Besides the familiar x ray, another common diagnostic imaging method is magnetic resonance imaging, which uses giant magnets that create radio waves, rather than radiation, to form an image. Not all imaging technologies use ionizing radiation or radio waves, however. Sonography, or ultrasonography, is the use of sound waves to generate an image for the assessment and diagnosis of various medical conditions. Many people associate sonography with obstetrics and the viewing of the fetus in the womb, but this technology has many other applications in the diagnosis and treatment of medical conditions.

Diagnostic medical sonographers, also known as *ultrasonographers*, use special equipment to direct nonionizing, high frequency sound waves into areas of the patient's body. Sonographers operate the equipment, which collects reflected echoes and forms an image that may be videotaped, transmitted, or photographed for interpretation and diagnosis by a physician.

Sonographers begin by explaining the procedure to the patient and recording any medical history that may be relevant to the condition being viewed. They then select appropriate equipment settings and direct the patient to move into positions that will provide the best view. To perform the exam, sonographers use a transducer, which transmits sound waves in a cone- or rectangle-shaped beam. Although techniques vary with the area being examined, sonographers usually spread a special gel on the skin to aid the transmission of sound waves.

Viewing the screen during the scan, sonographers look for subtle visual cues that contrast healthy areas with unhealthy ones. They decide whether the images are satisfactory for diagnostic purposes and select which ones to show to the physician.

Diagnostic medical sonographers may specialize in obstetric and gynecologic sonography (the female reproductive system), abdominal sonography (the liver, kidneys, gallbladder, spleen, and pancreas), neurosonography (the brain), or ophthalmologic sonography (the eyes). In addition, sonographers may specialize in vascular technology or echocardiography. (Vascular technologists and echocardiographers are covered in the *Handbook* statement on cardiovascular technologists and technicians.)

Obstetric and gynecologic sonographers specialize in the study of the female reproductive system. Included in the discipline is one of the more well-known uses of sonography: examining the fetus of a pregnant woman to track its growth and health.

Abdominal sonographers inspect a patient's abdominal cavity to help diagnose and treat conditions involving primarily the gallbladder, bile ducts, kidneys, liver, pancreas, and spleen. Abdominal sonographers also are able to scan parts of the chest, although studies of the heart using sonography usually are done by echocardiographers.

Neurosonographers focus on the nervous system, including the brain. In neonatal care, neurosonographers study and diagnose neurological and nervous system disorders in premature infants. They also may scan blood vessels to check for abnormalities indicating a stroke in infants diagnosed with sickle-cell anemia. Like other sonographers, neurosonographers operate transducers to perform the sonogram, but use frequencies and beam shapes different from those used by obstetric and abdominal sonographers.

Ophthalmologic sonographers use sonography to study the eyes. Sonography aids in the insertion of prosthetic lenses by allowing accurate measurement of the eyes. Ophthalmologic sonography also helps diagnose and track tumors, blood supply conditions, separated retinas, and other ailments of the eye and the surrounding tissue. Ophthalmologic sonographers use high-frequency transducers, made exclusively to study the eyes, which are much smaller than those used in other specialties.

In addition to working directly with patients, diagnostic medical sonographers keep patient records and adjust and maintain equipment. They also may prepare work schedules, evaluate equipment purchases, or manage a sonography or diagnostic imaging department.

Working Conditions

Most full-time sonographers work about 40 hours a week. Hospital-based sonographers may have evening and weekend hours and times when they are on call and must be ready to report to work on short notice.

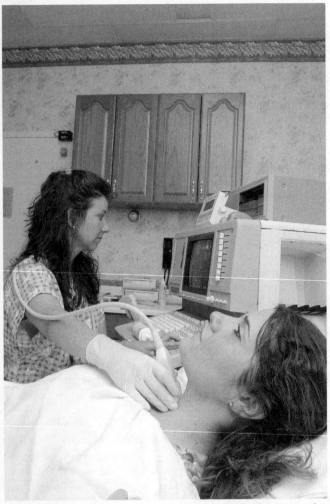

Using ultrasound equipment, a diagnostic medical sonographer creates an image of a patient's throat.

Sonographers typically work in healthcare facilities that are clean and well lighted. Some travel to patients in large vans equipped with sophisticated diagnostic equipment. Sonographers are on their feet for long periods and may have to lift or turn disabled patients. They work at diagnostic imaging machines, but also may perform some procedures at patients' bedsides.

Employment
Diagnostic medical sonographers held about 37,000 jobs in 2002. More than half of all sonographer jobs were in hospitals. Most of the rest were in offices of physicians or in medical and diagnostic laboratories, including diagnostic imaging centers. According to data from the Sonography Benchmark Survey conducted by the Society of Diagnostic Medical Sonography, about 3 out of 4 sonographers worked in urban areas.

Training, Other Qualifications, and Advancement
There are several avenues for entry into the field of diagnostic medical sonography. Sonographers may train in hospitals, vocational-technical institutions, colleges and universities, and the Armed Forces. Some training programs prefer applicants with a background in science or experience in other health professions, but also will consider high school graduates with courses in mathematics and science, as well as applicants with liberal arts backgrounds.

Colleges and universities offer formal training in both 2- and 4-year programs, culminating in an associate or a bachelor's degree. Two-year programs are most prevalent. Course work includes classes in anatomy, physiology, instrumentation, basic physics, patient care, and medical ethics. The Commission on Accreditation for Allied Health Education Programs accredits most formal training programs—about 102 programs in 2003.

Some health workers, such as obstetric nurses and radiologic technologists, increase their marketability by seeking training in fields such as sonography. This usually requires completion of an additional 1-year program that may result in a certificate. In addition, sonographers specializing in one particular discipline often seek competency in others; for example, obstetric sonographers might seek training in, and exposure to, abdominal sonography to broaden their opportunities.

Although no State requires licensure in diagnostic medical sonography, organizations such as the American Registry of Diagnostic Medical Sonographers (ARDMS) certify the competency of sonographers through registration. Because registration provides an independent, objective measure of an individual's professional standing, many employers prefer to hire registered sonographers. Registration with ARDMS requires passing a general physics and instrumentation examination, in addition to passing an exam in a specialty such as obstetric and gynecologic sonography, abdominal sonography, or neurosonography. To keep their registration current, sonographers must complete continuing education to stay abreast of technological advances related to the occupation.

Sonographers need good communication and interpersonal skills because they must be able to explain technical procedures and results to their patients, some of whom may be nervous about the exam or the problems it may reveal. Sonographers also should have a background in mathematics and science.

Job Outlook
Employment of diagnostic medical sonographers is expected to grow faster than the average for all occupations through 2012 as the population grows and ages, increasing the demand for diagnostic imaging and therapeutic technology. In addition to job openings due to growth, some job openings will arise from the need to replace sonographers who leave the occupation permanently.

Opportunities should be favorable because sonography is becoming an increasingly attractive alternative to radiologic procedures, as patients seek safer treatment methods. Unlike most diagnostic imaging methods, sonography does not involve radiation, so harmful side effects and complications from repeated use are rarer for both the patient and the sonographer. Sonographic technology is expected to evolve rapidly and to spawn many new sonography procedures, such as 3D-sonography for use in obstetric and ophthalmologic diagnosis. However, high costs may limit the rate at which some promising new technologies are adopted.

Hospitals will remain the principal employer of diagnostic medical sonographers. However, employment is expected to grow more rapidly in offices of physicians and in medical and diagnostic laboratories, including diagnostic imaging centers. Health facilities such as these are expected to grow very rapidly through 2012 due to the strong shift toward outpatient care, encouraged by third-party payers and made possible by technological advances that permit more procedures to be performed outside the hospital.

Earnings

Median annual earnings of diagnostic medical sonographers were $48,660 in 2002. The middle 50 percent earned between $41,420 and $56,020 a year. The lowest 10 percent earned less than $35,800, and the highest 10 percent earned more than $66,680. Median annual earnings of diagnostic medical sonographers in 2002 were $50,390 in offices of physicians and $47,530 in hospitals.

Related Occupations

Diagnostic medical sonographers operate sophisticated equipment to help physicians and other health practitioners diagnose and treat patients. Workers in related occupations include cardiovascular technologists and technicians, clinical laboratory technologists and technicians, nuclear medicine technologists, radiologic technologists and technicians, and respiratory therapists.

Sources of Additional Information

For information on a career as a diagnostic medical sonographer, contact:
➤ Society of Diagnostic Medical Sonography, 2745 Dallas Pkwy., Suite 350, Plano, TX 75093-8730. Internet: **http://www.sdms.org**

For information on becoming a registered diagnostic medical sonographer, contact:
➤ American Registry of Diagnostic Medical Sonographers, 51 Monroe St., Plaza East 1, Rockville, MD 20850-2400. Internet: **http://www.ardms.org**

For a current list of accredited education programs in diagnostic medical sonography, contact:
➤ Joint Review Committee on Education in Diagnostic Medical Sonography, 2025 Woodlane Dr., St. Paul, MN 55125-2998. Internet: **http://www.jrcdms.org**
➤ Commission on Accreditation for Allied Health Education Programs, 39 East Wacker Dr., Chicago, IL 60601. Internet: **http://www.caahep.org**

Emergency Medical Technicians and Paramedics

(0*NET 29-2041.00)

Significant Points

● Job stress is common because hours of work are irregular and workers often must treat patients in life-or-death situations.

● Formal training and certification are required, but State requirements vary.

● Employment is projected to grow faster than average as paid emergency medical technician positions replace unpaid volunteers.

● Competition will be greater for jobs in local fire, police, and rescue squad departments than in private ambulance services; opportunities will be best for those who have advanced certification.

Nature of the Work

People's lives often depend on the quick reaction and competent care of emergency medical technicians (EMTs) and paramedics—EMTs with additional advanced training to perform more difficult prehospital medical procedures. Incidents as varied as automobile accidents, heart attacks, drownings, childbirth, and gunshot wounds all require immediate medical attention. EMTs and paramedics provide this vital attention as they care for and transport the sick or injured to a medical facility.

In an emergency, EMTs and paramedics typically are dispatched to the scene by a 911 operator, and often work with police and fire department personnel. (Police and detectives and firefighting occupations are discussed elsewhere in the *Handbook*.) Once they arrive, they determine the nature and extent of the patient's condition while trying to ascertain whether the patient has preexisting medical problems. Following strict rules and guidelines, they give appropriate emergency care and, when necessary, transport the patient. Some paramedics are trained to treat patients with minor injuries on the scene of an accident or at their home without transporting them to a medical facility. Emergency treatment for more complicated problems is carried out under the direction of medical doctors by radio preceding or during transport.

EMTs and paramedics may use special equipment, such as backboards, to immobilize patients before placing them on stretchers and securing them in the ambulance for transport to a medical facility. Usually, one EMT or paramedic drives while the other monitors the patient's vital signs and gives additional care as needed. Some EMTs work as part of the flight crew of helicopters that transport critically ill or injured patients to hospital trauma centers.

At the medical facility, EMTs and paramedics help transfer patients to the emergency department, report their observations and actions to emergency room staff, and may provide additional emergency treatment. After each run, EMTs and paramedics replace used supplies and check equipment. If a transported patient had a contagious disease, EMTs and paramedics decontaminate the interior of the ambulance and report cases to the proper authorities.

Beyond these general duties, the specific responsibilities of EMTs and paramedics depend on their level of qualification and training. To determine this, the National Registry of Emergency Medical Technicians (NREMT) registers emergency medical service (EMS) providers at four levels: First Responder, EMT-Basic, EMT-Intermediate, and EMT-Paramedic. Some States, however, do their own certification and use numeric ratings from 1 to 4 to distinguish levels of proficiency.

The lowest-level workers—First Responders—are trained to provide basic emergency medical care because they tend to be the first persons to arrive at the scene of an incident. Many firefighters, police officers, and other emergency workers have this level of training. The EMT-Basic, also known as EMT-1, represents the first component of the emergency medical technician system. An EMT-1 is trained to care for patients at the scene of an accident and while transporting patients by ambulance to the hospital under medical direction. The EMT-1 has the emergency skills to assess a patient's condition and manage respiratory, cardiac, and trauma emergencies.

The EMT-Intermediate (EMT-2 and EMT-3) has more advanced training that allows the administration of intravenous fluids, the use of manual defibrillators to give lifesaving shocks to a stopped heart, and the application of advanced airway techniques and equipment to assist patients experiencing respiratory emergencies. EMT-Paramedics (EMT-4) provide the most extensive prehospital care. In addition to carrying out the procedures already described, paramedics may administer drugs

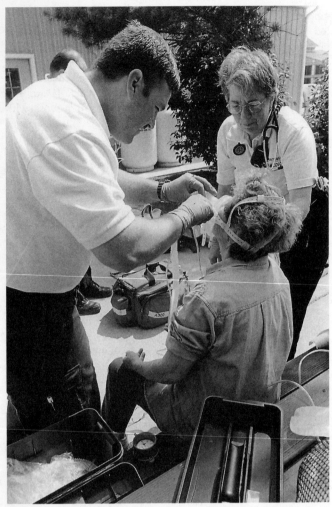

Emergency medical technicians provide medical care to patients at the scene of an emergency.

orally and intravenously, interpret electrocardiograms (EKGs), perform endotracheal intubations, and use monitors and other complex equipment.

Working Conditions

EMTs and paramedics work both indoors and outdoors, in all types of weather. They are required to do considerable kneeling, bending, and heavy lifting. These workers risk noise-induced hearing loss from sirens and back injuries from lifting patients. In addition, EMTs and paramedics may be exposed to diseases such as hepatitis-B and AIDS, as well as violence from drug overdose victims or mentally unstable patients. The work is not only physically strenuous, but also stressful, involving life-or-death situations and suffering patients. Nonetheless, many people find the work exciting and challenging and enjoy the opportunity to help others.

EMTs and paramedics employed by fire departments work about 50 hours a week. Those employed by hospitals frequently work between 45 and 60 hours a week, and those in private ambulance services, between 45 and 50 hours. Some of these workers, especially those in police and fire departments, are on call for extended periods. Because emergency services function 24 hours a day, EMTs and paramedics have irregular working hours that add to job stress.

Employment

EMTs and paramedics held about 179,000 jobs in 2002. Most career EMTs and paramedics work in metropolitan areas. There are many more volunteer EMTs and paramedics, especially in smaller cities, towns, and rural areas. These individuals volunteer for fire departments, emergency medical services (EMS), or hospitals, and may respond to only a few calls for service per month or may answer the majority of calls, especially in smaller communities. EMTs and paramedics work closely with firefighters, who often are certified as EMTs as well and act as first responders.

Full-time and part-time paid EMTs and paramedics were employed in a number of industries. About 4 out of 10 worked as employees of private ambulance services. About 3 out of 10 worked in local government for fire departments, public ambulance services, and EMS. Another 2 out 10 were found in hospitals, working full time within the medical facility or responded to calls in ambulances or helicopters to transport critically ill or injured patients. The remainder worked in various industries providing emergency services.

Training, Other Qualifications, and Advancement

Formal training and certification is needed to become an EMT or paramedic. All 50 States have a certification procedure. In most States and the District of Columbia, registration with the NREMT is required at some or all levels of certification. Other States administer their own certification examination or provide the option of taking the NREMT examination. To maintain certification, EMTs and paramedics must reregister, usually every 2 years. In order to reregister, an individual must be working as an EMT or paramedic and meet a continuing education requirement.

Training is offered at progressive levels: EMT-Basic, also known as EMT-1; EMT-Intermediate, or EMT-2 and EMT-3; and EMT-Paramedic, or EMT-4. EMT-Basic coursework typically emphasizes emergency skills, such as managing respiratory, trauma, and cardiac emergencies, and patient assessment. Formal courses are often combined with time in an emergency room or ambulance. The program also provides instruction and practice in dealing with bleeding, fractures, airway obstruction, cardiac arrest, and emergency childbirth. Students learn how to use and maintain common emergency equipment, such as backboards, suction devices, splints, oxygen delivery systems, and stretchers. Graduates of approved EMT basic training programs who pass a written and practical examination administered by the State certifying agency or the NREMT earn the title "Registered EMT-Basic." The course also is a prerequisite for EMT-Intermediate and EMT-Paramedic training.

EMT-Intermediate training requirements vary from State to State. Applicants can opt to receive training in EMT-Shock Trauma, wherein the caregiver learns to start intravenous fluids and give certain medications, or in EMT-Cardiac, which includes learning heart rhythms and administering advanced medications. Training commonly includes 35 to 55 hours of additional instruction beyond EMT-Basic coursework, and covers patient assessment as well as the use of advanced airway devices and intravenous fluids. Prerequisites for taking the EMT-Intermediate examination include registration as an EMT-Basic, required classroom work, and a specified amount of clinical experience.

The most advanced level of training for this occupation is EMT-Paramedic. At this level, the caregiver receives additional training in body function and learns more advanced skills. The Technology program usually lasts up to 2 years and results in an associate degree in applied science. Such education prepares the graduate to take the NREMT examination and become certified as an EMT-Paramedic. Extensive related coursework and clinical and field experience is required. Due to the longer training requirement, almost all EMT-Paramedics are in paid positions, rather than being volunteers. Refresher courses and continuing education are available for EMTs and paramedics at all levels.

EMTs and paramedics should be emotionally stable, have good dexterity, agility, and physical coordination, and be able to lift and carry heavy loads. They also need good eyesight (corrective lenses may be used) with accurate color vision.

Advancement beyond the EMT-Paramedic level usually means leaving fieldwork. An EMT-Paramedic can become a supervisor, operations manager, administrative director, or executive director of emergency services. Some EMTs and paramedics become instructors, dispatchers, or physician assistants, while others move into sales or marketing of emergency medical equipment. A number of people become EMTs and paramedics to assess their interest in healthcare, and then decide to return to school and become registered nurses, physicians, or other health workers.

Job Outlook
Employment of emergency medical technicians and paramedics is expected to grow faster than the average for all occupations through 2012. Population growth and urbanization will increase the demand for full-time paid EMTs and paramedics rather than for volunteers. In addition, a large segment of the population—the aging baby boomers—will further spur demand for EMT services as they become more likely to have medical emergencies. There will still be demand for part-time, volunteer EMTs and paramedics in rural areas and smaller metropolitan areas. In addition to those arising from job growth, openings will occur because of replacement needs; some workers leave the occupation because of stressful working conditions, limited potential for advancement, and the modest pay and benefits in private-sector jobs.

Most opportunities for EMTs and paramedics are expected to found in private ambulance services. Competition will be greater for jobs in local government, including fire, police, and independent third-service rescue squad departments, in which salaries and benefits tend to be slightly better. Opportunities will be best for those who have advanced certifications, such as EMT-Intermediate and EMT-Paramedic, as clients and patients demand higher levels of care before arriving at the hospital.

Earnings
Earnings of EMTs and paramedics depend on the employment setting and geographic location as well as the individual's training and experience. Median annual earnings of EMTs and paramedics were $24,030 in 2002. The middle 50 percent earned between $19,040 and $31,600. The lowest 10 percent earned less than $15,530, and the highest 10 percent earned more than $41,980. Median annual earnings in the industries employing the largest numbers of EMTs and paramedics in 2002 were:

Local government	$27,440
General medical and surgical hospitals	24,760
Other ambulatory health care services	22,180

Those in emergency medical services who are part of fire or police departments receive the same benefits as firefighters or police officers. For example, many are covered by pension plans that provide retirement at half pay after 20 or 25 years of service or if the worker is disabled in the line of duty.

Related Occupations
Other workers in occupations that require quick and level-headed reactions to life-or-death situations are air traffic controllers, firefighting occupations, physician assistants, police and detectives, and registered nurses.

Sources of Additional Information
General information about emergency medical technicians and paramedics is available from:
➤ National Association of Emergency Medical Technicians, P.O. Box 1400, Clinton, MS 39060-1400. Internet: **http://www.naemt.org**
➤ National Registry of Emergency Medical Technicians, Rocco V. Morando Bldg., 6610 Busch Blvd., P.O. Box 29233, Columbus, OH 43229. Internet: **http://www.nremt.org**
➤ National Highway Transportation Safety Administration, EMS Division, 400 7th St. SW., NTS-14, Washington, DC 20590. Internet: **http://www.nhtsa.dot.gov/people/injury/ems**

Licensed Practical and Licensed Vocational Nurses

(0*NET 29-2061.00)

Significant Points

● Training lasting about 1 year is available in about 1,100 State-approved programs, mostly in vocational or technical schools.

● Nursing care facilities will offer the most new jobs.

● Applicants for jobs in hospitals may face competition as the number of hospital jobs for LPNs declines.

Nature of the Work
Licensed practical nurses (LPNs), or licensed vocational nurses (LVNs), care for the sick, injured, convalescent, and disabled under the direction of physicians and registered nurses. (The work of *physicians and surgeons* and *registered nurses* is described elsewhere in the *Handbook*.)

Most LPNs provide basic bedside care, taking vital signs such as temperature, blood pressure, pulse, and respiration. They also prepare and give injections and enemas, monitor catheters, apply dressings, treat bedsores, and give alcohol rubs and massages. LPNs monitor their patients and report adverse reactions to medications or treatments. They collect samples for testing, perform routine laboratory tests, feed patients, and record food and fluid intake and output. To help keep patients comfortable, LPNs assist with bathing, dressing, and personal hygiene. In States where the law allows, they may administer prescribed medicines or start intravenous fluids. Some LPNs help deliver, care for, and feed infants. Experienced LPNs may supervise nursing assistants and aides.

In addition to providing routine beside care, LPNs in nursing care facilities help evaluate residents' needs, develop care plans, and supervise the care provided by nursing aides. In doctors' offices and clinics, they also may make appointments, keep records, and perform other clerical duties. LPNs who work in private homes may prepare meals and teach family members simple nursing tasks.

Working Conditions

Most licensed practical nurses in hospitals and nursing care facilities work a 40-hour week, but because patients need around-the-clock care, some work nights, weekends, and holidays. They often stand for long periods and help patients move in bed, stand, or walk.

LPNs may face hazards from caustic chemicals, radiation, and infectious diseases such as hepatitis. They are subject to back injuries when moving patients and shock from electrical equipment. They often must deal with the stress of heavy workloads. In addition, the patients they care for may be confused, irrational, agitated, or uncooperative.

Employment

Licensed practical nurses held about 702,000 jobs in 2002. About 28 percent of LPNs worked in hospitals, 26 percent in nursing care facilities, and another 12 percent in offices of physicians. Others worked for home healthcare services, employment services, community care facilities for the elderly, public and private educational services, outpatient care centers, and Federal, State, and local government agencies; about 1 in 5 worked part time.

Training, Other Qualifications, and Advancement

All States and the District of Columbia require LPNs to pass a licensing examination after completing a State-approved practical nursing program. A high school diploma or its equivalent usually is required for entry, although some programs accept candidates without a diploma or are designed as part of a high school curriculum.

In 2002, approximately 1,100 State-approved programs provided training in practical nursing. Almost 6 out of 10 students were enrolled in technical or vocational schools, while 3 out of 10 were in community and junior colleges. Others were in high schools, hospitals, and colleges and universities.

Most practical nursing programs last about 1 year and include both classroom study and supervised clinical practice (patient care). Classroom study covers basic nursing concepts and patient care-related subjects, including anatomy, physiology, medical-surgical nursing, pediatrics, obstetrics, psychiatric nursing, the administration of drugs, nutrition, and first aid. Clinical practice usually is in a hospital, but sometimes includes other settings.

LPNs should have a caring, sympathetic nature. They should be emotionally stable, because work with the sick and injured can be stressful. They also should have keen observational, decisionmaking, and communication skills. As part of a healthcare team, they must be able to follow orders and work under close supervision.

Licensed practical and licensed vocational nurses care for the sick, injured, convalescent, and disabled.

Job Outlook

Employment of LPNs is expected to grow about as fast as the average for all occupations through 2012 in response to the long-term care needs of an increasing elderly population and the general growth of healthcare. Replacement needs will be a major source of job openings, as many workers leave the occupation permanently.

Applicants for jobs in hospitals may face competition as the number of hospital jobs for LPNs declines. An increasing proportion of sophisticated procedures, which once were performed only in hospitals, is being performed in physicians' offices and in outpatient care centers such as ambulatory surgical and emergency medical centers, due largely to advances in technology. Consequently, employment of LPNs is projected to grow faster than average in these sectors as healthcare expands outside the traditional hospital setting.

Employment of LPNs in nursing care facilities is expected to grow faster than the average. Such facilities will offer the most new jobs for LPNs as the number of aged and disabled persons in need of long-term care rises. In addition to caring for the aged and the disabled, LPNs in nursing care facilities will care for the increasing number of patients who will have been discharged from the hospital, but have not recovered enough to return home.

Employment of LPNs is expected to grow much faster than average in home healthcare services. This growth is in response to an increasing number of older persons with functional disabilities, consumer preference for care in the home, and technological advances that make it possible to bring increasingly complex treatments into the home.

Earnings

Median annual earnings of licensed practical nurses were $31,440 in 2002. The middle 50 percent earned between $26,430 and $37,050. The lowest 10 percent earned less than $22,860, and the highest 10 percent earned more than $44,040. Median annual earnings in the industries employing the largest numbers of licensed practical nurses in 2002 were as follows:

Employment services	$40,550
Home health care services	32,850
Nursing care facilities	32,220
General medical and surgical hospitals	30,310
Offices of physicians	28,710

Related Occupations

LPNs work closely with people while helping them. So do emergency medical technicians and paramedics, social and human service assistants, surgical technologists, and teacher assistants.

Sources of Additional Information

For information about practical nursing, contact any of the following organizations:

➤ National League for Nursing, 61 Broadway, New York, NY 10006. Internet: **http://www.nln.org**

➤ National Federation of Licensed Practical Nurses, Inc., 605 Poole Dr., Garner, NC 27529.

Medical Records and Health Information Technicians

(0*NET 29-2071.00)

Significant Points

- This is one of the few health occupations in which there is little or no direct contact with patients.

- Medical records and health information technicians entering the field usually have an associate degree; courses include anatomy, physiology, medical terminology, and computer science.

- Job prospects should be very good, particularly in offices of physicians.

Nature of the Work

Every time a patient receives healthcare, a record is maintained of the observations, medical or surgical interventions, and treatment outcomes. This record includes information that the patient provides concerning his or her symptoms and medical history, the results of examinations, reports of x rays and laboratory tests, diagnoses, and treatment plans. Medical records and health information technicians organize and evaluate these records for completeness and accuracy.

Technicians begin to assemble patients' health information by first making sure their initial medical charts are complete. They ensure that all forms are completed and properly identified and signed, and that all necessary information is in the computer. They regularly communicate with physicians or other healthcare professionals to clarify diagnoses or to obtain additional information.

Medical records and health information technicians assign a code to each diagnosis and procedure. They consult classification manuals and also rely on their knowledge of disease processes. Technicians then use computer software to assign the patient to one of several hundred "diagnosis-related groups," or DRGs. The DRG determines the amount for which the hospital will be reimbursed if the patient is covered by Medicare or other insurance programs using the DRG system. Technicians who specialize in coding are called health information coders, medical record coders, coder/abstractors, or coding specialists. In addition to the DRG system, coders use other coding systems, such as those geared towards ambulatory settings or long-term care.

Technicians also use computer programs to tabulate and analyze data to help improve patient care, to control costs, for use in legal actions, in response to surveys, or for use in research studies. Cancer registrars compile, maintain, and review records of cancer patients to provide information to physicians and for use in research studies.

Medical records and health information technicians' duties vary with the size of the facility. In large to medium-sized facilities, technicians may specialize in one aspect of health information, or supervise health information clerks and transcriptionists while a medical records and health information administrator manages the department. (See the statement on medical and health services managers elsewhere in the *Handbook*.) In small facilities, a credentialed medical records and health information technician sometimes manages the department.

Working Conditions

Medical records and health information technicians usually work a 40-hour week. Some overtime may be required. In hospitals—where health information departments often are open 24 hours a day, 7 days a week—technicians may work day, evening, and night shifts.

Medical records and health information technicians work in pleasant and comfortable offices. This is one of the few health occupations in which there is little or no direct contact with patients. Because accuracy is essential in their jobs, technicians must pay close attention to detail. Technicians who work at computer monitors for prolonged periods must guard against eyestrain and muscle pain.

Employment

Medical records and health information technicians held about 147,000 jobs in 2002. Thirty-seven percent of all jobs were in hospitals. The rest were mostly in offices of physicians, nursing care facilities, outpatient care centers, and home healthcare services. Insurance firms that deal in health matters employ a small number of health information technicians to tabulate and analyze health information. Public health departments also hire technicians to supervise data collection from healthcare institutions and to assist in research.

Training, Other Qualifications, and Advancement

Medical records and health information technicians entering the field usually have an associate degree from a community or junior college. In addition to general education, coursework includes medical terminology, anatomy and physiology, legal aspects of health information, coding and abstraction of data, statistics, database management, quality improvement methods, and computer science. Applicants can improve their chances of admission into a program by taking biology, chemistry, health, and computer science courses in high school.

Hospitals sometimes advance promising health information clerks to jobs as medical records and health information technicians, although this practice may be less common in the future. Advancement usually requires 2 to 4 years of job experience and completion of a hospital's in-house training program.

Most employers prefer to hire Registered Health Information Technicians (RHIT), who must pass a written examination offered by the American Health Information Management Association (AHIMA). To take the examination, a person must graduate from a 2-year associate degree program accredited by the Commission on Accreditation of Allied Health Education Pro-

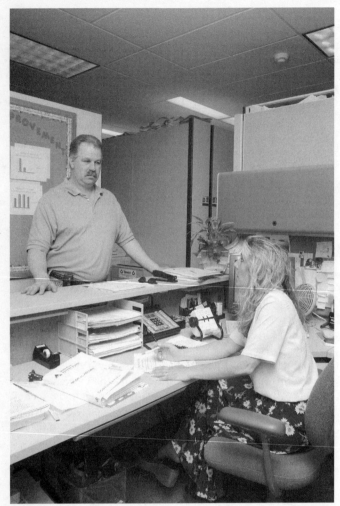

Medical records and health information technicians work in pleasant and comfortable offices.

grams (CAAHEP) of the American Medical Association. Technicians trained in non-CAAHEP-accredited programs, or on the job, are not eligible to take the examination. In 2003, CAAHEP accredited 182 programs for health information technicians. Technicians who specialize in coding may obtain voluntary certification.

Experienced medical records and health information technicians usually advance in one of two ways—by specializing or managing. Many senior technicians specialize in coding, particularly Medicare coding, or in cancer registry.

In large medical records and health information departments, experienced technicians may advance to section supervisor, overseeing the work of the coding, correspondence, or discharge sections, for example. Senior technicians with RHIT credentials may become director or assistant director of a medical records and health information department in a small facility. However, in larger institutions, the director is usually an administrator, with a bachelor's degree in medical records and health information administration.

Job Outlook
Job prospects should be very good. Employment of medical records and health information technicians is expected to grow much faster than the average for all occupations through 2012, due to rapid growth in the number of medical tests, treatments,

and procedures that will be increasingly scrutinized by third-party payers, regulators, courts, and consumers.

Although employment growth in hospitals will not keep pace with growth in other healthcare industries, many new jobs will nevertheless be created. The fastest employment growth and a majority of the new jobs are expected in offices of physicians, due to increasing demand for detailed records, especially in large group practices. Rapid growth also is expected in nursing care facilities, home healthcare services, and outpatient care centers. Additional job openings will result from the need to replace technicians who retire or leave the occupation permanently.

Earnings
Median annual earnings of medical records and health information technicians were $23,890 in 2002. The middle 50 percent earned between $19,550 and $30,600. The lowest 10 percent earned less than $16,460, and the highest 10 percent earned more than $38,640. Median annual earnings in the industries employing the largest numbers of medical records and health information technicians in 2002 were as follows:

Nursing care facilities	$25,160
General medical and surgical hospitals	24,910
Outpatient care centers	22,380
Offices of physicians	21,320

Related Occupations
Medical records and health information technicians need a strong clinical background to analyze the contents of medical records. Other workers who need knowledge of medical terminology, anatomy, and physiology, but have little or no direct contact with the patient, include medical secretaries and medical transcriptionists.

Sources of Additional Information
Information on careers in medical records and health information technology, including a list of programs accredited by the Commission on Accreditation of Allied Health Education Programs (CAAHEP), is available from:
➤ American Health Information Management Association, 233 N. Michigan Ave., Suite 2150, Chicago, IL 60601-5800. Internet: **http://www.ahima.org**

Nuclear Medicine Technologists

(0*NET 29-2033.00)

Significant Points

● Nuclear medicine technology programs range in length from 1 to 4 years and lead to a certificate, associate degree, or bachelor's degree.

● Faster-than-average growth will arise from an increase in the number of middle-aged and elderly persons, who are the primary users of diagnostic procedures.

Nature of the Work
Diagnostic imaging embraces several procedures that aid in diagnosing ailments, the most familiar being the x ray. Another

increasingly common diagnostic imaging method, called magnetic resonance imaging (MRI), uses giant magnets and radio waves, rather than radiation, to create an image. Not all imaging technologies use ionizing radiation or radio waves, however: In nuclear medicine, radionuclides—unstable atoms that emit radiation spontaneously—are used to diagnose and treat disease. Radionuclides are purified and compounded to form radiopharmaceuticals. Nuclear medicine technologists administer radiopharmaceuticals to patients and then monitor the characteristics and functions of tissues or organs in which the drugs localize. Abnormal areas show higher- or lower-than-expected concentrations of radioactivity.

Nuclear medicine technologists operate cameras that detect and map the radioactive drug in a patient's body to create diagnostic images. After explaining test procedures to patients, technologists prepare a dosage of the radiopharmaceutical and administer it by mouth, injection, or other means. They position patients and start a gamma scintillation camera, or "scanner," which creates images of the distribution of a radiopharmaceutical as it localizes in, and emits signals from, the patient's body. The images are produced on a computer screen or on film for a physician to interpret.

When preparing radiopharmaceuticals, technologists adhere to safety standards that keep the radiation dose to workers and patients as low as possible. Technologists keep patient records and record the amount and type of radionuclides received, used, and discarded.

Radiologic technologists and technicians, diagnostic medical sonographers, and cardiovascular technologists and technicians also operate diagnostic imaging equipment, but their equipment creates images by means of a different technology. (See the statements on these occupations elsewhere in the *Handbook*.)

Nuclear medicine technologists also perform radioimmunoassay studies that assess the behavior of a radioactive substance inside the body. For example, technologists may add radioactive substances to blood or serum to determine levels of hormones or of therapeutic drugs in the body. Some nuclear medicine studies, such as cardiac function studies, are processed with the aid of a computer.

Working Conditions

Nuclear medicine technologists generally work a 40-hour week, perhaps including evening or weekend hours in departments that operate on an extended schedule. Opportunities for part-time and shift work are also available. In addition, technologists in hospitals may have on-call duty on a rotational basis.

Because technologists are on their feet much of the day and may lift or turn disabled patients, physical stamina is important.

Although the potential for radiation exposure exists in this field, it is kept to a minimum by the use of shielded syringes, gloves, and other protective devices and by adherence to strict radiation safety guidelines. Technologists also wear badges that measure radiation levels. Because of safety programs, badge measurements rarely exceed established safety levels.

Employment

Nuclear medicine technologists held about 17,000 jobs in 2002. About two-thirds of all jobs were in hospitals. Most of the rest were in offices of physicians or in medical and diagnostic laboratories, including diagnostic imaging centers.

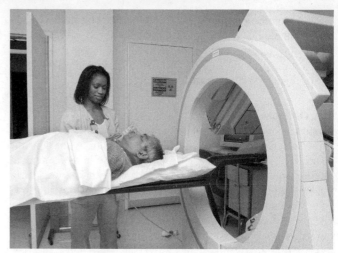

A nuclear medicine technologist readies a patient prior to a scan.

Training, Other Qualifications, and Advancement

Many employers and an increasing number of States require certification or licensure. Aspiring nuclear medicine technologists should check the requirements for the State in which they plan to work. Certification is available from the American Registry of Radiologic Technologists and from the Nuclear Medicine Technology Certification Board. Nuclear medicine technologists must meet the minimum Federal standards on the administration of radioactive drugs and the operation of radiation detection equipment.

Nuclear medicine technology programs range in length from 1 to 4 years and lead to a certificate, associate degree, or bachelor's degree. Generally, certificate programs are offered in hospitals, associate degree programs in community colleges, and bachelor's degree programs in 4-year colleges and universities. Courses cover the physical sciences, biological effects of radiation exposure, radiation protection and procedures, the use of radiopharmaceuticals, imaging techniques, and computer applications.

One-year certificate programs are for health professionals—especially radiologic technologists and diagnostic medical sonographers—who wish to specialize in nuclear medicine. They also attract medical technologists, registered nurses, and others who wish to change fields or specialize. Others interested in the nuclear medicine technology field have three options: a 2-year certificate program, a 2-year associate degree program, or a 4-year bachelor's degree program.

The Joint Review Committee on Education Programs in Nuclear Medicine Technology accredits most formal training programs in nuclear medicine technology. In 2002, there were 92 accredited programs in the continental United States and Puerto Rico.

Nuclear medicine technologists should be sensitive to patients' physical and psychological needs. They must pay attention to detail, follow instructions, and work as part of a team. In addition, operating complicated equipment requires mechanical ability and manual dexterity.

Technologists may advance to supervisor, then to chief technologist, and, finally, to department administrator or director. Some technologists specialize in a clinical area such as nuclear cardiology or computer analysis or leave patient care to take positions in research laboratories. Some become instructors or directors in nuclear medicine technology programs, a step that usually requires a bachelor's or master's degree in nuclear medicine technology. Others leave the occupation to work as sales or training representatives for medical equipment and radiopharmaceutical manufacturing firms or as radiation safety officers in regulatory agencies or hospitals.

Job Outlook

Employment of nuclear medicine technologists is expected to grow faster than the average for all occupations through the year 2012. Growth will arise from an increase in the number of middle-aged and older persons, who are the primary users of diagnostic procedures, including nuclear medicine tests. However, the number of openings each year will be relatively low because the occupation is small. Technologists who are also trained in other diagnostic methods, such as radiologic technology or diagnostic medical sonography, will have the best prospects.

Technological innovations may increase the diagnostic uses of nuclear medicine. One example is the use of radiopharmaceuticals in combination with monoclonal antibodies to detect cancer at far earlier stages than is customary today and without resorting to surgery. Another is the use of radionuclides to examine the heart's ability to pump blood. Wider use of nuclear medical imaging to observe metabolic and biochemical changes for neurology, cardiology, and oncology procedures also will spur demand for nuclear medicine technologists.

Nonetheless, cost considerations will affect the speed with which new applications of nuclear medicine grow. Some promising nuclear medicine procedures, such as positron emission tomography, are extremely costly, and hospitals contemplating these procedures will have to consider equipment costs, reimbursement policies, and the number of potential users.

Earnings

Median annual earnings of nuclear medicine technologists were $48,750 in 2002. The middle 50 percent earned between $41,460 and $57,200. The lowest 10 percent earned less than $35,870, and the highest 10 percent earned more than $68,710. Median annual earnings of nuclear medicine technologists in 2002 were $48,210 in general medical and surgical hospitals.

Related Occupations

Nuclear medical technologists operate sophisticated equipment to help physicians and other health practitioners diagnose and treat patients. Cardiovascular technologists and technicians, clinical laboratory technologists and technicians, diagnostic medical sonographers, radiation therapists, radiologic technologists and technicians, and respiratory therapists also perform similar functions.

Sources of Additional Information

Additional information on a career as a nuclear medicine technologist is available from:
➤ Society of Nuclear Medicine Technologists, 1850 Samuel Morse Dr., Reston, VA 20190-5316. Internet: **http://www.snm.org**

For career information, send a stamped, self-addressed, business-size envelope with your request to:
➤ American Society of Radiologic Technologists, 15000 Central Ave. SE., Albuquerque, NM 87123-3917. Telephone (tollfree): 800-444-2778. Internet: **http://www.asrt.org**

For a list of accredited programs in nuclear medicine technology, write to:
➤ Joint Review Committee on Educational Programs in Nuclear Medicine Technology, PMB 418, 1 2nd Ave. East, Suite C, Polson, MT 59860-2320. Internet: **http://www.jrcnmt.org**

Information on certification is available from:
➤ American Registry of Radiologic Technologists, 1255 Northland Dr., St. Paul, MN 55120-1155. Internet: **http://www.arrt.org**
➤ Nuclear Medicine Technology Certification Board, 2970 Clairmont Rd., Suite 935, Atlanta, GA 30329. Internet: **http://www.nmtcb.org**

Occupational Health and Safety Specialists and Technicians

(0*NET 29-9011.00, 29-9012.00)

Significant Points

● About 2 out of 5 worked in Federal, State, and local government agencies that enforce rules on health and safety.

● Many employers, including the Federal Government, require 4-year college degrees in safety or a related field for some specialist positions.

● Projected average employment growth reflects a balance of continuing public demand for a safe and healthy work environment against the desire for smaller government and fewer regulations.

Nature of the Work

Occupational health and safety specialists and technicians, also known as occupational health and safety inspectors, industrial hygienists, environmental protection officers, or ergonomists, help prevent harm to workers, property, and the environment, as well as the general public. They promote occupational health and safety within organizations by developing safer, healthier, and more efficient ways of working. (Industrial engineers, including health and safety—who have similar goals—are discussed elsewhere in the *Handbook*.)

Occupational health and safety specialists analyze work environments and design programs to control, eliminate, and prevent disease or injury caused by chemical, physical, and biological agents or ergonomic factors that involve the impact of equipment design on a worker's comfort or fatigue. They may conduct inspections and enforce adherence to laws, regulations, or employer policies governing worker health and safety.

Occupational health and safety technicians collect data on work environments for analysis by occupational health and safety specialists. Usually working under the supervision of specialists, they help implement and evaluate programs designed to limit risks to workers.

The specific responsibilities of occupational health and safety specialists and technicians vary by industry, workplace, and types of hazards affecting employees. In most settings, they initially focus on identifying hazardous conditions and practices. Sometimes they develop methods to predict hazards from experience, historical data, and other information sources. Then they identify potential hazards in systems, equipment, products, facilities, or processes planned for use in the future. After reviewing the causes or effects of hazards, they evaluate the probability and severity of accidents that may result. For example, they might uncover patterns in injury data that implicate a specific cause such as system failure, human error, incomplete or faulty decision making, or a weakness in existing policies or practices. Then they develop and help enforce a plan to eliminate hazards, conducting training sessions for management, supervisors, and workers on health and safety practices and regulations, as necessary. Lastly, they may check on the progress of the safety plan after its implementation. If improvements are not satisfactory, a new plan might be designed and put into practice.

Many occupational health and safety specialists examine and test machinery and equipment, such as lifting devices, machine guards, or scaffolding, to ensure the machinery and equipment meet appropriate safety regulations. They may check that personal protective equipment, such as masks, respirators, protective eyewear, or hardhats, is being used in workplaces according to regulations. They also check that dangerous materials are stored correctly. They test and identify work areas for potential accident and health hazards, such as toxic fumes and explosive gas-air mixtures, and may implement appropriate control measures, such as adjustments to ventilation systems. Their investigations might involve talking with workers and observing their work, as well as inspecting elements in their work environment, such as lighting, tools, and equipment.

To measure and control hazardous substances, such as the noise or radiation levels, occupational health and safety specialists and technicians prepare and calibrate scientific equipment. Samples of dust, gases, vapors, and other potentially toxic materials must be collected and handled properly to ensure safety and accurate test results.

If an accident occurs, occupational health and safety specialists help investigate unsafe working conditions, study possible causes, and recommend remedial action. Some occupational health and safety specialists and technicians assist with the rehabilitation of workers after accidents and injuries, and make sure they return to work successfully.

Frequent communication with management may be necessary to report on the status of occupational health and safety programs. Consultation with engineers or physicians also may be required.

Occupational health and safety specialists prepare reports including observations, analysis of contaminants, and recommendation for control and correction of hazards. Those who develop expertise in certain areas may develop occupational health and safety systems, including policies, procedures, and manuals.

Working Conditions

Occupational health and safety specialists and technicians work with many different people in a variety of environments. Their jobs often involve considerable fieldwork, and some travel frequently. Many occupational health and safety specialists and technicians work long and often irregular hours.

Occupational health and safety specialists and technicians may experience unpleasant, stressful, and dangerous working conditions. For example, health and safety inspectors are exposed to many of the same physically strenuous conditions and hazards as industrial employees, and the work may be performed in unpleasant, stressful, and dangerous working conditions.

About 2 out of 5 occupational health and safety specialists and technicians work for Federal, State, or local government agencies.

Health and safety inspectors may find themselves in adversarial roles when the organization or individual being inspected objects to the process or its consequences.

Employment

Occupational health and safety specialists and technicians held about 41,000 jobs in 2002, primarily in government agencies. Local governments employed 17 percent, State governments employed 14 percent, and the Federal Government—chiefly the Department of Labor—employed 6 percent. Other occupational health and safety specialists and technicians were employed in manufacturing firms; hospitals; educational services, including colleges, universities, and professional schools; employment services; management, scientific, and technical consulting services; management of companies and enterprises; electric power generation, transmission, and distribution; support activities for mining; scientific research and development services; and architectural, engineering, and related services.

Within the Federal government, most jobs are as Occupational Safety and Health Administration (OSHA) inspectors, who enforce U.S. Department of Labor regulations that ensure adequate safety principles, practices, and techniques are applied in workplaces. Employers may be fined for violation of OSHA standards. Within the U.S. Department of Health and Human Services, occupational health and safety specialists working for the National Institute of Occupational Safety and Health (NIOSH) provide private companies with an avenue to evaluate the health and safety of their employees without the risk of being fined. Most large government agencies also employ occupational health and safety specialists and technicians who work to protect agency employees.

Most private companies either employ their own occupational health and safety personnel or contract with occupational health and safety professionals to ensure OSHA compliance.

Training, Other Qualifications, and Advancement

Requirements for becoming an occupational health and safety specialist or technician include a combination of education, experience, and passing scores on written examinations. Many employers, including the Federal Government, require a 4-year college degree in safety or a related field for some specialist positions. Experience as an occupational health and safety professional is also a prerequisite for many positions.

All occupational health and safety specialists and technicians are trained in the applicable laws or inspection procedures through some combination of classroom and on-the-job training. In general, people who want to enter this occupation should be responsible and like detailed work. Occupational health and safety specialists and technicians should be able to communicate well. Recommended high school courses include English, mathematics, chemistry, biology, and physics.

Certification is available through the Board of Certified Safety Professionals (BCSP) and the American Board of Industrial Hygiene (ABIH). The BCSP offers the Certified Safety Professional (CSP) credential, while the ABIH offers the Certified Industrial Hygienist (CIH) and Certified Associate Industrial Hygienist (CAIH) credentials. Also, the Council on Certification of Health, Environmental, and Safety Technologists, a joint effort between the BCSP and ABIH, awards the Occupational Health and Safety Technologist (OHST) credential. Requirements for the OHST credential are less stringent than those for the CSP, CIH, or CAIH credentials. Once education and experience requirements have been met, certification may be obtained through an examination. Continuing education is required for recertification. Although voluntary, many employers encourage certification.

Federal Government occupational health and safety specialists and technicians whose job performance is satisfactory advance through their career ladder to a specified full-performance level. For positions above this level, usually supervisory positions, advancement is competitive and based on agency needs and individual merit. Advancement opportunities in State and local governments and the private sector are often similar to those in the Federal Government.

With additional experience or education, promotion to a managerial position is possible. Research or related teaching positions at the college level require advanced education.

Job Outlook

Employment of occupational health and safety specialists and technicians is expected to grow about as fast as the average for all occupations through 2012, reflecting a balance of continuing public demand for a safe and healthy work environment against the desire for smaller government and fewer regulations. Additional job openings will arise from the need to replace those who transfer to other occupations, retire, or leave the labor force for other reasons. In private industry, employment growth will reflect industry growth and the continuing self-enforcement of government and company regulations and policies.

Employment of occupational health and safety specialists and technicians is affected less by general economic fluctuations than employment in other occupations. Federal, State, and local governments, which employ about 2 out of 5 of all specialists and technicians, provide considerable job security.

Earnings

Median annual earnings of occupational health and safety specialists and technicians were $46,010 in 2002. The middle 50 percent earned between $34,280 and $58,230. The lowest 10 percent earned less than $25,080, and the highest 10 percent earned more than $71,450. Median annual earnings of occupational health and safety specialists and technicians in 2002 were $44,260 in State government and $42,430 in local government.

Most occupational health and safety specialists and technicians work for Federal, State, and local governments or in large private firms, most of which generally offer more generous benefits than smaller firms.

Related Occupations

Occupational health and safety specialists and technicians ensure that laws and regulations are obeyed. Others who enforce laws and regulations include agricultural inspectors, construction and building inspectors, correctional officers, financial examiners, fire inspectors, police and detectives, and transportation inspectors.

Sources of Additional Information

Information about jobs in Federal, State, and local government as well as in private industry is available from State employment service offices.

For information on a career as an industrial hygienist and a list of colleges and universities offering programs in industrial hygiene, contact:

➤ American Industrial Hygiene Association, 2700 Prosperity Ave., Suite 250, Fairfax, VA 22031. Internet: **http://www.aiha.org**

For information on the Certified Industrial Hygiene or Certified Associate Industrial Hygiene credential, contact:

➤ American Board of Industrial Hygiene, 6015 West St. Joseph Hwy., Suite 102, Lansing, MI 48917. Internet: **http://www.abih.org**

For more information on professions in safety and a list of colleges and universities offering safety and related degrees, including correspondence courses, contact:

➤ American Society of Safety Engineers, 1800 E Oakton St., Des Plaines, IL 60018. Internet: **http://www.asse.org**

For more information on professions in safety and the Certified Safety Professional credential, contact:

➤ Board of Certified Safety Professionals, 208 Burwash Ave., Savoy, IL 61874. Internet: **http://www.bcsp.org**

For information on the Occupational Health and Safety Technologist credential, contact:

➤ Council on Certification of Health, Environmental, and Safety Technologists, 208 Burwash Ave., Savoy, IL 61874. Internet: **http://www.cchest.org**

For additional career information, contact:

➤ U.S. Department of Health and Human Services, Center for Disease Control and Prevention, National Institute of Occupational Safety and Health, Hubert H. Humphrey Bldg., 200 Independence Ave. SW., Room 715H, Washington, DC 20201. Internet: **http://www.cdc.gov/niosh**

➤ U.S. Department of Labor, Occupational Safety and Health Administration, 200 Constitution Ave. NW., Washington, DC 20210. Internet: **http://www.osha.gov**

Information on obtaining positions as occupational health and safety specialists and technicians with the Federal Government is available from the Office of Personnel Management through a telephone-based system. Consult your telephone directory under U.S. Government for a local number or call (703) 724-1850; Federal Relay Service: (800) 877-8339. The first number is not tollfree, and charges may result. Information also is available from the Internet site: **http://www.usajobs.opm.gov.**

Opticians, Dispensing

(0*NET 29-2081.00)

Significant Points

● Most dispensing opticians receive training on the job or through apprenticeships lasting 2 or more years; twenty-one States require a license.

● Projected employment growth reflects steady demand for corrective lenses and eyeglass frames that are in fashion.

● The number of job openings will be limited because the occupation is small.

Nature of Work

Dispensing opticians fit eyeglasses and contact lenses, following prescriptions written by ophthalmologists or optometrists. (The work of optometrists is described in a statement elsewhere in the *Handbook.* See the statement on physicians and surgeons for information about ophthalmologists.)

Dispensing opticians examine written prescriptions to determine the specifications of lenses. They recommend eyeglass frames, lenses, and lens coatings after considering the prescription and the customer's occupation, habits, and facial features. Dispensing opticians measure clients' eyes, including the distance between the centers of the pupils and the distance between the surface and the lens. For customers without prescriptions, dispensing opticians may use a lensometer to record eyeglass measurements. They also may obtain a customer's previous record or verify a prescription with the examining optometrist or ophthalmologist.

Dispensing opticians prepare work orders that give ophthalmic laboratory technicians information needed to grind and insert lenses into a frame. The work order includes prescriptions for lenses and information on their size, material, color, and style. Some dispensing opticians grind and insert lenses themselves. After the glasses are made, dispensing opticians verify that the lenses have been ground to specifications. Then they may reshape or bend the frame, by hand or using pliers, so that the eyeglasses fit the customer properly and comfortably. Some also fix, adjust, and refit broken frames. They instruct clients about adapting to, wearing, or caring for eyeglasses.

Some dispensing opticians specialize in fitting contacts, artificial eyes, or cosmetic shells to cover blemished eyes. To fit contact lenses, dispensing opticians measure the shape and size of the eye, select the type of contact lens material, and prepare

work orders specifying the prescription and lens size. Fitting contact lenses requires considerable skill, care, and patience. Dispensing opticians observe customers' eyes, corneas, lids, and contact lenses with special instruments and microscopes. During several visits, opticians show customers how to insert, remove, and care for their contacts. Opticians do all this to ensure that the fit is correct.

Dispensing opticians keep records on customers' prescriptions, work orders, and payments; track inventory and sales; and perform other administrative duties.

Working Conditions

Dispensing opticians work indoors in attractive, well-lighted, and well-ventilated surroundings. They may work in medical offices or small stores where customers are served one at a time. Some work in large stores where several dispensing opticians serve a number of customers at once. Opticians spend a lot of time on their feet. If they prepare lenses, they need to take precautions against the hazards associated with glass cutting, chemicals, and machinery.

Most dispensing opticians work a 40-hour week, although some work longer hours. Those in retail stores may work evenings and weekends. Some work part time.

Employment

Dispensing opticians held about 63,000 jobs in 2002. About 2 out of 5 worked in health and personal care stores, including optical goods stores. Many of these stores offer one-stop shopping. Customers may have their eyes examined, choose frames, and have glasses made on the spot. Another 2 out of 5 dispensing opticians worked in offices of physicians or other health practitioners for ophthalmologists or optometrists who sell glasses directly to patients. Some work in optical departments of department stores or other general merchandise stores, such as warehouse clubs and superstores.

Training, Other Qualifications, and Advancement

Employers usually hire individuals with no background as an optician or those who have worked as ophthalmic laboratory

Dispensing opticians may work in medical offices or small stores where customers are served one at a time.

technicians. The employers then provide the required training. (See the statement on ophthalmic laboratory technicians elsewhere in the *Handbook*.) Most dispensing opticians receive training on the job or through apprenticeships lasting 2 or more years. Some employers, however, seek people with postsecondary training in the field.

Knowledge of physics, basic anatomy, algebra, geometry, and mechanical drawing is particularly valuable, because training usually includes instruction in optical mathematics, optical physics, and the use of precision measuring instruments and other machinery and tools. Dispensing opticians deal directly with the public, so they should be tactful, pleasant, and communicate well. Manual dexterity and the ability to do precision work are essential.

Large employers usually offer structured apprenticeship programs; small employers provide more informal, on-the-job training. In the 21 States that require dispensing opticians to be licensed, individuals without postsecondary training work from 2 to 4 years as apprentices. Apprenticeship or formal training is offered in most States as well.

Apprentices receive technical training and learn office management and sales. Under the supervision of an experienced optician, optometrist, or ophthalmologist, apprentices work directly with patients, fitting eyeglasses and contact lenses. In States requiring licensure, information about apprenticeships and licensing procedures is available from the State board of occupational licensing.

Formal training in the field is offered in community colleges and a few colleges and universities. In 2002, the Commission on Opticianry Accreditation accredited 22 programs that awarded 2-year associate degrees. There also are shorter programs of 1 year or less. Some States that offer a license to dispensing opticians allow graduates to take the licensure exam immediately upon graduation; others require a few months to a year of experience.

Dispensing opticians may apply to the American Board of Opticianry (ABO) and the National Contact Lens Examiners (NCLE) for certification of their skills. Certification must be renewed every 3 years through continuing education. Those licensed in States where licensing renewal requirements include continuing education credits may use proof of their renewed State license to meet the recertification requirements of the ABO. Likewise, the NCLE will accept proof of renewal from any State that has contact lens requirements.

Many experienced dispensing opticians open their own optical stores. Others become managers of optical stores or sales representatives for wholesalers or manufacturers of eyeglasses or lenses.

Job Outlook

Employment of dispensing opticians is expected to increase about as fast as the average for all occupations through 2012 as demand grows for corrective lenses. The number of middle-aged and elderly persons is projected to increase rapidly. Middle age is a time when many individuals use corrective lenses for the first time, and elderly persons generally require more vision care than others.

Fashion, too, influences demand. Frames come in a growing variety of styles and colors—encouraging people to buy more than one pair. Demand also is expected to grow in response to the availability of new technologies that improve the quality and look of corrective lenses, such as antireflective coatings and bifocal lenses without the line that is visible in old-style bifocals. Improvements in bifocal, extended-wear, and disposable contact lenses also will spur demand.

The need to replace those who leave the occupation will result in additional job openings. Nevertheless, the number of job openings will be limited because the occupation is small. Dispensing opticians are vulnerable to changes in the business cycle, because eyewear purchases often can be deferred for a time.

Earnings

Median annual earnings of dispensing opticians were $25,600 in 2002. The middle 50 percent earned between $19,960 and $33,530. The lowest 10 percent earned less than $16,310, and the highest 10 percent earned more than $43,490. Median annual earnings in the industries employing the largest numbers of dispensing opticians in 2002 were as follows:

Offices of physicians	$28,250
Health and personal care stores	25,860
Offices of other health practitioners	24,900

Related Occupations

Other workers who deal with customers and perform delicate work include jewelers and precious stone and metal workers, locksmiths and safe repairers, orthotists and prosthetists, and precision instrument and equipment repairers.

Sources of Additional Information

For general information about opticians and a list of home-study programs, seminars, and review materials, contact:
➤ National Academy of Opticianry, 8401 Corporate Dr., Suite 605, Landover, MD 20785. Telephone (tollfree): 800-229-4828. Internet: **http://www.nao.org**

For a list of accredited programs in opticianry, contact:
➤ Commission on Opticianry Accreditation, P.O. Box 3073, Merrifield, VA 22116-3073.

To learn about voluntary certification for opticians who fit eyeglasses, as well as a list of State licensing boards for opticians, contact:
➤ American Board of Opticianry, 6506 Loisdale Rd., Suite 209, Springfield, VA 22150. Internet: **http://www.abo.org**

For information on voluntary certification for dispensing opticians who fit contact lenses, contact:
➤ National Contact Lens Examiners, 6506 Loisdale Rd., Suite 209, Springfield, VA 22150. Internet: **http://www.abo.org**

Pharmacy Technicians

(0*NET 29-2052.00)

Significant Points

- Job opportunities are expected to be good, especially for those with certification or previous work experience.

- Many technicians work evenings, weekends, and holidays.

- Two-thirds of all jobs are in retail pharmacies.

Nature of the Work

Pharmacy technicians help licensed pharmacists provide medication and other healthcare products to patients. Technicians usually perform routine tasks to help prepare prescribed medication for patients, such as counting tablets and labeling bottles. Technicians refer any questions regarding prescriptions, drug information, or health matters to a *pharmacist*. (See the statement on pharmacists elsewhere in the *Handbook*.)

Pharmacy aides work closely with pharmacy technicians. They are often clerks or cashiers who primarily answer telephones, handle money, stock shelves, and perform other clerical duties. (See the statement on pharmacy aides elsewhere in the *Handbook*.) Pharmacy technicians usually perform more complex tasks than do pharmacy aides, although, in some States, their duties and job titles overlap.

Pharmacy technicians who work in retail or mail-order pharmacies have varying responsibilities, depending on State rules and regulations. Technicians receive written prescriptions or requests for prescription refills from patients. They also may receive prescriptions sent electronically from the doctor's office. They must verify that the information on the prescription is complete and accurate. To prepare the prescription, technicians must retrieve, count, pour, weigh, measure, and sometimes mix the medication. Then, they prepare the prescription labels, select the type of prescription container, and affix the prescription and auxiliary labels to the container. Once the prescription is filled, technicians price and file the prescription, which must be checked by a pharmacist before it is given to a patient. Technicians may establish and maintain patient profiles, prepare insurance claim forms, and stock and take inventory of prescription and over-the-counter medications.

In hospitals, nursing homes, and assisted-living facilities, technicians have added responsibilities. They read patient charts and prepare and deliver the medicine to patients. The pharmacist must check the order before it is delivered to the patient. The technician then copies the information about the prescribed medication onto the patient's profile. Technicians also may assemble a 24-hour supply of medicine for every patient. They package and label each dose separately. The package is then placed in the medicine cabinet of each patient until the supervising pharmacist checks it for accuracy. It is then given to the patient.

Working Conditions

Pharmacy technicians work in clean, organized, well-lighted, and well-ventilated areas. Most of their workday is spent on their feet. They may be required to lift heavy boxes or to use stepladders to retrieve supplies from high shelves.

Technicians work the same hours that pharmacists work. These may include evenings, nights, weekends, and holidays. Because some hospital and retail pharmacies are open 24 hours a day, technicians may work varying shifts. As their seniority increases, technicians often have increased control over the hours they work. There are many opportunities for part-time work in both retail and hospital settings.

Employment

Pharmacy technicians held about 211,000 jobs in 2002. Two-thirds of all jobs were in retail pharmacies, either independently owned or part of a drugstore chain, grocery store, department store, or mass retailer. About 22 percent of jobs were in hospitals and a small proportion was in mail-order and Internet pharmacies, clinics, pharmaceutical wholesalers, and the Federal Government.

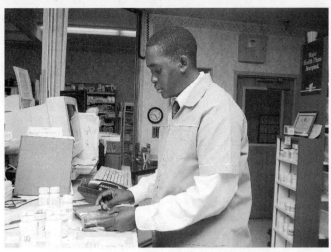

Pharmacy technicians frequently fill prescriptions.

Training, Other Qualifications, and Advancement

Although most pharmacy technicians receive informal on-the-job training, employers favor those who have completed formal training and certification. However, there are currently few State and no Federal requirements for formal training or certification of pharmacy technicians. Employers who have neither the time nor money to give on-the-job training often seek formally educated pharmacy technicians. Formal education programs and certification emphasize the technician's interest in and dedication to the work. In addition to the military, some hospitals, proprietary schools, vocational or technical colleges, and community colleges offer formal education programs.

Formal pharmacy technician education programs require classroom and laboratory work in a variety of areas, including medical and pharmaceutical terminology, pharmaceutical calculations, pharmacy recordkeeping, pharmaceutical techniques, and pharmacy law and ethics. Technicians also are required to learn medication names, actions, uses, and doses. Many training programs include internships, in which students gain hands-on experience in actual pharmacies. Students receive a diploma, a certificate, or an associate degree, depending on the program.

Prospective pharmacy technicians with experience working as an aide in a community pharmacy or volunteering in a hospital may have an advantage. Employers also prefer applicants with strong customer service and communication skills and with experience managing inventories, counting, measuring, and using computers. Technicians entering the field need strong mathematics, spelling, and reading skills. A background in chemistry, English, and health education also may be beneficial. Some technicians are hired without formal training, but under the condition that they obtain certification within a specified period to retain employment.

The Pharmacy Technician Certification Board administers the National Pharmacy Technician Certification Examination. This exam is voluntary in most States and displays the competency of the individual to act as a pharmacy technician. However, more States and employers are requiring certification as reliance on pharmacy technicians grows. Eligible candidates must have a high school diploma or GED and no felony convictions, and those who pass the exam earn the title of Certified Pharmacy Technician (CPhT). The exam is offered several times per year at various locations nationally. Employers, often pharmacists, know that individuals who pass the exam have a standardized body of knowledge and skills. Many employers will also reimburse the costs of the exam as an incentive for certification.

Certified technicians must be recertified every 2 years. Technicians must complete 20 contact hours of pharmacy-related topics within the 2-year certification period to become eligible for recertification. Contact hours are awarded for on-the-job training, attending lectures, and college coursework. At least 1 contact hour must be in pharmacy law. Contact hours can be earned from several different sources, including pharmacy associations, pharmacy colleges, and pharmacy technician training programs. Up to 10 contact hours can be earned when the technician is employed under the direct supervision and instruction of a pharmacist.

Successful pharmacy technicians are alert, observant, organized, dedicated, and responsible. They should be willing and able to take directions. They must enjoy precise work—details are sometimes a matter of life and death. Although a pharmacist must check and approve all their work, they should be able to work on their own without constant instruction from the pharmacist. Candidates interested in becoming pharmacy technicians cannot have prior records of drug or substance abuse.

Strong interpersonal and communication skills are needed because there is a lot of interaction with patients, coworkers, and healthcare professionals. Teamwork is very important because technicians are often required to work with pharmacists, aides, and other technicians.

Job Outlook
Good job opportunities are expected for full-time and part-time work, especially for technicians with formal training or previous experience. Job openings for pharmacy technicians will result from the expansion of retail pharmacies and other employment settings, and from the need to replace workers who transfer to other occupations or leave the labor force.

Employment of pharmacy technicians is expected to grow faster than the average for all occupations through 2012 due to the increased pharmaceutical needs of a larger and older population, and to the greater use of medication. The increased number of middle-aged and elderly people—who, on average, use more prescription drugs than do younger people—will spur demand for technicians in all practice settings. With advances in science, more medications are becoming available to treat more conditions.

Cost-conscious insurers, pharmacies, and health systems will continue to emphasize the role of technicians. As a result, pharmacy technicians will assume responsibility for more routine tasks previously performed by pharmacists. Pharmacy technicians also will need to learn and master new pharmacy technology as it surfaces. For example, robotic machines are used to dispense medicine into containers; technicians must oversee the machines, stock the bins, and label the containers. Thus, while automation is increasingly incorporated into the job, it will not necessarily reduce the need for technicians.

Almost all States have legislated the maximum number of technicians who can safely work under a pharmacist at one time. In some States, technicians have assumed more medication dispensing duties as pharmacists have become more involved in patient care, resulting in more technicians per pharmacist. Changes in these laws could directly affect employment.

Earnings
Median hourly earnings of wage and salary pharmacy technicians in 2002 were $10.70. The middle 50 percent earned between $8.74 and $13.19; the lowest 10 percent earned less than $7.44, and the highest 10 percent earned more than $15.82. Median hourly earnings in the industries employing the largest numbers of pharmacy technicians in 2002 were as follows:

General medical and surgical hospitals	$12.32
Grocery stores	11.34
Drugs and druggists' sundries merchant wholesalers	10.60
Health and personal care stores	9.70
Department stores	9.69

Certified technicians may earn more. Shift differentials for working evenings or weekends also can increase earnings. Some technicians belong to unions representing hospital or grocery store workers.

Related Occupations
This occupation is most closely related to pharmacists and pharmacy aides. Workers in other medical support occupations include dental assistants, licensed practical and licensed vocational nurses, medical transcriptionists, medical records and health information technicians, occupational therapist assistants and aides, physical therapist assistants and aides, and surgical technologists.

Sources of Additional Information
For information on the Certified Pharmacy Technician designation, contact:
➤ Pharmacy Technician Certification Board, 2215 Constitution Ave. NW., Washington DC 20037. Internet: **http://www.ptcb.org**

For a list of accredited pharmacy technician training programs, contact:
➤ American Society of Health-System Pharmacists, 7272 Wisconsin Ave., Bethesda, MD 20814. Internet: **http://www.ashp.org**

Radiologic Technologists and Technicians

(0*NET 29-2034.01, 29-2034.02)

Significant Points
- Formal training programs in radiography range in length from 1 to 4 years and lead to a certificate, associate degree, or bachelor's degree.
- Although hospitals will remain the primary employer, a greater number of new jobs will be found in physicians' offices and diagnostic imaging centers.
- Job opportunities are expected to be favorable; some employers report difficulty hiring sufficient numbers of radiologic technologists and technicians.

Nature of the Work
Radiologic technologists and technicians take x rays and administer nonradioactive materials into patients' bloodstreams for diagnostic purposes. Some specialize in diagnostic imaging technologies, such as computerized tomography (CT) and magnetic resonance imaging (MRI).

In addition to radiologic technologists and technicians, others who conduct diagnostic imaging procedures include cardiovascular technologists and technicians, diagnostic medical sonographers, and nuclear medicine technologists. (Each is discussed elsewhere in the *Handbook*.)

Radiologic technologists and technicians, also referred to as *radiographers*, produce x ray films (radiographs) of parts of the human body for use in diagnosing medical problems. They prepare patients for radiologic examinations by explaining the procedure, removing articles such as jewelry, through which x

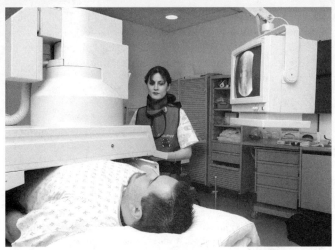

Radiologic technologists use advanced imaging technology to create diagnostic images for interpretation by a physician.

rays cannot pass, and positioning patients so that the parts of the body can be appropriately radiographed. To prevent unnecessary radiation exposure, these workers surround the exposed area with radiation protection devices, such as lead shields, or limit the size of the x ray beam. Radiographers position radiographic equipment at the correct angle and height over the appropriate area of a patient's body. Using instruments similar to a measuring tape, they may measure the thickness of the section to be radiographed and set controls on the x ray machine to produce radiographs of the appropriate density, detail, and contrast. They place the x ray film under the part of the patient's body to be examined and make the exposure. They then remove the film and develop it.

Experienced radiographers may perform more complex imaging procedures. For fluoroscopies, radiographers prepare a solution of contrast medium for the patient to drink, allowing the radiologist (a physician who interprets radiographs) to see soft tissues in the body. Some radiographers, called *CT technologists,* operate CT scanners to produce cross-sectional images of patients. Radiographers who operate machines that use strong magnets and radio waves, rather than radiation, to create an image are called *MRI technologists.*

Radiologic technologists and technicians must follow physicians' orders precisely and conform to regulations concerning the use of radiation to protect themselves, their patients, and their coworkers from unnecessary exposure.

In addition to preparing patients and operating equipment, radiologic technologists and technicians keep patient records and adjust and maintain equipment. They also may prepare work schedules, evaluate equipment purchases, or manage a radiology department.

Working Conditions

Most full-time radiologic technologists and technicians work about 40 hours a week; they may have evening, weekend, or on-call hours. Opportunities for part-time and shift work also are available.

Because technologists and technicians are on their feet for long periods and may lift or turn disabled patients, physical stamina is important. Technologists and technicians work at diagnostic machines, but may also perform some procedures at patients' bedsides. Some travel to patients in large vans equipped with sophisticated diagnostic equipment.

Although radiation hazards exist in this occupation, they are minimized by the use of lead aprons, gloves, and other shielding devices, as well as by instruments monitoring radiation exposure. Technologists and technicians wear badges measuring radiation levels in the radiation area, and detailed records are kept on their cumulative lifetime dose.

Employment

Radiologic technologists and technicians held about 174,000 jobs in 2002. Almost 1 in 5 worked part time. About half of all jobs were in hospitals. Most of the rest were in offices of physicians; medical and diagnostic laboratories, including diagnostic imaging centers; and outpatient care centers.

Training, Other Qualifications, and Advancement

Preparation for this profession is offered in hospitals, colleges and universities, vocational-technical institutes, and the U.S. Armed Forces. Hospitals, which employ most radiologic technologists and technicians, prefer to hire those with formal training.

Formal training programs in radiography range in length from 1 to 4 years and lead to a certificate, associate degree, or bachelor's degree. Two-year associate degree programs are most prevalent.

Some 1-year certificate programs are available for experienced radiographers or individuals from other health occupations, such as medical technologists and registered nurses, who want to change fields or specialize in CT or MRI. A bachelor's or master's degree in one of the radiologic technologies is desirable for supervisory, administrative, or teaching positions.

The Joint Review Committee on Education in Radiologic Technology accredits most formal training programs for the field. The committee accredited 587 radiography programs in 2003. Radiography programs require, at a minimum, a high school diploma or the equivalent. High school courses in mathematics, physics, chemistry, and biology are helpful. The programs provide both classroom and clinical instruction in anatomy and physiology, patient care procedures, radiation physics, radiation protection, principles of imaging, medical terminology, positioning of patients, medical ethics, radiobiology, and pathology.

Federal legislation protects the public from the hazards of unnecessary exposure to medical and dental radiation by ensuring operators of radiologic equipment are properly trained. Under this legislation, the Federal Government sets voluntary standards that the States, in turn, may use for accrediting training programs and certifying individuals who engage in medical or dental radiography.

In 2003, about 38 States licensed radiologic technologists and technicians. Voluntary registration is offered by the American Registry of Radiologic Technologists. To be eligible for registration, technologists generally must have graduated from an accredited program and pass an examination. Many employers prefer to hire registered radiographers. To be recertified, radiographers must complete 24 hours of continuing education every other year.

Radiologic technologists and technicians should be sensitive to patients' physical and psychological needs. They must pay attention to detail, follow instructions, and work as part of a team. In addition, operating complicated equipment requires mechanical ability and manual dexterity.

With experience and additional training, staff technologists may become specialists, performing CT scanning, angiography, and magnetic resonance imaging. Experienced technologists also may be promoted to supervisor, chief radiologic technologist, and, ultimately, department administrator or director. Depending on the institution, courses or a master's degree in business or health administration may be necessary for the director's position. Some technologists progress by leaving the occupation to become instructors or directors in radiologic technology programs; others take jobs as sales representatives or instructors with equipment manufacturers.

Job Outlook

Job opportunities are expected to be favorable. Some employers report difficulty hiring sufficient numbers of radiologic technologists and technicians. Imbalances between the demand for, and supply of, qualified workers should spur efforts to attract and retain qualified radiologic technologists and technicians. As an example of such efforts, employers may provide more flexible training programs or improve compensation and working conditions.

Radiologic technologists who also are experienced in more complex diagnostic imaging procedures, such as CT or MRI, will have better employment opportunities, as employers seek to control costs by using multiskilled employees.

Employment of radiologic technologists and technicians is expected to grow faster than the average for all occupations through 2012, as the population grows and ages, increasing the demand for diagnostic imaging. Although healthcare providers are enthusiastic about the clinical benefits of new technologies, the extent to which they are adopted depends largely on cost and reimbursement considerations. For example, digital imaging technology can improve quality and efficiency, but remains expensive. Some promising new technologies may not come into widespread use because they are too expensive and third-party payers may not be willing to pay for their use.

Hospitals will remain the principal employer of radiologic technologists and technicians. However, a greater number of new jobs will be found in offices of physicians and diagnostic imaging centers. Health facilities such as these are expected to grow rapidly through 2012, due to the strong shift toward outpatient care, encouraged by third-party payers and made possible by technological advances that permit more procedures to be performed outside the hospital. Some job openings also will arise from the need to replace technologists and technicians who leave the occupation.

Earnings

Median annual earnings of radiologic technologists and technicians were $38,970 in 2002. The middle 50 percent earned between $32,370 and $46,510. The lowest 10 percent earned less than $27,190, and the highest 10 percent earned more than $55,430. Median annual earnings in the industries employing the largest numbers of radiologic technologists and technicians in 2002 were as follows:

Medical and diagnostic laboratories	$42,470
General medical and surgical hospitals	39,580
Offices of physicians	36,490

Related Occupations

Radiologic technologists and technicians operate sophisticated equipment to help physicians, dentists, and other health practitioners diagnose and treat patients. Workers in related occupations include cardiovascular technologists and technicians, clinical laboratory technologists and technicians, diagnostic medical sonographers, nuclear medicine technologists, radiation therapists, and respiratory therapists.

Sources of Additional Information

For career information, send a stamped, self-addressed business-size envelope with your request to:
➤ American Society of Radiologic Technologists, 15000 Central Ave. SE., Albuquerque, NM 87123-3917. Telephone (tollfree): 800-444-2778. Internet: http://www.asrt.org

For the current list of accredited education programs in radiography, write to:
➤ Joint Review Committee on Education in Radiologic Technology, 20 N. Wacker Dr., Suite 900, Chicago, IL 60606-2901. Internet: http://www.jrcert.org

For information on certification, contact:
➤ American Registry of Radiologic Technologists, 1255 Northland Dr., St. Paul, MN 55120-1155. Internet: http://www.arrt.org

Surgical Technologists

(0*NET 29-2055.00)

Significant Points

● Training programs last 9 to 24 months and lead to a certificate, diploma, or associate degree.

● Job opportunities are expected to be favorable.

● Hospitals will continue to be the primary employer, although much faster employment growth is expected in offices of physicians and in outpatient care centers, including ambulatory surgical centers.

Nature of the Work

Surgical technologists, also called scrubs and surgical or operating room technicians, assist in surgical operations under the supervision of surgeons, registered nurses, or other surgical personnel. Surgical technologists are members of operating room teams, which most commonly include surgeons, anesthesiologists, and circulating nurses. Before an operation, surgical technologists help prepare the operating room by setting up surgical instruments and equipment, sterile drapes, and sterile solutions. They assemble both sterile and nonsterile equipment, as well as adjust and check it to ensure it is working properly. Technologists also get patients ready for surgery by washing, shaving, and disinfecting incision sites. They transport patients to the operating room, help position them on the operating table, and cover them with sterile surgical "drapes." Technologists also observe patients' vital signs, check charts, and assist the surgical team with putting on sterile gowns and gloves.

During surgery, technologists pass instruments and other sterile supplies to surgeons and surgeon assistants. They may hold retractors, cut sutures, and help count sponges, needles, supplies, and instruments. Surgical technologists help prepare, care for, and dispose of specimens taken for laboratory analysis and help apply dressings. Some operate sterilizers, lights, or suction machines, and help operate diagnostic equipment.

During surgery, surgical technologists pass instruments and other sterile supplies to surgeons and surgeon assistants.

After an operation, surgical technologists may help transfer patients to the recovery room and clean and restock the operating room.

Working Conditions

Surgical technologists work in clean, well-lighted, cool environments. They must stand for long periods and remain alert during operations. At times they may be exposed to communicable diseases and unpleasant sights, odors, and materials.

Most surgical technologists work a regular 40-hour week, although they may be on call or work nights, weekends and holidays on a rotating basis.

Employment

Surgical technologists held about 72,000 jobs in 2002. About three-quarters of jobs for surgical technologists were in hospitals, mainly in operating and delivery rooms. Other jobs were in offices of physicians or dentists who perform outpatient surgery and in outpatient care centers, including ambulatory surgical centers. A few, known as private scrubs, are employed directly by surgeons who have special surgical teams, like those for liver transplants.

Training, Other Qualifications, and Advancement

Surgical technologists receive their training in formal programs offered by community and junior colleges, vocational schools, universities, hospitals, and the military. In 2002, the Commission on Accreditation of Allied Health Education Programs (CAAHEP) recognized 361 accredited programs. High school graduation normally is required for admission. Programs last 9 to 24 months and lead to a certificate, diploma, or associate degree.

Programs provide classroom education and supervised clinical experience. Students take courses in anatomy, physiology, microbiology, pharmacology, professional ethics, and medical terminology. Other studies cover the care and safety of patients during surgery, sterile techniques, and surgical procedures. Students also learn to sterilize instruments; prevent and control infection; and handle special drugs, solutions, supplies, and equipment.

Most employers prefer to hire certified technologists. Technologists may obtain voluntary professional certification from the Liaison Council on Certification for the Surgical Technologist by graduating from a CAAHEP-accredited program and passing a national certification examination. They may then use the Certified Surgical Technologist (CST) designation. Continuing education or reexamination is required to maintain certification, which must be renewed every 4 years.

Certification may also be obtained from the National Center for Competency Testing. To qualify to take the exam, candidates follow one of three paths: complete an accredited training program, undergo a 2-year hospital on-the-job training program, or acquire seven years of experience working in the field. After passing the exam, individuals may use the designation Tech in Surgery-Certified, TS-C (NCCT). This certification may be renewed every 5 years through either continuing education or reexamination.

Surgical technologists need manual dexterity to handle instruments quickly. They also must be conscientious, orderly, and emotionally stable to handle the demands of the operating room environment. Technologists must respond quickly and know procedures well to have instruments ready for surgeons without having to be told. They are expected to keep abreast of new developments in the field. Recommended high school courses include health, biology, chemistry, and mathematics.

Technologists advance by specializing in a particular area of surgery, such as neurosurgery or open heart surgery. They also may work as circulating technologists. A circulating technologist is the "unsterile" member of the surgical team who prepares patients; helps with anesthesia; obtains and opens packages for the "sterile" persons to remove the sterile contents during the procedure; interviews the patient before surgery; keeps a written account of the surgical procedure; and answers the surgeon's questions about the patient during the surgery. With additional training, some technologists advance to first assistants, who help with retracting, sponging, suturing, cauterizing bleeders, and closing and treating wounds. Some surgical technologists manage central supply departments in hospitals, or take positions with insurance companies, sterile supply services, and operating equipment firms.

Job Outlook

Job opportunities are expected to be favorable. Employment of surgical technologists is expected to grow faster than the average for all occupations through the year 2012 as the volume of surgery increases. The number of surgical procedures is expected to rise as the population grows and ages. As members of the baby boom generation approach retirement age, the over-50 population, who generally require more surgical procedures, will account for a larger portion of the general population. Technological advances, such as fiber optics and laser technology, will also permit new surgical procedures to be performed.

Hospitals will continue to be the primary employer of surgical technologists, although much faster employment growth is expected in offices of physicians and in outpatient care centers, including ambulatory surgical centers.

Earnings

Median annual earnings of surgical technologists were $31,210 in 2002. The middle 50 percent earned between $26,000 and $36,740. The lowest 10 percent earned less than $21,920, and the highest 10 percent earned more than $43,470. Median annual earnings of surgical technologists in 2002 were $33,790 in offices of physicians and $30,590 in general medical and surgical hospitals.

Related Occupations

Other health occupations requiring approximately 1 year of training after high school include dental assistants, licensed practical and licensed vocational nurses, medical and clinical laboratory technicians, and medical assistants.

Sources of Additional Information

For additional information on a career as a surgical technologist and a list of CAAHEP-accredited programs, contact:

➤ Association of Surgical Technologists, 7108-C South Alton Way, Centennial, CO 80112. Internet: **http://www.ast.org**

For information on becoming a Certified Surgical Technologist, contact:

➤ Liaison Council on Certification for the Surgical Technologist, 128 S. Tejon St., Suite 301, Colorado Springs, CO 80903. Internet: **http://www.lcc-st.org**

For information on becoming a Tech in Surgery-Certified, contact:

➤ National Center for Competency Testing, 7007 College Blvd., Suite 250, Overland Park, KS 66211.

Veterinary Technologists and Technicians

(0*NET 29-2056.00)

Significant Points

- Animal lovers get satisfaction in this occupation, but aspects of the work can sometimes be unpleasant and physically and emotionally demanding.

- Entrants generally complete a 2-year or 4-year veterinary technology program, and must pass a State examination.

- Employment is expected to grow much faster than average.

- Keen competition is expected for jobs in zoos.

Nature of the Work

Owners of pets and other animals today expect state-of-the-art veterinary care. To provide this service, veterinarians use the skills of veterinary technologists and technicians, who perform many of the same duties for a veterinarian that a nurse would for a physician, including routine laboratory and clinical procedures. Although specific job duties vary by employer, there often is little difference between the tasks done by technicians and by technologists, despite some differences in formal education and training. As a result, most workers in this occupation are called technicians.

Veterinary technologists and technicians typically conduct clinical work in a private practice under the supervision of a veterinarian—often performing various medical tests along with treating and diagnosing medical conditions and diseases in animals. For example, they may perform laboratory tests such as urinalysis and blood counts, assist with dental prophylaxis, prepare tissue samples, take blood samples, or assist veterinarians

in a variety of tests and analyses in which they often utilize various items of medical equipment, such as test tubes and diagnostic equipment. While most of these duties are performed in a laboratory setting, many tasks are not. For example, some veterinary technicians obtain and record patient case histories, expose and develop x-rays, and provide specialized nursing care. Additionally, experienced veterinary technicians may discuss a pet's condition with its owners and train new clinic personnel. Veterinary technologists and technicians assisting small-animal practitioners usually care for companion animals, such as cats and dogs, but can perform a variety of duties with mice, rats, sheep, pigs, cattle, monkeys, birds, fish, and frogs. Very few veterinary technologists work in mixed animal practices where they care for both small companion animals and larger, nondomestic animals.

In addition to working in private clinics and animal hospitals, veterinary technologists and technicians also may work in research facilities. There, they may administer medications orally or topically, prepare samples for laboratory examinations, and record information on genealogy, diet, weight, medications, food intake, and clinical signs of pain and distress. Some may be required to sterilize laboratory and surgical equipment and provide routine postoperative care. At research facilities, veterinary technologists typically work under the guidance of veterinarians, physicians, and other laboratory technicians. Some veterinary technologists vaccinate newly admitted ani-

Many veterinary technologists and technicians assist veterinarians in routine laboratory and clinical procedures.

mals and occasionally are required to euthanize seriously ill, severely injured, or unwanted animals.

While the goal of most veterinary technologists and technicians goal is to promote animal health, some contribute to human health as well. Veterinary technologists occasionally assist veterinarians as they work with other scientists in medical-related fields such as gene therapy and cloning. Some find opportunities in biomedical research, wildlife medicine, the military, livestock management, or pharmaceutical sales.

Working Conditions

People who love animals get satisfaction from working with and helping them. However, some of the work may be unpleasant, physically and emotionally demanding, and sometimes dangerous. Veterinary technicians sometimes must clean cages and lift, hold, or restrain animals, risking exposure to bites or scratches. These workers must take precautions when treating animals with germicides or insecticides. The work setting can be noisy.

Veterinary technologists and technicians who witness abused animals or who euthanize unwanted, aged, or hopelessly injured animals may experience emotional stress. Those working for humane societies and animal shelters often deal with the public, some of whom might react with hostility to any implication that the owners are neglecting or abusing their pets. Such workers must maintain a calm and professional demeanor while they enforce the laws regarding animal care. In some animal hospitals, research facilities, and animal shelters, a veterinary technician is on duty 24 hours a day, which means some may work night shifts. Most full-time veterinary technologists and technicians work about 40 hours a week, while some work 50 or more hours a week.

Employment

Veterinary technologists and technicians held about 53,000 jobs in 2002. Most worked in veterinary services. The remainder worked in boarding kennels, animal shelters, stables, grooming shops, zoos, and local, State, and Federal agencies.

Training, Other Qualifications, and Advancement

There are primarily two levels of education and training for entry to this occupation—a 2-year program for veterinary technicians and a 4-year program for veterinary technologists. Most entry-level veterinary technicians have a 2-year degree, usually an associate degree, from an accredited community college program in veterinary technology, in which courses are taught in clinical and laboratory settings using live animals. A few colleges offer veterinary technology programs that are longer and that may culminate in a 4-year bachelor's degree in veterinary technology. These 4-year colleges, in addition to some vocational schools, also offer 2-year programs in laboratory animal science.

In 2003, more than 80 veterinary technology programs in 41 States were accredited by the American Veterinary Medical Association (AVMA). Graduation from an AVMA-accredited veterinary technology program allows students to take the credentialing exam in any State in the country. Each State regulates veterinary technicians and technologists differently; however, all States require them to pass a credentialing exam following coursework. Passing the State exam assures the public that

the technician or technologist has sufficient knowledge to work in a veterinary clinic or hospital. Candidates are tested for competency through an examination that includes oral, written, and practical portions. This process is regulated by the State Board of Veterinary Examiners, or the appropriate State agency. Depending on the State, candidates may become registered, licensed, or certified. Most States, however, use the National Veterinary Technician (NVT) exam. Prospects usually can have their passing scores transferred from one State to another, so long as both States utilize the same exam.

Employers recommend American Association for Laboratory Animal Science (AALAS) certification for those seeking employment in a research facility. AALAS offers certification for three levels of technician competence, with a focus on three principle areas—animal husbandry and welfare, facility administration and management, and animal health. Those who wish to become certified must satisfy a combination of education and experience requirements prior to taking an exam. Work experience must be directly related to the maintenance, health, and well-being of laboratory animals and must be gained in a laboratory animal facility as defined by AALAS. Candidates who meet the necessary criteria can begin pursuing the desired certification, based on their qualifications. The lowest level of certification is Animal Laboratory Assistant Technician (ALAT); the second level is Laboratory Animal Technician (LAT); and the highest level of certification is Laboratory Animal Technologist (LATG). The examination consists of multiple-choice questions and is longer and more difficult for higher levels of certification.

Persons interested in careers as veterinary technologists and technicians should take as many high school science, biology, and math courses as possible. Science courses taken beyond high school, in an associate or bachelor's degree program, should emphasize practical skills in a clinical or laboratory setting. Because veterinary technologists and technicians often deal with pet owners, communication skills are very important. Additionally, technologists and technicians should be able to work well with others, because teamwork with veterinarians is common. Organizational ability and the ability to pay attention to detail also are important.

Technologists and technicians usually begin work as trainees in routine positions under the direct supervision of a veterinarian. Entry-level workers whose training or educational background encompasses extensive hands-on experience with a variety of laboratory equipment, including diagnostic and medical equipment, usually require a shorter period of on-the-job training. As they gain experience, technologists and technicians take on more responsibility and carry out more assignments under only general veterinary supervision, and some eventually may become supervisors.

Job Outlook

Employment of veterinary technologists and technicians is expected to grow much faster than the average for all occupations through the year 2012. Job openings also will stem from the need to replace veterinary technologists and technicians who leave the occupation over the 2002-12 period. Keen competition is expected for veterinary technologist and technician jobs in zoos, due to expected slow growth in zoo capacity, low turnover among workers, the limited number of positions, and the fact that the occupation attracts many candidates.

Pet owners are becoming more affluent and more willing to pay for advanced care because many of them consider their pet to be part of the family, spurring employment growth for veterinary technologists and technicians. The number of dogs as pets, which also drives employment growth, is expected to increase more slowly during the projection period than in the previous decade. However, the rapidly growing number of cats as pets is expected to boost the demand for feline medicine, offsetting any reduced demand for veterinary care for dogs. The availability of advanced veterinary services, such as preventive dental care and surgical procedures, may provide opportunities for workers specializing in those areas. Biomedical facilities, diagnostic laboratories, wildlife facilities, humane societies, animal control facilities, drug or food manufacturing companies, and food safety inspection facilities will provide more jobs for veterinary technologists and technicians. Furthermore, demand for these workers will stem from the desire to replace veterinary assistants with more highly skilled technicians and technologists in animal clinics and hospitals, shelters, kennels, and humane societies.

Employment of veterinary technicians and technologists is relatively stable during periods of economic recession. Layoffs are less likely to occur among veterinary technologists and technicians than in some other occupations because animals will continue to require medical care.

Earnings
Median hourly earnings of veterinary technologists and technicians were $22,950 in 2002. The middle 50 percent earned between $19,210 and $27,890. The bottom 10 percent earned less than $16,170, and the top 10 percent earned more than $33,750.

Related Occupations
Others who work extensively with animals include animal care and service workers. Like veterinary technologists and technicians, they must have patience and feel comfortable with animals. However, the level of training required for these occupations is less than that needed by veterinary technologists and technicians. Veterinarians also work extensively with animals. They prevent, diagnose, and treat diseases, disorders, and injuries in animals.

Sources of Additional Information
For information on certification as a laboratory animal technician or technologist, contact:
➤ American Association for Laboratory Animal Science, 9190 Crestwyn Hills Dr., Memphis, TN 38125. Internet: **http://www.aalas.org**

For information on careers in veterinary medicine and a listing of AVMA-accredited veterinary technology programs, contact:
➤ American Veterinary Medical Assocation, 1931 N. Meacham Rd., Suite 100, Schaumburg, IL 60173-4360. Internet: **http://www.avma.org**

For information on veterinary technology programs, contact:
➤ Association of American Veterinary Medical Colleges, 1101 Vermont Ave. NW., Suite 710, Washington DC 20005. Internet: **http://www.aavmc.org**

For information on becoming a veterinary technician, contact:
➤ National Association of Veterinary Technicians in America, P.O. Box 224, Battle Ground, IN 47920. Internet: **http://www.navta.net**

Service Occupations

Healthcare Support Occupations

Dental Assistants

(0*NET 31-9091.00)

Significant Points

- Job prospects should be excellent.

- Dentists are expected to hire more assistants to perform routine tasks so that they may devote their own time to more profitable procedures.

- Most assistants learn their skills on the job, although an increasing number are trained in dental-assisting programs; most programs take 1 year or less to complete.

Nature of the Work

Dental assistants perform a variety of patient care, office, and laboratory duties. They work chairside as dentists examine and treat patients. They make patients as comfortable as possible in the dental chair, prepare them for treatment, and obtain their dental records. Assistants hand instruments and materials to dentists and keep patients' mouths dry and clear by using suction or other devices. Assistants also sterilize and disinfect instruments and equipment, prepare trays of instruments for dental procedures, and instruct patients on postoperative and general oral health care.

Some dental assistants prepare materials for impressions and restorations, take dental x rays, and process x-ray film as directed by a dentist. They also may remove sutures, apply topical anesthetics to gums or cavity-preventive agents to teeth, remove excess cement used in the filling process, and place rubber dams on the teeth to isolate them for individual treatment.

Those with laboratory duties make casts of the teeth and mouth from impressions, clean and polish removable appliances, and make temporary crowns. Dental assistants with office duties schedule and confirm appointments, receive patients, keep treatment records, send bills, receive payments, and order dental supplies and materials.

Dental assistants should not be confused with dental hygienists, who are licensed to perform different clinical tasks. (See the statement on dental hygienists elsewhere in the *Handbook*.)

Working Conditions

Dental assistants work in a well-lighted, clean environment. Their work area usually is near the dental chair so that they can arrange instruments, materials, and medication and hand them to the dentist when needed. Dental assistants must wear gloves, masks, eyewear, and protective clothing to protect themselves and their patients from infectious diseases. Following safety procedures also minimizes the risks associated with the use of x-ray machines.

About half of dental assistants have a 35- to 40-hour workweek, which may include work on Saturdays or evenings.

Employment

Dental assistants held about 266,000 jobs in 2002. Almost all jobs for dental assistants were in offices of dentists. A small number of jobs were in offices of physicians, educational services, and hospitals. About a third of dental assistants worked part time, sometimes in more than one dental office.

Training, Other Qualifications, and Advancement

Most assistants learn their skills on the job, although an increasing number are trained in dental-assisting programs offered by community and junior colleges, trade schools, technical institutes, or the Armed Forces. Assistants must be a second pair of hands for a dentist; therefore, dentists look for people who are reliable, can work well with others, and have good manual dexterity. High school students interested in a career as a dental assistant should take courses in biology, chemistry, health, and office practices.

The American Dental Association's Commission on Dental Accreditation approved 259 dental-assisting training programs in 2002. Programs include classroom, laboratory, and preclinical instruction in dental-assisting skills and related theory. In addition, students gain practical experience in dental schools, clinics, or dental offices. Most programs take 1 year or less to complete and lead to

Most dental assistants learn their skills on the job, although some are trained in dental-assisting programs.

a certificate or diploma. Two-year programs offered in community and junior colleges lead to an associate degree. All programs require a high school diploma or its equivalent, and some require science or computer-related courses for admission. A number of private vocational schools offer 4- to 6-month courses in dental assisting, but the Commission on Dental Accreditation does not accredit these programs.

Most States regulate the duties that dental assistants are allowed to perform through licensure or registration. Licensure or registration may require passing a written or practical examination. States offering licensure or registration have a variety of schools offering courses—approximately 10 to 12 months in length—that meet their State's requirements. Many States require continuing education to maintain licensure or registration. A few States allow dental assistants to perform any function delegated to them by the dentist.

Individual States have adopted different standards for dental assistants who perform certain advanced duties, such as radiological procedures. The completion of the Radiation Health and Safety examination offered by the Dental Assisting National Board (DANB) meets those standards in more than 30 States. Some States require the completion of a State-approved course in radiology as well.

Certification is available through DANB and is recognized or required in more than 30 States. Other organizations offer registration, most often at the State level. Certification is an acknowledgment of an assistant's qualifications and professional competence and may be an asset when one is seeking employment. Candidates may qualify to take the DANB certification examination by graduating from an accredited training program or by having 2 years of full-time, or 4 years of part-time, experience as a dental assistant. In addition, applicants must have current certification in cardiopulmonary resuscitation. For annual recertification, individuals must earn continuing education credits.

Without further education, advancement opportunities are limited. Some dental assistants become office managers, dental-assisting instructors, or dental product sales representatives. Others go back to school to become dental hygienists. For many, this entry-level occupation provides basic training and experience and serves as a steppingstone to more highly skilled and higher paying jobs.

Job Outlook

Job prospects for dental assistants should be excellent. Employment is expected to grow much faster than the average for all occupations through the year 2012. In fact, dental assistants is expected to be one of the fastest growing occupations through the year 2012.

In addition to job openings due to employment growth, numerous job openings will arise out of the need to replace assistants who transfer to other occupations, retire, or leave the labor force for other reasons. Many opportunities are for entry-level positions offering on-the-job training.

Population growth and greater retention of natural teeth by middle-aged and older people will fuel demand for dental services. Older dentists, who have been less likely to employ assistants, are leaving the occupation and will be replaced by recent graduates, who are more likely to use one or even two assistants. In addition, as dentists' workloads increase, they are expected to hire more assistants to perform routine tasks, so that they may devote their own time to more profitable procedures.

Earnings

Median hourly earnings of dental assistants were $13.10 in 2002. The middle 50 percent earned between $10.35 and $16.20 an hour. The lowest 10 percent earned less than $8.45, and the highest 10 percent earned more than $19.41 an hour.

Benefits vary substantially by practice setting and may be contingent upon full-time employment. According to the American Dental Association, almost all full-time dental assistants employed by private practitioners received paid vacation time. The ADA also found that 9 out of 10 full-time and part-time dental assistants received dental coverage.

Related Occupations

Other workers supporting health practitioners include medical assistants, occupational therapist assistants and aides, pharmacy aides, pharmacy technicians, and physical therapist assistants and aides.

Sources of Additional Information

Information about career opportunities and accredited dental assistant programs is available from:
➤ Commission on Dental Accreditation, American Dental Association, 211 E. Chicago Ave., Suite 1814, Chicago, IL 60611. Internet: **http://www.ada.org**

For information on becoming a Certified Dental Assistant and a list of State boards of dentistry, contact:
➤ Dental Assisting National Board, Inc., 676 North Saint Clair, Suite 1880, Chicago, IL 60611. Internet: **http://www.danb.org**

For more information on a career as a dental assistant and general information about continuing education, contact:
➤ American Dental Assistants Association, 35 East Wacker Drive, Suite 1730, Chicago, IL 60601. Internet: **http://www.dentalassistant.org**

For more information about continuing education courses, contact:
➤ National Association of Dental Assistants, 900 S. Washington Street, Suite G-13, Falls Church, VA 22046.

Medical Assistants

(O*NET 31-9092.00)

Significant Points

- Some medical assistants are trained on the job, but many complete 1- or 2-year programs in vocational-technical high schools, postsecondary vocational schools, and community and junior colleges.

- Medical assistants is projected to be the fastest growing occupation over the 2002-12 period.

- Job prospects should be best for medical assistants with formal training or experience, particularly those with certification.

Nature of the Work

Medical assistants perform routine administrative and clinical tasks to keep the offices of physicians, podiatrists, chiropractors, and other health practitioners running smoothly. They should not be confused with physician assistants, who examine, diagnose, and treat patients under the direct supervision of a physician. (Physician assistants are discussed elsewhere in the *Handbook*.)

The duties of medical assistants vary from office to office, depending on the location and size of the practice and the practitioner's specialty. In small practices, medical assistants usually are "generalists," handling both administrative and clinical duties and reporting directly to an office manager, physician, or other health practitioner. Those in large practices tend to specialize in a particular area, under the supervision of department administrators.

Medical assistants perform many administrative duties, including answering telephones, greeting patients, updating and filing patients' medical records, filling out insurance forms, handling correspondence, scheduling appointments, arranging for hospital admission and laboratory services, and handling billing and bookkeeping.

Clinical duties vary according to State law and include taking medical histories and recording vital signs, explaining treatment procedures to patients, preparing patients for examination, and assisting the physician during the examination. Medical assistants collect and prepare laboratory specimens or perform basic laboratory tests on the premises, dispose of contaminated supplies, and sterilize medical instruments. They instruct patients about medications and special diets, prepare and administer medications as directed by a physician, authorize drug refills as directed, telephone prescriptions to a pharmacy, draw blood, prepare patients for x rays, take electrocardiograms, remove sutures, and change dressings.

Medical assistants also may arrange examining-room instruments and equipment, purchase and maintain supplies and equipment, and keep waiting and examining rooms neat and clean.

Assistants who specialize have additional duties. *Podiatric medical assistants* make castings of feet, expose and develop x rays, and assist podiatrists in surgery. *Ophthalmic medical assistants* help ophthalmologists provide eye care. They conduct diagnostic tests, measure and record vision, and test eye muscle function. They also show patients how to insert, remove, and care for contact lenses, and they apply eye dressings. Under the direction of the physician, ophthalmic medical assistants may administer eye medications. They also maintain optical and surgical instruments and may assist the ophthalmologist in surgery.

Working Conditions

Medical assistants work in well-lighted, clean environments. They constantly interact with other people and may have to handle several responsibilities at once.

Most full-time medical assistants work a regular 40-hour week. Some work part time, evenings, or weekends.

Employment

Medical assistants held about 365,000 jobs in 2002. Almost 60 percent worked in offices of physicians; about 14 percent worked in public and private hospitals, including inpatient and outpatient facilities; and almost 10 percent worked in offices of other health practitioners, such as chiropractors and podiatrists. The rest worked mostly in outpatient care centers, public and private educational services, other ambulatory healthcare services, State and local government agencies, medical and diagnostic laboratories, nursing care facilities, and employment services.

Training, Other Qualifications, and Advancement

Most employers prefer graduates of formal programs in medical assisting. Such programs are offered in vocational-technical high schools, postsecondary vocational schools, and community and junior colleges. Postsecondary programs usually last either 1 year, resulting in a certificate or diploma, or 2 years, resulting in an associate degree. Courses cover anatomy, physiology, and medical terminology, as well as typing, transcription, recordkeeping, accounting, and insurance processing. Students learn laboratory techniques, clinical and diagnostic procedures, pharmaceutical principles, the administration of medications, and first aid. They study office practices, patient relations, medical law, and ethics. Accredited programs include an internship that provides practical experience in physicians' offices, hospitals, or other healthcare facilities.

Two agencies recognized by the U.S. Department of Education accredit programs in medical assisting: The Commission on Accreditation of Allied Health Education Programs (CAAHEP) and the Accrediting Bureau of Health Education Schools (ABHES). In 2002, there were 495 medical assisting programs accredited by CAAHEP and about 170 accredited by ABHES. The Committee on Accreditation for Ophthalmic Medical Personnel approved 14 programs in ophthalmic medical assisting.

Formal training in medical assisting, while generally preferred, is not always required. Some medical assistants are trained on the job, although this practice is less common than in the past. Applicants usually need a high school diploma or the equivalent. Recommended high school courses include mathematics, health, biology, typing, bookkeeping, computers, and office skills. Volunteer experience in the healthcare field also is helpful.

Although medical assistants are not licensed, some States require them to take a test or a course before they can perform certain tasks, such as taking x rays. Employers prefer to hire experienced workers or certified applicants who have passed a national examination, indicating that the medical assistant meets certain standards of competence. The American Association of Medical Assistants awards the Certified Medical Assistant credential; the American Medical Technologists awards the Registered Medical Assistant credential; the American Society of Podiatric Medical Assistants awards the Podiatric Medical Assistant Certified credential; and the Joint Commission on Allied Health Personnel in Ophthalmology awards credentials at three levels: Certified Ophthalmic Assistant, Certified Ophthalmic Technician, and Certified Ophthalmic Medical Technologist.

Medical assistants deal with the public; therefore, they must be neat and well groomed and have a courteous, pleasant manner. Medical assistants must be able to put patients at ease and explain physicians' instructions. They must respect the confidential nature of medical information. Clinical duties require a reasonable level of manual dexterity and visual acuity.

Medical assistants may be able to advance to office manager. They may qualify for a variety of administrative support occupations or may teach medical assisting. With additional education, some enter other health occupations, such as nursing and medical technology.

Medical assistants perform administrative and clinical duties in offices of physicians or other healthcare professionals.

Job Outlook

Employment of medical assistants is expected to grow much faster than the average for all occupations through the year 2012 as the health services industry expands because of technological advances in medicine, and a growing and aging population. Increasing utilization of medical assistants in the rapidly-growing healthcare industries will result in fast employment growth for the occupation. In fact, medical assistants is projected to be the fastest growing occupation over the 2002-12 period.

Employment growth will be driven by the increase in the number of group practices, clinics, and other healthcare facilities that need a high proportion of support personnel, particularly the flexible medical assistant who can handle both administrative and clinical duties. Medical assistants work primarily in outpatient settings, which are expected to exhibit much faster-than-average growth.

In view of the preference of many healthcare employers for trained personnel, job prospects should be best for medical assistants with formal training or experience, and particularly for those with certification.

Earnings

The earnings of medical assistants vary, depending on their experience, skill level, and location. Median annual earnings of medical assistants were $23,940 in 2002. The middle 50 percent earned between $20,260 and $28,410. The lowest 10 percent earned less than $17,640, and the highest 10 percent earned more than $34,130. Median annual earnings in the industries employing the largest numbers of medical assistants in 2002 were as follows:

General medical and surgical hospitals	$24,460
Offices of physicians	24,260
Outpatient care centers	23,980
Other ambulatory health care services	23,440
Offices of other health practitioners	21,620

Related Occupations

Workers in other medical support occupations include dental assistants, medical records and health information technicians, medical secretaries, occupational therapist assistants and aides, pharmacy aides, and physical therapist assistants and aides.

Sources of Additional Information

Information about career opportunities, educational programs in medical assisting accredited by the Commission on Accreditation of Allied Health Education Programs, and the Certified Medical Assistant exam is available from:

➤ American Association of Medical Assistants, 20 North Wacker Dr., Suite 1575, Chicago, IL 60606. Internet: **http://www.aama-ntl.org**

Information about career opportunities and the Registered Medical Assistant certification exam is available from:

➤ Registered Medical Assistants of American Medical Technologists, 710 Higgins Rd., Park Ridge, IL 60068-5765.

For a list of ABHES-accredited educational programs in medical assisting, contact:

➤ Accrediting Bureau of Health Education Schools, 7777 Leesburg Pike, Suite 314 N., Falls Church, VA 22043. Internet: **http://www.abhes.org**

Information about career opportunities, training programs, and the Certified Ophthalmic Assistant exam is available from:

➤ Joint Commission on Allied Health Personnel in Ophthalmology, 2025 Woodlane Dr., St. Paul, MN 55125-2998. Internet: **http://www.jcahpo.org**

Information about careers for podiatric assistants is available from:

➤ American Society of Podiatric Medical Assistants, 2124 S. Austin Blvd., Cicero, IL 60804. Internet: **http://www.aspma.org**

Medical Transcriptionists

(0*NET 31-9094.00)

Significant Points

- Job opportunities will be good.

- Employers prefer medical transcriptionists who have completed a postsecondary training program at a vocational school or community college.

- Many medical transcriptionists telecommute from home-based offices as employees or subcontractors for hospitals and transcription services or as self-employed, independent contractors.

- About 4 out of 10 worked in hospitals and another 3 out of 10 worked in offices of physicians.

Nature of the Work

Medical transcriptionists listen to dictated recordings made by physicians and other healthcare professionals and transcribe them into medical reports, correspondence, and other administrative material. They generally listen to recordings on a headset, using a foot pedal to pause the recording when necessary, and key the text into a personal computer or word processor, editing as necessary for grammar and clarity. The documents they produce include discharge summaries, history and physical examination reports, operative reports, consultation reports, autopsy reports, diagnostic imaging studies, progress notes, and referral letters. Medical transcriptionists return transcribed documents to the physicians or other healthcare professionals who dictated them for review and signature, or correction. These documents eventually become part of patients' permanent files.

To understand and accurately transcribe dictated reports into a format that is clear and comprehensible for the reader, medical transcriptionists must understand medical terminology, anatomy and physiology, diagnostic procedures, pharmacology, and treatment assessments. They also must be able to translate medical jargon and abbreviations into their expanded forms. To help identify terms appropriately, transcriptionists refer to standard medical reference materials—both printed and electronic; some of these are available over the Internet. Medical transcriptionists must comply with specific standards that apply to the style of medical records, in addition to the legal and ethical requirements involved with keeping patient information confidential.

Experienced transcriptionists spot mistakes or inconsistencies in a medical report and check to correct the information. Their ability to understand and correctly transcribe patient assessments and treatments reduces the chance of patients receiving ineffective or even harmful treatments and ensures high quality patient care.

Currently, most healthcare providers transmit dictation to medical transcriptionists using either digital or analog dictating equipment. The Internet has grown to be a popular mode for transmitting documentation. Many transcriptionists receive dictation over the Internet and are able to quickly return transcribed documents to clients for approval. Another emerging trend is the implementation of speech recognition technology, which electronically translates sound into text and creates drafts of reports. Reports are then formatted; edited for mistakes in translation, punctuation, or grammar; and checked for consistency and possible medical errors. Transcriptionists working in areas with standardized terminology, such as

Medical transcriptionists listen to dictated recordings made by physicians and other healthcare professionals and transcribe them into medical reports, correspondence, and other administrative material.

radiology or pathology, are more likely to encounter speech recognition technology. However, use of speech recognition technology will become more widespread as the technology becomes more sophisticated.

Medical transcriptionists who work in physicians' offices and clinics may have other office duties, such as receiving patients, scheduling appointments, answering the telephone, and handling incoming and outgoing mail. Medical secretaries, discussed in the statement on secretaries and administrative assistants elsewhere in the *Handbook*, may also transcribe as part of their jobs. Court reporters, also discussed elsewhere in the *Handbook*, have similar duties, but with a different focus. They take verbatim reports of speeches, conversations, legal proceedings, meetings, and other events when written accounts of spoken words are necessary for correspondence, records, or legal proof.

Working Conditions

The majority of these workers are employed in comfortable settings, such as hospitals, physicians' offices, transcription service offices, clinics, laboratories, medical libraries, government medical facilities, or at home. Many medical transcriptionists telecommute from home-based offices as employees or subcontractors for hospitals and transcription services or as self-employed, independent contractors.

Work in this occupation presents hazards from sitting in the same position for long periods, and workers can suffer wrist, back, neck, or eye problems due to strain and risk repetitive motion injuries such as carpal tunnel syndrome. The pressure to be accurate and productive also can be stressful.

Many medical transcriptionists work a standard 40-hour week. Self-employed medical transcriptionists are more likely to work irregular hours—including part time, evenings, weekends, or on-call at any time.

Employment

Medical transcriptionists held about 101,000 jobs in 2002. About 4 out of 10 worked in hospitals and another 3 out of 10 worked in offices of physicians. Others worked for business support services, offices of other health practitioners, medical and diagnostic laboratories, outpatient care centers, and home healthcare services.

Training, Other Qualifications, and Advancement

Employers prefer to hire transcriptionists who have completed postsecondary training in medical transcription, offered by many vocational schools, community colleges, and distance-learning programs. Completion of a 2-year associate degree or 1-year certificate program—including coursework in anatomy, medical terminology, legal issues relating to healthcare documentation, and English grammar and punctuation—is highly recommended, but not always required. Many of these programs include supervised on-the-job experience. Some transcriptionists, especially those already familiar with medical terminology due to previous experience as a nurse or medical secretary, become proficient through on-the-job training.

The American Association for Medical Transcription (AAMT) awards the voluntary designation, Certified Medical Transcriptionist (CMT), to those who earn passing scores on written and practical examinations. As in many other fields, certification is recognized as a sign of competence. Because medical terminology is constantly evolving, medical transcriptionists are encouraged to regularly update their skills. Every 3 years, CMTs must earn continuing education credits to be recertified.

In addition to understanding medical terminology, transcriptionists must have good English grammar and punctuation skills, as well as proficiency with personal computers and word processing software. Normal hearing acuity and good listening skills also are necessary. Employers often require applicants to take pre-employment tests.

With experience, medical transcriptionists can advance to supervisory positions, home-based work, editing, consulting, or teaching. With additional education or training, some become medical records and health information technicians, medical coders, or medical records and health information administrators.

Job Outlook

Job opportunities will be good. Employment of medical transcriptionists is projected to grow faster than the average for all occupations through 2012. Demand for medical transcription services will be spurred by a growing and aging population. Older age groups receive proportionately greater numbers of medical tests, treatments, and procedures that require documentation. A high level of demand for transcription services also will be sustained by the continued need for electronic documentation that can be easily shared among providers, third-party payers, regulators, and consumers. Growing numbers of medical transcriptionists will be needed to amend patients' records, edit for grammar, and identify discrepancies in medical records.

Contracting out transcription work overseas and advancements in speech recognition technology are not expected to significantly reduce the need for well-trained medical transcriptionists domestically. Contracting out transcription work abroad—to countries such as India—has grown more popular as transmitting confidential health information over the Internet has become more secure; however, the demand for overseas transcription services is expected to supplement the demand for well-trained domestic medical transcriptionists. Speech-recognition technology allows physicians and other health professionals to dictate medical reports to a computer that immediately creates an electronic document. In spite of the advances in this technology, it has been difficult for the software to grasp and analyze the human voice and the English language with all its diversity. As a result, there will continue to be a need for skilled medical transcriptionists to identify and appropriately edit the inevitable errors created by speech recognition systems, and create a final document.

Hospitals will continue to employ a large percentage of medical transcriptionists, but job growth there will not be as fast as in other industries. Increasing demand for standardized records should result in rapid employment growth in offices of physicians or other health practitioners, especially in large group practices.

Earnings
Medical transcriptionists had median hourly earnings of $13.05 in 2002. The middle 50 percent earned between $10.87 and $15.63. The lowest 10 percent earned less than $9.27, and the highest 10 percent earned more than $17.97. Median hourly earnings in the industries employing the largest numbers of medical transcriptionists in 2002 were as follows:

General medical and surgical hospitals $13.20
Offices of physicians 13.00
Business support services 12.42

Compensation methods for medical transcriptionists vary. Some are paid based on the number of hours they work or on the number of lines they transcribe. Others receive a base pay per hour with incentives for extra production. Employees of transcription services and independent contractors almost always receive production-based pay. Independent contractors earn more than transcriptionists who work for others but have higher expenses than their corporate counterparts, receive no benefits, and may face higher risk of termination than employed transcriptionists.

Related Occupations
A number of other workers type, record information, and process paperwork. Among these are court reporters; human resources assistants, except payroll and timekeeping; receptionists and information clerks; and secretaries and administrative assistants. Other workers who provide medical support include medical assistants and medical records and health information technicians.

Sources of Additional Information
For information on a career as a medical transcriptionist, send a self-addressed, stamped envelope to:
➤ American Association for Medical Transcription, 100 Sycamore Ave., Modesto, CA 95354-0550. Internet: **http://www.aamt.org**

State employment service offices can provide information about job openings for medical transcriptionists.

Nursing, Psychiatric, and Home Health Aides

(O*NET 31-1011.00, 31-1012.00, 31-1013.00)

Significant Points

- Most jobs are in nursing and residential care facilities, hospitals, and home healthcare services.
- Modest entry requirements, low pay, high physical and emotional demands, and lack of advancement opportunities characterize this occupation.
- Numerous job openings and excellent job opportunities are expected.

Nature of the Work
Nursing and psychiatric aides help care for physically or mentally ill, injured, disabled, or infirm individuals confined to hospitals,

nursing care facilities, and mental health settings. Home health aides' duties are similar, but they work in patients' homes or residential care facilities.

Nursing aides, also known as nursing assistants, geriatric aides, unlicensed assistive personnel, or hospital attendants, perform routine tasks under the supervision of nursing and medical staff. They answer patients' call lights, deliver messages, serve meals, make beds, and help patients eat, dress, and bathe. Aides also may provide skin care to patients; take their temperatures, pulse rate, respiration rate, and blood pressure; and help patients get in and out of bed and walk. They also may escort patients to operating and examining rooms, keep patients' rooms neat, set up equipment, store and move supplies, or assist with some procedures. Aides observe patients' physical, mental, and emotional conditions and report any change to the nursing or medical staff.

Nursing aides employed in nursing care facilities often are the principal caregivers, having far more contact with residents than other members of the staff. Because some residents may stay in a nursing care facility for months or even years, aides develop ongoing relationships with them and interact with them in a positive, caring way.

Home health aides help elderly, convalescent, or disabled persons live in their own homes instead of in a health facility. Under the direction of nursing or medical staff, they provide health-related services, such as administering oral medications. (*Personal and home care aides*, who provide mainly housekeeping and routine personal care services, are discussed elsewhere in the *Handbook*.) Like nursing aides, home health aides may check patients' pulse rates, temperatures, and respiration rates; help with simple prescribed exercises; keep patients' rooms neat; and help patients move from bed, bathe, dress, and groom. Occasionally, they change nonsterile dressings, give massages and alcohol rubs, or assist with braces and artificial limbs. Experienced home health aides also may assist with medical equipment such as ventilators, which help patients breathe.

Most home health aides work with elderly or disabled persons who need more extensive care than family or friends can provide. Some help discharged hospital patients who have relatively short-term needs.

In home health agencies, a registered nurse, physical therapist, or social worker usually assigns specific duties and supervises home health aides, who keep records of the services they perform and record patients' condition and progress. They report changes in patients' conditions to the supervisor or case manager.

Aides spend many hours standing and walking, and they often face heavy workloads.

Psychiatric aides, also known as mental health assistants or psychiatric nursing assistants, care for mentally impaired or emotionally disturbed individuals. They work under a team that may include psychiatrists, psychologists, psychiatric nurses, social workers, and therapists. In addition to helping patients dress, bathe, groom, and eat, psychiatric aides socialize with them and lead them in educational and recreational activities. Psychiatric aides may play games such as cards with the patients, watch television with them, or participate in group activities, such as sports or field trips. They observe patients and report any physical or behavioral signs that might be important for the professional staff to know. They accompany patients to and from examinations and treatment. Because they have such close contact with patients, psychiatric aides can have a great deal of influence on their patients' outlook and treatment.

Working Conditions
Most full-time aides work about 40 hours a week, but because patients need care 24 hours a day, some aides work evenings, nights, weekends, and holidays. Many work part time. Aides spend many hours standing and walking, and they often face heavy workloads. Because they may have to move patients in and out of bed or help them stand or walk, aides must guard against back injury. Aides also may face hazards from minor infections and major diseases, such as hepatitis, but can avoid infections by following proper procedures.

Aides often have unpleasant duties, such as emptying bedpans and changing soiled bed linens. The patients they care for may be disoriented, irritable, or uncooperative. Psychiatric aides must be prepared to care for patients whose illness may cause violent behavior. While their work can be emotionally demanding, many aides gain satisfaction from assisting those in need.

Home health aides may go to the same patient's home for months or even years. However, most aides work with a number of different patients, each job lasting a few hours, days, or weeks. Home health aides often visit multiple patients on the same day.

Home health aides generally work alone, with periodic visits by their supervisor. They receive detailed instructions explaining when to visit patients and what services to perform. Aides are individually responsible for getting to patients' homes, and they may spend a good portion of the working day traveling from one patient to another. Because mechanical lifting devices available in institutional settings are seldom available in patients' homes, home health aides are particularly susceptible to injuries resulting from overexertion when they assist patients.

Employment
Nursing, psychiatric, and home health aides held about 2.0 million jobs in 2002. Nursing aides held the most jobs—approximately 1.4 million. Home health aides held roughly 580,000 jobs and psychiatric aides held about 59,000 jobs. Around 2 in 5 nursing aides worked in nursing care facilities, and about one-fourth worked in hospitals. Most home health aides (about one-third) were employed by home healthcare services. Others were employed in social assistance agencies, nursing and residential care facilities, and employment services. More than half of all psychiatric aides worked in hospitals, primarily in psychiatric and substance abuse hospitals—although some also worked in the psychiatric units of general medical and surgical hospitals. Others were employed in State government agencies; residential mental retardation, mental health, and substance abuse facilities; individual and family services; and outpatient care centers.

Training, Other Qualifications, and Advancement
In many cases, neither a high school diploma nor previous work experience is necessary for a job as a nursing, psychiatric, or home health aide. A few employers, however, require some training or experience. Hospitals may require experience as a nursing aide or home health aide. Nursing care facilities often hire inexperienced workers who must complete a minimum of 75 hours of mandatory training and pass a competency evaluation program within 4 months of their employment. Aides who complete the program are certified and placed on the State registry of nursing aides. Some States require psychiatric aides to complete a formal training program.

The Federal Government has guidelines for home health aides whose employers receive reimbursement from Medicare. Federal law requires home health aides to pass a competency test covering 12 areas: Communication skills; documentation of patient status and care provided; reading and recording vital signs; basic infection control procedures; basic body functions; maintenance of a healthy environment; emergency procedures; physical, emotional, and developmental characteristics of patients; personal hygiene and grooming; safe transfer techniques; normal range of motion and positioning; and basic nutrition.

A home health aide may receive training before taking the competency test. Federal law suggests at least 75 hours of classroom and practical training, supervised by a registered nurse. Training and testing programs may be offered by the employing agency, but must meet the standards of the Center for Medicare and Medicaid Services. Training programs vary with State regulations.

The National Association for Home Care offers national certification for home health aides. The certification is a voluntary demonstration that the individual has met industry standards.

Nursing aide training is offered in high schools, vocational-technical centers, some nursing care facilities, and some community colleges. Courses cover body mechanics, nutrition, anatomy and physiology, infection control, communication skills, and resident rights. Personal care skills, such as how to help patients bathe, eat, and groom, also are taught.

Some employers other than nursing care facilities provide classroom instruction for newly hired aides, while others rely exclusively on informal on-the-job instruction from a licensed nurse or an experienced aide. Such training may last several days to a few months. From time to time, aides also may attend lectures, workshops, and inservice training.

These occupations can offer individuals an entry into the world of work. The flexibility of night and weekend hours also provides high school and college students a chance to work during the school year.

Applicants should be tactful, patient, understanding, emotionally stable, and dependable and should have a desire to help people. They also should be able to work as part of a team, have good communication skills, and be willing to perform repetitive, routine tasks. Home health aides should be honest and discreet, because they work in private homes.

Aides must be in good health. A physical examination, including State-regulated tests such as those for tuberculosis, may be required.

Opportunities for advancement within these occupations are limited. To enter other health occupations, aides generally need additional formal training. Some employers and unions provide opportunities by simplifying the educational paths to advancement. Experience as an aide also can help individuals decide whether to pursue a career in the health-care field.

Job Outlook

Numerous job openings for nursing, psychiatric, and home health aides will arise from a combination of fast employment growth and high replacement needs. High replacement needs in this large occupation reflect modest entry requirements, low pay, high physical and emotional demands, and lack of opportunities for advancement. For these same reasons, many people are unwilling to perform the kind of work required by the occupation. Therefore, persons who are interested in, and suited for, this work should have excellent job opportunities.

Overall employment of nursing, psychiatric, and home health aides is projected to grow faster than the average for all occupations through the year 2012, although individual occupational growth rates will vary. Employment of *home health aides* is expected to grow the fastest, as a result of both growing demand for home healthcare services from an aging population and efforts to contain healthcare costs by moving patients out of hospitals and nursing care facilities as quickly as possible. Consumer preference for care in the home and improvements in medical technologies for in-home treatment also will contribute to faster-than-average employment growth for home health aides.

Nursing aide employment will not grow as fast as home health aide employment, largely because nursing aides are concentrated in slower growing nursing care facilities. Nevertheless, employment of nursing aides is expected to grow faster than the average for all occupations in response to an increasing emphasis on rehabilitation and the long-term care needs of an increasing elderly population. Financial pressures on hospitals to discharge patients as soon as possible should produce more admissions to nursing care facilities. Modern medical technology also will increase the employment of nursing aides, because, as the technology saves and extends more lives, it increases the need for long-term care provided by aides.

Employment of *psychiatric aides*—the smallest of the three occupations—is expected to grow about as fast as the average for all occupations. The number of jobs for psychiatric aides in hospitals, where half of those in the occupation work, will grow slower than the average due to attempts to contain costs by limiting inpatient psychiatric treatment. Employment in other sectors will rise in response to growth in the number of older persons—many of whom will require mental health services, increasing public acceptance of formal treatment for substance abuse, and a lessening of the stigma attached to those receiving mental health care.

Earnings

Median hourly earnings of nursing aides, orderlies, and attendants were $9.59 in 2002. The middle 50 percent earned between $8.06 and $11.39 an hour. The lowest 10 percent earned less than $6.98, and the highest 10 percent earned more than $13.54 an hour. Median hourly earnings in the industries employing the largest numbers of nursing aides, orderlies, and attendants in 2002 were as follows:

Employment services	$11.38
Local government	10.33
General medical and surgical hospitals	10.09
Nursing care facilities	9.27
Community care facilities for the elderly	8.98

Nursing and psychiatric aides in hospitals generally receive at least 1 week's paid vacation after 1 year of service. Paid holidays and sick leave, hospital and medical benefits, extra pay for late-shift work, and pension plans also are available to many hospital, and some nursing care facility, employees.

Median hourly earnings of home health aides were $8.70 in 2002. The middle 50 percent earned between $7.54 and $10.37 an hour.

The lowest 10 percent earned less than $6.56, and the highest 10 percent earned more than $12.34 an hour. Median hourly earnings in the industries employing the largest numbers of home health aides in 2002 were as follows:

Employment services	$9.21
Residential mental retardation, mental health, and substance abuse facilities	8.91
Home health care services	8.46
Community care facilities for the elderly	8.36
Individual and family services	8.20

Home health aides receive slight pay increases with experience and added responsibility. Usually, they are paid only for the time worked in the home; normally, they are not paid for travel time between jobs. Most employers hire only on-call hourly workers and provide no benefits.

Median hourly earnings of psychiatric aides were $11.04 in 2002. The middle 50 percent earned between $8.97 and $13.74 an hour. The lowest 10 percent earned less than $7.52, and the highest 10 percent earned more than $16.16 an hour. Median hourly earnings in the industries employing the largest numbers of psychiatric aides in 2002 were as follows:

State government	$13.14
Psychiatric and substance abuse hospitals	11.32
General medical and surgical hospitals	11.04

Related Occupations

Nursing, psychiatric, and home health aides help people who need routine care or treatment. So do childcare workers, medical assistants, occupational therapist assistants and aides, personal and home care aides, and physical therapist assistants and aides.

Sources of Additional Information

Information about employment opportunities may be obtained from local hospitals, nursing care facilities, home health-care agencies, psychiatric facilities, State boards of nursing, and local offices of the State employment service.

General information about training, referrals to State and local agencies about job opportunities, a list of relevant publications, and information on certification of home health aides are available from:
➤ National Association for Home Care, 228 7th St. SE., Washington, DC 20003. Internet: **http://www.nahc.org**

Occupational Therapist Assistants and Aides

(0*NET 31-2011.00, 31-2012.00)

Significant Points

● Occupational therapist assistants generally must complete an associate degree or a certificate program; in contrast, occupational therapist aides usually receive most of their training on the job.

● Occupational therapists are expected to delegate more hands-on therapy work to occupational therapist assistants and aides.

● Employment is projected to increase much faster than the average, reflecting growth in the number of individuals with disabilities or limited function who require therapeutic services.

Nature of the Work

Occupational therapist assistants and aides work under the direction of occupational therapists to provide rehabilitative services to persons with mental, physical, emotional, or developmental impairments. The ultimate goal is to improve clients' quality of life and ability to perform daily activities. For example, occupational therapist assistants help injured workers re-enter the labor force by teaching them how to compensate for lost motor skills or help individuals with learning disabilities increase their independence.

Occupational therapist assistants help clients with rehabilitative activities and exercises outlined in a treatment plan developed in collaboration with an occupational therapist. Activities range from teaching the proper method of moving from a bed into a wheelchair to the best way to stretch and limber the muscles of the hand. Assistants monitor an individual's activities to make sure that they are performed correctly and to provide encouragement. They also record their client's progress for the occupational therapist. If the treatment is not having the intended effect, or the client is not improving as expected, the therapist may alter the treatment program in hopes of obtaining better results. In addition, occupational therapist assistants document the billing of the client's health insurance provider.

Occupational therapist aides typically prepare materials and assemble equipment used during treatment. They are responsible for a range of clerical tasks, including scheduling appointments, answering the telephone, restocking or ordering depleted supplies, and filling out insurance forms or other paperwork. Aides are not licensed, so the law does not allow them to perform as wide a range of tasks as occupational therapist assistants.

Working Conditions

The hours and days that occupational therapist assistants and aides work vary with the facility and with whether they are full- or part-time employees. Many outpatient therapy offices and clinics have evening and weekend hours, to help coincide with patients' personal schedules.

Occupational therapist assistants and aides need to have a moderate degree of strength, due to the physical exertion required in assisting patients with their treatment. For example, assistants and aides may need to lift patients. Constant kneeling, stooping, and standing for long periods also are part of the job.

Occupational therapist assistants and aides provide rehabilitative services to persons with mental, physical, emotional, or developmental impairments.

Employment

Occupational therapist assistants and aides held about 27,000 jobs in 2002. Occupational therapist assistants held about 18,000 jobs, and occupational therapist aides held approximately 8,300. Over 30 percent of jobs for assistants and aides were in hospitals, 23 percent were in offices of other health practitioners (which includes offices of occupational therapists), and 18 percent were in nursing care facilities. The rest were primarily in community care facilities for the elderly, home healthcare services, individual and family services, and State government agencies.

Training, Other Qualifications, and Advancement

An associate degree or a certificate from an accredited community college or technical school is generally required to qualify for occupational therapist assistant jobs. In contrast, occupational therapist aides usually receive most of their training on the job.

There were 161 accredited occupational therapist assistant programs in 2003. The first year of study typically involves an introduction to healthcare, basic medical terminology, anatomy, and physiology. In the second year, courses are more rigorous and usually include occupational therapist courses in areas such as mental health, adult physical disabilities, gerontology, and pediatrics. Students also must complete 16 weeks of supervised fieldwork in a clinic or community setting. Applicants to occupational therapist assistant programs can improve their chances of admission by taking high school courses in biology and health and by performing volunteer work in nursing care facilities, occupational or physical therapists' offices, or other healthcare settings.

Occupational therapist assistants are regulated in most States and must pass a national certification examination after they graduate. Those who pass the test are awarded the title "Certified Occupational Therapist Assistant."

Occupational therapist aides usually receive most of their training on the job. Qualified applicants must have a high school diploma, strong interpersonal skills, and a desire to help people in need. Applicants may increase their chances of getting a job by volunteering their services, thus displaying initiative and aptitude to the employer.

Assistants and aides must be responsible, patient, and willing to take directions and work as part of a team. Furthermore, they should be caring and want to help people who are not able to help themselves.

Job Outlook

Employment of occupational therapist assistants and aides is expected to grow much faster than the average for all occupations through 2012. The impact of proposed Federal legislation imposing limits on reimbursement for therapy services may adversely affect the job market for occupational therapist assistants and aides in the near term. However, over the long run, demand for occupational therapist assistants and aides will continue to rise, due to growth in the number of individuals with disabilities or limited function. Job growth will result from an aging population, including the baby-boom generation, which will need more occupational therapy services. Increasing demand also will result from advances in medicine that allow more people with critical problems to survive and then need rehabilitative therapy. Third-party payers, concerned with rising healthcare costs, are expected to encourage occupational therapists to delegate more hands-on therapy work to occupational therapist assistants and aides. By having assistants and aides work more closely with clients under the guidance of a therapist, the cost of therapy should decline.

Earnings

Median annual earnings of occupational therapist assistants were $36,660 in 2002. The middle 50 percent earned between $31,090 and $43,030. The lowest 10 percent earned less than $25,600, and the highest 10 percent earned more than $48,480.

Median annual earnings of occupational therapist aides were $22,040 in 2002. The middle 50 percent earned between $18,040 and $29,130. The lowest 10 percent earned less than $15,400, and the highest 10 percent earned more than $38,170.

Related Occupations

Occupational therapist assistants and aides work under the supervision and direction of occupational therapists. Other workers in the healthcare field who work under similar supervision include dental assistants, medical assistants, pharmacy aides, pharmacy technicians, and physical therapist assistants and aides.

Sources of Additional Information

For information on a career as an occupational therapist assistant or aide, and a list of accredited programs, contact:
➤ American Occupational Therapy Association, 4720 Montgomery Lane, Bethesda, MD 20824-1220. Internet: **http://www.aota.org**

Pharmacy Aides

(0*NET 31-9095.00)

Significant Points

● Many pharmacy aides work evenings, weekends, and holidays.

● Eighty percent of jobs are in retail pharmacies.

● Job opportunities are expected to be good, especially for those with related work experience.

Nature of the Work

Pharmacy aides help licensed pharmacists with administrative duties in running a pharmacy. Aides often are clerks or cashiers who primarily answer telephones, handle money, stock shelves, and perform other clerical duties. They work closely with pharmacy technicians. *Pharmacy technicians* usually perform more complex tasks than do aides, although, in some States, the duties and titles of the jobs overlap. (See the statement on pharmacy technicians elsewhere in the *Handbook*.) Aides refer any questions regarding prescriptions, drug information, or health matters to a pharmacist. (See the statement on pharmacists elsewhere in the *Handbook*.)

Aides have several important duties that help the pharmacy to function smoothly. They may establish and maintain patient profiles, prepare insurance claim forms, and stock and take inventory of prescription and over-the-counter medications. Accurate recordkeeping is necessary to help avert a potentially dangerous drug interaction. Because many people have medical insurance to help pay for the prescription, it is essential that pharmacy aides efficiently and correctly correspond with the third-party insurance providers to obtain payment. Pharmacy aides also maintain the inventory and inform the supervisor of stock needs so that the pharmacy has the vital medications for those who need them. Some also clean pharmacy equipment, help with the maintenance of equipment and supplies, and manage the cash register.

Working Conditions

Pharmacy aides work in clean, organized, well-lighted, and well-ventilated areas. Most of their workday is spent on their feet. They may be required to lift heavy boxes or to use stepladders to retrieve supplies from high shelves.

Aides work the same hours that pharmacists work. These include evenings, nights, weekends, and some holidays. Because some hospital and retail pharmacies are open 24 hours a day, aides may work varying shifts. There are many opportunities for part-time work in both retail and hospital settings.

Employment

Pharmacy aides held about 60,000 jobs in 2002. About 80 percent work in retail pharmacies either independently owned or part of a drug store chain, grocery store, department store, or mass retailer; the vast majority of these are in drug stores. About 1 in 10 work in hospitals, and the rest work in mail-order pharmacies, clinics, and pharmaceutical wholesalers.

Training, Other Qualifications, and Advancement

Most pharmacy aides receive informal on-the-job training, but employers favor those with at least a high school diploma. Prospective pharmacy aides with experience working as a cashier may have an advantage when applying for jobs. Employers also prefer applicants with strong customer service and communication skills and experience managing inventories and using a computer. Aides entering the field need strong spelling, reading, and mathematics skills.

Successful pharmacy aides are organized, dedicated, friendly, and responsible. They should be willing and able to take directions. Candidates interested in becoming pharmacy aides cannot have prior records of drug or substance abuse. Strong interpersonal and communication skills are needed because there is a lot of interaction with patients, coworkers, and healthcare professionals. Teamwork is very important because aides are often required to work with technicians and pharmacists.

Pharmacy aides almost always are trained on the job. They may begin by observing a more experienced worker. After they become familiar with the store's equipment, policies, and procedures, they begin to work on their own. Once they become experienced workers, they are not likely to receive additional training, except when new equipment is introduced or when policies or procedures change.

Pharmacy aides often take prescription orders from patients and ring up purchases.

To become a pharmacy aide, one should be able to perform repetitious work accurately. Aides need good basic mathematics skills and good manual dexterity. Because they deal constantly with the public, pharmacy aides should be neat in appearance and able to deal pleasantly and tactfully with customers. Some employers may prefer people with experience typing, handling money, or operating specialized equipment, including computers.

Advancement usually is limited, although some aides may decide to become pharmacy technicians or to enroll in pharmacy school to become pharmacists.

Job Outlook

Job opportunities for full-time and part-time work are expected to be good, especially for aides with related work experience in pharmacies, or as cashiers or stock clerks in other retail settings. Job openings will be created by employment growth and by the need to replace workers who transfer to other occupations or leave the labor force.

Employment of pharmacy aides is expected to grow about as fast as the average for all occupations through 2012 due to the increased use of medication in treating patients. In addition, a greater number of middle-aged and elderly people—who, on average, use more prescription drugs than do younger people—will spur demand for aides in all practice settings.

Cost-conscious insurers, pharmacies, and health systems will continue to employ aides. As a result, pharmacy aides will assume some responsibility for routine tasks previously performed by pharmacists and pharmacy technicians, thereby giving pharmacists more time to interact with patients and affording technicians more time to prepare medications. The number of pharmacy aides will not grow as fast as those of pharmacists and pharmacy technicians, however, because of legal limitations regarding their duties. Many smaller pharmacies that can afford only a small staff will favor pharmacy technicians because of their more extensive training and job skills.

Earnings

Median hourly wage and salary earnings of pharmacy aides were $8.86 in 2002. The middle 50 percent earned between $7.41 and $11.00; the lowest 10 percent earned less than $6.36, and the highest 10 percent earned more than $13.71. Median hourly earnings of pharmacy aides were $8.33 in health and personal care stores, $11.77 in general medical and surgical hospitals, and $9.08 in grocery stores in 2002.

Related Occupations

The work of pharmacy aides is closely related to that of pharmacy technicians, cashiers, and stock clerks and order fillers. Workers in other medical support occupations include dental assistants, licensed practical and licensed vocational nurses, medical transcriptionists, medical records and health information technicians, occupational therapist assistants and aides, physical therapist assistants and aides, and surgical technologists.

Sources of Additional Information

For information on employment opportunities, contact local employers or local offices of the State employment service.

Physical Therapist Assistants and Aides

(O*NET 31-2021.00, 31-2022.00)

Significant Points

- Employment in the occupation is projected to increase much faster than the average, reflecting the growing number of individuals with disabilities or limited function and the increasing use of physical therapist assistants to reduce the cost of therapeutic services.

- Physical therapist assistants generally have an associate degree, but physical therapist aides usually learn skills on the job.

- Almost three-fourths of all jobs were in hospitals or offices of physical therapists.

Nature of the Work

Physical therapist assistants and aides perform components of physical therapy procedures and related tasks selected by a supervising physical therapist. These workers assist physical therapists in providing services that help improve mobility, relieve pain, and prevent or limit permanent physical disabilities of patients suffering from injuries or disease. Patients include accident victims and individuals with disabling conditions such as low-back pain, arthritis, heart disease, fractures, head injuries, and cerebral palsy.

Physical therapist assistants perform a variety of tasks. Components of treatment procedures performed by these workers, under the direction and supervision of physical therapists, involve exercises, massages, electrical stimulation, paraffin baths, hot and cold packs, traction, and ultrasound. Physical therapist assistants record the patient's responses to treatment and report the outcome of each treatment to the physical therapist.

Physical therapist aides help make therapy sessions productive, under the direct supervision of a physical therapist or physical therapist assistant. They usually are responsible for keeping the treatment area clean and organized and for preparing for each patient's therapy. When patients need assistance moving to or from a treatment area, aides push them in a wheelchair or

Physical therapist assistants and aides perform physical therapy procedures and related tasks.

provide them with a shoulder to lean on. Because they are not licensed, aides do not perform the clinical tasks of a physical therapist assistant.

The duties of aides include some clerical tasks, such as ordering depleted supplies, answering the phone, and filling out insurance forms and other paperwork. The extent to which an aide or an assistant performs clerical tasks depends on the size and location of the facility.

Working Conditions

The hours and days that physical therapist assistants and aides work vary with the facility and with whether they are full- or part time employees. Many outpatient physical therapy offices and clinics have evening and weekend hours, to help coincide with patients' personal schedules.

Physical therapist assistants and aides need a moderate degree of strength because of the physical exertion required in assisting patients with their treatment. In some cases, assistants and aides need to lift patients. Constant kneeling, stooping, and standing for long periods also are part of the job.

Employment

Physical therapist assistants and aides held about 87,000 jobs in 2002. Physical therapist assistants held about 50,000 jobs, physical therapist aides approximately 37,000. Both work alongside physical therapists in a variety of settings. Almost three-fourths of all jobs were in hospitals or in offices of other health practitioners (which includes offices of physical therapists). Others worked primarily in nursing care facilities, offices of physicians, home healthcare services, and outpatient care centers.

Training, Other Qualifications, and Advancement

Physical therapist aides are trained on the job, but physical therapist assistants typically earn an associate degree from an accredited physical therapist assistant program. Not all States require licensure or registration in order for the physical therapist assistant to practice. The States that require licensure stipulate specific educational and examination criteria. Complete information on practice acts and regulations can be obtained from the State licensing boards. Additional requirements may include certification in cardiopulmonary resuscitation (CPR) and other first aid and a minimum number of hours of clinical experience.

According to the American Physical Therapy Association, there were 245 accredited physical therapist assistant programs in the United States as of 2003. Accredited physical therapist assistant programs are designed to last 2 years, or 4 semesters, and culminate in an associate degree. Programs are divided into academic study and hands-on clinical experience. Academic course work includes algebra, anatomy and physiology, biology, chemistry, and psychology. Many programs require that students complete a semester of anatomy and physiology and have certifications in CPR and other first aid even before they begin their clinical field experience. Both educators and prospective employers view clinical experience as integral to ensuring that students understand the responsibilities of a physical therapist assistant.

Employers typically require physical therapist aides to have a high school diploma, strong interpersonal skills, and a desire to

assist people in need. Most employers provide clinical on-the-job training.

Job Outlook

Employment of physical therapist assistants and aides is expected to grow much faster than the average through the year 2012. The impact of proposed Federal legislation imposing limits on reimbursement for therapy services may adversely affect the short-term job outlook for physical therapist assistants and aides. However, over the long run, demand for physical therapist assistants and aides will continue to rise, in accordance with growth in the number of individuals with disabilities or limited function. The growing elderly population is particularly vulnerable to chronic and debilitating conditions that require therapeutic services. These patients often need additional assistance in their treatment, making the roles of assistants and aides vital. The large baby-boom generation is entering the prime age for heart attacks and strokes, further increasing the demand for cardiac and physical rehabilitation. In addition, future medical developments should permit an increased percentage of trauma victims to survive, creating added demand for therapy services.

Physical therapists are expected to increasingly utilize assistants to reduce the cost of physical therapy services. Once a patient is evaluated and a treatment plan is designed by the physical therapist, the physical therapist assistant can provide many aspects of treatment, as prescribed by the therapist.

Earnings

Median annual earnings of physical therapist assistants were $36,080 in 2000. The middle 50 percent earned between $30,260 and $42,780. The lowest 10 percent earned less than $23,530, and the highest 10 percent earned more than $48,910. Median annual earnings of physical therapist assistants in 2002 were $35,870 in general medical and surgical hospitals and $35,750 in offices of other health practitioners.

Median annual earnings of physical therapist aides were $20,670 in 2002. The middle 50 percent earned between $17,430 and $24,560. The lowest 10 percent earned less than $15,290, and the highest 10 percent earned more than $29,990. Median annual earnings of physical therapist aides in 2002 were $20,690 in general medical and surgical hospitals and $19,840 in offices of other health practitioners.

Related Occupations

Physical therapist assistants and aides work under the supervision of physical therapists. Other workers in the healthcare field who work under similar supervision include dental assistants, medical assistants, occupational therapist assistants and aides, pharmacy aides, and pharmacy technicians.

Sources of Additional Information

Career information on physical therapist assistants and a list of schools offering accredited programs can be obtained from:
➤ The American Physical Therapy Association, 1111 North Fairfax St., Alexandria, VA 22314-1488. Internet: **http://www.apta.org**

Protective Service Occupations

Correctional Officers

(0*NET 33-1011.00, 33-3011.00, 33-3012.00)

Significant Points

- The work can be stressful and hazardous.
- Most correctional officers work in institutions located in rural areas with smaller inmate populations than those in urban jails.
- Job opportunities are expected to be excellent.

Nature of the Work

Correctional officers are responsible for overseeing individuals who have been arrested and are awaiting trial or who have been convicted of a crime and sentenced to serve time in a jail, reformatory, or penitentiary. They maintain security and inmate accountability to prevent disturbances, assaults, or escapes. Officers have no law enforcement responsibilities outside the institution where they work. (For more information on related occupations, see the statements on police and detectives, and probation officers and correctional treatment specialists, elsewhere in the *Handbook*.)

Police and sheriffs' departments in county and municipal jails or precinct station houses employ many correctional officers, also known as *detention officers*. Most of the approximately 3,300 jails in the United States are operated by county governments, with about three-quarters of all jails under the jurisdiction of an elected sheriff. Individuals in the jail population change constantly as some are released, some are convicted and transferred to prison, and new offenders are arrested and enter the system. Correctional officers in the U.S. jail system admit and process more than 11 million people a year, with about half a million offenders in jail at any given time. When individuals are first arrested, the jail staff may not know their true identity or criminal record, and violent detainees may be placed in the general population. This is the most dangerous phase of the incarceration process for correctional officers.

Most correctional officers are employed in large jails or State and Federal prisons, watching over the approximately one million offenders who are incarcerated at any given time. In addition to jails and prisons, a relatively small number of correctional officers oversee individuals being held by the U.S. Immigration and Naturalization Service before they are released or deported, or they work for correctional institutions that are run by private for-profit organizations. While both jails and prisons can be dangerous places to work, prison populations are more stable than jail populations, and correctional officers in prisons know the security and custodial requirements of the prisoners with whom they are dealing.

Regardless of the setting, correctional officers maintain order within the institution, and enforce rules and regulations. To help ensure that inmates are orderly and obey rules, correctional officers monitor the activities and supervise the work assignments of inmates. Sometimes, it is necessary for officers to search inmates and their living quarters for contraband like weapons or drugs, settle disputes between inmates, and enforce discipline. Correctional officers periodically inspect the facilities, check-

ing cells and other areas of the institution for unsanitary conditions, contraband, fire hazards, and any evidence of infractions of rules. In addition, they routinely inspect locks, window bars, grilles, doors, and gates for signs of tampering. Finally, officers inspect mail and visitors for prohibited items.

Correctional officers report orally and in writing on inmate conduct and on the quality and quantity of work done by inmates. Officers also report security breaches, disturbances, violations of rules, and any unusual occurrences. They usually keep a daily log or record of their activities. Correctional officers cannot show favoritism and must report any inmate who violates the rules. Should the situation arise, they help the responsible law enforcement authorities investigate crimes committed within their institution or search for escaped inmates.

In jail and prison facilities with direct supervision cellblocks, officers work unarmed. They are equipped with communications devices so that they can summon help if necessary. These officers often work in a cellblock alone, or with another officer, among the 50 to 100 inmates who reside there. The officers enforce regulations primarily through their interpersonal communications skills and the use of progressive sanctions, such as loss of some privileges.

In the highest security facilities where the most dangerous inmates are housed, correctional officers often monitor the activities of prisoners from a centralized control center with the aid of closed-circuit television cameras and a computer tracking system. In such an environment, the inmates may not see anyone but officers for days or weeks at a time and only leave their cells for showers, solitary exercise time, or visitors. Depending on the offender's security classification within the institution, correctional officers may have to restrain inmates in handcuffs and leg irons to safely escort them to and from cells and other areas to see authorized visitors. Officers also escort prisoners between the institution and courtrooms, medical facilities, and other destinations outside the institution.

Working Conditions

Working in a correctional institution can be stressful and hazardous. Every year, a number of correctional officers are injured

A correctional officer uses a metal-detecting wand to inspect a visitor before allowing the person into the facility.

in confrontations with inmates. Correctional officers may work indoors or outdoors. Some correctional institutions are well lighted, temperature controlled, and ventilated, while others are old, overcrowded, hot, and noisy. Correctional officers usually work an 8-hour day, 5 days a week, on rotating shifts. Prison and jail security must be provided around the clock, which often means that officers work all hours of the day and night, weekends, and holidays. In addition, officers may be required to work paid overtime.

Employment

Correctional officers held about 476,000 jobs in 2002. About 3 of every 5 jobs were in State correctional institutions such as prisons, prison camps, and youth correctional facilities. Most of the remaining jobs were in city and county jails or other institutions run by local governments. About 16,000 jobs for correctional officers were in Federal correctional institutions, and about 16,000 jobs were in privately owned and managed prisons.

There are 118 jail systems in the United States that house over 1,000 inmates, all of which are located in urban areas. A significant number work in jails and other facilities located in law enforcement agencies throughout the country. However, most correctional officers work in institutions located in rural areas with smaller inmate populations than those in urban jails.

Training, Other Qualifications, and Advancement

Most institutions require correctional officers to be at least 18 to 21 years of age and a U.S. citizen; have a high school education or its equivalent; demonstrate job stability, usually by accumulating two years of work experience; and have no felony convictions. Promotion prospects may be enhanced through obtaining a postsecondary education.

Correctional officers must be in good health. Candidates for employment are generally required to meet formal standards of physical fitness, eyesight, and hearing. In addition, many jurisdictions use standard tests to determine applicant suitability to work in a correctional environment. Good judgment and the ability to think and act quickly are indispensable. Applicants are typically screened for drug abuse, subject to background checks, and required to pass a written examination.

Federal, State, and some local departments of corrections provide training for correctional officers based on guidelines established by the American Correctional Association and the American Jail Association. Some States have regional training academies which are available to local agencies. All States and local correctional agencies provide on-the-job training at the conclusion of formal instruction, including legal restrictions and interpersonal relations. Many systems require firearms proficiency and self-defense skills. Officer trainees typically receive several weeks or months of training in an actual job setting under the supervision of an experienced officer. However, specific entry requirements and on-the-job training vary widely from agency to agency.

Academy trainees generally receive instruction on a number of subjects, including institutional policies, regulations, and operations, as well as custody and security procedures. As a condition of employment, new Federal correctional officers must undergo 200 hours of formal training within the first year of employment. They also must complete 120 hours of specialized training at the U.S. Federal Bureau of Prisons residential training center at Glynco, Georgia within the first 60 days after appointment. Experienced officers receive annual in-service training to keep abreast of new developments and procedures.

Some correctional officers are members of prison tactical response teams, which are trained to respond to disturbances, riots, hostage situations, forced cell moves, and other potentially dangerous confrontations. Team members receive training and practice with weapons, chemical agents, forced entry methods, crisis management, and other tactics.

With education, experience, and training, qualified officers may advance to correctional sergeant. Correctional sergeants supervise correctional officers and usually are responsible for maintaining security and directing the activities of other officers during an assigned shift or in an assigned area. Ambitious and qualified correctional officers can be promoted to supervisory or administrative positions all the way up to warden. Officers sometimes transfer to related areas, such as probation officer, parole officer, or correctional treatment specialist.

Job Outlook

Job opportunities for correctional officers are expected to be excellent. The need to replace correctional officers who transfer to other occupations, retire, or leave the labor force, coupled with rising employment demand, will generate thousands of job openings each year. In the past, some local and State corrections agencies have experienced difficulty in attracting and keeping qualified applicants, largely due to relatively low salaries and the concentration of jobs in rural locations. This situation is expected to continue.

Employment of correctional officers is expected to increase faster than the average for all occupations through 2012, as additional officers are hired to supervise and control a growing inmate population. The adoption of mandatory sentencing guidelines calling for longer sentences and reduced parole for inmates will continue to spur demand for correctional officers. Moreover, expansion and new construction of corrections facilities also are expected to create many new jobs for correctional officers, although State and local government budgetary constraints could affect the rate at which new facilities are built and staffed. Some employment opportunities also will arise in the private sector as public authorities contract with private companies to provide and staff corrections facilities.

Layoffs of correctional officers are rare because of increasing offender populations. While officers are allowed to join bargaining units, they are not allowed to strike.

Earnings

Median annual earnings of correctional officers and jailers were $32,670 in 2002. The middle 50 percent earned between $25,950 and $42,620. The lowest 10 percent earned less than $22,010, and the highest 10 percent earned more than $52,370. Median annual earnings in the public sector were $40,900 in the Federal Government, $33,260 in State government, and $31,380 in local government. In the management and public relations industry, where the relatively small number of officers employed by privately operated prisons are classified, median annual earnings were $21,390. According to the Federal Bureau of Prisons, the starting salary for Federal correctional officers was about $23,000 a year in 2003. Starting Federal salaries were slightly higher in selected areas where prevailing local pay levels were higher.

Median annual earnings of first-line supervisors/managers of correctional officers were $44,940 in 2002. The middle 50 percent earned between $33,730 and $59,160. The lowest 10 percent earned less than $29,220, and the highest 10 percent earned more than $69,370. Median annual earnings were $43,240 in State government and $49,120 in local government.

Median annual earnings of bailiffs were $32,710 in 2002. The middle 50 percent earned between $22,960 and $44,280. The lowest 10 percent earned less than $16,870, and the highest 10 percent earned more than $55,270. Median annual earnings were $27,470 in local government.

In addition to typical benefits, correctional officers employed in the public sector usually are provided with uniforms or a clothing allowance to purchase their own uniforms. Civil service systems or merit boards cover officers employed by the Federal Government and most State governments. Their retirement coverage entitles them to retire at age 50 after 20 years of service or at any age with 25 years of service.

Related Occupations

A number of options are available to those interested in careers in protective services and security. Security guards and gaming surveillance officers protect people and property against theft, vandalism, illegal entry, and fire. Police and detectives maintain law and order, prevent crime, and arrest offenders. Probation officers and correctional treatment specialists monitor and counsel offenders in the community and evaluate their progress in becoming productive members of society.

Sources of Additional Information

Information about correctional jobs in a jail setting is available from:

➤ American Jail Association, 1135 Professional Ct., Hagerstown, MD 21740.

Information on entrance requirements, training, and career opportunities for correctional officers at the Federal level may be obtained from the Federal Bureau of Prisons. Internet: **http://www.bop.gov**

Information on obtaining a position as a correctional officer with the Federal Government is available from the Office of Personnel Management (OPM) through a telephone-based system. Consult your telephone directory under U.S. Government for a local number or call (703) 724-1850; Federal Relay Service: (800) 877-8339. The first number is not tollfree and charges may result. Information also is available from the OPM Internet site: **http://www.usajobs.opm.gov**.

Firefighting Occupations

(0*NET 33-1021.01, 33-1021.02, 33-2011.01, 33-2011.02, 33-2021.01, 33-2021.02, 33-2022.00)

Significant Points

● Firefighting involves hazardous conditions and long, irregular hours.

● About 9 out of 10 firefighting workers were employed by municipal or county fire departments.

● Applicants for municipal firefighting jobs generally must pass written, physical, and medical examinations.

● Keen competition for jobs is expected.

Nature of the Work

Every year, fires and other emergencies take thousands of lives and destroy property worth billions of dollars. Firefighters help protect the public against these dangers by rapidly responding to a variety of emergencies. They are frequently the first emergency personnel at the scene of a traffic accident or medical emergency and may be called upon to put out a fire, treat injuries, or perform other vital functions.

During duty hours, firefighters must be prepared to respond immediately to a fire or any other emergency that arises. Because fighting fires is dangerous and complex, it requires organization and teamwork. At every emergency scene, firefighters perform specific duties assigned by a superior officer. At fires, they connect hose lines to hydrants, operate a pump to send water to high pressure hoses, and position ladders to enable them to deliver water to the fire. They also rescue victims and provide emergency medical attention as needed, ventilate smoke-filled areas, and attempt to salvage the contents of buildings. Their duties may change several times while the company is in action. Sometimes they remain at the site of a disaster for days at a time, rescuing trapped survivors and assisting with medical treatment.

Firefighters have assumed a range of responsibilities, including emergency medical services. In fact, most calls to which firefighters respond involve medical emergencies, and about half of all fire departments provide ambulance service for victims. Firefighters receive training in emergency medical procedures, and many fire departments require them to be certified as emergency medical technicians. (For more information, see the *Handbook* statement on emergency medical technicians and paramedics.)

Firefighters work in a variety of settings, including urban and suburban areas, airports, chemical plants, other industrial sites, and rural areas like grasslands and forests. In addition, some firefighters work in hazardous materials units that are trained for the control, prevention, and cleanup of oil spills and other hazardous materials incidents. (For more information, see the *Handbook* statement on hazardous material removal workers.) Workers in urban and suburban areas, airports, and industrial sites typically use conventional firefighting equipment and tactics, while forest fires and major hazardous materials spills call for different methods.

In national forests and parks, *forest fire inspectors and prevention specialists* spot fires from watchtowers and report their findings to headquarters by telephone or radio. Forest rangers patrol to ensure travelers and campers comply with fire regulations. When fires break out, crews of firefighters are brought in to suppress the blaze using heavy equipment, handtools, and water hoses. Forest firefighting, like urban firefighting, can be rigorous work. One of the most effective means of battling the blaze is by creating fire lines through cutting down trees and digging out grass and all other combustible vegetation, creating bare land in the path of the fire that deprives it of fuel. Elite firefighters, called smoke jumpers, parachute from airplanes to reach otherwise inaccessible areas. This can be extremely hazardous because the crews have no way to escape if the wind shifts and causes the fire to burn toward them.

Between alarms, firefighters clean and maintain equipment, conduct practice drills and fire inspections, and participate in physical fitness activities. They also prepare written reports on fire incidents and review fire science literature to keep abreast of technological developments and changing administrative practices and policies.

Most fire departments have a fire prevention division, usually headed by a fire marshall and staffed by *fire inspectors*. Workers in this division conduct inspections of structures to prevent fires and ensure fire code compliance. These firefighters also work with developers and planners to check and approve

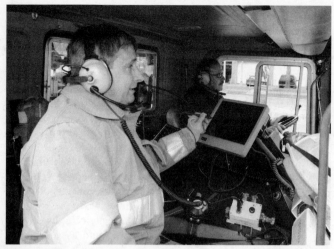

Firefighters use a variety of technologies to ensure prompt and effective responses to emergency situations.

plans for new buildings. Fire prevention personnel often speak on these subjects in schools and before public assemblies and civic organizations.

Some firefighters become *fire investigators*, who determine the origin and causes of fires. They collect evidence, interview witnesses, and prepare reports on fires in cases where the cause may be arson or criminal negligence. They often are called upon to testify in court.

Working Conditions

Firefighters spend much of their time at fire stations, which usually have features common to a residential facility like a dormitory. When an alarm sounds, firefighters respond rapidly, regardless of the weather or hour. Firefighting involves risk of death or injury from sudden cave-ins of floors, toppling walls, traffic accidents when responding to calls, and exposure to flames and smoke. Firefighters may also come in contact with poisonous, flammable, or explosive gases and chemicals, as well as radioactive or other hazardous materials that may have immediate or long-term effects on their health. For these reasons, they must wear protective gear that can be very heavy and hot.

Work hours of firefighters are longer and vary more widely than hours of most other workers. Many work more than 50 hours a week, and sometimes they may work even longer. In some agencies, they are on duty for 24 hours, then off for 48 hours, and receive an extra day off at intervals. In others, they work a day shift of 10 hours for 3 or 4 days, a night shift of 14 hours for 3 or 4 nights, have 3 or 4 days off, and then repeat the cycle. In addition, firefighters often work extra hours at fires and other emergencies and are regularly assigned to work on holidays. Fire lieutenants and fire captains often work the same hours as the firefighters they supervise. Duty hours include time when firefighters study, train, and perform fire prevention duties.

Employment

Employment figures in this *Handbook* statement include only paid career firefighters—they do not cover volunteer firefighters, who perform the same duties and may comprise the majority of firefighters in a residential area. According the United States Fire Administration, nearly 70 percent of fire companies are staffed by volunteer fire fighters. Paid career firefighters held about 282,000 jobs in 2002. First-line supervisors/managers of

firefighting and prevention workers held about 63,000 jobs; and fire inspectors held about 14,000.

About 9 out of 10 firefighting workers were employed by municipal or county fire departments. Some large cities have thousands of career firefighters, while many small towns have only a few. Most of the remainder worked in fire departments on Federal and State installations, including airports. Private firefighting companies employ a small number of firefighters and usually operate on a subscription basis.

In response to the expanding role of firefighters, some municipalities have combined fire prevention, public fire education, safety, and emergency medical services into a single organization commonly referred to as a public safety organization. Some local and regional fire departments are being consolidated into countywide establishments in order to reduce administrative staffs and cut costs, and to establish consistent training standards and work procedures.

Training, Other Qualifications, and Advancement

Applicants for municipal firefighting jobs generally must pass a written exam; tests of strength, physical stamina, coordination, and agility; and a medical examination that includes drug screening. Workers may be monitored on a random basis for drug use after accepting employment. Examinations are generally open to persons who are at least 18 years of age and have a high school education or the equivalent. Those who receive the highest scores in all phases of testing have the best chances for appointment. The completion of community college courses in fire science may improve an applicant's chances for appointment. In recent years, an increasing proportion of entrants to this occupation have had some postsecondary education.

As a rule, entry-level workers in large fire departments are trained for several weeks at the department's training center or academy. Through classroom instruction and practical training, the recruits study firefighting techniques, fire prevention, hazardous materials control, local building codes, and emergency medical procedures, including first aid and cardiopulmonary resuscitation. They also learn how to use axes, chain saws, fire extinguishers, ladders, and other firefighting and rescue equipment. After successfully completing this training, they are assigned to a fire company, where they undergo a period of probation.

A number of fire departments have accredited apprenticeship programs lasting up to 5 years. These programs combine formal, technical instruction with on-the-job training under the supervision of experienced firefighters. Technical instruction covers subjects such as firefighting techniques and equipment, chemical hazards associated with various combustible building materials, emergency medical procedures, and fire prevention and safety. Fire departments frequently conduct training programs, and some firefighters attend training sessions sponsored by the U.S. National Fire Academy. These training sessions cover topics including executive development, anti-arson techniques, disaster preparedness, hazardous materials control, and public fire safety and education. Some States also have extensive firefighter training and certification programs. In addition, a number of colleges and universities offer courses leading to 2- or 4-year degrees in fire engineering or fire science. Many fire departments offer firefighters incentives such as tuition reimbursement or higher pay for completing advanced training.

Among the personal qualities firefighters need are mental alertness, self-discipline, courage, mechanical aptitude, endurance, strength, and a sense of public service. Initiative and good judgment are also extremely important because firefighters make quick decisions in emergencies. Because members of a crew live and work closely together under conditions of stress and danger for extended periods, they must be dependable and able to get along well with others. Leadership qualities are necessary for officers, who must establish and maintain discipline and efficiency, as well as direct the activities of firefighters in their companies.

Most experienced firefighters continue studying to improve their job performance and prepare for promotion examinations. To progress to higher level positions, they acquire expertise in advanced firefighting equipment and techniques, building construction, emergency medical technology, writing, public speaking, management and budgeting procedures, and public relations.

Opportunities for promotion depend upon written examination results, job performance, interviews, and seniority. Increasingly, fire departments use assessment centers, which simulate a variety of actual job performance tasks, to screen for the best candidates for promotion. The line of promotion usually is to engineer, lieutenant, captain, battalion chief, assistant chief, deputy chief, and finally to chief. Many fire departments now require a bachelor's degree, preferably in fire science, public administration, or a related field, for promotion to positions higher than battalion chief. A master's degree is required for executive fire officer certification from the National Fire Academy and for State chief officer certification.

Job Outlook
Prospective firefighters are expected to face keen competition for available job openings. Many people are attracted to firefighting because it is challenging and provides the opportunity to perform an essential public service, a high school education is usually sufficient for entry, and a pension is guaranteed upon retirement after 20 years. Consequently, the number of qualified applicants in most areas exceeds the number of job openings, even though the written examination and physical requirements eliminate many applicants. This situation is expected to persist in coming years.

Employment of firefighters is expected to grow about as fast as the average for all occupations through 2012 as fire departments continue to compete with other public safety providers for funding. Most job growth will occur as volunteer firefighting positions are converted to paid positions. In addition to job growth, openings are expected to result from the need to replace firefighters who retire, stop working for other reasons, or transfer to other occupations.

Layoffs of firefighters are uncommon. Fire protection is an essential service, and citizens are likely to exert considerable pressure on local officials to expand or at least preserve the level of fire protection. Even when budget cuts do occur, local fire departments usually cut expenses by postponing equipment purchases or not hiring new firefighters, rather than through staff reductions.

Earnings
Median hourly earnings of firefighters were $17.42 in 2002. The middle 50 percent earned between $12.53 and $22.96. The lowest 10 percent earned less than $8.51, and the highest 10 percent earned more than $28.22. Median hourly earnings were $17.92 in local government, $15.96 in the Federal Government, and $13.58 in State government.

Median annual earnings of first-line supervisors/managers of firefighting and prevention workers were $55,450 in 2002. The middle 50 percent earned between $43,920 and $68,480. The lowest 10 percent earned less than $34,190, and the highest 10 percent earned more than $84,730. First-line supervisors/managers of firefighting and prevention workers employed in local government earned about $56,390 a year in 2002.

Median annual earnings of fire inspectors were $44,250 in 2002. The middle 50 percent earned between $33,880 and $56,100 a year. The lowest 10 percent earned less than $26,350, and the highest 10 percent earned more than $69,060. Fire inspectors and investigators employed in local government earned about $46,820 a year.

According to the International City-County Management Association, average salaries in 2002 for sworn full-time positions were as follows:

	Minimum annual base salary	Maximum annual base salary
Fire chief	$64,134	$82,225
Deputy chief	56,522	72,152
Assistant fire chief	55,645	69,036
Battalion chief	54,935	68,673
Fire captain	45,383	54,463
Fire lieutenant	41,800	49,404
Fire prevention/code inspector	40,387	51,531
Engineer	38,656	48,678

Firefighters who average more than a certain number of hours a week are required to be paid overtime. The hours threshold is determined by the department during the firefighter's work period, which ranges from 7 to 28 days. Firefighters often earn overtime for working extra shifts to maintain minimum staffing levels or for special emergencies.

Firefighters receive benefits that usually include medical and liability insurance, vacation and sick leave, and some paid holidays. Almost all fire departments provide protective clothing (helmets, boots, and coats) and breathing apparatus, and many also provide dress uniforms. Firefighters are generally covered by pension plans, often providing retirement at half pay after 25 years of service or if disabled in the line of duty.

Related Occupations
Like firefighters, emergency medical technicians and paramedics and police and detectives respond to emergencies and save lives.

Sources of Additional Information
Information about a career as a firefighter may be obtained from local fire departments and from:
➤ International Association of Firefighters, 1750 New York Ave. NW., Washington, DC 20006. Internet: **http://www.iaff.org**
➤ U.S. Fire Administration, 16825 South Seton Ave., Emmitsburg, MD 21727. Internet: **http://www.usfa.fema.gov**

Information about firefighter professional qualifications and a list of colleges and universities offering 2-year or 4-year degree programs in fire science or fire prevention may be obtained from:
➤ National Fire Academy, 16825 South Seton Ave., Emmitsburg, MD 21727. Internet: **http://www.usfa.fema.gov/nfa/index.htm**

Police and Detectives

(O*NET 33-1012.00, 33-3021.01, 33-3021.02, 33-3021.03, 33-3021.04, 33-3021.05, 33-3031.00, 33-3051.01, 33-3051.02, 33-3051.03, 33-3052.00)

Significant Points

- Police work can be dangerous and stressful.

- Civil service regulations govern the appointment of police and detectives.

- Competition should remain keen for higher paying jobs with State and Federal agencies and police departments in affluent areas; opportunities will be better in local and special police departments that offer relatively low salaries or in urban communities where the crime rate is relatively high.

- Applicants with college training in police science or military police experience should have the best opportunities.

Nature of the Work

People depend on police officers and detectives to protect their lives and property. Law enforcement officers, some of whom are State or Federal special agents or inspectors, perform these duties in a variety of ways, depending on the size and type of their organization. In most jurisdictions, they are expected to exercise authority when necessary, whether on or off duty.

Uniformed police officers who work in municipal police departments of various sizes, small communities, and rural areas have general law enforcement duties including maintaining regular patrols and responding to calls for service. They may direct traffic at the scene of a fire, investigate a burglary, or give first aid to an accident victim. In large police departments, officers usually are assigned to a specific type of duty. Many urban police agencies are becoming more involved in community policing—a practice in which an officer builds relationships with the citizens of local neighborhoods and mobilizes the public to help fight crime.

Police agencies are usually organized into geographic districts, with uniformed officers assigned to patrol a specific area, such as part of the business district or outlying residential neighborhoods. Officers may work alone, but in large agencies they often patrol with a partner. While on patrol, officers attempt to become thoroughly familiar with their patrol area and remain alert for anything unusual. Suspicious circumstances and hazards to public safety are investigated or noted, and officers are dispatched to individual calls for assistance within their district. During their shift, they may identify, pursue, and arrest suspected criminals, resolve problems within the community, and enforce traffic laws.

Public college and university police forces, public school district police, and agencies serving transportation systems and facilities are examples of special police agencies. These agencies have special geographic jurisdictions or enforcement responsibilities in the United States. Most sworn personnel in special agencies are uniformed officers, a smaller number are investigators.

Some police officers specialize in such diverse fields as chemical and microscopic analysis, training and firearms instruction, or handwriting and fingerprint identification. Others work with

special units such as horseback, bicycle, motorcycle or harbor patrol, canine corps, or special weapons and tactics (SWAT) or emergency response teams. A few local and special law enforcement officers primarily perform jail-related duties or work in courts. Regardless of job duties or location, police officers and detectives at all levels must write reports and maintain meticulous records that will be needed if they testify in court.

Sheriffs and deputy sheriffs enforce the law on the county level. Sheriffs are usually elected to their posts and perform duties similar to those of a local or county police chief. Sheriffs' departments tend to be relatively small, most having fewer than 25 sworn officers. A deputy sheriff in a large agency will have law enforcement duties similar to those of officers in urban police departments. Police and sheriffs' deputies who provide security in city and county courts are sometimes called bailiffs. (For information on other officers who work in jails and prisons, see correctional officers elsewhere in the *Handbook.*)

State police officers (sometimes called *State troopers* or *highway patrol officers*) arrest criminals Statewide and patrol highways to enforce motor vehicle laws and regulations. Uniformed officers are best known for issuing traffic citations to motorists who violate the law. At the scene of accidents, they may direct traffic, give first aid, and call for emergency equipment. They also write reports used to determine the cause of the accident. State police officers are frequently called upon to render assistance to other law enforcement agencies, especially those in rural areas or small towns.

State law enforcement agencies operate in every State except Hawaii. Most full-time sworn personnel are uniformed officers who regularly patrol and respond to calls for service. Others are investigators, perform court-related duties, or work in administrative or other assignments.

Detectives are plainclothes investigators who gather facts and collect evidence for criminal cases. Some are assigned to interagency task forces to combat specific types of crime. They conduct interviews, examine records, observe the activities of suspects, and participate in raids or arrests. Detectives and State and Federal agents and inspectors usually specialize in one of a wide variety of violations such as homicide or fraud. They are assigned cases on a rotating basis and work on them until an arrest and conviction occurs or the case is dropped.

The Federal Government maintains a high profile in many areas of law enforcement. *Federal Bureau of Investigation (FBI) agents* are the Government's principal investigators, responsible for investigating violations of more than 260 statutes and conducting sensitive national security investigations. Agents may conduct surveillance, monitor court-authorized wiretaps, examine business records, investigate white-collar crime, track the interstate movement of stolen property, collect evidence of espionage activities, or participate in sensitive undercover assignments. The FBI investigates organized crime, public corruption, financial crime, fraud against the government, bribery, copyright infringement, civil rights violations, bank robbery, extortion, kidnapping, air piracy, terrorism, espionage, interstate criminal activity, drug trafficking, and other violations of Federal statutes.

U.S. Drug Enforcement Administration (DEA) agents enforce laws and regulations relating to illegal drugs. Not only is the DEA the lead agency for domestic enforcement of Federal drug laws, it also has sole responsibility for coordinating and pursuing U.S. drug investigations abroad. Agents may conduct complex criminal investigations, carry out surveillance of criminals, and infiltrate illicit drug organizations using undercover techniques.

U.S. marshals and deputy marshals protect the Federal courts and ensure the effective operation of the judicial system. They provide protection for the Federal judiciary, transport Federal prisoners, protect Federal witnesses, and manage assets seized from criminal enterprises. They enjoy the widest jurisdiction of any Federal law enforcement agency and are involved to some degree in nearly all Federal law enforcement efforts. In addition, U.S. marshals pursue and arrest Federal fugitives.

U.S. Immigration and Naturalization Service (INS) agents and inspectors facilitate the entry of legal visitors and immigrants to the U.S. and detain and deport those arriving illegally. They consist of border patrol agents, immigration inspectors, criminal investigators and immigration agents, and detention and deportation officers. *U.S. Border Patrol agents* protect more than 8,000 miles of international land and water boundaries. Their missions are to detect and prevent the smuggling and unlawful entry of undocumented foreign nationals into the U.S., apprehend those persons found in violation of the immigration laws, and interdict contraband, such as narcotics. *Immigration inspectors* interview and examine people seeking entrance to the U.S. and its territories. They inspect passports to determine whether people are legally eligible to enter the United States. Immigration inspectors also prepare reports, maintain records, and process applications and petitions for immigration or temporary residence in the United States.

Bureau of Alcohol, Tobacco, Firearms, and Explosives agents regulate and investigate violations of Federal firearms and explosives laws, as well as Federal alcohol and tobacco tax regulations. *Customs agents* investigate violations of narcotics smuggling, money laundering, child pornography, customs fraud, and enforcement of the Arms Export Control Act. Domestic and foreign investigations involve the development and use of informants, physical and electronic surveillance, and examination of records from importers/exporters, banks, couriers, and manufacturers. They conduct interviews, serve on joint task forces with other agencies, and get and execute search warrants.

Customs inspectors inspect cargo, baggage, and articles worn or carried by people and carriers including vessels, vehicles, trains and aircraft entering or leaving the U.S. to enforce laws governing imports and exports. These inspectors examine, count, weigh, gauge, measure, and sample commercial and noncommercial cargoes entering and leaving the United States. Customs inspectors seize prohibited or smuggled articles, intercept contraband, and apprehend, search, detain, and arrest violators of U.S. laws.

U.S. Secret Service special agents protect the President, Vice President, and their immediate families; Presidential candidates; former Presidents; and foreign dignitaries visiting the United States. Secret Service agents also investigate counterfeiting, forgery of Government checks or bonds, and fraudulent use of credit cards.

The U.S. Department of State *Bureau of Diplomatic Security special agents* are engaged in the battle against terrorism. Overseas, they advise ambassadors on all security matters and manage a complex range of security programs designed to protect personnel, facilities, and information. In the U.S., they investigate passport and visa fraud, conduct personnel security investigations, issue security clearances, and protect the Secretary of State and a number of foreign dignitaries. They also train foreign civilian police and administer a counter-terrorism reward program.

Other Federal agencies employ police and special agents with sworn arrest powers and the authority to carry firearms. These agencies include the Postal Service, the Bureau of Indian Affairs Office of Law Enforcement, the Forest Service, the National Park Service, and the Federal Air Marshals.

Working Conditions

Police work can be very dangerous and stressful. In addition to the obvious dangers of confrontations with criminals, officers need to be constantly alert and ready to deal appropriately with a number of other threatening situations. Many law enforcement officers witness death and suffering resulting from accidents and criminal behavior. A career in law enforcement may take a toll on officers' private lives.

Uniformed officers, detectives, agents, and inspectors are usually scheduled to work 40-hour weeks, but paid overtime is common. Shift work is necessary because protection must be provided around the clock. Junior officers frequently work weekends, holidays, and nights. Police officers and detectives are required to work at any time their services are needed and may work long hours during investigations. In most jurisdictions, whether on or off duty, officers are expected to be armed and to exercise their arrest authority whenever necessary.

The jobs of some Federal agents such as U.S. Secret Service and DEA special agents require extensive travel, often on very short notice. They may relocate a number of times over the

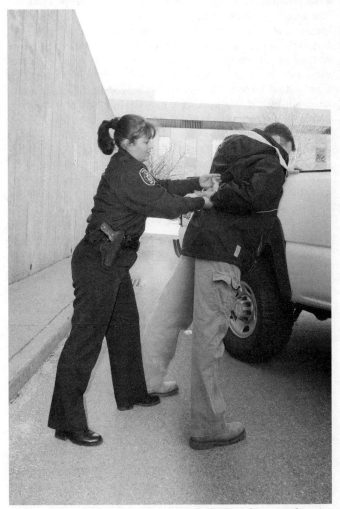

Police officers take every precaution during the apprehension of suspected criminals.

course of their careers. Some special agents in agencies such as the U.S. Border Patrol work outdoors in rugged terrain for long periods and in all kinds of weather.

Employment

Police and detectives held about 840,000 jobs in 2002. About 81 percent were employed by local governments. State police agencies employed about 11 percent and various Federal agencies employed about 6 percent. A small proportion worked for educational services, rail transportation, and contract investigation and security services.

According to the U.S. Bureau of Justice Statistics, police and detectives employed by local governments primarily worked in cities with more than 25,000 inhabitants. Some cities have very large police forces, while thousands of small communities employ fewer than 25 officers each.

Training, Other Qualifications, and Advancement

Civil service regulations govern the appointment of police and detectives in practically all States, large municipalities, and special police agencies, as well as in many smaller ones. Candidates must be U.S. citizens, usually at least 20 years of age, and must meet rigorous physical and personal qualifications. In the Federal Government, candidates must be at least 21 years of age but less than 37 years of age at the time of appointment. Physical examinations for entrance into law enforcement often include tests of vision, hearing, strength, and agility. Eligibility for appointment usually depends on performance in competitive written examinations and previous education and experience. In larger departments, where the majority of law enforcement jobs are found, applicants usually must have at least a high school education. Federal and State agencies typically require a college degree. Candidates should enjoy working with people and meeting the public.

Because personal characteristics such as honesty, sound judgment, integrity, and a sense of responsibility are especially important in law enforcement, candidates are interviewed by senior officers, and their character traits and backgrounds are investigated. In some agencies, candidates are interviewed by a psychiatrist or a psychologist, or given a personality test. Most applicants are subjected to lie detector examinations or drug testing. Some agencies subject sworn personnel to random drug testing as a condition of continuing employment.

Before their first assignments, officers usually go through a period of training. In State and large local departments, recruits get training in their agency's police academy, often for 12 to 14 weeks. In small agencies, recruits often attend a regional or State academy. Training includes classroom instruction in constitutional law and civil rights, State laws and local ordinances, and accident investigation. Recruits also receive training and supervised experience in patrol, traffic control, use of firearms, self-defense, first aid, and emergency response. Police departments in some large cities hire high school graduates who are still in their teens as police cadets or trainees. They do clerical work and attend classes, usually for 1 to 2 years, at which point they reach the minimum age requirement and may be appointed to the regular force.

Police officers usually become eligible for promotion after a probationary period ranging from 6 months to 3 years. In a large department, promotion may enable an officer to become a detective or specialize in one type of police work, such as working with juveniles. Promotions to corporal, sergeant, lieutenant,

and captain usually are made according to a candidate's position on a promotion list, as determined by scores on a written examination and on-the-job performance.

To be considered for appointment as an FBI agent, an applicant either must be a graduate of an accredited law school or a college graduate with a major in accounting, fluency in a foreign language, or 3 years of related full-time work experience. All new agents undergo 16 weeks of training at the FBI academy on the U.S. Marine Corps base in Quantico, Virginia.

Applicants for special agent jobs with the U.S. Secret Service and the Bureau of Alcohol, Tobacco, and Firearms must have a bachelor's degree or a minimum of 3 years' related work experience. Prospective special agents undergo 10 weeks of initial criminal investigation training at the Federal Law Enforcement Training Center in Glynco, Georgia, and another 17 weeks of specialized training with their particular agencies.

Applicants for special agent jobs with the U.S. Drug Enforcement Administration (DEA) must have a college degree and either 1 year of experience conducting criminal investigations, 1 year of graduate school, or have achieved at least a 2.95 grade point average while in college. DEA special agents undergo 14 weeks of specialized training at the FBI Academy in Quantico, Virginia.

U.S. Border Patrol agents must be U.S. citizens, younger than 37 years of age at the time of appointment, possess a valid driver's license, and pass a three-part examination on reasoning and language skills. A bachelor's degree or previous work experience that demonstrates the ability to handle stressful situations, make decisions, and take charge is required for a position as a Border Patrol agent. Applicants may qualify through a combination of education and work experience.

Postal inspectors must have a bachelor's degree and 1 year of related work experience. It is desirable that they have one of several professional certifications, such as that of certified public accountant. They also must pass a background suitability investigation, meet certain health requirements, undergo a drug screening test, possess a valid State driver's license, and be a U.S. citizen between 21 and 36 years of age when hired.

Law enforcement agencies are encouraging applicants to take postsecondary school training in law enforcement-related subjects. Many entry-level applicants for police jobs have completed some formal postsecondary education and a significant number are college graduates. Many junior colleges, colleges, and universities offer programs in law enforcement or administration of justice. Other courses helpful in preparing for a career in law enforcement include accounting, finance, electrical engineering, computer science, and foreign languages. Physical education and sports are helpful in developing the competitiveness, stamina, and agility needed for many law enforcement positions. Knowledge of a foreign language is an asset in many Federal agencies and urban departments.

Continuing training helps police officers, detectives, and special agents improve their job performance. Through police department academies, regional centers for public safety employees established by the States, and Federal agency training centers, instructors provide annual training in self-defense tactics, firearms, use-of-force policies, sensitivity and communications skills, crowd-control techniques, relevant legal developments, and advances in law enforcement equipment. Many agencies pay all or part of the tuition for officers to work toward degrees in criminal justice, police science, administration of justice, or public administration, and pay higher salaries to those who earn such a degree.

Job Outlook

The opportunity for public service through law enforcement work is attractive to many because the job is challenging and involves much personal responsibility. Furthermore, law enforcement officers in many agencies may retire with a pension after 20 or 25 years of service, allowing them to pursue a second career while still in their 40s. Because of relatively attractive salaries and benefits, the number of qualified candidates exceeds the number of job openings in Federal law enforcement agencies and in most State police departments—resulting in increased hiring standards and selectivity by employers. Competition should remain keen for higher paying jobs with State and Federal agencies and police departments in more affluent areas. Opportunities will be better in local and special police departments, especially in departments that offer relatively low salaries, or in urban communities where the crime rate is relatively high. Applicants with college training in police science, military police experience, or both should have the best opportunities.

Employment of police and detectives is expected to grow faster than the average for all occupations through 2012. A more security-conscious society and concern about drug-related crimes should contribute to the increasing demand for police services.

The level of government spending determines the level of employment for police and detectives. The number of job opportunities, therefore, can vary from year to year and from place to place. Layoffs, on the other hand, are rare because retirements enable most staffing cuts to be handled through attrition. Trained law enforcement officers who lose their jobs because of budget cuts usually have little difficulty finding jobs with other agencies. The need to replace workers who retire, transfer to other occupations, or stop working for other reasons will be the source of many job openings.

Earnings

Police and sheriff's patrol officers had median annual earnings of $42,270 in 2002. The middle 50 percent earned between $32,300 and $53,500. The lowest 10 percent earned less than $25,270, and the highest 10 percent earned more than $65,330. Median annual earnings were $47,090 in State government, $42,020 in local government, and $41,600 in Federal Government.

In 2002, median annual earnings of police and detective supervisors were $61,010. The middle 50 percent earned between $47,210 and $74,610. The lowest 10 percent earned less than $36,340, and the highest 10 percent earned more than $90,070. Median annual earnings were $78,230 in Federal Government, $64,410 in State government, and $59,830 in local government.

In 2002, median annual earnings of detectives and criminal investigators were $51,410. The middle 50 percent earned between $39,010 and $65,980. The lowest 10 percent earned less than $31,010, and the highest 10 percent earned more than $80,380. Median annual earnings were $66,500 in Federal Government, $47,700 in local government, and $46,600 in State government.

Federal law provides special salary rates to Federal employees who serve in law enforcement. Additionally, Federal special agents and inspectors receive law enforcement availability pay (LEAP)—equal to 25 percent of the agent's grade and step—awarded because of the large amount of overtime that these agents are expected to work. For example, in 2003 FBI agents enter Federal service as GS-10 employees on the pay scale at a base salary of $39,115, yet earned about $48,890 a year with availability pay. They can advance to the GS-13 grade level in field nonsupervisory assignments at a base salary of $61,251, which is worth $76,560 with availability pay. FBI supervisory, management, and executive positions in grades GS-14 and GS-15 pay a base salary of about $72,381 or $85,140 a year, respectively, and equaled $90,480 or $106,430 per year including availability pay. Salaries were slightly higher in selected areas where the prevailing local pay level was higher. Because Federal agents may be eligible for a special law enforcement benefits package, applicants should ask their recruiter for more information.

According to the International City-County Management Association's annual Police and Fire Personnel, Salaries, and Expenditures Survey, average salaries for sworn full-time positions in 2002 were as follows:

	Minimum annual base salary	Maximum annual base salary
Police chief	$68,337	$87,037
Deputy chief	59,790	75,266
Police captain	56,499	70,177
Police lieutenant	52,446	63,059
Police sergeant	46,805	55,661
Police corporal	39,899	9,299

Total earnings for local, State, and special police and detectives frequently exceed the stated salary because of payments for overtime, which can be significant. In addition to the common benefits—paid vacation, sick leave, and medical and life insurance—most police and sheriffs' departments provide officers with special allowances for uniforms. Because police officers usually are covered by liberal pension plans, many retire at half-pay after 20 or 25 years of service.

Related Occupations

Police and detectives maintain law and order, collect evidence and information, and conduct investigations and surveillance. Workers in related occupations include correctional officers, private detectives and investigators, and security guards and gaming surveillance officers.

Sources of Additional Information

Information about entrance requirements may be obtained from Federal, State, and local law enforcement agencies.

Further information about qualifications for employment as a FBI Special Agent is available from the nearest State FBI office. The address and phone number are listed in the local telephone directory. Internet: **http://www.fbi.gov**

Information on career opportunities, qualifications, and training for U.S. Secret Service Special Agents is available from the Secret Service Personnel Division at (202) 406-5800, (888) 813-8777 or (888) 813-USSS. Internet: **http://www.treas.gov/usss**

Information about qualifications for employment as a DEA Special Agent is available from the nearest DEA office, or call (800) DEA-4288. Internet: **http://www.usdoj.gov/dea**

Information about career opportunities, qualifications, and training to become a deputy marshal is available from:
➤ U.S. Marshals Service, Human Resources Division—Law Enforcement Recruiting, Washington, DC 20530-1000. Internet: **http://www.usdoj.gov/marshals**

For information on operations and career opportunities in the U.S. Bureau of Alcohol, Tobacco, Firearms, and Explosives operations, contact:

➤ U.S. Bureau of Alcohol, Tobacco, Firearms, and Explosives Personnel Division, 650 Massachusetts Ave. NW., Room 4100, Washington, DC 20226. Internet: **http://www.atf.treas.gov**

Information about careers in U.S. Customs and Border Protection is available from:

➤ U.S. Customs and Border Protection, 1300 Pennsylvania Ave., NW., Washington, DC 20229. Internet: **http://www.cbp.gov**

Private Detectives and Investigators

(0*Net 33-9021.00)

Significant Points

- Work hours often are irregular, and the work can be dangerous.

- About a third were self-employed.

- Applicants typically have related experience in areas such as law enforcement, insurance, the military, or government investigative or intelligence jobs.

- Keen competition is expected because of the large number of qualified people who are attracted to this occupation; opportunities will be best for entry-level jobs with detective agencies or as store detectives on a part-time basis.

Nature of the Work

Private detectives and investigators use many means to determine the facts in a variety of matters. To carry out investigations, they may use various types of surveillance or searches. To verify facts, such as an individual's place of employment or income, they may make phone calls or visit a subject's workplace. In other cases, especially those involving missing persons and background checks, investigators often interview people to gather as much information as possible about an individual. In all cases, private detectives and investigators assist attorneys, businesses, and the public with a variety of legal, financial, and personal problems.

Private detectives and investigators offer many services, including executive, corporate, and celebrity protection; pre-employment verification; and individual background profiles. They also provide assistance in civil liability and personal injury cases, insurance claims and fraud, child custody and protection cases, and premarital screening. Increasingly, they are hired to investigate individuals to prove or disprove infidelity.

Most detectives and investigators are trained to perform physical surveillance, often for long periods, in a car or van. They may observe a site, such as the home of a subject, from an inconspicuous location. The surveillance continues using still and video cameras, binoculars, and a cell phone, until the desired evidence is obtained. They also may perform computer database searches, or work with someone who does. Computers allow detectives and investigators to quickly obtain massive amounts of information on individuals' prior arrests, convictions, and civil legal judgments; telephone numbers; motor vehicle registrations; association and club memberships; and other matters.

The duties of private detectives and investigators depend on the needs of their client. In cases for employers involving workers' fraudulent compensation claims, for example, investigators may carry out long-term covert observation of subjects. If an investigator observes a subject performing an activity that contradicts injuries stated in a workers' compensation claim, the investigator would take video or still photographs to document the activity and report it to the client.

Private detectives and investigators often specialize. Those who focus on intellectual property theft, for example, investigate and document acts of piracy, help clients stop the illegal activity, and provide intelligence for prosecution and civil action. Other investigators specialize in developing financial profiles and asset searches. Their reports reflect information gathered through interviews, investigation and surveillance, and research, including review of public documents.

Legal investigators specialize in cases involving the courts and are normally employed by law firms or lawyers. They frequently assist in preparing criminal defenses, locating witnesses, serving legal documents, interviewing police and prospective witnesses, and gathering and reviewing evidence. Legal investigators also may collect information on the parties to the litigation, take photographs, testify in court, and assemble evidence and reports for trials.

Corporate investigators conduct internal and external investigations for corporations other than investigative firms. In internal investigations, they may investigate drug use in the workplace, ensure that expense accounts are not abused, or determine if employees are stealing merchandise or information. External investigations typically prevent criminal schemes originating outside the corporation, such as theft of company assets through fraudulent billing of products by suppliers.

Financial investigators may be hired to develop confidential financial profiles of individuals or companies who are prospective parties to large financial transactions. They often are Certified Public Accountants (CPAs) and work closely with investment bankers and accountants. They search for assets in order to recover damages awarded by a court in fraud or theft cases.

Detectives who work for retail stores or hotels are responsible for loss control and asset protection. *Store detectives*, also known as *loss prevention agents*, safeguard the assets of retail

Some private detectives and investigators work for insurance companies or law firms providing information on criminal activity or financial misconduct.

stores by apprehending anyone attempting to steal merchandise or destroy store property. They prevent theft by shoplifters, vendor representatives, delivery personnel, and even store employees. Store detectives also conduct periodic inspections of stock areas, dressing rooms, and restrooms, and sometimes assist in opening and closing the store. They may prepare loss prevention and security reports for management and testify in court against persons they apprehend. *Hotel detectives* protect guests of the establishment from theft of their belongings and preserve order in hotel restaurants and bars. They also may keep undesirable individuals, such as known thieves, off the premises.

Working Conditions

Private detectives and investigators often work irregular hours because of the need to conduct surveillance and contact people who are not available during normal working hours. Early morning, evening, weekend, and holiday work is common.

Many detectives and investigators spend time away from their offices conducting interviews or doing surveillance, but some work in their office most of the day conducting computer searches and making phone calls. Those who have their own agencies and employ other investigators may work primarily in an office and have normal business hours.

When working on a case away from the office, the environment might range from plush boardrooms to seedy bars. Store and hotel detectives work in the businesses that they protect. Investigators generally work alone, but they sometimes work with others during surveillance or when following a subject in order to avoid detection by the subject.

Some of the work involves confrontation, so the job can be stressful and dangerous. Some situations call for the investigator to be armed, such as certain bodyguard assignments for corporate or celebrity clients. Detectives and investigators who carry handguns must be licensed by the appropriate authority. In most cases, however, a weapon is not necessary because the purpose of their work is gathering information and not law enforcement or criminal apprehension. Owners of investigative agencies have the added stress of having to deal with demanding and sometimes distraught clients.

Employment

Private detectives and investigators held about 48,000 jobs in 2002. About a third were self-employed, including many who held a secondary job as a self-employed private detective. Almost a fifth jobs were found in investigation and security services, including private detective agencies, while another fifth were in department or other general merchandise stores. The rest worked mostly in State and local government, legal services firms, employment services, insurance carriers, and credit intermediation and related activities, including banks and other depository institutions.

Training, Other Qualifications, and Advancement

There are no formal education requirements for most private detective and investigator jobs, although many private detectives have college degrees. Private detectives and investigators typically have previous experience in other occupations. Some work initially for insurance or collections companies or in the private security industry. Many investigators enter the field after serving in law enforcement, the military, govern-

ment auditing and investigative positions, or Federal intelligence jobs.

Former law enforcement officers, military investigators, and government agents often become private detectives or investigators as a second career because they are frequently able to retire after 20 years of service. Others enter from such diverse fields as finance, accounting, commercial credit, investigative reporting, insurance, and law. These individuals often can apply their prior work experience in a related investigative specialty. A few enter the occupation directly after graduation from college, generally with associate or bachelor's degrees in criminal justice or police science.

The majority of States and the District of Colombia require private detectives and investigators to be licensed. Licensing requirements vary widely, but convicted felons cannot receive a license in most States and a growing number of States are enacting mandatory training programs for private detectives and investigators. Some States have few requirements, and 6 States— Alabama, Alaska, Colorado, Idaho, Mississippi, and South Dakota—have no statewide licensing requirements while others have stringent regulations. For example, the Bureau of Security and Investigative Services of the California Department of Consumer Affairs requires private investigators to be 18 years of age or older; have a combination of education in police science, criminal law, or justice, and experience equaling 3 years (6,000 hours) of investigative experience; pass an evaluation by the Federal Department of Justice and a criminal history background check; and receive a qualifying score on a 2-hour written examination covering laws and regulations. There are additional requirements for a firearms permit.

For private detective and investigator jobs, most employers look for individuals with ingenuity, persistence, and assertiveness. A candidate must not be afraid of confrontation, should communicate well, and should be able to think on his or her feet. Good interviewing and interrogation skills also are important and usually are acquired in earlier careers in law enforcement or other fields. Because the courts often are the ultimate judge of a properly conducted investigation, the investigator must be able to present the facts in a manner a jury will believe.

Training in subjects such as criminal justice is helpful to aspiring private detectives and investigators. Most corporate investigators must have a bachelor's degree, preferably in a business-related field. Some corporate investigators have master's degrees in business administration or law, while others are certified public accountants. Corporate investigators hired by large companies may receive formal training from their employers on business practices, management structure, and various finance-related topics. The screening process for potential employees typically includes a background check of criminal history.

Some investigators receive certification from a professional organization to demonstrate competency in a field. For example, the National Association of Legal Investigators (NALI) confers the Certified Legal Investigator designation to licensed investigators who devote a majority of their practice to negligence or criminal defense investigations. To receive the designation, applicants must satisfy experience, educational, and continuing training requirements, and must pass written and oral exams administered by the NALI.

Most private detective agencies are small, with little room for advancement. Usually there are no defined ranks or steps, so advancement takes the form of increases in salary and assignment status. Many detectives and investigators work for detective agencies at the beginning of their careers and, after a few years, start their own firms. Corporate and legal investigators may rise to supervisor or manager of the security or investigations department.

Job Outlook

Keen competition is expected because private detective and investigator careers attract many qualified people, including relatively young retirees from law enforcement and military careers. Opportunities will be best for entry-level jobs with detective agencies or as store detectives on a part-time basis. Those seeking store detective jobs have the best prospects with large chains and discount stores.

Employment of private detectives and investigators is expected to grow faster than the average for all occupations through 2012. In addition to growth, replacement of those who retire or leave the occupation for other reasons should create many job openings. Increased demand for private detectives and investigators will result from fear of crime, increased litigation, and the need to protect confidential information and property of all kinds. More private investigators also will be needed to assist attorneys working on criminal defense and civil litigation. Growing financial activity worldwide will increase the demand for investigators to control internal and external financial losses, and to monitor competitors and prevent industrial spying.

Earnings

Median annual earnings of salaried private detectives and investigators were $29,300 in 2002. The middle 50 percent earned between $21,980 and $41,710. The lowest 10 percent earned less than $17,290, and the highest 10 percent earned more than $57,370. In 2002, median annual earnings were $29,030 in investigation and security services, and $22,250 in department stores.

Earnings of private detectives and investigators vary greatly depending on their employer, specialty, and the geographic area in which they work. According to a study by Abbott, Langer & Associates, security/loss prevention directors and vice presidents had a median income of $77,500 per year in 2002; investigators, $39,800; and store detectives, $25,000. In addition to typical benefits, most corporate investigators received profit-sharing plans.

Related Occupations

Private detectives and investigators often collect information and protect the property and other assets of companies and individuals. Others with related duties include bill and account collectors; claims adjusters, appraisers, examiners, and investigators; police and detectives; and security guards and gaming surveillance officers. Investigators who specialize in conducting financial profiles and asset searches perform work closely related to that of accountants and auditors and financial analysts and personal finance advisors.

Sources of Additional Information

For information on local licensing requirements, contact your State Department of Public Safety, State Division of Licensing, or local or State police headquarters.

For information on a career as a legal investigator, contact:
➤ National Association of Legal Investigators, 908 21st St., Sacramento, CA, 95814-3118.

Security Guards and Gaming Surveillance Officers

(0*NET 33-9031.00, 33-9032.00)

Significant Points

- Opportunities for most jobs should be favorable, but competition is expected for higher paying positions at facilities requiring longer periods of training and a high level of security, such as nuclear power plants and weapons installations.

- Because of limited formal training requirements and flexible hours, this occupation attracts many individuals seeking a second or part-time job.

- Some positions, such as those of armored car guards, are hazardous.

Nature of the Work

Guards, who are also called *security officers*, patrol and inspect property to protect against fire, theft, vandalism, terrorism, and illegal activity. These workers protect their employer's investment, enforce laws on the property, and deter criminal activity or other problems. They use radio and telephone communications to call for assistance from police, fire, or emergency medical services as the situation dictates. Security guards write comprehensive reports outlining their observations and activities during their assigned shift. They may also interview witnesses or victims, prepare case reports, and testify in court.

Although all security guards perform many of the same duties, specific duties vary based on whether the guard works in a "static" security position or on a mobile patrol. Guards assigned to static security positions usually serve the client at one location for a specific length of time. These guards must become closely acquainted with the property and people associated with it and often monitor alarms and closed-circuit TV cameras. In contrast, guards assigned to mobile patrol duty drive or walk from location to location and conduct security checks within an assigned geographical zone. They may detain or arrest criminal violators, answer service calls concerning criminal activity or problems, and issue traffic violation warnings.

Specific job responsibilities also vary with the size, type, and location of the employer. In department stores, guards protect people, records, merchandise, money, and equipment. They often work with undercover store detectives to prevent theft by customers or store employees and help in the apprehension of shoplifting suspects prior to arrival by police. Some shopping centers and theaters have officers mounted on horses or bicycles who patrol their parking lots to deter car theft and robberies. In office buildings, banks, and hospitals, guards maintain order and protect the institutions' property, staff, and customers. At air, sea, and rail terminals and other transportation facilities, guards protect people, freight, property, and equipment. They may screen passengers and visitors for weapons and explosives using metal detectors and high-tech equipment, ensure nothing is stolen while being loaded or unloaded, and watch for fires and criminals.

Guards who work in public buildings such as museums or art galleries protect paintings and exhibits by inspecting people and packages entering and leaving the building. In factories, laboratories, government buildings, data processing centers, and military bases, security officers protect information, products, computer codes, and defense secrets and check the credentials of people and vehicles entering and leaving the premises. Guards working at universities, parks, and sports stadiums perform crowd control, supervise parking and seating, and direct traffic. Security guards stationed at the entrance to bars and places of adult entertainment, such as nightclubs, prevent access by minors, collect cover charges at the door, maintain order among customers, and protect property and patrons.

Armored car guards protect money and valuables during transit. In addition, they protect individuals responsible for making commercial bank deposits from theft or bodily injury. When the armored car arrives at the door of a business, an armed guard enters, signs for the money, and returns to the truck with the valuables in hand. Carrying money between the truck and the business can be extremely hazardous for guards. Because of this risk, armored car guards usually wear bullet-proof vests.

All security officers must show good judgment and common sense, follow directions and directives from supervisors, accurately testify in court, and follow company policy and guidelines. Guards should have a professional appearance and attitude and be able to interact with the public. They also must be able to take charge and direct others in emergencies or other dangerous incidents. In a large organization, the security manager is often in charge of a trained guard force divided into shifts; whereas in a small organization, a single worker may be responsible for all security.

Gaming surveillance officers and gaming investigators act as security agents for casino managers and patrons. They observe casino operations for irregular activities, such as cheating or theft, by either employees or patrons. To do this, surveillance officers and investigators often monitor activities from a catwalk over one-way mirrors located above the casino floor. Many casinos use audio and video equipment, allowing surveillance officers and investigators to observe these same areas via monitors. Recordings are kept as a record and are sometimes used as evidence against alleged criminals in police investigations.

Working Conditions

Most security guards and gaming surveillance officers spend considerable time on their feet, either assigned to a specific post or patrolling buildings and grounds. Guards may be stationed

Security guards are often responsible for checking visitors at a main gate and directing them to their destination.

at a guard desk inside a building to monitor electronic security and surveillance devices or to check the credentials of persons entering or leaving the premises. They also may be stationed at a guardhouse outside the entrance to a gated facility or community and use a portable radio or cellular telephone that allows them to be in constant contact with a central station. The work usually is routine, but guards must be constantly alert for threats to themselves and the property they are protecting. Guards who work during the day may have a great deal of contact with other employees and members of the public. Gaming surveillance often takes place behind a bank of monitors controlling several cameras in a casino, which can cause eyestrain.

Guards usually work at least 8-hour shifts for 40 hours per week and often are on call in case an emergency arises. Some employers have three shifts, and guards rotate to equally divide daytime, weekend, and holiday work. Guards usually eat on the job instead of taking a regular break away from the site. More than 1 in 7 guards worked part time, and many individuals held a second job as a guard to supplement their primary earnings.

Employment

Security guards and gaming surveillance officers held more than 1.0 million jobs in 2002. More than half of jobs for security guards were in investigation and security services, including guard and armored car services. These organizations provide security services on a contract basis, assigning their guards to buildings and other sites as needed. Most other security officers were employed directly by educational services, hospitals, food services and drinking places, traveler accommodation (hotels), department stores, manufacturing firms, lessors of real estate (residential and nonresidential buildings), and governments. Guard jobs are found throughout the country, most commonly in metropolitan areas. Gaming surveillance officers worked primarily in gambling industries; traveler accommodation, which includes casino hotels; and local government. Gaming surveillance officers were employed only in those States and Indian reservations where gambling has been legalized.

A significant number of law enforcement officers work as security guards when off-duty to supplement their incomes. Often working in uniform and with the official cars assigned to them, they add a high profile security presence to the establishment with which they have contracted. At construction sites and apartment complexes, for example, their presence often prevents trouble before it starts. (Police and detectives are discussed elsewhere in the *Handbook*.)

Training, Other Qualifications, and Advancement

Most States require that guards be licensed. To be licensed as a guard, individuals must usually be at least 18 years old, pass a background check, and complete classroom training in such subjects as property rights, emergency procedures, and detention of suspected criminals. Drug testing often is required, and may be random and ongoing.

Many employers of unarmed guards do not have any specific educational requirements. For armed guards, employers usually prefer individuals who are high school graduates or hold an equivalent certification. Many jobs require a driver's license. For positions as armed guards, employers often seek people who have had responsible experience in other occupations.

Guards who carry weapons must be licensed by the appropriate government authority, and some receive further certification as special police officers, which allows them to make limited types of arrests while on duty. Armed guard positions have more stringent background checks and entry requirements than those of unarmed guards because of greater insurance liability risks. Compared to unarmed security guards, armed guards and special police typically enjoy higher earnings and benefits, greater job security, more advancement potential, and usually are given more training and responsibility.

Rigorous hiring and screening programs consisting of background, criminal record, and fingerprint checks are becoming the norm in the occupation. Applicants are expected to have good character references, no serious police record, and good health. They should be mentally alert, emotionally stable, and physically fit in order to cope with emergencies. Guards who have frequent contact with the public should communicate well.

The amount of training guards receive varies. Training requirements are higher for armed guards because their employers are legally responsible for any use of force. Armed guards receive formal training in areas such as weapons retention and laws covering the use of force.

Many employers give newly hired guards instruction before they start the job and also provide on-the-job training. An increasing number of States are making ongoing training a legal requirement for retention of certification. Guards may receive training in protection, public relations, report writing, crisis deterrence, and first aid, as well as specialized training relevant to their particular assignment.

Guards employed at establishments placing a heavy emphasis on security usually receive extensive formal training. For example, guards at nuclear power plants undergo several months of training before being placed on duty under close supervision. They are taught to use firearms, administer first aid, operate alarm systems and electronic security equipment, and spot and deal with security problems. Guards authorized to carry firearms may be periodically tested in their use.

Although guards in small companies may receive periodic salary increases, advancement opportunities are limited. Most large organizations use a military type of ranking that offers the possibility of advancement in position and salary. Some guards may advance to supervisor or security manager positions. Guards with management skills may open their own contract security guard agencies.

In addition to the keen observation skills required to perform their jobs, gaming surveillance officers and gaming investigators must have excellent verbal and writing abilities to document violations or suspicious behavior. They also need to be physically fit and have quick reflexes because they sometimes must detain individuals until local law enforcement officials arrive.

Surveillance officers and investigators usually do not need a bachelor's degree, but some training beyond high school is required; previous security experience is a plus. Several educational institutes offer certification programs. Training classes usually are conducted in a casino-like atmosphere using surveillance camera equipment.

Job Outlook

Opportunities for security guards and gaming surveillance officers should be favorable. Numerous job openings will stem from employment growth attributable to the desire for increased security, and from the need to replace those who leave this large

occupation each year. In addition to full-time job opportunities, the limited training requirements and flexible hours attract many persons seeking part-time or second jobs. However, competition is expected for higher paying positions that require longer periods of training; these positions usually are found at facilities that require a high level of security, such as nuclear power plants or weapons installations.

Employment of security guards and gaming surveillance officers is expected to grow faster than the average for all occupations through 2012 as concern about crime, vandalism, and terrorism continue to increase the need for security. Demand for guards also will grow as private security firms increasingly perform duties—such as monitoring crowds at airports and providing security in courts—which were formerly handled by government police officers and marshals. Because enlisting the services of a security guard firm is easier and less costly than assuming direct responsibility for hiring, training, and managing a security guard force, job growth is expected to be concentrated among contract security guard agencies. Casinos will continue to hire more surveillance officers as more States legalize gambling and as the number of casinos increases in States where gambling is already legal. Additionally, casino security forces will employ more technically trained personnel as technology becomes increasingly important in thwarting casino cheating and theft.

Earnings

Median annual earnings of security guards were $19,140 in 2002. The middle 50 percent earned between $15,910 and $23,920. The lowest 10 percent earned less than $13,740, and the highest 10 percent earned more than $31,540. Median annual earnings in the industries employing the largest numbers of security guards in 2002 were as follows:

Elementary and secondary schools	$24,470
General medical and surgical hospitals	24,050
Local government	22,120
Traveler accommodation	21,390
Investigation and security services	17,910

Gaming surveillance officers and gaming investigators had median annual earnings of $23,110 in 2002. The middle 50 percent earned between $19,620 and $28,420. The lowest 10 percent earned less than $15,930, and the highest 10 percent earned more than $35,170.

Related Occupations

Guards protect property, maintain security, and enforce regulations and standards of conduct in the establishments at which they work. Related security and protective service occupations include correctional officers, police and detectives, and private detectives and investigators.

Sources of Additional Information

Further information about work opportunities for guards is available from local security and guard firms and State employment service offices. Information about licensing requirements for guards may be obtained from the State licensing commission or the State police department. In States where local jurisdictions establish licensing requirements, contact a local government authority such as the sheriff, county executive, or city manager.

Food Preparation and Serving Related Occupations

Chefs, Cooks, and Food Preparation Workers

(0*NET 35-1011.00, 35-2011.00, 35-2012.00, 35-2013.00, 35-2014.00, 35-2015.00, 35-2021.00)

Significant Points

- Many young people worked as cooks and food preparation workers—almost 20 percent were between 16 and 19 years old.

- More than 2 out of 5 food preparation workers were employed part time.

- Job openings are expected to be plentiful, primarily reflecting substantial replacement needs in this large occupation.

Nature of the Work

Chefs, cooks, and food preparation workers prepare, season, and cook a wide range of foods—from soups, snacks, and salads to entrees, side dishes, and desserts—in a variety of restaurants and other food services establishments. Chefs and cooks create recipes and prepare meals, while food preparation workers peel and cut vegetables, trim meat, prepare poultry, and perform other duties such as keeping work areas clean and monitoring temperatures of ovens and stovetops.

In general, *chefs* and *cooks* measure, mix, and cook ingredients according to recipes, using a variety of pots, pans, cutlery, and other equipment, including ovens, broilers, grills, slicers, grinders, and blenders. Chefs and head cooks also are responsible for directing the work of other kitchen workers, estimating food requirements, and ordering food supplies.

Larger restaurants and food services establishments tend to have varied menus and larger kitchen staffs. They often include several chefs and cooks, sometimes called assistant or line cooks, along with other lesser skilled kitchen workers, such as *food preparation workers*. Each chef or cook works an assigned station that is equipped with the types of stoves, grills, pans, and ingredients needed for the foods prepared at each station. Job titles often reflect the principal ingredient prepared or the type of cooking performed—*vegetable cook, fry cook, or grill cook*.

Executive chefs and *head cooks* coordinate the work of the kitchen staff and direct the preparation of meals. They determine serving sizes, plan menus, order food supplies, and oversee kitchen operations to ensure uniform quality and presentation of meals. The terms chef and cook often are used interchangeably, but generally reflect the different types of chefs and the organizational structure of the kitchen staff. For example, an *executive chef* is in charge of all food service operations and also may supervise the many kitchens of a hotel, restaurant group, or corporate dining operation. A *chef de cuisine* reports to an executive chef and is responsible for the daily operations of a single kitchen. A *sous chef*, or sub chef, is the second-in-command and runs the kitchen in the absence of the chef. Chefs tend to be more highly skilled and better trained than cooks. Many chefs earn fame both for themselves and for their kitchens because of the quality and distinctive nature of the food they serve.

The specific responsibilities of most cooks are determined by a number of factors, including the type of restaurant in which they work. *Institution and cafeteria cooks*, for example, work in the kitchens of schools, cafeterias, businesses, hospitals, and other institutions. For each meal, they prepare a large quantity of a limited number of entrees, vegetables, and desserts. *Restaurant cooks* usually prepare a wider selection of dishes, cooking most orders individually. *Short-order cooks* prepare foods in restaurants and coffee shops that emphasize fast service and quick food preparation. They grill and garnish hamburgers, prepare sandwiches, fry eggs, and cook French fries, often working on several orders at the same time. *Fast-food cooks* prepare a limited selection of menu items in fast-food restaurants. They cook and package batches of food, such as hamburgers and fried chicken, to be kept warm until served. (*Combined food preparation and service workers,* who both prepare and serve items in fast-food restaurants, are included in the *Handbook* statement on food and beverage serving and related workers.) *Private household cooks* plan and prepare meals in private homes according to the client's tastes or dietary needs. They order

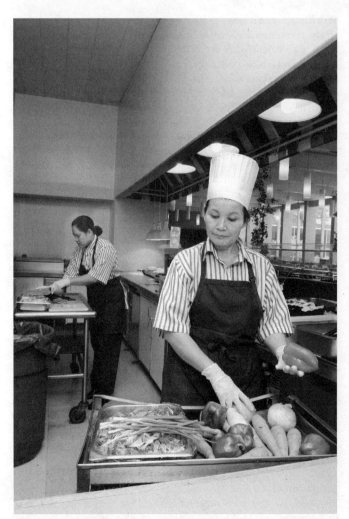

Food preparation workers slice and dice large quantities of vegetables and other foodstuffs for use in salads and other more complex dishes.

groceries and supplies, clean the kitchen and wash dishes and utensils. They also may serve meals.

Food preparation workers perform routine, repetitive tasks such as readying ingredients for complex dishes, slicing and dicing vegetables, and composing salads and cold items, under the direction of chefs and cooks. They weigh and measure ingredients, go after pots and pans, and stir and strain soups and sauces. Food preparation workers may cut and grind meats, poultry, and seafood in preparation for cooking. Their responsibilities also include cleaning work areas, equipment, utensils, dishes, and silverware.

The number and types of workers employed in kitchens depends on the type of establishment. For example, fast-food establishments offer only a few items, which are prepared by fast-food cooks. Small, full-service restaurants offering casual dining often feature a limited number of easy-to-prepare items supplemented by short-order specialties and ready-made desserts. Typically, one cook prepares all the food with the help of a short-order cook and one or two other kitchen workers.

Grocery and specialty food stores employ chefs, cooks, and food preparation workers to develop recipes and prepare meals to go. Typically, entrees, side dishes, salads, or other items are prepared in large quantities and stored at an appropriate temperature. Servers portion and package items according to customer orders for serving at home.

Working Conditions
Many restaurant and institutional kitchens have modern equipment, convenient work areas, and air conditioning, but kitchens in older and smaller eating places are often not as well designed. Kitchens must be well ventilated, appropriately lit, and properly equipped with sprinkler systems to protect against fires. Kitchen staffs invariably work in small quarters against hot stoves and ovens. They are under constant pressure to prepare meals quickly, while ensuring quality is maintained and safety and sanitation guidelines are observed.

Working conditions vary with the type and quantity of food prepared and the local laws governing food service operations. Workers usually must withstand the pressure and strain of standing for hours at a time, lifting heavy pots and kettles, and working near hot ovens and grills. Job hazards include slips and falls, cuts, and burns, but injuries are seldom serious.

Work hours in restaurants may include early mornings, late evenings, holidays, and weekends. Work schedules of chefs, cooks and other kitchen workers in factory and school cafeterias may be more regular. In 2002, about 33 percent of cooks and 45 percent of food preparation workers had part-time schedules, compared to 16 percent of workers throughout the economy.

The wide range in dining hours and the need for fully-staffed kitchens during all open hours creates work opportunities for individuals seeking supplemental income, flexible work hours, or variable schedules. For example, almost 20 percent of cooks and food preparation workers were 16-19 years old in 2002, and almost 10 percent had variable schedules. Kitchen workers employed by schools may work during the school year only, usually for 9 or 10 months. Similarly, resort establishments usually only offer seasonal employment.

Employment
Chefs, cooks and food preparation workers held nearly 3.0 million jobs in 2002. The distribution of jobs among the various types of chefs, cooks, and food preparation workers was as follows:

Food preparation workers	850,000
Cooks, restaurant	727,000
Cooks, fast food	588,000
Cooks, institution and cafeteria	436,000
Cooks, short order	227,000
Chefs and head cooks	132,000
Cooks, private household	8,000

More than three-fifths of all chefs, cooks, and food preparation workers were employed in restaurants and other food services and drinking places. Nearly one-fifth worked in institutions such as schools, universities, hospitals, and nursing care facilities. Grocery stores, hotels, gasoline stations with convenience stores, and other organizations employed the remainder.

Training, Other Qualifications, and Advancement
Most fast-food or short-order cooks and food preparation workers require little education or training; most skills are learned on the job. Training generally starts with basic sanitation and workplace safety subjects and continues with instruction on food handling, preparation, and cooking procedures.

A high school diploma is not required for beginning jobs, but it is recommended for those planning a career as a cook or chef. High school or vocational school programs may offer courses in basic food safety and handling procedures and general business and computer classes for those who want to manage or open their own place. Many school districts, in cooperation with State departments of education, provide on-the-job training and summer workshops for cafeteria kitchen workers who aspire to become cooks. Large corporations in the food services and hospitality industries also offer paid internships and summer jobs to those just starting out in the field. Internships provide valuable experience and can lead to placement in more formal chef training programs.

Executive chefs and head cooks who work in fine restaurants require many years of training and experience and an intense desire to cook. Some chefs and cooks may start their training in high school or post-high school vocational programs. Others may receive formal training through independent cooking schools, professional culinary institutes, or 2- or 4-year college degree programs in hospitality or culinary arts. In addition, some large hotels and restaurants operate their own training and job-placement programs for chefs and cooks. Most formal training programs require some form of apprenticeship, internship, or out placement program that are jointly offered by the school and affiliated restaurants. Professional culinary institutes, industry associations, and trade unions also may sponsor formal apprenticeship programs in coordination with the U.S. Department of Labor. Many chefs are trained on the job, receiving real work experience and training from chef mentors in the restaurants where they work.

People who have had courses in commercial food preparation may start in a cook or chef job without spending a lot of time in lower-skilled kitchen jobs. Their education may give them an advantage when looking for jobs in better restaurants. Some vocational programs in high schools may offer training, but employers usually prefer training given by trade schools, vocational centers, colleges, professional associations, or trade unions. Postsecondary courses range from a few months to 2 years or more. Degree-granting programs are open only to high school graduates. Chefs also may compete and test for certification as master chefs. Although certification is not required to enter the field, it can be a measure of accomplishment and lead to further advancement and higher-paying positions. The U.S. Armed Forces also are a good source of training and experience.

Although curricula may vary, students in formal culinary training programs spend most of their time in kitchens learning to use the appropriate equipment and to prepare meals through actual practice. They learn good knife techniques, safe food-handling procedures, and proper use and care of kitchen equipment. Training programs often include courses in nutrition, menu planning, portion control, purchasing and inventory methods, proper food storage procedures, and use of leftover food to minimize waste. Students also learn sanitation and public health rules for handling food. Training in food service management, computer accounting and inventory software, and banquet service are featured in some training programs.

The number of formal and informal culinary training programs continues to increase to meet demand. Formal programs, which may offer training leading to a certificate or a 2- or 4-year degree, are geared more for training chefs for fine-dining or upscale restaurants. They offer a wider array of training options and specialties, such as advanced cooking techniques or foods and cooking styles from around the world.

The American Culinary Federation accredits over 100 formal training programs and sponsors apprenticeship programs around the country. Typical apprenticeships last three years and combine classroom training and work experience. Accreditation is an indication that a culinary program meets recognized standards regarding course content, facilities, and quality of instruction. The American Culinary Federation also certifies pastry professionals and culinary educators in addition to various levels of chefs. Certification standards are based primarily on experience and formal training.

Vocational or trade-school programs typically offer more basic training in preparing food, such as food handling and sanitation procedures, nutrition, slicing and dicing methods for various kinds of meats and vegetables, and basic cooking methods, such as baking, broiling, and grilling.

Important characteristics for chefs, cooks, and food preparation workers include working well as part of a team, having a keen sense of taste and smell, and working efficiently to turn out meals rapidly. Personal cleanliness is essential, because most States require health certificates indicating that workers are free from communicable diseases. Knowledge of a foreign language may improve communication with other restaurant staff, vendors, and the restaurant's clientele.

Advancement opportunities for chefs, cooks, and food preparation workers depend on their training, work experience, and ability to perform more responsible and sophisticated tasks. Many food preparation workers, for example, may move into assistant or line cook positions. Chefs and cooks who demonstrate an eagerness to learn new cooking skills and to accept greater responsibility may move up within the kitchen and take on responsibility for training or supervising newer or lesser skilled kitchen staff. Others may move from one kitchen or restaurant to another.

Some chefs and cooks go into business as caterers or open their own restaurant. Others become instructors in culinary training programs. A number of cooks and chefs advance to executive chef positions or food service management positions, particularly in hotels, clubs, or larger, more elegant restaurants. (See the statement on food service managers elsewhere in the *Handbook*.)

Job Outlook

Job openings for chefs, cooks, and food preparation workers are expected to be plentiful through 2012; however, competition for jobs in the top kitchens of higher end restaurants should be keen. While job growth will create new positions, the overwhelming majority of job openings will stem from the need to replace workers who leave this large occupational group. Minimal education and training requirements, combined with a large number of part-time positions, make employment as chefs, cooks, and food preparation workers attractive to people seeking first-time or short-term employment, a source of additional income, or a flexible schedule. Many of these workers will transfer to other occupations or stop working, creating numerous openings for those entering the field.

Overall employment of chefs, cooks, and food preparation workers is expected to increase about as fast as the average for all occupations over the 2002-12 period. Employment growth will be spurred by increases in population, household income, and leisure time that will allow people to dine out and take vacations more often. In addition, growth in the number of two-income households will lead more families to opt for the convenience of dining out.

Projected employment growth, however, varies by specialty. The number of higher-skilled chefs and cooks working in full-service restaurants—those that offer table service and more varied menus—is expected to increase about as fast as the average. Much of the increase in this segment, however, will come from more casual rather than up-scale full-service restaurants. Dining trends suggest increasing numbers of meals eaten away from home, growth in family dining restaurants, and greater limits on expense-account meals.

Employment of fast-food cooks is expected to grow more slowly than the average. Duties of cooks in fast-food restaurants are limited; most workers are likely to be combined food preparation and serving workers, rather than fast-food cooks. Employment of short-order cooks is expected to increase about as fast as the average. Short-order cooks may work a grill or sandwich station in a full-line restaurant, but also may work in lunch counters or coffee shops that specialize in meals served quickly.

Employment of institution and cafeteria chefs and cooks will show little or no growth. Their employment will not keep pace with the rapid growth in the educational and health services industries—where their employment is concentrated. In an effort to make "institutional food" more attractive to office workers, students, staff, visitors, and patients, offices, schools and hospitals increasingly contract out their food services. Many of the contracted food service companies emphasize simple menu items and employ short-order cooks, instead of institution and cafeteria cooks, reducing the demand for these workers.

Employment of chefs, cooks, and food preparation workers who prepare meals-to-go, such as those who work in the prepared foods sections of grocery or specialty food stores, should increase faster than the average as people continue to demand quality meals and convenience.

Earnings

Wages of chefs, cooks, and food preparation workers vary greatly according to region of the country and the type of food services establishment in which they work. Wages usually are highest in elegant restaurants and hotels, where many executive chefs are employed, and in major metropolitan areas.

Median hourly earnings of chefs and head cooks were $13.43 in 2002. The middle 50 percent earned between $9.86 and $19.03. The lowest 10 percent earned less than $7.66, and the highest 10 percent earned more than $25.86 per hour. Median hourly earnings in the industries employing the largest number of head cooks and chefs in 2002 were:

Other amusement and recreation industries	$18.31
Traveler accommodation	17.03
Special food services	13.98
Full-service restaurants	12.70
Limited-service eating places	10.49

Median hourly earnings of restaurant cooks were $9.16 in 2002. The middle 50 percent earned between $7.64 and $10.93. The lowest 10 percent earned less than $6.58, and the highest 10 percent earned more than $13.21 per hour. Median hourly earnings in the industries employing the largest number of restaurant cooks in 2002 were:

Traveler accommodation	$10.49
Other amusement and recreation industries	10.45
Special food services	9.77
Full-service restaurants	9.14
Drinking places (alcoholic beverages)	9.03
Limited-service eating places	8.08

Median hourly earnings of institution and cafeteria cooks were $8.72 in 2002. The middle 50 percent earned between $7.06 and $10.83. The lowest 10 percent earned less than $6.10, and the highest 10 percent earned more than $13.34 per hour. Median hourly earnings in the industries employing the largest number of institution and cafeteria cooks in 2002 were:

General medical and surgical hospitals	$10.01
Special food services	9.89
Community care facilities for the elderly	9.10
Nursing care facilities	8.95
Elementary and secondary schools	7.89

Median hourly earnings of food preparation workers were $7.85 in 2002. The middle 50 percent earned between $6.72 and $9.43. The lowest 10 percent earned less than $5.96, and the highest 10 percent earned more than $11.37 per hour. Median hourly earnings in the industries employing the largest number of food preparation workers in 2002 were:

Elementary and secondary schools	$8.74
Grocery stores	8.43
Nursing care facilities	7.94
Full-service restaurants	7.66
Limited-service eating places	7.07

Median hourly earnings of short-order cooks were $7.82 in 2002. The middle 50 percent earned between $6.69 and $9.59. The lowest 10 percent earned less than $5.93, and the highest 10 percent earned more than $11.25 per hour. Median hourly earnings in the industries employing the largest number of short-order cooks in 2002 were:

Full-service restaurants	$8.29
Drinking places (alcoholic beverages)	7.85
Other amusement and recreation industries	7.74
Gasoline stations	7.04
Limited-service eating places	6.97

Median hourly earnings of fast-food cooks were $6.90 in 2002. The middle 50 percent earned between $6.16 and $8.03. The lowest 10 percent earned less than $5.68, and the highest 10 percent earned more than $9.13 per hour. Median hourly

earnings in the industries employing the largest number of fast-food cooks in 2002 were:

Special food services	$7.79
Full-service restaurants	7.19
Gasoline stations	7.02
Limited-service eating places	6.84

Some employers provide employees with uniforms and free meals, but Federal law permits employers to deduct from their employees' wages the cost or fair value of any meals or lodging provided, and some employers do so. Chefs, cooks, and food preparation workers who work full time often receive typical benefits, but part-time workers usually do not.

In some large hotels and restaurants, kitchen workers belong to unions. The principal unions are the Hotel Employees and Restaurant Employees International Union and the Service Employees International Union.

Related Occupations
Workers who perform tasks similar to those of chefs, cooks, and food preparation workers include food processing occupations, such as butchers and meat cutters, and bakers. Many executive chefs have primary responsibility for selecting menu items and share other tasks with food service managers.

Sources of Additional Information
Information about job opportunities may be obtained from local employers and local offices of the State employment service.

Career information about chefs, cooks, and other kitchen workers, as well as a directory of 2- and 4-year colleges that offer courses or programs that prepare persons for food service careers, is available from:
➤ National Restaurant Association, 1200 17th St. NW., Washington, DC 20036-3097. Internet: **http://www.restaurant.org**

For information on the American Culinary Federation's apprenticeship and certification programs for cooks, as well as a list of accredited culinary programs, send a self-addressed, stamped envelope to:
➤ American Culinary Federation, 180 Center Place Way, St. Augustine, FL 32095. Internet: **http://www.acfchefs.org**

For general information on hospitality careers, contact:
➤ International Council on Hotel, Restaurant, and Institutional Education, 2613 North Parham Rd., 2nd Floor, Richmond, VA 23294. Internet: **http://www.chrie.org**

Food and Beverage Serving and Related Workers

(O*NET 35-3011.00, 35-3021.00, 35-3022.00, 35-3031.00, 35-3041.00, 35-9011.00, 35-9021.00, 35-9031.00, 35-9099.99)

Significant Points

- Most jobs are part time and many opportunities exist for young people—around one-fourth of these workers were 16 to 19 years old, about 5 times the proportion for all workers.

- Job openings are expected to be abundant through 2012, reflecting substantial replacement needs.

- Tips comprise a major portion of earnings, so keen competition is expected for jobs where potential earnings from tips are greatest—bartenders, waiters and waitresses, and other jobs in popular restaurants and fine dining establishments.

Nature of the Work

Food and beverage serving and related workers are the front line of customer service in restaurants, coffee shops, and other food service establishments. These workers greet customers, escort them to seats and hand them menus, take food and drink orders, and serve food and beverages. They also answer questions, explain menu items and specials, and keep tables and dining areas clean and set for new diners. Most work as part of a team, helping coworkers during busy times to improve workflow and customer service.

Waiters and waitresses, the largest group of these workers, take customers' orders, serve food and beverages, prepare itemized checks, and sometimes accept payment. Their specific duties vary considerably, depending on the establishment. In coffee shops serving routine, straightforward fare, such as salads, soups, and sandwiches, servers are expected to provide fast, efficient, and courteous service. In fine dining restaurants, where more complicated meals are prepared and often served over several courses, waiters and waitresses provide more formal service emphasizing personal, attentive treatment and a more leisurely pace. They may recommend certain dishes and identify ingredients or explain how various items on the menu are prepared. Some prepare salads, desserts, or other menu items tableside. Additionally, they may check the identification of patrons to ensure they meet the minimum age requirement for the purchase of alcohol and tobacco products.

Waiters and waitresses sometimes perform the duties of other food and beverage service workers. These tasks may include escorting guests to tables, serving customers seated at counters, clearing and setting up tables, or operating a cash register. However, full-service restaurants frequently hire other staff, such as hosts and hostesses, cashiers, or dining room attendants, to perform these duties.

Bartenders fill drink orders either taken directly from patrons at the bar or through waiters and waitresses who place drink orders for dining room customers. Bartenders check identification of customers seated at the bar, to ensure they meet the minimum age requirement for the purchase of alcohol and tobacco products. They prepare mixed drinks, serve bottled or draught beer, and pour wine or other beverages. Bartenders must know a wide range of drink recipes and be able to mix drinks accurately, quickly, and without waste. Besides mixing and serving drinks, bartenders stock and prepare garnishes for drinks; maintain an adequate supply of ice, glasses, and other bar supplies; and keep the bar area clean for customers. They also may collect payment, operate the cash register, wash glassware and utensils, and serve food to customers seated at the bar. Bartenders usually are responsible for ordering and maintaining an inventory of liquor, mixes, and other bar supplies.

The majority of bartenders directly serve and interact with patrons. Bartenders should be friendly and enjoy mingling with customers. Bartenders at service bars, on the other hand, have less contact with customers. They work in small bars often located off the kitchen in restaurants, hotels, and clubs where only waiters and waitresses place drink orders. Some establishments, especially larger, higher volume ones, use equipment that automatically pours and mixes drinks at the push of a button. Bartenders who use this equipment, however, still must work quickly to handle a large volume of drink orders and be familiar with the ingredients for special drink requests. Much of a bartender's work still must be done by hand to fill each individual order.

Hosts and hostesses welcome guests and maintain reservation or waiting lists. They may direct patrons to coatrooms, restrooms, or to a place to wait until their table is ready. Hosts and hostesses assign guests to tables suitable for the size of their group, escort patrons to their seats, and provide menus. They also schedule dining reservations, arrange parties, and organize any special services that are required. In some restaurants, they act as cashiers.

Dining room and cafeteria attendants and bartender helpers assist waiters, waitresses, and bartenders by cleaning tables, removing dirty dishes, and keeping serving areas stocked with supplies. Sometimes called backwaiters or runners, they bring meals out of the kitchen and assist waiters and waitresses by distributing dishes to individual diners. They also replenish the supply of clean linens, dishes, silverware, and glasses in the dining room and keep the bar stocked with glasses, liquor, ice, and drink garnishes. Dining room attendants set tables with clean tablecloths, napkins, silverware, glasses, and dishes and serve ice water, rolls, and butter. At the conclusion of meals, they remove dirty dishes and soiled linens from tables. Cafeteria attendants stock serving tables with food, trays, dishes, and silverware and may carry trays to dining tables for patrons. *Bartender helpers* keep bar equipment clean and wash glasses. *Dishwashers* clean dishes, cutlery, and kitchen utensils and equipment.

Counter attendants take orders and serve food in cafeterias, coffee shops, and carryout eateries. In cafeterias, they serve food displayed on steam tables, carve meat, dish out vegetables, ladle sauces and soups, and fill beverage glasses. In lunchrooms and coffee shops, counter attendants take orders from customers seated at the counter, transmit orders to the kitchen, and pick up and serve food. They also fill cups with coffee, soda, and other beverages and prepare fountain specialties, such as milkshakes and ice cream sundaes. Counter attendants also take carryout orders from diners and wrap or place items in containers. They clean counters, write itemized checks, and sometimes accept payment. Some counter attendants may prepare short-order items, such as sandwiches and salads.

Some food and beverage serving workers take orders from customers at counters or drive-through windows at fast-food restaurants. They assemble orders, hand them to customers, and accept payment. Many of these are *combined food preparation and serving workers* who also cook and package food, make coffee, and fill beverage cups using drink-dispensing machines.

Waiters and waitresses serve food and beverages to diners.

Other workers serve food to patrons outside of a restaurant environment, such as in hotels, hospital rooms, or cars.

Working Conditions

Food and beverage service workers are on their feet most of the time and often carry heavy trays of food, dishes, and glassware. During busy dining periods, they are under pressure to serve customers quickly and efficiently. The work is relatively safe, but care must be taken to avoid slips, falls, and burns.

Part-time work is more common among food and beverage serving and related workers than among workers in almost any other occupation. In 2002, those on part-time schedules included half of all waiters and waitresses, and 2 out of 5 bartenders.

Food service and drinking establishments typically maintain long dining hours and offer flexible and varied work opportunities. Many food and beverage serving and related workers work evenings, weekends, and holidays. Some work split shifts—they work for several hours during the middle of the day, take a few hours off in the afternoon, and then return to their jobs for evening hours. Many students and teenagers seek part time or seasonal work as food and beverage serving and related workers as a first job to gain work experience or to earn spending money while in school. Around one-fourth of food and beverage serving and related workers were 16 to 19 years old—about 5 times the proportion for all workers.

Employment

Food and beverage serving and related workers held 6.5 million jobs in 2002. The distribution of jobs among the various food and beverage serving workers was as follows:

Waiters and waitresses 2,097,000
Combined food preparation and serving workers, including
    fast food 1,990,000
Dishwashers 505,000
Counter attendants, cafeteria, food concession, and coffee 467,000
Bartenders 463,000
Dining room and cafeteria attendants and bartender helpers . 409,000
Hosts and hostesses, restaurant, lounge, and coffee shop 298,000
Food servers, nonrestaurant 195,000
All other food preparation and serving related workers 117,000

The overwhelming majority of jobs for food and beverage serving and related workers were found in food services and drinking places, such as restaurants, coffee shops, and bars. Other jobs were found primarily in traveler accommodation (hotels); amusement, gambling, and recreation industries; educational services; grocery stores; nursing care facilities; civic and social organizations; and hospitals.

Jobs are located throughout the country but are typically plentiful in large cities and tourist areas. Vacation resorts offer seasonal employment, and some workers alternate between summer and winter resorts, instead of remaining in one area the entire year.

Training, Other Qualifications, and Advancement

There are no specific educational requirements for food and beverage service jobs. Many employers prefer to hire high school graduates for waiter and waitress, bartender, and host and hostess positions, but completion of high school usually is not required for fast-food workers, counter attendants, dishwashers, and dining room attendants and bartender helpers. A job as a food and beverage service worker serves as a source of immediate income, rather than a career, for many people. Many entrants

to these jobs are in their late teens or early twenties and have a high school education or less. Usually, they have little or no work experience. Many are full-time students or homemakers. Food and beverage service jobs are a major source of part-time employment for high school and college students.

Restaurants rely on good food and quality customer service to retain loyal customers and succeed in a competitive industry. Food and beverage serving and related workers who exhibit excellent personal qualities, such as a neat clean appearance, a well-spoken manner, an ability to work as a member of team, and a pleasant way with patrons, will be highly sought after.

Waiters and waitresses need a good memory to avoid confusing customers' orders and to recall faces, names, and preferences of frequent patrons. These workers also should be comfortable using computers to place orders and generate customers' bills. Some may need to be quick at arithmetic so they can total bills manually. Knowledge of a foreign language is helpful to communicate with a diverse clientele and staff. Prior experience waiting on tables is preferred by restaurants and hotels that have rigid table service standards. Jobs at these establishments often offer higher wages and have greater income potential from tips, but they may also have stiffer employment requirements, such as higher education or training standards, than other establishments.

Usually, bartenders must be at least 21 years of age, but employers prefer to hire people who are 25 or older. Bartenders should be familiar with State and local laws concerning the sale of alcoholic beverages.

Most food and beverage serving and related workers pick up their skills on the job by observing and working with more experienced workers. Some employers, particularly those in fast-food restaurants, use self-instruction programs with audio-visual presentations and instructional booklets to teach new employees food preparation and service skills. Some public and private vocational schools, restaurant associations, and large restaurant chains provide classroom training in a generalized food service curriculum.

Some bartenders acquire their skills by attending a bartending or vocational and technical school. These programs often include instruction on State and local laws and regulations, cocktail recipes, attire and conduct, and stocking a bar. Some of these schools help their graduates find jobs. Although few employers require any minimum level of educational attainment, some specialized training is usually needed in food handling and legal issues surrounding serving alcoholic beverages and tobacco. Employers are more likely to hire and promote based on people skills and personal qualities rather than education.

Due to the relatively small size of most food-serving establishments, opportunities for promotion are limited. After gaining experience, some dining room and cafeteria attendants and bartender helpers advance to waiter, waitress, or bartender jobs. For waiters, waitresses, and bartenders, advancement usually is limited to finding a job in a busier or more expensive restaurant or bar where prospects for tip earnings are better. A few bartenders open their own businesses. Some hosts and hostesses and waiters and waitresses advance to supervisory jobs, such as maitre d'hotel, dining room supervisor, or restaurant manager. In larger restaurant chains, food and beverage service workers who excel at their work often are invited to enter the company's formal management training program. (For more information, see the *Handbook* statement on food service managers.)

Job Outlook

Job openings are expected to be abundant for food and beverage serving and related workers. Overall employment of these workers is expected to increase about as fast as the average over the 2002-12 period, stemming from increases in population, personal incomes, and leisure time. While employment growth will account for many new jobs, the overwhelming majority of openings will arise from the need to replace the high proportion of workers who leave the occupations each year. There is substantial movement into and out of these occupations because education and training requirements are minimal, and the predominance of part-time jobs is attractive to people seeking a short-term source of income rather than a career. However, keen competition is expected for bartender, waiter and waitress, and other food and beverage service jobs in popular restaurants and fine dining establishments, where potential earnings from tips are greatest.

Projected employment growth between 2002 and 2012 varies by type of job. Employment of combined food preparation and serving workers, which includes fast-food workers, is expected to increase faster than the average in response to the continuing fast-paced lifestyle of many Americans and the addition of healthier foods at many fast-food restaurants. Increases in the number of families and the more affluent, 55-and-older population will result in more restaurants that offer table service and more varied menus—leading to average growth for waiters and waitresses and hosts and hostesses. Employment of dining room attendants and dishwashers will grow more slowly than other food and beverage serving and related workers, because diners increasingly are eating at more casual dining spots, such as coffee bars and sandwich shops, rather than at the full-service restaurants that employ more of these workers. Slower than average employment growth is expected for bartenders.

Earnings

Food and beverage serving and related workers derive their earnings from a combination of hourly wages and customer tips. Earnings vary greatly, depending on the type of job and establishment. For example, fast-food workers and hosts and hostesses usually do not receive tips, so their wage rates may be higher than those of waiters and waitresses and bartenders in full-service restaurants, who typically earn more from tips than from wages. In some restaurants, workers contribute a portion of their tips to a tip pool, which is distributed among qualifying workers. Tip pools allow workers who don't usually receive tips directly from customers, such as dining room attendants, to share in the rewards of good service.

In 2002, median hourly earnings (including tips) of waiters and waitresses were $6.80. The middle 50 percent earned between $6.13 and $8.00. The lowest 10 percent earned less than $5.70, and the highest 10 percent earned more than $11.00 an hour. For most waiters and waitresses, higher earnings are primarily the result of receiving more in tips rather than higher hourly wages. Tips usually average between 10 and 20 percent of guests' checks; waiters and waitresses working in busy, expensive restaurants earn the most.

Bartenders had median hourly earnings (including tips) of $7.21 in 2002. The middle 50 percent earned between $6.33 and $9.02. The lowest 10 percent earned less than $5.76, and the highest 10 percent earned more than $11.96 an hour. Like waiters and waitresses, bartenders employed in public bars may receive more than half of their earnings as tips. Service bartenders often are paid higher hourly wages to offset their lower tip earnings.

Median hourly earnings (including tips) of dining room and cafeteria attendants and bartender helpers were $6.99 in 2002. The middle 50 percent earned between $6.33 and $8.10. The lowest 10 percent earned less than $5.80, and the highest 10 percent earned more than $9.70 an hour. Most received over half of their earnings as wages; the rest of their income was a share of the proceeds from tip pools.

Median hourly earnings of hosts and hostesses were $7.36 in 2002. The middle 50 percent earned between $6.54 and $8.58. The lowest 10 percent earned less than $5.89, and the highest 10 percent earned more than $10.32 an hour. Wages comprised the majority of their earnings. In some cases, wages were supplemented by proceeds from tip pools.

Median hourly earnings of combined food preparation and serving workers, including fast food, were $6.97 in 2002. The middle 50 percent earned between $6.23 and $8.08. The lowest 10 percent earned less than $5.74, and the highest 10 percent earned more than $9.33 an hour. Although some combined food preparation and serving workers receive a part of their earnings as tips, fast-food workers usually do not.

Median hourly earnings of counter attendants in cafeterias, food concessions, and coffee shops (including tips) were $7.32 in 2002. The middle 50 percent earned between $6.52 and $8.53 an hour. The lowest 10 percent earned less than $5.87, and the highest 10 percent earned more than $10.39 an hour.

Median hourly earnings of dishwashers were $7.15 in 2002. The middle 50 percent earned between $6.40 and $8.28. The lowest 10 percent earned less than $5.82, and the highest 10 percent earned more than $9.41 an hour.

Median hourly earnings of nonrestaurant food servers were $7.52 in 2002. The middle 50 percent earned between $6.51 and $9.36. The lowest 10 percent earned less than $5.87, and the highest 10 percent earned more than $11.72 an hour.

Many beginning or inexperienced workers start earning the Federal minimum wage of $5.15 an hour. However, a few States set minimum wages higher than the Federal minimum. Also, various minimum wage exceptions apply under specific circumstances to disabled workers, full-time students, youth under age 20 in their first 90 days of employment, tipped employees, and student-learners. Tipped employees are those who customarily and regularly receive more than $30 a month in tips. The employer may consider tips as part of wages, but the employer must pay at least $2.13 an hour in direct wages. Employers also are permitted to deduct from wages the cost, or fair value, of any meals or lodging provided. Many employers, however, provide free meals and furnish uniforms. Food and beverage service workers who work full time often receive typical benefits, while part-time workers usually do not.

In some large restaurants and hotels, food and beverage serving and related workers belong to unions—principally the Hotel Employees and Restaurant Employees International Union and the Service Employees International Union.

Related Occupations

Other workers whose job involves serving customers and handling money include flight attendants, gaming services workers, and retail salespersons.

Sources of Additional Information

Information about job opportunities may be obtained from local employers and local offices of State employment services agencies.

A guide to careers in restaurants plus a list of 2- and 4-year colleges offering food service programs and related scholarship information is available from:

➤ National Restaurant Association, 1200 17th St. NW., Washington, DC 20036-3097. Internet: **http://www.restaurant.org**

For general information on hospitality careers, contact:

➤ International Council on Hotel, Restaurant, and Institutional Education, 2613 North Parham Rd., 2nd Floor, Richmond, VA 23294. Internet: **http://www.chrie.org**

Building and Grounds Cleaning and Maintenance Occupations

Building Cleaning Workers

(0*NET 37-1011.01, 37-1011.02, 37-2011.00, 37-2012.00)

Significant Points

- This very large occupation requires few skills to enter and has one of the largest numbers of job openings of any occupation each year.

- Most job openings result from the need to replace the many workers who leave these jobs due to their limited opportunities for training or advancement, low pay, and high incidence of only part-time or temporary work.

- Businesses providing janitorial and cleaning services on a contract basis are expected to be one of the fastest-growing employers of these workers.

Nature of the Work

Building cleaning workers—including janitors, maids, housekeeping cleaners, window washers, and rug shampooers—keep office buildings, hospitals, stores, apartment houses, hotels, and residences clean and in good condition. Some only do cleaning, while others have a wide range of duties.

Janitors and cleaners perform a variety of heavy cleaning duties, such as cleaning floors, shampooing rugs, washing walls and glass, and removing rubbish. They may fix leaky faucets, empty trash cans, do painting and carpentry, replenish bathroom supplies, mow lawns, and see that heating and air-conditioning equipment works properly. On a typical day, janitors may wet- or dry-mop floors, clean bathrooms, vacuum carpets, dust furniture, make minor repairs, and exterminate insects and rodents. They also clean snow or debris from sidewalks in front of buildings and notify management of the need for major repairs. While janitors typically perform most of the duties mentioned, cleaners tend to work for companies that specialize in one type of cleaning activity, such as washing windows.

Maids and housekeeping cleaners perform any combination of light cleaning duties to maintain private households or commercial establishments, such as hotels, restaurants, and hospitals, clean and orderly. In hotels, aside from cleaning and maintaining the premises, maids and housekeeping cleaners may deliver ironing boards, cribs, and rollaway beds to guests' rooms. In hospitals, they also may wash bedframes, brush mattresses, make beds, and disinfect and sterilize equipment and supplies with germicides and sterilizing equipment.

Janitors, maids, and cleaners use various equipment, tools, and cleaning materials. For one job they may need a mop and bucket, for another an electric polishing machine and a special cleaning solution. Improved building materials, chemical cleaners, and power equipment have made many tasks easier and less time consuming, but cleaning workers must learn the proper use of equipment and cleaners to avoid harming floors, fixtures, and themselves.

Cleaning supervisors coordinate, schedule, and supervise the activities of janitors and cleaners. They assign tasks and

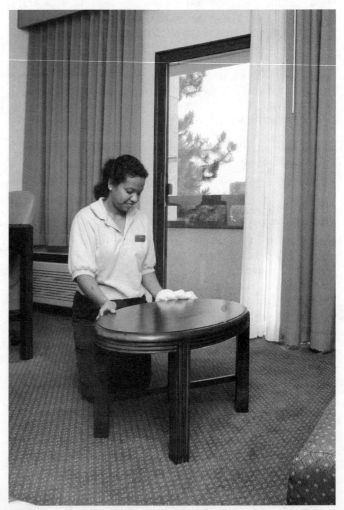

Housekeeping cleaners perform light housekeeping duties, mainly for hotels and motels, residential care facilities, hospitals, and private homes.

inspect building areas to see that work has been done properly, issue supplies and equipment, and inventory stocks to ensure that an adequate amount of supplies is present. They also screen and hire job applicants, train new and experienced employees, and recommend promotions, transfers, or dismissals. Supervisors may prepare reports concerning the occupancy of rooms, hours worked, and department expenses. Some also perform cleaning duties.

Cleaners and servants in private households dust and polish furniture; sweep, mop, and wax floors; vacuum; and clean ovens, refrigerators, and bathrooms. They also may wash dishes, polish silver, and change and make beds. Some wash, fold, and iron clothes; a few wash windows. General houseworkers also may take clothes and laundry to the cleaners, buy groceries, and perform many other errands.

Working Conditions
Because most office buildings are cleaned while they are empty, many cleaning workers work evening hours. Some, however, such as school and hospital custodians, work in the daytime. When there is a need for 24-hour maintenance, janitors may be assigned to shifts. Most full-time building cleaners work about 40 hours a week. Part-time cleaners usually work in the evenings and on weekends.

Building cleaning workers in large office and residential buildings often work in teams consisting of workers who specialize in vacuuming, picking up trash, and cleaning rest rooms, among other things. Supervisors conduct inspections to ensure that the building is cleaned properly and the team is functioning efficiently.

Building cleaning workers usually work inside heated, well-lighted buildings. However, they sometimes work outdoors, sweeping walkways, mowing lawns, or shoveling snow. Working with machines can be noisy, and some tasks, such as cleaning bathrooms and trash rooms, can be dirty and unpleasant. Janitors may suffer cuts, bruises, and burns from machines, handtools, and chemicals. They spend most of their time on their feet, sometimes lifting or pushing heavy furniture or equipment. Many tasks, such as dusting or sweeping, require constant bending, stooping, and stretching. As a result, janitors also may suffer back injuries and sprains.

Employment
Building cleaning workers held nearly 4 million jobs in 2002. More than 6 percent were self-employed.

Janitors and cleaners work in nearly every type of establishment and held about 2.3 million jobs. They accounted for about 57 percent of all building cleaning workers. About 28 percent worked for firms supplying building maintenance services on a contract basis, 21 percent were employed in educational institutions, and 2 percent worked in hotels. Other employers included hospitals, restaurants, religious institutions, manufacturing firms, government agencies, and operators of apartment buildings, office buildings, and other types of real estate.

First-line supervisors of housekeeping and janitorial workers held about 230,000 jobs. Approximately 22 percent worked in firms supplying building maintenance services on a contract basis, 14 percent were employed in hotels, 7 percent held jobs in nursing and other residential care facilities, and 5 percent worked in hospitals. Other employers included educational institutions and amusement and recreation facilities.

Maids and housekeepers held about 1.5 million jobs. Hotels, motels, and other traveler accommodations employed the

most maids and housekeepers—27 percent—while private households employed the second most: 25 percent. Eight percent were employed in hospitals; and, a similar percentage worked in nursing and other residential care facilities. Although cleaning jobs can be found in all cities and towns, most are located in highly populated areas where there are many office buildings, schools, apartment houses, nursing homes, and hospitals.

Training, Other Qualifications, and Advancement
No special education is required for most janitorial or cleaning jobs, but beginners should know simple arithmetic and be able to follow instructions. High school shop courses are helpful for jobs involving repair work.

Most building cleaners learn their skills on the job. Usually, beginners work with an experienced cleaner, doing routine cleaning. As they gain more experience, they are assigned more complicated tasks.

In some cities, programs run by unions, government agencies, or employers teach janitorial skills. Students learn how to clean buildings thoroughly and efficiently, how to select and safely use various cleansing agents, and how to operate and maintain machines, such as wet and dry vacuums, buffers, and polishers. Students learn to plan their work, to follow safety and health regulations, to interact positively with people in the buildings they clean, and to work without supervision. Instruction in minor electrical, plumbing, and other repairs also may be given. Those who come in contact with the public should have good communication skills. Employers usually look for dependable, hard-working individuals who are in good health, follow directions well, and get along with other people.

Building cleaners usually find work by answering newspaper advertisements, applying directly to organizations where they would like to work, contacting local labor unions, or contacting State employment service offices.

Advancement opportunities for workers usually are limited in organizations where they are the only maintenance worker. Where there is a large maintenance staff, however, cleaning workers can be promoted to supervisor and to area supervisor or manager. A high school diploma improves the chances for advancement. Some janitors set up their own maintenance or cleaning businesses.

Supervisors usually move up through the ranks. In many establishments, they are required to take some inservice training to improve their housekeeping techniques and procedures and to enhance their supervisory skills.

A small number of cleaning supervisors and managers are members of the International Executive Housekeepers Association, which offers two kinds of certification programs to cleaning supervisors and managers: Certified Executive Housekeeper (CEH) and Registered Executive Housekeeper (REH). The CEH designation is offered to those with a high school education, while the REH designation is offered to those who have a 4-year college degree. Both designations are earned by attending courses and passing exams, and both must be renewed every 2 years to ensure that workers keep abreast of new cleaning methods. Those with the REH designation usually oversee the cleaning services of hotels, hospitals, casinos, and other large institutions that rely on well-trained experts for their cleaning needs.

Job Outlook
Overall employment of building cleaning workers is expected to grow about as fast as the average for all occupations through 2012, as more office complexes, apartment houses, schools,

factories, hospitals, and other buildings requiring cleaning are built to accommodate a growing population and economy. As many firms reduce costs by contracting out the cleaning and maintenance of buildings, businesses providing janitorial and cleaning services on a contract basis are expected to be one of the faster growing employers of these workers. Although there have been some improvements in productivity in the way buildings are cleaned and maintained—using teams of cleaners, for example, and better cleaning supplies—it is still very much a labor-intensive job. Average growth is expected among janitors and cleaners and among cleaning supervisors, but less-than-average growth is projected for maids and housekeeping cleaners. In addition to job openings arising due to growth, numerous openings should result from the need to replace those who leave this very large occupation each year. Limited formal education and training requirements, low pay, and numerous part-time and temporary jobs induce many to leave the occupation, thereby contributing to the number of job openings and the need to replace these workers.

Much of the growth in these occupations will come from cleaning residential properties. As families become more pressed for time, they increasingly are hiring cleaning and handyman services to perform a variety of tasks in their homes. Also, as the population ages, older people will need to hire cleaners to help maintain their houses. In addition, housekeeping cleaners will be needed to clean the growing number of residential care facilities for the elderly. These facilities, including assisted-living arrangements, generally provide housekeeping services as part of the rent.

Earnings
Median annual earnings of janitors and cleaners, except maids and housekeeping cleaners, were $18,250 in 2002. The middle 50 percent earned between $14,920 and $23,650. The lowest 10 percent earned less than $12,920, and the highest 10 percent earned more than $30,700. Median annual earnings in 2002 in the industries employing the largest numbers of janitors and cleaners, except maids and housekeeping cleaners, were as follows:

Elementary and secondary schools	$22,820
Local government	22,770
Colleges, universities, and professional schools	21,540
Lessors of real estate	20,240
Services to buildings and dwellings	16,370

Median annual earnings of maids and housekeepers were $16,440 in 2002. The middle 50 percent earned between $14,210 and $19,400. The lowest 10 percent earned less than $12,560, and the highest 10 percent earned more than $23,750. Median annual earnings in 2002 in the industries employing the largest numbers of maids and housekeepers were as follows:

General medical and surgical hospitals	$18,050
Community care facilities for the elderly	16,470
Nursing care facilities	16,440
Services to buildings and dwellings	16,210
Traveler accommodation	15,740

Median annual earnings of first-line supervisors and managers of housekeeping and janitorial workers were $28,140 in 2002. The middle 50 percent earned between $21,520 and $36,940. The lowest 10 percent earned less than $17,490, and the highest 10 percent earned more than $46,570. Median annual earnings in 2002 in the industries employing the largest numbers of first-

line supervisors and managers of housekeeping and janitorial workers were as follows:

Elementary and secondary schools	$33,080
General medical and surgical hospitals	29,000
Nursing care facilities	26,960
Services to buildings and dwellings	25,410
Traveler accommodation	22,710

Related Occupations
Workers who specialize in one of the many job functions of janitors and cleaners include pest control workers; industrial machinery installation, repair, and maintenance workers; and grounds maintenance workers.

Sources of Additional Information
Information about janitorial jobs may be obtained from State employment service offices.

For information on certification in executive housekeeping, contact
➤ International Executive Housekeepers Association, Inc., 1001 Eastwind Dr., Suite 301, Westerville, OH 43081-3361. Internet: **http://www.ieha.org**

Grounds Maintenance Workers

(O*NET 37-1012.01, 37-1012.02, 37-3011.00, 37-3012.00, 37-3013.00)

Significant Points

- Opportunities should be excellent, especially for workers willing to work seasonal or variable schedules, due to significant job turnover and increasing demand by landscaping services companies.

- Many beginning jobs have low earnings and are physically demanding.

- Most workers learn through short-term on-the-job training.

Nature of the Work
Attractively designed, healthy, and well-maintained lawns, gardens, and grounds create a positive first impression, establish a peaceful mood, and increase property values. Grounds maintenance workers perform the variety of tasks necessary to achieve a pleasant and functional outdoor environment. They also care for indoor gardens and plantings in commercial and public facilities, such as malls, hotels, and botanical gardens.

The duties of *landscaping workers* and *groundskeeping workers* are similar and often overlap. Landscaping workers physically install and maintain landscaped areas. They grade property, install lighting or sprinkler systems, and build walkways, terraces, patios, decks, and fountains. In addition to initially transporting and planting new vegetation, they transplant, mulch, fertilize, and water flowering plants, trees, and shrubs and mow and water lawns. A growing number of residential and commercial clients, such as managers of office buildings, shopping malls, multiunit residential buildings, and hotels and motels, favor full-service landscape maintenance. Landscaping workers perform a range of duties, including mowing, edging, trimming, fertilizing, dethatching, and mulching, for such clients on a regular basis during the growing season.

Groundskeeping workers, also called *groundskeepers*, maintain a variety of facilities, including athletic fields, golf courses, cemeteries, university campuses, and parks. In addition to caring for sod, plants, and trees, they rake and mulch leaves, clear snow from walkways and parking lots, and use irrigation methods to adjust the amount of water consumption and prevent waste. They see to the proper upkeep and repair of sidewalks, parking lots, groundskeeping equipment, pools, fountains, fences, planters, and benches.

Groundskeeping workers who care for athletic fields keep those with natural and those with artificial turf in top condition and mark out boundaries and paint turf with team logos and names before events. They must make sure that the underlying soil on fields with natural turf has the required composition to allow proper drainage and to support the grasses used on the field. Groundskeeping workers mow, water, fertilize, and aerate the fields regularly. They also vacuum and disinfect synthetic turf after its use, in order to prevent the growth of harmful bacteria, and they remove the turf and replace the cushioning pad periodically.

Workers who maintain golf courses are called *greenskeepers*. Greenskeepers do many of the same things that other groundskeepers do. In addition, greenskeepers periodically relocate the holes on putting greens to eliminate uneven wear of the turf and to add interest and challenge to the game. Greenskeepers also keep canopies, benches, ball washers, and tee markers repaired and freshly painted.

Some groundskeeping workers specialize in caring for cemeteries and memorial gardens. They dig graves to specified depths, generally using a backhoe. They mow grass regularly, apply fertilizers and other chemicals, prune shrubs and trees, plant flowers, and remove debris from graves.

Groundskeeping workers in parks and recreation facilities care for lawns, trees, and shrubs, maintain athletic fields and playgrounds, clean buildings, and keep parking lots, picnic areas, and other public spaces free of litter. They also may remove snow and ice from roads and walkways, erect and dismantle snow fences, and maintain swimming pools. These workers inspect buildings and equipment, make needed repairs, and keep everything freshly painted.

Supervisors of landscaping and groundskeeping workers perform various functions. They prepare cost estimates, schedule work for crews on the basis of weather conditions or the availability of equipment, perform spot checks to ensure the quality of the service, and suggest changes in work procedures. In addition, supervisors train workers in their tasks; keep employees' time records and record work performed; and even assist workers when deadlines are near.

Landscaping and groundskeeping workers use handtools such as shovels, rakes, pruning and regular saws, hedge and brush trimmers, and axes, as well as power lawnmowers, chain saws, snowblowers, and electric clippers. Some use equipment such as tractors and twin-axle vehicles. Landscaping and groundskeeping workers at parks, schools, cemeteries, and golf courses may use sod cutters to harvest sod that will be replanted elsewhere.

Pesticide handlers, sprayers, and applicators, vegetation, mix or apply pesticides, herbicides, fungicides, or insecticides through sprays, dusts, vapors, incorporation into the soil, or application of chemicals onto trees, shrubs, lawns, or botanical crops. Those working for chemical lawn service firms are more specialized, inspecting lawns for problems and applying fertilizers , herbicides, pesticides, and other chemicals to stimulate

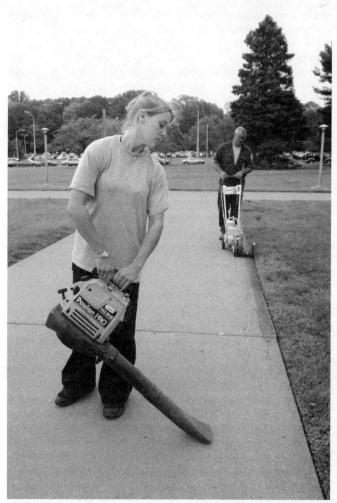

Grounds maintenance workers use a variety of equipment to maintain lawns, athletic fields, and other landscaped areas.

growth and prevent or control weeds, diseases, or insect infestation. Many practice integrated pest-management techniques.

Tree trimmers and pruners cut away dead or excess branches from trees or shrubs either to maintain rights-of-way for roads, sidewalks, or utilities or to improve the appearance, health, and value of trees. Tree trimmers also may fill cavities in trees to promote healing and prevent deterioration. Workers who specialize in pruning trim and shape ornamental trees and shrubs for private residences, golf courses, or other institutional grounds. Tree trimmers and pruners use handsaws, pruning hooks, shears, and clippers. When trimming near power lines, they usually use truck-mounted lifts and power pruners.

Working Conditions

Many of the jobs for grounds maintenance workers are seasonal, meaning that they are in demand mainly in the spring, summer, and fall, when most planting, mowing, trimming, and cleanup are necessary. The work, most of which is performed outdoors in all kinds of weather, can be physically demanding and repetitive, involving much bending, lifting, and shoveling. Workers in landscaping and groundskeeping may be under pressure to get the job completed, especially when they are preparing for scheduled events such as athletic competitions.

Those who work with pesticides, fertilizers, and other chemicals, as well as dangerous equipment and tools such as power lawnmowers, chain saws, and power clippers, must exercise safety precautions. Workers who use motorized equipment must take care to protect themselves against hearing damage.

Employment

Grounds maintenance workers held about 1.3 million jobs in 2002. Employment was distributed as follows:

Landscaping and groundskeeping workers 1,074,000
First-line supervisors/managers of landscaping, lawn service,
    and groundskeeping workers 150,000
Tree trimmers and pruners 59,000
Pesticide handlers, sprayers, and applicators, vegetation 27,000

About one-third of the workers in grounds maintenance were employed in companies providing landscaping services to buildings and dwellings. Others worked for property management and real-estate development firms, lawn and garden equipment and supply stores, and amusement and recreation facilities, such as golf courses and racetracks. Some were employed by local governments, installing and maintaining landscaping for parks, schools, hospitals, and other public facilities.

Almost 1 out of every 4 grounds maintenance workers was self-employed, providing landscape maintenance directly to customers on a contract basis. About 1 of every 6 worked part time; about a tenth were of school age.

Training, Other Qualifications, and Advancement

There usually are no minimum educational requirements for entry-level positions in grounds maintenance, although a diploma is necessary for some jobs. In 2002, most workers had a high school education or less. Short-term on-the-job training generally is sufficient to teach new hires how to operate equipment such as mowers, trimmers, leaf blowers, and small tractors and to follow correct safety procedures. Entry-level workers must be able to follow directions and learn proper planting procedures. If driving is an essential part of a job, employers look for applicants with a good driving record and some experience driving a truck. Employers also look for responsible, self-motivated individuals because grounds maintenance workers often work with little supervision. Workers who deal directly with customers must get along well with people.

Laborers who demonstrate a willingness to work hard and quickly, have good communication skills, and take an interest in the business may advance to crew leader or other supervisory positions. Advancement or entry into positions such as grounds manager and landscape contractor usually requires some formal education beyond high school and several years of progressively more responsible experience.

Most States require certification for workers who apply pesticides. Certification requirements vary, but usually include passing a test on the proper and safe use and disposal of insecticides, herbicides, and fungicides. Some States require that landscape contractors be licensed.

The Professional Grounds Management Society (PGMS) offers certification to grounds managers who have a combination of 8 years of experience and formal education beyond high school and who pass an examination covering subjects such as equipment management, personnel management, environmental issues, turf care, ornamentals, and circulatory systems. The PGMS also offers certification to groundskeepers who have a high school diploma or equivalent, plus 2 years of experience in the grounds maintenance field.

The Associated Landscape Contractors of America (ALCA) offers the designations "Certified Landscape Professional (Ex-

terior and Interior)" and "Certified Landscape Technician (Exterior or Interior)" to those who meet established education and experience standards and who pass a specific examination. The hands-on test for technicians covers areas such as the operation of maintenance equipment and the installation of plants by reading a plan. A written safety test also is administered. The Professional Lawn Care Association of America (PLCAA) offers the designations "Certified Turfgrass Professional" (CTP) and "Certified Ornamental Landscape Professional" (COLP), which require written exams.

Some workers with groundskeeping backgrounds may start their own businesses after several years of experience.

Job Outlook

Those interested in grounds maintenance occupations should find plentiful job opportunities in the future. Demand for their services is growing, and because wages for beginners are low and the work is physically demanding, many employers have difficulty attracting enough workers to fill all openings, creating favorable job opportunities. High turnover will generate a large number of job openings to replace workers who leave the occupation.

More workers also will be needed to keep up with increasing demand by lawn care and landscaping companies. Employment of grounds maintenance workers is expected to grow faster than the average for all occupations through the year 2012. Expected growth in the construction of all types of buildings requiring lawn care and maintenance, from office buildings to shopping malls and residential housing, plus more highways and parks, will contribute to demand for grounds maintenance workers. In addition, the upkeep and renovation of existing landscaping and grounds are continuing sources of demand for grounds maintenance workers. Owners of many buildings and facilities recognize the importance of "curb appeal" in attracting business and maintaining the value of the property and are expected to use grounds maintenance services more extensively to maintain and upgrade their properties.

Homeowners are a growing source of demand for grounds maintenance workers. Because many two-income households lack the time to take care of the lawn, they are increasingly hiring people to maintain it for them. They also know that a nice yard will increase the property's value. In addition, there is a growing interest by homeowners in their backyards, as well as a desire to make the yards more attractive for outdoor entertaining. With many newer homes having more and bigger windows overlooking the yard, it becomes more important to maintain and beautify the grounds. Also, as the population ages, more elderly homeowners will require lawn care services to help maintain their yards.

Job opportunities for nonseasonal work are more numerous in regions with temperate climates, where landscaping and lawn services are required all year. However, opportunities may vary with local economic conditions.

Earnings

Median hourly earnings in 2002 of grounds maintenance workers were as follows:

First-line supervisors/managers of landscaping, lawn service,
    and groundskeeping workers $15.89
Tree trimmers and pruners 12.07
Pesticide handlers, sprayers, and applicators, vegetation 11.94
Landscaping and groundskeeping workers 9.51

Median hourly earnings in the industries employing the largest numbers of landscaping and groundskeeping workers in 2002 were as follows:

Elementary and secondary schools	$13.36
Local government	11.81
Services to buildings and dwellings	9.38
Other amusement and recreation industries	8.92
Lessors of real estate	8.65
Employment services	8.05

Related Occupations

Grounds maintenance workers perform most of their work outdoors and have some knowledge of plants and soils. Others whose jobs may require that they work outdoors are agricultural workers; farmers, ranchers, and agricultural managers; forest, conservation, and logging workers; landscape architects; and biological scientists.

Sources of Additional Information

For career and certification information on tree trimmers and pruners, contact

➤ Tree Care Industry Association, 3 Perimeter Rd., Unit I, Manchester, NH 03103-3341. Internet: **http://www.TreeCareIndustry.org**

For information on work as a landscaping and groundskeeping worker, contact either of the following organizations:

➤ Professional Lawn Care Association of America, 1000 Johnson Ferry Rd. NE., Suite C-135, Marietta, GA, 30068-2112. Internet: **http://www.plcaa.org**

➤ Associated Landscape Contractors of America, 150 Elden St., Suite 270, Herndon, VA, 20170. Internet: **http://www.alca.org**

For information on becoming a licensed pesticide applicator, contact your State's Department of Agriculture or Department of Environmental Protection (or Conservation), most of which are accessible from the following Web site: **http://aapco.ceris.purdue.edu/doc/statedirs/offltabl.html**

Pest Control Workers

(0*NET 37-2021.00)

Significant Points

● Use of pest control products requires proper safety training.

● Federal and State laws require licensure through training and examination.

● Job prospects should be favorable for qualified applicants because of high turnover in the occupation.

Nature of the Work

Roaches, rats, mice, spiders, termites, fleas, ants, and bees—few people welcome them into their homes or offices. Unwanted creatures that infest households, buildings, or surrounding areas are pests that can pose serious risks to human health and safety. It is a pest control worker's job to eliminate them.

Pest control workers locate, identify, destroy, control, and repel pests. They use their knowledge of pests' biology and habits, along with an arsenal of pest management techniques—applying chemicals, setting traps, operating equipment, and even modifying structures—to alleviate pest problems.

Part of pest control may require pesticide application. Pest control workers use two different types of pesticides—general use and restricted use. General use pesticides are the most widely used and are readily available; in diluted concentrations, they are available to the public. Restricted use pesticides are available only to certified professionals for controlling the most severe infestations. Their registration, labeling, and application are regulated by Federal law, interpreted by the U.S. Environmental Protection Agency (EPA), because of their potential harm to pest control workers, customers, and the environment.

Pesticides are not pest control workers' only tool, however. Pest control workers increasingly use a combination of pest management techniques, known as integrated pest management. One method involves using proper sanitation and creating physical barriers, for pests cannot survive without food and will not infest a building if they cannot enter it. Another method involves using baits, some of which destroy the pests, and others that prevent them from reproducing. Yet another method involves using mechanical devices, such as traps, that remove pests from the immediate environment.

Integrated pest management is becoming popular for several reasons. First, pesticides can pose environmental and health risks. Second, some pests are becoming more resistant to pesticides in certain situations. Finally, an integrated pest management plan is more effective in the long term than use of a pesticide alone.

New technology is being introduced that allows pest control workers to conduct home inspections, mainly of termites, in much less time. The technology works by implanting microchips in baiting stations, which emit signals that can tell pest control workers if there is termite activity at one of the baiting stations. Workers pick up the signals using a device similar to a metal detector and it allows them to assess much more quickly whether termites are present.

Most pest control workers are employed as pest control technicians, applicators, or supervisors. Position titles vary by State, but the hierarchy—based on training and responsibility required—remains consistent.

Pest control technicians identify potential pest problems, conduct inspections, and design control strategies. They work directly with the customer. Some technicians require a higher level of training depending on their task. If certain products are used, the technician may be required to become a certified *applicator*.

Applicators that specialize in controlling termites are called termite control technicians. They use chemicals and modify structures to eliminate termites and prevent reinfestation. To treat infested areas, termite control technicians drill holes and cut openings into buildings to access infestations, install physical barriers, or bait systems around the structure. Some termite control technicians even repair structural damage caused by termites.

Fumigators are applicators who control pests using poisonous gases called fumigants. Fumigators pretreat infested buildings by examining, measuring, and sealing the buildings. Then, using cylinders, hoses, and valves, they fill structures with the proper amount and concentration of fumigant. They also monitor the premises during treatment for leaking gas. To prevent accidental fumigant exposure, fumigators padlock doors and post warning signs.

Pest control supervisors, also known as operators, direct service technicians and certified applicators. Supervisors are licensed to apply pesticides, but they usually are more involved

Pest control workers often are called in to eradicate pests in people's homes.

in running the business. Supervisors are responsible for ensuring that employees obey rules regarding pesticide use, and they must resolve any problems that arise with regulatory officials or customers. Most States require each pest control establishment to have a supervisor; self-employed business owners usually are supervisors.

Working Conditions

Pest control workers must kneel, bend, reach, and crawl to inspect, modify, and treat structures. They work both indoors and out, in all weather conditions. During warm weather, applicators may be uncomfortable wearing the heavy protective gear—such as respirators, gloves, and goggles—required for working with pesticides.

More than a third of all pest control workers work a 40-hour week, but 17% work more hours. Pest control workers often work evenings and weekends, but many work consistent shifts.

There are health risks associated with pesticide use. Various pest control chemicals are toxic and could be harmful if not used properly. Extensive training required for certification and the use of recommended protective equipment minimizes these health risks, resulting in fewer reported cases of lost work. Because pest control workers travel to visit clients, the potential risk of motor vehicle accidents is another occupational hazard.

Employment

Pest control workers held about 62,000 jobs in 2002; 86 percent of workers were employed in the services to buildings and dwellings industry. They are concentrated in States with warmer climates. About 9 percent were self-employed.

Training, Other Qualifications, and Advancement

A high school diploma or equivalent is the minimum qualification for most pest control jobs. Although a college degree is not required, almost half of all pest control workers have either attended college or earned a degree.

Pest control workers must have basic skills in math, chemistry, and writing, either learned at school or through employer. Because of the extensive interaction that pest control workers have with their customers, employers prefer to hire people who have good communication and interpersonal skills. In addition, most pest control companies require their employees to have a good driving record. Pest control workers must be in good health because of the physical demands of the job, and

they also must be able to withstand extreme conditions—such as the heat of climbing into an attic in the summertime or the chill of sliding into a crawlspace during winter.

Both Federal and State laws regulate pest control workers. These laws require them to be certified through training and examination, for which most pest control firms help their employees prepare. Workers may receive both formal classroom and on-the-job training, but they also must study on their own. Because the pest control industry is constantly changing, workers must attend continuing education classes to maintain their certification.

Requirements for pest control workers vary by State. Pest control workers usually begin their careers as apprentice technicians. Before performing any pest control services, apprentices must attend general training in pesticide safety and use. In addition, they must train in each pest control category in which they wish to practice. Categories may include general pest control, rodent control, termite control, fumigation, and ornamental and turf control.

Training usually involves spending 10 hours in the classroom and 60 hours on the job for each category. After completing the required training, apprentices can provide supervised pest control services. To be eligible to become applicators, technicians must have a combination of experience and education and pass a test. This requirement is sometimes waived for individuals who have either a college degree in biological sciences or extensive related work experience. To become certified as applicators, technicians must pass an additional set of category exams. Depending on the State, applicators must attend additional classes every 1 to 6 years to be recertified.

Applicators with several years of experience often become supervisors. To qualify as a pest control supervisor, applicators may have to pass State-administered exams and have experience in the industry, usually a minimum of 2 years.

Job Outlook

Job prospects should be favorable for qualified applicants because many people do not find pest control work appealing and turnover in this occupation is high. Thus, in addition to job openings arising from employment growth, opportunities will result from workers who transfer or leave the occupation and need to be replaced. Employment growth of pest control workers is expected to be as fast as the average for all occupations through 2012. One factor limiting growth in this occupation, however, is the lack of workers willing to go into this field.

Demand for pest control workers is projected to increase for a number of reasons. Growth in the population will generate new residential and commercial buildings that will require inspections by pest control workers. Also, more people are expected to use pest control services as environmental and health concerns, greater numbers of dual-income households, and improvements in the standard of living convince more people to hire professionals rather than attempt pest control work themselves. In addition, tougher regulations limiting pesticide use will demand more complex integrated pest management strategies.

Concerns about the effects of pesticide use in schools have increasingly prompted more school districts to investigate alternative means of pest control, such as integrated pest management. Furthermore, use of some newer materials for insulation around foundations has made many homes more susceptible to pest infestation. Finally, continuing population shifts to the more pest-prone sunbelt States should increase the number of households in need of pest control.

Earnings

Median hourly earnings of full-time wage and salary pest control workers were $11.90 in 2002. The middle 50 percent earned between $9.46 and $14.93. The lowest 10 percent earned less than $7.53, and the top 10 percent earned over $18.63. Pest control supervisors usually earn the most and technicians the least, with earnings of certified applicators falling somewhere in between. Some pest control workers earn commissions based on the number of contracts for pest control services they sell. Others may earn bonuses for exceeding performance goals.

Related Occupations

Pesticide handlers also apply pesticides in a safe manner to lawns, trees, and other plants. Pest control workers visit homes and places of business to provide building services. Other workers who provide services to buildings include building cleaning workers; various construction trades workers, including carpenters and electricians; and heating, air-conditioning, and refrigeration mechanics and installers.

Sources of Additional Information

Private employment agencies and State employment services offices have information about available job opportunities for pest control workers.

For information about the training and certification required in your State, contact your local office of the U.S. Department of Agriculture or your State's Environmental Protection Agency (or Conservation), most of which are accessible from the following Web site:

http://aapco.ceris.purdue.edu/doc/statedirs/offltabl.html

Personal Care and Service Occupations

Animal Care and Service Workers

(0*NET 39-2011.00, 39-2021.00)

Significant Points

- Animal lovers get satisfaction in this occupation, but the work can be unpleasant and physically and emotionally demanding.

- Most workers are trained on the job, but advancement depends on experience, formal training, and continuing education.

- Good employment opportunities are expected for most positions; however, keen competition is expected for jobs as zookeepers.

- Starting salaries are significantly lower than those in many other fields.

Nature of the Work

Many people like animals. But, as pet owners can attest, taking care of them is hard work. Animal care and service workers—which include animal caretakers and animal trainers—train, feed, water, groom, bathe, and exercise animals, and clean, disinfect, and repair their cages. They also play with the animals, provide companionship, and observe behavioral changes that could indicate illness or injury. Boarding kennels, animal shelters, veterinary hospitals and clinics, stables, laboratories, aquariums, and zoological parks all house animals and employ animal care and service workers. Job titles and duties vary by employment setting.

Kennel attendants care for pets while their owners are working or traveling out of town. Beginning attendants perform basic tasks, such as cleaning cages and dog runs, filling food and water dishes, and exercising animals. Experienced attendants may provide basic animal healthcare, as well as bathe animals, trim nails, and attend to other grooming needs. Attendants who work in kennels also may sell pet food and supplies, assist in obedience training, help with breeding, or prepare animals for shipping.

Animal caretakers who specialize in grooming or maintaining a pet's—usually a dog's or cat's—appearance are called *groomers*. Some groomers work in kennels, veterinary clinics, animal shelters, or pet-supply stores. Others operate their own grooming business, typically at a salon, or sometimes by making house calls. Groomers answer telephones, schedule appointments, discuss pets' grooming needs with clients, and collect information on the pet's disposition and its veterinarian. Groomers often are the first to notice a medical problem, such as an ear or skin infection, that requires veterinary care.

Grooming the pet involves several steps: an initial brush-out is followed by an initial clipping of hair or fur using electric clippers, combs, and grooming shears; the groomer then cuts the nails, cleans the ears, bathes, and blow-dries the animal, and ends with a final clipping and styling.

Animal caretakers in animal shelters perform a variety of duties and work with a wide variety of animals. In addition to attending to the basic needs of the animals, caretakers also must keep records of the animals received and discharged and any tests or treatments done. Some vaccinate newly admitted animals under the direction of a veterinarian or veterinary technician, and euthanize (painlessly put to death) seriously ill, severely injured, or unwanted animals. Animal caretakers in animal shelters also interact with the public, answering telephone inquiries, screening applicants for animal adoption, or educating visitors on neutering and other animal health issues.

Caretakers in stables are called *grooms*. They saddle and unsaddle horses, give them rubdowns, and walk them to cool them off after a ride. They also feed, groom, and exercise the horses; clean out stalls and replenish bedding; polish saddles; clean and organize the tack (harness, saddle, and bridle) room; and store supplies and feed. Experienced grooms may help train horses.

In zoos, animal care and service workers, called *keepers*, prepare the diets and clean the enclosures of animals, and sometimes assist in raising them when they are very young. They watch for any signs of illness or injury, monitor eating patterns or any changes in behavior, and record their observations. Keepers also may answer questions and ensure that the visiting public behaves responsibly toward the exhibited animals. Depending on the zoo, keepers may be assigned to work with a broad

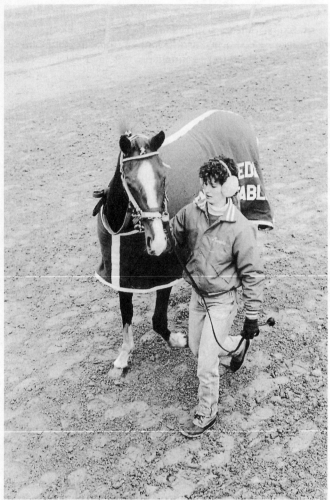

Animal care and service workers who work with horses in stables are called grooms; they saddle and unsaddle horses, give them rubdowns, and walk them to cool them off after a ride.

group of animals such as mammals, birds, or reptiles, or they may work with a limited collection of animals such as primates, large cats, or small mammals.

Animal trainers train animals for riding, security, performance, obedience, or assisting persons with disabilities. Animal trainers do this by accustoming the animal to human voice and contact, and conditioning the animal to respond to commands. Trainers use several techniques to help them train animals. One technique, known as a bridge, is a stimulus that a trainer uses to communicate the precise moment an animal does something correctly. When the animal responds correctly, the trainer gives positive reinforcement in a variety of ways: food, toys, play, rubdowns, or speaking the word "good." Animal training takes place in small steps, and often takes months and even years of repetition. During the conditioning process, trainers provide animals mental stimulation, physical exercise, and husbandry care. In addition to their hands-on work with the animals, trainers often oversee other aspects of the animal's care, such as diet preparation. Trainers often work in competitions or shows, such as the circus or marine parks. Trainers who work in shows also may participate in educational programs for visitors and guests.

Working Conditions
People who love animals get satisfaction from working with and helping them. However, some of the work may be unpleas-

ant, physically and emotionally demanding, and sometimes dangerous. Most animal care and service workers have to clean animal cages and lift, hold, or restrain animals, risking exposure to bites or scratches. Their work often involves kneeling, crawling, repeated bending, and lifting heavy supplies like bales of hay or bags of feed. Animal caretakers must take precautions when treating animals with germicides or insecticides. The work setting can be noisy. Caretakers of show and sports animals travel to competitions.

Animal care and service workers who witness abused animals or who assist in the euthanizing of unwanted, aged, or hopelessly injured animals may experience emotional stress. Those working for private humane societies and municipal animal shelters often deal with the public, some of whom might react with hostility to any implication that the owners are neglecting or abusing their pets. Such workers must maintain a calm and professional demeanor while they enforce the laws regarding animal care.

Animal care and service workers may work outdoors in all kinds of weather. Hours are irregular. Animals must be fed every day, so caretakers often work weekend and holiday shifts. In some animal hospitals, research facilities, and animal shelters, an attendant is on duty 24 hours a day, which means night shifts.

Employment
Animal care and service workers held 151,000 jobs in 2002. Over 80 percent worked as nonfarm animal caretakers; the remainder worked as animal trainers. Nonfarm animal caretakers worked primarily in boarding kennels, animal shelters, stables, grooming shops, animal hospitals, and veterinary offices. A significant number also worked for animal humane societies, racing stables, dog and horse racetrack operators, zoos, theme parks, circuses, and other amusement and recreations services. In 2002, 1 out of every 4 nonfarm animal caretakers was self-employed.

Employment of animal trainers was concentrated in animal services that specialize in training horses, pets, and other animal specialties; and in commercial sports, training racehorses and dogs. Over 2 in 5 animal trainers were self-employed.

Training, Other Qualifications, and Advancement
Most animal care and service workers are trained on the job. Employers generally prefer to hire people with some experience with animals. Some training programs are available for specific types of animal caretakers, such as groomers, but formal training is usually not necessary for entry-level positions. Animal trainers often need to possess a high school diploma or GED equivalent. However, some animal training jobs may require a bachelor's degree and additional skills. For example, a marine mammal trainer usually needs a bachelor's degree in biology, marine biology, animal science, psychology, zoology, or related field, plus strong swimming skills and SCUBA certification. All animal trainers need patience, sensitivity, and experience with problem-solving and animal obedience. Certification is not mandatory for animal trainers, but several organizations offer training programs and certification for prospective animal trainers.

Most pet groomers learn their trade by completing an informal apprenticeship, usually lasting 6 to 10 weeks, under the guidance of an experienced groomer. Prospective groomers also may attend one of the 50 State-licensed grooming schools throughout the country, with programs varying in length from 2 to 18 weeks. The National Dog Groomers Association of

America certifies groomers who pass a written examination consisting of 400 questions, including some on cats, with a separate part testing practical skills. Beginning groomers often start by taking on one duty, such as bathing and drying the pet. They eventually assume responsibility for the entire grooming process, from the initial brush-out to the final clipping. Groomers who work in large retail establishments or kennels may, with experience, move into supervisory or managerial positions. Experienced groomers often choose to open their own shops.

Beginning animal caretakers in kennels learn on the job, and usually start by cleaning cages and feeding and watering animals. Kennel caretakers may be promoted to kennel supervisor, assistant manager, and manager, and those with enough capital and experience may open up their own kennels. The American Boarding Kennels Association (ABKA) offers a three-stage, home-study program for individuals interested in pet care. The first two stages address basic and advanced principles of animal care, while the third stage focuses on indepth animal care and good business procedures. Those who complete the third stage and pass oral and written examinations administered by the ABKA become Certified Kennel Operators (CKO).

Some zoological parks may require their caretakers to have a bachelor's degree in biology, animal science, or a related field. Most require experience with animals, preferably as a volunteer or paid keeper in a zoo. Zookeepers may advance to senior keeper, assistant head keeper, head keeper, and assistant curator, but very few openings occur, especially for the higher level positions.

Animal caretakers in animal shelters are not required to have any specialized training, but training programs and workshops are increasingly available through the Humane Society of the United States, the American Humane Association, and the National Animal Control Association. Workshop topics include cruelty investigations, appropriate methods of euthanasia for shelter animals, proper guidelines for capturing animals, and techniques for preventing problems with wildlife. With experience and additional training, caretakers in animal shelters may become adoption coordinators, animal control officers, emergency rescue drivers, assistant shelter managers, or shelter directors.

Job Outlook
Good job opportunities are expected for most positions because many workers leave this occupation each year. The need to replace workers leaving the field will create the overwhelming majority of job openings. Many animal caretaker jobs require little or no training and have flexible work schedules, attracting people seeking their first job, students, and others looking for temporary or part-time work. The outlook for caretakers in zoos, however, is not favorable due to slow growth in zoo capacity and keen competition for the few positions. Job opportunities for animal care and service workers may vary from year to year, because the strength of the economy affects demand for these workers. Pet owners tend to spend more on animal services when the economy is strong.

In addition to replacement needs, employment of animal care and service workers is expected to grow faster than the average for all occupations through 2012. The pet population—which drives employment of animal caretakers in kennels, grooming shops, animal shelters, and veterinary clinics and hospitals—is expected to increase. Pet owners—including a large number of baby boomers, whose disposable income is expected to increase as they age— are expected to increasingly take advantage of grooming services, daily and overnight boarding services, training services, and veterinary services, resulting in more jobs for animal care and service workers. As many pet owners increasingly consider their pet as part of the family, their demand for luxury animal services and willingness to spend greater amounts of money on their pet will continue to grow.

Demand for animal care and service workers in animal shelters is expected to remain steady. Communities are increasingly recognizing the connection between animal abuse and abuse toward humans, and will probably continue to commit funds to animal shelters, many of which are working hand-in-hand with social service agencies and law enforcement teams. Employment growth of personal and group animal trainers will stem from an increased number of animal owners seeking training services for their pets, including behavior modification and feline behavior training.

Earnings
Median hourly earnings of nonfarm animal caretakers were $8.21 in 2002. The middle 50 percent earned between $6.95 and $10.26. The bottom 10 percent earned less than $6.13, and the top 10 percent earned more than $13.39. Median hourly earnings in the industries employing the largest numbers of nonfarm animal caretakers in 2002 were as follows:

Other personal services	$8.39
Spectator sports	8.24
Social advocacy organizations	7.79
Other miscellaneous store retailers	7.62
Other professional, scientific, and technical services	7.55

Median hourly earnings of animal trainers were $11.03 in 2002. The middle 50 percent earned between $8.21 and $15.96. The lowest 10 percent earned less than $6.87, and the top 10 percent earned more than $21.65.

Related Occupations
Others who work extensively with animals include farmers, ranchers, and agricultural managers; agricultural workers; veterinarians; veterinary technologists and technicians; veterinary assistants; biological scientists; and medical scientists.

Sources of Additional Information
For more information on jobs in animal caretaking and control, and the animal shelter and control personnel training program, write to:
➤ The Humane Society of the United States, 2100 L St. NW., Washington, DC 20037-1598. Internet: **http://www.hsus.org**

For career information and information on training, certification, and earnings of animal control officers at Federal, State, and local levels, contact:
➤ National Animal Control Association, P.O. Box 480851, Kansas City, MO 64148-0851. Internet: **http://www.nacanet.org**

To obtain a listing of State-licensed grooming schools, send a stamped, self-addressed, business-size envelope to:
➤ National Dog Groomers Association of America, P.O. Box 101, Clark, PA 16113. For information on certification, see the following Internet site: **http://www.nauticom.net/www/ndga**

For information on becoming an advanced pet care technician at a kennel, contact:
➤ The American Boarding Kennels Association, 1702 East Pikes Peak Ave., Colorado Springs, CO 80909.

Barbers, Cosmetologists, and Other Personal Appearance Workers

(O*NET 39-5011.00, 39-5012.00, 39-5091.00, 39-5092.00, 39-5093.00, 39-5094.00)

Significant Points

- Job opportunities generally should be good, but competition is expected for jobs and clients at higher paying salons; opportunities will be best for those licensed to provide a broad range of services.

- Barbers, cosmetologists, and most other personal appearance workers must be licensed.

- Almost half of all barbers, cosmetologists, and other personal appearance workers are self-employed; many also work flexible schedules.

Nature of the Work

Barbers and cosmetologists, also called *hairdressers* and *hairstylists*, help people look neat and well-groomed. Other personal appearance workers, such as *manicurists and pedicurists*, *shampooers*, and *skin care specialists* provide specialized services that help clients look and feel their best.

Barbers cut, trim, shampoo, and style hair. Also, they fit hairpieces and offer scalp treatments and facial massages. In many States, barbers are licensed to color, bleach, or highlight hair and offer permanent-wave services. Many barbers also provide skin care and nail treatments.

Hairdressers, hairstylists, and cosmetologists provide beauty services, such as shampooing, cutting, coloring, and styling hair. They may advise clients on how to care for their hair, straighten hair or give it a permanent wave, or lighten or darken hair color. Additionally, cosmetologists may train to give manicures, pedicures, and scalp and facial treatments; provide makeup analysis; and clean and style wigs and hairpieces.

A number of workers offer specialized services. *Manicurists and pedicurists*, called *nail technicians* in some States, work exclusively on nails and provide manicures, pedicures, coloring, and nail extensions to clients. Another group of specialists is *skin care specialists*, or *estheticians*, who cleanse and beautify the skin by giving facials, full-body treatments, and head and neck massages and by removing hair through waxing. *Electrologists* use an electrolysis machine to remove hair. Finally, in some larger salons, *shampooers* specialize in shampooing and conditioning clients' hair.

In addition to their work with clients, personal appearance workers are expected to maintain clean work areas and sanitize all work implements. They may make appointments and keep records of hair color and permanent-wave formulas used by their regular clients. A growing number actively sell hair products and other cosmetic supplies. Barbers, cosmetologists, and other personal appearance workers who operate their own salons have managerial duties that include hiring, supervising, and firing workers, as well as keeping business and inventory records, ordering supplies, and arranging for advertising.

Working Conditions

Barbers, cosmetologists, and other personal appearance workers usually work in clean, pleasant surroundings with good lighting and ventilation. Good health and stamina are important, because these workers are on their feet for most of their shift. Because prolonged exposure to some hair and nail chemicals may cause irritation, special care is taken to use protective clothing, such as plastic gloves or aprons.

Most full-time barbers, cosmetologists, and other personal appearance workers put in a 40-hour week, but longer hours are common in this occupation, especially among self-employed workers. Work schedules may include evenings and weekends, the times when beauty salons and barbershops are busiest. Because barbers and cosmetologists generally will be working on weekends and during lunch and evening hours, they may arrange to take breaks during less popular times. About 30 percent of cosmetologists and 19 percent of barbers work part time and 14 percent of cosmetologists and 13 percent of barbers have variable schedules.

Employment

Barbers, cosmetologists, and other personal appearance workers held about 754,000 jobs in 2002. Of these, barbers, hairdressers, hairstylists, and cosmetologists held 651,000 jobs; manicurists and pedicurists, 51,000; skin care specialists, 25,000; and shampooers, 25,000.

Most of these workers are employed in beauty salons or barber shops, but they are also found in nail salons, department stores, nursing and other residential care homes, and drug and cosmetics stores. Nearly every town has a barbershop or beauty

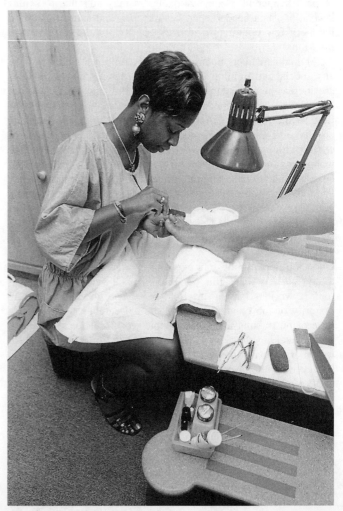

Barbers, cosmetologists, and most other personal appearance workers must be licensed.

salon, but employment in this occupation is concentrated in the most populous cities and States.

Almost half of all barbers, cosmetologists, and other personal appearance workers are self-employed. Many own their own salon, but a growing number lease booth space or a chair from the salon's owner.

Training, Other Qualifications, and Advancement

All States require barbers, cosmetologists, and most other personal appearance workers to be licensed. Qualifications for a license, however, vary. Generally, a person must have graduated from a State-licensed barber or cosmetology school and be at least 16 years old. A few States require applicants to pass a physical examination. Some States require graduation from high school while others require as little as an eighth-grade education. In a few States, the completion of an apprenticeship can substitute for graduation from a school, but very few barbers or cosmetologists learn their skills in this way. Applicants for a license usually are required to pass a written test and demonstrate an ability to perform basic barbering or cosmetology services.

Some States have reciprocity agreements that allow licensed barbers and cosmetologists to obtain a license in a different State without additional formal training. Other States do not recognize training or licenses obtained in another State; consequently, persons who wish to work in a particular State should review the laws of that State before entering a training program.

Public and private vocational schools offer daytime or evening classes in barbering and cosmetology. Full-time programs in barbering and cosmetology usually last 9 to 24 months, but training for manicurists and pedicurists, skin care specialists, and electrologists requires significantly less time. An apprenticeship program can last from 1 to 3 years. Shampooers generally do not need formal training or a license. Formal training programs include classroom study, demonstrations, and practical work. Students study the basic services—cutting hair, shaving customers, providing facial massages, and giving hair and scalp treatments—and, under supervision, practice on customers in school "clinics." Most schools also teach unisex hairstyling and chemical styling. Students attend lectures on the use and care of instruments, sanitation and hygiene, chemistry, anatomy, physiology, and the recognition of simple skin ailments. Instruction also is provided in communication, sales, and general business practices. Experienced barbers and cosmetologists may take advanced courses in hairstyling, coloring, and the sale and service of hairpieces.

After graduating from a training program, students can take the State licensing examination, which consists of a written test and, in some cases, a practical test of styling skills based on established performance criteria. A few States include an oral examination in which the applicant is asked to explain the procedures he or she is following while taking the practical test. In many States, cosmetology training may be credited toward a barbering license, and vice versa. A few States combine the two licenses into one hairstyling license. Many States require separate licensing examinations for manicurists, pedicurists, and skin care specialists.

For many barbers, cosmetologists, and other personal appearance workers, formal training and a license are only the first steps in a career that requires years of continuing education. Because hairstyles change, new products are developed, and services expand to meet clients' needs, personal appearance workers must keep abreast of the latest fashions and beauty techniques. They attend training at salons, cosmetology schools, or product shows. Through workshops and demonstrations of the latest techniques, industry representatives introduce cosmetologists to a wide range of products and services. As retail sales become an increasingly important part of salons' revenue, the ability to be an effective salesperson becomes vital for salon workers.

Successful personal appearance workers should have an understanding of fashion, art, and technical design. They should enjoy working with the public and be willing and able to follow clients' instructions. Communication, image, and attitude play an important role in career success. Some cosmetology schools consider "people skills" to be such an integral part of the job that they require coursework in this area. Business skills are important for those who plan to operate their own salons.

During their first months on the job, new workers are given relatively simple tasks or are assigned the simpler hairstyling patterns. Once they have demonstrated their skills, they are gradually permitted to perform more complicated tasks, such as coloring hair or applying a permanent wave. As they continue to work in the field, more training is usually required to learn the techniques used in each salon and to build on the basics learned in cosmetology school.

Advancement usually takes the form of higher earnings as barbers and cosmetologists gain experience and build a steady clientele. Some barbers and cosmetologists manage large salons or open their own after several years of experience. Others teach in barber or cosmetology schools, or provide training through vocational schools. Still others advance to become sales representatives, image or fashion consultants, or examiners for State licensing boards.

Job Outlook

Overall employment of barbers, cosmetologists, and other personal appearance workers is projected to grow about as fast as the average for all occupations through 2012, because of increasing population, incomes, and demand for personal appearance services. In addition to those arising from job growth, numerous job openings will arise from the need to replace workers who transfer to other occupations, retire, or leave the labor force for other reasons. As a result, job opportunities generally should be good. However, competition is expected for jobs and clients at higher paying salons, as applicants compete with a large pool of licensed and experienced cosmetologists for these positions. Opportunities will be best for those licensed to provide a broad range of services.

Employment trends are expected to vary among the different specialties within this grouping of occupations. For example, more slowly than average growth is expected in employment of barbers due to a large number of retirements and the relatively small number of cosmetology school graduates opting to obtain barbering licenses. On the other hand, employment of hairdressers, hairstylists, and cosmetologists should grow about as fast as average, because many now cut and style both men's and women's hair and because the demand for coloring services and other hair treatments, such as permanent waves, by teens and aging baby boomers is expected to remain steady or even grow.

Continued growth in the number of nail salons and full-service day spas will generate numerous job openings for manicurists, pedicurists, skin care specialists, and shampooers. Nail salons specialize in providing manicures and pedicures. Day spas typically provide a full range of services, including beauty wraps, manicures and pedicures, facials, and massages.

Earnings

Barbers, cosmetologists, and other personal appearance workers receive income from a variety of sources. They may receive commissions based on the price of the service or a salary based on number of hours worked. All receive tips, and many receive commissions on the products they sell. In addition, some salons pay bonuses to employees who bring in new business.

Median annual earnings in 2002 for salaried hairdressers, hairstylists, and cosmetologists, including tips and commission, were $18,960. The middle 50 percent earned between $15,010 and $25,600. The lowest 10 percent earned less than $13,020, and the highest 10 percent earned more than $35,240.

Median annual earnings in 2002 for salaried barbers, including tips, were $19,550. The middle 50 percent earned between $14,540 and $27,290. The lowest 10 percent earned less than $12,720, and the highest 10 percent earned more than $37,370.

Among skin care specialists, median annual earnings, including tips, were $22,450; for manicurists and pedicurists, $17,330; and $14,360 for shampooers.

A number of factors determine the total income of barbers, cosmetologists, and other personal appearance workers, including the size and location of the salon, the number of hours worked, clients' tipping habits, and competition from other barber shops and salons. Cosmetologists or barber's initiative and ability to attract and hold regular clients also are key factors in determining his or her earnings. Earnings for entry-level workers are usually low; however, for those who stay in the profession, earnings can be considerably higher.

Although some salons offer paid vacations and medical benefits, many self-employed and part-time workers in this occupation do not enjoy such common benefits.

Related Occupations

Other workers who provide a personal service to clients and usually must be professionally licensed or certified include massage therapists, fitness trainers, and aerobics instructors.

Sources of Additional Information

A list of licensed training schools and licensing requirements for cosmetologists may be obtained from:

➤ National Accrediting Commission of Cosmetology Arts and Sciences, 4401 Ford Ave., Suite 1300, Alexandria, VA 22302. Internet: **http://www.naccas.org**

Information about a career in cosmetology is available from:

➤ National Cosmetology Association, 401 N. Michigan Ave., 22nd floor, Chicago, IL 60611. Internet: **http://www.salonprofessionals.org**

For details on State licensing requirements and approved barber or cosmetology schools, contact the State boards of barber or cosmetology examiners in your State capital.

Childcare Workers

(O*NET 39-9011.00)

Significant Points

● About 2 out of 5 childcare workers are self-employed; most of these are family childcare providers.

● A high school diploma and little or no experience are adequate for many jobs, but training requirements vary from a high school diploma to a college degree.

● Large numbers of workers leave these jobs every year, creating good job opportunities.

Nature of the Work

Childcare workers nurture and teach children of all ages in childcare centers, nursery schools, preschools, public schools, private households, family childcare homes, and before- and afterschool programs. These workers play an important role in a child's development by caring for the child when parents are at work or away for other reasons. Some parents enroll their children in nursery schools or childcare centers primarily to provide them with the opportunity to interact with other children. In addition to attending to children's basic needs, these workers organize activities that stimulate the children's physical, emotional, intellectual, and social growth. They help children to explore their interests, develop their talents and independence, build self-esteem, and learn how to get along with others.

Private household workers who are employed on an hourly basis usually are called *babysitters*. These childcare workers bathe, dress, and feed children; supervise their play; wash their clothes; and clean their rooms. They also may put them to bed and waken them, read to them, involve them in educational games, take them for doctors' visits, and discipline them. Those who are in charge of infants, sometimes called infant nurses, also prepare bottles and change diapers.

Nannies generally take care of children from birth to age 10 or 12, tending to the child's early education, nutrition, health, and other needs. They also may perform the duties of a general housekeeper, including general cleaning and laundry duties.

Childcare workers spend most of their day working with children. However, they do maintain contact with parents or guardians through informal meetings or scheduled conferences to discuss each child's progress and needs. Many childcare workers keep records of each child's progress and suggest ways in which parents can stimulate their child's learning and development at home. Some preschools, childcare centers, and before- and after-school programs actively recruit parent volunteers to work with the children and participate in administrative decisions and program planning.

Most childcare workers perform a combination of basic care and teaching duties. Through many basic care activities, childcare workers provide opportunities for children to learn. For example, a worker who shows a child how to tie a shoelace teaches the child while also providing for that child's basic care needs. Childcare programs help children to learn about trust and to gain a sense of security.

Young children learn mainly through play. Recognizing the importance of play, childcare workers build their program around it. They capitalize on children's play to further language development (storytelling and acting games), improve social skills (working together to build a neighborhood in a sandbox), and introduce scientific and mathematical concepts (balancing and counting blocks when building a bridge or mixing colors when painting). Thus, a less structured approach is used to teach preschool children, including small-group lessons, one-on-one instruction, and learning through creative activities, such as art, dance, and music.

Interaction with peers is an important part of a child's early development. Preschool children in childcare centers have an opportunity to engage in conversation and discussions, and to learn to play and work cooperatively with their classmates. Childcare workers play a vital role in preparing children to build the skills they will need in school. (Teacher assistants as well as teachers—preschool, kindergarten, elementary, middle, and secondary school are discussed elsewhere in the *Handbook*.)

Childcare workers in preschools greet young children as they arrive, help them to remove outer garments, and select an activity of interest. When caring for infants, they feed and change them. To ensure a well-balanced program, childcare workers prepare daily and long-term schedules of activities. Each day's activities balance individual and group play, and quiet and active time. Children are given some freedom to participate in activities in which they are interested.

Concern over school-age children being home alone before and after school has spurred many parents to seek alternative ways for their children to constructively spend their time. The purpose of before- and afterschool programs is to watch over school-age children during the gap between school hours and their parents' work hours. These programs also may operate during the summer and on weekends. Workers in before- and after-school programs may help students with their homework or engage them in other extracurricular activities. These activities may include field trips, learning about computers, painting, photography, and participating in sports. Some childcare workers may be responsible for taking children to school in the morning and picking them up from school in the afternoon. Before- and afterschool programs may be operated by public school systems, local community centers, or other private organizations.

Helping to keep young children healthy is an important part of the job. Childcare workers serve nutritious meals and snacks and teach good eating habits and personal hygiene. They ensure that children have proper rest periods. They identify children who may not feel well or who show signs of emotional or developmental problems and discuss these matters with their supervisor and the child's parents. In some cases, childcare workers help parents to locate programs that will provide basic health services.

Early identification of children with special needs—such as those with behavioral, emotional, physical, or learning disabilities—is important to improve their future learning ability. Special education teachers often work with these preschool children to provide the individual attention they need. (Special education teachers are discussed elsewhere in the *Handbook*.)

Working Conditions
Preschool or childcare facilities include private homes, schools, religious institutions, workplaces in which employers provide care for employees' children, and private buildings. Individu-

Childcare workers help children to explore their interests and learn how to get along with others.

als who provide care in their own homes generally are called family childcare providers.

Nannies and babysitters usually work in the pleasant and comfortable homes or apartments of their employers. Most are day workers who live in their own homes and travel to work. Some live in the home of their employer, generally with their own room and bath. They often become part of their employer's family, and may derive satisfaction from caring for them.

Watching children grow, learn, and gain new skills can be very rewarding. While working with children, childcare workers often improve the child's communication, learning, and other personal skills. The work is sometimes routine; however, new activities and challenges mark each day. Childcare can be physically and emotionally taxing, as workers constantly stand, walk, bend, stoop, and lift to attend to each child's interests and problems.

To ensure that children receive proper supervision, State or local regulations may require a certain ratio of workers to children. The ratio varies with the age of the children. Child development experts generally recommend that a single caregiver be responsible for no more than 3 or 4 infants (less than 1 year old), 5 or 6 toddlers (1 to 2 years old), or 10 preschool-age children (between 2 and 5 years old). In before- and afterschool programs, workers may be responsible for many school-age children at one time.

The work hours of childcare workers vary widely. Childcare centers usually are open year round, with long hours so that parents can drop off and pick up their children before and after work. Some centers employ full-time and part-time staff with staggered shifts to cover the entire day. Some workers are unable to take regular breaks during the day due to limited staffing. Public and many private preschool programs operate during the typical 9- or 10-month school year, employing both full-time and part-time workers. Family childcare providers have flexible hours and daily routines, but may work long or unusual hours to fit parents' work schedules. Live-in nannies usually work longer hours than do those who have their own homes. However, if they work evenings or weekends, they may get other time off.

Replacement needs in this occupation are high. Many childcare workers leave the occupation temporarily to fulfill family responsibilities, to study, or for other reasons. Some workers leave permanently because they are interested in pursuing other occupations or because of dissatisfaction with hours, low pay and benefits, and stressful conditions.

Employment
Childcare workers held about 1.2 million jobs in 2002. Many worked part time. About 2 out of 5 childcare workers were self-employed; most of these were family childcare providers.

Sixteen percent of all childcare workers are found in child daycare services, and about 14 percent work for private households. The remainder worked primarily in local government educational services, nursing and residential care facilities, religious organizations, other amusement and recreation industries, private educational services, civic and social organizations, individual and family services, and local government, excluding education and hospitals. Some childcare programs are for-profit centers; some of these are affiliated with a local or national chain. Religious institutions, community agencies, school systems, and State and local governments operate nonprofit programs. Only a very small percentage of private industry establishments operate onsite childcare centers for the children of their employees.

Training, Other Qualifications, and Advancement

The training and qualifications required of childcare workers vary widely. Each State has its own licensing requirements that regulate caregiver training; these range from a high school diploma, to community college courses, to a college degree in child development or early-childhood education. Many States require continuing education for workers in this field. However, State requirements often are minimal. Childcare workers generally can obtain employment with a high school diploma and little or no experience. Local governments, private firms, and publicly funded programs may have more demanding training and education requirements.

Some employers prefer to hire childcare workers with a nationally recognized childcare development credential, secondary or postsecondary courses in child development and early childhood education, or work experience in a childcare setting. Other employers require their own specialized training. An increasing number of employers require an associate degree in early childhood education. Schools for nannies teach early childhood education, nutrition, and childcare.

Childcare workers must anticipate and prevent problems, deal with disruptive children, provide fair but firm discipline, and be enthusiastic and constantly alert. They must communicate effectively with the children and their parents, as well as other teachers and childcare workers. Workers should be mature, patient, understanding, and articulate, and have energy and physical stamina. Skills in music, art, drama, and storytelling also are important. Self-employed childcare workers must have business sense and management abilities.

Opportunities for advancement are limited. However, as childcare workers gain experience, some may advance to supervisory or administrative positions in large childcare centers or preschools. Often, these positions require additional training, such as a bachelor's or master's degree. Other workers move on to work in resource and referral agencies, consulting with parents on available child services. A few workers become involved in policy or advocacy work related to childcare and early childhood education. With a bachelor's degree, workers may become preschool teachers or become certified to teach in public or private schools. Some workers set up their own childcare businesses.

Job Outlook

High replacement needs should create good job opportunities for childcare workers. Many childcare workers must be replaced each year as they leave the occupation to take other jobs, to meet family responsibilities, or for other reasons. Qualified persons who are interested in this work should have little trouble finding and keeping a job. Opportunities for nannies should be especially good, as many workers prefer not to work in other people's homes.

Employment of childcare workers is projected to increase about as fast as the average for all occupations through the year 2012. The number of women of childbearing age (widely considered to be ages 15 to 44) in the labor force and the number of children under 5 years of age is expected to rise gradually over the projected 2002-12 period. Also, the proportion of youngsters enrolled full or part time in childcare and preschool programs is likely to continue to increase, spurring demand for additional childcare workers.

Changes in perceptions of preprimary education may lead to increased public and private spending on childcare. If more parents believe that some experience in center-based care and preschool is beneficial to children, enrollment will increase. Concern about the behavior of school-age children during nonschool hours should increase demand for before- and afterschool programs. In addition, the difficulty of finding suitable nannies or private household workers also may force many families to seek out alternative childcare arrangements in centers and family childcare programs. Government policy often favors increased funding of early childhood education programs, and that trend will probably continue. Government funding for before- and afterschool programs also is expected to be steady over the projection period. The growing availability of government-funded center-based care and preschool programs may induce some parents to enroll their children who otherwise would not do so. Some States also are increasing subsidization of the child daycare services industry in response to welfare reform legislation. This reform might cause some mothers to enter the workforce during the projection period as their welfare benefits are reduced or eliminated.

Earnings

Pay depends on the educational attainment of the worker and the type of establishment. Although the pay generally is very low, more education usually means higher earnings. Median hourly earnings of wage and salary childcare workers were $7.86 in 2002. The middle 50 percent earned between $6.66 and $9.65. The lowest 10 percent earned less than $5.91, and the highest 10 percent earned more than $11.46. Median hourly earnings in the industries employing the largest numbers of childcare workers in 2002 were as follows:

Other residential care facilities	$9.51
Elementary and secondary schools	9.04
Civic and social organizations	7.25
Child daycare services	7.18
Other amusement and recreation industries	7.09

Earnings of self-employed childcare workers vary depending on the hours worked, the number and ages of the children, and the location.

Benefits vary, but are minimal for most childcare workers. Many employers offer free or discounted childcare to employees. Some offer a full benefits package, including health insurance and paid vacations, but others offer no benefits at all. Some employers offer seminars and workshops to help workers learn new skills. A few are willing to cover the cost of courses taken at community colleges or technical schools. Live-in nannies get free room and board.

Related Occupations

Childcare work requires patience; creativity; an ability to nurture, motivate, teach, and influence children; and leadership, organizational, and administrative skills. Others who work with children and need these qualities and skills include teacher assistants; teachers—preschool, kindergarten, elementary, middle, and secondary; and teachers—special education.

Sources of Additional Information

For an electronic question-and-answer service on childcare, information on becoming a childcare provider, and other resources for persons interested in childcare work, contact:

➤ National Child Care Information Center, 243 Church St. NW., 2nd floor, Vienna, VA 22180. Telephone (tollfree): 800-424-4310. Internet: **http://www.nccic.org**

For information on becoming a family childcare provider, send a stamped, self-addressed envelope to:
➤ The Children's Foundation, 725 15th St. NW., Suite 505, Washington, DC 20005-2109. Internet: **http://www.childrensfoundation.net**

For eligibility requirements and a description of the Child Development Associate credential, contact:
➤ Council for Professional Recognition, 2460 16th St. NW., Washington, DC 20009-3575. Internet: **http://www.cdacouncil.org**

For eligibility requirements and a description of the Certified Childcare Professional designation, contact:
➤ National Childcare Association, 1016 Rosser St., Conyers, GA 30012. Internet: **http://www.nccanet.org**

For information about a career as a nanny, contact:
➤ International Nanny Association, 191 Clarksville Rd., Princeton Junction, NJ 08550-3111. Telephone (tollfree): 888-878-1477. Internet: **http://www.nanny.org**

State Departments of Human Services or Social Services can supply State regulations and training requirements for childcare workers.

Flight Attendants

(0*NET 39-6031.00)

Significant Points

- Job duties are learned through intensive formal training after workers are hired.

- Competition for positions will remain strong because the opportunity for travel attracts more applicants than there are jobs, with only the most qualified being hired.

- Although applicants must be high school graduates or hold a GED, many airlines today prefer a college degree.

Nature of the Work

Major airlines are required by law to provide flight attendants for the safety of the traveling public. Although the primary job of the flight attendants is to ensure that safety regulations are followed, they also try to make flights comfortable and enjoyable for passengers.

At least 1 hour before each flight, attendants are briefed by the captain—the pilot in command—on such things as emergency evacuation procedures, coordination of the crew, the length of the flight, expected weather conditions, and special issues having to do with passengers. Flight attendants make sure that first-aid kits and other emergency equipment are aboard and in working order and that the passenger cabin is in order, with adequate supplies of food, beverages, and blankets. As passengers board the plane, flight attendants greet them, check their tickets, and tell them where to store coats and carry-on items.

Before the plane takes off, flight attendants instruct all passengers in the use of emergency equipment and check to see that seat belts are fastened, seat backs are in upright positions, and all carry-on items are properly stowed. In the air, helping passengers in the event of an emergency is the most important responsibility of a flight attendant. Safety-related actions may range from reassuring passengers during occasional encounters with strong turbulence to directing passengers who must evacuate a plane following an emergency landing. Flight attendants

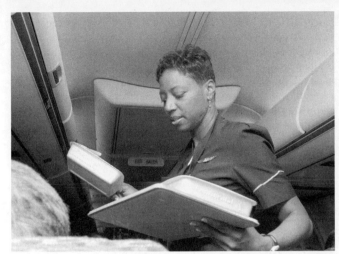

Although safety is their primary concern, flight attendants also try to make flights comfortable and enjoyable for airline passengers.

also answer questions about the flight; distribute reading material, pillows, and blankets; and help small children, elderly or disabled persons, and any others needing assistance. They may administer first aid to passengers who become ill. Flight attendants generally serve beverages and other refreshments and, on many flights, heat and distribute precooked meals or snacks. Prior to landing, flight attendants take inventory of headsets, alcoholic beverages, and moneys collected. They also report any medical problems passengers may have had, the condition of cabin equipment, and lost and found articles.

Lead, or first, flight attendants, sometimes known as pursers, oversee the work of the other attendants aboard the aircraft, while performing most of the same duties.

Working Conditions

Because airlines operate around-the-clock, year-round, flight attendants may work nights, holidays, and weekends. In most cases, agreements between the airline and the employees' union determine the total daily and monthly working time. On-duty time is usually limited to 12 hours per day, with a daily maximum of 14 hours. Attendants usually fly 65 to 85 hours a month and, in addition, generally spend about 50 hours a month on the ground preparing planes for flights, writing reports following completed flights, and waiting for planes to arrive. They may be away from their home base at least one-third of the time. During this period, the airlines provide hotel accommodations and an allowance for meal expenses.

Flight attendants must be flexible, reliable, and willing to relocate. Home bases and routes worked are bid for on a seniority basis. The longer the flight attendant has been employed, the more likely he or she is to work on chosen flights. Almost all flight attendants start out working on reserve status or on call. On small corporate airlines, flight attendants often work on an as-needed basis and must adapt to varying environments and passengers.

The combination of free time and discount airfares provides flight attendants the opportunity to travel and see new places. However, the work can be strenuous and trying. Short flights require speedy service if meals are served, and turbulent flights can make serving drinks and meals difficult. Flight attendants stand during much of the flight and must remain pleasant and efficient, regardless of how tired they are or how demanding passengers may be. Occasionally, flight attendants must deal with disruptive passengers.

Flight attendants are susceptible to injuries because of the job demands in a moving aircraft. Back injuries and mishaps incurred by opening overhead compartments are common. In addition, medical problems can arise from irregular sleeping and eating patterns, dealing with stressful passengers, working in a pressurized environment, and breathing recycled air.

Employment

Flight attendants held about 104,000 jobs in 2002. Commercial airlines employed the vast majority of flight attendants, most of who lived in their employer's home base city. A small number of flight attendants worked for large companies that operated company aircraft for business purposes.

Training, Other Qualifications, and Advancement

Airlines prefer to hire poised, tactful, and resourceful people who can interact comfortably with strangers and remain calm under duress. Applicants usually must be at least 18 to 21 years old. Some carriers may have higher minimum-age requirements. Flight attendants must have excellent health and the ability to speak clearly. All U.S. airlines require that applicants be citizens of the United States or registered aliens with legal rights to obtain employment in the United States.

In addition, airlines usually have physical and appearance requirements. There are height requirements for the purposes of reaching overhead bins, and most airlines want candidates with weight proportionate to height. Vision is required to be correctable to 20/30 or better with glasses or contact lenses (uncorrected no worse than 20/200). Men must have their hair cut above the collar and be clean shaven. Airlines prefer applicants with no visible tattoos, body piercing, or unusual hairstyles or makeup.

Applicants must be high school graduates. Those with several years of college and experience in dealing with the public are preferred. More and more flight attendants being hired are college graduates. Applicants who attend schools and colleges that offer flight attendant training may have an advantage over other applicants. Highly desirable areas of concentration include people-oriented disciplines such as psychology and education. Flight attendants for international airlines generally must speak a foreign language fluently. For their international flights, some of the major airlines prefer candidates who can speak two major foreign languages.

Once hired, all candidates must undergo a period of formal training. The length of training, ranging from 3 to 8 weeks, depends on the size and type of carrier and takes place at the airline's flight training center. Airlines that do not operate training centers generally send new employees to the center of another airline. Airlines may provide transportation to the training centers and an allowance for board, room, and school supplies. However, new trainees are not considered employees of the airline until they successfully complete the training program. Some airlines charge individuals for training. Trainees learn emergency procedures such as evacuating an airplane, operating emergency systems and equipment, administering first aid, and water-survival tactics. In addition, trainees are taught how to deal with disruptive passengers and with hijacking and terrorist situations. New hires learn flight regulations and duties, company operations and policies, and receive instruction on personal grooming and weight control. Trainees for the international routes get additional instruction in passport and

customs regulations. Many drills and duties must be performed alone, in front of the training staff. Tests are given throughout training to eliminate unsuccessful trainees. Toward the end of their training, students go on practice flights. Flight attendants also are required to go through periodic retraining and pass an FAA safety examination in order to continue flying.

After completing initial training, flight attendants are assigned to one of their airline's bases. New flight attendants are placed on "reserve status" and are called on either to staff extra flights or to fill in for crewmembers who are sick, on vacation, or rerouted. When they are not on duty, reserve flight attendants must be available to report for flights on short notice. They usually remain on reserve for at least 1 year, but, in some cities, it may take 5 to 10 years or longer to advance from reserve status. Flight attendants who no longer are on reserve bid monthly for regular assignments. Because assignments are based on seniority, usually only the most experienced attendants get their choice of assignments. Advancement takes longer today than in the past, because experienced flight attendants are remaining in this career longer than they used to.

Some flight attendants become supervisors or take on additional duties such as recruiting and instructing. Their experience also may qualify them for numerous airline-related jobs involving contact with the public, such as reservation ticket agent or public-relations specialist.

Job Outlook

In the long run, opportunities for persons seeking flight attendant jobs should improve as the airline industry recovers from the aftereffects of September 11 and the downturn in the economy. Employment of flight attendants is expected to grow about as fast as the average for all occupations through the year 2012. Population growth and an improving economy are expected to boost the number of airline passengers. As airlines enlarge their capacity to meet rising demand by increasing the number and size of planes in operation, more flight attendants will be needed. However, over the next decade, one can expect that demand for flight attendants will fluctuate with the demand for air travel, which is highly sensitive to swings in the economy. During downturns, as air traffic declines, the hiring of flight attendants declines, and some experienced attendants may be laid off until traffic recovers.

Despite the improving outlook, competition is expected to be keen because this job usually attracts more applicants than there are jobs, with only the most qualified eventually being hired. Those applicants with at least 2 years of college and who have experience in dealing with the public should have the best chance of being hired. Also, job opportunities may be better with the faster growing regional and low-fare airlines.

The majority of job openings through the year 2012 will arise from the need to replace flight attendants who leave the labor force or transfer to other occupations, often for higher earnings or a more stable lifestyle. However, with the job now viewed increasingly as a profession, fewer flight attendants are leaving their jobs and job turnover is not as high as in the past. The average job tenure of attendants is currently more than 7 years and is increasing.

Earnings

Median annual earnings of flight attendants were $43,140 in 2002. The middle 50 percent earned between $31,660 and $66,260. The lowest 10 percent earned less than $20,890, and the highest 10 percent earned more than $91,050.

According to data from the Association of Flight Attendants, beginning flight attendants had median earnings of about $15,338 a year in 2002. However, beginning pay scales for flight attendants vary by carrier. New hires usually begin at the same pay scale regardless of experience, and all flight attendants receive the same future pay increases. Flight attendants receive extra compensation for night and international flights and for increased hours. Further, some airlines offer incentive pay for working holidays or taking positions that require additional responsibility or paperwork. Most airlines guarantee a minimum of 65 to 85 flight hours per month, with the option to work additional hours. Flight attendants also receive a "per diem" allowance for meal expenses while on duty away from home. In addition, flight attendants and their immediate families are entitled to free fares on their own airline and reduced fares on most other airlines.

Flight attendants are required to purchase uniforms and wear them while on duty. The airlines usually pay for uniform replacement items, and may provide a small allowance to cover cleaning and upkeep of the uniforms.

The majority of flight attendants hold union membership, primarily with the Association of Flight Attendants. Others may be members of the Transport Workers Union of America, the International Brotherhood of Teamsters, or other unions.

Related Occupations
Other jobs that involve helping people as a safety professional, while requiring the ability to be calm even under trying circumstances, include emergency medical technicians and paramedics and firefighting occupations.

Sources of Additional Information
Information about job opportunities and qualifications required for work at a particular airline may be obtained by writing to the airline's human resources office.

Gaming Services Occupations

(O*NET 39-1011.00, 39-1012.00, 39-3011.00, 39-3012.00, 39-3019.99, 39-3099.99)

Significant Points

- These occupations have no common minimum educational requirements; each casino establishes its own requirements for education, training, and experience.

- Workers need a license issued by a regulatory agency, such as a State casino control board or commission; licensure requires proof of residency in the State in which gaming workers are employed.

- Job prospects are best for those with a degree or certification in gaming or a hospitality-related field, previous training or experience in casino gaming, and strong interpersonal and customer service skills.

Nature of the Work
Legalized gambling in the United States today includes casino gaming, State lotteries, parimutuel wagering on contests such as horse or dog racing, and charitable gaming. Gaming, the playing of games of chance, is a multibillion-dollar industry that is responsible for the creation of a number of unique service occupations.

The majority of all gaming services workers are employed in casinos. Their duties and titles may vary from one establishment to another. Despite differences in job title and task, however, workers perform many of the same basic functions in all casinos. Some positions are associated with oversight and direction—supervision, surveillance, and investigation—while others involve working with the games or patrons themselves, performing such activities as tending slot machines, handling money, writing and running tickets, and dealing cards or running games.

Like nearly every business establishment, casinos have workers who direct and oversee day-to-day operations. *Gaming supervisors* oversee the gaming operations and personnel in an assigned area. They circulate among the tables and observe the operations to ensure that all of the stations and games are covered for each shift. It is not uncommon for gaming supervisors to explain and interpret the operating rules of the house to patrons who may have difficulty understanding the rules. Gaming supervisors also may plan and organize activities to create a friendly atmosphere for the guests staying in their hotels or in casino hotels. Periodically, they address and adjust complaints about service.

Some gaming occupations demand specially acquired skills—dealing blackjack, for example—that are unique to casino work. Others require skills common to most businesses, such as the ability to conduct financial transactions. In both capacities, the workers in these jobs interact directly with patrons in attending to slot machines, making change, cashing or selling tokens and coins, writing and running for other games, and dealing cards at table games. Part of their responsibility is to make those interactions enjoyable.

Slot key persons, also called slot attendants or slot technicians, coordinate and supervise the slot department and its workers. Their duties include verifying and handling payoff winnings to patrons, resetting slot machines after completing the payoff, and refilling machines with money. Slot key persons must be familiar with a variety of slot machines and be able to make minor repairs and adjustments to the machines as needed. If major repairs are required, slot key persons determine whether the slot machine should be removed from the floor. Working the

Slot key persons must be familiar with a variety of slot machines and be able to make minor repairs and adjustments to the machines as needed.

floor as frontline personnel, they enforce safety rules and report hazards.

Gaming and sportsbook writers and runners assist in the operations of games such as bingo and keno, in addition to taking bets on sporting events. They scan tickets presented by patrons and calculate and distribute winnings. Some writers and runners operate the equipment that randomly selects the numbers. Others may announce numbers selected, pick up tickets from patrons, collect bets, or receive, verify, and record patrons' cash wagers.

Gaming dealers operate table games such as craps, blackjack, and roulette. Standing or sitting behind the table, dealers provide dice, dispense cards to players, or run the equipment. Some dealers also monitor the patrons for infractions of casino rules. Gaming dealers must be skilled in customer service and in executing their game. Dealers determine winners, calculate and pay winning bets, and collect losing bets. Because of the fast-paced work environment, most gaming dealers are competent in at least two games, usually blackjack and craps.

Working Conditions

The atmosphere in casinos is generally filled with fun and often considered glamorous. However, casino work can also be physically demanding. Most occupations require that workers stand for long periods; some require the lifting of heavy items. The "glamorous" atmosphere exposes casino workers to certain hazards, such as cigarette, cigar, and pipe smoke. Noise from slot machines, gaming tables, and talking workers and patrons may be distracting to some, although workers wear protective headgear in areas where loud machinery is used to count money.

Most casinos are open 24 hours a day, seven day a week and offer three staggered shifts.

Employment

Gaming services' occupations held 192,000 jobs in 2002. Employment by occupational specialty was distributed as follows:

Gaming dealers	78,000
Gaming supervisors	39,000
Slot key persons	21,000
Gaming and sports book writers & runners	14,000
All other gaming service workers	40,000

Gaming services workers are found mainly in the traveler accommodation and gaming industries. Most are employed in commercial casinos, including land-based or riverboat casinos, in 11 States: Colorado, Illinois, Indiana, Iowa, Louisiana, Michigan, Mississippi, Missouri, Nevada, New Jersey, and South Dakota. The largest number works in land-based casinos in Nevada, and the second-largest group works in similar establishments in New Jersey. Mississippi, which boasts the greatest number of riverboat casinos in operation, employs the most workers in that venue. In addition, there are 23 States with Indian casinos. Legal lotteries are held in 40 States and the District of Columbia, and parimutuel wagering is legal in 41 States. Forty-seven States and the District of Columbia also allow charitable gaming.

For most workers, gaming licensure requires proof of residency in the State in which gaming workers are employed. But some gaming services workers do not limit themselves to one State or even one country, finding jobs on the small number of casinos located on luxury cruise liners that travel the world. These individuals live and work aboard the vessel.

Training, Other Qualifications, and Advancement

There usually are no minimum educational requirements for entry-level gaming jobs, although most employers prefer a high school diploma or GED. However, entry-level gaming services workers are required to have a license issued by a regulatory agency, such as a State casino control board or commission. Applicants for a license must provide photo identification, offer proof of residency in the State in which they anticipate working, and pay a fee. Age requirements vary by State. The licensing application process also includes a background investigation.

In addition to possessing a license, gaming services workers need superior customer service skills. Casino gaming workers provide entertainment and hospitality to patrons, and the quality of their service contributes to an establishment's success or failure. Therefore, gaming workers need good communication skills, an outgoing personality, and the ability to maintain their composure even when dealing with angry or demanding patrons. Personal integrity also is important, because workers handle large amounts of money.

Each casino establishes its own requirements for education, training, and experience. Almost all provide some in-house training in addition to requiring certification. The type and quantity of classes needed may vary.

Many institutions of higher learning give training toward certification in gaming, as well as offering an associate's, bachelor's, or master's degree in a hospitality-related field such as hospitality management, hospitality administration, or hotel management. Some schools offer training in games, gaming supervision, slot attendant and slot repair technician work, slot department management, and surveillance and security.

Gaming services workers who manage money should have some experience handling cash or using calculators or computers. For such positions, most casinos administer a math test to assess an applicant's level of competency.

Most casino supervisory staff have an associate's or bachelor's degree. Supervisors who do not have a degree usually substitute hands-on experience for formal education. Regardless of their educational background, most supervisors gain experience in other gaming occupations before moving into supervisory positions, because knowledge of games and casino operations is essential for these workers. Gaming supervisors must have leadership qualities and good communication skills to supervise employees effectively and to deal with patrons in a way that encourages return visits.

Slot key persons do not need to meet formal educational requirements to enter the occupation, but completion of slot attendant or slot technician training is helpful. As with most other gaming workers, slot key persons receive on-the-job training during the first several weeks of employment. Most slot key positions are entry level, so a desire to learn is important. Slot key persons need good communication skills and an ability to remain calm, even when dealing with angry or demanding patrons. Personal integrity also is important, because these workers handle large sums of money.

Gaming and sportsbook writers and runners must have at least a high school diploma or GED. Most of these workers receive on-the-job training. Because gaming and sportsbook writers and runners work closely with patrons, they need excellent customer service skills.

Nearly all gaming dealers are certified. Certification is available through 2- or 4-year programs in gaming or a hospitality-related field. Experienced dealers, who often are able to attract new or return business, have the best job prospects. Dealers with more experience are placed at the "high-roller" tables.

Advancement opportunities in casino gaming depend less on workers' previous casino duties and titles than on their ability and eagerness to learn new jobs. For example, an entry-level gaming worker eventually might advance to become a dealer or card room manager or to assume some other supervisory position.

Job Outlook

With demand for gaming showing no sign of waning, employment in gaming services occupations is projected to grow faster than the average for all occupations through 2012. Even during the recent downturn in the economy, profits at casinos have risen. With many States benefiting from casino gambling in the form of tax revenue or compacts with Indian tribes, additional States are rethinking their opposition to legalized gambling and will likely approve the building of more casinos and other gaming formats during the next decade. Job prospects in gaming services occupations will be best for those with a degree or certification in gaming or a hospitality-related field, previous casino gaming training or experience, and strong interpersonal and customer service skills. As a direct result of increasing demand for additional table games in gaming establishments, the most rapid growth is expected among gaming dealers. In addition to job openings arising from employment growth, opportunities will result from the need to replace workers transferring to other occupations or leaving the labor force.

The increase in gaming reflects growth in the population and in its disposable income, both of which are expected to continue. Also, more domestic and international competition for gaming patrons and higher expectations among gaming patrons for customer service should result in more jobs for gaming services workers. Job growth is expected in established gaming areas such as Las Vegas, Nevada, and Atlantic City, New Jersey, as well as in other States and areas that may legalize gaming in the coming years, including Indian tribal lands.

Earnings

Wage earnings for gaming services workers vary according to occupation, level of experience, training, location, and size of the gaming establishment. The following were median earnings for various gaming services occupations in 2002:

Gaming supervisors	$39,290
Slot key persons	22,870
Gaming and sports book writers and runners	18,660
Gaming dealers	14,090

Related Occupations

Many other occupations provide hospitality and customer service. Some examples of related occupations are security guards and gaming surveillance officers, recreation and fitness workers, sales worker supervisors, cashiers, gaming change persons and booth cashiers, retail salespersons, gaming cage workers, and tellers.

Sources of Additional Information

For additional information on careers in gaming, visit your public library and your State gaming regulatory agency or casino control commission.

Information on careers in gaming also is available from:
➤ American Gaming Association, 555 13th St. NW., Suite 1010 East, Washington, DC 20004. Internet: **http://www.americangaming.org**

Personal and Home Care Aides

(0*NET 39-9021.00)

Significant Points

● Excellent job opportunities are expected, due to rapid employment growth and high replacement needs.

● Almost a third of personal and home care aides work part time; most aides work with a number of different clients, each job lasting a few hours, days, or weeks.

● Occupational characteristics include low skill requirements, low pay, and high emotional demands.

Nature of the Work

Personal and home care aides help elderly, disabled, and ill persons live in their own homes or in residential care facilities instead of in a health facility. Most personal and home care aides work with elderly or disabled clients who need more extensive personal and home care than family or friends can provide. Some aides work with families in which a parent is incapacitated and small children need care. Others help discharged hospital patients who have relatively short-term needs. *(Home health aides—who provide health-related services, rather than*

Personal and home care aides help patients live in their own homes or in residential care facilities, instead of in a health facility.

mainly housekeeping and routine personal care—are discussed in the statement on nursing, psychiatric, and home health aides, elsewhere in the *Handbook*.)

Personal and home care aides—also called homemakers, caregivers, companions, and personal attendants—provide housekeeping and routine personal care services. They clean clients' houses, do laundry, and change bed linens. Aides may plan meals (including special diets), shop for food, and cook. Aides also may help clients move from bed, bathe, dress, and groom. Some accompany clients outside the home, serving as a guide and companion.

Personal and home care aides provide instruction and psychological support to their patients. They may advise families and patients on such things as nutrition, cleanliness, and household tasks. Aides also may assist in toilet training a severely mentally handicapped child, or they may just listen to clients talk about their problems.

In home healthcare agencies, a registered nurse, physical therapist, or social worker assigns specific duties and supervises personal and home care aides. Aides keep records of services performed and of clients' condition and progress. They report changes in the client's condition to the supervisor or case manager. In carrying out their work, aides cooperate with other healthcare professionals, including registered nurses, therapists, and other medical staff.

Working Conditions

The personal and home care aide's daily routine may vary. Aides may go to the same home every day for months or even years. However, most aides work with a number of different clients, each job lasting a few hours, days, or weeks. Aides often visit four or five clients on the same day.

Surroundings differ from case to case. Some homes are neat and pleasant, whereas others are untidy or depressing. Some clients are pleasant and cooperative; others are angry, abusive, depressed, or otherwise difficult.

Personal and home care aides generally work on their own, with periodic visits by their supervisor. They receive detailed instructions explaining when to visit clients and what services to perform for them. Almost a third of aides work part time, and some work weekends or evenings to suit the needs of their clients.

Aides are individually responsible for getting to the client's home. They may spend a good portion of the working day traveling from one client to another. Because mechanical lifting devices that are available in institutional settings are seldom available in patients' homes, aides must be careful to avoid overexertion or injury when they assist clients.

Employment

Personal and home care aides held about 608,000 jobs in 2002. The majority of jobs were in home healthcare services, individual and family services, private households, and residential mental retardation, mental health, and substance abuse facilities. Self-employed aides have no agency affiliation or supervision and accept clients, set fees, and arrange work schedules on their own.

Training, Other Qualifications, and Advancement

In some States, this occupation is open to individuals who have no formal training. On-the-job training is then generally provided. Other States may require formal training. The National Association for Home Care offers national certification for per-

sonal and home care aides. Certification is a voluntary demonstration that the individual has met industry standards.

Successful personal and home care aides like to help people and do not mind hard work. They should be responsible, compassionate, emotionally stable, and cheerful. In addition, aides should be tactful, honest, and discreet, because they work in private homes. Aides also must be in good health. A physical examination, including State-mandated tests, such as those for tuberculosis, may be required.

Advancement for personal and home care aides is limited. In some agencies, workers start out performing homemaker duties, such as cleaning. With experience and training, they may take on personal care duties.

Job Outlook

Excellent job opportunities are expected for this occupation, as rapid employment growth and high replacement needs produce a large number of job openings.

Employment of personal and home care aides is projected to grow much faster than the average for all occupations through the year 2012. The number of elderly people, an age group characterized by mounting health problems and requiring some assistance, is projected to rise substantially. In addition to the elderly, however, patients in other age groups will increasingly rely on home care, a trend that reflects several developments, including efforts to contain costs by moving patients out of hospitals and nursing care facilities as quickly as possible, the realization that treatment can be more effective in familiar rather than clinical surroundings, and the development and improvement of medical technologies for in-home treatment.

In addition to job openings created by the increase in demand for these workers, replacement needs are expected to produce numerous openings. The relatively low skill requirements, low pay, and high emotional demands of the work result in high replacement needs. For these same reasons, many people are reluctant to seek jobs in the occupation. Therefore, persons who are interested in and suited for this work—particularly those with experience or training as personal care, home health, or nursing aides—should have excellent job opportunities.

Earnings

Median hourly earnings of personal and home care aides were $7.81 in 2002. The middle 50 percent earned between $6.65 and $9.06 an hour. The lowest 10 percent earned less than $5.90, and the highest 10 percent earned more than $10.67 an hour. Median hourly earnings in the industries employing the largest numbers of personal and home care aides in 2002 were as follows:

Residential mental retardation, mental health and substance abuse facilities	$8.63
Vocational rehabilitation services	8.40
Community care facilities for the elderly	8.14
Individual and family services	8.12
Home health care services	6.72

Most employers give slight pay increases with experience and added responsibility. Aides usually are paid only for the time they work in the home and normally are not paid for travel time between jobs. Employers often hire on-call hourly workers and provide no benefits.

Related Occupations

Personal and home care aide is a service occupation combining the duties of caregivers and social service workers. Workers in related occupations that involve personal contact to help others include childcare workers; nursing, psychiatric, and home health aides; occupational therapist assistants and aides; and physical therapist assistants and aides.

Sources of Additional Information

General information about training, referrals to State and local agencies about job opportunities, a list of relevant publications, and information on certification for personal and home care aides are available from:

➤ National Association for Home Care, 228 7th St. SE., Washington, DC 20003. Internet: **http://www.nahc.org**

Recreation and Fitness Workers

(O*NET 39-9031.00, 39-9032.00)

Significant Points

● Educational requirements for recreation workers range from a high school diploma to a graduate degree, whereas fitness workers usually need certification.

● Competition will remain keen for full-time career positions in recreation; however, job prospects for fitness workers will be more favorable.

● The recreation field offers many part-time and seasonal job opportunities.

Nature of the Work

People spend much of their leisure time participating in a wide variety of organized recreational activities, such as aerobics, arts and crafts, the performing arts, camping, and sports. Recreation and fitness workers plan, organize, and direct these activities in local playgrounds and recreation areas, parks, community centers, health clubs, fitness centers, religious organizations, camps, theme parks, and tourist attractions. Increasingly, recreational and fitness workers also are found in workplaces, where they organize and direct leisure activities and athletic programs for employees of all ages.

Recreation workers hold a variety of positions at different levels of responsibility. *Recreation leaders,* who are responsible for a recreation program's daily operation, primarily organize and direct participants. They may lead and give instruction in dance, drama, crafts, games, and sports; schedule use of facilities; keep records of equipment use; and ensure that recreation facilities and equipment are used properly. Workers who provide instruction and coach groups in specialties such as art, music, drama, swimming, or tennis may be called *activity specialists. Recreation supervisors* oversee recreation leaders and plan, organize, and manage recreational activities to meet the needs of a variety of populations. These workers often serve as liaisons between the director of the park or recreation center and the recreation leaders. Recreation supervisors with more specialized responsibilities also may direct special activities or events or oversee a major activity, such as aquatics, gymnastics, or performing arts. *Directors of recreation and parks* develop and manage comprehensive recreation programs in parks, playgrounds, and other settings. Directors usually serve as technical advisors to State and local recreation and park commissions and may be responsible for recreation and park budgets. (Workers in a related occupation, *recreational therapists,* help individuals to recover from or adjust to illness, disability, or specific social problems; this occupation is described elsewhere in the *Handbook.*)

Camp counselors lead and instruct children and teenagers in outdoor-oriented forms of recreation, such as swimming, hiking, horseback riding, and camping. In addition, counselors provide campers with specialized instruction in subjects such as archery, boating, music, drama, gymnastics, tennis, and computers. In resident camps, counselors also provide guidance and supervise daily living and general socialization. *Camp directors* typically supervise camp counselors, plan camp activities or programs, and perform the various administrative functions of a camp.

Fitness workers instruct or coach groups or individuals in various exercise activities. Because gyms and health clubs offer a variety of exercise activities such as weightlifting, yoga, aerobics, and karate, fitness workers typically specialize in only a few areas. *Fitness trainers* help clients to assess their level of physical fitness and help them to set and reach fitness goals. They also demonstrate various exercises and help clients to improve their exercise techniques. They may keep records of their clients' exercise sessions in order to assess their progress towards physical fitness. *Personal trainers* work with clients on a one-on-one basis in either a gym or the client's home. *Aerobics instructors* conduct group exercise sessions that involve aerobic exercise, stretching, and muscle conditioning. Some fitness workers may perform the duties of both aerobics instructors and fitness trainers. *Fitness directors* oversee the operations of a health club or fitness center. Their work involves creating and maintaining programs that meet the needs of the club's members. (Workers in a related occupation—*athletes, coaches, umpires, and related workers*—participate in organized sports; this occupation is described elsewhere in the *Handbook.*)

Working Conditions

Recreation and fitness workers may work in a variety of settings—for example, a health club, cruise ship, woodland recreational park, or playground in the center of a large urban community. Regardless of setting, most recreation workers spend

Fitness trainers demonstrate various exercises and help clients to improve their exercise techniques.

much of their time outdoors and may work in a variety of weather conditions, whereas most fitness workers spend their time indoors at fitness centers and health clubs. Recreation and fitness directors and supervisors, however, typically spend most of their time in an office, planning programs and special events. Directors and supervisors generally engage in less physical activity than do lower level recreation and fitness workers. Nevertheless, recreation and fitness workers at all levels risk suffering injuries during physical activities.

Many recreation and fitness workers work about 40 hours a week. People entering this field, especially camp counselors, should expect some night and weekend work and irregular hours. About 36 percent work part time and many recreation jobs are seasonal.

Employment

Recreation and fitness workers held about 485,000 jobs in 2002, and many additional workers held summer jobs in this occupation. About 62 percent were recreation workers; the rest were fitness trainers and aerobics instructors. Of those with year-round jobs as recreation workers, almost 40 percent worked for local governments, primarily in the park and recreation departments. Around 14 percent of recreation workers were employed in civic and social organizations, such as the Boy or Girl Scouts or Red Cross. Another 12 percent of recreation workers were employed by nursing and other personal care facilities.

Almost all fitness trainers and aerobics instructors worked in physical fitness facilities, health clubs, and fitness centers, mainly within the amusement and recreation services industry or civic and social organizations. About 5 percent of fitness workers were self-employed; many of these were personal trainers.

The recreation field has an unusually large number of part-time, seasonal, and volunteer jobs. These jobs include summer camp counselors, craft specialists, and afterschool and weekend recreation program leaders. In addition, many teachers and college students accept jobs as recreation and fitness workers when school is not in session. The vast majority of volunteers serve as activity leaders at local day-camp programs, or in youth organizations, camps, nursing homes, hospitals, senior centers, and other settings.

Training, Other Qualifications, and Advancement

Educational requirements for recreation workers range from a high school diploma—or sometimes less for many summer jobs—to graduate degrees for some administrative positions in large public recreation systems. Full-time career professional positions usually require a college degree with a major in parks and recreation or leisure studies, but a bachelor's degree in any liberal arts field may be sufficient for some jobs in the private sector. In industrial recreation, or "employee services" as it is more commonly called, companies prefer to hire those with a bachelor's degree in recreation or leisure studies and a background in business administration.

Specialized training or experience in a particular field, such as art, music, drama, or athletics, is an asset for many jobs. Some jobs also require certification. For example, a lifesaving certificate is a prerequisite for teaching or coaching water-related activities. Graduates of associate degree programs in parks and recreation, social work, and other human services disciplines also enter some career recreation positions. High school graduates occasionally enter career positions, but this is not common. Some college students work part time as recreation workers while earning degrees.

A bachelor's degree and experience are preferred for most recreation supervisor jobs and required for higher level administrative jobs. However, an increasing number of recreation workers who aspire to administrative positions obtain master's degrees in parks and recreation or related disciplines. Certification in the recreation field may be helpful for advancement. Also, many persons in other disciplines, including social work, forestry, and resource management, pursue graduate degrees in recreation.

Programs leading to an associate or bachelor's degree in parks and recreation, leisure studies, or related fields are offered at several hundred colleges and universities. Many also offer master's or doctoral degrees in the field. In 2002, 100 bachelor's degree programs in parks and recreation were accredited by the National Recreation and Park Association (NRPA). Accredited programs provide broad exposure to the history, theory, and practice of park and recreation management. Courses offered include community organization; supervision and administration; recreational needs of special populations, such as the elderly or disabled; and supervised fieldwork. Students may specialize in areas such as therapeutic recreation, park management, outdoor recreation, industrial or commercial recreation, or camp management. Certification in the recreation field is offered by the NRPA National Certification Board. Continuing education is necessary to remain certified.

Generally, fitness trainers and aerobics instructors must obtain a certification in the fitness field to obtain employment. Certification may be offered in various areas of exercise such as personal training, weight training, and aerobics. There are many organizations that offer certification testing in the fitness field, some of which are listed in the Sources of Additional Information section of this statement. Certification generally is good for 2 years, after which workers must become recertified. Recertification is accomplished by attending continuing education classes. Most fitness workers are required to maintain a cardiopulmonary resuscitation (CPR) certification. Some employers also require workers to be certified in first aid.

An increasing number of employers require fitness workers to have a bachelor's degree in a field related to health or fitness, such as exercise science or physical education. Some employers allow workers to substitute a college degree for certification, while others require both a degree and certification. A bachelor's degree and, in some cases, a master's degree in exercise science, physical education, or a related area, along with experience, usually is required to advance to management positions in a health club or fitness center. Many fitness workers become personal trainers, in addition to their main job in a fitness center, or as a full-time job. Some workers go into business for themselves and open up their own fitness centers.

Persons planning recreation and fitness careers should be outgoing, good at motivating people, and sensitive to the needs of others. Excellent health and physical fitness are required due to the physical nature of the job. Volunteer experience, part-time work during school, or a summer job can lead to a full-time career as a recreation worker. As in many fields, managerial skills are needed to advance to supervisory or managerial positions. College courses in management, business administration, accounting, and personnel management are helpful for advancement to supervisory or managerial jobs.

Job Outlook

Competition will be keen for career positions as recreation workers because the field attracts many applicants and because the number of career positions is limited compared with the number of lower level seasonal jobs. Opportunities for staff positions should be best for persons with formal training and experience gained in part-time or seasonal recreation jobs. Those with graduate degrees should have the best opportunities for supervisory or administrative positions. Opportunities are expected to be better for fitness trainers and aerobics instructors because of relatively rapid growth in employment. Job openings for both recreation and fitness workers also will stem from the need to replace the large numbers of workers who leave these occupations each year.

Overall employment of recreation and fitness workers is expected to grow faster than the average for all occupations through 2012, as an increasing number of people spend more time and money on recreation, fitness, and leisure services and as more businesses recognize the benefits of recreation and fitness programs and other services such as wellness programs. Average employment growth is projected for recreation workers—reflecting growth in local government and civic and social organizations, industries that employ just over half of all recreation workers. Employment growth among recreation workers may be inhibited, however, by budget constraints that some local governments may face over the 2002-12 projection period. Employment of fitness workers—who are concentrated in the rapidly growing arts, entertainment and recreation industry—is expected to increase much faster than average due to rising interest in personal training, aerobics instruction, and other fitness activities.

The recreation field provides a large number of temporary, seasonal jobs. These positions, which typically are filled by high school or college students, generally do not have formal education requirements and are open to anyone with the desired personal qualities. Employers compete for a share of the vacationing student labor force and, although salaries in recreation often are lower than those in other fields, the nature of the work and the opportunity to work outdoors are attractive to many.

Earnings
Median hourly earnings of recreation workers who worked full time in 2002 were $8.69. The middle 50 percent earned between about $7.09 and $11.36, while the top 10 percent earned $15.72 or more. However, earnings of recreation directors and others in supervisory or managerial positions can be substantially higher. Most public and private recreation agencies provide full-time recreation workers with typical benefits; part-time workers receive few, if any, benefits. Median hourly earnings in the industries employing the largest numbers of recreation workers in 2002 were:

Nursing care facilities	$9.30
Local government	8.98
Individual and family services	8.71
Civic and social organizations	7.73
Other amusement and recreation industries	7.53

Median hourly earnings of fitness trainers and aerobics instructors in 2002 were $11.51. The middle 50 percent earned between $8.06 and $18.18, while the top 10 percent earned $26.22 or more. Earnings of successful self-employed personal trainers can be much higher. Median hourly earnings in the industries employing the largest numbers of recreation workers in 2002 were:

Other amusement and recreation industries	$13.81
Civic and social organizations	9.24
Other schools and instruction	8.93

Related Occupations
Recreation workers must exhibit leadership and sensitivity when dealing with people. Other occupations that require similar personal qualities include counselors, probation officers and correctional treatment specialists, psychologists, recreational therapists, and social workers. Occupations that focus on physical fitness, as do fitness workers, include athletes, coaches, umpires, and related workers.

Sources of Additional Information
For information on jobs in recreation, contact employers such as local government departments of parks and recreation, nursing and personal care facilities, the Boy or Girl Scouts, or local social or religious organizations.

For information on careers, certification, and academic programs in parks and recreation, contact:
➤ National Recreation and Park Association, Division of Professional Services, 22377 Belmont Ridge Rd., Ashburn, VA 20148-4501. Internet: **http://www.nrpa.org**

For career information about camp counselors, contact:
➤ American Camping Association, 5000 State Road 67 North, Martinsville, IN 46151-7902. Internet: **http://www.acacamps.org**

For information on careers and certification in the fitness field, contact:
➤ American Council on Exercise, 4851 Paramount Dr., San Diego, CA 92123. Internet: **http://www.acefitness.org**
➤ National Strength and Conditioning Association, 4575 Galley Rd., Suite 400B, Colorado Springs, CO 80915. Internet: **http://www.nsca-lift.org**
➤ American College of Sports Medicine, PO Box 1440, Indianapolis, IN 46206-1440. Internet: **http://www.acsm.org**

Sales and Related Occupations

Cashiers

(O*NET 41-2011.00, 41-2012.00)

Significant Points

- Cashiers are trained on the job; this occupation provides opportunities for many young people with no previous work experience.
- Nearly one-half of all cashiers work part time.
- Good employment opportunities are expected because of the large number of workers who leave this occupation each year.
- Many cashiers start at the Federal minimum wage.

Nature of the Work

Supermarkets, department stores, gasoline service stations, movie theaters, restaurants, and many other businesses employ cashiers to register the sale of their merchandise. Most cashiers total bills, receive money, make change, fill out charge forms, and give receipts.

Although specific job duties vary by employer, cashiers usually are assigned to a register at the beginning of their shifts and are given drawers containing a specific amount of money with which to start—their "banks." They must count their banks to ensure that they contain the correct amount of money and adequate supplies of change. At the end of their shifts, they once again count the drawers' contents and compare the totals with sales data. An occasional shortage of small amounts may be overlooked but, in many establishments, repeated shortages are grounds for dismissal.

In addition to counting the contents of their drawers at the end of their shifts, cashiers usually separate and total charge forms, return slips, coupons, and any other noncash items. Cashiers also handle returns and exchanges. They must ensure that returned merchandise is in good condition, and determine where and when it was purchased and what type of payment was used.

After entering charges for all items and subtracting the value of any coupons or special discounts, cashiers total the customer's bill and take payment. Acceptable forms of payment include cash, personal checks, credit cards, and debit cards. Cashiers must know the store's policies and procedures for each type of payment the store accepts. For checks and charges, they may request additional identification from the customer or call in for an authorization. They must verify the age of customers purchasing alcohol or tobacco. When the sale is complete, cashiers issue a receipt to the customer and return the appropriate change. They may also wrap or bag the purchase.

Cashiers traditionally have totaled customers' purchases using cash registers—manually entering the price of each product bought. However, most establishments now use more sophisticated equipment, such as scanners and computers. In a store with scanners, a cashier passes a product's Universal Product Code over the scanning device, which transmits the code number to a computer. The computer identifies the item and its price. In other establishments, cashiers manually enter codes into computers, and descriptions of the items and their prices appear on the screen.

Cashiers are expected to have good employment opportunities because of the large number of workers who leave this occupation each year.

Depending on the type of establishment, cashiers may have other duties as well. In many supermarkets, for example, cashiers weigh produce and bulk food, as well as return unwanted items to the shelves. In convenience stores, cashiers may be required to know how to use a variety of machines other than cash registers, and how to furnish money orders and sell lottery tickets. Operating ticket-dispensing machines and answering customers' questions are common duties for cashiers who work at movie theaters and ticket agencies. In casinos, *gaming change persons* and *booth cashiers* exchange coins and tokens and may issue payoffs. They may also operate a booth in the slot-machine area and furnish change persons with a money bank at the start of the shift, or count and audit money in drawers

Working Conditions

Nearly one-half of all cashiers work part time. Hours of work often vary depending on the needs of the employer. Generally, cashiers are expected to work weekends, evenings, and holidays to accommodate customers' needs. However, many employers offer flexible schedules. For example, full-time workers who work on weekends may receive time off during the week. Because the holiday season is the busiest time for most retailers, many employers restrict the use of vacation time from Thanksgiving through the beginning of January.

Most cashiers work indoors, usually standing in booths or behind counters. In addition, they often are unable to leave their workstations without supervisory approval because they are responsible for large sums of money. The work of cashiers can be very repetitious, but improvements in workstation design are being made to combat problems caused by repetitive motion. In addition, the work can sometimes be dangerous; cashiers' risk from workplace homicides is much higher than that of the total workforce.

Employment

Cashiers held about 3.5 million jobs in 2002. Although cashiers are employed in almost every industry, 26 percent of all jobs were in food and beverage stores. Gasoline stations, department stores, other retail establishments, and restaurants also employed large numbers of these workers. Outside of retail establishments, many cashiers worked in amusement, gambling, and recreation industries, local government, and personal and laundry services. Because cashiers are needed in businesses and organizations of all types and sizes, job opportunities are found throughout the country.

Training, Other Qualifications, and Advancement

Cashier jobs tend to be entry-level positions requiring little or no previous work experience. Although there are no specific educational requirements, employers filling full-time jobs often prefer applicants with high school diplomas.

Nearly all cashiers are trained on the job. In small businesses, an experienced worker often trains beginners. The trainee spends the first day observing the operation and becoming familiar with the store's equipment, policies, and procedures. After this, trainees are assigned to a register—frequently under the supervision of an experienced worker. In larger businesses, trainees spend several days in classes before being placed at cash registers. Topics typically covered in class include a description of the industry and the company, store policies and procedures, equipment operation, and security.

Training for experienced workers is not common, except when new equipment is introduced or when procedures change. In these cases, the employer or a representative of the equipment manufacturer trains workers on the job.

Persons who want to become cashiers should be able to do repetitious work accurately. They also need basic mathematics skills and good manual dexterity. Because cashiers deal constantly with the public, they should be neat in appearance and able to deal tactfully and pleasantly with customers. In addition, some businesses prefer to hire persons who can operate specialized equipment or who have business experience, such as typing, selling, or handling money.

Advancement opportunities for cashiers vary. For those working part time, promotion may be to a full-time position. Others advance to head cashier or cash-office clerk. In addition, this job offers a good opportunity to learn about an employer's business and can serve as a steppingstone to a more responsible position.

Job Outlook

Opportunities for full-time and part-time cashier jobs should continue to be good, because of employment growth and the need to replace the large number of workers who transfer to other occupations or leave the labor force. There is substantial movement into and out of the occupation because education and training requirements are minimal, and the predominance of part-time jobs is attractive to people seeking a short-term source of income rather than a full-time career. Historically, workers under the age of 25 have filled many of the openings in this occupation—in 2002, one-half of all cashiers were 24 years of age or younger. Some establishments have begun hiring elderly and disabled persons to fill some of their job openings.

Cashier employment is expected to grow about as fast as the average for all occupations through the year 2012 because of expanding demand for goods and services by a growing population. The rising popularity of electronic commerce, which does not require a cashier to complete a transaction or accept payment, may reduce the employment growth of cashiers. However, electronic commerce will have a limited impact on this large occupation, as many consumers lack Internet access or still prefer the traditional method of purchasing goods at stores. The growing use of self-service check-out systems in retail trade, especially at grocery stores, may also have an adverse effect on employment of cashiers. This

trend, however, will largely depend on the public's acceptance of the new self-service technology.

Job opportunities may vary from year to year, because the strength of the economy affects demand for cashiers. Companies tend to hire more persons for such jobs when the economy is strong. Seasonal demand for cashiers also causes fluctuations in employment.

Earnings

Many cashiers start at the Federal minimum wage, which was $5.15 an hour in 2003. Some State laws set the minimum wage higher, and establishments must pay at least that amount. Wages tend to be higher in areas in which there is intense competition for workers.

Median hourly earnings of cashiers, except gaming in 2002 were $7.41. The middle 50 percent earned between $6.51 and $8.73 an hour. The lowest 10 percent earned less than $5.86, and the highest 10 percent earned more than $10.97 an hour. Median hourly earnings in the industries employing the largest numbers of cashiers in 2002 were as follows:

Grocery stores	$7.57
Department stores	7.55
Other general merchandise store	7.27
Gasoline stations	7.18
Health and personal care stores	7.08

Benefits for full-time cashiers tend to be better than those for cashiers working part time. In addition to typical benefits, those working in retail establishments often receive discounts on purchases, and cashiers in restaurants may receive free or low-cost meals. Some employers also offer employee stock-option plans and education-reimbursement plans.

Related Occupations

Cashiers accept payment for the purchase of goods and services. Other workers with similar duties include tellers, counter and rental clerks, food and beverage serving and related workers, gaming cage workers, Postal Service workers, and retail salespersons, all of whom are discussed elsewhere in the *Handbook*.

Sources of Additional Information

General information on retailing is available from:
➤ National Retail Federation, 325 7th St. NW., Suite 1100, Washington, DC 20004.

For information about employment opportunities as a cashier, contact:
➤ National Association of Convenience Stores, 1605 King St., Alexandria, VA 22314-2792.
➤ United Food and Commercial Workers International Union, Education Office, 1775 K St. NW., Washington, DC 20006-1502.

Counter and Rental Clerks

(0*NET 41-2021.00)

Significant Points

● Jobs are primarily entry-level and require little or no experience and minimal formal education.

● Faster-than-average employment growth is expected as businesses strive to improve customer service.

● Part-time employment opportunities should be plentiful.

Nature of the Work

Whether renting videotapes, air compressors, or moving vans, or dropping off clothes to be drycleaned or appliances to be serviced, we rely on counter and rental clerks to handle these transactions efficiently. Although the specific duties of these workers vary by establishment, counter and rental clerks answer questions involving product availability, cost, and rental provisions. Counter and rental clerks also take orders, calculate fees, receive payments, and accept returned merchandise. (Cashiers and retail salespersons, two occupations with similar duties, are discussed elsewhere in the *Handbook*.)

Regardless of where they work, counter and rental clerks must be knowledgeable about the company's services, policies, and procedures. Depending on the type of establishment, counter and rental clerks use their special knowledge to give advice on a wide variety of products and services, ranging from hydraulic tools to shoe repair. For example, in the car rental industry, these workers inform customers about the features of different types of automobiles, as well as daily and weekly rental costs. They also ensure that customers meet age and other requirements for renting cars, and they indicate when and in what condition the cars must be returned. Those in the equipment rental industry have similar duties, but must also know how to operate and care for the machinery rented. In drycleaning establishments, counter clerks inform customers when items will be ready and what the effects, if any, of the chemicals used on garments are. In video rental stores, counter clerks advise

Counter and rental clerks must be knowledgeable about the products and services that their firm provides.

customers about the use of video and game players and the length of a rental, scan returned movies and games, restock shelves, handle money, and log daily reports.

When taking orders, counter and rental clerks use various types of equipment. In some establishments, they write out tickets and order forms, although most use computers or bar-code scanners. Most of these computer systems are user friendly, require very little data entry, and are customized for the firm. Scanners read the product code and display a description of the item on a computer screen. However, clerks must ensure that the data on the screen pertain to the product.

Working Conditions

Firms employing counter and rental clerks usually operate nights and weekends for the convenience of their customers. However, many employers offer flexible schedules. Some counter and rental clerks work 40-hour weeks, but about half are on part-time schedules—usually during rush periods, such as weekends, evenings, and holidays.

Working conditions usually are pleasant; most stores and service establishments are clean, well lighted, and temperature controlled. However, clerks are on their feet much of the time and may be confined behind a small counter area or be exposed to harmful chemicals. The job requires constant interaction with the public and can be stressful, especially during busy periods.

Employment

Counter and rental clerks held 436,000 jobs in 2002. About 21 percent of clerks worked in consumer goods rental, which includes video rental stores. Other large employers included drycleaning and laundry services; automotive equipment rental and leasing services; automobile dealers; amusement, gambling, and recreation industries; and grocery stores.

Counter and rental clerks are employed throughout the country, but are concentrated in metropolitan areas, where personal services and renting and leasing services are in greater demand.

Training, Other Qualifications, and Advancement

Counter and rental clerk jobs are primarily at the entry level and require little or no experience and minimal formal education. However, many employers prefer workers with at least a high school diploma.

In most companies, counter and rental clerks are trained on the job, sometimes through the use of videotapes, brochures, and pamphlets. Clerks usually learn how to operate a firm's equipment and become familiar with the firm's policies and procedures under the observation of a more experienced worker. However, some employers have formal classroom training programs lasting from a few hours to a few weeks. Topics covered in this training include the nature of the industry, the company and its policies and procedures, operation of equipment, sales techniques, and customer service. Counter and rental clerks also must become familiar with the different products and services rented or provided by their company in order to give customers the best possible service.

Counter and rental clerks should enjoy working with people and should have the ability to deal tactfully with difficult customers. They also should be able to handle several tasks at once, while continuing to provide friendly service. In addition, good oral and written communication skills are essential.

Advancement opportunities depend on the size and type of company. Many establishments that employ counter or rental clerks tend to be small businesses, making advancement difficult. But in larger establishments with a corporate structure, jobs such as counter and rental clerks offer good opportunities for workers to learn about their company's products and business practices. These jobs can lead to more responsible positions. It is common in many establishments to promote counter and rental clerks to event planner, assistant manager, or salesperson. Workers may choose to pursue related positions, such as mechanic, or even establish their own business.

In certain industries, such as equipment repair, counter and rental jobs may be an additional or alternative source of income for workers who are unemployed or semiretired. For example, retired mechanics could prove invaluable at tool rental centers because of their knowledge of, and familiarity with, tools.

Job Outlook

Employment of counter and rental clerks is expected to increase about faster than the average for all occupations through the year 2012, as all types of businesses strive to improve customer service by hiring more clerks. In addition, some industries employing counter and rental clerks—for example, rental and leasing services and amusement and recreation industries—are expected to grow rapidly. Nevertheless, most job openings will arise from the need to replace experienced workers who transfer to other occupations or leave the labor force. Part-time employment opportunities are expected to be plentiful.

Earnings

Counter and rental clerks typically start at the minimum wage, which, in establishments covered by Federal law, was $5.15 an hour in 2003. In some States, the law sets the minimum wage higher, and establishments must pay at least that amount. Wages also tend to be higher in areas where there is intense competition for workers. In addition to wages, some counter and rental clerks receive commissions, based on the number of contracts they complete or services they sell.

Median hourly earnings of counter and rental clerks in 2002 were $8.31. The middle 50 percent earned between $6.89 and $10.91 an hour. The lowest 10 percent earned less than $6.03 an hour, and the highest 10 percent earned more than $15.10 an hour. Median hourly earnings in the industries employing the largest number of counter and rental clerks in 2002 were as follows:

Automobile dealers	$16.09
Automotive equipment rental and leasing	9.69
Lessors of real estate	9.19
Drycleaning and laundry services	7.34
Amusement and recreation services	7.30

Full-time workers typically receive health and life insurance, paid vacation, and sick leave. Benefits for counter and rental clerks who work part time or for independent stores tend to be significantly less than for those who work full time. Many companies offer discounts to both full-time and part-time employees on the services they provide.

Related Occupations

Counter and rental clerks take orders and receive payment for services rendered. Other workers with similar duties include tellers, cashiers, food- and beverage-serving and related workers, gaming cage workers, Postal Service workers, and retail salespersons.

Sources of Additional Information

For general information on employment in the equipment rental industry, contact
➤ American Rental Association, 1900 19th St., Moline, IL 61265. Internet: http://www.ararental.org

For more information about the work of counter clerks in drycleaning and laundry establishments, contact:
➤ International Fabricare Institute, 12251 Tech Rd., Silver Spring, MD 20904. Internet: http://www.ifi.org

Demonstrators, Product Promoters, and Models

(0*NET 41-9011.00, 41-9012.00)

Significant Points

● Job openings should be plentiful for demonstrators and product promoters, but keen competition is expected for modeling jobs.

● Most jobs are part time or have variable work schedules, and many jobs require frequent travel.

● Formal training and education requirements are limited.

Nature of the Work

Demonstrators, product promoters, and models create public interest in buying products such as clothing, cosmetics, food items, and housewares. The information they provide helps consumers make educated choices among the wide variety of products and services available.

Demonstrators and product promoters create public interest in buying a product by demonstrating it to prospective customers and answering their questions. They may sell the demonstrated merchandise, or gather names of prospects to contact at a later date or to pass on to a sales staff. *Demonstrators* promote sales of a product to consumers, while *product promoters* try to induce retail stores to sell particular products and market them effectively. Product demonstration is an effective technique used by both to introduce new products or promote sales of old products because it allows face-to-face interaction with potential customers.

Demonstrators and product promoters build current and future sales of both sophisticated and simple products, ranging from computer software to mops. They attract an audience by offering samples, administering contests, distributing prizes, and using direct-mail advertising. They must greet and catch the attention of

Demonstrators, product promoters, and models create public interest in buying products and services.

possible customers and quickly identify those who are interested and qualified. They inform and educate customers about the features of products and demonstrate their use with apparent ease to inspire confidence in the product and its manufacturer. They also distribute information, such as brochures and applications. Some demonstrations are intended to generate immediate sales through impulse buying, while others are considered an investment to generate future sales and increase brand awareness.

Demonstrations and product promotions are conducted in retail and grocery stores, shopping malls, trade shows, and outdoor fairs. Locations are selected based on both the nature of the product and the type of audience. Demonstrations at large events may require teams of demonstrators to efficiently handle large crowds. Some demonstrators promote products on videotape or on television programs, such as "infomercials" or home shopping programs.

Demonstrators and product promoters may prepare the content of a presentation and alter it to target a specific audience or to keep it current. They may participate in the design of an exhibit or customize exhibits for particular audiences. Results obtained by demonstrators and product promoters are analyzed, and presentations are adjusted to make them more effective. Demonstrators and product promoters also may be involved in transporting, assembling, and disassembling materials used in demonstrations.

A demonstrator's presentation may include visuals, models, case studies, testimonials, test results, and surveys. The equipment used for a demonstration varies with the product being demonstrated. A food product demonstration might require the use of cooking utensils, while a software demonstration could require the use of a multimedia computer. Demonstrators must be familiar with the product to be able to relate detailed information to customers and to answer any questions that arise before, during, or after a demonstration. Therefore, they may research the product to be presented, the products of competitors, and the interests and concerns of the target audience before conducting a demonstration. Demonstrations of complex products can require practice.

Models pose for photos or as subjects for paintings or sculptures. They display clothing, such as dresses, coats, underclothing, swimwear, and suits, for a variety of audiences and in various types of media. They model accessories, such as handbags, shoes, and jewelry, and promote beauty products, including fragrances and cosmetics. The most successful models, called supermodels, hold celebrity status and often use their image to sell products such as books, calendars, and fitness videos. In addition to modeling, they may appear in movies and television shows.

Models' clients use printed publications, live modeling, and television to advertise and promote products and services. There are different categories of modeling jobs within these media, and the nature of a model's work may vary with each. Most modeling jobs are for printed publications, and models usually do a combination of editorial, commercial, and catalog work. Editorial print modeling uses still photographs of models for fashion magazine covers and to accompany feature articles, but does not include modeling for advertisements. Commercial print modeling includes work for advertisements in magazines and newspapers, and for outdoor advertisements such as billboards. Catalog models appear in department store and mail order catalogs.

During a photo shoot, a model poses to demonstrate the features of clothing and products. Models make small changes in posture and facial expression to capture the look desired by the client. As they shoot film, photographers instruct models to pose in certain positions and to interact with their physical surroundings. Models work closely with photographers, hair and clothing stylists, makeup artists, and clients to produce the desired look and to finish the photo

shoot on schedule. Stylists and makeup artists prepare the model for the photo shoot, provide touchups, and change the look of models throughout the day. If stylists are not provided, models must apply their own makeup and bring their own clothing. Because the client spends time and money planning for and preparing an advertising campaign, the client usually is present to ensure that the work is satisfactory. The client also may offer suggestions.

Editorial printwork generally pays less than other types of modeling, but provides exposure for a model and can lead to commercial modeling opportunities. Often, beginning fashion models work in foreign countries where fashion magazines are more plentiful.

Live modeling is done in a variety of locations. Live models stand, turn, and walk to demonstrate clothing to a variety of audiences. At fashion shows and in showrooms, garment buyers are the primary audience. Runway models display clothes that either are intended for direct sale to consumers or are the artistic expressions of the designer. High fashion, or haute couture, runway models confidently walk a narrow runway before an audience of photographers, journalists, designers, and garment buyers. Live modeling also is done in apparel marts, department stores, and fitting rooms of clothing designers. In retail establishments, models display clothing directly for shoppers and may be required to describe the features and price of the clothing. Other models pose for sketching artists, painters, and sculptors.

Models may compete with actors and actresses for work in television and may even receive speaking parts. Television work includes commercials, cable television programs, and even game shows. However, competition for television work is intense because of the potential for high earnings and extensive exposure.

Because advertisers need to target very specific segments of the population, models may specialize in a certain area. Petite and plus-size fashions are modeled by women whose dress size is smaller or larger than that worn by the typical model. Models who are disabled may be used to model fashions or products for disabled consumers. "Parts" models have a body part, such as a hand or foot, that is particularly well-suited to model products such as fingernail polish or shoes.

Almost all models work through agents. Agents provide a link between models and clients. Clients pay models, while the agency receives a portion of the model's earnings for its services. Agents scout for new faces, advise and train new models, and promote them to clients. A typical modeling job lasts only 1 day, so modeling agencies differ from other employment agencies in that they maintain an ongoing relationship with the model. Agents find and nurture relationships with clients, arrange auditions called "gosees," and book shoots if a model is hired. They also provide bookkeeping and billing services to models and may offer them financial planning services. Relatively short careers and high incomes make financial planning an important issue for successful models.

With the help of agents, models spend a considerable amount of time promoting and developing themselves. Models assemble and maintain portfolios, print composite cards, and travel to go-sees. A portfolio is a collection of a model's previous work that is carried to all go-sees and bookings. A composite card, or comp card, contains the best photographs from a model's portfolio, along with his or her measurements.

Models must gather information before a job. From an agent, they learn the pay, date, time, and length of the shoot. Also, models need to ask if hair, makeup, and clothing stylists will be provided. It is helpful to know what product is being promoted and what image they should project. Some models research the client and the product being modeled to prepare for a shoot. Models use a document called a voucher to record the rate of pay and the actual duration of the job. The voucher is used for billing purposes after both the client and model sign it. Once a job is completed, models must check in with their agency and plan for the next appointment.

Working Conditions

More than half of all demonstrators, product promoters, and models work part time and almost one-third have variable work schedules. Many positions last 6 months or less.

Demonstrators and product promoters may work long hours while standing or walking, with little opportunity to rest. Some of them travel frequently, and night and weekend work often is required. The atmosphere of a crowded trade show or State fair is often hectic, and demonstrators and product promoters may feel pressure to influence the greatest number of consumers possible in a very limited amount of time. However, many enjoy the opportunity to interact with a variety of people.

The work of models is both glamorous and difficult, and they may work under a variety of conditions. The coming season's fashions may be modeled in a comfortable, climate-controlled studio or in a cold, damp outdoor location. Schedules can be demanding, and models must keep in constant touch with an agent so that they do not miss an opportunity for work. Being away from friends and family, and needing to focus on the photographer's instructions despite constant interruption for touchups, clothing, and set changes can be stressful. Yet, successful models interact with a variety of people and enjoy frequent travel. They may meet potential clients at several go-sees in one day and often travel to work in distant cities, foreign countries, and exotic locations.

Employment

Demonstrators, product promoters, and models held about 179,000 jobs in 2002. Models alone held only about 4,600 jobs in 2002. About 18 percent of all salaried jobs for demonstrators, product promoters, and models were in retail trade, especially general merchandise stores, and 11 percent were in administrative and support services—which includes employment services. Other jobs were found in advertising and related services.

Demonstrator and product promoter jobs may be found in communities throughout the Nation, but modeling jobs are concentrated in New York, Miami, and Los Angeles.

Training, Other Qualifications, and Advancement

Formal training and education requirements are limited for demonstrators, product promoters, and models. Training usually is moderate term, lasting a month or more. Postsecondary education, while helpful, usually is not required. Only about one-quarter have a bachelor's degree or higher.

Demonstrators and product promoters usually receive on-the-job training. Training is primarily product oriented because a demonstrator must be familiar with the product to demonstrate it properly. The length of training varies with the complexity of the product. Experience with the product or familiarity with similar products may be required for demonstration of complex products, such as computers. During the training process, demonstrators may be introduced to the manufacturer's corporate philosophy and preferred methods for dealing with customers.

Employers look for demonstrators and product promoters with good communication skills and a pleasant appearance and personality. Demonstrators and product promoters must be comfortable with public speaking. They should be able to entertain an audience and use humor, spontaneity, and personal interest in the product as promotional tools. Foreign language skills are helpful.

While no formal training is required to begin a modeling career, models should be photogenic and have a basic knowledge of hair styling, makeup, and clothing. Some local governments require models under the age of 18 to hold a work permit. An attractive physical appearance is necessary to become a successful model. A model should have flawless skin, healthy hair, and attractive facial features. Models must be within certain ranges for height, weight, and dress or coat size in order to meet the practical needs of fashion designers, photographers, and advertisers. Requirements may change slightly from time to time as our society's perceptions about physical beauty change; however, most fashion designers feel that their clothing looks its best on tall, thin models. Although physical requirements may be relaxed for some types of modeling jobs, opportunities are limited for those who do not meet these basic requirements.

Because a model's career depends on preservation of his or her physical characteristics, models must control their diet, exercise regularly, and get enough sleep in order to stay healthy. Haircuts, pedicures, and manicures are necessary work-related expenses for models.

In addition to being attractive, models must be photogenic. The ability to relate to the camera in order to capture the desired look on film is essential, and agents test prospective models using snapshots or professional photographs. For photographic and runway work, models must be able to move gracefully and confidently. Training in acting, voice, and dance is useful and allows a model to be considered for television work. Foreign language skills are useful because successful models travel frequently to foreign countries.

Because models must interact with a large number of people, personality plays an important role in success. Models must be professional, polite, and prompt; every contact could lead to future employment. Organizational skills are necessary to manage personal lives, financial matters, and busy work and travel schedules. Because competition for jobs is stiff and clients' needs are very specific, patience and persistence are essential.

Modeling schools provide training in posing, walking, makeup application, and other basic tasks, but attending such schools does not necessarily lead to job opportunities. In fact, many agents prefer beginning models with little or no previous experience and discourage models from attending modeling schools and purchasing professional photographs. A model's selection of an agency is an important factor for advancement in the occupation. The better the reputation and skill of the agency, the more assignments a model is likely to get. Because clients prefer to work with agents, it is very difficult for a model to pursue a freelance career.

Agents continually scout for new faces, and many of the top models are discovered in this way. Most agencies review snapshots or have "open calls", during which models are seen in person; this service usually is provided free of charge. Some agencies sponsor modeling contests and searches. Very few people who send in snapshots or attend open calls are offered contracts.

Agencies advise models on how to dress, wear makeup, and conduct themselves properly during go-sees and bookings. Because models' advancement depends on their previous work, development of a good portfolio is key to getting assignments. Models accumulate and display current tear sheets—examples of a model's editorial print work—and photographs in the portfolio. The higher the quality and currency of the photos in the portfolio, the more likely it is that the model will find work.

Demonstrators and product promoters who perform well and show leadership ability may advance to other marketing and sales occupations or open their own businesses. Because modeling careers are relatively short, most models eventually transfer to other occupations.

Job Outlook

Employment of demonstrators, product promoters, and models is expected to grow fast as the average for all occupations through 2012. Job growth should be driven by increases in the number and size of trade shows and greater use of these workers in department stores and various retail shops for in-store promotions. Additional job openings will arise from the need to replace demonstrators, product promoters, and models that transfer to other occupations, retire, or stop working for other reasons.

Job openings should be plentiful for demonstrators and product promoters. Employers may have difficulty finding qualified demonstrators who are willing to fill part-time, short-term positions. Product demonstration is considered a very effective marketing tool. New jobs should arise as firms devote a greater percentage of marketing budgets to product demonstration.

On the other hand, modeling is considered a glamorous occupation, with limited formal entry requirements. Consequently, those who wish to pursue a modeling career can expect keen competition for jobs. The modeling profession typically attracts many more jobseekers than there are job openings available. Only models who closely meet the unique requirements of the occupation will achieve regular employment. The increasing diversification of the general population should boost demand for models more representative of diverse racial and ethnic groups. Work for male models also should increase as society becomes more receptive to the marketing of men's fashions. Because fashions change frequently, demand for a model's look may fluctuate. Most models experience periods of unemployment.

Employment of demonstrators, product promoters, and models is affected by downturns in the business cycle. Many firms tend to reduce advertising budgets during recessions.

Earnings

Demonstrators and product promoters had median hourly earnings of $9.80 in 2002. The middle 50 percent earned between $7.99 and $13.83. The lowest 10 percent earned less than $7.04, and the highest 10 percent earned more than $20.59. Median hourly earnings in the industries that employed the largest numbers of demonstrators and product promoters in 2002 were as follows:

Employment services	$10.41
Other support services	8.60
Advertising and related services	8.27

Employers of demonstrators, product promoters, and models generally pay for job-related travel expenses.

Median hourly earnings of models were $10.29 in 2002. The middle 50 percent earned between $8.01 and $13.65. The lowest 10 percent earned less than $6.70, and the highest 10 percent earned more than $17.62. Earnings vary for different types of modeling, and depend on the experience and reputation of the model. Female models typically earn more than male models for similar work. Hourly earnings can be relatively high, particularly for supermodels and others in high demand, but models may not have work every day, and jobs may last only a few hours. Models occasionally receive clothing or clothing discounts instead of, or in addition to, regular earnings. Almost all models work with agents, and pay 15 to 20 percent of their earnings in return for an agent's services. Models who do not find immediate work may receive payments, called advances, from agents to cover promotional and living expenses. Models must provide their own health and retirement benefits.

Related Occupations

Demonstrators, product promoters, and models create public interest in buying clothing, products, and services. Others who create interest in a product or service include actors, producers, and directors; insurance sales agents; real estate brokers; retail salespersons; sales representatives, wholesale and manufacturing; and reservation and transportation ticket agents and travel clerks.

Sources of Additional Information

For information about modeling schools and agencies in your area, contact a local consumer affairs organization such as the Better Business Bureau.

Insurance Sales Agents

(O*NET 41-3021.00)

Significant Points

- Despite slower-than-average growth, job opportunities should be good for college graduates and persons with proven sales ability or success in other occupations.

- Successful agents often have high earnings, but many who assume agent jobs fail to earn enough from commissions to meet their income goals and eventually transfer to other careers.

- In addition to offering insurance policies, agents are beginning to sell more financial products, such as mutual funds, retirement funds, and securities.

Nature of the Work

Most people have their first contact with an insurance company through an insurance sales agent. These workers help individuals, families, and businesses select insurance policies that provide the best protection for their lives, health, and property. Insurance sales agents who work exclusively for one insurance company are referred to as captive agents. Independent insurance agents, or brokers, represent several companies and place insurance policies for their clients with the company that offers the best rate and coverage. In either case, agents prepare reports, maintain records, seek out new clients, and, in the event of a loss, help policyholders settle their insurance claims. Increasingly, some are also offering their clients financial analysis or advice on ways the clients can minimize risk.

Insurance sales agents, commonly referred to as "producers" in the insurance industry, sell one or more types of insurance, such as property and casualty, life, health, disability, and long-term care. Property and casualty insurance agents sell policies that protect individuals and businesses from financial loss resulting from automobile accidents, fire, theft, storms, and other events that can damage property. For businesses, property and casualty insurance can also cover injured workers' compensation, product liability claims, or medical malpractice claims.

Life insurance agents specialize in selling policies that pay beneficiaries when a policyholder dies. Depending on the policyholder's circumstances, a cash-value policy can be designed to provide retirement income, funds for the education of children, or other benefits. Life insurance agents also sell annuities that promise a retirement income. Health insurance agents sell health insurance policies that cover the costs of medical care and loss of income due to illness or injury. They also may sell dental insurance and short- and long-term-disability insurance policies.

An increasing number of insurance sales agents are offering comprehensive financial planning services to their clients, such as retirement planning, estate planning, or assistance in setting up pension plans for businesses. As a result, many insurance agents are involved in "cross-selling" or "total account development." Besides offering insurance, these agents may become licensed to sell mutual funds, variable annuities, and other securities. This practice is most common with life insurance agents who already sell annuities; however, property and casualty agents also sell financial products. (See the statement on securities, commodities, and financial services sales representatives elsewhere in the *Handbook*.)

Technology has greatly affected the insurance agency, making it much more efficient and giving the agent the ability to take on more clients. Agents' computers are now linked directly to the insurance carriers via the Internet, making the tasks of obtaining price quotes and processing applications and service requests faster and easier. Computers also allow agents to be better informed about new products that the insurance carriers may be offering.

The growth of the Internet in the insurance industry is gradually altering the relationship between agent and client. In the past, agents devoted much of their time to marketing and selling products to new clients, a practice that is now changing. Increasingly, clients are obtaining insurance quotes from a company's Web site and then contacting the company directly to purchase policies. This interaction gives the client a more active role in selecting a policy at the best price, while reducing the amount of time agents spend actively seeking new clients. Because insurance sales agents also obtain many new accounts through referrals, it is important that they maintain regular contact with their clients to ensure that the clients' financial needs are being met. Developing a satisfied clientele that will recommend an agent's services to other potential customers is a key to success in this field.

Increasing competition in the insurance industry has spurred carriers and agents to find new ways to keep their clients satisfied. One solution is to increase the use of call centers, which usually are accessible to clients 24 hours a day, 7 days a week. Insurance carriers and sales agents also are hiring customer service representatives to

Insurance sales agents maintain regular contact with their clients in order to ensure that their financial needs are being met.

handle routine tasks such as answering questions, making changes in policies, processing claims, and selling more products to clients. The opportunity to cross-sell new products to clients will help agents' businesses grow. The use of call centers also allows agents to concentrate their efforts on seeking out new clients and maintaining relationships with old ones. (See separate *Handbook* statements on customer service representatives and on claims adjusters, appraisers, examiners, and investigators.)

Working Conditions
Most insurance sales agents are based in small offices, from which they contact clients and provide information on the policies they sell. However, much of their time may be spent outside their offices, traveling locally to meet with clients, close sales, or investigate claims. Agents usually determine their own hours of work and often schedule evening and weekend appointments for the convenience of clients. Although most agents work a 40-hour week, some work 60 hours a week or longer. Commercial sales agents, in particular, may meet with clients during business hours and then spend evenings doing paperwork and preparing presentations to prospective clients.

Employment
Insurance sales agents held about 381,000 jobs in 2002. Most insurance sales agents employed in wage and salary positions work for insurance agencies and brokerages. A decreasing number work directly for insurance carriers. Although most insurance agents specialize in life and health or property and casualty insurance, a growing number of "multiline" agents sell all lines of insurance. A small number of agents work for banks and securities brokerages as a result of the increasing integration of the financial services industries. Approximately 1 out of 4 insurance sales agents is self-employed.

Insurance sales agents are employed throughout the country, but most work in or near large urban centers. Some are employed in the headquarters of insurance companies, but the majority work out of local offices or independent agencies.

Training, Other Qualifications, and Advancement
For insurance sales agent jobs, most companies and independent agencies prefer to hire college graduates—especially those who have majored in business or economics. High school graduates are occasionally hired if they have proven sales ability or have been successful in other types of work. In fact, many entrants to insurance sales agent jobs transfer from other occupations. In selling commercial insurance, technical experience in a particular field can help sell policies to those in the same profession. As a result, new agents tend to be older than entrants in many other occupations.

College training may help agents grasp the technical aspects of insurance policies and the fundamentals and procedures of selling insurance. Many colleges and universities offer courses in insurance, and a few schools offer a bachelor's degree in the field. College courses in finance, mathematics, accounting, economics, business law, marketing, and business administration enable insurance sales agents to understand how social and economic conditions relate to the insurance industry. Courses in psychology, sociology, and public speaking can prove useful in improving sales techniques. In addition, because computers provide instantaneous information on a wide variety of financial products and greatly improve agents' efficiency, familiarity with computers and popular software packages has become very important.

Insurance sales agents must obtain a license in the States where they plan to do their selling. Separate licenses are required for agents to sell life and health insurance and property and casualty insurance. In most States, licenses are issued only to applicants who complete specified prelicensing courses and who pass State examinations covering insurance fundamentals and State insurance laws. As a result of the Gramm-Leach-Bliley Act of 1999, the industry is increasingly moving toward uniform State licensing standards and reciprocal licensing, allowing agents who earn a license in one State to become licensed in other States upon passing the appropriate courses and examination.

A number of organizations offer professional designation programs that certify one's expertise in specialties such as life, health, and property and casualty insurance, as well as financial consulting. Although voluntary, such programs assure clients and employers that an agent has a thorough understanding of the relevant specialty. Agents are usually required to complete a specified number of hours of continuing education to retain their designation.

Employers also are placing greater emphasis on continuing professional education as the diversity of financial products sold by insurance agents increases. It is important for insurance agents to keep up to date on issues concerning clients. Changes in tax laws, government benefits programs, and other State and Federal regulations can affect the insurance needs of clients and the way in which agents conduct business. Agents can enhance their selling skills and broaden their knowledge of insurance and other financial services by taking courses at colleges and universities and by attending institutes, conferences, and seminars sponsored by insurance organizations. Most State licensing authorities also have mandatory continuing education requirements focusing on insurance laws, consumer protection, and the technical details of various insurance policies.

As the demand for financial products and financial planning increases, many insurance agents are choosing to gain the proper licensing and certification to sell securities and other financial products. Doing so, however, requires substantial study and passing an additional examination—either the Series 6 or Series 7 licensing exam, both of which are administered by the National Association of Securities Dealers (NASD). The Series 6 exam is for individuals who wish to sell only mutual funds and variable annuities, whereas the Series 7 exam is the main NASD series license that qualifies agents as general securities sales representatives. In addition, to further demonstrate competency in the area of financial planning, many agents find it worthwhile to earn the designation "Certified Financial Planner" or "Chartered Financial Consultant."

Insurance sales agents should be flexible, enthusiastic, confident, disciplined, hard working, and willing to solve problems. They should communicate effectively and inspire customer confidence. Because they usually work without supervision, sales agents must be able to plan their time well and have the initiative to locate new clients.

An insurance sales agent who shows ability and leadership may become a sales manager in a local office. A few advance to agency superintendent or executive positions. However, many who have built up a good clientele prefer to remain in sales work. Some—particularly in the property and casualty field—establish their own independent agencies or brokerage firms.

Job Outlook

Although slower-than-average employment growth is expected among insurance agents through 2012, opportunities for agents will be favorable for persons with the right qualifications and skills.

Among such persons are flexible and ambitious people who enjoy competitive sales work, have excellent interpersonal skills, and possess expertise in a wide range of insurance and financial services. Multilingual agents also should be in high demand because they can serve a wider range of customers. Insurance language tends to be quite technical, so it is important for insurance sales agents to have a firm understanding of relevant technical and legal terms. Because many beginners find it difficult to establish a sufficiently large clientele in this commission-based occupation, many eventually leave for other jobs. Most job openings are likely to result from the need to replace agents who leave the occupation or retire. A large number of agents are expected to retire in coming years.

Future demand for insurance sales agents depends largely on the volume of sales of insurance and other financial products. Sales of health and long-term-care insurance are expected to rise sharply as the population ages. In addition, a growing population will increase demand for insurance for automobiles, homes, and high-priced valuables and equipment. As new businesses emerge and existing firms expand their insurance coverage, sales of commercial insurance also should increase, including coverage such as product liability, workers' compensation, employee benefits, and pollution liability insurance.

Employment of agents will not keep up with the rising level of insurance sales, however. Many insurance carriers are trying to contain costs. As a result, many are shedding their captive agents—those agents working directly for insurance carriers—and are relying more on independent agents or direct marketing through the mail, by phone, or on the Internet.

Agents who incorporate new technology into their existing businesses will remain competitive. Agents who use the Internet to market their products will reach a broader client base and expand their businesses, but because most clients value their relationship with their agent, the Internet should not threaten jobs, given that many individuals still prefer discussing their policies directly with their agents, rather than through a computer. Also, the automation of policy and claims processing is allowing insurance agents to take on more clients.

Agents may face increased competition from traditional securities brokers and bankers as they begin to sell insurance policies. Because of increasing consolidation among insurance companies, banks, and brokerage firms, and due to increasing demands from clients for more comprehensive financial planning, insurance sales agents will need to expand the products and services they offer.

Agents who offer better customer service also will remain competitive. Call centers are another important way carriers and agents are offering better service to customers, because such centers provide greater access to their policies and more prompt services.

Insurance and investments are becoming more complex, and many people and businesses lack the time and expertise to buy insurance without the advice of an agent. Moreover, most individuals and businesses consider insurance a necessity, regardless of economic conditions. Therefore, agents are not likely to face unemployment because of a recession.

Earnings

The median annual earnings of wage and salary insurance sales agents were $40,750 in 2002. The middle 50 percent earned between $ 28,860 and $ 64,450. The lowest 10 percent had earnings of $21,730 or less, while the highest 10 percent earned more than $101,460. Median annual earnings in 2002 in the two industries employing the largest number of insurance sales agents were $40,480 for insurance agencies, brokerages, and other insurance related activities and $42,130 for insurance carriers.

Many independent agents are paid by commission only, whereas sales workers who are employees of an agency or an insurance carrier may be paid in one of three ways: salary only, salary plus commission, or salary plus bonus. In general, commissions are the most common form of compensation, especially for experienced agents. The amount of the commission depends on the type and amount of insurance sold and on whether the transaction is a new policy or a renewal. Bonuses usually are awarded when agents meet their sales goals or when an agency meets its profit goals. Some agents involved with financial planning receive a fee for their services, rather than a commission.

Company-paid benefits to insurance sales agents usually include continuing education, training to qualify for licensing, group insurance plans, office space, and clerical support services. Some companies also may pay for automobile and transportation expenses, attendance at conventions and meetings, promotion and marketing expenses, and retirement plans. Independent agents working for insurance agencies receive fewer benefits, but their commissions may be higher to help them pay for marketing and other expenses.

Related Occupations

Other workers who provide or sell financial products or services include real estate sales agents and brokers; securities, commodities, and financial services sales agents; financial analysts and personal financial advisors; and financial managers. Other occupations in the insurance industry include insurance underwriters; claims adjusters, examiners, and investigators; and insurance appraisers.

Sources of Additional Information

Occupational information about insurance sales agents is available from the home office of many life and casualty insurance companies. Information on State licensing requirements may be obtained from the department of insurance at any State capital.

For information about insurance sales careers and training, contact either of the following sources:

➤ Independent Insurance Agents of America, 127 S. Peyton St., Alexandria, VA 22314. Internet: **http://www.iiaa.org**

➤ Insurance Vocational Education Student Training (InVEST), 127 S. Peyton St., Alexandria, VA 22314. Internet: **http://www.investprogram.org**

For information about health insurance sales careers, contact

➤ National Association of Health Underwriters, 2000 N. 14th St., Suite 450, Arlington, VA 22201. Internet: **http://www.nahu.org**

For general information on the property and casualty field, contact

➤ Insurance Information Institute, 110 William St., New York, NY 10038. Internet: **http://www.iii.org**

For information about professional designation programs, contact either of the following organizations:

➤ The American Institute for Chartered Property and Casualty Underwriters/Insurance Institute of America, 720 Providence Rd., P.O. Box 3016, Malvern, PA 19355-0716. Internet: **http://www.aicpcu.org**

➤ The American College, 270 Bryn Mawr Ave., Bryn Mawr, PA 19010-2195. Internet: **http://www.amercoll.edu**

Real Estate Brokers and Sales Agents

(0*NET 41-9021.00, 41-9022.00)

Significant Points

● Real estate brokers and sales agents often work evenings and weekends and usually are on call to suit the needs of clients.

● A license is required in every State and the District of Columbia.

● Although gaining a job as a real estate agent or broker may be relatively easy, beginning agents and brokers may face competition from well-established, more experienced agents and brokers in obtaining listings and in closing a sufficient number of sales.

Nature of the Work

One of the most complex and important financial events in peoples' lives is the purchase or sale of a home or investment property. Because of this complexity and importance, people usually seek the help of real estate brokers and sales agents when buying or selling real estate.

Real estate brokers and sales agents have a thorough knowledge of the real estate market in their community. They know which neighborhoods will best fit clients' needs and budgets. They are familiar with local zoning and tax laws and know where to obtain financing. Agents and brokers also act as intermediaries in price negotiations between buyers and sellers.

Real estate agents usually are independent sales workers who provide their services to a licensed real estate broker on a contract basis. In return, the broker pays the agent a portion of the commission earned from the agent's sale of the property. Brokers are independent businesspeople who sell real estate owned by others; they also may rent or manage properties for a fee. When selling real estate, brokers arrange for title searches and for meetings between buyers and sellers wherein details of the transactions are agreed upon and the new owners take possession of the property. A broker may help to arrange favorable financing from a lender for the prospective buyer; often, this makes the difference between success and failure in closing a sale. In some cases, brokers and agents assume primary responsibility for closing sales; in others, lawyers or lenders do so. Brokers supervise agents who may have many of the same job duties. Brokers also manage their own offices, advertise properties, and handle other business matters. Some combine other types of work, such as selling insurance or practicing law, with their real estate business.

Besides making sales, agents and brokers must have properties to sell. Consequently, they spend a significant amount of time obtaining listings—agreements by owners to place properties for sale with the firm. When listing a property for sale, agents and brokers compare the listed property with similar properties that recently sold, in order to determine a competitive market price for the property. Once the property is sold, the agent who sold it and the agent who obtained the listing both receive a portion of the commission. Thus, agents who sell a property that they themselves have listed can increase their commission.

Most real estate brokers and sales agents sell residential property. A small number, usually employed in large or specialized firms, sell commercial, industrial, agricultural, or other types of real estate.

Every specialty requires knowledge of that particular type of property and clientele. Selling or leasing business property requires an understanding of leasing practices, business trends, and the location of the property. Agents who sell or lease industrial properties must know about the region's transportation, utilities, and labor supply. Whatever the type of property, the agent or broker must know how to meet the client's particular requirements.

Before showing residential properties to potential buyers, agents meet with them to get a feeling for the type of home the buyers would like. In this prequalifying phase, the agent determines how much the buyers can afford to spend. In addition, the agent and the buyer usually sign a loyalty contract which states the agent will be the only one to show houses to the buyers. An agent or broker uses a computer to generate lists of properties for sale, their location and description, and available sources of financing. In some cases, agents and brokers use computers to give buyers a virtual tour of properties in which they are interested. With a computer, buyers can view interior and exterior images or floor plans without leaving the real estate officc.

Agents may meet several times with prospective buyers to discuss and visit available properties. Agents identify and emphasize the most pertinent selling points. To a young family looking for a house, they may emphasize the convenient floor plan, the area's low crime rate, and the proximity to schools and shopping centers. To a potential investor, they may point out the tax advantages of owning a rental property and the ease of finding a renter. If bargaining over price becomes necessary, agents must follow their client's instructions carefully and may have to present counteroffers in order to get the best possible price.

Once both parties have signed the contract, the real estate broker or agent must make sure that all special terms of the contract are met before the closing date. For example, the agent must make sure that the mandated and agreed-upon inspections, including that of the home and termite and radon inspections, take place. Also, if the seller agrees to any repairs, the broker or agent must see that they are made. Increasingly, brokers and agents are handling environmental problems as well, by making sure that the properties they sell meet environmental regulations. For example, they may be responsible for dealing with lead paint on the walls. While loan officers, attorneys, or other persons handle many details, the agent must ensure that they are completed.

When a buyer is ready to purchase a property, the real estate agent or broker drafts a contract that details the terms of the buyer's offer.

Working Conditions

Advances in telecommunications and the ability to retrieve data about properties over the Internet allow many real estate brokers and sales agents to work out of their homes instead of real estate offices. Even with this convenience, much of the time of these workers is spent away from their desks—showing properties to customers, analyzing properties for sale, meeting with prospective clients, or researching the state of the market.

Agents and brokers often work more than a standard 40-hour week. They usually work evenings and weekends and are always on call to suit the needs of clients. Business usually is slower during the winter season. Although the hours are long and frequently irregular, most agents and brokers have the freedom to determine their own schedule. Consequently, they can arrange their work so that they can have time off when they want it.

Employment

In 2002, real estate brokers held about 99,000 jobs; real estate sales agents held 308,000. Many worked part time, combining their real estate activities with other careers. Almost 6 out of 10 real estate agents and brokers were self-employed. Real estate is sold in all areas, but employment is concentrated in large urban areas and in smaller, but rapidly growing communities.

Most real estate firms are relatively small; indeed, some are one-person businesses. By contrast, some large real estate firms have several hundred agents operating out of numerous branch offices. Many brokers have franchise agreements with national or regional real estate organizations. Under this type of arrangement, the broker pays a fee in exchange for the privilege of using the more widely known name of the parent organization. Although franchised brokers often receive help in training sales staff and running their offices, they bear the ultimate responsibility for the success or failure of their firms.

Real estate brokers and sales agents are older, on average, than most other workers. Historically, many homemakers and retired persons were attracted to real estate sales by the flexible and part-time work schedules characteristic of the field. These individuals could enter, leave, and later reenter the occupation, depending on the strength of the real estate market, their family responsibilities, or other personal circumstances. Recently, however, the attractiveness of part-time real estate work has declined, as increasingly complex legal and technological requirements are raising startup costs associated with becoming an agent.

Training, Other Qualifications, and Advancement

In every State and the District of Columbia, real estate brokers and sales agents must be licensed. Prospective agents must be high school graduates, at least 18 years old, and pass a written test. The examination—more comprehensive for brokers than for agents—includes questions on basic real estate transactions and laws affecting the sale of property. Most States require candidates for the general sales license to complete between 30 and 90 hours of classroom instruction. Those seeking a broker's license need between 60 and 90 hours of formal training and a specific amount of experience selling real estate, usually 1 to 3 years. Some States waive the experience requirements for the broker's license for applicants who have a bachelor's degree in real estate.

State licenses typically must be renewed every 1 or 2 years, usually without having to take an examination. However, many States require continuing education for license renewals. Prospective agents and brokers should contact the real estate licensing commission of the State in which they wish to work in order to verify exact licensing requirements.

As real estate transactions have become more legally complex, many firms have turned to college graduates to fill positions. A large number of agents and brokers have some college training. College courses in real estate, finance, business administration, statistics, economics, law, and English are helpful. For those who intend to start their own company, business courses such as marketing and accounting are as important as those in real estate or finance.

Personality traits are equally as important as academic background. Brokers look for applicants who possess a pleasant personality, are honest, and present a neat appearance. Maturity, tact, trustworthiness, and enthusiasm for the job are required in order to motivate prospective customers in this highly competitive field. Agents should be well organized, be detail oriented, and have a good memory for names, faces, and business particulars.

Those interested in jobs as real estate agents often begin in their own communities. Their knowledge of local neighborhoods is a clear advantage. Under the direction of an experienced agent, beginners learn the practical aspects of the job, including the use of computers to locate or list available properties and identify sources of financing.

Many firms offer formal training programs for both beginners and experienced agents. Larger firms usually offer more extensive programs than smaller firms. More than a thousand universities, colleges, and junior colleges offer courses in real estate. At some, a student can earn an associate's or bachelor's degree with a major in real estate; several offer advanced degrees. Many local real estate associations that are members of the National Association of Realtors sponsor courses covering the fundamentals and legal aspects of the field. Advanced courses in mortgage financing, property development and management, and other subjects also are available through various affiliates of the National Association of Realtors.

Advancement opportunities for agents may take the form of higher rates of commission. As agents gain knowledge and expertise, they become more efficient in closing a greater number of transactions and increase their earnings. In many large firms, experienced agents can advance to sales manager or general manager. Persons who have received their broker's license may open their own offices. Others with experience and training in estimating property value may become real estate appraisers, and people familiar with operating and maintaining rental properties may become property managers. (See the statement on property, real estate, and community association managers elsewhere in the *Handbook*.) Experienced agents and brokers with a thorough knowledge of business conditions and property values in their localities may enter mortgage financing or real estate investment counseling.

Job Outlook

Employment of real estate brokers and sales agents is expected to grow more slowly than the average for all occupations through the year 2012. Increasing use of information technology will continue to raise the productivity of agents and brokers, limiting the potential for job growth to a certain extent. Prospective customers often can conduct their own searches for properties that meet their criteria by accessing real estate information on the Internet. Real estate companies often use computer-generated images to show houses to customers without leaving the office. In addition, cellular phones can send and receive large amounts of data, allowing agents and brokers to become more efficient and to serve a greater number of customers. However, most people still want and need the services of real estate agents and brokers to handle the actual sale. The use of technology may eliminate some marginal agents, such as those

practicing real estate part-time or temporarily between jobs. Such workers generally are not able to compete with full-time agents who have invested in the technology. Changing legal requirements, such as disclosure laws, may also dissuade some who are not serious about practicing full time from continuing to work part time.

Real estate agents and brokers will continue to experience some employment growth due to the increasing housing needs of a growing population, as well as the perception that real estate is a good investment Low interest rates should continue to stimulate sales of real estate, resulting in the need for more agents and brokers. In addition, a large number of job openings will arise each year from the need to replace workers who transfer to other occupations or leave the labor force. This occupation is relatively easy to enter and is attractive, due to the flexible working conditions, the high interest in, and knowledge of, local real estate markets that entrants often have, and the potential for high earnings. Therefore, although gaining a job as a real estate agent or broker may be relatively easy, beginning agents and brokers may face competition from well-established, more experienced agents and brokers in obtaining listings and in closing a sufficient number of sales. Well-trained, ambitious people who enjoy selling, especially those with extensive social and business connections in their communities, should have the best chance for success.

Employment of real estate brokers and sales agents often is sensitive to swings in the economy, especially interest rates. During periods of declining economic activity and increasing interest rates, the volume of sales and the resulting demand for sales workers falls. As a result, the earnings of agents and brokers decline, and many work fewer hours or leave the occupation altogether.

Earnings

The median annual earnings of salaried real estate agents, including commissions, were $30,930 in 2002. The middle 50 percent earned between $21,010 and $52,860 a year. The lowest 10 percent earned less than $15,480, and the highest 10 percent earned more than $83,780.

Median annual earnings of salaried real estate brokers, including commission, were $50,330 in 2002. The middle 50 percent earned between $29,240 and $90,170 a year. The lowest 10 percent earned less than $17,920, and the highest 10 percent earned more than $145,600 a year.

Commissions on sales are the main source of earnings of real estate agents and brokers. The rate of commission varies according to whatever the agent and broker agree on, the type of property, and its value. The percentage paid on the sale of farm and commercial properties or unimproved land usually is higher than the percentage paid for selling a home.

Commissions may be divided among several agents and brokers. The broker or agent who obtained the listing usually shares their commission when the property is sold with the broker or agent who made the sale, and also with the firm that employs them. Although an agent's share varies greatly from one firm to another, often it is about half of the total amount received by the firm. Agents who both list and sell a property maximize their commission.

Income usually increases as an agent gains experience, but individual ability, economic conditions, and the type and location of the property also affect earnings. Sales workers who are active in community organizations and in local real estate associations can broaden their contacts and increase their earnings. A beginner's earnings often are irregular, because a few weeks or even months may go by without a sale. Although some brokers allow an agent to draw against future earnings from a special account, the practice is not usual with new employees. The beginner, therefore, should have enough money to live for about 6 months or until commissions increase.

Related Occupations

Selling expensive items such as homes requires maturity, tact, and a sense of responsibility. Other sales workers who find these character traits important in their work include insurance sales agents; retail salespersons; sales representatives, wholesale and manufacturing; and securities, commodities, and financial services sales agents. The work of property, real estate, and community association managers, although not involving sales, requires a knowledge of real estate.

Sources of Additional Information

Information on license requirements for real estate brokers and sales agents is available from most local real estate organizations or from the State real estate commission or board.

More information about opportunities in real estate is available on the Internet site of the following organization:

➤ National Association of Realtors. Internet: **http://www.realtor.org**

Retail Salespersons

(0*NET 41-2031.00)

Significant Points

● Good employment opportunities are expected because of the need to replace the large number of workers who leave the occupation each year.

● Many salespersons work evenings, weekends, and long hours from Thanksgiving through the beginning of January, during sales, and in other peak retail periods.

● Opportunities for part-time and temporary work are plentiful, attracting people looking to supplement their income; however, most of those selling high-priced items work full time and have substantial experience.

● There are no formal education requirements, although a high school diploma is preferred; employers look for people who enjoy working with others and who have tact, patience, an interest in sales work, a neat appearance, and the ability to communicate clearly.

Nature of the Work

Whether selling shoes, computer equipment, or automobiles, retail salespersons assist customers in finding what they are looking for and try to interest them in buying the merchandise. They describe a product's features, demonstrate its use, or show various models and colors. For some sales jobs, particularly those involving expensive and complex items, retail salespersons need special knowledge or skills. For example, salespersons who sell automobiles must be able to explain the features of various models, information about warranties, the meaning of manufacturers' specifications, and the types of options and financing available.

Consumers spend millions of dollars every day on merchandise and often form their impression of a store by evaluating its sales force. Therefore, retailers stress the importance of providing courteous and efficient service in order to remain competitive. When, for example, a customer wants an item that is not on the sales floor,

the salesperson may check the stock room, place a special order, or call another store to locate the item.

In addition to selling, most retail salespersons—especially those who work in department and apparel stores—make out sales checks; receive cash, checks, and charge payments; bag or package purchases; and give out change and receipts. Depending on the hours they work, retail salespersons may have to open or close cash registers. This work may include counting the money in the register; separating charge slips, coupons, and exchange vouchers; and making deposits at the cash office. Salespersons often are held responsible for the contents of their registers, and repeated shortages are cause for dismissal in many organizations. (Cashiers, who have similar job duties, are discussed elsewhere in the *Handbook*.)

Salespersons also may handle returns and exchanges of merchandise, wrap gifts, and keep their work areas neat. In addition, they may help stock shelves or racks, arrange for mailing or delivery of purchases, mark price tags, take inventory, and prepare displays.

Frequently, salespersons must be aware of special sales and promotions. They also must recognize security risks and thefts and know how to handle or prevent such situations.

Working Conditions

Most salespersons in retail trade work in clean, comfortable, well-lighted stores. However, they often stand for long periods and may need supervisory approval to leave the sales floor.

The Monday-through-Friday, 9-to-5 workweek is the exception rather than the rule in retail trade. Most salespersons work evenings and weekends, particularly during sales and other peak retail periods. Because the holiday season is the busiest time for most retailers, many employers restrict the use of vacation time to some period other than Thanksgiving through the beginning of January.

The job can be rewarding for those who enjoy working with people. Patience and courtesy are required, especially when the work is repetitive and the customers are demanding.

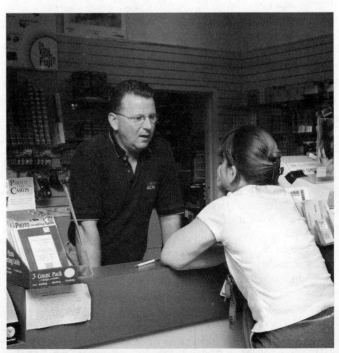

Jobs as retail salespersons can be rewarding to those who enjoy working with people.

Employment

Retail salespersons held about 4.1 million wage and salary jobs in 2002. They worked in stores ranging from small specialty shops employing a few workers to giant department stores with hundreds of salespersons. In addition, some were self-employed representatives of direct-sales companies and mail-order houses. The largest employers of retail salespersons are department stores, clothing and accessories stores, building material and garden equipment and supplies dealers, and motor vehicle dealers.

This occupation offers many opportunities for part-time work and is especially appealing to students, retirees, and others seeking to supplement their income. However, most of those selling "big-ticket" items, such as cars, jewelry, furniture, and electronic equipment, work full time and have substantial experience.

Because retail stores are found in every city and town, employment is distributed geographically in much the same way as the population.

Training, Other Qualifications, and Advancement

There usually are no formal education requirements for this type of work, although a high school diploma or equivalent is preferred. Employers look for people who enjoy working with others and who have the tact and patience to deal with difficult customers. Among other desirable characteristics are an interest in sales work, a neat appearance, and the ability to communicate clearly and effectively. The ability to speak more than one language may be helpful for employment in communities where people from various cultures tend to live and shop. Before hiring a salesperson, some employers may conduct a background check, especially for a job selling high-priced items.

In most small stores, an experienced employee or the proprietor instructs newly hired sales personnel in making out sales checks and operating cash registers. In large stores, training programs are more formal and are usually conducted over several days. Topics generally discussed are customer service, security, the store's policies and procedures, and how to work a cash register. Depending on the type of product they are selling, employees may be given additional specialized training by manufacturers' representatives. For example, those working in cosmetics receive instruction on the types of products the store has available and for whom the cosmetics would be most beneficial. Likewise, salespersons employed by motor vehicle dealers may be required to participate in training programs designed to provide information on the technical details of standard and optional equipment available on new models. Because providing the best service to customers is a high priority for many employers, employees often are given periodic training to update and refine their skills.

As salespersons gain experience and seniority, they usually move to positions of greater responsibility and may be given their choice of departments in which to work. This often means moving to areas with potentially higher earnings and commissions. The highest earnings potential usually is found in selling big-ticket items, although such a position often requires the most knowledge of the product and the greatest talent for persuasion.

Opportunities for advancement vary in small stores. In some establishments, advancement is limited because one person—often the owner—does most of the managerial work. In others, some salespersons are promoted to assistant managers.

Traditionally, capable salespersons without college degrees could advance to management positions. Today, however, large retail businesses usually prefer to hire college graduates as management trainees, making a college education increasingly important. Despite this trend, motivated and capable employees without college degrees still may advance to administrative or supervisory positions in large establishments.

Retail selling experience may be an asset when one is applying for sales positions with larger retailers or in other industries, such as financial services, wholesale trade, or manufacturing.

Job Outlook

As in the past, employment opportunities for retail salespersons are expected to be good because of the need to replace the large number of workers who transfer to other occupations or leave the labor force each year. In addition, many new jobs will be created for retail salespersons. Employment is expected to grow about as fast as the average for all occupations through the year 2012, reflecting rising retail sales stemming from a growing population. Opportunities for part-time work should be abundant, and demand will be strong for temporary workers during peak selling periods, such as the end-of-year holiday season. The availability of part-time and temporary work attracts many people seeking to supplement their income.

During economic downturns, sales volumes and the resulting demand for sales workers usually decline. Purchases of costly items, such as cars, appliances, and furniture, tend to be postponed during difficult economic times. In areas of high unemployment, sales of many types of goods decline. However, because turnover among retail salespersons is high, employers often can adjust employment levels simply by not replacing all those who leave.

Despite the growing popularity of electronic commerce, Internet sales have not decreased the need for retail salespersons. Retail stores commonly use an online presence just to complement their in-store sales—there are very few Internet—only apparel and specialty stores. Retail salespersons will remain important in assuring customers that they will receive specialized service and in improving customer satisfaction, something Internet services cannot do. Therefore, the impact of electronic commerce on employment of retail salespersons will be minimal.

Earnings

The starting wage for many retail sales positions is the Federal minimum wage, which was $5.15 an hour in 2002. In areas where employers have difficulty attracting and retaining workers, wages tend to be higher than the legislated minimum.

Median hourly earnings of retail salespersons, including commission, were $8.51 in 2002. The middle 50 percent earned between $7.08 and $11.30 an hour. The lowest 10 percent earned less than $6.18, and the highest 10 percent earned more than $16.96 an hour. Median hourly earnings in the industries employing the largest numbers of retail salespersons in 2002 were as follows:

Automobile dealers	$18.25
Building material and supplies dealers	10.41
Department stores	8.12
Other general merchandise stores	7.84
Clothing stores	7.77

Compensation systems vary by type of establishment and merchandise sold. Salespersons receive hourly wages, commissions, or a combination of wages and commissions. Under a commission system, salespersons receive a percentage of the sales that they make. This system offers sales workers the opportunity to increase their earnings considerably, but they may find that their earnings strongly depend on their ability to sell their product and on the ups and downs of the economy. Employers may use incentive programs such as awards, banquets, bonuses, and profit-sharing plans to promote teamwork among the sales staff.

Benefits may be limited in smaller stores, but benefits in large establishments usually are comparable to those offered by other employers. In addition, nearly all salespersons are able to buy their store's merchandise at a discount, with the savings depending upon the type of merchandise.

Related Occupations

Salespersons use sales techniques, coupled with their knowledge of merchandise, to assist customers and encourage purchases. Workers in a number of other occupations who use these same skills include sales representatives, wholesale and manufacturing; securities, commodities, and financial services sales agents; counter and rental clerks; real estate brokers and sales agents; purchasing managers, buyers, and purchasing agents; insurance sales agents; sales engineers; and cashiers.

Sources of Additional Information

Information on careers in retail sales may be obtained from the personnel offices of local stores or from State merchants' associations.

General information about retailing is available from:

➤ National Retail Federation, 325 7th St. NW., Suite 1100, Washington, DC 20004.

Information about retail sales employment opportunities is available from:

➤ Retail, Wholesale, and Department Store Union, 30 East 29th St., 4th Floor, New York, NY 10016. Internet: **http://www.rwdsu.org**

Information about training for a career in automobile sales is available from:

➤ National Automobile Dealers Association, Public Relations Department, 8400 Westpark Dr., McLean, VA 22102-3591. Internet: **http://www.nada.org**

Sales Engineers

(0*NET 41-9031.00)

Significant Points

● A bachelor's degree in engineering is required; many sales engineers have previous work experience in an engineering specialty.

● Projected employment growth stems from the increasing number and technical nature of products to be sold.

● More job opportunities are expected in independent agencies.

● Earnings are based on a combination of salary and commission.

Nature of the Work

Many products and services, especially those purchased by large companies and institutions, are highly complex. Sales engineers, using their engineering skills, help customers determine which products or services provided by the sales engineer's employer best suit their needs. Sales engineers—who also may be called manufacturers' agents, sales representatives, or technical sales support workers—often work with both the customer and the production, engineering, or research and development departments of their company, or of independent firms, to determine how products and services could be designed or modified to best suit the customer's needs.

They also may advise the customer on how to best utilize the products or services being provided.

Selling, of course, is an important part of the job. Sales engineers use their technical skills to demonstrate to potential customers how and why the products or services they are selling would suit the customer better than competitors' products. Often, there may not be a directly competitive product. In these cases, the job of the sales engineer is to demonstrate to the customer the usefulness of the product or service—for example, how much money new production machinery would save.

Most sales engineers have a bachelor's degree in engineering and some have previous work experience in an engineering specialty. Engineers apply the theories and principles of science and mathematics to technical problems. Their work is the link between scientific discoveries and commercial applications. Many sales engineers specialize in an area related to an engineering specialty. For example, sales engineers selling chemical products may have chemical engineering backgrounds, while those selling electrical products may have degrees in electrical engineering. (Information on engineers and 14 engineering specialties appears elsewhere in the *Handbook*.)

Many of the job duties of sales engineers are similar to those of other salespersons. They must interest the client in purchasing their products, many of which are durable manufactured products such

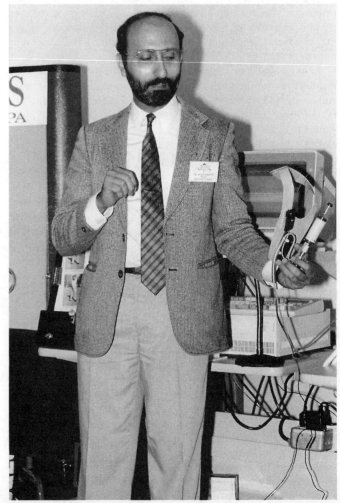

Sales engineers may use a consultative selling style, focusing on the client's problem and showing how it could be solved or mitigated with their product or service.

as turbines. Sales engineers are often teamed with other salespersons who concentrate on the marketing and sales, enabling the sales engineer to concentrate on the technical aspects of the job. By working as a sales team, each member is able to utilize his or her strengths and knowledge. (Information on other sales occupations, including sales representatives, wholesale and manufacturing, appears elsewhere in the *Handbook*.)

Sales engineers tend to employ selling techniques that are different from those used by most other sales workers. They may use a "consultative" style; that is, they focus on the client's problem and show how it could be solved or mitigated with their product or service. This selling style differs from the "benefits and features" method, whereby the product is described and the customer is left to decide how the product would be useful.

In addition to maintaining current clients and attracting new ones, sales engineers help clients solve any problems that arise when the product is installed, and may continue to serve as a liaison between the client and their company. In addition, using their familiarity with client needs, sales engineers may help identify and develop new products.

Sales engineers may work directly for manufacturers or service providers, or in small independent firms. In an independent firm, they may sell complimentary products from several different suppliers and be paid on a commission basis.

Working Conditions

Many sales engineers work more than 40 hours per week to meet sales goals and their clients' needs. Selling can be stressful because sales engineers' income and job security often directly depend on their success in sales and customer service.

Some sales engineers have large territories and travel extensively. Because sales regions may cover several States, sales engineers may be away from home for several days or even weeks at a time. Others work near their "home base" and travel mostly by automobile. International travel, to secure contracts with foreign customers, is becoming more important.

Although the hours may be long and are often irregular, many sales engineers have the freedom to determine their own schedule. Consequently, they often can arrange their appointments so that they can have time off when they want it. However, most independent sales workers do not earn any income while on vacation.

Employment

Sales engineers held about 82,000 jobs in 2002. About 32 percent were employed in the manufacturing industries and another 28 percent were employed in wholesale trade. Unlike workers in many other sales occupations, very few sales engineers are self-employed.

Training, Other Qualifications, and Advancement

A bachelor's degree in engineering is usually required to become a sales engineer. However, some workers with previous experience in sales combined with technical experience or training sometimes hold the title of sales engineer. Also, workers who have a degree in a science, such as chemistry, or even a degree in business with little or no previous sales experience, may be termed sales engineers.

Admissions requirements for undergraduate engineering schools include a solid background in mathematics (algebra, geometry, trigonometry, and calculus), physical sciences (biology, chemistry, and physics), and courses in English, social studies, humanities, and computer science. University programs vary in content. For example, some programs emphasize industrial practices, preparing students for a job in industry, whereas others are more theoretical and prepare students for graduate school. Therefore, students should

investigate curriculums and check accreditations carefully before making a selection. Once a university has been selected, a student must choose an area of engineering in which to specialize. Some programs offer a general engineering curriculum; students then specialize in graduate school or on the job. Most engineering degrees are granted in electrical, mechanical, or civil engineering. However, engineers trained in one branch may work in related branches.

Many sales engineers first worked as engineers. For some, the engineering experience was necessary to obtain the technical background needed to effectively sell their employers' products or services. Others moved into the occupation because it offered better earnings and advancement potential or because they were looking for a new challenge.

New graduates with engineering degrees may need sales experience and training to obtain employment directly as a sales engineer. This may involve teaming with a sales mentor who is familiar with the business practices, customers, and company procedures and culture. After the training period has been completed, the sales engineer may continue to partner with someone who lacks technical skills, yet excels in the art of sales.

Promotion may include a higher commission rate, larger sales territory, or elevation to the position of supervisor or marketing manager. In other cases, sales engineers may leave their companies and form an independent firm that may offer higher commissions and more freedom. Independent firms tend to be small, although relatively few sales engineers are self-employed.

It is important for sales engineers to continue their education throughout their careers because much of their value to their employers depends on their knowledge of the latest technology. Sales engineers in high-technology areas, such as information technology or advanced electronics, may find that technical knowledge can become obsolete rapidly.

Job Outlook

Employment of sales engineers is expected to grow about as fast as the average for all occupations through the year 2012. Projected employment growth stems from the increasing variety and number of goods to be sold. Competitive pressures and advancing technology will force companies to improve and update product designs more frequently and to optimize their manufacturing and sales processes. In addition to new positions created as companies expand their sales force, some openings will arise each year from the need to replace sales workers who transfer to other occupations or leave the labor force.

Manufacturers are expected to continue contracting out more of their sales functions to independent sales agencies in an attempt to control their costs. This should mean more job opportunities for sales engineers in independent agencies and for self-employed independent sales engineers.

Employment opportunities and earnings may fluctuate from year to year because sales are affected by changing economic conditions, legislative issues, and consumer preferences. Prospects will be best for those with the appropriate knowledge or technical expertise, as well as the personal traits necessary for successful sales work.

Earnings

Compensation varies significantly by the type of firm and product sold. Most employers use a combination of salary and commission or salary plus bonus. Commissions usually are based on the amount of sales, whereas bonuses may depend on individual performance, on the performance of all sales workers in the group or district, or on the company's performance. Earnings from commissions and bonuses may vary greatly from year to year, depending on sales ability, the demand for the company's products or services, and the overall economy.

Median annual earnings of sales engineers, including commissions, were $63,660 in 2002. The middle 50 percent earned between $48,650 and $84,880 a year. The lowest 10 percent earned less than $37,430, and the highest 10 percent earned more than $108,080 a year. Median annual earnings employed by firms in the computer systems design and related services industry in 2002 were $77,100; earnings for sales engineers in the professional and commercial equipment and supplies merchant wholesalers industry were $53,170.

In addition to their earnings, sales engineers who work for manufacturers are usually reimbursed for expenses such as transportation, meals, hotels, and customer entertainment. In addition to typical benefits, sales engineers often get personal use of a company car and frequent-flyer mileage. Some companies offer incentives such as free vacation trips or gifts for outstanding performance. Sales engineers who work in independent firms may have higher but less stable earnings and, often, relatively few benefits.

Related Occupations

Sales engineers must have sales ability and knowledge of the products they sell, as well as technical and analytical skills. Other occupations that require similar skills include advertising, marketing, promotions, public relations, and sales managers; engineers; insurance sales agents; purchasing managers, buyers, and purchasing agents; real estate brokers and sales agents; sales representatives, wholesale and manufacturing; and securities, commodities, and financial services sales agents.

Sources of Additional Information

Information on careers for manufacturers' representatives and agents is available from:

➤ Manufacturers' Agents National Association, P.O. Box 3467, Laguna Hills, CA 92654-3467. Internet: **http://www.manaonline.org**

➤ Manufacturers' Representatives Educational Research Foundation, P.O. Box 247, Geneva, IL 60134. Internet: **http://www.mrerf.org**

Sales Representatives, Wholesale and Manufacturing

(0*NET 41-4011.01, 41-4011.02, 41-4011.03, 41-4011.04, 41-4011.05, 41-4011.06, 41-4012.00)

Significant Points

● Earnings of sales representatives usually are based on a combination of salary and commission.

● Many individuals with previous sales experience enter the occupation without a college degree; however, a bachelor's degree increasingly is required.

● Prospects will be best for those with the appropriate knowledge or technical expertise, and the personal traits necessary for successful selling.

Nature of the Work

Sales representatives are an important part of manufacturers' and wholesalers' success. Regardless of the type of product they sell, their primary duties are to interest wholesale and retail buyers and purchasing agents in their merchandise, and to address any of the client's questions or concerns. Sales representatives represent one or several manufacturers or wholesale distributors by selling one product or a complimentary line of products. Sales representatives also advise clients on methods to reduce costs, use their products, and increase sales. They market their company's products to manufacturers, wholesale and retail establishments, construction contractors, government agencies, and other institutions. (Retail salespersons, who sell directly to consumers, and sales engineers, who specialize in sales of technical products and services, are discussed elsewhere in the *Handbook.*)

Depending on where they work, sales representatives have different job titles. Those employed directly by a manufacturer or wholesaler often are called *sales representatives*. *Manufacturers' agents* or *manufacturers' representatives* are self-employed sales workers or independent firms who contract their services to all types of manufacturing companies. However, many of these titles are used interchangeably.

Sales representatives spend much of their time traveling to and visiting with prospective buyers and current clients. During a sales call, they discuss the client's needs and suggest how their merchandise or services can meet those needs. They may show samples or catalogs that describe items their company stocks and inform customers about prices, availability, and ways in which their products can save money and improve productivity. Because a vast number of manufacturers and wholesalers sell similar products, sales representatives must emphasize any unique qualities of their products and services. Manufacturers' agents or manufacturers' representatives might sell several complimentary products made by different manufacturers and, thus, take a broad approach to their customers' business. Sales representatives may help install new equipment and train employees. They also take orders and resolve any problems with or complaints about the merchandise.

Obtaining new accounts is an important part of the job. Sales representatives follow leads from other clients, track advertisements in trade journals, participate in trade shows and conferences, and may visit potential clients unannounced. In addition, they may spend time meeting with and entertaining prospective clients during evenings and weekends.

In a process that can take several months, sales representatives present their product and negotiate the sale. Aided by a laptop computer connected to the Internet, they often can answer technical and nontechnical questions immediately.

Frequently, sales representatives who lack technical expertise work as a team with a technical expert. In this arrangement, the

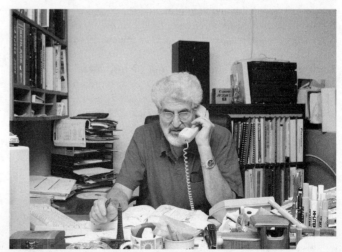

Obtaining new accounts is an important part of a sales representative's job.

technical expert—sometimes a sales engineer—will attend the sales presentation to explain the product and answer questions or concerns. The sales representative makes the preliminary contact with customers, introduces the company's product, and closes the sale. The representative is then able to spend more time maintaining and soliciting accounts and less time acquiring technical knowledge. After the sale, representatives may make followup visits to ensure that the equipment is functioning properly and may even help train customers' employees to operate and maintain new equipment. Those selling consumer goods often suggest how and where merchandise should be displayed. Working with retailers, they may help arrange promotional programs, store displays, and advertising.

Sales representatives have several duties beyond selling products. They also analyze sales statistics; prepare reports; and handle administrative duties, such as filing their expense account reports, scheduling appointments, and making travel plans. They study literature about new and existing products and monitor the sales, prices, and products of their competitors.

Manufacturers' agents who operate a sales agency must also manage their business. This requires organizational and general business skills, as well as knowledge of accounting, marketing, and administration.

Working Conditions
Some sales representatives have large territories and travel considerably. A sales region may cover several States, so they may be away from home for several days or weeks at a time. Others work near their "home base" and travel mostly by automobile. Due to the nature of the work and the amount of travel, sales representatives may work more than 40 hours per week.

Although the hours are long and often irregular, most sales representatives have the freedom to determine their own schedule. Sales representatives often are on their feet for long periods and may carry heavy sample products, which necessitates some physical stamina.

Dealing with different types of people can be stimulating but demanding. Sales representatives often face competition from representatives of other companies. Companies usually set goals or quotas that representatives are expected to meet. Because their earnings depend on commissions, manufacturers' agents are also under the added pressure to maintain and expand their clientele.

Employment
Manufacturers' and wholesale sales representatives held about 1.9 million jobs in 2002. About half of all salaried representatives worked in wholesale trade. Others were employed in manufacturing and mining. Due to the diversity of products and services sold, employment opportunities are available in every part of the country in a wide range of industries.

In addition to those working directly for a firm, many sales representatives are self-employed manufacturers' agents. They often form small sales firms and work for a straight commission based on the value of their own sales. However, manufacturers' agents usually gain experience and recognition with a manufacturer or wholesaler before becoming self-employed.

Training, Other Qualifications, and Advancement
The background needed for sales jobs varies by product line and market. Many employers hire individuals with previous sales experience who do not have a college degree, but often prefer those with some college education. Increasingly employers prefer or require a bachelor's degree as the job requirements have become more technical and analytical. Nevertheless, for some consumer products, factors such as sales ability, personality, and familiarity with brands are more important than educational background. On the other hand, firms selling complex, technical products may require a technical degree in addition to some sales experience. Many sales representatives attend seminars in sales techniques or take courses in marketing, economics, communication, or even a foreign language to provide the extra edge needed to make sales. In general, companies are looking for the best and brightest individuals who have the personality and desire to sell. Sales representatives need to be familiar with computer technology as computers are increasingly used in the workplace to place and track orders and to monitor inventory levels.

Many companies have formal training programs for beginning sales representatives lasting up to 2 years. However, most businesses are accelerating these programs to reduce costs and expedite the returns from training. In some programs, trainees rotate among jobs in plants and offices to learn all phases of production, installation, and distribution of the product. In others, trainees take formal classroom instruction at the plant, followed by on-the-job training under the supervision of a field sales manager.

New workers may get training by accompanying experienced workers on their sales calls. As they gain familiarity with the firm's products and clients, these workers are given increasing responsibility until they are eventually assigned their own territory. As businesses experience greater competition, increased pressure is placed upon sales representatives to produce sales.

Sales representatives stay abreast of new products and the changing needs of their customers in a variety of ways. They attend trade shows at which new products and technologies are showcased. They also attend conferences and conventions to meet other sales representatives and clients and discuss new product developments. In addition, the entire sales force may participate in company-sponsored meetings to review sales performance, product development, sales goals, and profitability.

Those who want to become sales representatives should be goal-oriented and persuasive, and work well both independently and as part of a team. A pleasant personality and appearance, the ability to communicate well with people, and problem-solving skills are highly valued. Furthermore, completing a sale can take several months and thus requires patience and perseverance.

Frequently, promotion takes the form of an assignment to a larger account or territory where commissions are likely to be greater. Experienced sales representatives may move into jobs as sales trainers, who instruct new employees on selling techniques and company policies and procedures. Those who have good sales records and leadership ability may advance to higher-level positions such as sales supervisor, district manager, or vice president of sales. In addition to advancement opportunities within a firm, some manufacturers' agents go into business for themselves. Others find opportunities in purchasing, advertising, or marketing research.

Job Outlook
Employment of sales representatives, wholesale and manufacturing, is expected to grow about as fast as the average for all occupations through the year 2012 due to continued growth in the variety and number of goods to be sold. Also, many job openings will result from the need to replace workers who transfer to other occupations or leave the labor force.

Prospective customers will still require sales workers to demonstrate or illustrate the particulars of a good or service. However, computer technology makes sales representatives more effective and productive, for example, by allowing them to provide accurate and current information to customers during sales presentations.

Job prospects for wholesale sales representatives will be better than those for manufacturing sales representatives because manufacturers are expected to continue contracting out sales duties to independent agents rather than using in-house or direct selling personnel. Agents are paid only if they sell, which reduces the overhead cost to their clients. Also, by using an agent who usually contracts his or her services to more than one company, companies can share costs with the other companies involved with that agent. As their customers and manufacturers continue to merge with other companies, independent agents and other wholesale trade firms will, in response, also merge with each other to better serve their clients. Although the demand for independent sales agents will increase over the 2002-12 projection period, the supply is expected to remain stable or decline because of the difficulties associated with self-employment. This factor could lead to many opportunities for sales representatives to start their own independent sales agencies.

Those interested in this occupation should keep in mind that direct selling opportunities in manufacturing are likely to be best for products for which there is strong demand. Furthermore, jobs will be most plentiful in small wholesale and manufacturing firms because a growing number of these companies will rely on agents to market their products as a way to control their costs and expand their customer base.

Employment opportunities and earnings may fluctuate from year to year because sales are affected by changing economic conditions, legislative issues, and consumer preferences. Job prospects will be best for persons with the appropriate knowledge or technical expertise as well as the personal traits necessary for successful selling.

Earnings

Compensation methods vary significantly by the type of firm and product sold. Most employers use a combination of salary and commission or salary plus bonus. Commissions usually are based on the amount of sales, whereas bonuses may depend on individual performance, on the performance of all sales workers in the group or district, or on the company's performance.

Median annual earnings of sales representatives, wholesale and manufacturing, technical and scientific products, were $55,740, including commission, in 2002. The middle 50 percent earned between $39,480 and $79,380 a year. The lowest 10 percent earned less than $28,770, and the highest 10 percent earned more than $108,010 a year. Median annual earnings in the industries employing the largest numbers of sales representatives, technical and scientific products, in 2002 were as follows:

Wholesale electronic markets and agents and brokers	$64,070
Professional and commercial equipment and supplies merchant wholesalers	60,890
Drugs and druggists' sundries merchant wholesalers	57,890
Machinery, equipment, and supplies merchant wholesalers	53,140
Electrical and electronic goods merchant wholesalers	50,550

Median annual earnings of sales representatives, wholesale and manufacturing, except technical and scientific products, were $42,730, including commission, in 2002. The middle 50 percent earned between $30,660 and $60,970 a year. The lowest 10 percent earned less than $22,610, and the highest 10 percent earned more than $88,990 a year. Median annual earnings in the industries employing the largest numbers of sales representatives, except technical and scientific products, in 2002 were as follows:

Wholesale electronic markets and agents and brokers	$48,320
Machinery, equipment, and supplies merchant wholesalers	44,030
Professional and commercial equipment and supplies merchant wholesalers	43,880
Grocery and related product wholesalers	41,840
Miscellaneous nondurable goods merchant whoelsalers	37,940

In addition to their earnings, sales representatives usually are reimbursed for expenses such as transportation costs, meals, hotels, and entertaining customers. They often receive benefits such as health and life insurance, pension plan, vacation and sick leave, personal use of a company car, and frequent flyer mileage. Some companies offer incentives such as free vacation trips or gifts for outstanding sales workers.

Unlike those working directly for a manufacturer or wholesaler, manufacturers' agents are paid strictly on commission and usually are not reimbursed for expenses. Depending on the type of product or products they are selling, their experience in the field, and the number of clients, their earnings can be significantly higher or lower than those working in direct sales.

Related Occupations

Sales representatives, wholesale and manufacturing, must have sales ability and knowledge of the products they sell. Other occupations that require similar skills include advertising, marketing, promotions, and public relations, and sales managers; insurance sales agents; purchasing managers, buyers, and purchasing agents; real estate brokers and sales agents; retail salespersons; sales engineers; and securities, commodities, and financial services sales agents.

Sources of Additional Information

Information on careers for manufacturers' representatives and agents is available from:

➤ Manufacturers' Agents National Association, P.O. Box 3467, Laguna Hills, CA 92654-3467. Internet: **http://www.manaonline.org**

➤ Manufacturers' Representatives Educational Research Foundation, P.O. Box 247, Geneva, IL 60134. Internet: **http://www.mrerf.org**

Sales Worker Supervisors

(0*NET 41-1011.00, 41-1012.00)

Significant Points

- Applicants with retail experience should have the best job opportunities in this occupation.

- Overall employment is projected to grow more slowly than average; the number of self-employed sales worker supervisors is expected to decline.

- Long, irregular hours, including evenings and weekends, are common.

- In many retail establishments, managers are promoted from within the company; a postsecondary degree may speed a sales worker supervisor's advancement into management.

Nature of the Work

Sales worker supervisors oversee the work of sales and related workers, such as retail salespersons, cashiers, customer service representatives, stock clerks and order fillers, sales engineers, and wholesale and manufacturing sales representatives. Sales worker supervisors are responsible for interviewing, hiring, and training employees, as well as for preparing work schedules and assigning workers to specific duties. Many of these workers hold job titles such as *sales manager* or *department manager*. Under the occupational classification system used in the *Handbook*, however, workers with the title *manager* who mainly supervise nonsupervisory workers are called *supervisors* rather than *managers*, even though many of these workers often perform numerous managerial functions. (Sales worker supervisors oversee retail salespersons, cashiers, customer service representatives, stock clerks and order fillers, sales engineers, and wholesale and manufacturing sales representatives, all of whom are discussed elsewhere in the *Handbook*.)

In retail establishments, sales worker supervisors ensure that customers receive satisfactory service and quality goods. They also answer customers' inquiries, deal with complaints, and sometimes handle purchasing, budgeting, and accounting. Their responsibilities vary with the size and type of establishment. As the size of retail stores and the types of goods and services increase, these workers tend to specialize in one department or one aspect of merchandising. (Managers in eating and drinking places are discussed in the *Handbook* statement on food service managers.)

Sales worker supervisors in large retail establishments, often referred to as department managers, provide day-to-day oversight of individual departments, such as shoes, cosmetics, or housewares in large department stores; produce and meat in grocery stores; and sales in automotive dealerships. These workers establish and implement policies, goals, objectives, and procedures for their specific departments; coordinate activities with other department heads; and strive for smooth operations within their departments. They supervise employees who price and ticket goods and place them on display; clean and organize shelves, displays, and inventories in stockrooms; and inspect merchandise to ensure that nothing is outdated. Sales worker supervisors also review inventory and sales records, develop merchandising techniques, and coordinate sales promotions. In addition, they may greet and assist customers and promote sales and good public relations.

Sales worker supervisors in nonretail establishments supervise and coordinate the activities of sales workers who sell industrial products, automobiles, or services such as advertising or Internet services. They may prepare budgets, make personnel decisions, devise sales-incentive programs, assign sales territories, or approve sales contracts.

Sales worker supervisors answer customers' inquiries, deal with complaints, and may handle purchasing, budgeting, and accounting.

In small or independent companies and retail stores, sales worker supervisors not only directly supervise sales associates, but also are responsible for the operation of the entire company or store. Some are self-employed business or store owners.

Working Conditions
Most sales worker supervisors have offices. In retail trade, their offices are within the stores, usually close to the areas they oversee. Although they spend some time in the office completing merchandise orders or arranging work schedules, a large portion of their workday is spent on the sales floor, supervising employees or selling.

Work hours of supervisors vary greatly among establishments, because work schedules usually depend on customers' needs. Supervisors generally work at least 40 hours a week. Long, irregular hours are common, particularly during sales, holidays, busy shopping hours, and times when inventory is taken. Supervisors are expected to work evenings and weekends, but usually are compensated with a day off during the week. Hours can change weekly, and managers sometimes must report to work on short notice, especially when employees are absent. Independent owners can often set their own schedules, but hours must be convenient to customers.

Employment
Sales worker supervisors held about 2.4 million jobs in 2002. Approximately 36 percent were self-employed, most of whom were store owners. Additionally, 43 percent of wage and salary sales worker supervisors are employed in the retail sector. Some of the largest employers are grocery stores, department stores, motor vehicle dealerships, and clothing and accessory stores. The remainder works in nonretail establishments.

Training, Other Qualifications, and Advancement
Sales worker supervisors usually acquire knowledge of management principles and practices—an essential requirement for a supervisory or managerial position in retail trade—through work experience. Many supervisors begin their careers on the sales floor as salespersons, cashiers, or customer service representatives. In these positions, they learn merchandising, customer service, and the basic policies and procedures of the company.

The educational backgrounds of sales worker supervisors vary widely. Regardless of the education they receive, recommended courses include accounting, marketing, management, and sales, as well as psychology, sociology, and communication. Supervisors also must be computer literate, because almost all cash registers, inventory control systems, and sales quotes and contracts are computerized.

Supervisors who have postsecondary education often hold associate's or bachelor's degrees in liberal arts, social sciences, business, or management. To gain experience, many college students participate in internship programs that usually are developed jointly by individual schools and firms.

The type and amount of training available to supervisors varies from company to company. Many national retail chains and companies have formal training programs for management trainees that include both classroom and on-site training. Training time may be as brief as 1 week, but may also last up to 1 year or more, because many organizations require that trainees gain experience during all sales seasons.

Ordinarily, classroom training includes topics such as interviewing and customer service skills, employee and inventory management, and scheduling. Management trainees may work in one specific department while training on the job, or they may rotate through several departments to gain a well-rounded knowledge of the company's operation. Training programs for retail franchises are generally extensive, covering all functions of the company's operation, including budgeting, marketing, management, finance, purchasing, product preparation, human resource management, and compensation. College graduates usually can enter management training programs directly.

Sales worker supervisors must get along with all types of people. They need initiative, self-discipline, good judgment, and decisiveness. Patience and a mild temperament are necessary when dealing with demanding customers. Sales worker supervisors also must be able to motivate, organize, and direct the work of subordinates and communicate clearly and persuasively with customers and other supervisors.

Individuals who display leadership and team-building skills, self-confidence, motivation, and decisiveness become candidates for promotion to assistant manager or manager. A postsecondary degree may speed a sales worker supervisor's advancement into management, because it is viewed by employers as a sign of motivation and maturity—qualities deemed important for promotion to more responsible positions. In many retail establishments, managers are promoted from within the company. In small retail establishments, where the number of positions is limited, advancement to a higher management position may come slowly. Large establishments often have extensive career ladder programs and may offer supervisors the opportunity to transfer to another store in the chain or to the central office if an opening occurs. Although promotions may occur more quickly in large establishments, some managers may need to relocate every several years in order to advance. Supervisors also can become advertising, marketing, promotions, public relations, and sales managers (workers who coordinate marketing plans, monitor sales, and propose advertisements and promotions) or purchasing managers, buyers, or purchasing agents (workers who purchase goods and supplies for their organization or for resale). (These occupations are covered elsewhere in the *Handbook*.)

Some supervisors who have worked in their industry for a long time open their own stores or sales firms. However, retail trade and sales occupations are highly competitive, and although many independent owners succeed, some fail to cover expenses and eventually go out of business. To prosper, owners usually need good business sense and strong customer service and public relations skills.

Job Outlook
Candidates who have retail experience—as a retail salesperson, cashier, or customer service representative, for example—will have the best opportunities for jobs as sales worker supervisors. As in other fields, competition is expected for supervisory jobs, particularly those with the most attractive earnings and working conditions.

Employment of sales worker supervisors is expected to grow more slowly than the average for all occupations through the year 2012. Growth in the occupation will be restrained somewhat as retail companies hire more sales staff and increase the responsibilities of sales worker supervisors. Many job openings will occur as experienced supervisors move into higher levels of management, transfer to other occupations, or leave the labor force. However, as with other supervisory and managerial occupations, job turnover is relatively low.

The Internet and electronic commerce are creating new opportunities to reach and communicate with potential customers. Some firms are hiring Internet sales managers, who are in charge of maintaining an Internet site and answering inquiries relating to the product, to prices, and to the terms of delivery—a trend that will increase demand for these supervisors. Overall, Internet sales and electronic commerce may reduce the number of additional sales

workers needed, thus reducing the number of additional supervisors required. However, the impact of electronic commerce on employment of sales worker supervisors should be minimal.

Projected employment growth of sales worker supervisors will mirror, in part, the patterns of employment growth in the industries in which they work. For example, faster-than-average employment growth is expected in many of the rapidly growing services industries. The number of self-employed sales worker supervisors is expected to decline as independent retailers face increasing competition from national chains.

Unlike middle- and upper-level managers, store-level retail supervisors generally will not be affected by the restructuring and consolidation taking place at the corporate and headquarters levels of many retail chains.

Earnings
Salaries of sales worker supervisors vary substantially, depending upon the level of responsibility the individual has; the person's length of service; and the type, size, and location of the firm.

In 2002, median annual earnings of salaried sales worker supervisors of retail sales workers, including commissions, were $29,700. The middle 50 percent earned between $22,790 and $40,100 a year. The lowest 10 percent earned less than $18,380, and the highest 10 percent earned more than $55,810 a year. Median annual earnings in the industries employing the largest numbers of salaried supervisors of retail sales workers in 2002 were as follows:

Building material and supplies dealers	$32,780
Grocery stores	29,940
Clothing stores	28,060
Department stores	27,390
Gasoline stations	25,000

In 2002, median annual earnings of salaried sales worker supervisors of nonretail sales workers, including commission, were $53,020. The middle 50 percent earned between $37,680 and $77,690 a year. The lowest 10 percent earned less than $26,780, and the highest 10 percent earned more than $114,210 a year. Median annual earnings in the industries employing the largest numbers of salaried supervisors of nonretail sales workers in 2002 were as follows:

Wholesale electronic markets and agents and brokers	$74,000
Professional and commercial equipment and supplies merchant wholesalers	72,970
Insurance carriers	63,220
Machinery, equipment, and supplies merchant wholesalers	60,450
Federal Government	50,570

Compensation systems vary by type of establishment and merchandise sold. Many supervisors receive a commission or a combination of salary and commission. Under a commission system, supervisors receive a percentage of department or store sales. Thus, supervisors have the opportunity to increase their earnings considerably, but they may find that their earnings depend on their ability to sell their product and the condition of the economy. Those who sell large amounts of merchandise or exceed sales goals often receive bonuses or other awards.

Related Occupations
Sales worker supervisors serve customers, supervise workers, and direct and coordinate the operations of an establishment. Others with similar responsibilities include financial managers, food service managers, lodging managers, and medical and health services managers.

Sources of Additional Information

Information on employment opportunities for sales worker supervisors may be obtained from the employment offices of various retail establishments or State employment service offices.

General information on management careers in retail establishments is available from:

➤ National Retail Federation, 325 7th St. NW., Suite 1100, Washington, DC 20004.

Information on management careers in grocery stores and on schools offering related programs is available from:

➤ International Food Service Distributors Association, 201 Park Washington Ct., Falls Church, VA 22046-4521.

Information about management careers and training programs in the motor vehicle dealers industry is available from:

➤ National Automobile Dealers Association, Public Relations Dept., 8400 Westpark Dr., McLean, VA 22102-3591. Internet: **http://www.nada.org**

Information about management careers in convenience stores is available from:

➤ National Association of Convenience Stores, 1600 Duke St., Alexandria, VA 22314-3436.

Securities, Commodities, and Financial Services Sales Agents

(0*NET 41-3031.01, 41-3031.02)

Significant Points

● Employment is expected to grow as fast as the average, and competition for entry-level jobs is expected to be keen because sales agents who succeed often have high earnings.

● A college degree, sales ability, good interpersonal and communication skills, and a strong desire to succeed are important qualifications for this profession.

● Beginning securities and commodities sales agents must pass a licensing exam to sell securities and commodities.

Nature of the Work

Most investors, whether they are individuals with a few hundred dollars to invest or large institutions with millions, use *securities, commodities, and financial services sales agents* when buying or selling stocks, bonds, shares in mutual funds, insurance annuities, or other financial products. In addition, many clients seek out these agents for advice on investments, estate planning, and other financial matters.

Securities and commodities sales agents, also called brokers, stockbrokers, registered representatives, account executives, or financial consultants, perform a variety of tasks, depending on their specific job duties. When an investor wishes to buy or sell a security, for example, sales agents may relay the order through their firm's computers to the floor of a securities exchange, such as the New York Stock Exchange. There, securities and commodities sales agents known as *floor brokers* negotiate the price with other floor brokers, make the sale, and forward the purchase price to the sales agents. If a security is not traded on an exchange, as in the case of bonds and over-the-counter stocks, the broker sends the order to the firm's trading department. Here, using their own funds or those of the firm, other securities sales agents, known as *dealers*, buy and sell securities directly from other dealers, with the intention of re-

selling the security to customers at a profit. After the transaction has been completed, the broker notifies the customer of the final price.

Securities and commodities sales agents also provide many related services for their customers. They may explain stock market terms and trading practices, offer financial counseling or advice on the purchase or sale of particular securities, and design an individual client's financial portfolio, which could include securities, life insurance, corporate and municipal bonds, mutual funds, certificates of deposit, annuities, and other investments.

Not all customers have the same investment goals. Some individuals prefer long-term investments, for capital growth or to provide income over a number of years; others might want to invest in speculative securities, which they hope will quickly rise in price. On the basis of each customer's objectives, securities and commodities sales agents furnish information about the advantages and disadvantages of an investment. They also supply the latest price quotes on any securities, as well as information on the activities and financial positions of the corporations issuing the securities.

Most securities and commodities sales agents serve individual investors; others specialize in institutional investors, such as banks and pension funds. In institutional investing, sales agents usually concentrate on a specific financial product, such as stocks, bonds, options, annuities, or commodity futures. At other times, they may also handle the sale of new issues, such as corporate securities issued to finance the expansion of a plant.

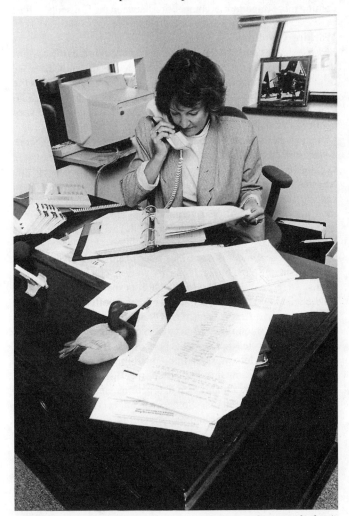

Securities sales agents recommend investment products on the basis of their clients' goals.

The most important part of a sales representative's job is finding clients and building a customer base. Thus, beginning securities and commodities sales agents spend much of their time searching for customers—relying heavily on telephone solicitation. They also may meet clients through business and social contacts. Many sales agents find it useful to contact potential clients by teaching adult education investment courses or by giving lectures at libraries or social clubs. Brokerage firms may give sales agents lists of people with whom the firm has done business in the past. Some agents inherit the clients of agents who have retired. After an agent is established, referrals from satisfied clients are an important source of new business.

Financial services sales agents sell a wide variety of banking and related services. They contact potential customers to explain their services and to ascertain customers' banking and other financial needs. In doing so, they discuss services such as loans, deposit accounts, lines of credit, sales or inventory financing, certificates of deposit, cash management, mutual funds, or investment services. They also may solicit businesses to participate in consumer credit card programs. Financial services sales agents who serve all the financial needs of a single affluent individual or a business often are called private bankers or relationship managers.

With deregulation of the financial services industry, the distinctions among sales agents are becoming less clear as securities firms, banks, and insurance companies venture further and further into each other's products and services. The agents' jobs also are becoming more important as competition between the firms intensifies.

Working Conditions

Most securities and commodities sales agents work in offices under fairly stressful conditions. They have access to "quote boards" or computer terminals that continually provide information on the prices of securities. When sales activity increases, due perhaps to unanticipated changes in the economy, the pace can become very hectic.

Established securities and commodities sales agents usually work a standard 40-hour week. Beginners who are seeking customers usually work longer hours. New brokers spend a great deal of time learning the firm's products and services and studying for exams in order to qualify to sell other products, such as insurance and commodities. Most securities and commodities sales agents accommodate customers by meeting with them in the evenings or on weekends.

A growing number of securities sales agents, employed mostly by discount or online brokerage firms, work in call-center environments. In these centers, hundreds of agents spend much of the day on the telephone taking orders from clients or offering advice and information on different securities. Often, such call centers operate 24 hours a day, requiring agents to work in shifts.

Financial services sales agents normally work 40 hours a week in a comfortable, less stressful office environment. They may spend considerable time outside the office, meeting with current and prospective clients, attending civic functions, and participating in trade association meetings. Some financial services sales agents work exclusively inside banks, providing service to walk-in customers.

Employment

Securities, commodities, and financial services sales agents held about 300,000 jobs in 2002. More than half of jobs were found in securities, commodity contracts, and other financial investments and related activities. One in 5 worked in depository and nondepository credit intermediation, including commercial banks, savings institu-

tions, and credit unions. Although securities and commodities sales agents are employed by firms in all parts of the country, many work for a small number of large securities and investment banking firms headquartered in New York City. About 1 securities, commodities, and financial services sales agent in 8 was self-employed.

Training, Other Qualifications, and Advancement

Because securities and commodities sales agents must be knowledgeable about economic conditions and trends, a college education is important, especially in larger securities firms. In fact, the overwhelming majority of workers in this occupation are college graduates. Although employers seldom require specialized academic training, courses in business administration, economics, and finance are helpful.

Many employers consider personal qualities and skills more important than academic training. Employers seek applicants who have considerable sales ability, good interpersonal and communication skills, and a strong desire to succeed. Some employers also make sure that applicants have a good credit history and a clean record. Self-confidence and an ability to handle frequent rejections are important ingredients for success.

Because maturity and the ability to work independently are important, many employers prefer to hire those who have achieved success in other jobs. Some firms prefer candidates with sales experience, particularly those who have worked on commission in areas such as real estate or insurance. Therefore, most entrants to this occupation transfer from other jobs. Some begin working as securities and commodities sales agents following retirement from other fields.

Securities and commodities sales agents must meet State licensing requirements, which usually include passing an examination and, in some cases, furnishing a personal bond. In addition, sales agents must register as representatives of their firm with the National Association of Securities Dealers, Inc. (NASD). Before beginners can qualify as registered representatives, they must pass the General Securities Registered Representative Examination (Series 7 exam), administered by the NASD, and be an employee of a registered firm for at least 4 months.

Most States require a second examination: the Uniform Securities Agents State Law Examination. This test measures the prospective representative's knowledge of the securities business in general, of customer protection requirements, and of recordkeeping procedures. Many take correspondence courses in preparation for the securities examinations. Within 2 years, brokers are encouraged to take additional licensing exams in order to sell mutual funds, insurance, and commodities.

Most employers provide on-the-job training to help securities and commodities sales agents meet the registration requirements for certification. In most firms, the training period takes about 4 months.

Trainees in large firms may receive classroom instruction in securities analysis, effective speaking, and the finer points of selling, may take courses offered by business schools and associations, and may undergo a period of on-the-job training lasting up to 2 years. Many firms like to rotate their trainees among various departments, to give them a broad perspective of the securities business. In small firms, sales agents often receive training in outside institutions and on the job.

Securities and commodities sales agents must understand the basic characteristics of the wide variety of financial products offered by brokerage firms. Brokers periodically take training through their firms or outside institutions in order to keep abreast of new financial products and improve their sales techniques. Computer training also is important, because the securities sales business is highly automated. Since 1995, it has become mandatory for all registered securities and commodities sales agents to attend periodic continuing education classes to maintain their licenses. Courses consist of computer-based training in regulatory matters and company training on new products and services.

The principal form of advancement for securities and commodities sales agents is an increase in the number and size of the accounts they handle. Although beginners usually service the accounts of individual investors, they may eventually handle very large institutional accounts, such as those of banks and pension funds. After taking a series of tests, some brokers become portfolio managers and have greater authority to make investment decisions regarding an account. Some experienced sales agents become branch office managers and supervise other sales agents while continuing to provide services for their own customers. A few agents advance to top management positions or become partners in their firms.

Banks and other credit institutions prefer to hire college graduates for financial services sales jobs. A business administration degree with a specialization in finance or a liberal arts degree that includes courses in accounting, economics, and marketing serves as excellent preparation for this job. Often, financial services sales agents learn their jobs through on-the-job training under the supervision of bank officers. However, those who wish to sell mutual funds and insurance products may need to undergo formal training and pass some of the same exams required of securities sales agents.

Job Outlook

Employment of securities, commodities, and financial services sales agents is expected to grow about as fast as the average for all occupations through 2012. As people's incomes continue to climb, they will increasingly seek the advice and services of securities, commodities, and financial services sales agents to realize their financial goals. Growth in the volume of trade in stocks over the Internet will reduce the need for brokers for many transactions. Nevertheless, the overall increase in investment is expected to spur employment growth among these workers, with a majority of transactions still requiring the advice and services of securities, commodities, and financial services sales agents.

Baby boomers in their peak savings years will fuel much of this increase in investment. Saving for retirement has been made much easier by the government, which continues to offer a number of tax-favorable pension plans, such as the 401(k) and the Roth IRA. The participation of more women in the workforce also means higher household incomes and more women qualifying for pensions. Many of these pensions are self-directed, meaning that the recipient has the responsibility for investing the money. With such large amounts of money to invest, sales agents, in their role as financial advisors, will be in great demand.

Other factors that will affect the demand for brokers are the increasing number and complexity of investment products, as well as the effects of globalization. As the public and businesses become more sophisticated about investing, they are venturing into the options and futures markets. Brokers are needed to buy or sell these products, which are not traded online. Also, markets for investment are expanding with the increase in global trading of stocks and bonds. Furthermore, the New York Stock Exchange has extended its trading hours to accommodate trading in foreign stocks and compete with foreign exchanges.

Employment of brokers is adversely affected by downturns in the stock market or the economy. Turnover is high for beginning brokers, who often are unable to establish a sizable clientele even in good times. Once established, securities and commodities sales agents have a very strong attachment to their occupation because of their high earnings and the considerable investment in training. Competition usually is intense, especially in larger companies with more applicants than jobs. Opportunities for beginning brokers should be better in smaller firms.

The number of financial services sales agents in banks will increase faster than average as banks expand their product offerings in order to compete directly with other investment firms.

Earnings

Median annual earnings of securities, commodities, and financial services sales agents were $60,990 in 2002. The middle half earned between $36,180 and $117,050.

Median annual earnings in the industries employing the largest numbers of securities and financial services sales agents in 2002 were as follows:

Securities and commodity contracts intermediation and brokerage	$78,140
Other financial investment activities	75,110
Management of companies and enterprises	54,730
Nondepository credit intermediation	43,220
Depository credit intermediation	39,870

Stockbrokers, who provide personalized service and more guidance with respect to a client's investments, usually are paid a commission based on the amount of stocks, bonds, mutual funds, insurance, and other products they sell. Earnings from commissions are likely to be high when there is much buying and selling, low when there is a slump in market activity. Most firms provide sales agents with a steady income by paying a "draw against commission"—a minimum salary based on commissions they can be expected to earn. Securities and commodities sales agents who can provide their clients with the most thorough financial services should enjoy the greatest income stability. Trainee brokers usually are paid a salary until they develop a client base. The salary gradually decreases in favor of commissions as the broker gains clients. A small, but increasing, number of full-service brokers are paid a percentage of the assets they oversee. This fee often covers a certain number of trades done for free.

Brokers who work for discount brokerage firms that promote the use of telephone and online trading services usually are paid a salary, sometimes boosted by bonuses that reflect the profitability of the office. Financial services sales agents usually are paid a salary also; however, bonuses or commissions from sales are starting to account for a larger share of their income.

Related Occupations

Other jobs requiring knowledge of finance and an ability to sell include insurance sales agents, real estate brokers and sales agents, and financial analysts and personal financial advisors.

Sources of Additional Information

For general information on the securities industry, contact:
➤ Securities Industry Association, 120 Broadway, New York, NY 10271.

For information about job opportunities for financial services sales agents in various States, contact State bankers' associations or write directly to a particular bank.

Travel Agents

(O*NET 41-3041.00)

Significant Points

- Travel benefits, such as reduced rates for transportation and lodging, attract many people to this occupation.

- Training at a postsecondary vocational school, college, or university is increasingly important.

- Industry consolidation and increasing use of the Internet to book travel will result in a decline in the employment of travel agents.

- Keen competition for jobs is expected.

Nature of the Work

Constantly changing airfares and schedules, thousands of available vacation packages, and a vast amount of travel information on the Internet can make travel planning frustrating and time-consuming. To sort out the many travel options, tourists and business people often turn to travel agents, who assess their needs and help them make the best possible travel arrangements. Also, many major cruise lines, resorts, and specialty travel groups use travel agents to promote travel packages to millions of people every year.

In general, travel agents give advice on destinations and make arrangements for transportation, hotel accommodations, car rentals, tours, and recreation. They also may advise on weather conditions, restaurants, tourist attractions, and recreation. For international travel, agents also provide information on customs regulations, required papers (passports, visas, and certificates of vaccination), and currency exchange rates.

Travel agents consult a variety of published and computer-based sources for information on departure and arrival times, fares, and hotel ratings and accommodations. They may visit hotels, resorts, and restaurants to evaluate comfort, cleanliness, and quality of food and service so that they can base recommendations on their own travel experiences or those of colleagues or clients.

Travel agents also promote their services, using telemarketing, direct mail, and the Internet. They make presentations to social and special-interest groups, arrange advertising displays, and suggest company-sponsored trips to business managers. Depending

Travel agents often recommend places to stay, eat, and visit to travelers.

on the size of the travel agency, an agent may specialize by type of travel, such as leisure or business, or destination, such as Europe or Africa.

Working Conditions

Travel agents spend most of their time behind a desk conferring with clients, completing paperwork, contacting airlines and hotels for travel arrangements, and promoting group tours. During vacation seasons and holiday periods, they may be under a great deal of pressure. Many agents, especially those who are self-employed, frequently work long hours. With advanced computer systems and telecommunication networks, some travel agents are able to work at home.

Employment

Travel agents held about 118,000 jobs in 2002 and are found in every part of the country. More than 8 out of 10 agents worked for travel agencies. Nearly 1 in 10 was self-employed.

Training, Other Qualifications, and Advancement

The minimum requirement for those interested in becoming a travel agent is a high school diploma or equivalent. Technology and computerization are having a profound effect on the work of travel agents, however, and formal or specialized training is increasingly important. Many vocational schools offer full-time travel agent programs that last several months, as well as evening and weekend programs. Travel agent courses also are offered in public adult education programs and in community and 4-year colleges. A few colleges offer bachelor's or master's degrees in travel and tourism. Although few college courses relate directly to the travel industry, a college education sometimes is desired by employers to establish a background in fields such as computer science, geography, communication, foreign languages, and world history. Courses in accounting and business management also are important, especially for those who expect to manage or start their own travel agencies.

The American Society of Travel Agents (ASTA) offers a correspondence course that provides a basic understanding of the travel industry. Travel agencies also provide on-the-job training for their employees, a significant part of which consists of computer instruction. All employers require computer skills of workers whose jobs involve the operation of airline and centralized reservation systems.

Experienced travel agents can take advanced self-study or group-study courses from the Travel Institute that lead to the Certified Travel Counselor (CTC) designation. The Travel Institute also offers marketing and sales skills development programs and destination specialist programs, which provide a detailed knowledge of regions such as North America, Western Europe, the Caribbean, and the Pacific Rim.

Personal travel experience or experience as an airline reservation agent is an asset because knowledge about a city or foreign country often helps to influence a client's travel plans. Patience and the ability to gain the confidence of clients also are useful qualities. Travel agents must be well-organized, accurate, and meticulous to compile information from various sources and plan and organize their clients' travel itineraries. As the Internet has become an important tool for making travel arrangements, more travel agencies are using Web sites to provide their services to clients. This trend has increased the importance of computer skills in this occupation. Other desirable qualifications include good writing, interpersonal, and sales skills.

Some employees start as reservation clerks or receptionists in travel agencies. With experience and some formal training, they can take on greater responsibilities and eventually assume travel agent duties. In agencies with many offices, travel agents may advance to office manager or to other managerial positions.

Those who start their own agencies generally have had experience in an established agency. Before they can receive commissions, these agents usually must gain formal approval from suppliers or corporations, such as airlines, ship lines, or rail lines. The Airlines Reporting Corporation and the International Airlines Travel Agency Network, for example, are the approving bodies for airlines. To gain approval, an agency must be financially sound and employ at least one experienced manager or travel agent.

There are no Federal licensing requirements for travel agents. However, nine States—California, Florida, Hawaii, Illinois, Iowa, Ohio, Oregon, Rhode Island, and Washington—require some form of registration or certification of retail sellers of travel services. More information may be obtained by contacting the Office of the Attorney General or Department of Commerce in each State.

Job Outlook

Employment of travel agents is expected to decline through 2012. Most openings will occur as experienced agents transfer to other occupations or leave the labor force. Because of the projected decline and the fact that a number of people are attracted by the travel benefits associated with this occupation, keen competition for jobs is expected.

An increasing reliance on the Internet to book travel, as well as industry consolidation, will continue to reduce the need for travel agents. The Internet increasingly allows people to access travel information from their personal computers, enabling them to research and plan their own trips, make their own reservations and travel arrangements, and purchase their own tickets. Also, airlines no longer pay commissions to travel agencies, which has reduced revenues and caused some agencies to go out of business. However, many consumers still prefer to use a professional travel agent to ensure reliability, to save time, and, in some cases, to save money.

Moderating the employment decline, however, are projections for increased spending on tourism and travel over the next decade. With rising household incomes, smaller families, and an increasing number of older people who are more likely to travel, more people are expected to travel on vacation—and to do so more frequently—than in the past. Business travel also should bounce back from recession and terrorism related lows as business activity expands. Further, as U.S. businesses open more foreign operations, and businesses, in general, increasingly sell their goods and services worldwide, more business travel is anticipated.

There are other factors spurring demand for travel agents that will moderate any decline. Most notable is the increasing affordability of air travel. Greater competition between airlines, especially from low-cost carriers, has resulted in bringing airfares within the budgets of more people. In addition, American travel agents now organize more tours for the growing number of foreign visitors. Also, travel agents often are able to offer various travel packages at a substantial discount.

The travel business is sensitive to economic downturns and international political crises, when travel plans are likely to be deferred. Therefore, the number of job opportunities for travel agents fluctuates. The best opportunities will be for those travel agents that can utilize the Internet for their own operations to reduce costs and better compete with travel suppliers.

Earnings

Experience, sales ability, and the size and location of the agency determine the salary of a travel agent. Median annual earnings of travel agents were $26,630 in 2002. The middle 50 percent earned between $20,800 and $33,580. The lowest 10 percent earned less than $16,530, while the top 10 percent earned more than $41,660.

Salaried agents usually enjoy standard employer-paid benefits that self-employed agents must provide for themselves. Among agencies, those focusing on corporate sales pay higher salaries and provide more extensive benefits, on average, than do those that focus on leisure sales. When they travel for personal reasons, agents usually get reduced rates for transportation and accommodations. In addition, agents sometimes take "familiarization" trips, at no cost to themselves, to learn about various vacation sites. These benefits attract many people to this occupation.

Earnings of travel agents who own their agencies depend mainly on commissions from travel-related bookings and service fees they charge clients. Often it takes time to acquire a sufficient number of clients to have adequate earnings, so it is not unusual for new self-employed agents to have low earnings. Established agents may have lower earnings during economic downturns.

Related Occupations

Travel agents organize and schedule business, educational, or recreational travel or activities. Other workers with similar responsibilities include tour and travel guides, and reservation and transportation ticket agents and travel clerks.

Sources of Additional Information

For further information on training opportunities, contact:
➤ American Society of Travel Agents, Education Department, 1101 King St., Alexandria, VA 22314.

For information on training and certification qualifications, contact:
➤ The Travel Institute, 148 Linden St., Suite 305, Wellesley, MA 02482.

Office and Administrative Support Occupations

Communications Equipment Operators

(O*NET 43-2011.00, 43-2021.01, 43-2021.02, 43-2099.99)

Significant Points

- Switchboard operators hold 3 out of 4 jobs.
- Workers train on the job.
- Employment is expected to decline.

Nature of the Work

Most communications equipment operators work as *switchboard operators* for a wide variety of businesses, such as hospitals, business support services, and employment services. Switchboard operators operate private branch exchange (PBX) or voiceover Internet protocol (VoIP) switchboards to relay incoming, outgoing, and interoffice calls, usually for a single organization. They also may handle other clerical duties, such as supplying information, taking messages, and announcing visitors. Technological improvements have automated many of the tasks handled by switchboard operators. New systems automatically connect outside calls to the correct destination or automated directories, and voice-mail systems take messages without the assistance of an operator.

Some communications equipment operators work as *telephone operators*, assisting customers in making telephone calls. Although most calls are connected automatically, callers sometimes require the assistance of an operator. *Central office operators* help customers to complete local and long-distance calls. *Directory assistance operators* provide customers with information such as telephone numbers or area codes.

When callers dial "0," they usually reach a central office operator, also known as a *local*, *long-distance*, or *call completion operator*. Most of these operators work for telephone companies, and many of their responsibilities have been automated. For example, callers can make international, collect, and credit card calls without the assistance of a central office operator. Other tasks previously handled by these operators, such as billing calls to third parties and monitoring the cost of a call, also have been automated.

Callers still need a central office operator for a limited number of tasks, including placing person-to-person calls or interrupting busy lines if an emergency warrants the disruption. When natural disasters such as storms or earthquakes occur, central office operators provide callers with emergency phone contacts. They also assist callers who are having difficulty with automated phone systems. An operator monitoring an automated system that aids a caller in placing collect calls, for example, may intervene if a caller needs assistance with the system.

Directory assistance operators provide callers with information such as telephone numbers or area codes. Most directory assistance operators work for telephone companies; increasingly, they also work for companies that provide business services. Automated systems now handle many of the responsibilities once performed by directory assistance operators. The systems prompt callers for a listing

Switchboard operators also may handle clerical duties.

and may even connect the call after providing the telephone number. However, directory assistance operators monitor many of the calls received by automated systems. The operators listen to recordings of the customer's request and then key information into electronic directories to access the correct telephone numbers. Directory assistance operators also provide personal assistance to customers having difficulty using the automated system.

Other communications equipment operators include workers who operate satellite communications equipment, telegraph equipment, and a wide variety of other communications equipment.

Working Conditions

Most communications equipment operators work in pleasant, well-lighted surroundings. Because telephone operators spend much time seated at keyboards and video monitors, employers often provide workstations designed to decrease glare and other physical discomforts. Such improvements reduce the incidence of eyestrain, back discomfort, and injury due to repetitive motion.

Switchboard operators generally work the same hours as other clerical employees at their company. In most organizations, full-time operators work regular business hours over a 5-day workweek. Work schedules are more irregular in hotels, hospitals, and other organizations that require round-the-clock operator services. In these companies, switchboard operators may work in the evenings and on holidays and weekends.

Central office and directory assistance operators must be accessible to customers 24 hours a day; therefore, they work a variety of shifts. Some operators work split shifts, coming on duty during peak calling periods in the late morning and early evening and going off duty during the intervening hours. Telephone companies normally assign shifts by seniority, allowing the most experienced operators first choice of schedules. As a result, entry-level operators may have less desirable schedules, including late evening, split-shift, and weekend work. Telephone company operators may work overtime during emergencies.

Approximately 1 in 5 communications equipment operators works part time. Because of the irregular nature of telephone operator schedules, many employers seek part-time workers for those shifts that are difficult to fill.

An operator's work may be quite repetitive and the pace hectic during peak calling periods. To maintain operators' efficiency, supervisors at telephone companies often monitor their performance, including the amount of time they spend on each call. The rapid pace of the job and frequent monitoring may cause stress.

Employment

Communications equipment operators held about 304,000 jobs in 2002. About 3 out of 4 worked as switchboard operators. Employment was distributed as follows:

Switchboard operators, including answering service 236,000
Telephone operators 50,000
All other communications equipment operators 19,000

Most switchboard operators worked for services establishments, such as employment services, hospitals, and hotels and motels.

Training, Other Qualifications, and Advancement

Communications equipment operators receive their training on the job. At large telecommunications companies, entry-level central office and directory assistance operators may receive both classroom and on-the-job instruction that can last several weeks. At small telecommunications companies, operators usually receive shorter, less formal training. These operators may be paired with experienced personnel who provide hands-on instruction. Switchboard operators also may receive short-term, informal training, sometimes provided by the manufacturer of their switchboard equipment.

New employees are trained in the operation of their equipment and in procedures designed to maximize efficiency. They are familiarized with company policies, including the expected level of customer service. Instructors monitor both the time and quality of trainees' responses to customer requests. Supervisors may continue to monitor new employees closely after they complete their initial training session.

Employers generally require a high school diploma for operator positions. Applicants should have clear speech, good hearing, and strong reading, spelling, and numerical skills. Computer literacy and typing skills also are important, and familiarity with a foreign language is helpful because of the increasing diversity of the population. Candidates for positions may be required to take an examination covering basic language and math skills. Most companies emphasize customer service and seek operators who will remain courteous to customers while working at a fast pace.

After 1 or 2 years on the job, communications equipment operators may advance to other positions within a company. Many enter clerical occupations in which their operator experience is valuable, such as customer service representative, dispatcher, and receptionist. (See the *Handbook* statements on these occupations.) Operators interested in more technical work may take training classes and advance into positions having to do with installing and repairing equipment. (See the *Handbook* statements on radio and telecommunications equipment installers and repairers, and line installers and repairers.) Promotion to supervisory positions also is possible.

Job Outlook

Employment of communications equipment operators is projected to decline through 2012, due largely to new labor-saving communications technologies, the movement of jobs to foreign countries, and consolidation of telephone operator jobs into fewer locations, often staffed by business support or employment services firms. Virtually all job openings will result from the need to replace com-

munications equipment operators who transfer to other occupations or leave the labor force.

Developments in communications technologies—in particular, voice recognition systems that are accessible and easy to use—will continue to have a significant impact on the demand for switchboard operators. Voice recognition technology allows automated telephone systems to recognize human speech. Callers speak directly to the system, which interprets the speech and then connects the call. Because voice recognition systems do not require callers to input data through a telephone keypad, they are easier to use than touch-tone systems. Voice recognition systems are increasingly able to understand sophisticated vocabulary and grammatical structures; however, many companies will continue to employ operators so that those callers who do have problems can access a "live" employee if they desire.

Electronic communication through the Internet or e-mail provides alternatives to telephone communication and requires no operators. Internet directory assistance services are reducing the need for directory assistance operators. Local telephone companies currently have the most reliable telephone directory data; however, Internet services provide information such as addresses and maps, in addition to telephone numbers. As the functions of telephones and computers converge, the convenience of Internet directory assistance is expected to attract many customers, reducing the need for telephone operators to provide this service.

Consolidations among telephone companies also will reduce the need for operators. As communications technologies improve and the prices of long-distance service fall, telephone companies will contract out and consolidate telephone operator jobs, often to other countries. Operators will be employed at fewer locations and will serve larger customer populations.

Earnings

Median hourly earnings of switchboard operators, including answering service, were $10.19 in 2002. The middle 50 percent earned between $8.41 and $12.27. The lowest 10 percent earned less than $7.13, and the highest 10 percent earned more than $14.59. Median hourly earnings in the industries employing the largest numbers of switchboard operators in 2002 are given in the following tabulation:

General medical and surgical hospitals $10.20
Offices of physicians 10.20
Traveler accommodation 9.69
Employment services 9.43
Business support services 8.37

Median hourly earnings of telephone operators in 2002 were $13.75. The middle 50 percent earned between $9.86 and $18.35. The lowest 10 percent earned less than $8.09, and the highest 10 percent earned more than $20.80.

Some telephone operators working at telephone companies are members of the Communications Workers of America or the International Brotherhood of Electrical Workers. For these operators, union contracts govern wage rates, wage increases, and the time required to advance from one pay step to the next. It normally takes 4 years to rise from the lowest paying nonsupervisory operator position to the highest. Contracts call for extra pay for work beyond the normal 6-1/2 to 7-1/2 hours a day or 5 days a week, for Sunday and holiday work, and for bilingual positions. A pay differential also is guaranteed for night work and split shifts. Many contracts provide for a 1-week vacation after 6 months of service, 2 weeks after 1 year, 3 weeks after 7 years, 4 weeks after 15 years, and 5 weeks after 25 years. Holidays range from 9 to 11 days a year.

Median hourly earnings of communication equipment operators, all other, in 2002 were $15.21. The middle 50 percent earned between $10.79 and $17.90. The lowest 10 percent earned less than $8.36, and the highest 10 percent earned more than $21.82.

Related Occupations

Other workers who provide information to the general public include dispatchers; hotel, motel, and resort desk clerks; information and record clerks; customer service representatives; receptionists and information clerks; and reservation and transportation ticket agents and travel clerks.

Sources of Additional Information

For more details about employment opportunities, contact a telephone company or temporary help agency, or write to either of the following unions:

➤ Communications Workers of America, 501 3rd St. NW., Washington, DC 20001.

➤ International Brotherhood of Electrical Workers, Telecommunications Department, 1125 15th St. NW., Room 807, Washington, DC 20005.

Computer Operators

(0*NET 43-9011.00)

Significant Points

● Computer operators usually receive on-the-job training; the length of training varies with the job and the experience of the worker.

● Employment is expected to decline sharply due to advances in technology.

● Opportunities will be best for operators who have formal computer-related education, are familiar with a variety of operating systems, and keep up-to-date with the latest technology.

Nature of the Work

Computer operators oversee the operation of computer hardware systems, ensuring that these machines are used as efficiently as possible. They may work with mainframes, minicomputers, or networks of personal computers. Computer operators must anticipate problems and take preventive action, as well as solve problems that occur during operations.

The duties of computer operators vary with the size of the installation, the type of equipment used, and the policies of the employer. Generally, operators control the console of either a mainframe digital computer or a group of minicomputers. Working from operating instructions prepared by programmers, users, or operations managers, computer operators set controls on the computer and on peripheral devices required to run a particular job.

Computer operators load equipment with tapes, disks, and paper, as needed. While the computer is running—which may be 24 hours a day for large computers—computer operators monitor the control console and respond to operating and computer messages. Messages indicate the individual specifications of each job being run. If an error message occurs, operators must locate and solve the problem or terminate the program. Operators also maintain logbooks or operating records, listing each job that is run and events, such as machine malfunctions, that occur during their shift. In ad-

Computer operators set controls on computers and peripheral devices required to run a particular job.

dition, computer operators may help programmers and systems analysts test and debug new programs. (See the statements on computer programmers; and systems analysts, computer scientists, and database administrators elsewhere in the *Handbook.*)

As the trend toward networking computers accelerates, a growing number of computer operators are working on personal computers (PCs) and minicomputers. In many offices, factories, and other work settings, PCs and minicomputers are connected in networks, often referred to as local area networks (LANs) or multiuser systems. Whereas users in the area operate some of these computers, many require the services of full-time operators. The tasks performed on PCs and minicomputers are very similar to those performed on large computers.

As organizations continue to look for opportunities to increase productivity, automation is expanding into additional areas of computer operations. Sophisticated software, coupled with robotics, enables a computer to perform many routine tasks formerly done by computer operators. Scheduling, loading and downloading programs, mounting tapes, rerouting messages, and running periodic reports can be done without the intervention of an operator. Consequently, these improvements will change what computer operators do in the future. As technology advances, the responsibilities of many computer operators are shifting to areas such as network operations, user support, and database maintenance.

Working Conditions

Computer operators generally work in well-lighted, well-ventilated, comfortable rooms. Because many organizations use their computers 24 hours a day, 7 days a week, computer operators may be required to work evening or night shifts and weekends. Shift assignments usually are made based on seniority. However, increasingly automated operations will lessen the need for shift work, because many companies can let the computer take over operations during less desirable working hours. In addition, advances in telecommuting technologies—such as faxes, modems, and e-mail—and data center automation, such as automated tape libraries, enable some operators to monitor batch processes, check systems performance, and record problems for the next shift.

Because computer operators generally spend a lot of time in front of a computer monitor, as well as performing repetitive tasks such as loading and unloading printers, they may be susceptible to eyestrain, back discomfort, and hand and wrist problems.

Employment

Computer operators held about 182,000 jobs in 2002. Jobs are found in various industries such as government, wholesale and retail trade, manufacturing, data processing services and other information industries, and finance and insurance. A number of computer operators are employed by firms in computer systems design and related services, as more companies contract out their data processing operations.

Training, Other Qualifications, and Advancement

Computer operators usually receive on-the-job training in order to become acquainted with their employer's equipment and routines. The length of training varies with the job and the experience of the worker. However, previous work experience is the key to obtaining an operator job in many large establishments. Employers generally look for specific, hands-on experience with the type of equipment and related operating systems they use. Additionally, formal computer-related training, perhaps through a community college or technical school, is recommended. Related training also can be obtained through the U.S. Armed Forces and from some computer manufacturers. As computer technology changes and data processing centers become more automated, employers will increasingly require candidates to have formal training and experience for operator jobs. And, although not required, a bachelor's degree in a computer-related field can be helpful when one is seeking employment as a computer operator or advancement to a managerial position.

Because computer technology changes so rapidly, operators must be adaptable and willing to learn. Analytical and technical expertise also are needed, particularly by operators who work in automated data centers, to deal with unique or high-level problems that a computer is not programmed to handle. Operators must be able to communicate well, and to work effectively with programmers, users, and other operators. Computer operators also must be able to work independently because they may have little or no direct supervision.

A few computer operators may advance to supervisory jobs, although most management positions within data processing or computer operations centers require advanced formal education, such as a bachelor's or higher degree. Through on-the-job experience and additional formal education, some computer operators may advance to jobs in areas such as network operations or support. As they gain experience in programming, some operators may advance to jobs as programmers or analysts. A move into these types of jobs is becoming much more difficult, as employers increasingly require candidates for more skilled computer jobs to possess at least a bachelor's degree.

Job Outlook

Employment of computer operators is expected to decline through the year 2012. Experienced operators are expected to compete for job openings that will arise each year to replace workers who transfer to other occupations or leave the labor force. Opportunities will be best for operators who have formal computer-related education, are familiar with a variety of operating systems, and keep up to date with the latest technology.

Advances in technology have reduced both the size and cost of computer equipment, while increasing the capacity for data storage and processing automation. Sophisticated computer hardware and software are now used in practically every industry, in such areas as factory and office automation, telecommunications, medicine, edu-cation, and administration. The expanding use of software that automates computer operations gives companies the option of making systems more user-friendly, greatly reducing the need for operators. Such improvements require operators to monitor a greater number of operations at the same time and be capable of solving a broader range of problems that may arise. The result is that fewer operators will be needed to perform more highly skilled work.

Computer operators who are displaced by automation may be reassigned to support staffs that maintain personal computer networks or assist other members of the organization. Operators who keep up with changing technology, by updating their skills and enhancing their training, should have the best prospects of moving into other areas such as network administration and technical support. Others may be retrained to perform different job duties, such as supervising an operations center, maintaining automation packages, or analyzing computer operations to recommend ways in which to increase productivity. In the future, operators who wish to work in the computer field will need to know more about programming, automation software, graphics interface, client/server environments, and open systems in order to take advantage of changing job opportunities.

Earnings

Median annual earnings of computer operators were $29,650 in 2002. The middle 50 percent earned between about $23,040 and $37,950 a year. The highest 10 percent earned more than $46,780, and the lowest 10 percent earned less than $18,610. Median annual earnings in the industries employing the largest numbers of computer operators in 2002 are shown below:

Management of companies and enterprises	$32,770
Computer systems design and related services	30,280
General medical and surgical hospitals	28,130
Data processing, hosting, and related services	27,440
Depository credit intermediation	24,160

The average salary for computer operators employed by the Federal Government was $41,117 in 2003.

According to Robert Half International, the average starting salaries for computer operators ranged from $28,250 to $38,500 in 2003. Salaries generally are higher in large organizations than in small ones.

Related Occupations

Other occupations involving work with computers include computer software engineers; computer programmers; computer support specialists and systems administrators; and computer systems analysts, database administrators, and computer scientists. Other occupations in which workers operate electronic office equipment include data entry and information processing workers, as well as secretaries and administrative assistants.

Sources of Additional Information

For information about a career as a computer operator, contact:
➤ Association of Computer Operations Management (AFCOM), 722 E. Chapman Ave., Orange, CA 92860.

For information about work opportunities in computer operations, contact establishments with large computer centers, such as banks, manufacturing firms, insurance companies, colleges and universities, and data processing service organizations. The local office of the State employment service can supply information about employment and training opportunities.

Customer Service Representatives

(0*NET 43-4051.01, 43-4051.02)

Significant Points

- Job prospects are expected to be excellent.
- Most jobs require only a high school diploma.
- Strong verbal communication and listening skills are important.

Nature of the Work

Customer service representatives are employed by many different types of companies throughout the country to serve as a direct point of contact for customers. They are responsible for ensuring that their company's customers receive an adequate level of service or help with their questions and concerns. These customers may be individual consumers or other companies, and the nature of their service needs can vary considerably.

All customer service representatives interact with customers to provide information in response to inquiries about products or services and to handle and resolve complaints. They communicate with customers through a variety of means—either in person; by telephone, e-mail or regular mail correspondence, or fax; or even over the Internet. Some customer service representatives handle general questions and complaints, whereas others specialize in a particular area.

Many customer inquiries involve routine questions and requests. For example, customer service representatives may be asked to provide a customer with a bank account balance, or to check on the status of an order that has been placed. Obtaining the answers to such questions usually requires simply looking up information on their computer. Other questions are more involved, and may call for additional research or further explanation on the part of the customer service representative. In handling customers' complaints, customer service representatives must attempt to resolve the problem according to guidelines established by the company. These procedures may involve asking questions to determine the validity of a complaint, offering possible solutions, or providing customers with refunds, exchanges, or other offers such as discounts or coupons. In some cases, customer service representatives are required to follow up with an individual customer until a question is answered or an issue is resolved.

Some customer service representatives help people decide what types of products or services would best suit their needs. They may even aid customers in completing purchases or transactions. Although the primary function of customer service representatives is not sales, some may spend a part of their time with customers attempting to convince them to purchase additional products or services. (For information on workers whose primary function is sales, see the statements on sales and related occupations elsewhere in the *Handbook*.) Customer service representatives may also make changes or updates to a customer's profile or account information. They may keep records of transactions and update and maintain databases of information.

Most customer service representatives use computers and telephones extensively in their work. Customer service representatives frequently enter information into a computer as they are speaking to customers. Often, companies have large amounts of data, such as account information, that can be pulled up on a computer screen while the representative is talking to a customer so that he or she can answer specific questions relating to the account. Customer service representatives also may have access to information such as answers to the most common customer questions, or guidelines for dealing with complaints. In the event that they encounter a question or situation to which they do not know how to respond, workers consult with a supervisor to determine the best course of action. Customer service representatives use multiline telephones systems, which often route calls directly to the most appropriate representative. However, at times, a customer service representative will need to transfer a call to someone who may be better able to respond to the customer's needs.

In some organizations, customer service representatives spend their entire day on the telephone. In others, they may spend part of their day answering e-mails and the remainder of the day taking calls. For some, most of their contact with the customer is face to face. Customer service representatives need to remain aware of the amount of time spent with each customer, in order to fairly distribute their time among the people who require their assistance. This is particularly important for customer service representatives whose primary activities are answering telephone calls, and conversations often are required to be kept within set time limits. For customer service representatives working in call centers, there is usually very little time between telephone calls; as soon as they have finished with one call they must immediately move on to another. When working in call centers, customer service representatives are likely to be under close supervision. Telephone calls may be taped and

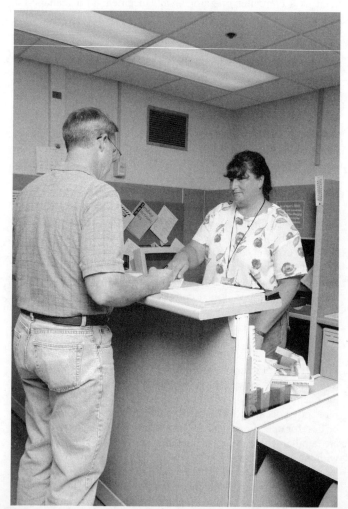

Customer service representatives respond to customers' questions and concerns.

reviewed by supervisors to ensure that company policies and procedures are being followed, or a supervisor may listen in on conversations.

Job responsibilities can differ, depending on the industry in which a customer service representative is employed. For example, a customer service representative working in the branch office of a bank may assume the responsibilities of other workers, such as teller or new account clerk, as needed. In insurance agencies, a customer service representative interacts with agents, insurance companies, and policyholders. These workers handle much of the paperwork related to insurance policies, such as policy applications and changes and renewals to existing policies. They answer questions regarding issues such as policy coverage, help with reporting claims, and do anything else that may need to be done. Although they must know as much as insurance agents about insurance products, and usually must have credentials equal to those of an agent in order to sell products and make changes to policies, the duties of a customer service representative differ from those of an agent in that customer service representatives are not responsible for actively seeking potential customers. Customer service representatives employed by communications and utilities companies assist individuals interested in opening accounts for various utilities such as electricity and gas, or for communication services such as cable television and telephone. They explain various options and receive orders for services to be installed, turned on, turned off, or changed. They may also look into and resolve complaints about billing and service provided by telephone, cable television, and utility companies.

Working Conditions
Although customer service representatives can work in a variety of settings, most work in areas that are clean and well lit. Many work in call or customer contact centers. In this type of environment, workers generally have their own workstation or cubicle space and are equipped with a telephone, headset, and computer. Because many call centers are open extended hours, beyond the traditional 9-to-5 business day, or are staffed around the clock, these positions may require workers to take on early morning, evening, or late night shifts. Weekend or holiday work also may be necessary. As a result, the occupation is well-suited to flexible work schedules. About 1 out of 7 customer service representatives work part time. The occupation also offers the opportunity for seasonal work in certain industries, often through temporary help agencies.

Call centers may be crowded and noisy, and work may be repetitious and stressful, with little time in between calls. Workers usually must attempt to minimize the length of each call, while still providing excellent service. To ensure that these procedures are followed, conversations may be monitored by supervisors, which can be stressful. Also, long periods spent sitting, typing, or looking at a computer screen may cause eye and muscle strain, backaches, headaches, and repetitive motion injuries.

Customer service representatives working outside of a call center environment may interact with customers through several different means. For example, workers employed by an insurance agency or in a grocery store may have customers approach them in person or contact them by telephone, computer, mail, or fax. Many of these customer service representatives will work a standard 40-hour week; however, their hours generally will depend on the hours of operation of the establishment in which they are employed. Work environments outside of a call center also will vary accordingly. Most customer service representatives will work either in an office or at a service or help desk.

For virtually all types of customer service representatives, dealing with difficult or irate customers can be a trying task; however,

the ability to directly help and resolve customers' problems has the potential to be very rewarding.

Employment
Customer service representatives held about 1.9 million jobs in 2002. Although they were found in a variety of industries, more than 1 in 4 customer service representatives worked in finance and insurance. The largest numbers were employed by insurance carriers, insurance agencies and brokerages, and banks and credit unions.

Nearly 1 in 8 customer service representatives were employed in administrative and support services. These workers were concentrated in the industries business support services—which includes telephone call centers—and employment services—which includes temporary help services and employment placement agencies. Another 1 in 8 customer service representatives were employed in retail trade establishments such as general merchandise stores, food and beverage stores, or nonstore retailers. Other industries that employ significant numbers of customer service representatives include information, particularly the telecommunications industry; manufacturing, such as printing and related support activities; and wholesale trade.

Although they are found in all States, customer service representatives who work in call centers tend to be concentrated geographically. Four States make up over 30 percent of total employment—California, Texas, Florida, and New York. Delaware, South Dakota, Utah, and Arizona have the highest concentration of workers in this occupation, with customer service representatives comprising over 2 percent of total employment in these States.

Training, Other Qualifications, and Advancement
A high school diploma or the equivalent is the most common educational requirement for customer service representatives. Basic computer knowledge and good interpersonal skills also are important qualities for people who wish to be successful in the field. Because customer service representatives constantly interact with the public, strong communication and problem-solving skills are a must, particularly strong verbal communication and listening skills. Additionally, for those workers who communicate through e-mail, good typing, spelling, and written communication skills are necessary. High school courses in computers, English, or business are helpful in preparing for a job in customer service.

Customer service representatives play a critical role in providing an interface between the customer and the company that employs them, and for this reason employers seek out people who are able to come across in a friendly and professional manner. The ability to deal patiently with problems and complaints and to remain courteous when faced with difficult or angry people is very important. Also, a customer service representative needs to be able to work independently within specified time constraints. Workers should have a clear and pleasant speaking voice and be fluent in the English language. However, the ability to speak a foreign language is becoming increasingly necessary, and bilingual skills are considered a plus.

Training requirements vary by industry. Almost all customer service representatives are provided with some training prior to beginning work and training continues once on the job. This training generally will cover four primary components: Training on customer service and phone skills, training on products and services or common customer problems, training on the use or operation of the telephone and/or computer systems, and training on company policies and regulations. Length of training varies, but it usually lasts at least several weeks. Because of a constant need to update skills and knowledge, most customer service representatives continue to receive instruction and training throughout their career. This is particularly true of workers in industries such as banking, in which regulations and products are continually changing.

Although some positions may require previous industry, office, or customer service experience, many customer service jobs are entry level. Customer service jobs are often good introductory positions into a company or an industry. In some cases, experienced workers can move up within the company into supervisory or managerial positions or they may move into areas such as product development, in which they can use their knowledge to improve products and services.

Within insurance agencies and brokerages, however, a customer service representative job is usually not an entry-level position. Workers must have previous experience in insurance and are often required by State regulations to be licensed like insurance sales agents. A variety of designations are available to demonstrate that a candidate has sufficient knowledge and skill, and continuing education and training are often offered through the employer. As they gain more knowledge of industry products and services, customer service representatives in insurance may advance to other, higher level positions, such as insurance sales agent.

Job Outlook
Prospects for obtaining a job in this field are expected to be excellent, with more job openings than jobseekers. Bilingual jobseekers, in particular, may enjoy favorable job prospects. In addition to many new openings occurring as businesses and organizations expand, numerous job openings will result from the need to replace experienced customer service representatives who transfer to other occupations or leave the labor force. Replacement needs are expected to be significant in this large occupation because many young people work as customer service representatives before switching to other jobs. This occupation is well-suited to flexible work schedules, and many opportunities for part-time work will continue to be available, particularly as organizations attempt to cut labor costs by hiring more temporary workers.

Employment of customer service representatives is expected to increase faster than the average for all occupations through the year 2012. Beyond growth stemming from expansion of the industries in which customer service representatives are employed, a need for additional customer service representatives is likely to result from heightened reliance on these workers. Customer service is critical to the success of any organization that deals with customers, and strong customer service can build sales and visibility as companies try to distinguish themselves from competitors. In many industries, the need to gain a competitive edge and retain customers will become increasingly important over the next decade. This is particularly true in industries such as financial services, communications, and utilities that already employ numerous customer service representatives. As the trend towards consolidation within industries continues, centralized call centers will provide an effective method for delivering a high level of customer service. As a result, employment of customer service representatives may grow at a faster rate in call centers than in other areas; however, this growth may be tempered as a variety of factors, including technological improvements, make it increasingly feasible and cost-effective for call centers to be built or relocated outside of the United States. Technology is impacting the occupation in many ways. Advancements such as the Internet and automated teller machines have provided customers with means of obtaining information and conducting transactions that do not entail interacting with another person. Technology also allows for a greater streamlining of processes, while at the same time increasing the productivity of workers. Use of computer soft-

ware to filter e-mails, generating automatic responses or directing messages to the appropriate representative, and use of similar systems to answer or route telephone inquiries are likely to become more prevalent in the future.

Despite such developments, the need for customer service representatives is expected to remain strong. In many ways, technology has heightened consumers' expectations for information and services, and availability of information online seems to have generated more need for customer service representatives, particularly to respond to e-mail. Also, technology cannot replace the need for human skills. As more sophisticated technologies are able to resolve many customers' questions and concerns, the nature of the inquiries to be handled by customer service representatives is likely to become increasingly complex.

Furthermore, the job responsibilities of customer service representatives are expanding. As companies downsize or look to increase profitability, workers are being trained to perform additional duties such as opening bank accounts or cross-selling products. As a result, employers may increasingly prefer customer service representatives who have education beyond high school, such as some college or even a college degree.

While jobs in some industries, such as retail trade, may be impacted by economic downturns, the occupation is generally resistant to major fluctuations in employment.

Earnings
In 2002, median annual earnings for wage and salary customer service representatives were $26,240. The middle 50 percent earned between $20,960 and $33,540. The lowest 10 percent earned less than $17,230, and the highest 10 percent earned more than $42,990.

Earnings for customer service representatives vary according to level of skill required, experience, training, location, and size of firm. Median annual earnings in the industries employing the largest numbers of these workers in 2002 are shown below:

Wired telecommunications carriers	$38,980
Insurance carriers	28,560
Agencies, brokerages, and other insurance related activities	28,270
Management of companies and enterprises	27,990
Nondepository credit intermediation	25,600
Depository credit intermediation	24,850
Employment services	22,510
Electronic shopping and mail-order houses	21,530
Business support services	21,130
Grocery stores	17,230

In addition to receiving an hourly wage, full-time customer service representatives who work evenings, nights, weekends, or holidays may receive shift differential pay. Also, because call centers are often open during extended hours, or even 24 hours a day, some customer service representatives have the benefit of being able to work a schedule that does not conform to the traditional workweek. Other benefits can include life and health insurance, pensions, bonuses, employer-provided training, or discounts on the products and services the company offers.

Related Occupations
Customer service representatives interact with customers to provide information in response to inquiries about products and services and to handle and resolve complaints. Other occupations in which workers have similar dealings with customers and the public are information and record clerks; financial clerks, such as tellers and new-account clerks; insurance sales agents; securities, commodities, and financial services sales agents; retail salespersons; computer support specialists; and gaming services workers.

Sources of Additional Information
State employment service offices can provide information about employment opportunities for customer service representatives.

Data Entry and Information Processing Workers

(0*NET 43-9021.00, 43-9022.00)

Significant Points

- Employers generally hire high school graduates who meet their requirements for keyboarding speed.

- Although overall employment is projected to decline, the need to replace workers who leave this large occupation each year should produce many job openings.

- Job prospects should be best for those with expertise in appropriate computer software applications.

Nature of the Work
Organizations need to process a rapidly growing amount of information. Data entry and information processing workers help ensure the smooth and efficient handling of information. By typing text, entering data into a computer, operating a variety of office machines, and performing other clerical duties, these workers help organizations keep up with the rapid changes that are characteristic of today's "Information Age." In addition to the job titles discussed below—such as word processors, typists, and data entry keyers—data entry and information processing workers are known by various other titles, including electronic data processors, keypunch technicians, and transcribers.

Word processors and *typists* usually set up and prepare reports, letters, mailing labels, and other textual material. *Typists* make neat, typed copies of materials written by other clerical, professional, or managerial workers. As entry-level workers, typists may begin by typing headings on form letters, addressing envelopes, or preparing standard forms on typewriters or computers. As they gain experience, they often are assigned tasks requiring a higher degree of accuracy and independent judgment. Senior typists may work with highly technical material, plan and type complicated statistical tables, combine and rearrange materials from different sources, or prepare master copies.

Most keyboarding is now done on word processing equipment—usually a personal computer or part of a larger computer system—which normally includes a keyboard, video display terminal, and printer, which may have "add-on" capabilities such as optical character recognition readers. *Word processors* use this equipment to record, edit, store, and revise letters, memos, reports, statistical tables, forms, and other printed materials. Although it is becoming less common, some word processing workers are employed on centralized word processing teams that handle transcription and typing for several departments.

In addition to fulfilling the duties mentioned above, word processors and typists often perform other office tasks, such as answering telephones, filing, and operating copiers or other office machines. Job titles of these workers frequently vary to reflect these duties. Clerk typists, for example, combine typing with filing, sorting mail,

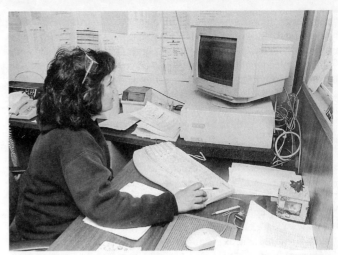

Although overall employment of data entry and information processing workers is projected to decline, the need to replace workers who leave this large occupation each year should produce many job openings.

answering telephones, and other general office work. Note readers transcribe stenotyped notes of court proceedings into standard formats.

Data entry keyers usually input lists of items, numbers, or other data into computers or complete forms that appear on a computer screen. They also may manipulate existing data, edit current information, or proofread new entries to a database for accuracy. Some examples of data sources include customers' personal information, medical records, and membership lists. Usually, this information is used internally by a company and may be reformatted before other departments or customers utilize it.

Keyers use various types of equipment to enter data. Many use a machine that converts the information they type to magnetic impulses on tapes or disks for entry into a computer system. Others prepare materials for printing or publication by using data entry composing machines. Some keyers operate online terminals or personal computers. Data entry keyers increasingly also work with nonkeyboard forms of data entry, such as scanners and electronically transmitted files. When using the new character recognition systems, data entry keyers often enter only those data which cannot be recognized by machines. In some offices, keyers also operate computer peripheral equipment such as printers and tape readers, act as tape librarians, and perform other clerical duties.

Working Conditions
Data entry and information processing workers usually work a standard 40-hour week in clean offices. They sit for long periods and sometimes must contend with high noise levels caused by various office machines. These workers are susceptible to repetitive strain injuries, such as carpal tunnel syndrome, neck and back injuries, and eye strain. To help prevent these conditions, many offices have scheduled exercise breaks, ergonomically designed keyboards, and workstations that allow workers to stand or sit as they wish.

Employment
Data entry and information processing workers held about 633,000 jobs in 2002 and were employed in every sector of the economy; 392,000 were data entry keyers and 241,000 were word processors

and typists. Some workers telecommute, working from their homes on personal computers linked by telephone lines to those in the main office. This arrangement enables them to type material at home while still being able to produce printed copy in their offices.

About 1 out of 5 data entry and information processing workers held jobs in firms providing administrative and support services, including temporary help and word processing agencies, and another 1 in 5 worked for State or local government.

Training, Other Qualifications, and Advancement

Employers generally hire high school graduates who meet their requirements for keyboarding speed. Increasingly, employers also are expecting applicants to have training or experience in word processing or data entry tasks. Spelling, punctuation, and grammar skills are important, as is familiarity with standard office equipment and procedures.

Students acquire skills in keyboarding and in the use of word processing, spreadsheet, and database management computer software packages through high schools, community colleges, business schools, temporary help agencies, or self-teaching aids such as books, tapes, and Internet tutorials.

For many people, a job as a data entry and information processing worker is their first job after graduating from high school or after a period of full-time family responsibilities. This work frequently serves as a steppingstone to higher paying jobs with increased responsibilities. Large companies and government agencies usually have training programs to help administrative employees upgrade their skills and advance to higher level positions. It is common for data entry and information processing workers to transfer to other administrative jobs, such as secretary, administrative assistant, or statistical clerk or to be promoted to a supervisory job in a word processing or data entry center.

Job Outlook

Overall employment of data entry and information processing workers is projected to decline through 2012. Nevertheless, the need to replace those who transfer to other occupations or leave this large occupation for other reasons will produce numerous job openings each year. Job prospects will be most favorable for those with the best technical skills—in particular, expertise in appropriate computer software applications. Data entry and information processing workers must be willing to upgrade their skills continuously in order to remain marketable.

Although data entry and information processing workers are affected by productivity gains stemming from organizational restructuring and the implementation of new technologies, projected growth differs among these workers. Employment of word processors and typists is expected to decline due to the proliferation of personal computers, which allows other workers to perform duties formerly assigned to word processors and typists. Most professionals and managers, for example, now use desktop personal computers to do their own word processing. However, because technologies affecting data entry keyers tend to be costlier to implement, employment of these workers will decline less than word processors and typists.

Employment growth of data entry keyers will still be dampened by productivity gains, as various data-capturing technologies, such as bar code scanners, voice recognition technologies, and sophisticated character recognition readers, become more prevalent. These technologies can be applied to a variety of business transactions, such as inventory tracking, invoicing, and placing orders. More-

over, as telecommunications technology improves, many organizations will increasingly take advantage of computer networks that allow data to be transmitted electronically. These networks will allow more data to be entered automatically into computers, reducing the demand for data entry keyers.

In addition to being affected by technology, employment of data entry and information processing workers will be adversely affected by businesses that are increasingly contracting out their work. Many organizations have reduced or even eliminated permanent in-house staff—for example, in favor of temporary employment and staffing services firms. Some large data entry and information processing firms increasingly employ workers in nations with low wages to enter data. As international trade barriers continue to fall and telecommunications technology improves, this transfer of jobs will mean reduced demand for data entry keyers in the United States.

Earnings

Median annual earnings of word processors and typists in 2002 were $26,730. The middle 50 percent earned between $21,540 and $32,950. The lowest 10 percent earned less than $17,750, while the highest 10 percent earned more than $40,450. The salaries of these workers vary by industry and by region. In 2002, median annual earnings in the industries employing the largest numbers of word processors and typists were as follows:

Local government	$27,840
State government	26,440
Elementary and secondary schools	24,960
Business support services	24,140
Employment services	24,050

Median annual earnings of data entry keyers in 2002 were $22,390. The middle 50 percent earned between $18,810 and $26,840. The lowest 10 percent earned less than $15,910, and the highest 10 percent earned more than $26,840. The following are median annual earnings for 2002 in the industries employing the largest numbers of data entry keyers:

Federal Government	$25,750
Insurance carriers	22,870
Employment services	21,150
Accounting, tax preparation, bookkeeping, and payroll services	19,950
Data processing, hosting, and related services	19,720

Related Occupations

Data entry and information processing workers must transcribe information quickly. Other workers who deliver information in a timely manner are dispatchers and communications equipment operators. Data entry and information processing workers also must be comfortable working with office automation, and in this regard they are similar to court reporters, medical records and health information technicians, secretaries and administrative assistants, and computer operators.

Sources of Additional Information

For information about job opportunities for data entry and information processing workers, contact the nearest office of the State employment service.

Desktop Publishers

(0*NET 43-9031.00)

Significant Points

- Desktop publishers are expected to experience faster than average employment growth.

- Two out of three worked in firms that handle newspaper, periodical, book, and directory publishing, or printing and related support activities.

- Although formal training is not always required, those with certificates or degrees will have the best job opportunities.

Nature of the Work

Using computer software, desktop publishers format and combine text, numerical data, photographs, charts, and other visual graphic elements to produce publication-ready material. Depending on the nature of a particular project, desktop publishers may write and edit text, create graphics to accompany text, convert photographs and drawings into digital images and then manipulate those images, design page layouts, create proposals, develop presentations and advertising campaigns, typeset and do color separation, and translate electronic information onto film or other traditional forms. Materials produced by desktop publishers include books, business cards, calendars, magazines, newsletters and newspapers, packaging, slides, and tickets. As companies have brought the production of marketing, promotional, and other kinds of materials in-house, they increasingly have employed people who can produce such materials.

Desktop publishers use a keyboard to enter and select formatting properties, such as the size and style of type, column width, and spacing, and store them in the computer, which then displays and arranges columns of type on a video display terminal or computer monitor. An entire newspaper, catalog, or book page, complete with artwork and graphics, can be created on the screen exactly as it will appear in print. Operators transmit the pages for production either into film and then into printing plates, or directly into plates.

Desktop publishing is a rapidly changing field that encompasses a number of different kinds of jobs. Personal computers enable desktop publishers to perform publishing tasks that would otherwise require complicated equipment and human effort. Advances in computer software and printing technology continue to change and enhance desktop-publishing work. Instead of receiving simple typed text from customers, desktop publishers get the material over the Internet or on a computer disk. Other innovations in the occupation include digital color page-makeup systems, electronic page-layout systems, and off-press color-proofing systems. In addition, because most materials today often are published on the Internet, desktop publishers may need to know electronic-publishing technologies, such as Hypertext Markup Language (HTML), and may be responsible for converting text and graphics to an Internet-ready format.

Typesetting and page layout have been affected by the technological changes shaping desktop publishing. Increasingly, desktop publishers are using computers to do much of the typesetting and page-layout work formerly done by prepress workers, posing new challenges for the printing industry. The old "hot type" method of text composition—which used molten lead to create individual letters, paragraphs, and full pages of text—is nearly extinct. Today,

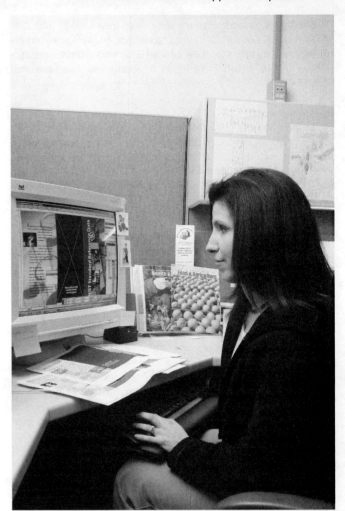

Using computer software, desktop publishers capture photographs, images, or art as digital data that can be incorporated directly into electronic page layouts.

composition work is done primarily with computers. Improvements in desktop-publishing software also allow customers to do much more of their own typesetting.

Desktop publishers use scanners to capture photographs, images, or art as digital data that can be either incorporated directly into electronic page layouts or further manipulated with the use of computer software. The desktop publisher then can correct mistakes or compensate for deficiencies in the original color print or transparency. Digital files are used to produce printing plates. Like photographers and multimedia artists and animators, desktop publishers also can create special effects or other visual images, using film, video, computers, or other electronic media. (Separate statements on photographers and on artists and related workers appear elsewhere in the *Handbook*.)

Depending on the establishment employing these workers, desktop publishers also may be referred to as publications specialists, electronic publishers, DTP operators, desktop-publishing editors, electronic prepress technicians, electronic-publishing specialists, image designers, typographers, compositors, layout artists, and web publications designers.

Working Conditions

Desktop publishers usually work in clean, air-conditioned office areas with little noise. They generally work an 8-hour day, 5 days a week. Some workers work night shifts, weekends, and holidays.

Desktop publishers often are subject to stress and the pressures of short deadlines and tight work schedules. Like other workers who spend long hours working in front of a computer monitor, they may be susceptible to eyestrain, back discomfort, and hand and wrist problems.

Employment

Desktop publishers held about 35,000 jobs in 2002. Two out of three worked in the newspaper, periodical, book, and directory publishing, and printing and related support activities; the rest worked in a wide variety of industries.

Firms in the publishing industry employ most desktop publishers. These firms publish newspapers, periodicals, books, directory and mailing lists, and greeting cards. A large number of desktop publishers also work for printing and related support activities firms, which print a wide range of products—newspapers, books, labels, business cards, stationary, inserts, catalogs, pamphlets, and advertisements—while business form establishments print material such as sales receipts and business forms and perform support activities such as data imaging and bookbinding. Establishments in printing and related support activities typically perform custom composition, platemaking, and related prepress services. (A separate statement on prepress technicians and workers appears elsewhere in the *Handbook*.) Other desktop publishers print or publish materials in-house or in-plant for business services firms, government agencies, hospitals, or universities, typically in a reproduction or publications department that operates within the organization.

The printing and publishing industries are two of the most geographically dispersed industries in the United States, and desktop-publishing jobs are found throughout the country. However, most jobs are in large metropolitan cities.

Training, Other Qualifications, and Advancement

Most workers qualify for jobs as desktop publishers by taking classes or completing certificate programs at vocational schools, universities, and colleges or through the Internet. Programs range in length, but the average certificate program takes approximately 1 year. However, some desktop publishers train on the job to develop the necessary skills. The length of on-the-job training varies by company. An internship or part-time desktop-publishing assignment is another way to gain experience as a desktop publisher.

Students interested in pursuing a career in desktop publishing may obtain an associate's degree in applied science or a bachelor's degree in graphic arts, graphic communications, or graphic design. Graphic arts programs are a good way to learn about desktop publishing software used to format pages, assign type characteristics, and import text and graphics into electronic page layouts to produce printed materials such as advertisements, brochures, newsletters, and forms. Applying this knowledge of graphic arts techniques and computerized typesetting usually is intended for students who may eventually move into management positions, while 2-year associate's degree programs are designed to train skilled workers. Students also develop finely tuned skills in typography, print media, packaging, branding and identity, Web-site design, and motion graphics. The programs teach print and graphic design fundamentals and provide an extensive background in imaging, prepress operations, print reproduction, and emerging media. Courses in other aspects of printing also are available at vocational-technical institutes, industry-sponsored update and retraining programs, and private trade and technical schools.

Although formal training is not always required, those with certificates or degrees will have the best job opportunities. Most employers prefer to hire people who have at least a high school diploma and who possess good communication skills, basic computer skills, and a strong work ethic. Desktop publishers should be able to deal courteously with people, because, in small shops, they may have to take customers' orders. They also may have to add, subtract, multiply, divide, and compute ratios to estimate job costs. Persons interested in working for firms using advanced printing technology need to know the basics of electronics and computers.

Desktop publishers need good manual dexterity, and they must be able to pay attention to detail and work independently. Good eyesight, including visual acuity, depth perception, a wide field of view, color vision, and the ability to focus quickly also are assets. Artistic ability often is a plus. Employers also seek persons who are even tempered and adaptable—important qualities for workers who often must meet deadlines and learn how to operate new equipment.

Workers with limited training and experience may start as helpers. They begin with instruction from an experienced desktop publisher and advance on the basis of their demonstrated mastery of skills at each level. All workers should expect to be retrained from time to time to handle new, improved software and equipment. As workers gain experience, they advance to positions with greater responsibility. Some move into supervisory or management positions. Other desktop publishers may start their own company or work as independent consultants, while those with more artistic talent and further education may find opportunities in graphic design or commercial art.

Job Outlook

Employment of desktop publishers is expected to grow faster than the average for all occupations through 2012, as more page layout and design work is performed in-house using computers and sophisticated publishing software. Desktop publishing is replacing much of the prepress work done by compositors and typesetters, enabling organizations to reduce costs while increasing production speeds. Many new jobs for desktop publishers are expected to emerge in commercial printing and publishing establishments. However, more companies also are turning to in-house desktop publishers, as computers with elaborate text and graphics capabilities have become common, and desktop publishing software has become cheaper and easier to use. In addition to employment growth, many job openings for desktop publishers also will result from the need to replace workers who move into managerial positions, transfer to other occupations, or who leave the labor force.

Printing and publishing costs represent a significant portion of a corporation's expenses, and firms are finding it more profitable to print their own newsletters and other reports than to send them out to trade shops. Desktop publishing reduces the time needed to complete a printing job and allows commercial printers to make inroads into new markets that require fast turnaround.

Most employers prefer to hire experienced desktop publishers. As more people gain desktop-publishing experience, however, competition for jobs may increase. Among persons without experience, opportunities should be best for those with computer backgrounds who are certified or who have completed postsecondary programs in desktop publishing or graphic design. Many employers prefer graduates of these programs because the comprehensive training they receive helps them learn the page-layout process and adapt more rapidly to new software and techniques.

Earnings

Earnings for desktop publishers vary according to level of experience, training, location, and size of firm. Median annual earnings of desktop publishers were $31,620 in 2002. The middle 50 percent earned between $24,030 and $41,280. The lowest 10 percent earned less than $18,670, and the highest 10 percent earned more than $52,540 a year. Median annual earnings in the industries employing the largest numbers of these workers in 2002 are presented in the following tabulation:

Printing and related support activities $35,140
Newspaper, periodical, book, and directory publishers 28,050

Related Occupations
Desktop publishers use artistic and editorial skills in their work. These skills also are essential for artists and related workers; designers; news analysts, reporters, and correspondents; prepress technicians and workers; public relations specialists; and writers and editors.

Sources of Additional Information
Details about apprenticeship and other training programs may be obtained from local employers such as newspapers and printing shops or from local offices of the State employment service.

For information on careers and training in printing, desktop publishing, and graphic arts, write to either of the following sources:
➤ Graphic Communications Council, 1899 Preston White Dr., Reston, VA 20191. Internet: **http://www.npes.org/edcouncil/**
➤ Graphic Arts Technical Foundation, 200 Deer Run Rd., Sewickley, PA 15143. Internet: **http://www.gatf.org**

For information on benefits and compensation in desktop publishing, write to:
➤ Printing Industries of America, Inc., 100 Daingerfield Rd., Alexandria, VA 22314. Internet: **http://www.gain.org**

Financial Clerks

(0*NET 43-3011.00, 43-3021.01, 43-3021.02, 43-3021.03, 43-3031.00, 43-3041.00, 43-3051.00, 43-3061.00, 43-3071.00)

Significant Points

● Most jobs in this occupation require only a high school diploma.

● Numerous job opportunities should arise due to high turnover.

● Slower-than-average growth is expected in overall employment, reflecting the spread of computers and other office automation, as well as organizational restructuring.

Nature of the Work
Financial clerks keep track of money, recording all amounts coming into or leaving an organization. Their records are vital to an organization's need to keep track of all revenues and expenses. While most financial clerks work in offices, maintaining and processing various accounting records, some deal directly with customers, taking in and paying out money. When bills are not paid on time, financial clerks must contact customers to find out why and attempt to resolve the problem. Other clerks keep track of a store's inventory and order replacement stock when supplies are low. (Additional information about specific financial clerks appears in separate statements that follow this introductory statement.)

Depending on their specific titles, these workers perform a wide variety of financial recordkeeping duties. *Bill and account collectors* notify customers with delinquent accounts in order to solicit payment. *Billing and posting clerks and machine operators* prepare bills and invoices. *Bookkeeping, accounting, and auditing clerks* maintain financial data in computer and paper files. *Payroll and timekeeping clerks* compute wages for payroll records and review employee timecards. *Procurement clerks* prepare purchase orders and monitor purchase requests. *Tellers* receive and pay out money for financial institutions, while *gaming cage workers* perform many of the same services for casinos.

The duties of financial clerks vary with the size of the firm. In a small business, a bookkeeper may handle all financial records and transactions, as well as payroll and billing duties. A large firm, by contrast, may employ specialized accounting, payroll, and billing clerks. In general, however, clerical staffs in firms of all sizes are increasingly performing a broader variety of tasks than in the past.

Another change in these occupations is the growing use of financial software to enter and manipulate data. Computer programs automatically perform calculations that previously were done manually. Computers also enable clerks to access data within files more quickly and even generate statements automatically. Nevertheless, most workers still keep backup paper records for research, auditing, and reference purposes, although a paperless office is increasingly the goal for many organizations.

Despite the growing use of automation, interaction with the public and with coworkers remains a basic part of the job for many financial clerks. Payroll clerks, for example, answer questions concerning employee benefits, tellers and gaming cage workers help customers with their financial needs, and procurement clerks often have to deal with an organization's suppliers.

Working Conditions
With the exception of gaming cage workers, financial clerks typically are employed in an office environment. Bill collectors who work for third-party collection agencies may spend most of their days on the phone in a call-center environment. However, a growing number of financial clerks—particularly medical billers—work at home, and many work part time.

Because the majority of financial clerks use computers on a daily basis, these workers may experience eye and muscle strain, backaches, headaches, and repetitive motion injuries. Also, clerks who review detailed data may have to sit for extended periods.

Most financial clerks work regular business hours. However, because most casinos are open 24 hours a day, gaming cage workers often work in shifts, including nights and weekends. Tellers can work some evenings and Saturday mornings, while bill collectors often have to work evenings and weekends, when it usually is easier to reach people. Accounting clerks may work longer hours to meet deadlines at the end of the fiscal year, during tax time, or when monthly and yearly accounting audits are performed. Billing, bookkeeping, and accounting clerks in hotels, restaurants, and stores may work overtime during peak holiday and vacation seasons.

Employment
Financial clerks held more than 3.7 million jobs in 2002. The following tabulation shows employment in individual occupations:

Bookkeeping, accounting, and auditing clerks 1,983,000
Tellers 530,000
Billing and posting clerks and machine operators 507,000
Bill and account collectors 413,000
Payroll and timekeeping clerks 198,000
Procurement clerks 77,000
Gaming cage workers 18,000

These workers are employed in virtually every industry, including manufacturing, business and health services, and government. However, it is becoming more common for financial clerks to work for companies that specialize in performing specific financial services, such as bookkeeping, bill collection, medical billing, and payroll services, as companies seek to cut costs and outsource many administrative functions. Also, more financial clerks are finding jobs with personnel supply agencies, as companies increasingly hire temporary workers for peak periods.

All financial clerk occupations have some part-time workers, but tellers and bookkeeping, accounting, and auditing clerks have the most, with more than one-fourth working part time.

Training, Other Qualifications, and Advancement

Most financial clerks are required to have at least a high school diploma. However, having completed some college is becoming increasingly important, particularly for those occupations requiring knowledge of accounting. For occupations such as bookkeepers, accounting clerks, and procurement clerks, an associate's degree in business or accounting often is required. Some financial clerks have bachelor's degrees in business, accounting, or liberal arts. Although a degree is rarely required, many graduates accept entry-level clerical positions to get into a particular company or to enter the finance or accounting field with the hope of being promoted to professional or managerial positions. Some companies have a set plan of advancement that tracks college graduates from entry-level clerical jobs into managerial positions. Workers with bachelor's degrees are likely to start at higher salaries and advance more easily than those without degrees.

Experience in a related job also is recommended for a number of these positions. For example, cash-handling experience is important for gaming cage workers and tellers, and telemarketing experience is useful for bill and account collectors. For other financial clerks, experience working in an office environment or in customer service is always beneficial. Regardless of the type of work, most employers prefer workers with good communication skills and who are computer literate; knowledge of word-processing and spreadsheet software is especially valuable.

Gaming cage workers have additional requirements. They must be at least 21 years old and they are required to obtain a license by the State gaming commission or another regulatory body. In addition to a fee, applicants must provide a photograph and proof of age and residence. A background check is conducted to make sure that applicants do not have a criminal history.

Once hired, financial clerks usually receive on-the-job training. Under the guidance of a supervisor or some other senior worker, new employees learn company procedures. Some formal classroom training also may be necessary, such as training in specific computer software. Bill and account collectors generally receive training in telephone techniques, negotiation skills, and the laws governing the collection of debt. Financial clerks must be careful, orderly, and detail oriented in order to avoid making errors and to recognize errors made by others. These workers also should be discreet and trustworthy, because they frequently come in contact with confidential material. In addition, all financial clerks should have a strong aptitude for numbers.

Bookkeepers—particularly those who handle all the recordkeeping for companies—may find it beneficial to become certified. The "Certified Bookkeeper" designation, awarded by the American Institute of Professional Bookkeepers, assures employers that individuals have the skills and knowledge required to carry out all the bookkeeping and accounting functions up through the adjusted trial balance, including payroll functions. For certifica-tion, candidates must have at least 2 years of bookkeeping experience, pass three tests, and adhere to a code of ethics.

Payroll clerks also may find it useful to become certified. The American Payroll Association offers two certifications: the Fundamental Payroll Certification (FPC) and the Certified Payroll Professional (CPP). The FPC is mainly for beginning payroll workers and certifies that one has a basic knowledge of payroll issues. The CPP is meant for payroll professionals who are required to have several years of experience dealing with payroll issues before they can become certified. Either certification requires several courses and passing an examination. Tellers can prepare for better jobs by taking courses offered throughout the country by banking and financial institutes, colleges and universities, and private training institutions.

Financial clerks usually advance by taking on more duties in the same occupation for higher pay or by transferring to a closely related occupation. For example, procurement clerks with the appropriate experience often become buyers. Most companies fill office and administrative support supervisory and managerial positions by promoting individuals from within the organization, so financial clerks who acquire additional skills, experience, and training improve their advancement opportunities. With appropriate experience and education, some clerks may become accountants, human resource specialists, or buyers.

Job Outlook

Overall employment of financial clerks is expected to experience slower-than-average growth through 2012. Despite continued growth in the volume of business transactions, rising productivity stemming from the spread of office automation, as well as company downsizing, will adversely affect demand for financial clerks. Turnover in this large occupation, however, will provide the most job openings. As a result, opportunities for full-time and part-time employment should be plentiful as financial clerks transfer to other occupations or leave the labor force.

Many basic data-entry accounting and clerical jobs already have become heavily automated. Productivity has risen significantly, as workers increasingly are using personal computers instead of manual entry and time-consuming equipment such as typewriters, adding machines, and calculators. The growing use of barcode readers, point-of-sale terminals, automated teller machines, and optical scanners that record transactions reduces much of the data entry handled by financial clerks. In addition, the use of local area networks is facilitating electronic data interchange—the sending of data from computer to computer—thereby abolishing the need for clerks to reenter the data. To further eliminate duplicate functions, many large companies are consolidating their clerical operations in a central office where accounting, billing, personnel, and payroll functions are performed for all offices—main and satellite—within the organization. In addition, as more companies merge or are acquired, accounting departments are usually merged as well, reducing the number of financial clerks. More companies also are outsourcing their financial and accounting functions to specialized companies that can do the job more efficiently.

Despite the relatively slow growth of the occupation, some financial clerks will fare better than others. The number of bill collectors is expected to increase as timely payments become a more important goal of companies and more companies offer credit to customers. The health-care services industry is projected to hire more financial clerks—particularly billing clerks—to match the explosive growth of that sector and to process the large amounts of paperwork having to do with patient claims. Tellers also will be needed as banks expand their hours.

Earnings

Salaries of financial clerks vary considerably. The region of the country, size of the city, and type and size of the establishment all influence salary levels. Also, the level of expertise required and the complexity and uniqueness of a clerk's responsibilities may affect earnings. Some companies may offer higher salaries to those who are certified in their profession. Median hourly earnings of full-time financial clerks in 2002 were as follows:

Procurement clerks	$14.23
Payroll and timekeeping clerks	13.94
Bookkeeping, accounting, and auditing clerks	13.16
Bill and account collectors	12.88
Billing and posting clerks and machine operators	12.55
Gaming cage workers	10.47
Tellers	9.81

In addition to earning their salaries, some bill and account collectors receive commissions or bonuses based on the number of cases they close.

Related Occupations

Financial clerks enter data into a computer, handle cash, and keep track of business and other financial transactions. Higher level financial clerks can generate reports and analyze the data. Other occupations that perform these duties include brokerage clerks; cashiers; credit authorizers, checkers, and clerks; loan interviewers and clerks; new-accounts clerks; order clerks; and secretaries and administrative assistants.

For more information on financial clerks, see the statements on bill and account collectors; billing and posting clerks and machine operators; bookkeeping, accounting, and auditing clerks; gaming cage workers; payroll and timekeeping clerks; procurement clerks; and tellers, all following this statement on financial clerks.

Bill and Account Collectors

(0*NET 43-3011.00)

Nature of the Work

Bill and account collectors, called simply *collectors*, keep track of accounts that are overdue and attempt to collect payment on them. Some are employed by third-party collection agencies, while others—known as "in-house collectors"—work directly for the original creditors, such as department stores, hospitals, or banks.

The duties of bill and account collectors are similar in the many different organizations in which they are employed. First, collectors are called upon to locate and notify customers of delinquent accounts, usually over the telephone, but sometimes by letter. When customers move without leaving a forwarding address, collectors may check with the post office, telephone companies, credit bureaus, or former neighbors to obtain the new address. The attempt to find the new address is called "skip tracing."

Once collectors find the debtor, they inform him or her of the overdue account and solicit payment. If necessary, they review the terms of the sale, service, or credit contract with the customer. Collectors also may attempt to learn the cause of the delay in payment. Where feasible, they offer the customer advice on how to pay off the debts, such as by taking out a bill consolidation loan. However, the collector's prime objective is always to ensure that the customer pays the debt in question.

If a customer agrees to pay, collectors record this commitment and check later to verify that the payment was indeed made. Col-

lectors may have authority to grant an extension of time if customers ask for one. If a customer fails to respond, collectors prepare a statement indicating the customer's action for the credit department of the establishment. In more extreme cases, collectors may initiate repossession proceedings, disconnect the customer's service, or hand the account over to an attorney for legal action. Most collectors handle other administrative functions for the accounts assigned to them, including recording changes of addresses and purging the records of the deceased.

Collectors use computers and a variety of automated systems to keep track of overdue accounts. Typically, collectors work at video display terminals that are linked to computers. In sophisticated predictive dialer systems, a computer dials the telephone automatically, and the collector speaks only when a connection has been made. Such systems eliminate time spent calling busy or nonanswering numbers. Many collectors use regular telephones, but others wear headsets like those used by telephone operators.

Employment

Bill and account collectors held about 413,000 jobs in 2002. About 1 in 5 collectors works for collection agencies. Many others work in banks, retail stores, government, hospitals, and other institutions that lend money and extend credit.

Job Outlook

Employment of bill and account collectors is expected to grow faster than the average for all occupations through 2012. Cash flow is becoming increasingly important to companies, which are now placing greater emphasis on collecting bad debts sooner. Thus, the workload for collectors is up as they seek to collect, not only debts that are relatively old, but ones that are more recent. Also, as more companies in a wide range of industries get involved in lending money and issuing their own credit cards, they will need to hire collectors, because debt levels will inevitably rise. Hospitals and physicians' offices are two of the fastest-growing areas requiring collectors. With insurance reimbursements not keeping up with cost increases, the health-care industry is seeking to recover more money from patients. Government agencies also are making more use of collectors to collect on everything from parking tickets to child-support payments and past-due taxes. Finally, the Internal Revenue Service (IRS) is looking into outsourcing the collection of overdue Federal taxes to third-party collection agencies. If the IRS does outsource, more collectors will be required for this large job.

Bill and account collectors notify people when payments are overdue and negotiate settlements.

Despite the increasing demand for bill collectors, an increasing number of mergers between collection agencies may result in fewer collectors being hired. Small, less automated agencies are being bought by larger, more computerized firms, resulting in greater productivity. Contrary to the pattern in most occupations, employment of bill and account collectors tends to rise during recessions, reflecting the difficulty that many people have in meeting their financial obligations. However, collectors usually have more success at getting people to repay their debts when the economy is good.

Sources of Additional Information

Career information on bill and account collectors is available from
➤ Association of Credit and Collection Professionals, P.O. Box 39106, Minneapolis, MN 55439. Internet: **http://www.acainternational.org** (Information on working conditions, training requirements, and earnings appears in the introduction to financial clerk occupations.)

Billing and Posting Clerks and Machine Operators

(0*NET 43-3021.01, 43-3021.02, 43-3021-03)

Nature of the Work

Billing and posting clerks and machine operators, commonly called *billing clerks*, compile records of charges for services rendered or goods sold, calculate and record the amounts of these services and goods, and prepare invoices to be mailed to customers.

Billing clerks review purchase orders, sales tickets, hospital records, or charge slips to calculate the total amount due from a customer. They must take into account any applicable discounts, special rates, or credit terms. A billing clerk for a trucking company often needs to consult a rate book to determine shipping costs of machine parts, for example. A hospital's billing clerk may need to contact an insurance company to determine what items will be reimbursed and for how much. In accounting, law, consulting, and similar firms, billing clerks calculate client fees based on the actual time required to perform the task. They keep track of the accumulated hours and dollar amounts to charge to each job, the type of job performed for a customer, and the percentage of work completed.

After billing clerks review all necessary information, they compute the charges, using calculators or computers. They then prepare itemized statements, bills, or invoices used for billing and recordkeeping purposes. In one organization, the clerk might prepare a bill containing the amount due and the date and type of service; in another, the clerk would produce a detailed invoice with codes for all goods and services provided. This latter form might list the items sold, the terms of credit, the date of shipment or the dates services were provided, a salesperson's or doctor's identification, if necessary, and the sales total.

Computers and specialized billing software allow many clerks to calculate charges and prepare bills in one step. Computer packages prompt clerks to enter data from handwritten forms, and to manipulate the necessary entries of quantities, labor, and rates to be charged. Billing clerks verify the entry of information and check for errors before the computer prints the bill. After the bills are printed, billing clerks check them again for accuracy. In offices that are not automated, *billing machine operators* run off the bill on a billing machine to send to the customer.

In addition to producing invoices, billing clerks may be asked to handle follow-up questions from customers and resolve any discrepancies or errors. And, finally, all changes must be entered in the accounting records.

Employment

In 2002, billing and posting clerks and machine operators held about 507,000 jobs. Although all industries employ billing clerks, the health services industry employs the most. About 1 in 3 billing clerks works in health services. Wholesale trade and retail trade industries also employ a large number of billing clerks.

Job Outlook

Employment of billing and posting clerks and machine operators is expected to grow more slowly than the average for all occupations through the year 2012. At the same time that computers are greatly simplifying the billing process and reducing the need for billing clerks, companies are putting greater emphasis on getting bills out faster in order to get paid more quickly. In addition, the fact that most billing clerks work in the fastest-growing sector of our economy (the health care sector) will generate more jobs for billing clerks in the future. But as the process becomes simplified, other people, particularly accounting and bookkeeping clerks, are taking on the billing function. In addition to employment growth, many job openings will occur as workers transfer to other occupations or leave the labor force. Turnover in the occupation is relatively high, a not unexpected characteristic of an entry-level occupation requiring only a high school diploma.

Most of the employment growth will occur in the expanding health services industries and in accounting firms and other billing services companies, as a result of increased outsourcing of the

Billing clerks check invoice amounts for accuracy before mailing the invoice.

service. Other areas will see declines as the billing function becomes increasingly automated and invoices and statements are automatically generated upon delivery of the service or shipment of goods. Bills also will increasingly be delivered electronically over the Internet, eliminating the production and mailing of paper bills. The health services area will see increasing automation, with more medical billers using electronic billing software to submit insurance claims to the insurer. Doing this speeds up the process and eliminates many of the coding errors to which medical bills are prone. The standardization of codes in the medical field also is expected to simplify medical bills and reduce errors.

Sources of Additional Information

Information on employment opportunities for billing clerks is available from local offices of the State employment service.

(See the introductory statement on financial clerks for information on working conditions, training requirements, and earnings.)

Bookkeeping, Accounting, and Auditing Clerks

(0*NET 43-3031.00)

Nature of the Work

Bookkeeping, accounting, and auditing clerks are an organization's financial recordkeepers. They update and maintain one or more accounting records, including those which tabulate expenditures, receipts, accounts payable and receivable, and profit and loss. They have a wide range of skills and knowledge from full-charge bookkeepers who can maintain an entire company's books to accounting clerks who handle specific accounts. All of these clerks make numerous computations each day and increasingly must be comfortable using computers to calculate and record data.

In small establishments, *bookkeeping clerks* handle all financial transactions and recordkeeping. They record all transactions, post debits and credits, produce financial statements, and prepare reports and summaries for supervisors and managers. Bookkeepers also prepare bank deposits by compiling data from cashiers, verifying and balancing receipts, and sending cash, checks, or other forms of payment to the bank. They also may handle payroll, make purchases, prepare invoices, and keep track of overdue accounts.

In large offices and accounting departments, *accounting clerks* have more specialized tasks. Their titles often reflect the type of accounting they do, such as accounts payable clerk or accounts receivable clerk. In addition, their responsibilities vary by level of experience. Entry-level accounting clerks post details of transactions, total accounts, and compute interest charges. They also may monitor loans and accounts, to ensure that payments are up to date.

More advanced accounting clerks may total, balance, and reconcile billing vouchers; ensure completeness and accuracy of data on accounts; and code documents, according to company procedures. These workers post transactions in journals and on computer files and update the files when needed. Senior clerks also review computer printouts against manually maintained journals and make necessary corrections. They may review invoices and statements to ensure that all the information appearing on them is accurate and complete, and they may reconcile computer reports with operating reports.

Auditing clerks verify records of transactions posted by other workers. They check figures, postings, and documents to ensure that they are correct, mathematically accurate, and properly coded.

Bookkeeping and accounting clerks prepare a wide range of financial statements and reports.

They also correct or note errors for accountants or other workers to adjust.

As organizations continue to computerize their financial records, many bookkeeping, accounting, and auditing clerks are using specialized accounting software on personal computers. With manual posting to general ledgers becoming obsolete, these clerks increasingly are posting charges to accounts on computer spreadsheets and databases. They now enter information from receipts or bills into computers, and the information is then stored either electronically, as computer printouts, or both. The widespread use of computers also has enabled bookkeeping, accounting, and auditing clerks to take on additional responsibilities, such as payroll, procurement, and billing. Many of these functions require these clerks to write letters, make phone calls to customers or clients, and interact with colleagues. Therefore, good communication skills are becoming increasingly important in the occupation.

Employment

Bookkeeping, accounting, and auditing clerks held about 2 million jobs in 2002. They are found in all industries and at all levels of government, with the most employed in local government and in the accounting, tax preparation, bookkeeping, and payroll services industry. A growing number work for employment services firms, the result of an increase in outsourcing of the occupation. Approximately 1 out of 4 bookkeeping, accounting, and auditing clerks worked part time in 2002.

Job Outlook

Slower than average growth is expected in the employment of book-keeping, accounting, and auditing clerks through 2012. More job openings will stem from replacement needs. Each year, numerous jobs will become available as these clerks transfer to other occupations or leave the labor force. The large size of this occupation ensures plentiful job openings, including many opportunities for temporary and part-time work.

Although a growing economy will result in more financial transactions and other activities that require these clerical workers, the continuing spread of office automation will lift worker productivity and contribute to the stagnant employment growth. In addition, organizations of all sizes will continue to downsize and consolidate various recordkeeping functions, thus reducing the demand for book-keeping, accounting, and auditing clerks. Specialized clerks will be in much less demand than those who can carry out a wider range of accounting activities. Demand for full-charge bookkeepers is expected to increase, because they are called upon to do much of the work of accountants, as well as perform a wider variety of financial transactions, from payroll to billing. Those with several years of accounting or bookkeeper certification will have the best job prospects.

Sources of Additional Information

For information on the "Certified Bookkeeper" designation, contact

➤ The American Institute of Professional Bookkeepers, 6001 Montrose Rd., Suite 500, Rockville, MD 20852. Internet: **http://www.aipb.org**

(See the introductory statement on financial clerks for information on working conditions, training requirements, and earnings.)

Gaming Cage Workers

(0*NET 43-3041.00)

Nature of the Work

Gaming cage workers, more commonly called *cage cashiers*, work in casinos and other gaming establishments. The "cage" where these workers can be found is the central depository for money, gaming chips, and paperwork necessary to support casino play.

Cage workers carry out a wide range of financial transactions and handle any paperwork that may be required. They perform credit checks and verify credit references for people who want to open a house credit account. They cash checks according to rules established by the casino. Cage workers sell gambling chips, tokens, or tickets to patrons or to other workers for resale to patrons and exchange chips and tokens for cash. They may use cash registers, adding machines, or computers to calculate and record transactions. At the end of their shift, cage cashiers must balance the books.

Because the industry is scrutinized closely, cage workers must follow a number of rules and regulations related to their handling of money. Large cash transactions, for example, must be reported to the Internal Revenue Service. Also, in determining when to extend credit or cash a check, cage workers must follow highly detailed procedures.

Employment

Gaming cage workers held about 18,000 jobs in 2002. All of these individuals work in the gaming industry, which is heavily concentrated in Nevada and Atlantic City, New Jersey. However, a growing number of States and Indian reservations have legalized gambling, and gaming establishments can now be found in many parts of the country.

Job Outlook

Employment of gaming cage workers is expected to increase about as fast as the average for all occupations through 2012. Opportunities for gaming cage workers depend on the health of the gaming industry. The industry as a whole is strong, and demand will remain high as gambling becomes a more popular and acceptable leisure pursuit. New casinos will continue to be built on Indian reservations and in States that currently do not have any casinos. Gaming cage workers, however, will not fare as well as others in the gaming industry, because many of the newer casinos are going cashless and using debitlike cards instead. However, a fair number of job openings will result from high turnover in this occupation due to the high level of scrutiny workers receive and the need to be accurate. Persons with good mathematics abilities, some background in accounting or bookkeeping, and good customer service skills should have the best opportunities.

Sources of Additional Information

Information on employment opportunities for gaming cage workers is available from local offices of the State employment service.

(See the introductory statement on financial clerks for information on working conditions, training requirements, and earnings.)

Gaming cage workers need good mathematical and customer service skills.

Payroll and Timekeeping Clerks

(O*NET 43-3051.00)

Nature of the Work

Payroll and timekeeping clerks perform a vital function: ensuring that employees are paid on time and that their paychecks are accurate. If inaccuracies arise, such as monetary errors or incorrect amounts of vacation time, these workers research and correct the records. In addition, they may perform various other clerical tasks. Automated timekeeping systems that allow employees to enter the number of hours they have worked directly into a computer have eliminated much of the data entry and review by timekeepers and have elevated the job of payroll clerk. In offices that have not automated this function, however, payroll and timekeeping clerks still perform many of the functions listed next.

The fundamental task of *timekeeping clerks* is distributing and collecting timecards each pay period. These workers review employee work charts, timesheets, and timecards to ensure that information is properly recorded and that records have the signatures of authorizing officials. In companies that bill for the time spent by staff, such as law or accounting firms, timekeeping clerks make sure that the hours recorded are charged to the correct job so that clients can be properly billed. These clerks also review computer reports listing timecards that cannot be processed because of errors, and they contact the employee or the employee's supervisor to resolve the problem. In addition, timekeeping clerks are responsible for informing managers and other employees about procedural changes in payroll policies.

Payroll clerks, also called payroll technicians, screen timecards for calculating, coding, or other errors. They compute pay by subtracting allotments, including Federal and State taxes and contributions to retirement, insurance, and savings plans, from gross earnings. Increasingly, computers are performing these calculations and alerting payroll clerks to problems or errors in the data. In small organizations or for new employees whose records are not yet entered into a computer system, clerks may perform the necessary calculations manually. In some small offices, clerks or other employees in the accounting department process payroll.

Payroll clerks record changes in employees' addresses; close out files when workers retire, resign, or transfer; and advise employees on income tax withholding and other mandatory deductions. They also issue and record adjustments to workers' pay because of previous errors or retroactive increases. Payroll clerks need to follow changes in tax and deduction laws, so they are aware of the most recent revisions. Finally, they prepare and mail earnings and tax-withholding statements for employees' use in preparing income tax returns.

In small offices, payroll and timekeeping duties are likely to be included in the duties of a general office clerk, a secretary, or an accounting clerk. However, large organizations employ specialized payroll and timekeeping clerks to perform these functions. In offices that have automated timekeeping systems, payroll clerks perform more analysis of the data, examine trends, and work with computer systems. They also spend more time answering employees' questions and processing unique data.

Employment

Payroll and timekeeping clerks held about 198,000 jobs in 2002. They can be found in every industry, but a growing number work for employment services companies as temporary employees, or for accounting, tax preparation, bookkeeping, and payroll services firms, which are increasingly taking on the payroll function as a service to other companies. Approximately 16 percent of all payroll and timekeeping clerks worked part time in 2002.

Job Outlook

Employment of payroll and timekeeping clerks is expected to grow more slowly than the average through 2012, due mainly to automation and increased outsourcing. Both of these trends allow payroll workers to handle more payroll recordkeeping functions with fewer people. Nevertheless, a number of job openings will arise in coming years as payroll and timekeeping clerks leave the labor force or transfer to other occupations. Those with payroll certifications indicating that they can handle more complex payroll issues will have an advantage in the job market.

As entering payroll and timekeeping information becomes more simplified, the job itself is becoming more complex, with companies now offering a greater variety of pension, 401(k), and other investment plans to their employees. Also, the growing use of garnishment of wages for child support is adding to the complexity. These transactions must be recorded and kept track of, requiring payroll clerks to implement changes. In contrast to this trend, the other one is that computers are doing much of the recordkeeping, allowing payroll clerks to handle more records. Also, the greater complexity of the job, coupled with the automation of records that is simplifying data entry, is resulting in payroll professionals, not clerks, doing more of the work.

Another factor leading to the slow growth in employment of payroll clerks is that companies are increasingly outsourcing the function of producing payroll to firms that specialize in the task. Many of these companies are data-processing facilities, but accounting firms also are taking on the payroll function to supplement their accounting work. This growing specialization of the payroll function should lead to more productive payroll clerks.

Computerization is still the number one factor that is slowing the demand for payroll and timekeeping clerks. For example, automated timeclocks, which calculate employee hours, allow large organizations to centralize their timekeeping duties in one location. At individual sites, employee hours are increasingly tracked by computer and verified by managers. This information is then compiled and sent to a central office to be processed by payroll clerks, eliminat-

Payroll clerks make sure that workers get paid the correct amount.

ing the need to have these clerks at every site. In addition, the growing use of direct deposit eliminates the need to draft paychecks, because these funds are automatically transferred each pay period. Also, a growing number of organizations are allowing employees to update their payroll records automatically. Furthermore, in smaller organizations, payroll and timekeeping duties are increasingly being distributed to secretaries, general office clerks, or accounting clerks.

Sources of Additional Information

Information on employment opportunities for payroll and timekeeping clerks is available from local offices of the State employment service.

(See the introductory statement on financial clerks for information on working conditions, training requirements, and earnings.)

Procurement Clerks

(O*NET 43-3061.00)

Nature of the Work

Procurement clerks compile requests for materials, prepare purchase orders, keep track of purchases and supplies, and handle inquiries about orders. Usually called *purchasing clerks* or *purchasing technicians*, they perform a variety of tasks related to the ordering of goods and supplies for an organization and make sure that what was purchased arrives on schedule and meets the purchaser's specifications.

Automation is having a profound effect on this occupation. Orders for goods now can be placed electronically when supplies are low. For example, computers integrated with cash registers at stores record purchases and automatically reorder goods when supplies reach a certain target level. However, automation is still years away for many firms, and the role of the procurement clerk is unchanged in many organizations.

Procurement clerks perform a wide range of tasks and also have a wide range of responsibilities. Some clerks act more like buyers, particularly at small to medium-sized companies, while others perform strictly clerical functions. In general, procurement clerks process requests for purchases. They first determine whether there is any of the requested product left in inventory and may go through catalogs or to the Internet to find suppliers. They may prepare invitation-to-bid forms and mail them to suppliers or distribute them for public posting. Once suppliers are found, procurement clerks may interview them to check on prices and specifications and thereby put together spreadsheets with price comparisons and other facts about each supplier. Upon the organization's approval of a supplier, purchase orders are prepared, mailed, and entered into computers. Procurement clerks keep track of orders and determine the causes of any delays. If the supplier has questions, clerks try to answer them and resolve any problems. When the shipment arrives, procurement clerks may reconcile the purchase order with the shipment, making sure that they match; notify the vendors when invoices are not received; and verify that the bills concur with the purchase orders.

Some purchasing departments, particularly in small companies, are responsible for overseeing the organization's inventory control system. At these organizations, procurement clerks monitor in-house inventory movement and complete inventory transfer forms for bookkeeping purposes. They may keep inventory spreadsheets and place orders when materials on hand are insufficient.

Employment

In 2002, procurement clerks held about 77,000 jobs. Procurement clerks are found in every industry, including manufacturing, retail and wholesale trade, health care, and government. Nearly 1 in 5 procurement clerks works for the Federal government.

Job Outlook

Employment of procurement clerks is expected to decline through 2012 as a result of increasing automation. The need for procurement clerks will be reduced as the use of computers to place orders directly with suppliers—called electronic data interchange—and as ordering over the Internet—known as "e-procurement"—become more commonplace. In addition, procurement authority for some purchases is now being given to employees in the departments originating the purchase. These departments may be issued procurement cards, which are similar to credit cards, that enable a department to charge purchases up to a specified amount.

Although employment in the occupation is expected to decline overall, job opportunities will vary by type of employer. As the manufacturing sector continues to decline, fewer procurement clerks will be needed in that sector. In contrast, procurement clerks will be increasingly employed by companies in the service sector, which are beginning to realize that a centralized procurement department may be more cost effective than units making purchases independently, as many service companies had been doing. However, most job openings will arise out of the need to replace workers who transfer to other occupations or leave the labor force. Persons with good writing and communication skills, along with computer skills, will have the best opportunities for employment.

Sources of Additional Information

Information on employment opportunities for procurement clerks is available from local offices of the State employment service.

(See the introductory statement on financial clerks for information on working conditions, training requirements, and earnings.)

Procurement clerks prepare purchase orders and make sure that the shipment and the bills agree with the order.

Tellers

(0*NET 43-3071.00)

Nature of the Work

The teller is the person most people associate with a bank. Tellers make up approximately one-fourth of bank employees and conduct most of a bank's routine transactions. Among the responsibilities of tellers are cashing checks, accepting deposits and loan payments, and processing withdrawals. They also may sell savings bonds, accept payment for customers' utility bills and charge cards, process necessary paperwork for certificates of deposit, and sell travelers' checks. Some tellers specialize in handling foreign currencies or commercial or business accounts.

Being a teller requires a great deal of attention to detail. Before cashing a check, a teller must verify the date, the name of the bank, the identity of the person who is to receive payment, and the legality of the document. A teller also must make sure that the written and numerical amounts agree and that the account has sufficient funds to cover the check. The teller then must carefully count cash to avoid errors. Sometimes a customer withdraws money in the form of a cashier's check, which the teller prepares and verifies. When accepting a deposit, tellers must check the accuracy of the deposit slip before processing the transaction.

Prior to starting their shifts, tellers receive and count an amount of working cash for their drawers. A supervisor—usually the head teller—verifies this amount. Tellers use this cash for payments during the day and are responsible for its safe and accurate handling. Before leaving, tellers count their cash on hand, list the currency-received tickets on a balance sheet, make sure that the accounts balance, and sort checks and deposit slips. Over the course of a workday, tellers also may process numerous mail transactions. Some tellers replenish their cash drawers and corroborate deposits and payments to automated teller machines (ATMs).

In most banks, head tellers are responsible for the teller line. They set work schedules, ensure that the proper procedures are adhered to, and act as a mentor to less experienced tellers. In addition, head tellers may perform the typical duties of a teller, as needed, and may deal with the more difficult customer problems. They may access the vault, ensure that the correct cash balance is in the vault, and oversee large cash transactions. Technology continues to play a large role in the job duties of all tellers. In most banks, for example,

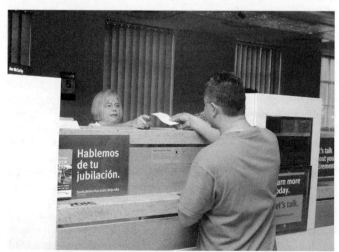

Part-time teller jobs will become more common as bank branches increase the hours during which they are open.

tellers use computer terminals to record deposits and withdrawals. These terminals often give tellers quick access to detailed information on customer accounts. Tellers can use this information to tailor the bank's services to fit a customer's needs or to recommend an appropriate bank product or service.

As banks begin to offer more and increasingly complex financial services, tellers are being trained to identify sales opportunities. This task requires them to learn about the various financial products and services the bank offers so that they can briefly explain them to customers and refer interested customers to appropriate specialized sales personnel. In addition, tellers in many banks are being cross-trained to perform some of the functions of customer service representatives. (Customer service representatives are discussed separately in another section of the *Handbook*.)

Employment

Tellers held about 530,000 jobs in 2002; approximately 1 out of 3 worked part time. The overwhelming majority worked in commercial banks, savings institutions, or credit unions. The remainder was employed in a variety of other financial service companies.

Job Outlook

Employment prospects for tellers have improved of late. Employment is projected to grow, but less than the average for all occupations. Banks are looking at their branch offices as places to attract customers for the increasing number and variety of financial products the banks sell. As recently as a few years ago, to cut costs, banks were closing branch offices and discouraging the use of tellers, but in a turnaround, banks are now opening branch offices in more and more locations. They also are keeping them open longer during the day and on weekends, which is expected to increase opportunities for tellers, particularly those who work part time. Most job openings will arise from replacement needs because turnover is high—a characteristic typical of large occupations that normally require little formal education and offer relatively low pay. Tellers who have excellent customer service skills, are knowledgeable about a variety of financial services, and can sell those services will be in greater demand in the future.

Despite the improved outlook, automation and technology will continue to reduce the need for tellers who perform only routine transactions. For example, ATMs and the increased use of direct deposit of paychecks and benefit checks have reduced the need for bank customers to interact with tellers for routine transactions. In addition, electronic banking is spreading rapidly throughout the banking industry. This type of banking, conducted over the telephone or the Internet, also will reduce the number of tellers over the long run.

Employment of tellers also is being affected by the increasing use of 24-hour telephone centers by many large banks. These centers allow a customer to interact with a bank representative at a distant location, either by telephone or by video terminal. Such centers usually are staffed by customer service representatives, who can handle a wider variety of transactions than tellers can, including applications for loans and credit cards.

Sources of Additional Information

Information on employment opportunities for tellers is available from local offices of the State employment service.

(See the introductory statement on financial clerks for information on working conditions, training requirements, and earnings.)

Information and Record Clerks

(O*NET 43-4011.00, 43-4021.00, 43-4031.01, 43-4031.02, 43-4031.03, 43-4041.01, 43-4041.02, 43-4051.01, 43-4051.02, 43-4061.01, 43-4061.02, 43-4071.00, 43-4081.00, 43-4111.00, 43-4121.00, 43-4131.00, 43-4141.00, 43-4151.00, 43-4161.00, 43-4171.00, 43-4181.01, 43-4181.02)

Significant Points

- Numerous job openings should arise for most types of information and record clerks, due to employment growth and the need to replace workers who leave this large occupational group.

- A high school diploma or its equivalent is the most common educational requirement.

- Because many information and record clerks deal directly with the public, a professional appearance and a pleasant personality are imperative.

- These occupations are well suited to flexible work schedules.

Nature of the Work

Information and record clerks are found in nearly every industry in the Nation, gathering data and providing information to the public. The specific duties of these clerks vary as widely as the job titles they hold.

Although their day-to-day duties differ considerably, many information and record clerks greet customers, guests, or other visitors. Many also answer telephones and either obtain information from, or provide information to, the public. Most clerks use multiline telephones, fax machines, and personal computers. *Hotel, motel, and resort desk clerks,* for example, are a guest's first contact for check-in, check-out, and other services within hotels, motels, and resorts. *Interviewers, except eligibility and loan,* found most often in medical facilities, research firms, and financial institutions, assist the public in completing forms, applications, or questionnaires. *Eligibility interviewers, government programs* determine the eligibility of individuals applying for assistance. *Receptionists and information clerks* often are a visitor's or caller's first contact within an organization, providing information and routing calls. *Reservation and transportation ticket agents and travel clerks* assist the public in making travel plans, reserving seats, and purchasing tickets for a variety of transportation services. (*Customer service representatives* provide information in response to inquiries about products or services and handle and resolve complaints. While these workers are classified as information and record clerks and are included in the estimate of employment for this occupational group, they are discussed in detail elsewhere in the *Handbook*).

Court, municipal, and license clerks perform administrative duties in courts of law, municipalities, and governmental licensing agencies and bureaus. Court clerks prepare the docket of cases to be called, secure information for judges, and contact witnesses, attorneys, and litigants to obtain information for the court. Municipal clerks prepare draft agendas or bylaws for town or city councils, answer official correspondence, and keep fiscal records and accounts. License clerks issue licenses or permits, record data, administer tests, and collect fees.

New-account clerks interview individuals desiring to open bank accounts. Their principal tasks include handling customer inquiries, explaining the institution's products and services to people, and referring customers to the appropriate sales personnel. If a customer wants to open a checking or savings account or an individual retirement account, the new-account clerk will interview the customer and enter the required information into a computer for processing.

Other information and record clerks focus on maintaining, updating, and processing a variety of records, ranging from payrolls to information on the shipment of goods or bank statements. They ensure that other workers get paid on time, that customers' questions are answered, and that records of all transactions are kept.

Depending on their specific titles, these workers perform a wide variety of recordkeeping duties. *Brokerage clerks* prepare and maintain the records generated when stocks, bonds, and other types of investments are traded. *File clerks* store and retrieve various kinds of office information for use by staff members. *Human resources assistants, except payroll and timekeeping* maintain employee records. *Library assistants, clerical* assist library patrons. *Order clerks* process incoming orders for goods and services. *Correspondence clerks* reply to customers regarding claims of damage, delinquent accounts, incorrect billings, complaints of unsatisfactory service, and requests for exchanges or returns of merchandise. *Loan interviewers and clerks* and *credit authorizers, checkers, and clerks* review applicants' credit history and obtain the information needed to determine the creditworthiness of those who apply for credit cards.

The duties of record clerks vary with the size of the firm. In a small business, a bookkeeping clerk may handle all financial records and transactions, as well as have payroll and personnel duties. A large firm, by contrast, may employ specialized accounting, payroll, and human resources clerks. In general, however, clerical staffs in firms of all sizes increasingly are performing a broader variety of tasks than in the past. This is especially true for clerical occupations involving accounting work. As the growing use of computers enables bookkeeping, accounting, and auditing clerks to become more productive, these workers may assume billing, payroll, and timekeeping duties.

Another way in which computers affect these occupations is the growing use of financial software to enter and manipulate data. Computer programs automatically perform calculations on data that were previously calculated manually. Computers also enable clerks to access data within files more quickly than they would using the former method of reviewing stacks of paper. Nevertheless, most workers still keep backup paper records for research, auditing, and reference purposes. Despite the growing use of automation, interaction with the public and coworkers remains a basic part of the job of many record clerks.

Working Conditions

Working conditions vary for different types of information and record clerks, but most clerks work in areas that are clean, well lit, and relatively quiet. This is especially true for information clerks who greet customers and visitors and usually work in highly visible areas that are furnished to make a good impression. Reservation agents and interviewing clerks who spend much of their day talking on the telephone, however, commonly work away from the public, often in large centralized reservation or phone centers. Because a number of agents or clerks may share the same workspace, it may be crowded and noisy. Interviewing clerks may conduct surveys on the street or in shopping malls, or they may go door to door.

Although most information and record clerks work a standard 40-hour week, about 1 out of 5 works part time. Some high school and college students work part time in these occupations, after school or during vacations. Some jobs—such as those in the transportation industry, hospitals, and hotels, in particular—may require working evenings, late-night shifts, weekends, and holidays. Interviewing clerks conducting surveys or other research may work mainly evenings or weekends. In general, employees with the least seniority tend to be assigned the least desirable shifts.

The work performed by information clerks may be repetitious and stressful. For example, many receptionists spend all day answering telephones while performing additional clerical or secretarial tasks. Reservation agents and travel clerks work under stringent time constraints or have quotas on the number of calls answered or reservations made. Additional stress is caused by technology that enables management to electronically monitor employees' use of computer systems, tape-record telephone calls, or limit the time spent on each call.

The work of hotel, motel, and resort desk clerks and transportation ticket agents also can be stressful when these workers are trying to serve the needs of difficult or angry customers. When flights are canceled, reservations mishandled, or guests dissatisfied, these clerks must bear the brunt of the customers' anger. Hotel desk clerks and ticket agents may be on their feet most of the time, and ticket agents may have to lift heavy baggage. In addition, prolonged exposure to a video display terminal may lead to eyestrain for the many information clerks who work with computers.

Employment

Information and record clerks held 5.1 million jobs in 2002. The following tabulation shows employment for the individual occupations:

Customer service representatives	1,894,000
Receptionists and information clerks	1,100,000
Order clerks	330,000
File clerks	265,000
Interviewers, except eligibility and loan	193,000
Hotel, motel, and resort desk clerks	178,000
Reservation and transportation ticket agents and travel clerks	177,000
Human resource assistants, except payroll and timekeeping	174,000
Loan interviewers and clerks	170,000
Library assistants, clerical	120,000
Court, municipal, and license clerks	106,000
New account clerks	99,000
Eligibility interviewers, government programs	94,000
Credit authorizers, checkers, and clerks	80,000
Brokerage clerks	78,000
Correspondence clerks	33,000

Although information and record clerks are found in a variety of industries, employment is concentrated in health services; finance, insurance, and real estate; transportation, communications, and utilities; and business services.

Training, Other Qualifications, and Advancement

Despite the fact that hiring requirements for information and record clerk jobs vary from industry to industry, a high school diploma or its equivalent is the most common educational requirement. Increasingly, familiarity or experience with computers and good interpersonal skills are becoming equally important as the diploma to employers. Although many employers prefer to hire information and record clerks with a higher level of education, only a few of these clerical occupations require such a level of education. For example, brokerage firms usually seek college graduates for brokerage clerk jobs, and order clerks in high-technology firms often need to understand scientific and mechanical processes, which may require some college education. For new-account clerks and airline

reservation and ticket agent jobs, some college education may be preferred.

Many information and record clerks deal directly with the public, so a professional appearance and a pleasant personality are important. A clear speaking voice and fluency in the English language also are essential, because these employees frequently use the telephone or public-address systems. Good spelling and computer literacy often are needed, particularly because most work involves considerable use of the computer. In addition, speaking a foreign language fluently is becoming increasingly helpful for those wishing to enter the lodging or travel industry.

With the exception of airline reservation and transportation ticket agents, information and record clerks generally receive orientation and training on the job. For example, orientation for hotel and motel desk clerks usually includes an explanation of the job duties and information about the establishment, such as the locations of rooms and the available services. New employees learn job tasks through on-the-job training under the guidance of a supervisor or an experienced clerk. They often need additional training in how to use the computerized reservation, room assignment, and billing systems and equipment. Most clerks continue to receive instruction on new procedures and on company policies after their initial training ends.

Receptionists usually receive on-the-job training that may include procedures for greeting visitors, for operating telephone and computer systems, and for distributing mail, fax, and parcel deliveries. Some employers look for applicants who already possess certain skills, such as computer and word-processing experience, or who have previous formal education. These workers must possess strong communication skills, because they are constantly interacting with customers.

Most airline reservation and ticket agents learn their skills through formal company training programs. In a classroom setting, they learn company and industry policies, computer systems, and ticketing procedures. They also learn to use the airline's computer system to obtain information on schedules, the availability of seats, and fares; to reserve space for passengers; and to plan passenger itineraries. In addition, they must become familiar with airport and airline code designations, regulations, and safety procedures, on all of which they may be tested. After completing classroom instruction, new agents work on the job with supervisors or experienced agents for a period during which the supervisors may monitor telephone conversations to improve the quality of customer service. Agents are expected to provide good service while limiting the time spent on each call, without being discourteous to customers. In contrast to the airlines, automobile clubs, bus lines, and railroads tend to train their ticket agents or travel clerks on the job through short in-house classes that last several days.

Most banks prefer to hire college graduates for new-account clerk positions. Nevertheless, many new-account clerks without college degrees start out as bank tellers and are promoted by demonstrating excellent communication skills and the motivation to learn new skills. If a new-account clerk has not been a teller before, he or she often will receive such training and work for several months as a teller. In either case, new-account clerks undergo formal training regarding the bank's procedures, products, and services.

Some information and record clerks learn the skills they need in high schools, business schools, and community colleges. Business education programs offered by these institutions typically include courses in typing, word processing, shorthand, business communications, records management, and office systems and procedures. Order clerks in specialized technical positions obtain their training from technical institutes and 2- and 4-year colleges.

Some entry-level clerks are college graduates with degrees in business, finance, or liberal arts. Although a degree rarely is required, many graduates accept entry-level clerical positions to get into a particular company or to enter a particular field. Some companies, such as brokerage and accounting firms, have a set plan of advancement that tracks college graduates from entry-level clerical jobs into managerial positions. Workers with college degrees are likely to start at higher salaries and advance more easily than those without degrees.

Regardless of their level of educational attainment, clerks usually receive on-the-job training. Under the guidance of a supervisor or other senior workers, new employees learn company procedures. Some formal classroom training also may be necessary, such as training in specific computer software.

Advancement for information and record clerks usually comes by transfer to a position with more responsibilities or by promotion to a supervisory position. Most companies fill office and administrative support supervisory and managerial positions by promoting individuals within their organization, so information and record clerks who acquire additional skills, experience, and training improve their opportunities for advancement. Receptionists, interviewers, and new-account clerks with word-processing or other clerical skills may advance to a better paying job as a secretary or administrative assistant. Within the airline industry, a ticket agent may advance to lead worker on the shift.

Additional training is helpful in preparing information clerks for promotion. In the lodging industry, clerks can improve their chances for advancement by taking home-study or group-study courses in lodging management, such as those sponsored by the Educational Institute of the American Hotel and Motel Association. In some industries—such as lodging, banking, insurance, or air transportation—workers commonly are promoted through the ranks. Information and record clerk positions offer good opportunities for qualified workers to get started in a business of their choice. In a number of industries, a college degree may be required for advancement to management ranks.

Job Outlook

Overall employment of information and record clerks is expected grow about as fast as the average for all occupations through 2012. In addition to many openings occurring as businesses and organizations expand, numerous job openings for information and record clerks will result from the need to replace experienced workers who transfer to other occupations or leave the labor force. Replacement needs are expected to be significant in this large occupational group, because many young people work as clerks for a few years before switching to other, higher paying jobs. These occupations are well suited to flexible work schedules, and many opportunities for part-time work will continue to be available, particularly as organizations attempt to cut labor costs by hiring more part-time or temporary workers.

The outlook for different types of information and record clerks is expected to vary in the coming decade. Economic growth and general business expansion are expected to stimulate faster-than-average growth among receptionists and information clerks. Positions as hotel, motel, and resort desk clerks are expected to grow faster than the average, as the occupational composition of the lodging industry changes and services provided by these workers expand. Employment of interviewers, except eligibility and loan, is expected to grow faster than average, with these workers benefiting from rapid growth in the health and social assistance sector. Library assistants are also expected to grow faster than the average as these workers take on more responsibilities.

Human resource assistants and new-account clerks are expected to grow about as fast as average; despite computer technology that increases their productivity, these workers will be needed to perform duties that are important to their organization. Average employment growth is expected for court, municipal, and license clerks as the number of court cases and demand for citizen services continues to increase. Employment of reservation and transportation ticket agents and travel clerks also is expected to grow about as fast as average, due to rising demand for travel services.

Employment of other information and record clerks is expected to experience little or no growth or decline. File clerks are expected are expected to have little or no growth; despite rising demand for file clerks to record and retrieve information, job growth will be slowed by productivity gains stemming from office automation and the consolidation of clerical jobs. As government programs, such as welfare, continue to be reformed, employment of eligibility interviewers will decline. Employment of correspondence clerks, as well as credit authorizers, checkers, and clerks is expected to decline due to automation and the consolidation of recordkeeping functions across all industries. Employment of both brokerage clerks and loan interviewers is expected to decline as online trading and other technological innovations continue to automate more of this type of work. With advances in electronic commerce continuing to increase the efficiency of transactions among businesses, consumers, and government, employment of order clerks also is expected to decline.

Earnings

Earnings vary widely by occupation and experience. Annual earnings in 2002 ranged from less than $13,020 for the lowest-paid 10 percent of hotel clerks to more than $53,410 for the top 10 percent of brokerage clerks. Salaries of human resource assistants tend to be higher than for other information and record clerks, while hotel, motel, and resort desk clerks tend to earn quite a bit less, as the following tabulation of median annual earnings shows:

Brokerage clerks	$33,210
Eligibility interviewers, government programs	31,010
Human resource assistants, except payroll and timekeeping	30,410
Loan interviewers and clerks	27,830
Court, municipal, and license clerks	27,300
Credit authorizers, checkers, and clerks	26,690
Customer service representatives	26,240
Correspondence clerks	25,960
Reservation and transportation ticket agents and travel clerks	25,350
New-account clerks	25,200
Order clerks	24,810
Interviewers, except eligibility and loan	21,690
Receptionists and information clerks	21,150
File clerks	20,020
Library assistants, clerical	19,450
Hotel, motel, and resort desk clerks	17,370

Earnings of hotel and motel desk clerks also vary considerably, depending on the location, size, and type of establishment in which they work. For example, clerks at large luxury hotels and at those located in metropolitan and resort areas generally are paid more than clerks at less exclusive or "budget" establishments and than those working at hotels and motels in less populated areas.

In 2003, the Federal Government typically paid salaries ranging from $19,898 to $23,555 a year to beginning receptionists with a high school diploma or 6 months of experience. The average annual salary for all receptionists employed by the Federal Government was about $25,704 in 2003.

In addition to their hourly wage, full-time information and record clerks who work evenings, nights, weekends, or holidays may receive shift differential pay. Some employers offer educational assistance to their employees. Reservation and transportation ticket agents and travel clerks receive free or reduced fares for travel on their company's carriers for themselves, their immediate families, and, in some companies, friends.

Related Occupations

A number of other workers deal with the public, receive and provide information, or direct people to others who can assist them. Among these workers are customer service representatives, dispatchers, security guards and gaming surveillance workers, tellers, and counter and rental clerks.

For more information on information and record clerks, see the statements on brokerage clerks; credit authorizers, checkers, and clerks; file clerks; hotel, motel, and resort desk clerks; human resources assistants; interviewers; library assistants; order clerks; receptionists and information clerks; and reservation and transportation ticket agents and travel clerks following this statement.

Brokerage Clerks

(0*NET 43-4011.00)

Nature of the Work

Brokerage clerks perform a number of different jobs with wide-ranging responsibilities; all involve computing and recording data pertaining to securities transactions. Brokerage clerks also may contact customers, take orders, and inform clients of changes to their accounts. Some of these jobs are more clerical and require only a high school diploma, while others are considered entry-level positions for which a bachelor's degree is needed. Brokerage clerks, who work in the operations departments of securities firms, on trading floors, and in branch offices, also are called margin clerks, dividend clerks, transfer clerks, and broker's assistants.

The broker's assistant, also called sales assistant, is the most common type of brokerage clerk. These workers typically assist two brokers, for whom they take calls from clients, write up order tickets, process the paperwork for opening and closing accounts, record a client's purchases and sales, and inform clients of changes in their accounts. All broker's assistants must be knowledgeable about investment products so that they can communicate clearly with clients. Those with a "Series 7" license can make recommendations to clients at the instruction of the broker. The Series 7 license, issued to securities and commodities sales representatives by the National Association of Securities Dealers, allows them to provide advice on securities to the public. (Securities, commodities, and financial services sales agents are discussed elsewhere in the *Handbook*.)

Brokerage clerks in the operations areas of securities firms perform many duties to facilitate the sale and purchase of stocks, bonds, commodities, and other kinds of investments. These clerks produce the necessary records of all transactions that occur in their area of the business. Job titles for many of these clerks depend upon the type of work that they perform. Purchase-and-sale clerks, for example, match orders to buy with orders to sell. They balance and verify trades of stock by comparing the records of the selling firm with those of the buying firm. Dividend clerks ensure timely payments of stock or cash dividends to clients of a particular brokerage firm. Transfer clerks execute customer requests for changes to security registration and examine stock certificates for adherence to

Brokerage clerks verify stock trades by comparing the records of sellers and buyers.

banking regulations. Receive-and-deliver clerks facilitate the receipt and delivery of securities among firms and institutions. Margin clerks record and monitor activity in customers' accounts to ensure that clients make payments and stay within legal boundaries concerning their purchases of stock.

Technology is changing the nature of many of these jobs. A significant and growing number of brokerage clerks use custom-designed software programs to process transactions more quickly. Only a few customized accounts are still handled manually. Furthermore, the rapid expansion of online trading reduces the amount of paperwork because brokerage clerks are able to make trades electronically.

Employment

Brokerage clerks held about 78,000 jobs in 2002. Most worked in firms that sell securities and commodities.

Job Outlook

Employment of brokerage clerks is expected to decline through the year 2012, as technological advancements continue to automate many of their job duties. With people increasingly investing in securities, brokerage clerks will still be required to process larger volumes of transactions. Moreover, some brokerage clerks will still be needed to update records, enter changes to customers' accounts, and verify transfers of securities. However, the emergence of online trading and widespread automation in the securities and commodities industry will limit demand for brokerage clerks in the coming decade. All job openings will stem from the need to replace clerks who transfer to other occupations or leave the labor force.

(See the introductory statement on information and record clerks for information on working conditions, training requirements, and earnings.)

Credit Authorizers, Checkers, and Clerks

(0*NET 43-4041.01, 43-4041.02)

Nature of the Work

Credit authorizers, checkers, and clerks review credit history and obtain the information needed to determine the creditworthiness of individuals or businesses applying for credit. They spend much of their day on the telephone, obtaining information from credit bureaus, employers, banks, credit institutions, and other sources to determine applicants' credit history and ability to pay back the charge.

Credit authorizers, checkers, and clerks process and authorize applications for credit, including applications for credit cards. Although the distinctions among the three job titles are disappearing, some general differences remain. *Credit clerks* typically handle the processing of credit applications by verifying the information on the application, calling applicants if additional data are needed, contacting credit bureaus for a credit rating, and obtaining any other information necessary to determine applicants' creditworthiness. If the clerk works in a department store or other establishment that offers instant credit, he or she enters the applicant's information into a computer at the point of sale. A credit rating will then be transmitted from a central office within seconds to indicate whether the application should be rejected or approved.

Credit checkers investigate the credit history and current credit standing of a person or business prior to the issuance of a loan or line of credit. Credit checkers also may telephone or write to credit departments of businesses and service companies to obtain information about an applicant's credit standing. Credit-reporting agencies and bureaus hire a number of checkers to secure, update, and verify information for credit reports. These workers often are called credit investigators or reporters.

Credit authorizers spend much of their day obtaining information on the telephone.

Credit authorizers approve charges against customers' existing accounts. Most charges are approved automatically by computer. However, when accounts are past due, overextended, or invalid, or when they show a change of address, salespersons refer the associated transactions to credit authorizers located in a central office. These authorizers evaluate the customers' computerized credit records and payment histories and quickly decide whether to approve new charges.

Employment
Credit authorizers, checkers, and clerks held about 80,000 jobs in 2002. Almost half of these workers were employed by finance and insurance industries, mainly firms in credit intermediation and related activities which includes commercial and savings banks, credit unions, and mortgage, finance, and loan companies. Credit bureaus and collection agencies and establishments in wholesale and retail trade also employ these clerks.

Job Outlook
Employment of credit authorizers, checkers, and clerks is expected to decline through 2012. Despite a projected increase in the number of credit applications, technology will allow these applications to be processed, checked, and authorized by fewer workers than were required in the past.

Credit scoring is a major development that has improved the productivity of credit authorizers, checkers, and clerks, thus limiting employment growth in the occupation. Companies and credit bureaus now can purchase software that quickly analyzes an applicant's creditworthiness and summarizes it into a "score." Credit issuers then can easily decide whether to accept or reject an application on the basis of its score, speeding up the authorization of loans or credit. Obtaining credit ratings also has become much easier for credit checkers and authorizers, because businesses now have computer systems that are directly linked to credit bureaus that provide immediate access to a person's credit history.

The job outlook for credit authorizers, checkers, and clerks is sensitive to overall economic activity. A downturn in the economy or a rise in interest rates usually leads to a decline in demand for credit. Even in slow economic times, however, job openings will arise from the need to replace workers who leave the occupation for various reasons.

(See the introductory statement on information and record clerks for information on working conditions, training requirements, and earnings.)

File Clerks

(0*NET 43-4071.00)

Nature of the Work
The amount of information generated by organizations continues to grow rapidly. File clerks classify, store, retrieve, and update this information. In many small offices, they often have additional responsibilities, such as entering data, performing word processing, sorting mail, and operating copying or fax machines. File clerks are employed across the Nation by organizations of all types.

File clerks, also called records, information, or record-center clerks, examine incoming material and code it numerically, alphabetically, or by subject matter. They then store paper forms, letters, receipts, or reports, or enter necessary information into other storage devices. Some clerks operate mechanized files that rotate to bring the needed records to them; others convert documents to film

File clerks examine and classify material numerically, alphabetically, or by subject matter.

that is then stored on microforms, such as microfilm or microfiche. A growing number of file clerks use imaging systems that scan paper files or film and store the material on optical disks.

In order for records to be useful, they must be up to date and accurate. File clerks ensure that new information is added to files in a timely manner and may discard outdated file materials or transfer them to inactive storage. They also check files at regular intervals to make sure that all items are correctly sequenced and placed. Whenever records cannot be found, the file clerk attempts to locate the missing material. As an organization's needs for information change, file clerks implement changes to the filing system established by supervisory personnel.

When records are requested, file clerks locate them and give them to the person requesting them. A record may be a sheet of paper stored in a file cabinet or an image on microform. In the former case, the clerk retrieves the document manually and hands or forwards it to the requester. In the latter case, the clerk retrieves the microform and displays it on a microform reader. If necessary, file clerks make copies of records and distribute them. In addition, they keep track of materials removed from the files, to ensure that borrowed files are returned.

Increasingly, file clerks are using computerized filing and retrieval systems that have a variety of storage devices, such as a mainframe computer, CD-ROM, or floppy disk. To retrieve a document in these systems, the clerk enters the document's identification code, obtains the location of the document, and gets the document for the patron. Accessing files in a computer database is much quicker than locating and physically retrieving paper files. Still, even when files are stored electronically, backup paper or electronic copies usually are also kept.

Employment

File clerks held about 265,000 jobs in 2002. Although file clerk jobs are found in nearly every sector of the economy, more than 85 percent of these workers are employed in service-providing industries, including government. Health care establishments employed around 1 out of every 4 file clerks. About 1 out of every 3 worked part time in 2002.

Job Outlook

Employment of file clerks is expected to experience little or no growth through the year 2012. Projected job growth stems from rising demand for file clerks to record and retrieve information in

organizations across the economy. This growth will be slowed, however, by productivity gains stemming from office automation and the consolidation of clerical jobs. Nonetheless, job opportunities for file clerks should be plentiful because a large number of workers will be needed to replace workers who leave the occupation each year. Job turnover among file clerks reflects the lack of formal training requirements, limited advancement potential, and relatively low pay.

Jobseekers who have typing and other secretarial skills and who are familiar with a wide range of office machines, especially personal computers, should have the best job opportunities. File clerks should find opportunities for temporary or part-time work, especially during peak business periods.

(See the introductory statement on information and record clerks for information on working conditions, training requirements, and earnings.)

Hotel, Motel, and Resort Desk Clerks

(O*NET 43-4081.00)

Nature of the Work

Hotel, motel, and resort desk clerks perform a variety of services for guests of hotels, motels, and other lodging establishments. Regardless of the type of accommodation, most desk clerks have similar responsibilities. Primarily, they register arriving guests, assign rooms, and check out guests at the end of their stay. They also keep records of room assignments and other registration-related information on computers. When guests check out, desk clerks prepare and explain the charges, as well as process payments.

Front-desk clerks always are in the public eye and, through their attitude and behavior, greatly influence the public's impressions of the establishment. When answering questions about services, check-out times, the local community, or other matters of public interest, clerks must be courteous and helpful. Should guests report problems with their rooms, clerks contact members of the housekeeping or maintenance staff to correct the problems.

In some smaller hotels and motels, clerks may have a variety of additional responsibilities that usually are performed by specialized employees in larger establishments. In the smaller places, desk

Hotel and motel clerks perform a variety of services for guests.

clerks often are responsible for all front-office operations, information, and services. For example, they may perform the work of a bookkeeper, advance reservation agent, cashier, laundry attendant, and telephone switchboard operator.

Employment

Hotel, motel, and resort desk clerks held about 178,000 jobs in 2002. The occupation is well suited to flexible work schedules, as nearly 1 in 4 hotel clerks worked part time in 2002. Because hotels and motels need to be staffed 24 hours a day, evening and weekend work is common.

Job Outlook

Employment of hotel, motel, and resort desk clerks is expected to grow faster than the average for all occupations through 2012, as more hotels, motels, and other lodging establishments are built and occupancy rates rise. Job opportunities for hotel and motel desk clerks also will result from a need to replace workers, because many of these clerks either transfer to other occupations that offer better pay and advancement opportunities or simply leave the workforce altogether. Opportunities for part-time work should continue to be plentiful, with front desks often staffed 24 hours a day, 7 days a week.

Employment of hotel and motel desk clerks should benefit from an increase in business and leisure travel. Shifts in preferences away from long vacations and toward long weekends and other, more frequent, shorter trips also should boost demand for these workers, because such stays increase the number of nights spent in hotels. The expansion of budget and extended-stay hotels relative to larger, luxury establishments reflects a change in the composition of the hotel and motel industry. As employment shifts from luxury hotels to those extended-stay establishments offering larger rooms with kitchenettes and laundry services, the proportion of hotel desk clerks should increase in relation to staff such as waiters and waitresses and recreation workers. Desk clerks are able to handle more of the guest's needs in these establishments, answering the main switchboard, providing business services, and coordinating services such as dry cleaning or grocery shopping.

New technologies automating check-in and checkout procedures now allow some guests to bypass the front desk in many larger establishments, reducing staffing needs. As some of the more traditional duties are automated, however, many desk clerks are assuming a wider range of responsibilities.

Employment of desk clerks is sensitive to cyclical swings in the economy. During recessions, vacation and business travel declines, and hotels and motels need fewer clerks. Similarly, employment is affected by seasonal fluctuations in tourism and travel.

Sources of Additional Information

Information on careers in the lodging industry, as well as information about professional development and training programs, may be obtained from:

➤ Educational Institute of the American Hotel and Lodging Association, 800 N. Magnolia Ave., Suite 1800, Orlando, FL 32803. Internet: **http://www.ei-ahma.org**

(See the introductory statement on information and record clerks for information on working conditions, training requirements, and earnings.)

Human Resources Assistants, Except Payroll and Timekeeping

(0*NET 43-4161.00)

Nature of the Work

Human resources assistants maintain the personnel records of an organization's employees. These records include information such as name, address, job title, and earnings, benefits such as health and life insurance, and tax withholding. On a daily basis, these assistants record information and answer questions about employee absences and supervisory reports on employees' job performance. When an employee receives a promotion or switches health insurance plans, the human resources assistant updates the appropriate form. Human resources assistants also may prepare reports for managers elsewhere within the organization. For example, they might compile a list of employees eligible for an award.

In smaller organizations, some human resources assistants perform a variety of other clerical duties, including answering telephone or written inquiries from the public, sending out announcements of job openings or job examinations, and issuing application forms. When credit bureaus and finance companies request confirmation of a person's employment, the human resources assistant provides authorized information from the employee's personnel records. He or she may also contact payroll departments and insurance companies to verify changes to records.

Some human resources assistants are involved in hiring. They screen job applicants to obtain information such as their education and work experience; administer aptitude, personality, and interest tests; explain the organization's employment policies and refer qualified applicants to the employing official; and request references from present or past employers. Also, human resources assistants inform job applicants, by telephone or letter, of their acceptance for or denial of employment.

In some job settings, human resources assistants have specific job titles. For example, *assignment clerks* notify a firm's existing employees of upcoming vacancies, identify applicants who qualify for the vacancies, and assign those who are qualified to various positions. They also keep track of vacancies that arise throughout the organization, and they complete and distribute forms advertising vacancies. When filled-out applications are returned, these clerks

Human resources assistants screen job applicants and request references.

review and verify the information in them, using personnel records. After a selection for a position is made, they notify all of the applicants of their acceptance or rejection.

As another example, *identification clerks* are responsible for security matters at defense installations. They compile and record personal data about vendors, contractors, and civilian and military personnel and their dependents. The identification clerk's job duties include interviewing applicants, corresponding with law enforcement authorities, and preparing badges, passes, and identification cards.

Employment

Human resources assistants held about 174,000 jobs in 2002. Although these workers are found in most industries, about 1 in every 4 is employed by a government agency. Colleges and universities, hospitals, department stores, and banks also employ large numbers of human resources assistants.

Job Outlook

Employment of human resources assistants is expected to grow about as fast as the average for all occupations through the year 2012, as assistants continue to take on more responsibilities. For example, workers conduct Internet research to locate resumes, must be able to scan resumes of job candidates quickly and efficiently, and must be increasingly sensitive to confidential information such as salaries and Social Security numbers. In a favorable job market, more emphasis is placed on human resources departments, thus increasing the demand for assistants. However, even in economic downturns, there is demand, as human resources departments in all industries try to make their organizations more efficient by determining what type of employees to hire and strategically filling job openings. Human resources assistants may play an instrumental role in their organization's human resources policies. For example, they may talk to staffing firms and consulting firms, conduct other research, and then offer their ideas on issues such as whether to hire temporary contract workers or full-time staff.

As with other office and administrative support occupations, the growing use of computers in human resources departments means that much of the data entry that is done by human resources assistants can be eliminated, as employees themselves enter the data and send the electronic file to the human resources office. Such an arrangement, which is most feasible in large organizations with multiple human resources offices, could limit job growth among human resources assistants.

In addition to positions arising from job growth, replacement needs will account for many job openings for human resources assistants as they advance within the human resources department, take jobs unrelated to human resources administration, or leave the labor force.

(See the introductory statement on information and record clerks for information on working conditions, training requirements, and earnings.)

Interviewers

(O*NET 43-4061.01, 43-4061.02, 43-4111.00, 43-4131.00)

Nature of the Work

Interviewers obtain information from individuals and business representatives who are opening bank accounts, trying to obtain loans, seeking admission to medical facilities, participating in consumer surveys, applying to receive aid from government programs, or providing data for various other purposes. By mail, telephone, or in person, these workers solicit and verify information, create files, and perform a number of other related tasks.

The specific duties and job titles of *interviewers, except eligibility and loan* depend upon the type of employer. In doctors' offices and other health-care facilities, for example, *interviewing clerks* also are known as *admitting interviewers* or *patient representatives*. These workers obtain all preliminary information required for a patient's record or for his or her admission to a hospital, such as the patient's name, address, age, medical history, present medications, previous hospitalizations, religion, persons to notify in case of emergency, attending physician, and party responsible for payment. In some cases, interviewing clerks may be required to verify that an individual is eligible for health benefits or to work out financing options for those who might need them.

Other duties of interviewers in health care include assigning patients to rooms and summoning escorts to take patients to their rooms; sometimes, interviewers may escort patients themselves. Using the facility's computer system, they schedule laboratory work, x rays, and surgeries, prepare admission and discharge records, and route them to appropriate departments. They also may bill patients, receive payments, and answer the telephone. In an outpatient or office setting, interviewers schedule appointments, keep track of cancellations, and provide general information about care. In addition, the role of the admissions staff, particularly in hospitals, is expanding to include a wide range of patient services, from assisting patients with financial and medical questions to helping family members find hotel rooms.

Interviewing clerks who conduct market research surveys and polls for research firms have somewhat different responsibilities. These interviewers ask a series of prepared questions, record the responses, and forward the results to management. They may ask individuals questions about their occupation and earnings, political preferences, buying habits, satisfaction with certain goods or services sold to them, or other aspects of their lives. Although most interviews are conducted over the telephone, some are conducted in focus groups or by randomly polling people in a public place. More recently, the Internet is being used to elicit people's opinions. Almost all interviewers use computers or similar devices to enter the responses to questions.

Eligibility interviewers, government programs determine the eligibility of individuals applying to receive government assistance such as welfare, unemployment benefits, social security benefits, and public housing. These interviewers gather the relevant personal and financial information on an applicant and, on the basis of the rules and regulations of the particular government program, grant, modify, deny, or terminate an individual's eligibility for the program in question. They also are involved in the detection of fraud committed by persons who try to obtain benefits they are not eligible to receive.

Loan interviewers and clerks review individuals' credit history and obtain the information needed to determine the creditworthiness of applicants for loans and credit cards. These workers spend much of their day on the telephone, obtaining information from credit bureaus, employers, banks, credit institutions, and other sources to determine an applicant's credit history and ability to pay back a loan or charge.

Loan clerks, also called *loan processing clerks*, *loan closers*, or *loan service clerks*, assemble documents pertaining to a loan, process the paperwork associated with the loan, and ensure that all in-

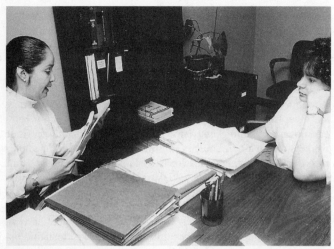

Interviewers obtain various types of information from individuals, and verify that information.

formation is complete and verified. Mortgage loans are the primary type of loan handled by loan clerks, who also may have to order appraisals of the property, set up escrow accounts, and secure any additional information required to transfer the property.

The specific duties of loan clerks vary by specialty. Loan closers, for example, complete the loan process by gathering the proper documents for signature at the closing, including deeds of trust, property insurance papers, and title commitments. They set the time and place for the closing, make sure that all parties are present, and ensure that all conditions for settlement have been met. After settlement, the loan closer records all of the documents involved and submits the final package to the owner of the loan. Loan service clerks maintain the payment records on a loan once it is issued. These clerical workers process the paperwork for payment of fees to insurance companies and tax authorities and also may record changes in clients' addresses and ownership of a loan. When necessary, they answer calls from customers with routine inquiries as well.

Loan interviewers have duties that are similar to those of loan clerks. They interview potential borrowers, help them fill out applications for loans, and then investigate the applicant's background and references, verify the information on the application, and forward any findings, reports, or documents to the company's appraisal department. Finally, interviewers inform the applicant as to whether the loan has been accepted or denied.

Employment

Interviewers held about 457,000 jobs in 2002. Approximately 193,000 were interviewers, except eligibility and loan; 170,000 were loan interviewers and clerks; and 94,000 were eligibility interviewers, government programs. Almost 1 out of every 5 interviewers worked in health care and social assistance industries, while most loan interviewers and clerks worked in financial institutions. Around 3 out of every 10 interviewers, except eligibility and loan, worked part time.

Job Outlook

Employment of interviewers is expected to grow more slowly than the average for all occupations through 2012. However, the projected change in employment varies by specialty. Most job openings should arise from the need to replace the numerous interview-

ers who leave the occupation or the labor force each year. Prospects for filling these openings will be best for applicants with a broad range of job skills, such as good customer service, math, and telephone skills. In addition to openings for full-time jobs, opportunities also should be available for part-time and temporary jobs.

The number of interviewers, except eligibility and loan, is projected to grow faster than average, reflecting growth in the health care and social assistance sector. This sector will hire more admissions interviewers as health-care facilities consolidate staff and expand the role of the admissions staff and as an aging and growing population requires more visits to health-care practitioners. In addition, an increasing use of market research will create more jobs requiring interviewers to collect data. In the future, though, more market research is expected to be conducted over the Internet, thus reducing the need for telephone interviewers to make individual calls.

The number of loan interviewers and clerks is projected to decline due to advances in technology that are making these workers more productive. Despite a projected increase in the number of applications for loans, automation will increase productivity, so that fewer workers will be required to process, check, and authorize applications than in the past. The effects of automation on employment will be moderated, however, by the many interpersonal aspects of the job. Mortgage loans, for example, require loan processors to personally verify financial data on the application, and loan closers are needed to assemble documents and prepare them for settlement. Employment, however, also will be adversely affected by changes in the financial services industry. For example, significant consolidation has occurred among mortgage loan-servicing companies. As a result, fewer mortgage banking companies are involved in servicing loans, making the function more efficient and reducing the need for loan service clerks.

The job outlook for loan interviewers and clerks is sensitive to overall economic activity. A downturn in the economy or a rise in interest rates usually leads to a decline in the demand for loans, particularly mortgage loans, and can result in layoffs. Even in slow economic times, however, job openings will arise from the need to replace workers who leave the occupation for various reasons.

Like that of loan interviewers and clerks, employment of eligibility interviewers for government programs also is projected to decline, due to advances in technology and the transformation of government aid programs over the last decade. Automation should have a significant effect on these workers because, as with credit and loan ratings, eligibility for government aid programs can be determined instantaneously by entering information into a computer. The job outlook for eligibility interviewers, however, also is sensitive to overall economic activity; a severe slowdown in the economy will cause more people to apply for government aid programs, increasing demand for eligibility interviewers.

Sources of Additional Information

State employment service offices can provide information about employment opportunities for interviewers.

For specific information on a career as a loan processor or loan closer, contact:

➤ Mortgage Bankers Association of America, 1919 Pennsylvania Ave., Washington, DC 20006. Internet: **http://www.mbaa.org**

(See the introductory statement on information and record clerks for information on working conditions, training requirements, and earnings.)

Library Assistants, Clerical

(0*NET 43-4121.00)

Nature of the Work

Library assistants assist librarians and, in some cases, library technicians in organizing library resources and making them available to users. (Librarians and library technicians are discussed elsewhere in the *Handbook*.)

Library assistants, clerical—sometimes referred to as library media assistants, library aides, or circulation assistants—register patrons so that they can borrow materials from the library. They record the borrower's name and address from an application and then issue a library card. Most library assistants enter patrons' records into computer databases.

At the circulation desk, library assistants lend and collect books, periodicals, videotapes, and other materials. When an item is borrowed, assistants stamp the due date on the material and record the patron's identification from his or her library card. They inspect returned materials for damage, check due dates, and compute fines for overdue material. Library assistants review records, compile a list of overdue materials, and send out notices reminding patrons that their materials are overdue. They also answer patrons' questions and refer those they cannot answer to a librarian.

Throughout the library, assistants sort returned books, periodicals, and other items and put them on their designated shelves, in the appropriate files, or in storage areas. They locate materials to be loaned, to either a patron or another library. Many card catalogues are computerized, so library assistants must be familiar with computers. If any materials have been damaged, these workers try to repair them. For example, they use tape or paste to repair torn pages or book covers and other specialized processes to repair more valuable materials.

Some library assistants specialize in helping patrons who have vision problems. Sometimes referred to as library, talking-books, or braille-and-talking-books clerks, they review the borrower's list of desired reading materials. They locate those materials or closely related substitutes from the library collection of large-type or braille volumes, tape cassettes, and open-reel talking books, complete the requisite paperwork, and give or mail the materials to the borrower.

Library assistants organize library materials and make them available to users.

Employment

Library assistants held about 120,000 jobs in 2002. More than one half of these workers were employed by local government in public libraries; most of the remaining employees worked in school libraries. Opportunities for flexible schedules are abundant; nearly half of these workers were on part-time schedules.

Job Outlook

Opportunities should be good through 2012 for persons interested in jobs as library assistants. Turnover of these workers is quite high, reflecting the limited investment in training and subsequent weak attachment to this occupation. The work is attractive to retirees, students, and others who want a part-time schedule, and there is a lot of movement into and out of the occupation. Many openings will become available each year to replace workers who transfer to another occupation or who leave the labor force. Some positions become available as library assistants move within the organization. Library assistants can be promoted to library technicians and, eventually, supervisory positions in public-service or technical-service areas. Advancement opportunities are greater in larger libraries.

Employment is expected to grow faster than the average for all occupations through 2012. The vast majority of library assistants work in public or school libraries. Efforts to contain costs in local governments and academic institutions of all types may result in more hiring of library support staff than librarians. Also, due to changing roles within libraries, library assistants are taking on more responsibility. Because most are employed by public institutions, library assistants are not directly affected by the ups and downs of the business cycle. Some of these workers may lose their jobs, however, if there are cuts in government budgets.

Sources of Additional Information

Information about a career as a library assistant can be obtained from either of the following organizations:

➤ Council on Library/Media Technology, 100 W. Broadway, Columbia, MO 65203. Internet: **http://colt.ucr.edu**

➤ American Library Association, 50 East Huron St., Chicago, IL 60611. Internet: **http://www.ala.org/hrdr**

Public libraries and libraries in academic institutions also can provide information about job openings for library assistants.

(See the introductory statement on information and record clerks for information on working conditions, training requirements, and earnings.)

Order Clerks

(0*NET 43-4151.00)

Nature of the Work

Order clerks receive and process incoming orders for a wide variety of goods or services, such as spare parts for machines, consumer appliances, gas and electric power connections, film rentals, and articles of clothing. They sometimes are called order-entry clerks, sales representatives, order processors, or order takers.

Orders for materials, merchandise, or services can come from inside or from outside of an organization. In large companies with many worksites, such as automobile manufacturers, clerks order parts and equipment from the company's warehouses. Inside order clerks receive orders from other workers employed by the same company or from salespersons in the field.

Many other order clerks, however, receive orders from outside companies or individuals. Order clerks in wholesale businesses, for

Order clerks receive and process incoming orders for a wide variety of goods and services.

instance, receive orders from retail establishments for merchandise that the retailer, in turn, sells to the public. An increasing number of order clerks are working for catalogue companies and online retailers, receiving orders from individual customers by telephone, fax, regular mail, or e-mail. Order clerks dealing primarily with the public sometimes are referred to as outside order clerks.

Computers provide order clerks with ready access to information such as stock numbers, prices, and inventory. The successful filling of an order frequently depends on having the right products in stock and being able to determine which products are most appropriate for the customer's needs. Some order clerks—especially those in industrial settings—must be able to give price estimates for entire jobs, not just single parts. Others must be able to take special orders, give expected arrival dates, prepare contracts, and handle complaints.

Many order clerks receive orders directly by telephone, entering the required information as the customer places the order. However, a rapidly increasing number of orders now are received through computer systems, the Internet, faxes, and e-mail. In some cases, these orders are sent directly from the customer's terminal to the order clerk's terminal. Orders received by regular mail are sometimes scanned into a database that is instantly accessible to clerks.

Clerks review orders for completeness and clarity. They may fill in missing information or contact the customer for the information. Clerks also contact customers if the customers need additional information, such as prices or shipping dates, or if delays in filling the order are anticipated. For orders received by regular mail, clerks extract checks or money orders, sort them, and send them for processing.

After an order has been verified and entered, the customer's final cost is calculated. The clerk then routes the order to the proper department—such as the warehouse—which actually sends out or delivers the item in question.

In organizations with sophisticated computer systems, inventory records are adjusted automatically, as sales are made. In less automated organizations, order clerks may adjust inventory records. Clerks also may notify other departments when inventories are low or when filling certain orders would deplete supplies.

Some order clerks must establish priorities in filling orders. For example, an order clerk in a blood bank may receive a request from a hospital for a certain type of blood. The clerk must first find out whether the request is routine or an emergency and then take appropriate action.

Employment

Order clerks held about 330,000 jobs in 2002. More than half were employed in wholesale and retail trade establishments, and about 1 in 6 order clerks were employed in manufacturing firms. Other jobs for order clerks were in various industries such as information, warehousing and storage, couriers, and business support services.

Job Outlook

Job openings for order clerks should be limited, as improvements in technology and office automation continue to increase worker productivity. While overall employment of order clerks is expected to decline through the year 2012, numerous openings will become available each year to replace order clerks who transfer to other occupations or leave the labor force completely. Many of these openings will be for seasonal work, especially in catalogue companies or online retailers catering to holiday gift buyers.

The growth in online retailing and in business-to-business electronic commerce, as well as the use of automated systems that make placing orders easy and convenient, will decrease demand for order clerks. The spread of electronic data interchange, which enables computers to communicate directly with each other, allows orders within establishments to be placed with little human intervention. In addition, internal systems allowing a firm's employees to place orders directly are becoming increasingly common. Outside orders placed over the Internet often are entered directly into the computer by the customer; thus, the order clerk is not involved at all in placing the order. Some companies also use automated phone menus that are accessible with a touch-tone phone to receive orders, and others use answering machines. Developments in voice recognition technology may further reduce the demand for order clerks.

Furthermore, increased automation will allow current order clerks to be more productive, with each clerk being able to handle an increasingly higher volume of orders. Sophisticated inventory control and automatic billing systems permit companies to track inventory and accounts with much less help from order clerks than in the past.

(See the introductory statement on information and record clerks for information on working conditions, training requirements, and earnings.)

Receptionists and Information Clerks

(O*NET 43-4171.00)

Nature of the Work

Receptionists and information clerks are charged with a responsibility that may have a lasting impact on the success of an organization: making a good first impression. These workers often are the first representatives of an organization a visitor encounters, so they need to be courteous, professional, and helpful. Receptionists answer telephones, route calls, greet visitors, respond to inquiries from the public, and provide information about the organization. Some receptionists are responsible for the coordination of all mail into and out of the office. In addition, receptionists contribute to the security of an organization by helping to monitor the access of visitors—a function that has become increasingly important in recent years.

Whereas some tasks are common to most receptionists and information clerks, the specific responsibilities of receptionists vary with the type of establishment in which they work. For example, receptionists in hospitals and in doctors' offices may gather patients' personal and financial information and direct them to the proper

A large number of receptionists are employed by healthcare establishments.

waiting rooms. In beauty or hair salons, by contrast, receptionists arrange appointments, direct customers to the hairstylist, and may serve as cashiers. In factories, large corporations, and government offices, they may provide identification cards and arrange for escorts to take visitors to the proper office. Those working for bus and train companies respond to inquiries about departures, arrivals, stops, and other related matters.

Increasingly, receptionists are using multiline telephone systems, personal computers, and fax machines. Despite the widespread use of automated answering systems or voice mail, many receptionists still take messages and inform other employees of visitors' arrivals or cancellation of an appointment. When they are not busy with callers, most receptionists are expected to perform a variety of office duties, including opening and sorting mail, collecting and distributing parcels, transmitting and delivering facsimiles, updating appointment calendars, preparing travel vouchers, and performing basic bookkeeping, word processing, and filing.

Employment

Receptionists and information clerks held about 1.1 million jobs in 2002. Almost 90 percent worked in service-providing industries. Among service-providing industries, health care and social assistance industries—including doctors' and dentists' offices, hospitals, nursing homes, urgent-care centers, surgical centers, and clinics—employed one-third of all receptionists and information clerks. Manufacturing, wholesale and retail trade, government, and real-estate industries also employed large numbers of receptionists and information clerks. About 3 of every 10 receptionists and information clerks worked part time.

Job Outlook

Employment of receptionists and information clerks is expected to grow faster than the average for all occupations through 2012. This increase will result from rapid growth in services industries—including physicians' offices, law firms, temporary-help agencies, and consulting firms—where most are employed. In addition, turnover in this large occupation will create numerous openings as receptionists and information clerks transfer to other occupations or leave the labor force altogether. Opportunities should be best for persons with a wide range of clerical and technical skills, particularly those with related work experience.

Technology should have conflicting effects on the demand for receptionists and information clerks. The increasing use of voice mail and other telephone automation reduces the need for receptionists by allowing one receptionist to perform work that formerly required several. However, the increasing use of other technology has caused a consolidation of clerical responsibilities and growing demand for workers with diverse clerical and technical skills. Because receptionists and information clerks may perform a wide variety of clerical tasks, they should continue to be in demand. Further, they perform many tasks that are interpersonal in nature and are not easily automated, ensuring continued demand for their services in a variety of establishments.

Sources of Additional Information

State employment offices can provide information on job openings for receptionists.

(See introductory statement on information and record clerks for information on working conditions, training requirements, and earnings.)

Reservation and Transportation Ticket Agents and Travel Clerks

(0*NET 43-4181.01, 43-4181.02)

Nature of the Work

Each year, millions of Americans travel by plane, train, ship, bus, and automobile. Many of these travelers rely on the services of reservation and transportation ticket agents and travel clerks, who perform functions as varied as selling tickets, confirming reservations, checking baggage, and providing tourists with useful travel information.

Most *reservation agents* work for large hotel chains or airlines, helping people to plan trips and make reservations. They usually work in large reservation centers, answering telephone or e-mail inquiries and offering suggestions and information about travel arrangements, such as routes, schedules, rates, and types of accommodation. Reservation agents quote fares and room rates, provide travel information, and make and confirm transportation and hotel reservations. Most agents use proprietary networks to obtain, as quickly as possible, information needed to make, change, or cancel reservations for customers.

Transportation ticket agents are sometimes known as passenger service agents, passenger booking clerks, reservation clerks, airport service agents, ticket clerks, or ticket sellers. They work in airports, train, and bus stations, selling tickets, assigning seats to passengers, and checking baggage. In addition, they may answer inquiries and give directions, examine passports and visas, or check in pets. Other ticket agents, more commonly known as *gate* or *station agents*, work in airport terminals, assisting passengers boarding airplanes. These workers direct passengers to the correct boarding area, check tickets and seat assignments, make boarding announcements, and provide special assistance to young, elderly, or disabled passengers when they board or disembark.

Most *travel clerks* are employed by membership organizations, such as automobile clubs. These workers, sometimes called *member services counselors* or *travel counselors*, plan trips, calculate mileage, and offer travel suggestions, such as the best route from the point of origin to the destination, to club members. Travel clerks also may prepare an itinerary indicating points of interest, restaurants, overnight accommodations, and availability of emergency services during a trip. In some cases, they make rental car, hotel, and restaurant reservations for club members.

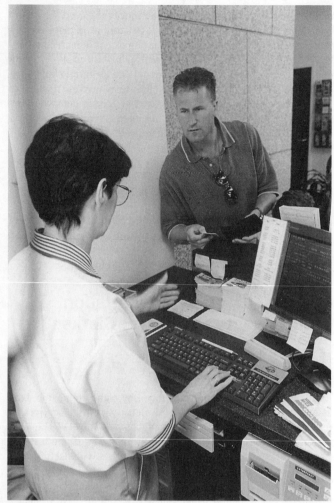

Ticket agents sell tickets, confirm reservations, check baggage, and provide travelers with useful information.

Passenger rate clerks generally work for bus companies. They sell tickets for regular bus routes and arrange nonscheduled or chartered trips. They plan travel routes, compute rates, and keep customers informed of appropriate details. They also may arrange travel accommodations.

Employment
Reservation and transportation ticket agents and travel clerks held about 177,000 jobs in 2002. More than 6 of every 10 are employed by airlines. Others work for membership organizations, such as automobile clubs; hotels and other lodging places; railroad companies; buslines; and other companies that provide transportation services.

Although agents and clerks are found throughout the country, most work in large metropolitan airports, downtown ticket offices, large reservation centers, and train or bus stations. The remainder work in small communities served only by intercity bus or railroad lines.

Job Outlook
Applicants for reservation and transportation ticket agent jobs are likely to encounter considerable competition, because the supply of qualified applicants exceeds the expected number of job openings. Entry requirements for these jobs are minimal, and many people seeking to get into the airline industry or travel business often start out in such positions. The jobs provide excellent travel benefits,

and many people view airline and other travel-related jobs as glamorous.

Employment of reservation and transportation ticket agents and travel clerks is expected to grow about as fast as the average for all occupations through 2012. Although a growing population will demand additional travel services, employment of these workers will grow more slowly than this demand because of the significant impact of technology on productivity. Automated reservations and ticketing, as well as "ticketless" travel, for example, are reducing the need for some workers. Most train stations and airports now have satellite ticket printer locations, called kiosks, that enable passengers to make reservations and purchase tickets themselves. Many passengers also are able to check flight times and fares, make reservations, and purchase tickets on the Internet. Nevertheless, not all travel-related passenger services can be fully automated, primarily for safety and security reasons. As a result, job openings will continue to become available as the occupation grows and as workers transfer to other occupations, retire, or leave the labor force altogether.

Employment of reservation and transportation ticket agents and travel clerks is sensitive to cyclical swings in the economy. During recessions, discretionary passenger travel declines, and transportation service companies are less likely to hire new workers and may even resort to layoffs.

Sources of Additional Information
For information about job opportunities as reservation and transportation ticket agents and travel clerks, write the personnel manager of individual transportation companies. Addresses of airlines are available from:
➤ Air Transport Association of America, 1301 Pennsylvania Ave. NW., Suite 1100, Washington, DC 20004-1707. Internet: **http://www.airlines.org**
(See the introductory statement on information and record clerks for information on working conditions, training requirements, and earnings.)

Material-Recording, -Scheduling, -Dispatching, and -Distributing Occupations

(0*NET 43-5011.00, 43-5021.00, 43-5031.00, 43-5032.00, 43-5041.00, 43-5051.00, 43-5052.00, 43-5053.00, 43-5061.00, 43-5071.00, 43-5081.01, 43-5081.02, 43-5081.03, 43-5081.04, 43-5111.00)

Significant Points

● Many of these occupations are at the entry level and do not require more than a high school diploma.

● Workers develop the necessary skills through on-the-job training lasting from several days to a few months; dispatchers usually require the most extensive training.

● Numerous job openings will arise each year from the need to replace workers who leave this very large occupational group.

Nature of the Work
Workers in this group are responsible for a variety of communications, recordkeeping, and scheduling operations. Typically, they coordinate, expedite, and track orders for personnel, materials, and equipment.

Cargo and freight agents route and track cargo and freight shipments, whether from airline, train, or truck terminals or from shipping docks. They keep records of any missing or damaged items and any excess supplies. The agents sort cargo according to its destination and separate items that cannot be packed together. They also coordinate payment schedules with customers and arrange for the pickup or delivery of freight.

Couriers and messengers deliver letters, important business documents, or packages within a firm to other businesses or to customers. They usually keep records of deliveries and sometimes obtain the recipient's signature. Couriers and messengers travel by car, van, or bicycle, or even by foot when making nearby deliveries.

Dispatchers receive requests for service and initiate action to provide that service. Duties vary with the needs of the employer. Police, fire, and ambulance dispatchers, also called public-safety dispatchers, handle calls from people reporting crimes, fires, and medical emergencies. Truck, bus, and train dispatchers schedule and coordinate the movement of these vehicles to ensure that they arrive at the appointed time. Taxicab dispatchers relay requests for cabs to individual drivers, tow-truck dispatchers take calls for emergency road service, and utility company dispatchers handle calls related to utility and telephone service. Courier and messenger service dispatchers route drivers, riders, and walkers around a (usually urban) designated area. They distribute work by radio, e-mail, or phone, making sure that service deadlines are met.

Meter readers read meters and record the consumption of electricity, gas, water, or steam. They serve a variety of consumers and travel along designated routes to track consumption. Although numerous meters still are read at the house or building that receives the utility's service, many newer meters can be read remotely from a central point. Meter readers also look for evidence of unauthorized utility usage.

Production, planning, and expediting clerks coordinate and expedite the flow of information, work, and materials, usually according to a production or work schedule. They gather information for reports on the progress of work and on production problems. They also may schedule workers or shipments of parts, estimate costs, and keep inventories of materials.

Shipping, receiving, and traffic clerks track all incoming and outgoing shipments of goods transferred among businesses, suppliers, and customers. These clerks may be required to lift cartons of various sizes. Shipping clerks assemble, address, stamp, and ship merchandise or materials. Receiving clerks unpack, verify, and record information on incoming merchandise. Traffic clerks record the destination, weight, and cost of all incoming and outgoing shipments. In a small company, one clerk may perform all of these tasks. (Postal Service workers sort and deliver mail for the United States Postal Service. While these workers are classified as material-recording, -scheduling, -dispatching, and -distributing workers and are included in the estimate of employment for this occupational group, they are discussed in detail elsewhere in the *Handbook*.)

Stock clerks and order fillers receive, unpack, and store materials and equipment, and maintain and distribute inventories. In wholesale and retail establishments, inventories may include merchandise; in other kinds of organizations, inventory may include equipment, supplies, or materials. In small firms, stock clerks and order fillers may perform all of the preceding tasks, as well as those usually handled by shipping and receiving clerks. In large establishments, stock clerks and order fillers may be responsible for only one task.

Weighers, measurers, checkers, and samplers check and record the weight and measurement of various materials and equipment.

They use scales, measuring and counting devices, and calculators to compare weights, measurements, or other specifications against bills or invoices. They also prepare reports on inventory levels.

(This introductory section is followed by sections that provide more detail on cargo and freight agents; couriers and messengers; dispatchers; utility meter readers; production, planning, and expediting clerks; shipping, receiving, and traffic clerks; stock clerks and order fillers; and weighers, measurers, checkers, and samplers.)

Working Conditions

Working conditions vary considerably by occupation and employment setting. Couriers and messengers spend most of their time alone, making deliveries, and usually are not closely supervised. Those who deliver by bicycle must be physically fit and are exposed to all weather conditions, as well as to the many hazards associated with heavy traffic. Car, van, and truck couriers must sometimes carry heavy loads, either manually or with the aid of a handtruck. They also have to deal with difficult parking situations, as well as traffic jams and road construction. The pressure of making as many deliveries as possible to increase one's earnings can be stressful and may lead to unsafe driving or bicycling practices.

Meter readers, usually working 40 hours a week, work outdoors in all types of weather as they travel through communities and neighborhoods, taking readings.

The work of dispatchers can be very hectic when many calls come in at the same time. The job of public-safety dispatcher is particularly stressful because a slow or an improper response to a call can result in serious injury or further harm. Also, callers who are anxious or afraid may become excited and be unable to provide needed information; some may even become abusive. Despite provocations, dispatchers must remain calm, objective, and in control of the situation.

Dispatchers sit for long periods, using telephones, computers, and two-way radios. Much of their time is spent at video display terminals, viewing monitors and observing traffic patterns. As a result of working for long stretches with computers and other electronic equipment, dispatchers can experience significant eyestrain and back discomfort. Generally, dispatchers work a 40-hour week; however, rotating shifts and compressed work schedules are common. Alternative work schedules are necessary to accommodate evening, weekend, and holiday work, as well as 24-hour-per-day, 7-day-per-week operations.

Other workers in this group—cargo and freight agents; shipping, receiving, and traffic clerks; stock clerks and order fillers; production, planning, and expediting clerks; and weighers, measurers, checkers, and samplers—work in a wide variety of businesses, institutions, and industries. Some work in warehouses, stockrooms, or shipping and receiving rooms that may not be temperature controlled. Others may spend time in cold storage rooms or outside on loading platforms, where they are exposed to the weather.

Production, planning, and expediting clerks work closely with supervisors who must approve production and work schedules. Most jobs for shipping, receiving, and traffic clerks, stock clerks and order fillers, and cargo and freight agents involve frequent standing, bending, walking, and stretching. Some lifting and carrying of smaller items also may be involved. Although automated devices have lessened the physical demands of this occupation, their use remains somewhat limited. The work still can be strenuous, even though mechanical material-handling equipment is employed to move heavy items.

The typical workweek is Monday through Friday; however, evening and weekend hours are common in some jobs, such as stock clerks and order fillers in retail trade and couriers and messengers, and may be required in other jobs when large shipments are involved or when inventory is taken.

Employment

In 2002, material-recording, -scheduling, -dispatching, and -distributing workers held about 4 million jobs, distributed among detailed occupations as follows:

Stock clerks and order fillers	1,628,000
Shipping, receiving, and traffic clerks	803,000
Postal service mail carriers	334,000
Production, planning, and expediting clerks	288,000
Postal service mail sorters, processors, and processing machine operators	253,000
Dispatchers, except police, fire, and ambulance	170,000
Couriers and messengers	132,000
Police, fire, and ambulance dispatchers	92,000
Weighers, measurers, checkers, and samplers, recordkeeping	81,000
Postal service clerks	77,000
Cargo and freight agents	59,000
Meter readers, utilities	54,000
All other material recording, scheduling, dispatching, and distributing workers	34,000

About 86 percent of material-recording, -scheduling, -dispatching, and -distributing jobs were in the service-providing sector. Most of the rest were in manufacturing. Although workers in these jobs are found throughout the country, most work near population centers where retail stores, warehouses, factories, and large communications centers are concentrated.

Training, Other Qualifications, and Advancement

Many material-recording, -scheduling, -dispatching, and -distributing occupations are at the entry level and do not require more than a high school diploma. Employers, however, prefer to hire those familiar with computers and other electronic office and business equipment. Applicants who have taken business courses or have previous business, dispatching, or specific job-related experience may be preferred. Because communication with other people is an integral part of some jobs in the occupation, good oral and written communications skills are essential. Typing, filing, recordkeeping, and other clerical skills also are important.

State or local government civil-service regulations usually govern police, fire, emergency medical, and ambulance dispatching jobs. Candidates for these positions may have to pass written, oral, and performance tests. Also, they may be asked to attend training classes and attain the proper certification in order to qualify for advancement.

Workers usually develop the necessary skills on the job. This informal training lasts from several days to a few months, depending on the complexity of the job. Dispatchers usually require the most extensive training. Working with an experienced dispatcher, they monitor calls and learn how to operate a variety of communications equipment, including telephones, radios, and various wireless devices. As trainees gain confidence, they begin to handle calls themselves. In smaller operations, dispatchers sometimes act as customer service representatives, processing orders. Many public-safety dispatchers also participate in structured training programs sponsored by their employer. Increasingly, public-safety dispatchers receive training in stress and crisis management, as well as family counseling. Employers are recognizing the toll this work has on daily living and the potential impact that stress has on the job, on the work environment, and in the home.

Communication skills and the ability to work under pressure are important personal qualities for dispatchers. Residency in the city or county of employment frequently is required for public-safety dispatchers. Dispatchers in transportation industries must be able to deal with sudden influxes of shipments and disruptions of shipping schedules caused by bad weather, road construction, or accidents.

Although there are no mandatory licensing or certification requirements, some States require that public-safety dispatchers possess a certificate to work on a State network, such as the Police Information Network. The Association of Public Safety Communications Officials, International and the National Academies of Emergency Dispatch offer certification programs. Many dispatchers participate in these programs in order to improve their prospects for career advancement.

Couriers and messengers usually learn on the job, training with a veteran for a short time. Those who work as independent contractors for a messenger or delivery service may be required to have a valid driver's license, a registered and inspected vehicle, a good driving record, and insurance coverage. Many couriers and messengers who are employees, rather than independent contractors, also are required to provide and maintain their own vehicle. Although some companies have spare bicycles or mopeds that their riders may rent for a short period, almost all two-wheeled couriers own their own bicycle, moped, or motorcycle. A good knowledge of the geographic area in which they travel, as well as a good sense of direction, also are important.

Utility meter readers usually work with a more experienced meter reader until they feel comfortable doing the job on their own. They learn how to read the meters and determine the consumption rate. They also must learn the route that they need to travel in order to read all their customers' meters.

Production, planning, and expediting clerks; weighers, measurers, checkers, and samplers; stock clerks and order fillers; and shipping, receiving, and traffic clerks usually learn the job by doing routine tasks under close supervision. They learn how to count and mark stock, and then they start keeping records and taking inventory. Strength, stamina, good eyesight, and an ability to work at repetitive tasks, sometimes under pressure, are important characteristics. Production, planning, and expediting clerks must learn both how their company operates and the company's priorities before they can begin to write production and work schedules efficiently. Stock clerks, whose sole responsibility is to bring merchandise to the sales floor to stock shelves and racks, need little training. Shipping, receiving, and traffic clerks and stock clerks and order fillers who handle jewelry, liquor, or drugs may be bonded.

Shipping, receiving, and traffic clerks, as well as cargo and freight agents, start out by checking items to be shipped and then attaching labels to them and making sure that the addresses are correct. Training in the use of automated equipment usually is done informally, on the job. As these occupations become more automated, however, workers in them may need longer periods of training in order to master the use of the equipment.

Advancement opportunities for material-recording, -scheduling, -dispatching, and -distributing workers vary with the place of employment. Dispatchers who work for private firms, which usually are small, will find few opportunities for advancement. In contrast, public-safety dispatchers may become a shift or divisional supervisor or chief of communications, or they may move to higher paying administrative jobs. Some become police officers or firefighters. Couriers and messengers—especially those who work for messenger or courier services—have limited advancement opportunities; a small fraction move into the office to learn dispatching or to take service requests by phone. In large firms, stock clerks can advance to invoice clerk, stock control clerk, or procurement clerk.

Shipping, receiving, and traffic clerks are promoted to head clerk, and those with a broad understanding of shipping and receiving may enter a related field, such as industrial traffic management. With additional training, some stock clerks and order fillers and shipping, receiving, and traffic clerks advance to jobs as warehouse manager or purchasing agent.

Job Outlook

Overall employment of material-recording, -scheduling, -dispatching, and -distributing workers is expected to show little or no change through 2012. However, numerous job openings will arise each year from the need to replace workers who leave this very large occupational group.

Projected employment growth varies by detailed occupation. Meter readers will experience a decline in employment due to automated meter reading systems that greatly increase productivity. New technologies will enable stock clerks and order fillers to handle more stock, resulting in declining employment in this occupation as well. The use of e-mail and fax will contribute to slow growth for couriers and messengers. Employment of shipping, receiving, and traffic clerks also will grow more slowly than average due to the increasing use of automated devices and systems that enable these workers to handle materials and shipments more efficiently and more accurately.

Employment of dispatchers; production, planning, and expediting clerks; weighers, measurers, checkers, and samplers; and cargo and freight agents is projected to grow about as fast as the average for all occupations through 2012. Population growth, as well as an expanded role for dispatchers stemming from advances in telecommunications, should boost employment levels. Employment of production, planning, and expediting clerks and cargo and freight agents should benefit from more emphasis on efficiency in the production and shipping processes, while a growing need for accurate inventory records should spur employment of weighers, measurers, checkers, and samplers.

Earnings

Earnings of material-recording, -scheduling, -dispatching, and -distributing occupations vary somewhat by occupation and industry. The range of median hourly earnings in 2002 is shown in the following tabulation:

Production, planning, and expediting clerks	$16.18
Cargo and freight agents	15.10
Dispatchers, except police, fire, and ambulance	14.56
Meter readers, utilities	13.86
Police, fire, and ambulance dispatchers	13.30
Weighers, measurers, checkers, and samplers, recordkeeping	11.62
Shipping, receiving, and traffic clerks	11.26
Couriers and messengers	9.32
Stock clerks and order fillers	9.26
All other material recording, scheduling, dispatching, and distributing workers	12.45

Workers in material-recording, -scheduling, -dispatching, and -distributing occupations usually receive the same benefits as most other workers. If uniforms are required, employers generally provide them or offer an allowance to purchase them.

The sections that follow provide more information on cargo and freight agents; couriers and messengers; dispatchers; meter readers, utilities; production, planning, and expediting clerks; shipping, receiving, and traffic clerks; stock clerks and order fillers; and weighers, measurers, checkers, and samplers.

Cargo and Freight Agents

(O*NET 43-5011.00)

Nature of the Work

Cargo and freight agents arrange for and track incoming and outgoing cargo and freight shipments in airline, train, or trucking terminals or on shipping docks. They expedite the movement of shipments by determining the route that shipments are to take and by preparing all necessary shipping documents. The agents take orders from customers and arrange for the pickup of freight or cargo for delivery to loading platforms. Cargo and freight agents may keep records of the properties of the cargo, such as its amount, type, weight, and dimensions. They keep a tally of missing items, record the conditions of damaged items, and document any excess supplies.

Cargo and freight agents arrange cargo according to its destination. They also determine the shipping rates and other charges that can sometimes apply to the freight. For imported or exported freight, they verify that the proper customs paperwork is in order. Cargo and freight agents often track shipments electronically, using bar codes, and answer customers' inquiries on the status of their shipments.

Employment

Cargo and freight agents held about 59,000 jobs in 2002. Most jobs were in transportation. Approximately 13 percent worked in the air transportation industry, and 9 percent worked in the truck transportation industry. Couriers employed another 14 percent. In addition, about 45 percent worked for firms engaged in support activities for the transportation industry.

Job Outlook

Employment of cargo and freight agents is expected to grow about as fast as the average for all occupations through 2012. Although cargo traffic is expected to grow faster than it has in the past, employment of cargo and freight agents will not quite keep pace, because of technological advances. For example, the increasing use of bar codes on cargo and freight allows agents and customers to track these shipments quickly over the Internet, rather than manually tracking their location. In addition, customs and insurance pa-

Cargo and freight agents expedite the movement of shipments by determining the route that shipments are to take and by preparing all necessary documents.

perwork now can be completed over the Internet by customers, reducing the need for cargo and freight agents.

Despite these advances in technology that dampen job growth among cargo and freight agents, job openings will continue to arise, due to increases in buying over the Internet, which will result in more shipments. Jobs also will open up because of the increasing importance of same-day delivery, which expands the role of agents. In addition, many job openings will be created to replace cargo and freight agents who leave the occupation.

Related Occupations
Cargo and freight agents plan and coordinate shipments of cargo by airlines, trains, and trucks. They also arrange freight pickup with customers. Others who do similar work are couriers and messengers; shipping, receiving, and traffic clerks; weighers, measurers, checkers, and samplers; truck drivers and driver/sales workers; and Postal Service workers.

Sources of Additional Information
Information about job opportunities may be obtained from local employers and local offices of the State employment service.

(See the introduction to the section on material-recording, -scheduling, -dispatching, and -distributing occupations for information on working conditions, training requirements, and earnings.)

Couriers and Messengers

(0*NET 43-5021.00)

Nature of the Work
Couriers and messengers move and distribute information, documents, and small packages for businesses, institutions, and government agencies. They pick up and deliver letters, important business documents, or packages that need to be sent or received quickly within a local area. Trucks and vans are used for larger deliveries, such as legal caseloads and conference materials. By sending an item by courier or messenger, the sender ensures that it reaches its destination the same day or even within the hour. Couriers and messengers also deliver items that the sender is unwilling to entrust to other means of delivery, such as important legal or financial documents, passports, airline tickets, or medical samples to be tested.

Couriers and messengers receive their instructions either in person—by reporting to their office—or by telephone, two-way radio, or wireless data service. Then they pick up the item and carry it to its destination. After each pickup or delivery, they check in with their dispatcher to receive instructions. Sometimes the dispatcher will contact them while they are between stops, and they may be routed to go past a stop that recently called in a delivery. Because most couriers and messengers work on commission, they are carrying more than one package at any given time of the day. Consequently, most couriers and messengers spend much of their time outdoors or in their vehicle. They usually maintain records of deliveries and often obtain signatures from the persons receiving the items.

Most couriers and messengers deliver items within a limited geographic area, such as a city or metropolitan area. Items that need to go longer distances usually are sent by mail or by an overnight delivery service. Some couriers and messengers carry items only for their employer, which typically might be a law firm, bank, or financial institution. Others may act as part of an organization's internal mail system and carry items mainly within the organization's build-

Most couriers and messengers deliver items within a limited geographic area, such as a city or metropolitan area.

ings or entirely within one building. Many couriers and messengers work for messenger or courier services; for a fee, they pick up items from anyone and deliver them to specified destinations within a local area. Most are paid on a commission basis.

Couriers and messengers reach their destination by several methods. Many drive vans or cars or ride motorcycles. A few travel by foot, especially in urban areas or when making deliveries nearby. In congested urban areas, messengers often use bicycles to make deliveries. Bicycle messengers usually are employed by messenger or courier services. Although e-mail and fax machines can deliver information faster than couriers and messengers can, and although a great deal of information is available over the Internet, an electronic copy cannot substitute for the original document in many types of business transactions.

Employment
Couriers and messengers together held about 132,000 jobs in 2002. Approximately 28 percent were employed in the couriers and messengers industry. About 13 percent worked in health-care services, and around 9 percent worked in the legal services industry. Another 8 percent were employed in finance and insurance firms. Technically, many messengers are self-employed independent contractors, because they provide their own vehicles and, to a certain extent, set their own schedules. In many respects, however, they are like employees, because they usually work for one company.

Job Outlook
Employment of couriers and messengers is expected to grow more slowly than average through 2012, despite an increasing volume of parcels, business documents, promotional materials, and other written information that must be handled and delivered as the economy expands. However, some jobs will arise out of the need to replace couriers and messengers who leave the occupation.

Employment of couriers and messengers will continue to be adversely affected by the more widespread use of electronic information-handling technology, such as e-mail and fax. Many documents, forms, and other materials that people used to have delivered by hand are now downloaded from the Internet. Many legal and financial documents, which used to be delivered by hand because they required a handwritten signature, can now be delivered electronically with online signatures. However, couriers and messengers still will be needed to transport materials that cannot be sent electronically—such as blueprints and other oversized materials, securities, and passports. Also, they still will be required by medical and dental laboratories to pick up and deliver medical samples, specimens, and other materials.

Related Occupations

Messengers and couriers deliver letters, parcels, and other items. They also keep accurate records of their work. Others who do similar work are Postal Service workers; truck drivers and driver/sales workers; shipping, receiving, and traffic clerks; and cargo and freight agents.

Sources of Additional Information

Information about job opportunities may be obtained from local employers and local offices of the State employment service. Persons interested in courier and messenger jobs also may contact messenger and courier services, mail-order firms, banks, printing and publishing firms, utility companies, retail stores, or other large companies.

(See the introduction to the section on material-recording, -scheduling, -dispatching, and -distributing occupations for information on working conditions, training requirements, and earnings.)

Dispatchers

(O*NET 43-5031.00, 43-5032.00)

Nature of the Work

Dispatchers schedule and dispatch workers, equipment, or service vehicles for the conveyance of materials or passengers. They keep records, logs, and schedules of the calls they receive, the transportation vehicles they monitor and control, and the actions they take. They maintain information on each call and then prepare a detailed report on all activities occurring during their shifts. Many dispatchers employ computer-aided dispatch systems to accomplish these tasks. The work of dispatchers varies greatly, depending on the industry in which they work.

Regardless of where they work, all dispatchers are assigned a specific territory and have responsibility for all communications within that area. Many work in teams, especially those dispatchers in large communications centers or companies. One person usually handles all dispatching calls to the response units or company drivers, while the other members of the team usually receive the incoming calls and deal with the public.

Police, fire, and ambulance dispatchers, also called public safety dispatchers, monitor the location of emergency services personnel from any one or all of the jurisdiction's emergency services departments. These workers dispatch the appropriate type and number of units in response to calls for assistance. Dispatchers, or call takers, often are the first people the public contacts when emergency assistance is required. If certified for emergency medical services, the dispatcher may provide medical instruction to those on the scene of the emergency until the medical staff arrives.

Police, fire, and ambulance dispatchers work in a variety of settings: a police station, a fire station, a hospital, or, increasingly, a centralized communications center. In many areas, the police department serves as the communications center. In these situations, all emergency calls go to the police department, where a dispatcher handles the police calls and screens the others before transferring them to the appropriate service.

When handling calls, dispatchers question each caller carefully to determine the type, seriousness, and location of the emergency. The information obtained is posted either electronically by computer or, with decreasing frequency, by hand. It is communicated immediately to uniformed or supervisory personnel, who quickly decide on the priority of the incident, the kind and number of units needed, and the location of the closest and most suitable units available. Typically, a team answers calls and relays the information to be dispatched. Responsibility then shifts to the dispatchers, who send response units to the scene and monitor the activity of the public safety personnel answering the dispatched message. During the course of the shift, dispatchers may rotate these functions.

When appropriate, dispatchers stay in close contact with other service providers—for example, a police dispatcher would monitor the response of the fire department when there is a major fire. In a medical emergency, dispatchers keep in close touch not only with the dispatched units, but also with the caller. They may give extensive first-aid instructions before the emergency personnel arrive, while the caller is waiting for the ambulance. Dispatchers continuously give updates on the patient's condition to the ambulance personnel and often serve as a link between the medical staff in a hospital and the emergency medical technicians in the ambulance. (A separate statement on emergency medical technicians and paramedics appears elsewhere in the *Handbook.*)

Other dispatchers coordinate deliveries, service calls, and related activities for a variety of firms. *Truck dispatchers,* who work for local and long-distance trucking companies, coordinate the movement of trucks and freight between cities. They direct the pickup and delivery activities of drivers, receive customers' requests for the pickup and delivery of freight, consolidate freight orders into truckloads for specific destinations, assign drivers and trucks, and draw up routes and pickup and delivery schedules. *Bus dispatchers* make sure that local and long-distance buses stay on schedule. They handle all problems that may disrupt service, and they dispatch other buses or arrange for repairs in order to restore service and schedules. *Train dispatchers* ensure the timely and efficient movement of trains according to orders and schedules. They must be aware of track switch positions, track maintenance areas, and the location of other trains running on the track. *Taxicab dispatchers,* or starters, dispatch taxis in response to requests for service and keep logs on all road service calls. *Tow-truck dispatchers* take calls for emergency road service. They relay the nature of the problem to a nearby service station or a tow-truck service and see to it that the road service is completed. *Gas and water service dispatchers* monitor gaslines and water mains and send out service trucks and crews to take care of emergencies.

Dispatchers schedule and dispatch workers, equipment, or service vehicles for the conveyance of materials or passengers.

Employment

Dispatchers held 262,000 jobs in 2002. About one-third were police, fire, and ambulance dispatchers, almost all of whom worked for State and local governments—primarily local police and fire departments. About one-quarter of all dispatchers worked in the transportation and warehousing industry, and the rest worked in a wide variety of mainly service-providing sector industries.

Although dispatching jobs are found throughout the country, most dispatchers work in urban areas, where large communications centers and businesses are located.

Job Outlook

Employment of dispatchers is expected to grow about as fast as the average for all occupations through 2012. In addition to those positions resulting from job growth, many openings will arise from the need to replace workers who transfer to other occupations or leave the labor force.

Population growth and economic expansion are expected to spur employment growth for all types of dispatchers. The growing and aging population will increase demand for emergency services and stimulate employment growth of police, fire, and ambulance dispatchers. Many districts are consolidating their communications centers into a shared areawide facility. Individuals with computer skills and experience will have a greater opportunity for employment as public-safety dispatchers.

Employment of some dispatchers is more adversely affected by economic downturns than that of other dispatchers. For example, when economic activity falls, demand for transportation services declines. As a result, taxicab, train, and truck dispatchers may experience layoffs or a shortened workweek, and jobseekers may have some difficulty finding entry-level jobs. Employment of tow-truck dispatchers, by contrast, is seldom affected by general economic conditions, because of the emergency nature of their business.

Related Occupations

Other occupations that involve directing and controlling the movement of vehicles, freight, and personnel, as well as distributing information and messages, include air traffic controllers, communications equipment operators, customer service representatives, and reservation and transportation ticket agents and travel clerks.

Sources of Additional Information

For further information on training and certification for police, fire, and emergency dispatchers, contact either of the following organizations:

➤ National Academies of Emergency Dispatch, 139 East South Temple, Suite 530, Salt Lake City, UT 84111. Internet: **http://www.emergencydispatch.org**

➤ Association of Public Safety Communications Officials, International, 351 N. Williamson Blvd., Daytona Beach, FL 32114-1112. Internet: **http://www.apco911.org**

Information on job opportunities for police, fire, and emergency dispatchers is available from personnel offices of State and local governments or police departments. Information about work opportunities for other types of dispatchers is available from local employers and State employment service offices.

(See the introduction to the section on material-recording, -scheduling, -dispatching, and -distributing occupations for information on working conditions, training requirements, and earnings.)

Meter Readers, Utilities

(0*NET 43-5041.00)

Nature of the Work

Meter readers read electric, gas, water, or steam consumption meters and record the volume used. They serve both residential and commercial consumers, either walking or driving along the designated route. Their duties include inspecting the meters and their connections for any defects or damage, supplying repair and maintenance workers with the necessary information to fix damaged meters, keeping track of the average usage, and recording reasons for any extreme fluctuations in volume.

Meter readers are constantly aware of any abnormal behavior or consumption that might indicate an unauthorized connection. They may turn off service for questionable behavior or nonpayment of charges, and they also are responsible for turning on service for new occupants. These workers usually keep a record of the fact that the meters on which they have completed work have been serviced.

Employment

Meter readers held about 54,000 jobs in 2002. About 43 percent were employed by electric, gas, and water utilities. Most of the rest were employed in local government, reading water meters or meters for other government-owned utilities.

Job Outlook

Employment of meter readers is expected to decline through 2012. New automated meter reading (AMR) systems allow meters to be monitored and billed from a central point, reducing the need for meter readers. However, because it will be many years before AMR systems can be implemented in all locations, there still will be some openings for meter readers, mainly to replace workers who leave the occupation.

Related Occupations

Other workers responsible for the distribution and control of utilities include powerplant operators, distributors, and dispatchers.

Sources of Additional Information

Information about job opportunities may be obtained from local employers and local offices of the State employment service.

New automated meter-reading systems allow meters to be monitored and billed from a central point, reducing the need for meter readers.

(See the introduction to the section on material-recording, -scheduling, -dispatching, and -distributing occupations for information on working conditions, training requirements, and earnings.)

Production, Planning, and Expediting Clerks

(0*NET 43-5061.00)

Nature of the Work

Production, planning, and expediting clerks coordinate and expedite the flow of information, work, and materials within or among offices. Most of their work is done according to production, work, or shipment schedules that are devised by supervisors who determine work progress and completion dates. Production, planning, and expediting clerks compile reports on the progress of work and on production problems. They also may schedule workers, estimate costs, schedule the shipment of parts, keep an inventory of materials, inspect and assemble materials, and write special orders for services and merchandise. In addition, they may route and deliver parts to ensure that production quotas are met and that merchandise is delivered on the date promised.

Production and planning clerks compile records and reports on various aspects of production, such as materials and parts used, products produced, machine and instrument readings, and frequency of defects. These workers prepare work tickets or other production guides and distribute them to other workers. Production and planning clerks coordinate, schedule, monitor, and chart production and its progress, either manually or with electronic equipment. They also gather information from customers' orders or other specifications and use the information to prepare a detailed production sheet that serves as a guide in assembling or manufacturing the product.

Expediting clerks contact vendors and shippers to ensure that merchandise, supplies, and equipment are forwarded on the specified shipping dates. They communicate with transportation companies to prevent delays in transit, and they may arrange for the distribution of materials upon their arrival. They may even visit work areas of vendors and shippers to check the status of orders. Expediting clerks locate and distribute materials to specified production areas. They may inspect products for quality and quantity to ensure their adherence to specifications. They also keep a chronological list of due dates and may move work that does not meet the production schedule to the front of the list.

Employment

In 2002, production, planning, and expediting clerks held 288,000 jobs. Jobs in manufacturing made up 45 percent. Another 13 percent were in wholesale and retail trade establishments.

Job Outlook

Employment of production, planning, and expediting clerks is expected to grow about as fast as the average for all occupations through 2012. As increasing pressure is put on firms to manufacture and deliver their goods more quickly and efficiently, the need for production, planning, and expediting clerks will grow. The work of production, planning, and expediting clerks is less likely to be automated than the work of many other administrative support occupations. In addition to openings due to employment growth, job openings will arise from the need to replace production, planning, and expediting clerks who leave the labor force or transfer to other occupations.

Related Occupations

Other workers who coordinate the flow of information to assist the production process include cargo and freight agents; shipping, receiving, and traffic clerks; stock clerks and order fillers; and weighers, measurers, checkers, and samplers, recordkeeping.

Sources of Additional Information

Information about job opportunities may be obtained from local employers and local offices of the State employment service.

(See the introduction to the section on material-recording, -scheduling, -dispatching, and -distributing occupations for information on working conditions, training requirements, and earnings.)

Shipping, Receiving, and Traffic Clerks

(0*NET 43-5071.00)

Nature of the Work

Shipping, receiving, and traffic clerks keep records of all goods shipped and received. Their duties depend on the size of the establishment and the level of automation used. Larger companies typically are better able to finance the purchase of computers and other equipment to handle some or all of a clerk's responsibilities. In smaller companies, a clerk maintains records, prepares shipments, and accepts deliveries. In both environments, shipping, receiving, and traffic clerks may lift cartons of various sizes.

Shipping clerks keep records of all outgoing shipments. They prepare shipping documents and mailing labels and make sure that orders have been filled correctly. Also, they record items taken from inventory and note when orders were filled. Sometimes they fill the order themselves, obtaining merchandise from the stockroom, noting when inventories run low, and wrapping or packing the goods in shipping containers. They also address and label packages, look up and compute freight or postal rates, and record the weight and cost of each shipment. In addition, shipping clerks may prepare invoices and furnish information about shipments to other parts of the company, such as the accounting department. Once a shipment is checked and ready to go, shipping clerks may move the goods from the plant—sometimes by forklift—to the shipping dock and direct its loading.

Production, planning, and expediting clerks coordinate and expedite the flow of information, work, and materials within or among offices.

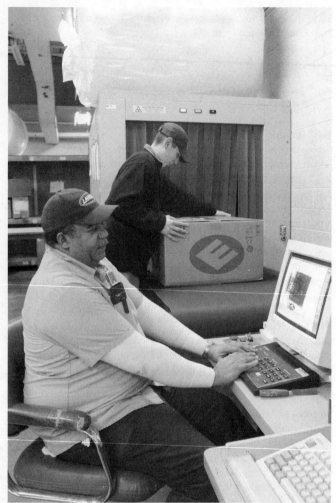

Shipping, receiving, and traffic clerks typically use computers to keep records of all goods shipped and received.

Receiving clerks perform tasks similar to those of shipping clerks. They determine whether orders have been filled correctly by verifying incoming shipments against the original order and the accompanying bill of lading or invoice. They make a record of the shipment and the condition of its contents. In many firms, receiving clerks either use hand-held scanners to record barcodes on incoming products or enter the information into a computer. These data then can be transferred to the appropriate departments. The shipment is checked for any discrepancies in quantity, price, and discounts. Receiving clerks may route or move shipments to the proper department, warehouse section, or stockroom. They also may arrange for adjustments with shippers whenever merchandise is lost or damaged. Receiving clerks in small businesses may perform some duties similar to those of stock clerks. In larger establishments, receiving clerks may control all receiving-platform operations, such as scheduling of trucks, recording of shipments, and handling of damaged goods.

Traffic clerks maintain records on the destination, weight, and charges on all incoming and outgoing freight. They verify rate charges by comparing the classification of materials with rate charts. In many companies, this work may be automated. Information either is scanned or is entered by hand into a computer for use by the accounting department or other departments within the company. Traffic clerks also keep a file of claims for overcharges and for damage to goods in transit.

Employment

Shipping, receiving, and traffic clerks held about 803,000 jobs in 2002. About three-fourths were employed in manufacturing or by wholesale and retail establishments. Although jobs for shipping, receiving, and traffic clerks are found throughout the country, most clerks work in urban areas, where shipping depots in factories and wholesale establishments usually are located. (For information on workers who perform duties similar to those of shipping, receiving, and traffic clerks and who are employed by the U.S. Postal Service, see the statement on Postal Service workers elsewhere in the *Handbook*).

Job Outlook

Employment of shipping, receiving, and traffic clerks is expected to grow more slowly than the average for all occupations through 2012. Job growth will continue to be limited by automation as all but the smallest firms move to reduce labor costs by using computers to store and retrieve shipping and receiving records.

Methods of handling materials have changed significantly in recent years. Large warehouses are increasingly becoming automated, with equipment such as computerized conveyor systems, robots, computer-directed trucks, and automatic data storage and retrieval systems. Automation, coupled with the growing use of hand-held scanners and personal computers in shipping and receiving departments, has increased the productivity of these workers.

Despite technology, job openings will continue to arise due to increasing economic and trade activity and because certain tasks cannot be automated. As an example of the latter circumstance, someone needs to check shipments before they go out and when they arrive, to ensure that everything is in order. In addition to those arising from job growth, openings will occur because of the need to replace shipping, receiving, and traffic clerks who leave the occupation. Because this is an entry-level occupation, many vacancies are created by a worker's normal career progression.

Related Occupations

Shipping, receiving, and traffic clerks record, check, and often store materials that a company receives. They also process and pack goods for shipment. Other workers who perform similar duties are stock clerks and order fillers; production, planning, and expediting clerks; cargo and freight agents; and Postal Service workers.

Sources of Additional Information

Information about job opportunities may be obtained from local employers and local offices of the State employment service.

(See the introduction to the section on material recording, -scheduling, -dispatching, and -distributing occupations for information on working conditions, training requirements, and earnings.)

Stock Clerks and Order Fillers

(0*NET 43-5081.01, 43-5081.02, 43-5081.03, 43-5081.04)

Nature of the Work

Stock clerks and order fillers receive, unpack, check, store, and track merchandise or materials. They keep records of items entering or leaving the stockroom and inspect damaged or spoiled goods. They sort, organize, and mark items with identifying codes, such as price, stock, or inventory control codes, so that inventories can be located quickly and easily. They also may be required to lift cartons of various sizes. In larger establishments, where they may be responsible for only one task, they may be called *stock-control clerks*,

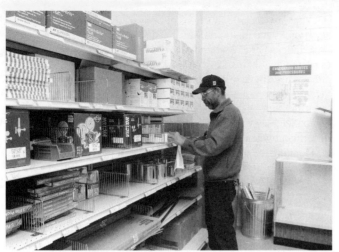

Stock clerks and order fillers keep records of items entering or leaving the stockroom.

merchandise distributors, or *property custodians*. In smaller firms, they also may perform tasks usually handled by shipping and receiving clerks. (A separate statement on shipping, receiving, and traffic clerks appears elsewhere in this section of the *Handbook*.)

In many firms, stock clerks and order fillers use hand-held scanners connected to computers to keep inventories up to date. In retail stores, stock clerks bring merchandise to the sales floor and stock shelves and racks. In stockrooms and warehouses, stock clerks store materials in bins, on floors, or on shelves. Instead of putting the merchandise on the sales floor or on shelves, order fillers take customers' orders and either hold the merchandise until the customers can pick it up or send it to them.

Employment

Stock clerks and order fillers held about 1.6 million jobs in 2002; they were, by far, the largest material-recording, -scheduling, -dispatching, and -distributing occupation. About 75 percent work in wholesale and retail trade. The greatest numbers are found in grocery stores, followed by department stores. Jobs for stock clerks are found in all parts of the country, but most work in large urban areas that have many large suburban shopping centers, warehouses, and factories.

Job Outlook

Employment of stock clerks and order fillers is projected to decline through 2012, due to the use of automation in factories and stores. Because the occupation is very large and many jobs are entry level, however, numerous job openings will occur each year to replace those who transfer to other jobs or leave the labor force.

The growing use of computers for inventory control and the installation of new, automated equipment are expected to inhibit growth in demand for stock clerks and order fillers, especially in manufacturing and wholesale trade industries whose operations are most easily automated. In addition to utilizing computerized inventory control systems, firms in these industries are relying more on sophisticated conveyor belts and automatic high stackers to store and retrieve goods. Also, expanded use of battery-powered, driverless, automatically guided vehicles can be expected.

Employment of stock clerks and order fillers who work in grocery, general merchandise, department, apparel, and accessories stores is expected to be somewhat less affected by automation, because much of their work is done manually and is difficult to automate. In addition, the increasing role of large retail outlets and

warehouses, as well as catalogue, mail, telephone, and Internet shopping services, should bolster employment of stock clerks and order fillers in these sectors of retail trade.

Related Occupations

Workers who also handle, move, organize, store, and keep records of materials include shipping, receiving, and traffic clerks; production, planning, and expediting clerks; cargo and freight agents; and procurement clerks.

Sources of Additional Information

State employment service offices can provide information about job openings for stock clerks and order fillers. Also, see office and administrative support occupations and sales occupations, elsewhere in the *Handbook*, for sources of additional information.

(See introduction to the section on material-recording, -scheduling, -dispatching, and -distributing occupations for information on working conditions, training requirements, and earnings.)

Weighers, Measurers, Checkers, and Samplers, Recordkeeping

(0*NET 43-5111.00)

Nature of the Work

Weighers, measurers, checkers, and samplers weigh, measure, and check materials, supplies, and equipment in order to keep relevant records. Most of their duties are clerical. Using either manual or automated data processing systems, they verify the quantity, quality, and overall value of the items within their purview and check the condition of items purchased, sold, or produced against records, bills, invoices, or receipts. They check the items to ensure the accuracy of the recorded data. They prepare reports on warehouse inventory levels and on uses of parts. Weighers, measurers, checkers, and samplers also check for any defects in the items and record the severity of the defects they find.

These workers use weight scales, counting devices, tally sheets, and calculators to record information about the products. They usually move objects to and from the scales with a handtruck or forklift. They issue receipts for the products when needed or requested.

Using either manual or automated data-processing systems, weighers, measurers, checkers, and samplers check and document items.

Employment

Weighers, measurers, checkers, and samplers held about 81,000 jobs in 2002. Their employment is spread across many industries. Retail trade accounted for 18 percent of those jobs, manufacturing accounted for about 29 percent, and wholesale trade employed another 13 percent.

Job Outlook

Employment of weighers, measurers, checkers, and samplers is expected to grow about as fast as the average for all occupations through 2012. The desire for accurate measurements and high-quality materials, as well as the use of records for verifying information, is increasing the need for weighers, measurers, checkers, and samplers. Furthermore, automation should not have a significant effect on employment in this occupation, because most of its duties need to be performed manually. In addition to job openings resulting from job growth, openings should arise from the need to replace workers who leave the labor force or transfer to other occupations.

Related Occupations

Other workers who determine and document characteristics of materials or equipment include cargo and freight agents; production, planning, and expediting clerks; shipping, receiving, and traffic clerks; stock clerks and order fillers; and procurement clerks.

Sources of Additional Information

Information about job opportunities may be obtained from local employers and local offices of the State employment service.

(See the introduction to the section on material-recording, -scheduling, -dispatching, and -distributing occupations for information on working conditions, training requirements, and earnings.)

Office and Administrative Support Worker Supervisors and Managers

(0*NET 43-1011.01, 43-1011.02)

Significant Points

- Most jobs are filled by promoting office or administrative support workers from within the organization.

- Office automation will cause employment in some office and administrative support occupations to grow slowly or even decline, resulting in slower-than-average growth among supervisors and managers.

- Like those seeking other supervisory and managerial occupations, applicants are likely to encounter keen competition because their number should greatly exceed the number of job openings.

Nature of the Work

All organizations need timely and effective office and administrative support to operate efficiently. Office and administrative support supervisors and managers coordinate this support. These workers are employed in virtually every sector of the economy, working in positions as varied as teller supervisor, customer services manager, or shipping-and-receiving supervisor.

Although specific functions of office and administrative support supervisors and managers vary considerably, they share many common duties. For example, supervisors perform administrative tasks to ensure that their staffs can work efficiently. Equipment and machinery used in their departments must be in good working order. If the computer system goes down or a facsimile machine malfunctions, the supervisors must try to correct the problem or alert repair personnel. They also request new equipment or supplies for their department when necessary.

Planning the work and supervising the staff are key functions of this job. To do these effectively, the supervisor must know the strengths and weaknesses of each member of the staff, as well as the results required from and time allotted to each job. Supervisors must make allowances for unexpected staff absences and other disruptions by adjusting assignments or performing the work themselves if the situation requires it.

After allocating work assignments and issuing deadlines, office and administrative support supervisors and managers oversee the work to ensure that it is proceeding on schedule and meeting established quality standards. This may involve reviewing each person's work on a computer—as in the case of accounting clerks—or listening to how a worker deals with customers—as in the case of customer services representatives. When supervising long-term projects, the supervisor may meet regularly with staff members to discuss their progress.

Office and administrative support supervisors and managers also evaluate each worker's performance. If a worker has done a good job, the supervisor records it in the employee's personnel file and may recommend a promotion or other award. Alternatively, if a worker is performing poorly, the supervisor discusses the problem with the employee to determine the cause and helps the worker to improve his or her performance. This might require sending the employee to a training course or arranging personal counseling. If the situation does not improve, the supervisor may recommend a transfer, demotion, or dismissal.

Office and administrative support supervisors and managers usually interview and evaluate prospective clerical employees. When new workers arrive on the job, the supervisor greets them and provides orientation to acquaint them with the organization and its operating routines. Some supervisors may be actively involved in recruiting new workers—for example, by making presentations at high schools and business colleges. They also may serve as the primary liaisons between their offices and the general public through direct contact and by preparing promotional information.

Supervisors help train new employees in organization and office procedures. They may teach new employees how to use the telephone system and operate office equipment. Because much clerical work is computerized, they also must teach new employees to use the organization's computer system. When new office equipment or updated computer software is introduced, supervisors train experienced employees to use it efficiently. If this is not possible, they may arrange for special outside training for their employees.

Office and administrative support supervisors and managers often act as liaisons between the clerical staff and the professional, technical, and managerial staff. This may involve implementing new company policies or restructuring the workflow in their departments. They must also keep their superiors informed of their progress and any potential problems. Often, this communication takes the form of research projects and progress reports. Because supervisors and managers have access to information such as their department's performance records, they may compile and present these data for use in planning or designing new policies.

Administrative support worker supervisors and managers plan work and supervise staff to ensure that the work remains on schedule.

Office and administrative support supervisors and managers also may have to resolve interpersonal conflicts among the staff. In organizations covered by union contracts, supervisors must know the provisions of labor-management agreements and run their departments accordingly. They may meet with union representatives to discuss work problems or grievances.

Working Conditions

Office and administrative support supervisors and managers are employed in a wide variety of work settings, but most work in clean, well-lit, offices that usually are comfortable.

Most work a standard 40-hour week. Because some organizations operate around the clock, office and administrative support supervisors and managers may have to work nights, weekends, and holidays. Sometimes, supervisors rotate among the 8-hour three shifts in a workday; in other cases, shifts are assigned on the basis of seniority.

Employment

Office and administrative support supervisors and managers held 1.5 million jobs in 2002. Although jobs for office and administrative support supervisors and managers are found in practically every industry, the largest number are found in organizations with a large administrative support workforce, such as banks, wholesalers, government agencies, retail establishments, business service firms, healthcare facilities, schools, and insurance companies. Because of most organizations' need for continuity of supervision, few office and administrative support supervisors and managers work on a temporary or part-time basis.

Training, Other Qualifications, and Advancement

Most firms fill office and administrative support supervisory and managerial positions by promoting office or administrative support workers from within their organizations. To become eligible for promotion to a supervisory position, clerical or administrative support workers must prove they are capable of handling additional responsibilities. When evaluating candidates, superiors look for strong teamwork, problem-solving, leadership, and communication skills, as well as determination, loyalty, poise, and confidence. They also look for more specific supervisory attributes, such as the ability to organize and coordinate work efficiently, to set priorities, and to motivate others. Increasingly, supervisors need a broad base of office skills coupled with personal flexibility to adapt to changes in

organizational structure and move among departments when necessary.

In addition, supervisors must pay close attention to detail in order to identify and correct errors made by the staff they oversee. Good working knowledge of the organization's computer system also is an advantage. Many employers require postsecondary training—in some cases, an associate or even a bachelor's degree.

A clerk with potential supervisory abilities may be given occasional supervisory assignments. To prepare for full-time supervisory duties, he or she may attend in-house training or take courses in time management or interpersonal relations.

Some office and administrative support supervisor positions are filled with people from outside the organization. These positions may serve as entry-level training for potential higher level managers. New college graduates may rotate through departments of an organization at this level to learn the work of the organization.

Job Outlook

Like those seeking other supervisory and managerial occupations, applicants for jobs as office and administrative support worker supervisors and managers are likely to encounter keen competition because the number of applicants should greatly exceed the number of job openings. Employment is expected to grow more slowly than the average for all occupations through 2012. In addition to the job openings arising from growth, a larger number of openings will stem from the need to replace workers who transfer to other occupations or leave this large occupation for other reasons.

Employment of office and administrative support supervisors and managers is determined largely by the demand for administrative support workers. Continuing office automation due to new technology should increase office and administrative support workers' productivity and allow a wider variety of tasks to be performed by more people in professional positions. These trends will cause employment in some clerical occupations to grow slowly or even decline. Supervisors will direct smaller permanent staffs—supplemented by increased use of temporary clerical staff—and perform more professional tasks. Office and administrative support managers will coordinate the increasing amount of administrative work and make sure that the technology is applied and running properly. However, organizational restructuring should continue to reduce employment in some managerial positions, distributing more responsibility to office and administrative support supervisors.

Earnings

Median annual earnings of office and administrative support supervisors and managers were $38,820 in 2002; the middle 50 percent earned between $29,960 and $50,660. The lowest paid 10 percent earned less than $23,630, while the highest paid 10 percent earned more than $65,180. In 2002, median annual earnings in the industries employing the largest numbers of office and administrative support supervisors and managers were:

Insurance carriers	$48,720
Management of companies and enterprises	45,090
Local government	40,500
Offices of physicians	37,510
Depository credit intermediation	35,500

In addition to typical benefits, some office and administrative support supervisors and managers, particularly in the private sector, may receive additional compensation in the form of bonuses and stock options.

Related Occupations

Office and administrative support supervisors and managers must understand and sometimes perform the work of those whom they oversee, including bookkeeping, accounting, and auditing clerks; cashiers; communications equipment operators; customer service representatives; data entry and information processing workers; general office clerks; receptionists and information clerks; stock clerks and order fillers; order clerks; and tellers. Their supervisory and administrative duties are similar to those of other supervisors and managers.

Sources of Additional Information

For a wide variety of information related to management occupations, including educational programs and certified designations, contact:

➤ American Management Association, 1601 Broadway, New York, NY 10019-7420. Internet: **http://www.amanet.org**

➤ National Management Association, 2210 Arbor Blvd., Dayton, OH 45439. Internet: **http://www.nma1.org**

➤ International Association of Administrative Professionals, 10502 NW Ambassador Dr., P.O. Box 20404, Kansas City, MO 64195-0404. Internet: **http://www.iaap-hq.org**

Office Clerks, General

(0*NET 43-9061.00)

Significant Points

- Although most jobs are entry level, applicants with previous office experience, computer skills, and sound communication abilities may have an advantage.

- Part-time and temporary positions are common.

- Plentiful job opportunities will stem from employment growth, the large size of the occupation, and high replacement needs.

Nature of the Work

Rather than performing a single specialized task, general office clerks often have daily responsibilities that change with the needs of the specific job and the employer. Whereas some clerks spend their days filing or typing, others enter data at a computer terminal. They also can be called upon to operate photocopiers, fax machines, and other office equipment; prepare mailings; proofread copies; and answer telephones and deliver messages.

The specific duties assigned to a clerk vary significantly, depending upon the type of office in which he or she works. An office clerk in a doctor's office, for example, would not perform the same tasks that a clerk in a large financial institution or in the office of an auto-parts wholesaler would perform. Although they may sort checks, keep payroll records, take inventory, and access information, clerks also perform duties unique to their employer, such as organizing medications, making transparencies for a presentation, or filling orders received by fax machine.

The specific duties assigned to a clerk also vary by level of experience. Whereas inexperienced employees make photocopies, stuff envelopes, or record inquiries, experienced clerks usually are given additional responsibilities. For example, they may maintain financial or other records, set up spreadsheets, verify statistical reports for accuracy and completeness, handle and adjust customer complaints, work with vendors, make travel arrangements, take inventory of equipment and supplies, answer questions on departmental services and functions, or help prepare invoices or budgetary requests. Senior office clerks may be expected to monitor and direct the work of lower level clerks.

Working Conditions

For the most part, general office clerks work in comfortable office settings. Those on full-time schedules usually work a standard 40-hour week; however, some work shifts or overtime during busy periods. About 1 in 4 clerks works part time.

Employment

General office clerks held about 3 million jobs in 2002. Most are employed in relatively small businesses. Although they work in every sector of the economy, almost half worked in local government; health care and social assistance; administrative and support services; finance and insurance; or professional, scientific, and technical services industries.

Training, Other Qualifications, and Advancement

Although most office clerk jobs are entry-level administrative support positions, employers may prefer or require previous office or business experience. Employers usually require a high school diploma, and some require typing, basic computer skills, and other general office skills. Familiarity with computer word-processing software and applications is becoming increasingly important.

Training for this occupation is available through business education programs offered in high schools, community and junior colleges, and postsecondary vocational schools. Courses in office practices, word processing, and other computer applications are particularly helpful.

Because general office clerks usually work with other office staff, they should be cooperative and able to work as part of a team. Employers prefer individuals who are able to perform a variety of tasks and satisfy the needs of the many departments within a company. In addition, applicants should have good communication skills, be detail-oriented, and be adaptable.

General office clerks who exhibit strong communication, interpersonal, and analytical skills may be promoted to supervisory positions. Others may move into different, more senior clerical or administrative jobs, such as receptionist, secretary, or administrative assistant. After gaining some work experience or specialized skills, many workers transfer to jobs with higher pay or greater advancement potential. Advancement to professional occupations

General office clerks have daily responsibilities that change with the needs of the specific job and the employer.

within an establishment normally requires additional formal education, such as a college degree.

Job Outlook

Employment growth, the large size of the occupation, and high replacement needs should result in plentiful job opportunities for general office clerks. In addition to those for full-time jobs, many job openings are expected for part-time and temporary general office clerks. Prospects should be brightest for those who have knowledge of basic computer applications and office machinery, such as fax machines and scanners, and good writing and communication skills. As general clerical duties continue to be consolidated, employers will increasingly seek well-rounded individuals with highly developed communication skills and the ability to perform multiple tasks.

Employment of general office clerks is expected to grow about as fast as average for all occupations through the year 2012. The employment outlook for these workers will be affected by the increasing use of computers, expanding office automation, and the consolidation of clerical tasks. Automation has led to productivity gains, allowing a wide variety of duties to be performed by fewer office workers. However, automation also has led to a consolidation of clerical staffs and a diversification of job responsibilities. This consolidation increases the demand for general office clerks, because they perform a variety of clerical tasks. It will become increasingly common within small businesses to find a single general office clerk in charge of all clerical work.

Job opportunities may vary from year to year, because the strength of the economy affects demand for general office clerks. Companies tend to hire more workers when the economy is strong. Industries least likely to be affected by economic fluctuation tend to be the most stable places for employment.

Earnings

Median annual earnings of general office clerks were $22,280 in 2002; the middle 50 percent earned between $17,630 and $28,190 annually. The lowest 10 percent earned less than $14,260, and the highest 10 percent earned more than $34,890. Median annual salaries in the industries employing the largest numbers of general office clerks in 2002 are shown below:

Local government	$25,020
Elementary and secondary schools	23,310
General medical and surgical hospitals	23,250
Colleges, universities, and professional schools	22,540
Employment services	20,630

Related Occupations

The duties of general office clerks can include a combination of bookkeeping, typing, office machine operation, and filing. Other office and administrative support workers who perform similar duties include financial clerks, information and records clerks, secretaries and administrative assistants, and data entry and information processing workers. Nonclerical entry-level workers include cashiers, counter and rental clerks, and food and beverage serving and related workers.

Sources of Additional Information

State employment service offices and agencies can provide information about job openings for general office clerks.

Postal Service Workers

(0*NET 43-5051.00, 43-5052.00, 43-5053.00)

Significant Points

- Qualification is based on an examination.
- Overall employment within the U.S. Postal Service is expected to shrink due to declining mail volume and increasing automation.
- Keen competition is expected because the number of qualified applicants should continue to exceed the number of job openings.

Nature of the Work

Each week, the U.S. Postal Service delivers billions of pieces of mail, including letters, bills, advertisements, and packages. To do this in an efficient and timely manner, the Postal Service employs about 845,000 individuals. Most Postal Service workers are clerks, mail carriers, or mail sorters, processors, and processing machine operators. Postal clerks wait on customers at post offices, whereas mail sorters, processors, and processing machine operators sort incoming and outgoing mail at post offices and mail processing centers. Mail carriers deliver mail to urban and rural residences and businesses throughout the United States.

Postal service clerks, also known as window clerks, sell stamps, money orders, postal stationary, and mailing envelopes and boxes. They also weigh packages to determine postage and check that packages are in satisfactory condition for mailing. These clerks register, certify, and insure mail and answer questions about postage rates, post office boxes, mailing restrictions, and other postal matters. Window clerks also help customers file claims for damaged packages.

Postal service mail sorters, processors, and processing machine operators prepare incoming and outgoing mail for distribution. These workers are commonly referred to as mail handlers, distribution clerks, mail processors, or mail processing clerks. They load and unload postal trucks and move mail around a mail processing center with forklifts, small electric tractors, or hand-pushed carts. They also load and operate mail processing, sorting, and canceling machinery.

Postal service mail carriers deliver mail, once it has been processed and sorted. Although carriers are classified by their type of route—either city or rural—duties of city and rural carriers are similar. Most travel established routes, delivering and collecting mail. Mail carriers start work at the post office early in the morning, when they arrange the mail in delivery sequence. Automated equipment has reduced the time that carriers need to sort the mail, allowing them to spend more time delivering it.

Mail carriers cover their routes on foot, by vehicle, or a combination of both. On foot, they carry a heavy load of mail in a satchel or push it on a cart. In most urban and rural areas, they use a car or small truck. Although the Postal Service provides vehicles to city carriers, most rural carriers must use their own automobiles. Deliveries are made house-to-house, to roadside mailboxes, and to large buildings such as offices or apartments, which generally have all of their tenants' mailboxes in one location.

Besides delivering and collecting mail, carriers collect money for postage-due and COD (cash-on-delivery) fees and obtain signed receipts for registered, certified, and insured mail. If a customer is not home, the carrier leaves a notice that tells where special mail is being held. After completing their routes, carriers return to the post

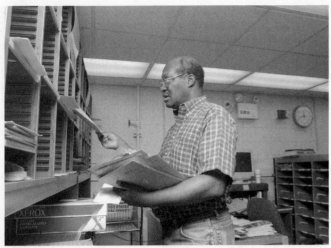

Depending on the size of the post office in which they work, window clerks also may be required to sort mail.

office with mail gathered from street collection boxes, homes, and businesses and turn in the mail, receipts, and money collected during the day.

Some city carriers may have specialized duties such as delivering only parcels or picking up mail from mail collection boxes. In contrast to city carriers, rural carriers provide a wider range of postal services, in addition to delivering and picking up mail. For example, rural carriers may sell stamps and money orders and register, certify, and insure parcels and letters. All carriers, however, must be able to answer customers' questions about postal regulations and services and provide change-of-address cards and other postal forms when requested.

Working Conditions
Window clerks usually work in the public portion of clean, well-ventilated, and well-lit buildings. They have a variety of duties and frequent contact with the public, but they rarely work at night. However, they may have to deal with upset customers, stand for long periods, and be held accountable for an assigned stock of stamps and funds. Depending on the size of the post office in which they work, they also may be required to sort mail.

Despite the use of automated equipment, the work of mail sorters, processors, and processing machine operators can be physically demanding. Workers may have to move heavy sacks of mail around a mail processing center. These workers usually are on their feet, reaching for sacks and trays of mail or placing packages and bundles into sacks and trays. Processing mail can be tiring and boring. Many sorters, processors, and machine operators work at night or on weekends, because most large post offices process mail around the clock, and the largest volume of mail is sorted during the evening and night shifts. Workers can experience stress as they process ever-larger quantities of mail under tight production deadlines and quotas.

Most carriers begin work early in the morning—those with routes in a business district can start as early as 4 a.m. Overtime hours are frequently required for urban carriers. A carrier's schedule has its advantages, however. Carriers who begin work early in the morning are through by early afternoon and spend most of the day on their own, relatively free from direct supervision. Carriers spend most of their time outdoors, delivering mail in all kinds of weather. Even those who drive often must walk periodically when making deliveries and must lift heavy sacks of parcel post items when loading their vehicles. In addition, carriers must be cautious of poten-

tial hazards on their routes. Wet and icy roads and sidewalks can be treacherous, and each year dogs attack numerous carriers.

Employment
The U.S. Postal Service employed 77,000 clerks; 334,000 mail carriers; and 253,000 mail sorters, processors, and processing machine operators in 2002. Most of them worked full time. Most postal clerks provided window service at post office branches. Many mail sorters, processors, and processing machine operators sorted mail at major metropolitan post offices; others worked at mail processing centers. The majority of mail carriers worked in cities and suburbs, while the rest worked in rural areas.

Postal Service workers are classified as casual, part-time flexible, part-time regular, or full time. Casuals are hired for 90 days at a time to help process and deliver mail during peak mailing or vacation periods. Part-time flexible workers do not have a regular work schedule or weekly guarantee of hours but are called as the need arises. Part-time regulars have a set work schedule of fewer than 40 hours per week, often replacing regular full-time workers on their scheduled day off. Full-time postal employees work a 40-hour week over a 5-day period.

Training, Other Qualifications, and Advancement
Postal Service workers must be at least 18 years old. They must be U.S. citizens or have been granted permanent resident-alien status in the United States, and males must have registered with the Selective Service upon reaching age 18. Applicants should have a basic competency of English. Qualification is based on a written examination that measures speed and accuracy at checking names and numbers and the ability to memorize mail distribution procedures. Applicants must pass a physical examination and drug test, and may be asked to show that they can lift and handle mail sacks weighing 70 pounds. Applicants for mail carrier positions must have a driver's license and a good driving record, and must receive a passing grade on a road test.

Jobseekers should contact the post office or mail processing center where they wish to work to determine when an exam will be given. Applicants' names are listed in order of their examination scores. Five points are added to the score of an honorably discharged veteran and 10 points are added to the score of a veteran who was wounded in combat or is disabled. When a vacancy occurs, the appointing officer chooses one of the top three applicants; the rest of the names remain on the list to be considered for future openings until their eligibility expires—usually 2 years after the examination date.

Relatively few people become postal clerks or mail carriers on their first job, because of keen competition and the customary waiting period of 1 to 2 years or more after passing the examination. It is not surprising, therefore, that most entrants transfer from other occupations.

New Postal Service workers are trained on the job by experienced workers. Many post offices offer classroom instruction on safety and defensive driving. Workers receive additional instruction when new equipment or procedures are introduced. In these cases, workers usually are trained by another postal employee or a training specialist.

Postal clerks and mail carriers should be courteous and tactful when dealing with the public, especially when answering questions or receiving complaints. A good memory and the ability to read rapidly and accurately are important. Good interpersonal skills also are vital, because mail distribution clerks work closely with other postal workers, frequently under the tension and strain of meeting dispatch or transportation deadlines and quotas.

Postal Service workers often begin on a part-time, flexible basis and become regular or full time in order of seniority, as vacancies occur. Full-time workers may bid for preferred assignments, such as the day shift or a high-level nonsupervisory position. Carriers can look forward to obtaining preferred routes as their seniority increases. Postal Service workers can advance to supervisory positions on a competitive basis.

Job Outlook

Employment of Postal Service workers is expected to decline through 2012. Still, many jobs will become available because of the need to replace those who retire or leave the occupation. Those seeking jobs as Postal Service workers can expect to encounter keen competition. The number of applicants should continue to exceed the number of job openings due to low entry requirements and attractive wages and benefits.

A small decline in employment is expected among window clerks over the 2002-12 projection period. Efforts by the Postal Service to provide better service may somewhat increase the demand for window clerks, but the demand for such clerks will be offset by the use of electronic communications technologies and private delivery companies. Employment of mail sorters, processors, and processing machine operators is expected to decline because of the increasing use of automated materials handling equipment and optical character readers, barcode sorters, and other automated sorting equipment.

Several factors are expected to influence demand for mail carriers. The competition from alternative delivery systems and new forms of electronic communication could decrease the total volume of mail handled. Most of the decrease is expected to consist of first-class mail. The Postal Service expects an increase in package deliveries due to the rising number of purchases made through the Internet. Although total mail volume may decrease, the number of addresses to which mail must be delivered will continue to grow. However, increased use of the "delivery point sequencing" system, which allows machines to sort mail directly by the order of delivery, should reduce the amount of time that carriers spend sorting their mail, allowing them more time to handle longer routes. In addition, the Postal Service is moving toward more centralized mail delivery, such as the use of cluster boxes, to cut down on the number of door-to-door deliveries. These trends are expected to increase carrier productivity, resulting in a small decline in employment among mail carriers over the projection period. The increasing number of delivery points may result in greater demand for rural mail carriers than for city mail carriers, as much of the increase in delivery points will be seen in less urbanized areas.

Currently, the role of the Postal Service as a government-approved monopoly is a topic of debate. Any legislative changes that would privatize or deregulate the Postal Service might affect employment of all its workers. Employment and schedules in the Postal Service fluctuate with the demand for its services. When mail volume is high, full-time workers work overtime, part-time workers get additional hours, and casual workers may be hired. When mail volume is low, overtime is curtailed, part-timers work fewer hours, and casual workers are discharged.

Earnings

Median annual earnings of postal mail carriers were $39,530 in 2002. The middle 50 percent earned between $36,020 and $43,040. The lowest 10 percent had earnings of less than $31,180, while the top 10 percent earned over $47,500. Rural mail carriers are reimbursed for mileage put on their own vehicles while delivering mail.

Median annual earnings of Postal Service clerks were $39,700 in 2002. The middle 50 percent earned between $37,160 and $42,230. The lowest 10 percent had earnings of less than $35,640, while the top 10 percent earned more than $43,750.

Median annual earnings of mail sorters, processors, and processing machine operators were $38,150 in 2002. The middle 50 percent earned between $30,140 and $41,450. The lowest 10 percent had earnings of less than $21,680, while the top 10 percent earned more than $43,430.

Postal Service workers enjoy a variety of employer-provided benefits similar to those enjoyed by Federal Government workers. The American Postal Workers Union, the National Association of Letter Carriers, the National Postal Mail Handlers Union, and the National Rural Letter Carriers Association together represent most of these workers.

Related Occupations

Other occupations with duties similar to those of postal clerks include cashiers; counter and rental clerks; file clerks; and shipping, receiving, and traffic clerks. Others with duties related to those of mail carriers include couriers and messengers, and truck drivers and driver/sales workers. Occupations whose duties are related to those of mail sorters, processors, and processing machine operators include inspectors, testers, sorters, samplers, and weighers, and material-moving occupations.

Sources of Additional Information

Local post offices and State employment service offices can supply details about entrance examinations and specific employment opportunities for Postal Service workers.

Secretaries and Administrative Assistants

(0*NET 43-6011.00, 43-6012.00, 43-6013.00, 43-6014.00)

Significant Points

- Increasing office automation and organizational restructuring will lead to slow growth in overall employment of secretaries and administrative assistants.

- Numerous job openings will result from the need to replace workers who leave this very large occupation each year.

- Opportunities should be best for applicants with extensive knowledge of software applications.

Nature of the Work

As the reliance on technology continues to expand in offices across the Nation, the role of the office professional has greatly evolved. Office automation and organizational restructuring have led secretaries and administrative assistants to assume a wider range of new responsibilities once reserved for managerial and professional staff. Many secretaries and administrative assistants now provide training and orientation for new staff, conduct research on the Internet, and operate and troubleshoot new office technologies. In the midst of these changes, however, their core responsibilities have remained much the same—performing and coordinating an office's administrative activities, and storing, retrieving, and integrating information for dissemination to staff and clients.

Secretaries and administrative assistants are responsible for a variety of administrative and clerical duties necessary to run an organization efficiently. They serve as an information manager for an office, plan and schedule meetings and appointments, organize and maintain paper and electronic files, manage projects, conduct research, and provide information by using the telephone, postal mail, and e-mail. They also may handle travel arrangements.

Secretaries and administrative assistants are aided in these tasks by a variety of office equipment, such as facsimile machines, photocopiers, and telephone systems. In addition, secretaries and administrative assistants use personal computers to create spreadsheets, compose correspondence, manage databases, and create presentations, reports, and documents by using desktop publishing software and digital graphics—all tasks previously handled by managers and professionals. At the same time, these other office workers have assumed many tasks traditionally assigned to secretaries and administrative assistants, such as word processing and answering the telephone. Because secretaries and administrative assistants often are not responsible for dictation and typing, they have time to support more members of the executive staff. In a number of organizations, secretaries and administrative assistants work in teams in order to work flexibly and share their expertise.

Specific job duties vary with experience and titles. *Executive secretaries and administrative assistants*, for example, perform fewer clerical tasks than do other secretaries. In addition to arranging conference calls and scheduling meetings, they may handle more complex responsibilities such as conducting research, preparing statistical reports, training employees, and supervising other clerical staff.

Some secretaries and administrative assistants, such as legal and medical secretaries, perform highly specialized work requiring knowledge of technical terminology and procedures. For instance, *legal secretaries* prepare correspondence and legal papers such as summonses, complaints, motions, responses, and subpoenas under the supervision of an attorney or paralegal. They also may review legal journals and assist in other ways with legal research, as by verifying quotes and citations in legal briefs. *Medical secretaries* transcribe dictation, prepare correspondence, and assist physicians or medical scientists with reports, speeches, articles, and conference proceedings. They also record simple medical histories, arrange for patients to be hospitalized, and order supplies. Most medical secretaries need to be familiar with insurance rules, billing

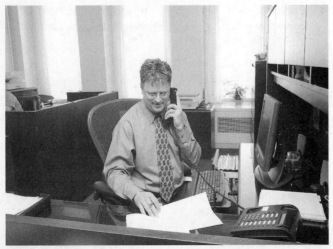

Secretaries and administrative assistants are responsible for a variety of administrative and clerical duties necessary to run an organization efficiently.

practices, and hospital or laboratory procedures. Other technical secretaries who assist engineers or scientists may prepare correspondence, maintain the technical library, and gather and edit materials for scientific papers.

Working Conditions

Secretaries and administrative assistants usually work in schools, hospitals, corporate settings, or legal and medical offices. Their jobs often involve sitting for long periods. If they spend a lot of time typing, particularly at a video display terminal, they may encounter problems of eyestrain, stress, and repetitive motion, such as carpal tunnel syndrome.

Office work can lend itself to alternative or flexible working arrangements, such as part-time work or telecommuting—especially if the job requires extensive computer use. About 1 secretary in 6 works part time and many others work in temporary positions. A few participate in job-sharing arrangements in which two people divide responsibility for a single job. The majority of secretaries, however, are full-time employees who work a standard 40-hour week.

Employment

Secretaries and administrative assistants held about 4.1 million jobs in 2002, ranking among the largest occupations in the U.S. economy. The following tabulation shows the distribution of employment by secretarial specialty:

Secrecretaries, except legal, medical, and executive 1,975,000
Executive secretaries and administrative assistants 1,526,000
Medical secretaries 339,000
Legal secretaries 264,000

Secretaries and administrative assistants are employed in organizations of every type. Around 9 out of 10 secretaries and administrative assistants are employed in service-providing industries, ranging from education and health to government and retail trade. Most of the rest work for firms engaged in manufacturing or construction.

Training, Other Qualifications, and Advancement

High school graduates who have basic office skills may qualify for entry-level secretarial positions. However, employers increasingly require extensive knowledge of software applications, such as word processing, spreadsheets, and database management. Secretaries and administrative assistants should be proficient in keyboarding and good at spelling, punctuation, grammar, and oral communication. Because secretaries and administrative assistants must be tactful in their dealings with people, employers also look for good customer service and interpersonal skills. Discretion, good judgment, organizational or management ability, initiative, and the ability to work independently are especially important for higher level administrative positions.

As office automation continues to evolve, retraining and continuing education will remain an integral part of secretarial jobs. Changes in the office environment have increased the demand for secretaries and administrative assistants who are adaptable and versatile. Secretaries and administrative assistants may have to attend classes or participate in online education in order to learn how to operate new office technologies, such as information storage systems, scanners, the Internet, or new updated software packages. They may also get involved in selecting and maintaining equipment.

Secretaries and administrative assistants acquire skills in various ways. Training ranges from high school vocational education programs that teach office skills and keyboarding to 1- and 2-year programs in office administration offered by business schools, vocational-technical institutes, and community colleges. Many temporary placement agencies also provide formal training in computer and office skills. However, many skills tend to be acquired through on-the-job instruction by other employees or by equipment and software vendors. Specialized training programs are available for students planning to become medical or legal secretaries or administrative technology specialists. Bachelor's degrees and professional certifications are becoming increasingly important as business continues to become more global.

Testing and certification for proficiency in entry-level office skills is available through organizations such as the International Association of Administrative Professionals; NALS, Inc.; and Legal Secretaries International, Inc. As secretaries and administrative assistants gain experience, they can earn several different designations. Prominent designations include the Certified Professional Secretary (CPS) or the Certified Administrative Professional (CAP) designations, which can be earned by meeting certain experience and/or educational requirements and passing an examination. Similarly, those with 1 year of experience in the legal field, or who have concluded an approved training course and who want to be certified as a legal support professional, can acquire the Accredited Legal Secretary (ALS) designation through a testing process administered by NALS. NALS also offers two additional designations; an examination to confer the Professional Legal Secretary (PLS) designation, considered an advanced certification for legal support professionals, as well as a paralegal examination and designation for proficiency as a paralegal. Legal Secretaries International confers the Certified Legal Secretary Specialist (CLSS) designation in areas such as intellectual property, criminal law, civil litigation, probate, and business law, to those who have 5 years of law-related experience and pass an examination. In some instances, certain requirements may be waived.

Secretaries generally advance by being promoted to other administrative positions with more responsibilities. Qualified secretaries who broaden their knowledge of a company's operations and enhance their skills may be promoted to other positions such as senior or executive secretary, clerical supervisor, or office manager. Secretaries with word processing or data entry experience can advance to jobs as word processing or data entry trainers, supervisors, or managers within their own firms or in a secretarial, word processing, or data entry service bureau. Secretarial experience can also lead to jobs such as instructor or sales representative with manufacturers of software or computer equipment. With additional training, many legal secretaries become paralegals.

Job Outlook
Overall employment of secretaries and administrative assistants is expected to grow more slowly than the average for all occupations over the 2002-12 period. In addition to those resulting from growth, numerous job openings will result from the need to replace workers who transfer to other occupations or leave this very large occupation for other reasons each year. Opportunities should be best for applicants, particularly experienced secretaries, with extensive knowledge of software applications.

Projected employment of secretaries will vary by occupational specialty. Employment growth in the health care and social assistance and legal services industries should lead to average growth for medical and legal secretaries. Employment of executive secretaries and administrative assistants is projected to grow more slowly than the average for all occupations. Rapidly growing industries—such as administrative and support services, health care and social assistance, educational services (private), and professional, scientific, and technical services—will continue to generate most new

job opportunities. A decline in employment is expected for all other secretaries, except legal, medical, or executive. They account for almost half of all secretaries and administrative assistants.

Increasing office automation and organizational restructuring will continue to make secretaries and administrative assistants more productive in coming years. Personal computers, e-mail, scanners, and voice message systems will allow secretaries to accomplish more in the same amount of time. The use of automated equipment is also changing the distribution of work in many offices. In some cases, such traditional secretarial duties as keyboarding, filing, photocopying, and bookkeeping are being assigned to workers in other units or departments. Professionals and managers increasingly do their own word processing and data entry, and handle much of their own correspondence rather than submit the work to secretaries and other support staff. Also, in some law and medical offices, paralegals and medical assistants are assuming some tasks formerly done by secretaries. As other workers assume more of these duties, there is a trend in many offices for professionals and managers to "share" secretaries and administrative assistants. The traditional arrangement of one secretary per manager is becoming less prevalent; instead, secretaries and administrative assistants increasingly support systems, departments, or units. This approach often means that secretaries and administrative assistants assume added responsibilities and are seen as valuable members of a team, but it also contributes to the projected decline in the overall number of secretaries and administrative assistants.

Developments in office technology are certain to continue, and they will bring about further changes in the work of secretaries and administrative assistants. However, many secretarial and administrative duties are of a personal, interactive nature and, therefore, not easily automated. Responsibilities such as planning conferences, working with clients, and instructing staff require tact and communication skills. Because technology cannot substitute for these personal skills, secretaries and administrative assistants will continue to play a key role in most organizations.

Earnings
Median annual earnings of executive secretaries and administrative assistants were $33,410 in 2002. The middle 50 percent earned between $26,980 and $41,350. The lowest 10 percent earned less than $22,270, and the highest 10 percent earned more than $50,420. Median annual earnings in the industries employing the largest numbers of executive secretaries and administrative assistants in 2002 were:

Management of companies and enterprises	$36,770
Local government	34,600
Colleges, universities, and professional schools	32,210
State government	31,220
Employment services	29,700

Median annual earnings of legal secretaries were $35,020 in 2002. The middle 50 percent earned between $27,540 and $44,720. The lowest 10 percent earned less than $21,990, and the highest 10 percent earned more than $54,810. Medical secretaries earned a median annual salary of $25,430 in 2002. The middle 50 percent earned between $21,090 and $31,070. The lowest 10 percent earned less than $18,310, and the highest 10 percent earned more than $37,550. Median annual earnings of secretaries, except legal, medical, and executive, were about $25,290 in 2002.

Salaries vary a great deal, however, reflecting differences in skill, experience, and level of responsibility. Salaries also vary in different parts of the country; earnings are usually lowest in southern cities, and highest in northern and western cities. Certification in this field usually is rewarded by a higher salary.

Related Occupations
A number of other workers type, record information, and process paperwork. Among them are bookkeeping, accounting, and auditing clerks; receptionists and information clerks; court reporters; human resources assistants, except payroll and timekeeping; computer operators; data entry and information processing workers; paralegals and legal assistants; medical assistants; and medical records and health information technicians. A growing number of secretaries share in managerial and human resource responsibilities. Occupations requiring these skills include office and administrative support supervisors and managers, computer and information systems managers, administrative services managers, and human resources, training, and labor relations managers and specialists.

Sources of Additional Information
State employment offices provide information about job openings for secretaries.

For information on the Certified Professional Secretary or Certified Administrative Professional designations, contact:

➤ International Association of Administrative Professionals, 10502 NW Ambassador Dr., P.O. Box 20404, Kansas City, MO 64195-0404. Internet: **http://www.iaap-hq.org**

Information on the Certified Legal Secretary Specialist (CLSS) designation can be obtained from:

➤ Legal Secretaries International Inc., Internet: **http://www.legalsecretaries.org**

Information on the Accredited Legal Secretary (ALS), Professional Legal Secretary (PLS), and Paralegal certifications is available from:

➤ NALS, Inc., 314 East 3rd St., Suite 210, Tulsa, OK 74120. Internet: **http://www.nals.org**

Farming, Fishing, and Forestry Occupations

Agricultural Workers

(0*NET 45-2011.00, 45-2041.00, 45-2091.00, 45-2092.01, 45-2092.02, 45-2093.00, and 45-2099.99)

Significant Points

● Duties and working conditions vary widely, from working in greenhouses, to producing crops and raising livestock outdoors, to inspecting agricultural products in plants.

● Most workers learn through short-term on-the-job training; agricultural inspectors need work experience or a college degree in a related field.

● Most farmworkers receive low pay and often must perform strenuous work outdoors in all kinds of weather, but many prefer to work and live in a rural area.

● Employment is projected to grow more slowly than average.

Nature of the Work

Agricultural workers play a large role in getting food, plants, and other agricultural products to market. Working mostly on farms or ranches or in nurseries, slaughterhouses, or ports of entry, these workers have numerous and diverse duties. Among their activities are planting and harvesting crops, installing irrigation, delivering animals, and making sure that our food is safe.

More than 4 out of 5 agricultural workers are farmworkers and laborers. *Farmworkers and laborers, crop, nursery, and greenhouse* perform numerous activities related to growing and harvesting grains, fruits, vegetables, nuts, fiber, trees, shrubs, and other crops. Among their activities are planting and seeding, pruning, irrigating, harvesting, and packing and loading crops for shipment. Farmworkers also apply pesticides, herbicides, and fertilizers to crops; repair fences; and help with irrigation. Nursery and greenhouse workers prepare land or greenhouse beds for growing horticultural products, such as trees, plants, flowers, and sod. Their duties include planting, watering, pruning, weeding, and spraying the plants. They may cut, roll, and stack sod; stake trees; tie, wrap, and pack plants to fill orders; and dig up or move field-grown and containerized shrubs and trees.

Farmworkers, farm and ranch animals care for live farm, ranch, or aquacultural animals that may include cattle, sheep, swine, goats, horses, poultry, finfish, shellfish, and bees. The animals are usually raised to supply such products as meat, fur, skins, feathers, eggs, milk, and honey. The farmworkers' duties may include feeding, watering, herding, grazing, castrating, branding, debeaking, weighing, catching, and loading animals. On dairy farms, farmworkers operate milking machines; they also may maintain records on animals, examine animals to detect diseases and injuries, assist in delivering animals at their birth, and administer medications, vaccinations, or insecticides as appropriate. Daily duties of such farmworkers include cleaning and maintaining animal housing areas.

Other farmworkers known as *agricultural equipment operators* operate a variety of farm equipment used in plowing, sowing, main-taining, and harvesting agricultural products. The equipment may include tractors, fertilizer spreaders, haybines, raking equipment, balers, combines, and threshers, as well as trucks. These farmworkers also operate machines used in moving and treating crops after their harvest, such as conveyor belts, loading machines, separators, cleaners, and dryers. In addition, they may make adjustments and minor repairs to equipment. When not operating machines, agricultural equipment operators may perform other farm duties that are not typical of other farmworkers.

Agricultural inspectors, another type of agricultural worker, are employed by Federal and State governments to ensure compliance with laws and regulations governing the health, quality, and safety of agricultural commodities. Inspectors also make sure that the facilities and equipment used in processing the commodities meet quality standards. Meat safety is one of their prime responsibilities, and they try to ensure that the meat we eat is free of harmful ingredients or bacteria. In meat-processing facilities, inspectors may collect samples of suspected diseased animals or materials and send the samples to a laboratory for identification and analysis. They also may inspect livestock to help determine the effectiveness of medication and feeding programs. Some inspectors are stationed at export and import sites to weigh and inspect agricultural shipments leaving and entering the country, to ensure the quality and quantity of the shipments. A few work at logging sites, making sure that safety regulations are enforced.

Graders and sorters of agricultural products examine agricultural commodities being prepared to be packed for market and classify them according to quality or size guidelines. They grade, sort, or classify unprocessed food and other agricultural products by size, weight, color, or condition and discard inferior or defective products. For example, graders sort eggs are by color and size and also examine the fat content, or marbling, of beef, assigning a grade of "Prime," "Choice," or something else, as appropriate. The grade that is assigned determines the price at which the commodity may be sold.

Working Conditions

Working conditions for agricultural workers vary widely. Much of the work of farmworkers and laborers on farms and ranches takes

Many agricultural workers work in nurseries and greenhouses.

473

place outdoors in all kinds of weather and is physical in nature. Harvesting fruits and vegetables, for example, may require much bending, stooping, and lifting. Workers may lack adequate sanitation facilities while working in the field, and their drinking water may be limited. The year-round nature of much livestock production work means that ranch workers must be out in the heat of summer, as well as the cold of winter. While some of these workers enjoy the day-to-day variability of the work, the rural setting, working on the land, and raising animals, the work hours are generally uneven and often long; work cannot be delayed when crops must be planted and harvested or when animals must be sheltered and fed. Weekend work is common, and farmworkers may work a 6- or 7-day week during planting and harvesting seasons. Because much of the work is seasonal in nature, many workers also obtain other jobs during slow seasons. Migrant farmworkers, who move from location to location as crops ripen, live an unsettled lifestyle, which can be stressful.

Work also is seasonal for farmworkers in nurseries; spring and summer are the busiest times of the year. Greenhouse workers enjoy relatively comfortable working conditions while tending to plants indoors. However, during the busy seasons, when landscape contractors need plants, work schedules may be more demanding, requiring weekend work. Moreover, the transition from warm weather to cold weather means that nursery workers might have to work overtime with little notice given, in order to move plants indoors in case of a frost.

Federal meat inspectors may work in highly mechanized plants or with poultry or livestock in confined areas with extremely cold temperatures and slippery floors. The duties often require working with sharp knives, moderate lifting, and walking or standing for long periods. Many inspectors work long and often irregular hours. Inspectors may find themselves in adversarial roles when the organization or individual being inspected objects to the inspection or its potential consequences. Some inspectors travel frequently to visit farms and processing facilities. Others work at ports, inspecting cargo on the docks or on boats.

Graders and sorters may work with similar products for an entire shift, or they may be assigned a variety of items. They may be on their feet all day and may have to lift heavy objects, whereas others may sit during most of their shift and do little strenuous work. Some graders work in clean, air-conditioned environments, suitable for carrying out controlled tests. Some may work evenings or weekends because of the perishable nature of the products. Overtime may be required to meet production goals.

Farmworkers in crop production risk exposure to pesticides and other hazardous chemicals sprayed on crops or plants. However, exposure is relatively minimal if safety procedures are followed. Those who work on mechanized farms must take precautions to avoid injury when working with tools and heavy equipment. Those who work directly with animals risk being bitten or kicked.

Employment

Agricultural workers held about 795,000 jobs in 2002. Of these, farmworkers were the most numerous, holding 670,000 jobs. Graders and sorters held 49,000 jobs, agricultural inspectors 16,000 jobs, and agricultural equipment operators 61,000 jobs. Approximately 69 percent of all agricultural workers worked for crop and livestock producers, while almost 5 percent worked for agricultural service providers, mostly farm labor contractors.

Training, Other Qualifications, and Advancement

Farmworkers learn through short-term on-the-job training. Most do not have a high school diploma. The preponderance of workers without a high school diploma is particularly high in the crop production sector, where there are more labor-intensive establishments employing migrant farmworkers.

In nurseries, entry-level workers must be able to follow directions and learn proper planting procedures. If driving is an essential part of a job, employers look for applicants with a good driving record and some experience driving a truck. Workers who deal directly with customers must get along well with people. Employers also look for responsible, self-motivated individuals, because nursery workers sometimes work with little supervision.

For graders and sorters, training requirements vary on the basis of their responsibilities. For those who perform tests on various agricultural products, a high school diploma is preferred and may be required. Simple jobs requiring mostly visual inspection may be filled by beginners provided with short-term on-the-job training.

Becoming an agricultural inspector requires relevant work experience or some college course work in a field such as biology or agricultural science. Inspectors are trained in the applicable laws or inspection procedures through some combination of classroom and on-the-job training. In general, people who want to enter this occupation should be responsible, like detailed work, and be able to communicate well. Federal Government inspectors whose job performance is satisfactory advance through a career ladder to a specified full-performance level. For positions above this level—usually supervisory positions—advancement is competitive and based on agency needs and individual merit. Advancement opportunities in State and local governments and in the private sector often are similar to those in the Federal Government.

Advancement of agricultural workers depends on motivation and experience. Farmworkers who work hard and quickly, have good communication skills, and take an interest in the business may advance to crew leader or other supervisory positions. Some agricultural workers may aspire to become farm, ranch, and other agricultural managers, or farmers or ranchers themselves. (Farmers, ranchers, and agricultural managers are discussed elsewhere in the *Handbook*.) In addition, their knowledge of raising and harvesting produce may provide an excellent background for becoming purchasing agents and buyers of farm products. Knowledge of working a farm as a business can help agricultural workers become farm and home management advisors. Those who earn a college degree in agricultural science could become agricultural and food scientists.

Job Outlook

Overall employment of agricultural workers is projected to grow more slowly than the average for all occupations over the 2002-12 period, primarily reflecting the outlook for farmworkers, who make up the large majority of all agricultural workers. Low wages, the physical demands of the work, and high job turnover should result in abundant job opportunities, however.

Continued consolidation of farms and technological advancements in farm equipment will dampen employment growth. Nevertheless, those farms remaining in operation will still need workers to help with their operations, and farm labor contractors' employment of farmworkers is expected to increase steadily. Nursery and greenhouse workers should have the most rapid job growth, reflecting the increasing demand for landscaping services.

Slower-than-average employment growth also is anticipated for agricultural inspectors. Governments at all levels are not expected to hire significant numbers of new inspectors, choosing to leave more of the routine inspection to businesses. Slower-than-average growth also is expected for graders and sorters, and agricultural equipment operators, reflecting the agriculture industry's continuing ability to produce more with fewer workers.

Earnings

Median hourly earnings of the more numerous farmworkers in crops, nurseries, and greenhouses were $7.24 in 2002. The middle 50 percent earned between $6.85 and $8.37 an hour, while the lowest 10 percent earned less than $6.24 and the highest 10 percent earned more than $10.32.

Median hourly earnings for farmworkers who work with livestock were $8.22. The middle 50 percent earned between $6.98 and $10.32 an hour, while the lowest 10 percent earned less than $6.27 and the highest 10 percent earned more than $13.01.

Median hourly earnings of graders and sorters of agricultural products were $7.67 in 2002. The middle 50 percent earned between $6.88 and $9.30. The lowest 10 percent earned less than $6.22, and the highest 10 percent earned more than $11.80.

Median hourly earnings of agricultural inspectors were $13.76 in 2002. The middle 50 percent earned between $10.44 and $18.79. The lowest 10 percent earned less than $9.10, and the highest 10 percent earned more than $23.94.

Median hourly earnings for agricultural equipment operators in 2002 were $8.31. The middle 50 percent earned between $6.96 and $10.78. The lowest 10 percent earned less than $6.11, the highest 10 percent more than $13.89.

Few agricultural workers are members of unions.

Related Occupations

The duties of farmworkers who perform outdoor labor are related to the work of fishers and operators of fishing vessels; forest, conservation, and logging workers; and grounds maintenance workers. Farmworkers who work with farm and ranch animals perform work related to that of animal care and service workers.

Sources of Additional Information

Information on agricultural worker jobs is available from

➤ National FFA Organization, The National FFA Center, Career Information Requests, P.O. Box 68690, Indianapolis, IN, 46268-0960. Internet: **http://www.ffa.org**

Information on farmworker jobs is available from

➤ The New England Small Farm Institute, 275 Jackson St., Belchertown, MA 01007. Internet: **http://www.smallfarm.org/newoof/newoof.html**

Information on obtaining a position as an agricultural inspector with the Federal Government is available from the Office of Personnel Management (OPM) through a telephone-based system. Consult your telephone directory under "U.S. Government" for a local number, or call (703) 724-1850; Federal Relay Service: (800) 877-8339. The first number is not toll free, and charges may result. Information also is available from the OPM Internet site: **http://www.usajobs.opm.gov**

Fishers and Fishing Vessel Operators

(0*NET 45-3011.00)

Significant Points

● More than half of all workers are self-employed, among the highest proportion in the workforce.

● Many jobs require strenuous work and long hours and provide only seasonal employment.

● Employment is projected to decline, due to the depletion of fish stocks and new Federal and State laws restricting both commercial and recreational fishing.

Nature of the Work

Fishers and fishing vessel operators catch and trap various types of marine life for human consumption, animal feed, bait, and other uses. (Aquaculture—the raising and harvesting, under controlled conditions, of fish and other aquatic life in ponds or confined bodies of water—is covered in the *Handbook* statement on farmers, ranchers, and agricultural managers.)

Fishing hundreds of miles from shore with commercial fishing vessels—large boats capable of hauling a catch of tens of thousands of pounds of fish—requires a crew that includes a captain, or skipper, a first mate and sometimes a second mate, a boatswain (called a deckboss on some smaller boats), and deckhands with specialized skills.

The *fishing boat captain* plans and oversees the fishing operation—the fish to be sought, the location of the best fishing grounds, the method of capture, the duration of the trip, and the sale of the catch.

The captain ensures that the fishing vessel is seaworthy; oversees the purchase of supplies, gear, and equipment, such as fuel, netting, and cables; obtains the required fishing permits and licenses; and hires qualified crew members and assigns their duties. The captain plots the vessel's course, often using electronic navigational equipment such as autopilots, loran systems, and satellite navigation systems. However, traditional navigational equipment (for example, compasses, sextants, and charts) is still in use. Ships also use radar to avoid obstacles and utilize depth sounders to indicate the water depth and whether there is marine life between the vessel and sea bottom. Sophisticated tracking technology allows captains to better locate and analyze schools of fish. The captain directs the fishing operation through the officers' actions and records daily activities in the ship's log. Upon returning to port, the captain arranges for the sale of the catch—directly to buyers or through a fish auction—and ensures that each crew member receives the prearranged portion of adjusted net proceeds from the sale of the catch. Some captains have begun buying and selling fish via the Internet, and as electronic commerce grows as a method of finding buyers for fresh catch, more captains may use computers.

The *first mate*—the captain's assistant, who must be familiar with navigation requirements and the operation of all electronic equipment—assumes control of the vessel when the captain is off duty. Duty shifts, called watches, usually last 6 hours. The mate's regular duty, with the help of the boatswain and under the captain's oversight, is to direct the fishing operations and sailing responsibilities of the deckhands, including the operation, maintenance, and repair of the vessel and the gathering, preservation, stowing, and unloading of the catch.

The *boatswain*, a highly experienced deckhand with supervisory responsibilities, directs the *deckhands* as they carry out the sailing and fishing operations. Before departure, the boatswain directs the deckhands to load equipment and supplies, either by hand or with hoisting equipment, and to untie lines from other boats and the dock. When necessary, boatswains repair fishing gear, equipment, nets, and accessories. They operate the fishing gear, letting out and pulling in nets and lines, and extract the catch, such as pollock, flounder, and tuna, from the nets or the lines' hooks. Deckhands use dip nets to prevent the escape of small fish and gaffs to facilitate the landing of large fish. They then wash, salt, ice, and stow away the catch. Deckhands also must ensure that decks are clear and clean at all times and that the vessel's engines and equipment are kept in good working order. Upon return to port, they secure the vessel's lines to and from the docks and other vessels. Unless "lumpers" (laborers or longshore workers) are hired, the deckhands unload the catch.

Large fishing vessels that operate in deep water generally have technologically advanced equipment, and some may have facilities on board where the fish are processed and prepared for sale. Such vessels are equipped for long stays at sea and can perform the work of several smaller boats.

Some full-time and many part-time fishers work on small boats in relatively shallow waters, often in sight of land. Navigation and communication needs are vital and constant for almost all types of boats. Crews are small—usually, only one or two people collaborate on all aspects of the fishing operation, which may include placing gill nets across the mouths of rivers or inlets, entrapment nets in bays and lakes, or pots and traps for fish or shellfish such as lobsters and crabs. Dredges and scrapes are sometimes used to gather shellfish such as oysters and scallops. A very small proportion of commercial fishing is conducted as diving operations. Depending upon the water's depth, divers—wearing regulation diving suits with an umbilical (air line) or a scuba outfit and equipment—use spears to catch fish and use nets and other equipment to gather shellfish, coral, sea urchins, abalone, and sponges. In very shallow waters, fish are caught from small boats having an outboard motor, from rowboats, or by wading or seining from shore. Fishers use a wide variety of hand-operated equipment—for example, nets, tongs, rakes, hoes, hooks, and shovels—to gather fish and shellfish; catch amphibians and reptiles such as frogs and turtles; and harvest marine vegetation such as Irish moss and kelp.

Although most fishers are involved in commercial fishing, some captains and deckhands use their expertise in fishing for sport or recreational purposes. For this type of fishing, a group of people charter a fishing vessel for periods ranging from several hours to a number of days and embark upon sportfishing, socializing, and relaxation, employing a captain and possibly several deckhands.

Working Conditions
Fishing operations are conducted under various environmental conditions, depending on the region of the country and the kind of species sought. Storms, fog, and wind may hamper fishing vessels or cause them to suspend fishing operations and return to port. Divers are affected by murky water and unexpected shifts in underwater currents. In relatively busy fisheries, smaller boats have to take care not to be hit by larger vessels.

Fishers and fishing vessel operators work under some of the most hazardous conditions of any occupation, and often help is not

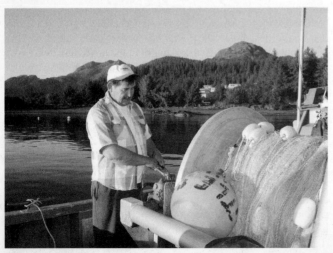

Fishing vessel operators must check their gear before heading out.

readily available when injuries occur. Malfunctioning navigation or communication equipment may lead to collisions or shipwrecks. The crew must be on guard against the danger of injury from malfunctioning fishing gear, entanglement in fishing nets and gear, slippery decks resulting from fish-processing operations, ice formation in the winter, or being swept overboard—a fearsome situation. Also, treatment for any serious injuries may have to await transfer to a hospital. Divers must guard against entanglement of air lines, malfunction of scuba equipment, decompression problems, and attacks by predatory fish.

Fishers and fishing vessel operators face strenuous outdoor work and long hours. Commercial fishing trips may require a stay of several weeks or even months—hundreds of miles away from one's home port. The pace of work may vary, but even during travel between the home port and the fishing grounds, deckhands on smaller boats try to finish their cleaning duties so that there are no chores remaining to be done at port. However, lookout watches are a regular responsibility, and crew members must be prepared to stand watch at prearranged times of the day or night. Although fishing gear has improved, and operations have become more mechanized, netting and processing fish are strenuous activities. Whereas newer vessels have improved living quarters and amenities such as television and shower stalls, crews still experience the aggravations of confined quarters, continuous close personal contact, and the absence of family.

Employment
Fishers and fishing vessel operators held an estimated 36,000 jobs in 2002. More than 5 out of 10 were self-employed. Most fishing takes place off the coasts, with Alaska, Louisiana, Virginia, California, and Washington bringing in the greatest volume of fish. While fishing off the New England coast has declined in recent years because of restrictions on catching certain species, it still ranks high in total value of fish caught, according to the National Marine Fisheries Society.

Training, Other Qualifications, and Advancement
Fishers usually acquire their occupational skills on the job, many as members of families involved in fishing activities. No formal academic requirements exist. Operators of large commercial fishing vessels are required to complete a Coast Guard-approved training course. Students can expedite their entrance into these occupations by enrolling in 2-year vocational-technical programs offered by secondary schools. In addition, some community colleges and universities offer fishery technology and related programs that include courses in seamanship, vessel operations, marine safety, navigation, vessel repair and maintenance, health emergencies, and fishing gear technology. Courses include hands-on experience. Secondary and postsecondary programs are normally offered in or near coastal areas.

Experienced fishers may find short-term workshops offered through various postsecondary institutions especially useful. These programs provide a good working knowledge of electronic equipment used in navigation and communication and offer the latest improvements in fishing gear.

Captains and mates on large fishing vessels of at least 200 gross tons must be licensed. Captains of sportfishing boats used for charter, regardless of the boats' size, must also be licensed. Crew members on certain fish-processing vessels may need a merchant mariner's document. The U.S. Coast Guard issues these documents and licenses to individuals who meet the stipulated health, physical, and academic requirements. (For information about merchant marine occupations, see the statement on water transportation occupations elsewhere in the *Handbook*.)

Fishers must be in good health and possess physical strength. Good coordination, mechanical aptitude, and the ability to work under difficult or dangerous conditions are necessary to operate, maintain, and repair equipment and fishing gear. Fishers need stamina to work long hours at sea, often under difficult conditions. On large vessels, they must be able to work as members of a team. Fishers must be patient, yet always alert, to overcome the boredom of long watches when they are not engaged in fishing operations. The ability to assume any deckhand's functions on short notice is important. As supervisors, mates must be able to assume all duties, including the captain's, when necessary. The captain must be highly experienced, mature, and decisive and also must possess the business skills needed to run business operations.

On fishing vessels, most fishers begin as deckhands. Deckhands who acquire experience and whose interests are in ship engineering—the maintenance and repair of ship engines and equipment—can eventually become licensed chief engineers on large commercial vessels after meeting the Coast Guard's experience, physical, and academic requirements. Experienced, reliable deckhands who display supervisory qualities may become boatswains, who, in turn, may become second mates, first mates, and, finally, captains. Almost all captains become self-employed, and the overwhelming majority eventually own, or have an interest in, one or more fishing ships. Some may choose to run a sport or recreational fishing operation. When their seagoing days are over, experienced individuals may work in or, with the necessary capital, own stores selling fishing and marine equipment and supplies. Some captains may assume advisory or administrative positions in industry trade associations or government offices, such as harbor development commissions, or in teaching positions in industry-sponsored workshops or educational institutions. Divers in fishing operations can enter a commercial diving activity—for example, repairing ships or maintaining piers and marinas—usually after the completion of a certified training program sponsored by an educational institution or industry association.

Job Outlook

Employment of fishers and fishing vessel operators is expected to decline through the year 2012. These workers depend on the natural ability of fish stocks to replenish themselves through growth and reproduction, as well as on governmental regulation of fisheries. Many operations are currently at or beyond the maximum sustainable yield, partially because of habitat destruction, and the number of workers who can earn an adequate income from fishing is expected to decline. Many fishers and fishing vessel operators leave the occupation because of the strenuous and hazardous nature of the job and the lack of steady, year-round income. Some job openings will nevertheless arise from the need to replace workers who leave the occupation or retire.

The use of sophisticated electronic equipment for navigation, for communication, and for locating fish has raised the efficiency of finding fish stocks. Also, improvements in fishing gear and the use of highly automated floating processors, where the catch is processed aboard the vessel, have greatly increased fish hauls. In many areas, particularly the North Atlantic and Pacific Northwest, damage to spawning grounds and excess fishing capacity have adversely affected the stock of fish and, consequently, the employ-

ment opportunities for fishers. Some States have issued various types of restrictions on harvesting, to allow stocks of fish and shellfish to replenish themselves, thereby idling many fishers. In addition, low prices for some species and rising seafood imports are adversely affecting fishing income. Sportfishing boats, however, will continue to provide some job opportunities.

Governmental efforts to replenish stocks are having positive results, which should increase the stock of fish at some point in the future. Furthermore, efforts by private fishers' associations on the West Coast to increase government monitoring of the fisheries may help significantly to prevent the type of decline in fish stocks found in waters off the East Coast. Nevertheless, fewer fishers and fishing vessel operators are expected to make their living from the Nation's waters in the years ahead.

Earnings

Based on limited information, the majority of full-time wage and salary fishers earn between $300 and $700 per week. Earnings of fishers and fishing vessel operators normally are highest in the summer and fall—when demand for services peaks and environmental conditions are favorable—and lowest during the winter. Many full-time and most part-time workers supplement their income by working in other activities during the off-season. For example, fishers may work in seafood-processing plants, in establishments selling fishing and marine equipment, in construction, or in a number of unrelated seasonal occupations.

Earnings of fishers vary widely, depending upon their position, their ownership percentage of the vessel, the size of their ship, and the amount and value of the catch. The costs of the fishing operation—the physical aspects of operating the ship, such as the fuel costs, repair and maintenance of gear and equipment, and the crew's supplies—are deducted from the sale of the catch. Net proceeds are distributed among the crew members in accordance with a prearranged percentage. Generally, the ship's owner—usually its captain—receives half of the net proceeds. From this amount, the owner pays for depreciation, maintenance and repair, and replacement and insurance costs of the ship and its equipment; the money that remains is the owner's profit.

Related Occupations

Other occupations that involve outdoor work with fish and watercraft include water transportation occupations and fish and game wardens.

Sources of Additional Information

Names of postsecondary schools offering fishing and related marine educational programs are available from

➤ Marine Technology Society, 5565 Sterrett Place, Suite 108, Columbia, MD 21044. Internet: **http://www.mtsociety.org**

Information on licensing of fishing vessel captains and mates and on requirements for merchant mariner documentation is available from the U.S. Coast Guard Marine Inspection Office or Marine Safety Office in your State. Or contact either of the following agencies:

➤ Office of Compliance, Commandant (G-MOC-3) 2100 Second St. SW., Washington, DC 20593. Internet:
http://www.access.gpo.gov/nara/cfr/waisidx_01/46cfr28_01.html

➤ Licensing and Evaluation Branch, National Maritime Center, 4200 Wilson Blvd., Suite 630, Arlington, VA 22203-1804.

Forest, Conservation, and Logging Workers

(O*NET 45-4011.00, 45-4021.00, 45-4022.01, 45-4023.00)

Significant Points

- Workers spend all their time outdoors, sometimes in poor weather and often in isolated areas.
- Most jobs are physically demanding and can be hazardous.
- A small decline in overall employment is expected in the occupation.

Nature of the Work

The Nation's forests are a rich natural resource, providing beauty and tranquility, varied recreational areas, and wood for commercial use. Managing forests and woodlands requires many different kinds of workers. Forest and conservation workers help develop, maintain, and protect the forests by growing and planting new seedlings, fighting insects and diseases that attack trees, and helping to control soil erosion. Timber-cutting and logging workers harvest thousands of acres of forests each year for the timber that provides the raw material for countless consumer and industrial products.

Forest and conservation workers perform a variety of tasks to reforest and conserve timberlands and maintain forest facilities, such as roads and campsites. Some forest workers, called tree planters, use digging and planting tools called "dibble bars" and "hoedads" to plant seedlings to reforest timberland areas. Forest workers also remove diseased or undesirable trees with power saws or handsaws, spray trees with insecticides and fungicides to kill insects and to protect against disease, and apply herbicides on undesirable brush and trees to reduce competing vegetation. Forest workers in private industry usually work for professional foresters and paint boundary lines, assist with prescribed burning, and aid in marking and measuring trees by keeping a tally of those examined and counted. Forest workers who work for State and local governments or who are under contract to the Federal Government also clear away brush and debris from camp trails, roadsides, and camping areas under their employers' jurisdiction. Some clean kitchens and rest rooms at recreational facilities and campgrounds.

Other forest and conservation workers work in forest nurseries, sorting out tree seedlings and discarding those not meeting prescribed standards of root formation, stem development, and condition of foliage.

Some forest workers are employed on tree farms, where they plant, cultivate, and harvest many different kinds of trees. Their duties vary with the type of farm. Those who work on specialty farms, such as farms growing Christmas or ornamental trees for nurseries, are responsible for shearing treetops and limbs to control the growth of the trees under their care, to increase the density of limbs, and to improve the shapes of the trees. In addition, these workers' duties include planting the seedlings, spraying to control surrounding weed growth and insects, and harvesting the trees.

Other forest workers gather, by hand or with the use of handtools, products from the woodlands, such as decorative greens, tree cones and barks, moss, and other wild plant life. Still others tap trees for sap to make syrup or to produce chemicals.

The timber-cutting and logging process is carried out by a variety of workers who make up a logging crew. *Fallers* cut down trees with hand-held power chain saws or, occasionally, axes. Usually using gas-powered chain saws, *buckers* trim off the tops and branches and buck (cut) the resulting logs into specified lengths.

Choke setters fasten chokers (steel cables or chains) around logs to be skidded (dragged) by tractors or forwarded by the cable-yarding system to the landing or deck area, where the logs are separated by species and type of product, such as pulpwood, sawlogs, or veneer logs, and loaded onto trucks. *Rigging slingers* and *chasers* set up and dismantle the cables and guy wires of the yarding system. *Log sorters*, *markers*, *movers*, and *debarkers* sort, mark, and move logs, based on species, size, and ownership, and tend machines that debark logs.

Logging equipment operators on a logging crew perform a number of duties. They use tree harvesters to shear the tops off of trees, cut and limb the trees, and then cut the logs into desired lengths. They drive tractors mounted on crawler tracks called crawlers, and self-propelled machines called skidders or forwarders, which drag or transport logs from the felling site in the woods to the log landing area for loading. They operate grapple loaders, which lift and load logs into trucks, and tree fellers or shears, which cut the trees. Some logging equipment operators use tracked or wheeled equipment similar to a forklift to unload logs and pulpwood off of trucks or gondola railroad cars, usually in a sawmill or a pulp-mill woodyard. Some newer, more efficient logging equipment is now equipped with state-of-the-art computer technology, requiring more skilled operators with more training.

Log graders and *scalers* inspect logs for defects, measure logs to determine their volume, and estimate the marketable content or value of logs or pulpwood. These workers often use hand-held data collection terminals to enter data about individual trees; later, the data can be downloaded or sent from the scaling area to a central computer via modem.

Other timber-cutting and logging workers have a variety of responsibilities. Some hike through forests to assess logging conditions. Some clear areas of brush and other growth to prepare for logging activities or to promote the growth of desirable species of trees.

The timber-cutting and logging industry is characterized by a large number of small crews of four to eight workers. A typical crew might consist of one or two fallers or one feller machine operator, one bucker, two logging tractor operators to drag cut trees to the loading deck, and one equipment operator to load the logs onto trucks. Most crews work for self-employed logging contractors who possess substantial logging experience, the capital to purchase

Most forestry and logging jobs are physically demanding and often require the use of dangerous equipment.

equipment, and the skills needed to run a small business successfully. Most contractors work alongside their crews as supervisors and often operate one of the logging machines, such as the grapple loader or the tree harvester. Many manage more than one crew and function as owners-supervisors.

Although timber-cutting and logging equipment has greatly improved and operations are becoming increasingly mechanized, many logging jobs still are labor intensive. These jobs require various levels of skill, ranging from the unskilled task of manually moving logs, branches, and equipment to skillfully using chain saws, peavies (hooked poles), and log jacks to cut and position logs for further processing or loading. To keep costs down, some timber-cutting and logging workers maintain and repair the equipment they use. A skillful, experienced logger is expected to handle a variety of logging operations.

Working Conditions

Forestry and logging jobs are physically demanding. Workers spend all their time outdoors, sometimes in poor weather and often in isolated areas. The increased use of enclosed machines has decreased some of the discomforts caused by inclement weather. A few lumber camps in Alaska house workers in bunkhouses or company towns. Workers in sparsely populated western States commute long distances between their homes and logging sites. In the more densely populated eastern and southern States, commuting distances are much shorter.

Most logging occupations involve lifting, climbing, and other strenuous activities, although machinery has eliminated some of the heavy labor. Loggers work under unusually hazardous conditions. Falling trees and branches are a constant menace, as are the dangers associated with log-handling operations and the use of sawing equipment, especially delimbing devices. Special care must be taken during strong winds, which can even halt operations. Slippery or muddy ground and hidden roots or vines not only reduce efficiency, but also present a constant danger, especially in the presence of moving vehicles and machinery. Poisonous plants, brambles, insects, snakes, heat, and humidity are minor annoyances. If safety precautions are not taken, the high noise level of sawing and skidding operations over long periods may impair one's hearing. Experience, the exercise of caution, and the use of proper safety measures and equipment—such as hardhats, eye and ear protection, and safety clothing and boots—are extremely important to avoid injury.

The jobs of forest and conservation workers generally are much less hazardous than those of loggers. It may be necessary for some forestry aides or forest workers to walk long distances through densely wooded areas to do their work.

Employment

Forest, conservation, and logging workers held about 81,000 jobs in 2002, distributed among the following occupations:

Logging equipment operators	43,000
Forest and conservation workers	14,000
Fallers	14,000
Log graders and scalers	10,000

Most wage and salary fallers and logging equipment operators are employed in logging camps and in the logging contractors industry, although some work in sawmills and planing mills. Employment of log graders and scalers is concentrated largely in sawmills and planing mills.

More than half of all forest and conservation workers work for government, primarily at the State and local level. Twenty percent are employed by companies that operate timber tracts, tree farms,

or forest nurseries, or for contractors that supply services to agriculture and forestry industries. Some of those employed in forestry services work on a contract basis for the U.S. Department of Agriculture's Forest Service. A small number of forest and conservation workers work in sawmills and planing mills. Although forest and conservation workers are located in every State, employment is concentrated in the West and Southeast, where many national and private forests and parks are located.

Self-employed forestry, conservation, and logging workers account for almost 3 of every 10 such workers—a much higher proportion of self-employment than in most other occupations.

Seasonal demand for forest, conservation, and logging workers varies by region. For example, in the northern States, winter work is common because the frozen ground facilitates logging. In the Southeast, logging and related activities occur year-round.

Training, Other Qualifications, and Advancement

Most forest, conservation, and logging workers develop skills through on-the-job training, with instruction coming primarily from experienced workers. Logging workers must familiarize themselves with the character and dangers of the forest environment and the operation of logging machinery and equipment. However, large logging companies and trade associations, such as the Northeastern Loggers Association and the Forest Resources Association, Inc., offer special programs, particularly for workers training to operate large, expensive machinery and equipment. Often, a representative of the manufacturer or company spends several days in the field explaining and overseeing the operation of newly purchased machinery. Safety training is a vital part of the instruction of all logging workers.

Many State forestry or logging associations provide training sessions for fallers, whose job duties require more skill and experience than do other positions on the logging team. Sessions may take place in the field, where trainees, under the supervision of an experienced logger, have the opportunity to practice various felling techniques. Fallers learn how to manually cut down extremely large or expensive trees safely and with minimal damage to the felled or surrounding trees.

Training programs for loggers and foresters are becoming common in many States, largely in response to a collaborative effort by the American Forest & Paper Association and others in the forestry industry. Such programs are designed to encourage the health and productivity of the Nation's forests through the Sustainable Forest Initiative program. Logger training programs vary by State, but generally include some type of classroom or field training in a number of areas: best management practices, safety, endangered species, reforestation, and business management. Some programs lead to certification as a logger.

Experience in other occupations can expedite one's entry into some logging occupations. For example, equipment operators, such as truckdrivers and bulldozer and crane operators, can assume skidding and yarding functions. Some loggers have worked in sawmills or on family farms with extensive wooded areas. Some logging contractors were formerly crew members of family-owned businesses operated over several generations.

Generally, little formal education is required for most forest, conservation, and logging occupations. Many secondary schools, including vocational and technical schools and some community colleges, offer courses or a 2-year degree in general forestry, wildlife, conservation, and forest harvesting, which could be helpful in obtaining a job. A curriculum that includes field trips to observe or participate in forestry or logging activities provides a particularly good background. There are no educational requirements for forest worker jobs. Many of these workers are high school or college students who are hired on a part-time or seasonal basis to perform short-term, labor-intensive tasks, such as planting tree seedlings.

Forest, conservation, and logging workers must be in good health and able to work outdoors every day. They also must be able to work as part of a team. Many logging occupations require physical strength and stamina. Maturity and good judgment are important in making quick, intelligent decisions in dealing with hazards as they arise. Mechanical aptitude and coordination are necessary qualities for operators of machinery and equipment, who often are responsible for repair and maintenance as well. Initiative and managerial and business skills are necessary for success as a self-employed logging contractor.

Experience working at a nursery or as a laborer can be useful in obtaining a job as a forest or conservation worker. Logging workers generally advance from occupations involving primarily manual labor to those involving the operation of expensive, sometimes complicated, machinery and other equipment. Inexperienced entrants usually begin as laborers, carrying tools and equipment, clearing brush, and loading and unloading logs and brush. For some, familiarization with logging operations may lead to jobs such as log-handling equipment operator. Further experience may lead to jobs involving the operation of more complicated machinery and yarding towers to transport, load, and unload logs. Those who have the motor skills required for the efficient use of power saws and other equipment may become fallers and buckers.

Job Outlook

Overall employment of forest, conservation, and logging workers is expected to decline slightly through the year 2012. Most job openings will result from replacement needs. Many logging workers transfer to other jobs that are less physically demanding and dangerous, or else they retire. In addition, some forestry workers are youths who are not committed to the occupation on a long-term basis. Some take jobs to earn money for school; others work in this occupation only until they find a better paying job.

Employment of forest and conservation workers is expected to grow more slowly than the average for all occupations. Setting aside more land to protect natural resources or wildlife habitats helps to create demand for more forest and conservation workers. In addition, under the latest farm bill, small, private farmowners were offered incentives to convert all or part of their land to forest for ecological purposes. This conversion may indirectly cause the hiring of forest and conservation workers to work on the property.

Despite steady demand for lumber and other wood products, employment of timber-cutting and logging occupations is expected to decline, primarily because of increased mechanization and increasing imports. New federal policy allowing some access to federal timberland may moderate any decline, however, and job opportunities also will arise from owners of privately owned forests and tree farms. However, domestic timber producers face increasing competition from foreign producers, who can harvest the same amount of timber at lower cost. As competition increases, the logging industry is expected to continue to consolidate in order to reduce costs, thereby eliminating some jobs.

Increased mechanization of logging operations and improvements in logging equipment will continue to depress demand for many timber-cutting and logging workers. Employment of fallers, buckers, choke setters, and other workers—whose jobs are labor intensive—should decline as safer laborsaving machinery and other equipment are increasingly used. Employment of machinery and equipment operators, such as logging tractor and log-handling equipment operators, should be less adversely affected.

Weather can force the curtailment of logging operations during the muddy spring season and the cold winter months, depending on the geographic region. Changes in the level of construction, particularly residential construction, also affect logging activities in the short term. In addition, logging operations must be relocated when timber in a particular area has been completely harvested. During prolonged periods of inactivity, some workers may stay on the job to maintain or repair logging machinery and equipment; others are forced to find jobs in other occupations or be without work.

Earnings

Earnings vary with the particular forestry or logging occupation and with experience. Earnings range from the minimum wage in some beginning forestry and conservation positions to about $28.23 an hour for some experienced fallers. Median hourly earnings in 2002 for forest, conservation, and logging occupations were as follows:

Fallers	$13.54
Log graders and scalers	13.08
Logging equipment operators	12.88
Forest and conservation workers	9.12

Earnings of logging workers vary by size of establishment and by geographic area. Workers in the largest establishments earn more than those in the smallest ones. Workers in Alaska and the Northwest earn more than those in the South, where the cost of living is generally lower.

Forest and conservation workers who work for State and local governments or for large, private firms generally enjoy more generous benefits than do workers in smaller firms. Small logging contractors generally offer timber-cutting and logging workers few benefits. However, some employers offer full-time workers basic benefits, such as medical coverage, and provide safety apparel and equipment.

Related Occupations

Other occupations concerned with the care of trees and their environment include conservation scientists and foresters, forest and conservation technicians, and grounds maintenance workers. Logging equipment operators have skills similar to material-moving equipment operators, such as industrial truck and tractor operators and crane and tower operators.

Sources of Additional Information

For information about timber-cutting and logging careers and about secondary and postsecondary programs offering training for logging occupations, contact either of the following sources:

➤ Northeastern Loggers Association, P.O. Box 69, Old Forge, NY 13420. Internet: **http://www.loggertraining.com**

➤ Forest Resources Association, Inc., 600 Jefferson Plaza, Suite 350, Rockville, MD 20852. Internet: **http://www.forestresources.org**

For information on the Sustainable Forestry Initiative training programs, contact

➤ American Forest & Paper Association, 1111 19th St. NW., Suite 800, Washington, DC 20036. Internet: **http://www.afandpa.org**

A list of State forestry associations and other forestry-related State associations is available at most public libraries. Schools of forestry at States' land-grant colleges or universities also should be useful sources of information.

Boilermakers

(0*NET 47-2011.00)

Significant Points

- A formal apprenticeship is the best way to learn this trade.
- Little or no employment growth is expected, but many openings will be created by the need to replace experienced workers who leave this occupation.

Nature of the Work

Boilermakers and *boilermaker mechanics* make, install, and repair boilers, vats, and other large vessels that hold liquids and gases. Boilers supply steam to drive huge turbines in electric powerplants and to provide heat and power in buildings, factories, and ships. Tanks and vats are used to process and store chemicals, oil, beer, and hundreds of other products.

Boilers and other high-pressure vessels usually are made in sections, by casting each piece out of molten iron or steel. Manufacturers are increasingly automating this process to increase the quality of these vessels. Boiler sections are then welded together, often using automated orbital welding machines, which make more consistent welds than are possible by hand. Small boilers may be assembled in the manufacturing plant; larger boilers usually are assembled on site.

Following blueprints, boilermakers locate and mark reference points on the boiler foundation, using straightedges, squares, transits, and tape measures. Boilermakers attach rigging and signal crane operators to lift heavy frame and plate sections and other parts into place. They align sections, using plumb bobs, levels, wedges, and turnbuckles. Boilermakers use hammers, files, grinders, and cutting torches to remove irregular edges, so that edges fit properly. They then bolt or weld edges together. Boilermakers align and at-tach water tubes, stacks, valves, gauges, and other parts and test complete vessels for leaks or other defects. They also install refractory brick and other heat-resistant materials in fireboxes or pressure vessels. Usually, they assemble large vessels temporarily in a fabrication shop to ensure a proper fit before final assembly on the permanent site.

Because boilers last a long time—35 years or more—boilermakers regularly maintain them and update components, such as burners and boiler tubes, to increase efficiency. Boilermaker mechanics maintain and repair boilers and similar vessels. They inspect tubes, fittings, valves, controls, and auxiliary machinery and clean or supervise the cleaning of boilers using scrapers, wire brushes, and cleaning solvents. They repair or replace defective parts, using hand and power tools, gas torches, and welding equipment, and may operate metalworking machinery to repair or make parts. They also dismantle leaky boilers, patch weak spots with metal stock, replace defective sections, and strengthen joints.

Working Conditions

Boilermakers often use potentially dangerous equipment, such as acetylene torches and power grinders, handle heavy parts, and work on ladders or on top of large vessels. Work is physically demanding and may be done in cramped quarters inside boilers, vats, or tanks that are often damp and poorly ventilated. In some instances, work may be done at high elevations for an extended period. To reduce the chance of injuries, boilermakers may wear hardhats, harnesses, protective clothing, safety glasses and shoes, and respirators. Boilermakers may experience extended periods of overtime when equipment is shut down for maintenance. Overtime work also may be necessary to meet construction or production deadlines.

Employment

Boilermakers held about 25,000 jobs in 2002. Nearly 7 out of 10 worked in the construction industry, assembling and erecting boilers and other vessels. More than 1 in 10 worked in manufacturing, primarily in boiler manufacturing shops, iron and steel plants, petroleum refineries, chemical plants, and shipyards. Some also worked for boiler repair firms or railroads.

Training, Other Qualifications, and Advancement

Many boilermakers learn this trade through a formal apprenticeship. Others become boilermakers through a combination of trade or technical school training and employer-provided training. Apprenticeship programs usually consist of 4 years of on-the-job training, supplemented by a minimum of 144 hours of classroom instruction each year in subjects such as set-up and assembly rigging, welding of all types, blueprint reading, and layout. Experienced boilermakers often attend apprenticeship classes or seminars to learn about new equipment, procedures, and technology. When an apprenticeship becomes available, the local union publicizes the opportunity by notifying local vocational schools and high school vocational programs.

Some boilermakers advance to supervisory positions. Because of their broader training, apprentices usually have an advantage in promotion.

Many boilermakers learn their trade through a formal apprenticeship

Job Outlook

Little or no growth in employment of boilermakers is expected through the year 2012, but many openings will be created by the need to replace experienced workers who leave this occupation; boilermakers tend to retire early, partly due to the physically demanding nature of the work. Because the number of persons seeking entry to the occupation is relatively low, some areas currently are experiencing a shortage of applicants for apprenticeship programs.

Growth may be limited by the trend toward repairing and retrofitting, rather than replacing, existing boilers; the use of small boilers, which require less onsite assembly; and automation of production technologies. However, demand for more boilermakers may stem from environmental upgrades required by Federal regulations such as the Clean Air Act.

Most industries that purchase boilers are sensitive to economic conditions. Therefore, during economic downturns, boilermakers in the construction industry may be laid off. However, because maintenance and repairs of boilers must continue even during economic downturns, boilermaker mechanics in manufacturing and other industries generally have stable employment.

Earnings

In 2002, the median hourly earnings of boilermakers were about $20.17. The middle 50 percent earned between $16.24 and $25.09. The lowest 10 percent earned less than $12.24, and the highest 10 percent earned more than $28.96. Apprentices generally start at about half of journey wages, with wages gradually increasing to the journey wage as progress is made in the apprenticeship.

About two-thirds of boilermakers belong to labor unions. The principal union is the International Brotherhood of Boilermakers. Other boilermakers are members of the International Association of Machinists, the United Automobile Workers, or the United Steelworkers of America.

Related Occupations

Workers in a number of other occupations assemble, install, or repair metal equipment or machines. These occupations include assemblers and fabricators; machinists; industrial machinery installation, repair, and maintenance workers, except millwrights; millwrights; pipelayers, plumbers, pipefitters, and steamfitters; sheet metal workers; tool-and-die makers; and welding, soldering, and brazing workers.

Sources of Additional Information

For further information regarding boilermaking apprenticeships or other training opportunities, contact local offices of the unions previously mentioned, local construction companies and boiler manufacturers, or the local office of your State employment service.

For information on apprenticeships and the boilermaking occupation, contact:

➤ International Brotherhood of Boilermakers, Iron Ship Builders, Blacksmiths, Forgers, and Helpers, 753 State Ave., Suite 570, Kansas City, KS 66101.

There are more than 500 occupations registered by the U.S. Department of Labor's National Apprenticeship system. For more information on the Labor Department's registered apprenticeship system and links to State apprenticeship programs, check their website: **http://www.doleta.gov**

Brickmasons, Blockmasons, and Stonemasons

(0*NET 47-2021.00, 47-2022.00)

Significant Points

- Job prospects are expected to be excellent.
- Most entrants learn informally on the job, but apprenticeship programs provide the most thorough training.
- The work is usually outdoors and involves lifting heavy materials and working on scaffolds.
- More than 1 out of 4 are self-employed.

Nature of the Work

Brickmasons, blockmasons, and stonemasons work in closely related trades creating attractive, durable surfaces and structures. The work varies in complexity, from laying a simple masonry walkway to installing an ornate exterior on a highrise building. *Brickmasons and blockmasons*—who often are called simply *bricklayers*—build and repair walls, floors, partitions, fireplaces, chimneys, and other structures with brick, precast masonry panels, concrete block, and other masonry materials. Some brickmasons specialize in installing firebrick linings in industrial furnaces. *Stonemasons* build stone walls, as well as set stone exteriors and floors. They work with two types of stone—natural cut stone, such as marble, granite, and limestone; and artificial stone made from concrete, marble chips, or other masonry materials. Stonemasons usually work on nonresidential structures, such as houses of worship, hotels, and office buildings.

When building a structure, brickmasons use 1 of 2 methods, the corner lead or the corner pole. Using the corner lead method, they begin by constructing a pyramid of bricks at each corner—called a lead. After the corner leads are complete, less experienced brickmasons fill in the wall between the corners, using a line from corner to corner to guide each course, or layer, of brick. Due to the precision needed, corner leads are time-consuming to erect and require the skills of experienced bricklayers.

Because of the expense associated with building corner leads, most brickmasons use corner poles, also called masonry guides, that enable them to build an entire wall at the same time. They fasten the corner poles (posts) in a plumb position to define the wall line and stretch a line between them. This line serves as a guide for each course of brick. Brickmasons then spread a bed of mortar (a cement, sand, and water mixture) with a trowel (a flat, bladed metal tool with a handle), place the brick on the mortar bed, and press and tap the brick into place. Depending on blueprint specifications, brickmasons either cut bricks with a hammer and chisel or saw them to fit around windows, doors, and other openings. Mortar joints are then finished with jointing tools for a sealed, neat, uniform appearance. Although brickmasons typically use steel supports, or lintels, at window and door openings, they sometimes build brick arches, which support and enhance the beauty of the brickwork.

Stonemasons often work from a set of drawings, in which each stone has been numbered for identification. Helpers may locate and carry these prenumbered stones to the masons. A derrick operator using a hoist may be needed to lift large stone pieces into place.

When building a stone wall, masons set the first course of stones into a shallow bed of mortar. They then align the stones with wedges, plumblines, and levels, and work them into position with a hard rubber mallet. Masons continue to build the wall by alternating layers of mortar and courses of stone. As the work progresses, masons remove the wedges, fill the joints between stones, and use a pointed metal tool, called a tuck pointer, to smooth the mortar to an attractive finish. To hold large stones in place, stonemasons attach brackets to the stone and weld or bolt these brackets to anchors in the wall. Finally, masons wash the stone with a cleansing solution to remove stains and dry mortar.

When setting stone floors, which often consist of large and heavy pieces of stone, masons first use a trowel to spread a layer of damp mortar over the surface to be covered. Using crowbars and hard rubber mallets for aligning and leveling, they then set the stone in the mortar bed. To finish, workers fill the joints and wash the stone slabs.

Masons use a special hammer and chisel to cut stone. They cut stone along the grain to make various shapes and sizes, and valuable pieces often are cut with a saw that has a diamond blade. Some masons specialize in setting marble, which, in many respects, is similar to setting large pieces of stone. Brickmasons and stonemasons also repair imperfections and cracks, and replace broken or missing masonry units in walls and floors.

Most nonresidential buildings now are built with walls made of concrete block, brick veneer, stone, granite, marble, tile, or glass. In the past, masons doing nonresidential interior work mainly built block partition walls and elevator shafts, but because many types of masonry and stone are used in the interiors of today's nonresiden-

tial structures, these workers now must be more versatile. For example, some brickmasons and blockmasons now install structural insulated wall panels and masonry accessories used in many highrise buildings.

Refractory masons are brickmasons who specialize in installing firebrick and refractory tile in high-temperature boilers, furnaces, cupolas, ladles, and soaking pits in industrial establishments. Most of these workers are employed in steel mills, where molten materials flow on refractory beds from furnaces to rolling machines.

Working Conditions

Brickmasons, blockmasons, and stonemasons usually work outdoors and are exposed to the elements. They stand, kneel, and bend for long periods and often have to lift heavy materials. Common hazards include injuries from tools and falls from scaffolds, but these can often be avoided when proper safety equipment is used and safety practices are followed.

Employment

Brickmasons, blockmasons, and stonemasons held 165,000 jobs in 2002. The vast majority were brickmasons. Workers in these crafts are employed primarily by building, specialty trade, or general contractors. Brickmasons, blockmasons, and stonemasons work throughout the country but, like the general population, are concentrated in metropolitan areas.

More than 1 out of 4 brickmasons, blockmasons, and stonemasons are self-employed. Many of the self-employed specialize in contracting to work on small jobs, such as patios, walkways, and fireplaces.

Training, Other Qualifications, and Advancement

Most brickmasons, blockmasons, and stonemasons pick up their skills informally, observing and learning from experienced workers. Many others receive training in vocational education schools or from industry-based programs that are common throughout the country. Another way to learn these skills is through an apprenticeship program, which generally provides the most thorough training.

Individuals who learn the trade on the job usually start as helpers, laborers, or mason tenders. These workers carry materials, move scaffolds, and mix mortar. When the opportunity arises, they learn from experienced craftworkers how to spread mortar, lay brick and block, or set stone. As they gain experience, they make the transition to full-fledged craftworkers. The learning period on the job may last longer than an apprenticeship program. Industry-based training programs offered through companies usually last between 2 and 4 years.

Apprenticeships for brickmasons, blockmasons, and stonemasons usually are sponsored by local contractors, trade associations, or by local union-management committees. The apprenticeship program requires 3 years of on-the-job training, in addition to a minimum 144 hours of classroom instruction each year in subjects such as blueprint reading, mathematics, layout work, and sketching.

Apprentices often start by working with laborers, carrying materials, mixing mortar, and building scaffolds. This period generally lasts about a month and familiarizes the apprentice with job routines and materials. Next, apprentices learn to lay, align, and join brick and block. They also learn to work with stone and concrete, which enables them to be certified to work with more than one masonry material.

Applicants for apprenticeships must be at least 17 years old and in good physical condition. A high school education is preferable; and courses in mathematics, mechanical drawing, and shop are helpful. The Associated Builders and Contractors and International

More than 1 out of 4 brickmasons, blockmasons, and stonemasons are self-employed.

Masonry Institute (IMI), a joint trust of the International Union of Bricklayers and Allied Craftsworkers and the contractors who employ its members, operates training centers in several large cities that help jobseekers develop the skills needed to successfully complete the formal apprenticeship program. In order to attract more entrants, IMI has expanded these centers in recent years to recruit and train workers before they enter apprenticeship programs. In addition, the IMI has a national training and education center at Fort Ritchie, MD. The national center's programs teach basic job skills for brick, stone, tile, terrazzo, refractory, and restoration work, as well as safety and scaffolding training.

Bricklayers who work in nonresidential construction usually work for large contractors and receive well-rounded training—normally through apprenticeship in all phases of brick or stone work. Those who work in residential construction usually work primarily for small contractors and specialize in only one or two aspects of the job.

With additional training, brickmasons, blockmasons, and stonemasons may become supervisors for masonry contractors. Some eventually become owners of businesses employing many workers and may spend most of their time as managers rather than as brickmasons, blockmasons, or stonemasons. Others move into closely related areas such as construction management or building inspection.

Job Outlook

Job opportunities for brickmasons, blockmasons, and stonemasons are expected to be excellent through 2012. Many openings will result from the need to replace workers who retire, transfer to other occupations, or leave these trades for other reasons. There may be fewer applicants than needed because many potential workers prefer to work under less strenuous, more comfortable conditions.

Employment of brickmasons, blockmasons, and stonemasons is expected to increase about as fast as the average for all occupations over the 2002-12 period, as population and business growth create a need for new houses, industrial facilities, schools, hospitals, offices, and other structures. Also stimulating demand will be the need to restore a growing stock of old masonry buildings, as well as the increasing use of brick and stone for decorative work on building fronts and in lobbies and foyers. Brick exteriors should remain very popular, reflecting a growing preference for durable exterior materials requiring little maintenance.

Employment of brickmasons, blockmasons, and stonemasons, like that of many other construction workers, is sensitive to changes in the economy. When the level of construction activity falls, workers in these trades can experience periods of unemployment.

Earnings

Median hourly earnings of brickmasons and blockmasons in 2002 were $20.11. The middle 50 percent earned between $15.36 and $25.32. The lowest 10 percent earned less than $11.55, and the highest 10 percent earned more than $30.66. Median hourly earnings in the industries employing the largest number of brickmasons in 2002 are shown below:

Nonresidential building construction	$22.12
Foundation, structure, and building exterior contractors	20.26

Median hourly earnings of stonemasons in 2002 were $16.36. The middle 50 percent earned between $12.06 and $20.76. The lowest 10 percent earned less than $9.43, and the highest 10 percent earned more than $26.59.

Earnings for workers in these trades can be reduced on occasion because poor weather and downturns in construction activity limit the time they can work. Apprentices or helpers usually start at about 50 percent of the wage rate paid to experienced workers. Pay increases as apprentices gain experience and learn new skills.

Some brickmasons, blockmasons, and stonemasons are members of the International Union of Bricklayers and Allied Craftsworkers.

Related Occupations

Brickmasons, blockmasons, and stonemasons combine a thorough knowledge of brick, concrete block, stone, and marble with manual skill to erect attractive, yet highly durable, structures. Workers in other occupations with similar skills include carpet, floor, and tile installers and finishers; cement masons, concrete finishers, segmental pavers, and terrazzo workers; and plasterers and stucco masons.

Sources of Additional Information

For details about apprenticeships or other work opportunities in these trades, contact local bricklaying, stonemasonry, or marble-setting contractors; the Associated Builders and Contractors; a local of the International Union of Bricklayers and Allied Craftsworkers; a local joint union-management apprenticeship committee; or the nearest office of the State employment service or apprenticeship agency.

For general information about the work of brickmasons, blockmasons, or stonemasons, contact:

➤ International Union of Bricklayers and Allied Craftworkers, 1776 I St. NW., Washington, DC. 20006.

For information on training for brickmasons, blockmasons, and stonemasons, contact:

➤ Associated Builders and Contractors, Workforce Development Department, 4250 North Fairfax Dr., 9th Floor, Arlington, VA 22203.

➤ International Masonry Institute, Apprenticeship and Training, The James Brice House, 42 East St., Annapolis, MD 21401. Internet: **http://www.imiweb.org**

Information about the work of bricklayers also can be obtained from:

➤ Associated General Contractors of America, Inc., 333 John Carlyle St., Alexandria, VA 22314. Internet: **http://www.agc.org**

➤ Brick Industry Association, 11490 Commerce Park Dr., Reston, VA 22091-1525. Internet: **http://www.brickinfo.org**

➤ National Association of Home Builders, 1201 15th St. NW., Washington, DC 20005. Internet: **http://www.nahb.org**

➤ Home Builders Institute, 1201 15th St. NW., Washington, DC 20005. Internet **http://www.hbi.org**

➤ National Concrete Masonry Association, 13750 Sunrise Valley Dr., Herndon, VA 20171-3499. Internet: **http://www.ncma.org**

There are more than 500 occupations registered by the U.S. Department of Labor's National Apprenticeship system. For more information on the Labor Department's registered apprenticeship system and links to State apprenticeship programs, check their website: **http://www.doleta.gov**

Carpenters

(O*NET 47-2031.01, 47-2031.02, 47-2031.03, 47-2031.04, 47-2031.05, 47-2031.06)

Significant Points

● About 30 percent of all carpenters—the largest construction trade in 2002—were self-employed.

● Job opportunities should be excellent.

● Carpenters with all-round skills will have the best opportunities for steady work.

Nature of the Work

Carpenters are involved in many different kinds of construction activity. They cut, fit, and assemble wood and other materials for the construction of buildings, highways, bridges, docks, industrial plants, boats, and many other structures. Carpenters' duties vary by type of employer. Builders increasingly are using specialty trade contractors who, in turn, hire carpenters who specialize in just one or two activities. Such activities include setting forms for concrete construction; erecting scaffolding; or doing finishing work, such as installing interior and exterior trim. However, a carpenter directly employed by a general building contractor often must perform a variety of the tasks associated with new construction, such as framing walls and partitions, putting in doors and windows, building stairs, laying hardwood floors, and hanging kitchen cabinets. Carpenters also build brattices (ventilation walls or partitions) in underground passageways to control the proper circulation of air through these passageways and to worksites.

Because local building codes often dictate where certain materials can be used, carpenters must know these regulations. Each carpentry task is somewhat different, but most involve the same basic steps. Working from blueprints or instructions from supervisors, carpenters first do the layout—measuring, marking, and arranging materials. They cut and shape wood, plastic, fiberglass, or drywall, using hand and power tools, such as chisels, planes, saws, drills, and sanders. They then join the materials with nails, screws, staples, or adhesives. In the final step, carpenters check the accuracy of their work with levels, rules, plumb bobs, and framing squares, and make any necessary adjustments. When working with prefabricated components, such as stairs or wall panels, the carpenter's task is somewhat simpler than above, because it does not require as much layout work or the cutting and assembly of as many pieces. Prefabricated components are designed for easy and fast installation and generally can be installed in a single operation.

Carpenters who remodel homes and other structures must be able to do all aspects of a job—not just one task. Thus, individuals with good basic overall training are at a distinct advantage, because they can switch from residential building to commercial construction or remodeling work, depending on which offers the best work opportunities.

Carpenters employed outside the construction industry perform a variety of installation and maintenance work. They may replace panes of glass, ceiling tiles, and doors, as well as repair desks, cabinets, and other furniture. Depending on the employer, carpenters install partitions, doors, and windows; change locks; and repair broken furniture. In manufacturing firms, carpenters may assist in moving or installing machinery. (For more information on workers who install machinery, see the discussion of millwrights as well as industrial machinery installation, repair, and maintenance workers, except millwrights, elsewhere in the *Handbook*.)

Working Conditions

As is true of other building trades, carpentry work is sometimes strenuous. Prolonged standing, climbing, bending, and kneeling often are necessary. Carpenters risk injury working with sharp or rough materials, using sharp tools and power equipment, and working in situations where they might slip or fall. Additionally, many carpenters work outdoors.

Some carpenters change employers each time they finish a construction job. Others alternate between working for a contractor and working as contractors themselves on small jobs.

Employment

Carpenters, who make up the largest building trades occupation, held about 1.2 million jobs in 2002. One-third worked for general building contractors and one-fifth worked for special trade contractors. Most of the rest of the wage and salary workers worked for manufacturing firms, government agencies, retail establishments and a wide variety of other industries. About 30 percent of all carpenters were self-employed.

Carpenters are employed throughout the country in almost every community.

Training, Other Qualifications, and Advancement

Carpenters learn their trade through on-the-job training, as well as formal training programs. Most pick up skills informally by working under the supervision of experienced workers. Many acquire skills through vocational education. Others participate in employer training programs or apprenticeships.

Most employers recommend an apprenticeship as the best way to learn carpentry. Apprenticeship programs are administered by local joint union-management committees of the United Brotherhood of Carpenters and Joiners of America, the Associated General Contractors, Inc., and the National Association of Home Builders. In addition, training programs are administered by local chapters of the Associated Builders and Contractors and by local chapters of the Associated General Contractors, Inc. These programs combine on-the-job training with related classroom instruction.

On the job, apprentices learn elementary structural design and become familiar with common carpentry jobs, such as layout, form building, rough framing, and outside and inside finishing. They also learn to use the tools, machines, equipment, and materials of the trade. Apprentices receive classroom instruction in safety, first aid, blueprint reading, freehand sketching, basic mathematics, and different carpentry techniques. Both in the classroom and on the job, they learn the relationship between carpentry and the other building trades.

Usually, apprenticeship applicants must be at least 18 years old and meet local requirements. For example, some union locals test an applicant's aptitude for carpentry. The length of the program, usually 3 to 4 years, varies with the apprentice's skill. Because the number of apprenticeship programs is limited, however, only a small proportion of carpenters learn their trade through these programs.

Informal on-the-job training is normally less thorough than an apprenticeship. The degree of training and supervision often depends on the size of the employing firm. A small contractor specializing in homebuilding may provide training only in rough

Carpenters employed outside the construction industry perform a variety of installation and maintenance work.

framing. In contrast, a large general contractor may provide training in several carpentry skills. Although specialization is becoming increasingly common, it is important to try to acquire skills in all aspects of carpentry and to have the flexibility to perform any kind of work.

A high school education is desirable, including courses in carpentry, shop, mechanical drawing, and general mathematics. Manual dexterity, eye-hand coordination, physical fitness, and a good sense of balance are important. The ability to solve arithmetic problems quickly and accurately also is helpful. Employers and apprenticeship committees generally view favorably any construction-related training and work experience obtained in the Armed Services or Job Corps.

Carpenters may advance to carpentry supervisor or general construction supervisor positions. Carpenters usually have greater opportunities than most other construction workers to become general construction supervisors, because carpenters are exposed to the entire construction process. Some carpenters become independent contractors. To advance, these workers should be able to identify and estimate the quantity of materials needed to properly complete a job. In addition, they must be able to accurately estimate how long a job should take to complete and what it will cost.

Job Outlook

Job opportunities for carpenters are expected to be excellent over the 2002-12 period, largely due to the numerous openings arising each year as experienced carpenters leave this large occupation. Contributing to this favorable job market is the fact that many potential workers prefer work that is less strenuous and that has more comfortable working conditions. Because there are no strict training requirements for entry, many people with limited skills take jobs as carpenters but eventually leave the occupation because they dislike the work or cannot find steady employment.

Employment of carpenters is expected to increase about as fast as average for all occupations through 2012. Construction activity should increase in response to demand for new housing and commercial and industrial plants and the need to renovate and modernize existing structures. The demand for larger homes with more amenities and for second homes will continue to rise, especially as the baby boomers reach their peak earning years and can afford to spend more on housing. At the same time, the demand for manufactured housing, starter homes, and rental apartments also is expected to increase as the number of immigrants grows and as the relatively small baby bust generation, which followed the baby boom generation, is replaced by echo boomers (the children of the baby boomers) in the young adult age groups.

However, some of the demand for carpenters will be offset by expected productivity gains resulting from the increasing use of prefabricated components, such as prehung doors and windows and prefabricated wall panels and stairs, which can be installed very quickly. Prefabricated walls, partitions, and stairs are lifted into place in one operation; beams—and, in some cases, entire roof assemblies—are lifted into place using a crane. As prefabricated components become more standardized, builders will use them more often. In addition, improved adhesives will reduce the time needed to join materials, and lightweight, cordless, and pneumatic tools—such as nailers and drills—all make carpenters more efficient.

Carpenters can experience periods of unemployment because of the short-term nature of many construction projects and the cyclical nature of the construction industry. Building activity depends on many factors—interest rates, availability of mortgage funds, the season, government spending, and business investment—that vary with the state of the economy. During economic downturns, the number of job openings for carpenters declines. New and improved tools, equipment, techniques, and materials have vastly increased carpenter versatility. Therefore, carpenters with all-round skills will have better opportunities for steady work than carpenters who can do only a few relatively simple, routine tasks.

Job opportunities for carpenters also vary by geographic area. Construction activity parallels the movement of people and businesses and reflects differences in local economic conditions. Therefore, the number of job opportunities and apprenticeship opportunities in a given year may vary widely from area to area.

Earnings

In 2002, median hourly earnings of carpenters were $16.44. The middle 50 percent earned between $12.59 and $21.91. The lowest 10 percent earned less than $9.95, and the highest 10 percent earned more than $27.97. Median hourly earnings in the industries employing the largest numbers of carpenters in 2002 are shown below:

Nonresidential building construction	$18.31
Building finishing contractors	17.30
Residential building construction	16.02
Foundation, structure, and building exterior contractors	16.01
Employment services	12.58

Earnings can be reduced on occasion, because carpenters lose worktime in bad weather and during recessions when jobs are unavailable.

Some carpenters are members of the United Brotherhood of Carpenters and Joiners of America.

Related Occupations

Carpenters are skilled construction workers. Other skilled construction occupations include brickmasons, blockmasons, and stonemasons; cement masons, concrete finishers, segmental pavers, and terrazzo workers; electricians; pipelayers, plumbers, pipefitters, and steamfitters; and plasterers and stucco masons.

Sources of Additional Information

For information about carpentry apprenticeships or other work opportunities in this trade, contact local carpentry contractors, locals of the union mentioned above, local joint union-contractor apprenticeship committees, or the nearest office of the State employment service or apprenticeship agency.

For information on training opportunities and carpentry in general, contact:

➤ Associated Builders and Contractors, Workforce Development Department, 4250 North Fairfax Dr., 9th Floor, Arlington, VA 22203.

➤ Associated General Contractors of America, Inc., 333 John Carlyle St., Suite 200, Alexandria VA, 22314. Internet: http://www.agc.org

➤ Home Builders Institute, 1201 15th St. NW., Washington, DC 20005. Internet: http://www.hbi.org

➤ National Association of Home Builders, 1201 15th St. NW., Washington, DC 20005. Internet: http://www.nahb.org

➤ United Brotherhood of Carpenters and Joiners of America, 50 F St. NW., Washington, DC 20001. Internet: http://www.carpenters.org

There are more than 500 occupations registered by the U.S. Department of Labor's National Apprenticeship system. For more information on the Labor Department's registered apprenticeship system and links to State apprenticeship programs, check the Web site: http://www.doleta.gov

Carpet, Floor, and Tile Installers and Finishers

(O*NET 47-2041.00, 47-2042.00, 47-2043.00, 47-2044.00)

Significant Points

- Forty-three percent of all carpet, floor, and tile installers and finishers are self-employed, compared with 19 percent of all construction trades workers.

- Most workers learn on the job.

- Carpet installers, the largest specialty, should have the best job opportunities.

- The employment of carpet, floor, and tile installers and finishers is less sensitive to fluctuations in construction activity than that of other construction trades workers.

Nature of the Work

Carpet, tile, and other types of floor coverings not only serve an important basic function in buildings, but their decorative qualities also contribute to the appeal of the buildings. Carpet, floor, and tile installers and finishers lay these floor coverings in homes, offices, hospitals, stores, restaurants, and many other types of buildings. Tile also is installed on walls and ceilings.

Before installing carpet, *carpet installers* first inspect the surface to be covered to determine its condition and, if necessary, correct any imperfections that could show through the carpet or cause the carpet to wear unevenly. They must measure the area to be carpeted and plan the layout, keeping in mind expected traffic patterns and placement of seams for best appearance and maximum wear.

When installing wall-to-wall carpet without tacks, installers first fasten a tackless strip to the floor, next to the wall. They then install the padded cushion or underlay. Next, they roll out, measure, mark, and cut the carpet, allowing for 2 to 3 inches of extra carpet for the final fitting. Using a device called a "knee kicker," they position the carpet, stretching it to fit evenly on the floor and snugly against each wall and door threshold. They then cut off the excess carpet. Finally, using a power stretcher, they stretch the carpet, hooking it to the tackless strip to hold it in place. The installers then finish the edges using a wall trimmer.

Because most carpet comes in 12-foot widths, wall-to-wall installations require installers to join carpet sections together for large rooms. The installers join the sections using heat-taped seams—seams held together by a special plastic tape that is activated by heat.

On special upholstery work, such as stairs, carpet may be held in place with staples. Also, in commercial installations, carpet often is glued directly to the floor or to padding that has been glued to the floor.

Carpet installers use handtools such as hammers, drills, staple guns, carpet knives, and rubber mallets. They also may use carpetlaying tools, such as carpet shears, knee kickers, wall trimmers, loop pile cutters, heat irons, and power stretchers.

Floor installers, or *floor layers*, apply blocks, strips, or sheets of shock-absorbing, sound-deadening, or decorative coverings to floors and cabinets using rollers, knives, trowels, sanding machines, and other tools. Some floor covering materials are designed to be purely decorative. Others have more specialized purposes, such as to deaden sound, to absorb shocks, or to create air-tight environments. Before installing the floor, floor layers inspect the surface to be covered and, if necessary, correct any imperfections in order to start with a smooth, clean foundation. They measure and cut floor covering materials, such as rubber, vinyl, linoleum, or cork, and any foundation material, such as felt, according to designated blueprints. Next, they may nail or staple a wood underlayment to the surface or may use an adhesive to cement the foundation material to the floor; the foundation helps to deaden sound and prevents the top floor covering from wearing at board joints. Finally, floor layers install the top covering. They join sections of sheet covering by overlapping adjoining edges and cutting through both layers with a knife to form a tight joint.

Floor sanders and finishers scrape and sand wooden floors to smooth surfaces using floor-sanding machines. They then inspect the floor for smoothness and remove excess glue from joints using a knife or wood chisel and may sand wood surfaces by hand, using sandpaper. Finally, they apply coats of finish.

Tile installers, *tilesetters*, and *marble setters* apply hard tile and marble to floors, walls, ceilings, and roof decks. Tile is durable, impervious to water, and easy to clean, making it a popular building material in hospitals, tunnels, lobbies of buildings, bathrooms, and kitchens.

Prior to installation, tilesetters use measuring devices and levels to ensure that the tile is placed in a consistent manner. To set tile, which generally ranges in size from 1 inch to 12 or more inches square, tilesetters use cement or "mastic," a very sticky paste. When using cement, tilesetters nail a support of metal mesh to the wall or ceiling to be tiled. They use a trowel to apply a cement mortar—called a "scratch coat"—onto the metal screen, and scratch the surface of the soft mortar with a small tool similar to a rake. After the scratch coat has dried, tilesetters apply another coat of mortar to level the surface, and then apply mortar to the back of the tile and place it onto the surface.

To set tile in mastic or a cement adhesive, called "thin set," tilesetters need a flat, solid surface such as drywall, concrete, plaster, or wood. They use a tooth-edged trowel to spread mastic on the surface or apply cement adhesive, and then properly position the tile.

Because tile varies in color, shape, and size, workers sometimes prearrange tiles on a dry floor according to a specified design. This allows workers to examine the pattern and make changes. In order to cover all exposed areas, including corners and around pipes, tubs, and wash basins, tilesetters cut tiles to fit with a machine saw or a special cutting tool. Once the tile is placed, they gently tap the

Prior to installing tile, tilesetters use measuring devices and levels to ensure that the tile is placed in a consistent manner.

surface with their trowel handle or a small block of wood to seat the tile evenly.

When the cement or mastic has set, tilesetters fill the joints with "grout," which is very fine cement. They then scrape the surface with a rubber-edged device called a grout float or a grouting trowel to dress the joints and remove excess grout. Before the grout sets, they finish the joints with a damp sponge for a uniform appearance. Marble setters cut and set marble slabs in floors and walls of buildings. They trim and cut marble to specified size using a power wet saw, other cutting equipment, or handtools. After setting the marble in place, they polish the marble to high luster using power tools or by hand.

Working Conditions

Carpet, floor, and tile installers and finishers generally work indoors and have regular daytime hours. However, when floor covering installers work in occupied stores or offices, they may work evenings and weekends to avoid disturbing customers or employees. Installers and finishers usually work under better conditions than do most other construction workers. By the time workers install carpets, flooring, or tile in a new structure, most construction has been completed and the work area is relatively clean and uncluttered. Installing these materials is labor intensive; workers spend much of their time bending, kneeling, and reaching—activities that require endurance. Carpet installers frequently lift heavy rolls of carpet and may move heavy furniture. Safety regulations may require that they wear kneepads or safety goggles when using certain tools. Carpet and floor layers may be exposed to fumes from various kinds of glue and to fibers of certain types of carpet.

Although workers are subject to cuts from tools or materials, falls from ladders, and strained muscles, the occupation is not as hazardous as some other construction occupations.

Employment

Carpet, floor, and tile installers and finishers held about 164,000 jobs in 2002. Forty-three percent of all carpet, floor, and tile installers and finishers were self-employed, compared with 19 percent of all construction trades workers. The following tabulation shows 2002 wage and salary employment by specialty:

Carpet installers	82,000
Tile and marble setters	33,000
Floor layers, except carpet, wood, and hard tiles	31,000
Floor sanders and finishers	17,000

Many carpet installers worked for flooring contractors or floor covering retailers. Most salaried tilesetters were employed by tilesetting contractors who work mainly on nonresidential construction projects, such as schools, hospitals, and office buildings. Most self-employed tilesetters work on residential projects.

Although carpet, floor, and tile installers and finishers are employed throughout the Nation, they tend to be concentrated in populated areas where there are high levels of construction activity.

Training, Other Qualifications, and Advancement

The vast majority of carpet, floor, and tile installers and finishers learn their trade informally, on the job, as helpers to experienced workers. Others learn through formal apprenticeship programs, which include on-the-job training as well as related classroom instruction.

Informal training for carpet installers often is sponsored by individual contractors. Workers start as helpers, and begin with simple assignments, such as installing stripping and padding, or helping to stretch newly installed carpet. With experience, helpers take on more difficult assignments, such as measuring, cutting, and fitting.

Persons who wish to begin a career in carpet installation as a helper or apprentice should be at least 18 years old and have good manual dexterity. Many employers prefer applicants with a high school diploma; courses in general mathematics and shop are helpful. Some employers may require a driver's license and a criminal background check. Because carpet installers frequently deal directly with customers, they should be courteous and tactful.

Many tile and floor layers learn their job through on-the-job training and begin by learning about the tools of the trade. They next learn to prepare surfaces to receive flooring. As they progress, tilesetters, marble setters, and floor layers learn to cut and install tile, marble, and floor coverings. Tile and marble setters also learn to apply grout and to do finishing work.

Apprenticeship programs and some contractor-sponsored programs provide comprehensive training in all phases of the tilesetting and floor layer trades. Most apprenticeship programs are union-sponsored and consist of weekly classes and on-the-job training usually lasting 3 to 4 years.

When hiring apprentices or helpers for floor layer and tilesetter jobs, employers usually prefer high school graduates who have had courses in general mathematics, mechanical drawing, and shop. Good physical condition, manual dexterity, and a good sense of color harmony also are important assets.

Carpet, floor, and tile installers and finishers may advance to positions as supervisors or become salespersons or estimators. Some carpet installers may become managers for large installation firms. Many carpet, floor, and tile installers and finishers who begin working for a large contractor eventually go into business for themselves as independent subcontractors.

Job Outlook

Employment of carpet, floor, and tile installers and finishers is expected to grow about as fast as the average for all occupations through the year 2012, reflecting the continued need to renovate and refurbish existing structures. However, employment of one specialty— floor sanders and finishers—is projected to grow more slowly than average due to the increasing use of prefinished hardwood and similar flooring. Carpet installers, the largest specialty, should have the best job opportunities.

Carpet as a floor covering continues to be popular and its use is expected to grow in structures such as schools, offices, hospitals, and industrial plants. Employment of carpet installers also is expected to grow because wall-to-wall carpeting is a necessity in the many houses built with plywood, rather than hardwood, floors. Similarly, offices, hotels, and stores often cover concrete floors with wall-to-wall carpet, which must be periodically replaced.

Demand for tile and marble setters will stem from population and business growth, which should result in more construction of shopping malls, hospitals, schools, restaurants, and other structures in which tile is used extensively. Tile is expected to continue to increase in popularity as a building material and to be used more extensively, particularly in the growing number of more expensive homes, leading to faster than average growth for tile and marble setters. Demand for floor layers and sanders and finishers will expand as a result of growth in construction activity, particularly that related to residential homes and commercial buildings, and as some people decide to replace their plywood floors with hardwood floors. Job opportunities for tile and marble setters and for floor layers and sanders, relatively small specialties, will not be as plentiful as those for carpet installers.

The employment of carpet, floor, and tile installers and finishers is less sensitive to changes in construction activity than is that of most other construction occupations because much of the work involves replacing carpet and other flooring in existing buildings. As a result, these workers tend to be sheltered from the business fluctuations that often occur in new construction activity.

Earnings

In 2002, the median hourly earnings of carpet installers were $15.67. The middle 50 percent earned between $11.39 and $21.03. The lowest 10 percent earned less than $8.90, and the top 10 percent earned more than $27.15. In 2002, median hourly earnings of carpet installers working for building finishing contractors were $16.09, and in home furnishings stores, $14.64.

Carpet installers are paid either on an hourly basis, or by the number of yards of carpet installed. The rates vary widely depending on the geographic location and whether the installer is affiliated with a union.

Median hourly earnings of floor layers were $16.15 in 2002. The middle 50 percent earned between $11.42 and $20.81. The lowest 10 percent earned less than $8.58, and the top 10 percent earned more than $26.87.

Median hourly earnings of floor sanders and finishers were $13.22 in 2002. The middle 50 percent earned between $10.38 and $16.97. The lowest 10 percent earned less than $8.96, and the top 10 percent earned more than $22.51.

Median hourly earnings of tile and marble setters were $17.20 in 2002. The middle 50 percent earned between $12.96 and $22.39. The lowest 10 percent earned less than $10.21, and the top 10 percent earned more than $28.22. Earnings of tile and marble setters also vary greatly by geographic location and by union membership status.

Apprentices and other trainees usually start out earning about half of what an experienced worker earns, although their wage rate increases as they advance through the training program.

Some carpet, floor, and tile installers and finishers belong to the United Brotherhood of Carpenters and Joiners of America. Some tilesetters belong to the International Union of Bricklayers and Allied Craftsmen, while some carpet installers belong to the International Brotherhood of Painters and Allied Trades.

Related Occupations

Carpet, floor, and tile installers and finishers measure, cut, and fit materials to cover a space. Workers in other occupations involving similar skills, but using different materials, include brickmasons, blockmasons, and stonemasons; carpenters; cement masons, concrete finishers, segmental pavers, and terrazzo workers; drywall installers, ceiling tile installers, and tapers; painters and paperhangers; roofers; and sheet metal workers.

Sources of Additional Information

For details about apprenticeships or work opportunities, contact local flooring or tilesetting contractors or retailers, locals of the unions previously mentioned, or the nearest office of the State apprenticeship agency or employment service.

For general information about the work of carpet installers and floor layers, contact:

➤ Floor Covering Installation Contractors Association, 7439 Milwood Dr., West Bloomfield, MI 48322.

Additional information on training for carpet installers and floor layers is available from:

➤ International Union of Painters and Allied Trades, 1750 New York Ave. NW., Washington, DC 20006. Internet: **http://www.iupat.org**

For general information about the work of tile installers and finishers, contact:

➤ International Union of Bricklayers and Allied Craftworkers, 1776 I St. NW., Washington, DC. 20006.

➤ International Masonry Institute, James Brice House, 42 East St. Annapolis, MD 21401. Internet: **http://www.imiweb.org**

➤ Home Builders Institute, 1201 15th St. NW., Washington, DC 20005. Internet: **http://www.hbi.org**

➤ National Association of Home Builders, 1201 15th St. NW., Washington, DC 20005. Internet: **http://www.nahb.org**

For more information about tile setting and tile training, contact:

➤ National Tile Contractors Association, P.O. Box 13629, Jackson MS 39236.

For information concerning training of carpet, floor, and tile installers and finishers, contact:

➤ United Brotherhood of Carpenters and Joiners of America, 50 F St. NW., Washington, DC 20001. Internet: **http://www.carpenters.org**

There are more than 500 occupations registered by the U.S. Department of Labor's National Apprenticeship system. For more information on the Labor Department's registered apprenticeship system and links to State apprenticeship programs, check the Internet site: **http://www.doleta.gov**.

Cement Masons, Concrete Finishers, Segmental Pavers, and Terrazzo Workers

(0*NET 47-2051.00, 47-2053.00, 47-4091.00)

Significant Points

● Job opportunities are expected to be favorable.

● Most learn on the job, either through formal 3-year or 4-year apprenticeship programs or by working as helpers.

● Like many other construction trades, these workers may experience reduced earnings and layoffs during downturns in construction activity.

● Cement masons often work overtime, with premium pay, because once concrete has been placed, the job must be completed.

Nature of the Work

Cement masons, concrete finishers, and terrazzo workers all work with concrete, one of the most common and durable materials used in construction. Once set, concrete—a mixture of Portland cement, sand, gravel, and water—becomes the foundation for everything from decorative patios and floors to huge dams or miles of roadways.

Cement masons and *concrete finishers* place and finish the concrete. They also may color concrete surfaces; expose aggregate (small stones) in walls and sidewalks; or fabricate concrete beams, columns, and panels. In preparing a site for placing concrete, cement masons first set the forms for holding the concrete and properly align them. They then direct the casting of the concrete and supervise laborers who use shovels or special tools to spread it. Masons then guide a straightedge back and forth across the top of the forms to "screed," or level, the freshly placed concrete. Immediately after leveling the concrete, masons carefully smooth the concrete surface with a "bull float," a long-handled tool about 8 by 48 inches that covers the coarser materials in the concrete and brings a rich mixture of fine cement paste to the surface.

After the concrete has been leveled and floated, concrete finishers press an edger between the forms and the concrete and guide it along the edge and the surface. This produces slightly rounded edges and helps prevent chipping or cracking. Concrete finishers use a special tool called a "groover" to make joints or grooves at specific intervals that help control cracking. Next, they trowel the surface using either a powered or hand trowel, a small, smooth, rectangular metal tool.

Sometimes, cement masons perform all the steps of laying concrete, including the finishing. As the final step, they retrowel the concrete surface back and forth with powered and hand trowels to create a smooth finish. For a coarse, nonskid finish, masons brush the surface with a broom or stiff-bristled brush. For a pebble finish, they embed small gravel chips into the surface. They then wash any excess cement from the exposed chips with a mild acid solution. For color, they use colored premixed concrete. On concrete surfaces that will remain exposed after the forms are stripped, such as columns, ceilings, and wall panels, cement masons cut away high spots and loose concrete with hammer and chisel, fill any large indentations with a Portland cement paste, and smooth the surface with a carborundum stone. Finally, they coat the exposed area with a rich Portland cement mixture, using either a special tool or a coarse cloth to rub the concrete to a uniform finish.

Throughout the entire process, cement masons must monitor how the wind, heat, or cold affects the curing of the concrete. They must have a thorough knowledge of concrete characteristics so that, by using sight and touch, they can determine what is happening to the concrete and take measures to prevent defects.

Segmental pavers lay out, cut, and install pavers, which are flat pieces of masonry usually made from compacted concrete or brick. Pavers are used to pave paths, patios, playgrounds, driveways, and steps. They are manufactured in various textures and often interlock together to form an attractive pattern. Segmental pavers first prepare the site by removing the existing pavement or soil. They grade the remaining soil to the proper depth and determine the amount of base material that is needed, which depends on the local soil conditions. They then install and compact the base material, a granular material that compacts easily, and lay the pavers from the center out, so that any trimmed pieces will be on the outside rather than in the center. Then, they install edging materials to prevent the pavers from shifting and fill the spaces between the pavers with dry sand.

Terrazzo workers create attractive walkways, floors, patios, and panels by exposing marble chips and other fine aggregates on the surface of finished concrete. Much of the preliminary work of terrazzo workers is similar to that of cement masons. Attractive, marble-chip terrazzo requires three layers of materials. First, cement masons or terrazzo workers build a solid, level concrete foundation that is 3 to 4 inches deep. After the forms are removed from the foundation, workers add a 1-inch layer of sandy concrete. Before this layer sets, terrazzo workers partially embed metal divider strips in the concrete wherever there is to be a joint or change of color in the terrazzo. For the final layer, terrazzo workers blend and place into each of the panels a fine marble chip mixture that may be color-pigmented. While the mixture is still wet, workers toss additional marble chips of various colors into each panel and roll a lightweight roller over the entire surface.

When the terrazzo is thoroughly dry, helpers grind it with a terrazzo grinder, which is somewhat like a floor polisher, only much heavier. Slight depressions left by the grinding are filled with a matching grout material and hand-troweled for a smooth, uniform

Sometimes, cement masons perform all the steps of laying concrete, including the finishing.

surface. Terrazzo workers then clean, polish, and seal the dry surface for a lustrous finish.

Working Conditions

Concrete, segmental paving, or terrazzo work is fast-paced and strenuous, and requires continuous physical effort. Because most finishing is done at floor level, workers must bend and kneel often. Many jobs are outdoors, and work is generally halted during inclement weather. The work, either indoors or outdoors, may be in areas that are muddy, dusty, or dirty. To avoid chemical burns from uncured concrete and sore knees from frequent kneeling, many workers wear kneepads. Workers usually also wear water-repellent boots while working in wet concrete.

Employment

Cement masons, concrete finishers, segmental pavers, and terrazzo workers held about 190,000 jobs in 2002; segmental pavers and terrazzo workers accounted for only a small portion of the total. Most cement masons and concrete finishers worked for concrete contractors or for general contractors on projects such as highways; bridges; shopping malls; or large buildings such as factories, schools, and hospitals. A small number were employed by firms that manufacture concrete products. Most segmental pavers and terrazzo workers worked for special trade contractors who install decorative floors and wall panels.

Only about 1 out of 20 cement masons, concrete finishers, segmental pavers, and terrazzo workers were self-employed, a smaller proportion than in other building trades. Most self-employed masons specialized in small jobs, such as driveways, sidewalks, and patios.

Training, Other Qualifications, and Advancement

Most cement masons, concrete finishers, segmental pavers, and terrazzo workers learn their trades either through on-the-job training as helpers, or through 3-year or 4-year apprenticeship programs. Many masons and finishers first gain experience as construction laborers. (See the statement on construction laborers elsewhere in the *Handbook*.)

When hiring helpers and apprentices, employers prefer high school graduates who are at least 18 years old and in good physical condition, and who have a driver's license. The ability to get along with others also is important because cement masons frequently work in teams. High school courses in general science, vocational-technical subjects, mathematics, blueprint reading, or mechanical drawing provide a helpful background.

On-the-job training programs consist of informal instruction, in which experienced workers teach helpers to use the tools, equipment, machines, and materials of the trade. Trainees begin with tasks such as edging, jointing, and using a straightedge on freshly placed concrete. As training progresses, assignments become more complex, and trainees can usually do finishing work within a short time.

Three-year or four-year apprenticeship programs, usually jointly sponsored by local unions and contractors, provide on-the-job training in addition to a recommended minimum of 144 hours of classroom instruction each year. A written test and a physical exam may be required. In the classroom, apprentices learn applied mathematics, blueprint reading, and safety. Apprentices generally receive special instruction in layout work and cost estimation. Some workers learn their jobs by attending trade or vocational-technical schools.

Cement masons, concrete finishers, segmental pavers, and terrazzo workers should enjoy doing demanding work. They should take pride in craftsmanship and be able to work without close supervision.

With additional training, cement masons, concrete finishers, segmental pavers, or terrazzo workers may become supervisors for masonry contractors. Some eventually become owners of businesses employing many workers and may spend most of their time as managers rather than practicing their original trade. Others move into closely related areas such as construction management, building inspection, or contract estimation.

Job Outlook

Opportunities for cement masons, concrete finishers, segmental pavers, and terrazzo workers are expected to be favorable as the demand meets the supply of workers trained in this craft. In addition, many potential workers may prefer work that is less strenuous and has more comfortable working conditions.

Employment of cement masons, concrete finishers, segmental pavers, and terrazzo workers is expected to grow faster than the average for all occupations through 2012. These workers will be needed to build highways, bridges, subways, factories, office buildings, hotels, shopping centers, schools, hospitals, and other structures. In addition, the increasing use of concrete as a building material will add to the demand. More cement masons also will be needed to repair and renovate existing highways, bridges, and other structures. In addition to job growth, other openings will become available as experienced workers transfer to other occupations or leave the labor force.

Employment of cement masons, concrete finishers, segmental pavers, and terrazzo workers, like that of many other construction workers, is sensitive to the fluctuations of the economy. Workers in these trades may experience periods of unemployment when the overall level of construction falls. On the other hand, shortages of these workers may occur in some areas during peak periods of building activity.

Earnings

In 2002, the median hourly earnings of cement masons and concrete finishers were $14.74. The middle 50 percent earned between $11.52 and $20.02. The top 10 percent earned over $26.02, and the bottom 10 percent earned less than $9.31. Median hourly earnings in the industries employing the largest numbers of cement masons and concrete finishers in 2002 are shown below:

Nonresidential building construction	$16.24
Highway, street, and bridge construction	15.37
Other specialty trade contractors	15.19
Foundation, structure, and building exterior contractors	14.52
Residential building construction	14.44

In 2002, the median hourly earnings of terrazzo workers and finishers were $13.42. The middle 50 percent earned between $10.46 and $17.72. The top 10 percent earned over $23.70, and the bottom 10 percent earned less than $8.94.

Like those of other construction trades workers, earnings of cement masons, concrete finishers, segmental pavers, and terrazzo workers may be reduced on occasion because poor weather and downturns in construction activity limit the amount of time they can work. Cement masons often work overtime, with premium pay, because once concrete has been placed, the job must be completed.

Many cement masons, concrete finishers, segmental pavers, and terrazzo workers belong to the Operative Plasterers' and Cement Masons' International Association of the United States and Canada, or to the International Union of Bricklayers and Allied Craftworkers. Some terrazzo workers belong to the United Brotherhood of Carpenters and Joiners of the United States. Nonunion workers generally have lower wage rates than do union workers. Apprentices usually start at 50 to 60 percent of the rate paid to experienced workers.

Related Occupations

Cement masons, concrete finishers, segmental pavers, and terrazzo workers combine skill with knowledge of building materials to construct buildings, highways, and other structures. Other occupations involving similar skills and knowledge include brickmasons, blockmasons, and stonemasons; carpet, floor, and tile installers and finishers; drywall installers, ceiling tile installers, and tapers; and plasterers and stucco masons.

Sources of Additional Information

For information about apprenticeships and work opportunities, contact local concrete or terrazzo contractors, locals of unions previously mentioned, a local joint union-management apprenticeship committee, or the nearest office of the State employment service or apprenticeship agency.

For general information about cement masons, concrete finishers, segmental pavers, and terrazzo workers, contact:

➤ Associated Builders and Contractors, Workforce Development Department, 4250 North Fairfax Dr., 9th Floor, Arlington, VA 22203.

➤ Associated General Contractors of America, Inc., 333 John Carlyle St., Alexandria, VA 22314. Internet: **http://www.agc.org**

➤ International Union of Bricklayers and Allied Craftworkers, International Masonry Institute, The James Brice House, 42 East St., Annapolis, MD 21401. Internet: **http://www.imiweb.org**

➤ Operative Plasterers' and Cement Masons' International Association of the United States and Canada, 14405 Laurel Place, Suite 300, Laurel, MD 20707. Internet: **http://www.opcmia.org**

➤ National Terrazzo and Mosaic Association, 110 E. Market St., Suite 200 A, Leesburg, VA 20176.

➤ Portland Cement Association, 5420 Old Orchard Rd., Skokie, IL 60077. Internet: **http://www.portcement.org**

➤ United Brotherhood of Carpenters and Joiners of America, 50 F St. NW., Washington, DC 20001. Internet: **http://www.carpenters.org**

For general information about cement masons and concrete finishers, contact:

➤ National Concrete Masonry Association, 13750 Sunrise Valley Dr., Herndon, VA 20171-3499. Internet: **http://www.ncma.org**

There are more than 500 occupations registered by the U.S. Department of Labor's National Apprenticeship system. For more information on the Labor Department's registered apprenticeship system and links to State apprenticeship programs, check their website: **http://www.doleta.gov**

Construction and Building Inspectors

(0*NET 47-4011.00)

Significant Points

- Almost half of all inspectors worked for local governments, primarily municipal or county building departments.

- Opportunities should be best for experienced construction supervisors and craftworkers who have some college education, engineering or architectural training, or certification as construction inspectors or plan examiners.

- Home inspection is becoming a standard practice in the home purchasing process, creating more opportunities for home inspectors.

Nature of the Work

Construction and building inspectors examine the construction, alteration, or repair of buildings, highways and streets, sewer and water systems, dams, bridges, and other structures to ensure compliance with building codes and ordinances, zoning regulations, and contract specifications. Building codes and standards are the primary means by which building construction is regulated in the United States for the health and safety of the general public. Inspectors make an initial inspection during the first phase of construction, and followup inspections throughout the construction project to monitor compliance with regulations. However, no inspection is ever exactly the same. In areas where certain types of severe weather or natural disasters—such as earthquakes or hurricanes—are more common, inspectors monitor compliance with additional safety regulations designed to protect structures and occupants during these events.

In the past, most localities based their building codes on regional model codes established by the Building Officials and Code Administration (BOCA), the International Conference of Building Officials (ICBO), or the Southern Building Code Congress International (SBCCI). Therefore, building inspectors in one region who were experts in one code found it difficult to move to an area of the country in which another code was used. To eliminate differences among the three sets of codes, these organizations jointly created the International Code Council (ICC) in 1994 and released the Nation's first set of uniform building code regulations in 2000. In 2003, BOCA, ICBO and SBCCI consolidated their operations into the ICC. All code development and support services are now provided by the ICC. This makes it much easier for construction and building inspectors to work in different regions within the United States.

There are many types of inspectors. *Building inspectors* inspect the structural quality and general safety of buildings. Some specialize in such areas as structural steel or reinforced concrete structures. Before construction begins, *plan examiners* determine whether the plans for the building or other structure comply with building code regulations and if they are suited to the engineering and environmental demands of the building site. Inspectors visit the worksite before the foundation is poured to inspect the soil condition and positioning and depth of the footings. Later, they return to the site to inspect the foundation after it has been completed. The size and type of structure, as well as the rate of completion, determine the number of other site visits they must make. Upon completion of the project, they make a final, comprehensive inspection.

In addition to structural characteristics, a primary concern of building inspectors is fire safety. They inspect structures' fire sprinklers, alarms, and smoke control systems, as well as fire exits. Inspectors assess the type of construction, building contents, adequacy of fire protection equipment, and risks posed by adjoining buildings.

Electrical inspectors examine the installation of electrical systems and equipment to ensure that they function properly and comply with electrical codes and standards. They visit worksites to inspect new and existing sound and security systems, wiring, lighting, motors, and generating equipment. They also inspect the installation of the electrical wiring for heating and air-conditioning systems, appliances, and other components.

Elevator inspectors examine lifting and conveying devices such as elevators, escalators, moving sidewalks, lifts and hoists, inclined railways, ski lifts, and amusement rides.

Mechanical inspectors inspect the installation of the mechanical components of commercial kitchen appliances, heating and air-conditioning equipment, gasoline and butane tanks, gas and oil piping, and gas-fired and oil-fired appliances. Some specialize in boilers or ventilating equipment as well.

Plumbing inspectors examine plumbing systems, including private disposal systems, water supply and distribution systems, plumbing fixtures and traps, and drain, waste, and vent lines.

Public works inspectors ensure that Federal, State, and local government construction of water and sewer systems, highways, streets, bridges, and dams conforms to detailed contract specifications. They inspect excavation and fill operations, the placement of forms for concrete, concrete mixing and pouring, asphalt paving, and grading operations. They record the work and materials used so that contract payments can be calculated. Public works inspectors may specialize in highways, structural steel, reinforced concrete, or ditches. Others specialize in dredging operations required for bridges and dams or for harbors.

Home inspectors conduct inspections of newly built or previously owned homes. Home inspection is becoming a standard practice in the home purchasing process. Prospective home buyers hire home inspectors to inspect and report the condition of a home's systems, components, and structure. They typically are hired either immediately prior to a purchase offer on a home, or as a contingency to a sales contract. In addition to structural quality, home inspectors inspect all home systems and features, including roofing as well as plumbing, electrical, and heating or cooling systems.

The owner of a building or structure under construction employs *specification inspectors* to ensure that work is done according to design specifications. They represent the owner's interests, not those of the general public. Insurance companies and financial institutions also may use the services of specification inspectors.

Details concerning construction projects, building and occupancy permits, and other documentation generally are stored on computers so that they can easily be retrieved, kept accurate, and updated. For example, inspectors may use laptop computers to record their findings while inspecting a site. Most inspectors use computers to help them monitor the status of construction inspection activities and keep track of issued permits. Many inspectors also use a paper checklist to detail their findings.

Although inspections are primarily visual, inspectors may use tape measures, survey instruments, metering devices, and test equipment such as concrete strength measurers. They keep a log of their work, take photographs, file reports, and, if necessary, act on their findings. For example, construction inspectors notify the construction contractor, superintendent, or supervisor when they discover a code or ordinance violation or something that does not comply with

Home inspection is becoming a standard practice in the home-purchasing process.

the contract specifications or approved plans. If the problem is not corrected within a reasonable or specified period, government inspectors have authority to issue a "stop-work" order.

Many inspectors also investigate construction or alterations being done without proper permits. Inspectors who are employees of municipalities enforce laws pertaining to the proper design, construction, and use of buildings. They direct violators of permit laws to obtain permits and submit to inspection.

Working Conditions

Construction and building inspectors usually work alone. However, several may be assigned to large, complex projects, particularly because inspectors tend to specialize in different areas of construction. Although they spend considerable time inspecting construction worksites, inspectors also spend time in a field office reviewing blueprints, answering letters or telephone calls, writing reports, and scheduling inspections.

Inspection sites are dirty and may be cluttered with tools, materials, or debris. Inspectors may have to climb ladders or many flights of stairs, or crawl around in tight spaces. Although their work generally is not considered hazardous, inspectors, like other construction workers, wear hard hats and adhere to other safety requirements while at a construction site.

Inspectors normally work regular hours. However, they may work additional hours during periods when a lot of construction is taking place. Also, if an accident occurs at a construction site, inspectors must respond immediately and may work additional hours to complete their report. Nongovernment inspectors may have a varied work schedule. At times, they may work evenings and weekends.

Employment

Construction and building inspectors held about 84,000 jobs in 2002. Local governments, primarily municipal or county building departments, employed 48 percent. Employment of local government inspectors is concentrated in cities and in suburban areas undergoing rapid growth. Local governments employ large inspection staffs, including many plan examiners or inspectors who specialize in structural steel, reinforced concrete, boiler, electrical, and elevator inspection.

Another 21 percent of construction and building inspectors worked for architectural and engineering services firms, conducting inspections for a fee or on a contract basis. Many of these were home inspectors working on behalf of potential real estate purchas-

ers. Most of the remaining inspectors were employed in other services industries or by State governments.

Training, Other Qualifications, and Advancement

Although requirements vary considerably depending upon where one is employed, construction and building inspectors should have a thorough knowledge of construction materials and practices in either a general area, such as structural or heavy construction, or a specialized area, such as electrical or plumbing systems, reinforced concrete, or structural steel. Applicants for construction or building inspection jobs need several years of experience as a construction manager, supervisor, or craftworker. Many inspectors previously worked as carpenters, electricians, plumbers, or pipefitters.

Because inspectors must possess the right mix of technical knowledge, experience, and education, employers prefer applicants who have formal training as well as experience. Most employers require at least a high school diploma or equivalent, even for workers with considerable experience. More often, employers look for persons who have studied engineering or architecture, or who have a degree from a community or junior college, with courses in building inspection, home inspection, construction technology, drafting, and mathematics. Many community colleges offer certificate or associate degree programs in building inspection technology. Courses in blueprint reading, algebra, geometry, and English also are useful.

Construction and building inspectors must be in good physical condition in order to walk and climb about construction sites. They must also have a driver's license. In addition, Federal, State, and many local governments may require that inspectors pass a civil service exam.

Construction and building inspectors usually receive much of their training on the job, although they must learn building codes and standards on their own. Working with an experienced inspector, they learn about inspection techniques; codes, ordinances, and regulations; contract specifications; and recordkeeping and reporting duties. They may begin by inspecting less complex types of construction, such as residential buildings, and then progress to more difficult assignments. An engineering or architectural degree is often required for advancement to supervisory positions.

Because they advise builders and the general public on building codes, construction practices, and technical developments, construction and building inspectors must keep abreast of changes in these areas. Continuing education is imperative in this field. Many employers provide formal training programs to broaden inspectors' knowledge of construction materials, practices, and techniques. Inspectors who work for small agencies or firms that do not conduct training programs can expand their knowledge and upgrade their skills by attending State-sponsored training programs, by taking college or correspondence courses, or by attending seminars sponsored by various related organizations, such as the building code organization.

Most States and cities require some type of certification for employment; even if not required, certification can enhance an inspector's opportunities for employment and advancement to more responsible positions. To become certified, inspectors with substantial experience and education must pass stringent examinations on code requirements, construction techniques, and materials. The ICC offers voluntary certification, as do other professional membership associations. In most cases, there are no education or experience prerequisites, and certification consists of passing an examination in a designated field. Many categories of certification are awarded for inspectors and plan examiners in a variety of disciplines, including the Certified Building Official (CBO) designation.

Job Outlook

Job opportunities in construction and building inspection should be best for highly experienced supervisors and construction craftworkers who have some college education, engineering or architectural training, or certification as inspectors or plan examiners. Thorough knowledge of construction practices and skills in areas such as reading and evaluating blueprints and plans is essential.

Employment of construction and building inspectors is expected to grow about as fast as the average for all occupations through 2012. Growing concern for public safety and improvements in the quality of construction should continue to stimulate demand for construction and building inspectors. In addition to the expected employment growth, some job openings will arise from the need to replace inspectors who transfer to other occupations or leave the labor force.

Inspectors are involved in all phases of construction, including maintenance and repair work, and are therefore less likely to lose jobs when new construction slows during recessions. As the population grows and the volume of real estate transactions increases, greater emphasis on home inspections should result in strong demand for home inspectors. In addition, there should be job opportunities for inspectors in firms specializing in architectural, engineering, and related services as governments—particularly Federal and State—contract out inspection work, and as private inspection services grow.

Earnings

Median annual earnings of construction and building inspectors were $41,620 in 2002. The median hourly earnings were $20.01. The middle 50 percent earned between $15.81 and $25.05. The lowest 10 percent earned less than $12.53, and the highest 10 percent earned more than $30.10. Median annual earnings in the industries employing the largest numbers of construction and building inspectors in 2002 were:

Local government	$42,260
Architectural, engineering, and related services	40,770
State government	39,610

Generally, building inspectors, including plan examiners, earn the highest salaries. Salaries in large metropolitan areas are substantially higher than those in small jurisdictions.

Related Occupations

Construction and building inspectors combine knowledge of construction principles and law with an ability to coordinate data, diagnose problems, and communicate with people. Workers in other occupations using a similar combination of skills include architects, except landscape and naval; construction managers; civil engineers; cost estimators; drafters; engineering technicians; and surveyors, cartographers, photogrammetrists, and surveying technicians.

Sources of Additional Information

Information about certification and a career as a construction or building inspector is available from the following model code organization:

➤ International Code Conference, 5203 Leesburg Pike, Suite 600, Falls Church, VA 22041. Internet: **http://www.iccsafe.org**

For more information about construction inspectors, contact:

➤ Association of Construction Inspectors, 1224 North Nokomis NE., Alexandria, MN 56308. Internet: **http://www.iami.org/aci**

For more information about training and requirements for electrical inspectors, contact:

➤ International Association of Electrical Inspectors, 901 Waterfall Way, Suite 602, Richardson, TX 75080-7702. Internet: **http://www.iaei.org**

For information about becoming a home inspector, contact:

➤ American Society of Home Inspectors, 932 Lee St., Suite 101, Des Plaines, IL 60016. Internet: **http://www.ashi.org**

➤ National Association of Certified Home Inspectors, 1220 Valley Forge Rd., Building 47, P.O. Box 987, Valley Forge, PA 19482-0987. Internet: **http://www.nachi.org**

➤ Housing Inspection Foundation, 1224 North Nokomis NE., Alexandria, MN 56308. Internet: **http://www.iami.org/hif.cfm**

➤ National Association of Home Inspectors, 4248 Park Glen Rd., Minneapolis, MN, 55416. Internet: **http://www.nahi.org**

For information about a career as a State or local government construction or building inspector, contact your State or local employment service.

Construction Equipment Operators

(0*NET 47-2071.00, 47-2072.00, 47-2073.01, 47-2073.02)

Significant Points

- Many construction equipment operators acquire their skills on the job, but formal apprenticeship programs provide more comprehensive training.

- Job opportunities are expected to be good, with as fast as average employment growth.

- Hourly pay is relatively high but, because some construction equipment operators cannot work in inclement weather, total annual earnings may be reduced.

Nature of the Work

Construction equipment operators use machinery to move construction materials, earth, and other heavy materials and to apply asphalt and concrete to roads and other structures. Operators control equipment by moving levers or foot pedals, operating switches, or turning dials. The operation of much of this equipment is becoming more complex as a result of computerized controls. Construction equipment operators may also set up and inspect equipment, make adjustments, and perform some maintenance and minor repairs.

Construction equipment operators include operating engineers and other construction equipment operators; paving, surfacing, and tamping equipment operators; and piledriver operators. *Operating engineers and other construction equipment operators* operate one or several types of power construction equipment. They may operate excavation and loading machines equipped with scoops, shovels, or buckets that dig sand, gravel, earth, or similar materials and load it into trucks or onto conveyors. In addition to the familiar bulldozers, they operate trench excavators, road graders, and similar equipment. Sometimes, they may drive and control industrial trucks or tractors equipped with forklifts or booms for lifting materials or with hitches for pulling trailers. They also may operate and maintain air compressors, pumps, and other power equipment at construction sites. Construction equipment operators who are classified as operating engineers are capable of operating several different types of construction equipment.

Paving and surfacing equipment operators use levers and other controls to operate machines that spread and level asphalt or spread and smooth concrete for roadways or other structures. *Asphalt paving machine operators* turn valves to regulate the temperature and flow of asphalt onto the roadbed. They must take care that the machine distributes the paving material evenly and without voids, and be dangerous. As with most machinery, accidents generally can be avoided by observing proper operating procedures and safety practices. Construction equipment operators are cold in the winter and hot in the summer, and often get dirty, greasy, muddy, or dusty.

Operators may have irregular hours because work on some construction projects continues around the clock or must be performed late at night or early in the morning. Some operators work in remote locations on large construction projects, such as highways and dams, or in factory or mining operations.

Employment

Construction equipment operators held about 416,000 jobs in 2002. Jobs were found in every section of the country and were distributed among various types of operators as follows:

Operating engineers and other construction equipment operators	353,000
Paving, surfacing, and tamping equipment operators	58,000
Pile-driver operators	5,200

About three out of five construction equipment operators worked in the construction industry. Many equipment operators worked in heavy construction, building highways, bridges, or railroads. About one out of five of all construction equipment operators worked in State and local government. Others—mostly grader, bulldozer, and scraper operators—worked in mining. Some also worked in manufacturing and for utility companies. Less than one in twenty construction equipment operators were self-employed.

Training, Other Qualifications, and Advancement

Construction equipment operators usually learn their skills on the job. However, it is generally accepted that formal training provides more comprehensive skills. Some construction equipment operators train in formal 3-year operating engineer apprenticeship programs administered by union-management committees of the International Union of Operating Engineers and the Associated General Contractors of America. Because apprentices learn to operate a wider variety of machines than do other beginners, they usually have better job opportunities. Apprenticeship programs consist of at least 3 years, or 6,000 hours, of on-the-job training and 144 hours a year of related classroom instruction.

Employers of construction equipment operators generally prefer to hire high school graduates, although some employers may train nongraduates to operate some types of equipment. Technologically advanced construction equipment has computerized controls and improved hydraulics and electronics, requiring more skill to operate. Operators of such equipment may need more training and some understanding of electronics. Mechanical aptitude and high school training in automobile mechanics are helpful because workers may perform some maintenance on their machines. Also, high school courses in science and mechanical drawing are useful. Experience operating related mobile equipment, such as farm tractors or heavy equipment, in the Armed Forces or elsewhere is an asset.

Private vocational schools offer instruction in the operation of certain types of construction equipment. Completion of such a program may help a person get a job as a trainee or apprentice. However, persons considering such training should check the school's reputation among employers in the area.

Beginning construction equipment operators handle light equipment under the guidance of an experienced operator. Later, they may operate heavier equipment such as bulldozers and cranes. Operators need to be in good physical condition and have a good sense of balance, the ability to judge distance, and eye-hand-foot

Operating engineers and other construction equipment operators operate one or several types of power construction equipment.

make sure that there is a constant flow of asphalt going into the hopper. *Concrete paving machine operators* control levers and turn handwheels to move attachments that spread, vibrate, and level wet concrete within forms. They must observe the surface of concrete to identify low spots into which workers must add concrete. They use other attachments to smooth the surface of the concrete, spray on a curing compound, and cut expansion joints. *Tamping equipment operators* operate tamping machines that compact earth and other fill materials for roadbeds. They also may operate machines with interchangeable hammers to cut or break up old pavement and drive guardrail posts into the earth.

Piledriver operators operate piledrivers—large machines, mounted on skids, barges, or cranes, that hammer piles into the ground. Piles are long heavy beams of wood or steel driven into the ground to support retaining walls, bulkheads, bridges, piers, or building foundations. Some piledriver operators work on offshore oil rigs. Piledriver operators move hand and foot levers and turn valves to activate, position, and control the pile-driving equipment.

Working Conditions

Many construction equipment operators work outdoors, in nearly every type of climate and weather condition, although in many areas of the country, construction operations must be suspended in winter and during periods of extremely wet weather. Bulldozers, scrapers, and especially tampers and piledrivers are noisy and shake or jolt the operator. Operating heavy construction equipment can coordination. Some operator positions require the ability to work at heights.

Job Outlook
Job opportunities for construction equipment operators are expected to be good through 2012—due, in part, to the shortage of adequate training programs. In addition, many potential workers may choose not to enter training programs because they prefer work that is less strenuous and has more comfortable working conditions.

Employment of construction equipment operators is expected to increase as fast as the average for all occupations through the year 2012 even with improvements in equipment expected to continue to raise worker productivity and to moderate demand for these workers. Employment is expected to increase as population and business growth create a need for new houses, industrial facilities, schools, hospitals, offices, and other structures. More construction equipment operators also will be needed as a result of expected growth in highway, bridge, and street construction. Bridge construction is expected to grow the fastest, due to the need to repair or replace structures before they become unsafe. Poor highway conditions also will spur demand for highway maintenance and repair. In the last several years, Congress has passed substantial public works bills to provide money for such construction projects, including mass transit systems. In addition to job growth, many job openings will arise because of the need to replace experienced construction equipment operators who transfer to other occupations or leave the labor force.

Like that of other construction workers, employment of construction equipment operators is sensitive to fluctuations in the economy. Workers may experience periods of unemployment when the level of construction activity falls.

Earnings
Earnings for construction equipment operators vary. In 2002, median hourly earnings of operating engineers and other construction equipment operators were $16.94. The middle 50 percent earned between $12.96 and $22.98. The lowest 10 percent earned less than $10.61, and the highest 10 percent earned more than $28.93. Median hourly earnings in the industries employing the largest numbers of operating engineers in 2002 were:

Highway, street, and bridge construction	$19.81
Other specialty trade contractors	17.56
Utility system construction	17.48
Other heavy and civil engineering construction	16.89
Local government	14.88

Median hourly earnings of paving, surfacing, and tamping equipment operators were $13.87 in 2002. The middle 50 percent earned between $10.73 and $19.12. The lowest 10 percent earned less than $9.07, and the highest 10 percent earned more than $25.99. Median hourly earnings in the industries employing the largest numbers of paving, surfacing, and tamping equipment operators in 2002 were:

Highway, street, and bridge construction	$14.46
Other specialty trade contractors	14.40
Local government	13.07

In 2002, median hourly earnings of piledriver operators were $21.84. The middle 50 percent earned between $14.89 and $29.24. The lowest 10 percent earned less than $11.73, and the highest 10 percent earned more than $33.97.

Pay scales generally are higher in large metropolitan areas. Annual earnings of some workers may be lower than hourly rates would indicate because worktime may be limited by bad weather.

Related Occupations
Other workers who operate heavy mechanical equipment include bus drivers; truck drivers and driver/sales workers; farmers, ranchers, and agricultural managers; agricultural workers; and forest, conservation, and logging workers.

Sources of Additional Information
For further information about apprenticeships or work opportunities for construction equipment operators, contact a local of the International Union of Operating Engineers, a local apprenticeship committee, or the nearest office of the State apprenticeship agency or employment service. For general information about the work of construction equipment operators, contact:

➤ National Center for Construction Education and Research, University of Florida, P.O. Box 141104, Gainesville, FL 32614-1104. Internet: **http://www.nccer.org**
➤ Associated General Contractors of America, 333 John Carlyle St., Suite 200, Alexandria, VA 22314. Internet: **http://www.agc.org**
➤ International Union of Operating Engineers, 1125 17th St. NW., Washington, DC 20036. Internet: **http://www.iuoe.org**

There are more than 500 occupations registered by the U.S. Department of Labor's National Apprenticeship system. For more information on the Labor Department's registered apprenticeship system and links to State apprenticeship programs, check their website: **http://www.doleta.gov**

Construction Laborers

(0*NET 47-2061.00)

Significant Points

- Job opportunities should be good.
- The work can be physically demanding and sometimes dangerous.
- Most construction laborers learn through informal on-the-job training, but formal apprenticeship programs provide more thorough preparation.
- Like many other construction occupations, employment opportunities are affected by the cyclical nature of the construction industry and can vary greatly by State and locality.

Nature of the Work
Construction laborers perform a wide range of physically demanding tasks involving building and highway construction, tunnel and shaft excavation, hazardous waste removal, environmental remediation, and demolition. Although the term "laborer" implies work that requires relatively little skill or training, many tasks that these workers perform require a fairly high level of training and experience. Construction laborers clean and prepare construction sites to eliminate possible hazards, dig trenches, mix and place concrete, and set braces to support the sides of excavations. They load, unload, identify, and distribute building materials to the appropriate location according to project plans and specifications on building construction projects. They also tend machines; for example, they may mix concrete using a portable mixer or tend a machine that pumps concrete, grout, cement, sand, plaster, or stucco through a spray gun for application to ceilings and walls. Construction laborers often help other craftworkers, including carpenters, plasterers, operating engineers, and masons.

At heavy and highway construction sites, construction laborers clear and prepare highway work zones and rights of way; install traffic barricades, cones, and markers; and control traffic passing near, in, and around work zones. They also install sewer, water, and storm drain pipes, and place concrete and asphalt on roads.

At hazardous waste removal sites, construction laborers prepare the site and safely remove asbestos, lead, radioactive waste, and other hazardous materials. They operate, read, and maintain air monitoring and other sampling devices in confined and/or hazardous environments. They also safely sample, identify, handle, pack, and transport hazardous and/or radioactive materials and clean and decontaminate equipment, buildings, and enclosed structures. Other highly specialized tasks include operating laser guidance equipment to place pipes, operating air, electric, and pneumatic drills, and transporting and setting explosives for tunnel, shaft, and road construction.

Construction laborers operate a variety of equipment including pavement breakers; jackhammers; earth tampers; concrete, mortar, and plaster mixers; electric and hydraulic boring machines; torches; small mechanical hoists; laser beam equipment; and surveying and measuring equipment. They may use computers and other high-tech input devices to control robotic pipe cutters and cleaners. To perform their jobs effectively, construction laborers must be familiar with the duties of other craftworkers and with the materials, tools, and machinery they use.

Construction laborers often help other craftworkers, including carpenters, plasterers, operating engineers, and masons.

Construction laborers often work as part of a team with other skilled craftworkers, jointly carrying out assigned construction tasks. At other times, construction laborers may work alone, reading and interpreting instructions, plans, and specifications with little or no supervision.

While most construction laborers tend to specialize in a type of construction, such as highway or tunnel construction, they are generalists who perform many different tasks during all stages of construction. However, construction laborers who work in underground construction (such as in tunnels) or in demolition are more likely to specialize in only those areas.

Working Conditions
Most laborers do physically demanding work. They may lift and carry heavy objects, and stoop, kneel, crouch, or crawl in awkward positions. Some work at great heights, or outdoors in all weather conditions. Some jobs expose workers to harmful materials or chemicals, fumes, odors, loud noise, or dangerous machinery. To avoid injury, workers in these jobs wear safety clothing, such as gloves, hardhats, protective chemical suits, and devices to protect their eyes, respiratory system, or hearing. While working in underground construction, construction laborers must be especially alert to safely follow procedures and must deal with a variety of hazards.

Construction laborers generally work 8-hour shifts, although longer shifts also are common. They may work only during certain seasons, when the weather permits construction activity.

Employment
Construction laborers held about 938,000 jobs in 2002. They worked throughout the country but, like the general population, were concentrated in metropolitan areas. Almost all construction laborers work in the construction industry and almost one-third work for special trade contractors. About 14 percent were self-employed in 2002.

Training, Other Qualifications, and Advancement
Many construction laborer jobs require no experience or training related to the occupation. Although many workers enter the occupation with few skills, training is encourage and available through apprenticeships and laborer training centers. However, the work requires more strength and stamina than do most occupations, as well as a basic education. The willingness to work outdoors or in confined spaces also is needed. Basic literacy is a must if a worker is to read and comprehend warning signs and labels and understand instructions and specifications.

Most construction laborers learn their skills informally, observing and learning from experienced workers. Individuals who learn the trade on the job usually start as helpers. These workers perform routine tasks, such as cleaning and preparing the worksite and unloading materials. When the opportunity arises, they learn how to do more difficult tasks, such as operating tools and equipment, from experienced craftworkers. Becoming a fully skilled construction laborer by training on the job normally takes longer than the 2 to 4 years required to complete a construction craft laborer apprenticeship program.

Formal apprenticeship programs provide more thorough preparation for jobs as construction laborers than does on-the-job training. Local apprenticeship programs are operated under guidelines established by the Laborers-Associated General Contractors of America Education and Training Fund. These programs typically require at least 4,000 hours of supervised on-the-job training and approximately 400 hours of classroom training. Depending on the availability of work and on local training schedules, it can take an individual from 2 to 4 years to complete the apprenticeship. A core curriculum consisting of basic construction skills such as blueprint reading, the correct use of tools and equipment, and knowledge of safety and health procedures comprises the first 200 hours. The remainder of the curriculum consists of specialized skills training in three of the largest segments of the construction industry: Building construction, heavy/highway construction, and environmental remediation (cleaning up debris, landscaping, and restoring the environment to its original state). Workers who use dangerous equipment or handle toxic chemicals usually receive specialized training in safety awareness and procedures. Apprentices must complete a minimum 144 hours of classroom work each year.

Most apprenticeship programs require workers to be at least 18 years old and physically able to perform the work. Many apprenticeship programs require a high school diploma or equivalent. High school and junior college courses in science, physics, chemistry, and mathematics are helpful. Vocational classes in welding, construction, and other general building skills can give anyone wishing to become a construction laborer a significant head start.

Experience and training is helpful but usually is not necessary to obtain a job. Relevant work experience that provides construction-related job skills can often reduce or eliminate a wide range of training and apprenticeship requirements. Finally, most apprenticeship programs, local unions, and employers look very favorably on military service and/or service in the Job Corps, as veterans and Job Corps graduates have already demonstrated a high level of responsibility and reliability and may have gained many valuable job skills.

Construction laborers need good manual dexterity, hand-eye coordination, and balance. They also need the ability to read and comprehend all warning signs and labels on a construction site and reading skills sufficient to understand and interpret plans, drawings, and written instructions and specifications. They should be capable of working as a member of a team and have basic problem-solving and math skills. Employers want workers who are hard-working, reliable, and diligent about being on time. Additionally, construction laborers who wish to work in environmental remediation must pass a physical test that measures the ability to wear protective equipment such as respirators. Computer skills also are important as construction becomes increasingly mechanized and computerized.

Experience in many construction laborer jobs may allow some workers to advance to positions such as supervisor or construction superintendent. Some construction laborers become skilled craftworkers, either through extensive on the job training or apprenticeships in a craft. A few become independent contractors.

Job Outlook

Job opportunities for construction laborers are expected to be good due to the numerous openings arising each year as laborers leave the occupation. In addition, many potential workers are not attracted to the occupation because they prefer work that is less strenuous and has more comfortable working conditions. Opportunities will be best for workers who are willing to relocate to different worksites.

Employment of construction laborers is expected to grow about as fast as the average for all occupations through the year 2012. New jobs will arise from a continuing emphasis on environmental remediation and on rebuilding infrastructure—roads, airports, bridges, tunnels, and communications facilities, for example. How-

ever, employment growth will be adversely affected by automation as some jobs are replaced by new machines and equipment that improve productivity and quality.

Employment of construction laborers, like that of many other construction workers, can be variable or intermittent due to the limited duration of construction projects and the cyclical nature of the construction industry. Employment opportunities can vary greatly by State and locality. During economic downturns, job openings for construction laborers decrease as the level of construction activity declines.

Earnings

Median hourly earnings of construction laborers in 2002 were $11.90. The middle 50 percent earned between $9.33 and $17.06. The lowest 10 percent earned less than $7.58, and the highest 10 percent earned more than $23.36. Median hourly earnings in the industries employing the largest number of construction laborers in 2002 were as follows:

Highway, street, and bridge construction	$14.48
Nonresidential building construction	12.97
Other specialty trade contractors	12.35
Foundation, structure, and building exterior contractors	11.89
Residential building construction	11.42

Earnings for construction laborers can be reduced by poor weather or by downturns in construction activity, which sometimes result in layoffs.

Apprentices or helpers usually start at about 50 percent of the wage rate paid to experienced workers. Pay increases as apprentices gain experience and learn new skills.

Some laborers belong to the Laborers' International Union of North America.

Related Occupations

The work of construction laborers is closely related to other construction occupations. Other workers who perform similar physical work include persons in material-moving occupations; forest, conservation, and logging workers; and grounds maintenance workers.

Sources of Additional Information

For information about jobs as construction laborers, contact local building or construction contractors, local joint labor-management apprenticeship committees, apprenticeship agencies, or the local office of your State Employment Service.

For general information about the work of construction laborers, contact:

➤ Laborers' International Union of North America, 905 16th St. NW., Washington, DC 20006. Internet: **http://www.liuna.org**

For information on education programs for laborers, contact:

➤ Laborers-AGC Education and Training Fund, 37 Deerfield Road, P.O. Box 37, Pomfret Center, CT 06259. Internet: **http://www.laborerslearn.org**

➤ National Center for Construction Education and Research, P.O. Box 141104, Gainesville FL 32614-1104. Internet: **http://www.nccer.org**

There are more than 500 occupations registered by the U.S. Department of Labor's National Apprenticeship system. For more information on the Labor Department's registered apprenticeship system and links to State apprenticeship programs, check their website: **http://doleta.gov**

Drywall Installers, Ceiling Tile Installers, and Tapers

(0*NET 47-2081.01, 47-2081.02, 47-2082.00)

Significant Points

- Most workers learn the trade on the job, either by working as helpers or through a formal apprenticeship.
- Job prospects are expected to be good.
- Inclement weather seldom interrupts work, but workers may be idled when downturns in the economy slow new construction activity.

Nature of the Work

Drywall consists of a thin layer of gypsum between two layers of heavy paper. It is used for walls and ceilings in most buildings today because it is both faster and cheaper to install than plaster.

There are two kinds of drywall workers—installers and tapers—although many workers do both types of work. Installers, also called *applicators* or *hangers*, fasten drywall panels to the inside framework of residential houses and other buildings. *Tapers*, or *finishers*, prepare these panels for painting by taping and finishing joints and imperfections.

Because drywall panels are manufactured in standard sizes—usually 4 feet by 8 or 12 feet—drywall installers must measure, cut, and fit some pieces around doors and windows. They also saw or cut holes in panels for electrical outlets, air-conditioning units, and plumbing. After making these alterations, installers may glue, nail, or screw the wallboard panels to the wood or metal framework. Because drywall is heavy and cumbersome, a helper generally assists the installer in positioning and securing the panel. Workers often use a lift when placing ceiling panels.

After the drywall is installed, tapers fill joints between panels with a joint compound. Using the wide, flat tip of a special trowel, they spread the compound into and along each side of the joint with brush-like strokes. They immediately use the trowel to press a paper tape—used to reinforce the drywall and to hide imperfections—into the wet compound and to smooth away excess material. Nail and screw depressions also are covered with this compound, as are imperfections caused by the installation of air-conditioning vents and other fixtures. On large projects, finishers may use automatic taping tools that apply the joint compound and tape in one step. Tapers apply second and third coats of the compound, sanding the treated areas where needed after each coat to make them as smooth as the rest of the wall surface. This results in a very smooth and almost perfect surface. Some tapers apply textured surfaces to walls and ceilings with trowels, brushes, or spray guns.

Ceiling tile installers, or *acoustical carpenters*, apply or mount acoustical tiles or blocks, strips, or sheets of shock-absorbing materials to ceilings and walls of buildings to reduce reflection of sound or to decorate rooms. First, they measure and mark the surface according to blueprints and drawings. Then, they nail or screw moldings to the wall to support and seal the joint between the ceiling tile and the wall. Finally, they mount the tile, either by applying a cement adhesive to the back of the tile and then pressing the tile into place, or by nailing, screwing, stapling, or wire-tying the lath directly to the structural framework.

Lathers also are included in this occupation. Lathers fasten metal or rockboard lath to walls, ceilings, and partitions of buildings. Lath forms the support base for plaster, fireproofing, or acoustical mate-

Because drywall is heavy and cumbersome, a helper generally assists the installer in positioning and securing the panel.

rials. At one time, lath was made of wooden strips. Now, lathers work mostly with wire, metal mesh, or rockboard lath. Metal lath is used where the plaster application will be exposed to weather or water or for curved or irregular surfaces for which drywall is not a practical material. Using handtools and portable power tools, lathers nail, screw, staple, or wire-tie the lath directly to the structural framework.

Working Conditions

As in many other construction trades, the work sometimes is strenuous. Drywall installers, ceiling tile installers, and tapers spend most of the day on their feet, either standing, bending, or kneeling. Some tapers use stilts to tape and finish ceiling and angle joints. Installers have to lift and maneuver heavy panels. Hazards include falls from ladders and scaffolds and injuries from power tools and from working with sharp materials. Because sanding a joint compound to a smooth finish creates a great deal of dust, some finishers wear masks for protection.

Employment

Drywall installers, ceiling tile installers, and tapers held about 176,000 jobs in 2002. Most worked for contractors specializing in drywall and ceiling tile installation; others worked for contractors doing many kinds of construction. About 33,000 were self-employed independent contractors.

Most installers and tapers are employed in populous areas. In other areas, where there may not be enough work to keep a drywall or ceiling tile installer employed full time, carpenters and painters usually do the work.

Training, Other Qualifications, and Advancement

Most drywall installers, ceiling tile installers, and tapers start as helpers and learn their skills on the job. Installer helpers start by carrying materials, lifting and holding panels, and cleaning up debris. Within a few weeks, they learn to measure, cut, and install materials. Eventually, they become fully experienced workers. Taper apprentices begin by taping joints and touching up nail holes, scrapes, and other imperfections. They soon learn to install corner guards and to conceal openings around pipes. At the end of their training, drywall installers, ceiling tile installers, and tapers learn to estimate the cost of installing and finishing drywall.

Some drywall installers, ceiling tile installers, and tapers learn their trade in an apprenticeship program. The United Brotherhood of Carpenters and Joiners of America, in cooperation with local contractors, administers an apprenticeship program both in drywall installation and finishing and in acoustical carpentry. Apprenticeship programs consist of at least 3 years, or 6,000 hours, of on-the-job training and 144 hours a year of related classroom instruction. In addition, local affiliates of the Associated Builders and Contractors and the National Association of Home Builders conduct training programs for nonunion workers. The International Union of Painters and Allied Trades conducts an apprenticeship program in drywall finishing that lasts 2 to 3 years.

Employers prefer high school graduates who are in good physical condition, but they frequently hire applicants with less education. High school or vocational school courses in carpentry provide a helpful background for drywall work. Regardless of educational background, installers must be good at simple arithmetic. Other useful high school courses include English, wood shop, metal shop, blueprint reading, and mechanical drawing.

Drywall installers, ceiling tile installers, and tapers with a few years of experience and with leadership ability may become supervisors. Some workers start their own contracting businesses.

Job Outlook

Job opportunities for drywall installers, ceiling tile installers, and tapers are expected to be good. Many potential workers are not attracted to this occupation because they prefer work that is less strenuous and has more comfortable working conditions. Experienced workers will have especially favorable opportunities.

Employment is expected to increase faster than average for all occupations over the 2002-12 period, reflecting increases in the numbers of new construction and remodeling projects. In addition to jobs involving traditional interior work, drywall workers will find employment opportunities in the installation of insulated exterior wall systems, which are becoming increasingly popular.

Besides those resulting from job growth, many jobs will open up each year because of the need to replace workers who transfer to other occupations or leave the labor force. Some drywall installers, ceiling tile installers, and tapers with limited skills leave the occupation when they find that they dislike the work or fail to find steady employment.

Despite the growing use of exterior panels, most drywall installation and finishing is done indoors. Therefore, drywall workers lose less worktime because of inclement weather than do some other construction workers. Nevertheless, they may be unemployed between construction projects and during downturns in construction activity.

Earnings

In 2002, the median hourly earnings of drywall and ceiling tile installers were $16.21. The middle 50 percent earned between $12.43 and $21.50. The lowest 10 percent earned less than $9.76, and the highest 10 percent earned more than $28.03. The median hourly earnings in the industries employing the largest numbers of drywall and ceiling tile installers in 2002 were:

Building finishing contractors $16.50
Nonresidential building construction 14.66

In 2002, the median hourly earnings of tapers were $18.75. The middle 50 percent earned between $14.57 and $24.68. The lowest 10 percent earned less than $11.07, and the highest 10 percent earned more than $29.32.

Trainees usually started at about half the rate paid to experienced workers and received wage increases as they became more highly skilled.

Some contractors pay these workers according to the number of panels they install or finish per day; others pay an hourly rate. A 40-hour week is standard, but the workweek may sometimes be longer. Workers who are paid hourly rates receive premium pay for overtime.

Related Occupations

Drywall installers, ceiling tile installers, and tapers combine strength and dexterity with precision and accuracy to make materials fit according to a plan. Other occupations that require similar abilities include carpenters; carpet, floor, and tile installers and finishers; insulation workers; and plasterers and stucco masons.

Sources of Additional Information

For information about work opportunities in drywall application and finishing and ceiling tile installation, contact local drywall installation and ceiling tile installation contractors, a local of the unions previously mentioned, a local joint union-management apprenticeship committee, a State or local chapter of the Associated Builders and Contractors, or the nearest office of the State employment service or apprenticeship agency.

For details about job qualifications and training programs in drywall application and finishing and ceiling tile installation, contact:

➤ Associated Builders and Contractors, 1300 N. 17th St., Arlington, VA 22209.

➤ National Association of Home Builders, 1201 15th St. NW. Suite 800, Washington, DC 20005. Internet: **http://www.nahb.org**

➤ Home Builders Institute, 1201 15th St. NW., Washington, DC 20005. Internet: **http://www.hbi.org**

➤ International Union of Painters and Allied Trades, 1750 New York Ave. NW., Washington, DC 20006. Internet: **http://www.iupat.org**

➤ United Brotherhood of Carpenters and Joiners of America, 50 F St. NW., Washington, DC 20001. Internet: **http://www.carpenters.org**

There are more than 500 occupations registered by the U.S. Department of Labor's National Apprenticeship system. For more information on the Labor Department's registered apprenticeship system and links to State apprenticeship programs, check their Web site: **http://www.doleta.gov**.

Electricians

(0*NET 47-2111.00)

Significant Points

● Job opportunities are expected to be good.

● Most electricians acquire their skills by completing an apprenticeship program lasting 3 to 5 years.

● More than one-quarter of wage and salary electricians work in industries other than construction.

Nature of the Work

Electricity is essential for light, power, air-conditioning, and refrigeration. Electricians install, connect, test, and maintain electrical systems for a variety of purposes, including climate control, security, and communications. They also may install and maintain the electronic controls for machines in business and industry. Although most electricians specialize in construction or maintenance, a growing number do both.

Electricians work with blueprints when they install electrical systems in factories, office buildings, homes, and other structures. Blueprints indicate the locations of circuits, outlets, load centers, panel boards, and other equipment. Electricians must follow the National Electric Code and comply with State and local building codes when they install these systems. In factories and offices, they first place conduit (pipe or tubing) inside designated partitions, walls, or other concealed areas. They also fasten to the walls small metal or plastic boxes that will house electrical switches and outlets. They then pull insulated wires or cables through the conduit to complete circuits between these boxes. In lighter construction, such as residential, plastic-covered wire usually is used instead of conduit.

Regardless of the type of wire used, electricians connect it to circuit breakers, transformers, or other components. They join the wires in boxes with various specially designed connectors. After they finish the wiring, they use testing equipment, such as ohmmeters, voltmeters, and oscilloscopes, to check the circuits for proper connections, ensuring electrical compatibility and safety of components.

Electricians also may install low voltage wiring systems in addition to wiring a building's electrical system. Low voltage wiring involves voice, data, and video wiring systems, such as those for telephones, computers and related equipment, intercoms, and fire alarm and security systems. Electricians also may install coaxial or fiber optic cable for computers and other telecommunications equipment and electronic controls for industrial equipment.

Maintenance work varies greatly, depending on where the electrician is employed. Electricians who specialize in residential work may rewire a home and replace an old fuse box with a new circuit breaker box to accommodate additional appliances. Those who work in large factories may repair motors, transformers, generators, and electronic controllers on machine tools and industrial robots. Those in office buildings and small plants may repair all types of electrical equipment.

Maintenance electricians spend much of their time doing preventive maintenance. They periodically inspect equipment, and locate and correct problems before breakdowns occur. Electricians may also advise management whether continued operation of equipment could be hazardous. When needed, they install new electrical equipment. When breakdowns occur, they must make the necessary repairs as quickly as possible in order to minimize inconvenience. Electricians may replace items such as circuit breakers, fuses, switches, electrical and electronic components, or wire. When working with complex electronic devices, they may work with engineers, engineering technicians, or industrial machinery installa-

tion, repair, and maintenance workers. (Statements on these occupations appear elsewhere in the *Handbook*.)

Electricians use handtools such as screwdrivers, pliers, knives, hacksaws, and wire strippers. They also use a variety of power tools as well as testing equipment such as oscilloscopes, ammeters, and test lamps.

Working Conditions
Electricians' work is sometimes strenuous. They bend conduit, stand for long periods, and frequently work on ladders and scaffolds. Their working environment varies, depending on the type of job. Some may work in dusty, dirty, hot, or wet conditions, or in confined areas, ditches, or other uncomfortable places. Electricians risk injury from electrical shock, falls, and cuts; to avoid injuries, they must follow strict safety procedures. Some electricians may have to travel great distances to jobsites.

Most electricians work a standard 40-hour week, although overtime may be required. Those in maintenance work may work nights or weekends, and be on call. Maintenance electricians may also have periodic extended overtime during scheduled maintenance or retooling periods. Companies that operate 24 hours a day may employ three shifts of electricians.

Employment
Electricians held about 659,000 jobs in 2002. More than one-quarter of wage and salary workers were employed in the construction industry; while the remainder worked as maintenance electricians employed outside the construction industry. In addition, about one in ten electricians were self-employed.

Because of the widespread need for electrical services, jobs for electricians are found in all parts of the country.

Training, Other Qualifications, and Advancement
Most people learn the electrical trade by completing an apprenticeship program lasting 3 to 5 years. Apprenticeship gives trainees a thorough knowledge of all aspects of the trade and generally improves their ability to find a job. Although electricians are more likely to be trained through apprenticeship than are workers in other construction trades, some still learn their skills informally on the job. Others train to be residential electricians in a 3-year program.

Apprenticeship programs may be sponsored by joint training committees made up of local unions of the International Brotherhood of Electrical Workers and local chapters of the National Electrical Contractors Association; company management committees of individual electrical contracting companies; or local chapters of the Associated Builders and Contractors and the Independent Electrical Contractors Association. Because of the comprehensive training received, those who complete apprenticeship programs qualify to do both maintenance and construction work.

The typical large apprenticeship program provides at least 144 hours of classroom instruction and 2,000 hours of on-the-job training each year. In the classroom, apprentices learn blueprint reading, electrical theory, electronics, mathematics, electrical code requirements, and safety and first aid practices. They also may receive specialized training in welding, communications, fire alarm systems, and cranes and elevators. On the job, under the supervision of experienced electricians, apprentices must demonstrate mastery of the electrician's work. At first, they drill holes, set anchors, and set up conduit. Later, they measure, fabricate, and install conduit, as well as install, connect, and test wiring, outlets, and switches. They also learn to set up and draw diagrams for entire electrical systems.

After finishing an apprenticeship, journeymen often continue to learn about related electrical systems, such as low voltage voice,

Electricians join the wires in boxes with specially designed connectors.

data, and video systems. Many builders and owners want to work with only one contractor who can install or repair both regular electrical systems and low voltage systems.

Those who do not enter a formal apprenticeship program can begin to learn the trade informally by working as helpers for experienced electricians. While learning to install conduit, connect wires, and test circuits, helpers also learn safety practices. Many helpers supplement this training with trade school or correspondence courses.

Regardless of how one learns the trade, previous training is very helpful. High school courses in mathematics, electricity, electronics, mechanical drawing, science, and shop provide a good background. Special training offered in the U.S. Armed Forces and by postsecondary technical schools also is beneficial. All applicants should be in good health and have at least average physical strength. Agility and dexterity also are important. Good color vision is needed because workers frequently must identify electrical wires by color.

Most apprenticeship sponsors require applicants for apprentice positions to be at least 18 years old, have a high school diploma or its equivalent, and be able to pass a skills test. For those interested in becoming maintenance electricians, a background in electronics is increasingly important because of the growing use of complex electronic controls on manufacturing equipment.

Most localities require electricians to be licensed. Although licensing requirements vary from area to area, electricians usually must pass an examination that tests their knowledge of electrical theory, the National Electrical Code, and local electric and building codes. Electricians periodically take courses offered by their employer or union to keep abreast of changes in the National Electrical Code, materials, or methods of installation.

Experienced electricians can become supervisors and then superintendents. Those with sufficient capital and management skills may start their own contracting business, although this may require an electrical contractor's license. Many electricians become electrical inspectors.

Job Outlook

Job opportunities for electricians are expected to be good. Numerous openings will arise each year as experienced electricians leave the occupation. In addition, many potential workers may choose not to enter training programs because they prefer work that is less strenuous and has more comfortable working conditions.

Employment of electricians is expected to increase faster than the average for all occupations through the year 2012. As the population and economy grow, more electricians will be needed to install and maintain electrical devices and wiring in homes, factories, offices, and other structures. New technologies also are expected to continue to stimulate the demand for these workers. For example, buildings will be prewired during construction to accommodate use of computers and telecommunications equipment. More factories will be using robots and automated manufacturing systems. Additional jobs will be created by rehabilitation and retrofitting of existing structures.

In addition to jobs created by increased demand for electrical work, many openings will occur each year as electricians transfer to other occupations, retire, or leave the labor force for other reasons. Because the training for this occupation is long and difficult and the earnings are relatively high, a smaller proportion of electricians than of other craftworkers leave the occupation each year. The number of retirements is expected to rise, however, as more electricians reach retirement age.

Employment of construction electricians, like that of many other construction workers, is sensitive to changes in the economy. This results from the limited duration of construction projects and the cyclical nature of the construction industry. During economic downturns, job openings for electricians are reduced as the level of construction activity declines. Apprenticeship opportunities also are less plentiful during these periods.

Although employment of maintenance electricians is steadier than that of construction electricians, those working in the automotive and other manufacturing industries that are sensitive to cyclical swings in the economy may be laid off during recessions. Also, efforts to reduce operating costs and increase productivity through the increased use of contracting out for electrical services may limit opportunities for maintenance electricians in many industries. However, this should be partially offset by increased job opportunities for electricians in electrical contracting firms.

Job opportunities for electricians also vary by area. Employment opportunities follow the movement of people and businesses among States and local areas, and reflect differences in local economic conditions. The number of job opportunities in a given year may fluctuate widely from area to area.

Earnings

In 2002, median hourly earnings of electricians were $19.90. The middle 50 percent earned between $14.95 and $26.50. The lowest 10 percent earned less than $11.81, and the highest 10 percent earned more than $33.21. Median hourly earnings in the industries employing the largest numbers of electricians in 2002 are shown below:

Motor vehicle parts manufacturing	$28.72
Local government	21.15
Building equipment contractors	19.54
Nonresidential building construction	19.36
Employment services	15.46

Depending on experience, apprentices usually start at between 40 and 50 percent of the rate paid to fully trained electricians. As apprentices become more skilled, they receive periodic increases throughout the course of their training. Many employers also provide training opportunities for experienced electricians to improve their skills.

Many construction electricians are members of the International Brotherhood of Electrical Workers. Among unions organizing maintenance electricians are the International Brotherhood of Electrical Workers; the International Union of Electronic, Electrical, Salaried, Machine, and Furniture Workers; the International Association of Machinists and Aerospace Workers; the International Union, United Automobile, Aircraft and Agricultural Implement Workers of America; and the United Steelworkers of America.

Related Occupations

To install and maintain electrical systems, electricians combine manual skill and knowledge of electrical materials and concepts. Workers in other occupations involving similar skills include heating, air-conditioning, and refrigeration mechanics and installers; line installers and repairers; electrical and electronics installers and repairers; electronic home entertainment equipment installers and repairers; and elevator installers and repairers.

Sources of Additional Information

For details about apprenticeships or other work opportunities in this trade, contact the offices of the State employment service, the State apprenticeship agency, local electrical contractors or firms that employ maintenance electricians, or local union-management electrician apprenticeship committees. This information also may be available from local chapters of the Independent Electrical Contractors, Inc.; the National Electrical Contractors Association; the Home

Builders Institute; the Associated Builders and Contractors; and the International Brotherhood of Electrical Workers.

For information about union apprenticeship programs, contact:

➤ National Joint Apprenticeship Training Committee (NJATC), 301 Prince George's Blvd., Upper Marlboro, MD 20774. Internet: **http://www.njatc.org**

➤ National Electrical Contractors Association (NECA), 3 Metro Center, Suite 1100, Bethesda, MD 20814. Internet: **http://www.necanet.org**

➤ International Brotherhood of Electrical Workers (IBEW), 1125 15th St. NW., Washington, DC 20005. Internet: **http://www.ibew.org**

For information about independent apprenticeship programs, contact:

➤ Associated Builders and Contractors, Workforce Development Department, 4250 North Fairfax Dr., 9th Floor, Arlington, VA 22203.

➤ Independent Electrical Contractors, Inc., 4401 Ford Ave., Suite 1100, Alexandria, VA 22302. Internet: **http://www.ieci.org**

➤ National Association of Home Builders, 1201 15th St. NW., Washington, DC 20005. Internet: **http://www.nahb.org**

➤ Home Builders Institute, 1201 15th St. NW., Washington, DC 20005. Internet: **http://www.hbi.org**

There are more than 500 occupations registered by the U.S. Department of Labor's National Apprenticeship system. For more information on the Labor Department's registered apprenticeship system and links to State apprenticeship programs, check their Web site: **http://www.doleta.gov**.

Elevator Installers and Repairers

(0*NET 47-4021.00)

Significant Points

● Workers learn the trade through 4 years of on-the-job training and classroom instruction.

● Job opportunities are expected to be limited in this small occupation; prospects should be best for those with postsecondary education in electronics.

● Elevator installers and repairers lose less worktime due to inclement weather than do other construction trades workers.

Nature of the Work

Elevator installers and repairers—also called *elevator constructors* or *elevator mechanics*—assemble, install, and replace elevators, escalators, dumbwaiters, moving walkways, and similar equipment in new and old buildings. Once the equipment is in service, they maintain and repair it as well. They also are responsible for modernizing older equipment.

To install, repair, and maintain modern elevators, which are almost all electronically controlled, elevator installers and repairers must have a thorough knowledge of electronics, electricity, and hydraulics. Many elevators are controlled with microprocessors, which are programmed to analyze traffic conditions in order to dispatch elevators in the most efficient manner. With these computer controls, it is possible to get the greatest amount of service with the least number of cars.

When installing a new elevator, installers and repairers begin by studying blueprints to determine the equipment needed to install rails, machinery, car enclosures, motors, pumps, cylinders, and plunger foundations. Once this has been done, they begin equipment installation. Working on scaffolding or platforms, installers bolt or weld steel rails to the walls of the shaft to guide the elevator.

Elevator installers put in electrical wires and controls by running tubing, called conduit, along a shaft's walls from floor to floor. Once the conduit is in place, mechanics pull plastic-covered electrical wires through it. They then install electrical components and related devices required at each floor and at the main control panel in the machine room.

Installers bolt or weld together the steel frame of an elevator car at the bottom of the shaft; install the car's platform, walls, and doors; and attach guide shoes and rollers to minimize the lateral motion of the car as it travels through the shaft. They also install the outer doors and door frames at the elevator entrances on each floor.

For cabled elevators, these workers install geared or gearless machines with a traction drive wheel that guides and moves heavy steel cables connected to the elevator car and counterweight. (The counterweight moves in the opposite direction from the car and balances most of the weight of the car to reduce the weight that the elevator's motor must lift.) Elevator installers also install elevators in which a car sits on a hydraulic plunger that is driven by a pump. The plunger pushes the elevator car up from underneath, similar to a lift in an auto service station.

Installers and repairers also install escalators. They put in place the steel framework, the electrically powered stairs, and the tracks, and install associated motors and electrical wiring. In addition to elevators and escalators, installers and repairers also may install devices such as dumbwaiters and material lifts—which are similar to elevators in design—as well as moving walkways, stair lifts, and wheelchair lifts.

The most highly skilled elevator installers and repairers, called "adjusters," specialize in fine-tuning all the equipment after installation. Adjusters make sure that an elevator is working according to specifications and is stopping correctly at each floor within a specified time. Once an elevator is operating properly, it must be maintained and serviced regularly to keep it in safe working condition. Elevator installers and repairers generally do preventive maintenance—such as oiling and greasing moving parts, replacing worn parts, testing equipment with meters and gauges, and adjusting equipment for optimal performance. They also troubleshoot and may be called to do emergency repairs.

A service crew usually handles major repairs—for example, replacing cables, elevator doors, or machine bearings. This may require the use of cutting torches or rigging equipment—tools that an elevator repairer normally would not carry. Service crews also do

Once an elevator is operating properly, it must be maintained and serviced regularly to keep it in safe working condition.

major modernization and alteration work, such as moving and replacing electrical motors, hydraulic pumps, and control panels.

Elevator installers and repairers usually specialize in installation, maintenance, or repair work. Maintenance and repair workers generally need greater knowledge of electricity and electronics than do installers, because a large part of maintenance and repair work is troubleshooting. Similarly, adjusters need a thorough knowledge of electricity, electronics, and computers to ensure that newly installed elevators operate properly.

Working Conditions
Most elevator installers and repairers work a 40-hour week. However, overtime is required when essential elevator equipment must be repaired, and some workers are on 24-hour call. Unlike most elevator installers, workers who specialize in elevator maintenance are on their own most of the day and typically service the same elevators periodically.

Elevator installers lift and carry heavy equipment and parts, and may work in cramped spaces or awkward positions. Potential hazards include falls, electrical shock, muscle strains, and other injuries related to handling heavy equipment. Because most of their work is performed indoors in buildings under construction or in existing buildings, elevator installers and repairers lose less worktime due to inclement weather than do other construction trades workers.

Employment
Elevator installers and repairers held about 21,000 jobs in 2002. Most were employed by special trade contractors. Others were employed by field offices of elevator manufacturers, wholesale distributors, small-elevator maintenance and repair contractors, government agencies, or businesses that do their own elevator maintenance and repair.

Training, Other Qualifications, and Advancement
Most elevator installers and repairers apply for their jobs through a local of the International Union of Elevator Constructors. Applicants for apprenticeship positions must be at least 18 years old, have a high school diploma or equivalent, and pass an aptitude test. Good physical condition and mechanical aptitude also are important.

Elevator installers and repairers learn their trade in a program administered by local joint educational committees representing the employers and the union. These programs, through which the apprentice learns everything from installation to repair, combine on-the-job training with classroom instruction in blueprint reading, electrical and electronic theory, mathematics, applications of physics, and safety. In nonunion shops, workers may complete training programs sponsored by independent contractors.

Generally, apprentices must complete a 6-month probationary period. After successful completion, they work toward becoming fully qualified within 4 years. To be classified as a fully qualified elevator installer or repairer, union trainees must pass a standard examination administered by the National Elevator Industry Educational Program. Most States and cities also require elevator installers and repairers to pass a licensing examination. Both union and nonunion technicians may take the Certified Elevator Technician (CET) course offered by the National Association of Elevator Contractors.

Most apprentices assist experienced elevator installers and repairers. Beginners carry materials and tools, bolt rails to walls, and assemble elevator cars. Eventually, apprentices learn more difficult tasks such as wiring, which requires knowledge of local and national electrical codes.

High school courses in electricity, mathematics, and physics provide a useful background. As elevators become increasingly sophisticated, workers may find it necessary to acquire more advanced formal education—for example, in postsecondary technical school or junior college—with an emphasis on electronics. Workers with more formal education, such as an associate degree, usually advance more quickly than do their counterparts.

Many elevator installers and repairers also receive training from their employers or through manufacturers to become familiar with a particular company's equipment. Retraining is very important if a worker is to keep abreast of technological developments in elevator repair. In fact, union elevator installers and repairers typically receive continual training throughout their careers, through correspondence courses, seminars, or formal classes. Although voluntary, this training greatly improves one's chances for promotion.

Some installers may receive further training in specialized areas and advance to the position of mechanic-in-charge, adjuster, supervisor, or elevator inspector. Adjusters, for example, may be picked for their position because they possess particular skills or are electronically inclined. Other workers may move into management, sales, or product design jobs.

Job Outlook
Job opportunities are expected to be limited in this small occupation. A large proportion of elevator installer and repairer jobs are unionized and involve a significant investment in training. As a result, workers tend to stay in this occupation for a long time. This investment in training, as well as good benefits and relatively high wages, results in fewer openings due to turnover, thus reducing job opportunities. Job prospects should be best for those with postsecondary education in electronics.

Employment of elevator installers and repairers is expected to increase about as fast as the average for all occupations through the year 2012. Job growth is related to the growth of nonresidential construction, such as commercial office buildings and stores that have elevators and escalators. The need to continually update and modernize old equipment, expand and access, improve appearance, and install increasingly sophisticated equipment and computerized controls also should add to the demand for elevator installers and repairers.

Because it is desirable that equipment always be kept in good working condition, economic downturns will have less of an effect on employment of elevator installers and repairers than on other construction trades.

Earnings
Median hourly earnings of elevator installers and repairers were $25.99 in 2002. The middle 50 percent earned between $20.08 and $31.72. The lowest 10 percent earned less than $14.60, and the top 10 percent earned more than $36.81. In 2002, median hourly earnings in the miscellaneous special trade contractors industry were $26.62. In addition to free continuing education, elevator installers and repairers receive basic benefits enjoyed by most other workers.

Related Occupations
Elevator installers and repairers combine electrical and mechanical skills with construction skills, such as welding, rigging, measuring, and blueprint reading. Other occupations that require many of these skills are boilermakers; electricians; electrical and electronics installers and repairers; industrial machinery installation, repair, and maintenance workers; sheet metal workers; and structural and reinforcing iron and metal workers.

Sources of Additional Information

For further information on opportunities as an elevator installer and repairer, contact:

➤ International Union of Elevator Constructors, 7154 Columbia Gateway Dr., Columbia, MD 21046. Internet: **http://www.iuec.org**

For additional information about the Certified Elevator Technician (CET) program, contact:

➤ National Association of Elevator Contractors,1298 Wellbrook Circle, Suite A, Conyers, GA 30012. Internet: **http://www.naec.org**

There are more than 500 occupations registered by the U.S. Department of Labor's National Apprenticeship system. For more information on the Labor Department's registered apprenticeship system and links to State apprenticeship programs, check their Web site: **http://www.doleta.gov**.

Glaziers

(O*NET 47-2121.00)

Significant Points

● Many glaziers learn the trade by working as helpers to experienced glaziers; however, employers recommend a 3- to 4-year apprenticeship program.

● Job opportunities are expected to be excellent.

Nature of the Work

Glass serves many uses in modern life. Insulated and specially treated glass keeps in warmed or cooled air and provides good condensation and sound control qualities; tempered and laminated glass makes doors and windows more secure. In large commercial buildings, glass panels give office buildings a distinctive look while reducing the need for artificial lighting. The creative use of large windows, glass doors, skylights, and sunroom additions makes homes bright, airy, and inviting.

Glaziers are responsible for selecting, cutting, installing, replacing, and removing all types of glass. They generally work on one of several types of projects. Residential glazing involves work such as replacing glass in home windows; installing glass mirrors, shower doors, and bathtub enclosures; and fitting glass for tabletops and display cases. On commercial interior projects, glaziers install items such as heavy, often etched, decorative room dividers or security windows. Glazing projects also may involve replacement of storefront windows for establishments such as supermarkets, auto dealerships, or banks. In the construction of large commercial buildings, glaziers build metal framework extrusions and install glass panels or curtain walls.

Besides working with glass, glaziers also may work with plastics, granite, marble, similar materials used as glass substitutes, and films or laminates that improve the durability or safety of the glass. They may mount steel and aluminum sashes or frames and attach locks and hinges to glass doors. For most jobs, the glass is precut and mounted in frames at a factory or a contractor's shop. It arrives at the jobsite ready for glaziers to position and secure it in place. They may use a crane or hoist with suction cups to lift large, heavy pieces of glass. They then gently guide the glass into position by hand.

Once glaziers have the glass in place, they secure it with mastic, putty, or other pastelike cement, or with bolts, rubber gaskets, glazing compound, metal clips, or metal or wood moldings. When they secure glass using a rubber gasket—a thick, molded rubber half-tube with a split running its length—they first secure the gasket around the perimeter within the opening, then set the glass into the split side of the gasket, causing it to clamp to the edges and hold the glass firmly in place.

When they use metal clips and wood moldings, glaziers first secure the molding to the opening, place the glass in the molding, and then force springlike metal clips between the glass and the molding. The clips exert pressure and keep the glass firmly in place.

When a glazing compound is used, glaziers first spread it neatly against and around the edges of the molding on the inside of the opening. Next, they install the glass. Pressing it against the compound on the inside molding, workers screw or nail outside molding that loosely holds the glass in place. To hold it firmly, they pack the space between the molding and the glass with glazing compound and then trim any excess material with a glazing knife.

For some jobs, the glazier must cut the glass manually at the jobsite. To prepare the glass for cutting, glaziers rest it either on edge on a rack, or "A-frame," or flat against a cutting table. They then measure and mark the glass for the cut.

Glaziers cut glass with a special tool that has a small, very hard metal wheel. Using a straightedge as a guide, the glazier presses the cutter's wheel firmly on the glass, guiding and rolling it carefully to make a score just below the surface. To help the cutting tool move smoothly across the glass, workers brush a thin layer of oil along the line of the intended cut or dip the cutting tool in oil. Immediately after cutting, the glazier presses on the shorter end of the glass to break it cleanly along the cut.

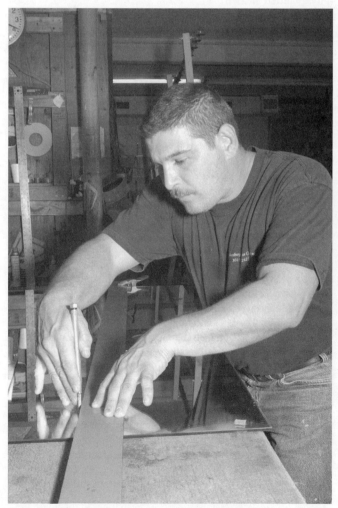

For some jobs, the glazier must cut the glass manually at the jobsite.

In addition to handtools such as glasscutters, suction cups, and glazing knives, glaziers use power tools such as saws, drills, cutters, and grinders. An increasing number of glaziers use computers in the shop or at the jobsite to improve their layout work and reduce the amount of glass that is wasted.

Working Conditions

Glaziers often work outdoors, sometimes in inclement weather. At times, they work on scaffolds at great heights. They do a considerable amount of bending, kneeling, lifting, and standing. Glaziers may be injured by broken glass or cutting tools, by falls from scaffolds, or by improperly lifting heavy glass panels.

Employment

Glaziers held 49,000 jobs in 2002. Almost two-thirds of glaziers worked for glazing contractors engaged in new construction, alteration, and repair. About 1 in 5 glaziers worked in retail glass shops that install or replace glass and for wholesale distributors of products containing glass.

Training, Other Qualifications, and Advancement

Many glaziers learn the trade informally on the job. They usually start as helpers, carrying glass and cleaning up debris in glass shops. They often practice cutting on discarded glass. After a while, they are given an opportunity to cut glass for a job. Eventually, helpers assist experienced workers on simple installation jobs. By working with experienced glaziers, they eventually acquire the skills of a fully qualified glazier.

Employers recommend that glaziers learn the trade through a formal apprenticeship program that lasts 3 to 4 years. Apprenticeship programs, which are administered by the National Glass Association and local union-management committees or local contractors' associations, consist of on-the-job training and a minimum of 144 hours of classroom instruction or home study each year. On the job, apprentices learn to use the tools and equipment of the trade; handle, measure, cut, and install glass and metal framing; cut and fit moldings; and install and balance glass doors. In the classroom, they are taught basic mathematics, blueprint reading and sketching, general construction techniques, safety practices, and first aid. Learning the trade through an apprenticeship program usually takes less time and provides more complete training than acquiring skills informally on the job, but opportunities to obtain apprenticeships are declining.

Local apprenticeship administrators determine the physical, age, and educational requirements needed by applicants for apprenticeships and for helper positions. In general, applicants must be in good physical condition and be at least 18 years old. High school or vocational school graduates are preferred. In some areas, applicants must take mechanical-aptitude tests. Courses in general mathematics, blueprint reading or mechanical drawing, general construction, and shop provide a good background.

Standards for acceptance into apprenticeship programs are rising to reflect changing skill requirements associated with the use of new products and equipment. In addition, the growing use of computers in glass layout requires that glaziers be familiar with personal computers.

Because many glaziers do not learn the trade through a formal apprenticeship program, some associations offer a series of written examinations that certify an individual's competency to perform glazier work at three progressively more difficult levels of proficiency. These levels include Level I, Glazier; Level II, Commercial Interior/Residential Glazier or Storefront/Curtainwall Glazier; and Level III, Master Glazier. There also is a certification program for auto-glass repair.

Advancement generally consists of increases in pay for most glaziers; some advance to supervisory jobs or become contractors or estimators.

Job Outlook

Job opportunities are expected to be excellent for glaziers, largely due to the numerous openings arising each year as experienced glaziers leave the occupation. In addition, many potential workers may choose not to enter this occupation because they prefer work that is less strenuous and has more comfortable working conditions.

Employment of glaziers is expected to increase about as fast as the average for all occupations through the year 2012, as a result of growth in residential and nonresidential construction. Demand for glaziers will be spurred by the continuing need to modernize and repair existing structures and the popularity of glass in bathroom and kitchen design. Improved glass performance related to insulation, privacy, safety, condensation control, and noise reduction also are expected to contribute to the demand for glaziers in both residential and nonresidential remodeling. A continuing emphasis on energy management, which encourages people to replace their old windows and doors with high-efficiency products, also should result in more jobs for glaziers. The increased level of security consciousness should spur demand for specialized safety glass in many commercial and government buildings.

Like other construction trades workers, glaziers employed in the construction industry should expect to experience periods of unemployment resulting from the limited duration of construction projects and the cyclical nature of the construction industry. During bad economic times, job openings for glaziers are reduced as the level of construction declines. Because construction activity varies from area to area, job openings and apprenticeship opportunities fluctuate with local economic conditions. Employment and apprenticeship opportunities should be greatest in metropolitan areas, where most glazing contractors and glass shops are located.

Earnings

In 2002, median hourly earnings of glaziers were $15.20. The middle 50 percent earned between $11.56 and $20.53. The lowest 10 percent earned less than $9.14, and the highest 10 percent earned more than $28.18. Median hourly earnings in the industries employing the largest numbers of glaziers in 2002 are shown below:

Foundation, structure, and building exterior contractors $16.36
Building material and supplies dealers 13.13

Glaziers covered by union contracts generally earn more than their nonunion counterparts. Apprentice wage rates usually start at 40 to 50 percent of the rate paid to experienced glaziers and increase as they gain experience in the field. Because glaziers can lose time due to weather conditions and fluctuations in construction activity, their overall earnings may be lower than their hourly wages suggest.

Many glaziers employed in construction are members of the International Union of Painters and Allied Trades.

Related Occupations

Glaziers use their knowledge of construction materials and techniques to install glass. Other construction workers whose jobs also involve skilled, custom work are brickmasons, blockmasons, and stonemasons; carpenters; carpet, floor, and tile installers and finishers; cement masons, concrete finishers, segmental pavers, and terrazzo workers; and painters and paperhangers. Other related occupations include automotive body and related repairers who install broken or damaged glass on vehicles that they repair.

Sources of Additional Information

For more information about glazier apprenticeships or work opportunities, contact local glazing or general contractors, a local of the International Union of Painters and Allied Trades, a local joint union-management apprenticeship agency, or the nearest office of the State employment service or State apprenticeship agency.

For general information about the work of glaziers, contact:

➤ International Union of Painters and Allied Trades, 1750 New York Ave. NW., Washington, DC 20006. Internet: **http://www.iupat.org**

For information concerning training for glaziers, contact:

➤ National Glass Association, Education and Training Department, 8200 Greensboro Dr., Suite 302, McLean, VA 22102-3881. Internet: **http://www.glass.org**

➤ Associated Builders and Contractors, Workforce Development Department, 4250 North Fairfax Dr., 9th Floor, Arlington, VA 22203.

Hazardous Materials Removal Workers

(0*NET 47-4041.00)

Significant Points

● Working conditions can be hazardous, and the use of protective clothing often is required.

● Formal education beyond high school is not required, but a training program leading to a Federal license is mandatory.

● Good job opportunities are expected.

Nature of the Work

Increased public awareness and Federal and State regulations are resulting in the removal of hazardous materials from buildings, facilities, and the environment to prevent further contamination of natural resources and to promote public health and safety. Hazardous materials removal workers identify, remove, package, transport, and dispose of various hazardous materials, including asbestos, lead, and radioactive and nuclear materials. The removal of hazardous materials, or "hazmats," from public places and the environment also is called abatement, remediation, and decontamination.

Hazardous materials removal workers use a variety of tools and equipment, depending on the work at hand. Equipment ranges from brooms to personal protective suits that completely isolate workers from the hazardous material. The equipment required varies with the threat of contamination and can include disposable or reusable coveralls, gloves, hardhats, shoe covers, safety glasses or goggles, chemical-resistant clothing, face shields, and devices to protect one's hearing. Most workers also are required to wear respirators while working, to protect them from airborne particles. The respirators range from simple versions that cover only the mouth and nose to self-contained suits with their own air supply.

In the past, asbestos was used to fireproof roofing and flooring, for heat insulation, and for a variety of other purposes. Today, asbestos is rarely used in buildings, but there still are structures that contain the material. Embedded in materials, asbestos is fairly harmless; airborne, however, it can cause several lung diseases, including lung cancer and asbestosis. Similarly, lead was a common building component found in paint and plumbing fixtures and pipes until the late 1970s. Because lead is easily absorbed into the bloodstream, often from breathing lead dust or from eating chips of paint containing lead, it can cause serious health risks, especially in children.

Due to these risks, it has become necessary to remove lead-based products and asbestos from buildings and structures.

Asbestos abatement workers and *lead abatement workers* remove asbestos, lead, and other materials from buildings scheduled to be renovated or demolished. Using a variety of hand and power tools, such as vacuums and scrapers, these workers remove the asbestos and lead from surfaces. A typical residential lead abatement project involves the use of a chemical to strip the lead-based paint from the walls of the home. Lead abatement workers apply the compound with a putty knife and allow it to dry. Then they scrape the hazardous material into an impregnable container for transport and storage. They also use sandblasters and high-pressure water sprayers to remove lead from large structures. The vacuums utilized by asbestos abatement workers have special, highly efficient filters designed to trap the asbestos, which later is disposed of or stored. During the abatement, special monitors measure the amount of asbestos and lead in the air, to protect the workers; in addition, lead abatement workers wear a personal air monitor that indicates the amount of lead to which a worker has been exposed. Workers also use monitoring devices to identify the asbestos, lead, and other materials that need to be removed from the surfaces of walls and structures.

Transportation of hazardous materials is safer today than it was in the past, but accidents still occur. *Emergency and disaster response workers* clean up hazardous materials after train derailments and trucking accidents. These workers also are needed when an immediate cleanup is required, as would be the case after an attack by biological or chemical weapons.

Radioactive materials are classified as either high- or low-level wastes. High-level wastes are primarily nuclear-reactor fuels used to produce electricity. Low-level wastes include any radioactively contaminated protective clothing, tools, filters, medical equipment, and other items. *Decontamination technicians* perform duties similar to those of janitors and cleaners. They use brooms, mops, and other tools to clean exposed areas and remove exposed items for decontamination or disposal. With experience, these workers can advance to *radiation-protection technician* jobs and use radiation survey meters to locate and evaluate materials, operate high-pressure cleaning equipment for decontamination, and package radioactive materials for transportation or disposal.

Decommissioning and decontamination workers remove and treat radioactive materials generated by nuclear facilities and power plants. With a variety of handtools, they break down contaminated items such as "gloveboxes," which are used to process radioactive materials. At decommissioning sites, the workers clean and decontaminate the facility, as well as remove any radioactive or contaminated materials.

Treatment, storage, and disposal workers transport and prepare materials for treatment or disposal. To ensure proper treatment of the materials, laws require these workers to be able to verify shipping manifests. At incinerator facilities, treatment, storage, and disposal workers transport materials from the customer or service center to the incinerator. At landfills, they follow a strict procedure for the processing and storage of hazardous materials. They organize and track the location of items in the landfill and may help change the state of a material from liquid to solid in preparation for its storage. These workers typically operate heavy machinery, such as forklifts, earthmoving machinery, and large trucks and rigs.

Mold remediation is a new and growing part of the work of some hazardous materials removal workers. Some types of mold can cause allergic reactions, especially in people who are susceptible to them. Although mold is present in almost all structures, some mold—especially the types that cause allergic reactions—can infest a building to such a degree that extensive efforts must be taken to remove it

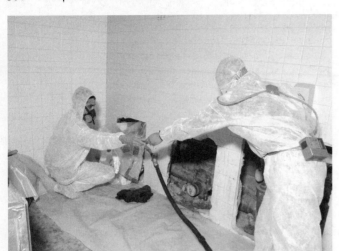

Most hazardous materials removal workers are required to wear respirators to protect them from airborne particles.

safely. Mold typically grows in damp areas, in heating and air-conditioning ducts, within walls, and in attics and basements. Although some mold remediation work is undertaken by other construction workers, mold often must be removed by hazardous materials removal workers, who take special precautions to protect themselves and surrounding areas from being contaminated.

Hazardous materials removal workers also may be required to construct scaffolding or erect containment areas prior to abatement or decontamination. In most cases, government regulation dictates that hazardous materials removal workers be closely supervised on the worksite. The standard usually is 1 supervisor to every 10 workers. The work is highly structured, sometimes planned years in advance, and team oriented. There is a great deal of cooperation among supervisors and workers. Because of the hazard presented by the materials being removed, work areas are restricted to licensed hazardous materials removal workers, thus minimizing exposure to the public.

Working Conditions

Hazardous materials removal workers function in a highly structured environment, to minimize the danger they face. Each phase of an operation is planned in advance, and workers are trained to deal with safety breaches and hazardous situations. Crews and supervisors take every precaution to ensure that the worksite is safe. Whether they work in asbestos, mold, or lead abatement or in radioactive decontamination, hazardous materials removal workers must stand, stoop, and kneel for long periods. Some must wear fully enclosed personal protective suits for several hours at a time; these suits may be hot and uncomfortable and may cause some individuals to experience claustrophobia.

Hazardous materials removal workers face different working conditions, depending on their area of expertise. Although many work a standard 40-hour week, overtime and shift work are common, especially in asbestos and lead abatement. Asbestos abatement and lead abatement workers are found primarily in structures such as office buildings and schools. Because they are under pressure to complete their work within certain deadlines, workers may experience fatigue. Completing projects frequently requires night and weekend work, because hazardous materials removal workers often work around the schedules of others. Treatment, storage, and disposal workers are employed primarily at facilities such as landfills, incinerators, boilers, and industrial furnaces. These facilities often are located in remote areas, due to the kinds of work being

done. As a result, workers employed by treatment, storage, or disposal facilities may commute long distances to their jobs.

Decommissioning and decontamination workers, decontamination technicians, and radiation protection technicians work at nuclear facilities and electric power plants. Like treatment, storage, and disposal facilities, these sites often are far from urban areas. Workers, who often perform jobs in cramped conditions, may need to use sharp tools to dismantle contaminated objects. A hazardous materials removal worker must have great self-control and a level head to cope with the daily stress associated with handling hazardous materials.

Hazardous materials removal workers may be required to travel outside their normal working areas in order to respond to emergencies, the cleanup of which sometimes take several days or weeks to complete. During the cleanup, workers may be away from home for the entire time.

Employment

Hazardous materials removal workers held about 38,000 jobs in 2002. About 7 in 10 were employed in waste management and remediation services. About 6 percent were employed by specialty trade contractors, primarily in asbestos abatement and lead abatement. A small number worked at nuclear and electric plants as decommissioning and decontamination workers and radiation safety and decontamination technicians.

Training, Other Qualifications, and Advancement

No formal education beyond a high school diploma is required for a person to become a hazardous materials removal worker. Federal regulations require an individual to have a license to work in the occupation, although, at present, there are few laws regulating mold removal. Most employers provide technical training on the job, but a formal 32- to 40-hour training program must be completed if one is to be licensed to as an asbestos abatement and lead abatement worker or a treatment, storage, and disposal worker. The program covers health hazards, personal protective equipment and clothing, site safety, recognition and identification of hazards, and decontamination. In some cases, workers discover one hazardous material while abating another. If they are not licensed to work with the newly discovered material, they cannot continue to work with it. Many experienced workers opt to take courses in additional disciplines to avoid this situation. Some employers prefer to hire workers licensed in multiple disciplines.

For decommissioning and decontamination workers employed at nuclear facilities, training is more extensive. In addition to the standard 40-hour training course in asbestos, lead, and hazardous waste, workers must take courses dealing with regulations governing nuclear materials and radiation safety. These courses add up to approximately 3 months of training, although most are not taken consecutively. Many agencies, organizations, and companies throughout the country provide training programs that are approved by the U.S. Environmental Protection Agency, the U.S. Department of Energy, and other regulatory bodies. Workers in all fields are required to take refresher courses every year in order to maintain their license.

Workers must be able to perform basic mathematical conversions and calculations, and should have good physical strength and manual dexterity. Because of the nature of the work and the time constraints sometimes involved, employers prefer people who are dependable, prompt, and detail-oriented. Because much of the work is done in buildings, a background in construction is helpful.

Job Outlook

Job opportunities are expected to be good for hazardous materials removal workers. The occupation is characterized by a relatively high rate of turnover, resulting in a number of job openings each year stemming from experienced workers leaving the occupation. In addition, many potential workers are not attracted to this occupation, because they may prefer work that is less strenuous and has safer working conditions. Experienced workers will have especially favorable opportunities, particularly in the private sector, as more State and local governments contract out hazardous materials removal work to private companies.

Employment of hazardous materials removal workers is expected to grow much faster than the average for all occupations through the year 2012, reflecting increasing concern for a safe and clean environment. Special-trade contractors will have strong demand for the largest segment of these workers, namely, asbestos abatement and lead abatement workers; lead abatement should offer particularly good opportunities. Mold remediation is an especially rapidly growing part of the occupation at the present time, but it is unclear whether its rapid growth will continue: until a few years ago, mold remediation was not considered a significant problem, and perhaps a few years from now, less attention will be paid to it again.

Employment of decontamination technicians, radiation safety technicians, and decommissioning and decontamination workers is expected to grow in response to increased pressure for safer and cleaner nuclear and electric generator facilities. In addition, the number of closed facilities that need decommissioning may continue to grow, due to Federal legislation. These workers also are less affected by economic fluctuations, because the facilities in which they work must operate, regardless of the state of the economy.

Earnings

Median hourly earnings of hazardous materials removal workers were $15.61 in 2002. The middle 50 percent earned between $12.37 and $22.18 per hour. The lowest 10 percent earned less than $10.29 per hour, and the highest 10 percent earned more than $26.60 per hour. The median hourly earnings in remediation and other waste management services, the largest industry employing hazardous materials removal workers in 2002, were $14.92 in 2002.

According to the limited data available, treatment, storage, and disposal workers usually earn slightly more than asbestos abatement and lead abatement workers. Decontamination and decommissioning workers and radiation protection technicians, though constituting the smallest group, tend to earn the highest wages.

Related Occupations

Asbestos abatement workers and lead abatement workers share skills with other construction trades workers, including painters and paperhangers; insulation workers; and sheet metal workers. Treatment, storage, and disposal workers, decommissioning and decontamination workers, and decontamination and radiation safety technicians work closely with plant and system operators, such as power-plant operators, distributors, and dispatchers and water and wastewater treatment plant operators.

Sources of Additional Information

For more information on hazardous materials removal workers, including information on training, contact

➤ Laborers-AGC Education and Training Fund, 37 Deerfield Rd., P.O. Box 37, Pomfret, CT 06259. Internet: **http://www.laborerslearn.org**

There are more than 500 occupations registered by the U.S. Department of Labor's National Apprenticeship system. For more information on the Labor Department's registered apprenticeship system, and links to State apprenticeship programs, check their website: **http:// www.doleta.gov**.

Insulation Workers

(0*NET 47-2131.00, 47-2132.00)

Significant Points

- Workers must follow strict safety guidelines to protect themselves from the dangers of insulating irritants.
- Most insulation workers learn their work informally on the job; others complete formal apprenticeship programs.
- Job opportunities in the occupation are expected to be excellent.

Nature of the Work

Properly insulated buildings reduce energy consumption by keeping heat in during the winter and out in the summer. Refrigerated storage rooms, vats, tanks, vessels, boilers, and steam and hot-water pipes also are insulated to prevent the wasteful transfer of heat. Insulation workers install the materials used to insulate buildings and equipment.

Insulation workers cement, staple, wire, tape, or spray insulation. When covering a steampipe, for example, insulation workers measure and cut sections of insulation to the proper length, stretch it open along a cut that runs the length of the material, and slip it over the pipe. They fasten the insulation with adhesive, staples, tape, or wire bands. Sometimes, they wrap a cover of aluminum, plastic, or canvas over the insulation and cement or band the cover in place. Insulation workers may screw on sheet metal around insulated pipes to protect the insulation from weather conditions or physical abuse.

When covering a wall or other flat surface, workers may use a hose to spray foam insulation onto a wire mesh that provides a rough surface to which the foam can cling and that adds strength to the finished surface. Workers may then install drywall or apply a final coat of plaster for a finished appearance.

In attics or exterior walls of uninsulated buildings, workers blow in loose-fill insulation. A helper feeds a machine with fiberglass, cellulose, or rock-wool insulation, while another worker blows the insulation with a compressor hose into the space being filled.

In new construction or on major renovations, insulation workers staple fiberglass or rock-wool batts to exterior walls and ceilings before drywall, paneling, or plaster walls are put in place. In making major renovations to old buildings or when putting new insulation around pipes and industrial machinery, insulation workers often must first remove the old insulation. In the past, asbestos—now known to cause cancer in humans-was used extensively in walls and ceilings and to cover pipes, boilers, and various industrial equipment. Because of this danger, U.S. Environmental Protection Agency regulations require that asbestos be removed before a building undergoes major renovations or is demolished. When asbestos is present, specially trained workers must remove the asbestos before insulation workers can install the new insulating materials. (See the statement on hazardous materials removal workers elsewhere in the *Handbook*.)

Insulation workers install the materials used to insulate buildings and equipment.

Insulation workers use common handtools—trowels, brushes, knives, scissors, saws, pliers, and stapling guns. They use power saws to cut insulating materials, welding machines to join sheet metal or secure clamps, and compressors to blow or spray insulation.

Working Conditions
Insulation workers generally work indoors. They spend most of the workday on their feet, either standing, bending, or kneeling. Sometimes, they work from ladders or in tight spaces. The work requires more coordination than strength. Insulation work often is dusty and dirty, and the summer heat can make the insulation worker very uncomfortable. Minute particles from insulation materials, especially when blown, can irritate the eyes, skin, and respiratory system. Workers must follow strict safety guidelines to protect themselves from the dangers of insulating irritants. They keep work areas well ventilated; wear protective suits, masks, and respirators; and take decontamination showers when necessary.

Employment
Insulation workers held about 53,000 jobs in 2002. The construction industry employed 4 out of 5 workers; most worked for building finishing contractors. Small numbers of insulation workers held jobs in the Federal Government, in wholesale trade, and in shipbuilding and other manufacturing industries that have extensive installations for power, heating, and cooling. Most worked in urban areas. In less populated areas, carpenters, heating and air-conditioning installers or drywall installers may do insulation work.

Training, Other Qualifications, and Advancement
Most insulation workers learn their trade informally on the job, although some complete formal apprenticeship programs. For entry-level jobs, insulation contractors prefer high school graduates who are in good physical condition and licensed to drive. High school courses in blueprint reading, shop mathematics, science, sheet metal layout, woodworking, and general construction provide a helpful background. Applicants seeking apprenticeship positions should have a high school diploma or its equivalent and be at least 18 years old.

Trainees who learn on the job receive instruction and supervision from experienced insulation workers. Trainees begin with simple tasks, such as carrying insulation or holding material while it is fastened in place. On-the-job training can take up to 2 years, depending on the nature of the work. A certification program is being developed by insulation contractor organizations to help all workers prove their skills and knowledge. Learning to install insulation in homes generally requires less training than does learning to apply insulation in commercial and industrial settings. As they gain experience, trainees receive less supervision, more responsibility, and higher pay.

In contrast, trainees in formal apprenticeship programs receive indepth instruction in all phases of insulation. Apprenticeship programs may be provided by a joint committee of local insulation contractors and the local union of the International Association of Heat and Frost Insulators and Asbestos Workers, to which many insulation workers belong. Programs normally consist of 4 years of on-the-job training coupled with classroom instruction, and trainees must pass practical and written tests to demonstrate their knowledge of the trade.

Skilled insulation workers may advance to supervisor, shop superintendent, or insulation contract estimator, or they may set up their own insulation business.

Job Outlook
Job opportunities are expected to be excellent for insulation workers. Because there are no strict training requirements for entry, many people with limited skills work as insulation workers for a short time and then move on to other types of work, creating many job openings. In addition, many potential workers may prefer work that is less strenuous and that has more comfortable working conditions. Other opportunities will arise from the need to replace workers who leave the labor force.

In addition to opening up as a result of replacement needs, new jobs will arise as employment of insulation workers increases about as fast as the average for all occupations through the year 2012, due to growth in residential and nonresidential construction. Demand for insulation workers will be spurred by continuing concerns about the efficient use of energy to heat and cool buildings, resulting in increased demand for these workers in the construction of new residential, industrial, and commercial buildings. In addition, renovation and efforts to improve insulation in existing structures will increase demand.

Insulation workers in the construction industry may experience periods of unemployment because of the short duration of many construction projects and the cyclical nature of construction activity. Workers employed in industrial plants generally have more stable employment because maintenance and repair must be done on a continuing basis. Most insulation is applied after buildings are enclosed, so weather conditions have less effect on the employment of insulation workers than on that of some other construction occupations.

Earnings
In 2002, median hourly earnings of insulation workers were $13.91. The middle 50 percent earned between $10.58 and $18.36. The lowest 10 percent earned less than $8.45, and the highest 10 percent earned more than $26.29. Median hourly earnings in the industries employing the largest numbers of insulation workers in 2002 are shown in the following tabulation:

Building equipment contractors	$15.30
Building finishing contractors	12.97

Union workers tend to earn more than nonunion workers. Apprentices start at about one-half of the journey worker's wage. Insulation workers doing commercial and industrial work earn substantially more than those working in residential construction, which does not require as much skill.

Related Occupations

Insulation workers combine their knowledge of insulation materials with the skills of cutting, fitting, and installing materials. Workers in occupations involving similar skills include carpenters; carpet, floor, and tile installers and finishers; drywall installers, ceiling tile installers, and tapers; roofers; and sheet metal workers.

Sources of Additional Information

For information about training programs or other work opportunities in this trade, contact a local insulation contractor, the nearest office of the State employment service or apprenticeship agency, or either of the following organizations:

➤ National Insulation Association, 99 Canal Center Plaza, Suite 222, Alexandria, VA 22314. Internet: **http://www.insulation.org/**

➤ Insulation Contractors Association of America, 1321 Duke St., Suite 303, Alexandria, VA 22314. Internet: **http://www.insulate.org**

Painters and Paperhangers

(O*NET 47-2141.00, 47-2142.00)

Significant Points

- Largely due to worker turnover, employment prospects should be good.

- Most workers learn informally on the job as helpers; however, training authorities recommend completion of an apprenticeship program.

- Two in five painters and paperhangers are self-employed, compared with one in five of all construction trades workers.

- Working conditions can be hazardous.

Nature of the Work

Paint and wall coverings make surfaces clean, attractive, and bright. In addition, paints and other sealers protect exterior surfaces from wear caused by exposure to the weather. Apprentices learn both painting and paperhanging, even though each requires different skills.

Painters apply paint, stain, varnish, and other finishes to buildings and other structures. They choose the right paint or finish for the surface to be covered, taking into account durability, ease of handling, method of application, and customers' wishes. Painters first prepare the surfaces to be covered, so that the paint will adhere properly. This may require removing the old coat of paint by stripping, sanding, wire brushing, burning, or water and abrasive blasting. Painters also wash walls and trim to remove dirt and grease, fill nail holes and cracks, sandpaper rough spots, and brush off dust. On new surfaces, they apply a primer or sealer to prepare the surface for the finish coat. Painters also mix paints and match colors, relying on knowledge of paint composition and color harmony. In large paint shops or hardware stores, these functions are automated.

There are several ways to apply paint and similar coverings. Painters must be able to choose the right paint applicator for each job, depending on the surface to be covered, the characteristics of the finish, and other factors. Some jobs need only a good bristle brush with a soft, tapered edge; others require a dip or fountain pressure roller; still others can best be done using a paint sprayer. Many jobs need several types of applicators. The right tools for each job not only expedite the painter's work but also produce the most attractive surface.

When working on tall buildings, painters erect scaffolding, including "swing stages," scaffolds suspended by ropes, or cables attached to roof hooks. When painting steeples and other conical structures, they use a bosun's chair, a swing-like device.

Paperhangers cover walls and ceilings with decorative wall coverings made of paper, vinyl, or fabric. They first prepare the surface to be covered by applying "sizing," which seals the surface and makes the covering stick better. When redecorating, they may first remove the old covering by soaking, steaming, or applying solvents. When necessary, they patch holes and take care of other imperfections before hanging the new wall covering.

After the surface has been prepared, paperhangers must prepare the paste or other adhesive. Then, they measure the area to be covered, check the covering for flaws, cut the covering into strips of the proper size, and closely examine the pattern in order to match it when the strips are hung. Much of this process can now be handled by specialized equipment.

The next step is to brush or roll the adhesive onto the back of the covering and to then place the strips on the wall or ceiling, making sure the pattern is matched, the strips are hung straight, and the edges are butted together to make tight, closed seams. Finally, paperhangers smooth the strips to remove bubbles and wrinkles, trim the top and bottom with a razor knife, and wipe off any excess adhesive.

Working Conditions

Most painters and paperhangers work 40 hours a week or less; about one-quarter have variable schedules or work part time. Painters and paperhangers must stand for long periods. Their jobs also require a considerable amount of climbing and bending. These workers must have stamina, because much of the work is done with their arms raised overhead. Painters often work outdoors but seldom in wet, cold, or inclement weather.

Painters and paperhangers risk injury from slips or falls off ladders and scaffolds. They sometimes may work with materials that can be hazardous if masks are not worn or if ventilation is poor. Some painting jobs can leave a worker covered with paint. In some cases, painters may work in a sealed self-contained suit to prevent inhalation of or contact with hazardous materials.

Self-employed independent painting contractors accounted for 2 in 5 of all painters and paperhangers, double the 1 in 5 of construction trades workers in general.

Employment

Painters and paperhangers held about 468,000 jobs in 2002; most were painters. Around 42 percent of painters and paperhangers work for contractors engaged in new construction, repair, restoration, or remodeling work. In addition, organizations that own or manage large buildings—such as apartment complexes—employ maintenance painters, as do some schools, hospitals, factories, and government agencies.

Self-employed independent painting contractors accounted for two in five of all painters and paperhangers, significantly greater than the one in five of construction trades workers in general.

Training, Other Qualifications, and Advancement

Painting and paperhanging are learned through apprenticeship or informal, on-the-job instruction. Although training authorities recommend completion of an apprenticeship program as the best way to become a painter or paperhanger, most painters learn the trade informally on the job as a helper to an experienced painter. Limited opportunities for informal training exist for paperhangers because few paperhangers need helpers.

The apprenticeship for painters and paperhangers consists of 2 to 4 years of on-the-job training, in addition to 144 hours of related classroom instruction each year. Apprentices receive instruction in color harmony, use and care of tools and equipment, surface preparation, application techniques, paint mixing and matching, characteristics of different finishes, blueprint reading, wood finishing, and safety.

Whether a painter learns the trade through a formal apprenticeship or informally as a helper, on-the-job instruction covers similar skill areas. Under the direction of experienced workers, trainees carry supplies, erect scaffolds, and do simple painting and surface preparation tasks while they learn about paint and painting equipment. As they gain experience, trainees learn to prepare surfaces for painting and paperhanging, to mix paints, and to apply paint and wall coverings efficiently and neatly. Near the end of their training, they may learn decorating concepts, color coordination, and cost-estimating techniques. In addition to learning craft skills, painters must become familiar with safety and health regulations so that their work complies with the law.

Apprentices or helpers generally must be at least 18 years old and in good physical condition. A high school education or its equivalent, with courses in mathematics, usually is required to enter an apprenticeship program. Applicants should have good manual dexterity and color sense.

Painters and paperhangers may advance to supervisory or estimating jobs with painting and decorating contractors. Many establish their own painting and decorating businesses.

Job Outlook

Job prospects should be good, as thousands of painters and paperhangers transfer to other occupations or leave the labor force each year. Because there are no strict training requirements for entry, many people with limited skills work as painters or paperhangers for a short time and then move on to other types of work. Many fewer openings will arise for paperhangers because the number of these jobs is comparatively small.

In addition to the need to replace experienced workers, new jobs will be created. Employment of painters and paperhangers is expected to grow about as fast as the average for all occupations through the year 2012, reflecting increases in the level of new construction and in the stock of buildings and other structures that require maintenance and renovation. Painting is very labor-intensive and not susceptible to technological changes that might make workers more productive and, thus, restrict employment growth.

Jobseekers considering these occupations should expect some periods of unemployment, especially until they gain experience. Many construction projects are of short duration, and construction activity is cyclical and seasonal in nature. Remodeling, restoration, and maintenance projects, however, often provide many jobs for painters and paperhangers even when new construction activity declines. The most versatile painters and skilled paperhangers generally are best able to keep working steadily during downturns in the economy.

Earnings

In 2002, median hourly earnings of painters, construction and maintenance, were $13.98. The middle 50 percent earned between $11.08 and $18.00. The lowest 10 percent earned less than $9.10, and the highest 10 percent earned more than $23.90. Median hourly earnings in the industries employing the largest numbers of painters in 2002 are shown below:

Local government	$17.46
Residential building construction	14.01
Building finishing contractors	14.00
Lessors of real estate	11.62
Employment services	10.21

In 2002, median earnings for paperhangers were $15.22. The middle 50 percent earned between $11.52 and $20.38. The lowest 10 percent earned less than $9.04, and the highest 10 percent earned more than $25.64.

Earnings for painters may be reduced on occasion because of bad weather and the short-term nature of many construction jobs. Hourly wage rates for apprentices usually start at 40 to 50 percent of the rate for experienced workers and increase periodically.

Some painters and paperhangers are members of the International Brotherhood of Painters and Allied Trades. Some maintenance painters are members of other unions.

Related Occupations

Painters and paperhangers apply various coverings to decorate and protect wood, drywall, metal, and other surfaces. Other construction occupations in which workers do finishing work include carpenters; carpet, floor, and tile installers and finishers; drywall installers, ceiling tile installers, and tapers; painting and coating workers, except construction and maintenance; and plasterers and stucco masons.

Sources of Additional Information

For details about painting and paperhanging apprenticeships or work opportunities, contact local painting and decorating contractors, a local of the International Union of Painters and Allied Trades, a local joint union-management apprenticeship committee, or an office of the State apprenticeship agency or employment service.

For information about the work of painters and paperhangers and training opportunities, contact:

➤ International Union of Painters and Allied Trades, 1750 New York Ave. NW., Washington, DC 20006. Internet: **http://www.iupat.org**

➤ Associated Builders and Contractors, Workforce Development Department, 4250 North Fairfax Dr., 9th Floor, Arlington, VA 22203.

➤ Painting and Decorating Contractors of America, 3913 Old Lee Hwy., Fairfax, VA, 22030. Internet: **http://www.pdca.org**

There are more than 500 occupations registered by the U.S. Department of Labor's National Apprenticeship system. For more information on the Labor Department's registered apprenticeship system and links to State apprenticeship programs, check their Web site: **http://www.doleta.gov**.

Pipelayers, Plumbers, Pipefitters, and Steamfitters

(0*NET 47-2151.00, 47-2152.01, 47-2152.02, 47-2152.03)

Significant Points

- Job opportunities should be excellent because not enough people are seeking training.
- Most workers learn the trade through 4 or 5 years of formal apprenticeship training.
- Pipelayers, plumbers, pipefitters, and steamfitters make up one of the largest and highest paid construction occupations.

Nature of the Work

Most people are familiar with plumbers, who come to their home to unclog a drain or install an appliance. In addition to these activities, however, pipelayers, plumbers, pipefitters, and steamfitters install, maintain, and repair many different types of pipe systems. For example, some systems move water to a municipal water treatment plant and then to residential, commercial, and public buildings. Other systems dispose of waste, provide gas to stoves and furnaces, or supply air-conditioning. Pipe systems in powerplants carry the steam that powers huge turbines. Pipes also are used in manufacturing plants to move material through the production process. Specialized piping systems are very important in both pharmaceutical and computer-chip manufacturing.

Although pipelaying, plumbing, pipefitting, and steamfitting sometimes are considered a single trade, workers generally specialize in one of the four areas. *Pipelayers* lay clay, concrete, plastic, or cast-iron pipe for drains, sewers, water mains, and oil or gas lines. Before laying the pipe, pipelayers prepare and grade the trenches either manually or with machines. *Plumbers* install and repair the water, waste disposal, drainage, and gas systems in homes and commercial and industrial buildings. Plumbers also install plumbing fixtures—bathtubs, showers, sinks, and toilets—and appliances such as dishwashers and water heaters. *Pipefitters* install and repair both high- and low-pressure pipe systems used in manufacturing, in the generation of electricity, and in heating and cooling buildings. They also install automatic controls that are increasingly being used to regulate these systems. Some pipefitters specialize in only one type of system. *Steamfitters*, for example, install pipe systems that move liquids or gases under high pressure. *Sprinklerfitters* install automatic fire sprinkler systems in buildings.

Pipelayers, plumbers, pipefitters, and steamfitters use many different materials and construction techniques, depending on the type of project. Residential water systems, for example, incorporate copper, steel, and plastic pipe that can be handled and installed by one or two workers. Municipal sewerage systems, on the other hand, are made of large cast-iron pipes; installation normally requires crews of pipefitters. Despite these differences, all pipelayers, plumbers, pipefitters, and steamfitters must be able to follow building plans or blueprints and instructions from supervisors, lay out the job, and work efficiently with the materials and tools of the trade. Computers often are used to create blueprints and plan layouts.

When construction plumbers install piping in a house, for example, they work from blueprints or drawings that show the planned location of pipes, plumbing fixtures, and appliances. Recently, plumbers have become more involved in the design process. Their knowledge of codes and the operation of plumbing systems can cut costs. They first lay out the job to fit the piping into the structure of the house with the least waste of material. Then they measure and mark areas in which pipes will be installed and connected. Construction plumbers also check for obstructions such as electrical wiring and, if necessary, plan the pipe installation around the problem.

Sometimes, plumbers have to cut holes in walls, ceilings, and floors of a house. For some systems, they may hang steel supports from ceiling joists to hold the pipe in place. To assemble a system, plumbers—using saws, pipe cutters, and pipe-bending machines—cut and bend lengths of pipe. They connect lengths of pipe with fittings, using methods that depend on the type of pipe used. For plastic pipe, plumbers connect the sections and fittings with adhesives. For copper pipe, they slide a fitting over the end of the pipe and solder it in place with a torch.

After the piping is in place in the house, plumbers install the fixtures and appliances and connect the system to the outside water or sewer lines. Finally, using pressure gauges, they check the system to ensure that the plumbing works properly.

Working Conditions

Because pipelayers, plumbers, pipefitters, and steamfitters frequently must lift heavy pipes, stand for long periods, and sometimes work

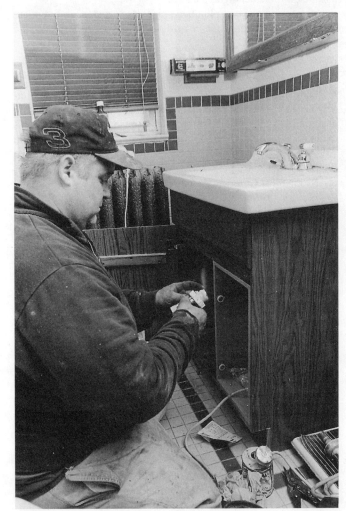

Pipelayers, plumbers, pipefitters, and steamfitters use many different materials and construction techniques, depending on the type of project.

in uncomfortable or cramped positions, they need physical strength as well as stamina. They also may have to work outdoors in inclement weather. In addition, they are subject to possible falls from ladders, cuts from sharp tools, and burns from hot pipes or soldering equipment.

Pipelayers, plumbers, pipefitters, and steamfitters engaged in construction generally work a standard 40-hour week; those involved in maintaining pipe systems, including those who provide maintenance services under contract, may have to work evening or weekend shifts, as well as be on call. These maintenance workers may spend quite a bit of time traveling to and from worksites.

Employment

Pipelayers, plumbers, pipefitters, and steamfitters constitute one of the largest construction occupations, holding about 550,000 jobs in 2002. About 7 in 10 worked for plumbing, heating, and air-conditioning contractors engaged in new construction, repair, modernization, or maintenance work. Others did maintenance work for a variety of industrial, commercial, and government employers. For example, pipefitters were employed as maintenance personnel in the petroleum and chemical industries, in which manufacturing operations require the moving of liquids and gases through pipes. About 1 of every 10 pipelayers, plumbers, pipefitters, and steamfitters was self-employed. One in three pipelayers, plumbers, pipefitters, and steamfitters belong to a union.

Jobs for pipelayers, plumbers, pipefitters, and steamfitters are distributed across the country in about the same proportion as the general population.

Training, Other Qualifications, and Advancement

Virtually all pipelayers, plumbers, pipefitters, and steamfitters undergo some type of apprenticeship training. Many apprenticeship programs are administered by local union-management committees made up of members of the United Association of Journeymen and Apprentices of the Plumbing and Pipefitting Industry of the United States and Canada, and local employers who are members of either the Mechanical Contractors Association of America, the National Association of Plumbing-Heating-Cooling Contractors, or the National Fire Sprinkler Association.

Nonunion training and apprenticeship programs are administered by local chapters of the Associated Builders and Contractors, the National Association of Plumbing-Heating-Cooling Contractors, the American Fire Sprinkler Association, or the Home Builders Institute of the National Association of Home Builders.

Apprenticeships—both union and nonunion—consist of 4 or 5 years of on-the-job training, in addition to at least 144 hours per year of related classroom instruction. Classroom subjects include drafting and blueprint reading, mathematics, applied physics and chemistry, safety, and local plumbing codes and regulations. On the job, apprentices first learn basic skills, such as identifying grades and types of pipe, using the tools of the trade, and safely unloading materials. As apprentices gain experience, they learn how to work with various types of pipe and how to install different piping systems and plumbing fixtures. Apprenticeship gives trainees a thorough knowledge of all aspects of the trade. Although most pipelayers, plumbers, pipefitters, and steamfitters are trained through apprenticeship, some still learn their skills informally on the job.

Applicants for union or nonunion apprentice jobs must be at least 18 years old and in good physical condition. Apprenticeship committees may require applicants to have a high school diploma or its equivalent. Armed Forces training in pipelaying, plumbing, and pipefitting is considered very good preparation. In fact, persons with this background may be given credit for previous experience when entering a civilian apprenticeship program. Secondary or postsecondary courses in shop, plumbing, general mathematics, drafting, blueprint reading, computers, and physics also are good preparation.

Although there are no uniform national licensing requirements, most communities require plumbers to be licensed. Licensing requirements vary from area to area, but most localities require workers to pass an examination that tests their knowledge of the trade and of local plumbing codes.

With additional training, some pipelayers, plumbers, pipefitters, and steamfitters become supervisors for mechanical and plumbing contractors. Others, especially plumbers, go into business for themselves, often starting as a self-employed plumber working from home. Some eventually become owners of businesses employing many workers and may spend most of their time as managers rather than as plumbers. Others move into closely related areas such as construction management or building inspection.

Job Outlook

Job opportunities are expected to be excellent, as demand for skilled pipelayers, plumbers, pipefitters, and steamfitters is expected to outpace the supply of workers trained in this craft. Many potential workers may prefer work that is less strenuous and has more comfortable working conditions.

Employment of pipelayers, plumbers, pipefitters, and steamfitters is expected to grow about as fast as the average for all occupations through the year 2012. Demand for plumbers will stem from building renovation, including the increasing installation of sprinkler systems; repair and maintenance of existing residential systems; and maintenance activities for places having extensive systems of pipes, such as powerplants, water and wastewater treatment plants, pipelines, office buildings, and factories. The enforcement of laws pertaining to the certification requirements of workers on jobsites will create additional opportunities and demand for skilled workers. However, the number of new jobs will be limited by the growing use of plastic pipe and fittings, which are much easier to install and repair than other types, and by increasingly efficient sprinkler systems. In addition to new positions resulting from employment growth, many jobs will become available each year because of the need to replace experienced workers who retire or leave the occupation for other reasons.

Traditionally, many organizations with extensive pipe systems have employed their own plumbers or pipefitters to maintain equipment and keep systems running smoothly. But, to reduce labor costs, many of these firms no longer employ a full-time, in-house plumber or pipefitter. Instead, when they need a plumber, they rely on workers provided under service contracts by plumbing and pipefitting contractors.

Construction projects provide only temporary employment. So, when a project ends, pipelayers, plumbers, pipefitters, and steamfitters working on the project may experience bouts of unemployment. Because construction activity varies from area to area, job openings, as well as apprenticeship opportunities, fluctuate with local economic conditions. However, employment of pipelayers, plumbers, pipefitters, and steamfitters generally is less sensitive to changes in economic conditions than is employment of some other construction trades. Even when construction activity declines, maintenance, rehabilitation, and replacement of existing piping systems, as well as the increasing installation of fire sprinkler systems, provide many jobs for pipelayers, plumbers, pipefitters, and steamfitters.

Earnings

Pipelayers, plumbers, pipefitters, and steamfitters are among the highest paid construction occupations. In 2002, median hourly earnings of pipelayers were $13.70. The middle 50 percent earned between $10.96 and $18.43. The lowest 10 percent earned less than $9.20, and the highest 10 percent earned more than $24.31. Also in 2002, median hourly earnings of plumbers, pipefitters, and steamfitters were $19.31. The middle 50 percent earned between $14.68 and $25.87. The lowest 10 percent earned less than $11.23, and the highest 10 percent earned more than $32.27. Median hourly earnings in the industries employing the largest numbers of plumbers, pipefitters, and steamfitters in 2002 are shown below:

Nonresidential building construction	$19.65
Building equipment contractors	19.52
Utility system construction	17.81
Ship and boat building	16.62
Local government	16.21

Apprentices usually begin at about 50 percent of the wage rate paid to experienced pipelayers, plumbers, pipefitters, and steamfitters. Wages increase periodically as skills improve. After an initial waiting period, apprentices receive the same benefits as experienced pipelayers, plumbers, pipefitters, and steamfitters.

Many pipelayers, plumbers, pipefitters, and steamfitters are members of the United Association of Journeymen and Apprentices of the Plumbing and Pipefitting Industry of the United States and Canada.

Related Occupations

Other occupations in which workers install and repair mechanical systems in buildings are boilermakers; electricians; elevator installers and repairers; heating, air-conditioning, and refrigeration mechanics and installers; industrial machinery installation, repair, and maintenance workers, except millwrights; millwrights; sheet metal workers; and stationary engineers and boiler operators. Other related occupations include construction managers and construction and building inspectors.

Sources of Additional Information

For information about apprenticeships or work opportunities in pipelaying, plumbing, pipefitting, and steamfitting, contact local plumbing, heating, and air-conditioning contractors; a local or State chapter of the National Association of Plumbing, Heating, and Cooling Contractors; a local chapter of the Mechanical Contractors Association; a local chapter of the United Association of Journeymen and Apprentices of the Plumbing and Pipefitting Industry of the United States and Canada; or the nearest office of your State employment service or apprenticeship agency.

For information about apprenticeship opportunities for pipelayers, plumbers, pipefitters, and steamfitters, contact:

➤ United Association of Journeymen and Apprentices of the Plumbing and Pipefitting Industry, 901 Massachusetts Ave. NW., Washington, DC 20001. Internet: **http://www.ua.org**

For more information about training programs for pipelayers, plumbers, pipefitters, and steamfitters, contact:

➤ Associated Builders and Contractors, Workforce Development Department, 4250 North Fairfax Dr., 9th Floor, Arlington, VA 22203.
➤ National Association of Home Builders, 1201 15th St. NW., Washington, DC 20005. Internet: **http://www.nahb.org**
➤ Home Builders Institute, 1201 15th St., NW., Washington, DC 20005. Internet: **http://www.hbi.org**

For general information about the work of pipelayers, plumbers, and pipefitters, contact:

➤ Mechanical Contractors Association of America, 1385 Piccard Dr., Rockville, MD 20850. Internet: **http://www.mcaa.org**
➤ National Association of Plumbing-Heating-Cooling Contractors, 180 S. Washington St, Falls Church, VA 22040. Internet: **http://www.phccweb.org**

For general information about the work of sprinklerfitters, contact:

➤ American Fire Sprinkler Association, Inc., 9696 Skillman St. Suite 300, Dallas, TX 75243-8264. Internet: **http://www.firesprinkler.org**
➤ National Fire Sprinkler Association, P.O. Box 1000, Patterson, NY 12563. Internet: **http://www.nfsa.org**

There are more than 500 occupations registered by the U.S. Department of Labor's National Apprenticeship system. For more information on the Labor Department's registered apprenticeship system and links to State apprenticeship programs, check their website: **http://www.doleta.gov**

Plasterers and Stucco Masons

(0*NET 47-2161.00)

Significant Points

● Plastering is physically demanding.

● Plastering is learned on the job, either through a formal apprenticeship program or by working as a helper.

● Job opportunities are expected to be good, particularly in the South and Southwest.

Nature of the Work

Plastering—one of the oldest crafts in the building trades—is enjoying resurgence in popularity because of the introduction of newer, less costly materials and techniques. Plasterers apply plaster to interior walls and ceilings to form fire-resistant and relatively soundproof surfaces. They also apply plaster veneer over drywall to create smooth or textured abrasion-resistant finishes. In addition, plasterers install prefabricated exterior insulation systems over existing walls—for good insulation and interesting architectural effects—and cast ornamental designs in plaster. Stucco masons apply durable plasters, such as polymer-based acrylic finishes and stucco, to exterior surfaces. Plasterers and stucco masons should not be confused with drywall installers, ceiling tile installers, and tapers—discussed elsewhere in the *Handbook*—who use drywall instead of plaster when erecting interior walls and ceilings.

Plasterers can plaster either solid surfaces, such as concrete block, or supportive wire mesh called lath. When plasterers work with interior surfaces, such as concrete block and concrete, they first apply a brown coat of gypsum plaster that provides a base, which is followed by a second, or finish, coat—also called "white coat"—made of a lime-based plaster. When plastering metal lath foundations, they apply a preparatory, or "scratch," coat with a trowel. They spread this rich plaster mixture into and over the metal lath. Before the plaster sets, plasterers scratch its surface with a rake-like tool to produce ridges, so that the subsequent brown coat will bond tightly.

Laborers prepare a thick, smooth plaster for the brown coat. Plasterers spray or trowel this mixture onto the surface, then finish by smoothing it to an even, level surface.

For the finish coat, plasterers prepare a mixture of lime, plaster of paris, and water. They quickly apply this to the brown coat using

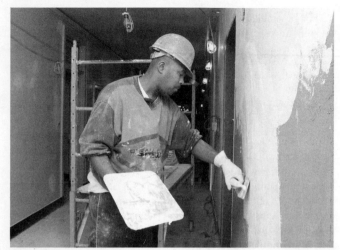

Most plasterers and stucco masons work for independent contractors.

a "hawk"—a light, metal plate with a handle—trowel, brush, and water. This mixture, which sets very quickly, produces a very smooth, durable finish.

Plasterers also work with a plaster material that can be finished in a single coat. This "thin-coat" or gypsum veneer plaster is made of lime and plaster of paris and is mixed with water at the jobsite This plaster provides a smooth, durable, abrasion-resistant finish on interior masonry surfaces, special gypsum baseboard, or drywall prepared with a bonding agent.

Plasterers create decorative interior surfaces as well. They do this by pressing a brush or trowel firmly against a wet plaster surface and using a circular hand motion to create decorative swirls.

For exterior work, stucco masons usually apply stucco—a mixture of Portland cement, lime, and sand—over cement, concrete, masonry, or lath. Stucco may also be applied directly to a wire lath with a scratch coat, followed by a brown coat and then a finish coat. Stucco masons may also embed marble or gravel chips into the finish coat to achieve a pebblelike, decorative finish.

Increasingly, plasterers apply insulation to the exteriors of new and old buildings. They cover the outer wall with rigid foam insulation board and reinforcing mesh, and then trowel on a polymer-based or polymer-modified base coat. They may apply an additional coat of this material with a decorative finish.

Plasterers sometimes do complex decorative and ornamental work that requires special skill and creativity. For example, they may mold intricate wall and ceiling designs. Following an architect's blueprint, plasterers pour or spray a special plaster into a mold and allow it to set. Workers then remove the molded plaster and put it in place, according to the plan.

Working Conditions

Most plastering jobs are indoors; however, plasterers and stucco masons work outside when applying stucco or exterior wall insulation and decorative finish systems. Sometimes, plasterers work on scaffolds high above the ground.

Plastering is physically demanding, requiring considerable standing, bending, lifting, and reaching overhead. The work can be dusty and dirty, soiling shoes and clothing, and can irritate the skin and eyes.

Employment

Plasterers and stucco masons held about 59,000 jobs in 2002. Most plasterers and stucco masons work on new construction sites, par-

ticularly where special architectural and lighting effects are required. Some repair and renovate older buildings. Many plasterers and stucco masons are employed in Florida, California, and the Southwest, where exterior stucco with decorative finishes is very popular.

Most plasterers and stucco masons work for independent contractors. About 1out of every 10 plasterers and stucco masons is self-employed.

Training, Other Qualifications, and Advancement

Although most employers recommend apprenticeship as the best way to learn plastering, many people learn the trade by working as helpers for experienced plasterers and stucco masons. Those who learn the trade informally as helpers usually start by carrying materials, setting up scaffolds, and mixing plaster. Later, they learn to apply the scratch, brown, and finish coats.

Apprenticeship programs, sponsored by local joint committees of contractors and unions, generally consist of 2 or 3 years of on-the-job training, in addition to at least 144 hours annually of classroom instruction in drafting, blueprint reading, and mathematics for layout work.

In the classroom, apprentices start with a history of the trade and the industry. They also learn about the uses of plaster, estimating materials and costs, and casting ornamental plaster designs. On the job, they learn about lath bases, plaster mixes, methods of plastering, blueprint reading, and safety. They also learn how to use various tools, such as hand and powered trowels, floats, brushes, straightedges, power tools, plaster-mixing machines, and piston-type pumps. Some apprenticeship programs allow individuals to obtain training in related occupations, such as cement masonry and bricklaying.

Applicants for apprentice or helper jobs normally must be at least 18 years old, in good physical condition, and have good manual dexterity. Applicants who have a high school education are preferred. Courses in general mathematics, mechanical drawing, and shop provide a useful background.

With additional training and experience, plasterers and stucco masons may advance to positions as supervisors, superintendents, or estimators for plastering contractors. Many become self-employed contractors. Others become building inspectors.

Job Outlook

Job opportunities for plasterers and stucco masons are expected to be good through 2012. Many potential workers may choose not to enter this occupation because they prefer work that is less strenuous and has more comfortable working conditions. The best employment opportunities should continue to be in Florida, California, and the Southwest, where exterior plaster and decorative finishes are expected to remain popular.

Employment of plasterers and stucco masons is expected to increase about as fast as the average for all occupations through the year 2012. Jobs will become available as plasterers and stucco masons transfer to other occupations or leave the labor force.

In past years, employment of plasterers declined as more builders switched to drywall construction. This decline has halted, however, and employment of plasterers is expected to continue growing as a result of the appreciation for the durability and attractiveness that troweled finishes provide. Thin-coat plastering—or veneering—in particular is gaining wide acceptance as more builders recognize its ease of application, durability, quality of finish, and soundproofing and fire-retarding qualities, although the increased use of fire sprinklers will reduce the demand for fire-resistant plaster work.

Prefabricated wall systems and new polymer-based or polymer-modified acrylic exterior insulating finishes also are gaining popularity, particularly in the South and Southwest regions of the country. This is not only because of their durability, attractiveness, and insulating properties, but also because of their relatively low cost. In addition, plasterers will be needed to renovate plasterwork in old structures and to create special architectural effects, such as curved surfaces, which are not practical with drywall materials.

Most plasterers and stucco masons work in construction, where prospects fluctuate from year to year due to changing economic conditions. Bad weather affects plastering less than other construction trades because most work is indoors. On exterior surfacing jobs, however, plasterers and stucco masons may lose time because plastering materials cannot be applied under wet or freezing conditions.

Earnings

In 2002, median hourly earnings of plasterers and stucco masons were $15.91. The middle 50 percent earned between $12.33 and $20.67. The lowest 10 percent earned less than $9.94, and the top 10 percent earned more than $26.81.

The median hourly earnings in the largest industries employing plasterers and stucco masons in 2002 were $15.99 in building finishing contractors, and $14.94 in foundation, structure, and building exterior contractors.

Apprentice wage rates start at about half the rate paid to experienced plasterers and stucco masons. Annual earnings for plasterers and stucco masons and apprentices can be less than the hourly rate would indicate, because poor weather and periodic declines in construction activity can limit work hours.

Related Occupations

Other construction workers who use a trowel as their primary tool include brickmasons, blockmasons, and stonemasons; cement masons, concrete finishers, segmental pavers, and terrazzo workers; and drywall installers, ceiling tile installers, and tapers.

Sources of Additional Information

For information about apprenticeships or other work opportunities, contact local plastering contractors, locals of the unions mentioned below, a local joint union-management apprenticeship committee, or the nearest office of your State apprenticeship agency or employment service.

For general information about the work of plasterers and stucco masons, contact:
➤ International Union of Bricklayers and Allied Craftworkers, 1776 I St. NW., Washington, DC 20006.
➤ Association of Wall and Ceiling Industries International, 803 West Broad St., Falls Church, VA 22046. Internet: **http://www.awci.org**

For information about plasterers, contact:
➤ Operative Plasterers' and Cement Masons' International Association of the United States and Canada, 14405 Laurel Place, Suite 300, Laurel, MD 20707.

For information on the training of plasterers and stucco masons, contact:
➤ International Masonry Institute, The James Brice House, 42 East St., Annapolis, MD 21401. Internet: **http://www.imiweb.org**

There are more than 500 occupations registered by the U.S. Department of Labor's National Apprenticeship system. For more information on the Labor Department's registered apprenticeship system and links to State apprenticeship programs, check their website: **http://www.doleta.gov**

Roofers

(O*NET 47-2181.00)

Significant Points

- Most roofers acquire their skills informally on the job; some roofers train through 3-year apprenticeship programs.

- Jobs for roofers should be plentiful because the work is hot, strenuous, and dirty, resulting in higher job turnover than in most construction trades.

- Demand for roofers is less susceptible to downturns in the economy than demand for other construction trades because most roofing work consists of repair and reroofing.

Nature of the Work

A leaky roof can damage ceilings, walls, and furnishings. To protect buildings and their contents from water damage, roofers repair and install roofs made of tar or asphalt and gravel; rubber or thermoplastic; metal; or shingles made of asphalt, slate, fiberglass, wood, tile, or other material. Repair and reroofing—replacing old roofs on existing buildings—provide many job opportunities for these workers. Roofers also may waterproof foundation walls and floors.

There are two types of roofs—flat and pitched (sloped). Most commercial, industrial, and apartment buildings have flat or slightly sloping roofs. Most houses have pitched roofs. Some roofers work on both types; others specialize.

Most flat roofs are covered with several layers of materials. Roofers first put a layer of insulation on the roof deck. Over the insulation, they then spread a coat of molten bitumen, a tarlike substance. Next, they install partially overlapping layers of roofing felt—a fabric saturated in bitumen—over the surface. Roofers use a mop to spread hot bitumen over the surface and under the next layer. This seals the seams and makes the surface watertight. Roofers repeat these steps to build up the desired number of layers, called "plies." The top layer either is glazed to make a smooth finish or has gravel embedded in the hot bitumen to create a rough surface.

An increasing number of flat roofs are covered with a single-ply membrane of waterproof rubber or thermoplastic compounds. Roofers roll these sheets over the roof's insulation and seal the seams.

About 1 out of every 3 roofers is self-employed.

Adhesive, mechanical fasteners, or stone ballast hold the sheets in place. The building must be of sufficient strength to hold the ballast.

Most residential roofs are covered with shingles. To apply shingles, roofers first lay, cut, and tack 3-foot strips of roofing felt lengthwise over the entire roof. Then, starting from the bottom edge, they staple or nail overlapping rows of shingles to the roof. Workers measure and cut the felt and shingles to fit intersecting roof surfaces and to fit around vent pipes and chimneys. Wherever two roof surfaces intersect, or shingles reach a vent pipe or chimney, roofers cement or nail flashing-strips of metal or shingle over the joints to make them watertight. Finally, roofers cover exposed nailheads with roofing cement or caulking to prevent water leakage. Roofers who use tile, metal shingles, or shakes follow a similar process.

Some roofers also waterproof and dampproof masonry and concrete walls and floors. To prepare surfaces for waterproofing, they hammer and chisel away rough spots, or remove them with a rubbing brick, before applying a coat of liquid waterproofing compound. They also may paint or spray surfaces with a waterproofing material, or attach waterproofing membrane to surfaces. When dampproofing, they usually spray a bitumen-based coating on interior or exterior surfaces.

Working Conditions

Roofing work is strenuous. It involves heavy lifting, as well as climbing, bending, and kneeling. Roofers work outdoors in all types of weather, particularly when making repairs. These workers risk slips or falls from scaffolds, ladders, or roofs, or burns from hot bitumen. In addition, roofs become extremely hot during the summer.

Employment

Roofers held about 166,000 jobs in 2002. Almost all wage and salary roofers worked for roofing contractors. About 1 out of every 3 roofers was self-employed. Many self-employed roofers specialized in residential work.

Training, Other Qualifications, and Advancement

Most roofers acquire their skills informally by working as helpers for experienced roofers. Safety training is increasing to reduce the number of accidents on the job and is one of the first classes that a worker takes. Trainees scart by carrying equipment and material, and erecting scaffolds and hoists. Within 2 or 3 months, trainees are taught to measure, cut, and fit roofing materials and, later, to lay asphalt or fiberglass shingles. Because some roofing materials are used infrequently, it can take several years to get experience working on all the various types of roofing applications.

Some roofers train through 3-year apprenticeship programs administered by local union-management committees representing roofing contractors and locals of the United Union of Roofers, Waterproofers, and Allied Workers. The apprenticeship program generally consists of a minimum of 2,000 hours of on-the-job training annually, plus a minimum of 144 hours of classroom instruction a year in subjects such as tools and their use, arithmetic, and safety. On-the-job training for apprentices is similar to that for helpers, except that the apprenticeship program is more structured. Apprentices also learn to dampproof and waterproof walls.

Good physical condition and good balance are essential for roofers. A high school education, or its equivalent, is helpful, as are courses in mechanical drawing and basic mathematics. Most apprentices are at least 18 years old. Experience with metal-working is helpful for workers who install metal roofing.

Roofers may advance to supervisor or estimator for a roofing contractor, or become contractors themselves.

Job Outlook

Jobs for roofers should be plentiful through the year 2012, primarily because of the need to replace workers who transfer to other occupations or leave the labor force. Turnover is higher than in most construction trades—roofing work is hot, strenuous, and dirty, and a significant number of workers treat roofing as a temporary job until something better comes along. Some roofers leave the occupation to go into other construction trades.

Employment of roofers is expected to grow as fast as the average for all occupations through the year 2012. Roofs deteriorate faster and are more susceptible to weather damage than most other parts of buildings and periodically need to be repaired or replaced. Roofing has a much higher proportion of repair and replacement work than most other construction occupations. As a result, demand for roofers is less susceptible to downturns in the economy than demand for other construction trades. In addition to repair and reroofing work on the growing stock of buildings, new construction of industrial, commercial, and residential buildings will add to the demand for roofers. Jobs should be easiest to find during spring and summer when most roofing is done.

Earnings

In 2002, median hourly earnings of roofers were $14.51. The middle 50 percent earned between $11.23 and $19.56. The lowest 10 percent earned less than $9.15, and the highest 10 percent earned more than $25.35. The median hourly earnings of roofers in the foundation, structure, and building exterior contractors industry were $14.57 in 2002.

Apprentices usually start at about 40 percent to 50 percent of the rate paid to experienced roofers and receive periodic raises as they acquire the skills of the trade. Earnings for roofers are reduced on occasion because poor weather often limits the time they can work.

Some roofers are members of the United Union of Roofers, Waterproofers, and Allied Workers.

Related Occupations

Roofers use shingles, bitumen and gravel, single-ply plastic or rubber sheets, or other materials to waterproof building surfaces. Workers in other occupations who cover surfaces with special materials for protection and decoration include carpenters; carpet, floor, and tile installers and finishers; cement masons, concrete finishers, segmental pavers, and terrazzo workers; drywall installers, ceiling tile installers, and tapers; and plasterers and stucco masons.

Sources of Additional Information

For information about apprenticeships or job opportunities in roofing, contact local roofing contractors, a local chapter of the roofers union, a local joint union-management apprenticeship committee, or the nearest office of your State employment service or apprenticeship agency.

For information about the work of roofers, contact:

➤ National Roofing Contractors Association, 10255 W. Higgins Rd., Suite 600, Rosemont, IL 60018-5607. Internet: **http://www.nrca.net**

➤ United Union of Roofers, Waterproofers, and Allied Workers, 1660 L St. NW., Suite 800, Washington, DC 20036. Internet: **http://www.unionroofers.org**

There are more than 500 occupations registered by the U.S. Department of Labor's National Apprenticeship system. For more information on the Labor Department's registered apprenticeship system and links to State apprenticeship programs, check their website: **http://www.doleta.gov**

Sheet Metal Workers

(0*NET 47-2211.00)

Significant Points

- Nearly two-thirds of the jobs are found in the construction industry; about one quarter are in manufacturing.
- Apprenticeship programs lasting 4 or 5 years are considered the best training.
- Job opportunities in construction should be good.

Nature of the Work

Sheet metal workers make, install, and maintain heating, ventilation, and air-conditioning duct systems; roofs; siding; rain gutters; downspouts; skylights; restaurant equipment; outdoor signs; railroad cars; tailgates; customized precision equipment; and many other products made from metal sheets. They also may work with fiberglass and plastic materials. Although some workers specialize in fabrication, installation, or maintenance, most do all three jobs. Sheet metal workers do both construction-related sheet metal work and mass production of sheet metal products in manufacturing.

Sheet metal workers first study plans and specifications to determine the kind and quantity of materials they will need. They then measure, cut, bend, shape, and fasten pieces of sheet metal to make ductwork, countertops, and other custom products. In an increasing number of shops, sheet metal workers use computerized metalworking equipment. This enables them to perform their tasks more quickly and to experiment with different layouts to find the one that results in the least waste of material. They cut, drill, and form parts with computer-controlled saws, lasers, shears, and presses.

In shops without computerized equipment, and for products that cannot be made on such equipment, sheet metal workers use hand calculators to make the required calculations and use tapes, rulers, and other measuring devices for layout work. They then cut or stamp the parts on machine tools.

Before assembling pieces, sheet metal workers check each part for accuracy using measuring instruments such as calipers and micrometers and, if necessary, finish it by using hand, rotary, or squaring shears and hacksaws. After the parts have been inspected, workers fasten seams and joints together with welds, bolts, cement, rivets, solder, specially formed sheet metal drive clips, or other connecting devices. They then take the parts to the construction site, where they further assemble the pieces as they install them. These workers install ducts, pipes, and tubes by joining them end to end and hanging them with metal hangers secured to a ceiling or a wall. They also use shears, hammers, punches, and drills to make parts at the worksite or to alter parts made in the shop.

Some jobs are done completely at the jobsite. When installing a metal roof, for example, sheet metal workers measure and cut the roofing panels that are needed to complete the job. They secure the first panel in place and interlock and fasten the grooved edge of the next panel into the grooved edge of the first. Then, they nail or weld the free edge of the panel to the structure. This two-step process is repeated for each additional panel. Finally, the workers fasten machine-made molding at joints, along corners, and around windows and doors for a neat, finished effect.

In addition to installation, some sheet metal workers specialize in testing, balancing, adjusting, and servicing existing air-conditioning and ventilation systems to make sure they are functioning properly and to improve their energy efficiency. Properly installed duct systems are a key component to heating, ventilation, and air-conditioning (HVAC) systems, which causes duct installers to sometimes be referred to as *HVAC technicians*. A duct system allows for even air distribution while minimizing leaks and temperature differentiation that can cause other problems, such as mold.

Sheet metal workers in manufacturing plants make sheet metal parts for products such as aircraft or industrial equipment. Although some of the fabrication techniques used in large-scale manufacturing are similar to those used in smaller shops, the work may be highly automated and repetitive. Sheet metal workers doing such work may be responsible for reprogramming the computer control systems of the equipment they operate.

Working Conditions

Sheet metal workers usually work a 40-hour week. Those who fabricate sheet metal products work in shops that are well-lighted and well-ventilated. However, they stand for long periods and lift heavy materials and finished pieces. Sheet metal workers must follow safety practices because working around high-speed machines can be dangerous. They also are subject to cuts from sharp metal, burns from soldering and welding, and falls from ladders and scaffolds. They usually wear safety glasses but must not wear jewelry or loose-fitting clothing that could easily be caught in a machine. They may work at a variety of different production stations to reduce the repetitiveness of the work.

Those performing installation work do considerable bending, lifting, standing, climbing, and squatting, sometimes in close quarters or in awkward positions. Although duct systems and kitchen equipment are installed indoors, the installation of siding, roofs, and gutters involves much outdoor work, requiring sheet metal workers to be exposed to various kinds of weather.

Employment

Sheet metal workers held about 205,000 jobs in 2002. Nearly two-thirds of all sheet metal workers were found in the construction industry. Of those employed in construction, almost half worked for plumbing, heating, and air-conditioning contractors; most of the rest worked for roofing and sheet metal contractors. Some worked for other special trade contractors and for general contractors engaged in residential and commercial building. One-quarter of all sheet metal workers work outside of construction and are found in

In addition to performing installation, some sheet metal workers specialize in testing, balancing, adjusting, and servicing existing air-conditioning and ventilation systems to make sure that they are functioning properly and to improve their energy efficiency.

manufacturing industries, such as the fabricated metal products, machinery, and aerospace products and parts industries. Some work for the Federal Government.

Compared with workers in most construction craft occupations, relatively few sheet metal workers are self-employed.

Training, Other Qualifications, and Advancement

Apprenticeship generally is considered to be the best way to learn this trade. The apprenticeship program consists of 4 or 5 years of on-the-job training and an average of 200 hours per year of classroom instruction. Apprenticeship programs provide comprehensive instruction in both sheet metal fabrication and installation. They may be administered by local joint committees composed of the Sheet Metal Workers' International Association and local chapters of the Sheet Metal and Air-Conditioning Contractors National Association.

On the job, apprentices learn the basics of pattern layout and how to cut, bend, fabricate, and install sheet metal. They begin by learning to install and maintain basic ductwork and gradually advance to more difficult jobs, such as making more complex ducts, commercial kitchens, and decorative pieces. They also use materials such as fiberglass, plastics, and other nonmetallic materials. Some workers may focus on exterior or architectural sheet metal installation.

In the classroom, apprentices learn drafting, plan and specification reading, trigonometry and geometry applicable to layout work, the use of computerized equipment, welding, and the principles of heating, air-conditioning, and ventilating systems. Safety is stressed throughout the program. In addition, apprentices learn the relationship between sheet metal work and other construction work.

Some persons pick up the trade informally, usually by working as helpers to experienced sheet metal workers. Most begin by carrying metal and cleaning up debris in a metal shop while they learn about materials and tools and their uses. Later, they learn to operate machines that bend or cut metal. In time, helpers go out on the jobsite to learn installation. Those who acquire their skills this way often take vocational school courses in mathematics or sheet metal fabrication to supplement their work experience. To be promoted to the journey level, helpers usually must pass the same written examination as apprentices. Most sheet metal workers in large-scale manufacturing receive on-the-job training, with additional classwork or in-house training when necessary.

Applicants for jobs as apprentices or helpers should be in good physical condition and have mechanical and mathematical aptitude as well as good reading skills. Good eye-hand coordination, spatial and form perception, and manual dexterity also are important. Local apprenticeship committees require a high school education or its equivalent. Courses in algebra, trigonometry, geometry, mechanical drawing, and shop provide a helpful background for learning the trade, as does related work experience obtained in the Armed Services.

It is important for experienced sheet metal workers to keep abreast of new technological developments, such as the growing use of computerized layout and laser-cutting machines. Workers often take additional training, provided by the union or by their employer, to improve existing skills or to acquire new ones.

Sheet metal workers in construction may advance to supervisory jobs. Some of these workers take additional training in welding and do more specialized work. Others go into the contracting business for themselves. Because a sheet metal contractor must have a shop with equipment to fabricate products, this type of contracting business is more expensive to start than other types of construction contracting. Sheet metal workers in manufacturing may advance to positions as supervisors or quality inspectors. Some of these workers may move into other management positions.

Job Outlook

Job opportunities are expected to be good for sheet metal workers in the construction industry and in construction-related sheet metal fabrication, reflecting both employment growth and openings arising each year as experienced sheet metal workers leave the occupation. In addition, many potential workers may prefer work that is less strenuous and that has more comfortable working conditions, thus limiting the number of applicants for sheet metal jobs. Opportunities should be particularly good for individuals who acquire apprenticeship training. Job prospects in manufacturing will not be as good because construction is expected to grow faster than the manufacturing industries that employ sheet metal workers. Because some sheet metal manufacturing is labor-intensive, manufacturers sometimes move production to lower wage areas or countries.

Employment of sheet metal workers in construction is expected to increase about as fast as the average for all occupations through 2012, reflecting growth in the demand for sheet metal installations as more industrial, commercial, and residential structures are built. The need to install energy-efficient air-conditioning, heating, and ventilation systems in the increasing stock of old buildings and to perform other types of renovation and maintenance work also should boost employment. In addition, the popularity of decorative sheet metal products and increased architectural restoration are expected to add to the demand for sheet metal workers. On the other hand, slower-than-average job growth is projected for sheet metal workers in manufacturing.

Sheet metal workers in construction may experience periods of unemployment, particularly when construction projects end and economic conditions dampen construction activity. Nevertheless, employment of sheet metal workers is less sensitive to declines in new construction than is the employment of some other construction workers, such as carpenters. Maintenance of existing equipment—which is less affected by economic fluctuations than is new construction—makes up a large part of the work done by sheet metal workers. Installation of new air-conditioning and heating systems in existing buildings continues during construction slumps, as individuals and businesses adopt more energy-efficient equipment to cut utility bills. In addition, a large proportion of sheet metal installation and maintenance is done indoors, so sheet metal workers usually lose less worktime due to bad weather than other construction workers do.

Earnings

In 2002, median hourly earnings of sheet metal workers were $16.62. The middle 50 percent earned between $12.15 and $23.03. The lowest 10 percent of all sheet metal workers earned less than $9.50, and the highest 10 percent earned more than $29.53. The median hourly earnings of the largest industries employing sheet metal workers in 2002 are shown below:

Federal Government	$19.73
Building equipment contractors	17.47
Building finishing contractors	16.77
Foundation, structure, and building exterior contractors	15.48
Architectural and structural metals manufacturing	14.60

Apprentices normally start at about 40 to 50 percent of the rate paid to experienced workers. As apprentices acquire more skills throughout the course of their training, they receive periodic increases until their pay approaches that of experienced workers. In addition, union workers in some areas receive supplemental wages from the union when they are on layoff or shortened workweeks.

Related Occupations

To fabricate and install sheet metal products, sheet metal workers combine metalworking skills and knowledge of construction materials and techniques. Other occupations in which workers lay out and fabricate metal products include assemblers and fabricators; machinists; machine setters, operators, and tenders—metal and plastic; and tool and die makers. Construction occupations requiring similar skills and knowledge include glaziers and heating, air-conditioning, and refrigeration mechanics and installers.

Sources of Additional Information

For more information about apprenticeships or other work opportunities, contact local sheet metal contractors or heating, refrigeration, and air-conditioning contractors; a local of the Sheet Metal Workers International Association; a local of the Sheet Metal and Air-Conditioning Contractors National Association; a local joint union-management apprenticeship committee; or the nearest office of your State employment service or apprenticeship agency.

For general and training information about sheet metal workers, contact:

➤ International Training Institute for the Sheet Metal and Air-Conditioning Industry, 601 N. Fairfax St., Suite 240, Alexandria, VA 22314. Internet: **http://www.sheetmetal-iti.org**

➤ Sheet Metal and Air-Conditioning Contractors National Association, 4201 Lafayette Center Dr., Chantilly, VA 20151-1209. Internet: **http://www.smacna.org**

➤ Sheet Metal Workers International Association, 1750 New York Ave. NW., Washington, DC 20006. Internet: **http://www.smwia.org**

There are more than 500 occupations registered by the U.S. Department of Labor's National Apprenticeship system. For more information on the Labor Department's registered apprenticeship system and links to State apprenticeship programs, check their Web site: **http://www.doleta.gov**.

Structural and Reinforcing Iron and Metal Workers

(O*NET 47-2171.00, 47-2221.00)

Significant Points

- Most employers recommend a 3- or 4-year apprenticeship.
- During economic downturns, workers can experience high rates of unemployment.
- The danger of injuries due to falls is high; those who work at great heights do not work during wet, icy, or extremely windy conditions.

Nature of the Work

Structural and reinforcing iron and metal workers place and install iron or steel girders, columns, and other construction materials to form buildings, bridges, and other structures. They also position and secure steel bars or mesh in concrete forms in order to reinforce the concrete used in highways, buildings, bridges, tunnels, and other structures. In addition, they repair and renovate older buildings and structures. Even though the primary metal involved in this work is steel, these workers often are known as *ironworkers*.

Before construction can begin, ironworkers must erect steel frames and assemble the cranes and derricks that move structural steel, reinforcing bars, buckets of concrete, lumber, and other materials and equipment around the construction site. Once this job has been completed, workers begin to connect steel columns, beams, and girders according to blueprints and instructions from supervisors and superintendents. Structural steel, reinforcing rods, and ornamental iron generally come to the construction site ready for erection—cut to the proper size, with holes drilled for bolts and numbered for assembly.

Ironworkers at the construction site unload and stack the prefabricated steel so that it can be hoisted easily when needed. To hoist the steel, ironworkers attach cables (slings) to the steel and to the crane or derrick. One worker directs the hoist operator with hand signals while another worker holds a rope (tag line) attached to the steel to prevent it from swinging. The crane or derrick hoists steel into place in the framework, whereupon several ironworkers position the steel with connecting bars and jacks. Workers using driftpins or the handle of a spud wrench—a long wrench with a pointed handle—align the holes in the steel with the holes in the framework. Before the bolts are permanently tightened, ironworkers check vertical and horizontal alignment with plumb bobs, laser equipment, transits, or levels; then they bolt or weld the piece permanently in place.

Reinforcing iron and rebar workers set reinforcing bars (often called rebar) in the forms that hold concrete, following blueprints showing the location, size, and number of bars. They then fasten the bars together by tying wire around them with pliers. When reinforcing floors, ironworkers place spacers under the rebar to hold the bars off the deck. Although these materials usually arrive ready to use, ironworkers occasionally must cut bars with metal shears or acetylene torches, bend them by hand or machine, or weld them with arc-welding equipment. Some concrete is reinforced with welded wire fabric. Using hooked rods, workers cut and fit the fabric, and while a concrete crew places the concrete, ironworkers properly position the fabric into the concrete. Posttensioning is another technique used in reinforcing concrete. In this technique, workers

Even though the primary metal involved in this work is steel, these workers often are known as ironworkers.

substitute cables for reinforcing bars. When the concrete is poured, the ends of the cables are left exposed. After the concrete cures, ironworkers tighten the cables with jacking equipment specially designed for the purpose. Posttensioning allows designers to create larger open areas in a building, because supports can be placed further apart. This technique is commonly employed in parking garages and arenas.

Ornamental ironworkers install elevator shafts, stairs, curtain walls (the nonstructural walls and window frames of many large buildings), and other ornamentation after the structure of the building has been completed. As they hoist pieces into position, ornamental ironworkers make sure that the pieces are properly fitted and aligned before bolting, brazing, or welding them for a secure fit.

Working Conditions

Structural and reinforcing iron and metal workers usually work outside in all kinds of weather. However, those who work at great heights do not work during wet, icy, or extremely windy conditions. Because the danger of injuries due to falls is great, ironworkers use safety devices such as safety belts, scaffolding, and nets to reduce risk.

Some ironworkers fabricate structural metal in fabricating shops, which usually are located away from the construction site. These workers are covered in the statement on assemblers and fabricators found elsewhere in the *Handbook*.

Employment

Structural and reinforcing iron and metal workers held about 107,000 jobs in 2002. Around 4 out of 5 worked in construction, with nearly half working for foundation, structure, and building exterior contractors. Most of the remaining ironworkers worked for contractors specializing in the construction of homes; factories; commercial buildings; religious structures; schools; bridges and tunnels; and water, sewer, communications, and power lines.

Structural and reinforcing iron and metal workers are employed in all parts of the country, but most work in metropolitan areas, where the bulk of commercial and industrial construction takes place.

Training, Other Qualifications, and Advancement

Most employers recommend a 3- or 4-year apprenticeship consisting of on-the-job training and evening classroom instruction as the best way to learn this trade. Apprenticeship programs usually are administered by committees made up of representatives of local unions of the International Association of Bridge, Structural, Ornamental and Reinforcing Iron Workers or the local chapters of contractors' associations.

Ironworkers must be at least 18 years old. A high school diploma is preferred by employers and local apprenticeship committees. High school courses in general mathematics, mechanical drawing, and shop are helpful. Because materials used in iron working are heavy and bulky, ironworkers must be in good physical condition. They also need good agility, balance, eyesight, and depth perception to work safely at great heights on narrow beams and girders. Ironworkers should not be afraid of heights or suffer from dizziness.

In the classroom, apprentices study blueprint reading; mathematics for layout work; the basics of structural erecting, rigging, reinforcing, welding, and burning; ornamental erection; and assembling. Apprentices also study the care and safe use of tools and materials. On the job, apprentices work in all aspects of the trade, such as unloading and storing materials at the job site, rigging materials for movement by crane, connecting structural steel, and welding.

Some ironworkers learn the trade informally on the job, without completing an apprenticeship. These workers generally do not receive classroom training, although some large contractors have extensive training programs. On-the-job trainees usually begin by assisting experienced ironworkers on simple jobs, such as carrying various materials. With experience, trainees perform more difficult tasks, such as cutting and fitting different parts; however, learning through work experience alone may not provide training as complete as an apprenticeship program, and it usually takes longer.

Some experienced workers are promoted to supervisor. Others may go into the contracting business for themselves.

Job Outlook

Employment of structural and reinforcing iron and metal workers is expected to rise about as fast as the average for all occupations through the year 2012, largely on the basis of continued growth in industrial and commercial construction. The rehabilitation, maintenance, and replacement of a growing number of older buildings, factories, powerplants, highways, and bridges is expected to create employment opportunities. In addition to new jobs that arise, other job openings will result from the need to replace experienced ironworkers who transfer to other occupations or leave the labor force.

The number of job openings fluctuates from year to year with economic conditions and the level of construction activity. During economic downturns, ironworkers can experience high rates of unemployment. Similarly, job opportunities for ironworkers may vary widely by geographic area. Job openings for ironworkers usually are more abundant during the spring and summer months, when the level of construction activity increases.

Earnings

In 2002, median hourly earnings of structural iron and steel workers in all industries were $19.55. The middle 50 percent earned between $14.45 and $26.00. The lowest 10 percent earned less than $10.81, and the highest 10 percent earned more than $31.81. In 2002, median hourly earnings of reinforcing iron and rebar workers in all industries were $17.66. The middle 50 percent earned between $12.72 and $25.74. The lowest 10 percent earned less than $10.07, and the highest 10 percent earned more than $31.40.

Median hourly earnings of structural iron and steel workers in 2002 in foundation, structure, and building exterior contractors were $21.35 and in nonresidential building construction, $16.98. Reinforcing iron and rebar workers earned median hourly earnings of $18.46 in foundation, structure, and building exterior contractors in 2002.

Many workers in this trade are members of the International Association of Bridge, Structural, Ornamental, and Reinforcing Iron Workers. According to the union, average hourly earnings, including benefits, for structural and reinforcing metal workers who belonged to a union and worked full time were 34 percent higher than the hourly earnings of nonunion workers. Structural and reinforcing iron and metal workers in New York, Boston, San Francisco, Chicago, Los Angeles, Philadelphia, and other large cities received the highest wages.

Apprentices generally start at about 50 percent to 60 percent of the rate paid to experienced journey workers. Throughout the course of the apprenticeship program, as they acquire the skills of the trade, they receive periodic increases until their pay approaches that of experienced workers.

Earnings for ironworkers may be reduced on occasion because work can be limited by bad weather, the short-term nature of construction jobs, and economic downturns.

Related Occupations

Structural and reinforcing iron and metal workers play an essential role in erecting buildings, bridges, highways, power lines, and other structures. Others who work on these construction jobs include assemblers and fabricators; boilermakers; civil engineers; cement masons, concrete finishers, segmental pavers, and terrazzo workers; construction managers; and welding, soldering, and brazing workers.

Sources of Additional Information

For more information on apprenticeships or other work opportunities, contact local general contractors; a local of the International Association of Bridge, Structural, Ornamental, and Reinforcing Iron Workers Union; a local ironworkers' joint union-management apprenticeship committee; a local or State chapter of the Associated Builders and Contractors or the Associated General Contractors; or the nearest office of your State employment service or apprenticeship agency.

For apprenticeship information, contact

➤ International Association of Bridge, Structural, Ornamental, and Reinforcing Iron Workers, Apprenticeship Department, 1750 New York Ave. NW., Suite 400, Washington, DC 20006.

For general information about ironworkers, contact either of the following sources:

➤ Associated Builders and Contractors, Workforce Development Department, 4250 North Fairfax Dr., 9th Floor, Arlington, VA 22203.

➤ Associated General Contractors of America, 333 John Carlyle St., Suite 200, Alexandria, VA 22314. Internet: **http://www.agc.org**

More than 500 occupations are registered by the U.S. Department of Labor's National Apprenticeship system. For more information on the Labor Department's registered apprenticeship system and links to State apprenticeship programs, check the Department's website: **http://www.doleta.gov**

Installation, Maintenance, and Repair Occupations

Electrical and Electronic Equipment Mechanics, Installers, and Repairers

Computer, Automated Teller, and Office Machine Repairers

(0*NET 49-2011.01, 49-2011.02, 49-2011.03)

Significant Points

- Workers qualify for these jobs by receiving training in electronics from associate degree programs, the military, vocational schools, equipment manufacturers, or employers.

- Job growth reflects the increasing dependence of business and residential customers on computers and other sophisticated office machines.

- Job prospects will be best for applicants with knowledge of electronics, as well as repair experience; opportunities for computer repairers should be excellent, given that employers are reporting difficulty finding qualified applicants.

Nature of the Work

Computer repairers, also known as *computer service technicians or data-processing equipment repairers,* service mainframe, server, and personal computers; printers; and disc drives. These workers perform primarily hands-on repair, maintenance, and installation of computers and related equipment. Workers who provide technical assistance, in person or by telephone, to computer system users are known as computer support specialists or computer support technicians. (See the statement on computer support specialists and systems administrators elsewhere in the *Handbook.*)

Automated teller machines (ATMs) allow customers to carry out bank transactions without the assistance of a teller. ATMs now provide a growing variety of other services, including stamp, phone card, and ticket sales. *Automated teller machine servicers* repair and service these machines.

Office machine and cash register servicers work on photocopiers, cash registers, mail-processing equipment, and fax machines. Newer models of office machinery increasingly include computerized components that allow them to function more effectively than earlier models.

To install large equipment, such as mainframe computers and ATMs, repairers connect the equipment to power sources and communication lines that allow the transmission of information over computer networks. For example, when an ATM dispenses cash, it transmits the withdrawal information to the customer's bank. Workers also may install operating software and peripheral equipment, checking that all components are configured to function together correctly. The installation of personal computers and other small office machines is less complex and may be handled by the purchaser.

When equipment breaks down, many repairers travel to customers' workplaces or other locations to make the necessary repairs. These workers, known as *field technicians*, often have assigned areas in which they perform preventive maintenance on a regular basis. *Bench technicians* work in repair shops located in stores, factories, or service centers. In small companies, repairers may work both in repair shops and at customer locations.

Computer repairers usually replace subsystems instead of repairing them. Replacement is common because subsystems are inexpensive and businesses are reluctant to shut down their computers for time-consuming repairs. Subsystems commonly replaced by computer repairers include video cards, which transmit signals from the computer to the monitor; hard drives, which store data; and network cards, which allow communication over the network. Defective modules may be given to bench technicians, who use software programs to diagnose the problem and who may repair the modules, if possible.

When ATMs malfunction, computer networks recognize the problem and alert repairers. Common problems include worn magnetic heads on card readers, which prevent the equipment from recognizing customers' bankcards, and "pick failures," which prevent the equipment from dispensing the correct amount of cash. Field technicians travel to the locations of ATMs and usually repair equipment by removing and replacing defective components. Broken components are brought to a repair shop, where bench technicians make the necessary repairs. Field technicians perform routine maintenance on a regular basis, replacing worn parts and running diagnostic tests to ensure that the equipment functions properly.

Office machine repairers usually work on machinery at the customer's workplace; alternatively, if the machines are small enough, customers may bring them to a repair shop for maintenance.

Computer repairers usually replace defective components, such as video and network cards, instead of repairing them.

Common malfunctions include paper misfeeds, due to worn or dirty parts, and poor-quality copy, due to problems with lamps, lenses, or mirrors. These malfunctions usually can be resolved simply by cleaning the relevant components. Breakdowns also may result from the failure of commonly used parts. For example, heavy usage of a photocopier may wear down the printhead, which applies ink to the final copy. In such cases, the repairer usually replaces the part instead of repairing it.

Workers use a variety of tools for diagnostic tests and repair. To diagnose malfunctions, they use multimeters to measure voltage, current, resistance, and other electrical properties; signal generators to provide test signals; and oscilloscopes to monitor equipment signals. To diagnose computerized equipment, repairers use software programs. To repair or adjust equipment, workers use handtools, such as pliers, screwdrivers, soldering irons, and wrenches.

Working Conditions

Repairers usually work in clean, well-lighted surroundings. Because computers and office machines are sensitive to extreme temperatures and to humidity, repair shops usually are air conditioned and well ventilated. Field repairers must travel frequently to various locations to install, maintain, or repair customers' equipment. ATM repairers may have to perform their jobs in small, confined spaces that house the equipment.

Because computers and ATMs are critical for many organizations to function efficiently, data-processing equipment repairers and ATM field technicians often work around the clock. Their schedules may include evening, weekend, and holiday shifts, sometimes assigned on the basis of seniority. Office machine and cash register servicers usually work regular business hours because the equipment they repair is not as critical.

Although their job is not strenuous, repairers must lift equipment and work in a variety of postures. Repairers of computer monitors need to discharge voltage from the equipment to avoid electrocution. Workers may have to wear protective goggles.

Employment

Computer, automated teller, and office machine repairers held about 156,000 jobs in 2002. Wholesale trade establishments employed about one-third of the workers in this occupation; most of these establishments were wholesalers of professional and commercial equipment and supplies. Many workers also were employed in electronics, appliance, and office supplies stores. Others worked in electronic and precision equipment repair shops and computer systems design firms. A small number were found in computer and peripheral equipment manufacturing, government agencies, and internet service providers. About 1 computer, automated teller, and office machine repairer in 8 was self-employed, more than twice the proportion for all installation, maintenance, and repair occupations.

Training, Other Qualifications, and Advancement

Knowledge of electronics is necessary for employment as a computer, automated teller, or office machine repairer. Employers prefer workers who are certified as repairers or who have training in electronics from associate degree programs, the military, vocational schools, or equipment manufacturers. Employers generally provide some training to new repairers on specific equipment; however, workers are expected to arrive on the job with a basic understanding of equipment repair. Employers may send experienced workers to training sessions to keep up with changes in technology and service procedures.

Most office machine and ATM repairer positions require an associate degree in electronics. A basic understanding of mechanical equipment also is important, because many of the parts that fail in office machines and ATMs are mechanical, such as paper loaders. Entry-level employees at large companies normally receive on-the-job training lasting several months. Such training may include a week of classroom instruction, followed by a period of 2 weeks to several months assisting an experienced repairer.

Field technicians work closely with customers and must have good communications skills and a neat appearance. Employers normally require that field technicians have a driver's license.

Various organizations offer certification, including ACES International, the Computing Technology Industry Association, the Electronic Technicians Association International, and the International Society of Certified Electronics Technicians. Repairers may specialize in a variety of skill areas. To receive certification, repairers must pass qualifying examinations corresponding to their level of training and experience.

Newly hired computer repairers may work on personal computers or peripheral equipment. With experience, they can advance to positions maintaining more sophisticated systems, such as networking equipment and servers. Field repairers of ATMs may advance to bench-technician positions responsible for more complex repairs. Experienced workers may become specialists who help other repairers diagnose difficult problems or who work with engineers in designing equipment and developing maintenance procedures. Experienced workers also may move into management positions responsible for supervising other repairers.

Because of their familiarity with equipment, experienced repairers may move into customer service or sales positions. Some experienced workers open their own repair shops or become wholesalers or retailers of electronic equipment.

Job Outlook

Employment of computer, automated teller, and office machine repairers is expected to grow about as fast as the average for all occupations through 2012. Job growth will be driven by the increasing dependence of business and residential customers on computers and other sophisticated office machines. The need to maintain this equipment in working order will create new jobs for repairers. In addition, openings will result from the need to replace repairers who retire or transfer into new occupations.

Job prospects will be best for applicants with knowledge of electronics as well as repair experience; opportunities for computer repairers should be excellent, given that employers are reporting difficulty finding qualified applicants and that computers are increasingly being relied on. Although computer equipment continues to become less expensive and more reliable, malfunctions still occur and can cause severe problems for users, most of whom lack the knowledge to make repairs. Computers are critical to most businesses today and will become even more so to companies that do business on the Internet and to households that bank, pay bills, or make purchases online.

People also are becoming increasingly reliant on ATMs. Besides offering bank and retail transactions, ATMs provide an increasing number of other services, such as employee information processing and distribution of government payments. Improvements in ATM design have increased reliability and simplified repair tasks, reducing the number and extent of repairs. Opportunities for ATM repairers should be available, arising primarily from the need to replace workers who leave the specialty, rather than from employment growth.

Conventional office machines, such as calculators, are inexpensive, and often are replaced instead of repaired. However, digital copiers and other, newer office machines are more costly and complex. This equipment often is computerized, designed to work on a network, and able to perform multiple functions. The growing need for repairers to service such sophisticated equipment should result in job opportunities for office machine repairers.

Earnings

Median hourly earnings of computer, automated teller, and office machine repairers were $15.98 in 2002. The middle 50 percent earned between $12.44 and $20.38. The lowest 10 percent earned less than $9.99, and the highest 10 percent earned more than $25.06. Median hourly earnings in the industries employing the largest numbers of computer, automated teller, and office machine repairers in 2002 were as follows:

Computer systems design and related services	$17.33
Professional and commercial equipment and supplies merchant wholesalers	17.28
Office supplies, stationery, and gift stores	14.79
Electronics and appliance stores	13.89
Electronic and precision equipment repair and maintenance	13.46

Related Occupations

Workers in other occupations who repair and maintain electronic equipment include broadcast and sound engineering technicians and radio operators; electronic home entertainment equipment installers and repairers; electrical and electronics installers and repairers; industrial machinery installation, repair, and maintenance workers; and radio and telecommunications equipment installers and repairers.

Sources of Additional Information

For information on careers and certification, contact:

➤ ACES International, 5241 Princess Anne Rd., Suite 110, Virginia Beach, VA 23462. Internet: **http://www.acesinternational.org**

➤ Computing Technology Industry Association, 1815 S Meyers Rd., Suite 300, Oakbrook Terrace, IL 60181-5228. Internet: **http://www.comptia.org**

➤ Electronics Technicians Association International, 5 Depot St., Greencastle, IN 46135.

➤ International Society of Certified Electronics Technicians, 3608 Pershing Ave., Fort Worth, TX 76107-4527. Internet: **http://www.iscet.org**

Electrical and Electronics Installers and Repairers

(O*NET 49-2092.01, 49-2092.02, 49.2092.03, 49-2092.04, 49-2092.05, 49-2092.06, 49-2093.00, 49-2094.00, 49-2095.00, 49-2096.00)

Significant Points

- Knowledge of electrical equipment and electronics is necessary for employment; many applicants complete 1 to 2 years at vocational schools and community colleges, although some less skilled repairers may have only a high school diploma.

- Employment is projected to grow more slowly than average, but will vary by occupational specialty.

- Job opportunities will be best for applicants with a thorough knowledge of electrical and electronic equipment, as well as repair experience.

Nature of the Work

Businesses and other organizations depend on complex electronic equipment for a variety of functions. Industrial controls automatically monitor and direct production processes on the factory floor. Transmitters and antennae provide communication links for many organizations. Electric power companies use electronic equipment to operate and control generating plants, substations, and monitoring equipment. The Federal Government uses radar and missile control systems to provide for the national defense and to direct commercial air traffic. These complex pieces of electronic equipment are installed, maintained, and repaired by electrical and electronics installers and repairers.

Electrical equipment and electronic equipment are two distinct types of industrial equipment, although much equipment contains both electrical and electronic components. In general, electrical portions provide the power for the equipment, while electronic components control the device, although many types of equipment still are controlled with electrical devices. Electronic sensors monitor the equipment and the manufacturing process, providing feedback to the programmable logic control (PLC), which controls the equipment. The PLC processes the information provided by the sensors and makes adjustments to optimize output. To adjust the output, the PLC sends signals to the electrical, hydraulic, and pneumatic devices that power the machine—changing feed rates, pressures, and other variables in the manufacturing process. Many installers and repairers, known as *field technicians*, travel to factories or other locations to repair equipment. These workers often have assigned areas in which they perform preventive maintenance on a regular basis. When equipment breaks down, field technicians go to a customer's site to repair the equipment. *Bench technicians* work in repair shops located in factories and service centers, fixing components that cannot be repaired on the factory floor.

Some industrial electronic equipment is self-monitoring and alerts repairers to malfunctions. When equipment breaks down, repairers first check for common causes of trouble, such as loose connections or obviously defective components. If routine checks do not locate the trouble, repairers may refer to schematics and manufacturers' specifications that show connections and provide instructions on how to locate problems. Automated electronic control systems are increasing in complexity, making diagnosis more challenging. Repairers use software programs and testing equipment to diagnose malfunctions. Among their diagnostic tools are multimeters, which measure voltage, current, and resistance; and advanced multimeters, which measure capacitance, inductance, and current gain of transistors. Repairers also use signal generators, which provide test signals, and oscilloscopes, which display signals graphically. Finally, repairers use handtools such as pliers, screwdrivers, soldering irons, and wrenches to replace faulty parts and adjust equipment.

Because repairing components is a complex activity and factories cannot allow production equipment to stand idle, repairers on the factory floor usually remove and replace defective units, such as circuit boards, instead of fixing them. Defective units are discarded or returned to the manufacturer or a specialized shop for repair. Bench technicians at these locations have the training, tools, and parts needed to thoroughly diagnose and repair circuit boards or other complex components. These workers also locate and repair circuit defects, such as poorly soldered joints, blown fuses, or malfunctioning transistors.

Electrical and electronics installers often fit older manufacturing equipment with new automated control devices. Older manufacturing machines are frequently in good working order, but are limited by inefficient control systems for which replacement parts are no longer available. Installers replace old electronic control units with new PLCs. Setting up and installing a new PLC involves connecting it to different sensors and electrically powered devices (electric motors, switches, and pumps) and writing a computer program to operate the PLC. Electronics installers coordinate their efforts with those of other workers who are installing and maintaining equipment. (See the statement on industrial machinery installation, repair, and maintenance workers elsewhere in the *Handbook*.)

Electrical and electronics installers and repairers, transportation equipment install, adjust, or maintain mobile electronic communication equipment, including sound, sonar, security, navigation, and surveillance systems on trains, watercraft, or other mobile equipment. *Electrical and electronics repairers, powerhouse, substation, and relay* inspect, test, repair, or maintain electrical equipment in generating stations, substations, and in-service relays. These workers may be known as powerhouse electricians, relay technicians, or power transformer repairers. *Electric motor, power tool, and related repairers*—such as armature winders, generator mechanics, and electric golf cart repairers—specialize in repairing, maintaining, or installing electric motors, wiring, or switches.

Electronic equipment installers and repairers, motor vehicles have a significantly different job. They install, diagnose, and repair communication, sound, security, and navigation equipment in motor vehicles. Most installation work involves either new alarm or sound systems. New sound systems vary significantly in cost and complexity of installation. Replacing a head unit (radio) with a new computer disc (CD) player is quite simple, requiring the removal of a few screws and the connection of a few wires. Installing a new sound system with a subwoofer, amplifier, and fuses is far more complicated. The installer builds a fiberglass or wood box designed to hold the subwoofer and to fit inside the unique dimensions of the automobile. Installing sound-deadening material, which often is necessary with more powerful speakers, requires an installer to remove many parts of a car (for example, seats, carpeting, or interiors of doors), add sound-absorbing material in empty spaces, and reinstall the interior parts. The installer also runs new speaker and electrical cables. The new system may require additional fuses, a new electrical line to be run from the battery through a newly drilled hole in the firewall into the interior of the vehicle, or an additional or more powerful alternator or battery. Motor vehicle installers and repairers work with an increasingly complex range of electronic equipment, including DVD players, satellite navigation equipment, passive-security tracking systems, and active-security systems.

Electrical and electronic repairers use software and testing equipment to diagnose malfunctions.

Working Conditions

Many electrical and electronics installers and repairers work on factory floors, where they are subject to noise, dirt, vibration, and heat. Bench technicians work primarily in repair shops, where the surroundings are relatively quiet, comfortable, and well lighted.

Installers and repairers may have to do heavy lifting and work in a variety of positions. They must follow safety guidelines and often wear protective goggles and hardhats. When working on ladders or on elevated equipment, repairers must wear harnesses to prevent falls. Before repairing a piece of machinery, these workers must follow procedures to ensure that others cannot start the equipment during the repair process. They also must take precautions against electric shock by locking off power to the unit under repair.

Motor vehicle electronic equipment installers and repairers normally work indoors in well-ventilated and well-lighted repair shops. Minor cuts and bruises are common, but serious accidents usually are avoided when safety practices are observed.

Employment

Electrical and electronics installers and repairers held about 172,000 jobs in 2002. The following tabulation breaks down their employment by occupational specialty:

Electrical and electronics repairers, commercial and industrial equipment	85,000
Electric motor, power tool, and related repairers	31,000
Electrical and electronics repairers, powerhouse, substation, and relay	21,000
Electronic equipment installers and repairers, motor vehicles	18,000
Electrical and electronics installers and repairers, transportation equipment	18,000

Many repairers worked for utilities, building equipment contractors, machinery and equipment repair shops, wholesalers, the Federal Government, retailers of automotive parts and accessories, rail transportation companies, and manufacturers of electrical, electronic, and transportation equipment.

Training, Other Qualifications, and Advancement

Knowledge of electrical equipment and electronics is necessary for employment. Many applicants gain this knowledge through programs lasting 1 to 2 years at vocational schools or community colleges, although some less skilled repairers may have only a high school diploma. Entry-level repairers may work closely with more experienced technicians who provide technical guidance.

Installers and repairers should have good eyesight and color perception in order to work with the intricate components used in electronic equipment. Field technicians work closely with customers and should have good communication skills and a neat appearance. Employers also may require that field technicians have a driver's license.

Various organizations offer certification, including ACES International, the Consumer Electronics Association, the Electronics Technicians Association International, and the International Society of Certified Electronics Technicians. Repairers may specialize—in industrial electronics, for example. To receive certification, repairers must pass qualifying exams corresponding to their level of training and experience.

Experienced repairers with advanced training may become specialists or troubleshooters who help other repairers diagnose difficult problems. Workers with leadership ability may become supervisors of other repairers. Some experienced workers open their own repair shops.

Job Outlook

Job opportunities should be best for applicants with a thorough knowledge of electrical equipment and electronics, as well as with repair experience. Overall employment of electrical and electronics installers and repairers is expected to grow more slowly than the average for all occupations over the 2002-12 period, but varies by occupational specialty. In addition to employment growth, many job openings should result from the need to replace workers who transfer to other occupations or leave the labor force.

Average employment growth is projected for electrical and electronics installers and repairers of commercial and industrial equipment. This equipment will become more sophisticated and will be used more frequently as businesses strive to lower costs by increasing and improving automation. Companies will install electronic controls, robots, sensors, and other equipment to automate processes such as assembly and testing. As prices decline, applications will be found across a number of industries, including services, utilities, and construction, as well as manufacturing. Improved reliability of equipment should not constrain employment growth, however: companies increasingly will rely on repairers because any malfunction that idles commercial and industrial equipment is costly.

Employment of motor vehicle electronic equipment installers and repairers also is expected to grow as fast as the average. However, motor vehicle manufacturers will install more and better sound, security, entertainment, and navigation systems in new vehicles, limiting employment growth for aftermarket electronic equipment installers. In addition, newer electronic systems are more reliable and require less maintenance.

Employment of electric motor, power tool, and related repairers is expected to grow more slowly than average. Improvements in electrical and electronic equipment design should limit job growth by simplifying repair tasks. More parts are being designed to be easily disposable, further reducing employment growth.

Employment of electrical and electronic installers and repairers of transportation equipment is expected to grow more slowly than the average, due to declining industry employment in rail transportation, aerospace product and parts manufacturing, and ship- and boatbuilding.

Employment of electrical and electronics installers and repairers, powerhouse, substation, and relay is expected to decline slightly. Consolidation and privatization in utilities industries should improve productivity, reducing employment. Newer equipment will be more reliable and easier to repair, further limiting employment.

Earnings

Median hourly earnings of electrical and electronics repairers, commercial and industrial equipment were $19.77 in 2002. The middle 50 percent earned between $15.13 and $24.03. The lowest 10 percent earned less than $11.71, and the highest 10 percent earned more than $27.08. In 2002, median hourly earnings were $23.68 in the Federal government and $16.87 in building equipment contractors, the industries employing the largest numbers of electrical and electronics repairers, commercial and industrial equipment.

Median hourly earnings of electric motor, power tool, and related repairers were $15.49 in 2002. The middle 50 percent earned between $11.82 and $19.99. The lowest 10 percent earned less than $9.32, and the highest 10 percent earned more than $25.34. In 2002, median hourly earnings were $14.05 in commercial and industrial machinery and equipment (except automotive and electronic) repair and maintenance, the industry employing the largest number of electronic motor, power tool, and related repairers.

Median hourly earnings of electrical and electronics repairers, powerhouse, substation, and relay were $24.85 in 2002. The middle 50 percent earned between $20.81 and $27.90. The lowest 10 percent earned less than $15.92, and the highest 10 percent earned more than $32.08. In 2002, median hourly earnings were $25.69 in electric power generation, transmission, and distribution—the industry employing the largest number of electrical and electronics repairers, powerhouse, substation, and relay.

Median hourly earnings of electronics installers and repairers, motor vehicles were $12.51 in 2002. The middle 50 percent earned between $9.97 and $16.02. The lowest 10 percent earned less than $8.47, and the highest 10 percent earned more than $19.45.

Median hourly earnings of electrical and electronics repairers, transportation equipment were $18.56 in 2002. The middle 50 percent earned between $13.85 and $22.96. The lowest 10 percent earned less than $10.68, and the highest 10 percent earned more than $26.87.

Related Occupations

Workers in other occupations who install and repair electronic equipment include broadcast and sound technicians and radio operators; computer, automated teller, and office machine repairers; electronic home entertainment equipment installers and repairers; and radio and telecommunications equipment installers and repairers. Industrial machinery installation, repair, and maintenance workers also install, maintain, and repair industrial machinery.

Sources of Additional Information

For information on careers and certification, contact any of the following organizations:

➤ ACES International, 5241 Princess Anne Rd., Suite 110, Virginia Beach, VA 23462. Internet: **http://www.acesinternational.org**

➤ Consumer Electronics Association, 2500 Wilson Blvd, Arlington VA. 22201-3834. Internet: **http://www.ce.org**

➤ Electronics Technicians Association International, 5 Depot St., Greencastle, IN 46135.

➤ International Society of Certified Electronics Technicians, 3608 Pershing Ave., Fort Worth, TX 76107-4527. Internet: **http://www.iscet.org**

Electronic Home Entertainment Equipment Installers and Repairers

(O*NET 49-2097.00)

Significant Points

● Employment is expected to grow more slowly than the average for all occupations, because it often is cheaper to replace equipment than to repair it.

● Job opportunities will be best for applicants with knowledge of electronics and with related hands-on experience.

Nature of the Work

Electronic home entertainment equipment installers and repairers, also called *service technicians*, repair a variety of equipment, including televisions and radios, stereo components, video and audio disc players, video cameras, and video recorders. They also install and repair home security systems, intercom equipment, satellite television dishes, and home theater systems, which consist of large-screen televisions and sophisticated surround-sound audio components.

Customers usually bring small, portable equipment to repair shops for servicing. Repairers at these locations, known as *bench technicians*, are equipped with a full array of electronic tools and parts. When larger, less mobile equipment breaks down, customers may pay repairers to come to their homes. These repairers, known as *field technicians*, travel with a limited set of tools and parts, and attempt to complete the repair at the customer's location. If the job is complex, technicians may bring defective components back to the shop for thorough diagnosis and repair.

When equipment breaks down, repairers check for common causes of trouble, such as dirty or defective components. Many repairs consist simply of cleaning and lubricating equipment. If routine checks do not locate the trouble, repairers may refer to schematics and manufacturers' specifications that provide instructions on how to locate problems. Repairers use a variety of test equipment to diagnose and identify malfunctions. Multimeters detect short circuits, failed capacitors, and blown fuses by measuring voltage, current, and resistance. Color-bar and dot generators provide onscreen test patterns, signal generators to test signals, and oscilloscopes and digital storage scopes to measure complex waveforms produced by electronic equipment. Repairs may involve removing and replacing a failed capacitor, transistor, or fuse. Repairers use handtools such as pliers, screwdrivers, soldering irons, and wrenches to replace faulty parts. They also make adjustments to equipment, such as focusing and converging the picture of a television set or balancing the audio on a surround-sound system.

Improvements in technology have miniaturized and digitized many audio and video recording devices. Miniaturization has made repairwork significantly more difficult, because both the components and the acceptable tolerances are smaller. For example, an analog video camera operates at 1800 revolutions per minute (rpm), while a digital video camera may operate at 9,000 rpm. Also, components now are mounted on the surface of circuit boards, instead of plugged into slots, requiring more precise soldering when a new part is installed. Improved technologies have lowered the price of electronic home entertainment equipment, to the point where customers often replace broken equipment instead of repairing it.

Working Conditions

Most repairers work in well-lighted electrical repair shops. Field technicians, however, spend much time traveling in service vehicles and working in customers' residences.

Most electronic home entertainment equipment installers and repairers work in retail stores or repair shops.

Repairers may have to work in a variety of positions and carry heavy equipment. Although the work of repairers is comparatively safe, they must take precautions against minor burns and electric shock. Because television monitors carry high voltage even when they are turned off, repairers need to discharge the voltage before servicing such equipment.

Employment

Electronic home entertainment equipment installers and repairers held about 43,000 jobs in 2002. Most repairers worked in electronics and appliance stores that sell and service electronic home entertainment products or in electronic and precision equipment repair and maintenance shops. About 1 electronic home entertainment equipment installer and repairer in 4 was self-employed, more than 4 times the proportion for all installation, maintenance, and repair occupations.

Training, Other Qualifications, and Advancement

Employers prefer applicants who have basic knowledge and skills in electronics. Applicants should be familiar with schematics and have some hands-on experience repairing electronic equipment. Many applicants gain these skills at vocational training programs and community colleges. Training programs should include both hands-on experience and theoretical education in digital consumer electronics. Entry-level repairers may work closely with more experienced technicians, who provide technical guidance.

Field technicians work closely with customers and must have good communication skills and a neat appearance. Employers also may require that field technicians have a driver's license.

Various organizations offer certification for electronic home entertainment equipment installers and repairers, including ACES International, the Custom Electronic Design and Installation Association, the Electronic Technicians Association International, and the International Society of Certified Electronics Technicians. Repairers may specialize in a variety of skill areas, including consumer electronics. To receive certification, repairers must pass qualifying exams corresponding to their level of training and experience.

Experienced repairers with advanced training may become specialists or troubleshooters, helping other repairers diagnose difficult problems. Workers with leadership ability may become supervisors of other repairers. Some experienced workers open their own repair shops.

Job Outlook

Employment of electronic home entertainment equipment installers and repairers is expected to grow more slowly than average through 2012, due to decreased demand for repair work. In addition to job openings arising from employment growth, some will also result from the need to replace workers who retire or who transfer to higher paying jobs in other occupations requiring electronics experience. Opportunities will be best for applicants with hands-on experience and knowledge of electronics.

The need for repairers is expected to grow slowly because home entertainment equipment is less expensive than in the past. As technological developments have lowered the price and improved the reliability of equipment, the demand for repair services has slackened. When malfunctions do occur, it often is cheaper for consumers to replace equipment rather than to pay for repairs.

Employment growth will be spurred somewhat by the introduction of sophisticated digital equipment, such as DVDs, digital televisions, and digital camcorders. So long as the price of such equipment remains high, purchasers will be willing to hire repairers when malfunctions occur.

Earnings

Median hourly earnings of electronic home entertainment equipment installers and repairers were $13.08 in 2002. The middle 50 percent earned between $10.20 and $17.00. The lowest 10 percent earned less than $8.18, and the highest 10 percent earned more than $21.48. In 2002, median hourly earnings of electronic home entertainment equipment installers and repairers were $12.73 in electronics and appliance stores and $11.99 in electronic and precision equipment repair and maintenance.

Related Occupations

Other workers who repair and maintain electronic equipment include broadcast and sound engineering technicians and radio operators; computer, automated teller, and office machine repairers; electrical and electronics installers and repairers; and radio and telecommunications equipment installers and repairers.

Sources of Additional Information

For information on careers and certification, contact:
➤ ACES International, 5241 Princess Anne Rd., Suite 110, Virginia Beach, VA 23462. Internet: **http://www.acesinternational.org**
➤ Custom Electronic Design and Installation Association, 7150 Winton Dr., Suite 300, Indianapolis, IN 46268. Internet: **http://www.cedia.org**
➤ Electronics Technicians Association International, 5 Depot St., Greencastle, IN 46135.
➤ International Society of Certified Electronics Technicians, 3608 Pershing Ave., Fort Worth, TX 76107-4527. Internet: **http://www.iscet.org**

Radio and Telecommunications Equipment Installers and Repairers

(O*NET 49-2021.00, 49-2022.01, 49-2022.02, 49-2022.03, 49-2022.04, 49-2022.05)

Significant Points

● Employment is projected to decline.

● Applicants with electronics training and computer skills should have the best opportunities.

● Weekend and holiday hours are common; repairers may be on call around the clock in case of emergencies.

Nature of the Work

Telephones and radios depend on a variety of equipment to transmit communications signals. Electronic switches route telephone signals to their destinations. Switchboards direct telephone calls within a single location or organization. Radio transmitters and receivers relay signals from wireless phones and radios to their destinations. Newer telecommunications equipment is computerized and can communicate a variety of information, including data, graphics, and video. The workers who set up and maintain this sophisticated equipment are radio and telecommunications equipment installers and repairers.

Central office installers set up switches, cables, and other equipment in central offices. These locations are the hubs of a telecommunications network—they contain the switches and routers that direct packets of information to their destinations. Although most telephone lines connecting houses to central offices and switching stations are still copper, the lines connecting these central hubs are fiber optic. Fiber optic lines have led to a revolution in switching

equipment. The greatly increased transmission capacity of each line has allowed a few fiber optic lines to replace many copper lines. Packet switching equipment is evolving rapidly, ever increasing the amount of information that a single fiber optic line can carry. These switches and routers have the ability to transmit, process, amplify, and direct a massive amount of information. Installing and maintaining this equipment requires a high level of technical knowledge.

The increasing reliability of telephone switches and routers has simplified maintenance. New telephone switches are self-monitoring and alert repairers to malfunctions. Some switches allow repairers to diagnose and correct problems from remote locations. When faced with a malfunction, the repairer may refer to manufacturers' manuals that provide maintenance instructions.

When problems with telecommunications equipment arise, telecommunications equipment repairers diagnose the source of the problem by testing each of the different parts of the equipment, which requires an understanding of how the software and hardware interact. Repairers often use spectrum and/or network analyzers to locate the problem. A network analyzer sends a signal through the equipment to detect any distortion in the signal. The nature of the signal distortion often directs the repairer to the source of the problem. To fix the equipment, repairers may use small handtools, including pliers and screwdrivers, to remove and replace defective components such as circuit boards or wiring. Newer equipment is easier to repair because whole boards and parts are designed to be quickly removed and replaced. Repairers also may install updated software or programs that maintain existing software.

PBX installers and repairers set up private branch exchange (PBX) switchboards, which relay incoming, outgoing, and interoffice calls within a single location or organization. To install switches and switchboards, installers first connect the equipment to power lines and communications cables and install frames and supports. They test the connections to ensure that adequate power is available and that the communication links function. They also install equipment such as power systems, alarms, and telephone sets. New switches and switchboards are computerized; workers install software or program the equipment to provide specific features. For example, as a cost-cutting feature, an installer may program a PBX switchboard to route calls over different lines at different times of the day. However, other workers, such as computer support specialists generally handle complex programming. (The work of computer support specialists is described in the *Handbook* statement on computer support specialists and systems administrators.) Finally, the installer performs tests to verify that the newly installed equipment functions properly. If a problem arises, PBX repairers determine whether it is located within the PBX system or originates in the telephone lines maintained by the local phone company.

Due to rapidly developing technologies, PBX installers must adapt and learn new technologies. Instead of installing PBX systems, many companies are choosing to install voice-over Internet protocol (VoIP) systems. VoIP systems operate like a PBX system, but they use a company's computer wiring to run Internet access, network applications, and telephone communications. Specialized phones have their own Internet protocol (IP) addresses. The phones can be plugged into any port in the system and still use the same number.

Station installers and repairers, telephone—commonly known as *telephone installers and repairers* or *telecommunications service technicians*—install and repair telephone wiring and equipment on customers' premises. They install telephone or digital subscriber line (DSL) service by connecting customers' telephone wires to outside service lines. These lines run on telephone poles or in underground conduits. The installer may climb poles or ladders to

Telecommunications equipment repairers set up, adjust, and maintain central-office switches and routers.

make the connections. Once the connection is made, the line is tested. When a maintenance problem occurs, repairers test the customers' lines to determine if the problem is located in the customers' premises or in the outside service lines. When onsite procedures fail to resolve installation or maintenance problems, repairers may request support from their technical service center. Line installers and repairers, covered elsewhere in the *Handbook*, install the wires and cables that connect customers with central offices.

Radio mechanics install and maintain radio transmitting and receiving equipment. This includes stationary equipment mounted on transmission towers and mobile equipment, such as radio communications systems in service and emergency vehicles. Radio mechanics do not work on cellular communications towers and equipment. Newer radio equipment is self-monitoring and may alert mechanics to potential malfunctions. When malfunctions occur, these mechanics examine equipment for damaged components and loose or broken wires. They use electrical measuring instruments to monitor signal strength, transmission capacity, interference, and signal delay, as well as handtools to replace defective components and parts and to adjust equipment so that it performs within required specifications.

Working Conditions

Radio and telecommunications equipment installers and repairers generally work in clean, well-lighted, air-conditioned surroundings, such as a telephone company's central office, a customer's PBX location, or an electronic repair shop or service center. Telephone installers and repairers work on rooftops, ladders, and telephone poles. Telephone and PBX installers must travel to a customer's location. Radio mechanics may maintain equipment located on the tops of transmissions towers. While working outdoors, these workers are subject to a variety of weather conditions.

Nearly all radio and telecommunications equipment installers and repairers work full time. Many work regular business hours to meet the demand for repair services during the workday. Schedules are more irregular at companies that need repair services 24 hours a day or where installation and maintenance must take place after business hours. At these locations, mechanics work a variety of shifts, including weekend and holiday hours. Repairers may be on call around the clock, in case of emergencies, and may have to work overtime.

The work of most repairers involves lifting, reaching, stooping, crouching, and crawling. Adherence to safety precautions is impor-

tant in order to guard against work hazards. These hazards include falls, minor burns, electrical shock, and contact with hazardous materials.

Employment

Radio and telecommunications equipment installers and repairers held about 226,000 jobs in 2002. About 219,000 were telecommunications equipment installers and repairers, except line installers, mostly working in the telecommunications industry, and the rest were radio mechanics. Radio mechanics worked in electronic and precision equipment repair and maintenance, telecommunications, electronics and appliance stores, and many other industries.

Training, Other Qualifications, and Advancement

Most employers seek applicants with postsecondary training in electronics and a familiarity with computers. Training sources include 2- and 4-year college programs in electronics or communications, trade schools, and equipment and software manufacturers. Military experience with communications equipment is valued by many employers. Many equipment repairers begin working in telecommunications companies as line-installers or telephone installers, before moving up to the job of central office installer and other more complex work.

Newly hired repairers usually receive some training from their employers. This may include formal classroom training in electronics, communications systems, or software and informal hands-on training assisting an experienced repairer. Large companies may send repairers to outside training sessions to keep them informed about new equipment and service procedures. As networks have become more sophisticated—often including equipment from a variety of companies—the knowledge needed for installation and maintenance also has increased.

Telecommunications equipment companies provide much of the training on specific equipment. With the rapid advances in switches, routers, and other equipment, repairers need to continually take courses and work to obtain manufacturers' certifications on the latest technology.

Repairers must be able to distinguish colors, because wires are color-coded, and they must be able to hear distinctions in the various tones on a telephone system. For positions that require climbing poles and towers, workers must be in good physical shape. Repairers who handle assignments alone at a customer's site must be able to work without close supervision. For workers who frequently contact customers, a pleasant personality, neat appearance, and good communications skills also are important.

Experienced repairers with advanced training may become specialists or troubleshooters who help other repairers diagnose difficult problems, or may work with engineers in designing equipment and developing maintenance procedures. Because of their familiarity with equipment, repairers are particularly well qualified to become manufacturers' sales workers. Workers with leadership ability also may become maintenance supervisors or service managers. Some experienced workers open their own repair services or shops, or become wholesalers or retailers of electronic equipment.

Job Outlook

Employment of radio and telecommunications equipment installers and repairers is expected to decline through 2012. Although the need for installation work will remain as companies seek to upgrade their telecommunications networks, there will be a declining need for maintenance work—performed by telecommunications equipment installers and repairers, except line installers—because of increasingly reliable self-monitoring and self-diagnosing equipment and because installation of higher capacity equipment will reduce the amount of equipment needed. The replacement of two-way radio systems with wireless systems, especially in service vehicles, will eliminate the need in many companies for onsite radio mechanics. The increased reliability of wireless equipment and the use of self-monitoring systems also will continue to lessen the need for radio mechanics. Applicants with electronics training and computer skills should have the best opportunities for radio and telecommunications equipment installer and repairer jobs.

Job opportunities will vary by specialty. For example, opportunities should be available for central office and PBX installers and repairers experienced in current technology, as the growing popularity of VoIP, expanded multimedia offerings such as video on demand, and other telecommunications services continue to place additional demand on telecommunications networks. These new services require high data transfer rates, which can be achieved only by installing new optical switching and routing equipment. Extending high-speed communications from central offices to customers also will require the installation of more advanced switching and routing equipment. Whereas increased reliability and automation of switching equipment will limit opportunities, these effects will be somewhat offset by the demand for installation and upgrading of switching equipment.

Station installers and repairers can expect keen competition. Prewired buildings and the increasing reliability of telephone equipment will reduce the need for installation and maintenance of customers' telephones. Upgrading internal lines in businesses and the wiring of new homes and businesses with fiber optic lines should offset some of these losses. As cellular telephones have increased in popularity, the number of pay phones is declining, which also will adversely affect employment of station installers and repairers as pay phone installation and maintenance is one of their major functions.

Earnings
In 2002, median hourly earnings of telecommunications equipment installers and repairers, except line installers were $22.78. The middle 50 percent earned between $18.07 and $26.38. The bottom 10 percent earned less than $13.27, whereas the top 10 percent earned more than $29.09. Median hourly earnings in the wired telecommunications carriers (telephone) industry were $24.07 in 2002.

Median hourly earnings of radio mechanics in 2002 were $17.42. The middle 50 percent earned between $13.17 and $22.78. The bottom 10 percent earned less than $10.34, whereas the top 10 percent earned more than $28.38.

Related Occupations
Related occupations that involve work with electronic equipment include broadcast and sound engineering technicians and radio operators; computer, automated teller, and office machine repairers; electronic home entertainment equipment installers and repairers; and electrical and electronics installers and repairers. Line installers and repairers also set up and install telecommunications equipment. Engineering technicians also may repair electronic equipment as part of their duties.

Sources of Additional Information
For information on career and training opportunities, contact:
➤ International Brotherhood of Electrical Workers, Telecommunications Department, 1125 15th St. NW., Room 807, Washington, DC 20005.
➤ Communications Workers of America, 501 3rd St. NW., Washington, DC 20001.

For information on careers and schools, contact:
➤ Electronics Technicians Association International, 5 Depot St., Greencastle, IN 46135.

For information on training and professional certifications for those already employed by cable telecommunications firms, contact:
➤ Society of Cable Telecommunications Engineers, Certification Department, 140 Phillips Rd., Exton, PA 19341-1318. Internet: http://www.scte.org

Vehicle and Mobile Equipment Mechanics, Installers, and Repairers

Aircraft and Avionics Equipment Mechanics and Service Technicians

(O*NET 49-2091.00, 49-3011.01, 49-3011.02, 49-3011.03)

Significant Points

● The majority of these workers learn their job in 1 of about 200 trade schools certified by the Federal Aviation Administration.

● Opportunities should be excellent, but competition is likely for the best paying airline jobs.

Nature of the Work
To keep aircraft in peak operating condition, aircraft and avionics equipment mechanics and service technicians perform scheduled maintenance, make repairs, and complete inspections required by the Federal Aviation Administration (FAA).

Many aircraft mechanics, also called airframe, powerplant, and avionics aviation maintenance technicians, specialize in preventive maintenance. They inspect engines, landing gear, instruments, pressurized sections, accessories—brakes, valves, pumps, and air-conditioning systems, for example—and other parts of the aircraft, and do the necessary maintenance and replacement of parts. Inspections take place following a schedule based on the number of hours the aircraft has flown, calendar days since the last inspection, cycles of operation, or a combination of these factors. Large, sophisticated planes are equipped with aircraft monitoring systems, consisting of electronic boxes and consoles that monitor the aircraft's basic operations and provide valuable diagnostic information to the mechanic. To examine an engine, aircraft mechanics work through specially designed openings while standing on ladders or scaffolds, or use hoists or lifts to remove the entire engine from the craft. After taking an engine apart, mechanics use precision instruments to measure parts for wear and use x-ray and magnetic inspection equipment to check for invisible cracks. Worn or defective parts are repaired or replaced. Mechanics may also repair sheet metal or composite surfaces, measure the tension of control cables, and check for corrosion, distortion, and cracks in the fuselage, wings, and tail. After completing all repairs, they must test the equipment to ensure that it works properly.

Mechanics specializing in repairwork rely on the pilot's description of a problem to find and fix faulty equipment. For example, during a preflight check, a pilot may discover that the aircraft's fuel gauge does not work. To solve the problem, mechanics may troubleshoot the electrical system, using electrical test equipment to make sure that no wires are broken or shorted out, and replace any defective electrical or electronic components. Mechanics work as fast as safety permits so that the aircraft can be put back into service quickly.

Some mechanics work on one or many different types of aircraft, such as jets, propeller-driven airplanes, and helicopters. Others specialize in one section of a particular type of aircraft, such as the engine, hydraulics, or electrical system. *Powerplant mechanics* are authorized to work on engines and do limited work on propellers. *Airframe mechanics* are authorized to work on any part of the aircraft except the instruments, powerplants, and propellers. *Combination airframe-and-powerplant mechanics*—called A & P mechanics—work on all parts of the plane, except instruments. The majority of mechanics working on civilian aircraft today are A & P mechanics. In small, independent repair shops, mechanics usually inspect and repair many different types of aircraft.

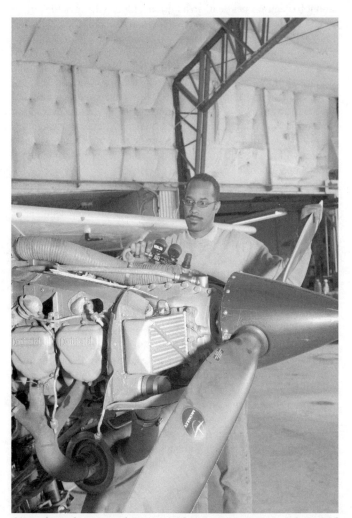

Aircraft mechanics and service technicians inspect, maintain, and repair airplanes in accordance with Federal Aviation Administration regulations.

Avionics systems are now an integral part of aircraft design and have vastly increased aircraft capability. *Avionics technicians* repair and maintain components used for aircraft navigation and radio communications, weather radar systems, and other instruments and computers that control flight, engine, and other primary functions. These duties may require additional licenses, such as a radiotelephone license issued by the U.S. Federal Communications Commission (FCC). Because of technological advances, an increasing amount of time is spent repairing electronic systems, such as computerized controls. Technicians also may be required to analyze and develop solutions to complex electronic problems.

Working Conditions

Mechanics usually work in hangars or in other indoor areas, although they can work outdoors—sometimes in unpleasant weather—when hangars are full or when repairs must be made quickly. Mechanics often work under time pressure to maintain flight schedules or, in general aviation, to keep from inconveniencing customers. At the same time, mechanics have a tremendous responsibility to maintain safety standards, and this can cause the job to be stressful.

Frequently, mechanics must lift or pull objects weighing as much as 70 pounds. They often stand, lie, or kneel in awkward positions and occasionally must work in precarious positions on scaffolds or ladders. Noise and vibration are common when engines are being tested, so ear protection is necessary. Aircraft mechanics usually work 40 hours a week on 8-hour shifts around the clock. Overtime work is frequent.

Employment

Aircraft and avionics equipment mechanics and service technicians held about 154,000 jobs in 2002; about 1 in 6 of these workers was an avionics technician. Nearly 40 percent of aircraft and avionics equipment mechanics and technicians worked for air transportation companies and close to 20 percent worked for private maintenance and repair facilities. About 20 percent worked for the Federal Government, and about 13 percent worked for aerospace products and parts manufacturing firms. Most of the rest worked for companies that operate their own planes to transport executives and cargo. Few mechanics and technicians were self-employed.

Most airline mechanics and service technicians work at major airports near large cities. Civilian mechanics employed by the U.S. Armed Forces work at military installations. Large proportions of mechanics who work for aerospace manufacturing firms are located in California or in Washington State. Others work for the FAA, many at the facilities in Oklahoma City, Atlantic City, Wichita, or Washington, DC. Mechanics for independent repair shops work at airports in every part of the country.

Training, Other Qualifications, and Advancement

The majority of mechanics who work on civilian aircraft are certificated by the FAA as "airframe mechanic," "powerplant mechanic," or "avionics repair specialist." Mechanics who also have an inspector's authorization can certify work completed by other mechanics and perform required inspections. Uncertificated mechanics are supervised by those with certificates.

The FAA requires at least 18 months of work experience for an airframe, powerplant, or avionics repairer's certificate. For a combined A & P certificate, at least 30 months of experience working with both engines and airframes is required. Completion of a program at an FAA-certified mechanic school can substitute for the work experience requirement. Applicants for all certificates also must pass written and oral tests and demonstrate that they can do the work authorized by the certificate. To obtain an inspector's authorization, a mechanic must have held an A & P certificate for at least 3 years. Most airlines require that mechanics have a high school diploma and an A & P certificate.

Although a few people become mechanics through on-the-job training, most learn their job in 1 of about 200 trade schools certified by the FAA. About one-third of these schools award 2- and 4-year degrees in avionics, aviation technology, or aviation maintenance management.

FAA standards established by law require that certified mechanic schools offer students a minimum of 1,900 actual class hours. Coursework in these trade schools normally lasts from 24 to 30 months and provides training with the tools and equipment used on the job. Aircraft trade schools are placing more emphasis on technologies such as turbine engines, composite materials—including graphite, fiberglass, and boron—and aviation electronics, which are increasingly being used in the construction of new aircraft. Additionally, employers prefer mechanics who can perform a variety of tasks.

Some aircraft mechanics in the Armed Forces acquire enough general experience to satisfy the work experience requirements for the FAA certificate. With additional study, they may pass the certifying exam. In general, however, jobs in the military services are too specialized to provide the broad experience required by the FAA. Most Armed Forces mechanics have to complete the entire training program at a trade school, although a few receive some credit for the material they learned in the service. In any case, military experience is a great advantage when seeking employment; employers consider trade school graduates who have this experience to be the most desirable applicants.

Courses in mathematics, physics, chemistry, electronics, computer science, and mechanical drawing are helpful, because they demonstrate many of the principles involved in the operation of aircraft, and knowledge of these principles is often necessary to make repairs. Courses that develop writing skills also are important because mechanics are often required to submit reports.

FAA regulations require current experience to keep the A & P certificate valid. Applicants must have at least 1,000 hours of work experience in the previous 24 months or take a refresher course. As new and more complex aircraft are designed, more employers are requiring mechanics to take ongoing training to update their skills. Recent technological advances in aircraft maintenance necessitate a strong background in electronics—both for acquiring and retaining jobs in this field. FAA certification standards also make ongoing training mandatory. Every 24 months, mechanics are required to take at least 16 hours of training to keep their certificate. Many mechanics take courses offered by manufacturers or employers, usually through outside contractors.

Aircraft mechanics must do careful and thorough work that requires a high degree of mechanical aptitude. Employers seek applicants who are self-motivated, hard-working, enthusiastic, and able to diagnose and solve complex mechanical problems. Agility is important for the reaching and climbing necessary to do the job. Because they may work on the tops of wings and fuselages on large jet planes, aircraft mechanics must not be afraid of heights.

As aircraft mechanics gain experience, they may advance to lead mechanic (or crew chief), inspector, lead inspector, or shop supervisor positions. Opportunities are best for those who have an aircraft inspector's authorization. In the airlines, where promotion often is determined by examination, supervisors sometimes advance to executive positions. Those with broad experience in maintenance and overhaul might become inspectors with the FAA. With additional business and management training, some open their own aircraft maintenance facilities. Mechanics learn many different skills in their training that can be applied to other jobs, and some transfer to other skilled repairer occupations or electronics technician jobs.

Job Outlook

Opportunities for aircraft and avionics equipment mechanics and service technician jobs should be excellent for persons who have completed aircraft mechanic training programs. Employment of aircraft mechanics is expected to increase about as fast as the average for all occupations through the year 2012, and large numbers of additional job openings should arise from the need to replace experienced mechanics who retire. Avionics technicians are projected to increase at a slower than average rate. Despite the long-term forecast, these occupations are currently in a period of little to no growth. Reduced passenger traffic resulting from a weak economy and the events of September 11, 2001, have forced airlines to cut back flights and take aircraft out of service. As the economy improves and public reluctance to board aircraft decreases, a growing population should increase passenger traffic and create the need for more aircraft mechanics and service technicians over the next decade. If the number of graduates from aircraft mechanic training programs continues to fall short of employer needs, opportunities for graduates of mechanic training programs should be excellent.

Most job openings for aircraft mechanics through the year 2012 will stem from replacement needs. A large number of mechanics are expected to retire over the next decade and create several thousand job openings per year. In addition, others will leave to work in related fields, such as automobile repair, as much of their skills are transferable to other maintenance and repair occupations. Also contributing to favorable future job opportunities for mechanics is the long-term trend towards fewer students entering technical schools to learn skilled maintenance and repair trades. Many of the students who have the ability and aptitude to work on planes are choosing to go to college, work in computer-related fields, or go into other repair and maintenance occupations with better working conditions. If the trend continues, the supply of trained aviation mechanics will not be able to keep up with air transportation industry needs when growth resumes in the industry.

Job opportunities are likely to be the best at small commuter and regional airlines, at FAA repair stations, and in general aviation. Commuter and regional airlines are the fastest growing segment of the air transportation industry, but wages in these companies tend to be lower than those in the major airlines, so they attract fewer job applicants. Also, some jobs will become available as experienced mechanics leave for higher paying jobs with the major airlines or transfer to another occupation. At the same time, general aviation aircraft are becoming increasingly sophisticated, boosting the demand for qualified mechanics. Mechanics will face more competition for jobs with large airlines because the high wages and travel benefits that these jobs offer generally attract more qualified applicants than there are openings. In spite of this, job opportunities with the airlines are expected to be better than they have been in the past. But, in general, prospects will be best for applicants with experience. Mechanics who keep abreast of technological advances in electronics, composite materials, and other areas will be in greatest demand. The number of job openings for aircraft mechanics in the Federal Government should decline as the government increasingly contracts out service and repair functions to private repair companies.

Earnings

Median hourly earnings of aircraft mechanics and service technicians were about $20.71 in 2002. The middle 50 percent earned between $16.94 and $25.23. The lowest 10 percent earned less than

$13.16, and the highest 10 percent earned more than $28.92. Median hourly earnings in the industries employing the largest numbers of aircraft mechanics and service technicians in 2002 were:

Air transportation, scheduled	$23.48
Federal Government	20.59
Air transportation, nonscheduled	19.84
Aerospace product and parts manufacturing	19.68
Support activities for air transportation	17.64

Median hourly earnings of avionics technicians were about $20.21 in 2002. The middle 50 percent earned between $17.44 and $23.91. The lowest 10 percent earned less than $14.01, and the highest 10 percent earned more than $27.00.

Mechanics who work on jets for the major airlines generally earn more than those working on other aircraft. Airline mechanics and their immediate families receive reduced-fare transportation on their own and most other airlines.

Almost 4 in 10 aircraft and avionics equipment mechanics and service technicians are members of or covered by union agreements. The principal unions are the International Association of Machinists and Aerospace Workers and the Transport Workers Union of America. Some mechanics are represented by the International Brotherhood of Teamsters.

Related Occupations

Workers in some other occupations that involve similar mechanical and electrical work are electricians, electrical and electronics installers and repairers, and elevator installers and repairers.

Sources of Additional Information

Information about jobs with a particular airline can be obtained by writing to the personnel manager of the company.

For general information about aircraft and avionics equipment mechanics and service technicians, write to:

➤ Professional Aviation Maintenance Association, 717 Princess St., Alexandria, VA 22314. Internet: **http://www.pama.org**

For information on jobs in a particular area, contact employers at local airports or local offices of the State employment service.

Automotive Body and Related Repairers

(O*NET 49-3021.00, 49-3022.00)

Significant Points

● Both formal and on-the-job training are suggested if a worker wants to become a fully skilled automotive body repairer, because advances in technology have greatly changed the structure, components, and materials used in automobiles.

● Repairers need good reading ability and basic mathematics and computer skills in order to follow instructions and diagrams in print and computer-based technical manuals.

Nature of the Work

Thousands of motor vehicles are damaged in traffic accidents every day. Although some of these vehicles are beyond repair, others can be made to look and drive like new. Automotive body repairers straighten bent bodies, remove dents, and replace crumpled parts

that cannot be fixed. They repair all types of vehicles, but work mostly on cars and small trucks, although some work on large trucks, buses, or tractor-trailers.

Automotive body repairers use special equipment to restore damaged metal frames and body sections. Repairers chain or clamp frames and sections to alignment machines that use hydraulic pressure to align damaged components. "Unibody" vehicles—designs built without frames—must be restored to precise factory specifications for the vehicle to operate correctly. To do so, repairers use benchmark systems to make accurate measurements of how much each section is out of alignment and hydraulic machinery to return the vehicle to its original shape.

Body repairers remove badly damaged sections of body panels with a pneumatic metal-cutting gun or by other means and weld in replacement sections. Repairers pull out less serious dents with a hydraulic jack or hand prying bar or knock them out with handtools or pneumatic hammers. They smooth out small dents and creases in the metal by holding a small anvil against one side of the damaged area while hammering the opposite side. Repairers also remove very small pits and dimples with pick hammers and punches in a process called metal finishing.

Body repairers also repair or replace the plastic body parts that are increasingly being used on new-model vehicles. They remove damaged panels and identify the type and properties of the plastic used on the vehicle. With most types of plastic, repairers can apply heat from a hot-air welding gun or by immersion in hot water and press the softened panel back into its original shape by hand. They replace plastic parts that are badly damaged or very difficult to repair.

Body repairers use plastic or solder to fill small dents that cannot be worked out of the plastic or metal panel. On metal panels, they file or grind the hardened filler to the original shape and clean the surface with a media blaster before painting. In many shops, automotive painters do the painting. (These workers are discussed in the *Handbook* statement on painting and coating workers, except construction and maintenance.) In small shops, workers often do both body repairing and painting. A few body repairers specialize in repairing fiberglass car bodies.

The advent of assembly-line repairs in large shops enables the establishment to move away from the one-vehicle, one-repairer method to a team approach and allows body repairers to specialize in one type of repair, such as straightening frames or repairing doors and fenders. Some body repairers specialize in installing and

Automotive body repairers use their broad knowledge of automotive construction and repair techniques.

repairing glass in automobiles and other vehicles. *Automotive glass installers and repairers* remove broken, cracked, or pitted windshields and window glass. Glass installers apply a moisture-proofing compound along the edges of the glass, place the glass in the vehicle, and install rubber strips around the sides of the windshield or window to make it secure and weatherproof.

Body repair work has variety and challenges: each damaged vehicle presents a different problem. Using their broad knowledge of automotive construction and repair techniques, repairers must develop appropriate methods for each job. They usually work alone, with only general directions from supervisors. In some shops, helpers or apprentices assist experienced repairers.

Working Conditions

Most automotive body repairers work a standard 40-hour week, although some, including the self-employed, work more than 40 hours a week. Repairers work indoors in body shops that are noisy with the clatters of hammers against metal and the whine of power tools. Most shops are well ventilated, in order to disperse dust and paint fumes. Body repairers often work in awkward or cramped positions, and much of their work is strenuous and dirty. Hazards include cuts from sharp metal edges, burns from torches and heated metal, injuries from power tools, and fumes from paint. However, serious accidents usually are avoided when the shop is kept clean and orderly and when safety practices are observed.

Employment

Automotive body and related repairers held about 220,000 jobs in 2002; about 1 in 10 specialized in automotive glass installation and repair. Most repairers worked for automotive repair and maintenance shops or automobile dealers. Others worked for organizations that maintain their own motor vehicles, such as trucking companies. A small number worked for wholesalers of motor vehicles, parts, and supplies. More than 1 automotive body repairer in 10 was self-employed, almost twice the proportion for all installation, maintenance, and repair occupations.

Training, Other Qualifications, and Advancement

Most employers prefer to hire persons who have completed formal training programs in automotive body repair, but these programs supply only a portion of employers' needs. Therefore, most new repairers receive primarily on-the-job training, supplemented, when available, with short-term training sessions given by vehicle, parts, and equipment manufacturers. Some degree of training is necessary because advances in technology have greatly changed the structure, components, and materials used in automobiles. As a result, proficiency in new repair techniques is necessary. For example, bodies of many newer automobiles are a combination of materials—traditional steel, aluminum, and a growing variety of metal alloys and plastics. Each of these materials or composites requires the use of somewhat different techniques to reshape parts and smooth out dents and small pits. Many high schools, vocational schools, private trade schools, and community colleges offer automotive body repair training as part of their automotive service programs.

A fully skilled automotive body repairer must have good reading ability and basic mathematics and computer skills. Restoring unibody automobiles to their original form requires body repairers to follow instructions and diagrams in technical manuals in order to make precise three-dimensional measurements of the position of one body section relative to another.

A new repairer begins by assisting experienced body repairers in tasks such as removing damaged parts, sanding body panels, and installing repaired parts. Novices learn to remove small dents and

to make other minor repairs. They then progress to more difficult tasks, such as straightening body parts and returning them to their correct alignment. Generally, to become skilled in all aspects of body repair requires 3 to 4 years of on-the-job training.

Certification by the National Institute for Automotive Service Excellence (ASE), although voluntary, is the recognized standard of achievement for automotive body repairers. ASE offers a series of four exams for collision repair professionals twice a year. Repairers may take from one to four ASE Master Collision Repair and Refinish Exams. Repairers who pass at least one exam and have 2 years of hands-on work experience earn ASE certification. The completion of a postsecondary program in automotive body repair may be substituted for 1 year of work experience. Those who pass all four exams become ASE Master Collision Repair and Refinish Technicians. Automotive body repairers must retake the examination at least every 5 years to retain their certification.

Continuing education is required throughout a career in automotive body repair. Automotive parts, body materials, and electronics continue to change and to become more complex and technologically advanced. To keep up with the technological advances, repairers must continue to gain new skills, read technical manuals, and attend seminars and classes.

As beginners increase their skills, learn new techniques, and complete work more rapidly, their pay increases. An experienced automotive body repairer with supervisory ability may advance to shop supervisor. Some workers open their own body repair shops. Others become automobile damage appraisers for insurance companies.

Job Outlook

Employment of automotive body repairers is expected to increase about as fast as the average for all occupations through the year 2012. The need to replace experienced repairers who transfer to other occupations or who retire or stop working for other reasons will account for the majority of job openings. Opportunities should be best for persons with formal training in automotive body repair and mechanics.

Demand for qualified body repairers will increase as the number of motor vehicles in operation continues to grow in line with the Nation's population. With each rise in the number of motor vehicles in use, the number of vehicles damaged in accidents also will grow. New automobile designs increasingly have body parts made of steel alloys, aluminum, and plastics—materials that are more difficult to work with than are traditional steel body parts. In addition, new automotive designs of lighter weight are prone to greater collision damage than are older, heavier designs and, consequently, more time is consumed in repair.

However, increasing demand due to growth in the number of vehicles in operation will be somewhat tempered by improvements in the quality of vehicles and technological innovations that enhance safety and reduce the likelihood of accidents. Employment growth also will be limited by changes in body shop management that will increase productivity, reduce overhead expenses, and improve standardization. Larger shops will employ a team approach to repairs to decrease repair time and expand their volume of work. Insurers are increasingly looking to shop networks for repair services. In addition, demand for repair services will grow slowly as more vehicles are declared a total loss after accidents. In many such cases, the vehicles are not repaired because of the high cost of fixing the extensive damage that results when airbags deploy and of replacing the increasingly complex parts and electronic components of new vehicles.

Employment growth will continue to be concentrated in automotive repair and maintenance shops and automobile dealers. The automotive repair business is not very sensitive to changes in economic conditions, and experienced body repairers are rarely laid off. However, although major body damage must be repaired if a vehicle is to be restored to safe operating condition, repair of minor dents and crumpled fenders often can be deferred during an economic slowdown. In times of economic contractions, most employers will hire few new workers, some unprofitable body shops may go out of business, and some dealers might consolidate body shops.

Earnings

Median hourly earnings of automotive body and related repairers, including incentive pay, were $15.71 in 2002. The middle 50 percent earned between $11.64 and $20.94 an hour. The lowest 10 percent earned less than $8.70, and the highest 10 percent earned more than $27.10 an hour. In 2002, median hourly earnings of automotive body and related repairers were $16.96 in automobile dealers and $15.45 in automotive repair and maintenance.

Median hourly earnings of automotive glass installers and repairers, including incentive pay, were $12.93 in 2002. The middle 50 percent earned between $9.90 and $16.58 an hour. The lowest 10 percent earned less than $7.91, and the highest 10 percent earned more than $20.24 an hour. Median hourly earnings in 2002 in automotive repair and maintenance shops, the industry employing the largest number of automotive glass installers and repairers, were $12.86.

The majority of body repairers employed by automotive dealers and repair shops are paid on an incentive basis. Under this method, body repairers are paid a predetermined amount for various tasks, and earnings depend on the amount of work assigned to the repairer and how fast it is completed. Employers frequently guarantee workers a minimum weekly salary. Body repairers who work for trucking companies, buslines, and other organizations that maintain their own vehicles usually receive an hourly wage.

Helpers and trainees typically earn from 30 percent to 60 percent of the earnings of skilled workers. Helpers and trainees usually receive an hourly rate, until they are skilled enough to be paid on an incentive basis.

Related Occupations

Repairing damaged motor vehicles often involves working on mechanical components, as well as vehicle bodies. Automotive body repairers often work closely with individuals in several related occupations, including automotive service technicians and mechanics, diesel service technicians and mechanics, auto damage insurance appraisers, and painting and coating workers, except construction and maintenance.

Sources of Additional Information

Additional details about work opportunities may be obtained from automotive body repair shops, automobile dealers, locals of the unions previously mentioned, or local offices of your State employment service. State employment services also are a source of information about training programs.

For general information about automotive body repairer careers, write to any of the following sources:

➤ Automotive Service Association, P.O. Box 929, Bedford, Texas 76095-0929. Internet: **http://www.asashop.org**

➤ National Automobile Dealers Association, 8400 Westpark Dr., McLean, VA 22102. Internet: **http://www.nada.org**

➤ Inter-Industry Conference On Auto Collision Repair Education Foundation (I-CAR), 3701 Algonquin Rd., Suite 400, Rolling Meadow, IL 60008. Telephone (tollfree): 800-422-7872.

For information on how to become a certified automotive body repairer, write to:

➤ National Institute for Automotive Service Excellence (ASE), 101 Blue Seal Dr. SE., Suite 101, Leesburg, VA 20175. Internet: **http://www.asecert.org**

For a directory of certified automotive body repairer programs, contact:

➤ National Automotive Technician Education Foundation, 101 Blue Seal Dr., SE., Suite 101, Leesburg, VA 20175. Internet: **http://www.natef.org**

For a directory of accredited private trade and technical schools that offer training programs in automotive body repair, contact:

➤ Accrediting Commission of Career Schools and Colleges of Technology, 2101 Wilson Blvd., Suite 302, Arlington, VA 22201. Internet: **http://www.accsct.org**

For a list of public automotive body repair training programs, contact:

➤ SkillsUSA-VICA, P.O. Box 3000, Leesburg, VA 20177-0300. Internet: **http://www.skillsusa.org**

Automotive Service Technicians and Mechanics

(O*NET 49-3023.01, 49-3023.02)

Significant Points

● Formal automotive technician training is the best preparation for these challenging technology-based jobs.

● Opportunities should be very good for automotive service technicians and mechanics with diagnostic and problem-solving skills and knowledge of electronics and mathematics.

● Automotive service technicians and mechanics must continually adapt to changing technology and repair techniques as vehicle components and systems become increasingly sophisticated.

Nature of the Work

Anyone whose car or light truck has broken down knows the importance of the jobs of automotive service technicians and mechanics. The ability to diagnose the source of a problem quickly and accurately requires good reasoning ability and a thorough knowledge of automobiles. Many technicians consider diagnosing hard-to-find troubles one of their most challenging and satisfying duties.

The work of automotive service technicians and mechanics has evolved from mechanical repair to a high technology job. Today, integrated electronic systems and complex computers run vehicles and measure their performance while on the road. Technicians must have an increasingly broad base of knowledge about how vehicles' complex components work and interact, as well as the ability to work with electronic diagnostic equipment and computer-based technical reference materials.

Automotive service technicians and mechanics use their high-tech skills to inspect, maintain, and repair automobiles and light trucks that have gasoline engines. The increasing sophistication of automotive technology now requires workers who can use computerized shop equipment and work with electronic components while maintaining their skills with traditional handtools. (Service technicians and mechanics who work on diesel-powered trucks, buses, and equipment are discussed in the *Handbook* statement on diesel service technicians and mechanics. Motorcycle mechanics—who repair and service motorcycles, motor scooters, mopeds, and, occasionally, small all-terrain vehicles—are discussed in the *Handbook* statement on small engine mechanics.)

When mechanical or electrical troubles occur, technicians first get a description of the symptoms from the owner or, if they work in a large shop, the repair service estimator who wrote the repair order. To locate the problem, technicians use a diagnostic approach. First, they test to see whether components and systems are proper and secure. Then, they isolate the components or systems that could not logically be the cause of the problem. For example, if an air-conditioner malfunctions, the technician's diagnostic approach can pinpoint a problem as simple as a low coolant level or as complex as a bad drive-train connection that has shorted out the air conditioner. Technicians may have to test drive the vehicle or use a variety of testing equipment, such as onboard and hand-held diagnostic computers or compression gauges, to identify the source of the problem. These tests may indicate whether a component is salvageable or whether a new one is required to get the vehicle back in working order.

During routine service inspections, technicians test and lubricate engines and other major components. In some cases, the technician may repair or replace worn parts before they cause breakdowns that could damage critical components of the vehicle. Technicians usually follow a checklist to ensure that they examine every critical part. Belts, hoses, plugs, brake and fuel systems, and other potentially troublesome items are among those closely watched.

Service technicians use a variety of tools in their work—power tools, such as pneumatic wrenches to remove bolts quickly; machine tools like lathes and grinding machines to rebuild brakes; welding and flame-cutting equipment to remove and repair exhaust systems, and jacks and hoists to lift cars and engines. They also use common handtools, such as screwdrivers, pliers, and wrenches, to work on small parts and in hard-to-reach places.

In modern repair shops, service technicians compare the readouts from diagnostic testing devices with the benchmarked standards given by the manufacturer of the components being tested. Deviations outside of acceptable levels are an indication to the technician that further attention to an area is necessary. The testing devices diagnose problems and make precision adjustments with calculations downloaded from large computerized databases. The computerized systems provide automatic updates to technical manuals and unlimited access to manufacturers' service information, technical service bulletins, and other databases that allow technicians to keep current on problem spots and to learn new procedures.

Automotive service technicians in large shops have increasingly become specialized. For example, *transmission technicians and rebuilders* work on gear trains, couplings, hydraulic pumps, and other parts of transmissions. Extensive knowledge of computer controls, the ability to diagnose electrical and hydraulic problems, and other specialized skills are needed to work on these complex components, which employ some of the most sophisticated technology used in vehicles. *Tuneup technicians* adjust the ignition timing and valves, and adjust or replace spark plugs and other parts to ensure efficient engine performance. They often use electronic testing equipment to isolate and adjust malfunctions in fuel, ignition, and emissions control systems.

Automotive air-conditioning repairers install and repair air-conditioners and service their components, such as compressors, condensers, and controls. These workers require special training in Federal and State regulations governing the handling and disposal of refrigerants. *Front-end mechanics* align and balance wheels and

Automotive service technicians work with computerized equipment and electronic components.

repair steering mechanisms and suspension systems. They frequently use special alignment equipment and wheel-balancing machines. *Brake repairers* adjust brakes, replace brake linings and pads, and make other repairs on brake systems. Some technicians and mechanics specialize in both brake and front-end work.

Working Conditions

About half of automotive service technicians work a standard 40-hour week, but almost 30 percent work more than 40 hours a week. Many of those working extended hours are self-employed technicians. To satisfy customer service needs, some service shops offer evening and weekend service. Generally, service technicians work indoors in well-ventilated and -lighted repair shops. However, some shops are drafty and noisy. Although they fix some problems with simple computerized adjustments, technicians frequently work with dirty and greasy parts, and in awkward positions. They often lift heavy parts and tools. Minor cuts, burns, and bruises are common, but technicians usually avoid serious accidents when the shop is kept clean and orderly and safety practices are observed.

Employment

Automotive service technicians and mechanics held about 818,000 jobs in 2002. The majority worked for automotive repair and maintenance shops, automobile dealers, and retailers and wholesalers of automotive parts, accessories, and supplies. Others found employment in gasoline stations; home and auto supply stores; automotive equipment rental and leasing companies; Federal, State, and local governments; and other organizations. About 16 percent of service technicians were self-employed, more than twice the proportion for all installation, maintenance, and repair occupations.

Training, Other Qualifications, and Advancement

Automotive technology is rapidly increasing in sophistication, and most training authorities strongly recommend that persons seeking automotive service technician and mechanic jobs complete a formal training program in high school or in a postsecondary vocational school. However, some service technicians still learn the trade solely by assisting and learning from experienced workers.

Many high schools, community colleges, and public and private vocational and technical schools offer automotive service technician training programs. The traditional postsecondary programs usually provide a thorough career preparation that expands upon the student's high school repair experience.

Postsecondary automotive technician training programs vary greatly in format, but normally provide intensive career preparation through a combination of classroom instruction and hands-on practice. Some trade and technical school programs provide concentrated training for 6 months to a year, depending on how many hours the student attends each week. Community college programs normally spread the training over 2 years; supplement the automotive training with instruction in English, basic mathematics, computers, and other subjects; and award an associate degree or certificate. Some students earn repair certificates and opt to leave the program to begin their career before graduation. Recently, some programs have added to their curriculums training on employability skills such as customer service and stress management. Employers find that these skills help technicians handle the additional responsibilities of dealing with the customers and parts vendors.

High school programs, while an asset, vary greatly in quality. The better programs, such as the Automotive Youth Education Service (AYES), with about 150 participating schools and more than 300 participating dealers, conclude with the students receiving their technician's certification and high school diploma. Other programs offer only an introduction to automotive technology and service for the future consumer or hobbyist. Still others aim to equip graduates with enough skills to get a job as a mechanic's helper or trainee mechanic.

The various automobile manufacturers and their participating dealers sponsor 2-year associate degree programs at postsecondary schools across the Nation. The Accrediting Commission of Career Schools and Colleges of Technology (ACCSCT) currently certifies a number of automotive and diesel technology schools. Schools update their curriculums frequently to reflect changing technology and equipment. Students in these programs typically spend alternate 6- to 12-week periods attending classes full time and working full time in the service departments of sponsoring dealers. At these dealerships, students get practical experience while assigned to an experienced worker who provides hands-on instruction and time-saving tips.

The National Automotive Technicians Education Foundation (NATEF), an affiliate of the National Institute for Automotive Service Excellence (ASE), establishes the standards by which training facilities become certified. Once the training facility achieves these minimal standards, NATEF recommends the facility to ASE for certification. The ASE certification is a nationally recognized standard for programs offered by high schools, postsecondary trade schools, technical institutes, and community colleges that train automobile service technicians. Automotive manufacturers provide ASE certified instruction, service equipment, and current-model cars on which students practice new skills and learn the latest automotive technology. While ASE certification is voluntary, it does signify that the program meets uniform standards for instructional facilities, equipment, staff credentials, and curriculum. To ensure that programs keep up with ever-changing technology, repair techniques, and ASE standards, the certified programs are subjected to periodic compliance reviews and mandatory recertification. NATEF program experts also review and update program standards to match the level of training and skill-level achievement necessary for success in the occupation. In 2002, about 1,200 high school and postsecondary automotive service technician training programs had been certified by ASE.

For trainee automotive service technician jobs, employers look for people with strong communication and analytical skills. Technicians need good reading, mathematics, and computer skills to study technical manuals and to keep abreast of new technology and learn new service and repair procedures and specifications.

Trainees also must possess mechanical aptitude and knowledge of how automobiles work. Most employers regard the successful completion of a vocational training program in automotive service technology as the best preparation for trainee positions. Experience working on motor vehicles in the Armed Forces or as a hobby also is valuable. Because of the complexity of new vehicles, a growing number of employers require completion of high school and additional postsecondary training. Courses in automotive repair, electronics, physics, chemistry, English, computers, and mathematics provide a good educational background for a career as a service technician.

Many new cars have several onboard computers, operating everything from the engine to the radio. Some of the more advanced vehicles have global positioning systems, Internet access, and other high-tech features integrated into the functions of the vehicle. Therefore, knowledge of electronics and computers has grown increasingly important for service technicians. Engine controls and dashboard instruments were among the first components to use electronics but, now, everything from brakes to transmissions and air-conditioning systems to steering systems is run primarily by computers and electronic components. In the past, a specialist usually handled any problems involving electrical systems or electronics. Now that electronics are so common, it is essential for service technicians to be familiar with at least the basic principles of electronics. Electrical components or a series of related components account for nearly all malfunctions in modern vehicles.

In addition to electronics and computers, automotive service technicians will have to learn and understand the science behind the alternate-fuel vehicles that have begun to enter the market. The fuel for these vehicles will come from the dehydrogenization of water, electric fuel cells, natural gas, solar power, and other nonpetroleum-based sources. Some vehicles will even capture the energy from brakes and use it as fuel. As vehicles with these new technologies become more common, technicians will need additional training to learn the science and engineering that makes them possible.

Beginners usually start as trainee technicians, mechanics' helpers, lubrication workers, or gasoline service station attendants, and gradually acquire and practice their skills by working with experienced mechanics and technicians. With a few months' experience, beginners perform many routine service tasks and make simple repairs. It usually takes 2 to 5 years of experience to become a journey-level service technician, who is expected to quickly perform the more difficult types of routine service and repairs. However, some graduates of postsecondary automotive training programs are often able to earn promotion to the journey level after only a few months on the job. An additional 1 to 2 years of experience familiarizes mechanics and technicians with all types of repairs. Difficult specialties, such as transmission repair, require another year or two of training and experience. In contrast, brake specialists may learn their jobs in considerably less time because they do not need a complete knowledge of automotive repair.

In the past, many persons became automotive service technicians through 3- or 4-year formal apprenticeship programs. However, apprenticeships have become rare, as formal vocational training programs in automotive service technology have become more common.

At work, the most important possessions of technicians and mechanics are their handtools. Technicians and mechanics usually provide their own tools, and many experienced workers have thousands of dollars invested in them. Employers typically furnish expensive power tools, engine analyzers, and other diagnostic equipment, but technicians accumulate handtools with experience. Some formal training programs have alliances with tool manufacturers that help entry-level technicians accumulate tools during their training period.

Employers increasingly send experienced automotive service technicians to manufacturer training centers to learn to repair new models or to receive special training in the repair of components, such as electronic fuel injection or air-conditioners. Motor vehicle dealers also may send promising beginners to manufacturer-sponsored mechanic training programs. Employers typically furnish this additional training to maintain or upgrade employees' skills and thus increase the employees' value to the dealership. Factory representatives also visit many shops to conduct short training sessions.

Voluntary certification by the National Institute for Automotive Service Excellence (ASE) has become a standard credential for automotive service technicians. Certification is available in 1 or more of 8 different service areas, such as electrical systems, engine repair, brake systems, suspension and steering, and heating and air-conditioning. For certification in each area, technicians must have at least 2 years of experience and pass a written examination. Completion of an automotive training program in high school, vocational or trade school, or community or junior college may be substituted for 1 year of experience. In some cases, graduates of ASE-certified programs achieve certification in up to three specialties. For certification as a master automotive mechanic, technicians must be certified in all eight areas. Mechanics and technicians must retake each examination at least once every 5 years to maintain their certifications.

Experienced technicians who have leadership ability sometimes advance to shop supervisor or service manager. Those who work well with customers may become automotive repair service estimators. Some with sufficient funds open independent repair shops.

Job Outlook

Job opportunities in this occupation are expected to be very good for persons who complete automotive training programs in high school, vocational and technical schools, or community colleges. Persons with good diagnostic and problem-solving skills, and whose training includes basic electronics skills, should have the best opportunities. For well-prepared people with a technical background, automotive service technician careers offer an excellent opportunity for good pay and the satisfaction of highly skilled work with vehicles incorporating the latest in high technology. However, persons without formal automotive training are likely to face competition for entry-level jobs.

Employment of automotive service technicians and mechanics is expected to increase about as fast as the average through the year 2012. Over the 2002-12 period, population growth will boost demand for motor vehicles, which will require regular maintenance and service. Growth of the labor force and in the number of families in which both spouses need vehicles to commute to work will contribute to increased vehicle sales and employment in this industry. As personal incomes continue to rise, greater numbers of persons will be able to afford the luxury of owning multiple vehicles, which also should increase the number of passenger cars in operation. However, a slowdown in the growth of the driving-age population, as the smaller post-baby boom generation comes of age, may curb demand for cars and trucks. In addition, increasing demand due to growth in the number of vehicles in operation will be partially offset by improvements in vehicle quality and durability that improve reliability and reduce the need for extensive repair and maintenance.

Employment growth will continue to be concentrated in automobile dealerships and independent automotive repair shops. Many new jobs also will be created in small retail operations that offer after-warranty repairs, such as oil changes, brake repair, air-conditioner service, and other minor repairs generally taking less than 4 hours to complete. Employment of automotive service technicians and mechanics in gasoline service stations will continue to decline, as fewer stations offer repair services.

In addition to job openings due to growth, a substantial number of openings will be created by the need to replace experienced technicians who transfer to other occupations or who retire or stop working for other reasons. Most persons who enter the occupation can expect steady work, because changes in general economic conditions and developments in other industries have little effect on the automotive repair business.

Earnings

Median hourly earnings of automotive service technicians and mechanics, including commission, were $14.71 in 2002. The middle 50 percent earned between $10.61 and $19.84. The lowest 10 percent earned less than $8.14, and the highest 10 percent earned more than $25.21. Median annual earnings in the industries employing the largest numbers of service technicians in 2002 were as follows:

Local government	$18.04
Automobile dealers	17.66
Gasoline stations	13.04
Automotive repair and maintenance	12.77
Automotive parts, accessories, and tire stores	12.60

Many experienced technicians employed by automobile dealers and independent repair shops receive a commission related to the labor cost charged to the customer. Under this method, weekly earnings depend on the amount of work completed. Employers frequently guarantee commissioned mechanics and technicians a minimum weekly salary.

Some automotive service technicians are members of labor unions such as the International Association of Machinists and Aerospace Workers; the International Union, United Automobile, Aerospace and Agricultural Implement Workers of America; the Sheet Metal Workers' International Association; and the International Brotherhood of Teamsters.

Related Occupations

Other workers who repair and service motor vehicles include automotive body and related repairers, diesel service technicians and mechanics, and small engine mechanics.

Sources of Additional Information

For more details about work opportunities, contact local automobile dealers and repair shops or local offices of the State employment service. The State employment service also may have information about training programs.

A list of certified automotive service technician training programs can be obtained from:
➤ National Automotive Technicians Education Foundation, 101 Blue Seal Dr., SE., Suite 101, Leesburg, VA 20175. Internet: **http://www.natef.org**

For a directory of accredited private trade and technical schools that offer programs in automotive service technician training, contact:
➤ Accrediting Commission of Career Schools and Colleges of Technology, 2101 Wilson Blvd., Suite 302, Arlington, VA 22201 Internet: **http://www.accsct.org**

For a list of public automotive service technician training programs, contact:
➤ SkillsUSA-VICA, P.O. Box 3000, Leesburg, VA 20177-0300. Internet: **http://www.skillsusa.org**

Information on automobile manufacturer-sponsored programs in automotive service technology can be obtained from:

➤ Automotive Youth Educational Systems (AYES), 50 W. Big Beaver, Suite 145, Troy, MI 48084. Internet: **http://www.ayes.org**

Information on how to become a certified automotive service technician is available from:

➤ National Institute for Automotive Service Excellence (ASE), 101 Blue Seal Dr. SE., Suite 101, Leesburg, VA 20175. Internet: **http://www.asecert.org**

For general information about a career as an automotive service technician, contact:

➤ National Automobile Dealers Association, 8400 Westpark Dr., McLean, VA 22102. Internet: **http://www.nada.org**

➤ Automotive Retailing Today, 8400 Westpark Dr., MS #2, McLean, VA 22102. Internet: **http://www.autoretailing.org**

Diesel Service Technicians and Mechanics

(O*NET 49-3031.00)

Significant Points

- A career as a diesel service technician or mechanic offers relatively high wages and the challenge of skilled repair work.

- Opportunities are expected to be good for persons who complete formal training programs.

- National certification is the recognized standard of achievement for diesel service technicians and mechanics.

Nature of the Work

The diesel engine is the workhorse powering the Nation's trucks and buses, because it delivers more power and is more durable than its gasoline-burning counterpart. Diesel-powered engines also are becoming more prevalent in light vehicles, including pickups and other work trucks.

Diesel service technicians and mechanics, also known as *bus and truck mechanics and diesel engine specialists*, repair and maintain the diesel engines that power transportation equipment such as heavy trucks, buses, and locomotives. Some diesel technicians and mechanics also work on heavy vehicles and mobile equipment, including bulldozers, cranes, road graders, farm tractors, and combines. A small number of technicians repair diesel-powered passenger automobiles, light trucks, or boats. (For information on technicians and mechanics working primarily on automobiles, heavy vehicles, mobile equipment, or boats, see the *Handbook* statements on automotive, heavy vehicle, and mobile equipment; and small engine service mechanics.

Technicians who work for organizations that maintain their own vehicles spend most of their time doing preventive maintenance, to ensure that equipment will operate safely. These workers also eliminate unnecessary wear on, and damage to, parts that could result in costly breakdowns. During a routine maintenance check on a vehicle, technicians follow a checklist that includes inspecting brake systems, steering mechanisms, wheel bearings, and other important parts. Following inspection, technicians repair or adjust parts that do not work properly or remove and replace parts that cannot be fixed.

Increasingly, technicians must be flexible, in order to adapt to customers' needs and new technologies. It is common for technicians to handle all kinds of repairs, from working on a vehicle's electrical system one day to doing major engine repairs the next. Diesel maintenance is becoming increasingly complex, as more electronic components are used to control the operation of an engine. For example, microprocessors now regulate and manage fuel timing, increasing the engine's efficiency. In modern shops, diesel service technicians use hand-held computers to diagnose problems and adjust engine functions. Technicians must continually learn about new techniques and advanced materials.

Diesel service technicians use a variety of tools in their work, including power tools, such as pneumatic wrenches, to remove bolts quickly; machine tools, such as lathes and grinding machines, to rebuild brakes; welding and flame-cutting equipment, to remove and repair exhaust systems; and jacks and hoists, to lift and move large parts. Common handtools—screwdrivers, pliers, and wrenches—are used to work on small parts and get at hard-to-reach places. Diesel service technicians and mechanics also use a variety of computerized testing equipment to pinpoint and analyze malfunctions in electrical systems and engines.

In large shops, technicians generally receive their assignments from shop supervisors or service managers. Most supervisors and managers are experienced technicians who also assist in diagnosing problems and maintaining quality standards. Technicians may work as a team or be assisted by an apprentice or helper when doing heavy work, such as removing engines and transmissions.

Working Conditions

Diesel technicians usually work indoors, although they occasionally make repairs to vehicles on the road. Diesel technicians may lift heavy parts and tools, handle greasy and dirty parts, and stand or lie in awkward positions to repair vehicles and equipment. Minor cuts, burns, and bruises are common, although serious accidents can usually be avoided if the shop is kept clean and orderly and if safety procedures are followed. Technicians normally work in well-lighted, heated, and ventilated areas; however, some shops are drafty and noisy. Many employers provide lockers and shower facilities.

Employment

Diesel service technicians and mechanics held about 267,000 jobs in 2002. About 20 percent serviced buses, trucks, and other diesel-powered equipment for customers of automotive repair and

Diesel service technicians use a variety of testing equipment to pinpoint and analyze malfunctions in electrical systems and engines.

maintenance shops, motor vehicle and parts wholesalers, or automotive equipment rental and leasing agencies. About 19 percent maintained the buses, trucks, and other equipment of buslines, public transit companies, school systems, or State and local governments, and another 17 percent worked for freight trucking companies. The remaining technicians maintained vehicles and other equipment for manufacturing, construction, or other companies. A relatively small number were self-employed. Nearly every section of the country employs diesel service technicians and mechanics, although most work in towns and cities where trucking companies, buslines, and other fleet owners have large operations.

Training, Other Qualifications, and Advancement

Although many persons qualify for diesel service technician and mechanic jobs through years of on-the-job training, authorities recommend the completion of a formal diesel engine training program. Employers prefer to hire graduates of formal training programs because those workers often have a head start in training and are able to advance quickly to the journey level.

Many community colleges and trade and vocational schools offer programs in diesel repair. These programs, lasting 6 months to 2 years, lead to a certificate of completion or an associate degree. Programs vary in the degree of hands-on training they provide on equipment. Some offer about 30 hours per week on equipment, whereas others offer more lab or classroom instruction. Training provides a foundation in the latest diesel technology and instruction in the service and repair of the vehicles and equipment that technicians will encounter on the job. Training programs also improve the skills needed to interpret technical manuals and to communicate with coworkers and customers. In addition to the hands-on aspects of the training, many institutions teach communication skills, customer service, basic understanding of physics, and logical thought. Increasingly, employers work closely with representatives of training programs, providing instructors with the latest equipment, techniques, and tools and offering jobs to graduates.

Whereas most employers prefer to hire persons who have completed formal training programs, some technicians and mechanics continue to learn their skills on the job. Unskilled beginners generally are assigned tasks such as cleaning parts, fueling and lubricating vehicles, and driving vehicles into and out of the shop. Beginners usually are promoted to trainee positions as they gain experience and as vacancies become available. In some shops, beginners with experience in automobile service start as trainee technicians.

Most trainees perform routine service tasks and make minor repairs after a few months' experience. These workers advance to increasingly difficult jobs as they prove their ability and competence. After technicians master the repair and service of diesel engines, they learn to work on related components, such as brakes, transmissions, and electrical systems. Generally, technicians with at least 3 to 4 years of on-the-job experience will qualify as journey-level diesel technicians. The completion of a formal training program speeds advancement to the journey level.

For unskilled entry-level jobs, employers usually look for applicants who have mechanical aptitude and strong problem-solving skills and who are at least 18 years of age and in good physical condition. Nearly all employers require the completion of high school. Courses in automotive repair, electronics, English, mathematics, and physics provide a strong educational background for a career as a diesel service technician or mechanic. Technicians need a State commercial driver's license to test-drive trucks or buses on public roads. Many companies also require applicants to pass a drug test. Practical experience in automobile repair at a gasoline

service station, in the Armed Forces, or as a hobby is valuable as well.

Employers often send experienced technicians and mechanics to special training classes conducted by manufacturers and vendors, in which workers learn the latest technology and repair techniques. Technicians constantly receive updated technical manuals and instructions outlining changes in techniques and standards for repair. It is essential for technicians to read, interpret, and comprehend service manuals in order to keep abreast of engineering changes.

Voluntary certification by the National Institute for Automotive Service Excellence (ASE) is recognized as the standard of achievement for diesel service technicians and mechanics. Technicians may be certified as master truck technicians or in specific areas of truck repair, such as gasoline engines, drivetrains, brakes, suspension and steering, electrical and electronic systems, or preventive maintenance and inspection.

For certification in each area, a technician must pass one or more of the ASE-administered exams and present proof of 2 years of relevant hands-on work experience. Two years of relevant formal training from a high school, vocational or trade school, or community or junior college program may be substituted for up to 1 year of the work experience requirement. To remain certified, technicians must be retested every 5 years. Retesting ensures that service technicians and mechanics keep up with changing technology. Diesel service technicians and mechanics also may opt for ASE certification as master school bus technicians or master truck equipment technicians.

The most important work possessions of technicians and mechanics are their handtools. Technicians and mechanics usually provide their own tools, and many experienced workers have thousands of dollars invested in them. Employers typically furnish expensive power tools, computerized engine analyzers, and other diagnostic equipment, but individual workers ordinarily accumulate handtools with experience.

Experienced technicians and mechanics with leadership ability may advance to shop supervisor or service manager. Technicians and mechanics with sales ability sometimes become sales representatives. Some open their own repair shops.

Job Outlook

Employment of diesel service technicians and mechanics is expected to increase about as fast as the average for all occupations through the year 2012. Besides openings resulting from employment growth, opportunities will be created by the need to replace workers who retire or transfer to other occupations.

Employment of diesel service technicians and mechanics is expected to grow as freight transportation by truck increases. Additional trucks will be needed to keep pace with the increasing volume of freight shipped nationwide. Trucks also serve as intermediaries for other forms of transportation, such as rail and air. Due to the greater durability and economy of the diesel engine relative to the gasoline engine, buses and trucks of all sizes are expected to be increasingly powered by diesels. In addition, diesel service technicians will be needed to maintain and repair the growing number of schoolbuses in operation.

Careers as diesel service technicians attract many because they offer relatively high wages and the challenge of skilled repair work. Opportunities should be good for persons who complete formal training in diesel mechanics at community and junior colleges or vocational and technical schools. Applicants without formal training may face stiffer competition for entry-level jobs.

Most persons entering this occupation can expect relatively steady work, because changes in economic conditions have less of an effect on the diesel repair business than on other sectors of the economy. During a downturn in the economy, however, some employers may lay off workers or be reluctant to hire new workers.

Earnings

Median hourly earnings of bus and truck mechanics and diesel engine specialists, including incentive pay, were $16.53 in 2002. The middle 50 percent earned between $13.13 and $20.54 an hour. The lowest 10 percent earned less than $10.66, and the highest 10 percent earned more than $24.61 an hour. Median hourly earnings in the industries employing the largest numbers of bus and truck mechanics and diesel engine specialists in 2002 were as follows:

Local government	$19.58
Motor vehicle and motor vehicle parts and supplies merchant wholesalers	16.80
General freight and trucking	15.62
Automotive repair and maintenance	15.36
Elementary and secondary schools	15.10

Because many experienced technicians employed by truck fleet dealers and independent repair shops receive a commission related to the labor cost charged to the customer, weekly earnings depend on the amount of work completed. Beginners usually earn from 50 to 75 percent of the rate of skilled workers and receive increases as they become more skilled, until they reach the rates of skilled service technicians.

The majority of service technicians work a standard 40-hour week, although some work longer hours, particularly if they are self-employed. A growing number of shops have expanded their hours, either to perform repairs and routine service in a more timely fashion or as a convenience to customers. Those technicians employed by truck and bus firms providing service around the clock may work evenings, nights, and weekends, usually at a higher rate of pay than those working traditional hours.

Many diesel service technicians and mechanics are members of labor unions, including the International Association of Machinists and Aerospace Workers; the Amalgamated Transit Union; the International Union, United Automobile, Aerospace and Agricultural Implement Workers of America; the Transport Workers Union of America; the Sheet Metal Workers' International Association; and the International Brotherhood of Teamsters.

Related Occupations

Diesel service technicians and mechanics repair trucks, buses, and other diesel-powered equipment. Related technician and mechanic occupations include aircraft and avionics equipment mechanics and service technicians, automotive service technicians and mechanics, heavy vehicle and mobile equipment service technicians and mechanics, and small engine mechanics.

Sources of Additional Information

More details about work opportunities for diesel service technicians and mechanics may be obtained from local employers such as trucking companies, truck dealers, or buslines; locals of the unions previously mentioned; and local offices of your State employment service. Local State employment service offices also may have information about training programs. State boards of postsecondary career schools have information on licensed schools with training programs for diesel service technicians and mechanics.

For general information about a career as a diesel service technician or mechanic, write:

➤ Detroit Diesel, Personnel Director, MS B39, 13400 West Outer Dr., Detroit, MI 48239.

Information on how to become a certified diesel technician of medium to heavy-duty vehicles or a certified bus technician is available from:

➤ National Institute for Automotive Service Excellence (ASE), 101 Blue Seal Dr. SE, Suite 101, Leesburg, VA 20175. Internet: **http://www.asecert.org**

For a directory of accredited private trade and technical schools with training programs for diesel service technicians and mechanics, contact:

➤ Accrediting Commission of Career Schools and Colleges of Technology, 2101 Wilson Blvd., Suite 302, Arlington, VA 22201. Internet: **http://www.accsct.org**

➤ National Automotive Technicians Education Foundation, 101 Blue Seal Dr., SE., Suite 101, Leesburg, VA 20175. Internet: **http://www.natef.org**

For a list of public training programs for diesel service technicians and mechanics, contact:

➤ SkillsUSA-VICA, P.O. Box 3000, Leesburg, VA 20177-0300. Internet: **http://www.skillsusa.org**

Heavy Vehicle and Mobile Equipment Service Technicians and Mechanics

(O*NET 49-3041.00, 49-3042.00, 49-3043.00)

Significant Points

- Opportunities should be good for persons with formal postsecondary training in diesel or heavy equipment mechanics, especially if they also have training in basic electronics and hydraulics.

- This occupation offers relatively high wages and the challenge of skilled repair work.

- Skill in using computerized diagnostic equipment is becoming more important.

Nature of the Work

Heavy vehicles and mobile equipment are indispensable to many industrial activities, from construction to railroads. Various types of equipment move materials, till land, lift beams, and dig earth to pave the way for development and production. *Heavy vehicle and mobile equipment service technicians and mechanics* repair and maintain engines and hydraulic, transmission, and electrical systems powering farm equipment, cranes, bulldozers, and railcars. (For more detailed information on service technicians specializing in diesel engines, see the statement on diesel service technicians and mechanics elsewhere in the *Handbook*.)

Service technicians perform routine maintenance checks on diesel engines and on fuel, brake, and transmission systems to ensure peak performance, safety, and longevity of the equipment. Maintenance checks and comments from equipment operators usually alert technicians to problems. With many types of modern heavy and mobile equipment, technicians can plug hand-held diagnostic computers into onboard computers to diagnose any component needing adjustment or repair. After locating the problem, these technicians rely on their training and experience to use the best possible technique to solve the problem. If necessary, they may partially dismantle the component to examine parts for damage or excessive wear. Then, using hand-held tools, they repair, replace, clean, and lubricate parts as necessary. In some cases, technicians calibrate systems by typing codes into the onboard computer. After reassembling the component and testing it for safety, they put it back into the equipment and return the equipment to the field.

Many types of heavy and mobile equipment use hydraulics, to raise and lower movable parts. When hydraulic components malfunction, technicians examine them for fluid leaks, ruptured hoses, or worn gaskets on fluid reservoirs. Occasionally, the equipment requires extensive repairs, as when a defective hydraulic pump is replaced.

In addition to conducting routine maintenance checks, service technicians perform a variety of other repairs. They diagnose electrical problems and adjust or replace defective components. They also disassemble and repair undercarriages and track assemblies. Occasionally, technicians weld broken equipment frames and structural parts, using electric or gas welders.

It is common for technicians in large shops to specialize in one or two types of repair. For example, a shop may have individual specialists in major engine repair, transmission work, electrical systems, and suspension or brake systems. The technology used in heavy equipment is becoming more sophisticated with the increased use of electronic and computer-controlled components. Training in electronics is essential for these technicians to make engine adjustments and diagnose problems. Training in the use of hand-held computers also is necessary, because computers help technicians diagnose problems and adjust the functions of components.

Service technicians use a variety of tools in their work: power tools, such as pneumatic wrenches, to remove bolts quickly; machine tools, like lathes and grinding machines, to rebuild brakes; welding and flame-cutting equipment, to remove and repair exhaust systems; and jacks and hoists, to lift and move large parts. Service technicians also use common handtools—screwdrivers, pliers, and wrenches—to work on small parts and to get at hard-to-reach places. They may use a variety of computerized testing equipment to pinpoint and analyze malfunctions in electrical systems and other essential systems. For example, tachometers and dynamometers serve to locate engine malfunctions. Service technicians also use ohmmeters, ammeters, and voltmeters when working on electrical systems.

Mobile heavy equipment mechanics and service technicians keep construction and surface mining equipment, such as bulldozers, cranes, crawlers, draglines, graders, excavators, and other equipment, in working order. Typically, these workers are employed by equipment wholesale distribution and leasing firms, large construction and mining companies, local and Federal governments, and other organizations operating and maintaining heavy machinery and

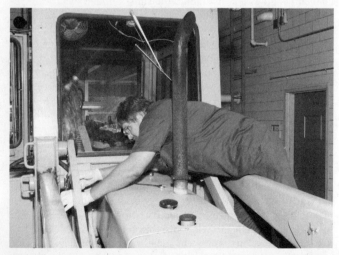

With many types of modern heavy and mobile equipment, technicians can plug hand-held diagnostic computers into onboard computers to diagnose components needing adjustment or repair.

equipment fleets. Service technicians employed by the Federal Government may work on tanks and other armored equipment.

Farm equipment mechanics service, maintain, and repair farm equipment, as well as smaller lawn and garden tractors sold to suburban homeowners. What typically was a general repairer's job around the farm has evolved into a specialized technical career. Farmers have increasingly turned to farm equipment dealers to service and repair their equipment because the machinery has grown in complexity. Modern equipment uses more electronics and hydraulics, making it difficult to perform repairs without some specialized training.

Farm equipment mechanics work mostly on equipment brought into the shop for repair and adjustment. During planting and harvesting seasons, they may travel to farms to make emergency repairs to minimize delays in farm operations.

Railcar repairers specialize in servicing railroad locomotives and other rolling stock, streetcars and subway cars, or mine cars. Most work for railroads, public and private transit companies, and railcar manufacturers.

Working Conditions
Service technicians usually work indoors, although many make repairs at the worksite. To repair vehicles and equipment, technicians often lift heavy parts and tools, handle greasy and dirty parts, and stand or lie in awkward positions. Minor cuts, burns, and bruises are common; serious accidents normally are avoided when the shop is kept clean and orderly and when safety practices are observed. Technicians usually work in well-lighted, heated, and ventilated areas. However, some shops are drafty and noisy. Many employers provide uniforms, locker rooms, and shower facilities.

When heavy or mobile equipment breaks down at a construction site, it may be too difficult or expensive to bring it into a repair shop, so the shop often sends a field service technician to the site to make repairs. Field service technicians work outdoors and spend much of their time away from the shop. Generally, the more experienced service technicians specialize in field service. They usually drive trucks specially equipped with replacement parts and tools. On occasion, they must travel many miles to reach disabled machinery. Field technicians normally earn a higher wage than their counterparts, because they are required to make on-the-spot decisions that are necessary to serve their customers.

The hours of work for farm equipment mechanics vary according to the season of the year. During the busy planting and harvesting seasons, mechanics often work 6 or 7 days a week, 10 to 12 hours daily. In slow winter months, however, mechanics may work fewer than 40 hours a week.

Employment
Heavy vehicle and mobile equipment service technicians and mechanics held about 176,000 jobs in 2002. Approximately 126,000 were mobile heavy equipment mechanics, 35,000 were farm equipment mechanics, and 15,000 were railcar repairers. About a third were employed by machinery, equipment, and supplies merchant wholesalers. More than 12 percent were employed by Federal, State, and local governments, and another 12 percent worked in construction, primarily for specialty trade contractors and highway, street, and bridge construction companies. Other service technicians worked in agriculture; mining; rail transportation and support activities; and commercial and industrial machinery and equipment rental, leasing, and repair. A small number repaired equipment for machinery and railroad rolling stock manufacturers or lawn and garden equipment and supplies stores. Less than 5 percent of service technicians were self-employed.

Nearly every section of the country employs heavy and mobile equipment service technicians and mechanics, although most work in towns and cities where equipment dealers, equipment rental and leasing companies, and construction companies have repair facilities.

Training, Other Qualifications, and Advancement

Many persons qualify for service technician jobs through years of on-the-job training, but most employers prefer that applicants complete a formal diesel or heavy equipment mechanic training program after graduating from high school. They seek persons with mechanical aptitude who are knowledgeable about the fundamentals of diesel engines, transmissions, electrical systems, and hydraulics. In addition, the constant change in equipment technology makes it necessary for technicians to be flexible and have the capacity to learn new skills quickly.

Many community colleges and vocational schools offer programs in diesel technology. Some tailor programs to heavy equipment mechanics. These programs educate the student in the basics of analytical and diagnostic techniques, electronics, and hydraulics. The increased use of electronics and computers makes training in the fundamentals of electronics essential for new heavy and mobile equipment mechanics. Some 1- to 2-year programs lead to a certificate of completion, whereas others lead to an associate degree in diesel or heavy equipment mechanics. These programs not only provide a foundation in the components of diesel and heavy equipment technology, but also enable trainee technicians to advance more rapidly to the journey, or experienced worker, level.

A combination of formal and on-the-job training prepares trainee technicians with the knowledge to service and repair equipment handled by a shop. After a few months' experience, most beginners perform routine service tasks and make minor repairs. As they prove their ability and competence, they advance to harder jobs. After trainees master the repair and service of diesel engines, they learn to work on related components, such as brakes, transmissions, and electrical systems. Generally, a service technician with at least 3 to 4 years of on-the-job experience is accepted as fully qualified.

Many employers send trainee technicians to training sessions conducted by heavy equipment manufacturers. The sessions, which typically last up to 1 week, provide intensive instruction in the repair of the manufacturer's equipment. Some sessions focus on particular components found in the equipment, such as diesel engines, transmissions, axles, and electrical systems. Other sessions focus on particular types of equipment, such as crawler-loaders and crawler-dozers. As they progress, trainees may periodically attend additional training sessions. When appropriate, experienced technicians attend training sessions to gain familiarity with new technology or equipment.

High school courses in automobile repair, physics, chemistry, and mathematics provide a strong foundation for a career as a service technician or mechanic. It is also essential for technicians to be able to read and interpret service manuals in order to keep abreast of engineering changes. Experience working on diesel engines and heavy equipment acquired in the Armed Forces is valuable as well.

Voluntary certification by the National Institute for Automotive Service Excellence is recognized as the standard of achievement for heavy vehicle and mobile equipment service technicians, who may be certified as a master heavy-duty diesel technician or in a specific area of heavy-duty equipment repair, such as brakes, gasoline engines, diesel engines, drivetrains, electrical systems, or suspension and steering. For certification in each area, technicians must pass a written examination and have at least 2 years' experience. High school, vocational or trade school, or community or junior college training in gasoline or diesel engine repair may substitute for up to 1 year's experience. To remain certified, technicians must be retested every 5 years. Retesting ensures that service technicians keep up with changing technology. However, there are currently no certification programs for other heavy vehicle and mobile equipment repair specialties.

The most important work possessions of technicians are their handtools. Service technicians typically buy their own handtools, and many experienced technicians have thousands of dollars invested in them. Employers typically furnish expensive power tools, computerized engine analyzers, and other diagnostic equipment, but handtools are normally accumulated with experience.

Experienced technicians may advance to field service jobs, wherein they have a greater opportunity to tackle problems independently and earn additional pay. Technicians with leadership ability may become shop supervisors or service managers. Some technicians open their own repair shops or invest in a franchise.

Job Outlook

Opportunities for heavy vehicle and mobile equipment service technicians and mechanics should be good for those who have completed formal training programs in diesel or heavy equipment mechanics. Persons without formal training are expected to encounter growing difficulty entering these jobs.

Employment of heavy vehicle and mobile equipment service technicians and mechanics is expected to grow slower than the average for all occupations through the year 2012. Most job openings will arise from the need to replace experienced repairers who retire. Employers report difficulty finding candidates with formal postsecondary training to fill available service technician positions, because many young people with mechanic training and experience opt to take jobs as automotive service technicians, diesel service technicians, or industrial machinery repairers—jobs that offer more openings and a wider variety of locations in which to work.

Faster employment growth is expected for mobile heavy equipment mechanics than for farm equipment mechanics or railcar repairers. Increasing numbers of heavy duty and mobile equipment service technicians will be required to support growth in the construction industry, equipment dealers, and rental and leasing companies. Because of the nature of construction activity, demand for service technicians follows the Nation's economic cycle. As the economy expands, construction activity increases, resulting in the use of more mobile heavy equipment to grade construction sites, excavate basements, and lay water and sewer lines. The increased use of such equipment increases the need for periodic service and repair. In addition, the construction and repair of highways and bridges requires more technicians to service equipment. As equipment becomes more complicated, repairs increasingly must be made by specially trained technicians. Job openings for farm equipment mechanics and railcar repairers are expected to arise mostly because of replacement needs.

Construction and mining are particularly sensitive to changes in the level of economic activity; therefore, heavy and mobile equipment may be idled during downturns. In addition, winter is traditionally the slow season for construction and farming activity, particularly in cold regions. Few technicians may be needed during periods when equipment is used less; however, employers usually try to retain experienced workers. Employers may be reluctant to hire inexperienced workers during slow periods.

Earnings

Median hourly earnings of mobile heavy equipment mechanics were $17.29 in 2002. The middle 50 percent earned between $14.13 and $20.88. The lowest 10 percent earned less than $11.54, and the highest 10 percent earned more than $24.90. Median hourly earnings in the industries employing the largest numbers of mobile heavy equipment mechanics in 2002 were as follows:

Federal Government	$19.44
Local government	18.03
Other specialty trade contractors	17.72
Machinery, equipment, and supplies merchant wholesalers	17.10
Commercial and industrial machinery and equipment rental and leasing	15.81

Median hourly earnings of farm equipment mechanics were $13.03 in 2002. The middle 50 percent earned between $10.50 and $16.01. The lowest 10 percent earned less than $8.73, and the highest 10 percent earned more than $18.86.

Median hourly earnings of railcar repairers were $18.78 in 2002. The middle 50 percent earned between $15.65 and $21.18. The lowest 10 percent earned less than $12.07, and the highest 10 percent earned more than $23.76. In 2002, median hourly earnings were $19.72 in rail transportation, the industry employing the largest number of railcar repairers.

Many heavy vehicle and mobile equipment service technicians and mechanics are members of unions, including the International Association of Machinists and Aerospace Workers, the International Union of Operating Engineers, and the International Brotherhood of Teamsters.

Related Occupations

Workers in related repair occupations include aircraft and avionics equipment mechanics and service technicians; automotive service technicians and mechanics; diesel service technicians and mechanics; heating, air-conditioning, and refrigeration mechanics and installers; and small engine mechanics.

Sources of Additional Information

More details about job openings for heavy vehicle and mobile equipment service technicians and mechanics may be obtained from local heavy and mobile equipment dealers and distributors, construction contractors, and government agencies. Local offices of the State employment service also may have information on job openings and training programs.

For general information about a career as a heavy vehicle and mobile equipment service technician or mechanic, contact:
➤ The Equipment Maintenance Counsel, P.O. Box 1368, Glenwood Springs, CO 81602. Internet: **http://www.equipment.org**
➤ The AED Foundation (Associated Equipment Dealers affiliate), 615 W. 22nd St., Oak Brook, IL 60523. Internet: **http://www.aednet.org/aed_foundation**

For a directory of public training programs in heavy and mobile equipment mechanics, contact:
➤ SkillsUSA-VICA, P.O. Box 3000, Leesburg, VA 20177-0300. Internet: **http://www.skillsusa.org**

A list of certified diesel service technician training programs can be obtained from:
➤ National Automotive Technician Education Foundation (NATEF), 101 Blue Seal Dr., Suite 101, Leesburg, VA 20175. Internet: **http://www.natef.org**

Information on certification as a heavy-duty diesel service technician is available from:
➤ National Institute for Automotive Service Excellence (ASE), 101 Blue Seal Dr. SE., Suite 101, Leesburg, VA 20175. Internet: **http://www.asecert.org**

Small Engine Mechanics

(O*NET 49-3051.00, 49-3052.00, 49-3053.00)

Significant Points

● Employment is expected to grow as fast as the average for all occupations, and persons with formal training as a mechanic should enjoy good job prospects.

● The use of motorcycles, motorboats, and outdoor power equipment is seasonal in many areas, so mechanics may service other types of equipment or work reduced hours in the winter.

Nature of the Work

Small engines powering motorcycles, motorboats, and outdoor power equipment share many characteristics with their larger counterparts, including breakdowns. Small engine mechanics repair and service power equipment ranging from racing motorcycles to chain saws.

Like large engines, small engines require periodic service to minimize the chance of breakdowns and to keep them operating at peak performance. During routine equipment maintenance, mechanics follow a checklist that includes the inspection and cleaning of brakes, electrical systems, fuel injection systems, plugs, carburetors, and other parts. Following inspection, mechanics usually repair or adjust parts that do not work properly or replace unfixable parts. Routine maintenance is normally a major part of the mechanic's work.

When a piece of equipment breaks down, mechanics use various techniques to diagnose the source and extent of the problem. The mark of a skilled mechanic is the ability to diagnose mechanical, fuel, and electrical problems and to make repairs in a minimal amount of time. Quick and accurate diagnosis requires problem-solving ability and a thorough knowledge of the equipment's operation.

In larger repair shops, mechanics may use special computerized diagnostic testing equipment as a preliminary tool in analyzing equipment. This computerized equipment provides a systematic performance report of various components to compare against normal ratings. After pinpointing the problem, the mechanic makes the needed adjustments, repairs, or replacements. Some jobs require minor adjustments or the replacement of a single item, such as a carburetor or fuel pump. In contrast, a complete engine overhaul requires a number of hours to disassemble the engine and replace worn valves, pistons, bearings, and other internal parts. Some highly skilled mechanics use highly specialized components and the latest computerized equipment to customize and tune motorcycles and motorboats for racing.

Small engine mechanics use common handtools, such as wrenches, pliers, and screwdrivers. They also utilize power tools, such as drills and grinders, when customized repairs warrant their use. Computerized engine analyzers, compression gauges, ammeters and voltmeters, and other testing devices help mechanics locate faulty parts and tune engines. Hoists may be used to lift heavy equipment such as motorcycles, snowmobiles, or motorboats. Mechanics often refer to service manuals for detailed directions and specifications while performing repairs.

Motorcycle mechanics repair and overhaul motorcycles, motor scooters, mopeds, dirt bikes, and all-terrain vehicles. Besides repairing engines, they may work on transmissions, brakes, and ignition systems and make minor body repairs. Mechanics usually

Small engine mechanics inspect and clean engine parts during routine equipment maintenance.

specialize in the service and repair of one type of equipment, although they may work on closely related products. Mechanics may service just a few makes and models of motorcycles, because dealers usually service only the products they sell.

Motorboat mechanics, or *marine equipment mechanics,* repair and adjust the electrical and mechanical equipment of inboard and outboard boat engines. Most small boats have portable outboard engines that are removed and brought into the repair shop. Larger craft, such as cabin cruisers and commercial fishing boats, are powered by diesel or gasoline inboard or inboard-outboard engines, which are removed only for major overhauls. Most of these repairs are performed at the docks or marinas. Motorboat mechanics also may work on propellers, steering mechanisms, marine plumbing, and other boat equipment.

Outdoor power equipment and other small engine mechanics service and repair outdoor power equipment, such as lawnmowers, garden tractors, edge trimmers, and chain saws. They also may occasionally work on portable generators and gocarts. In addition, small engine mechanics in northern parts of the country may work on snowblowers and snowmobiles, but demand for this type of repair is seasonal.

Working Conditions

Small engine mechanics usually work in repair shops that are well lighted and ventilated, but are sometimes noisy when engines are tested. Motorboat mechanics may work outdoors at docks or marinas, as well as in all weather conditions, when making repairs aboard boats. They may work in cramped or awkward positions to reach a boat's engine.

During the winter months in the northern United States, mechanics may work fewer than 40 hours a week, because the amount of repair and service work declines when lawnmowers, motorboats, and motorcycles are not in use. Many mechanics work only during the busy spring and summer seasons. However, many schedule time-consuming engine overhauls or work on snowmobiles and snowblowers during winter downtime. Mechanics may work considerably more than 40 hours a week when demand is strong.

Employment

Small engine mechanics held about 67,000 jobs in 2002. Motorcycle mechanics held around 15,000 jobs. Motorboat mechanics held approximately 22,000 and outdoor power equipment and other small engine mechanics about 30,000. Almost half worked for other motor vehicle dealers, an industry that includes retail dealers of motorcycles, boats, and miscellaneous vehicles; or for retail hardware, lawn, and garden stores. Most of the remainder were employed by independent repair shops, marinas and boatyards, equipment rental companies, wholesale distributors, and landscaping services. About 15 percent were self-employed, compared to about 6 percent of workers in all installation, maintenance, and repair occupations.

Training, Other Qualifications, and Advancement

Due to the increasing complexity of motorcycles and motorboats, most employers prefer to hire mechanics who graduate from formal training programs for small engine mechanics. Because the number of these specialized postsecondary programs is limited, most mechanics learn their skills on the job or while working in related occupations. For trainee jobs, employers hire persons with mechanical aptitude who are knowledgeable about the fundamentals of small two- and four-stroke engines. Many trainees develop an interest in mechanics and acquire some basic skills through working on automobiles, motorcycles, motorboats, or outdoor power equipment as a hobby. Others may be introduced to mechanics through vocational automotive training in high school or one of many postsecondary institutions.

Trainees learn routine service tasks under the guidance of experienced mechanics by replacing ignition points and spark plugs or by taking apart, assembling, and testing new equipment. As they gain experience and proficiency, trainees progress to more difficult tasks, such as advanced computerized diagnosis and engine overhauls. Up to 3 years of on-the-job training may be necessary before a novice worker becomes competent in all aspects of the repair of motorcycle and motorboat engines.

Employers often send mechanics and trainees to special courses conducted by motorcycle, motorboat, and outdoor power equipment manufacturers or distributors. These courses, which last as long as 2 weeks, upgrade the worker's skills and provide information on repairing new models. They are usually a prerequisite for any mechanic who performs warranty work for manufacturers or insurance companies.

Most employers prefer to hire high school graduates for trainee mechanic positions, but will accept applicants with less education if they possess adequate reading, writing, and arithmetic skills. Many equipment dealers employ students part time and during the summer to help assemble new equipment and perform minor repairs. Helpful high school courses include small engine repair, automobile mechanics, science, and business arithmetic.

Knowledge of basic electronics is essential for small engine mechanics, because electronic components control an engine's performance, the vehicle's instrument displays, and a variety of other functions of motorcycles, motorboats, and outdoor power equipment.

The most important work possessions of mechanics are their handtools. Mechanics usually provide their own tools, and many experienced mechanics have invested thousands of dollars in them. Employers typically furnish expensive power tools, computerized engine analyzers, and other diagnostic equipment, but mechanics accumulate handtools with experience.

The skills used as a small engine mechanic generally transfer to other occupations, such as automobile, diesel, or heavy vehicle and mobile equipment mechanics. Experienced mechanics with leadership ability may advance to shop supervisor or service manager jobs. Mechanics with sales ability sometimes become sales representatives or open their own repair shops.

Job Outlook

Employment of small engine mechanics is expected to grow about as fast as the average for all occupations through the year 2012. Most of the job openings are expected to be replacement jobs, because many experienced small engine mechanics are expected to transfer to other occupations, retire, or stop working for other reasons. Job prospects should be especially favorable for persons who complete mechanic training programs.

Growth of personal disposable income over the 2002-12 period should provide consumers with more discretionary dollars to buy motorboats, lawn and garden power equipment, and motorcycles. This type of spending will require more mechanics to keep the growing amount of equipment in operation. In addition, routine service will always be a significant source of work for mechanics. While advancements in technology will lengthen the interval between checkups, the need for qualified mechanics to perform this service will increase.

Employment of motorcycle mechanics should increase as the popularity of motorcycles rebounds. Motorcycle usage should continue to be popular with persons between 18 and 24 years, an age group that historically has had the greatest proportion of motorcycle enthusiasts. Motorcycles also are becoming increasingly popular with persons over the age of 40. Traditionally, this group has more disposable income to spend on recreational equipment such as motorcycles and motorboats.

Over the next decade, more people will be entering the 40-and-older age group, the group responsible for the largest segment of marine craft purchases. These potential buyers will help expand the market for motorboats, while maintaining the demand for qualified mechanics.

The construction of new single-family houses will result in an increase in the lawn and garden equipment in operation, increasing the need for mechanics. However, equipment growth will be slowed by trends toward smaller lawns and the contracting out of maintenance to lawn service firms. Growth also will be tempered by the tendency of many consumers to dispose of and replace relatively inexpensive items rather than have them repaired.

Earnings

Median hourly earnings of motorcycle mechanics were $13.03 in 2002. The middle 50 percent earned between $10.14 and $16.65. The lowest 10 percent earned less than $8.17, and the highest 10 percent earned more than $21.04. Median hourly earnings in 2002 in other motor vehicle dealers, the industry employing the largest number of motorcycle mechanics, were $13.00.

Median hourly earnings of motorboat mechanics were $13.97 in 2002. The middle 50 percent earned between $10.91 and $17.32. The lowest 10 percent earned less than $8.89, and the highest 10 percent earned more than $21.20. Median hourly earnings in 2002 in other motor vehicle dealers, the industry employing the largest number of motorboat mechanics, were $13.43.

Median hourly earnings of outdoor power equipment and other small engine mechanics were $11.93 in 2002. The middle 50 percent earned between $9.45 and $14.99. The lowest 10 percent earned less than $7.39, and the highest 10 percent earned more than $18.24. Median hourly earnings in 2002 in lawn and garden equipment and supplies stores, the industry employing the largest number of outdoor power equipment and other small engine mechanics, were $10.97.

Small engine mechanics tend to receive few benefits in small shops, but those employed in larger shops often receive paid vacations, sick leave, and health insurance. Some employers also pay for work-related training and provide uniforms.

Related Occupations

Mechanics and repairers who work on mobile equipment other than small engines include automotive service technicians and mechanics, diesel service technicians and mechanics, and heavy vehicle and mobile equipment service technicians and mechanics.

Sources of Additional Information

For more details about work opportunities, contact local motorcycle, motorboat, and lawn and garden equipment dealers, boatyards, and marinas. Local offices of the State employment service also may have information about employment and training opportunities.

General information about motorcycle mechanic careers may be obtained from:

➤ American Motorcycle Institute, 3042 West International Speedway Blvd., Daytona Beach, FL 32124. Telephone (toll free): 800-881-2264.
➤ Motorcycle Mechanics Institute, 2844 West Deer Valley Rd., Phoenix, AZ 85027. Telephone (toll free): 800-528-7995.

General information about motorboat mechanic careers is available from:

➤ American Marine and Watercraft Institute, 3042 West International Speedway Blvd., Daytona Beach, FL 32124. Telephone (toll free): 800-881-2264.
➤ Marine Mechanics Institute, 9751 Delegates Dr., Orlando, FL 32827. Telephone (toll free): 800-342-9253.

Other Installation, Maintenance, and Repair Occupations

Coin, Vending, and Amusement Machine Servicers and Repairers

(0*NET 49-9091.00)

Significant Points

● Most workers in this occupation learn their skills on the job.

● Opportunities should be especially good for persons with some knowledge of electronics.

Nature of the Work

Coin, vending, and amusement machines are a familiar sight in offices, convenience stores, arcades, and casinos. These coin-operated machines give out change, dispense refreshments, test our gaming skills, and spit out lottery tickets nearly everywhere we turn. Coin, vending, and amusement machine servicers and repairers install, service, and stock such machines and keep them in good working order.

Vending machine servicers, often called route drivers, visit machines that dispense soft drinks, candy and snacks, and other items. They collect money from the machines, restock merchandise, and change labels to indicate new selections. They also keep the machines clean and appealing.

Vending machine repairers, often called mechanics or technicians, make sure that the machines operate correctly. When checking complicated electrical and electronic machines, such as beverage dispensers, they ascertain whether the machines mix drinks properly and whether the refrigeration and heating units work correctly. If the machines are not in good working order, the mechanics repair them. On the relatively simple gravity-operated machines, repairers check the keypads, motors, and merchandise chutes. They also test coin, bill, and change-making mechanisms.

When installing machines, vending machine repairers make the necessary water and electrical connections and check the machines for proper operation. They also make sure that the installation complies with local plumbing and electrical codes. Because many vending machines dispense food, these workers, along with vending machine servicers, must comply with State and local public health and sanitation standards.

Amusement machine servicers and repairers work on jukeboxes, video games, pinball machines, and slot machines. They make sure that the various levers, joysticks, and mechanisms function properly, so that the games remain fair and the jukebox selections are accurate. They update selections, repair or replace malfunctioning parts, and rebuild existing equipment. Those who work in the gaming industry must adhere to strict guidelines, because Federal and State agencies regulate many gaming machines.

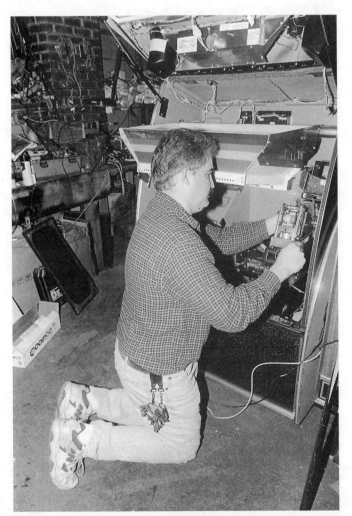

When servicing electronic machines, repairers use hand-held diagnostic computers to determine the extent and location of any problem.

Preventive maintenance—avoiding trouble before it starts—is a major job of repairers. For example, they periodically clean refrigeration condensers, lubricate mechanical parts, and adjust machines so that they perform properly.

If a machine breaks down, vending and amusement machine repairers inspect it for obvious problems, such as loose electrical wires, malfunctions of the coin mechanism or bill validator, and leaks. When servicing electronic machines, repairers test them with hand-held diagnostic computers that determine the extent and location of any problem. Repairers may only have to replace a circuit board or other component to fix the problem. However, if the problem cannot be readily located, these workers refer to technical manuals and wiring diagrams and use testing devices, such as electrical circuit testers, to find defective parts. Repairers decide whether they must replace a part and whether they can fix the malfunction onsite or whether they have to send the machine to the repair shop.

In the repair shop, vending and amusement machine repairers use power tools, such as grinding wheels, saws, and drills, as well as voltmeters, ohmmeters, oscilloscopes, and other testing equipment. They also use ordinary repair tools, such as screwdrivers, pliers, and wrenches.

Vending machine servicers and repairers employed by small companies may both fill and fix machines on a regular basis. These combination servicers-repairers stock machines, collect money, fill coin and currency changers, and repair machines when necessary.

Servicers and repairers also do some paperwork, such as filing reports, preparing repair cost estimates, ordering parts, and keeping daily records of merchandise distributed and money collected. However, new machines with computerized inventory controls reduce the paperwork that a servicer must complete.

Working Conditions

Some vending and amusement machine repairers work primarily in company repair shops, but many spend substantial time on the road, visiting machines wherever they have been placed. Repairers generally work a total of 40 hours a week. However, vending and amusement machines operate around the clock, so repairers may be on call to work at night and on weekends and holidays.

Vending and amusement machine repair shops generally are quiet, are well lighted, and have adequate workspace. However, when machines are serviced on location, the work may be done where pedestrian traffic is heavy, such as in busy supermarkets, industrial complexes, offices, casinos, or arcades. Repair work is relatively safe, although servicers and repairers must take care to avoid hazards such as electrical shocks and cuts from sharp tools and other metal objects. They also must follow safe work procedures, especially when moving heavy vending and amusement machines.

Employment

Coin, vending, and amusement machine servicers and repairers held about 43,000 jobs in 2002. Most repairers work for vending machine operators that sell food and other items through machines. Others work for beverage manufacturing companies that have their own coin-operated machines. A growing number of servicers and repairers work for amusement, gambling, and recreation establishments that own video games, pinball machines, jukeboxes, slot machines, and similar types of amusement equipment. Although vending and amusement machine servicers and repairers are employed throughout the country, most are located in areas with large populations and, thus, many vending and amusement machines.

Training, Other Qualifications, and Advancement

Most workers learn their skills on the job. New workers are trained informally on the job to fill and fix machines by observing, working with, and receiving instruction from experienced repairers. Employers normally prefer to hire high school graduates; high school or vocational school courses in electricity, refrigeration, and machine repair are an advantage in qualifying for entry-level jobs. Employers usually require applicants to demonstrate mechanical ability, either through work experience or by scoring well on mechanical-aptitude tests.

Because coin, vending, and amusement machine servicers and repairers sometimes handle thousands of dollars in merchandise and cash, employers hire persons who seem to have a record of honesty. Also, the ability to deal tactfully with people is important, because the servicers and repairers play a significant role in relaying customers' requests and concerns. A driver's license and a good driving record are essential for most vending and amusement machine servicer and repairer jobs. Some employers require their servicers to be bonded.

As electronics become more prevalent in vending and amusement machines, employers will increasingly prefer applicants who have some training in electronics. Technologically advanced machines with features such as multilevel pricing, inventory control, and scrolling messages use electronics and microchip computers extensively. Some vocational high schools and junior colleges offer 1- to 2-year training programs in basic electronics.

Beginners start training with simple jobs, such as cleaning or stocking machines. They then learn to rebuild machines by removing defective parts and repairing, adjusting, and testing the machines. Next, they accompany an experienced repairer on service calls and, finally, make visits on their own. This learning process takes from 6 months to 2 years, depending on the individual's abilities, previous education, types of machines serviced, and quality of instruction.

The National Automatic Merchandising Association has a self-study technician training program for vending machine repairers. Manuals give instruction in subjects such as customer relations, safety, electronics, and reading schematics. Upon completion of the program, repairers must pass a written test to become certified as a technician or journeyman.

To learn about new machines, repairers and servicers sometimes attend training sessions sponsored by manufacturers and distributors that may last from a few days to several weeks. Both trainees and experienced workers sometimes take evening courses in basic electricity, electronics, microwave ovens, refrigeration, and other related subjects to stay on top of new techniques and equipment. Skilled servicers and repairers may be promoted to supervisory jobs or go into business for themselves.

Job Outlook

Employment of coin, vending, and amusement machine servicers and repairers is expected to grow about as fast as the average for all occupations through the year 2012, primarily because of the increasing number of vending and amusement machines in operation. Job openings for coin, vending, and amusement machine servicers and repairers will arise from employment growth and from the need to replace experienced workers who transfer to other occupations or leave the labor force.

Establishments are likely to install additional vending machines in industrial plants, hospitals, stores, and schools to meet the public demand for inexpensive snacks and other food items. Also, there is an increased need for vending machines in businesses with few employees. The range of products dispensed by the machines

is expected to increase, as vending machines continue to become increasingly automated and begin to incorporate microwave ovens, minirefrigerators, and freezers. In addition, casinos, arcades, and other amusement establishments are becoming an increasing source of entertainment. State and multi-State lotteries are increasingly using coin-operated machines to sell scratch-off tickets in grocery stores and other public places.

Opportunities should be especially good for persons with some knowledge of electronics, because electronic circuitry is an important component of vending and amusement machines. If firms cannot find trained or experienced workers for these jobs, they are likely to train qualified route drivers or hire inexperienced people who have acquired some mechanical, electrical, or electronics training by taking high school or vocational courses.

Improved technology in newer machines will moderate employment growth because these machines require maintenance less frequently than do older ones. The new machines will need repairing and restocking less often, and they contain computers that record sales and inventory data, reducing the amount of time-consuming paperwork that otherwise would have to be filled out. The Internet is beginning to play a large role in the monitoring of vending machines from remote locations. In addition, some new machines use wireless data transmitters to signal the vending machine company when the machine needs restocking or repairing. This allows servicers and repairers to be dispatched only when needed, instead of having to check each machine on a regular schedule.

Earnings

Median hourly earnings of coin, vending, and amusement machine servicers and repairers were $13.16 in 2002. The middle 50 percent earned between $10.31 and $16.43 an hour. The lowest 10 percent earned less than $8.07 an hour, and the highest 10 percent earned more than $20.12 an hour. Median hourly earnings were $11.69 in vending machine operators, the industry employing the largest number of coin, vending, and amusement machine servicers and repairers in 2002.

Typically, States with some form of legalized gaming have the highest wages. Most coin, vending, and amusement machine servicers and repairers work 8 hours a day, 5 days a week, and receive premium pay for overtime. Some union contracts stipulate higher pay for night work and for emergency repair jobs on weekends and holidays than for regular hours. Some vending machine repairers and servicers are members of the International Brotherhood of Teamsters.

Related Occupations

Other workers who repair equipment with electrical and electronic components include electrical and electronics installers and repairers; electronic home-entertainment equipment installers and repairers; heating, air-conditioning, and refrigeration mechanics and installers; and home appliance repairers.

Sources of Additional Information

Information on job opportunities in this field can be obtained from local vending machine firms and local offices of your State employment service. For general information on vending machine repair, contact:

➤ National Automatic Merchandising Association, 20 N. Wacker Dr., Suite 3500, Chicago, IL 60606-3102. Internet: **http://www.vending.org**

➤ Automatic Merchandiser Vending Group, Cygnus Business Media, P.O. Box 803, 1233 Janesville Ave., Fort Atkinson, WI 53538-0803.

Heating, Air-Conditioning, and Refrigeration Mechanics and Installers

(0*NET 49-9021.01, 49-9021.02)

Significant Points

- Job prospects for heating, air-conditioning, and refrigeration mechanics and installers are expected to be good, particularly for those with technical school or formal apprenticeship training.

- The Air-Conditioning Excellence program, offered through North American Technician Excellence, is the standard for certification of experienced technicians.

Nature of the Work

What would those living in Chicago do without heating, those in Miami do without air-conditioning, or blood banks all over the country do without refrigeration? Heating and air-conditioning systems control the temperature, humidity, and the total air quality in residential, commercial, industrial, and other buildings. Refrigeration systems make it possible to store and transport food, medicine, and other perishable items. Heating, air-conditioning, and refrigeration mechanics and installers—also called technicians—install, maintain, and repair such systems. Because heating, ventilation, air-conditioning, and refrigeration systems often are referred to as HVACR systems, these workers also may be called HVACR technicians.

Heating, air-conditioning, and refrigeration systems consist of many mechanical, electrical, and electronic components, such as motors, compressors, pumps, fans, ducts, pipes, thermostats, and switches. In central heating systems, for example, a furnace heats air that is distributed throughout the building via a system of metal or fiberglass ducts. Technicians must be able to maintain, diagnose, and correct problems throughout the entire system. To do this, they adjust system controls to recommended settings and test the performance of the entire system using special tools and test equipment.

Technicians often specialize in either installation or maintenance and repair, although they are trained to do both. Some specialize in one type of equipment—for example, oil burners, solar panels, or commercial refrigerators. Technicians may work for large or small contracting companies or directly for a manufacturer or wholesaler. Those working for smaller operations tend to do both installation and servicing, and work with heating, cooling, and refrigeration equipment. Service contracts—which involve heating, air-conditioning, and refrigeration work for particular customers on a regular basis—are becoming more common. Service agreements help to reduce the seasonal fluctuations of this work.

Heating and air-conditioning mechanics install, service, and repair heating and air-conditioning systems in both residences and commercial establishments. *Furnace installers*, also called *heating equipment technicians*, follow blueprints or other specifications to install oil, gas, electric, solid-fuel, and multiple-fuel heating systems. *Air-conditioning mechanics* install and service central air-conditioning systems. After putting the equipment in place, they install fuel and water supply lines, air ducts and vents, pumps, and other components. They may connect electrical wiring and controls and check the unit for proper operation. To ensure the proper functioning of the system, furnace installers often use combustion test equipment, such as carbon dioxide and oxygen testers.

After a furnace has been installed, heating equipment technicians often perform routine maintenance and repair work to keep the system operating efficiently. During the fall and winter, for example, when the system is used most, they service and adjust burners and blowers. If the system is not operating properly, they check the thermostat, burner nozzles, controls, or other parts to diagnose and then correct the problem.

During the summer, when the heating system is not being used, heating equipment technicians do maintenance work, such as replacing filters, ducts, and other parts of the system that may accumulate dust and impurities during the operating season. During the winter, air-conditioning mechanics inspect the systems and do required maintenance, such as overhauling compressors.

Refrigeration mechanics install, service, and repair industrial and commercial refrigerating systems and a variety of refrigeration equipment. They follow blueprints, design specifications, and manufacturers' instructions to install motors, compressors, condensing units, evaporators, piping, and other components. They connect this equipment to the ductwork, refrigerant lines, and electrical power source. After making the connections, they charge the system with refrigerant, check it for proper operation, and program control systems.

When heating, air-conditioning, and refrigeration mechanics service equipment, they must use care to conserve, recover, and recycle chlorofluorocarbon (CFC) and hydrochlorofluorocarbon

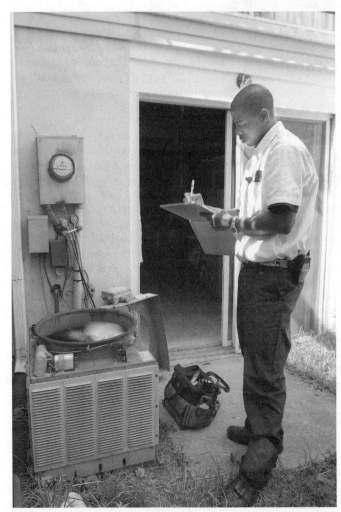

Service contracts—which involve heating, air-conditioning, and refrigeration maintenance on a regular basis—are becoming more common.

(HCFC) refrigerants used in air-conditioning and refrigeration systems. The release of CFCs and HCFCs contributes to the depletion of the stratospheric ozone layer, which protects plant and animal life from ultraviolet radiation. Technicians conserve the refrigerant by making sure that there are no leaks in the system; they recover it by venting the refrigerant into proper cylinders; and they recycle it for reuse with special filter-dryers.

Heating, air-conditioning, and refrigeration mechanics and installers are adept at using a variety of tools, including hammers, wrenches, metal snips, electric drills, pipe cutters and benders, measurement gauges, and acetylene torches, to work with refrigerant lines and air ducts. They use voltmeters, thermometers, pressure gauges, manometers, and other testing devices to check airflow, refrigerant pressure, electrical circuits, burners, and other components.

Other craftworkers sometimes install or repair cooling and heating systems. For example, on a large air-conditioning installation job, especially where workers are covered by union contracts, ductwork might be done by sheet metal workers and duct installers; electrical work by electricians; and installation of piping, condensers, and other components by pipelayers, plumbers, pipefitters, and steamfitters. Home appliance repairers usually service room air-conditioners and household refrigerators. (Additional information about each of these occupations appears elsewhere in the *Handbook*.)

Working Conditions

Heating, air-conditioning, and refrigeration mechanics and installers work in homes, stores of all kinds, hospitals, office buildings, and factories—anywhere there is climate-control equipment. They may be assigned to specific jobsites at the beginning of each day, or if they are making service calls, they may be dispatched to jobs by radio, telephone, or pager. Increasingly, employers are using cell phones to coordinate technicians' schedules.

Technicians may work outside in cold or hot weather or in buildings that are uncomfortable because the air-conditioning or heating equipment is broken. In addition, technicians might have to work in awkward or cramped positions and sometimes are required to work in high places. Hazards include electrical shock, burns, muscle strains, and other injuries from handling heavy equipment. Appropriate safety equipment is necessary when handling refrigerants because contact can cause skin damage, frostbite, or blindness. Inhalation of refrigerants when working in confined spaces also is a possible hazard.

The majority of mechanics and installers work at least a 40-hour week. During peak seasons they often work overtime or irregular hours. Maintenance workers, including those who provide maintenance services under contract, often work evening or weekend shifts and are on call. Most employers try to provide a full workweek year-round by scheduling both installation and maintenance work, and many manufacturers and contractors now provide or even require service contracts. In most shops that service both heating and air-conditioning equipment, employment is stable throughout the year.

Employment

Heating, air-conditioning, and refrigeration mechanics and installers held about 249,000 jobs in 2002; almost half worked for cooling and heating contractors. The remainder was employed in a variety of industries throughout the country, reflecting a widespread dependence on climate-control systems. Some worked for fuel oil dealers, refrigeration and air-conditioning service and repair shops, schools, and stores that sell heating and air-conditioning systems. Local governments, the Federal Government, hospitals, office build-

ings, and other organizations that operate large air-conditioning, refrigeration, or heating systems employed others. About 15 percent of mechanics and installers were self-employed.

Training, Other Qualifications, and Advancement

Because of the increasing sophistication of heating, air-conditioning, and refrigeration systems, employers prefer to hire those with technical school or apprenticeship training. Many mechanics and installers, however, still learn the trade informally on the job.

Many secondary and postsecondary technical and trade schools, junior and community colleges, and the U.S. Armed Forces offer 6-month to 2-year programs in heating, air-conditioning, and refrigeration. Students study theory, design, and equipment construction, as well as electronics. They also learn the basics of installation, maintenance, and repair.

Apprenticeship programs frequently are run by joint committees representing local chapters of the Air-Conditioning Contractors of America, the Mechanical Contractors Association of America, the National Association of Plumbing-Heating-Cooling Contractors, and locals of the Sheet Metal Workers' International Association or the United Association of Journeymen and Apprentices of the Plumbing and Pipefitting Industry of the United States and Canada. Other apprenticeship programs are sponsored by local chapters of the Associated Builders and Contractors and the National Association of Home Builders. Formal apprenticeship programs normally last 3 to 5 years and combine on-the-job training with classroom instruction. Classes include subjects such as the use and care of tools, safety practices, blueprint reading, and the theory and design of heating, ventilation, air-conditioning, and refrigeration systems. Applicants for these programs must have a high school diploma or equivalent. Math and reading skills are essential.

Those who acquire their skills on the job usually begin by assisting experienced technicians. They may begin by performing simple tasks such as carrying materials, insulating refrigerant lines, or cleaning furnaces. In time, they move on to more difficult tasks, such as cutting and soldering pipes and sheet metal and checking electrical and electronic circuits.

Courses in shop math, mechanical drawing, applied physics and chemistry, electronics, blueprint reading, and computer applications provide a good background for those interested in entering this occupation. Some knowledge of plumbing or electrical work also is helpful. A basic understanding of electronics is becoming more important because of the increasing use of this technology in equipment controls. Because technicians frequently deal directly with the public, they should be courteous and tactful, especially when dealing with an aggravated customer. They also should be in good physical condition because they sometimes have to lift and move heavy equipment.

All technicians who purchase or work with refrigerants must be certified in their proper handling. To become certified to purchase and handle refrigerants, technicians must pass a written examination specific to the type of work in which they specialize. The three possible areas of certification are: Type I—servicing small appliances, Type II—high-pressure refrigerants, and Type III—low-pressure refrigerants. Exams are administered by organizations approved by the U.S. Environmental Protection Agency, such as trade schools, unions, contractor associations, or building groups.

Several organizations have begun to offer basic self-study, classroom, and Internet courses for individuals with limited experience. In addition to understanding how systems work, technicians must be knowledgeable about refrigerant products and the legislation and regulations that govern their use. The Air-Conditioning Excellence program, which is offered through North American Technician Excellence (NATE), generally has been adopted as the standard for certification of experienced technicians.

Advancement usually takes the form of higher wages. Some technicians, however, may advance to positions as supervisor or service manager. Others may move into areas such as sales and marketing. Still others may become building superintendents, cost estimators, or, with the necessary certification, teachers. Those with sufficient money and managerial skill can open their own contracting business.

Job Outlook

Job prospects for heating, air-conditioning, and refrigeration mechanics and installers are expected to be good, particularly for those with technical school or formal apprenticeship training. Employment of heating, air-conditioning, and refrigeration mechanics and installers is expected to increase faster than the average for all occupations through the year 2012. As the population and economy grow, so does the demand for new residential, commercial, and industrial climate-control systems. Technicians who specialize in installation work may experience periods of unemployment when the level of new construction activity declines, but maintenance and repair work usually remains relatively stable. People and businesses depend on their climate-control systems and must keep them in good working order, regardless of economic conditions.

Renewed concern for energy conservation should continue to prompt the development of new energy-saving heating and air-conditioning systems. An emphasis on better energy management should lead to the replacement of older systems and the installation of newer, more efficient systems in existing homes and buildings. Also, demand for maintenance and service work should increase as businesses and homeowners strive to keep systems operating at peak efficiency. Regulations prohibiting the discharge of CFC and HCFC refrigerants took effect in 1993, and regulations banning CFC production became effective in 2000. Consequently, these regulations should continue to result in demand for technicians to replace many existing systems, or modify them to use new environmentally safe refrigerants. In addition, the continuing focus on improving indoor air quality should contribute to the creation of more jobs for heating, air-conditioning, and refrigeration technicians. Also, growth of business establishments that use refrigerated equipment—such as supermarkets and convenience stores—will contribute to a growing need for technicians. In addition to job openings created by employment growth, thousands of openings will result from the need to replace workers who transfer to other occupations or leave the labor force.

Earnings

Median hourly earnings of heating, air-conditioning, and refrigeration mechanics and installers were $16.78 in 2002. The middle 50 percent earned between $12.95 and $21.37 an hour. The lowest 10 percent earned less than $10.34, and the top 10 percent earned more than $26.20. Median hourly earnings in the industries employing the largest numbers of heating, air-conditioning, and refrigeration mechanics and installers in 2002 were as follows:

Hardware, and plumbing and heating equipment and supplies merchant wholesalers	$18.78
Commercial and industrial machinery and equipment (except automotive and electronic) repair and maintenance	17.16
Direct selling establishments	17.14
Elementary and secondary schools	16.80
Building equipment contractors	16.03

Apprentices usually begin at about 50 percent of the wage rate paid to experienced workers. As they gain experience and improve their skills, they receive periodic increases until they reach the wage rate of experienced workers.

Heating, air-conditioning, and refrigeration mechanics and installers enjoy a variety of employer-sponsored benefits. In addition to typical benefits such as health insurance and pension plans, some employers pay for work-related training and provide uniforms, company vans, and tools.

About 20 percent of heating, air-conditioning, and refrigeration mechanics and installers are members of a union. The unions to which the greatest numbers of mechanics and installers belong are the Sheet Metal Workers' International Association and the United Association of Journeymen and Apprentices of the Plumbing and Pipefitting Industry of the United States and Canada.

Related Occupations

Heating, air-conditioning, and refrigeration mechanics and installers work with sheet metal and piping, and repair machinery, such as electrical motors, compressors, and burners. Other workers who have similar skills include boilermakers; home appliance repairers; electricians; sheet metal workers; and pipelayers, plumbers, pipefitters, and steamfitters.

Sources of Additional Information

For more information about opportunities for training, certification, and employment in this trade, contact local vocational and technical schools; local heating, air-conditioning, and refrigeration contractors; a local of the unions or organizations previously mentioned; a local joint union-management apprenticeship committee; or the nearest office of the State employment service or apprenticeship agency.

For information on career opportunities, training, and technician certification, contact:

➤ Air-Conditioning Contractors of America (ACCA), 2800 Shirlington Rd., Suite 300, Arlington, VA 22206. Internet: **http://www.acca.org**
➤ Refrigeration Service Engineers Society (RSES), 1666 Rand Rd., Des Plaines, IL 60016-3552. Internet: **http://www.rses.org**
➤ Plumbing-Heating-Cooling Contractors (PHCC), 180 S. Washington St., P.O. Box 6808, Falls Church, VA 22046. Internet: **http://www.phccweb.org**
➤ Sheet Metal and Air-Conditioning Contractors' National Association, 4201 Lafayette Center Dr., Chantilly, VA 20151-1209. Internet: **http://www.smacna.org**

For information on technician testing and certification, contact:
➤ North American Technician Excellence (NATE), 4100 North Fairfax Dr., Suite 210, Arlington, VA 22203. Internet: **http://www.natex.org**

For information on career opportunities and training, contact:
➤ Associated Builders and Contractors, Workforce Development Department, 4250 North Fairfax Dr., 9th Floor, Arlington, VA 22203.
➤ Home Builders Institute, 1201 15th St. NW., 6th Floor, Washington, DC 20005-2800. Internet: **http://www.hbi.org**
➤ Mechanical Contractors Association of America, 1385 Piccard Dr., Rockville, MD 20850-4329. Internet: **http://www.mcaa.org**
➤ Air-Conditioning and Refrigeration Institute, 4100 North Fairfax Dr., Suite 200, Arlington, VA 22203. Internet: **http://www.coolcareers.org** or **http://www.ari.org**

There are more than 500 occupations registered by the U.S. Department of Labor's National Apprenticeship System. For more information on the Labor Department's registered apprenticeship system and links to State apprenticeship programs, check their Web site: **http://www.doleta.gov**

Home Appliance Repairers

(O*NET 49-9031.01, 49-9031.02)

Significant Points

- Repairers of small appliances commonly learn the trade on the job; repairers of large household appliances often receive their training in a formal trade school, community college, or directly from the appliance manufacturer.

- Knowledge of electronics is increasingly important.

- Job prospects are expected to be good as job openings will continue to outnumber jobseekers.

Nature of the Work

Anyone whose washer, dryer, or refrigerator has ever broken knows the importance of a dependable repair person. Home appliance repairers, often called service technicians, keep home appliances working and help prevent unwanted breakdowns. Some repairers work specifically on small appliances such as microwaves and vacuum cleaners; others specialize in major appliances such as refrigerators, dishwashers, washers, and dryers.

Home appliance repairers visually inspect appliances and check for unusual noises, excessive vibration, fluid leaks, or loose parts to determine why the appliances fail to operate properly. They use service manuals, troubleshooting guides, and experience to diagnose particularly difficult problems. Repairers disassemble the appliance to examine its internal parts for signs of wear or corrosion. They follow wiring diagrams and use testing devices such as ammeters, voltmeters, and wattmeters to check electrical systems for shorts and faulty connections.

After identifying problems, home appliance repairers replace or repair defective belts, motors, heating elements, switches, gears, or other items. They tighten, align, clean, and lubricate parts as necessary. Repairers use common handtools, including screwdrivers, wrenches, files, and pliers, as well as soldering guns and special tools designed for particular appliances. When repairing appliances with electronic parts, they may replace circuit boards or other electronic components.

Home appliance repairers keep home appliances working and help to prevent unwanted breakdowns.

When repairing refrigerators and window air-conditioners, repairers must use care to conserve, recover, and recycle chlorofluorocarbon (CFC) and hydrochlorofluorocarbon (HCFC) refrigerants used in the cooling systems, as required by law. Repairers conserve the refrigerant by making sure there are no leaks in the system; they recover the refrigerant by venting it into proper cylinders; and they recycle the refrigerant, with special filter-dryers, so that it can be used again. Federal regulations also require that home appliance repairers document the capture and disposal of refrigerants.

Home appliance repairers generally install household durable goods such as refrigerators, washing machines, and cooking products. They may have to install pipes in a customer's home to connect the appliances to the gas line. They measure, lay out, cut, and thread pipe and connect it to a feeder line and to the appliance. They may have to saw holes in walls or floors and hang steel supports from beams or joists to hold gas pipes in place. Once the gas line is in place, they turn on the gas and check for leaks. *Gas appliance repairers* check the heating unit and replace tubing, thermocouples, thermostats, valves, and indicator spindles. They also answer emergency calls about gas leaks.

Repairers also answer customers' questions about the care and use of appliances. For example, they demonstrate how to load automatic washing machines, arrange dishes in dishwashers, or sharpen chain saws to maximize performance.

Repairers write up estimates of the cost of repairs for customers, keep records of parts used and hours worked, prepare bills, and collect payments. Self-employed repairers also deal with the original appliance manufacturers to recoup monetary claims for work performed on appliances still under warranty.

Working Conditions

Home appliance repairers who handle portable appliances usually work in repair shops that are generally quiet and adequately lighted and ventilated. Those who repair major appliances usually make service calls to customers' homes. They carry their tools and a number of commonly used parts with them in a truck or van for use on their service calls. Repairers may spend several hours a day driving to and from appointments and emergency calls. They may work in clean comfortable rooms such as kitchens, or in damp, dirty, or dusty areas of a home. Repairers sometimes work in cramped and uncomfortable positions when they are replacing parts in hard-to-reach areas of appliances. Repairer jobs generally are not hazardous, but workers must exercise care and follow safety precautions to avoid electrical shocks and injuries when lifting and moving large appliances. When repairing gas appliances and microwave ovens, repairers must be aware of the dangers of gas and radio frequency energy leaks.

Home appliance repairers usually work with little or no direct supervision, a feature of the job that is appealing to many people. Many home appliance repairers work a standard 40-hour week but may work overtime and weekend hours in the summer months, when they are in high demand to fix air-conditioners and refrigerators. Some repairers work early morning, evening, and weekend shifts and may remain oncall in case of emergency.

Employment

Home appliance repairers held nearly 42,000 jobs in 2002. About 41 percent of salaried repairers worked in retail trade establishments such as department stores and electronics and appliance stores. About 17 percent of repairers are self-employed. Almost every community in the country employs appliance repairers; a high concentration of jobs is found in more populated areas.

Training, Other Qualifications, and Advancement

Employers generally require a high school diploma for home appliance repairer jobs. Repairers of small appliances commonly learn the trade on the job; repairers of large household appliances often receive their training in a formal trade school, community college, or directly from the appliance manufacturer. Mechanical and electrical aptitudes are desirable, and those who work in customers' homes must be courteous and tactful.

Employers prefer to hire people with formal training in appliance repair and electronics. Many repairers complete 1- or 2-year formal training programs in appliance repair and related subjects in high schools, private vocational schools, and community colleges. Courses in basic electricity and electronics are increasingly important as more manufacturers install circuit boards and other electronic control systems in home appliances.

Whether their basic skills are developed through formal training or on the job, trainees usually receive additional training from their employer and from manufacturers. In shops that fix portable appliances, they work on a single type of appliance, such as a vacuum cleaner, until they master its repair. Then they move on to others, until they can repair all those handled by the shop. In companies that repair major appliances, beginners assist experienced repairers on service visits. They may also study on their own. They learn to read schematic drawings, analyze problems, determine whether to repair or replace parts, and follow proper safety procedures. Up to 3 years of on-the-job training may be needed for a technician to become skilled in all aspects of repair.

Some appliance manufacturers and department store chains have formal training programs that include home study and shop classes, in which trainees work with demonstration appliances and other training equipment. Many repairers receive supplemental instruction through 2- or 3-week seminars conducted by appliance manufacturers. Experienced repairers also often attend training classes and study service manuals. Repairers authorized for warranty work by manufacturers are required to attend periodic training sessions.

The U.S. Environmental Protection Agency (EPA) has mandated that all repairers who buy or work with refrigerants must be certified in their proper handling; a technician must pass a written examination to become certified to buy and handle refrigerants. Exams are administered by organizations approved by the EPA, such as trade schools, unions, and employer associations. There are even EPA-approved take-home certification exams. Though no formal training is required for certification, many of these organizations offer training programs designed to prepare workers for the certification examination.

In addition to certification required by the EPA, home appliance repairers may exhibit their competence by passing a certification examination offered by various organizations. Although voluntary, such certification can be helpful when one is seeking employment. The National Appliance Service Technician Certification (NASTeC), which is administered by the International Society of Certified Electronics Technicians (ISCET), requires repairers to pass a comprehensive examination testing their competence in the diagnosis, repair, and maintenance of major home appliances. Examinations are given in three specialty areas of appliance repair: Refrigeration and air-conditioning, cooking, or laundry and dishwashing. Although the NASTeC credential does not expire, continuing education classes are available so repairers can keep abreast of technological changes. The Professional Service Association (PSA) also administers a certification program, with goals similar to the NASTeC program. Those who pass the PSA examination earn the Certified Appliance Professional (CAP) designation, which is valid for 4 years. If certified repairers complete at least 60 credit hours of instruction every year during the 4 years, they need not take the recertification examination. Otherwise, they must take the examination again.

Repairers in large shops or service centers may be promoted to supervisor, assistant service manager, or service manager. Some repairers advance to managerial positions such as regional service manager or parts manager for appliance or tool manufacturers. Preference is given to those who demonstrate technical competence and show an ability to get along with other workers and customers. Experienced repairers who have sufficient funds and knowledge of small-business management may open their own repair shop.

Job Outlook

Good job prospects are expected as job openings will continue to outnumber jobseekers. Many potential workers may choose not to enter this occupation because they prefer work that is less strenuous and that has more comfortable working conditions. Employment of home appliance repairers is expected to increase more slowly than average for all occupations through the year 2012. Although employment of self-employed home appliance repairers is projected to decline, employment of wage and salary workers will increase about as fast as average.

The number of home appliances in use is expected to increase with growth in the numbers of households and businesses. Appliances are also becoming more technologically advanced and will increasingly require a skilled technician to diagnose and fix problems. In recent years, many consumers have tended to purchase new appliances when existing warranties expired rather than invest in repairs on old appliances. However, over the next decade, as more consumers purchase higher priced appliances designed to have much longer lives, they will be more likely to use repair service than to purchase new appliances. Employment is relatively steady during economic downturns because there is still demand for appliance repair services. In addition to new jobs created over the 2002-12 period, openings will arise as home appliance repairers retire or transfer to other occupations.

Self employment of home appliance repairers will continue to decline due to the availability of manufacturer-sponsored training programs. Manufacturers often make these programs available only to large equipment dealers, thereby discouraging repairers from becoming self-employed or working for small shops. Many self-employed repairers are forced to join larger shops so that they can stay abreast of developments in the industry. Jobs are expected to be increasingly concentrated in larger companies as the numbers of smaller shops and family-owned businesses decline. However, repairers who maintain strong industry relationships may still go into business for themselves.

Earnings

Median annual earnings, including commission, of home appliance repairers were $30,390 in 2002. The middle 50 percent earned between $22,900 and $39,800 a year. The lowest 10 percent earned less than $18,210, and the highest 10 percent earned more than $48,170 a year. Median annual earnings of home appliance repairers in 2002 in the electronics and appliance stores industry, which employs the largest number of these workers was $27,340.

Earnings of home appliance repairers vary according to the skill level required to fix equipment, geographic location, and the type of equipment repaired. Because many repairers receive commission along with their salary, earnings increase along with the number of jobs a repairer can complete in a day.

Many larger dealers, manufacturers, and service stores offer typical benefits such as health insurance coverage, sick leave, and retirement and pension programs. Some home appliance repairers belong to the International Brotherhood of Electrical Workers.

Related Occupations

Other workers who repair electrical and electronic equipment include electrical and electronics installers and repairers; electronic home entertainment equipment installers and repairers; small-engine mechanics; coin, vending, and amusement machine servicers and repairers; and heating, air-conditioning, and refrigeration mechanics and installers.

Sources of Additional Information

For general information about the work of home appliance repairers, contact:

➤ North American Retail Dealers Association, 10 E. 22nd St., Suite 310, Lombard, IL 60148.

➤ National Appliance Service Association, P.O. Box 2514, Kokomo, IN 46904.

➤ United Servicers Association, Inc., 6428 Coldwater Canyon Ave., North Hollywood, CA 91606.

For information on the NASTeC certification program, contact:

➤ International Society of Certified Electronics Technicians, 3608 Pershing Ave., Fort Worth, TX 76107. Internet: **http://www.iscet.org**

For information on the Certified Appliance Professional program, contact:

➤ Professional Service Association, 71 Columbia St., Cohoes, NY 12047.

Industrial Machinery Installation, Repair, and Maintenance Workers, Except Millwrights

(0*NET 49-9041.00, 49-9043.00)

Significant Points

- Highly skilled mechanics usually learn their trade through a 4-year apprenticeship program, while lower skilled maintenance workers receive short-term on-the-job training.

- Employment is projected to grow more slowly than average, but applicants with broad skills in machine repair and maintenance should have favorable job prospects.

- Unlike many other manufacturing occupations, these workers usually are not affected by seasonal changes in production.

Nature of the Work

A wide range of employees is required to keep sophisticated industrial machinery running smoothly—from highly skilled industrial machinery mechanics to lower skilled machinery maintenance workers who perform routine tasks. Their work is vital to the success of industrial facilities, not only because an idle machine will delay production, but also because a machine that is not properly repaired and maintained may damage the final product or injure an operator.

The most basic tasks in this process are performed by *machinery maintenance workers*. These employees are responsible for cleaning and lubricating machinery, performing basic diagnostic tests,

checking performance, and testing damaged machine parts to determine whether major repairs are necessary. In carrying out these tasks, maintenance workers must follow machine specifications and adhere to maintenance schedules. Maintenance workers may perform minor repairs, but major repairs are generally left to machinery mechanics.

Industrial machinery mechanics, also called industrial machinery repairers or maintenance machinists, are highly skilled workers who maintain and repair machinery in a plant or factory. To do this effectively, they must be able to detect minor problems and correct them before they become major problems. For example, after hearing a vibration from a machine, the mechanic must decide whether it is due to worn belts, weak motor bearings, or some other problem. Computerized maintenance, vibration analysis techniques, and self-diagnostic systems are aiding in this task, but mechanics still need years of training and experience to perform effectively.

After diagnosing the problem, the industrial machinery mechanic disassembles the equipment to repair or replace the necessary parts. When repairing electronically controlled machinery, mechanics may work closely with electronic repairers or electricians who maintain the machine's electronic parts. (Statements on electrical and electronic installers and repairers, as well as electricians, appear elsewhere in the *Handbook*.) Increasingly, mechanics need electronic and computer skills in order to repair sophisticated equipment on

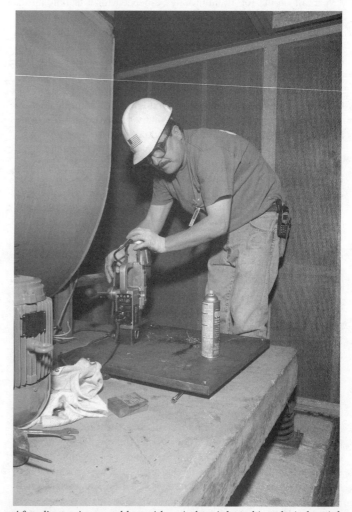

After diagnosing a problem with an industrial machine, the industrial machinery mechanic disassembles the equipment and repairs or replaces the problem parts.

their own. Once a repair is made, mechanics perform tests to ensure that the machine is running smoothly.

Although repairing machines is the primary responsibility of industrial machinery mechanics, they also may perform preventive maintenance and install new machinery. For example, they adjust and calibrate automated manufacturing equipment, such as industrial robots. As plants retool and invest in new equipment, they increasingly rely on mechanics to properly situate and install the machinery. In many plants, this has traditionally been the job of millwrights, but mechanics are increasingly called upon to carry out this task. (See the statement on millwrights elsewhere in the *Handbook*.)

Industrial machinery mechanics and machinery maintenance workers use a variety of tools to perform repairs and preventive maintenance. They may use a screwdriver and wrench to adjust a motor, or a hoist to lift a printing press off the ground. When replacements for broken or defective parts are not readily available, or when a machine must be quickly returned to production, mechanics may sketch a part to be fabricated by the plant's machine shop. Mechanics use catalogs to order replacement parts and often follow blueprints and engineering specifications to maintain and fix equipment. By keeping complete and up-to-date records, mechanics try to anticipate trouble and service equipment before factory production is interrupted.

Working Conditions
In production facilities, these workers are subject to common shop injuries such as cuts, bruises, and strains. They also may work in awkward positions, including on top of ladders or in cramped conditions under large machinery, which exposes them to additional hazards. They often use protective equipment such as hardhats, safety glasses, steel-tipped shoes, hearing protectors, and belts.

Because factories and other facilities cannot afford to have industrial machinery out of service for long periods, mechanics may be called to the plant at night or on weekends for emergency repairs. Overtime is common among industrial machinery mechanics; about 33 percent work over 40 hours a week.

Employment
Industrial machinery installation, repair, and maintenance workers, except millwrights held about 289,200 jobs in 2002. Of these, 197,300 were held by the more highly skilled industrial machinery mechanics, while machinery maintenance workers accounted for 91,900 jobs. Two out of three workers were employed in the manufacturing sector, in industries such as food processing, textile mills, chemicals, fabricated metal products, motor vehicles, and primary metals. Others worked for government agencies, public utilities, mining companies, and other establishments in which industrial machinery is used.

Training, Other Qualifications, and Advancement
Machinery maintenance workers typically receive short-term on-the-job training in order to perform routine tasks, such as setting up, cleaning, lubricating, and starting machinery. This training may be offered by experienced workers, professional trainers, or product representatives.

Industrial machinery mechanics, on the other hand, often learn their trade through 4-year apprenticeship programs that combine classroom instruction with on-the-job-training. These programs usually are sponsored by a local trade union. Other mechanics start as helpers and learn the skills of the trade informally or by taking courses offered by machinery manufacturers and community colleges.

Mechanics learn from experienced repairers how to operate, disassemble, repair, and assemble machinery. Classroom instruction focuses on subjects such as shop mathematics, blueprint reading, welding, electronics, and computer training.

Employers prefer to hire those who have completed high school or technical college and have taken courses in mechanical drawing, mathematics, blueprint reading, computers, and electronics. Mechanical aptitude and manual dexterity are important characteristics for workers in this trade. Good physical conditioning and agility also are necessary because repairers sometimes have to lift heavy objects or climb to reach equipment.

Opportunities for advancement are limited. Machinery maintenance workers may gain additional skills to make more complex repairs to machinery or work as supervisors. Industrial machinery mechanics also may advance either by working with more complicated equipment or by becoming supervisors. The most highly skilled repairers can be promoted to master mechanic or can become machinists, millwrights, or tool and die makers.

Job Outlook
Employment of industrial machinery installation, repair, and maintenance workers, except millwrights is projected to grow more slowly than the average for all occupations through 2012. Nevertheless, applicants with broad skills in machine repair and maintenance should have favorable job prospects. Many mechanics are expected to retire in coming years, and employers have reported difficulty in recruiting young workers with the necessary skills to be industrial machinery mechanics. Most job openings will stem from the need to replace workers who transfer to other occupations or who retire or leave the labor force for other reasons.

As more firms introduce automated production equipment, these workers will be needed to ensure that these machines are properly maintained and consistently in operation. However, many new machines are capable of self-diagnosis, increasing their reliability and somewhat reducing the need for repairers. Increasing imports and the relocation of production facilities abroad also are expected to dampen employment growth for these workers.

Unlike many other manufacturing occupations, industrial machinery installation, repair, and maintenance workers, except millwrights are not usually affected by seasonal changes in production. During slack periods, when some plant workers are laid off, mechanics often are retained to do major overhaul jobs and to keep expensive machinery in working order. Although these workers may face layoff or a reduced workweek when economic conditions are particularly severe, they usually are less affected than other workers because machines have to be maintained regardless of production level.

Earnings
Median hourly earnings of industrial machinery mechanics were $18.26 in 2002. The middle 50 percent earned between $14.62 and $22.95. The lowest 10 percent earned less than $11.91, and the highest 10 percent earned more than $27.48.

Machinery maintenance workers earned less than the higher skilled machinery mechanics. Median hourly earnings of machinery maintenance workers were $15.63 in 2002. The middle 50 percent earned between $12.11 and $19.81. The lowest 10 percent earned less than $9.57, and the highest 10 percent earned more than $24.19.

Earnings vary by industry and geographic region. Median hourly earnings in the industries employing the largest numbers of industrial machinery mechanics in 2002 are shown below:

Electric power generation, transmission, and distribution	$26.25
Motor vehicle parts manufacturing	22.02
Local government	19.14
Converted paper products manufacturing	18.04
Machinery, equipment, and supplies merchant wholesalers	15.93

About 26 percent of industrial machinery installation, repair, and maintenance workers, except millwrights are union members. Labor unions that represent these workers include the United Steelworkers of America; the United Automobile, Aerospace, and Agricultural Implement Workers of America; the International Association of Machinists and Aerospace Workers; the United Brotherhood of Carpenters and Joiners of America; and the International Union of Electronic, Electrical, Salaried, Machine, and Furniture Workers.

Related Occupations
Other occupations that involve repairing and maintaining machinery include aircraft and avionics equipment mechanics and service technicians; automotive service technicians and mechanics; diesel service technicians and mechanics; elevator installers and repairers; heating, air-conditioning, and refrigeration mechanics and installers; heavy vehicle and mobile equipment service technicians and mechanics; machinists; maintenance and repair workers, general; millwrights; and small engine mechanics.

Sources of Additional Information
Information about employment and apprenticeship opportunities may be obtained from local employers, from local offices of the State employment service, or from:

➤ United Brotherhood of Carpenters and Joiners of America, 101 Constitution Ave. NW., Washington, DC 20001. Internet: **http://www.carpenters.org**

➤ National Tooling and Machining Association, 9300 Livingston Rd., Fort Washington, MD 20744. Internet: **http://www.ntma.org**

Line Installers and Repairers

(0*NET 49-9051.00, 49-9052.00)

Significant Points

● Line installers and repairers work outdoors; conditions can be hazardous.

● Line installers and repairers are trained on the job; employers prefer applicants with a technical knowledge of electricity and electronics.

● Employment is expected to grow about as fast as average.

● Earnings are higher than in most other occupations that do not require postsecondary education.

Nature of the Work
Vast networks of wires and cables provide customers with electrical power and communications services. Networks of electrical power lines deliver electricity from generating plants to customers. Communications networks of telephone and cable television lines provide voice, video, and other communications services. These networks are constructed and maintained by line installers and repairers.

Line installers, or *line erectors*, install new lines by constructing utility poles, towers, and underground trenches to carry the wires and cables. Line erectors use a variety of construction equipment, including digger derricks, trenchers, cable plows, and borers. Digger derricks are trucks equipped with augers and cranes; workers use augers to dig holes in the ground, and cranes are used to set utility poles in place. Trenchers and cable plows are used to cut openings in the earth for the laying of underground cables. Borers, which tunnel under the earth, are used to install tubes for the wire without opening a trench in the soil.

When construction is complete, line installers string cable along the poles, towers, tunnels, and trenches. While working on poles and towers, installers first use truck-mounted buckets to reach the top of the structure or physically climb the pole or tower. Next, they pull up cable from large reels mounted on trucks. The line is then set in place and pulled so that it has the correct amount of tension. Finally, line installers attach the cable to the structure using hand and hydraulic tools. When working with electrical power lines, installers bolt or clamp insulators onto the poles before attaching the cable. Underground cable is laid directly in a trench, pulled through a tunnel, or strung through a conduit running through a trench.

Other installation duties include setting up service for customers and installing network equipment. To set up service, line installers string cable between the customers' premises and the lines running on poles or towers or in trenches. They install wiring to houses and check the connection for proper voltage readings. Line installers also may install a variety of equipment. Workers on telephone and cable television lines install amplifiers and repeaters that maintain the strength of communications transmissions. Workers on electrical powerlines install and replace transformers, circuitbreakers, switches, fuses, and other equipment to control and direct the electrical current.

In addition to installation, line installers and repairers also are responsible for maintenance of electrical, telecommunications, and cable television lines. Workers periodically travel in trucks, helicopters, and airplanes to visually inspect the wires and cables. Sensitive monitoring equipment can automatically detect malfunctions on the network, such as loss of current flow. When line repairers identify a problem, they travel to the location of the malfunction and repair or replace defective cables or equipment. Bad weather or natural disasters can cause extensive damage to networks. Line installers and repairers must respond quickly to these emergencies to restore critical utility and communications services. This can often involve working outdoors in adverse weather conditions.

Installation and repair work may require splicing, or joining together, separate pieces of cable. Each cable contains numerous individual wires; splicing the cables together requires that each wire in one piece of cable be joined to another wire in the matching piece. Line installers splice cables using small handtools, epoxy, or mechanical equipment. At each splice, they place insulation over the conductor and seal the splice with moistureproof covering.

Many communications networks now use fiber optic cables instead of conventional wire or metal cables. Fiber optic cables are made of hair-thin strands of glass, which convey pulses of light. These cables can carry much more information at higher speeds than can conventional cables. The higher transmission capacity of fiber optic cable has allowed communication networks to offer upgraded services, such as high-speed Internet access. Splicing fiber optic cable requires specialized equipment that carefully slices, matches, and aligns individual glass fibers. The fibers are joined

Line installers work on both telecommunications and electrical lines.

by either electrical fusion (welding) or a mechanical fixture and gel (glue).

Working Conditions

Line installers and repairers must climb and maintain their balance while working on poles and towers. They lift equipment and work in a variety of positions, such as stooping or kneeling. Their work often requires that they drive utility vehicles, travel long distances, and work outdoors under a variety of weather conditions. Many line installers and repairers work a 40-hour week; however, emergencies may require overtime work. For example, when severe weather damages electrical and communications lines, line installers and repairers may work long and irregular hours to restore service.

Line installers and repairers encounter serious hazards on their jobs and must follow safety procedures to minimize potential danger. They wear safety equipment when entering utility holes and test for the presence of gas before going underground. Electric powerline workers have the most hazardous jobs. High-voltage powerlines can cause electrocution, and line installers and repairers must consequently use electrically insulated protective devices and tools when working with live cables. Powerlines are typically higher than telephone and cable television lines, increasing the risk of severe injury due to falls. To prevent these injuries, line installers and repairers must use fall-protection equipment when working on poles or towers.

Employment

Line installers and repairers held about 268,000 jobs in 2002. Approximately 167,000 were telecommunications line installers and repairers; the remainder were electrical powerline installers and repairers. Nearly all line installers and repairers worked for telecommunications, construction or electric power generation, transmission, and distributions companies. Approximately 9,300 line installers and repairers were self-employed.

Training, Other Qualifications, and Advancement

Line installers and repairers are trained on the job, and employers require at least a high school diploma. Employers also prefer a technical knowledge of electricity, electronics, and experience obtained through vocational/technical programs, community colleges, or the Armed Forces. Prospective employees should possess a basic knowledge of algebra and trigonometry, and mechanical ability. Customer service and interpersonal skills also are important. Because the work entails lifting heavy objects (many employers require applicants to be able to lift at least 50 pounds), climbing, and other physical activity, applicants should have stamina, strength, and coordination, and must be unafraid of heights. The ability to distinguish colors is necessary because wires and cables may be color-coded.

Many community or technical colleges offer programs in telecommunications, electronics, and/or electricity. These programs often are operated with assistance from local employers and unions. Some schools, working with local companies, offer 1-year certificate programs that emphasize hands-on field work; graduates get preferential treatment in the hiring process at companies participating in the program. More advanced 2-year associate degree programs provide students with a broader knowledge of telecommunications and electrical utilities technology through courses in electricity, electronics, fiber optics, and microwave transmission.

Electrical line installers and repairers complete formal apprenticeships or employer training programs. These are sometimes administered jointly by the employer and the union representing the workers. The unions include the International Brotherhood of Electrical Workers, the Communications Workers of America, and the Utility Workers Union of America. Apprenticeship programs last up to 5 years and combine formal instruction with on-the-job training. Government safety regulations strictly define the training and education requirements for apprentice electrical line installers.

Line installers and repairers in telephone and cable television companies receive several years of on-the-job training. They also may attend training or take online courses provided by equipment manufacturers, schools, unions, or industry training organizations. The Society of Cable Television Engineers (SCTE) provides certification programs for line installers and repairers. Applicants for certification must be employed in the cable television industry and attend training sessions at local SCTE chapters.

Entry-level line installers may be hired as ground workers, helpers, or tree trimmers, who clear branches from telephone and power lines. These workers may advance to positions stringing cable and performing service installations. With experience, they may advance to more sophisticated maintenance and repair positions responsible for increasingly larger portions of the network. Promotion to supervisory or training positions also is possible, but more advanced supervisory positions often require a college diploma.

Job Outlook

Overall employment of line installers and repairers is expected to grow about as fast as the average for all occupations through 2012. Much of this increase will result from growth in the construction and telecommunications industries. With the increasing competition in electrical distribution, many companies are contracting out construction of new lines. The introduction of new technologies, especially fiber optic cable, has increased the transmission capacity of telephone and cable television networks. This higher capacity has allowed the creation of new and popular services, such as high-speed Internet access. At the same time, deregulation of the telecommunications industry has reduced barriers to competition. Competition for local phone service and demand for high-speed Internet access is forcing former local telephone companies to update and modernize their networks. In some regions, underground telephone lines may be up to 50 years old and incapable of providing advanced services. Job growth also will stem from the maintenance and modernization of telecommunications networks. Besides those due to employment growth, many job openings will result from the need to replace the large number of older workers reaching retirement age.

Employment of telecommunications line installers and repairers is expected to grow about as fast as average as telephone and cable television companies expand and improve networks that provide customers with high-speed access to data, video, and graphics. Line installers and repairers will be needed not only to construct and install networks, but also to maintain the ever-growing systems of wires and cables. The average residential customer already has more than two telephone lines. Increased demand for high-speed Internet access and multiple telephone lines will require the improvement and expansion of local telephone-line networks. However, excess transmission capacity due to the overexpansion of fiber optic lines, especially long-distance lines, in recent years should significantly reduce employment demand. The need for maintenance work will be reduced by the improved reliability of fiber optic lines. The demand for additional telephone lines also will be tempered by the increasing use of wireless telephones. Wireless networks do not require as many technicians to maintain and expand their systems, a characteristic that will reduce job growth in the industry.

Little or no growth in employment of electrical powerline installers and repairers is expected through 2012. The demand for electricity has been consistently rising, driving the expansion of powerline networks, which tends to increase employment. However, industry deregulation is pushing companies to cut costs and maintenance, which tends to reduce employment. Most new jobs are expected to arise in the construction industry. Because electrical power companies have reduced hiring and training in past years, opportunities are best for workers who possess experience and training.

Earnings

Earnings for line installers and repairers are higher than those in most other occupations that do not require postsecondary education. Median hourly earnings for electrical powerline installers and repairers were $23.33 in 2002. The middle 50 percent earned between $18.02 and $27.43. The lowest 10 percent earned less than $13.22, and the highest 10 percent earned more than $32.08. Median hourly earnings in the industries employing the largest numbers of electrical powerline installers and repairers in 2002 are shown below:

Electric power generation, transmission and distribution	$24.72
Wired telecommunications carriers	23.80
Local government	22.07
Utility system construction	17.22
Building equipment contractors	16.27

Median hourly earnings for telecommunications line installers and repairers were $19.06 in 2002. The middle 50 percent earned between $13.36 and $24.70. The lowest 10 percent earned less than $10.31, and the highest 10 percent earned more than $27.70. Median hourly earnings in the industries employing the largest numbers of telephone and cable television line installers and repairers in 2002 are shown below:

Wired telecommunications carriers	$24.20
Cable and other subscription programming	18.48
Cable and other program distribution	15.01
Building equipment contractors	15.00
Utility system construction	13.58

Most line installers and repairers belong to unions, principally the Communications Workers of America, the International Brotherhood of Electrical Workers, and the Utility Workers Union of America. For these workers, union contracts set wage rates, wage increases, and the time needed to advance from one job level to the next.

Related Occupations

Other workers who install and repair electrical and electronic equipment include broadcast and sound engineering technicians and radio operators, electricians, and radio and telecommunications equipment installers and repairers.

Sources of Additional Information

For more details about employment opportunities, contact the telephone, cable television, or electrical power companies in your community. For general information and some educational resources on line installer and repairer jobs, write to:

➤ Communications Workers of America, 501 3rd St. NW., Washington, DC 20001.

➤ International Brotherhood of Electrical Workers, Telecommunications Department, 1125 15th St. NW., Washington, DC 20005.

For training and professional certifications for those already employed by cable telecommunications firms, contact:

➤ Society of Cable Telecommunications Engineers, Certification Department, 140 Phillips Rd., Exton, PA 19341-1318. Internet: **http://www.scte.org**

Maintenance and Repair Workers, General

(0*NET 49-9042.00)

Significant Points

● General maintenance and repair workers are employed in almost every industry.

● Most workers are trained on the job; others learn by working as helpers to other repairers or to construction workers such as carpenters, electricians, or machinery repairers.

● Job openings should be plentiful due to significant turnover in this large occupation.

Nature of the Work

Most craft workers specialize in one kind of work, such as plumbing or carpentry. General maintenance and repair workers, however, have skills in many different crafts. They repair and maintain machines, mechanical equipment, and buildings and work on plumbing, electrical, and air-conditioning and heating systems. They build partitions, make plaster or drywall repairs, and fix or paint roofs, windows, doors, floors, woodwork, and other parts of building structures. They also maintain and repair specialized equipment and machinery found in cafeterias, laundries, hospitals, stores, offices, and factories. Typical duties include troubleshooting and fixing faulty electrical switches, repairing air-conditioning motors, and unclogging drains. New buildings sometimes have computer-controlled systems, requiring workers to acquire basic computer skills. For example, new air-conditioning systems often can be controlled from a central computer terminal. In addition, light sensors can be electronically controlled to turn off lights automatically after a set amount of time.

General maintenance and repair workers inspect and diagnose problems and determine the best way to correct them, frequently checking blueprints, repair manuals, and parts catalogs. They obtain supplies and repair parts from distributors or storerooms. Using common hand and power tools such as screwdrivers, saws,

General maintenance and repair workers in small establishments, where they are often the only maintenance worker, do all repairs except for very large or difficult jobs.

drills, wrenches, and hammers, as well as specialized equipment and electronic testing devices, these workers replace or fix worn or broken parts, where necessary, or make adjustments to correct malfunctioning equipment and machines.

General maintenance and repair workers also perform routine preventive maintenance and ensure that machines continue to run smoothly, building systems operate efficiently, and the physical condition of buildings does not deteriorate. Following a checklist, they may inspect drives, motors, and belts, check fluid levels, replace filters, and perform other maintenance actions. Maintenance and repair workers keep records of their work.

Employees in small establishments, where they are often the only maintenance worker, make all repairs, except for very large or difficult jobs. In larger establishments, their duties may be limited to the general maintenance of everything in a workshop or a particular area.

Working Conditions

General maintenance and repair workers often carry out several different tasks in a single day, at any number of locations. They may work inside of a single building or in several different buildings. They may have to stand for long periods, lift heavy objects, and work in uncomfortably hot or cold environments, in awkward and cramped positions, or on ladders. They are subject to electrical shock, burns, falls, cuts, and bruises. Most general maintenance workers work a 40-hour week. Some work evening, night, or weekend shifts or are on call for emergency repairs.

Those employed in small establishments often operate with only limited supervision. Those working in larger establishments frequently are under the direct supervision of an experienced worker.

Employment

General maintenance and repair workers held 1.3 million jobs in 2002. They were employed in almost every industry. Around 1 in 5 worked in manufacturing industries, almost evenly distributed through all sectors. About 17 percent worked for different government bodies. Others worked for wholesale and retail firms and for real-estate firms that operate office and apartment buildings.

Training, Other Qualifications, and Advancement

Many general maintenance and repair workers learn their skills informally on the job. They start as helpers, watching and learning from skilled maintenance workers. Helpers begin by doing simple jobs, such as fixing leaky faucets and replacing lightbulbs, and progress to more difficult tasks, such as overhauling machinery or building walls. Some learn their skills by working as helpers to other repair or construction workers, including carpenters, electricians, or machinery repairers.

Necessary skills also can be learned in high school shop classes and postsecondary trade or vocational schools. It generally takes from 1 to 4 years of on-the-job training or school, or a combination of both, to become fully qualified, depending on the skill level required. Because a growing number of new buildings rely on computers to control various of their systems, general maintenance and repair workers may need basic computer skills, such as how to log onto a central computer system and navigate through a series of menus. Usually, companies that install computer-controlled equipment provide on-site training for general maintenance and repair workers.

Graduation from high school is preferred for entry into this occupation. High school courses in mechanical drawing, electricity, woodworking, blueprint reading, science, mathematics, and computers are useful. Mechanical aptitude, the ability to use shop mathematics, and manual dexterity are important. Good health is necessary because the job involves much walking, standing, reaching, and heavy lifting. Difficult jobs require problem-solving ability, and many positions require the ability to work without direct supervision.

Many general maintenance and repair workers in large organizations advance to maintenance supervisor or become a craftworker such as an electrician, a heating and air-conditioning mechanic, or a plumber. Within small organizations, promotion opportunities are limited.

Job Outlook

Job openings should be plentiful. General maintenance and repair is a large occupation with significant turnover, and many job openings should result from the need to replace workers who transfer to other occupations or stop working for other reasons.

Employment of general maintenance and repair workers is expected to grow about as fast as average for all occupations through 2012. Employment is related to the number of buildings-for example, office and apartment buildings, stores, schools, hospitals, hotels, and factories-and the amount of equipment needing maintenance and repair. However, as machinery becomes more advanced and requires less maintenance, the need for general maintenance and repair workers diminishes.

Earnings

Median hourly earnings of general maintenance and repair workers were $14.12 in 2002. The middle 50 percent earned between $10.61 and $18.48. The lowest 10 percent earned less than $8.25, and the highest 10 percent earned more than $22.78. Median hourly earnings in the industries employing the largest numbers of general maintenance and repair workers in 2002 are shown in the following tabulation:

Local government	$14.83
Elementary and secondary schools	14.01
Activities related to real estate	11.79
Lessors of real estate	11.64
Traveler accommodation	10.58

Some general maintenance and repair workers are members of unions, including the American Federation of State, County, and Municipal Employees and the United Automobile Workers.

Related Occupations
Some duties of general maintenance and repair workers are similar to those of carpenters; pipelayers, plumbers, pipefitters, and steamfitters; electricians; and heating, air-conditioning, and refrigeration mechanics. Other duties are similar to those of coin, vending, and amusement machine servicers and repairers; electrical and electronics installers and repairers; electronic home entertainment equipment installers and repairers; and radio and telecommunications equipment installers and repairers.

Sources of Additional Information
Information about job opportunities may be obtained from local employers and local offices of the State Employment Service.

Millwrights

(0*NET 49-9044.00)

Significant Points

● Training through apprenticeship programs, or through community colleges coupled with on-the-job training, generally lasts 4 years.

● Despite projected slower-than-average employment growth, skilled applicants should have good job opportunities.

● About 6 in 10 millwrights belong to labor unions, one of the highest rates of membership in the economy.

Nature of the Work
Millwrights install, repair, replace, and dismantle the machinery and heavy equipment used in many industries. The wide range of facilities and the development of new technology require millwrights to continually update their skills—from blueprint reading and pouring concrete to diagnosing and solving mechanical problems.

The millwright's responsibilities begin when machinery arrives at the jobsite. New equipment must be unloaded, inspected, and moved into position. To lift and move light machinery, millwrights use rigging and hoisting devices, such as pulleys and cables. With heavier equipment, they may require the assistance of hydraulic lift-truck or crane operators to position the machinery. Because millwrights often decide which device to use for moving machinery, they must know the load-bearing properties of rope, cables, hoists, and cranes.

Millwrights consult with production managers and others to determine the optimal placement of machines in a plant. When this placement requires building a new foundation, millwrights either prepare the foundation themselves or supervise its construction. As a result, they must know how to read blueprints and work with a variety of building materials.

To assemble machinery, millwrights fit bearings, align gears and wheels, attach motors, and connect belts, according to the manufacturer's blueprints and drawings. Precision leveling and alignment are important in the assembly process, so millwrights measure angles, material thickness, and small distances with tools such as squares, calipers, and micrometers. When a high level of precision is required, devices such as lasers and ultrasonic measur-

Most millwrights who work with complicated machinery need mechanical aptitude.

ing tools may be used. Millwrights also work with hand and power tools, such as cutting torches, welding machines, and soldering guns, and with metalworking equipment, including lathes and grinding machines.

In addition to installing and dismantling machinery, many millwrights work with mechanics and maintenance workers to repair and maintain equipment. This includes preventive maintenance, such as lubrication and fixing or replacing worn parts. (For further information on machinery maintenance, see the statement on industrial machinery installation, repair, and maintenance workers, except millwrights, elsewhere in the *Handbook*.)

Increasingly sophisticated automation means more complicated machines for millwrights to install and maintain. For example, millwrights may install and maintain numerical control equipment—computer-controlled machine tools that fabricate manufacturing parts. This machinery requires special care and knowledge, so millwrights often work closely with computer or electronics experts, electricians, engineers, and manufacturers' representatives to install it. (Statements on electrical and electronics installers and repairers, as well as electricians, appear elsewhere in the *Handbook*.)

Working Conditions
Working conditions vary by industry. Millwrights employed in manufacturing often work in a typical shop setting and use protective equipment to avoid common hazards. For example, protective devices, such as safety belts, protective glasses, and hardhats may

be worn to prevent injuries from falling objects or machinery. Those employed in construction may work outdoors in difficult weather conditions.

Millwrights work independently or as part of a team. Their tasks must be performed quickly and precisely, because disabled machinery costs a company time and money. Many millwrights work overtime; about 1 in 3 full-time millwrights report working more than 40 hours during a typical week. During power outages or other emergencies, millwrights are often assigned overtime and shift work.

Employment

Millwrights held about 69,000 jobs in 2002. Most work in manufacturing, primarily in durable goods industries, such as motor vehicle and parts manufacturing and iron and steel mills. About 36 percent of all millwrights are employed in construction, where most work for contracting firms. Although millwrights work in every State, employment is concentrated in heavily industrialized areas.

Training, Other Qualifications, and Advancement

Millwrights normally receive training for 4 years, through apprenticeship programs that combine on-the-job training with classroom instruction or through community college coupled with informal on-the-job training. These programs include training in dismantling, moving, erecting, and repairing machinery. Trainees also may work with concrete and receive instruction in related skills, such as carpentry, welding, and sheet-metal work. Classroom instruction is provided in mathematics, blueprint reading, hydraulics, electricity, computers, and electronics.

Employers prefer applicants with a high school diploma or equivalency and some vocational training or experience. Courses in science, mathematics, mechanical drawing, computers, and machine shop practice are useful. Millwrights are expected to keep their skills up-to-date and may need additional training on technological advances, such as laser shaft alignment and vibration analysis.

Because millwrights assemble and disassemble complicated machinery, mechanical aptitude is very important. Strength and agility also are necessary for lifting and climbing. Millwrights need good interpersonal and communication skills to work as part of a team and to effectively give detailed instructions to others.

Advancement for millwrights usually takes the form of higher wages. Some advance to the position of supervisor or superintendent, while others may become self-employed contractors.

Job Outlook

Employment of millwrights is projected to grow more slowly than the average for all occupations through the year 2012. Because millwrights will be needed to maintain and repair existing machinery, dismantle old machinery, and install new equipment, skilled applicants should have good job opportunities. Prospects will be best for millwrights with training in installing new production technologies. In addition to employment growth, many job openings for these workers will stem from the need to replace experienced millwrights who transfer to other occupations or retire.

Employment of millwrights has historically been cyclical, rising and falling in line with investments in automation in the Nation's factories and production facilities. To remain competitive in coming years, firms will continue to require the services of millwrights to dismantle old equipment and install new machinery. Employment growth from new automation will be dampened somewhat by foreign competition and the introduction of new technologies, such as hydraulic torque wrenches, ultrasonic measuring tools, and laser shaft alignment, which allow fewer millwrights to perform more work. In addition, the demand for millwrights may be adversely affected as lower paid workers, such as electronics technicians and industrial machinery mechanics and maintenance workers, assume some installation and maintenance duties.

Earnings

Median hourly earnings of millwrights were $20.19 in 2002. The middle 50 percent earned between $15.77 and $25.48. The lowest 10 percent earned less than $12.39, and the highest 10 percent earned more than $29.49. Earnings vary by industry and geographic location. Median hourly earnings in the industries employing the largest numbers of millwrights in 2002 are shown below.

Motor vehicle parts manufacturing	$28.14
Building equipment contractors	19.33
Nonresidential building construction	18.98

About 60 percent of millwrights belong to labor unions, one of the highest rates of membership in the economy.

Related Occupations

To set up machinery for use in a plant, millwrights must know how to use hoisting devices and how to assemble, disassemble, and sometimes repair machinery. Other workers with similar job duties include industrial machinery installation, repair, and maintenance workers, except millwrights; aircraft and avionics equipment mechanics and service technicians; structural and reinforcing iron and metal workers; assemblers and fabricators; and heavy vehicle and mobile equipment service technicians and mechanics.

Sources of Additional Information

For further information on apprenticeship programs, write to the Apprenticeship Council of your State's labor department, local offices of your State employment service, or local firms that employ millwrights. In addition, you may contact:

➤ United Brotherhood of Carpenters and Joiners of America, 101 Constitution Ave. NW., Washington DC 20001. Internet: **http://www.carpenters.org**

➤ Associated General Contractors of America, 333 John Carlyle St., Suite 200, Alexandria, VA 22314. Internet: **http://www.agc.org**

➤ National Tooling and Machining Association, 9300 Livingston Rd., Fort Washington, MD 20744. Internet: **http://www.ntma.org**

Precision Instrument and Equipment Repairers

(O*NET 49-9061.00, 49.9062.00, 49-9063.01, 49-9063.02, 49-9063.03, 49-9063.04, 49-9064.00, 49-9069.99)

Significant Points

- Training requirements include a high school diploma and, in some cases, postsecondary education, coupled with significant on-the-job training.

- Good opportunities are expected for most types of jobs.

- Overall employment is expected to grow more slowly than average, but projected growth varies by detailed occupation.

- About 1 out of 5 is self-employed.

Nature of the Work

Repairing and maintaining watches, cameras, musical instruments, medical equipment, and other precision instruments requires a high level of skill and attention to detail. For example, some devices contain tiny gears that must be manufactured to within one one-hundredth of a millimeter of design specifications, and other devices contain sophisticated electronic controls.

Camera and photographic equipment repairers work through a series of steps in fixing a camera. The first step is determining whether a repair should be attempted, because many inexpensive cameras cost more to repair than to replace. Of the problems for which repair seems worthwhile, the most complicated or expensive are referred back to the manufacturer. If the repairers decide to proceed with the job themselves, they diagnose the problem, often by disassembling numerous small parts in order to reach the source. They then make needed adjustments or replace a defective part. Many problems are caused by the electronic circuits used in many cameras, which require an understanding of electronics. Camera repairers also maintain cameras by removing and replacing broken or worn parts and cleaning and lubricating gears and springs. Because many of the components and parts involved are extremely small, repairers must have a great deal of manual dexterity. Frequently, older camera parts are no longer available, requiring repairers to build replacement parts or to strip junked cameras. When machining new parts, workers often use a small lathe, a grinding wheel, and other metalworking tools.

Camera repairers also repair the increasingly popular digital cameras. Repairs on such cameras are similar to those for most modern cameras, but, because digital cameras have no film to wind, they have fewer moving parts.

Watch and clock repairers work almost exclusively on expensive and antique timepieces, as moderately priced timepieces are cheaper to replace than to repair. Electrically powered clocks and quartz watches and clocks function with almost no moving parts, limiting necessary maintenance to replacing the battery. Many expensive timepieces still employ old-style mechanical movements and a manual or automatic winding mechanism. This type of timepiece must be regularly adjusted and maintained. Repair and maintenance work on a mechanical timepiece requires using handtools to disassemble many fine gears and components. Each part is inspected for signs of wear. Some gears or springs may need to be replaced or machined. Exterior portions of the watch may require polishing and buffing. Specialized machines are used to clean all of the parts with ultrasonic waves and a series of baths in cleaning agents. Reassembling a watch requires lubricating key parts.

As with older cameras, replacement parts are frequently unavailable for antique watches or clocks. In such cases, watch repairers must machine their own parts. They employ small lathes and other machines in creating tiny parts.

Musical instrument repairers and tuners combine their love of music with a highly skilled craft. Musical instrument repairers and tuners, often referred to as technicians, work in four specialties: Band instruments, pianos and organs, violins, and guitars. (Repairers and tuners who work on electronic organs are discussed in the *Handbook* statement on electronic home entertainment equipment installers and repairers.)

Band instrument repairers, brass and wind instrument repairers, and percussion instrument repairers focus on woodwind, brass, reed, and percussion instruments damaged through deterioration or by accident. They move mechanical parts or play scales to find problems. They may unscrew and remove rod pins, keys, worn cork pads, and pistons and remove soldered parts using gas torches. They repair dents in metal and wood using filling techniques or a mallet.

These repairers use gas torches, grinding wheels, lathes, shears, mallets, and small handtools and are skilled in metalworking and woodworking. Percussion instrument repairers often must install new drumheads, which are cut from animal skin.

Violin repairers and guitar repairers adjust and repair stringed instruments. Some repairers work on both stringed and band instruments. Initially, repairers play and inspect the instrument to find any defects. They replace or repair cracked or broken sections and damaged parts. They also restring the instruments and repair damage to their finish.

Piano tuners and repairers use similar techniques, skills, and tools. Most workers in this group are piano tuners, tuning and making minor repairs. Tuning involves tightening and loosening different strings to achieve the proper tone or pitch. Because pianos are difficult to transport, tuners normally make house calls. Some repairers specialize in restoring older pianos. Restoration is complicated work, often involving replacing many of the more than 12,000 parts in some pianos. With proper maintenance and restoration, pianos often survive more than 100 years.

Pipe organ repairers do work similar to that of piano repairers, but on a larger scale. Additionally, they assemble new organs. Because pipe organs are too large to transport, they must be assembled onsite. Even with repairers working in teams or with assistants, the organ assembly process can take several weeks or even months, depending upon the size of the organ.

Medical equipment repairers and *other precision instrument and equipment repairers* maintain, adjust, calibrate, and repair electronic, electromechanical, and hydraulic equipment. They use various tools, including multimeters, specialized software, and computers designed to communicate with specific pieces of hardware. Some of their tools are specialized, such as equipment designed to simulate water or air pressure. These repairers use handtools, soldering irons, and other electronic tools to repair and adjust the equipment. Faulty circuit boards and other parts are normally removed and replaced. Medical equipment and other precision instrument repairers must maintain careful, detailed logs of all maintenance and repair on each piece of equipment.

Medical equipment repairers, often called *biomedical equipment technicians,* work on medical equipment such as defibrillators, heart monitors, medical imaging equipment (x rays, CAT scanners, and ultrasound equipment), and electric wheelchairs.

Other precision instrument and equipment repairers service, repair, and replace a wide range of equipment associated with automated or instrument-controlled manufacturing processes. A precision instrument repairer working at an electric powerplant, for example, would repair and maintain instruments that monitor the operation of the plant, such as pressure and temperature gauges. Replacement parts are not always available, so repairers sometimes machine or fabricate a new part. Preventive maintenance involves regular lubrication, cleaning, and adjustment of many measuring devices.

Working Conditions

Camera, watch, and musical instrument repairers work under fairly similar solitary, low-stress conditions with minimal supervision. A quiet, well-lighted workshop or repair shop is typical, while a few of these repairers travel to the instrument being repaired, such as a piano, organ, or grandfather clock.

Medical equipment and precision instrument and equipment repairers normally work daytime hours, but are often expected to be on call. But, like other hospital and factory employees, some repairers work irregular hours. Precision instrument repairers work under a wide array of conditions, from hot, dirty, noisy factories to air-conditioned workshops to outdoor fieldwork. Attention to safety is essential, as the work sometimes involves dangerous machinery or toxic chemicals. Due to the individual nature of the work, supervision is fairly minimal.

Employment

Precision instrument and equipment repairers held 64,000 jobs in 2002. Medical equipment repairers often work for hospitals or wholesale equipment suppliers, while precision instrument repairers, all other, often work for manufacturing companies and durable goods wholesalers. About 1 out of 5 precision instrument and equipment repairers was self-employed-they may own jewelry, camera, medical equipment, or music stores. The following tabulation presents employment by detailed occupation:

Medical equipment repairers	29,000
Camera and photographic equipment repairers	6,900
Musical instrument repairers and tuners	6,200
Watch repairers	4,800
All other precision instrument and equipment repairers	17,000

Training, Other Qualifications, and Advancement

Most employers require at least a high school diploma for beginning precision instrument and equipment repairers. Many employers prefer applicants with some postsecondary education. Much training takes place on the job. The ability to read and understand

Some musical instrument repairers and tuners specialize in stringed instruments.

technical manuals is important. Necessary physical qualities include good fine motor skills and vision. Also, precision equipment repairers must be able to pay close attention to details, enjoy problem solving, and have the desire to disassemble machines to see how they work. Most precision equipment repairers must be able to work alone with minimal supervision.

The educational background required for camera and photographic equipment repairers varies, but some knowledge of electronics is necessary. Some workers complete postsecondary training, such as an associate degree, in this field. The job requires the ability to read an electronic schematic diagram and comprehend other technical information, in addition to good manual dexterity. New employees are trained on the job in two stages over about a year. First, they assist a senior repairer for about 6 months. Then, they refine their skills by performing repairs on their own for an additional 6 months. Finally, repairers continually hone and improve their skills by attending manufacturer-sponsored seminars on the specifics of particular models.

Training also varies for watch and clock repairers. Several associations, including the American Watchmakers-Clockmakers Institute (AWI) and the National Association of Watch and Clock Collectors, offer certifications. Some certifications can be completed in a few months; some require simply passing an examination; and the most demanding certifications require 3,000 hours, over 2 years, of classroom time in technical institutes or colleges. Clock repairers generally require less training than do watch repairers because watches have smaller components and require greater precision. Some repairers opt to learn through assisting a master watch repairer. Nevertheless, developing proficiency in watch or clock repair requires several years of education and experience.

For musical instrument repairers and tuners, employers prefer people with post-high school training in music repair technology. According to a Piano Technicians Guild membership survey, the overwhelming majority of respondents had completed at least some college work; most had a bachelor's or higher degree, although not always in music repair technology. Almost all repairers have a strong musical background. A basic ability to play the instruments being repaired is helpful, but not always required. A few technical schools and colleges offer courses in instrument repair, and correspondence courses also are common. Graduates of these programs normally receive additional training on the job, working with an experienced repairer. A few musical instrument repairers and tuners begin learning their trade on the job as assistants or apprentices. Trainees perform a variety of tasks around the shop. Full qualification usually requires 2 to 5 years of training and practice.

Medical equipment repairers are trained in a similar manner. An associate degree in electronics or medical technology is helpful, but not always required. The required training varies by specialty. On-the-job training, for those with a background in electronics, is more common for workers repairing less critical equipment such as hospital beds or electric wheelchairs. An associate or even a bachelor's degree, often in medical technology or engineering, and a passing grade on a certification exam is likely to be required of persons repairing more critical equipment such as CAT scanners and defibrillators. Some repairers are trained in the military. New repairers begin by observing and assisting an experienced worker over a period of 3 to 6 months. Gradually, they begin working independently, while still under close supervision.

Educational requirements for other precision instrument and equipment repair jobs also vary, but include a high school diploma, with a focus on mathematics and science courses. Most employers require an associate or sometimes a bachelor's degree in instrumentation and control, electronics, or a related engineering field, as repairers need to understand blueprints, electrical schematic diagrams, and electrical, hydraulic, and electromechanical systems. In addition to formal education, a year or two of on-the-job training is required before a repairer is considered fully qualified. Some advancement opportunities exist, but many supervisory positions require a bachelor's degree.

Job Outlook

Good opportunities are expected for most types of precision instrument and equipment repairer jobs. Overall employment growth is projected to be slower than the average for all occupations over the 2002-12 period. However, projected growth varies by detailed occupation.

Job growth among medical equipment repairers should be about as fast as the average for all occupations over the projected period. The rapidly expanding healthcare industry and elderly population should spark demand for increasingly sophisticated medical equipment and, in turn, create good employment opportunities in this occupation.

On the other hand, employment of musical instrument repairers is expected to increase more slowly than the average. Replacement needs will provide the most job opportunities as many repairers and tuners are expected to retire. While an increase in the number of school-age children involved with music should spur demand for repairers, music must compete with other extracurricular activities and interests. Without new musicians, there will be a slump in instrument rentals, purchases, and repairs. Because training in the repair of musical instruments is difficult to obtain—there are only a few schools that offer training programs, and few experienced workers are willing to take on apprentices—opportunities should be good for those who receive training.

Employment of camera and photographic equipment repairers is expected to decline. The popularity of inexpensive cameras adversely affects employment in this occupation, as most point-and-shoot cameras are cheaper to replace than repair. The rapid technological progress in digital cameras also has hurt the job prospects of repairers. When a digital camera breaks, not only is replacing the camera often not much more expensive, but the new model is also far more advanced.

Employment of watch repairers is expected to increase more slowly than the average. Over the past few decades, changes in technology, including the invention of digital and quartz watches that need few repairs, caused a significant decline in the demand for watch repairers. In recent years, this trend was somewhat reversed, as the growing popularity of expensive mechanical watches increased the need for watch repairers. While the demand for watch repairers has risen, however, few new repairers have entered the field. The small number of entrants, coupled with the fact that a large proportion of watch and clock repairers are approaching retirement age, should result in very good job opportunities in this field.

The projected slower-than-average employment growth of other precision instrument and equipment repairers reflects the expected lack of employment growth in manufacturing and other industries in which they are employed. Nevertheless, good employment opportunities are expected for these precision instrument and equipment repairers due to the relatively small number of people entering the occupation and the need to replace repairers who retire.

Earnings

The following tabulation shows median hourly earnings for various precision instrument and equipment repairers in 2002. Earnings ranged from less than $7.59 for the lowest 10 percent of watch repairers, to more than $30.68 for the highest 10 percent of precision instrument and equipment repairers, all other. Median hourly earnings of all precision instrument and equipment repairers by occupation are:

Precision instrument and equipment repairers, all other	$21.20
Medical equipment repairers	17.49
Camera and photographic equipment repairers	15.09
Musical instrument repairers and tuners	14.15
Watch repairers	12.77

Earnings within the different occupations vary significantly, depending upon skill levels. For example, a watch and clock repairer may simply change batteries and replace worn wrist straps, while highly skilled watch and clock repairers, with years of training and experience, may rebuild and replace worn parts. According to a survey by the American Watchmakers-Clockmakers Institute, the median annual earnings of highly skilled watch and clock repairers were about $42,500 in 2001.

Related Occupations

Many precision instrument and equipment repairers work with precision mechanical and electronic equipment. Other workers who repair precision mechanical and electronic equipment include computer, automated teller, and office machine repairers and coin, vending, and amusement machine servicers and repairers. Other workers who make precision items include dental laboratory technicians and ophthalmic laboratory technicians. Some precision instrument and equipment repairers work with a wide array of industrial equipment. Their work environment and responsibilities are similar to those of industrial machinery installation, maintenance, and repair workers. Much of the work of watch repairers is similar to that of jewelers and precious stone and metal workers. Camera repairers' work is similar to that of electronic home entertainment equipment installers and repairers; both occupations work with consumer electronics that are based around a circuit board, but that also involve numerous moving mechanical parts.

Sources of Additional Information

For more information about camera repair careers, contact:

➤ National Association of Photographic Equipment Technicians (NAPET), 3000 Picture Pl., Jackson, MI 49201.

For information on musical instrument repair, including schools offering training, contact:

➤ National Association of Professional Band Instrument Repair Technicians (NAPBIRT), P.O. Box 51, Normal, IL 61761. Internet: **http://www.napbirt.org**

For additional information on piano tuning and repairwork, contact:

➤ Piano Technicians Guild, 3930 Washington St., Kansas City, MO 64111-2963. Internet: **http://www.ptg.org**

For information about training, mentoring programs, employers, and schools with programs in precision instrumentation, automation, and control, contact:

➤ ISA-The Instrumentation, Systems, and Automation Society, 67 Alexander Dr., P.O. Box 12277, Research Triangle Park, NC 27709. Internet: **http://www.isa.org**

For information about watch and clock repair and a list of schools with related programs of study, contact:

➤ American Watchmakers-Clockmakers Institute (AWI), 701 Enterprise Dr., Harrison, OH 45030-1696. Internet: **http://www.awi-net.org**

For information about medical equipment technicians and a list of schools with related programs of study, contact:

➤ Association for the Advancement of Medical Instrumentation (AAMI), 1110 North Glebe Rd., Arlington, VA 22201-4795. Internet: **http://www.aami.org**

Production Occupations

Assemblers and Fabricators

(0*NET 51-2011.01, 51.2011.02, 51-2011.03, 51-2021.00, 51-2022.00, 51-2023.00, 51-2031.00, 51-2041.01, 51-2041.02, 51-2091.00, 51-2092.00, 51-2093.00, 51-2099.99)

Significant Points

- A decline in employment is expected, reflecting increasing automation and the shift of assembly to countries with lower labor costs.

- Work areas may be noisy, and many assemblers may have to sit or stand for long periods.

- A high school diploma is preferred for most positions; specialized training is required for some assembly jobs.

Nature of the Work

Assemblers and fabricators produce a wide range of finished goods from manufactured parts or subassemblies. They produce intricate manufactured products, such as aircraft, automobile engines, computers, and electrical and electronic components.

Assemblers may work on subassemblies or the final assembly of an array of finished products or components. For example, *electrical and electronic equipment assemblers* put together or modify missile control systems, radio or test equipment, computers, machine-tool numerical controls, radar, or sonar, and prototypes of these and other products. *Electromechanical equipment assemblers* prepare and test equipment or devices such as appliances, dynamometers, or ejection-seat mechanisms. *Coil winders, tapers, and finishers* wind wire coil used in resistors, transformers, generators, and electric motors. *Engine and other machine assemblers* construct, assemble, or rebuild engines and turbines, and office, agricultural, construction, oilfield, rolling mill, textile, woodworking, paper, and food-wrapping machinery. *Aircraft structure, surfaces, rigging, and systems assemblers* put together and install parts of airplanes, space vehicles, or missiles, such as landing gear. *Structural metal fabricators and fitters* cut, align, and fit structural metal parts according to detailed specifications prior to welding or riveting.

Assemblers and fabricators involved in product development read and interpret engineering specifications from text, drawings, and computer-aided drafting systems. They also may use a variety of tools and precision measuring instruments. Some experienced assemblers work with engineers and technicians, assembling prototypes or test products.

As technology changes, so too does the manufacturing process. For example, automated manufacturing systems include applications of robotics, computers, programmable motion control, and various sensing technologies. These systems change the way in which goods are made and affect the jobs of those who make them.

The concept of "lean" manufacturing, for example, places a greater premium on teamwork and communication within "cells" of workers than it does on the assembly line process. *Team assemblers* perform all of the assembly tasks assigned to their teams, rotating through the different tasks, rather than specializing in a single task. They also may decide how the work is to be assigned and how different tasks are to be performed. This worker flexibility helps companies to cover for absent workers, and increases their ability to respond to changes in demand by shifting labor from one product line to another. For example, if demand for a product drops, companies may reduce the number of workers involved, while individual workers perform more stages of the assembly process. Some aspects of lean production, such as rotating tasks, are becoming more common to all assembly and fabrication occupations.

Working Conditions

The working conditions for assemblers and fabricators vary from plant to plant and from industry to industry. Work areas may be noisy, and many assemblers may have to sit or stand for long periods. Both electronic and electromechanical equipment assemblers, for example, sit at tables to perform much of their work, although their surroundings are generally clean, well-lit, and free from dust. Some electrical and electronics assemblers come in contact with soldering fumes, but ventilation systems and fans normally minimize this problem. Assemblers of equipment that is vulnerable to dust and dirt, such as transmissions, may work in clean rooms that are designed to minimize contamination. Aircraft assemblers, however, usually come in contact with oil and grease, and their working areas may be quite noisy. They also may have to lift and fit heavy objects. In many cases, improvements in workstation design and the increased use of overhead cranes and other power-lifting equipment have improved working conditions.

Most full-time assemblers work a 40-hour week, although overtime and shiftwork is fairly common in some industries. Work schedules of assemblers may vary at plants with more than one shift.

Employment

Most of the 2.1 million assembler and fabricator jobs in 2002 were in manufacturing; most of the 7 percent who were employed by employment services firms also worked in manufacturing plants. Team assemblers, the largest specialty, accounted for 55 percent of

Most assemblers and fabricators work in manufacturing.

567

assembler and fabricator jobs. The distribution of employment among the various types of assemblers was as follows:

Team assemblers	1,174,000
Electrical and electronic equipment assemblers	281,000
Structural metal fabricators and fitters	89,000
Electromechanical equipment assemblers	60,000
Engine and other machine assemblers	50,000
Fiberglass laminators and fabricators	37,000
Coil winders, tapers, and finishers	36,000
Aircraft structure, surfaces, rigging, and systems assemblers	27,000
Timing device assemblers, adjusters, and calibrators	6,500
All other assemblers and fabricators	361,000

Manufacturing industries employ 80 percent of assemblers and fabricators. Assembly of computers and electronic products accounted for 13 percent of all jobs. Assembly of transportation equipment, such as aircraft, autos, trucks, and buses accounted for 19 percent of all jobs. Other industries that employ many assemblers and fabricators were machinery manufacturing (heating and air-conditioning equipment; agriculture, construction, and mining machinery; and engine, turbine, and power transmission equipment); electrical equipment, appliance, and component manufacturing (lighting, household appliances, and electrical equipment); and fabricated metal products.

The following tabulation shows wage and salary employment in manufacturing industries employing the most assemblers and fabricators in 2002.

Transportation equipment manufacturing	397,000
Computer and electronic product manufacturing	285,000
Machinery manufacturing	209,000
Electrical equipment, appliance, and component manufacturing	160,000
Fabricated metal product manufacturing	155,000

Training, Other Qualifications, and Advancement

New assemblers and fabricators are normally entry-level employees. The ability to do accurate work at a rapid pace and to follow detailed instructions are key job requirements. A high school diploma is preferred for most positions. Following detailed assembly instructions requires basic reading skills, although many instructions rely on pictures and diagrams.

Applicants need specialized training for some assembly jobs. For example, employers may require that applicants for electrical or electronic assembler jobs be technical school graduates or have equivalent military training. Other positions require only on-the-job training, sometimes including employer-sponsored classroom instruction, in the broad range of assembly duties that employees may be required to perform.

Good eyesight, with or without glasses, is required for assemblers and fabricators who work with small parts. Plants that make electrical and electronic products may test applicants for color vision, because many of their products contain many differently colored wires. Manual dexterity and the ability to carry out complex, repetitive tasks quickly and methodically also are important.

As assemblers and fabricators become more experienced, they may progress to jobs that require greater skill and be given more responsibility. Experienced assemblers may become product repairers if they have learned the many assembly operations and understand the construction of a product. These workers fix assembled articles that operators or inspectors have identified as defective. Assemblers also can advance to quality control jobs or be promoted to supervisor. Experienced assemblers and fabricators also may become members of research and development teams, working with engineers and other project designers to design, develop, and build prototypes, and test new product models. In some companies, assemblers can become trainees for one of the skilled trades, such as machinist. Those with a background in math, science, and computers may advance to become programmers or operators of more highly automated production equipment.

Job Outlook

Employment of assemblers and fabricators is expected to decline through the year 2012, reflecting increasing automation and the shift of assembly to countries with lower labor costs. As manufacturers strive to improve precision and productivity, automated machinery increasingly will be used to perform work more economically and more efficiently. Technological advances should continue raising the productivity of assembly workers and adversely affecting their employment. In addition to new jobs stemming from growth, many job openings will result from the need to replace workers leaving this large occupational group.

The effects of automation will be felt more among some types of assemblers and fabricators than among others. Automated manufacturing systems are expensive, and a large volume of repetitive work is required to justify their purchase. Also, where the assembly parts involved are irregular in size or location, new technology only now is beginning to make inroads. For example, much assembly in the aerospace industry is done in hard-to-reach locations—inside airplane fuselages or gear boxes, for example—which are unsuited to robots; as a result, aircraft assemblers will not be easily replaced by automated processes, although employment of aircraft assemblers is still expected to decline due to the projected employment decline in the aerospace industry. On the other hand, automation increasingly will be used in the precision assembly of electronic goods, in which a significant number of electronics assemblers are employed.

Many producers send their assembly functions to countries where labor costs are lower. This trend in assembly, promoted by more liberal trade and investment policies, results in shifts in the composition of America's manufacturing workforce. Decisions by American corporations to move assembly to other nations should limit employment growth for assemblers in some industries, such as electronics assembly, but a free trade environment also may lead to growth in the export of goods assembled in the United States.

Earnings

Earnings vary by industry, geographic region, skill, educational level, and complexity of the machinery operated. In 2002, median hourly earnings were $ 18.71 for aircraft structure, surfaces, rigging, and systems assemblers; $14.02 for engine and other machine assemblers; $11.07 for coil winders, tapers, and finishers; $11.83 for fiberglass laminators and finishers; $11.63 for timing device assemblers, calibrators, and adjusters; $12.15 for electromechanical equipment assemblers; and $11.00 for all other assemblers.

Median hourly earnings of team assemblers were $10.90 in 2002. The middle 50 percent earned between $8.81 and $13.84. The lowest 10 percent earned less than $7.41, and the highest 10 percent earned $17.73. Median hourly earnings in the manufacturing industries employing the largest numbers of team assemblers in 2002 are shown below:

Motor vehicle parts manufacturing	$12.36
Other wood product manufacturing	10.44
Plastics product manufacturing	10.24
Other miscellaneous manufacturing	9.58
Employment services	8.30

Median hourly earnings of electrical and electronic equipment assemblers were $11.03 in 2002. The middle 50 percent earned between $9.02 and $13.84. The lowest 10 percent earned less than $7.57, and the highest 10 percent earned more than $17.38. Mcdian hourly earnings in the manufacturing industries employing the largest numbers of electrical and electronic equipment assemblers in 2002 are shown below:

Navigational, measuring, electromedical, and control
    instruments manufacturing $12.21
Computer and peripheral equipment manufacturing 12.01
Electrical equipment manufacturing 11.95
Communications equipment manufacturing 10.87
Semiconductor and other electronic component
    manufacturing 10.77

Many assemblers and fabricators are members of labor unions. These unions include the International Association of Machinists and Aerospace Workers; the United Electrical, Radio and Machine Workers of America; the United Automobile, Aerospace and Agricultural Implement Workers of America; the International Brotherhood of Electrical Workers; and the United Steelworkers of America.

Related Occupations

Other occupations that involve operating machines and tools and assembling products include welding, soldering, and brazing workers; and machine setters, operators, and tenders—metal and plastic. Assemblers and fabricators also are responsible for some quality control and product testing, as is the case for inspectors, testers, sorters, samplers, and weighers.

Sources of Additional Information

Information about employment opportunities for assemblers is available from local offices of the State employment service and from locals of the unions mentioned earlier.

Food Processing Occupations

(0*NET 51-3011.01, 51-3011.02, 51.3021.00, 51.3022.00, 51.3023.00, 51-3091.00, 51-3092.00, 51-3093.00)

Significant Points

- Workers in meatpacking plants have among the highest incidences of injury and illness of all workers.

- Most employees in manual food-processing jobs require little or no training prior to being hired.

- Job growth will be concentrated among lower skilled workers, who are found mostly in manufacturing plants.

Nature of the Work

Food-processing occupations include many different types of workers who process raw food products into the finished goods sold by grocers or wholesalers, restaurants, or institutional food services. These workers perform a variety of tasks and are responsible for producing many of the food products found in every household.

Butchers and meat, poultry, and fish cutters and trimmers are employed at different stages in the process by which animal carcasses are converted into manageable pieces of meat, known as boxed meat, that are suitable for sale to wholesalers and retailers. Meat, poultry, and fish cutters and trimmers commonly work in animal slaughtering and processing plants, while butchers and meatcutters usually are employed at the retail level. As a result, the nature of these jobs varies significantly.

In animal slaughtering and processing plants, *slaughterers and meatpackers* slaughter cattle, hogs, goats, and sheep and cut the carcasses into large wholesale cuts, such as rounds, loins, ribs, and chucks, to facilitate the handling, distribution, and marketing of meat. In some of these plants, slaughterers and meatpackers also further process the large parts into cuts that are ready for retail use. These workers also produce hamburger meat and meat trimmings, which are used to prepare sausages, luncheon meats, and other fabricated meat products. Slaughterers and meatpackers usually work on assembly lines, with each individual responsible for only a few of the many cuts needed to process a carcass. Depending on the type of cut, they use knives, cleavers, meat saws, bandsaws, or other, often dangerous, equipment.

In grocery stores, wholesale establishments that supply meat to restaurants, and institutional food service facilities, *butchers and meatcutters* separate wholesale cuts of meat into retail cuts or individually sized servings. They cut meat into steaks and chops, shape and tie roasts, and grind beef for sale as chopped meat. Boneless cuts are prepared with the use of knives, slicers, or power cutters, while bandsaws are required to carve bone-in pieces. Butchers and meatcutters in retail food stores also may weigh, wrap, and label the cuts of meat, arrange them in refrigerated cases for display, and prepare special cuts to fill unique orders.

Poultry cutters and trimmers slaughter and cut up chickens, turkeys, and other types of poultry. Although the poultry-processing industry is becoming increasingly automated, many jobs, such as trimming, packing, and deboning, are still done manually. As in the animal slaughtering and processing industry, most poultry cutters and trimmers perform routine cuts on poultry as it moves along production lines.

Unlike some of the other occupations just listed, *fish cutters and trimmers,* also called *fish cleaners,* are likely to be employed in both manufacturing and retail establishments. These workers primarily scale, cut, and dress fish by removing the head, scales, and other inedible portions and cutting the fish into steaks or fillets. In retail markets, they may also wait on customers and clean fish to order.

Meat, poultry, and fish cutters and trimmers also prepare ready-to-heat foods. This often entails filleting meat or fish or cutting it into bite-sized pieces, preparing and adding vegetables, or applying sauces, marinades, or breading.

Bakers mix and bake ingredients in accordance with recipes to produce varying quantities of breads, pastries, and other baked goods. Bakers commonly are employed in grocery stores and specialty shops and produce small quantities of breads, pastries, and other baked goods for consumption on premises or for sale as specialty baked goods. In manufacturing, bakers produce goods in large quantities, using high-volume mixing machines, ovens, and other equipment. Goods produced in large quantities usually are available for sale through distributors, grocery stores, or manufacturer's outlets.

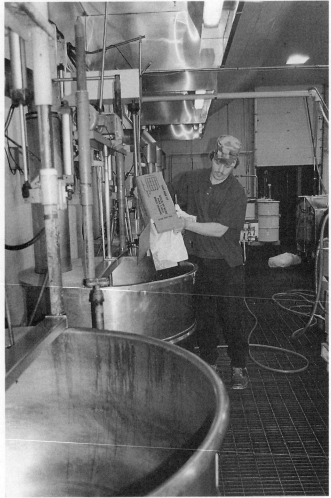

Food batchmakers set up and operate equipment that mixes, blends, or cooks ingredients used in the manufacture of food products

Others in food-processing occupations include *food batchmakers,* who set up and operate equipment that mixes, blends, or cooks ingredients used in the manufacture of food products, according to formulas or recipes; *food cooking machine operators and tenders,* who operate or tend cooking equipment such as steam cooking vats, deep-fry cookers, pressure cookers, kettles, and boilers to prepare food products such as meat, sugar, cheese, and grain; and *food and tobacco roasting, baking, and drying machine operators and tenders,* who use equipment to reduce the moisture content of food or tobacco products or to process food in preparation for canning. Some of the machines that are used include hearth ovens, kiln driers, roasters, char kilns, steam ovens, and vacuum drying equipment.

Working Conditions

Working conditions vary by type and size of establishment. In animal slaughtering and processing plants and large retail food establishments, butchers and meatcutters work in large meatcutting rooms equipped with power machines and conveyors. In small retail markets, the butcher or fish cleaner may work in a cramped space behind the meat or fish counter. To prevent viral and bacterial infections, work areas must be kept clean and sanitary.

Butchers and meatcutters, poultry and fish cutters and trimmers, and slaughterer and meatpackers often work in cold, damp rooms, which are refrigerated to prevent meat from spoiling and are damp because meat cutting generates large amounts of blood, condensation, and fat. Cool, damp floors increase the likelihood of slips and falls. In addition, cool temperatures, long periods of standing, and repetitious physical tasks make the work tiring. As a result, butchers and meat, poultry, and fish cutters are more susceptible to injury than are most other workers. In fact, meatpacking plants had one of the highest incidences of work-related injury and illness of any industry in 2002. Nearly 1 in 7 employees in such plants experienced a work-related injury or illness that year.

Injuries include cuts and occasional amputations, which occur when knives, cleavers, or power tools are used improperly. Also, repetitive slicing and lifting often lead to cumulative trauma injuries, such as carpal tunnel syndrome. To reduce the incidence of cumulative trauma injuries, some employers have reduced employee workloads, added prescribed rest periods, redesigned jobs and tools, and promoted increased awareness of early warning signs so that steps can be taken to prevent further injury. Nevertheless, workers in the occupation still face the serious threat of disabling injuries.

Most traditional bakers work in bakeries, cake shops, hot-bread shops, hotels, restaurants, and cafeterias. They also may work in the bakery departments of supermarkets and cruise ships. Bakers may work under hot and noisy conditions. Also, bakers typically work under strict order deadlines and critical time-sensitive baking requirements, both of which can induce stress. Bakers usually work in shifts and may work early mornings, evenings, weekends, and holidays. While many bakers often work as part of a team, they also may work alone when baking particular items. They may supervise assistants and teach apprentices and trainees. Bakers in retail establishments may be required to serve customers.

Other food-processing workers, such as food batchmakers, food and tobacco roasting, baking, and drying machine operators, and food cooking machine operators and tenders, typically work in production areas that are specially designed for food preservation or processing. Food batchmakers, in particular, work in kitchen-type, assembly-line production facilities. Because this work involves food, work areas must meet governmental sanitary regulations. The ovens, as well as the motors of blenders, mixers, and other equipment, often make work areas very warm and noisy. There are some hazards, such as burns, created by the equipment that these workers use. Food batchmakers; food and tobacco roasting, baking, and drying machine operators; and food cooking machine operators and tenders spend a great deal of time on their feet and generally work a regular 40-hour week that may include evening and night shifts.

Employment

Food-processing workers held 757,000 jobs in 2002. Employment among the various types of food-processing occupations was distributed as follows:

Bakers	173,000
Meat, poultry, and fish cutters and trimmers	154,000
Butchers and meat cutters	132,000
Slaughterers and meat packers	128,000
Food batchmakers	74,000
All other food processing workers	42,000
Food cooking machine operators and tenders	34,000
Food and tobacco roasting, baking, and drying machine operators and tenders	19,000

About 36 percent of all food-processing workers were employed in animal slaughtering and processing plants. Another 21 percent were employed at grocery stores. Most of the remainder worked in food manufacturing. Butchers, meatcutters, and bakers are employed in almost every city and town in the Nation, while most other food-processing jobs are concentrated in communities with food-processing plants.

Training, Other Qualifications, and Advancement

Training varies widely among food-processing occupations. However, most manual food-processing workers require little or no training prior to being hired.

Most butchers and poultry and fish cutters and trimmers acquire their skills on the job through formal and informal training programs. The length of training varies significantly. Simple cutting operations require a few days to learn, while more complicated tasks, such as eviscerating slaughtered animals, generally require several months to learn. The training period for highly skilled butchers at the retail level may be 1 or 2 years.

Generally, on-the-job trainees begin by doing less difficult jobs, such as making simple cuts or removing bones. Under the guidance of experienced workers, trainees learn the proper use and care of tools and equipment and how to prepare various cuts of meat. After demonstrating skill with various meatcutting tools, trainees learn to divide carcasses into wholesale cuts and wholesale cuts into retail and individual portions. Trainees also may learn to roll and tie roasts, prepare sausage, and cure meat. Those employed in retail food establishments often are taught operations such as inventory control, meat buying, and recordkeeping. In addition, growing concern about the safety of meats has led employers to offer numerous safety seminars and extensive training in food safety to employees.

Skills that are important to meat, poultry, and fish cutters and trimmers include manual dexterity, good depth perception, color discrimination, and good hand-eye coordination. Physical strength often is needed to lift and move heavy pieces of meat. Butchers and fish cleaners who wait on customers should have a pleasant personality, a neat appearance, and the ability to communicate clearly. In some States, a health certificate is required for employment.

Bakers often start as apprentices or trainees. Apprentice bakers usually start in craft bakeries, while in-store bakeries, such as those in supermarkets, often employ trainees. Bakers need to be skilled in baking, icing, and decorating. They also need to be able to follow instructions, have an eye for detail, and communicate well with others. Knowledge of bakery products and ingredients, as well as mechanical mixing and baking equipment, is important. Many apprentice bakers participate in correspondence study and may work towards a certificate in baking. Working as a baker's assistant or at other activities that involve handling food also is a useful tool for training. The complexity of the skills required for certification as a baker often is underestimated. Bakers need to know about applied chemistry, ingredients and nutrition, government health and sanitation regulations, business concepts, and production processes, including how to operate and maintain machinery. Modern food plants typically use high-speed, automated equipment that often is operated by computers.

Food-machine operators and tenders usually are trained on the job. They learn to run the different types of equipment by watching and helping other workers. Training can last anywhere from a month to a year, depending on the complexity of the tasks and the number of products involved. A degree in the appropriate area—dairy processing for those working in diary product operations, for example—is helpful for advancement to a lead worker or a supervisory role. Most food batchmakers participate in on-the-job training, usually from about a month to a year. Some food batchmakers learn their trade through an approved apprenticeship program.

Food-processing workers in retail or wholesale establishments may progress to supervisory jobs, such as department managers or team leaders in supermarkets. A few of these workers may become buyers for wholesalers or supermarket chains. Some open their own markets or bakeries. In processing plants, workers may advance to supervisory positions or become team leaders.

Job Outlook

Overall employment in the food-processing occupations is expected to grow as fast as average for all occupations through 2012. Increasingly, cheaper meat imports from abroad will have a negative effect on domestic employment in many food-processing occupations. Job growth will be concentrated at the manufacturing level, as more cutting and processing of meat shifts from retail stores to food-processing plants. Nevertheless, job opportunities should be available at all levels of the occupation due to the need to replace experienced workers who transfer to other occupations or leave the labor force.

As the Nation's population grows, the demand for meat, poultry, and seafood should continue to increase. Successful marketing by the poultry industry is likely to increase demand for chicken and ready-to-heat products. Similarly, the development of prepared food products that are lower in fat and more nutritious promises to stimulate the consumption of red meat. The trend toward preparing case-ready meat at the processing level also should contribute to demand for animal slaughterers and meatpackers.

Employment growth of lesser skilled meat, poultry, and fish cutters and trimmers—who work primarily in animal slaughtering and processing plants—is expected to increase about as fast as the average for all occupations in coming years. With the growing popularity of labor-intensive, ready-to-heat poultry products, demand for poultry workers should remain firm. Fish cutters also will be in demand, as the task of preparing ready-to-heat fish goods gradually shifts from retail stores to processing plants. Also, advances in fish farming, or "aquaculture," should help meet the growing demand for fish and produce opportunities for fish cutters.

Employment of more highly skilled butchers and meatcutters, who work primarily in retail stores, is expected to continue to decline. Automation and the consolidation of the animal slaughtering and processing industries are enabling employers to transfer employment from higher paid butchers to lower wage slaughterers and meatpackers in meatpacking plants. At present, most red meat arrives at grocery stores partially cut up, but a growing share of meat is being delivered prepackaged, with additional fat removed, to wholesalers and retailers. This trend is resulting in less work and, thus, fewer jobs for retail butchers.

While high-volume production equipment limits the demand for bakers in manufacturing, overall employment of bakers is expected to increase about as fast as average due to growing numbers of large wholesale bakers, in-store and specialty shops, and traditional bakeries. In addition to the growing numbers of cookie, muffin, and cinnamon roll bakeries, the numbers of specialty bread and bagel shops have been growing, spurring demand for bread and pastry bakers.

Employment of food batchmakers, food and tobacco cooking and roasting machine operators and tenders, is expected to grow more slowly than average. As more of this work is being done at the manufacturing level rather than at the retail level, potential employment gains will be offset by productivity gains from automated cooking and roasting equipment. All other food processing workers should experience about as fast as average growth.

Earnings

Earnings vary by industry, skill, geographic region, and educational level. Median annual earnings of butchers and meatcutters were

$25,500 in 2002. The middle 50 percent earned between $19,440 and $34,140. The highest-paid 10 percent earned more than $42,330 annually, while the lowest 10 percent earned less than $15,490. Butchers and meatcutters employed at the retail level typically earn more than those in manufacturing. Median annual earnings in the industries employing the largest numbers of butchers and meatcutters in 2002 were as follows:

Other general merchandise stores	$30,670
Grocery stores	27,230
Specialty food stores	22,280
Animal slaughtering and processing	20,630

Meat, poultry, and fish cutters and trimmers typically earn less than butchers and meatcutters. In 2002, median annual earnings for these lower skilled workers were $17,820. The middle 50 percent earned between $15,800 and $21,170. The highest 10 percent earned more than $24,840, while the lowest 10 percent earned less than $14,270. Median annual earnings in the industries employing the largest numbers of meat, poultry, and fish cutters and trimmers in 2002 are shown in the following tabulation:

Grocery stores	$20,900
Grocery and related product wholesalers	18,440
Animal slaughtering and processing	17,710
Seafood product preparation and packaging	15,660

Median annual earnings of bakers were $20,580 in 2002. The middle 50 percent earned between $16,420 and $26,610. The highest 10 percent earned more than $33,470, and the lowest 10 percent earned less than $14,100. Median annual earnings in the industries employing the largest numbers of bakers in 2002 are given in the following tabulation:

Bakeries and tortilla manufacturing	$22,030
Other general merchandise stores	21,650
Grocery stores	20,470
Full-service restaurants	19,650
Limited-service eating places	17,830

Median annual earnings of food batchmakers were $21,920 in 2002. The middle 50 percent earned between $16,720 and $28,740. The highest 10 percent earned more than $35,110, and the lowest 10 percent earned less than $13,930. Median annual earnings in the industries employing the largest numbers of food batchmakers in 2002 are presented in the following tabulation:

Dairy product manufacturing ,..	$26,330
Fruit and vegetable preserving and specialty food manufacturing	22,980
Other food manufacturing	22,850
Bakeries and tortilla manufacturing	22,530
Sugar and confectionary product manufacturing	21,390

In 2002, median annual earnings for slaughterers and meatpackers were $20,370. The middle 50 percent earned between $17,650 and $22,900. The highest 10 percent earned more than $26,270, and the lowest 10 percent earned less than $15,350. Median annual earnings in animal slaughtering and processing, the industry employing the largest number of food processing workers, were $20,410 in 2002.

Median annual earnings for food cooking machine operators and tenders were $21,860 in 2002. The middle 50 percent earned between $16,900 and $28,160. The highest 10 percent earned more than $34,890, and the lowest 10 percent earned less than $14,380. Median annual earnings in fruit and vegetable preserving and specialty food manufacturing, the industry employing the largest number of food cooking machine operators and tenders, were $25,320 in 2002.

In 2002, median annual earnings for food and tobacco roasting, baking, and drying machine operators and tenders were $23,260 and for all other food processing workers, $19,410.

Food-processing workers generally received typical benefits, including pension plans for union members or those employed by grocery stores. However, poultry workers rarely earned substantial benefits. In 2002, 25 percent of all butchers and other meat, poultry, and fish processing workers were union members or were covered by a union contract. Sixteen percent of all bakers and 18 percent of all food batchmakers also were union members or were covered by a union contract. Many food-processing workers are members of the United Food and Commercial Workers International Union.

Related Occupations
Food-processing workers must be skilled at both hand and machine work and must have some knowledge of processes and techniques that are involved in handling and preparing food. Other occupations that require similar skills and knowledge include chefs, cooks, and food preparation workers.

Sources of Additional Information
State employment service offices can provide information about job openings for food-processing occupations.

Metal Workers and Plastic Workers

Computer-Control Programmers and Operators

(0*NET 51-4011.01, 51-4012.00)

Significant Points

● Workers learn in apprenticeship programs, informally on the job, and in secondary, vocational, or postsecondary schools; many entrants have previously worked as machinists or machine setters, operators, and tenders.

● Job opportunities should be excellent, as employers are expected to continue to have difficulty finding qualified workers.

Nature of the Work

Computer-control programmers and operators use computer numerically controlled (CNC) machines to cut and shape precision products, such as automobile parts, machine parts, and compressors. CNC machines include machining tools such as lathes, multiaxis spindles, milling machines, and electrical discharge machines (EDM), but the functions formerly performed by human operators are performed by a computer-control module. CNC machines cut away material from a solid block of metal, plastic, or glass—known as a workpiece—to form a finished part. Computer-control programmers and operators normally produce large quantities of one part, although they may produce small batches or one-of-a-kind items. They use their knowledge of the working properties of metals and their skill with CNC programming to design and carry out the operations needed to make machined products that meet precise specifications.

Before CNC programmers—also referred to as numerical tool and process control programmers—machine a part, they must carefully plan and prepare the operation. First, these workers review three-dimensional computer aided/automated design (CAD) blueprints of the part. Next, they calculate where to cut or bore into the workpiece, how fast to feed the metal into the machine, and how much metal to remove. They then select tools and materials for the job and plan the sequence of cutting and finishing operations.

Next, CNC programmers turn the planned machining operations into a set of instructions. These instructions are translated into a computer aided/automated manufacturing (CAM) program containing a set of commands for the machine to follow. These commands normally are a series of numbers (hence, numerical control) that describes where cuts should occur, what type of cut should be used, and the speed of the cut. CNC programmers and operators check new programs to ensure that the machinery will function properly and that the output will meet specifications. Because a problem with the program could damage costly machinery and cutting tools, computer simulations may be used to check the program instead of a trial run. If errors are found, the program must be changed and retested until the problem is resolved. In addition, growing connectivity between CAD/CAM software and CNC machine tools is raising productivity by automatically translating designs into instructions for the computer controller on the machine tool. These new CAM technologies enable programs to be easily modified for use on other jobs with similar specifications.

After the programming work is completed, CNC operators—also referred to as computer-controlled machine tool operators, metal and plastic—perform the necessary machining operations. The CNC operators transfer the commands from the server to the CNC control module using a computer network link or floppy disk. Many advanced control modules are conversational, meaning that they ask the operator a series of questions about the nature of the task. CNC operators position the metal stock on the CNC machine tool—spindle, lathe, milling machine, or other—set the controls, and let the computer make the cuts. Heavier objects may be loaded with the assistance of other workers, autoloaders, a crane, or a forklift. During the machining process, computer-control operators constantly monitor the readouts from the CNC control module, checking to see if any problems exist. Machine tools have unique characteristics, which can be problematic. During a machining operation, the operator modifies the cutting program to account for any problems encountered. Unique, modified CNC programs are saved for every different machine that performs a task.

CNC operators detect some problems by listening for specific sounds—for example, a dull cutting tool or excessive vibration. Dull cutting tools are removed and replaced. Machine tools rotate at high speeds, which can create problems with harmonic vibrations in the workpiece. Vibrations cause the machine tools to make minor cutting errors, hurting the quality of the product. Operators listen for vibrations and then adjust the cutting speed to compensate. In older, slower machine tools, the cutting speed would be reduced to eliminate the vibrations, but the amount of time needed to finish the product would increase as a result. In newer, high-speed CNC machines, increasing the cutting speed normally eliminates the vibrations and reduces production time. CNC operators also ensure that the workpiece is being properly lubricated and cooled, because the machining of metal products generates a significant amount of heat.

Working Conditions

Most machine shops are clean, well lit, and ventilated. Most modern CNC machines are partially or totally enclosed, minimizing the exposure of workers to noise, debris, and the lubricants used to cool workpieces during machining. Nevertheless, working around

Using specialized control modules, computer control programmers and operators make adjustments to the machining process.

high-speed machine tools presents certain dangers, and workers must follow safety precautions. Computer-controlled machine tool operators, metal and plastic, wear protective equipment, such as safety glasses to shield against bits of flying metal and earplugs to dampen machinery noise. They also must exercise caution when handling hazardous coolants and lubricants. The job requires stamina because operators stand most of the day and, at times, may need to lift moderately heavy workpieces.

Numerical tool and process control programmers work on desktop computers in offices that typically are near, but separate from, the shop floor. These work areas usually are clean, well lit, and free of machine noise. Numerical tool and process control programmers occasionally need to enter the shop floor to monitor CNC machining operations. On the shop floor, CNC programmers encounter the same hazards and exercise the same safety precautions as do CNC operators.

Most computer-control programmers and operators work a 40-hour week. CNC operators increasingly work evening and weekend shifts as companies justify investments in more expensive machinery by extending hours of operation. Overtime is common during peak production periods.

Employment

Computer-control programmers and operators held about 151,000 jobs in 2002, mostly working in machine shops, plastics products manufacturing, or machinery manufacturing. Although computer-control programmers and operators work in all parts of the country, jobs are most plentiful in the areas where manufacturing is concentrated.

Training, Other Qualifications, and Advancement

Computer-control programmers and operators train in various ways—in apprenticeship programs, informally on the job, and in secondary, vocational, or postsecondary schools. Due to a shortage of qualified applicants, many employers teach introductory courses, which provide a basic understanding of metalworking machines, safety, and blueprint reading. A basic knowledge of computers and electronics also is helpful. Experience with machine tools is extremely important. In fact, many entrants to these occupations have previously worked as machinists or machine setters, operators, and tenders. Persons interested in becoming computer-control programmers or operators should be mechanically inclined and able to work independently and do highly accurate work.

High school or vocational school courses in mathematics (trigonometry and algebra), blueprint reading, computer programming, metalworking, and drafting are recommended. Apprenticeship programs consist of shop training and related classroom instruction. In shop training, apprentices learn filing, handtapping, and dowel fitting, as well as the operation of various machine tools. Classroom instruction includes math, physics, programming, blueprint reading, CAD software, safety, and shop practices. Skilled computer-control programmers and operators need an understanding of the machining process, including the complex physics that occur at the cutting point. Thus, most training programs teach CNC operators and programmers to perform operations on manual machines prior to operating CNC machines. A growing number of computer-control programmers and operators receive most of their formal training from community or technical colleges. Less skilled CNC operators may need only a couple of weeks of on-the-job training.

To boost the skill level of all metalworkers and to create a more uniform standard of competency, a number of training facilities and colleges have recently begun implementing curriculums incorporating national skills standards developed by the National Institute of Metalworking Skills (NIMS). After completing such a curriculum and passing a performance requirement and written exam, trainees are granted a NIMS credential that provides formal recognition of competency in a metalworking field. Completion of a formal certification program provides expanded career opportunities.

Qualifications for CNC programmers vary widely depending upon the complexity of the job. Employers often prefer skilled machinists or those with technical school training. For some specialized types of programming, such as that needed to produce complex parts for the aerospace or shipbuilding industries, employers may prefer individuals with a degree in engineering.

For those entering CNC programming directly, a basic knowledge of computers and electronics is necessary, and experience with machine tools is extremely helpful. Classroom training includes an introduction to computer numerical control, the basics of programming, and more complex topics, such as computer-aided manufacturing. Trainees start writing simple programs under the direction of an experienced programmer. Although machinery manufacturers are trying to standardize programming languages, there are numerous languages in use. Because of this, computer-control programmers and operators should be able to learn new programming languages.

As new automation is introduced, computer-control programmers and operators normally receive additional training to update their skills. This training usually is provided by a representative of the equipment manufacturer or a local technical school. Many employers offer tuition reimbursement for job-related courses.

Computer-control programmers and operators can advance in several ways. Experienced CNC operators may become CNC programmers, and some are promoted to supervisory or administrative positions in their firms. A few open their own shops.

Job Outlook

Computer-control programmers and operators should have excellent job opportunities. Due to the limited number of people entering training programs, employers are expected to continue to have difficulty finding workers with the necessary skills and knowledge. Employment of computer-controlled machine tool operators is projected to grow more slowly than the average for all occupations through 2012, but employment of numerical tool and process control programmers is expected to grow about as fast as the average for all occupations through 2012. Job growth in both occupations will be driven by the increasing use of CNC machine tools. Advances in CNC machine tools and manufacturing technology will further automate production, boosting CNC operator productivity and limiting employment growth. The demand for computer-control programmers will be negatively affected by the increasing use of software that automatically translates part and product designs into CNC machine tool instructions.

Employment levels of computer-control programmers and operators are influenced by economic cycles—as the demand for machined goods falls, programmers and operators involved in production may be laid off or forced to work fewer hours.

Earnings

Median hourly earnings of computer-controlled machine tool operators, metal and plastic, were $13.97 in 2002. The middle 50 percent earned between $11.07 and $17.43. The lowest 10 percent earned less than $9.14, whereas the top 10 percent earned more than $21.27. Median hourly earnings in the manufacturing industries employing the largest numbers of computer-controlled machine tool operators, metal and plastic, in 2002 were:

Metalworking machinery manufacturing $15.97
Other fabricated metal product manufacturing 15.14
Machine shops; turned product; and screw, nut, and bolt
  manufacturing 13.82
Motor vehicle parts manufacturing 13.08
Plastics product manufacturing 11.00

Median hourly earnings of numerical tool and process control programmers were $18.04 in 2002. The middle 50 percent earned between $14.52 and $22.23. The lowest 10 percent earned less than $11.53, while the top 10 percent earned more than $27.37.

Related Occupations

Occupations most closely related to computer-control programmers and operators are other metal worker occupations, which include machinists; tool and die makers; machine setters, operators, and tenders—metal and plastic; and welding, soldering, and brazing workers. Numerical tool and process control programmers apply their knowledge of machining operations, metals, blueprints, and machine programming to write programs that run machine tools. Computer programmers also write detailed programs to meet precise specifications.

Sources of Additional Information

For general information about computer-control programmers and operators, contact:

➤ Precision Machine Products Association, 6700 West Snowville Rd., Brecksville, OH 44141-3292. Internet: **http://www.pmpa.org**

For a list of training centers and apprenticeship programs, contact:

➤ National Tooling and Metalworking Association, 9300 Livingston Rd., Fort Washington, MD 20744. Internet: **http://www.ntma.org**

For general occupational information, including a list of training programs, contact:

➤ Precision Metalforming Association Educational Foundation, 6363 Oak Tree Blvd., Independence, OH 44131-2500. Internet: **http://www.pmaef.org**

Machinists

(O*NET 51-4041.00)

Significant Points

● Machinists learn in apprenticeship programs, informally on the job, and in high schools, vocational schools, or community or technical colleges.

● Many entrants previously have worked as machine setters, operators, or tenders.

● Job opportunities are expected to be excellent.

Nature of the Work

Machinists use machine tools, such as lathes, milling machines, and machining centers, to produce precision metal parts. Although they may produce large quantities of one part, precision machinists often produce small batches or one-of-a-kind items. They use their knowledge of the working properties of metals and their skill with machine tools to plan and carry out the operations needed to make machined products that meet precise specifications.

Before they machine a part, machinists must carefully plan and prepare the operation. These workers first review blueprints or writ-

ten specifications for a job. Next, they calculate where to cut or bore into the workpiece (the piece of metal that is being shaped), how fast to feed the metal into the machine, and how much metal to remove. They then select tools and materials for the job, plan the sequence of cutting and finishing operations, and mark the metal stock to show where cuts should be made.

After this layout work is completed, machinists perform the necessary machining operations. They position the metal stock on the machine tool—drill press, lathe, milling machine, or other type of machine—set the controls, and make the cuts. During the machining process, they must constantly monitor the feed rate and speed of the machine. Machinists also ensure that the workpiece is being properly lubricated and cooled, because the machining of metal products generates a significant amount of heat. The temperature of the workpiece is a key concern because most metals expand when heated; machinists must adjust the size of their cuts relative to the temperature. Some rare but increasingly popular metals, such as titanium, are machined at extremely high temperatures.

Machinists detect some problems by listening for specific sounds—for example, a dull cutting tool or excessive vibration. Dull cutting tools are removed and replaced. Cutting speeds are adjusted to compensate for harmonic vibrations, which can decrease the accuracy of cuts, particularly on newer high-speed spindles and lathes. After the work is completed, machinists use both simple and highly sophisticated measuring tools to check the accuracy of their work against blueprints.

Some machinists, often called production machinists, may produce large quantities of one part, especially parts requiring the use of complex operations and great precision. Many modern machine tools are computer numerically controlled (CNC). Frequently, machinists work with computer-control programmers to determine how the automated equipment will cut a part. (See the statement on computer control programmers and operators elsewhere in the *Handbook*.) The programmer may determine the path of the cut, while the machinist determines the type of cutting tool, the speed of the cutting tool, and the feed rate. Because most machinists train in CNC programming, they may write basic programs themselves and often modify programs in response to problems encountered during test runs. After the production process is designed, relatively simple and repetitive operations normally are performed by machine setters, operators, and tenders. (See the statement on machine setters, operators, and tenders—metal and plastic, elsewhere in the *Handbook*.)

Machinists replace worn cutting tools.

Some manufacturing techniques employ automated parts loaders, automatic tool changers, and computer controls, allowing machine tools to operate without anyone present. One production machinist, working 8 hours a day, might monitor equipment, replace worn cutting tools, check the accuracy of parts being produced, and perform other tasks on several CNC machines that operate 24 hours a day (lights-out manufacturing). During lights-out manufacturing, a factory may need only a few machinists to monitor the entire factory.

Other machinists do maintenance work—repairing or making new parts for existing machinery. To repair a broken part, maintenance machinists may refer to blueprints and perform the same machining operations that were needed to create the original part.

Working Conditions

Today, most machine shops are relatively clean, well lit, and ventilated. Many computer-controlled machines are partially or totally enclosed, minimizing the exposure of workers to noise, debris, and the lubricants used to cool workpieces during machining. Nevertheless, working around machine tools presents certain dangers, and workers must follow safety precautions. Machinists wear protective equipment, such as safety glasses to shield against bits of flying metal and earplugs to dampen machinery noise. They also must exercise caution when handling hazardous coolants and lubricants, although many common water-based lubricants present little hazard. The job requires stamina, because machinists stand most of the day and, at times, may need to lift moderately heavy workpieces. Modern factories extensively employ autoloaders and overhead cranes, reducing heavy lifting.

Most machinists work a 40-hour week. Evening and weekend shifts are becoming more common as companies justify investments in more expensive machinery by extending hours of operation. However, this trend is somewhat offset by the increasing use of lights-out manufacturing. Overtime is common during peak production periods.

Employment

Machinists held about 387,000 jobs in 2002. Most machinists work in small machining shops or in manufacturing industries, such as machinery manufacturing and transportation equipment manufacturing (motor vehicle parts and aerospace products and parts). Maintenance machinists work in most industries that use production machinery.

Training, Other Qualifications, and Advancement

Machinists train in apprenticeship programs, informally on the job, and in high schools, vocational schools, or community or technical colleges. Experience with machine tools is helpful. In fact, many entrants previously have worked as machine setters, operators, or tenders. Persons interested in becoming machinists should be mechanically inclined, have good problem-solving abilities, be able to work independently, and be able to do highly accurate work (tolerances may reach 1/10,000th of an inch) that requires concentration and physical effort.

High school or vocational school courses in mathematics (especially trigonometry), blueprint reading, metalworking, and drafting are highly recommended. Apprenticeship programs consist of shop training and related classroom instruction lasting up to 4 years. In shop training, apprentices work almost full time, and are supervised by an experienced machinist while learning to operate various machine tools. Classroom instruction includes math, physics, materials science, blueprint reading, mechanical drawing, and quality and safety practices. In addition, as machine shops have increased their use of computer-controlled equipment, training in the operation and programming of CNC machine tools has become essential. Apprenticeship classes are taught in cooperation with local community or vocational colleges. A growing number of machinists learn the trade through 2-year associate degree programs at community or technical colleges. Graduates of these programs still need significant on-the-job experience before they are fully qualified.

To boost the skill level of machinists and to create a more uniform standard of competency, a number of training facilities and colleges are implementing curriculums that incorporate national skills standards developed by the National Institute of Metalworking Skills (NIMS). After completing such a curriculum and passing a performance requirement and written exam, trainees are granted a NIMS credential, which provides formal recognition of competency in a metalworking field. Completing a recognized certification program provides a machinist with better career opportunities.

As new automation is introduced, machinists normally receive additional training to update their skills. This training usually is provided by a representative of the equipment manufacturer or a local technical school. Some employers offer tuition reimbursement for job-related courses.

Machinists can advance in several ways. Experienced machinists may become CNC programmers, tool and die makers, or mold makers, or be promoted to supervisory or administrative positions in their firms. A few open their own shops.

Job Outlook

Despite projected slower-than-average employment growth, job opportunities for machinists should continue to be excellent. Many young people with the necessary educational and personal qualifications needed to obtain machining skills may prefer to attend college or may not wish to enter production occupations. Therefore, the number of workers obtaining the skills and knowledge necessary to fill machinist jobs is expected to be less than the number of job openings arising each year from employment growth and from the need to replace experienced machinists who transfer to other occupations or retire.

Employment of machinists is expected to grow more slowly than the average for all occupations over the 2002-12 period because of rising productivity among these workers. Machinists will become more efficient as a result of the expanded use of and improvements in technologies such as CNC machine tools, autoloaders, and high-speed machining. This allows fewer machinists to accomplish the same amount of work previously performed by more workers. Technology is not expected to affect the employment of machinists as significantly as that of most other production occupations, however, because machinists monitor and maintain many automated systems. Due to modern production techniques, employers prefer workers, such as machinists, who have a wide range of skills and are capable of performing almost any task in a machine shop.

Employment levels in this occupation are influenced by economic cycles—as the demand for machined goods falls, machinists involved in production may be laid off or forced to work fewer hours. Employment of machinists involved in plant maintenance, however, often is more stable because proper maintenance and repair of costly equipment remain critical to manufacturing operations, even when production levels fall.

Earnings

Median hourly earnings of machinists were $15.66 in 2002. The middle 50 percent earned between $12.15 and $19.45. The lowest 10 percent earned less than $9.57, while the top 10 percent earned more than $23.17. Median hourly earnings in the manufacturing industries employing the largest number of machinists in 2002 were:

Metalworking machinery manufacturing	$16.75
Other general purpose machinery manufacturing	15.91
Machine shops; turned product; and screw, nut, and bolt manufacturing	15.45
Motor vehicle parts manufacturing	15.18
Employment services	9.41

Related Occupations

Occupations most closely related to that of machinist are other machining occupations, which include tool and die makers; machine setters, operators, and tenders—metal and plastic; and computer-control programmers and operators. Another occupation that requires precision and skill in working with metal is welding, soldering, and brazing.

Sources of Additional Information

For general information about machinists, contact:
➤ Precision Machine Products Association, 6700 West Snowville Rd., Brecksville, OH 44141-3292. Internet: **http://www.pmpa.org**

For a list of training centers and apprenticeship programs, contact:
➤ National Tooling and Machining Association, 9300 Livingston Rd., Fort Washington, MD 20744. Internet: **http://www.ntma.org**

For general occupational information and a list of training programs, contact:
➤ Precision Metalforming Association Educational Foundation, 6363 Oak Tree Blvd., Independence, OH 44131-2500. Internet: **http://www.pmaef.org**

Machine Setters, Operators, and Tenders—Metal and Plastic

(0*NET 51-4021.00, 51-4022.00, 51-4023.00, 51-4031.01, 51-4031.02, 51-4031.03, 51-4031.04, 51-4032.00, 51-4033.01, 51-4033.02, 51-4034.00, 51-4035.00, 51-4051.00, 51-4052.00, 51-4061.00, 51-4062.00, 51-4071.00, 51-4072.01, 51-4072.02, 51-4072.03, 51-4072.04, 51-4072.05, 51-4081.01, 51-4081.02, 51-4191.01, 51-4191.02, 51-4191.03, 51-4192.00, 51-4193.01, 51-4193.02, 51-4193.03, 51-4193.04, 51-4194.00, 51-4199.99)

Significant Points

- Machine setters, operators, and tenders—metal and plastic operate powerful, high-speed machines that can be dangerous if strict safety rules are not observed.

- A few weeks of on-the-job training is sufficient for most workers to learn basic machine operations, but several years are required to become a highly skilled operator or setter.

- Overall employment growth in the various machine setter, operator, and tender occupations will be slower than average, although employment trends among these occupations will diverge over the 2002-12 period.

Nature of the Work

Consider the parts of a toaster, such as the metal or plastic housing or the lever that lowers the toast. These parts, and many other metal and plastic products, are produced by machine setters, operators, and tenders—metal and plastic. In fact, machine tool operators in the metalworking and plastics industries play a major role in producing most of the consumer products on which we rely daily.

In general, these workers can be separated into two groups—those who set up machines for operation and those who tend the machines during production. Setup workers prepare the machines *prior* to production and may adjust the machinery during its operation. Operators and tenders primarily monitor the machinery *during* its operation, sometimes loading or unloading the machine or making minor adjustments to the controls. Many workers both set up and operate equipment. Because the setup process requires an understanding of the entire production process, setters usually have more training and are more highly skilled than those who simply operate or tend machinery. As new automation simplifies the setup process, however, less skilled workers also are increasingly able to set up machines for operation.

Setters, operators, and tenders usually are identified by the type of machine with which they work. Some examples of specific titles are drilling- and boring-machine toolsetters, milling- and planing-machine tenders, and lathe- and turning-machine tool operators. Job duties usually vary with the size of the firm and the type of machine being operated. Although some workers specialize in one or two types of machinery, many are trained to set up or operate a variety of machines. Newer production techniques, such as team-oriented "lean" manufacturing, require machine operators to rotate between different machines. Rotating assignments result in more varied work, but also require workers to have a wider range of skills.

Machine setters, operators, and tenders—metal set up and tend machines that cut and form all types of metal parts. Setup workers plan and set up the sequence of operations according to blueprints, layouts, or other instructions. They adjust the speed, feed, and other controls, choose the proper coolants and lubricants, and select the instruments or tools for each operation. Using micrometers, gauges, and other precision measuring instruments, they also may compare the completed work with the tolerance limits stated in the specifications.

Although there are many different types of metalworking machine tools that require specific knowledge and skills, most operators perform similar tasks. Whether tending grinding machines that remove excess material from the surface of machined products or presses that extrude metal through a die to form wire, operators usually perform simple, repetitive operations that can be learned quickly. Typically, these workers place metal stock in a machine on which the operating specifications have already been set. They may watch one or more machines and make minor adjustments according to their instructions. Regardless of the type of machine they operate, machine tenders usually depend on skilled setup workers for major adjustments when the machines are not functioning properly.

Machine setters, operators, and tenders—plastic set up and tend machines that transform plastic compounds—chemical-based products that can be produced in powder, pellet, or syrup form—into a wide variety of consumer goods such as toys, tubing, and auto parts. These products are manufactured by various methods, of which injection molding is the most common. The injection-molding machine heats and liquefies a plastic compound and forces it into a mold. After the part has cooled and hardened, the mold opens and the part is released. Many common kitchen products are produced with this method. To produce long parts such as pipes or window frames, an extruding machine usually is employed. These machines force a plastic compound through a die that contains an opening with the desired shape of the final product. Blow molding is another common plasticsworking technique. Blow-molding machines force hot air into a mold that contains a plastic tube. As the air

Machine setters, operators, and tenders operate some computer-controlled machines.

moves into the mold, the tube is inflated to the shape of the mold, and a plastic container is formed. The familiar 2-liter soft-drink bottles are produced by this method.

Workers in three distinct specialties—setters, operators, and tenders—operate injection-molding machines. Most other types of plastic machines function in a similar manner. A typical injection-molding machine may have 25 different controls that can be adjusted. Setters or technicians set up the machines prior to their operation. These workers are responsible for repairing any major problem. Operators monitor the many gauges on injection-molding machines, adjusting different inputs, pressures, and speeds to maintain quality. Tenders remove the cooled plastic from the mold, loading the product into boxes.

Working Conditions

Most machine setters, operators, and tenders—metal and plastic work in areas that are clean, well lit, and well ventilated. Nevertheless, many operators require stamina, because they are on their feet much of the day and may do moderately heavy lifting. Also, these workers operate powerful, high-speed machines that can be dangerous if strict safety rules are not observed. Most operators wear protective equipment, such as safety glasses and earplugs, to protect against flying particles of metal or plastic and against noise from the machines. However, many modern machines are enclosed, minimiz-

ing the exposure of workers to noise, dust, and lubricants used during machining. Other required safety equipment varies by work setting and machine. For example, those in the plastics industry who work near materials that emit dangerous fumes or dust must wear face masks or self-contained breathing apparatus.

Most workers in the occupation put in a 40-hour week, but overtime is common during periods of increased production. Because many metalworking and plastics working shops operate more than one shift daily, some operators work nights and weekends.

Employment

Machine setters, operators, and tenders—metal and plastic held about 1.3 million jobs in 2002. Approximately 9 of 10 jobs were found in manufacturing. About 38 percent of all employment was in these manufacturing industries: transportation equipment manufacturing, plastics and rubber products manufacturing, and machinery manufacturing. The following tabulation shows the distribution of employment of machine setters, operators, and tenders—metal and plastic by detailed occupation.

Cutting, punching, and press machine setters, operators, and tenders, metal and plastic	283,000
Molding, coremaking, and casting machine setters, operators, and tenders, metal and plastic	151,000
Grinding, lapping, polishing, and buffing machine tool setters, operators, and tenders, metal and plastic	104,000
Multiple machine tool setters, operators, and tenders, metal and plastic	99,000
Extruding and drawing machine setters, operators, and tenders, metal and plastic	98,000
Lathe and turning machine tool setters, operators, and tenders, metal and plastic	75,000
Drilling and boring machine tool setters, operators, and tenders, metal and plastic	53,000
Forging machine setters, operators, and tenders, metal and plastic	45,000
Rolling machine setters, operators, and tenders, metal and plastic	44,000
Plating and coating machine setters, operators, and tenders, metal and plastic	44,000
Milling and planing machine setters, operators, and tenders, metal and plastic	31,000
Heat treating equipment setters, operators, and tenders, metal and plastic	29,000
Tool grinders, filers, and sharpeners	26,000
Foundry mold and coremakers	23,000
Metal-refining furnace operators and tenders	18,000
Pourers and casters, metal	13,000
Lay-out workers, metal and plastic	13,000
Model makers, metal and plastic	8,500
Patternmakers, metal and plastic	6,500
All other metal workers and plastic workers	104,000

Training, Other Qualifications, and Advancement

Machine setters, operators, and tenders—metal and plastic learn their skills on the job. Trainees begin by observing and assisting experienced workers, sometimes in formal training programs. Under supervision, they may start as tenders, supplying materials, starting and stopping the machine, or removing finished products from it. Then they advance to the more difficult tasks performed by operators, such as adjusting feed speeds, changing cutting tools, or inspecting a finished product for defects. Eventually, they become responsible for their own machines.

The complexity of the equipment largely determines the time required to become an operator. Most operators learn the basic machine operations and functions in a few weeks, but they may need a year to become skilled operators or to advance to the more highly skilled job of setter. Although many operators learn on the job, some community colleges and other educational institutions offer courses and certifications in operating metal and plastics machines. In addition to providing on-the-job training, some employers send promising machine tenders to operator classes. Other employers prefer to hire workers who have completed, or currently are enrolled in, a training program.

Setters or technicians normally need a thorough knowledge of the machinery and of the products being manufactured, because they often plan the sequence of work, make the first production run, and determine which adjustments need to be made. Strong analytical abilities are particularly important for this job. Some companies have formal training programs for operators and setters; often, the programs combine classroom instruction with on-the-job training.

Although no special education is required for many jobs in the occupation, employers prefer to hire applicants with good basic skills. Many require employees to have a high school education and to read, write, and speak English. Because machinery is becoming more complex and shop-floor organization is changing, employers increasingly look for persons with good communication and interpersonal skills. Mechanical aptitude, manual dexterity, and experience working with machinery also are helpful. Those interested in becoming machine setters, operators, and tenders can improve their employment opportunities by completing high school courses in shop and blueprint reading and by gaining a working knowledge of the properties of metals and plastics. A solid math background, including courses in algebra, geometry, trigonometry, and basic statistics, also is useful.

Job opportunities and advancement can be enhanced as well by becoming certified in a particular machining skill. The National Institute for Metalworking Skills has developed standards for machine setters, operators, and tenders—metal. After taking a course approved by the organization and passing a written exam and performance requirement, the worker is issued a credential that signifies competence in a specific machining operation. The Society of Plastics Industry, the national trade association representing plastics manufacturers, also certifies workers in that industry. To achieve machine-operator certification, 2 years of experience operating a plastics-processing machine is recommended, and one must pass a computer-based exam.

Advancement for operators usually takes the form of higher pay, although there are some limited opportunities for operators to advance to new positions as well. For example, they can become multiple-machine operators, setup operators, or trainees for the more highly skilled position of machinist, tool and die maker, or computer-control programmer or operator. Some setup workers may advance to supervisory positions. (See the statements on machinists, computer-control programmers and operators, and tool and die makers elsewhere in the *Handbook*.)

Job Outlook

Overall employment growth in the various machine setter, operator, and tender occupations will be slower than average, although employment trends among these occupations will diverge over the 2002-12 period. In general, employment of workers in the occupation will be affected by the rate of technological implementation, the demand for the goods they produce, the effects of trade, and the reorganization of production processes. Employment of multiple-machine-tool operators; molding, coremaking, and casting-machine operators, metal and plastic; and a number of miscellaneous operating occupations is expected to grow. A decline in employment, however, is projected for some machine tool operators, including metal-refining furnace operators and tenders and pourers and casters, metal. Despite differing rates of employment change, a large number of machine setter, operator, and tender jobs will become available due to an expected surge in retirements as some baby boomers become eligible for retirement by the end of the decade.

One of the most important factors influencing employment change in this occupation is the implementation of labor-saving machinery. In order to remain competitive by improving quality and lowering production costs, many firms are adopting new technologies, such as computer-controlled machine tools and robots. Computer-controlled equipment allows operators to tend a greater number of machines simultaneously and often makes setup easier, thereby reducing the amount of time setup workers spend on each machine. Robots are being used to load and unload parts from machines. The lower skilled manual machine tool operators and tenders are more likely to be eliminated by these new technologies, because the functions they perform are more easily automated.

The demand for machine setters, operators, and tenders—metal and plastic largely mirrors the demand for the parts they produce. The consumption of plastic products has grown as they have been substituted for metal goods in many consumer and manufactured products in recent years. The process is likely to continue and should result in stronger demand for machine operators in plastics than in metal.

Both the plastics and metal industries, however, face stiff foreign competition that is limiting the demand for domestically produced parts. One way in which larger U.S. producers have responded to this competition is by moving production operations to other countries where labor costs are lower. These moves are likely to continue and will further reduce employment opportunities for many machine operators, setters, and tenders—metal and plastic in the United States. Another way domestic manufacturers compete with low-wage foreign competition is by increasing their use of automated systems, which can make manufacturing establishments more competitive by improving their productivity. However, increased automation also limits employment growth.

Workers with a thorough background in machine operations, exposure to a variety of machines, and a good working knowledge of the properties of metals and plastics will be best able to adjust to the changing environment. In addition, new shop-floor arrangements will reward workers with good basic mathematics and reading skills, good communication skills, and the ability and willingness to learn new tasks. As workers adapt to team-oriented production methods and operate more machines, the number of multiple-machine-tool operators, setters, and tenders—metal and plastic will continue to rise.

Earnings

Earnings for machine operators can vary by size of the company, union or nonunion status, industry, and skill level and experience of the operator. Also, temporary employees, who are being hired in greater numbers, usually get paid less than company-employed workers. The median hourly earnings in 2002 for a variety of machine setters, operators, and tenders—metal and plastic were as follows:

Model makers, metal and plastic	$18.27
Patternmakers, metal and plastic	16.09
Metal-refining furnace operators and tenders	14.79
Lay-out workers, metal and plastic	14.79
Lathe and turning machine tool setters, operators, and tenders, metal and plastic	14.55
Tool grinders, filers, and sharpeners	14.14
Milling and planing machine setters, operators, and tenders, metal and plastic	14.04
Multiple machine tool setters, operators, and tenders, metal and plastic	13.79
Rolling machine setters, operators, and tenders, metal and plastic	13.62
Heat treating equipment setters, operators, and tenders, metal and plastic	13.56
Pourers and casters, metal	13.40
Drilling and boring machine tool setters, operators, and tenders, metal and plastic	13.23
Forging machine setters, operators, and tenders, metal and plastic	12.64
Grinding, lapping, polishing, and buffing machine tool setters, operators, and tenders, metal and plastic	12.56
Foundry mold and coremakers	12.55
Extruding and drawing machine setters, operators, and tenders, metal and plastic	12.44
Plating and coating machine setters, operators, and tenders, metal and plastic	12.22
Cutting, punching, and press machine setters, operators, and tenders, metal and plastic	11.81
Molding, coremaking, and casting machine setters, operators, and tenders, metal and plastic	11.17
All other metal workers and plastic workers	13.65

Related Occupations

Workers in occupations closely related to machine setters, operators, and tenders—metal and plastic include machinists; tool and die makers; assemblers and fabricators; computer-control programmers and operators; and welding, soldering, and brazing workers. Often, machine operators are responsible for checking the quality of parts being produced, work similar to that of inspectors, testers, sorters, samplers, and weighers.

Sources of Additional Information

For general information about metal machine setters, operators, and tenders, contact any of the following organizations:
➤ National Tooling and Machining Association, 9300 Livingston Rd., Fort Washington, MD 20744. Internet: **http://www.ntma.org**
➤ Precision Metalforming Association Educational Foundation, 6363 Oak Tree Blvd., Independence, OH 44131. Internet: **http://www.pmaef.org**
➤ Precision Machine Products Association, 6700 West Snowville Rd., Brecksville, OH 44141-3292. Internet: **http://www.pmpa.org**

For information on schools and employers with training programs in plastics, contact
➤ Society of Plastics Industry, 1801 K St. NW., Suite 600K, Washington, DC 20006-1301. Internet: **http://www.socplas.org**

Tool and Die Makers

(O*NET 51-4111.00)

Significant Points

● Most tool and die makers train for 4 or 5 years in apprenticeships or postsecondary programs; employers typically recommend apprenticeship training.

● Jobseekers with the appropriate skills and background should enjoy excellent opportunities and very high earnings.

Nature of the Work

Tool and die makers are among the most highly skilled workers in manufacturing. These workers produce tools, dies, and special guiding and holding devices that enable machines to manufacture a variety of products we use daily—from clothing and furniture to heavy equipment and parts for aircraft.

Toolmakers craft precision tools and machines that are used to cut, shape, and form metal and other materials. They also produce jigs and fixtures (devices that hold metal while it is bored, stamped, or drilled) and gauges and other measuring devices. Die makers construct metal forms (dies) that are used to shape metal in stamping and forging operations. They also make metal molds for diecasting and for molding plastics, ceramics, and composite materials. Some tool and die makers craft prototypes of parts, and then determine how best to manufacture the part. In addition to developing, designing, and producing new tools and dies, these workers also may repair worn or damaged tools, dies, gauges, jigs, and fixtures.

To perform these functions, tool and die makers employ many types of machine tools and precision measuring instruments. They also must be familiar with the machining properties, such as hardness and heat tolerance, of a wide variety of common metals and alloys. As a result, tool and die makers are knowledgeable in machining operations, mathematics, and blueprint reading. In fact, tool and die makers often are considered highly specialized machinists. The main difference between tool and die makers and machinists is that machinists normally make a single part during the production process, while tool and die makers make parts and machines used in the production process. (See the statement on machinists elsewhere in the *Handbook*.)

Working from blueprints, tool and die makers first must plan the sequence of operations necessary to manufacture the tool or die. Next, they measure and mark the pieces of metal that will be cut to form parts of the final product. At this point, tool and die makers cut, drill, or bore the part as required, checking to ensure that the final product meets specifications. Finally, these workers assemble the parts and perform finishing jobs such as filing, grinding, and polishing surfaces.

Modern technology has changed the ways in which tool and die makers perform their jobs. Today, for example, these workers often use computer-aided design (CAD) to develop products and parts. Specifications entered into computer programs can be used to electronically develop drawings for the required tools and dies. Numerical tool and process control programmers use computer-aided manufacturing (CAM) programs to convert electronic drawings into computer programs that contain instructions for a sequence of cutting tool operations. (See the statement on computer-control programmers and operators elsewhere in the *Handbook*.) Once these programs are developed, computer numerically controlled (CNC) machines follow the set of instructions contained in the program to produce the part. Computer-controlled machine tool operators or machinists normally operate CNC machines; however, tool and die makers are trained in both operating CNC machines and writing CNC programs, and they may perform either task. CNC programs are stored electronically for future use, saving time and increasing worker productivity.

After machining the parts, tool and die makers carefully check the accuracy of the parts using many tools, including coordinate measuring machines (CMM), which use software and sensor arms to compare the dimensions of the part to electronic blueprints. Next, they assemble the different parts into a functioning machine. They file, grind, shim, and adjust the different parts to properly fit them together. Finally, the tool and die makers set up a test run using the

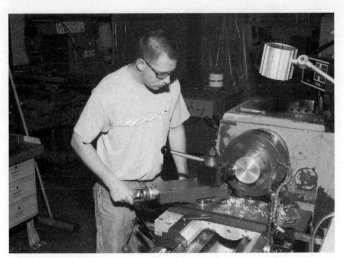

Tool and die makers sometimes machine parts manually.

tools or dies they have made to make sure that the manufactured parts meet specifications. If problems occur, they compensate by adjusting the tools or dies.

Working Conditions
Tool and die makers usually work in toolrooms. These areas are quieter than the production floor because there are fewer machines in use at one time. They also are generally kept clean and cool to minimize heat-related expansion of metal workpieces and to accommodate the growing number of computer-operated machines. To minimize the exposure of workers to moving parts, machines have guards and shields. Most computer-controlled machines are totally enclosed, minimizing the exposure of workers to noise, dust, and the lubricants used to cool workpieces during machining. Tool and die makers also must follow safety rules and wear protective equipment, such as safety glasses to shield against bits of flying metal, earplugs to protect against noise, and gloves and masks to reduce exposure to hazardous lubricants and cleaners. These workers also need stamina because they often spend much of the day on their feet and may do moderately heavy lifting.

Companies employing tool and die makers have traditionally operated only one shift per day. Overtime and weekend work are common, especially during peak production periods.

Employment
Tool and die makers held about 109,000 jobs in 2002. Most worked in industries that manufacture metalworking machinery, transportation equipment (such as motor vehicle parts and aerospace products), and fabricated metal products, as well as plastics product manufacturing. Although they are found throughout the country, jobs are most plentiful in the Midwest, Northeast, and West, where many of the metalworking industries are located.

Training, Other Qualifications, and Advancement
Most tool and die makers learn their trade through 4 or 5 years of education and training in formal apprenticeships or postsecondary programs. Apprenticeship programs include a mix of classroom instruction and job experience and often require 10,400 hours, or about 5 years to complete. According to most employers these apprenticeship programs are the best way to learn all aspects of tool and die making. A growing number of tool and die makers receive most of their formal classroom training from community and technical colleges, sometimes in conjunction with an apprenticeship program.

Even after completing their apprenticeship, tool and die makers still need years of experience to become highly skilled. Most specialize in making certain types of tools, molds, or dies.

Tool and die maker trainees learn to operate milling machines, lathes, grinders, wire electrical discharge machines, and other machine tools. They also learn to use handtools for fitting and assembling gauges, and other mechanical and metal-forming equipment. In addition, they study metalworking processes, such as heat treating and plating. Classroom training usually consists of mechanical drawing, tool designing, tool programming, blueprint reading, and mathematics courses, including algebra, geometry, trigonometry, and basic statistics. Tool and die makers increasingly must have good computer skills to work with CAD technology, CNC machine tools, and computerized measuring machines.

Workers who become tool and die makers without completing formal apprenticeships generally acquire their skills through a combination of informal on-the-job training and classroom instruction at a vocational school or community college. They often begin as machine operators and gradually take on more difficult assignments. Many machinists become tool and die makers.

Because tools and dies must meet strict specifications—precision to one ten-thousandth of an inch is common—the work of tool and die makers requires skill with precision measuring devices and a high degree of patience and attention to detail. Good eyesight is essential. Persons entering this occupation also should be mechanically inclined, able to work and solve problems independently, and capable of doing work that requires concentration and physical effort.

There are several ways for skilled workers to advance. Some move into supervisory and administrative positions in their firms; many obtain their college degree and go into engineering or tool design; and some may start their own shops.

Job Outlook
Applicants with the appropriate skills and background should enjoy excellent opportunities for tool and die maker jobs. The number of workers receiving training in this occupation is expected to continue to be fewer than the number of openings created each year by tool and die makers who retire or transfer to other occupations. As more of these highly skilled workers retire, employers in certain parts of the country report difficulty attracting well-trained applicants. A major factor limiting the number of people entering the occupation is that many young people who have the educational and personal qualifications necessary to learn tool and die making may prefer to attend college or may not wish to enter production-related occupations.

Despite expected excellent employment opportunities, little or no growth in employment of tool and die makers is projected over the 2002-12 period because advancements in automation, including CNC machine tools and computer-aided design, should improve worker productivity, thus limiting employment. On the other hand, tool and die makers play a key role in building and maintaining advanced automated manufacturing equipment. As firms invest in new equipment, modify production techniques, and implement product design changes more rapidly, they will continue to rely heavily on skilled tool and die makers for retooling.

Earnings
Median hourly earnings of tool and die makers were $20.54 in 2002. The middle 50 percent earned between $16.33 and $25.64. The lowest 10 percent had earnings of less than $12.97, while the top 10 percent earned more than $30.74. Median hourly earnings in the manufacturing industries employing the largest numbers of tool and die makers in 2002 are shown below.

Motor vehicle parts manufacturing $25.64
Metalworking machinery manufacturing 20.02
Forging and stamping 19.97
Plastics product manufacturing 19.79

Related Occupations

The occupations most closely related to the work of tool and die makers are other machining occupations. These include machinists; computer-control programmers and operators; and machine setters, operators, and tenders—metal and plastic. Another occupation that requires precision and skill in working with metal is welding, soldering, and brazing workers.

Like tool and die makers, assemblers and fabricators assemble complex machinery. When measuring parts, tool and die makers use some of the same tools and equipment that inspectors, testers, sorters, samplers, and weighers use in their jobs.

Sources of Additional Information

For career information and to have inquiries on training and employment referred to member companies, contact:

➤ Precision Machine Products Association, 6700 West Snowville Rd., Brecksville, OH 44141-3292. Internet: **http://www.pmpa.org**

For lists of schools and employers with tool and die apprenticeship and training programs, contact:

➤ National Tooling and Machining Association, 9300 Livingston Rd., Ft. Washington, MD 20744. Internet: **http://www.ntma.org**

For information on careers, education and training, earnings, and apprenticeship opportunities in metalworking, contact:

➤ Precision Metalforming Association Educational Foundation, 6363 Oak Tree Blvd., Independence, OH 44131-2500. Internet: **http://www.pmaef.org**

Welding, Soldering, and Brazing Workers

(0*NET 51-4121.01, 51-4121.02, 51-4121.03, 51-4121.04, 51-4121.05, 51-4122.01, 51-4122.02, 51-4122.03, 51.4122.04)

Significant Points

● Job prospects should be excellent.

● Training ranges from a few weeks of school or on-the-job training for low-skilled positions to several years of combined school and on-the-job training for highly skilled jobs.

Nature of the Work

Welding is the most common way of permanently joining metal parts. In this process, heat is applied to metal pieces, melting and fusing them to form a permanent bond. Because of its strength, welding is used in shipbuilding, automobile manufacturing and repair, aerospace applications, and thousands of other manufacturing activities. Welding also is used to join beams when constructing buildings, bridges, and other structures, and to join pipes in pipelines, power plants, and refineries.

Welders use many types of welding equipment set up in a variety of positions, such as flat, vertical, horizontal, and overhead. They may perform manual welding, in which the work is entirely controlled by the welder, or semiautomatic welding, in which the welder uses machinery, such as a wire feeder, to perform welding tasks.

Arc welding is the most common type of welding. Standard arc welding involves two large metal alligator clips that carry a strong

electrical current. One clip is attached to any part of the workpiece being welded. The second clip is connected to a thin welding rod. When the rod touches the workpiece, a powerful electrical circuit is created. The massive heat created by the electrical current causes both the workpiece and the steel core of the rod to melt together, cooling quickly to form a solid bond. During welding, the flux that surrounds the rod's core vaporizes, forming an inert gas that serves to protect the weld from atmospheric elements that might weaken it. Welding speed is important. Variations in speed can change the amount of flux applied, weakening the weld, or weakening the surrounding metal by increasing heat exposure.

Two common but advanced types of welding are Gas Tungsten Arc (TIG) and Gas Metal Arc (MIG) welding. TIG welding often is used with stainless steel or aluminum. While TIG uses welding rods, MIG uses a spool of continuously fed wire, which allows the welder to join longer stretches of metal without stopping to replace the rod. In TIG welding, the welder holds the welding rod in one hand and an electric torch in the other hand. The torch is used to simultaneously melt the rod and the workpiece. In MIG welding, the welder holds the wire feeder, which functions like the alligator clip in arc welding. Instead of using gas flux surrounding the rod, TIG and MIG protect the initial weld from the environment by blowing inert gas onto the weld.

Like arc welding, soldering and brazing use molten metal to join two pieces of metal. However, the metal added during the process has a melting point lower than that of the workpiece, so only the added metal is melted, not the workpiece. Soldering uses metals with a melting point below 800 degrees Fahrenheit; brazing uses metals with a higher melting point. Because soldering and brazing do not melt the workpiece, these processes normally do not create the distortions or weaknesses in the workpiece that can occur with welding. Soldering commonly is used to join electrical, electronic, and other small metal parts. Brazing produces a stronger joint than does soldering, and often is used to join metals other than steel, such as brass. Brazing can also be used to apply coatings to parts to reduce wear and protect against corrosion.

Skilled welding, soldering, and brazing workers generally plan work from drawings or specifications or use their knowledge of fluxes and base metals to analyze the parts to be joined. These workers then select and set up welding equipment, execute the planned welds, and examine welds to ensure that they meet standards or specifications. Highly skilled welders often are trained to work with a wide variety of materials in addition to steel, such as titanium, aluminum, or plastics. Some welders have more limited duties, however. They perform routine jobs that already have been planned and laid out and do not require extensive knowledge of welding techniques.

Automated welding is used in an increasing number of production processes. In these instances, a machine or robot performs the welding tasks while monitored by a welding machine operator. Welding, soldering, and brazing machine setters, operators, and tenders follow specified layouts, work orders, or blueprints. Operators must load parts correctly and constantly monitor the machine to ensure that it produces the desired bond.

The work of arc, plasma, and oxy-gas cutters is closely related to that of welders. However, instead of joining metals, cutters use the heat from an electric arc, a stream of ionized gas (plasma), or burning gases to cut and trim metal objects to specific dimensions. Cutters also dismantle large objects, such as ships, railroad cars, automobiles, buildings, or aircraft. Some operate and monitor cutting machines similar to those used by welding machine operators. Plasma cutting has been increasing in popularity because, unlike other methods, it can cut a wide variety of metals, including stainless steel, aluminum, and titanium.

Working Conditions

Welding, soldering, and brazing workers often are exposed to a number of hazards, including the intense light created by the arc, poisonous fumes, and very hot materials. They wear safety shoes, goggles, hoods with protective lenses, and other devices designed to prevent burns and eye injuries and to protect them from falling objects. They normally work in well-ventilated areas to limit their exposure to fumes. Automated welding, soldering, and brazing machine operators are not exposed to as many dangers, however, and a face shield or goggles usually provide adequate protection for these workers.

Welders and cutters may work outdoors, often in inclement weather, or indoors, sometimes in a confined area designed to contain sparks and glare. Outdoors, they may work on a scaffold or platform high off the ground. In addition, they may be required to lift heavy objects and work in a variety of awkward positions, while bending, stooping, or standing to perform work overhead.

Although about 55 percent of welders, solderers, and brazers work a 40-hour week, overtime is common, and some welders work up to 70 hours per week. Welders also may work in shifts as long as 12 hours. Some welders, solderers, brazers, and machine operators work in factories that operate around the clock, necessitating shift work.

Employment

Welding, soldering, and brazing workers held about 452,000 jobs in 2002. Of these jobs, about 2 of every 3 were found in manufacturing. Jobs were concentrated in transportation equipment manufacturing (motor vehicle body and parts and ship and boat building), machinery manufacturing (agriculture, construction, and mining machinery), and architectural and structural metals manufacturing. Most jobs for welding, soldering, and brazing machine setters, operators, and tenders were found in the same manufacturing industries as skilled welding, soldering, and brazing workers.

Training, Other Qualifications, and Advancement

Training for welding, soldering, and brazing workers can range from a few weeks of school or on-the-job training for low-skilled positions to several years of combined school and on-the-job training for highly skilled jobs. Formal training is available in high schools, vocational schools, and postsecondary institutions, such as vocational-technical institutes, community colleges, and private welding schools. The Armed Forces operate welding schools as well. Some employers provide training. Courses in blueprint reading, shop mathematics, mechanical drawing, physics, chemistry, and metallurgy are helpful. Knowledge of computers is gaining importance, especially for welding, soldering, and brazing machine operators, who are becoming responsible for the programming of computer-controlled machines, including robots.

Some welders become certified, a process whereby the employer sends a worker to an institution, such as an independent testing lab or technical school, to weld a test specimen according to specific codes and standards required by the employer. Testing procedures are based on the standards and codes set by one of several industry associations with which the employer may be affiliated. If the welding inspector at the examining institution determines that the worker has performed according to the employer's guidelines, the inspector will then certify the welder being tested as able to work with a particular welding procedure.

Some welding, soldering, and brazing workers are employed in ship and boat building.

Welding, soldering, and brazing workers need good eyesight, hand-eye coordination, and manual dexterity. They should be able to concentrate on detailed work for long periods and be able to bend, stoop, and work in awkward positions. In addition, welders increasingly need to be willing to receive training and perform tasks in other production jobs.

Welders can advance to more skilled welding jobs with additional training and experience. For example, they may become welding technicians, supervisors, inspectors, or instructors. Some experienced welders open their own repair shops.

Job Outlook

Job prospects should be excellent, as many potential entrants who could be welders may prefer to attend college or may prefer work that has more comfortable working conditions. Employment of welding, soldering, and brazing workers is expected to grow about as fast as the average for all occupations over the 2002-12 period. In addition, many openings will arise as workers retire or leave the occupation for other reasons.

The major factor affecting employment of welders is the health of the industries in which they work. Because almost every manufacturing industry uses welding at some stage of manufacturing or in the repair and maintenance of equipment, a strong economy will keep demand for welders high. A downturn affecting industries such as auto manufacturing, construction, or petroleum, however, would have a negative impact on the employment of welders in those areas, and could cause some layoffs. Levels of government funding for shipbuilding as well as for infrastructure repairs and improvements are expected to be another important determinant of the future number of welding jobs.

Regardless of the state of the economy, the pressures to improve productivity and hold down labor costs are leading many companies to invest more in automation, especially computer-controlled and robotically-controlled welding machinery. This will reduce the demand for some low-skilled welders, solderers, and brazers because these simple, repetitive jobs are being automated. The growing use of automation, however, should increase demand for welding, soldering, and brazing machine setters, operators, and tenders. Welders working on construction projects or in equipment repair will not be affected by technology change to the same extent, because their jobs are not as easily automated.

Technology is helping to improve welding, creating more uses for welding in the workplace and expanding employment opportunities. For example, new ways are being developed to bond dissimilar materials and nonmetallic materials, such as plastics, composites, and new alloys. Also, laser beam and electron beam welding, new fluxes, and other new technologies and techniques are improving the results of welding, making it useful in a wider assortment of applications. Improvements in technology have also boosted welding productivity, making welding more competitive with other methods of joining materials.

Earnings

Median hourly earnings of welders, cutters, solderers, and brazers were $14.02 in 2002. The middle 50 percent earned between $11.41 and $17.34. The lowest 10 percent had earnings of less than $9.41, while the top 10 percent earned over $21.79. The range of earnings of welders reflects the wide range of skill levels. Median hourly earnings in the industries employing the largest numbers of welders, cutters, solderers, and brazers in 2002 were:

Motor vehicle parts manufacturing	$16.02
Agriculture, construction, and mining machinery manufacturing	13.74
Architectural and structural metals manufacturing	13.34
Commercial and industrial machinery and equipment (except automotive and electronic) repair and maintenance	13.06
Motor vehicle body and trailer manufacturing	12.83

Median hourly earnings of welding, soldering, and brazing machine setters, operators, and tenders were $13.90 in 2002. The middle 50 percent earned between $11.22 and $17.77. The lowest 10 percent had earnings of less than $9.36, while the top 10 percent earned over $24.60. Median hourly earnings in motor vehicle parts manufacturing, the industry employing the largest numbers of welding machine operators in 2002 were $18.29.

Many welders belong to unions. Among these are the International Association of Machinists and Aerospace Workers; the International Brotherhood of Boilermakers, Iron Ship Builders, Blacksmiths, Forgers and Helpers; the International Union, United Automobile, Aerospace and Agricultural Implement Workers of America; the United Association of Journeymen and Apprentices of the Plumbing, Pipefitting, Sprinkler Fitting Industry of the United States and Canada; and the United Electrical, Radio, and Machine Workers of America.

Related Occupations

Welding, soldering, and brazing workers are skilled metal workers. Other metal workers include machinists; machine setters, operators, and tenders—metal and plastic; computer-control programmers and operators; tool and die makers; sheet metal workers; and boilermakers. Assemblers and fabricators of electrical and electronic equipment often assemble parts using soldering.

Sources of Additional Information

For information on training opportunities and jobs for welding, soldering, and brazing workers, contact local employers, the local office of the State employment service, or schools providing welding, soldering, or brazing training.

Information on careers and educational opportunities in welding is available from:

➤ American Welding Society, 550 N.W. Lejeune Rd., Miami, FL 33126-5699. Internet: **http://www.aws.org**

Printing Occupations

Bookbinders and Bindery Workers

(0*NET 51-5011.01, 51-5011.02, 51-5012.00)

Significant Points

● Most bookbinders and bindery workers train on the job.

● Employment is expected to decline, reflecting increasingly productive bindery operations, changing business practices, and competition from imports.

● Opportunities for hand bookbinders are limited because only a small number of establishments do this highly specialized work.

Nature of the Work

The process of combining printed sheets into finished products such as books, magazines, catalogs, folders, directories, or product packaging is known as "binding." Binding involves cutting, folding, gathering, gluing, stapling, stitching, trimming, sewing, wrapping, and other finishing operations. Bindery workers setup, operate, and maintain the machines that perform these various tasks.

Job duties depend on the kind of material being bound. In firms that do *edition binding*, for example, workers bind books produced in large numbers, or "runs." *Job binding* workers bind books produced in smaller quantities. In firms specializing in *library binding*, workers repair books and provide other specialized binding services to libraries. *Pamphlet binding* workers produce leaflets and folders, and *manifold binding* workers bind business forms such as ledgers and books of sales receipts. *Blankbook binding* workers bind blank pages to produce notebooks, checkbooks, address books, diaries, calendars, and note pads.

Some types of binding and finishing consist of only one step. Preparing leaflets or newspaper inserts, for example, requires only folding. Binding of books and magazines, on the other hand, requires a number of steps.

Bookbinders and bindery workers assemble books and magazines from large, flat, printed sheets of paper. Skilled workers operate machines that first fold printed sheets into "signatures," which are groups of pages arranged sequentially. Bookbinders then sew, stitch, or glue the assembled signatures together, shape the book bodies with presses and trimming machines, and reinforce them with glued fabric strips. Covers are created separately, and glued, pasted, or stitched onto the book bodies. The books then undergo a variety of finishing operations, often including wrapping in paper jackets.

A small number of bookbinders work in hand binderies. These highly skilled workers design original or special bindings for limited editions, or restore and rebind rare books. The work requires creativity, knowledge of binding materials, and a thorough background in the history of binding. Hand bookbinding gives individuals the opportunity to work in the greatest variety of bindery jobs.

Bookbinders and bindery workers in small shops may perform many binding tasks, while those in large shops usually are assigned only one or a few operations, such as running complicated manual or electronic guillotine papercutters or folding machines. Others

Bindery work requires careful attention to detail because these workers are responsible for the final assembly of printed materials.

specialize in adjusting and preparing equipment, and may perform minor repairs as needed.

Working Conditions

Binderies often are noisy and jobs can be fairly strenuous, requiring considerable lifting, standing, and carrying. The jobs also may require stooping, kneeling, and crouching. Binding often resembles an assembly line on which workers perform repetitive tasks.

Employment

In 2002, bookbinders and bindery workers held about 98,400 jobs, including 7,400 as skilled bookbinders and 91,000 as bindery workers. Nearly one in ten work in the employment services industry, which contracts them out as temporary employees to companies that need their services .

Although some advertising agencies, and book, magazine, and newspaper publishers have their own bindery operations, employing some bookbinders and bindery workers, the majority of jobs are in commercial printing plants. The largest employers of bindery workers are bindery trade shops—these companies specialize in providing binding services for printers without binderies or whose printing production exceeds their binding capabilities. Few publishers maintain their own manufacturing facilities, so most contract out the printing and assembly of books to commercial printing plants or bindery trade shops.

Training, Other Qualifications, and Advancement

Most bookbinders and bindery workers learn the craft through on-the-job training. Inexperienced workers usually are assigned simple tasks such as moving paper from cutting machines to folding machines. They learn basic binding skills, including the characteristics of paper and how to cut large sheets of paper into different sizes with the least amount of waste. As workers gain experience, they advance to more difficult tasks, such as embossing and adding holograms, and learn to operate one or more pieces of equipment. Usually, it takes 1 to 3 months to learn to operate the simpler machines but it can take up to 1 year to become completely familiar with more complex equipment, such as computerized binding machines.

Formal apprenticeships are not as common as they used to be, but still are offered by some employers. Apprenticeships provide a more structured program that enables workers to acquire the high levels of specialization and skill needed for some bindery jobs. For example, a 4-year apprenticeship usually is necessary to teach workers how to restore rare books and to produce valuable collectors' items.

High school students interested in bindery careers should take shop courses or attend a vocational-technical high school. Occupational skill centers, usually operated by labor unions, also provide an introduction to a bindery career. To keep pace with changing technology, retraining is increasingly important for bindery workers. Students with computer skills and mechanical aptitude are especially in demand.

Bindery workers need basic mathematics and language skills. Bindery work requires careful attention to detail; accuracy, patience, neatness, and good eyesight also are important. Manual dexterity is essential in order to count, insert, paste, and fold. Mechanical aptitude is needed to operate the newer, more automated equipment. Artistic ability and imagination are necessary for hand bookbinding.

Training in graphic arts also can be an asset. Vocational-technical institutes offer postsecondary programs in the graphic arts, as do some skill-updating or retraining programs and community colleges. Some updating and retraining programs require students to have bindery experience; other programs are made available by unions to their members. Four-year colleges also offer programs, but their emphasis is on preparing people for careers as graphic artists, educators, or managers in the graphic arts field.

Without additional training, advancement opportunities outside of bindery work are limited. In large binderies, experienced bookbinders or bindery workers may advance to supervisory positions.

Job Outlook

Overall employment of bookbinders and bindery workers is expected to decline through 2012 as demand for printed material slows and productivity in bindery operations increases. Contributing to this situation is the trend toward outsourcing of work to firms in foreign countries, where books and other materials with long leadtimes can be produced more cheaply. Most job openings, however, will result from the need to replace experienced workers who leave the occupation, many of whom will be retiring in the next decade.

Computers have caused binding to become increasingly automated. New computer-operated "in-line" equipment performs a number of operations in sequence, beginning with raw stock and ending with a finished product. Technological advances such as automatic tabbers, counters, palletizers, and joggers reduce labor and improve the appearance of the finished product. These improvements are inducing printing companies to acquire in-house binding and finishing equipment that allows printing machine operators to perform bindery work during "downtimes."

Growth in demand for specialized bindery workers who assist skilled bookbinders will be slowed as binding machinery continues to become more efficient. New technology requires a considerable investment in capital expenditures and employee training, so computer skills and mechanical aptitude are increasingly important for bindery workers.

Because the number of establishments that do hand bookbinding is small, opportunities for hand bookbinders will be limited. Experienced workers will continue to have the best opportunities for these specialist jobs.

Earnings

Median hourly earnings of bookbinders were $13.31 in 2002. The middle 50 percent earned between $9.88 and $17.73 an hour. The lowest 10 percent earned less than $7.84, and the highest 10 percent earned more than $21.90.

Median hourly earnings of bindery workers were $10.51 in 2002. The middle 50 percent earned between $8.27 and $13.86 an hour.

The lowest 10 percent earned less than $6.95, and the highest 10 percent earned more than $17.95. Workers covered by union contracts usually had higher earnings.

Related Occupations

Other workers who set up and operate production machinery include prepress technicians and workers; printing machine operators; machine setters, operators, and tenders—metal and plastic; and various other precision machine operators.

Sources of Additional Information

Information about apprenticeships and other training opportunities may be obtained from local printing industry associations, local bookbinding shops, local offices of the Graphic Communications International Union, or local offices of the State employment service.

For general information on bindery occupations, write to:

➤ Bindery Industries Association, International, 100 Daingerfield Road, Alexandria, VA 22314.

➤ Graphic Communications International Union, 1900 L St. NW., Washington, DC 20036. Internet: **http://www.gciu.org**

For information on careers and training programs in printing and the graphic arts, contact:

➤ Graphic Communications Council, 1899 Preston White Dr., Reston, VA 20191. Internet: **http://www.npes.org/edcouncil/index.html**

➤ Printing Industries of America, 100 Daingerfield Rd., Alexandria, VA 22314. Internet: **http://www.gain.org/servlet/gateway/PIA_GATF/non_index.html**

➤ Graphic Arts Technical Foundation, 200 Deer Run Rd., Sewickley, PA 15143. Internet: **http://www.gatf.org**

Prepress Technicians and Workers

(0*NET 51.5021, 51-5022.01, 51-5022.02, 51-5022.03, 51-5022.04, 51-5022.05, 51-5022.06, 51-5022.07, 51-5022.08, 51-5022.09, 51-5022.10, 51-5022.11, 51-5022.12, 51-5022.13)

Significant Points

● Most workers train on the job; some complete formal graphics arts programs or other postsecondary programs in printing technology.

● Most employers prefer to hire workers with experience in the printing industry.

● Employment is projected to decline as the increased use of computers in typesetting and page layout eliminates many prepress jobs.

Nature of the Work

The printing process has three stages—prepress, press, and binding or postpress. In small print shops, *job printers* may be responsible for all three stages. They do the composition and page layout of the material received from the customer, check proofs for errors and print clarity and correct mistakes, print the job, and attach each copy's pages together. In most printing firms, however, each of the stages is the responsibility of a specialized group of workers. *Prepress technicians and workers* are responsible for the first stage, preparing the material for printing presses. They perform a variety of tasks involved with transforming text and pictures into finished pages and making printing plates of the pages.

Typesetting and page layout have been greatly affected by technological changes over the years and, today, advances in computer software and printing technology continue to change prepress work.

The old "hot type" method of text composition—in which molten lead was used to create individual letters, which were placed in frames to produce paragraphs and full pages of text—has become rare. Its successor, phototypesetting or "cold type" technology, is still used for some composition work, but it, in turn, is being rapidly replaced by computerized digital imaging technology. Customers today are able to provide printers with pages of material that look like the desired finished product they want printed and bound in volume. Using a process called "desktop publishing," customers are increasingly using their own computers to do much of the typesetting and page layout work formerly done by prepress technicians. Many regular customers employ workers called desktop publishers to do this work. (A separate statement on desktop publishers appears elsewhere in the *Handbook*.) Other customers employ in-house graphic designers who do desktop publishing as part of their work, or send the work out to freelance graphic designers. (Graphic designers are discussed in the statement on designers elsewhere in the *Handbook*.) It is increasingly common for prepress technicians or other printing workers to receive files from the customer on a computer disk or submitted by e-mail, that contains typeset material already laid out in pages.

The printing industry is doing more prepress work using complete "digital imaging." Using this technology, prepress technicians called "preflight technicians" take material received on computer disks from customers, check it for completeness, and format it into pages using electronic page layout systems; even though the pages may already be laid out, they still may have to be formatted to fit the dimensions of the paper stock to be used. When color printing is required, the technicians use digital color page-makeup systems to electronically produce an image of the printed pages, then use off-press color proofing systems to print a copy, or "proof," of the pages as they will appear when printed. The technician then has the proofs delivered or mailed to the customer for a final check. Once the customer gives the "OK to print," technicians use laser "imagesetters" to expose digital images of the pages directly onto thin aluminum printing plates.

Some customers continue to provide material to printers that is more suitable for cold type prepress technology. Cold type processing, which describes any of a variety of methods to create a printing plate without molten lead, has traditionally used "phototypesetting" to prepare text and pictures for printing. Although this method has many variations, all use photography to create images on paper. The images are assembled into page format and rephotographed to create film negatives from which the actual printing plates are made.

In one common form of phototypesetting, printed text received from the customer must first be entered into a computer programmed to hyphenate, space, and create columns of text. Typesetters or data entry clerks may do the keyboarding of text at the printing establishment. (See the *Handbook* statement on data entry and information processing workers.) The coded text then is transferred to a typesetting machine, which uses photography, a cathode-ray tube, or a laser to create an image on typesetting paper or film. Once it has been developed, the paper or film is sent to a lithographer who makes the actual printing plate.

With traditional photolithographic processes, the material to be printed is arranged and typeset, and then passed on to workers who further prepare it for the presses. *Camera operators* start the process of making a lithographic plate by photographing and developing film negatives or positives of the material to be printed. They adjust light and expose film for a specified length of time, and then develop the film in a series of chemical baths. They may load exposed film in machines that automatically develop and fix the image. The lithographic printing process requires that images be made up of tiny dots coming together to form a picture. Photographs cannot be printed without them. When normal "continuous-tone" photographs need to be reproduced, camera operators use halftone cameras to separate the photograph into an image containing the dots of varying sizes corresponding to the values of the original photograph

Color separation photography is more complex. In this process, camera operators produce four-color separation negatives from a continuous-tone color print or transparency. Because this is a complicated and time-consuming process, most of this separation work is instead being done electronically on scanners. *Scanner operators* use computerized equipment to capture photographs or art as digital data, or to create film negatives or positives of photographs or art. The computer controls the color separation of the scanning process and, with the help of the operator, corrects for mistakes or compensates for deficiencies in the original color print or transparency. Each scan produces a dotted image, or halftone, of the original in 1 of 4 primary printing colors—yellow, magenta, cyan, and black. The images are used to produce printing plates that print each of these colors, with transparent colored inks, one at a time. Superimposition of the images on the photos produces "secondary" color combinations of red, green, blue, and black that approximate the colors and hues of the original photograph.

Where this process is still being used, *film strippers* cut the film of text and images to the required size and arrange and tape the

Using computer software to design publications, a growing number of prepress technicians work in offices.

negatives onto "flats"—or layout sheets used by platemakers to make press plates. When completed, flats resemble large film negatives of the text in its final form. Platemakers use a photographic process to make printing plates. The flat is placed on top of a thin metal plate coated with a light-sensitive resin. Exposure to ultraviolet light activates the chemical in parts of the plate not protected by the film's dark areas. The plate then is developed in a solution that removes the unexposed nonimage area, exposing bare metal. The chemical on areas of the plate exposed to the light hardens and becomes water repellent. The hardened parts of the plate form the text and images to be printed.

During the printing process, the plate is first covered with a thin coat of water. The water adheres only to the bare metal nonimage areas, and is repelled by the hardened areas that were exposed to light. Next, the plate comes in contact with a rubber roller covered with oil-based ink. Because oil and water do not mix, the ink is repelled by the water-coated area and sticks to the hardened areas. The ink covering the hardened text is transferred to paper.

Working Conditions

Prepress technicians and workers usually work in clean, air-conditioned areas with little noise. Some workers may develop eyestrain from working in front of a video display terminal, or musculoskeletal problems such as backaches. Platemakers, who still work with toxic chemicals, face the hazard of skin irritations. Workers often are subject to stress and the pressures of short deadlines and tight work schedules.

Prepress employees usually work an 8-hour day. Some workers—particularly those employed by newspapers—work night shifts, weekends, and holidays.

Employment

Prepress technicians and workers overall held about 148,000 jobs in 2002. Of these, approximately 56,000 were employed as job printers; the remainder was employed as prepress technicians and other prepress workers. Most prepress jobs are found in the printing industry, while newspaper publishing employs the second largest number of prepress technicians and workers.

The printing and publishing industries are two of the most geographically dispersed in the United States, and prepress jobs are found throughout the country. However, jobs are concentrated in large metropolitan cities such as New York; Chicago; Los Angeles; Philadelphia; Washington, DC; and Dallas.

Training, Other Qualifications, and Advancement

Traditionally, prepress technicians and workers started as helpers and were trained on the job, the length of training varying by occupation. Some jobs required years of experience performing the detailed handwork to become skillful enough to perform even difficult tasks quickly. Instead of painstakingly taping pieces of photographic negatives to flats, today's prepress technicians increasingly use computer software skills to electronically modify and lay out the material; in some cases, the first time the material appears on paper is when the final product rolls off the printing press. As this digital imaging technology increasingly replaces cold type print technology, persons seeking to enter prepress technician jobs will require formal graphic communications training in the various types of computer software used in digital imaging.

Postsecondary graphic communications programs are available from a variety of sources. For beginners, 2-year associate degree programs offered by community and junior colleges and technical schools, and some 4-year bachelor's degree programs in graphic design colleges teach the latest prepress skills and allow students to practice applying them. However, bachelor's programs usually are intended for students who may eventually move into management positions in printing or design jobs. Community and junior colleges, 4-year colleges and universities, vocational-technical institutes, industry-sponsored update and retraining programs, and private trade and technical schools all also offer prepress-related courses for workers who do not wish to enroll in a degree program. Many workers with experience in other printing jobs take a few college graphic communications courses to upgrade their skills and qualify for prepress jobs. Prepress training designed to train skilled workers already employed in the printing industry also is offered through unions in the printing industry. Many employers view individuals with a combination of experience in the printing industry and formal training in the new digital technology as the best candidates for prepress jobs. The experience of these applicants in printing press operator or other jobs provides them with an understanding of how printing plants operate, familiarizes them with basic prepress functions, and demonstrates their reliability and interest in advancing in the industry.

Employers prefer workers with good communication skills, both oral and written, for prepress jobs. Prepress technicians and workers should be able to deal courteously with people because, when prepress problems arise, they sometimes have to contact the customer to resolve them. Also, in small shops, they may take customer orders. Persons interested in working for firms using advanced printing technology need to know the basics of electronics and computers. Mathematical skills also are essential for operating many of the software packages used to run modern, computerized prepress equipment. At times, prepress personnel may have to perform computations in order to estimate job costs.

Prepress technicians and workers need good manual dexterity, and they must be able to pay attention to detail and work independently. Good eyesight, including visual acuity, depth perception, field of view, color vision, and the ability to focus quickly, also are assets. Artistic ability is often a plus. Employers also seek persons who possess an even temperament and an ability to adapt, important qualities for workers who often must meet deadlines and learn how to use new software or operate new equipment.

Job Outlook

Overall employment of prepress technicians and workers is expected to decline through 2012. The number of job printers, however, is expected to grow, though at a rate slower than average. Demand for printed material should continue to grow, spurred by rising levels of personal income, increasing school enrollments, higher levels of educational attainment, and expanding markets. But increased use of computers in desktop publishing will contribute to the elimination of many jobs for prepress technicians.

Technological advances will have a varying effect on employment among the prepress occupations. This reflects the increasing proportion of page layout and design that will be performed using computers. Thus, the need for preflight technicians will remain strong. However, most prepress technicians and workers such as pasteup, composition and typesetting, photoengraving, platemaking, film stripping, and camera operator occupations are expected to experience declines as handwork becomes automated. Computer software that allows office workers to specify text typeface and style, and to format pages at a desktop computer terminal, already has eliminated most typesetting and composition jobs; more jobs will disappear in the years ahead.

Job prospects also will vary by industry. Changes in technology have shifted many prepress functions away from the tradi-

tional printing plants into advertising and public relations agencies, graphic design firms, and large corporations. Many companies are turning to in-house desktop publishing as page layout and graphic design capabilities of computer software have improved and become less expensive and more user-friendly. Some firms are finding it more profitable to prepare their own newsletters and other reports than to send them out to trade shops. At newspapers, writers and editors also are doing more composition using publishing software.

Some new jobs for prepress technicians and workers are expected to emerge in commercial printing establishments. New equipment should reduce the time needed to complete a printing job, and allow commercial printers to make inroads into new markets that require fast turnaround. Because small establishments predominate, commercial printing should provide the best opportunities for inexperienced workers who want to gain a good background in all facets of printing.

Employers in the printing industry prefer to hire workers experienced in all facets of printing. Among persons without experience, however, opportunities should be best for those with computer backgrounds who have completed postsecondary programs in printing technology or graphic communications. Many employers prefer graduates of these programs because the comprehensive training that they receive helps them to learn the printing process and to adapt more rapidly to new processes and techniques.

Earnings

Median hourly earnings of prepress technicians and workers were $14.98 in 2002. The middle 50 percent earned between $11.25 and $19.68 an hour. The lowest 10 percent earned less than $8.68, and the highest 10 percent earned more than $24.36 an hour.

For job printers, median hourly earnings were $14.47 in 2002. The middle 50 percent earned between $10.98 and $18.91 an hour. The lowest 10 percent earned less than $8.59, while the highest 10 percent earned more than $23.06 an hour.

Median hourly earnings in commercial printing, the industry employing the largest number of prepress technicians and workers, were $16.05 in 2002, while the figure for these workers in the newspaper, periodical, and book publishing industry was $13.07 an hour. For job printers, median hourly earnings in commercial printing in 2002 were $14.84, while in the newspaper, periodical, and book publishing industry median hourly earnings were $13.98.

Wage rates for prepress technicians and workers vary according to occupation, level of experience, training, location, size of firm, and union membership status.

Related Occupations

Prepress technicians and workers use artistic skills in their work. These skills also are essential for artists and related workers, graphic designers, and desktop publishers. Moreover, many of the skills used in Web site design also are employed in prepress technology.

In addition to typesetters, other workers who operate machines equipped with keyboards include data entry and information processing workers. Prepress technicians' work also is tied in closely with that of printing machine operators, including job printers.

Sources of Additional Information

Details about training programs may be obtained from local employers such as newspapers and printing shops, or from local offices of the State employment service.

For information on careers and training in printing and the graphic arts, write to:

➤ Printing Industries of America, 100 Daingerfield Rd., Alexandria, VA 22314. Internet: **http://www.gain.net**

➤ Graphic Communications Council, 1899 Preston White Dr., Reston, VA 20191. Internet: **http://www.teched.vt.edu/gcc**

➤ Graphic Communications International Union, 1900 L St. NW., Washington, DC 20036. Internet: **http://www.gciu.org**

➤ Graphic Arts Technical Foundation, 200 Deer Run Rd., Sewickley, PA 15143. Internet: **http://www.gatf.org**

Printing Machine Operators

(O*NET 51-5023.01, 51-5023.02, 51-5023.03, 51-5023.04, 51-5023.05, 51-5023.06, 51-5023.07, 51-5023.08, 51-5023.09)

Significant Points

● Most are trained informally on the job.

● Employment growth will be slowed by the increasing use of new, more efficient computerized printing presses that will facilitate movement towards printing-on-demand.

● Opportunities should be best for persons who qualify for formal apprenticeship training or who complete postsecondary training programs in printing.

Nature of the Work

Printing machine operators prepare, operate, and maintain the printing presses in a pressroom. Duties of printing machine operators vary according to the type of press they operate—offset lithography, gravure, flexography, screen printing, letterpress, and digital. Offset lithography, which transfers an inked impression from a rubber-covered cylinder to paper or other material, is the dominant printing process. With gravure, the recesses on an etched plate or cylinder are inked and pressed to paper. Flexography is a form of rotary printing in which ink is applied to a surface by a flexible rubber printing plate with a raised image area. Use of gravure and flexography should increase over the next decade, but letterpress, in which an inked, raised surface is pressed against paper, remains in existence only as specialty printing. In addition to the major printing processes, plateless or nonimpact processes are coming into general use. Plateless processes—including digital, electrostatic, and ink-jet printing—are used for copying, duplicating, and document and specialty printing, usually by quick and in-house printing shops, and increasingly by commercial printers for short-run jobs and variable data printing.

To prepare presses for printing, machine operators install and adjust the printing plate, adjust pressure, ink the presses, load paper, and adjust the press to the paper size. Press operators ensure that paper and ink meet specifications, and adjust margins and the flow of ink to the inking rollers accordingly. They then feed paper through the press cylinders and adjust feed and tension controls.

While printing presses are running, press operators monitor their operation and keep the paper feeders well stocked. They make adjustments to correct uneven ink distribution, speed, and temperatures in the drying chamber, if the press has one. If paper jams or tears and the press stops, which can happen with some offset presses, operators quickly correct the problem to minimize downtime. Similarly, operators working with other high-speed presses constantly look for problems, making quick corrections to avoid expensive losses of paper and ink. Throughout the run, operators may occasionally pull sheets to check for any printing imperfections, though much of this checking for quality is now being done by computers.

In most shops, press operators also perform preventive maintenance. They oil and clean the presses and make minor repairs.

Machine operators' jobs differ from one shop to another because of differences in the kinds and sizes of presses. Small commercial shops are operated by one person and tend to have relatively small presses, which print only one or two colors at a time. Operators who work with large presses have assistants and helpers. Large newspaper, magazine, and book printers use giant "in-line web" presses that require a crew of several press operators and press assistants. These presses are fed paper in big rolls, called "webs," up to 50 inches or more in width. Presses print the paper on both sides; trim, assemble, score, and fold the pages; and count the finished sections as they come off the press.

Most plants have or will soon have installed printing presses with computers and sophisticated instruments to control press operations, making it possible to set up for jobs in less time. Computers allow press operators to perform many of their tasks electronically. With this equipment, press operators monitor the printing process on a control panel or computer monitor, which allows them to adjust the press electronically.

Working Conditions

Operating a press can be physically and mentally demanding, and sometimes tedious. Printing machine operators are on their feet most of the time. Often, operators work under pressure to meet deadlines. Most printing presses are capable of high printing speeds, and adjustments must be made quickly to avoid waste. Pressrooms are noisy, and workers in certain areas wear ear protectors. Working with press machinery can be hazardous, but accidents can be avoided when press operators follow safe work practices. The threat of accidents has decreased with newer computerized presses because operators make most adjustments from a control panel. Many press operators, particularly those who work for newspapers, work weekends, nights, and holidays. They also may work overtime to meet deadlines.

Employment

Printing machine operators held about 199,000 jobs in 2002. Nearly one-half of operator jobs were in the printing industry, but newspaper publishers and paper product manufacturers also were large employers, having each about 10 percent of all printing machine operator jobs. Additional jobs were in the "in-plant" section of organizations and businesses that do their own printing—such as banks, insurance companies, government agencies, and universities.

Operating newer printing presses requires some computer skills and continual retraining.

The printing and newspaper publishing industries are two of the most geographically dispersed in the United States, and press operators can find jobs throughout the country. However, jobs are concentrated in large printing centers such as Dallas, Chicago, Los Angeles, New York, Philadelphia, and Washington, DC.

Training, Other Qualifications, and Advancement

Although completion of a formal apprenticeship or a postsecondary program in printing equipment operation continues to be the best way to learn the trade, most printing machine operators are trained informally on the job while they work as assistants or helpers to experienced operators. Beginning press operators load, unload, and clean presses. With time, they move up to operating one-color sheet-fed presses and eventually advance to multicolor presses. Operators are likely to gain experience on many kinds of printing presses during the course of their career.

Apprenticeships for press operators in commercial shops take 4 years. In addition to on-the-job instruction, apprenticeships include related classroom or correspondence school courses. Once the dominant method for preparing for this occupation, apprenticeships are becoming less prevalent.

In contrast, formal postsecondary programs in printing equipment operation offered by technical and trade schools and community colleges are growing in importance. Some postsecondary school programs require 2 years of study and award an associate degree, but most programs can be completed in 1 year or less. Postsecondary courses in printing are increasingly important because they provide the theoretical knowledge needed to operate advanced equipment.

Persons who wish to become printing machine operators need mechanical aptitude to make press adjustments and repairs. Oral and writing skills also are required. Operators should possess the mathematical skills necessary to compute percentages, weights, and measures, and to calculate the amount of ink and paper needed to do a job. Because of technical developments in the printing industry, courses in chemistry, electronics, color theory, and physics are helpful.

Technological changes have had a tremendous effect on the skills needed by printing machine operators. New presses now require operators to possess basic computer skills. Even experienced operators periodically receive retraining and skill updating. For example, printing plants that change from sheet-fed offset presses to digital presses have to retrain the entire press crew because skill requirements for the two types of presses are different.

Printing machine operators may advance in pay and responsibility by working on a more complex printing press. Through experience and demonstrated ability, for example, a one-color sheet-fed press operator may become a four-color sheet-fed press operator. Others may advance to pressroom supervisor and become responsible for an entire press crew. Their understanding of the prepress requirements needed to run a press smoothly allows some operators with several years of experience to transfer to jobs as prepress technicians.

Job Outlook

Employment of printing machine operators is expected to grow more slowly than the average through 2012. Despite the slow growth, looming retirements of printing machine operators and the need for workers trained on increasingly computerized printing equipment will create many job openings over the next decade. Opportunities to become printing machine operators are likely to be favorable for persons who qualify for formal apprenticeship training or who complete postsecondary training programs in printing.

The demand for, and the output of, printed materials is expected to grow over the 2002-12 period. Demand for books and magazines will increase as school enrollments rise, and as substantial growth in the middle-aged and older population spurs adult education and leisure reading. Additional growth should stem from increased foreign demand for domestic trade publications, professional and scientific works, and mass-market books such as paperbacks. Demand for commercial printing also will be driven by increased expenditures for print advertising materials. New market research techniques are leading advertisers to increase spending on messages targeted to specific audiences, and should continue to require the printing of a wide variety of newspaper inserts, catalogs, direct mail enclosures, and other kinds of print advertising. Other printing, such as newspapers, books, and greeting cards, also will continue to provide jobs.

Employment, however, will not grow in line with output because of the increased use of new computerized printing equipment. Also, new business practices within the publishing industry, such as printing-on-demand and electronic publishing, will cut into the production of printed materials. Printing-on-demand refers to the printing of materials as they are requested by customers, in contrast to printing thousands of publications prior to purchase, many of which are subsequently discarded. There are also expected to be fewer newspaper printing jobs as a result of mergers and consolidation within the industry.

Earnings

Median hourly earnings of printing machine operators were $13.95 in 2012. The middle 50 percent earned between $10.52 and $18.27 an hour. The lowest 10 percent earned less than $8.32, and the highest 10 percent earned more than $22.46 an hour. Median hourly earnings in the industries employing the largest numbers of printing machine operators in 2002 were:

Newspapers, periodicals, book, and directory publishers	$16.09
Commercial printing	15.02
Converted paper products	14.95
Plastic products	13.21
Business support services	10.60

The basic wage rate for a printing machine operator depends on the type of press being run and the geographic area in which the work is located. Workers covered by union contracts usually have higher earnings.

Related Occupations

Other workers who set up and operate production machinery include machine setters, operators, and tenders—metal and plastic; bookbinders and bindery workers; and various precision machine operators.

Sources of Additional Information

Details about apprenticeships and other training opportunities may be obtained from local employers, such as newspapers and printing shops, local offices of the Graphic Communications International Union, local affiliates of Printing Industries of America, or local offices of the State employment service.

For general information about press operators, write to:

➤ Graphic Communications International Union, 1900 L St. NW., Washington, DC 20036. Internet: **http://www.gciu.org**

For information on careers and training in printing and the graphic arts, write to:

➤ Printing Industries of America, 100 Daingerfield Rd., Alexandria, VA 22314. Internet:
http://www.gain.org/servlet/gateway/PIA_GATF/non_index.html

➤ Graphic Communications Council, 1899 Preston White Dr., Reston, VA 20191. Internet: **http://www.tcched.vt.edu/gcc**

➤ Graphic Arts Technical Foundation, 200 Deer Run Rd., Sewickley, PA 15143. Internet: **http://www.gatf.org**

Textile, Apparel, and Furnishings Occupations

(O*NET 51-6011.01, 51-6011.02, 51-6011.03, 51-6021.01, 51-6021.02,
51-6021.03, 51-6031.01, 51-6031.02, 51-6041.00, 51-6042.00,
51-6051.00, 51-6052.01, 51-6052.02, 51-6061.00, 51-6062.00, 51-6063.00,
51-6064.00, 51-6091.01, 51-6092.00, 51-6093.00, 51-6099.99)

Significant Points

- Most workers learn through on-the-job training.

- Employment is expected to decline in most detailed occupations in this group, due primarily to increased imports, the increased use of laborsaving machinery, and the creation of new fabrics that do not need as much processing.

- Earnings of most workers are low.

Nature of the Work

Textiles and leather clothe our bodies, cover our furniture, and adorn our homes. Textile, apparel, and furnishings workers produce these materials and fashion them into a wide range of products that we use in our daily lives. Jobs range from those which employ computers, to those in which the worker operates large industrial machinery and smaller power equipment, to those which involve substantial handwork.

Textile machine operators. Textile machine operators run machines that make textile products from fibers. Textiles are the basis of towels, bed linens, hosiery and socks, and nearly all clothing, but they also are a key ingredient of products ranging from roofing to tires. The first step in manufacturing textiles is preparing the natural or synthetic fibers. *Extruding and forming machine operators, synthetic and glass fibers* set up and operate machines that extrude— or force—liquid synthetic material such as rayon, fiberglass, or liquid polymers out through small holes and draw out filaments. Other operators put natural fibers such as cotton, wool, flax, or hemp through carding and combing machines that clean and align them into short lengths called "sliver." When sliver is produced, different types of natural fibers and synthetics filaments may be combined to give the product a desired texture, durability, or other characteristics. *Textile winding, twisting, and drawing-out machine operators* take the sliver and draw out, twist, and wind it to produce yarn, taking care to repair any breaks.

Textile bleaching and dyeing machine operators control machines that wash, bleach, or dye either yarn or finished fabrics and other products. *Textile knitting and weaving machine operators* put the yarn on machines that weave, knit, loop, or tuft it into a product. Woven fabrics are used to make apparel and other goods, while some knitted products (such as hosiery) and tufted products (such as carpeting) emerge in near-finished form. Different types of machines are used for these processes, but operators perform similar tasks, repairing breaks in the yarn and monitoring the yarn supply, while tending many machines at once. *Textile cutting machine operators* trim the fabric into various widths and lengths, depending on its intended use.

Apparel workers. Apparel workers cut fabric and other materials and sew it into clothing and related products. Workers in a variety of occupations fall under the heading of apparel workers. *Tailors, dressmakers, and sewers* make custom clothing and alter and repair garments for individuals. However, workers in most apparel occupations are found in manufacturing, performing specialized tasks in the production of large numbers of garments that are shipped to retail establishments for sale to the public.

Fabric and apparel patternmakers convert a clothing designer's original model of a garment into a pattern of separate parts that can be laid out on a length of fabric. After discussing the item with the designer, these skilled workers usually use a computer to outline the parts and draw in details to indicate the positions of pleats, buttonholes, and other features. (In the past, patternmakers laid out the parts on paper, using pencils and drafting instruments such as rulers.) Patternmakers then alter the size of the pieces in the pattern to produce garments of various sizes, and they may "mark" the fabric to show the best layout of pattern pieces to minimize waste of material.

Once an item's pattern has been made and marked, mass production of the garment begins. Cutters and trimmers take the patterns and cut out material, paying close attention to their work because mistakes are costly. Following the outline of the pattern, they place multiple layers of material on the cutting table and use an electric knife or other cutting tools to cut out the various pieces of the garment; delicate materials may be cut by hand. In some companies, computer-controlled machines do the cutting.

Sewing machine operators join the parts of a garment together, reinforce seams, and attach buttons, hooks, zippers, and accessories to produce clothing. After the product is sewn, other workers remove lint and loose threads and inspect and package the garments.

Shoe and leather workers. Shoe and leather workers are employed either in manufacturing or in personal services. In shoe manufacturing, *shoe machine operators and tenders* operate a variety of specialized machines that perform cutting, joining, and finishing functions. In personal services, *shoe and leather workers and repairers* perform a variety of repairs and custom leatherwork for members of the general public. They construct, decorate, or repair shoes, belts, purses, saddles, luggage, and other leather products. They also may repair some products made of canvas or plastic. When making custom shoes or modifying existing footwear for people with foot problems or special needs, shoe and leather workers and repairers cut pieces of leather, shape them over a form shaped like a foot, and sew them together. They then attach soles and heels, using sewing machines or cement and nails. They also dye and polish the items, utilizing a buffing wheel for a smooth surface and lustrous shine. When making luggage, they fasten leather to a frame and attach handles and other hardware. They also cut and secure linings inside the frames and sew or stamp designs onto the exterior

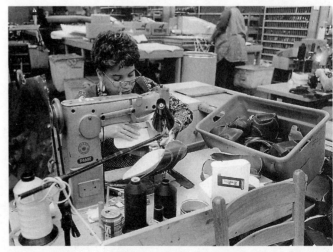

Shoe machine operators and other apparel and textile workers will see fewer jobs in the future as more work is outsourced abroad.

of the luggage. In addition to performing all of the preceding steps, saddle makers often apply leather dyes and liquid topcoats to produce a glossy finish on a saddle. They also may decorate the surface of the saddle by hand stitching or by stamping the leather with decorative patterns and designs. Shoe and leather workers and repairers who own their own shops keep records and supervise other workers.

Upholsterers. *Upholsterers* make, fix, and restore furniture that is covered with fabric. Using hammers and tack pullers upholsterers who restore furniture remove old fabric and stuffing to get back down to the springs and wooden frame. Then they reglue loose sections of the frame and refinish exposed wood. The springs sit on a cloth mat, called webbing, that is attached to the frame. Upholsterers replace torn webbing, examine the springs, and replace broken or bent ones.

Upholsterers who make new furniture start with a bare wooden frame. First, they install webbing, tacking it to one side of the frame, stretching it tight, and tacking it to the other side. Then, they tie each spring to the webbing and to its neighboring springs. Next, they cover the springs with filler, such as foam, a polyester batt, or similar fibrous batting material, to form a smooth, rounded surface. Then they measure and cut fabric for the arms, backs, seats, sides, and other surfaces, leaving as little waste as possible. Finally, sewing the fabric pieces together and attaching them to the frame with tacks, staples, or glue, they affix any ornaments, such as fringes, buttons, or rivets. Sometimes, upholsterers pick up and deliver the furniture they work on. They also help customers pick new coverings by providing samples of fabrics and pictures of finished pieces.

Laundry and drycleaning workers. *Laundry and drycleaning workers* clean cloth garments, linens, draperies, blankets, and other articles. They also may clean leather, suede, furs, and rugs. When necessary, they treat spots and stains on articles before laundering or drycleaning. They tend machines during cleaning and ensure that items are not lost or misplaced with those of another customer. *Pressers, textile, garment, and related materials* shape and remove wrinkles from items after steam pressing them or ironing them by hand. Workers then assemble each customer's items, box or bag them, and prepare an itemized bill for the customer.

Working Conditions

Most persons in textile, apparel, and furnishings occupations work a standard 5-day, 35- to 40-hour week. Evenings and weekend work is common for shoe and leather workers, laundry and drycleaning workers, and tailors, dressmakers, and sewers employed in retail stores. In manufacturing, some employers add second shifts to justify the expense of new machinery. Many textile and fiber mills often use rotating schedules of shifts so that employees do not continuously work nights or days. But these rotating shifts sometimes cause workers to have sleep disorders and stress-related problems.

While much of the work in apparel manufacturing still is based on a piecework system that allows for little interpersonal contact, some apparel firms are placing more emphasis on teamwork and cooperation. Under this new system, individuals work closely with one another, and each team or module often governs itself, increasing the overall responsibility of each operator.

Working conditions vary by establishment and by occupation. In manufacturing, machinery in textile mills often is noisy, as are areas in which sewing and pressing are performed in apparel factories; patternmaking and spreading areas tend to be much quieter. Many older factories are cluttered, hot, and poorly lit and ventilated, but more modern facilities usually have more workspace and are well lit and ventilated. Textile machinery operators use protective glasses and masks that cover their noses and mouths to protect against airborne materials. Many machines operate at high speeds, and textile machinery workers must be careful not to wear clothing or jewelry that could get caught in moving parts. In addition, extruding and forming machine operators wear protective shoes and clothing when working with certain chemical compounds.

Work in apparel production can be physically demanding. Some workers sit for long periods, and others spend many hours on their feet, leaning over tables and operating machinery. Operators must be attentive while running sewing machines, pressers, automated cutters, and the like. A few workers wear protective devices such as gloves. In some instances, new machinery and production techniques have decreased the physical demands upon workers. For example, newer pressing machines are operated by foot pedals or computer controls and do not require much strength to operate them.

Laundries and drycleaning establishments often are hot and noisy; those in retail stores, however, tend to be less noisy and more comfortable. Areas in which shoe and leather workers make or repair shoes and other leather items can be noisy, and odors from leather dyes and stains frequently are present. Workers need to pay close attention when working with machines, in order to avoid punctures, lacerations, and abrasions.

Upholstery work is not dangerous, but upholsterers usually wear protective gloves and clothing when using sharp tools and lifting and handling furniture or springs. Upholsterers stand most of the workday and may do a lot of bending and heavy lifting. They also may work in awkward positions for short periods.

Employment

Textile, apparel, and furnishings workers held over 1.1 million jobs in 2002. Employment in the detailed occupations that make up this group was distributed as follows:

Sewing machine operators	315,000
Laundry and drycleaning workers	231,000
Pressers, textile, garment, and related materials	91,000
Textile winding, twisting, and drawing out machine setters, operators, and tenders	66,000
All other textile, apparel, and furnishings workers	61,000
Upholsterers	56,000
Tailors, dressmakers, and sewers	53,000
Textile knitting and weaving machine setters, operators, and tenders	53,000
Textile cutting machine setters, operators, and tenders	34,000
Extruding and forming machine setters, operators, and tenders, synthetic and glass fibers	27,000
Textile bleaching and dyeing machine operators and tenders	27,000
Shoe and leather workers and repairers	16,000
Fabric and apparel patternmakers	11,000
Shoe machine operators and tenders	6,600

Manufacturing jobs are concentrated in California, New York, North Carolina, Pennsylvania, Tennessee, and Georgia. Jobs in reupholstery, shoe repair and custom leatherwork, and laundry and drycleaning establishments are found in cities and towns throughout the Nation. Overall, about 10 percent of all workers in textile, apparel, and furnishings occupations were self-employed; however, more than one-third of tailors, dressmakers, and sewers and more than one-quarter of upholsterers were self-employed.

Training, Other Qualifications, and Advancement

Most employers prefer to hire high school graduates for jobs in textile, apparel, and furnishings occupations. Entrants with postsecondary vocational training or previous work experience in apparel production usually have a better chance of getting a job and advancing to a supervisory position. Regardless of the setting, workers usually begin by performing simple tasks.

In manufacturing, textile and apparel workers need good hand-eye coordination, manual dexterity, physical stamina, and the ability to perform repetitive tasks for long periods. Machine operators usually are trained on the job by more experienced employees or by machinery manufacturers' representatives. As they gain experience, these workers are assigned more difficult operations. Further advancement is limited, however. Some production workers may become first-line supervisors, but most can advance only to more skilled operator jobs. As machinery in the industry continues to become more complex, knowledge of the basics of computers and electronics will increasingly be an asset. In addition, the trends toward cross-training of operators and working in teams will increase the time needed to become fully trained on all machines and require interpersonal skills to work effectively with others.

Retailers prefer to hire custom tailors, dressmakers, and sewers with previous experience in apparel manufacture, design, or alteration. Knowledge of fabrics, design, and construction is very important. Custom tailors sometimes learn these skills through courses in high school or a community college. A few private schools and colleges offer advanced training in sewing, draping, patternmaking, and design. Some experienced custom tailors open their own tailoring shop. Custom tailoring is a highly competitive field, however, and training in small-business operations can mean the difference between success and failure. Although laundries and drycleaners prefer entrants with previous work experience, they routinely hire inexperienced workers.

Precision shoe and leather workers and repairers generally learn their skills on the job. Manual dexterity and the mechanical aptitude to work with handtools and machines are important in shoe repair and leatherworking. Shoe and leather workers who produce custom goods should have artistic ability as well. Beginners start as helpers for experienced workers, but, in manufacturing, they may attend more formal in-house training programs. Beginners gradually take on more tasks until they are fully qualified workers, a process that takes about 2 years in an apprenticeship program or as a helper in a shop. In a vocational training program, it can take 6 months to a year. Learning to make saddles takes longer. Shoe repairers need to keep their skills up to date in order to work with the rapidly changing footwear styles and materials. Some do this by attending trade shows, while others attend specialized training seminars and workshops in custom shoe making, shoe repair, and other leatherwork sponsored by associations. Skilled workers who produce and modify prescription footwear may become certified as *pedorthists* by the Pedorthic Footwear Association after completing 120 hours of training and passing an examination. Some in the shoe and leather working occupations begin as workers or repairers and advance to salaried supervisory and managerial positions. Some open their own shop, but knowledge of business practices and management and a pleasant manner when dealing with customers are needed to stay in business.

Most upholsterers learn their skills on the job, but a few do so through apprenticeships. Inexperienced persons also may take training in basic upholstery in vocational schools and some community colleges. Upholsterers should have manual dexterity, good coordination, and the strength needed to lift heavy furniture. An eye for detail, a flair for color, and the ability to use fabrics creatively also are helpful. The length of training may vary from 6 weeks to 3 years. Upholsterers who work on custom-made pieces may train for 8 to 10 years. The primary forms of advancement for upholsterers are opening their own shop or moving into management. The upholstery business is highly competitive, so operating a shop successfully is difficult. In large shops and factories, experienced or

highly skilled upholsterers may become supervisors or samplemakers.

Job Outlook
Employment of textile, apparel, and furnishings workers is expected to decline through 2012. Apparel workers have been among the most rapidly declining occupational groups in the economy, and increasing imports, the use of offshore assembly, and greater productivity through new automation will contribute to additional job losses. Also, many new textiles require less production and processing. Because of the large size of this occupation, however, many thousands of job openings will arise each year from the need to replace persons who transfer to other occupations, retire, or leave the occupation for other reasons.

Employment in the domestic textile and apparel industries has declined in recent years as foreign producers have gained a greater share of the U.S. market. Domestic production—especially of apparel—will continue to move abroad, and imports to the U.S. market will increase. Declines in U.S. apparel production will cause reductions in domestic textile production because the apparel industry is the largest consumer of American-made textiles. Fierce competition in the market for apparel will keep domestic apparel and textile firms under intense pressure to cut costs and produce more with fewer workers.

The textile industry already is highly automated, but it will continue to seek to increase worker productivity through the introduction of laborsaving machinery and the invention of new fibers and fabrics that reduce production costs. Despite advances in technology, the apparel industry has had difficulty employing automated equipment extensively due to the soft properties of textile products. The industry produces a wide variety of apparel items that change frequently with changes in style and season. Technological developments, such as computer-aided marking and grading, computer-controlled cutters, semiautomatic sewing and pressing machines, and automated material-handling systems have increased output while reducing the need for some workers in larger firms. However, assembly and sewing continues to be the most labor-intensive step in the production of apparel, and increasing numbers of sewing machine operator jobs are expected to be lost to lower wage workers abroad. Still, improvements in productivity will allow many of the presewing functions of design, patternmaking, marking, and cutting to continue be done domestically, and employment of workers who perform these functions will not be as adversely affected.

Outside of the manufacturing sector, tailors, dressmakers, and sewers—the most skilled apparel workers—also are expected to experience declining employment. Demand for their services will continue to lessen as consumers become increasingly likely to buy new, mass-produced apparel instead of purchasing custom-made apparel or having clothes altered or repaired.

Employment of shoe and leather workers is expected to decline through 2012 due to growing imports of less expensive shoes and leather goods, increasing productivity of U.S. manufacturers, and the more frequent tendency to buy new shoes rather than repair worn or damaged ones. However, declines are expected to be somewhat offset as more people invest in expensive leather shoes that they will want repaired. Also, as the population continues to age, more people will need custom shoes for health reasons.

Employment of upholsterers is expected to decline through 2012 as new furniture and automotive seats use more durable coverings and as manufacturing firms continue to become more automated and efficient. Demand for the reupholstery of furniture also is expected to decline as the increasing manufacture of new, relatively inexpensive upholstered furniture causes many people simply to replace old, worn furniture. However, demand will continue to be steady for upholsterers who restore very valuable furniture. Most reupholstery work is labor intensive and not easily automated. Job opportunities for experienced upholsterers should be good because few young people enter the occupation and few shops offer training.

Earnings
Earnings of textile, apparel, and furnishings workers vary by occupation. Because many production workers in apparel manufacturing are paid according to the number of acceptable pieces they or their group produce, their total earnings depend on skill, speed, and accuracy. Workers covered by union contracts tend to have higher earnings. Median hourly earnings by occupation in 2002 were as follows:

Extruding and forming machine setters, operators, and tenders, synthetic and glass fibers	$13.22
Fabric and apparel patternmakers	12.67
Upholsterers	11.86
Textile knitting and weaving machine setters, operators, and tenders	11.05
Tailors, dressmakers, and custom sewers	10.68
Textile winding, twisting, and drawing out machine setters, operators, and tenders	10.54
Textile bleaching and dyeing machine operators and tenders	10.00
Shoe machine operators and tenders	9.90
Textile cutting machine setters, operators, and tenders	9.77
Shoe and leather workers and repairers	9.14
All other textile, apparel, and furnishings workers	9.01
Sewers, hand	8.69
Sewing machine operators	8.39
Pressers, textile, garment, and related materials	8.21
Laundry and drycleaning workers	8.07

Benefits also vary. A few large employers, for example, include childcare in their benefits package. Apparel workers in retail trade also may receive a discount on their purchases from the company for which they work. In addition, some of the larger manufacturers operate company stores from which employees can purchase apparel products at significant discounts. Some small firms, however, offer only limited benefits.

Related Occupations
Textile, apparel, and furnishings workers apply their knowledge of textiles and leathers to fashion products with use of handtools and machinery. Other occupations that produce products by means of handtools, machines, and their knowledge of the materials with which they work include assemblers and fabricators, dental laboratory technicians, food-processing workers, jewelers and precious stone and metal workers, and woodworkers.

Sources of Additional Information
Information about job opportunities in textile, apparel, and furnishings occupations is available from local employers and local offices of the State employment service.

For general information on careers, technology, and trade regulations in the textile industry, contact
➤ American Textile Manufacturers Institute, Inc., 1130 Connecticut Ave. NW., Suite 1200, Washington, DC 20036-3954.

To receive a list of technical schools with accredited programs in upholstery, contact
➤ Accrediting Commission of Career Schools and Colleges of Technology, 2101 Wilson Blvd., Suite 302, Arlington, VA 22201. Internet: **http://www.accsct.org**

Woodworkers

(0*NET 51-7011.00, 51-7021.00, 51-7031.00, 51-7032.00, 51-7041.01, 51-7041.02, 51-7042.01, 51-7042.02, 51-7099.99)

Significant Points

- Most woodworkers are trained on the job; basic machine operations may be learned in a few months, but becoming a skilled woodworker often requires 2 or more years.

- Employment of woodworkers is expected to grow more slowly than average through the year 2012. Little or no growth is expected among woodworking machine setters, operators, and tenders.

- Job prospects will be best for workers with knowledge of computerized numerical control machine tool operation.

Nature of the Work
Despite the development of sophisticated plastics and other materials, the demand for wood products continues unabated. Helping to meet this demand are woodworkers. Woodworkers are found in industries that produce wood, such as sawmills and plywood mills;

in industries that use wood to produce furniture, kitchen cabinets, musical instruments, and other fabricated wood products; or in small shops that make architectural woodwork, furniture, and many other specialty items.

All woodworkers are employed at some stage of the process through which logs of wood are transformed into finished products. Some of these workers produce the structural elements of buildings; others mill hardwood and softwood lumber; still others assemble finished wood products. They operate machines that cut, shape, assemble, and finish raw wood to make the doors, windows, cabinets, trusses, plywood, flooring, paneling, molding, and trim that are components of most homes. Others may fashion home accessories, such as beds, sofas, tables, dressers, and chairs. In addition to these household goods, woodworkers also make sporting goods, including baseball bats and oars, as well as musical instruments, toys, caskets, tool handles, and thousands of other wooden items.

Production woodworkers set up, operate, and tend woodworking machines such as power saws, planers, sanders, lathes, jointers, and routers that cut and shape components from lumber, plywood, and other wood products. In sawmills, *sawing machine operators and tenders* set up, operate, or tend wood sawing machines that cut logs into planks, timbers, or boards. In plants manufacturing wood products, woodworkers first determine the best method of shaping and assembling parts, working from blueprints, supervisors' instructions, or shop drawings that woodworkers themselves produce. Before cutting, they often must measure and mark the materials. They verify dimensions and may trim parts using handtools such as planes, chisels, wood files, or sanders to ensure a tight fit. *Woodworking machine operators and tenders* set up, operate, or tend specific woodworking machines, such as drill presses, lathes, shapers, routers, sanders, planers, and wood-nailing machines. Lower skilled operators may merely press a switch on a woodworking machine and monitor the automatic operation, whereas more highly skilled operators set up equipment, cut and shape wooden parts, and verify dimensions using a template, caliper, or rule.

The next step in the manufacturing process is the production of subassemblies using fasteners and adhesives. Next, the pieces are brought together to form a complete unit. The product is then finish-sanded, stained, and, if necessary, coated with a sealer, such as lacquer or varnish. Woodworkers may perform this work in teams or be assisted by a helper.

Woodworkers have been greatly affected by the introduction of computer-controlled machinery. This technology has raised worker productivity by allowing one operator to simultaneously tend a greater number of machines. With computerized numerical controls (CNC), an operator can program a machine to perform a sequence of operations automatically, resulting in greater precision and reliability. The integration of computers with equipment has improved production speeds and capabilities, simplified setup and maintenance requirements, and increased the demand for workers with computer skills.

While this costly equipment has had a great impact on workers in the largest, most efficient firms, precision or custom woodworkers—who generally work in smaller firms—have continued to employ the same production techniques they have used for many years. Workers such as *cabinetmakers and bench carpenters; model makers and patternmakers;* and *furniture finishers* work on a customized basis, often building one-of-a-kind items. These highly skilled precision woodworkers usually perform a complete cycle of tasks—cutting, shaping, and preparing surfaces, and assembling prepared parts of complex wood components into a finished wood product. For this reason, these workers normally need substantial training and an ability to work from detailed instructions and specifications. In addition, they often are required to exercise independent judgment when undertaking an assignment.

Working Conditions

Working conditions vary by industry and specific job duties. In logging and sawmills, for example, working conditions are physically demanding due to the handling of heavy, bulky material. Workers in these industries also may encounter excessive noise, dust, and other air pollutants. However, the use of earplugs and respirators may partially alleviate these problems. Also, rigid adherence to safety precautions minimizes risk of injury from contact with rough wood stock, sharp tools, and power equipment. The risk of injury also is lowered by the installation of computer-controlled equipment, which reduces the physical labor and hands-on contact with machinery.

In furniture and kitchen cabinet manufacturing, employees who operate machinery often must wear ear and eye protection. They also must follow operating safety instructions and use safety shields or guards to prevent accidents. Those who work in the finishing area must be provided with an appropriate dust or vapor mask or a complete protective safety suit, or must work in a finishing envi-

All woodworkers are employed at some stage of the process through

ronment that removes all vapors and dust particles from the atmosphere. Prolonged standing, lifting, and fitting of heavy objects are common characteristics of the job.

Employment

Woodworkers held about 374,000 jobs in 2002. Self-employed woodworkers, mostly cabinetmakers and furniture finishers, accounted for 10 percent of these jobs. Employment among detailed woodworking occupations was distributed as follows:

Cabinetmakers and bench carpenters	147,000
Woodworking machine setters, operators, and tenders, except sawing	95,000
Sawing machine setters, operators, and tenders, wood	56,000
Furniture finishers	39,000
Model makers, wood	4,400
Patternmakers, wood	4,200
All other woodworkers	29,000

About 3 out of 4 woodworkers were employed in manufacturing industries. Among these woodworkers, 41 percent were found in establishments fabricating household and office furniture and fixtures and 28 percent worked in wood product manufacturing, producing a variety of raw, intermediate, and finished wood stock. Wholesale and retail lumber dealers, furniture stores, reupholstery and furniture repair shops, and construction firms also employ woodworkers.

Woodworking jobs are found throughout the country. However, production jobs are concentrated in the South and Northwest, close to the supply of wood, whereas furniture makers are more prevalent in the East. Custom shops can be found everywhere, but generally are concentrated in or near highly populated areas.

Training, Other Qualifications, and Advancement

Most woodworkers are trained on the job, picking up skills informally from experienced workers. Most woodworkers learn basic machine operations and job tasks in a few months, but becoming a skilled woodworker often requires 2 or more years.

Some woodworkers acquire skills through vocational education or by working as carpenters on construction jobs. Others may attend colleges or universities that offer training in areas including wood technology, furniture manufacturing, wood engineering, and production management. These programs prepare students for positions in production, supervision, engineering, and management.

596 Occupational Outlook Handbook

Beginners usually observe and help experienced machine operators. They may supply material to, or remove fabricated products from, machines. Trainees also do simple machine operating jobs, while at first closely supervised by experienced workers. As beginners gain experience, they perform more complex jobs with less supervision. Some may learn to read blueprints, set up machines, and plan the sequence of the work.

Employers increasingly seek applicants with a high school diploma or the equivalent, because of the growing sophistication of machinery and the constant need for retraining. Persons seeking woodworking jobs can enhance their employment and advancement prospects by completing high school and receiving training in mathematics, science, and computer applications. Other important qualities for entrants in this occupation include mechanical ability, manual dexterity, and the ability to pay attention to detail.

Advancement opportunities often are limited and depend upon availability, seniority, and a worker's skills and initiative. Sometimes experienced woodworkers become inspectors or supervisors responsible for the work of a group of woodworkers. Production workers often can advance into these positions by assuming additional responsibilities and by attending workshops, seminars, or college programs. Those who are highly skilled may set up their own woodworking shops.

Job Outlook

Employment of woodworkers is expected to grow more slowly than average through the year 2012. Little or no growth is expected among woodworking machine setters, operators, and tenders. Employment of cabinetmakers and bench carpenters and furniture finishers is expected to grow more slowly than average and employment of model makers and patternmakers is expected to grow about as fast as the average for all occupations. Job openings also will arise each year because of the need to replace experienced woodworkers who transfer to other occupations or leave the labor force.

Demand for woodworkers will stem from increases in population, personal income, and business expenditures, in addition to the continuing need for repair and renovation of residential and commercial properties. Therefore, opportunities should be available for woodworkers who specialize in such items as moldings, cabinets, stairs, and windows. Due to increasingly automated manufacturing processes, job prospects will be best for highly skilled woodworkers with knowledge of computerized numerical control machine tool operation.

Several factors may limit the growth of woodworking occupations. Technological advances, such as robots and CNC machinery, will continue to increase productivity among woodworkers, preventing employment from rising as fast as the demand for wood products, particularly in the mills and manufacturing plants where many processes can be automated. In addition, more jobs in the United States will be lost as imports continue to grow and as U.S. firms move some production to other countries. Also, the demand for wood may be reduced somewhat, as materials such as metal, plastic, and fiberglass continue to be used in many products as alternatives to wood. Environmental measures designed to control various pollutants used in, or generated by, woodworking processes also may adversely impact employment.

Employment in all woodworking specialties is highly sensitive to economic cycles. During economic downturns, workers are subject to layoffs or reductions in hours.

Earnings

Median hourly earnings of cabinetmakers and bench carpenters were $11.54 in 2002. The middle 50 percent earned between $9.26 and $14.66. The lowest 10 percent earned less than $7.70, and the highest 10 percent earned more than $18.11. Median hourly earnings in the industries employing the largest numbers of cabinetmakers and bench carpenters in 2002 are shown below:

Office furniture (including fixtures) manufacturing	$13.02
Household and institutional furniture and kitchen cabinet manufacturing	11.19
Other wood product manufacturing	11.14

Median hourly earnings of sawing machine setters, operators, and tenders, wood were $10.62 in 2002. The middle 50 percent earned between $8.70 and $13.11. The lowest 10 percent earned less than $7.36, and the highest 10 percent earned more than $15.94. Median hourly earnings in the industries employing the largest numbers of sawing machine setters, operators, and tenders, wood in 2002 are shown below:

Sawmills and wood preservation	$11.59
Veneer, plywood, and engineered wood product manufacturing	10.91
Household and institutional furniture and kitchen cabinet manufacturing	10.40
Other wood product manufacturing	10.06

Median hourly earnings of woodworking machine setters, operators, and tenders, except sawing were $10.59 in 2002. The middle 50 percent earned between $8.72 and $13.03. The lowest 10 percent earned less than $7.39, and the highest 10 percent earned more than $15.93. Median hourly earnings in the industries employing the largest numbers of woodworking machine setters, operators, and tenders, except sawing in 2002 are shown below:

Office furniture (including fixtures) manufacturing	$11.00
Sawmills and wood preservation	10.99
Veneer, plywood, and engineered wood product manufacturing	10.99
Household and institutional furniture and kitchen cabinet manufacturing	10.54
Other wood product manufacturing	10.26

In 2002, median hourly earnings were $10.92 for furniture finishers and $10.11 for all other woodworkers.

Some woodworkers, such as those in logging or sawmills who are engaged in processing primary wood and building materials, are members of the International Association of Machinists. Others belong to the United Brotherhood of Carpenters and Joiners of America.

Related Occupations

Carpenters also work with wood. In addition, many woodworkers follow blueprints and drawings and use machines to shape and form raw wood into a final product. Workers who perform similar functions working with other materials include sheet metal workers, structural and reinforcing iron and metal workers, computer-control programmers and operators, machinists, and tool and die makers.

Sources of Additional Information

For information about woodworking occupations, contact local furniture manufacturers, sawmills and planing mills, cabinetmaking or millwork firms, lumber dealers, a local of one of the unions mentioned above, or the nearest office of the State employment service.

Plant and System Operators

Power Plant Operators, Distributors, and Dispatchers

(0*NET 51-8011.00, 51-8012.00, 51-8013.01, 51-8013.02)

Significant Points

- Most entry-level workers start as helpers or laborers, and several years of training and experience are required to become fully qualified.

- Applicants are expected to encounter keen competition for jobs.

- Opportunities will be best for operators with training in computers and automated equipment.

Nature of the Work

Electricity is vital for most everyday activities. From the moment you flip the first switch each morning, you are connecting to a huge network of people, electric lines, and generating equipment. Power plant operators control the machinery that generates electricity. Power plant distributors and dispatchers control the flow of electricity from the power plant, over a network of transmission lines, to industrial plants and substations, and, finally, over distribution lines to residential users.

Power plant operators control and monitor boilers, turbines, generators, and auxiliary equipment in power-generating plants. Operators distribute power demands among generators, combine the current from several generators, and monitor instruments to maintain voltage and regulate electricity flows from the plant. When power requirements change, these workers start or stop generators and connect or disconnect them from circuits. They often use computers to keep records of switching operations and loads on generators, lines, and transformers. Operators also may use computers to prepare reports of unusual incidents, malfunctioning equipment, or maintenance performed during their shift.

Operators in plants with automated control systems work mainly in a central control room and usually are called *control room opera-*

A power plant dispatcher uses a computer to control the flow of electricity.

tors and *control room operator trainees* or *assistants.* In older plants, the controls for the equipment are not centralized, and *swtchboard operators* control the flow of electricity from a central point, whereas *auxiliary equipment operators* work throughout the plant, operating and monitoring valves, switches, and gauges.

The Nuclear Regulatory Commission (NRC) licenses operators of nuclear power plants. *Reactor operators* are authorized to control equipment that affects the power of the reactor in a nuclear power plant. In addition, an NRC-licensed *senior reactor operator* must be on duty during each shift to act as the plant supervisor and supervise the operation of all controls in the control room.

Power distributors and dispatchers, also called *load dispatchers* or *systems operators,* control the flow of electricity through transmission lines to industrial plants and substations that supply residential electric needs. They monitor and operate current converters, voltage transformers, and circuit breakers. Dispatchers also monitor other distribution equipment and record readings at a pilot board—a map of the transmission grid system showing the status of transmission circuits and connections with substations and industrial plants.

Dispatchers also anticipate power needs, such as those caused by changes in the weather. They call control room operators to start or stop boilers and generators, to bring production into balance with needs. Dispatchers handle emergencies such as transformer or transmission line failures and route current around affected areas. In substations, they also operate and monitor equipment that increases or decreases voltage, and they operate switchboard levers to control the flow of electricity in and out of the substations.

Working Conditions

Because electricity is provided around the clock, operators, distributors, and dispatchers usually work one of three daily 8-hour shifts or one of two 12-hour shifts on a rotating basis. Shift assignments may change periodically, so that all operators can share duty on less desirable shifts. Work on rotating shifts can be stressful and fatiguing, because of the constant change in living and sleeping patterns. Operators, distributors, and dispatchers who work in control rooms generally sit or stand at a control station. This work is not physically strenuous, but it does require constant attention. Operators who work outside the control room may be exposed to danger from electric shock, falls, and burns.

Nuclear power plant operators are subject to random drug and alcohol tests, as are most workers at such plants.

Employment

Power plant operators, distributors, and dispatchers held about 51,000 jobs in 2002. Jobs were located throughout the country. About 86 percent of jobs were in utility companies and government agencies that produced electricity. Others worked for manufacturing establishments that produced electricity for their own use.

Training, Other Qualifications, and Advancement

Employers seek high school graduates for entry-level operator, distributor, and dispatcher positions. Candidates with strong mathematics and science skills are preferred. College-level courses or prior experience in a mechanical or technical job may be helpful. With computers now used to keep records, generate reports, and track maintenance, employers are increasingly requiring computer proficiency. Most entry-level workers start as helpers or laborers.

Depending on the results of aptitude tests, their own preferences, and the availability of openings, workers may be assigned to train for one of many utility positions.

Workers selected for training as a fossil-fueled power plant operator or distributor undergo extensive on-the-job and classroom instruction. Several years of training and experience are required to become a fully qualified control room operator or power plant distributor. With further training and experience, workers may advance to shift supervisor. Utilities generally promote from within; therefore, opportunities to advance by moving to another employer are limited.

Extensive training and experience are necessary to pass the NRC examinations for reactor operators and senior reactor operators. To maintain their license, licensed reactor operators must pass an annual practical plant operation exam and a biennial written exam administered by their employers. Training may include simulator and on-the-job training, classroom instruction, and individual study. Entrants to nuclear power plant operator trainee jobs must have strong mathematics and science skills. Experience in other power plants or with Navy nuclear propulsion plants also is helpful. With further training and experience, reactor operators may advance to senior reactor operator positions.

In addition to receiving preliminary training as a power plant operator, distributor, or dispatcher, most workers are given periodic refresher training—frequently in the case of nuclear power plant operators. Refresher training usually is taken on plant simulators designed specifically to replicate procedures and situations that might be encountered at the trainee's plant.

Job Outlook

People who want to become power plant operators, distributors, and dispatchers are expected to encounter keen competition for these high-paying jobs. Declining employment and very low replacement needs in the occupation will result in few job opportunities. The slow pace of construction of new plants also will limit opportunities for power plant operators, distributors, and dispatchers. In addition, the increasing use of automatic controls and more computerized equipment should boost productivity and decrease the demand for operators. As a result, individuals with training in computers and automated equipment will have the best job prospects.

A decline in employment of power plant operators, distributors, and dispatchers is expected through the year 2012, as the utilities industry continues to restructure in response to deregulation and increasing competition. The Energy Policy Act of 1992 continues to have an impact on the organization of the industry. The Act aims at increasing competition in power-generating utilities by allowing independent producers to sell power directly to industrial and other wholesale customers. Consequently, utilities, which historically operated as regulated local monopolies, are restructuring their operations in order to reduce costs and compete effectively; as a result, the number of jobs is decreasing.

Earnings

Median annual earnings of power plant operators were $49,920 in 2002. The middle 50 percent earned between $40,090 and $58,690. The lowest 10 percent earned less than $31,290, and the highest 10 percent earned more than $67,950. Median annual earnings of power plant operators in 2002 were $52,410 in electric power generation, transmission, and distribution and $44,200 in local government.

Median annual earnings of nuclear power reactor operators were $61,060 in 2002. The middle 50 percent earned between $53,060 and $70,580. The lowest 10 percent earned less than $48,060, and the highest 10 percent earned more than $79,880.

Median annual earnings of power distributors and dispatchers were $54,120 in 2002. The middle 50 percent earned between $43,750 and $65,390. The lowest 10 percent earned less than $34,640, and the highest 10 percent earned more than $75,420.

Related Occupations

Other workers who monitor and operate plant and system equipment include chemical plant and system operators; petroleum pump system operators, refinery operators, and gaugers; stationary engineers and boiler operators; and water and wastewater treatment plant and system operators.

Sources of Additional Information

For information about employment opportunities, contact local electric utility companies, locals of unions, and State employment service offices.

For general information about power plant operators, nuclear power reactor operators, and power plant distributors and dispatchers, contact:

➤ American Public Power Association, 2301 M St. NW., Washington, DC 20037-1484. Internet. http://www.appanet.org
➤ International Brotherhood of Electrical Workers, 1125 15th St. NW., Washington, DC 20005.

Stationary Engineers and Boiler Operators

(O*NET 51-8021.01, 51-8021.02)

Significant Points

- Applicants may face competition for jobs; opportunities will be best for workers with training in computerized controls and instrumentation.
- Stationary engineers and boiler operators usually acquire their skills through a formal apprenticeship program, or on-the-job training supplemented by courses at a trade or technical school.
- Most States and cities have licensing requirements.

Nature of the Work

Heating, air-conditioning, refrigeration, and ventilation systems keep large buildings and other commercial facilities comfortable all year long. Industrial plants often have facilities to provide electrical power, steam, or other services. Stationary engineers and boiler operators operate and maintain these systems, which include boilers, air-conditioning and refrigeration equipment, diesel engines, turbines, generators, pumps, condensers, and compressors. The equipment that stationary engineers and boiler operators control is similar to equipment operated by locomotive or marine engineers, except that it is not in a moving vehicle.

Stationary engineers and boiler operators start up, regulate, repair, and shut down equipment. They ensure that the equipment operates safely, economically, and within established limits by monitoring meters, gauges, and computerized controls. Stationary engineers and boiler operators control equipment manually and, if necessary, make adjustments. They also record relevant events and facts concerning the operation and maintenance of the equipment in a log. With regard to steam boilers, for example, they observe, control, and record the steam pressure, temperature, water level, chemistry, power output, fuel consumption, and emissions from the vessel. They watch and listen to machinery and routinely check safety devices, identifying and correcting any trouble that develops. They use hand and power tools to perform repairs and maintenance ranging from a complete overhaul to replacing defective valves, gaskets, or bearings. Service, troubleshooting, repair, and monitoring of modern systems require the use of sophisticated electrical and electronic test equipment.

Stationary engineers typically use computers to operate the mechanical, electrical, and fire safety systems of new buildings and plants. Engineers monitor, adjust, and diagnose these systems from a central location, using a computer linked into the buildings' communications network.

Routine maintenance, such as lubricating moving parts, replacing filters, and removing soot and corrosion that can reduce the boiler's operating efficiency, is a regular part of the work of stationary engineers and boiler operators. They test the water in the boiler and add chemicals to prevent corrosion and harmful deposits. In most facilities, stationary engineers are responsible for the maintenance and balancing of air systems, as well as hydronic systems that heat or cool buildings by circulating fluid (as water or vapor) in a closed system of pipes. They also may check the air quality of the ventilation system and make adjustments to keep the operation of the boiler within mandated guidelines.

In a large building or industrial plant, a stationary engineer may be in charge of all mechanical systems in the building. Engineers may supervise the work of assistant stationary engineers, turbine operators, boiler tenders, and air-conditioning and refrigeration operators and mechanics. Most stationary engineers perform other maintenance duties, such as carpentry, plumbing, locksmithing, and electrical repairs. In a small building or industrial plant, there may be only one stationary engineer.

Working Conditions

Stationary engineers and boiler operators generally have steady, year-round employment. The average workweek is 40 hours. In facilities that operate around the clock, engineers and operators usually work one of three daily 8-hour shifts on a rotating basis. Weekend and holiday work often is required.

Engine rooms, power plants, boiler rooms, mechanical rooms, and electrical rooms usually are clean and well lighted. Even under the most favorable conditions, however, some stationary engineers and boiler operators are exposed to high temperatures, dust, dirt, and high noise levels from the equipment. General maintenance duties also may require contact with oil, grease, or smoke. Workers

A stationary engineer adjusts a boiler's fuel pressure.

spend much of the time on their feet. They may also have to crawl inside boilers and work in crouching or kneeling positions to inspect, clean, or repair equipment.

Stationary engineers and boiler operators work around hazardous machinery, such as low and high pressure boilers and electrical equipment. They must follow procedures to guard against burns, electric shock, noise, moving parts, and exposure to hazardous materials, such as asbestos or certain chemicals.

Employment

Stationary engineers and boiler operators held about 55,000 jobs in 2002. Jobs were dispersed throughout a variety of industries. The majority of jobs were in State and local government facilities; hospitals; educational services; manufacturing firms, such as pulp, paper, and paperboard mills; and electric power generation, transmission and distribution facilities. Other jobs were in architectural, engineering, and related services; traveler accommodation (hotels); and lessors of real estate (apartment and commercial buildings). Some were employed as contractors to a building or plant.

Stationary engineers and boiler operators worked throughout the country, generally in the more heavily populated areas in which large industrial and commercial establishments are located.

Training, Other Qualifications, and Advancement

Stationary engineers and boiler operators usually acquire their skills through a formal apprenticeship program, or on-the-job training supplemented by courses at a trade or technical school. In addition, valuable experience can be obtained in the Navy or the merchant marine, because marine engineering plants are similar to many stationary power and heating plants. Most employers prefer to hire persons with at least a high school diploma or the equivalent, due to the increasing complexity of the equipment with which engineers and operators now work. Many stationary engineers and boiler operators have some form of continuing education including college. Mechanical aptitude, manual dexterity, and good physical condition also are important.

The International Union of Operating Engineers sponsors apprenticeship programs and is the principal union for stationary engineers and boiler operators. In selecting apprentices, most local labor-management apprenticeship committees prefer applicants with education or training in mathematics, computers, mechanical drawing, machine shop practice, physics, and chemistry. An apprenticeship usually lasts 4 years and includes 8,000 hours of on-the-job training. In addition, apprentices receive 600 hours of classroom instruction in subjects such as boiler design and operation, elementary physics, pneumatics, refrigeration, air-conditioning, electricity, and electronics.

Those who acquire their skills on the job usually start as boiler tenders or helpers to experienced stationary engineers and boiler operators. This practical experience may be supplemented by postsecondary vocational training in computerized controls and instrumentation. However, becoming an engineer or operator without completing a formal apprenticeship program usually requires many years of work experience.

Most large and some small employers encourage and pay for skill-improvement training for their employees. Training almost always is provided when new equipment is introduced or when regulations concerning some aspect of the workers' duties change.

Most States and cities have licensing requirements for stationary engineers and boiler operators. Applicants usually must be at least 18 years of age, reside for a specified period in the State or locality, meet experience requirements, and pass a written examination. A stationary engineer or boiler operator who moves from one State or city to another may have to pass an examination for a new license due to regional differences in licensing requirements.

There are several classes of stationary engineer licenses. Each class specifies the type and size of equipment the engineer can operate without supervision. A licensed first-class stationary engineer is qualified to run a large facility, supervise others, and operate equipment of all types and capacities. An applicant for this license may be required to have a high school education, apprenticeship or on-the-job training, and several years of experience. Licenses below first class limit the types or capacities of equipment the engineer may operate without supervision.

Stationary engineers and boiler operators advance by being placed in charge of larger, more powerful, or more varied equipment. Generally, engineers advance to these jobs as they obtain higher class licenses. Some stationary engineers and boiler operators advance to boiler inspectors, chief plant engineers, building and plant superintendents, or building managers. A few obtain jobs as examining engineers or technical instructors.

Job Outlook

Applicants may face competition for jobs as stationary engineers and boiler operators. Employment opportunities will be best for those with apprenticeship training or vocational school courses covering systems that are operated by computerized controls and instrumentation.

Employment of stationary engineers and boiler operators is expected to show little or no growth through the year 2012. Continuing commercial and industrial development will increase the amount of equipment to be operated and maintained. However, automated systems and computerized controls are making newly installed equipment more efficient, thus reducing the number of jobs needed for its operation. Furthermore, relatively few job openings will arise from the need to replace experienced workers who transfer to other occupations or leave the labor force. The low replacement rate in this occupation reflects its high wages.

Earnings

Median annual earnings of stationary engineers and boiler operators were $43,240 in 2002. The middle 50 percent earned between $33,860 and $54,550. The lowest 10 percent earned less than $26,340, and the highest 10 percent earned more than $65,290. Median annual earnings of stationary engineers and boiler operators in 2002 were $48,450 in local government and $40,800 in general medical and surgical hospitals.

Related Occupations

Workers who monitor and operate stationary machinery include chemical plant and system operators; gas plant operators; petroleum pump system operators, refinery operators, and gaugers; power plant operators, distributors, and dispatchers; and water and liquid waste treatment plant and system operators. Other workers who maintain the equipment and machinery in a building or plant are industrial machinery installation, repair, and maintenance workers, as well as millwrights.

Sources of Additional Information

Information about apprenticeships, vocational training, and work opportunities is available from State employment service offices, locals of the International Union of Operating Engineers, vocational schools, and State and local licensing agencies.

Specific questions about this occupation should be addressed to:

➤ International Union of Operating Engineers, 1125 17th St. NW., Washington, DC 20036. Internet: **http://www.iuoe.org**

➤ National Association of Power Engineers, Inc., 1 Springfield St., Chicopee, MA 01013.

➤ Building Owners and Managers Institute International, 1521 Ritchie Hwy., Arnold, MD 21012. Internet: **http://www.bomi-edu.org**

Water and Liquid Waste Treatment Plant and System Operators

(0*NET 51-8031.00)

Significant Points

● Employment is concentrated in local government and private water, sewage, and other systems utilities.

● The completion of an associate degree or 1-year certificate program is increasingly becoming an asset.

● Operators must pass exams certifying that they are capable of overseeing various treatment processes.

● Job prospects will be good for qualified individuals because the number of applicants in this field is normally low.

Nature of the Work

Clean water is essential for everyday life. *Water treatment plant and system operators* treat water so that it is safe to drink. *Liquid waste treatment plant and system operators*, also known as wastewater treatment plant and system operators, remove harmful pollutants from domestic and industrial liquid waste so that it is safe to return to the environment.

Water is pumped from wells, rivers, streams, and reservoirs to water treatment plants, where it is treated and distributed to customers. Liquid waste travels through customers' sewer pipes to liquid waste treatment plants, where it is either treated and returned to streams, rivers, and oceans or reused for irrigation and landscaping. Operators in both types of plants control equipment and processes that remove or destroy harmful materials, chemical compounds, and microorganisms from the water. They also control pumps, valves, and other equipment that moves the water or liquid waste through the various treatment processes, after which they dispose of the removed waste materials.

Operators read, interpret, and adjust meters and gauges to make sure that plant equipment and processes are working properly. Operators operate chemical-feeding devices, take samples of the water or liquid waste, perform chemical and biological laboratory analyses, and adjust the amounts of chemicals, such as chlorine, in the water. They use a variety of instruments to sample and measure water quality and common hand and power tools to make repairs. Operators also make minor repairs to valves, pumps, and other equipment.

Water and liquid waste treatment plant and system operators increasingly rely on computers to help monitor equipment, store the results of sampling, make process-control decisions, schedule and record maintenance activities, and produce reports. When equipment malfunctions, operators also may use computers to determine the cause of the malfunction and seek its solution.

Occasionally, operators must work during emergencies. A heavy rainstorm, for example, may cause large amounts of liquid waste to flow into sewers, exceeding a plant's treatment capacity. Emergencies also can be caused by conditions inside a plant, such as chlorine gas leaks or oxygen deficiencies. To handle these conditions, operators are trained to make an emergency management response and use special safety equipment and procedures to protect public health and the facility. During these periods, operators may work under extreme pressure to correct problems as quickly as possible. Because working conditions may be dangerous, operators must be extremely cautious.

The specific duties of plant operators depend on the type and size of plant. In smaller plants, one operator may control all of the machinery, perform tests, keep records, handle complaints, and perform repairs and maintenance. A few operators may handle both a water treatment and a liquid waste treatment plant. In larger plants with many employees, operators may be more specialized and monitor only one process. The staff also may include chemists, engineers, laboratory technicians, mechanics, helpers, supervisors, and a superintendent.

Water pollution standards have become increasingly stringent since the adoption of two major Federal environmental statutes: the Clean Water Act of 1972, which implemented a national system of regulation on the discharge of pollutants; and the Safe Drinking Water Act of 1974, which established standards for drinking water. Industrial facilities sending their wastes to municipal treatment plants must meet certain minimum standards to ensure that the wastes have been adequately pretreated and will not damage municipal treatment facilities. Municipal water treatment plants also must meet stringent drinking water standards. The list of contaminants regulated by these statutes has grown over time. As a result, plant operators must be familiar with the guidelines established by Federal regulations and how they

affect their plant. In addition to knowing and understanding the Federal regulations, operators must be aware of any guidelines imposed by the State or locality in which the plant operates.

Working Conditions
Water and liquid waste treatment plant and system operators work both indoors and outdoors and may be exposed to noise from machinery and to unpleasant odors. Operators' work is physically demanding and often is performed in unclean locations. Operators must pay close attention to safety procedures, due to the presence of hazardous conditions, such as slippery walkways, dangerous gases, and malfunctioning equipment. Plants operate 24 hours a day, 7 days a week; therefore, operators work one of three 8-hour shifts, including weekends and holidays, on a rotational basis. Operators may be required to work overtime.

Employment
Water and liquid waste treatment plant and system operators held about 99,000 jobs in 2002. About 3 in 4 operators worked for local governments. Others worked primarily for private water, sewage, and other systems utilities, and for private waste treatment and disposal companies. Private firms are increasingly providing operation and management services to local governments on a contract basis.

Water and liquid waste treatment plant and system operators were employed throughout the country, but most jobs were in larger towns and cities. Although nearly all operators worked full time, those in small towns may work only part time at the treatment plant, with the remainder of their time spent handling other municipal duties.

Training, Other Qualifications, and Advancement
A high school diploma usually is required for an individual to become a water or liquid waste treatment plant operator. Operators need mechanical aptitude and should be competent in basic mathematics, chemistry, and biology. They must have the ability to apply data to formulas prescribing treatment requirements, flow levels, and concentration levels. Some basic familiarity with computers also is necessary because of the trend toward computer-controlled equipment and more sophisticated instrumentation. Certain positions—particularly in larger cities and towns—are covered by civil service regulations. Applicants for these positions may be required to pass a written examination testing their mathematics skills, mechanical aptitude, and general intelligence.

The completion of an associate degree or a 1-year certificate program in water quality and liquid waste treatment technology increases an applicant's chances for employment and promotion because plants are becoming more complex. Offered throughout the country, these programs provide a good general knowledge of water and liquid waste treatment processes, as well as basic preparation for becoming an operator.

Trainees usually start as attendants or operators-in-training and learn their skills on the job under the direction of an experienced operator. They learn by observing and doing routine tasks such as recording meter readings, taking samples of liquid waste and sludge, and performing simple maintenance and repair work on pumps, electric motors, valves, and other plant equipment. Larger treatment plants generally combine this on-the-job training with formal classroom or self-paced study programs.

The Safe Drinking Water Act Amendments of 1996, enforced by the U.S. Environmental Protection Agency, specify national minimum standards for certification and recertification of operators of community and nontransient, noncommunity water systems. As a result, operators must pass an examination to certify that they are capable of overseeing liquid waste treatment plant operations. There are different levels of certification, depending on the operator's experience and training. Higher certification levels qualify the opera-

Operators take samples of water or liquid waste, perform laboratory analyses, and adjust the amounts of chemicals in the water.

tor for a wider variety of treatment processes. Certification requirements vary by State and by size of treatment plants. Although relocation may mean having to become certified in a new jurisdiction, many States accept other States' certifications.

Most State drinking water and water pollution control agencies offer courses to improve operators' skills and knowledge. The courses cover principles of treatment processes and process control, laboratory procedures, maintenance, management skills, collection systems, safety, chlorination, sedimentation, biological treatment, sludge treatment and disposal, and flow measurements. Some operators take correspondence courses on subjects related to water and liquid waste treatment, and some employers pay part of the tuition for related college courses in science or engineering.

As operators are promoted, they become responsible for more complex treatment processes. Some operators are promoted to plant supervisor or superintendent; others advance by transferring to a larger facility. Postsecondary training in water and liquid waste treatment, coupled with increasingly responsible experience as an operator, may be sufficient to qualify a worker for becoming superintendent of a small plant, where a superintendent also serves as an operator. However, educational requirements are rising as larger, more complex treatment plants are built to meet new drinking water and water pollution control standards. With each promotion, the operator must have greater knowledge of Federal, State, and local regulations. Superintendents of large plants generally need an engineering or a science degree.

A few operators get jobs as technicians with State drinking water or water pollution control agencies. In that capacity, they monitor and provide technical assistance to plants throughout the State. Vocational-technical school or community college training generally is preferred for technician jobs. Experienced operators may transfer to related jobs with industrial liquid waste treatment plants, water or liquid waste treatment equipment and chemical companies, engineering consulting firms, or vocational-technical schools.

Job Outlook
Employment of water and liquid waste treatment plant and system operators is expected to grow about as fast as the average for all occupations through the year 2012. Job prospects will be good for qualified individuals because the number of applicants in this field is normally low, due primarily to the unclean and physically demanding nature of the work.

The increasing population and growth of the economy are expected to boost demand for essential water and liquid waste treatment services. As new plants are constructed to meet this demand, employ-

ment of water and liquid waste treatment plant and system operators will increase. In addition, many job openings will occur as experienced operators leave the labor force or transfer to other occupations.

Local governments are the largest employers of water and liquid waste treatment plant and system operators. However, Federal certification requirements have increased utilities' reliance on private firms specializing in the operation and management of water and liquid waste treatment facilities. As a result, employment in privately owned facilities will grow faster than the average.

Earnings
Median annual earnings of water and liquid waste treatment plant and system operators were $33,390 in 2002. The middle 50 percent earned between $25,790 and $42,490. The lowest 10 percent earned less than $20,220, and the highest 10 percent earned more than $52,110. Median annual earnings of water and liquid waste treatment plant and systems operators in 2002 were $33,210 in local government and $32,190 in water, sewage, and other systems.

In addition to their annual salaries, water and liquid waste treatment plant and system operators usually receive benefits that may include health and life insurance, a retirement plan, and educational reimbursement for job-related courses.

Related Occupations
Other workers whose main activity consists of operating a system of machinery to process or produce materials include chemical plant and system operators; gas plant operators; petroleum pump system operators, refinery operators, and gaugers; power plant operators, distributors, and dispatchers; and stationary engineers and boiler operators.

Sources of Additional Information
For information on employment opportunities, contact State or local water pollution control agencies, State water and liquid waste operator associations, State environmental training centers, or local offices of the State employment service.

For information on certification, contact:
➤ Association of Boards of Certification, 208 Fifth St., Ames, IA 50010-6259. Internet: **http://www.abccert.org**

For educational information related to a career as a water or liquid waste treatment plant and system operator, contact:
➤ American Water Works Association, 6666 West Quincy Ave., Denver, CO 80235. Internet: **http://www.awwa.org**
➤ Water Environment Federation, 601 Wythe St., Alexandria, VA 22314-1994. Internet: **http://www.wef.org**

Other Production Occupations

Dental Laboratory Technicians

(0*NET 51-9081.00)

Significant Points

● Employment should increase slowly, as the public's improving dental health requires fewer dentures but more bridges and crowns.

● Dental laboratory technicians need artistic aptitude for detailed and precise work, a high degree of manual dexterity, and good vision.

Nature of the Work
Dental laboratory technicians fill prescriptions from dentists for crowns, bridges, dentures, and other dental prosthetics. First, dentists send a specification of the item to be manufactured, along with an impression (mold) of the patient's mouth or teeth. Then, dental laboratory technicians, also called dental technicians, create a model of the patient's mouth by pouring plaster into the impression and allowing it to set. Next, they place the model on an apparatus that mimics the bite and movement of the patient's jaw. The model serves as the basis of the prosthetic device. Technicians examine the model, noting the size and shape of the adjacent teeth, as well as gaps within the gumline. Based upon these observations and the dentist's specifications, technicians build and shape a wax tooth or

teeth model, using small hand instruments called wax spatulas and wax carvers. They use this wax model to cast the metal framework for the prosthetic device.

After the wax tooth has been formed, dental technicians pour the cast and form the metal and, using small hand-held tools, prepare the surface to allow the metal and porcelain to bond. They then apply porcelain in layers, to arrive at the precise shape and color of a tooth. Technicians place the tooth in a porcelain furnace to bake the porcelain onto the metal framework, and then adjust the shape and color, with subsequent grinding and addition of porcelain to achieve a sealed finish. The final product is a nearly exact replica of the lost tooth or teeth.

In some laboratories, technicians perform all stages of the work, whereas, in other labs, each technician does only a few. Dental laboratory technicians can specialize in 1 of 5 areas: Orthodontic appliances, crowns and bridges, complete dentures, partial dentures, or ceramics. Job titles can reflect specialization in these areas. For example, technicians who make porcelain and acrylic restorations are called *dental ceramists*.

Working Conditions

Dental laboratory technicians generally work in clean, well-lighted, and well-ventilated areas. Technicians usually have their own workbenches, which can be equipped with Bunsen burners, grinding and polishing equipment, and hand instruments, such as wax spatulas and wax carvers. Some technicians have computer-aided milling equipment to assist them with creating artificial teeth.

The work is extremely delicate and time consuming. Salaried technicians usually work 40 hours a week, but self-employed technicians frequently work longer hours.

Employment

Dental laboratory technicians held about 47,000 jobs in 2002. Around 7 out of 10 jobs were in medical equipment and supply manufacturing laboratories, which usually are small, privately owned businesses with fewer than five employees. However, some laboratories are large; a few employ more than 50 technicians.

Some dental laboratory technicians work in offices of dentists. Others work for hospitals providing dental services, including U.S. Department of Veterans Affairs hospitals. Some technicians work in dental laboratories in their homes, in addition to their regular job.

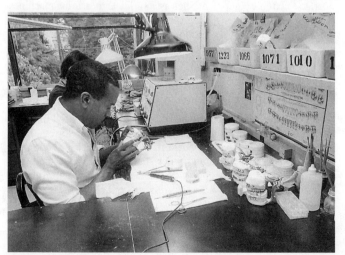

Dental laboratory technicians need a high degree of manual dexterity, good vision, and the ability to recognize very fine color shadings and variations in shape.

Training, Other Qualifications, and Advancement

Most dental laboratory technicians learn their craft on the job. They begin with simple tasks, such as pouring plaster into an impression, and progress to more complex procedures, such as making porcelain crowns and bridges. Becoming a fully trained technician requires an average of 3 to 4 years, depending upon the individual's aptitude and ambition, but it may take a few years more to become an accomplished technician.

Training in dental laboratory technology also is available through community and junior colleges, vocational-technical institutes, and the U.S. Armed Forces. Formal training programs vary greatly both in length and in the level of skill they impart.

In 2002, 25 programs in dental laboratory technology were approved (accredited) by the Commission on Dental Accreditation in conjunction with the American Dental Association (ADA). These programs provide classroom instruction in dental materials science, oral anatomy, fabrication procedures, ethics, and related subjects. In addition, each student is given supervised practical experience in a school or an associated dental laboratory. Accredited programs normally take 2 years to complete and lead to an associate degree. A few programs take about 4 years to complete and offer a bachelor's degree in dental technology.

Graduates of 2-year training programs need additional hands-on experience to become fully qualified. Each dental laboratory owner operates in a different way, and classroom instruction does not necessarily expose students to techniques and procedures favored by individual laboratory owners. Students who have taken enough courses to learn the basics of the craft usually are considered good candidates for training, regardless of whether they have completed a formal program. Many employers will train someone without any classroom experience.

The National Board for Certification, an independent board established by the National Association of Dental Laboratories, offers certification in dental laboratory technology. Certification, which is voluntary, can be obtained in five specialty areas: Crowns and bridges, ceramics, partial dentures, complete dentures, and orthodontic appliances.

In large dental laboratories, technicians may become supervisors or managers. Experienced technicians may teach or may take jobs with dental suppliers in such areas as product development, marketing, and sales. Still, for most technicians, opening one's own laboratory is the way toward advancement and higher earnings.

A high degree of manual dexterity, good vision, and the ability to recognize very fine color shadings and variations in shape are necessary. An artistic aptitude for detailed and precise work also is important. High school students interested in becoming dental laboratory technicians should take courses in art, metal and wood shop, drafting, and sciences. Courses in management and business may help those wishing to operate their own laboratories.

Job Outlook

Job opportunities for dental laboratory technicians should be favorable, despite expected slower-than-average growth in the occupation through the year 2012. Employers have difficulty filling trainee positions, probably because entry-level salaries are relatively low and because the public is not familiar with the occupation.

The overall dental health of the population has improved because of fluoridation of drinking water, which has reduced the incidence of dental cavities, and greater emphasis on preventive dental care since the early 1960s. As a result, full dentures will be less common, as most people will need only a bridge or crown. However, during the last few years, demand has arisen from an aging public that is growing increasingly interested in cosmetic prostheses. For example, many dental laboratories are filling orders for composite fillings that are the same shade of white as natural teeth to replace older, less attractive fillings.

Earnings

Median hourly earnings of dental laboratory technicians were $13.70 in 2002. The middle 50 percent earned between $10.51 and $18.40 an hour. The lowest 10 percent earned less than $8.16, and the highest 10 percent earned more than $23.65 an hour. Median hourly earnings of dental laboratory technicians in 2002 were $13.78 in medical equipment and supplies manufacturing and $12.98 in offices of dentists.

Technicians in large laboratories tend to specialize in a few procedures, and, therefore, tend to be paid a lower wage than those employed in small laboratories who perform a variety of tasks.

Related Occupations

Dental laboratory technicians manufacture artificial teeth, crowns and bridges, and orthodontic appliances, following specifications and instructions provided by dentists. Other workers who make and repair medical devices include dispensing opticians, ophthalmic laboratory technicians, orthotists and prosthetists, and precision instrument and equipment repairers.

Sources of Additional Information

For a list of accredited programs in dental laboratory technology, contact:

➤ Commission on Dental Accreditation, American Dental Association, 211 E. Chicago Ave., Chicago, IL 60611. Internet: **http://www.ada.org**

For information on requirements for certification, contact:

➤ National Board for Certification in Dental Technology, 1530 Metropolitan Blvd., Tallahassee, FL 32308. Internet: **http://www.nadl.org/html/certification.html**

For information on career opportunities in commercial laboratories, contact:

➤ National Association of Dental Laboratories, 1530 Metropolitan Blvd., Tallahassee, FL 32308. Internet: **http://www.nadl.org**

General information on grants and scholarships is available from dental technology schools.

Inspectors, Testers, Sorters, Samplers, and Weighers

(0*NET 51-9061.01, 51-9061.02, 51-9061.03, 51-9061.04, 51-9061.05)

Significant Points

- Seven out of 10 worked in manufacturing establishments.

- For workers who perform relatively simple tests of products, a high school diploma is sufficient; experienced production workers fill more complex inspecting positions.

- Employment is expected to grow more slowly than average, reflecting the growth of automated inspection and the redistribution of quality-control responsibilities from inspectors to other production workers.

Nature of the Work

Inspectors, testers, sorters, samplers, and weighers ensure that your food will not make you sick, that your car will run properly, and that your pants will not split the first time you wear them. These workers monitor or audit quality standards for virtually all manufactured products, including foods, textiles, clothing, glassware, motor vehicles, electronic components, computers, and structural steel. As product quality becomes increasingly important to the success of many manufacturing firms, daily duties of inspectors have changed. In some cases, the job titles of these workers also have been changed to *quality-control inspector* or a similar name, reflecting the growing importance of quality. (A separate statement on construction and building inspectors appears elsewhere in the *Handbook*.)

Regardless of title, all inspectors, testers, sorters, samplers, and weighers work to guarantee the quality of the goods their firms produce. Job duties, even within one company, vary by the type of products produced or the stage of production. Specific job duties also vary across the wide range of industries in which these workers are found. For example, inspectors may check products by sight, sound, feel, smell, or even taste to locate imperfections such as cuts, scratches, bubbles, missing pieces, misweaves, or crooked seams. These workers also may verify dimensions, color, weight, texture, strength, or other physical characteristics of objects. Machinery testers generally verify that parts fit, move correctly, and are properly lubricated; check the pressure of gases and the level of liquids; test the flow of electricity; and do a test run to check for proper operation. Some jobs involve only a quick visual inspection; others require a longer, detailed one. Sorters may separate goods according to length, size, fabric type, or color, while samplers test or inspect a sample taken from a batch or production run for malfunctions or defects. Weighers weigh quantities of materials for use in production.

Inspectors, testers, sorters, samplers, and weighers are involved at every stage of the production process. Some inspectors examine materials received from a supplier before sending them to the production line. Others inspect components and assemblies or perform a final check on the finished product. Depending on their skill level, inspectors also may set up and test equipment, calibrate precision instruments, repair defective products, or record data.

Inspectors, testers, sorters, samplers, and weighers rely on a number of tools to perform their jobs. Many use micrometers, calipers, alignment gauges, and other instruments to check and compare the dimensions of parts against the parts' specifications. They also may operate electronic equipment, such as coordinate measuring machines (CMMs), which use sensitive probes to measure a part's dimensional accuracy and compare the results with a computerized blueprint. Inspectors testing electrical devices may use voltmeters, ammeters, and oscilloscopes to test insulation, current flow, and resistance.

Inspectors mark, tag, or note problems. They may reject defective items outright, send them for repair or correction, or fix minor problems themselves. If the product is acceptable, inspectors may screw on a nameplate onto it, tag it, stamp it with a serial number, or certify it in some other way. Inspectors, testers, sorters, samplers, and weighers record the results of their inspections, compute the percentage of defects and other statistical measures, and prepare inspection and test reports. Some electronic inspection equipment automatically provides test reports containing these inspection results. When defects are found, inspectors notify supervisors and help to analyze and correct the production problems.

The emphasis on finding the root cause of defects is a basic tenet of modern management and production philosophies. Industrial production managers (see the statement on this occupation elsewhere in the *Handbook*) work closely with the inspectors to reduce defects and improve quality. In older production philosophies, it was considered acceptable to simply throw away or repair defective parts, but the root cause of the defects remained. A certain level of defects was considered acceptable because variations would always occur. Current philosophies emphasize constant quality improvement through analysis and correction of the causes of defects. The nature of inspectors' work has changed from merely checking for defects, to determining the cause of those defects.

Increased emphasis on quality control in manufacturing means that inspection is more fully integrated into the production process than in the past. Formerly, many companies considered quality control to be independent from the production work. Now, companies have integrated teams of inspection and production workers to jointly review and improve product quality. In addition, many companies now use self-monitoring production machines to ensure that the output is produced within quality standards. Self-monitoring machines can alert inspectors to production problems and automatically repair defects in some cases. Many firms have completely automated inspection with the help of advanced vision inspection systems, using machinery installed at one or several points in the production process. Inspectors in these firms calibrate and monitor the equipment, review output, and perform random product checks.

Testers repeatedly test existing products or prototypes under real-world conditions. For example, they may purposely abuse a machine by not changing its oil to see when failure occurs. They may devise automated machines to repeat a basic task thousands of times, such as opening and closing a car door. Through these tests, companies determine how long a product will last, what parts will break down first, and how to improve durability.

Working Conditions

Working conditions vary by industry and establishment size. As a result, some inspectors examine similar products for an entire shift, whereas others examine a variety of items. In manufacturing, it is common for most inspectors to remain at one workstation; in transportation, some travel from place to place to do inspections. Inspectors in some industries may be on their feet all day and may have to lift heavy objects, whereas, in other industries, they sit during most of their shift and do little strenuous work. Workers in heavy manufacturing plants may be exposed to the noise and grime of machinery; in other plants, inspectors work in clean, air-conditioned environments suitable for carrying out controlled tests.

Some inspectors work evenings, nights, or weekends. Shift assignments generally are made on the basis of seniority. Overtime may be required to meet production goals.

Inspectors calibrate scales.

Employment

Inspectors, testers, sorters, samplers, and weighers held about 515,000 jobs in 2002. About 7 out of 10 worked in manufacturing establishments that produced such products as motor vehicle parts, plastics products, semiconductor and other electronic components, and aerospace products and parts. Inspectors, testers, sorters, samplers, and weighers also were found in employment services, architectural, engineering, and related services, wholesale trade, and government agencies.

Training, Other Qualifications, and Advancement

Training requirements vary, based on the responsibilities of the inspector, tester, sorter, sampler, or weigher. For workers who perform simple "pass/fail" tests of products, a high school diploma generally is sufficient. Simple jobs may be filled by beginners provided with in-house training. Training for new inspectors may cover the use of special meters, gauges, computers, or other instruments; quality-control techniques; blueprint reading; safety; and reporting requirements. There are some postsecondary training programs in testing, but many employers prefer to train inspectors on the job.

Complex precision-inspecting positions are filled by experienced assemblers, machine operators, or mechanics who already have a thorough knowledge of the products and production processes. To advance to these positions, experienced workers may need training in statistical process control, new automation, or the company's quality assurance policies. As automated inspection equipment becomes more common, computer skills are increasingly important.

In general, inspectors, testers, sorters, samplers, and weighers need mechanical aptitude, math and communication skills, and good hand-eye coordination and vision. Advancement for these workers frequently takes the form of higher pay. They also may advance to inspector of more complex products, supervisor, or related positions such as purchaser of materials and equipment.

Job Outlook

Like that of many other occupations concentrated in manufacturing industries, employment of inspectors, testers, sorters, samplers, and weighers is expected to grow more slowly than average through the year 2012. The slower than average growth stems primarily from the growing use of automated inspection and the redistribution of quality-control responsibilities from inspectors to production workers. Numerous job openings also will arise due to turnover in this large occupation. Many of these jobs, however, will be open only to experienced production workers with advanced skills.

Employment of inspectors, testers, sorters, samplers, and weighers will be positively affected by the increased focus on quality in American industry. The emphasis on improving quality and productivity has led manufacturers to invest in automated inspection equipment, hire more inspectors, and to take a more systematic approach to quality inspection. Continued improvements in technologies, such as spectrophotometers and computer-assisted visual inspection systems, allow firms to effectively automate simple inspection tasks, increasing worker productivity and reducing the demand for inspectors.

Inspectors will continue to operate these automated machines and monitor the defects they detect. The increased emphasis on quality has increased the importance of inspection and the demand for inspectors. These two trends—increased emphasis on inspection and increased automation of inspection—have had opposite effects on the demand for inspectors.

Apart from automation, firms are integrating quality control into the production process. Many inspection duties are being redistributed from inspectors, testers, sorters, samplers, and weighers to other production workers who monitor quality at every stage of the process. In addition, the growing implementation of statistical process control is resulting in "smarter" inspection. Using this system, firms survey the sources and incidence of defects so that they can better focus their efforts on reducing production of defective products.

In many industries, however, automation is not being aggressively pursued as an alternative to manual inspection. Where key inspection elements are oriented toward size, such as length, width, or thickness, automation may play some role in the future. But where taste, smell, texture, appearance, fabric complexity, or product performance is important, inspection will probably continue to be done by workers. Employment of inspectors, testers, sorters, samplers, and weighers is expected to increase in the rapidly growing employment services industry, as more manufacturers and industrial firms hire temporary inspectors to increase the flexibility of their staffing strategies.

Earnings

Median hourly earnings of inspectors, testers, sorters, samplers, and weighers were $13.01 in 2002. The middle 50 percent earned between $9.84 and $17.46 an hour. The lowest 10 percent earned less than $7.81 an hour, and the highest 10 percent earned more than $23.56 an hour. Median hourly earnings in the industries employing the largest numbers of inspectors, testers, sorters, samplers, and weighers in 2002 were:

Aerospace product and parts manufacturing	$18.24
Motor vehicle parts manufacturing	16.49
Semiconductor and other electronic component manufacturing	12.86
Plastics product manufacturing	11.94
Employment services	8.85

Related Occupations

Other workers who conduct inspections include agricultural inspectors, construction and building inspectors, fire inspectors and investigators, forest fire inspectors and prevention specialists, occupational health and safety specialists and technicians, and transportation inspectors.

Sources of Additional Information

For general information about inspection and testing, contact:
➤ American Society for Quality, 600 North Plankinton Ave., Milwaukee, WI 53203. Internet: **http://www.asq.org**

Jewelers and Precious Stone and Metal Workers

(O*NET 51-9071.01, 51-9071.02, 51-9071.03, 51-9071.04, 51-9071.05, 51-9071.06)

Significant Points

- About one-fourth of all jewelers were self-employed.

- Jewelers usually learn their trade in vocational or technical schools, through distance-learning centers, or on the job.

- Prospects for new jewelers should be excellent; many employers have difficulty finding and retaining workers with the right skills to replace those who retire or who leave the occupation for other reasons.

Nature of the Work

Jewelers and precious stone and metal workers use a variety of common and specialized handtools and equipment to design and manufacture new pieces of jewelry; cut, set, and polish gem stones; and repair or adjust rings, necklaces, bracelets, earrings, and other jewelry. Jewelers usually specialize in one or more of these areas and may work for large jewelry-manufacturing firms, for small retail jewelry shops, or as owners of their own businesses. Regardless of the type of work done or the work setting, jewelers require a high degree of skill, precision, and attention to detail.

Some jewelers design or make their own jewelry. Following their own designs or those created by designers or customers, they begin by shaping the metal or by carving wax to make a model for casting the metal. The individual parts then are soldered together, and the jeweler may mount a diamond or other gem or may engrave a design into the metal. Others do finishing work, such as setting stones, polishing, or engraving. Typical repair work includes enlarging or reducing ring sizes, resetting stones, and replacing broken clasps and mountings.

In larger manufacturing businesses, jewelers usually specialize in a single operation. *Mold and model makers* create models or tools for the jewelry that is to be produced. *Assemblers* solder or fuse jewelry and their parts; they also may set stones. *Engravers* etch designs into the metal using specialized tools, and *polishers* bring a finished luster to the final product.

In small retail stores or repair shops, jewelers may be involved in all aspects of the work. Jewelers who own or manage stores or shops also hire and train employees; order, market, and sell merchandise; and perform other managerial duties.

Jewelers typically do the handiwork required to produce a piece of jewelry, while *gemologists* study the quality, characteristics, and value of gem stones. Gemologists usually sell jewelry and provide appraisal services. A few gemologists are employed by insurance companies that offer their own appraisal services for those customers who wish to insure certain pieces of jewelry. Many jewelers also study gemology in order to become familiar with the physical properties of the gem stones with which they work.

New technology is helping to produce jewelry of higher quality at a reduced cost and in a shorter amount of time. For example, lasers are often used for cutting and improving the quality of stones, for applying intricate engraving or design work, and for inscribing personal messages or identification on jewelry. Jewelers also use lasers to weld metals together in milliseconds with no seams or blemishes, improving the quality and appearance of the jewelry.

Some manufacturing firms use computer-aided design and manufacturing (CAD/CAM) to facilitate product design and automate some steps in the mold- and modelmaking process. CAD allows jewelers to create a virtual-reality model of a piece of jewelry. Using CAD, jewelers can modify the design, change the stone, or try a different setting and see the changes on a computer screen before cutting a stone or performing other costly steps. Once they are satisfied with the model, CAM produces it in a wax-like or other material. After the mold of the model is made, it is easier for manufacturing firms to produce numerous copies of a given piece of jewelry, which are then distributed to different retail establishments across the country. Similar techniques may be used in the retail setting, allowing individual customers to review their jewelry designs with the jeweler and make modifications before committing to the expense of a customized piece of jewelry.

Working Conditions

A jeweler's work involves a great deal of concentration and attention to detail. Working on precious stones and metals, while trying to satisfy customers' and employers' demands for speed and quality, can cause fatigue or stress. However, the use of more ergonomically correct jewelers' benches has eliminated most of the strain and discomfort caused by spending long periods bending over a workbench in one position.

Lasers require both careful handling, to avoid injury, and steady hands, to direct precision tasks. In larger manufacturing plants and some smaller repair shops, chemicals, sharp or pointed tools, and jewelers' torches pose safety threats and may cause injury if proper care is not taken. Most dangerous chemicals, however, have been replaced with synthetic, less toxic, products to meet safety requirements.

In repair shops, jewelers usually work alone, with little supervision. In retail stores, they may talk with customers about repairs, perform custom design work, and even do some selling. Because many of their materials are valuable, jewelers must observe strict security procedures, including working behind locked doors that are opened only by a buzzer, working on the other side of barred windows, making use of burglar alarms, and, in larger jewelry establishments, working in the presence of armed guards.

Jewelers and precious stone and metal workers must have excellent hand-eye coordination.

Employment

Jewelers and precious stone and metal workers held about 40,000 jobs in 2002. About one-fourth of these workers were self-employed; many operated their own store or repair shop, and some specialized in designing and creating custom jewelry.

About 3 out of 10 jobs for jewelers and precious stone and metal workers were in other miscellaneous manufacturing, which includes jewelry and silverware manufacturing. Another 3 out of 10 jobs were in retail trade, primarily in jewelry, luggage, and leather goods stores. A small number of jobs were in miscellaneous durable goods merchant wholesalers and in repair shops providing personal and household goods repair and maintenance. Although jewelry stores and repair shops were found in every city and in many small towns, most jobs were in larger metropolitan areas. In 2002, many jewelers employed in manufacturing worked in Rhode Island, New York, or California.

Training, Other Qualifications, and Advancement

Jewelers usually learn their trade in vocational or technical schools, through distance-learning centers, or on the job. Colleges and art and design schools also offer programs that can lead to a Bachelor of Fine Arts or Master of Fine Arts degree in jewelry design. Formal training in the basic skills of the trade enhances one's employment and advancement opportunities. Many employers prefer jewelers with design, repair, and sales skills.

For those interested in working in a jewelry store or repair shop, vocational and technical training or courses offered by public and private colleges are the best sources of training. In these programs, which can vary in length from 6 months to 1 year, students learn the use and care of jewelers' tools and machines and basic jewelry-making and -repairing skills, such as design, casting, stone setting, and polishing. Technical school courses also cover topics such as blueprint reading, math, and shop theory. To enter some technical school, and most college, programs, a high school diploma or its equivalent is required. However, some schools specializing in jewelry training do not require graduation from high school. Because computer-aided design is used increasingly in the jewelry field, it is recommended that students—especially those interested in design and manufacturing—obtain training in CAD.

Various institutes offer courses and programs in gemology and jewelry manufacturing and design. Programs cover a wide range of topics, including the identification and grading of diamonds and gem stones.

Most employers feel that vocational- and technical-school graduates need several more years of supervised on-the-job training or apprenticeship, in order to refine their repair skills and learn more about the operation of the store or shop. In addition, some employers encourage workers to improve their skills by enrolling in short-term technical school courses such as fabricating, jewelry design, jewelry manufacturing, wax carving, or gemology. Employers may pay all or part of the cost of this additional training.

In jewelry-manufacturing plants, workers traditionally develop their skills through informal apprenticeships and on-the-job training. The apprenticeship or training period lasts 3 to 4 years, depending on the difficulty of the specialty. Training usually focuses on casting, stone setting, modelmaking, or engraving. In recent years, a growing number of technical schools have begun to offer training designed for jewelers working in manufacturing. As a result, those in manufacturing now prefer graduates of these programs because they are familiar with the production process, requiring less on-the-job training.

The precise and delicate nature of jewelry work requires finger and hand dexterity, good hand-eye coordination, patience, and concentration. Artistic ability and fashion consciousness are major assets, because jewelry must be stylish and attractive. Those who work in jewelry stores have frequent contact with customers and should be neat, personable, and knowledgeable about the merchandise. In addition, employers require workers of good character, because jewelers work with valuable materials.

Advancement opportunities are limited and depend greatly on an individual's skill and initiative. In manufacturing, some jewelers advance to supervisory jobs, such as master jeweler or head jeweler, but, for most, advancement takes the form of higher pay for doing the same job. Jewelers who work in jewelry stores or repair shops may become managers; some open their own businesses.

Those interested in starting their own business should first establish themselves and build a reputation for their work within the jewelry trade. Once they obtain sufficient credit from jewelry suppliers and wholesalers, they can acquire the necessary inventory. Also, because the jewelry business is highly competitive, jewelers who plan to open their own store should have experience in selling, as well as knowledge of marketing and business management. Courses in these areas often are available from technical schools and community colleges.

Job Outlook

Employment of jewelers and precious stone and metal workers is expected to grow more slowly than the average through 2012. Employment opportunities, however, should be excellent, because jewelry sales are increasing. New jewelers also will be needed to replace those who retire or who leave the occupation for other reasons. When master jewelers retire, they take with them years of experience that require substantial time and financial resources to replace. Many employers have difficulty finding and retaining jewelers with the right skills and the necessary knowledge. Some technological advances have made jewelrymaking more efficient; however, many tasks cannot be fully automated. Jewelry work is a labor-intensive process that requires excellent handiwork.

The increasing numbers of affluent individuals, working women, double-income households, and fashion-conscious men are expected to keep jewelry sales strong. The population aged 45 and older, which accounts for a major portion of jewelry sales, also is on the rise.

Nontraditional jewelry marketers, such as discount stores, mail-order and catalogue companies, television shopping networks, and Internet retailers, have expanded the number of buying options and increased their sales volume. However, these establishments require fewer sales staff, limiting employment opportunities for jewelers and precious stone and metal workers who work mainly in sales. Because these marketers enjoy increases in sales, however, they will need highly skilled jewelers to make and repair the jewelry they sell.

Opportunities in jewelry stores and repair shops will be best for graduates from training programs for jewelers or gemologists. Despite an increase in sales by nontraditional jewelry marketers, traditional jewelers should not be affected greatly. Traditional jewelers have the advantage of being able to build client relationships based on trust. Many clients prefer to work directly with a jeweler, to ensure that the product is of the highest quality and meets their specifications. Many traditional jewelers expand their businesses as clients recommend their services to friends and relatives.

The jewelry industry can be cyclical. During economic downturns, demand for jewelry products and for jewelers tends to decrease. However, demand for repair workers should remain strong, even during economic slowdowns, because maintaining and repairing jewelry is an ongoing process. In fact, demand for jewelry repair may increase during recessions, as people repair or restore existing pieces rather than purchase new ones. Also, many nontraditional vendors typically do not offer repair services.

Within manufacturing, increasing automation will adversely affect employment of low-skilled occupations, such as assemblers and polishers. Automation will have a lesser impact on more creative, highly skilled positions, such as mold- and modelmakers. Furthermore, small manufacturers, which typify the industry, will have an increasingly difficult time competing with the larger manufacturers when it comes to supplying large retailers. Because of recent international trade agreements, exports are increasing modestly as manufacturers become more competitive in foreign markets. However, imports from foreign manufacturers are increasing more rapidly than exports, due to these same agreements.

Earnings

Median annual earnings for jewelers and precious stone and metal workers were $26,260 in 2002. The middle 50 percent earned between $19,550 and $35,310. The lowest 10 percent earned less than $15,030, and the highest 10 percent earned more than $45,620. In 2002, median annual earnings in the industries employing the largest numbers of jewelers and precious stone and metal workers were $30,000 in jewelry, luggage, and leather goods stores and $22,650 in other miscellaneous manufacturing.

Most jewelers start out with a base salary, but once they become more proficient, they may begin charging by the number of pieces completed. Jewelers who work in retail stores may earn a commission for each piece of jewelry sold, in addition to their base salary. Many jewelers also enjoy a variety of benefits, including reimbursement from their employers for work-related courses and discounts on jewelry purchases.

Related Occupations

Jewelers and precious stone and metal workers do precision handwork. Other skilled workers who do similar jobs include precision instrument and equipment repairers; welding, soldering, and brazing workers; and woodworkers. Some jewelers and precious stone and metal workers create their own jewelry designs. Other occupations that require visual arts abilities include artists and related workers, and designers. Finally, some jewelers and precious stone and metal workers are involved in the buying and selling of stones and metals or of the finished piece of jewelry. Similar occupations include retail salespersons and sales representatives in wholesale trade.

Sources of Additional Information

Information on job opportunities and training programs for jewelers is available from:

➤ Gemological Institute of America, 5345 Armada Dr., Carlsbad, CA 92008. Internet: **http://www.gia.org**

General career information is available from:

➤ Manufacturing Jewelers and Suppliers of America, 45 Royal Little Dr., Providence, RI 02904. Internet: **http://mjsa.polygon.net**

To receive a list of accredited technical schools that have programs in jewelry design, contact:

➤ Accrediting Commission of Career Schools and Colleges of Technology, 2101 Wilson Blvd., Suite 302, Arlington, VA 22201. Internet: **http://www.accsct.org**

Ophthalmic Laboratory Technicians

(O*NET 51-9083.01, 51-9083.02)

Significant Points

- Nearly all ophthalmic laboratory technicians learn their skills on the job.

- Employment is expected to grow more slowly than the average, reflecting the increasing use of automated machinery.

- Only a limited number of job openings will be created each year, because the occupation is small.

Nature of the Work

Ophthalmic laboratory technicians—also known as manufacturing opticians, optical mechanics, or optical goods workers—make prescription eyeglass or contact lenses. Prescription lenses are curved in such a way that light is correctly focused onto the retina of the patient's eye, improving his or her vision. Some ophthalmic laboratory technicians manufacture lenses for other optical instruments, such as telescopes and binoculars. Ophthalmic laboratory technicians cut, grind, edge, and finish lenses according to specifications provided by dispensing opticians, optometrists, or ophthalmologists and may insert lenses into frames to produce finished glasses. Although some lenses still are produced by hand, technicians are increasingly using automated equipment to make lenses.

Ophthalmic laboratory technicians should not be confused with workers in other vision care occupations. Ophthalmologists and optometrists are "eye doctors" who examine eyes, diagnose and treat vision problems, and prescribe corrective lenses. Ophthalmologists are physicians who perform eye surgery. Dispensing opticians, who also may do the work of ophthalmic laboratory technicians, help patients select frames and lenses, and adjust finished eyeglasses. (See the statement on physicians and surgeons, which includes ophthalmologists, as well as the statements on optometrists and opticians, dispensing, elsewhere in the *Handbook*.)

Ophthalmic laboratory technicians read prescription specifications, select standard glass or plastic lens blanks, and then mark them to indicate where the curves specified on the prescription should be ground. They place the lens in the lens grinder, set the dials for the prescribed curvature, and start the machine. After a minute or so, the lens is ready to be "finished" by a machine that rotates it against a fine abrasive, to grind it and smooth out rough edges. The lens is then placed in a polishing machine with an even finer abrasive, to polish it to a smooth, bright finish.

Next, the technician examines the lens through a lensometer, an instrument similar in shape to a microscope, to make sure that the degree and placement of the curve are correct. The technician then cuts the lenses and bevels the edges to fit the frame, dips each lens into dye if the prescription calls for tinted or coated lenses, polishes the edges, and assembles the lenses and frame parts into a finished pair of glasses.

In small laboratories, technicians usually handle every phase of the operation. In large ones, in which virtually every phase of the operation is automated, technicians may be responsible for operating computerized equipment. Technicians also inspect the final product for quality and accuracy.

Working Conditions

Ophthalmic laboratory technicians work in relatively clean and well-lighted laboratories and have limited contact with the public. Their

Although some lenses are still produced by hand, ophthalmic laboratory technicians increasingly use automated equipment to make lenses.

surroundings are relatively quiet despite the humming of machines. At times, technicians wear goggles to protect their eyes, and they may spend a great deal of time standing.

Most ophthalmic laboratory technicians work a 5-day, 40-hour week, which may include weekends, evenings, or, occasionally, some overtime. Some work part time.

Ophthalmic laboratory technicians need to take precautions against the hazards associated with cutting glass, handling chemicals, and working near machinery.

Employment

Ophthalmic laboratory technicians held about 33,000 jobs in 2002. Around 34 percent were in health and personal care stores, such as optical goods stores that manufacture and sell prescription glasses and contact lenses. About 29 percent were in medical equipment and supplies manufacturing, working for ophthalmic goods manufacturers that produce eyewear and contact lenses for sale by retail stores, as well as by ophthalmologists and optometrists. Most of the rest were in offices of other health practitioners, professional and commercial equipment and supplies merchant wholesalers, offices of physicians, employment services, or in commercial and service industry machine manufacturing firms that produce lenses for other optical instruments, such as telescopes and binoculars.

Training, Other Qualifications, and Advancement

Nearly all ophthalmic laboratory technicians learn their skills on the job. Employers filling trainee jobs prefer applicants who are high school graduates. Courses in science, mathematics, and computers are valuable; manual dexterity and the ability to do precision work are essential.

Technician trainees producing lenses by hand start on simple tasks, such as marking or blocking lenses for grinding, and then progress to grinding, cutting, edging, and beveling lenses, and, finally, to assembling the eyeglasses. Depending on individual aptitude, it may take up to 6 months to become proficient in all phases of the work.

Technicians using automated systems will find computer skills valuable. Training is completed on the job and varies in duration, depending on the type of machinery and the worker's aptitude.

A very small number of ophthalmic laboratory technicians learn their trade in the Armed Forces or in the few programs in optical technology offered by vocational-technical institutes or trade schools. These programs have classes in optical theory, surfacing and lens finishing, and the reading and applying of prescriptions. Programs vary in length from 6 months to 1 year and award certificates or diplomas.

Ophthalmic laboratory technicians can become supervisors and managers. Some become dispensing opticians, although further education or training generally is required in that occupation.

Job Outlook

Overall employment of ophthalmic laboratory technicians is expected to grow more slowly than the average for all occupations through the year 2012, reflecting the increasing use of automated machinery. Most job openings will arise from the need to replace technicians who transfer to other occupations or who leave the labor force. Only a limited number of job openings will be created each year, because the occupation is small.

Demographic trends make it likely that many more Americans will need vision care in the years ahead. Not only will the population grow, but also, the proportion of middle-aged and older adults is projected to increase rapidly. Middle age is a time when many people use corrective lenses for the first time, and elderly persons usually require more vision care than others.

Fashion also influences demand. Frames come in a variety of styles and colors, encouraging people to buy more than one pair. Demand is expected to grow as well in response to the availability of new technologies that improve the quality and look of corrective lenses, such as antireflective coatings and bifocal lenses without the line that is visible in traditional bifocals.

Earnings

Median hourly earnings of ophthalmic laboratory technicians were $10.46 in 2002. The middle 50 percent earned between $8.73 and $13.05 an hour. The lowest 10 percent earned less than $7.56, and the highest 10 percent earned more than $16.40 an hour. In 2002, median hourly earnings of ophthalmic laboratory technicians were $10.68 in medical equipment and supplies manufacturing and $10.15 in health and personal care stores.

Related Occupations

Workers in other precision production occupations include dental laboratory technicians; opticians, dispensing; orthotists and prosthetists; and precision instrument and equipment repairers.

Sources of Additional Information

For a list of accredited programs in ophthalmic laboratory technology, contact:

➤ Commission on Opticianry Accreditation, P.O. Box 3073, Merrifield, VA 22116-3073.

State employment service offices can provide information about job openings for ophthalmic laboratory technicians.

Painting and Coating Workers, Except Construction and Maintenance

(0*NET 51-9121.01, 51-9121.02, 51-9122.00, 51-9123.00)

Significant Points

- Nearly 70 percent of jobs are in manufacturing establishments.

- Most workers acquire their skills on the job; for most operators, training lasts from a few days to several months, but becoming skilled in all aspects of automotive painting usually requires 1 to 2 years.

- Employment growth for highly skilled transportation painters and automotive refinishers is projected to be faster than for lesser skilled painting, coating, and spraying machine operators, whose jobs are subject to automation.

Nature of the Work

Millions of items ranging from cars to candy are covered by paint, plastic, varnish, chocolate, or some other type of coating solution. Often, the protection provided by the paint or coating is essential to the product, as with the coating of insulating material covering wires and other electrical and electronic components. Many paints and coatings have dual purposes; for example, the paint finish on an automobile heightens the visual appearance of the vehicle while providing protection from corrosion.

Painting, coating, and spraying machine setters, operators, and tenders control the machinery that applies these paints and coatings to a wide range of manufactured products. Perhaps the most straightforward technique is simply dipping an item in a large vat of paint or other coating. This is the technique used by *dippers*, who immerse racks or baskets of articles in vats of paint, liquid plastic, or other solutions by means of a power hoist. Similarly, *tumbling barrel painters* deposit articles made of porous materials in a barrel of paint, varnish, or other coating, which is then rotated to ensure thorough coverage.

Another familiar technique is spraying products with a solution of paint or some other coating. *Spray machine operators* use spray guns to coat metal, wood, ceramic, fabric, paper, and food products with paint and other coating solutions. Following a formula, operators fill the equipment's tanks with a mixture of paints or chemicals, adding prescribed amounts of solution. They adjust nozzles on the spray guns to obtain the proper dispersion of the spray and hold or position the guns to direct the spray onto the article. Operators also check the flow and viscosity of the paint or solution and visually inspect the quality of the coating. When products are drying, these workers often must regulate the temperature and air circulation in drying ovens. Individuals who paint, coat, or decorate articles such as furniture, glass, pottery, toys, and books are known as *painting, coating, and decorating workers.*

Painting workers use various types of machines to coat a range of products. Frequently, their job title reflects the specialized nature of the machine or the coating being applied. For example, *enrobing machine operators* coat, or "enrobe," confectionery, bakery, and other food products with melted chocolate, cheese, oils, sugar, or other substances. *Paper coating machine operators* spray "size" on rolls of paper to give it its gloss or finish. *Silvering applicators* spray silver, tin, and copper solutions on glass in the manufacture of mirrors.

In response to concerns about air pollution and worker safety, manufacturers increasingly are using new types of paints and coatings on their products, instead of high-solvent paints. Water-based paints and powder coatings are two of the most common. These compounds do not emit as many volatile organic compounds into the air and can be applied to a variety of products. Powder coatings are sprayed much as are liquid paints and then are heated to melt and cure the coating.

The adoption of new types of paints often is accompanied by a conversion to more automated painting equipment that the operator sets and monitors. When using these machines, operators position the automatic spray guns, set the nozzles, and synchronize the action of the guns with the speed of the conveyor carrying articles through the machine and drying ovens. The operator also may add solvents or water to the paint vessel that prepares the paint for application. During operation, these workers tend painting machines, observe gauges on the control panel, and randomly check articles for evidence of any variation from specifications. The operator then uses a spray gun to "touch up" spots where necessary.

Although the majority of these workers are employed in manufacturing, the best known group refinishes old and damaged cars, trucks, and buses in automotive body repair and paint shops. *Transportation equipment* or *automotive painters* are among the most highly skilled manual spray operators, because they perform intricate, detailed work and mix paints to match the original color, a task that is especially difficult if the color has faded.

To prepare a vehicle for painting, painters or their helpers use power sanders and sandpaper to remove the original paint or rust and then fill small dents and scratches with body filler. They also remove or mask parts they do not want to paint, such as chrome trim, headlights, windows, and mirrors. Automotive painters use a spray gun to apply several coats of paint. They apply lacquer, enamel, or water-based primers to vehicles with metal bodies and flexible primers to newer vehicles with plastic body parts. Controlling the spray gun by hand, they apply successive coats until the finish of the repaired sections of the vehicle matches that of the original, undamaged portions. To speed drying between coats, they may place the freshly painted vehicle under heat lamps or in a special infrared oven. After each coat of primer dries, they sand the surface to remove any irregularities and to improve the adhesion of the next coat. Final sanding of the primers may be done by hand with a fine grade of sandpaper. A sealer then is applied and allowed to dry, followed by the final topcoat. When lacquer is used, painters or their helpers usually polish the finished surface after the final coat has dried.

Working Conditions

Painting and coating workers typically work indoors and may be exposed to dangerous fumes from paint and coating solutions. Although painting usually is done in special ventilated booths, many operators wear masks or respirators that cover their noses and

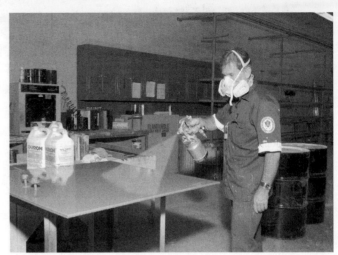

Spraying machine operators use spray guns to coat a variety of products and surfaces.

mouths. In addition, Federal legislation has led to a decrease in workers' exposure to hazardous chemicals by regulating emissions of volatile organic compounds from paints and other chemicals. This legislation also has led to increasing use of more sophisticated paint booths and fresh-air systems that provide a safer work environment.

Operators have to stand for long periods, and, when using a spray gun, they may have to bend, stoop, or crouch in uncomfortable positions to reach different parts of the article. Most operators work a normal 40-hour week, but self-employed automotive painters sometimes work more than 50 hours a week, depending on the number of vehicles customers want repainted.

Employment

Painting and coating workers held about 187,000 jobs in 2002. Lesser skilled coating, painting, and spraying machine setters, operators, and tenders accounted for about 103,000 jobs, while more skilled transportation equipment painters constituted about 50,000. About 34,000 workers were painting, coating, and decorating workers.

Nearly seventy percent of jobs for salaried workers were found in manufacturing establishments, where the workers applied coatings to items such as fabricated metal products, motor vehicles and related equipment, industrial machines, household and office furniture, and plastics, wood, and paper products. Other workers included automotive painters employed by independent automotive repair shops and body repair and paint shops operated by retail motor vehicle dealers. About 8 percent of painting workers were self-employed; most of these were transportation equipment painters.

Training, Other Qualifications, and Advancement

Most painting and coating workers acquire their skills on the job, usually by watching and helping other, more experienced workers. For most setters, operators, and tenders, as well as painting, coating, and decorating workers, training lasts from a few days to several months. Coating, painting, and spraying machine setters, operators, and tenders who modify the operation of computer-controlled equipment while it is running may require additional training in computer operations and minor programming.

Similarly, most transportation equipment painters start as helpers and gain their skills informally on the job. Becoming skilled in all aspects of automotive painting usually requires 1 to 2 years of on-the-job training. Beginning helpers usually remove trim, clean and sand surfaces to be painted, mask surfaces that they do not want painted, and polish finished work. As helpers gain experience, they progress to more complicated tasks, such as mixing paint to achieve a good match and using spray guns to apply primer coats or final coats to small areas.

Painters should have keen eyesight and a good sense of color. The completion of high school generally is not required, but is advantageous. Additional instruction is offered at many community colleges and vocational or technical schools. Such programs enhance one's employment prospects and can speed promotion to the next level.

Some employers sponsor training programs to help their workers become more productive. This training is available from manufacturers of chemicals, paints, or equipment or from other private sources. It may include safety and quality tips and impart knowledge of products, equipment, and general business practices. Some automotive painters are sent to technical schools to learn the intricacies of mixing and applying different types of paint.

Voluntary certification by the National Institute for Automotive Service Excellence is recognized as the standard of achievement for automotive painters. For certification, painters must pass a written examination and have at least 2 years of experience in the field. High school, trade or vocational school, or community or junior college training in automotive painting and refinishing may substitute for up to 1 year of experience. To retain their certification, painters must retake the examination at least every 5 years.

Experienced painting and coating workers with leadership ability may become team leaders or supervisors. Those who acquire practical experience, college, or other formal training may become sales or technical representatives for chemical or paint companies. Eventually, some automotive painters open their own shops.

Job Outlook

Overall employment of painting and coating workers is expected to grow about as fast as the average for all occupations through the year 2012. Employment growth for highly skilled transportation painters and automotive refinishers is projected to be faster than for lesser skilled painting, coating, and spraying machine operators. In addition to jobs arising from growth, some jobs will become available each year as employers replace experienced operators who transfer to other occupations or leave the labor force.

An increasing population demanding more manufactured goods will spur employment growth among coating, painting, and spraying machine operators. Similarly, increasing demand for hand-painted tiles and related specialty products will lead to growth among painting, coating, and decorating workers. Employment growth will be limited, however, by improvements in the automation of paint and coating applications that will raise worker productivity. For example, operators will be able to coat goods more rapidly as they use sophisticated industrial robots that move and aim spray guns increasingly as humans do; as the cost of robots continues to fall, they will be more widely used. Legislation has set limits on the emissions of ozone-forming volatile organic compounds and is expected to impede job growth among operators in manufacturing; as these firms switch to water-based and powder coatings to comply with the law, they will introduce more efficient automation.

Because the detailed work of refinishing automobiles in collision repair shops and motor vehicle dealerships does not lend itself to automation, painters employed in these establishments are projected to experience faster employment growth. As the demand for refinishing continues to grow, slower productivity growth among

these workers will lead to employment increases that are more in line with the growing demand for their services.

The number of job openings for painting and coating workers may fluctuate from year to year due to cyclical changes in economic conditions. When demand for manufactured goods lessen, production may be suspended or reduced, and workers may be laid off or face a shortened workweek. Automotive painters, by contrast, can expect relatively steady work because automobiles damaged in accidents require repair and refinishing regardless of the state of the economy.

Earnings

Median hourly earnings of coating, painting, and spraying machine setters, operators, and tenders were $12.16 in 2002. The middle 50 percent earned between $9.81 and $15.17 an hour. The lowest 10 percent earned less than $8.11, and the highest 10 percent earned more than $18.73 an hour.

Median hourly earnings of transportation equipment painters were $16.13 in 2002. The middle 50 percent earned between $12.31 and $21.40 an hour. The lowest 10 percent earned less than $9.70, and the highest 10 percent earned more than $26.48 an hour. Median hourly earnings of transportation equipment painters were $15.86 in automotive repair and maintenance shops and $23.23 in motor vehicle manufacturing.

Median hourly earnings of painting, coating, and decorating workers were $10.19 in 2002. The middle 50 percent earned between $8.16 and $13.08 an hour. The lowest 10 percent earned less than $7.04, and the highest 10 percent earned more than $16.72 an hour.

Many automotive painters employed by motor vehicle dealers and independent automotive repair shops receive a commission based on the labor cost charged to the customer. Under this method, earnings depend largely on the amount of work a painter does and how fast it is completed. Employers frequently guarantee commissioned painters a minimum weekly salary. Helpers and trainees usually receive an hourly rate until they become sufficiently skilled to work on commission. Trucking companies, bus lines, and other organizations that repair and refinish their own vehicles usually pay by the hour.

Many painting and coating machine operators belong to unions, including the International Brotherhood of Painters and Allied Trades, the Sheet Metal Workers International Association, and the International Brotherhood of Teamsters. Most union operators work for manufacturers and large motor vehicle dealers.

Related Occupations

Other occupations in which workers apply paints and coatings include painters and paperhangers, woodworkers, and machine setters, operators, and tenders—metal and plastic.

Sources of Additional Information

For more details about work opportunities, contact local manufacturers, automotive body repair shops, motor vehicle dealers, and vocational schools; locals of unions representing these workers; or the local office of the State employment service. The State employment service also may be a source of information about training programs.

Information on how to become a certified automotive painter is available from:

➤ National Institute for Automotive Service Excellence (ASE), 101 Blue Seal Dr. SE., Leesburg, VA 20175. Internet: **http://www.asecert.org**

Photographic Process Workers and Processing Machine Operators

(0*NET 51-9131.01, 51-9131.02, 51-9131.03, 51-9131.04, 51-9132.00)

Significant Points

● Little or no employment growth is expected as digital photography becomes commonplace.

● Most receive on-the-job training from their companies, manufacturers' representatives, and experienced workers.

● Job opportunities will be best for individuals with experience using computers and digital technology.

Nature of the Work

Both amateur and professional photographers rely heavily on photographic process workers and processing machine operators to develop film, make prints or slides, and do related tasks, such as enlarging or retouching photographs. *Photographic processing machine operators* operate various machines, such as mounting presses and motion picture film printing, photographic printing, and film developing machines. *Photographic process workers* perform more delicate tasks, such as retouching photographic negatives and prints to emphasize or correct specific features.

Photographic processing machine operators often have specialized jobs. *Film process technicians* operate machines that develop exposed photographic film or sensitized paper in a series of chemical and water baths to produce negative or positive images. First, technicians mix developing and fixing solutions, following a formula. They then load the film in the machine, which immerses the exposed film in a developer solution. This brings out the latent image. The next steps include immersing the negative in a stop-bath to halt the developer action, transferring it to a hyposolution to fix the image, and then immersing it in water to remove the chemicals. The technician then dries the film. In some cases, these steps are performed by hand.

Color printer operators control equipment that produces color prints from negatives. These workers read customer instructions to determine processing requirements. They load film into color printing equipment, examine negatives to determine equipment control settings, set controls, and produce a specified number of prints. Finally, they inspect the finished prints for defects, remove any that are found, and insert the processed negatives and prints into an envelope for return to the customer.

Photographic process workers, sometimes known as *digital imaging technicians*, use computer images of conventional negatives and specialized computer software to vary the contrast of images, remove unwanted background, or combine features from different photographs. Although computers and digital technology are replacing much manual work, some photographic process workers, especially those who work in portrait studios, still perform many specialized tasks by hand directly on the photo or negative. *Airbrush artists* restore damaged and faded photographs, and may color or shade drawings to create photographic likenesses using an airbrush. *Photographic retouchers* alter photographic negatives, prints, or images to accentuate the subject. *Colorists* apply oil colors to portrait photographs to create natural, lifelike appearances. *Photographic spotters* remove imperfections on photographic prints and images.

Film process technicians operate machines that develop exposed photographic film to produce negative or positive images.

Working Conditions

Photographic process workers and processing machine operators generally spend their work hours in clean, appropriately lighted, well-ventilated, and air-conditioned offices, photofinishing laboratories, or 1-hour minilabs. In recent years, more commercial photographic processing has been done on computers than in darkrooms, and this trend is expected to continue.

Some photographic process workers and processing machine operators are exposed to the chemicals and fumes associated with developing and printing. These workers must wear rubber gloves and aprons and take precautions against these hazards. Those who use computers for extended periods may experience back pain, eyestrain, or fatigue.

Photographic processing machine operators must do repetitive work at a rapid pace without any loss of accuracy. Photographic process workers do detailed tasks, such as airbrushing and spotting, which can contribute to eye fatigue.

Many photo laboratory employees work a 40-hour week, including evenings and weekends, and may work overtime during peak seasons. Almost one-fourth work part time.

Employment

Photographic process workers held about 28,000 jobs in 2002. Almost one in four photographic process workers were employed in photofinishing laboratories and 1-hour minilabs. More than one in six worked for portrait studios or commercial laboratories that specialize in processing the work of professional photographers for advertising and other industries. An additional one in six were employed by general merchandise stores, and one in ten in the printing, publishing, and motion picture industries.

Photographic processing machine operators held about 54,000 jobs in 2002. About four in ten worked in retail establishments, primarily in general merchandise stores and drug stores. About three in ten worked in photofinishing laboratories and 1-hour minilabs. Small numbers were employed in the printing industry and in portrait studios and commercial laboratories that process the work of professional photographers.

Employment fluctuates somewhat over the course of the year. Typically, employment peaks during school graduation and summer vacation periods, and again during the winter holiday season.

Training, Other Qualifications, and Advancement

Most photographic process workers and processing machine operators receive on-the-job training from their companies, manufacturers' representatives, and experienced workers. New employees gradually learn to use the machines and chemicals that develop and print film.

Employers prefer applicants who are high school graduates or those who have some experience in the field. Familiarity with computers is essential for photographic processing machine operators. The ability to perform simple mathematical calculations also is helpful. Photography courses that include instruction in film processing are valuable preparation. Such courses are available through high schools, vocational-technical institutes, private trade schools, and colleges and universities.

On-the-job training in photographic processing occupations can range from just a few hours for print machine operators to several months for photographic processing workers such as airbrush artists and colorists. Some workers attend periodic training seminars to maintain a high level of skill. Manual dexterity, good hand-eye coordination, and good vision, including normal color perception, are important qualifications for photographic process workers.

Photographic process machine workers can sometimes advance from jobs as machine operators to supervisory positions in laboratories or to management positions within retail stores.

Job Outlook

Slower-than-average growth is expected for photographic process workers and processing machine operators through the year 2012. Most openings will result from replacement needs, which are higher for machine operators than for photographic process workers.

In recent years, the use of digital cameras, which use electronic memory rather than film to record images, has grown rapidly among professional photographers and advanced amateurs. As the cost of digital photography drops, the use of such cameras will become more widespread among amateur photographers, reducing the demand for traditional photographic processing machine operators. However, conventional cameras, which use film to record images, are expected to continue to be the camera of choice among most casual photographers. Population growth and the popularity of amateur and family photography will contribute to a continuing need for photographic processing machine operators to process the film used in conventional cameras, including increasingly sophisticated disposable cameras. This need will prevent what otherwise would be even slower growth in the number of these workers.

Digital photography also will reduce demand for photographic process workers. Using digital cameras and technology, consumers who have a personal computer and the proper software will be able to download and view pictures on their computer, as well as manipulate, correct, and retouch their own photographs. No matter what improvements occur in camera technology, though, some photographic processing tasks will still require skillful manual treatment. Moreover, not all consumers will want to invest in the software. Job opportunities will be best for individuals with experience using computers and digital technology.

Earnings

Earnings of photographic process workers vary greatly depending on skill level, experience, and geographic location. Median hourly earnings for photographic process workers were $9.72 in 2002. The middle 50 percent earned between $7.84 and $13.08. The lowest 10 percent earned less than $6.79, and the highest 10 percent earned more than $17.43. Median hourly earnings were $9.75 in

photofinishing laboratories, the largest employer of photographic process workers.

Median hourly earning for photographic processing machine operators were $9.05 in 2002. The middle 50 percent earned between $7.53 and $11.63. The lowest 10 percent earned less than $6.53, and the highest 10 percent earned more than $15.60. Median hourly earnings in the two industries employing the largest numbers of photographic processing machine operators were $10.15 in photofinishing laboratories and $7.20 in health and personal care stores.

Related Occupations

Photographic process workers and processing machine operators need specialized knowledge of the photo developing process. Other workers who apply specialized technical knowledge include clinical laboratory technologists and technicians, computer operators, jewelers and precious stone and metal workers, prepress technicians and workers, printing machine operators, and science technicians.

Sources of Additional Information

For information about employment opportunities in photographic laboratories and schools that offer degrees in photographic technology, contact:

➤ Photo Marketing Association International, 3000 Picture Place, Jackson, MI 49201.

Semiconductor Processors

(0*NET 51-9141.00)

Significant Points

● Employment is expected to decline over the next 10 years because of rising imports of computer chips and increasing automation of fabrication plants in this country.

● An associate degree in a relevant curriculum is increasingly required.

Nature of the Work

Electronic semiconductors—also known as computer chips, microchips, or integrated circuits—are the miniature but powerful brains of high-technology equipment. Semiconductors are composed of a myriad of tiny aluminum or copper lines and electric switches, which manipulate the flow of electrical current. Semiconductor processors are responsible for many of the steps necessary in the manufacture of each semiconductor that goes into personal computers, missile guidance systems, and a host of other electronic equipment.

Semiconductor processors manufacture semiconductors in disks of varying sizes, generally eight to twelve inches wide. These disks, called wafers, are thin slices of silicon on which the circuitry of the microchips is layered. Each wafer is eventually cut into dozens or scores of individual chips.

Semiconductor processors make wafers by means of photolithography, a printing process for creating patterns from photographic images. Operating automated equipment, workers imprint precise microscopic patterns of the circuitry on the wafers, etch out the patterns with acids, and replace the patterns with metals that conduct electricity. Then, the wafers receive a chemical bath to make them smooth, and the imprint process begins again on a new layer with the next pattern. Wafers usually have from 8 to 20 such layers of microscopic, three-dimensional circuitry.

Semiconductors are produced in semiconductor-fabricating plants, or "fabs." Within fabs, the manufacture and cutting of wafers to create semiconductors takes place in "cleanrooms"—production areas that must be kept free of any airborne matter, because the least bit of dust can damage a semiconductor. All semiconductor processors working in cleanrooms—both operators and technicians—must wear special lightweight outer garments known as "bunny suits." These garments fit over clothing to prevent lint and other particles from contaminating semiconductor-processing worksites.

Operators, who make up the majority of the workers in cleanrooms, start and monitor the sophisticated equipment that performs the various tasks during the many steps of the semiconductor production sequence. They spend a great deal of time at computer terminals, monitoring the operation of the equipment to ensure that each of the tasks in the production of the wafer is performed correctly. Operators also may transfer wafer carriers from one development station to the next; in newer fabs, the lifting of heavy wafer carriers and the constant monitoring for quality control are increasingly being automated.

Once begun, the production of semiconductor wafers is continuous. Operators work to the pace of the machinery that has largely automated the production process. Operators are responsible for keeping the automated machinery within proper operating parameters.

Technicians account for a smaller percentage of the workers in cleanrooms, but they troubleshoot production problems and make equipment adjustments and repairs. They also take the lead in assuring quality control and in maintaining equipment. To keep equipment repairs to a minimum, technicians perform diagnostic analyses and run computations. For example, technicians may determine if a flaw in a chip is due to contamination, and peculiar to that wafer, or if the flaw is inherent in the manufacturing process.

Working Conditions

The work pace in cleanrooms is deliberately slow. Limited movement keeps the air in cleanrooms as free as possible of dust and other particles, which can destroy semiconductors during their production. Because the machinery sets operators' rate of work in the largely automated production process, workers maintain an easygoing pace. Although workers spend some time alone monitoring equipment, operators and technicians spend much of their time working in teams.

Technicians are on their feet most of the day, walking through the cleanroom to oversee production activities. Operators spend a great deal of time sitting or standing at workstations, monitoring computer readouts and gauges. Sometimes, they must retrieve wafers from one station and take them to another.

The temperature in the cleanrooms must be kept within a narrow range: usually, it is set at a comfortable 72 degrees Fahrenheit. Although bunny suits cover virtually the entire body, except perhaps the eyes (over which workers wear protective glasses), their lightweight fabric keeps the temperature inside fairly comfortable as well. Entry and exit of workers in bunny suits from the cleanroom are controlled to minimize contamination, and workers must be reclothed in a clean suit and decontaminated each time they return to the cleanroom.

Several highly toxic chemicals are used at various points in the process of manufacturing semiconductors. Workers who are exposed to such chemicals can be harmed. However, semiconductor fabrication plants are designed with safeguards to ensure that these chemicals are handled, used, and disposed of without exposure to workers or the surrounding environment. Toxic chemicals are applied to wafers by computer-controlled machine tools in sealed chambers and there is normally little risk of workers coming into contact with them.

Semiconductor-fabricating plants operate around the clock. For this reason, night and weekend work is common. In some plants, workers maintain standard 8-hour shifts, 5 days a week. In other plants, employees are on duty for 12-hour shifts to minimize the disruption of cleanroom operations brought about by changes in shift. In some plants, managers allow workers to alternate schedules, thereby distributing the "graveyard" shift equitably.

Employment

Electronic semiconductor processors held approximately 46,000 jobs in 2002. Nearly all of them were employed in facilities that manufacture semiconductors and other electronic components and accessories, though a small percentage worked in plants that primarily manufacture computers and office equipment.

Training, Other Qualifications, and Advancement

People interested in becoming semiconductor processors—either operators or technicians—need a solid background in mathematics and the physical sciences. In addition to applying these disciplines to the complex manufacturing processes performed in fabs, math

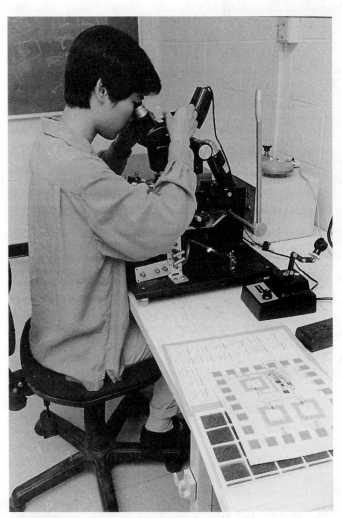

Semiconductor processors increasingly need at least an associate degree.

and science knowledge are essentials for pursuing higher education in semiconductor technology—and knowledge of both subjects is one of the best ways to advance in the semiconductor fabricating field.

Semiconductor processor workers must also be able to think analytically and critically to anticipate problems and avoid costly mistakes. Communication skills also are vital, as workers must be able to convey their thoughts and ideas both orally and in writing.

A high school diploma or equivalent is the minimum requirement for entry-level operator jobs in semiconductor fabrication plants. However, employers increasingly prefer persons who have completed associate degree programs for semiconductor processor jobs. While completion of a 1-year certificate program in semiconductor technology offered by some community colleges is an asset for most processor jobs, technicians must have at least an associate degree in electronics technology or a related field.

Degree or certificate candidates who get hands-on training while attending school look even more attractive to prospective employers. Semiconductor technology programs in a growing number of community colleges include an internship at a semiconductor fabricating plant; many students in these programs already hold full- or part-time jobs in the industry and work toward degrees in semiconductor technology in their spare time to update their skills or qualify for promotion to technician jobs. In addition, to ensure that operators and technicians keep their skills current, many employers provide 40 hours of formal training annually. Some employers also provide financial assistance to employees who want to earn associate and bachelor's degrees. Summer and part-time employment provide another option for getting started in the field for those who live near a semiconductor processing plant. Students often are hired to work during the summer, and some students are allowed to continue working part time during the school year. Students in summer and part-time semiconductor processor jobs learn what education they need to prosper in the field. They also gain valuable experience that may lead to full-time employment after graduation.

Some semiconductor processing technicians transfer to sales engineer jobs with suppliers of the machines that manufacture the semiconductors or become field support personnel.

Job Outlook

Between 2002 and 2012, employment of semiconductor processors is projected to decline. The two main reasons for this reversal are much higher productivity and rising imports. Companies are upgrading many of their older fabs to make larger 12" wafers, which produce twice as many chips as fabs making 8" wafers. These plants also are more automated, allowing them to sharply increase production with the same number of workers. A number of domestic companies also are building more fabs overseas, where costs are lower. In addition, imports of semiconductors from non-U.S. companies are on the rise and should continue to increase throughout the decade. Besides the creation of new jobs, additional openings will result from the need to replace workers who leave the occupation.

Despite the expected decline in employment of semiconductor processors, the demand for semiconductor chips remains very high stemming from the many existing and future applications for semiconductors in computers, appliances, machinery, biotechnology, vehicles, cell phones and other telecommunications devices, and other equipment. Moreover, the advent of the new 64-bit microchip is expected to provide the power of computer servers or workstations, onto desktop computers and open up a wealth of new applications, particularly in medical devices.

Industry development of semiconductors made from better materials means that semiconductors will become even smaller, more powerful, and more durable. For example, the industry has begun producing a new generation of microchips made with copper rather than aluminum wires, which will better conduct electricity. Also, technology to develop chips based on plastic, rather than on silicon, will make computers durable enough to be used in a variety of applications in which they could not easily have been used previously.

Job prospects will be best for people with postsecondary education in electronics or semiconductor technology.

Earnings

Median hourly earnings of electronic semiconductor processors were $13.14 in 2002. The middle 50 percent earned between $10.76 and $16.39 an hour. The lowest 10 percent earned less than $9.28, and the top 10 percent earned more than $20.35 an hour.

Technicians with an associate degree in electronics or semiconductor technology generally start at higher salaries than those with less education. Between a fourth and a half of all electronic semiconductor processors belong to a union, considerably higher than the rate for all occupations.

Related Occupations

Electronic semiconductor processors do production work that resembles the work of precision assemblers and fabricators of electrical and electronic equipment. Also, many electronic semiconductor processors have academic training in semiconductor technology, which emphasizes scientific and engineering principles. Other occupations that require some college or postsecondary vocational training emphasizing such principles are engineering technicians, electrical and electronics engineers, and science technicians.

Sources of Additional Information

For more information on semiconductor processor careers, contact:

➤ Semiconductor Industry Association, 181 Metro Dr., Suite 450, San Jose, CA 95110. Internet: **http://www.semichips.org**

➤ Maricopa Advanced Technology Education Center (MATEC), 2323 West 14th St., Suite 540, Tempe, AZ 85281. Internet: **http://matec.org/ops/career.shtml**

Transporation and Material Moving Occupations

Air Transportation Occupations

Aircraft Pilots and Flight Engineers

(O*NET 53-2011.00, 53-2012.00)

Significant Points

- The best opportunities for jobs will be with the regional airlines and business aviation.
- Pilots usually start with smaller commuter and regional airlines to acquire the experience needed to qualify for higher paying jobs with national airlines.
- Most pilots traditionally have learned to fly in the military, but growing numbers have college degrees with flight training from civilian flying schools that are certified by the Federal Aviation Administration (FAA).

Nature of the Work

Pilots are highly trained professionals who fly airplanes and helicopters to carry out a wide variety of tasks. Most are *airline pilots, copilots, and flight engineers* who transport passengers and cargo, but 1 out of 5 pilots is a *commercial pilot* involved in more unusual tasks, such as dusting crops, spreading seed for reforestation, testing aircraft, flying passengers and cargo to areas not served by regular airlines, directing firefighting efforts, tracking criminals, monitoring traffic, and rescuing and evacuating injured persons.

Except on small aircraft, two pilots usually make up the cockpit crew. Generally, the most experienced pilot, the *captain*, is in command and supervises all other crew members. The pilot and the copilot, often called the first officer, share flying and other duties, such as communicating with air traffic controllers and monitoring the instruments. Some large aircraft have a third pilot—the *flight engineer*—who assists the other pilots by monitoring and operating many of the instruments and systems, making minor in-flight repairs, and watching for other aircraft. New technology can perform many flight tasks, however, and virtually all new aircraft now fly with only two pilots, who rely more heavily on computerized controls.

Before departure, pilots plan their flights carefully. They thoroughly check their aircraft to make sure that the engines, controls, instruments, and other systems are functioning properly. They also make sure that baggage or cargo has been loaded correctly. They confer with flight dispatchers and aviation weather forecasters to find out about weather conditions en route and at their destination. Based on this information, they choose a route, altitude, and speed that will provide the fastest, safest, and smoothest flight. When flying under instrument flight rules—procedures governing the operation of the aircraft when there is poor visibility—the pilot in command, or the company dispatcher, normally files an instrument flight plan with air traffic control so that the flight can be coordinated with other air traffic.

Takeoff and landing are the most difficult parts of the flight, and require close coordination between the pilot and first officer. For example, as the plane accelerates for takeoff, the pilot concentrates on the runway while the first officer scans the instrument panel. To calculate the speed they must attain to become airborne, pilots consider the altitude of the airport, outside temperature, weight of the plane, and speed and direction of the wind. The moment the plane reaches takeoff speed, the first officer informs the pilot, who then pulls back on the controls to raise the nose of the plane.

Unless the weather is bad, the actual flight is relatively easy. Airplane pilots, with the assistance of autopilot and the flight management computer, steer the plane along their planned route and are monitored by the air traffic control stations they pass along the way. They regularly scan the instrument panel to check their fuel supply, the condition of their engines, and the air-conditioning, hydraulic, and other systems. Pilots may request a change in altitude or route if circumstances dictate. For example, if the ride is rougher than expected, they may ask air traffic control if pilots flying at other altitudes have reported better conditions. If so, they may request an altitude change. This procedure also may be used to find a stronger tailwind or a weaker headwind to save fuel and increase speed.

In contrast, helicopters are used for short trips at relatively low altitude, so pilots must be constantly on the lookout for trees, bridges, powerlines, transmission towers, and other dangerous obstacles. Regardless of the type of aircraft, all pilots must monitor warning devices designed to help detect sudden shifts in wind conditions that can cause crashes.

Pilots must rely completely on their instruments when visibility is poor. On the basis of altimeter readings, they know how high above ground they are and whether they can fly safely over mountains and other obstacles. Special navigation radios give pilots precise information that, with the help of special maps, tells them their exact position. Other very sophisticated equipment provides directions to a point just above the end of a runway and enables pilots to land completely "blind." Once on the ground, pilots must complete records on their flight for their organization and the FAA report.

The number of nonflying duties that pilots have depends on the employment setting. Airline pilots have the services of large support staffs, and consequently, perform few nonflying duties. Pilots employed by other organizations such as charter operators or businesses have many other duties. They may load the aircraft, handle all passenger luggage to ensure a balanced load, and supervise refueling; other nonflying responsibilities include keeping records, scheduling flights, arranging for major maintenance, and performing minor aircraft maintenance and repairwork.

Some pilots are instructors. They teach their students the principles of flight in ground-school classes and demonstrate how to operate aircraft in dual-controlled planes and helicopters. A few specially trained pilots are "examiners" or "check pilots." They periodically fly with other pilots or pilot's license applicants to make sure that they are proficient.

One in five pilots is a commercial pilot who performs a wide range of tasks, such as crop-dusting, firefighting, traffic monitoring, and policing from the air.

Working Conditions

By law, airline pilots cannot fly more than 100 hours a month or more than 1,000 hours a year. Most airline pilots fly an average of 75 hours a month and work an additional 75 hours a month performing nonflying duties. Most pilots have a variable work schedule, working several days on, then several days off. Most spend a considerable amount of time away from home because the majority of flights involve overnight layovers. When pilots are away from home, the airlines provide hotel accommodations, transportation between the hotel and airport, and an allowance for meals and other expenses. Airlines operate flights at all hours of the day and night, so work schedules often are irregular. Flight assignments are based on seniority.

Commercial pilots also may have irregular schedules, flying 30 hours one month and 90 hours the next. Because these pilots frequently have many nonflying responsibilities, they have much less free time than do airline pilots. Except for business pilots, most do not remain away from home overnight. They may work odd hours. Flight instructors may have irregular and seasonal work schedules, depending on their students' available time and the weather. Instructors frequently work in the evening or on weekends.

Airline pilots, especially those on international routes, often suffer jet lag—fatigue caused by many hours of flying through different time zones. To guard against excessive pilot fatigue that could result in unsafe flying conditions, the FAA requires airlines to allow pilots at least 8 hours of uninterrupted rest in the 24 hours before finishing their flight duty. The work of test pilots, who check the flight performance of new and experimental planes, may be dangerous. Pilots who are crop dusters may be exposed to toxic chemicals and seldom have the benefit of a regular landing strip. Helicopter pilots involved in rescue and police work may be subject to personal injury.

Although flying does not involve much physical effort, the mental stress of being responsible for a safe flight, regardless of the weather, can be tiring. Pilots must be alert and quick to react if something goes wrong, particularly during takeoff and landing.

Employment

Civilian aircraft pilots and flight engineers held about 100,000 jobs in 2002. About 79,000 worked as airline pilots, copilots, and flight engineers. The remainder were commercial pilots who worked as flight instructors at local airports or for large businesses that fly company cargo and executives in their own airplanes or helicopters.

Some commercial pilots flew small planes for air-taxi companies, usually to or from lightly traveled airports not served by major airlines. Others worked for a variety of businesses, performing tasks such as dusting crops, inspecting pipelines, or conducting sightseeing trips. Federal, State, and local governments also employed pilots. A few pilots were self-employed.

Pilots are located across the country, but airline pilots usually are based near major metropolitan airports or airports operating as hubs for the major airlines.

Training, Other Qualifications, and Advancement

All pilots who are paid to transport passengers or cargo must have a commercial pilot's license with an instrument rating issued by the FAA. Helicopter pilots must hold a commercial pilot's certificate with a helicopter rating. To qualify for these licenses, applicants must be at least 18 years old and have at least 250 hours of flight experience. The experience required can be reduced through participation in certain flight school curricula approved by the FAA. Applicants also must pass a strict physical examination to make sure that they are in good health and have 20/20 vision with or without glasses, good hearing, and no physical handicaps that could impair their performance. They must pass a written test that includes questions on the principles of safe flight, navigation techniques, and FAA regulations, and must demonstrate their flying ability to FAA or designated examiners.

To fly during periods of low visibility, pilots must be rated by the FAA to fly by instruments. Pilots may qualify for this rating by having 105 hours of flight experience, including 40 hours of experience in flying by instruments; they also must pass a written examination on procedures and FAA regulations covering instrument flying and demonstrate to an examiner their ability to fly by instruments.

Airline pilots must fulfill additional requirements. Pilots must have an airline transport pilot's license. Applicants for this license must be at least 23 years old and have a minimum of 1,500 hours of flying experience, including night and instrument flying, and must pass FAA written and flight examinations. Usually, they also have one or more advanced ratings, such as multiengine aircraft or aircraft-type ratings, dependent upon the requirements of their particular flying jobs. Because pilots must be able to make quick decisions and accurate judgments under pressure, many airline companies reject applicants who do not pass required psychological and aptitude tests. All licenses are valid so long as a pilot can pass the periodic physical and eye examinations and tests of flying skills required by Federal Government and company regulations.

The U.S. Armed Forces have always been an important source of trained pilots for civilian jobs. Military pilots gain valuable experience on jet aircraft and helicopters, and persons with this experience usually are preferred for civilian pilot jobs. This primarily reflects the extensive flying time military pilots receive. Persons without Armed Forces training may become pilots by attending flight schools or by taking lessons from individual FAA-certified flight instructors. The FAA has certified about 600 civilian flying schools, including some colleges and universities that offer degree credit for pilot training. Over the projection period, trained pilots leaving the military are not expected to increase very much in number as the need for pilots grows in civilian aviation. As a result, FAA-certified schools will train a larger share of pilots than in the past.

Although some small airlines will hire high school graduates, most airlines require at least 2 years of college and prefer to hire college graduates. In fact, most entrants to this occupation have a college degree. Because the number of college educated applicants continues to increase, many employers are making a college degree an educational requirement.

Depending on the type of aircraft, new airline pilots start as first officers or flight engineers. Although some airlines favor applicants who already have a flight engineer's license, they may provide flight engineer training for those who have only the commercial license. Many pilots begin with smaller regional or commuter airlines, where they obtain experience flying passengers on scheduled flights into busy airports in all weather conditions. These jobs often lead to higher paying jobs with bigger, national airlines.

Initial training for airline pilots includes a week of company indoctrination, 3 to 6 weeks of ground school and simulator training, and 25 hours of initial operating experience, including a check-ride with an FAA aviation safety inspector. Once trained and "on the line," pilots are required to attend recurrent training and simulator checks twice a year throughout their career.

Organizations other than airlines usually require less flying experience. However, a commercial pilot's license is a minimum requirement, and employers prefer applicants who have experience in the type of craft they will be flying. New employees usually start as first officers, or fly less sophisticated equipment. Test pilots often are required to have an engineering degree.

Advancement for all pilots usually is limited to other flying jobs. Many pilots start as flight instructors, building up their flying hours while they earn money teaching. As they become more experienced, these pilots occasionally fly charter planes or perhaps get jobs with small air transportation firms, such as air-taxi companies. Some advance to flying corporate planes. A small number get flight engineer jobs with the airlines.

In the airlines, advancement usually depends on seniority provisions of union contracts. After 1 to 5 years, flight engineers advance according to seniority to first officer and, after 5 to 15 years, to captain. Seniority also determines which pilots get the more desirable routes. In a nonairline job, a first officer may advance to pilot and, in large companies, to chief pilot or director of aviation in charge of aircraft scheduling, maintenance, and flight procedures.

Job Outlook

The passenger airline industry is undergoing many changes, with some airlines posting increases in passenger traffic and adding routes while others are cutting back. Overall, the employment of aircraft pilots is projected to increase about as fast as average for all occupations through 2012. In the long run, demand for air travel is expected to track increases in the population and growth of the economy. In the short run, however, employment of pilots is generally sensitive to cyclical swings in the economy. During recessions, when a decline in the demand for air travel forces airlines to curtail the number of flights, airlines may temporarily furlough some pilots.

After September 11, 2001, air travel was severely depressed. A number of the major airlines were forced to reduce schedules, layoff pilots, and even declare bankruptcy. At the same time, hiring continued at regional and low-fare airlines. It is expected that job opportunities will continue to be better with the regional airlines and low-fare carriers, which are growing faster than the more well-known major airlines. Opportunities with air cargo carriers also are expected to be good due to increasing security requirements for shipping freight on passenger airlines and growth in e-business.

Pilots attempting to get jobs at the major airlines will face strong competition, as those firms tend to attract many more applicants than they have jobs. They also will have to compete with laid off pilots for any available jobs. Pilots who have logged the greatest number of flying hours in the more sophisticated equipment typically have the best prospects. For this reason, military pilots often have an advantage over other applicants. However, prior to September 11, 2001, some airlines reported a shortage of qualified pilots to operate the most sophisticated aircraft. Thus, when hiring improves, jobseekers with the most FAA licenses will have a competitive advantage. Opportunities for pilot jobs should be better at smaller airlines and in corporate travel.

The number of flight engineers is projected to decline through 2012 as new planes needing only two pilots replace older planes that required flight engineers. Pilots also will experience some productivity improvements as airlines switch to larger planes and adopt the low-fare carrier model that emphasizes faster turnaround times for flights, keeping more pilots in the air rather than waiting on the ground.

Earnings

Earnings of aircraft pilots and flight engineers vary greatly depending whether they work as airline or commercial pilots. Earnings of airline pilots are among the highest in the Nation, and depend on factors such as the type, size, and maximum speed of the plane and the number of hours and miles flown. For example, pilots who fly jet aircraft usually earn higher salaries than do pilots who fly turboprops. Airline pilots and flight engineers may earn extra pay for night and international flights. In 2002, median annual earnings of airline pilots, copilots, and flight engineers were $109,580. The lowest 10 percent earned less than $55,800. More than 25 percent earned over $145,000.

Median annual earnings of commercial pilots were $47,970 in 2002. The middle 50 percent earned between $33,830 and $70,140. The lowest 10 percent earned less than $26,100, and the highest 10 percent earned more than $101,460.

Airline pilots usually are eligible for life and health insurance plans financed by the airlines. They also receive retirement benefits and, if they fail the FAA physical examination at some point in their careers, they get disability payments. In addition, pilots receive an expense allowance, or "per diem," for every hour they are away from home. Some airlines also provide allowances to pilots for purchasing and cleaning their uniforms. As an additional benefit, pilots and their immediate families usually are entitled to free or reduced-fare transportation on their own and other airlines.

More than half of all aircraft pilots are members of unions. Most of the pilots who fly for the major airlines are members of the Airline Pilots Association, International, but those employed by one major airline are members of the Allied Pilots Association. Some flight engineers are members of the Flight Engineers' International Association.

Related Occupations

Although they are not in the cockpit, air traffic controllers and airfield operation specialists also play an important role in making sure flights are safe and on schedule, and participate in many of the decisions that pilots must make.

Sources of Additional Information

Information about job opportunities, salaries for a particular airline, and qualifications required may be obtained by writing to the personnel manager of the airline.

For information on airline pilots, contact:

➤ Air Line Pilots Association, 533 Herndon Parkway, Herndon, VA 22070..

➤ Air Transport Association of America, Inc., 1301 Pennsylvania Ave. NW., Suite 1100, Washington, DC 20004.

For information on helicopter pilots, contact:

➤ Helicopter Association International, 1635 Prince Street, Alexandria, VA 22314.

For information about job opportunities in companies other than airlines, consult the classified section of aviation trade magazines and apply to companies that operate aircraft at local airports.

Air Traffic Controllers

(O*NET 53-2021.00)

Significant Points

- Nearly all air traffic controllers are employed by the Federal Aviation Administration, part of the Federal Government.

- Large numbers of air traffic controllers will be eligible to retire over the next decade, potentially creating many job openings.

- Aircraft controllers earn relatively high pay and have good benefits.

Nature of the Work

The air traffic control system is a vast network of people and equipment that ensures the safe operation of commercial and private aircraft. Air traffic controllers coordinate the movement of air traffic to make certain that planes stay a safe distance apart. Their immediate concern is safety, but controllers also must direct planes efficiently to minimize delays. Some regulate airport traffic; others regulate flights between airports.

Although *airport tower* or *terminal controllers* watch over all planes traveling through the airport's airspace, their main responsibility is to organize the flow of aircraft into and out of the airport. Relying on radar and visual observation, they closely monitor each plane to ensure a safe distance between all aircraft and to guide pilots between the hangar or ramp and the end of the airport's airspace. In addition, controllers keep pilots informed about changes in weather conditions such as wind shear—a sudden change in the velocity or direction of the wind that can cause the pilot to lose control of the aircraft.

During arrival or departure, several controllers direct each plane. As a plane approaches an airport, the pilot radios ahead to inform the terminal of the plane's presence. The controller in the radar room, just beneath the control tower, has a copy of the plane's flight plan and already has observed the plane on radar. If the path is clear, the controller directs the pilot to a runway; if the airport is busy, the plane is fitted into a traffic pattern with other aircraft waiting to land. As the plane nears the runway, the pilot is asked to contact the tower. There, another controller, who also is watching the plane on radar, monitors the aircraft the last mile or so to the runway, delaying any departures that would interfere with the plane's landing. Once the plane has landed, a ground controller in the tower directs it along the taxiways to its assigned gate. The ground controller usually works entirely by sight, but may use radar if visibility is very poor.

The procedure is reversed for departures. The ground controller directs the plane to the proper runway. The local controller then informs the pilot about conditions at the airport, such as weather, speed and direction of wind, and visibility. The local controller also issues runway clearance for the pilot to take off. Once in the air, the plane is guided out of the airport's airspace by the departure controller.

After each plane departs, airport tower controllers notify *enroute controllers* who will next take charge. There are 21 air route traffic control centers located around the country, each employing 300 to 700 controllers, with more than 150 on duty during peak hours at the busier facilities. Airplanes usually fly along designated routes; each center is assigned a certain airspace containing many different routes. Enroute controllers work in teams of up to three members,

depending on how heavy traffic is; each team is responsible for a section of the center's airspace. A team, for example, might be responsible for all planes that are between 30 to 100 miles north of an airport and flying at an altitude between 6,000 and 18,000 feet.

To prepare for planes about to enter the team's airspace, the radar associate controller organizes flight plans coming off a printer. If two planes are scheduled to enter the team's airspace at nearly the same time, location, and altitude, this controller may arrange with the preceding control unit for one plane to change its flight path. The previous unit may have been another team at the same or an adjacent center, or a departure controller at a neighboring terminal. As a plane approaches a team's airspace, the radar controller accepts responsibility for the plane from the previous controlling unit. The controller also delegates responsibility for the plane to the next controlling unit when the plane leaves the team's airspace.

The radar controller, who is the senior team member, observes the planes in the team's airspace on radar and communicates with the pilots when necessary. Radar controllers warn pilots about nearby planes, bad weather conditions, and other potential hazards. Two planes on a collision course will be directed around each other. If a pilot wants to change altitude in search of better flying conditions, the controller will check to determine that no other planes will be along the proposed path. As the flight progresses, the team responsible for the aircraft notifies the next team in charge of the airspace ahead. Through team coordination, the plane arrives safely at its destination.

Both airport tower and enroute controllers usually control several planes at a time; often, they have to make quick decisions about completely different activities. For example, a controller might direct a plane on its landing approach and at the same time provide pilots entering the airport's airspace with information about conditions at the airport. While instructing these pilots, the controller also would observe other planes in the vicinity, such as those in a holding pattern waiting for permission to land, to ensure that they remain well separated.

Some air traffic controllers regulate airport traffic, while others regulate flights between airports.

In addition to airport towers and enroute centers, air traffic controllers also work in flight service stations operated at more than 100 locations. These *flight service specialists* provide pilots with information on the station's particular area, including terrain, preflight and inflight weather information, suggested routes, and other information important to the safety of a flight. Flight service station specialists help pilots in emergency situations and initiate and coordinate searches for missing or overdue aircraft. However, they are not involved in actively managing air traffic.

Some air traffic controllers work at the Federal Aviation Administration's (FAA) Air Traffic Control Systems Command Center in Herndon, Virginia, where they oversee the entire system. They look for situations that will create bottlenecks or other problems in the system, then respond with a management plan for traffic into and out of the troubled sector. The objective is to keep traffic levels in the trouble spots manageable for the controllers working at enroute centers.

Currently, the FAA is implementing a new automated air traffic control system, called the National Airspace System (NAS) Architecture. The NAS Architecture is a long-term strategic plan that will allow controllers to more efficiently deal with the demands of increased air traffic. It encompasses the replacement of aging equipment and the introduction of new systems, technologies, and procedures to enhance safety and security and support future aviation growth.

Working Conditions

Controllers work a basic 40-hour week; however, they may work additional hours for which they receive overtime pay or equal time off. Because most control towers and centers operate 24 hours a day, 7 days a week, controllers rotate night and weekend shifts.

During busy times, controllers must work rapidly and efficiently. Total concentration is required to keep track of several planes at the same time and to make certain that all pilots receive correct instructions. The mental stress of being responsible for the safety of several aircraft and their passengers can be exhausting for some persons.

Employment

Air traffic controllers held about 26,000 jobs in 2002. The vast majority were employed by the FAA, which is part of the Federal Government. Air traffic controllers work at airports—in towers and flight service stations—and in air route traffic control centers. Some professional controllers conduct research at the FAA's national experimental center near Atlantic City, New Jersey. Others serve as instructors at the FAA Academy in Oklahoma City, Oklahoma. A small number of civilian controllers work for the U.S. Department of Defense. In addition to controllers employed by the Federal Government, some work for private air traffic control companies providing service to non-FAA towers.

Training, Other Qualifications, and Advancement

To become an air traffic controller, a person must enroll in an FAA-approved education program and pass a pre-employment test that measures his or her ability to learn the controller's duties in order to qualify for job openings in the air traffic control system. Exceptions are air traffic controllers with prior experience and military veterans. The pre-employment test is currently offered only to students in the FAA Air Traffic Collegiate Training Initiative (AT-CTI) Program or the Minneapolis Community & Technical College, Air Traffic Control Training Program. In addition, applicants must have 3 years of full-time work experience or 4 years of college, or a combination of both. In combining education and experience, 1 year of undergraduate study (30 semester or 45 quarter hours) is equivalent to 9 months of work experience.

Upon successful completion of an FAA-approved program, individuals who receive school recommendation and who meet the basic qualification requirements, including age limit and achievement of a qualifying score on the FAA authorized pre-employment test, become eligible for employment as an air traffic controller. Candidates also must pass a medical exam, drug screening, and security clearance before they can be hired.

Upon selection, employees attend the FAA Academy in Oklahoma City for 12 weeks of training, during which they learn the fundamentals of the airway system, FAA regulations, controller equipment, and aircraft performance characteristics, as well as more specialized tasks.

After graduation, it takes several years of progressively more responsible work experience, interspersed with considerable classroom instruction and independent study, to become a fully qualified controller. Controllers who fail to complete either the academy or the on-the-job portion of the training usually are dismissed. Controllers must pass a physical examination each year and a job performance examination twice each year. Failure to become certified in any position at a facility within a specified time also may result in dismissal. Controllers also are subject to drug screening as a condition of continuing employment.

Air traffic controllers must be articulate, because pilots must be given directions quickly and clearly. Intelligence and a good memory also are important because controllers constantly receive information that they must immediately grasp, interpret, and remember. Decisiveness also is required because controllers often have to make quick decisions. The ability to concentrate is crucial because controllers must make these decisions in the midst of noise and other distractions.

At airports, new controllers begin by supplying pilots with basic flight data and airport information. They then advance to the position of ground controller, then local controller, departure controller, and, finally, arrival controller. At an air route traffic control center, new controllers first deliver printed flight plans to teams, gradually advancing to radar associate controller and then radar controller.

Controllers can transfer to jobs at different locations or advance to supervisory positions, including management or staff jobs in air traffic control and top administrative jobs in the FAA. However, there are only limited opportunities for a controller to switch from a position in an enroute center to a tower.

Job Outlook

Employment of air traffic controllers is expected to grow about as fast as the average through the year 2012. Increasing air traffic will require more controllers to handle the additional work. Employment growth, however, is not expected to keep pace with growth in the number of aircraft flying because of the increasing automation of the air traffic control system and Federal budget constraints. New computerized systems will assist the controller by automatically making many of the routine decisions. This will allow controllers to handle more traffic, thus increasing their productivity. Federal budget constraints also may limit hiring of air traffic controllers.

More job openings are expected due to replacement needs. The majority of today's air traffic controllers will be eligible to retire over the next decade, although not all are expected to do so. Nevertheless, replacement needs will be substantial and will result in hundreds of job opportunities each year for those graduating from the FAA training programs. Despite the increasing number of jobs coming open, competition to get into the FAA training programs is expected to remain keen, as there generally are many more applicants to get into the schools than there are openings. But those that graduate have good prospects of getting a job as a controller.

Air traffic controllers who continue to meet the proficiency and medical requirements enjoy more job security than do most workers. The demand for air travel and the workloads of air traffic controllers decline during recessions, but controllers seldom are laid off.

Earnings
Median annual earnings of air traffic controllers in 2002 were $91,600. The middle 50 percent earned between $65,480 and $112,550. The lowest 10 percent earned less than $46,410, and the highest 10 percent earned more than $131,610.

The average annual salary, excluding overtime earnings, for air traffic controllers in the Federal Government—which employs 90 percent of the total—in nonsupervisory, supervisory, and managerial positions was $95,700 in 2002. Both the worker's job responsibilities and the complexity of the particular facility determine a controller's pay. For example, controllers who work at the FAA's busiest air traffic control facilities earn higher pay.

Depending on length of service, air traffic controllers receive 13 to 26 days of paid vacation and 13 days of paid sick leave each year, life insurance, and health benefits. In addition, controllers can retire at an earlier age and with fewer years of service than other Federal employees. Air traffic controllers are eligible to retire at age 50 with 20 years of service as an active air traffic controller or after 25 years of active service at any age. There is a mandatory retirement age of 56 for controllers who manage air traffic. However, Federal law provides for exemptions to the mandatory age of 56, up to age 61, for controllers having exceptional skills and experience.

Related Occupations
Airfield operations specialists also are involved in the direction and control of traffic in air transportation.

Sources of Additional Information
For further information on how to qualify and apply for a job as an air traffic controller, contact
➤ Federal Aviation Administration, 800 Independence Ave., SW., Washington, DC 20591. Internet: **http:www.faa.gov**

Motor Vehicle Operators

Bus Drivers

(0*NET 53-3021.00, 53-3022.00)

Significant Points
● Opportunities should be good, particularly for schoolbus driver jobs.
● A commercial driver's license is required to operate a bus.
● Work schedules vary considerably among various types of bus drivers.
● Bus drivers must possess strong customer service skills, including communication skills and the ability to manage large groups of people with varying needs.

Nature of the Work
Every day, millions of Americans every day leave the driving to bus drivers. Bus drivers are essential in providing passengers with an alternative to their automobiles or other forms of transportation. Intercity bus drivers transport people between regions of a State or of the country; local-transit bus drivers do so within a metropolitan area or county; motor coach drivers take customers on charter excursions and tours; and schoolbus drivers take children to and from schools and related events.

Drivers pick up and drop off passengers at bus stops, stations, or, in the case of students, at regularly scheduled neighborhood locations based on strict time schedules. Drivers must operate vehicles safely, especially when traffic is heavier than normal. However, they cannot let light traffic put them ahead of schedule so that they miss passengers.

Local-transit and *intercity bus drivers* report to their assigned terminal or garage, where they stock up on tickets or transfers and prepare trip report forms. In some transportation firms, maintenance departments are responsible for keeping vehicles in good condition. In others, drivers may check their vehicle's tires, brakes,

windshield wipers, lights, oil, fuel, and water supply before beginning their routes. Drivers usually verify that the bus has safety equipment, such as fire extinguishers, first aid kits, and emergency reflectors in case of an emergency.

During the course of their shift, local-transit and intercity bus drivers collect fares; answer questions about schedules, routes, and transfer points; and sometimes announce stops. Intercity bus drivers may make only a single one-way trip to a distant city or a round trip each day. They may stop at towns just a few miles apart or only at large cities hundreds of miles apart. Local-transit bus drivers may make several trips each day over the same city and suburban streets, stopping as frequently as every few blocks.

Local-transit bus drivers submit daily trip reports with a record of trips, significant schedule delays, and mechanical problems. Intercity drivers who drive across State or national boundaries must comply with U.S. Department of Transportation regulations. These include completing vehicle inspection reports and recording distances traveled and the periods they spend driving, performing other duties, and off duty.

Motorcoach drivers transport passengers on charter trips and sightseeing tours. Drivers routinely interact with customers and tour guides to make the trip as comfortable and informative as possible. They are directly responsible for keeping to strict schedules, adhering to the guidelines of the tours' itinerary, and ensuring the overall success of the trip. These drivers act as customer service representative, tour guide, program director, and safety guide. Trips frequently last more than 1 day. The driver may be away for more than a week if assigned to an extended tour. As with all drivers who drive across State or national boundaries, motorcoach drivers must comply with Department of Transportation regulations.

Schoolbus drivers usually drive the same routes each day, stopping to pick up pupils in the morning and return them to their homes in the afternoon. Some schoolbus drivers also transport students and teachers on field trips or to sporting events. In addition to driving, some schoolbus drivers work part time in the school system as janitors, mechanics, or classroom assistants when not driving buses.

Drivers must operate vehicles safely and still try to maintain their schedule.

Bus drivers must be alert in order to prevent accidents, especially in heavy traffic or in bad weather, and to avoid sudden stops or swerves that jar passengers. Schoolbus drivers must exercise particular caution when children are getting on or off the bus. They must maintain order on their bus and enforce school safety standards by allowing only students to board. In addition, they must know and enforce rules regarding student conduct used throughout the school system.

Schoolbus drivers do not always have to report to an assigned terminal or garage. In some cases, they have the choice of taking their bus home, or parking it in a more convenient area. Schoolbus drivers do not collect fares. Instead, they prepare weekly reports on the number of students, trips or "runs," work hours, miles, and fuel consumption. Their supervisors set time schedules and routes for the day or week.

Working Conditions

Driving a bus through heavy traffic while dealing with passengers is more stressful and fatiguing than physically strenuous. Many drivers enjoy the opportunity to work without direct supervision, with full responsibility for their bus and passengers. To improve working conditions and retain drivers, many buslines provide ergonomically designed seats and controls for drivers.

Intercity bus drivers may work nights, weekends, and holidays and often spend nights away from home, during which they stay in hotels at company expense. Senior drivers with regular routes have regular weekly work schedules, but others do not have regular schedules and must be prepared to report for work on short notice. They report for work only when called for a charter assignment or to drive extra buses on a regular route. Intercity bus travel and charter work tends to be seasonal. From May through August, drivers may work the maximum number of hours per week that regulations allow. During winter, junior drivers may work infrequently, except for busy holiday travel periods, and may be furloughed at times.

Schoolbus drivers work only when school is in session. Many work 20 hours a week or less, driving one or two routes in the morning and afternoon. Drivers taking field or athletic trips, or who also have midday kindergarten routes, may work more hours a week. As more students with a variety of physical and behavioral disabilities assimilate into mainstream schools, schoolbus drivers must learn how to accommodate their special needs.

Regular local-transit bus drivers usually have a 5-day workweek; Saturdays and Sundays are considered regular workdays. Some

drivers work evenings and after midnight. To accommodate commuters, many work "split shifts," for example, 6 a.m. to 10 a.m. and 3 p.m. to 7 p.m., with time off in between.

Tour and charter bus drivers may work any day and all hours of the day, including weekends and holidays. Their hours are dictated by the charter trips booked and the schedule and prearranged itinerary of tours. However, like all bus drivers, their weekly hours must be consistent with the Department of Transportation's rules and regulations concerning hours of service. For example, a driver may drive for 10 hours and work for up to 15 hours—including driving and nondriving duties—before having 8 hours off-duty. A driver may not drive after having worked for 70 hours in the past 8 days. Most drivers are required to document their time in a logbook.

Employment

Bus drivers held about 654,000 jobs in 2002. Over one-third worked part time. More than two-thirds of all bus drivers were schoolbus drivers working primarily for school systems or for companies providing schoolbus services under contract. Most of the remainder worked for private and local government transit systems; some also worked for intercity and charter buslines.

Training, Other Qualifications, and Advancement

Bus driver qualifications and standards are established by State and Federal regulations. All drivers must comply with Federal regulations and with any State regulations that exceed Federal requirements. Federal regulations require drivers who operate commercial motor vehicles to hold a commercial driver's license (CDL) from the State in which they live.

To qualify for a commercial driver's license, applicants must pass a written test on rules and regulations and then demonstrate that they can operate a bus safely. A national databank permanently records all driving violations incurred by persons who hold commercial licenses. A State may not issue a commercial driver's license to a driver who has already had a license suspended or revoked in another State. A driver with a CDL must accompany trainees until the trainees get their own CDL. Information on how to apply for a commercial driver's license may be obtained from State motor vehicle administrations.

While many States allow those who are 18 years of age and older to drive buses within State borders, the Department of Transportation establishes minimum qualifications for bus drivers engaged in interstate commerce. Federal Motor Carrier Safety Regulations require drivers to be at least 21 years old and to pass a physical examination once every 2 years. The main physical requirements include good hearing, at least 20/40 vision with or without glasses or corrective lenses, and a 70-degree field of vision in each eye. Drivers must not be colorblind. They must be able to hear a forced whisper in one ear at not less than 5 feet, with or without a hearing aide. Drivers must have normal use of arms and legs and normal blood pressure. They may not use any controlled substances, unless prescribed by a licensed physician. Persons with epilepsy or diabetes controlled by insulin are not permitted to be interstate bus drivers. Federal regulations also require employers to test their drivers for alcohol and drug use as a condition of employment, and require periodic random tests of the drivers while they are on duty. In addition, a driver must not have been convicted of a felony involving the use of a motor vehicle; a crime involving drugs; driving under the influence of drugs or alcohol; or hit-and-run driving that resulted in injury or death. All drivers must be able to read and speak English well enough to read road signs, prepare reports, and communicate with law enforcement officers and the public. In addition, drivers must take a written examination on the Motor Carrier Safety Regulations of the U.S. Department of Transportation.

Many employers prefer high school graduates and require a written test of ability to follow complex bus schedules. Many intercity and public transit bus companies prefer applicants who are at least 24 years of age; some require several years of experience driving a bus or truck. In some States, schoolbus drivers must pass a background investigation to uncover any criminal record or history of mental problems.

Because bus drivers deal with passengers, they must be courteous. They need an even temperament and emotional stability because driving in heavy, fast-moving, or stop-and-go traffic and dealing with passengers can be stressful. Drivers must have strong customer service skills, including communication skills and the ability to coordinate and manage large groups of people.

Most intercity bus companies and local-transit systems give driver trainees 2 to 8 weeks of classroom and "behind-the-wheel" instruction. In the classroom, trainees learn Department of Transportation and company work rules, safety regulations, State and municipal driving regulations, and safe driving practices. They also learn to read schedules, determine fares, keep records, and deal courteously with passengers.

Schoolbus drivers also are required to obtain a commercial driver's license from the State in which they live. Many persons who become school bus drivers have never driven any vehicle larger than an automobile. They receive between 1 and 4 weeks of driving instruction plus classroom training on State and local laws, regulations, and policies of operating schoolbuses; safe driving practices; driver-pupil relations; first aid; special needs of disabled and emotionally troubled students; and emergency evacuation procedures. Schoolbus drivers also must be aware of the school system's rules for discipline and conduct for bus drivers and the students they transport.

During training, bus drivers practice driving on set courses. They practice turns and zigzag maneuvers, backing up, and driving in narrow lanes. Then, they drive in light traffic and, eventually, on congested highways and city streets. They also make trial runs, without passengers, to improve their driving skills and learn the routes. Local-transit trainees memorize and drive each of the runs operating out of their assigned garage. New drivers begin with a "break-in" period. They make regularly scheduled trips with passengers, accompanied by an experienced driver who gives helpful tips, answers questions, and evaluates the new driver's performance.

New intercity and local-transit drivers are usually placed on an "extra" list to drive charter runs, extra buses on regular runs, and special runs (for example, during morning and evening rush hours and to sports events). They also substitute for regular drivers who are ill or on vacation. New drivers remain on the extra list, and may work only part time, for perhaps several years, until they have enough seniority to be given a regular run.

Senior drivers may bid for the runs that they prefer, such as those with more work hours, lighter traffic, weekends off, or, in the case of intercity bus drivers, higher earnings or fewer workdays per week.

Opportunities for promotion are generally limited. However, experienced drivers may become supervisors or dispatchers, assigning buses to drivers, checking whether drivers are on schedule, rerouting buses to avoid blocked streets or other problems, and dispatching extra vehicles and service crews to scenes of accidents and breakdowns. In transit agencies with rail systems, drivers may become train operators or station attendants. A few drivers become managers. Promotion in publicly owned bus systems is often by competitive civil service examination. Some motorcoach drivers purchase their own equipment and open their own business.

Job Outlook

Persons seeking jobs as bus drivers should encounter good opportunities. Individuals who have good driving records and who are willing to work a part-time or irregular schedule should have the best job prospects. Schoolbus driving jobs, particularly in rapidly growing suburban areas, should be easiest to acquire because most are part-time positions with high turnover and minimal training requirements. Those seeking higher paying intercity and public transit bus driver positions may encounter competition. Employment prospects for motorcoach drivers will fluctuate with the cyclical nature of the economy, as demand for motorcoach services is very dependent on tourism.

Employment of bus drivers is expected to increase about as fast as the average for all occupations through the year 2012, primarily to meet the transportation needs of the growing general population and the school-age population. Many additional job openings are expected to occur each year because of the need to replace workers who take jobs in other occupations or who retire or leave the occupation for other reasons.

The number of schoolbus drivers is expected to increase as a result of growth in elementary and secondary school enrollments. In addition, more schoolbus drivers will be needed as more of the Nation's population is concentrated in suburban areas, where students generally ride schoolbuses, and less in central cities, where transportation is not provided for most pupils.

Employment growth of local-transit bus drivers will be spurred by increases in the number of passengers and in funding levels. Funding levels for public transit may fluctuate as the public's interest in transportation changes. There may be competition for positions with more regular hours and steady driving routes.

Competition from other modes of transportation—airplane, train, or automobile—will temper job growth among intercity bus drivers. Most growth in intercity bus transportation will occur in group charters to locations not served by other modes of transportation. Like automobiles, buses have a far greater number of possible destinations than airplanes or trains. Due to greater cost savings and convenience over automobiles, buses usually are the most economical option for tour groups traveling to out-of-the-way destinations.

Full-time bus drivers are rarely laid off during recessions. However, employers might reduce hours of part-time local-transit and intercity bus drivers if the number of passengers decreases, because fewer extra buses would be needed. Seasonal layoffs are common. Many intercity bus drivers with little seniority, for example, are furloughed during the winter when regular schedule and charter business declines; schoolbus drivers seldom work during the summer or school holidays.

Earnings

Median hourly earnings of transit and intercity bus drivers were $14.22 in 2002. The middle 50 percent earned between $10.51 and $18.99 an hour. The lowest 10 percent earned less than $8.37, and the highest 10 percent earned more than $22.51 an hour. Median hourly earnings in the industries employing the largest numbers of transit and intercity bus drivers in 2002 were as follows:

Local government	$16.95
Interurban and rural bus transportation	15.15
Urban transit systems	15.02
School and employee bus transportation	11.29
Charter bus industry	10.64

Median hourly earnings of schoolbus drivers were $10.77 in 2002. The middle 50 percent earned between $7.73 and $13.53 an hour. The lowest 10 percent earned less than $6.24, and the highest 10 percent earned more than $16.44 an hour. Median hourly earnings in the industries employing the largest numbers of schoolbus drivers in 2002 were as follows:

School and employee bus transportation	$11.44
Local government	11.09
Elementary and secondary schools	10.50
Other transit and ground passenger transportation	9.79
Individual and family services	8.27

The benefits bus drivers receive from their employers vary greatly. Most intercity and local-transit bus drivers receive paid health and life insurance, sick leave, vacation leave, and free bus rides on any of the regular routes of their line or system. Schoolbus drivers receive sick leave, and many are covered by health and life insurance and pension plans. Because they generally do not work when school is not in session, they do not get vacation leave. In a number of States, local-transit and schoolbus drivers employed by local governments are covered by a statewide public employee pension system. Increasingly, school systems extend benefits to drivers who supplement their driving by working in the school system during off hours.

Most intercity and many local-transit bus drivers are members of the Amalgamated Transit Union. Local-transit bus drivers in New York and several other large cities belong to the Transport Workers Union of America. Some drivers belong to the United Transportation Union or the International Brotherhood of Teamsters.

Related Occupations

Other workers who drive vehicles on highways and city streets include taxi drivers and chauffeurs and truck drivers and driver/sales workers.

Sources of Additional Information

For information on employment opportunities, contact local-transit systems, intercity buslines, school systems, or the local offices of the State employment service.

General information on schoolbus driving is available from:
➤ National School Transportation Association, 625 Slaters Lane, Suite 205, Alexandria, VA 22314.

General information on local-transit bus driving is available from:
➤ American Public Transportation Association, 1666 K St. NW., Suite 1100, Washington, DC 20006.

General information on motorcoach driving is available from:
➤ United Motorcoach Association, 113 S. West St., 4th Floor, Alexandria, VA 22314.

Taxi Drivers and Chauffeurs

(0*NET 53-3041.00)

Significant Points

● Taxi drivers and chauffeurs may work any schedule, including full-time, part-time, night, evening, and weekend work.

● Many taxi drivers and chauffeurs like the independent, unsupervised work of driving their automobile.

● Local governments set license standards that include minimum qualifications for driving experience and training; many taxi and limousine companies set higher standards.

● Job opportunities will be good because of the need to replace the many people who work in this occupation for short periods and then leave.

Nature of the Work

Anyone who has been in a large city knows the importance of taxi and limousine service. *Taxi drivers*, also known as *cab drivers* help passengers get to and from their homes, workplaces, and recreational pursuits such as dining, entertainment, and shopping. They also help out-of-town business people and tourists get around in unfamiliar surroundings.

At the start of their driving shift, taxi drivers usually report to a taxicab service or garage where they are assigned a vehicle, most frequently a large, conventional automobile modified for commercial passenger transport. They record their name, work date, and cab identification number on a trip sheet. Drivers check the cab's fuel and oil levels, and make sure that the lights, brakes, and windshield wipers are in good working order. Drivers adjust rear and side mirrors and their seat for comfort. Any equipment or part not in good working order is reported to the dispatcher or company mechanic.

Taxi drivers pick up passengers in 1 of 3 ways: "Cruising" the streets to pick up random passengers; prearranging pickups; and picking up passengers from taxistands established in highly trafficked areas. In urban areas, the majority of passengers "wave down" drivers cruising the streets. Customers may also prearrange a pickup by calling a cab company and giving a location, approximate pickup time, and destination. The cab company dispatcher then relays the information to a driver by two-way radio, cellular telephone, or onboard computer. Outside of urban areas, the majority of trips are dispatched in this manner. Drivers also pick up passengers waiting at cabstands or in taxi lines at airports, train stations, hotels, restaurants, and other places where people frequently seek taxis.

Some drivers transport individuals with special needs, such as those with disabilities and the elderly. These drivers, also known as *paratransit drivers*, operate specially equipped vehicles designed to accommodate a variety of needs in nonemergency situations. Although special certification is not necessary, some additional training on the equipment and passenger needs may be required.

Drivers should be familiar with streets in the areas they serve so they can use the most efficient route to destinations. They should know the locations of frequently requested destinations, such as airports, bus and railroad terminals, convention centers, hotels, and other points of interest. In case of emergency, the driver should also know the location of fire and police stations and hospitals.

Upon reaching the destination, drivers determine the fare and announce it to the rider. Fares often consist of many parts. In many

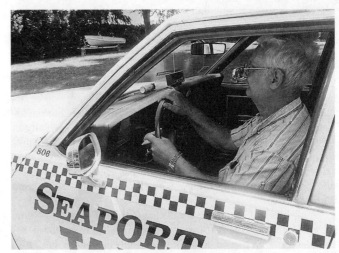

Customers may prearrange a pickup by calling a cab company and giving a location, approximate pickup time, and destination.

cabs, a taximeter measures the fare based on the length of the trip and the amount of time the trip took. Drivers turn the taximeter on when passengers enter the cab and turn it off when they reach the final destination. The fare also may include a surcharge for additional passengers, a fee for handling luggage, or a drop charge—an additional flat fee added for use of the cab. In some cases, fares are determined by a system of zones through which the taxi passes during a trip. Each jurisdiction determines the rate and structure of the fare system covering licensed taxis. Passengers generally add a tip or gratuity to the fare. The amount of the gratuity depends on the passengers' satisfaction with the quality and efficiency of the ride and courtesy of the driver. Drivers issue receipts upon request by the passenger. They enter onto the trip sheet all information regarding the trip, including the place and time of pickup and dropoff and the total fee. These logs help taxi company management check the driver's activity and efficiency. Drivers also must fill out accident reports when necessary.

Chauffeurs operate limousines, vans, and private cars for limousine companies, private businesses, government agencies, and wealthy individuals. Chauffeur service differs from taxi service in that all trips are prearranged. Many chauffeurs transport customers in large vans between hotels and airports, bus, or train terminals. Others drive luxury automobiles, such as limousines, to business events, entertainment venues, and social events. Still others provide full-time personal transportation for wealthy families and private companies.

At the start of the workday, chauffeurs prepare their automobiles or vans for use. They inspect the vehicle for cleanliness and, when needed, vacuum the interior and wash the exterior body, windows, and mirrors. They check fuel and oil levels and make sure the lights, tires, brakes, and windshield wipers work. Chauffeurs may perform routine maintenance and make minor repairs, such as changing tires or adding oil and other fluids when needed. If a vehicle requires more complicated repair, they take it to a professional mechanic.

Chauffeurs cater to passengers with attentive customer service and a special regard for detail. They help riders into the car by holding open doors, holding umbrellas when it is raining, and loading packages and luggage into the trunk of the car. They may perform errands for their employers such as delivering packages or picking up clients arriving at airports. Many chauffeurs offer conveniences and luxuries in their limousines to ensure a pleasurable ride, such as newspapers, magazines, music, drinks, televisions, and telephones. A growing number of chauffeurs work as full-service *executive assistants*, simultaneously acting as driver, secretary, and itinerary planner.

Working Conditions

Taxi drivers and chauffeurs occasionally have to load and unload heavy luggage and packages. Driving for long periods can be tiring and uncomfortable, especially in densely populated urban areas. Drivers must be alert to conditions on the road, especially in heavy and congested traffic or in bad weather. They must take precautions to prevent accidents and avoid sudden stops, turns, and other driving maneuvers that would jar passengers. Taxi drivers also risk robbery because they work alone and often carry large amounts of cash.

Work hours of taxi drivers and chauffeurs vary greatly. Some jobs offer full-time or part-time employment with work hours that can change from day to day or remain the same every day. It is often necessary for drivers to report to work on short notice. Chauffeurs who work for a single employer may be on call much of the time. Evening and weekend work are common for limousine and taxicab services.

The needs of the client or employer dictate the work schedule for chauffeurs. The work of taxi drivers is much less structured. Working free of supervision, they may break for a meal or a rest whenever their vehicle is unoccupied. Many taxi drivers and chauffeurs like the independent, unsupervised work of driving their automobile.

This occupation is attractive to individuals seeking flexible work schedules, such as college and postgraduate students, and to anyone seeking a second source of income. For example, other service workers, such as ambulance drivers and police officers, often consider moonlighting as taxi drivers and chauffeurs.

Full-time taxi drivers usually work one shift a day, which may last from 8 to 12 hours. Part-time drivers may work half a shift each day, or work a full shift once or twice a week. Drivers may work shifts at all times of the day and night, because most taxi companies offer services 24 hours a day. Early morning and late night shifts are common. Drivers work long hours during holidays, weekends, and other special times during which demand for their services may be heavier. Independent drivers, however, often set their own hours and schedules.

Design improvements in newer cabs have reduced the stress and increased the comfort and efficiency of drivers. Many regulatory bodies overseeing taxi and chauffeur services require standard amenities such as air-conditioning and general upkeep of the vehicles. Modern taxicabs also are sometimes equipped with sophisticated tracking devices, fare meters, and dispatching equipment. Satellites and tracking systems link many of these state-of-the-art vehicles with company headquarters. In a matter of seconds, dispatchers can deliver directions, traffic advisories, weather reports, and other important communications to drivers anywhere in the transporting area. The satellite link also allows dispatchers to track vehicle location, fuel consumption, and engine performance. Drivers can easily communicate with dispatchers to discuss delivery schedules and courses of action should there be mechanical problems. For instance, automated dispatch systems help dispatchers locate the closest driver to a customer in order to maximize efficiency and quality of service. When threatened with crime or violence, drivers may have special "trouble lights" to alert authorities of emergencies and guarantee that help arrives quickly.

Taxi drivers and chauffeurs meet many different types of people. Dealing with rude customers and waiting for passengers requires patience. Many municipalities and taxicab and chauffeur companies require taxi drivers to wear clean and neat clothes. Many chauffeurs wear formal attire such as a tuxedo, a coat and tie, a dress, or a uniform and cap.

Employment

Taxi drivers and chauffeurs held about 132,000 jobs in 2002. Over one quarter worked for taxi and limousine service companies. Many taxi drivers and chauffeurs were self-employed.

Training, Other Qualifications, and Advancement

Local governments set license standards and requirements for taxi drivers and chauffeurs that include minimum qualifications for driving experience and training. Many taxi and limousine companies set higher standards than required by law. It is common for companies to review applicants' medical, credit, criminal, and driving records. In addition, many companies require a higher minimum age than that which is legally required and prefer that drivers be high school graduates.

Persons interested in driving a limousine or taxicab must first have a regular automobile driver's license. They also must acquire a chauffeur or taxi driver's license, commonly called a "hack" license. Local authorities generally require applicants for a hack license to pass a written exam or complete a training program that may include up to 80 hours of classroom instruction. To qualify through either an exam or a training program, applicants must know local geography, motor vehicle laws, safe driving practices, regulations governing taxicabs, and display some aptitude for customer service. Many training programs include a test on English proficiency, usually in the form of listening comprehension; applicants who do not pass the English exam must take an English course along with the formal driving program. In addition, some classroom instruction includes route management, mapreading, and service for passengers with disabilities. Many taxicab or limousine companies sponsor applicants and give them a temporary permit that allows them to drive, although the applicant may not yet have finished the training program or passed the test. However, some jurisdictions, such as New York City, have discontinued this practice and now require driver applicants to complete the licensing process before operating a taxi or limousine.

Some taxi and limousine companies give new drivers on-the-job training. They show drivers how to operate the taximeter and communications equipment, and how to complete paperwork. Other topics covered may include driver safety and popular sightseeing and entertainment destinations. Many companies have contracts with social service agencies and transportation services to transport elderly and disabled citizens in nonemergency situations. To support these services, new drivers may get special training on how to handle wheelchair lifts and other mechanical devices.

Taxi drivers and chauffeurs should be able to get along with many different types of people. They must be patient when waiting for passengers or when dealing with rude customers. It is also helpful for drivers to be tolerant and have even tempers when driving in heavy and congested traffic. Drivers should be dependable because passengers expect to be picked up at a prearranged time and taken to the correct destination. To be successful, drivers must be responsible and self-motivated because they work with little supervision. Increasingly, companies encourage drivers to develop their own loyal customer base to improve their businesses.

Many taxi drivers and chauffeurs are called *lease drivers*. These drivers pay a daily, weekly, or monthly fee to the company allowing them to lease their vehicle. In the case of limousines, leasing also permits the driver access to the company's dispatch system. The fee also may include a charge for vehicle maintenance, insurance, and a deposit on the vehicle. Lease drivers may take their cars home with them when they are not on duty.

Opportunities for advancement are limited for taxi drivers and chauffeurs. Experienced drivers may obtain preferred routes or shifts. Some advance to dispatcher or manager jobs; others may start their own limousine company.

In small and medium-sized communities, drivers are sometimes able to buy their taxi, limousine, or other type of automobile and go into business for themselves. These independent owner-drivers require an additional permit allowing them to operate their vehicle as a company. Some big cities limit the number of operating permits. In these cities, drivers become owner-drivers by buying permits from owner-drivers who leave the business. Although many owner-drivers are successful, some fail to cover expenses and eventually lose their permit and automobile. Good business sense and courses in accounting, business, and business arithmetic can help an owner-driver to become successful. Knowledge of mechanics enables owner-drivers to perform their own routine maintenance and minor repairs to cut expenses.

Job Outlook

Persons seeking jobs as taxi drivers and chauffeurs should encounter good opportunities, because of the need to replace the many people who work in this occupation for short periods and then transfer to other occupations or leave the labor force. However, opportunities for drivers vary greatly in terms of earnings, work hours, and working conditions, depending on economic and regulatory conditions. Opportunities should be best for persons with good driving records and the ability to work flexible schedules.

Employment of taxi drivers and chauffeurs is expected to grow faster than the average for all occupations through the year 2012, as local and suburban travel increases with population growth. Employment growth also will stem from Federal legislation requiring services for persons with disabilities. Rapidly growing metropolitan areas should offer the best job opportunities.

The number of job openings can fluctuate with the cycle of the overall economy because the demand for taxi and limousine transportation depends on travel and tourism. During economic slowdowns, drivers are seldom laid off, but they may have to increase their work hours and earnings may decline. In economic upturns, job openings are numerous as many drivers transfer to other occupations. Extra drivers may be hired during holiday seasons and peak travel and tourist times.

Earnings

Earnings of taxi drivers and chauffeurs vary greatly, depending on factors such as the number of hours worked, customers' tips, and geographic location. Median hourly earnings of salaried taxi drivers and chauffeurs, including tips, were $8.91 in 2002. The middle 50 percent earned between $7.31 and $11.45 an hour. The lowest 10 percent earned less than $6.31, and the highest 10 percent earned more than $15.18 an hour. Median hourly earnings in the industries employing the largest numbers of taxi drivers and chauffeurs in 2002 were as follows:

Taxi and limousine service	$9.71
Other transit and ground passenger transportation	8.70
Individual and family services	8.14
Automotive equipment rental and leasing	7.99
Traveler accommodation	7.96

Related Occupations

Other workers who have similar jobs include bus drivers and truck drivers and driver/sales workers.

Sources of Additional Information

Information on licensing and registration of taxi drivers and chauffeurs is available from local government agencies that regulate taxicabs. For information about work opportunities as a taxi driver or chauffeur, contact local taxi or limousine companies or State employment service offices.

For general information about the work of limousine drivers, contact:

➤ National Limousine Association, 49 South Maple Ave., Marlton, NJ 08053. Internet: **http://www.limo.org**

Truck Drivers and Driver/Sales Workers

(0*NET 53-3031.00, 53-3032.01, 53-3032.02, 53-3033.00)

Significant Points

- Job opportunities should be favorable.
- Competition is expected for jobs offering the highest earnings or most favorable work schedules.
- A commercial driver's license is required to operate most larger trucks.

Nature of the Work

Truck drivers are a constant presence on the Nation's highways and interstates, delivering everything from automobiles to canned foods. Firms of all kinds rely on trucks for pickup and delivery of goods because no other form of transportation can deliver goods door to door. Even if goods travel in part by ship, train, or airplane, trucks carry nearly all goods at some point in their journey from producer to consumer.

Before leaving the terminal or warehouse, truck drivers check the fuel level and oil in their trucks. They also inspect the trucks to make sure the brakes, windshield wipers, and lights are working and that a fire extinguisher, flares, and other safety equipment are aboard and in working order. Drivers make sure their cargo is secure and adjust their mirrors so that both sides of the truck are visible from the driver's seat. Drivers report equipment that is inoperable, missing, or loaded improperly to the dispatcher.

Once under way, drivers must be alert to prevent accidents. Drivers can see farther down the road, because large trucks sit higher than most other vehicles. This allows drivers to seek traffic lanes that allow for a steady speed, while keeping sight of varying road conditions.

Delivery time varies according to the type of merchandise and its final destination. Local drivers may provide daily service for a specific route, while other drivers make intercity and interstate deliveries that take longer and may vary from job to job. The driver's responsibilities and assignments change according to the time spent on the road, the type of payloads transported, and vehicle size.

New technologies are changing the way truck drivers work, especially long-distance truck drivers. Satellites and Global Positioning Systems (GPS) link many trucks with company headquarters. Troubleshooting information, directions, weather reports, and other important communications can be delivered to the truck, anywhere, within seconds. Drivers can easily communicate with the dispatcher to discuss delivery schedules and courses of action in the event of mechanical problems. The satellite linkup also allows the dispatcher to track the truck's location, fuel consumption, and engine performance. Many drivers also work with computerized inventory tracking equipment. It is important for the producer, warehouse, and customer to know the product's location at all times, in order to keep costs low and the quality of service high.

Heavy truck and tractor-trailer drivers drive trucks or vans with a capacity of at least 26,000 pounds Gross Vehicle Weight (GVW). They transport goods including cars, livestock, and other materials in liquid, loose, or packaged form. Many routes are from city to city and cover long distances. Some companies use two drivers on very long runs—one drives while the other sleeps in a berth behind the cab. "Sleeper" runs may last for days, or even weeks, usually with the truck stopping only for fuel, food, loading, and unloading.

Some heavy truck and tractor-trailer drivers who have regular runs transport freight to the same city on a regular basis. Other drivers perform unscheduled runs because shippers request varying service to different cities every day.

After these truck drivers reach their destination or complete their operating shift, the U.S. Department of Transportation requires that they complete reports detailing the trip, the condition of the truck, and the circumstances of any accidents. In addition, Federal regulations require employers to subject drivers to random alcohol and drug tests while they are on duty.

Long-distance heavy truck and tractor-trailer drivers spend most of their working time behind the wheel, but may load or unload their cargo after arriving at the final destination. This is especially common when drivers haul specialty cargo, because they may be the only one at the destination familiar with procedures or certified to handle the materials. Auto-transport drivers, for example, position cars on the trailers at the manufacturing plant and remove them at the dealerships. When picking up or delivering furniture, drivers of long-distance moving vans hire local workers to help them load or unload.

Light or delivery services truck drivers drive trucks or vans with a capacity under 26,000 pounds GVW. They deliver or pick up merchandise and packages within a specific area. This may include short "turnarounds" to deliver a shipment to a nearby city, pick up another loaded truck or van, and drive it back to their home base the same day. These services may require use of electronic delivery tracking systems to track the whereabouts of the merchandise or packages. Light or delivery services truck drivers usually load or unload the merchandise at the customer's place of business. They may have helpers if there are many deliveries to make during the day, or if the load requires heavy moving. Typically, before the driver arrives for work, material handlers load the trucks and arrange items to improve delivery efficiency. Customers must sign receipts for goods and pay drivers the balance due on the merchandise if there is a cash-on-delivery arrangement. At the end of the day, drivers turn in receipts, money, records of deliveries made, and any reports on mechanical problems with their trucks.

Some local truck drivers have sales and customer service responsibilities. The primary responsibility of *driver/sales workers*, or *route drivers*, is to deliver and sell their firm's products over established routes or within an established territory. They sell goods such as food products, including restaurant takeout items, or pick

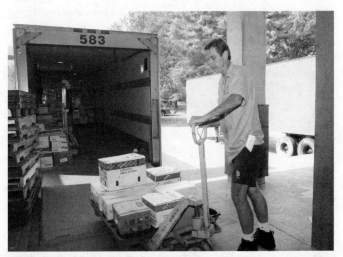

Even if goods travel in part by ship, train, or airplane, trucks carry nearly all goods at some point in their journey from producer to consumer.

up and deliver items such as laundry. Their response to customer complaints and requests can make the difference between a large order and a lost customer. Route drivers may also take orders and collect payments.

The duties of driver/sales workers vary according to their industry, the policies of their particular company, and the emphasis placed on their sales responsibility. Most have wholesale routes that deliver to businesses and stores, rather than to homes. For example, wholesale bakery driver/sales workers deliver and arrange bread, cakes, rolls, and other baked goods on display racks in grocery stores. They estimate how many of each item to stock by paying close attention to what is selling. They may recommend changes in a store's order or encourage the manager to stock new bakery products. Laundries that rent linens, towels, work clothes, and other items employ driver/sales workers to visit businesses regularly to replace soiled laundry. From time to time, they solicit new orders from businesses along their route.

After completing their route, driver/sales workers order items for the next delivery based on product sales trends, weather, and customer requests.

Working Conditions

Truck driving has become less physically demanding because most trucks now have more comfortable seats, better ventilation, and improved, ergonomically-designed cabs. Although these changes make the work environment more attractive, driving for many hours at a stretch, unloading cargo, and making many deliveries can be tiring. Local truck drivers, unlike long-distance drivers, usually return home in the evening. Some self-employed long-distance truck drivers who own and operate their trucks spend most of the year away from home.

Design improvements in newer trucks reduce stress and increase the efficiency of long-distance drivers. Many of the newer trucks are virtual mini-apartments on wheels, equipped with refrigerators, televisions, and bunks.

The U.S. Department of Transportation governs work hours and other working conditions of truck drivers engaged in interstate commerce. A long-distance driver cannot work more than 60 hours in any 7-day period. Federal regulations also require that truckers rest 10 hours for every 11 hours of driving. Many drivers, particularly on long runs, work close to the maximum time permitted because they typically are compensated according to the number of miles or hours they drive. Drivers on long runs may face boredom, loneliness, and fatigue. Drivers frequently travel at night, and on holidays and weekends, to avoid traffic delays and deliver cargo on time.

Local truck drivers frequently work 50 or more hours a week. Drivers who handle food for chain grocery stores, produce markets, or bakeries typically work long hours, starting late at night or early in the morning. Although most drivers have regular routes, some have different routes each day. Many local truck drivers, particularly driver/sales workers, load and unload their own trucks. This requires considerable lifting, carrying, and walking each day.

Employment

Truck drivers and driver/sales workers held about 3.2 million jobs in 2002. Of these workers, 431,000 were driver/sales workers and 2.8 million were truck drivers. Most truck drivers find employment in large metropolitan areas along major interstate roadways where major trucking, retail, and wholesale companies have distribution outlets. Some drivers work in rural areas, providing specialized services such as delivering newspapers to customers or coal to a railroad.

The truck transportation industry employed almost one-quarter of all truck drivers and driver/sales workers in the United States. Another quarter worked for companies engaged in wholesale or retail trade. The remaining truck drivers and driver/sales workers were distributed across many industries, including construction and manufacturing.

Over 10 percent of all truck drivers and driver/sales workers were self-employed. Of these, a significant number were owner-operators who either served a variety of businesses independently or leased their services and trucks to a trucking company.

Training, Other Qualifications, and Advancement

State and Federal regulations govern the qualifications and standards for truck drivers. All drivers must comply with Federal regulations and any State regulations that are stricter than Federal requirements. Truck drivers must have a driver's license issued by the State in which they live, and most employers require a clean driving record. Drivers of trucks designed to carry 26,000 pounds or more—including most tractor-trailers, as well as bigger straight trucks—must obtain a commercial driver's license (CDL) from the State in which they live. All truck drivers who operate trucks transporting hazardous materials must obtain a CDL, regardless of truck size. Federal regulations governing the CDL exempt certain groups, including farmers, emergency medical technicians, firefighters, some military drivers, and snow and ice removers. In many States, a regular driver's license is sufficient for driving light trucks and vans.

To qualify for a commercial driver's license, applicants must pass a written test on rules and regulations, and then demonstrate that they can operate a commercial truck safely. A national database permanently records all driving violations incurred by persons who hold commercial licenses. A State will check these records and deny a commercial driver's license to a driver who already has a license suspended or revoked in another State. Licensed drivers must accompany trainees until the trainees get their own CDL. Information on how to apply for a commercial driver's license may be obtained from State motor vehicle administrations.

While many States allow those who are at least 18 years old to drive trucks within their borders, the U.S. Department of Transportation establishes minimum qualifications for truck drivers engaged in interstate commerce. Federal Motor Carrier Safety Regulations require drivers to be at least 21 years old and to pass a physical examination once every 2 years. The main physical requirements include good hearing, at least 20/40 vision with glasses or corrective lenses, and a 70-degree field of vision in each eye. Drivers cannot be colorblind. Drivers must be able to hear a forced whisper in one ear at not less than 5 feet, with a hearing aide if needed. Drivers must have normal use of arms and legs and normal blood pressure. Drivers cannot use any controlled substances, unless prescribed by a licensed physician. Persons with epilepsy or diabetes controlled by insulin are not permitted to be interstate truck drivers. Federal regulations also require employers to test their drivers for alcohol and drug use as a condition of employment, and require periodic random tests of the drivers while they are on duty. In addition, drivers must have no criminal records such as felonies involving the use of a motor vehicle; any crime involving drugs, including driving under the influence of drugs or alcohol; and any hit-and-run accident that resulted in injury or death. All drivers must be able to read and speak English well enough to read road signs, prepare reports, and communicate with law enforcement officers and the public. Also, drivers must take a written examination on the Motor Carrier Safety Regulations of the U.S. Department of Transportation.

Many trucking operations have higher standards than those described. Many firms require that drivers be at least 22 years old, be able to lift heavy objects, and have driven trucks for 3 to 5 years. Many prefer to hire high school graduates and require annual physical examinations. Companies have an economic incentive to hire less risky drivers. Good drivers drive more efficiently, using less fuel and costing less to insure.

Taking driver-training courses is a desirable method of preparing for truck driving jobs and for obtaining a commercial driver's license. High school courses in driver training and automotive mechanics also may be helpful. Many private and public vocational-technical schools offer tractor-trailer driver training programs. Students learn to maneuver large vehicles on crowded streets and in highway traffic. They also learn to inspect trucks and freight for compliance with regulations. Some programs provide only a limited amount of actual driving experience, and completion of a program does not guarantee a job. Persons interested in attending a driving school should check with local trucking companies to make sure the school's training is acceptable. Some States require prospective drivers to complete a training course in basic truck driving before being issued their CDL. The Professional Truck Driver Institute (PTDI), a nonprofit organization established by the trucking industry, manufacturers, and others, certifies driver training programs at truck driver training schools that meet industry standards and Federal Highway Administration guidelines for training tractor-trailer drivers.

Drivers must get along well with people because they often deal directly with customers. Employers seek driver/sales workers who speak well and have self-confidence, initiative, tact, and a neat appearance. Employers also look for responsible, self-motivated individuals able to work with little supervision.

Training given to new drivers by employers is usually informal, and may consist of only a few hours of instruction from an experienced driver, sometimes on the new employee's own time. New drivers may also ride with and observe experienced drivers before assignment of their own runs. Drivers receive additional training to drive special types of trucks or handle hazardous materials. Some companies give 1 to 2 days of classroom instruction covering general duties, the operation and loading of a truck, company policies, and the preparation of delivery forms and company records. Driver/sales workers also receive training on the various types of products the company carries, so that they will be effective sales workers.

Although most new truck drivers are assigned immediately to regular driving jobs, some start as extra drivers, substituting for regular drivers who are ill or on vacation. They receive a regular assignment when an opening occurs.

New drivers sometimes start on panel trucks or other small straight trucks. As they gain experience and show competent driving skills, they may advance to larger and heavier trucks, and finally to tractor-trailers.

Advancement of truck drivers generally is limited to driving runs that provide increased earnings or preferred schedules and working conditions. For the most part, a local truck driver may advance to driving heavy or special types of trucks, or transfer to long-distance truck driving. Working for companies that also employ long-distance drivers is the best way to advance to these positions. A few truck drivers may advance to dispatcher, manager, or traffic work—for example, planning delivery schedules.

Some long-distance truck drivers purchase a truck and go into business for themselves. Although many of these owner-operators are successful, some fail to cover expenses and eventually go out of business. Owner-operators should have good business sense as well as truck driving experience. Courses in accounting, business, and business mathematics are helpful, and knowledge of truck mechanics can enable owner-operators to perform their own routine maintenance and minor repairs.

Job Outlook

Job opportunities should be favorable for truck drivers. In addition to growth in demand for truck drivers, numerous job openings will occur as experienced drivers leave this large occupation to transfer to other fields of work, retire, or leave the labor force for other reasons. Jobs vary greatly in terms of earnings, weekly work hours, number of nights spent on the road, and quality of equipment operated. Because this occupation does not require education beyond high school, competition is expected for jobs with the most attractive earnings and working conditions.

Overall employment of truck drivers and driver/sales workers is expected to increase as fast as the average for all occupations through the year 2012, due to growth in the economy and in the amount of freight carried by truck. The increased use of rail, air, and ship transportation requires truck drivers to pick up and deliver shipments. Demand for long-distance drivers will remain strong because these drivers transport perishable and time-sensitive goods more efficiently than do alternative modes of transportation, such as railroads. Job opportunities for truck drivers with less-than-truckload carriers will be more competitive than those with truckload carriers because of the more desirable working conditions for less-than-truckload carriers.

Faster than average growth of light and heavy truck driver employment will outweigh relatively slow growth in driver/sales worker jobs. The number of truck drivers with sales responsibilities is expected to increase more slowly than the average for all other occupations as companies increasingly shift sales, ordering, and customer service tasks to sales and office staffs, and use regular truck drivers to make deliveries to customers.

Job opportunities may vary from year to year, because the strength of the economy dictates the amount of freight moved by trucks. Companies tend to hire more drivers when the economy is strong and deliveries are in high demand. Consequently, when the economy slows, employers hire fewer drivers, or even lay off drivers. Independent owner-operators are particularly vulnerable to slowdowns. Industries least likely to be affected by economic fluctuation, such as grocery stores, tend to be the most stable places for employment.

Earnings

Median hourly earnings of heavy truck and tractor-trailer drivers were $15.97 in 2002. The middle 50 percent earned between $12.51 and $20.01 an hour. The lowest 10 percent earned less than $10.01, and the highest 10 percent earned more than $23.75 an hour. Median hourly earnings in the industries employing the largest numbers of heavy truck and tractor-trailer drivers in 2002 were as follows:

General freight trucking	$17.56
Grocery and related product wholesalers	16.90
Specialized freight trucking	15.79
Other specialty trade contractors	14.25
Cement and concrete product manufacturing	14.14

Median hourly earnings of light or delivery services truck drivers were $11.48 in 2002. The middle 50 percent earned between $8.75 and $15.57 an hour. The lowest 10 percent earned less than $7.03, and the highest 10 percent earned more than $20.68 an hour. Median hourly earnings in the industries employing the largest numbers of light or delivery services truck drivers in 2002 were as follows:

Couriers	$17.48
General freight trucking	14.92
Grocery and related product wholesalers	12.26
Building material and supplies dealers	10.83
Automotive parts, accessories, and tire stores	7.82

Median hourly earnings of driver/sales workers, including commission, were $9.92 in 2002. The middle 50 percent earned between $6.98 and $14.70 an hour. The lowest 10 percent earned less than $6.07, and the highest 10 percent earned more than $19.60 an hour. Median hourly earnings in the industries employing the largest numbers of driver/sales workers in 2002 were as follows:

Specialty food stores	$14.98
Drycleaning and laundry services	14.74
Grocery and related product wholesalers	12.66
Limited-service eating places	6.78
Full-service restaurants	6.47

As a general rule, local truck drivers receive an hourly wage and extra pay for working overtime, usually after 40 hours. Employers pay long-distance drivers primarily by the mile. Their rate per mile can vary greatly from employer to employer and may even depend on the type of cargo. Typically, earnings increase with mileage driven, seniority, and the size and type of truck driven. Most driver/sales workers receive a commission based on their sales in addition to an hourly wage.

Most self-employed truck drivers are primarily engaged in long-distance hauling. Many truck drivers are members of the International Brotherhood of Teamsters. Some truck drivers employed by companies outside the trucking industry are members of unions representing the plant workers of the companies for which they work.

Related Occupations
Other driving occupations include ambulance drivers and attendants, except emergency medical technicians; bus drivers; and taxi drivers and chauffeurs.

Sources of Additional Information
Information on truck driver employment opportunities is available from local trucking companies and local offices of the State employment service.

Information on career opportunities in truck driving may be obtained from:
➤ American Trucking Associations, Inc., 2200 Mill Rd., Alexandria, VA 22314. Internet: **http://www.trucking.org**

A list of certified tractor-trailer driver training courses may be obtained from:
➤ Professional Truck Driver Institute, 2200 Mill Rd., Alexandria, VA 22314. Internet: **http://www.ptdi.org**

Rail Transportation Occupations

(O*NET 53-4011.00, 53-4012.00, 53-4013.00, 53-4021.01, 53-4021.02, 53-4031.00, 53-4041.00, 53-4099.99)

Significant Points

● Most workers begin as yard laborers, and later may have the opportunity to train for engineer or conductor jobs.

● Employment of most rail transportation occupations is expected to decline; however, employment of subway and streetcar operators will have average growth.

● Competition for available job opportunities is expected to be keen.

● Nearly 3 out of 4 workers are members of unions, and earnings are relatively high.

Nature of the Work
More than a century ago, freight and passenger railroads were the ties binding the Nation together and the engine driving the economy. Today, rail transportation remains a vital link in our Nation's transportation network and economy. Railroads deliver billions of tons of freight and thousands of travelers to destinations throughout the Nation, while subways and light-rail systems transport millions of passengers within metropolitan areas.

Locomotive engineers are among the most experienced and skilled workers on the railroad. Locomotive engineers operate large trains carrying cargo and passengers between stations. Most engineers run diesel locomotives, while a few operate electrically powered locomotives.

Before and after each run, engineers check the mechanical condition of their locomotive and make minor adjustments on the spot. Engineers receive starting instructions from conductors and move controls such as throttles and airbrakes to drive the locomotive. They monitor gauges and meters that measure speed, amperage, battery charge, and air pressure, both in the brake lines and in the main reservoir.

On the open rail and in the yard, engineers confer with conductors and traffic control center personnel via two-way radio or mobile telephone to issue or receive information concerning stops, delays, and train locations. They interpret and comply with orders, signals, speed limits, and railroad rules and regulations. They must have a thorough knowledge of the signaling systems, yards, and terminals on routes over which they operate. Engineers must be constantly aware of the condition and makeup of their train, because trains react differently to acceleration, braking, and curves, depending on the grade and condition of the rail, the number of cars, the ratio of empty to loaded cars, and the amount of slack in the train.

Rail yard engineers, dinkey operators, and hostlers drive switching or small "dinkey" engines within railroad yards, industrial plants, mines and quarries, or construction projects.

Railroad conductors coordinate the activities of freight and passenger train crews. Railroad conductors assigned to freight trains review schedules, switching orders, waybills, and shipping records to obtain loading and unloading information regarding their cargo. Conductors assigned to passenger trains also ensure passenger safety and comfort as they go about collecting tickets and fares, making announcements for the benefit of passengers, and coordinating activities of the crew to provide passenger services.

Before a train leaves the terminal, the conductor and engineer discuss instructions received from the dispatcher concerning the train's route, timetable, and cargo. During the run, conductors use two-way radios and mobile telephones to communicate with dispatchers, engineers, and conductors of other trains. Conductors use dispatch or electronic monitoring devices that relay information about equipment problems on the train or the rail. They may arrange for the removal of defective cars from the train for repairs at the nearest station or stop. In addition, conductors may discuss alternative routes if there is a defect or obstruction on the rail.

Yardmasters coordinate activities of workers engaged in railroad traffic operations. These activities include making up or breaking up trains and switching inbound or outbound traffic to a specific section of the line. Some cars are sent to unload their cargo on special tracks, while other cars are moved to other tracks to await assemblage into new trains destined for different cities. Yardmasters inform engineers where to move the cars to fit the planned train configuration. Switches, many of them operated remotely by computer, divert the locomotive or cars to the proper track for coupling and uncoupling.

Railroad brake, signal, and switch operators perform a variety of activities, such as operating track switches to route cars to different sections of the yard. They may signal engineers and set warning signals, help to couple and uncouple rolling stock to make up or break up trains, or inspect couplings, airhoses, and handbrakes.

Traditionally, freight train crews included either one or two brake operators—one in the locomotive with the engineer and another who rode with the conductor in the rear car. Brake operators worked

Most railroad transportation workers begin as yard laborers, and later may have the opportunity to train for engineer or conductor jobs.

under the direction of conductors and did the physical work involved in adding and removing cars at railroad stations and assembling and disassembling trains in railroad yards. In an effort to reduce costs and take advantage of new technology, most railroads have phased out brake operators. Many modern freight trains use only an engineer and a conductor, stationed with the engineer, because new visual instrumentation and monitoring devices have eliminated the need for crewmembers located at the rear of the train.

In contrast to other rail transportation workers, subway and streetcar operators generally work for public transit authorities instead of railroads. *Subway operators* control trains that transport passengers throughout a city and its suburbs. The trains run in underground tunnels, on the surface, or on elevated tracks. Operators must stay alert to observe signals along the track that indicate when they must start, slow, or stop their train. They also make announcements to riders, may open and close the doors of the train, and ensure that passengers get on and off the subway safely.

To meet predetermined schedules, operators must control the train's speed and the amount of time spent at each station. Increasingly, however, these functions are controlled by computers and not by the operator. When breakdowns or emergencies occur, operators contact their dispatcher or supervisor and may have to evacuate cars.

Streetcar operators drive electric-powered streetcars, trolleys, or light-rail vehicles that are similar to streetcars that transport passengers in metropolitan areas. Some tracks may be recessed in city streets or have grade crossings, so operators must observe traffic signals and cope with car and truck traffic. Operators start, slow, and stop their cars so that passengers may get on and off with ease. Operators may collect fares and issue change and transfers. They also answer questions from passengers concerning fares, schedules, and routes.

Working Conditions

Many rail transportation employees work nights, weekends, and holidays because trains operate 24 hours a day, 7 days a week. Many work more than a 40-hour workweek. Seniority usually dictates who receives the more desirable shifts.

Most freight trains are unscheduled, and few workers on these trains have scheduled assignments. Instead, workers place their names on a list and wait for their turn to work. Jobs usually are assigned on short notice and often at odd hours. Those who work on trains operating between points hundreds of miles apart may spend several nights at a time away from home.

Workers on passenger trains ordinarily have regular and reliable shifts. Also, the appearance, temperature, and accommodations of passenger trains are more comfortable than those of freight trains.

Rail yard workers spend most of their time outdoors in varying weather. The work of conductors and engineers on local runs, on which trains frequently stop at stations to pick up and deliver cars, is physically demanding. Climbing up and down and getting off moving cars is strenuous and can be dangerous.

Employment

Rail transportation workers held 101,000 jobs in 2002, distributed among the detailed occupations as follows:

Railroad conductors and yardmasters	38,000
Locomotive engineers and firers	33,000
Railroad brake, signal, and switch operators	15,000
Subway, streetcar operators and all other rail transportation workers	15,000

Most rail transportation workers are employed in either the rail transportation industry or support activities for the industry. The rest work primarily for local governments as subway and streetcar operators and for mining and manufacturing establishments who operate their own locomotives and dinkey engines to move railcars containing ore, coal, and other bulk materials.

Training, Other Qualifications, and Advancement

Most railroad transportation workers begin as yard laborers and later may have the opportunity to train for engineer or conductor jobs. Railroads require that applicants have a minimum of a high school diploma or its equivalent. Applicants must have good hearing, eyesight, and color vision, as well as good hand-eye coordination, manual dexterity, and mechanical aptitude. Physical stamina is required for these entry-level jobs. Employers require railroad transportation job applicants to pass a physical examination, drug and alcohol screening, and a criminal background check. Under Federal law, all train crewmembers are subject to random drug and alcohol testing while on duty.

Applicants for locomotive engineer jobs must be at least 21 years old. Employers almost always fill engineer positions with workers who have experience in other railroad-operating occupations. Federal regulations require beginning engineers to complete a formal engineer training program, including classroom, simulator, and hands-on instruction in locomotive operation. The instruction usually is administered by the rail company in programs approved by the Federal Railroad Administration. At the end of the training period, engineers must pass a hearing and visual acuity test, a safety conduct background check, a railroad operation knowledge test, and a skills performance test. The company issues the engineer a license after the applicant passes the examinations. Other conditions and rules may apply to entry-level engineers and usually vary by employer.

To maintain certification, railroad companies must monitor their engineers. In addition, engineers must periodically pass an operational rules efficiency test. The test is an unannounced event requiring engineers to take active or responsive action in certain situations, such as maintaining a particular speed through a curve or yard.

Engineers undergo periodic physical examinations and drug and alcohol testing to determine their fitness to operate locomotives. In some cases, engineers who fail to meet these physical and conduct standards are restricted to yard service; in other instances, they may be disciplined, trained to perform other work, or discharged.

Conductor jobs generally are filled from the ranks of experienced rail transportation workers who have passed tests covering signals, timetables, operating rules, and related subjects. Seniority usually is the main factor in determining promotion to conductor. Entry-level conductors must generally be at least 21 years of age and are either trained by their employers or required to complete a formal conductor training program through a community college.

Newly trained engineers and conductors are placed on the "extra board" until permanent positions become available. Extra-board workers receive assignments only when the railroad needs substitutes for regular workers who are absent because of vacation, illness, or other personal reasons. Seniority rules may allow workers with greater seniority to select their type of assignment. For example, an engineer may move from an initial regular assignment in yard service to road service.

For subway and streetcar operator jobs, subway transit systems prefer applicants with a high school education. Most transit systems that operate subways and streetcars also operate buses. In these systems, subway or streetcar operators usually must start as bus drivers. Applicants also must be in good health, have good communication skills, and be able to make quick, responsible judgments. New operators generally complete training programs that last from a few weeks to 6 months. At the end of the period of classroom and on-the-job training, operators usually must pass qualifying examinations covering the operating system, troubleshooting, and evacuation and emergency procedures. Some operators with sufficient seniority can advance to station manager or other supervisory positions.

Job Outlook

Competition for available job opportunities is expected to be keen. Many persons qualify for rail transportation occupations because education beyond high school generally is not required. Rail transportation occupations attract more applicants than the number of available job openings, because the pay is good and the work is steady.

Employment of most railroad transportation occupations is expected to decline through the year 2012. The need to replace workers who transfer to other occupations or retire will be the main source of job openings. Employment in most rail occupations will continue to decline as both railroads and job duties are consolidated. Locomotive engineers and conductors will increasingly take on the job duties of other workers as railroads control labor costs to remain competitive with other modes of transportation. However, employment of subway and streetcar operators will grow about as fast as the average for all occupations, due to increased demand for light-rail transportation systems around the Nation.

Demand for railroad freight service will grow as the economy and the intermodal transportation of goods expand. Intermodal systems use trucks to pick up and deliver the shippers' sealed trailers or containers and employ trains to transport them long distance. This practice saves customers time and money because it carries goods across the country efficiently. For railroads, the benefit has been an increase in the efficiency of equipment use, allowing each train to make more runs each year. In order to compete with other modes of transportation, such as trucks, ships, and aircraft, railroads are improving delivery times and ontime service while reducing shipping rates.

However, growth in the number of railroad transportation workers will be adversely affected by innovations such as larger, faster, more fuel-efficient trains and computerized classification yards that make it possible to move freight more economically. Computers help to keep track of freight cars, match empty cars with the closest loads, and dispatch trains. Computer-assisted devices alert engineers to malfunctions, and work rules now allow trains to operate with two-person crews instead of the traditional three- to five-person crews.

Earnings

Median hourly earnings of rail transportation occupations in 2002 were relatively high, as indicated by the following tabulation:

Locomotive engineers and locomotive firers	$23.26
Subway and streetcar operators and all other rail transportation workers	21.48
Railroad conductors and yardmasters	21.39
Railroad brake, signal, and switch operators	20.93

Most railroad workers are paid according to miles traveled or hours worked, whichever leads to higher earnings. Full-time employees have steadier work, more regular hours, increased opportunities for overtime work, and higher earnings than do those assigned to the extra board.

Almost three-quarters of railroad transportation workers are members of unions. Many different railroad unions represent various crafts on the railroads. Most railroad engineers are members of the Brotherhood of Locomotive Engineers, while most other railroad transportation workers are members of the United Transportation

Union. Many subway operators are members of the Amalgamated Transit Union, while others belong to the Transport Workers Union of North America.

Related Occupations
Other related transportation workers include bus drivers, truck drivers and driver/sales workers, and those working in water transportation occupations.

Sources of Additional Information
To obtain information on employment opportunities, contact the employment offices of the various railroads and rail transit systems, or State employment service offices.

For general information about the rail transportation industry, contact either of the following organizations:
➤ Association of American Railroads, 50 F St. NW., Washington, DC 20001. Internet: **http://www.aar.org**
➤ Federal Railroad Administration, 1120 Vermont Ave. NW., Washington, DC 20590. Internet: **http://www.fra.dot.gov**

For general information about career opportunities in passenger transportation, contact:
➤ American Public Transportation Association, 1666 K St. NW., Suite 1100, Washington, DC 20006.

General information on career opportunities as a locomotive engineer is available from:
➤ Brotherhood of Locomotive Engineers, 1370 Ontario Ave., Cleveland, OH 44113-1702. Internet: **http://www.ble.org**

Water Transportation Occupations

(0*NET 53 5011.01, 53-5011.02, 53-5021.01, 53-5021.02, 53-5021.03, 53-5022.00, 53-5031.00)

Significant Points

● Many jobs in water transportation occupations require a merchant mariner's document or a license from the U.S. Coast Guard.

● Merchant mariners on oceangoing ships are hired for periods ranging from a single voyage to several continuous voyages and may be away from home continuously for months.

● Jobs aboard oceangoing vessels have high pay, but competition for them remains keen, and merchant mariners might have to wait months between work opportunities.

Nature of the Work
The movement of huge amounts of cargo, as well as passengers, between nations and within our Nation depends on workers in water transportation occupations, also known on commercial ships as merchant mariners. They operate and maintain deep-sea merchant ships, tugboats, towboats, ferries, dredges, excursion vessels, and other waterborne craft on the oceans, the Great Lakes, rivers, canals, and other waterways, as well as in harbors. (Workers who operate watercraft used in commercial fishing are described in the section on fishers and fishing vessel operators elsewhere in the *Handbook*.)

Captains, mates, and pilots of water vessels command or supervise the operations of ships and water vessels, both within domestic waterways and on the deep sea. *Captains* or *masters* are in overall command of the operation of a vessel, and they supervise the work of all other officers and crew. They determine the course and speed of the vessel, maneuver to avoid hazards, and continuously monitor the vessel's position with charts and navigational aides. Captains either direct or oversee crew members who steer the vessel, determine its location, operate engines, communicate with other vessels, perform maintenance, handle lines, or operate equipment on the vessel. Captains and their department heads ensure that proper procedures and safety practices are followed, check to make sure that machinery and equipment are in good working order, and oversee the loading and discharging of cargo or passengers. They also main-

tain logs and other records tracking the ships' movements, efforts at controlling pollution, and cargo and passengers carried.

Deck officers or *mates* direct the routine operation of the vessel for the captain during the shifts when they are on watch. All mates stand watch for specified periods, usually 4 hours on and 8 hours off. However, on smaller vessels, there may be only one mate (called a *pilot* on some inland towing vessels), who alternates watches with the captain. The mate would assume command of the ship if the captain became incapacitated. When more than one mate is necessary aboard a ship, they typically are designated chief mate or first mate, second mate, third mate, etc. Mates also supervise and coordinate activities of the crew aboard the ship. They inspect the cargo holds during loading to ensure that the load is stowed according to specifications and regulations. Mates supervise crew members engaged in maintenance and the primary upkeep of the vessel.

Pilots guide ships in and out of harbors, through straits, and on rivers and other confined waterways where a familiarity with local water depths, winds, tides, currents, and hazards such as reefs and shoals are of prime importance. Pilots on river and canal vessels usually are regular crew members, like mates. Harbor pilots are generally independent contractors who accompany vessels while they enter or leave port. Harbor pilots may pilot many ships in a single day. *Motorboat operators* operate small, motor-driven boats that carry six of fewer passengers on fishing charters. They also take depth soundings in turning basins and serve as liaisons between ships, between ship and shore, between harbors and beaches, or on area patrol.

Ship engineers operate, maintain, and repair propulsion engines, boilers, generators, pumps, and other machinery. Merchant marine vessels usually have four engineering officers: A chief engineer and a first, second, and third assistant engineer. Assistant engineers stand periodic watches, overseeing the safe operation of engines and machinery.

Marine oilers and more experienced *qualified members of the engine department*, or QMEDs, maintain the vessel in proper running order in the engine spaces below decks, under the direction of the ship's engineering officers. These workers lubricate gears, shafts, bearings, and other moving parts of engines and motors; read pressure and temperature gauges; record data; and sometimes assist with repairs and adjust machinery.

Sailors operate the vessel and its deck equipment under the direction of the ship's officers and keep the nonengineering areas in good condition. They stand watch, looking out for other vessels

Water transportation workers guide ships in and out of harbors, being careful to avoid other ships and other hazards.

and obstructions in the ship's path, as well as for navigational aids such as buoys and lighthouses. They also steer the ship, measure water depth in shallow water, and maintain and operate deck equipment such as lifeboats, anchors, and cargo-handling gear. On vessels handling liquid cargo, mariners designated as *pumpmen* hook up hoses, operate pumps, and clean tanks; on tugboats or tow vessels, they tie barges together into tow units, inspect them periodically, and disconnect them when the destination is reached. When docking or departing, they handle lines. They also perform routine maintenance chores, such as repairing lines, chipping rust, and painting and cleaning decks or other areas. Experienced sailors are designated *able seamen* on oceangoing vessels, but may be called simply *deckhands* on inland waters; larger vessels usually have a *boatswain*, or head seaman.

A typical deep-sea merchant ship has a captain, three deck officers or mates, a chief engineer and three assistant engineers, a radio operator, plus six or more unlicensed seamen, such as able seamen, oilers, QMEDs, and cooks or food handlers. The size and service of the ship determine the number of crewmembers for a particular voyage. Small vessels operating in harbors, on rivers, or along the coast may have a crew comprising only a captain and one deckhand. The cooking responsibilities usually fall under the deckhands' duties.

On larger coastal ships, the crew may include a captain, a mate or pilot, an engineer, and seven or eight seamen. Some ships may have special unlicensed positions for entry level apprentice trainees. Unlicensed positions on a large ship may include a full-time cook, an electrician, and machinery mechanics. On cruise ships, *bedroom stewards* keep passengers' quarters clean and comfortable.

Working Conditions

Merchant mariners spend extended periods at sea. Most deep-sea mariners are hired for one or more voyages that last for several months; there is no job security after that. The length of time between voyages varies depending on job availability and personal preference.

The rate of unionization for these workers is about 24 percent, much higher than the average for all occupations. Consequently, merchant marine officers and seamen, both veterans and beginners, are hired for voyages through union hiring halls or directly by shipping companies. Hiring halls rank the candidates by the length of time the person has been out of work and fill open slots accordingly. Hiring halls typically are found in major seaports.

At sea, these workers usually stand watch for 4 hours and are off for 8 hours, 7 days a week. Those employed on Great Lakes ships work 60 days and have 30 days off, but do not work in the winter when the lakes are frozen. Workers on rivers, on canals, and in harbors are more likely to have year-round work. Some work 8- or 12-hour shifts and go home every day. Others work steadily for a week or a month and then have an extended period off. When working, they usually are on duty for 6 or 12 hours and off for 6 or 12 hours. Those on smaller vessels are normally assigned to one vessel and have steady employment.

People in water transportation occupations work in all weather conditions. Although merchant mariners try to avoid severe storms while at sea, working in damp and cold conditions often is inevitable. While it is uncommon nowadays for vessels to suffer disasters such as fire, explosion, or a sinking, workers face the possibility that they may have to abandon their craft on short notice if it collides with other vessels or runs aground. They also risk injury or death from falling overboard and hazards associated with working with machinery, heavy loads, and dangerous cargo. However, modern safety management procedures, advanced emergency communications, and effective international rescue systems place modern mariners in a much safer position.

Most newer vessels are air conditioned, soundproofed from noisy machinery, and equipped with comfortable living quarters. For some mariners, these amenities have helped ease the sometimes difficult circumstances of long periods away from home. Also, modern communications, especially email, link modern mariners to their families. Nevertheless, some mariners dislike the long periods away from home and the confinement aboard ship and consequently leave the occupation.

Employment

Water transportation workers held about 97,000 jobs in 2002. The total number that worked at some point in the year was perhaps twice as large because many merchant marine officers and seamen worked only part of the year. The following tabulation shows employment in the occupations that make up this group:

Sailors and marine oilers	27,000
Captains, mates, and pilots of water vessels	25,000
Ship engineers	8,200
Motorboat operators	4,100
All other water transportation workers	3,600

About 30 percent of all workers were employed in water transportation services. About one half worked in inland water transportation—primarily the Mississippi River system—while the other half were employed in water transportation on the deep seas, along the coasts, and on the Great Lakes. About another 28 percent worked in establishments related to port and harbor operations, marine cargo handling, or navigational services to shipping. The Federal government employed approximately 5 percent of all water transportation workers, most of whom worked on supply ships and are Civilian Mariners of the Department Navy's Military Sealift Command.

Training, Other Qualifications

Entry, training, and educational requirements for most water transportation occupations are established and regulated by the U.S. Coast Guard, an agency of the U.S. Department of Homeland Security. All officers and operators of commercially operated vessels must be licensed by the Coast Guard, which offers various kinds of licenses, depending on the position and type of vessel.

There are two ways to qualify for a deck or engineering officer's license: applicants either must accumulate sea time and meet regulatory requirements or must graduate from the U.S. Merchant Marine Academy or one of the six State maritime academies. In both cases, applicants must pass a written examination. Federal regulations also require that an applicant pass a physical examination, a drug screening, and a National Driver Register Check before being considered. Persons without formal training can be licensed if they pass the written exam and possess sea service appropriate to the license for which they are applying. However, it is difficult to pass the examination without substantial formal schooling or independent study. Also, because seamen may work 6 or fewer months a year, it can take 5 to 8 years to accumulate the necessary experience. The academies offer a 4-year academic program leading to a bachelor-of-science degree, a license (issued only by the Coast Guard) as a third mate (deck officer) or third assistant engineer (engineering officer), and, if the person is qualified, a commission as ensign in the U.S. Naval Reserve, Merchant Marine Reserve, or Coast Guard Reserve. With experience and additional training, third officers may qualify for higher rank.

Sailors and unlicensed engineers working on U.S. flagged deep-sea and Great Lakes vessels must hold a Coast Guard-issued document. In addition, they must hold certification when working aboard liquid-carrying vessels. Able seamen also must hold government-issued certification. For employment in the merchant marine as an unlicensed seaman, a merchant mariner's document issued by the Coast Guard is needed. Most of the jobs must be filled by U.S. citizens; however, a small percentage of applicants for merchant mariner documents do not need to be U.S. citizens, but must at least be aliens legally admitted into the United States and holding a green card. A medical certificate of excellent health attesting to vision, color perception, and general physical condition is required for higher level deckhands and unlicensed engineers. While no experience or formal schooling is required, training at a union-operated school is the best source. Beginners are classified as ordinary seamen and may be assigned to any of the three unlicensed departments: Deck, engine, or steward. With experience at sea and perhaps union-sponsored training, an ordinary seaman can pass the able-seaman exam and move up with 3 years of service.

No special training or experience is needed to become a seaman or deckhand on vessels operating in harbors or on rivers or other waterways. Newly hired workers generally are given a short introductory course and then learn skills on the job. After sufficient experience, they are eligible to take a Coast Guard exam to qualify as a mate, pilot, or captain. Substantial knowledge gained through experience, courses taught at approved schools, and independent study is needed to pass the exam.

Harbor pilot training usually consists of an extended apprenticeship with a towing company or a pilots' association. Entrants may be able seamen or licensed officers.

Job Outlook

Keen competition is expected to continue for jobs in water transportation occupations. Overall, employment in these occupations is projected to grow more slowly than the average for all occupations through the year 2012. Opportunities will vary by sector, and some of the best opportunities will be in scenic transportation and sightseeing and deep sea, coastal, and Great Lakes transportation.

Employment in deep-sea shipping for American mariners is expected to stabilize after several years of decline. New international regulations have raised shipping standards with respect to safety, training, and working conditions. Consequently, competition from ships that sail under foreign *flags of convenience* should lessen as insurance rates rise for ships that do not meet the new standards.

Insuring ships under industrialized countries' flags, including that of the United States, should become less expensive, increasing the amount of international cargo carried by U.S. ships. A fleet of deep-sea U.S.-flagged ships is considered to be vital to the Nation's defense, so some receive Federal support through a maritime security subsidy and other provisions in laws that limit certain Federal cargoes to ships that fly the U.S. flag. Possible future developments include "fast ships"—oceangoing cargo vessels that use jet propulsion—which would decrease ocean-crossing times significantly. If such plans are successful, the industry will benefit in terms of increased business and employment.

Vessels on rivers and canals and on the Great Lakes carry mostly bulk products, such as coal, iron ore, petroleum, sand and gravel, grain, and chemicals. Although shipments of these products are expected to grow through the year 2012, current imports of steel are dampening employment on the Lakes, but actually leading to greater chances for overall employment for transport up the Mississippi River system. Employment in water transportation services is likely to rise, and efforts are underway at the Federal level that could lead to significantly greater use of ferries to handle commuter traffic around major metropolitan areas.

Employment growth also is expected in passenger cruise ships within U.S. waters. Vessels that operate between U.S. ports are required by law to be U.S.-flagged vessels. The building and staffing of several new cruise ships that will travel around the Hawaiian Islands will create new opportunities for employment at sea in the cruise line industry, which is composed mostly of foreign-flagged ships.

Openings within the traditional water transportation sector for mariners, although expanding only slightly, should be quite numerous because of the sizable need to replace those leaving the occupation Some experienced merchant mariners may continue to go without work for varying periods. However, this situation appears to be changing, with demand for licensed and unlicensed personnel rising. Maritime academy graduates who have not found licensed shipboard jobs in the U.S. merchant marine find jobs in related industries. Because they are commissioned as ensigns in the Naval or Coast Guard Reserve, some are selected for active duty in those branches of the Service. Some find jobs as seamen on U.S.-flagged or foreign-flagged vessels, tugboats, and other watercraft or enter civilian jobs with the U.S. Navy or Coast Guard. Some take land-based jobs with shipping companies, marine insurance companies, manufacturers of boilers or related machinery, or other related jobs.

Earnings

Earnings vary widely with the particular water transportation position and the worker's experience, ranging from the minimum wage for some beginning seamen or mate positions to more than $37.37 an hour for some experienced ship engineers. Median hourly earnings of water transportation occupations in 2002 were as follows:

Ship engineers	$24.61
Captains, mates, and pilots of water vessels	23.97
All other water transportation workers	14.67
Sailors and marine oilers	13.64
Motorboat operators	12.71

Annual pay for captains of larger vessels, such as container ships, oil tankers, or passenger ships, may exceed $100,000, but only after many years of experience. Similarly, captains of tugboats often earn more than the median reported here, with earnings dependent on the port and the nature of the cargo.

Related Occupations

Workers in other occupations who make their living on the seas and coastal waters include fishers and fishing vessel operators and some members of branches of the Armed Forces.

Sources of Additional Information

Information on a program called "Careers Afloat", which includes a substantial listing of training and employment descriptive information and contacts in the U.S., may be obtained through:

➤ Maritime Administration, U.S. Department of Transportation, 400 7th St. SW., Room 7302, Washington, DC 20590. Internet: **http://www.marad.dot.gov**

Information on merchant marine careers, training, and licensing requirements is available from any of the following organizations:

➤ Military Sealift Command, APMC, PO Box 120, Camp Pendleton, Virginia Beach, VA 23548-0120. Internet: **http://www.sealiftcommand.com**

➤ Seafarers' International Union, 5201 Auth Way, Camp Springs, MD 20746.

➤ Paul Hall Center for Maritime Training and Education, P.O. Box 75, Piney Point, MD 20674-0075. Internet: **http://www.seafarers.org/phc**

➤ International Organization of Masters, Mates, and Pilots, 700 Maritime Boulevard, Linthicum Heights, MD 21090-1941.

➤ U.S. Coast Guard National Maritime Center, 4200 Wilson Boulevard, Suite 630, Arlington, VA 22203-1804. Internet: **http://www.uscg.mil/stcw/index.htm**

Material Moving Occupations

(O*NET 53-1021.00, 53-7011.00, 53-7021.00, 53-7031.00, 53-7032.01, 53-7032.02, 53-7033.00, 53-7041.00, 53-7051.00, 53-7061.00, 53-7062.01, 53-7062.02, 53-7062.03, 53-7063.00, 53-7064.00, 53-7071.01, 53-7071.02, 53-7072.00, 53-7073.00, 53-7081.00, 53-7111.00, 53-7121.00, 53-7199.99)

Significant Points

● Job openings should be numerous because the occupation is very large and turnover is relatively high.

● Most jobs require little work experience or specific training.

● Pay is low, and the seasonal nature of the work may reduce earnings.

Nature of the Work

Material moving workers are categorized into two groups—operators and laborers. Operators use machinery to move construction materials, earth, petroleum products, and other heavy materials. Generally, they move materials over short distances—around a construction site, factory, or warehouse. Some move materials onto or off of trucks and ships. Operators control equipment by moving levers or foot pedals, operating switches, or turning dials. They may also set up and inspect equipment, make adjustments, and perform minor repairs when needed. Laborers and hand material movers manually handle freight, stock, or other materials; clean vehicles, machinery, and other equipment; feed materials into or remove materials from machines or equipment; and pack or package products and materials.

Material moving occupations are classified by the type of equipment they operate or goods they handle. Each piece of equipment requires different skills to move different types of loads. (For information on *operating engineers; paving, surfacing, and tamping equipment operators; and piledriver operators*, see the statement on construction equipment operators elsewhere in the *Handbook.*)

Industrial truck and tractor operators drive and control industrial trucks or tractors equipped to move materials around a warehouse, storage yard, factory, or construction site. A typical industrial truck, often called a forklift or lift truck, has a hydraulic lifting mechanism and forks. Industrial truck and tractor operators also may operate tractors that pull trailers loaded with materials, goods, or equipment within factories and warehouses, or around outdoor storage areas.

Excavating and loading machine and dragline operators operate or tend machinery equipped with scoops, shovels, or buckets, to dig and load sand, gravel, earth, or similar materials into trucks or onto conveyors. Construction and mining industries employ the majority of excavation and loading machine and dragline operators. *Dredge operators* excavate and maintain navigable channels in waterways by operating dredges to remove sand, gravel, or other materials from lakes, rivers, or streams. *Underground mining loading machine operators* operate underground loading machine to load coal, ore, or rock into shuttle or mine car or onto conveyors. Loading equipment may include power shovels, hoisting engines equipped with cable-drawn scraper or scoop, or machines equipped with gathering arms and conveyor.

Crane and tower operators operate mechanical boom and cable or tower and cable equipment to lift and move materials, machinery, or other heavy objects. They extend or retract a horizontally mounted boom to lower or raise a hook attached to the loadline. Most operators coordinate their maneuvers in response to hand signals and radioed instructions. Operators position the loads from the onboard console or from a remote console at the site. While crane and tower operators are noticeable at office building and other construction sites, the biggest group works in primary metal, metal fabrication, and transportation equipment manufacturing industries that use heavy, bulky materials. *Hoist and winch operators* control movement of cables, cages, and platforms to move workers and materials for manufacturing, logging, and other industrial operations. They work in such positions as derrick operators and hydraulic boom operators. Many hoist and winch operators are found in manufacturing or construction industries.

Pump operators and their helpers tend, control, or operate power-driven pumps and manifold systems that transfer gases, oil, or other materials to vessels or equipment. They maintain the equipment to regulate the flow of materials according to a schedule set up by petroleum engineers and production supervisors. *Gas compressor and gas pumping station operators* operate steam, gas, electric motor, or internal combustion engine-driven compressors. They transmit, compress, or recover gases, such as butane, nitrogen, hydrogen, and natural gas. *Wellhead pumpers* operate power pumps and auxiliary equipment to produce flow of oil or gas from wells in oilfields.

Tank, car, truck, and ship loaders operate ship loading and unloading equipment, conveyors, hoists, and other specialized material handling equipment such as railroad tank car unloading equipment. They may gauge or sample shipping tanks and test them for leaks.

Conveyor operators and tenders control or tend conveyor systems that move materials to or from stockpiles, processing stations, departments, or vehicles. *Shuttle car operators* operate diesel or electric-powered shuttle car in underground mine to transport materials from working face to mine cars or conveyor.

Laborers and hand freight, stock, and material movers manually move materials or perform other unskilled general labor. These workers move freight, stock, and other materials to and from storage and production areas, loading docks, delivery vehicles, ships, and containers. Their specific duties vary by industry and work setting. Specialized workers within this group include baggage and cargo handlers, who work in transportation industries, and truck loaders and unloaders. In factories, they may move raw materials or finished goods between loading docks, storage areas, and work areas as well as sort materials and supplies and prepare them according to their work orders

Hand packers and packagers manually pack, package, or wrap a variety of materials. They may inspect items for defects, label cartons, stamp information on products, keep records of items packed, and stack packages on loading docks. This group also includes order fillers, who pack materials for shipment, as well as grocery store courtesy clerks. In grocery stores, they may bag groceries, carry packages to customers' cars, and return shopping carts to designated areas.

Machine feeders and offbearers feed materials into or remove materials from automatic equipment or machines tended by other workers. *Cleaners of vehicles and equipment* clean machinery, vehicles, storage tanks, pipelines, and similar equipment using water and other cleaning agents, vacuums, hoses, brushes, cloths, and other cleaning equipment. *Refuse and recyclable material collectors* gather trash, garbage, and recyclables from homes and businesses along a regularly scheduled route, and deposit the refuse in their truck for transport to a dump, landfill, or recycling center. They lift and empty garbage cans or recycling bins by hand, or operate a hydraulic lift truck that picks up and empties dumpsters.

Working Conditions

Many material moving workers work outdoors in every type of climate and weather condition. The work tends to be repetitive and physically demanding. They may lift and carry heavy objects, and stoop, kneel, crouch, or crawl in awkward positions. Some work at great heights, or outdoors in all weather conditions. Some jobs expose workers to harmful materials or chemicals, fumes, odors, loud

Many material moving workers perform their duties outdoors in every type of climate and weather condition.

noise, or dangerous machinery. To avoid injury, these workers wear safety clothing, such as gloves and hardhats, and devices to protect their eyes, mouth, or hearing. These jobs have become much safer as safety equipment such as overhead guards on forklift trucks has become common. As with most machinery, accidents usually can be avoided by observing proper operating procedures and safety practices.

Material movers generally work 8-hour shifts, though longer shifts also are common. In many industries that work around the clock, material movers work evening or "graveyard" shifts. Some may work at night because the establishment may not want to disturb customers during normal business hours. Refuse and recyclable material collectors often work shifts starting at 5 or 6 a.m. Some material movers work only during certain seasons, such as when the weather permits construction activity.

Employment

Material movers held 4.9 million jobs in 2002. They were distributed among the detailed occupations as follows:

Laborers and freight, stock, and material movers, hand	2,231,000
Hand packers and packagers	920,000
Industrial truck and tractor operators	594,000
Cleaners of vehicles and equipment	344,000
Machine feeders and offbearers	164,000
First-line supervisors/managers of helpers, laborers, and material movers, hand	147,000
Refuse and recyclable material collectors	134,000
Excavating and loading machine and dragline operators	80,000
Conveyor operators and tenders	58,000
Crane and tower operators	50,000
Tank car, truck, and ship loaders	17,000
Pump operators, except wellhead pumpers	13,000
Wellhead pumpers	11,000
Hoist and winch operators	9,000
Gas compressor and gas pumping station operators	7,300
Loading machine operators, underground mining	4,000
Dredge operators	3,500
Shuttle car operators	3,200
All other material moving workers	78,000

About 29 percent of all material movers worked in the wholesale trade or retail trade industries. About 23 percent worked in manufacturing and 14 percent worked in transportation and warehousing. Significant numbers of material movers also worked in construction and mining. In addition, 13 percent of material moving workers were employed in the employment services industry where they are employed on a temporary or contract basis. For example, companies that need workers for only a few days, to move materials or to clean up a site, may contract with temporary help agencies specializing in providing suitable workers on a short-term basis. A small proportion of material movers were self-employed.

Material movers work in every part of the country. Some work in remote locations on large construction projects, such as highways and dams, or in factory or mining operations.

Training, Other Qualifications, and Advancement

Most material moving jobs require little work experience or specific training. Some employers prefer applicants with a high school diploma, but most simply require workers to be at least 18 years old and physically able to perform the work. For those jobs requiring physical exertion, employers may require that applicants pass a physical exam. Some employers also require drug testing or background checks before employment. These workers often are younger than workers in other occupations—reflecting the limited training but significant physical requirements of many of these jobs.

Material movers generally learn skills informally, on the job, from more experienced workers or supervisors. However, workers who use industrial trucks, other dangerous equipment, or handle toxic chemicals must receive specialized training in safety awareness and procedures. Many of the training requirements are standardized through the U.S. Occupational Safety and Health Administration (OSHA). This training usually is provided by the employer. Employers must also certify that each operator has received the training and evaluate each operator at least once every three years.

Material moving equipment operators need a good sense of balance, distance judgment, and eye-hand-foot coordination. For those jobs that involve dealing with the public, such as grocery store courtesy clerks, workers should be pleasant and courteous. Most jobs require reading and basic mathematics skills to read procedures manuals and billing and other documents. Mechanical aptitude and high school training in automobile or diesel mechanics are helpful because workers may perform some maintenance on their equipment. Experience operating mobile equipment, such as tractors on farms or heavy equipment in the Armed Forces, is an asset. As material moving equipment becomes more automated, many workers will need basic computer and technical knowledge to operate the equipment.

Experience in many of these jobs may allow workers to qualify or become trainees for jobs such as construction trades workers; assemblers or other production workers; motor vehicle operators; or vehicle and mobile equipment mechanics, installers, and repairers. In many workplaces, new workers often work in a material moving position before being promoted to a better paying and more highly skilled job. Some may eventually advance to become supervisors.

Job Outlook

Job openings should be numerous because the occupation is very large and turnover is relatively high—characteristic of occupations requiring little formal training. Many openings will arise from the need to replace workers who transfer to other occupations, or who retire or leave the labor force for other reasons.

Employment in material moving occupations will increase more slowly than average for all occupations through 2012. Employment growth will stem from an expanding economy and increased spending on the Nation's infrastructure, such as highways and bridges. However, equipment improvements, including the growing automation of material handling in factories and warehouses, will continue to raise productivity and moderate the demand for material movers.

Job growth for material movers largely depends on growth in the industries employing them and the type of equipment the workers operate or the materials they handle. For example, employment of operators in manufacturing will decline due to increased automation and efficiency in the production process. On the other hand, employment will grow rapidly in temporary help organizations as firms contract out material moving services. Employment also will grow in warehousing and storage as more firms contract out their warehousing functions to firms that specialize in them.

Both construction and manufacturing are very sensitive to changes in economic conditions, so the number of job openings in these industries may fluctuate from year to year. Although increasing automation may eliminate some manual tasks, new jobs will be created to operate and maintain material moving equipment.

Earnings

Median hourly earnings of material moving workers in 2002 were relatively low, as indicated by the following tabulation:

Gas compressor and gas pumping station operators	$20.44
First-line supervisors/managers of helpers, laborers, and material movers, hand	17.87
Pump operators, except wellhead pumpers	17.53
Crane and tower operators	17.47
Wellhead pumpers	16.24
Tank car, truck, and ship loaders	15.63
Excavating and loading machine and dragline operators	15.58
Hoist and winch operators	15.09
Industrial truck and tractor operators	12.54
Conveyor operators and tenders	11.66
Refuse and recyclable material collectors	11.60
Machine feeders and offbearers	10.50
Laborers and freight, stock, and material movers, hand	9.48
Cleaners of vehicles and equipment	8.20
Hand packers and packagers	8.03
All other material moving workers	12.58

Pay rates vary according to experience and job responsibilities. Pay usually is higher in metropolitan areas. The seasonality of work may reduce earnings.

Related Occupations

Other workers who operate mechanical equipment include bus drivers; construction equipment operators; machine setters, operators, and tenders—metal and plastic; rail transportation workers; and truck drivers and driver/sales workers. Other entry-level workers who perform mostly physical work are agricultural workers; building cleaning workers; construction laborers; forest, conservation, and logging workers; and grounds maintenance workers.

Sources of Additional Information

For information about job opportunities and training programs, contact local State employment service offices, building or construction contractors, manufacturers, and wholesale and retail establishments.

Information on safety and training requirements is available from:
➤ U.S. Department of Labor, Occupational Safety and Health Administration (OSHA), 200 Constitution Ave. NW., Washington, DC 20210. Internet: **http://www.osha.gov**

Information on industrial truck and tractor operators is available from:
➤ Industrial Truck Association, 1750 K St. NW., Suite 460, Washington, DC 20006.

Job Opportunities in the Armed Forces

(0*NET 55-1011.00, 55-1012.00, 55-1013.00, 55-1014.00, 55-1015.00, 55-1016.00, 55-1017.00, 55-1019.99, 55-2011.00, 55-2012.00, 55-2013.00, 55-3011.00, 55-3012.00, 55-3013.00, 55-3014.00, 55-3015.00, 55-3016.00, 55-3017.00, 55-3018.00, 55-3019.99)

Significant Points

- Opportunities should be good in all branches of the Armed Forces for applicants who meet designated standards.

- Most enlisted personnel need at least a high school diploma, while officers need a bachelor's or an advanced degree.

- Hours and working conditions can be arduous and vary substantially.

- Some training and duty assignments are hazardous, even in peacetime.

Nature of the Work

Maintaining a strong national defense encompasses such diverse activities as running a hospital, commanding a tank, programming computers, operating a nuclear reactor, or repairing and maintaining a helicopter. The military provides training and work experience in these and many other fields for more than 2.5 million people. More than 1.4 million people serve in the active Army, Navy, Marine Corps, and Air Force, and more than 1.1 million serve in their Reserve components, and the Air and Army National Guard. The Coast Guard, which is also discussed in this *Handbook* statement, is now part of the U.S. Department of Homeland Security.

The military distinguishes between enlisted and officer careers. Enlisted personnel, who make up about 85 percent of the Armed Forces, carry out the fundamental operations of the military in areas such as combat, administration, construction, engineering, health care, and human services. Officers, who make up the remaining 15 percent of the Armed Forces, are the leaders of the military, supervising and managing activities in every occupational specialty of the Armed Forces.

The sections that follow discuss the major occupational groups for enlisted personnel and officers.

Enlisted occupational groups

Administrative careers include a wide variety of positions. The military must keep accurate information for planning and managing its operations. Both paper and electronic records are kept on personnel and on equipment, funds, supplies, and other property of the military. Enlisted administrative personnel record information, type reports, maintain files, and review information to assist military officers. Personnel may work in a specialized area such as finance, accounting, legal affairs, maintenance, supply, or transportation. Some examples of administrative specialists are recruiting specialists, who recruit and place qualified personnel and provide information about military careers to young people, parents, schools, and local communities; training specialists and instructors, who provide the training programs necessary to help people perform their jobs effectively; and personnel specialists, who collect and store information about individuals in the military, including information on their training, job assignments, promotions, and health.

Combat specialty occupations refer to enlisted specialties, such as infantry, artillery, and special forces, whose members operate weapons or execute special missions during combat. Persons in these occupations normally specialize by the type of weapon system or combat operation. These personnel maneuver against enemy forces and position and fire artillery, guns, and missiles to destroy enemy positions. They also may operate tanks and amphibious assault vehicles in combat or scouting missions. When the military has difficult and dangerous missions to perform, they call upon special-operations teams. These elite combat forces maintain a constant state of readiness to strike anywhere in the world on a moment's notice. Team members from the special-operations forces conduct offensive raids, demolitions, intelligence, search-and-rescue missions, and other operations from aboard aircraft, helicopters, ships, or submarines.

Construction occupations in the military include personnel who build or repair buildings, airfields, bridges, foundations, dams, bunkers, and the electrical and plumbing components of these structures. Enlisted personnel in construction occupations operate bulldozers, cranes, graders, and other heavy equipment. Construction specialists also may work with engineers and other building specialists as part of military construction teams. Some personnel specialize in areas such as plumbing or electrical wiring. Plumbers and pipefitters install and repair the plumbing and pipe systems needed in buildings and on aircraft and ships. Building electricians install and repair electrical-wiring systems in offices, airplane hangars, and other buildings on military bases.

Electronic and electrical equipment repair personnel repair and maintain electronic and electrical equipment used in the military. Repairers normally specialize by type of equipment, such as avionics, computer, optical, communications, or weapons systems. For example, electronic instrument repairers install, test, maintain, and repair a wide variety of electronic systems, including navigational controls and biomedical instruments. Weapons maintenance technicians maintain and repair weapons used by combat forces; most of these weapons have electronic components and systems that assist in locating targets and in aiming and firing the weapon.

The military has many *engineering, science, and technical occupations*, whose members require specific knowledge to operate technical equipment, solve complex problems, or provide and interpret information. Enlisted personnel normally specialize in one area, such as space operations, emergency management, environmental health and safety, or intelligence. Space operations specialists use and repair ground-control command equipment having to do with spacecraft, including electronic systems that track the location and operation of a craft. Emergency management specialists prepare emergency procedures for all types of disasters, such as floods, tornadoes, and earthquakes. Environmental health and safety specialists inspect military facilities and food supplies for the presence of disease, germs, or other conditions hazardous to health and the environment. Intelligence specialists gather and study information by means of aerial photographs and various types of radar and surveillance systems.

Health-care personnel assist medical professionals in treating and providing services for men and women in the military. They may work as part of a patient-service team in close contact with doctors, dentists, nurses, and physical therapists to provide the necessary support functions within a hospital or clinic. Health-care specialists normally specialize in a particular area—emergency medical treatment, the operation of diagnostic tools such as x-ray and ultrasound equipment, laboratory testing of tissue and blood samples, or maintaining pharmacy supplies or patients' records, among others.

Human resources development specialists recruit and place qualified personnel and provide the training programs necessary to help people perform their jobs effectively. Personnel in this career area normally specialize by activity. For example, recruiting specialists provide information about military careers to young people, parents, schools, and local communities and explain the Armed Service's employment and training opportunities, pay and benefits, and service life. Personnel specialists collect and store information about the people in the military, including information on their previous and current training, job assignments, promotions, and health. Training specialists and instructors teach classes and give demonstrations to provide military personnel with the knowledge they need to perform their jobs.

Armed Forces personnel in *machine operator and production occupations* operate industrial equipment, machinery, and tools to fabricate and repair parts for a variety of items and structures. They may operate engines, turbines, nuclear reactors, and water pumps. Often, they specialize by type of work performed. Welders and metalworkers, for instance, work with various types of metals to repair or form the structural parts of ships, submarines, buildings, or other equipment. Survival equipment specialists inspect, maintain, and repair survival equipment such as parachutes and aircraft life support equipment. Dental and optical laboratory technicians construct and repair dental equipment and eyeglasses for military personnel.

Media and public affairs occupations deal with the public presentation and interpretation of military information and events. Enlisted media and public affairs personnel take and develop photographs; film, record, and edit audio and video programs; present news and music programs; and produce graphic artwork, drawings, and other visual displays. Other public affairs specialists act as interpreters and translators to convert written or spoken foreign languages into English or other languages.

Protective service personnel include those who enforce military laws and regulations, provide emergency response to natural and human-made disasters, and maintain food standards. These personnel normally specialize by function. For example, military police control traffic, prevent crime, and respond to emergencies. Other law enforcement and security specialists investigate crimes committed on military property and guard inmates in military correctional facilities. Firefighters put out, control, and help prevent fires in buildings, on aircraft, and aboard ships. Food service specialists prepare all types of food in dining halls, hospitals, and ships.

Transportation and material handling specialists ensure the safe transport of people and cargo. Most personnel within this occupational group are classified according to mode of transportation, such as aircraft, motor vehicle, or ship. Aircrew members operate equipment on board aircraft during operations. Vehicle drivers operate all types of heavy military vehicles, including fuel or water tank trucks, semi-trailers, heavy troop transports, and passenger buses. Quartermasters and boat operators navigate and pilot many types of small watercraft, including tugboats, gunboats, and barges. Cargo specialists load and unload military supplies, using equipment such as forklifts and cranes.

Vehicle and machinery mechanics conduct preventive and corrective maintenance on aircraft, ships, automotive and heavy equipment, heating and cooling systems, marine engines, and powerhouse station equipment. These workers typically specialize by the type of equipment that they maintain. For example, aircraft mechanics inspect, service, and repair helicopters and airplanes. Automotive and heavy-equipment mechanics maintain and repair vehicles such as jeeps, cars, trucks, tanks, self-propelled missile launchers, and other combat vehicles. They also repair bulldozers, power shovels, and other construction equipment. Heating and cooling mechanics install and repair air-conditioning, refrigeration, and heating equipment. Marine engine mechanics repair and maintain gasoline and diesel engines on ships, boats, and other watercraft. They also repair shipboard mechanical and electrical equipment. Powerhouse mechanics install, maintain, and repair electrical and mechanical equipment in power-generating stations.

Officer occupational groups

Combat specialty officers plan and direct military operations, oversee combat activities, and serve as combat leaders. This category includes officers in charge of tanks and other armored assault vehicles, artillery systems, special operations forces, and infantry. Combat specialty officers normally specialize by the type of unit that they lead. Within the unit, they may specialize by the type of weapon system. Artillery and missile system officers, for example, direct personnel as they target, launch, test, and maintain various types of missiles and artillery. Special-operations officers lead their units in offensive raids, demolitions, intelligence gathering, and search-and-rescue missions.

Engineering, science, and technical officers have a wide range of responsibilities based on their area of expertise. They lead or perform activities in areas such as space operations, environmental health and safety, and engineering. These officers may direct the operations of communications centers or the development of complex computer systems. Environmental health and safety officers study the air, ground, and water to identify and analyze sources of pollution and its effects. They also direct programs to control safety and health hazards in the workplace. Other personnel work as aerospace engineers to design and direct the development of military aircraft, missiles, and spacecraft.

Executive, administrative, and managerial officers oversee and direct military activities in key functional areas such as finance, accounting, health administration, international relations, and supply. Health services administrators, for instance, are responsible for the overall quality of care provided at the hospitals and clinics they

An Air Force mechanic maintains an aircraft.

An Army x-ray technician works with sophisticated equipment.

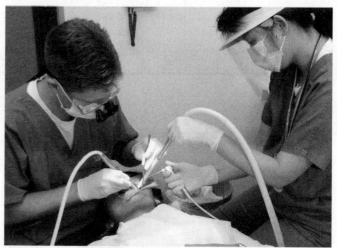

Navy dentist providing dental care.

operate. They must ensure that each department works together to provide the highest quality of care. As another example, purchasing and contracting managers negotiate and monitor contracts for the purchase of the billions of dollars worth of equipment, supplies, and services that the military buys from private industry each year.

Health-care officers provide health services at military facilities, on the basis of their area of specialization. Officers who assist in examining, diagnosing, and treating patients with illness, injury, or disease include physicians, registered nurses, and dentists. Other health-care officers provide therapy, rehabilitative treatment, and additional services for patients. Physical and occupational therapists plan and administer therapy to help patients adjust to disabilities, regain independence, and return to work. Speech therapists evaluate and treat patients with hearing and speech problems. Dietitians manage food service facilities and plan meals for hospital patients and for outpatients who need special diets. Pharmacists manage the purchase, storage, and dispensation of drugs and medicines. Physicians and surgeons in this occupational group provide the majority of medical services to the military and their families. Dentists treat diseases and disorders of the mouth. Optometrists treat vision problems by prescribing eyeglasses or contact lenses. Psychologists provide mental health care and also conduct research on behavior and emotions.

Media and affairs officers oversee the development, production, and presentation of information or events for the public. These officers may produce and direct motion pictures, videotapes, and television and radio broadcasts that are used for training, news, and entertainment. Some plan, develop, and direct the activities of military bands. Public information officers respond to inquiries about military activities and prepare news releases and reports to keep the public informed.

Protective service officers are responsible for the safety and protection of individuals and property on military bases and vessels. Emergency management officers plan and prepare for all types of natural and human-made disasters. They develop warning, control, and evacuation plans to be used in the event of a disaster. Law enforcement and security officers enforce all applicable laws on military bases and investigate crimes when the law has been broken.

Support services officers manage food service activities and perform services in support of the morale and well-being of military personnel and their families. Food services managers oversee the preparation and delivery of food services within dining facilities located on military installations and vessels. Social workers focus on improving conditions that cause social problems such as drug and alcohol abuse, racism, and sexism. Chaplains conduct worship services for military personnel and perform other spiritual duties covering the beliefs and practices of all religious faiths

Table 1. Military enlisted personnel by broad occupational category and branch of military service, June 2003

Occupational Group - Enlisted	Army	Air Force	Coast Guard	Marine Corps	Navy	Total, all services
Administrative occupations	15,175	25,674	1,775	8,642	21,225	72,491
Combat specialty occupations	104,876	253	745	33,070	3,316	142,260
Construction occupations	15,340	6,261		5,145	5,397	32,143
Electronic and electrical repair occupations	14,035	37,155	3,530	16,082	52,094	122,896
Engineering, science, and technical occupations	63,531	43,422	720	35,237	41,003	183,913
Health care occupations	26,660	17,108	685		23,818	68,271
Human resource development occupations	16,202	12,715		6,784	5,510	41,211
Machine operator and precision work occupations	4,528	7,783	2,079	1,710	23,485	39,585
Media and public affairs occupations	4,552	5,921	131	1,556	5,255	17,415
Protective service occupations	24,831	29,516	893	6,086	10,630	71,956
Support services occupations	13,687	1,535	1,213	3,704	11,570	31,709
Transportation and material handling occupations	54,140	33,835	6,423	23,908	39,272	157,578
Vehicle machinery mechanic occupations	48,043	48,433	5,654	18,473	50,266	170,869
Total, by service	405,600	269,611	23,848	160,397	292,841	1,152,297

SOURCE: U.S. Department of Defense, Defense Manpower Data Center East

Table 2. Military officer personnel by broad occupational category and branch of service, June 2003

Occupational Group - Officer	Army	Air Force	Coast Guard	Marine Corps	Navy	Total, all services
Combat specialty occupations	18,306	5,422	2	3,990	5,626	33,346
Engineering, science, and technical occupations	17,368	15,902	1,715	3,044	15,413	53,442
Executive, administrative, and managerial occupations	10,139	9,579	388	2,398	8,234	30,738
Health care occupations	9,775	9,247	10		6,531	25,563
Human resource development occupations	1,369	2,406	247	23	3,807	7,852
Media and public affairs occupations	177	503	15	131	932	1,758
Protective service occupations	2,174	1,838	172	174	855	5,213
Support services occupations	1,500	836		40	1,654	4,030
Transportation occupations	12,612	19,710	3,244	6,258	12,679	54,503
Total, by service	73,420	65,443	5,793	16,058	55,731	216,445

SOURCE: U.S. Department of Defense, Defense Manpower Data Center East

Officers in *transportation occupations* manage and perform activities related to the safe transport of military personnel and material by air and water. Officers normally specialize by mode of transportation or area of expertise, because, in many cases, they must meet licensing and certification requirements. Pilots in the military fly various types of specialized airplanes and helicopters to carry troops and equipment and to execute combat missions. Navigators use radar, radio, and other navigation equipment to determine their position and plan their route of travel. Officers on ships and submarines work as a team to manage the various departments aboard their vessels. Ships' engineers direct engineering departments aboard ships and submarines, including engine operations, maintenance, repair, heating, and power generation.

Employment

In 2003, more than 2.5 million people served in the Armed Forces. More than 1.4 million individuals were on active duty in the Armed Forces—about 490,000 in the Army, 377,000 in the Navy, 368,000 in the Air Force, and 179,000 in the Marine Corps. In addition, more than 1.1 million people served in their Reserve components, and the Air and Army National Guard. In addition, 38,000 individuals served in the Coast Guard, which is now part of the U.S. Department of Homeland Security. Table 1 shows the occupational composition of the 1.2 million active-duty enlisted personnel in 2003; table 2 presents similar information for the 216,000 active-duty officers.

Military personnel are stationed throughout the United States and in many countries around the world. More than half of all military jobs are located in California, Texas, North Carolina, Virginia, Florida, and Georgia. About 395,000 individuals were stationed outside the United States in 2002, including those assigned to ships at sea. Approximately 104,000 of these were stationed in Europe, mainly in Germany, and another 85,000 were assigned to East Asia and the Pacific area, mostly in Japan and the Republic of Korea.

Qualifications, Training, and Advancement

Enlisted personnel. In order to join the services, enlisted personnel must sign a legal agreement called an enlistment contract, which usually involves a commitment to 8 years of service. Depending on the terms of the contract, 2 to 6 years are spent on active duty, and the balance is spent in the reserves. The enlistment contract obligates the service to provide the agreed-upon job, rating, pay, cash bonuses for enlistment in certain occupations, medical and other benefits, occupational training, and continuing education. In return, enlisted personnel must serve satisfactorily for the period specified.

Requirements for each service vary, but certain qualifications for enlistment are common to all branches. In order to enlist, one must be between 17 and 35 years old, be a U.S. citizen or an alien holding permanent resident status, not have a felony record, and possess a birth certificate. Applicants who are aged 17 must have the consent of a parent or legal guardian before entering the service.

The Coast Guard is the Nation's leading maritime law enforcement agency.

The Marine Corps embarks on many dangerous missions.

Coast Guard enlisted personnel must enter active duty before their 28th birthday, whereas Marine Corps enlisted personnel must not be over the age of 29. Applicants must both pass a written examination—the Armed Services Vocational Aptitude Battery—and meet certain minimum physical standards, such as height, weight, vision, and overall health. All branches of the Armed Forces require high school graduation or its equivalent for certain enlistment options. In 2003, nearly 9 out of 10 recruits were high school graduates.

People thinking about enlisting in the military should learn as much as they can about military life before making a decision. Doing so is especially important if you are thinking about making the military a career. Speaking to friends and relatives with military experience is a good idea. Find out what the military can offer you and what it will expect in return. Then, talk to a recruiter, who can determine whether you qualify for enlistment, explain the various enlistment options, and tell you which military occupational specialties currently have openings. Bear in mind that the recruiter's job is to recruit promising applicants into his or her branch of military service, so the information that the recruiter gives you is likely to stress the positive aspects of military life in the branch in which he or she serves.

Ask the recruiter for the branch you have chosen to assess your chances of being accepted for training in the occupation of your choice, or, better still, take the aptitude exam to see how well you score. The military uses this exam as a placement exam, and test scores largely determine an individual's chances of being accepted into a particular training program. Selection for a particular type of training depends on the needs of the service, your general and technical aptitudes, and your personal preference. Because all prospective recruits are required to take the exam, those who do so before committing themselves to enlist have the advantage of knowing in advance whether they stand a good chance of being accepted for training in a particular specialty. The recruiter can schedule you for the Armed Services Vocational Aptitude Battery without any obligation. Many high schools offer the exam as an easy way for students to explore the possibility of a military career, and the test also affords an insight into career areas in which the student has demonstrated aptitudes and interests.

If you decide to join the military, the next step is to pass the physical examination and sign an enlistment contract. Negotiating the contract involves choosing, qualifying for, and agreeing on a number of enlistment options, such as the length of active-duty time, which may vary according to the option. Most active-duty programs have first-term enlistments of 4 years, although there are some 2-, 3-, and 6-year programs. The contract also will state the date of enlistment and other options—for example, bonuses and the types of training to be received. If the service is unable to fulfill any of its obligations under the contract, such as providing a certain kind of training, the contract may become null and void.

All branches of the Armed Services offer a "delayed-entry program" by which an individual can delay entry into active duty for up to 1 year after enlisting. High school students can enlist during their senior year and enter a service after graduation. Others choose this program because the job training they desire is not currently available, but will be within the coming year, or because they need time to arrange their personal affairs.

Women are eligible to enter most military specialties; for example, they may become mechanics, missile maintenance technicians, heavy-equipment operators, and fighter pilots, or they may enter into medical care, administrative support, and intelligence specialties. Generally, only occupations involving direct exposure to combat are excluded.

People planning to apply the skills gained through military training to a civilian career should first determine how good the prospects are for civilian employment in jobs related to the military specialty that interests them. Second, they should know the prerequisites for the related civilian job. Because many civilian occupations require a license, certification, or minimum level of education, it is important to determine whether military training is sufficient for a person to enter the civilian equivalent or, if not, what additional training will be required. Other *Handbook* statements discuss the job outlook, training requirements, and other aspects of civilian occupations for which military training and experience are helpful. Additional information often can be obtained from school counselors.

Following enlistment, new members of the Armed Forces undergo recruit training, better known as "basic" training. Through courses in military skills and protocol recruit training provides a 6- to 12-week introduction to military life. Days and nights are carefully structured and include rigorous physical exercise designed to improve strength and endurance and build each unit's cohesion.

Following basic training, most recruits take additional training at technical schools that prepare them for a particular military occupational specialty. The formal training period generally lasts from 10 to 20 weeks, although training for certain occupations—nuclear power plant operator, for example—may take as long as a year. Recruits not assigned to classroom instruction receive on-the-job training at their first duty assignment.

Many service people get college credit for the technical training they receive on duty, which, combined with off-duty courses, can lead to an associate degree through programs in community colleges such as the Community College of the Air Force. In addition to on-duty training, military personnel may choose from a variety of educational programs. Most military installations have tuition assistance programs for people wishing to take courses during off-duty hours. The courses may be correspondence courses or courses in degree programs offered by local colleges or universities. Tuition assistance pays up to 75 percent of college costs. Also available are courses designed to help service personnel earn high school equivalency diplomas. Each branch of the service provides opportunities for full-time study to a limited number of exceptional applicants. Military personnel accepted into these highly competitive programs—in law or medicine, for example—receive full pay, allowances, tuition, and related fees. In return, they must agree to serve an additional amount of time in the service. Other highly selective programs enable enlisted personnel to qualify as commissioned officers through additional military training.

Warrant officers. Warrant officers are technical and tactical leaders who specialize in a specific technical area; for example, Army aviators make up one group of warrant officers. The Army Warrant Officer Corps constitutes less than 5 percent of the total Army. Although the Corps is small in size, its level of responsibility is high. Its members receive extended career opportunities, worldwide leadership assignments, and increased pay and retirement benefits. Selection to attend the Warrant Officer Candidate School is highly competitive and restricted to those with the rank of E5 or higher (table 3.)

Officers. Officer training in the Armed Forces is provided through the Federal service academies (Military, Naval, Air Force, and Coast Guard); the Reserve Officers Training Corps (ROTC) program offered at many colleges and universities; Officer Candidate School (OCS) or Officer Training School (OTS); the National Guard (State Officer Candidate School programs); the Uniformed Services University of Health Sciences; and other programs. All are highly selective and are good options for those wishing to make the military a career. Persons interested in obtaining training through the Federal service academies must be single to enter and graduate, while those seeking training through OCS, OTS, or ROTC need not be single. Single parents with one or more minor dependents are not eligible to become commissioned officers.

Federal service academies provide a 4-year college program leading to a bachelor-of-science degree. Midshipmen or cadets are provided free room and board, tuition, medical and dental care, and a monthly allowance. Graduates receive regular or reserve commissions and have a 5-year active-duty obligation, or more if they are entering flight training.

To become a candidate for appointment as a cadet or midshipman in one of the service academies, applicants are required to obtain a nomination from an authorized source, usually a member of Congress. Candidates do not need to know a member of Congress personally to request a nomination. Nominees must have an academic record of the requisite quality, college aptitude test scores above an established minimum, and recommendations from teachers or school officials; they also must pass a medical examination. Appointments are made from the list of eligible nominees. Appointments to the Coast Guard Academy, however, are based strictly on merit and do not require a nomination.

ROTC programs train students in about 950 Army, approximately 70 Navy and Marine Corps, and around 1,000 Air Force units at participating colleges and universities. Trainees take 2 to 5 hours of military instruction a week, in addition to regular college courses. After graduation, they may serve as officers on active duty for a stipulated period. Some may serve their obligation in the Reserves or National Guard. In the last 2 years of a ROTC program, students receive a monthly allowance while attending school, as well as additional pay for summer training. ROTC scholarships for 2, 3, and 4 years are available on a competitive basis. All scholarships pay for tuition and have allowances for subsistence, textbooks, supplies, and other costs.

College graduates can earn a commission in the Armed Forces through OCS or OTS programs in the Army, Navy, Air Force, Marine Corps, Coast Guard, and National Guard. These officers generally must serve their obligation on active duty. Those with training in certain health professions may qualify for direct appointment as officers. In the case of persons studying for the health professions, financial assistance and internship opportunities are available from the military in return for specified periods of military service. Prospective medical students can apply to the Uniformed Services University of Health Sciences, which offers free tuition in a program leading to a doctor-of-medicine (M.D.) degree. In return, graduates must serve for 7 years in either the military or the U.S. Public Health Service. Direct appointments also are available for those qualified to serve in other specialty areas, such as the judge advocate general (legal) or chaplain corps. Flight training is available to commissioned officers in each branch of the Armed Forces.

Table 3. Military rank and employment for active duty personnel, June 2003

Grade   Rank and title

	Army	Navy and Coast Guard	Air Force	Marine Corps	Total Employment
Commissioned officers:					
O-10	General	Admiral	General	General	35
O-9	Lieutenant General	Vice Admiral	Lieutenant General	Lieutenant General	126
O-8	Major General	Rear Admiral Upper	Major General	Major General	282
O-7	Brigadier General	Rear Admiral Lower	Brigadier General	Brigadier General	446
O-6	Colonel	Captain	Colonel	Colonel	11,884
O-5	Lieutenant Colonel	Commander	Lieutenant Colonel	Lieutenant Colonel	28,565
O-4	Major	Lieutenant Commander	Major	Major	44,501
O-3	Captain	Lieutenant	Captain	Captain	69,184
O-2	1st Lieutenant	Lieutenant (JG)	1st Lieutenant	1st Lieutenant	29,416
O-1	2nd Lieutenant	Ensign	2nd Lieutenant	2nd Lieutenant	28,597
Warrant officers:					
W-5	Chief Warrant Officer	Chief Warrant Officer	—	Chief Warrant Officer	504
W-4	Chief Warrant Officer	Chief Warrant Officer	—	Chief Warrant Officer	2,082
W-3	Chief Warrant Officer	Chief Warrant Officer	—	Chief Warrant Officer	4,385
W-2	Chief Warrant Officer	Chief Warrant Officer	—	Chief Warrant Officer	6,118
W-1	Warrant Officer	Warrant Officer	—	Warrant Officer	2,603
Enlisted personnel:					
E-9	Sergeant Major	Master Chief Petty Officer	Chief Master Sergeant	Sergeant Major	10,869
E-8	1st Sergeant/Master Sergeant	Senior Chief Petty Officer	Senior Master Sergeant	Master Sergeant/1st Sergeant	26,545
E-7	Sergeant First Class	Chief Petty Officer	Master Sergeant	Gunnery Sergeant	100,002
E-6	Staff Sergeant	Petty Officer 1st Class	Technical Sergeant	Staff Sergeant	175,281
E-5	Sergeant	Petty Officer 2nd Class	Staff Sergeant	Sergeant	251,122
E-4	Corporal/Specialist	Petty Officer 3rd Class	Senior Airman	Corporal	268,606
E-3	Private First Class	Seaman	Airman 1st Class	Lance Corporal	218,219
E-2	Private	Seaman Apprentice	Airman	Private 1st Class	83,423
E-1	Private	Seaman Recruit	Airman Basic	Private	53,211

SOURCE: U.S. Department of Defense

In addition, the Army has a direct enlistment option to become a warrant officer aviator.

Each service has different criteria for promoting personnel. Generally, the first few promotions for both enlisted and officer personnel come easily; subsequent promotions are much more competitive. Criteria for promotion may include time in service and in grade, job performance, a fitness report (supervisor's recommendation), and the passing of written examinations. People who are passed over for promotion several times generally must leave the military. Table 3 shows the officer, warrant officer, and enlisted ranks by service.

Job Outlook

Opportunities should be good for qualified individuals in all branches of the Armed Forces through 2012. Many military personnel retire with a pension after 20 years of service, while they still are young enough to start a new career. More than 365,000 enlisted personnel and officers must be recruited each year to replace those who complete their commitment or retire. Since the end of the draft in 1973, the military has met its personnel requirements with volunteers. When the economy is good and civilian employment opportunities generally are more favorable, it is more difficult for all the services to meet their recruitment quotas. By contrast, it is much easier to do so during a recession.

America's strategic position is stronger than it has been in decades. Despite reductions in personnel due to the elimination of the threat from Eastern Europe and Russia, the number of active-duty personnel is expected to remain roughly constant through 2012. However, recent conflicts in other countries and the resulting strain on the Armed Forces may lead to an increasing number of active-duty personnel. The Armed Forces' current goal is to maintain a sufficient force to fight and win two major regional conflicts at the same time. Political events, however, could cause these plans to change.

Educational requirements will continue to rise as military jobs become more technical and complex. High school graduates and applicants with a college background will be sought to fill the ranks of enlisted personnel, while virtually all officers will need at least a bachelor's degree and, in some cases, an advanced degree as well.

Earnings

The earnings structure for military personnel is shown in table 4. Most enlisted personnel started as recruits at Grade E-1 in 2003; however, those with special skills or above-average education started as high as Grade E-4. Most warrant officers had started at Grade W-1 or W-2, depending upon their occupational and academic qualifications and the branch of service of which they were a member, but warrant officer is not an entry-level occupation and, consequently, these individuals all had previous military service. Most commissioned officers started at Grade O-1; some with advanced education started at Grade O-2, and some highly trained officers—for example, physicians and dentists—started as high as Grade O-3. Pay varies by total years of service as well as rank. Because it usually takes many years to reach the higher ranks, most personnel in higher ranks receive the higher pay rates awarded to those with many years of service.

In addition to receiving their basic pay, military personnel are provided with free room and board (or a tax-free housing and subsistence allowance), free medical and dental care, a military clothing allowance, military supermarket and department store shopping privileges, 30 days of paid vacation a year (referred to as leave), and travel opportunities. In many duty stations, military personnel may receive a housing allowance that can be used for off-base housing. This allowance can be substantial, but varies greatly by rank and

Table 4. Military basic monthly pay by grade for active duty personnel, June 1, 2003

Years of service

Grade	Less than 2	Over 4	Over 8	Over 12	Over 16	Over 20
O-10	—	—	—	—	—	$11,874.90
O-9	—	—	—	—	—	10,563.60
O-8	$7,474.50	$7,927.20	$8,468.70	$8,868.90	$9,238.20	10,008.90
O-7	6,210.90	6,739.20	7,120.80	7,559.40	8,468.70	9,051.30
O-6	4,603.20	5388.9	5,641.20	5672.1	6,564.30	7,233.30
O-5	3,837.60	4,678.50	4,977.00	5,403.00	5,991.90	6,329.10
O-4	3,311.10	4,145.70	4,637.70	5,201.40	5,471.10	—
O-3	2,911.20	3,883.50	4,273.50	4,623.30	—	—
O-2	2,515.20	3,410.00	—	—	—	—
O-1	2,183.70	2,746.80	—	—	—	—
W-5	—	—	—	—	—	5,169.30
W-4	3,088.10	3,420.60	3,733.50	4,044.60	4,356.00	4,664.40
W-3	2,747.10	3,017.70	3,281.70	3,580.50	3,915.60	4,201.50
W-2	2,416.50	2,763.00	2,993.10	3,264.00	3,453.90	3,705.90
W-1	2,133.90	2,501.10	2,782.20	3,006.90	3,203.40	3,409.50
E-9	—	—	—	3,645.00	3,687.00	4,180.80
E-8	—	—	2,975.40	3,141.30	3,342.00	3,625.50
E-7	2,068.50	2,428.20	2,667.90	2,838.30	3,066.30	3,182.70
E-6	1,770.60	2,117.10	2,400.90	2,562.30	2,663.10	2709.60
E-5	1,625.40	1,903.50	2,151.90	2,283.30	2,283.30	—
E-4	1,502.70	1,749.30	1824.00	—	—	—
E-3	1,356.90	1,528.80	—	—	—	—
E-2	1,290.00	—	—	—	—	—
E-1 4mos+	1,150.80	—	—	—	—	—
E-1 <4mos	1,064.70	—	—	—	—	—

SOURCE: U.S. Department of Defense — Defense Finance and Accounting Service duty station. For example, in July 2003, the housing allowance for an E-4 with dependents was $505 per month; for a comparable individual without dependents, it was $353. The allowance for an O-4 with dependents was $961 per month; for a person without dependents, it was $836. Other allowances are paid for foreign duty, hazardous duty, submarine and flight duty, and employment as a medical officer. Athletic and other facilities—such as gymnasiums, tennis courts, golf courses, bowling centers, libraries, and movie theaters—are available on many military installations. Military personnel are eligible for retirement benefits after 20 years of service.

The Veterans Administration (VA) provides numerous benefits to those who have served at least 2 years in the Armed Forces. Veterans are eligible for free care in VA hospitals for all service-related disabilities, regardless of time served; those with other medical problems are eligible for free VA care if they are unable to pay the cost of hospitalization elsewhere. Admission to a VA medical center depends on the availability of beds, however. Veterans also are eligible for certain loans, including loans to purchase a home. Veterans, regardless of health, can convert a military life insurance policy to an individual policy with any participating company in the veteran's State of residence. In addition, job counseling, testing, and placement services are available.

Veterans who participate in the New Montgomery GI Bill Program receive educational benefits. Under this program, Armed Forces personnel may elect to deduct up to $100 a month from their pay during the first 12 months of active duty, putting the money toward their future education. Veterans who serve on active duty for more than 2 years or who put in 2 years' active duty plus 4 years in the Selected Reserve will receive $528 a month in basic benefits for 36 months. Those who enlist and serve for 2 years will receive $429 a month for 36 months. In addition, each service provides its own contributions to the enlistee's future education. The sum of the amounts from all these sources becomes the service member's educational fund. Upon separation from active duty, the fund can be used to finance educational costs at any VA-approved institution. Among those institutions which are approved by the VA are many vocational, correspondence, certification, business, technical, and flight-training schools; community and junior colleges; and colleges and universities.

Sources of Additional Information

Each of the military services publishes handbooks, fact sheets, and pamphlets describing entrance requirements, training and advancement opportunities, and other aspects of military careers. These publications are widely available at all recruiting stations, at most State employment service offices, and in high schools, colleges, and public libraries. Information on educational and other veterans' benefits is available from VA offices located throughout the country.

In addition, the Defense Manpower Data Center, an agency of the U.S. Department of Defense, publishes *Military Career Guide Online*, a compendium of military occupational, training, and career information designed for use by students and jobseekers. This information is available on the Internet: **http://www.todaysmilitary.com**

Data for Occupations Not Studied in Detail

Employment in the hundreds of occupations covered in detail in the main body of the *Handbook* accounts for more than 126 million or 88 percent of all jobs in the economy. Although occupations covering the full spectrum of work are included, those requiring lengthy education or training generally are given the most attention.

This chapter presents summary data on 126 additional occupations, for which employment projections are prepared, but for which detailed occupational information is not developed. These occupations account for about 7 percent of all jobs. For each occupation, the Occupational Information Network (O*NET) code, a brief description of the nature of the work, the number of jobs in 2002, a phrase describing the projected employment change from 2002 to 2012, and the most significant source of education or training are presented. For a complete list of O*NET codes cited in the *Handbook*, refer to a later chapter, *Occupational Information Network (O*NET) Coverage*. For guidelines on interpreting the description of projected employment change, refer to a chapter in the front of the *Handbook*, Occupational Information Included in the *Handbook*.

The approximately 5 percent of all jobs not covered either in the detailed occupational descriptions in the main body of the *Handbook* or in the summary data presented in this chapter are mainly residual categories, such as "all other managers," for which little meaningful information could be developed.

Management, business, and financial occupations

Agents and business managers of artists, performers, and athletes

(O*NET 13-1011.00)

Represent and promote artists, performers, and athletes to prospective employers. May handle contract negotiations and other business matters for clients.

2002 employment: 15,000
Projected 2002-12 employment change: Faster than average
Most significant source of education or training: Bachelor's or higher degree, plus work experience

Appraisers and assessors of real estate

(O*NET 13-2021.01, 13-2021.02)

Appraise real property to determine its fair value. May assess taxes in accordance with prescribed schedules.

2002 employment: 88,000
Projected 2002-12 employment change: About as fast as average
Most significant source of education or training: Postsecondary vocational award

Compliance officers, except agriculture, construction, health and safety, and transportation

(O*NET 13-1041.01, 13-1041.02, 13-1041.03, 13-1041.04, 13-1041.05, 13-1041.06)

Examine, evaluate, and investigate eligibility for or conformity with laws and regulations governing contract compliance of licenses and permits, and other compliance and enforcement inspection activities not classified elsewhere. Exclude tax examiners, collectors, and revenue agents and financial examiners.

2002 employment: 158,000
Projected 2002-12 employment change: About as fast as average
Most significant source of education or training: Long-term on-the-job training

Credit analysts

(O*NET 13-2041.00)

Analyze current credit data and financial statements of individuals or firms to determine the degree of risk involved in extending credit or lending money. Prepare reports with this credit information for use in decisionmaking.

2002 employment: 66,000
Projected 2002-12 employment change: About as fast as average
Most significant source of education or training: Bachelor's degree

Emergency management specialists

(O*NET 13-1061.00)

Coordinate disaster response or crisis management activities, provide disaster preparedness training, and prepare emergency plans and procedures for natural (e.g. hurricanes, floods, earthquakes), wartime, or technological (e.g., nuclear power plant emergencies, hazardous materials spills) disasters or hostage situations.

2002 employment: 11,000
Projected 2002-12 employment change: Faster than average
Most significant source of education or training: Work experience in a related occupation

Financial examiners

(O*NET 13-2061.00)

Enforce or ensure compliance with laws and regulations governing financial and securities institutions and financial and real estate transactions. May examine, verify correctness of, or establish authenticity of records.

2002 employment: 25,000
Projected 2002-12 employment change: More slowly than average
Most significant source of education or training: Bachelor's degree

Gaming managers

(O*NET 11-9071.00)

Plan, organize, direct, control, or coordinate gaming operations in a casino. Formulate gaming policies for their area of responsibility.

2002 employment: 6,100
Projected 2002-12 employment change: About as fast as average
Most significant source of education or training: Work experience in a related occupation

Meeting and convention planners

(O*NET 13-1121.00)

Coordinate activities of staff and convention personnel to make arrangements for group meetings and conventions.

2002 employment: 37,000
Projected 2002-12 employment change: Faster than average
Most significant source of education or training: Bachelor's degree

Postmasters and mail superintendents

(O*NET 11-9131.00)

Direct and coordinate operational, administrative, management, and supportive services of a U.S. post office; or coordinate activities of workers engaged in postal and related work in assigned post office.

2002 employment: 25,000
Projected 2002-12 employment change: A decline
Most significant source of education or training: Work experience in a related occupation

Social and community service managers

(O*NET 11-9151.00)

Plan, organize, or coordinate the activities of a social service program or community outreach organization. Oversee the program or organization's budget and polices regarding participant involvement, program requirement, and benefits. Work may involve directing social workers, counselors, or probation officers.

2002 employment: 129,000
Projected 2002-12 employment change: Faster than average
Most significant source of education or training: Bachelor's degree

Tax preparers

(O*NET 13-2082.00)

Prepare tax returns for individuals or small businesses but do not have the background or responsibilities of an accredited or certified public accountant.

2002 employment: 79,000
Projected 2002-12 employment change: Faster than average
Most significant source of education or training: Moderate-term on-the-job training

Transportation, storage, and distribution managers

(O*NET 11-3071.01, 11-3071.02)

Plan, direct, or coordinate transportation, storage, or distribution activities in accordance with governmental policies and regulations. Includes logistics managers.

2002 employment: 111,000
Projected 2002-12 employment change: About as fast as average
Most significant source of education or training: Work experience in a related occupation

Professional and related occupations

Athletic trainers

(O*NET 29-9091.00)

Evaluate, advise, and treat athletes to assist recovery from injury, avoid injury, or maintain peak physical fitness.

2002 employment: 14,000
Projected 2002-12 employment change: Faster than average
Most significant source of education or training: Bachelor's degree

Audio-visual collections specialists

(O*NET 25-9011.00)

Prepare, plan, and operate audio-visual teaching aids for use in education. May record, catalogue, and file audio-visual materials.

2002 employment: 9,800
Projected 2002-12 employment change: About as fast as average
Most significant source of education or training: Moderate-term on-the-job training

Dietetic technicians

(O*NET 29-2051.00)

Assist dieticians in the provision of food service and nutritional programs. Under the supervision of dieticians, may plan and produce meals based on established guidelines, teach principles of food and nutrition, or counsel individuals.

2002 employment: 29,000
Projected 2002-12 employment change: About as fast as average
Most significant source of education or training: Moderate-term on-the-job training

Directors, religious activities and education

(O*NET 21-2021.00)

Direct and coordinate activities of a denominational group to meet religious needs of students. Plan, direct, or coordinate church school programs designed to promote religious education among church membership. May provide counseling and guidance relative to marital, health, financial, or religious problems.

2002 employment: 105,000
Projected 2002-12 employment change: Faster than average
Most significant source of education or training: Bachelor's degree

Farm and home management advisors

(O*NET 25-9021.00)

Advise, instruct, and assist individuals and families engaged in agriculture, agricultural-related processes, or home economics activities. Demonstrate procedures and apply research findings to solve problems; instruct and train in product development, sales, and the utilization of machinery and equipment to promote general welfare. Include county agricultural agents, feed and farm management advisors, home economists, and extension service advisors.

2002 employment: 16,000
Projected 2002-12 employment change: More slowly than average
Most significant source of education or training: Bachelor's degree

Health educators

(O*NET 21-1091.00)

Promote, maintain, and improve individual and community health by assisting individuals and communities to adopt healthy behaviors. Collect and analyze data to identify community needs prior to planning, implementing, monitoring, and evaluating programs designed to encourage healthy lifestyles, policies and environments. May also serve as a resource to assist individuals, other professionals, or the community, and may administer fiscal resources for health education programs.

2002 employment: 45,000
Projected 2002-12 employment change: Faster than average
Most significant source of education or training: Master's degree

Law clerks

(O*NET 23-2092.00)

Assist lawyers or judges by researching or preparing legal documents. May meet with clients or assist lawyers and judges in court. Excludes lawyers, and paralegal and legal assistants.

2002 employment: 48,000
Projected 2002-12 employment change: More slowly than average
Most significant source of education or training: Bachelor's degree

Orthotists and prosthetists

(O*NET 29-2091.00)

Assist patients with disabling conditions of limbs and spine or with partial or total absence of limb by fitting and preparing orthopedic braces and prostheses.

2002 employment: 4,600
Projected 2002-12 employment change: About as fast as average
Most significant source of education or training: Bachelor's degree

Psychiatric technicians

(O*NET 29-2053.00)

Care for mentally impaired or emotionally disturbed individuals, following physician instructions and hospital procedures. Monitor patients' physical and emotional well-being and report to medical staff. May participate in rehabilitation and treatment programs, help with personal hygiene, and administer oral medications and hypodermic injections.

2002 employment: 60,000
Projected 2002-12 employment change: More slowly than average
Most significant source of education or training: Moderate-term on-the-job training

Radiation therapists

(O*NET 29-1124.00)

Provide radiation therapy to patients as prescribed by a radiologist according to established practices and standards. Duties may include reviewing prescription and diagnosis; acting as a liaison with physician and supportive care personnel; preparing equipment, such as immobilization, treatment, and protection devices; and maintaining records, reports, and files. May assist in dosimetry procedures and tumor localization.

2002 employment: 14,000
Projected 2002-12 employment change: Faster than average
Most significant source of education or training: Associate degree

Title examiners, abstractors, and searchers

(O*NET 23-2093.01, 23-2093.02)

Search real estate records, examine titles, or summarize pertinent legal or insurance details for a variety of purposes. May compile lists of mortgages, contracts, and other instruments pertaining to titles by searching public and private records for law firms, real estate agencies, or title insurance companies.

2002 employment: 55,000
Projected 2002-12 employment change: A decline
Most significant source of education or training: Moderate-term on-the-job training

Service occupations

Amusement and recreation attendants

(O*NET 39-3091.00)

Perform a variety of attending duties at amusement or recreation facilities. May schedule use of recreations facilities, maintain and provide equipment to participants of sporting events or recreational pursuits, or operate amusement concessions and rides.

2002 employment: 234,000
Projected 2002-12 employment change: Faster than average
Most significant source of education or training: Short-term on-the-job training

Animal control workers

(O*NET 33-9011.00)

Handle animals for the purpose of investigations of mistreatment, or control of abandoned, dangerous, or unattended animals.

2002 employment: 11,000
Projected 2002-12 employment change: About as fast as average
Most significant source of education or training: Moderate-term on-the-job training

Baggage porters and bellhops

(O*NET 39-6011.00)

Handle baggage for travelers at transportation terminals or for guests at hotels or similar establishments.

2002 employment: 58,000
Projected 2002-12 employment change: About as fast as average
Most significant source of education or training: Short-term on-the-job training

Concierges

(O*NET 39-6012.00)

Assist patrons at hotel, apartment or office building with personal services. May take messages, arrange or give advice on transportation, business services or entertainment, or monitor guest requests for housekeeping and maintenance.

2002 employment: 17,000
Projected 2002-12 employment change: About as fast as average
Most significant source of education or training: Moderate-term on-the-job training

Costume attendants

(O*NET 39-3092.00)

Select, fit and take care of costumes for cast members, and aid entertainers.

2002 employment: 3,600
Projected 2002-12 employment change: Faster than average
Most significant source of education or training: Short-term on-the-job training

Crossing guards

(O*NET 33-9091.00)

Guide or control vehicular or pedestrian traffic at such places as streets, schools, railroad crossings, or construction sites.

2002 employment: 74,000
Projected 2002-12 employment change: About as fast as average
Most significant source of education or training: Short-term on-the-job training

Embalmers

(O*NET 39-4011.00)

Prepare bodies for interment in conformity with legal requirements.

2002 employment: 6,800
Projected 2002-12 employment change: More slowly than average
Most significant source of education or training: Postsecondary vocational award

First-line supervisors/managers of food preparation and serving workers

(O*NET 35-1012.00)

Supervise workers engaged in preparing and serving food.

2002 employment: 692,000
Projected 2002-12 employment change: About as fast as average
Most significant source of education or training: Work experience in a related occupation

First-line supervisors/managers of personal service workers

(O*NET 39-1021.00)

Supervise and coordinate activities of personal service workers, such as supervisors of flight attendants, hairdressers, or caddies.

2002 employment: 216,000
Projected 2002-12 employment change: More slowly than average
Most significant source of education or training: Work experience in a related occupation

First-line supervisors/managers, protective service workers, except police, fire, and corrections

(O*NET 33-1099.99)

All protective services supervisors who are not supervisors of protective service workers, correctional officers, police and detectives, or fire fighting and prevention workers.

2002 employment: 56,000
Projected 2002-12 employment change: Faster than average
Most significant source of education or training: Work experience in a related occupation

Funeral attendants

(O*NET 39-4021.00)

Perform a variety of tasks during a funeral, such as placing casket in parlor or chapel prior to service; arranging floral offerings or lights around casket; directing or escorting mourners; closing casket; and issuing and storing funeral equipment.

2002 employment: 26,000
Projected 2002-12 employment change: About as fast as average
Most significant source of education or training: Short-term on-the-job training

Locker room, coatroom and dressing room attendants

(O*NET 39-3093.00)

Provide personal items to patrons or customers in locker rooms, dressing rooms, or coatrooms.

2002 employment: 23,000
Projected 2002-12 employment change: Faster than average
Most significant source of education or training: Short-term on-the-job training

Massage therapists

(O*NET 31-9011.00)

Massage customers for hygienic or remedial purposes.

2002 employment: 92,000
Projected 2002-12 employment change: Faster than average
Most significant source of education or training: Postsecondary vocational award

Medical equipment preparers

(O*NET 31-9093.00)

Prepare, sterilize, install, or clean laboratory or healthcare equipment. May perform routine laboratory tasks and operate or inspect equipment.

2002 employment: 36,000
Projected 2002-12 employment change: About as fast as average
Most significant source of education or training: Short-term on-the-job training

Motion picture projectionists

(O*NET 39-3021.00)

Set up and operate motion picture projection and related sound reproduction equipment.

2002 employment: 9,400
Projected 2002-12 employment change: Little or no growth
Most significant source of education or training: Short-term on-the-job training

Parking enforcement workers

(O*NET 33-3041.00)

Patrol assigned area, such as public parking lot or section of city to issue tickets to overtime parking violators and illegally parked vehicles.

2002 employment: 11,000
Projected 2002-12 employment change: About as fast as average
Most significant source of education or training: Short-term on-the-job training

Residential advisors

(O*NET 39-9041.00)

Coordinate activities for residents of boarding schools, college fraternities or sororities, college dormitories, or similar establishments. Order supplies and determine need to maintenance, repairs, and furnishings. May maintain household records and assign rooms. May refer residents to counseling resources if needed.

2002 employment: 53,000
Projected 2002-12 employment change: Faster than average
Most significant source of education or training: Moderate-term on-the-job training

Tour guides and escorts

(O*NET 39-6021.00)

Escort individuals or groups on sightseeing tours or through places of interest, such as industrial establishments, public buildings, and art galleries.

2002 employment: 36,000
Projected 2002-12 employment change: About as fast as average
Most significant source of education or training: Moderate-term on-the-job training

Transportation attendants, except flight attendants and baggage porters

(O*NET 39-6032.00)

Provide services to ensure the safety and comfort of passengers aboard ships, buses, trains, or within the station or terminal. Perform duties, such as greeting passengers, explaining the use of safety equipment, serving meals or beverages, or answering questions related to travel.

2002 employment: 26,000
Projected 2002-12 employment change: About as fast as average
Most significant source of education or training: Short-term on-the-job training

Travel guides

(O*NET 39-6022.00)

Plan, organize, and conduct long distance cruises, tours, and expeditions for individuals or groups.

2002 employment: 6,400
Projected 2002-12 employment change: Little or no growth
Most significant source of education or training: Moderate-term on-the-job training

Ushers, lobby attendants, and ticket takers

(O*NET 39-3031.00)

Assist patrons at entertainment events by performing duties, such as collecting admission tickets and passes from patrons, assisting in finding seats, searching for lost articles, and locating such facilities as rest rooms and telephones.

2002 employment: 105,000
Projected 2002-12 employment change: About as fast as average
Most significant source of education or training: Short-term on-the-job training

Veterinary assistants and laboratory animal caretakers

(O*NET 31-9096.00)

Feed, water, and examine pets and other nonfarm animals for signs of illness, disease, or injury in laboratories and animal hospitals and clinics. Clean and disinfect cages and work areas, and sterilize laboratory and surgical equipment. May provide routine postoperative care, administer medication orally or topically, or prepare samples for laboratory examination under the supervision of veterinary or laboratory animal technologists or technicians, veterinarians, or scientists. Excludes nonfarm animal caretakers.

2002 employment: 63,000
Projected 2002-12 employment change: Faster than average
Most significant source of education or training: Short-term on-the-job training

Sales and related occupations

Advertising sales agents

(O*NET 41-3011.00)

Sell or solicit advertising, including graphic art, advertising space in publications, custom made signs, or TV and radio advertising time. May obtain leases for outdoor advertising sites or persuade retailer to use sales promotion display items.

2002 employment: 157,000
Projected 2002-12 employment change: About as fast as average
Most significant source of education or training: Moderate-term on-the-job training

Door-to-door sales workers, news and street vendors, and related workers

(O*NET 41-9091.00)

Sell goods or services door-to-door or on the street.

2002 employment: 155,000
Projected 2002-12 employment change: A decline
Most significant source of education or training: Short-term on-the-job training

Parts salespersons

(O*NET 41-2022.00)

Sell spare and replacement parts and equipment in repair shop or parts store.

2002 employment: 248,000
Projected 2002-12 employment change: A decline
Most significant source of education or training: Moderate-term on-the-job training

Telemarketers

(O*NET 41-9041.00)

Solicit orders for goods and services over the telephone.

2002 employment: 428,000
Projected 2002-12 employment change: A decline
Most significant source of education or training: Short-term on-the-job training

Office and administrative support occupations

Insurance claims and policy processing clerks

(O*NET 43-9041.01, 43-9041.02)

Process new insurance policies, modifications to existing policies, and claims forms. Obtain information from policyholders to verify the accuracy and completeness of information on claims forms, applications and related documents, and company records. Update existing policies and company records to reflect changes requested by policyholders and insurance company representatives. Excludes claims adjusters, examiners, and investigators.

2002 employment: 266,000
Projected 2002-12 employment change: More slowly than average
Most significant source of education or training: Moderate-term on-the-job training

Mail clerks and mail machine operators, except Postal Service

(O*NET 43-9051.01, 43-9051.02)

Prepare incoming and outgoing mail for distribution. Use hand or mail handling machines to time, stamp, open, read, sort, and route outgoing mail or packages. Duties may also include keeping necessary records and completed forms.

2002 employment: 170,000
Projected 2002-12 employment change: A decline
Most significant source of education or training: Short-term on-the-job training

Office machine operators, except computer

(O*NET 43-9071.01)

Operate one or more of a variety of office machines, such as photocopying, photographic, and duplicating machines, or other office machines. Excludes computer operators; mail clerks and mail machine operators; and billing and posting clerks and machine operators.

2002 employment: 96,000
Projected 2002-12 employment change: A decline
Most significant source of education or training: Short-term on-the-job training

Proofreaders and copy markers

(O*NET 43-9081.00)

Read transcript or proof type setup to detect and mark for correction any grammatical, typographical, or compositional errors. Excludes workers whose primary duty is editing copy. Includes proofreaders of Braille.

2002 employment: 27,000
Projected 2002-12 employment change: A decline
Most significant source of education or training: Short-term on-the-job training

Statistical assistants

(O*NET 43-9111.00)

Compile and compute data according to statistical formulas for use in statistical studies. May perform actuarial computations and compile charts and graphs for use by actuaries. Includes actuarial clerks.

2002 employment: 23,000
Projected 2002-12 employment change: A decline
Most significant source of education or training: Moderate-term on-the-job training

Farming, fishing, and forestry occupations

Animal breeders

(O*NET 45-2021.00)

Breed animals, including cattle, goats, horses, sheep, swine, poultry, dogs, cats, or pet birds. Select and breed animals according to their genealogy, characteristics, and offspring. May require a knowledge of artificial insemination techniques and equipment use. May involve keeping records on heats, birth intervals, or pedigree. Excludes nonfarm animal caretakers who may occasionally breed animals as part of their other caretaking duties. Excludes animal scientists whose primary function is research.

2002 employment: 9,000
Projected 2002-12 employment change: More slowly than average
Most significant source of education or training: Moderate-term on-the-job training

Hunters and trappers

(O*NET 45-3021.00)

Hunt and trap wild animals for human consumption, fur, feed, bait, or other purposes.

2002 employment: 1,500
Projected 2002-12 employment change: More slowly than average
Most significant source of education or training: Moderate-term on-the-job training

Supervisors, farming, fishing, and forestry workers

(O*NET 45-1011.01, 45-1011.02, 45-1011.03, 45-1011.04, 45-1011.05, 45-1011.06)

Directly supervise and coordinate the activities of agricultural, forestry, aquacultural, and related workers. Excludes first-line supervisors/ managers of landscaping, lawn service, and groundskeeping workers.

2002 employment: 52,000
Projected 2002-12 employment change: About as fast as average
Most significant source of education or training: Work experience in a related occupation

Construction and extraction occupations

Continuous mining machine operators

(O*NET 47-5041.00)

Operate self-propelled mining machines that rip coal, metal and nonmetal ores, rock, stone, or sand form the face and load it onto conveyors or into shuttle cars in a continuous operation.

2002 employment: 8,500
Projected 2002-12 employment change: A decline
Most significant source of education or training: Moderate-term on-the-job training

Derrick operators, oil and gas

(O*NET 47-5011.00)

Rig derrick equipment and operate pumps to circulate mud through drill hole.

2002 employment: 15,000
Projected 2002-12 employment change: Little or no growth
Most significant source of education or training: Moderate-term on-the-job training

Earth drillers, except oil and gas

(O*NET 47-5021.01, 47-5021.02)

Operate a variety of drills—such as rotary, churn, and pneumatic—to tap subsurface water and salt deposits, to remove core samples during mineral exploration or soil testing, and to facilitate the use of explosives in mining or construction. May use explosives. Includes horizontal and earth boring machine operators.

2002 employment: 23,000
Projected 2002-12 employment change: More slowly than average
Most significant source of education or training: Moderate-term on-the-job training

Explosives workers, ordnance handling experts, and blasters

(O*NET 47-5031.00)

Place and detonate explosives to demolish structures or to loosen, remove, or displace earth, rock, or other materials. May perform specialized handling, storage, and accounting procedures. Includes seismograph shooters. Excludes earth drillers, except oil and gas who may also work with explosives.

2002 employment: 5,100
Projected 2002-12 employment change: Little or no growth
Most significant source of education or training: Moderate-term on-the-job training

Fence erectors

(O*NET 47-4031.00)

Erect and repair metal and wooden fences and fence gates around highways, industrial establishments, residences, or farms, using hand and power tools.

2002 employment: 27,000
Projected 2002-12 employment change: About as fast as average
Most significant source of education or training: Moderate-term on-the-job training

First-line supervisors/managers of construction trades and extraction workers

(O*NET 47-1011.01, 47-1011.02)

Directly supervise and coordinate activities of construction or extraction workers.

2002 employment: 633,000
Projected 2002-12 employment change: About as fast as average
Most significant source of education or training: Work experience in a related occupation

Helpers—brickmasons, blockmasons, stonemasons, and tile and marble setters

(O*NET 47-3011.00)

Help brickmasons, blockmasons, stonemasons, or tile and marble setters by performing duties of lesser skill. Duties include using, supplying, or holding materials or tools, and cleaning work area and equipment. Excludes apprentice workers and report them with the appropriate skilled construction trade occupation. Excludes construction laborers who do not primarily assist brickmasons, blockmasons, and stonemasons or tile and marble setters.

2002 employment: 59,000
Projected 2002-12 employment change: Little or no growth
Most significant source of education or training: Short-term on-the-job training

Helpers—carpenters

(O*NET 47-3012.00)

Help carpenters by performing duties of lesser skill. Duties include using, supplying, or holding materials or tools, and cleaning work area and equipment. Excludes apprentice workers and report them with the appropriate skilled construction trade occupation. Excludes construction laborers who do not primarily assist carpenters.

2002 employment: 97,000
Projected 2002-12 employment change: About as fast as average
Most significant source of education or training: Short-term on-the-job training

Helpers—electricians

(O*NET 47-3013.00)

Help electricians by performing duties of lesser skill. Duties include using, supplying, or holding materials or tools, and cleaning work area and equipment. Excludes apprentice workers and report them with them with the appropriate skilled construction trade occupation. Excludes construction laborers who do not primarily assist electricians.

2002 employment: 99,000
Projected 2002-12 employment change: About as fast as average
Most significant source of education or training: Short-term on-the-job training

Helpers—extraction workers

(O*NET 47-5081.00)

Help extraction craft workers, such as earth drillers, blasters and explosives workers, derrick operators, and mining machine operators, by performing duties of lesser skill. Duties include supplying equipment or cleaning work area. Excludes apprentice workers.

2002 employment: 29,000
Projected 2002-12 employment change: More slowly than average
Most significant source of education or training: Short-term on-the-job training

Helpers—painters, paperhangers, plasterers, and stucco masons

(O*NET 47-3014.00)

Help painters, paperhangers, plasterers, or stucco masons by performing duties of lesser skill. Duties including using, supplying, or holding materials or tools, and cleaning work area and equipment. Excludes apprentice workers and report them with the appropriate skilled construction trade occupation. Excludes construction laborers who do not primarily assist painters, paperhangers, plasterers, or stucco masons.

2002 employment: 31,000
Projected 2002-12 employment change: About as fast as average
Most significant source of education or training: Short-term on-the-job training

Helpers—pipelayers, plumbers, pipefitters, and steamfitters

(O*NET 47-3015.00)

Help pipelayers, plumbers, pipefitters, or steamfitters by performing duties of lesser skill. Duties including using, supplying, or holding materials or tools, and cleaning work area and equipment. Excludes apprentice workers and report them with the appropriate skilled construction trade occupation. Excludes construction laborers who do not primarily assist pipelayers, plumbers, pipefitters or steamfitters.

2002 employment: 79,000
Projected 2002-12 employment change: About as fast as average
Most significant source of education or training: Short-term on-the-job training

Helpers—roofers

(O*NET 47-3016.00)

Help roofers by performing duties of lesser skill. Duties include using, supplying, or holding materials or tools, and cleaning work area and equipment. Excludes apprentice workers and report them with the appropriate skilled construction trade occupation. Excludes construction laborers who do not primarily assist roofers.

2002 employment: 21,000
Projected 2002-12 employment change: About as fast as average
Most significant source of education or training: Short-term on-the-job training

Highway maintenance workers

(O*NET 47-4051.00)

Maintain highways, municipal and rural roads, airport runways, and rights-of-way. Duties include patching broken or eroded pavement, repairing guard rails, highway markers, and snow fences. May also mow or clear brush from along road or plow snow from roadway. Excludes tree trimmers and pruners.

2002 employment: 154,000
Projected 2002-12 employment change: About as fast as average
Most significant source of education or training: Moderate-term on-the-job training

Mine cutting and channeling machine operators

(O*NET 47-5042.00)

Operate machinery—such as longwall shears, plows, and cutting machines—to cut or channel along the face or seams of coal mines, stone quarries, or other mining surfaces to facilitate blasting, separating, or removing minerals or materials from mines or from the earth's surface. Includes shale planers.

2002 employment: 5,200
Projected 2002-12 employment change: A decline
Most significant source of education or training: Moderate-term on-the-job training

Rail-track laying and maintenance equipment operators

(O*NET 47-4061.00)

Lay, repair, and maintain track for standard or narrow-gauge railroad equipment used in regular railroad service or in plant yards, quarries, sand and gravel pits, and mines. Includes ballast cleaning machine operators and railroad bed tamping machine operators.

2002 employment: 11,000
Projected 2002-12 employment change: A decline
Most significant source of education or training: Moderate-term on-the-job training

Rock splitters, quarry

(O*NET 47-5051.00)

Separate blocks of rough dimension stone from quarry mass using jackhammer and wedges.

2002 employment: 2,700
Projected 2002-12 employment change: About as fast as average
Most significant source of education or training: Moderate-term on-the-job training

Roof bolters, mining

(O*NET 47-5061.00)

Operate machinery to install roof support bolts in underground mine.

2002 employment: 4,200
Projected 2002-12 employment change: A decline
Most significant source of education or training: Moderate-term on-the-job training

Rotary drill operators, oil and gas

(O*NET 47-5012.00)

Set up or operate a variety of drills to remove petroleum products from the earth and to find and remove core samples for testing during oil and gas exploration.

2002 employment: 14,000
Projected 2002-12 employment change: Little or no growth
Most significant source of education or training: Moderate-term on-the-job training

Roustabouts, oil and gas

(O*NET 47-5071.00)

Assemble or repair oil field equipment using hand and power tools. Perform other tasks as needed.

2002 employment: 32,000
Projected 2002-12 employment change: More slowly than average
Most significant source of education or training: Moderate-term on-the-job training

Septic tank servicers and sewer pipe cleaners

(O*NET 47-4071.00)

Clean and repair septic tanks, sewer lines, or drains. May patch walls and partitions of tank, replace damaged drain tile, or repair breaks in underground piping.

2002 employment: 18,000
Projected 2002-12 employment change: Faster than average
Most significant source of education or training: Moderate-term on-the-job training

Service unit operators, oil, gas, and mining

(O*NET 47-5013.00)

Operate equipment to increase oil flow from producing wells or to remove stick pipe, casing, tools, or other obstructions from drilling wells. May also perform similar services in mining exploration operations. Includes fishing-tool technicians.

2002 employment: 13,000
Projected 2002-12 employment change: A decline
Most significant source of education or training: Moderate-term on-the-job training

Installation, maintenance, and repair occupations

Bicycle repairers

(O*NET 49-3091.00)

Repair and service bicycles.

2002 employment: 7,000
Projected 2002-12 employment change: About as fast as average
Most significant source of education or training: Moderate-term on-the-job training

Commercial divers

(O*NET 49-9092.00)

Work below surface of water, using scuba gear to inspect, repair, remove, or install equipment and structures. May use a variety of power and hand tools, such as drills, sledgehammers, torches, and welding equipment. May conduct tests or experiments, rig explosives, or photograph structures or marine life. Excludes fishers and related fishing workers, athletes and sports competitors, and police and sheriff's patrol officers.

2002 employment: 4,500
Projected 2002-12 employment change: About as fast as average
Most significant source of education or training: Moderate-term on-the-job training

Control and valve installers and repairers, except mechanical door

(O*NET 49-9012.01, 49-9012.02, 49-9012.03)

Install, repair, and maintain mechanical regulating and controlling devices, such as electric meters, gas regulators, thermostats, safety and flow valves, and other mechanical governors.

2002 employment: 38,000
Projected 2002-12 employment change: About as fast as average
Most significant source of education or training: Moderate-term on-the-job training

Fabric menders, except garment

(O*NET 49-9093.00)

Repair tears, holes, and other defects in fabrics, such as draperies, linens, parachutes, and tents.

2002 employment: 2,400
Projected 2002-12 employment change: A decline
Most significant source of education or training: Moderate-term on-the-job training

First-line supervisors/managers of mechanics, installers, and repairers

(O*NET 49-1011.00)

Supervise and coordinate the activities of mechanics, installers, and repairers. Excludes team or work leaders.

2002 employment: 444,000
Projected 2002-12 employment change: About as fast as average
Most significant source of education or training: Work experience in a related occupation

Helpers—installation, maintenance, and repair workers

(O*NET 49-9098.00)

Help installation, maintenance, and repair workers in maintenance, parts replacement, and repair of vehicles, industrial machinery, and electrical and electronic equipment. Perform duties, such as furnishing tools, materials, and supplies to other workers; cleaning work area, machines, and tools; and holding materials or tools for other workers.

2002 employment: 150,000
Projected 2002-12 employment change: About as fast as average
Most significant source of education or training: Short-term on-the-job training

Locksmiths and safe repairers

(O*NET 49-9094.00)

Repair and open locks; make keys; change locks and safe combinations; and install and repair locks.

2002 employment: 23,000
Projected 2002-12 employment change: Faster than average
Most significant source of education or training: Moderate-term on-the-job training

Manufactured building and mobile home installers

(O*NET 49-9095.00)

Move or install homes or prefabricated buildings.

2002 employment: 18,000
Projected 2002-12 employment change: Faster than average
Most significant source of education or training: Moderate-term on-the-job training

Mechanical door repairers

(O*NET 49-9011.00)

Install, service, or repair opening and closing mechanisms of automatic doors and hydraulic door closers. Includes garage door mechanics.

2002 employment: 11,000
Projected 2002-12 employent change: Faster than average
Most significant source of education or training: Moderate-term on-the-job training

Recreational vehicle service technicians

(O*NET 49-3092.00)

Diagnose, inspect, adjust, repair, or overhaul recreational vehicles including travel trailers. May specialize in maintaining gas, electrical, hydraulic, plumbing, or chassis/towing systems as well as repairing generators, appliances, and interior components. Includes workers who perform customized van conversions. Excludes automotive service technicians and mechanics, and bus and truck mechanics and diesel engine specialists who also work on recreation vehicles.

2002 employment: 13,000
Projected 2002-12 employment change: Faster than average
Most significant source of education or training: Long-term on-the-job training

Refractory materials repairers, except brickmasons

(O*NET 49-9045.00)

Build or repair furnaces, kilns, cupolas, boilers, converters, ladles, soaking pits, ovens, etc., using refractory materials.

2002 employment: 3,600
Projected 2002-12 employment change: More slowly than average
Most significant source of education or training: Moderate-term on-the-job training

Riggers

(O*NET 49-9096.00)

Set up or repair rigging for construction projects, manufacturing plants, logging yards, ships and shipyards, or for the entertainment industry.

2002 employment: 14,000
Projected 2002-12 employment change: About as fast as average
Most significant source of education or training: Short-term on-the-job training

Security and fire alarm systems installers

(O*NET 49-2098.00)

Install, program, maintain, and repair security and fire alarm wiring and equipment. Ensure that work is in accordance with relevant codes. Excludes electricians who do a broad range of electrical wiring.

2002 employment: 46,000
Projected 2002-12 employment change: Faster than average
Most significant source of education or training: Postsecondary vocational award

Signal and track switch repairers

(O*NET 49-9097.00)

Install, inspect, test, maintain, or repair electric gate crossings, signals, signal equipment, track switches, section lines, or intercommunications systems within a railroad system.

2002 employment: 7,900
Projected 2002-12 employment change: A decline
Most significant source of education or training: Moderate-term on-the-job training

Tire repairers and changers

(O*NET 49-3093.00)

Repair and replace tires.

2002 employment: 83,000
Projected 2002-12 employment change: More slowly than average
Most significant source of education or training: Short-term on-the-job training

Production occupations

Cementing and gluing machine operators and tenders

(O*NET 51-9191.00)

Operate or tend cementing and gluing machines to join items for further processing or to form a completed product. Processes include joining veneer sheets into plywood; gluing paper; joining rubber and rubberized fabric parts, plastic, simulated leather, or other materials. Excludes shoe machine operators and tenders.

2002 employment: 27,000
Projected 2002-12 employment change: Little or no growth
Most significant source of education or training: Moderate-term on-the-job training

Chemical equipment operators and tenders

(O*NET 51-9011.01, 51-9011.02)

Operate or tend equipment to control chemical changes or reactions in the processing of industrial or consumer products. Equipment used includes devulcanizers, steam-jacketed kettles, and reactor vessels. Excludes chemical plant and system operators.

2002 employment: 59,000
Projected 2002-12 employment change: A decline
Most significant source of education or training: Moderate-term on-the-job training

Chemical plant and system operators

(O*NET 51-8091.00)

Control or operate an entire chemical process or system of machines.

2002 employment: 58,000
Projected 2002-12 employment change: A decline
Most significant source of education or training: Long-term on-the-job training

Cleaning, washing, and metal pickling equipment operators and tenders

(O*NET 51-9192.00)

Operate or tend machines to wash or clean products, such as barrels or kegs, glass items, tin plate, food, pulp, coal, plastic, or rubber, to remove impurities.

2002 employment: 18,000
Projected 2002-12 employment change: More slowly than average
Most significant source of education or training: Moderate-term on-the-job training

Cooling and freezing equipment operators and tenders

(O*NET 51-9193.00)

Operate or tend equipment, such as cooling and freezing units, refrigerators, batch freezers, and freezing tunnels, to cool or freeze products, food, blood plasma, and chemicals.

2002 employment: 7,200
Projected 2002-12 employment change: More slowly than average
Most significant source of education or training: Moderate-term on-the-job training

Crushing, grinding, and polishing machine setters, operators, and tenders

(O*NET 51-9021.00)

Set up, operate, or tend machines to crush, grind, or polish materials, such as coal, glass, grain, stone, food, or rubber.

2002 employment: 45,000
Projected 2002-12 employment change: A decline
Most significant source of education or training: Moderate-term on-the-job training

Cutters and trimmers, hand

(O*NET 51-9031.00)

Use hand tools or hand-held power tools to cut and trim a variety of manufactured items, such as carpet, fabric, stone, glass, or rubber.

2002 employment: 31,000
Projected 2002-12 employment change: More slowly than average
Most significant source of education or training: Short-term on-the-job training

Cutting and slicing machine setters, operators, and tenders

(O*NET 51-9032.01, 51-9032.02, 51-9032.03, 51-9032.04)

Set up, operate, or tend machines that cut or slice materials, such as glass, stone, cork, rubber, tobacco, food, paper, or insulating material. Excludes woodworking machines setters, operators, and tenders; cutting, punching, and press machine setters, operators, and

tenders, metal and plastic; and textile cutting machine setters, operators, and tenders.

2002 employment: 77,000
Projected 2002-12 employment change: More slowly than average
Most significant source of education or training: Moderate-term on-the-job training

Etchers and engravers

(O*NET 51-9194.01, 51-9194.02, 51-9194.03, 51-9194.04, 51-9194.05, 51-9194.06)

Engrave or etch metal, wood, rubber, or other materials for identification or decorative purposes. Includes such workers as etcher-circuit processors, pantograph engravers, and silk screen etchers. Includes photoengravers with prepress technicians and workers.

2002 employment: 9,700
Projected 2002-12 employment change: More slowly than average
Most significant source of education or training: Long-term on-the-job training

Extruding, forming, pressing, and compacting machine setters, operators, and tenders

(O*NET 51-9041.01, 51-9041.02)

Set up, operate, or tend machines, such as glass forming machines, plodder machines, and tuber machines, to shape and form products, such as glassware, food, rubber, soap, brick, tile, clay, wax, tobacco, or cosmetics. Excludes paper goods machine setters, operators, and tenders; and shoe machine operators and tenders.

2002 employment: 73,000
Projected 2002-12 employment change: Little or no growth
Most significant source of education or training: Moderate-term on-the-job training

First-line supervisors/managers of production and operating workers

(O*NET 51-1011.00)

Supervise and coordinate the activities of production and operating workers, such as inspectors, precision workers, machine setters, and operators, assemblers, fabricators, and plant and system operators. Excludes team or work leaders.

2002 employment: 733,000
Projected 2002-12 employment change: About as fast as average
Most significant source of education or training: Work experience in a related occupation

Furnace, kiln, oven, drier, and kettle operators and tenders

(O*NET 51-9051.00)

Operate or tend heating equipment other than basic metal, plastic or food processing equipment. Includes activities, such as annealing glass, drying lumber, curing rubber, removing moisture from materials, or boiling soap.

2002 employment: 31,000
Projected 2002-12 employment change: A decline
Most significant source of education or training: Moderate-term on-the-job training

Gas plant operators

(O*NET 51-8092.01, 51-8092.02)

Distribute or process gas for utility companies and others by controlling compressors to maintain specified pressures on main pipelines.

2002 employment: 12,000
Projected 2002-12 employment change: More slowly than average
Most significant source of education or training: Long-term on-the-job training

Grinding and polishing workers, hand

(O*NET 51-9022.00)

Grind, sand, or polish, using hand tools or hand-held power tools, a variety of metal, wood, stone, clay, plastic, or glass objects. Includes chippers, buffers, and finishers.

2002 employment: 45,000
Projected 2002-12 employment change: More slowly than average
Most significant source of education or training: Moderate-term on-the-job training

Helpers—production workers

(O*NET 51-9198.01, 51-9198.02)

Help production workers by performing duties of lesser skill. Duties include supplying or holding materials or tools, and cleaning work area and equipment. Excludes apprentice workers.

2002 employment: 467,000
Projected 2002-12 employment change: More slowly than average
Most significant source of education or training: Short-term on-the-job training

Medical appliance technicians

(O*NET 51-9082.00)

Construct, fit, maintain, or repair medical supportive devices, such as braces, artificial limbs, joints, arch supports, and other surgical and medical appliances.

2002 employment: 14,000
Projected 2002-12 employment change: About as fast as average
Most significant source of education or training: Long-term on-the-job training

Mixing and blending machine setters, operators, and tenders

(O*NET 51-9023.00)

Set up, operate, or tend machines to mix or blend materials, such as chemicals, tobacco, liquids, color pigments, or explosive ingredients. Excludes food batchmakers.

2002 employment: 106,000
Projected 2002-12 employment change: A decline
Most significant source of education or training: Moderate-term on-the-job training

Molders, shapers, and casters, except metal and plastic

(O*NET 51-9195.01, 51-9195.02, 51-9195.03, 51-9195.04, 51-9195.05, 51-9195.06, 51-9195.07)

Mold, shape, form, cast, or carve products such as food products, figurines, tile, pipes, and candles consisting of clay, glass, plaster, concrete, stone, or combinations of materials.

2002 employment: 46,000
Projected 2002-12 employment change: More slowly than average
Most significant source of education or training: Moderate-term on-the-job training

Packaging and filling machine operators and tenders

(O*NET 51-9111.00)

Operate or tend machines to prepare industrial or consumer products for storage or shipment. Includes cannery workers who pack food products.

2002 employment: 387,000
Projected 2002-12 employment change: Faster than average
Most significant source of education or training: Short-term on-the-job training

Paper goods machine setters, operators, and tenders

(O*NET 51-9196.00)

Set up, operate, or tend paper goods machines that perform a variety of functions, such as converting, sawing, corrugating, banding, wrapping, boxing, stitching, forming, or sealing paper or paperboard sheets into products.

2002 employment: 117,000
Projected 2002-12 employment change: A decline
Most significant source of education or training: Moderate-term on-the-job training

Petroleum pump system operators, refinery operators, and gaugers

(O*NET 51-8093.01, 51-8093.02, 51-8093.03)

Control the operation of petroleum refining or processing units. May specialize in controlling manifold and pumping systems, gauging or testing oil in storage tanks, or regulating the flow of oil into pipelines.

2002 employment: 39,000
Projected 2002-12 employment change: A decline
Most significant source of education or training: Long-term on-the-job training

Separating, filtering, clarifying, precipitating, and still machine setters, operators and tenders

(O*NET 51-9012.00)

Set up, operate, or tend continuous flow or vat-type equipment; filter presses; shaker screens; centrifuges; condenser tubes; precipitating, fermenting, or evaporating tanks; scrubbing towers; or batch stills. These machines extract, sort, or separate liquids, gases, or solids from other materials to recover a refined product. Includes dairy processing equipment operators. Excludes chemical equipment operators and tenders.

2002 employment: 36,000
Projected 2002-12 employment change: Little or no growth
Most significant source of education or training: Moderate-term on-the-job training

Tire builders

(O*NET 51-9197.00)

Operate machines to build tires from rubber components.

2002 employment: 14,000
Projected 2002-12 employment change: More slowly than average
Most significant source of education or training: Moderate-term on-the-job training

Transportation and material moving occupations

Aircraft cargo handling supervisors

(O*NET 53-1011.00)

Direct ground crew in the loading, unloading, securing, and staging of aircraft cargo and baggage. Determine the quantity and orientation of cargo and compute aircraft center of gravity. May accompany aircraft as member of flight crew and monitor and handle cargo in flight, and assist and brief passengers on safety and emergency procedures. Includes loadmasters.

2002 employment: 8,900
Projected 2002-12 employment change: About as fast as average
Most significant source of education or training: Work experience in a related occupation

Airfield operations specialists

(O*NET 53-2022.00)

Ensure the safe takeoff and landing of commercial and military aircraft. Duties include coordination between air-traffic control and maintenance personnel; dispatching; using airfield landing and navigational aids; implementing airfield safety procedures; monitoring and maintaining flight records; and applying knowledge of weather information.

2002 employment: 6,100
Projected 2002-12 employment change: About as fast as average
Most significant source of education or training: Long-term on-the-job training

Ambulance drivers and attendants, except emergency medical technicians

(O*NET 53-3011.00)

Drive ambulance or assist ambulance drivers in transporting sick, injured, or convalescent patients. Assist in lifting patients.

2002 employment: 17,000
Projected 2002-12 employment change: Faster than average
Most significant source of education or training: Moderate-term on-the-job training

Bridge and lock tenders

(O*NET 53-6011.00)

Operate and tend bridges, canal locks, and lighthouses to permit marine passage on inland waterways, near shores, and at danger points in waterway passages. May supervise such operations. Includes drawbridge operators, lock tenders and operators, and slip bridge operators.

2002 employment: 4,100
Projected 2002-12 employment change: A decline
Most significant source of education or training: Short-term on-the-job training

First-line supervisors/managers of transportation and material moving machine and vehicle operators

(O*NET 53-1031.00)

Directly supervise and coordinate activities of transportation and material-moving machine and vehicle operators and helpers.

2002 employment: 207,000
Projected 2002-12 employment change: About as fast as average
Most significant source of education or training: Work experience in a related occupation

Parking lot attendants

(O*NET 53-6021.00)

Park automobiles or issue tickets for customers in parking lot or garage. May collect fee.

2002 employment: 107,000
Projected 2002-12 employment change: About as fast as average
Most significant source of education or training: Short-term on-the-job training

Service station attendants

(O*NET 53-6031.00)

Service automobiles, buses, trucks, boats, and other automotive or marine vehicles with fuel, lubricants, and accessories. Collect payment for services and supplies. May lubricate vehicle, change motor oil, install antifreeze, or replace lights or other accessories, such as windshield wiper blades or fan belts. May repair or replace tires.

2002 employment: 107,000
Projected 2002-12 employment change: Little or no growth
Most significant source of education or training: Short-term on-the-job training

Traffic technicians

(O*NET 53-6041.00)

Conduct field studies to determine traffic volume, speed, effectiveness of signals, adequacy of lighting, and other factors influencing traffic conditions, under direction of traffic engineer.

2002 employment: 5,600
Projected 2002-12 employment change: More slowly than average
Most significant source of education or training: Short-term on-the-job training

Transportation inspectors

(O*NET 53-6051.01, 53-6051.02, 53-6051.03, 53-6051.04, 53-6051.05, 53-6051.06)

Inspect equipment or goods in connection with the safe transport of cargo or people. Includes rail transport inspectors, such as freight inspectors, car inspectors, rail inspectors, and other nonprecision inspectors of other types of transportation vehicles.

2002 employment: 29,000
Projected 2002-12 employment change: More slowly than average
Most significant source of education or training: Work experience in a related occupation

Assumptions and Methods Used in Preparing Employment Projections

Occupational statements in the *Handbook* use 1 of 6 phrases to describe the projected change in employment between 2002 and 2012. (See page 20.) These phrases are based on numerical projections developed using the Bureau of Labor Statistics (BLS) employment projections model system. Projections of occupational employment are the sixth and final step in the system; the six steps are listed in the discussion of methods below. A full description, including numerical projections of employment, appears in the February 2004 *Monthly Labor Review* and in the BLS *Handbook of Methods*. The winter 2003-04 *Occupational Outlook Quarterly* presents the projections in a series of charts.

The projections reflect the knowledge and judgment of staff in the BLS Office of Occupational Statistics and Employment Projections and of knowledgeable people from other BLS offices, other government agencies, colleges and universities, industries, unions, professional societies, and trade associations, who furnished data and information, prepared reports, or reviewed the projections. BLS takes full responsibility, however, for the projections.

Assumptions. The information in the *Handbook* is based on an economic projection, which is characterized by labor force growth at the same rate (1.1-percent average annual growth) posted over the past 10-year period (1992-2002), strong productivity growth (2.1-percent average annual growth), a continued low unemployment rate (5.2-percent average annual rate), and increasing trade deficits. A Federal budget deficit is assumed, with modest growth in Federal defense and nondefense expenditures. Other assumptions include consumer spending on durable goods that grows faster than consumer spending on services and nondurable goods. Within nondurable goods, a large source of consumer spending is drugs and medicines, and is assumed to grow much faster than spending on other categories. Within services, consumer spending on medical care is expected to drive growth. Investment spending for production equipment—including communication equipment and computer software—will grow rapidly. Expenditures for construction of residential structures will grow at an average annual rate of 2.1 percent, significantly slower than during the 1992-2002 period. Spending on nonresidential construction will grow at an average annual rate of 6.6 percent, almost the same as during the 1992-2002 period.

Although BLS considers these assumptions reasonable, the economy may follow a different course, resulting in a different pattern of occupational growth. Real growth also could be different because most occupations are sensitive to a much wider variety of factors than those considered in the various projections models. Unforeseen changes in consumer, business, or government spending patterns and in the ways in which goods and services are produced could greatly alter the growth of individual occupations.

Methods. This section summarizes the steps involved in BLS projections of employment by occupation. BLS uses U.S. Census Bureau projections of the population by age, gender, and race, combined with projections of labor force participation rates—the percent of the specified group of the population working or seeking work—to arrive at estimates of the civilian labor force for the projected year.

BLS projections are developed in a series of six steps, each of which is based on separate projections procedures and models and various related assumptions. These six steps, or system components, deal with:

- Size and demographic composition of the labor force
- Growth of the aggregate economy
- Final demand or gross domestic product (GDP)
- Interindustry relationships (input-output)
- Industry output and employment
- Occupational employment

These components provide the overall analytical framework needed to develop detailed employment projections. Each component is developed in order, with the results of each used as input for successive components and with some results feeding back into earlier steps. Each step is repeated a number of times to ensure internal consistency as assumptions and results are reviewed and revised.

The projections of the labor force and assumptions about other demographic variables, fiscal policy, foreign economic activity, and energy prices and availability form the input to the macroeconomic model. This model projects GDP (sales to all final consuming sectors in the economy) and the distribution of GDP by its major demand components (consumer expenditures, investment, government purchases, and net exports). Estimating the intermediate flows of goods and services—for example, the steel incorporated into automobiles—is the next step in the projections process. The resulting estimates of demand for goods and services are used to project industry output of final products as well as total output by industry.

Industry output of goods and services is then converted to industry employment. Studies of trends in productivity and technology are used to estimate future output per worker hour, and regression analysis is used to estimate worker hours. These estimates, along with output projections, are used to develop the final industry employment projections.

An industry-occupation matrix is used to project employment for wage and salary workers. The matrix shows occupational staffing patterns—each occupation as a percent of employment in every industry. The matrix covering the 2002-12 period includes 284 detailed industries and 725 detailed occupations. Data for current staffing patterns in the matrix come from the BLS Occupational Employment Statistics surveys, which collect data from employers on a 3-year cycle.

The occupational staffing patterns for each industry were projected based on anticipated changes in the ways in which goods and services are produced, and were then applied to projected industry employment. The resulting employment was summed across industries to derive total wage and salary employment by occupation. Using this method, rapid employment growth is projected for healthcare workers while employment of rail transportation workers is expected to decline, reflecting the projected changes in the healthcare and railroad transportation industries, respectively.

Employment in an occupation also may grow or decline as a result of many other factors. For example, faster-than-average growth also is expected among computer support specialists as technology advances and organizations place more emphasis on network applications and maximizing the efficiency of their computer systems. On the other hand, automation, the expanding use of computers, and developments in computer software will result in declining employment among procurement clerks, order clerks, and word processors and typists. The projected-year matrix incorporates these expected changes.

Data on self-employed workers in each occupation come from the Current Population Survey. Numbers of self-employed workers were projected separately.

Replacement needs. In most occupations, replacement needs provide more job openings than growth. Replacement openings occur as people leave occupations. Some individuals transfer to other occupations as a step up the career ladder or to change careers; some stop working temporarily, perhaps to return to school or care for a family; other workers—retirees for example—leave the labor force permanently. A discussion of replacements and the methodology used to prepare estimates is presented in *Occupational Projections and Training Data, 2004-05 Edition,* BLS Bulletin 2572.

Occupational Information Network Coverage

The *Occupational Information Network* (O*NET), which replaced the Dictionary of Occupational Titles, is used by public employment service offices to classify and place jobseekers. The O*NET was developed by job analysts. Future information on job duties, knowledge and skills, education and training, and other occupational characteristics will come directly from workers and employers. Information on O*NET is available from O*NET Project, U.S. Department of Labor/ETA, 200 Constitution Ave. NW., Room N-5637, Washington, DC 20210-0001. Telephone (202) 693-3660. Internet: **http://www.doleta.gov/programs/onet**

The O*NET reflects the 2000 *Standard Occupational Classification* (SOC) system. With 822 detailed occupations, the SOC represents the Federal Government's most recent effort to analyze the occupational structure in the United States and to provide a universal occupational classification system. All Federal agencies that collect occupational data adhere to the SOC. Information on the SOC, including its occupational structure, is available on the Internet: **http://www.bls.gov/soc**

Occupational statements in this 2004-05 edition of the *Handbook* list the O*NET codes that relate to or match the definitions used in the Bureau's Occupational Employment Statistics (OES) survey-the principal source of occupational employment data in the Handbook. All numbers listed also appear in the table below. The table is arranged by the O*NET/SOC code, followed by the O*NET/SOC title and the page on which the corresponding *Handbook* statement begins.

Index

C

D

F

I

M

P

T